PENGUIN CLASSICS (P) DELUXE EDITION

THE HISTORIES

HERODOTUS was born around 480 BC in Halicarnassus, on the southwest coast of Asia Minor. Few facts are known about his life but he remains known through his life's work, *The Histories*, a groundbreaking account of the Greco-Persian Wars of 490 and 480–479 BC and the world in which they took place. He died around 425 BC, possibly in southern Italy. His reputation has varied greatly, but many believe he well deserves the title (given to him by Cicero) of "the Father of History."

TOM HOLLAND is an acclaimed translator and historian of the ancient world. He is the author of several works of nonfiction, including *Rubicon: The Triumph and Tragedy of the Roman Republic*, which won the Hessell-Tiltman Prize for History and was short-listed for the Samuel Johnson Prize, and *Persian Fire: The First World Empire and the Battle for the West*, which won the Anglo-Hellenic League's Runciman Award in 2006. He has adapted works by Homer, Herodotus, Thucydides, and Virgil for the BBC. In 2007, he won the Classical Association Prize, awarded to "the individual who has done most to promote the study of the language, literature and civilisation of Ancient Greece and Rome."

PAUL CARTLEDGE is A. G. Leventis Professor of Greek Culture Emeritus at the University of Cambridge and A. G. Leventis Senior Research Fellow at Clare College. His numerous books include *Sparta and Lakonia: A Regional History; 1300–362 BC* and *The Greeks: A Portrait of Self and Others*. He is an Honorary Citizen of Sparta and a recipient of the Gold Cross of the Order of Honour conferred by the president of the Hellenic Republic.

HERODOTUS

The Histories

Translated by TOM HOLLAND
Introduction and Notes by PAUL CARTLEDGE

PENGUIN BOOKS

PENGUIN BOOKS
Published by the Penguin Group
Penguin Group (USA) LLC
375 Hudson Street
New York, New York 10014

USA I Canada I UK I Ireland I Australia I New Zealand I India I South Africa I China
penguin.com
A Penguin Random House Company

First published in Great Britain by Penguin Books Ltd., 2013
First published in the United States of America by Viking Penguin,
a member of Penguin Group (USA) LLC, 2014
Published in Penguin Books 2015

Map illustrations by Jeff Edwards

ISBN 978-0-670-02489-6 (hc.)
ISBN 978-0-14-310754-5 (pbk.)

Printed in the United States of America
7   9   10   8   6

Contents

The Histories

Translator's Preface
Herodotus: A Historian for All Ages

Herodotus is the most entertaining of historians. Indeed, he is as entertaining as anyone who has ever written – historian or not. He has been my constant companion since I was twelve, and never once have I grown tired of him. His great work is many things – the first example of nonfiction, the text that underlies the entire discipline of history, the most important source of information we have for a vital episode in human affairs – but it is above all a treasure-trove of wonders. This, coming from a translator of *The Histories*, may sound like special pleading – but it is not. To spend as much time with Herodotus as I have done over these past years has been a rare privilege: a veritable labour of love. The Father of History he may be – but he is also very much more than that.

The ostensible goal of *The Histories* is to explain what would now be termed 'the clash of civilizations': the inability of the peoples of East and West to live together in peace. The theme was one fit to inspire a whole new genre. Herodotus was writing within living memory of events so epic that they continue to thrill and astonish to this day. In 490 BC, the King of Persia, Darius the Great, had dispatched an expedition to swat the buzzing of the Greek city of Athens. Since the empire he ruled was the largest that the world had ever seen, and since no Greek army had ever before defeated the Persians in battle, the King was confident of victory. His confidence, though, proved misplaced. The Athenians, marching out to a plain named Marathon, defeated the invaders. The respite this won for them, however, was only temporary. A decade later, the Persians were back. This time they came in overwhelming numbers, and were led in person by their new king, Xerxes. Many Greeks, convinced that they had no prospect of preserving their liberty, went over to the invaders. Only a few cities, headed by Athens and the peerless warrior-state of Sparta, refused to surrender. At Thermopylae, a pass to the north of Athens, a tiny Greek holding-force led by a Spartan king managed to keep the Persians at bay for two days, before the pass was finally forced. Athens was captured soon afterwards. The Acropolis was put to the torch. But then, in the waters off a nearby island called Salamis, the Greek fleet won an unexpected and decisive victory. A year later, in a great battle outside the city of Plataea, mainland Greece's liberty was definitively secured. To the Greeks themselves, and to many ages since, it seemed a barely believable triumph: the most astounding victory of all time.

That was certainly my opinion when I first read about the Persian Wars. To me, at the tender and impressionable age of twelve, the heroics of Marathon and Thermopylae, of Salamis and Plataea, seemed the very stuff of fantasy. Better than fantasy, even – for unlike *Star Wars* or *The Lord of the Rings* the victory of the Greeks, won against all the odds and achieved amid such drama, had actually happened. So it was I became obsessed. I read everything I could on the topic. It did not take me long to realize that, when it came to the study of the Persian Wars, all roads led back to the single source: Herodotus. This did give me momentary pause. I had never read a classic before. What would it be like to read a book by an actual ancient Greek? Screwing up my courage, I resolved to find out. *The Histories* began promisingly:

> Herodotus, from Halicarnassus, here displays his enquiries, that human achievement may be spared the ravages of time, and that everything great and astounding, and all the glory of those exploits which served to display Greeks and barbarians alike to such effect, be kept alive – and additionally, and most importantly, to give the reason they went to war.

Glorious exploits, of course, were exactly what I was after – and so on I read, my appetite duly whetted. Soon, though, I began to feel a trifle puzzled. For an author I had thought was meant to be telling me the story of the Persian Wars, Herodotus appeared to have a disconcerting habit of veering off-piste. Only a couple of pages in, he was giving me a strange tale about a king who wanted his bodyguard to have a peek at the queen while she was naked – with predictably fatal consequences. Then came a story about a musician who was captured by pirates, jumped into the sea as he played his lyre, and was promptly rescued by a dolphin. It took many pages more before Herodotus so much as mentioned a Persian king – and even then he was soon off again on a whole new tangent. Egypt, so he chattily observed, 'is a land which boasts an inordinate number of wonders, and possesses more monuments surpassing description than any other in the world. Reason enough, then, to describe it at some length' (2.35). Which Herodotus then proceeded to do. At great length.

Only in Book 5, halfway through *The Histories*, did his central narrative finally come into focus. Herodotus' account of the road to Marathon, and of the famous battles themselves, is more than thrilling enough to meet expectations; but anyone reading him to get the story of the Persian Wars, as I was when I first read him, is liable to find the first four books a surprise. At the time, he reminded me of those comedians whose entire act consists of a single joke of escalating and ever more tantric complexity, taking forever to reach its climax. Even now, when I wish that Herodotus had written many more digressions, I think the comparison a not wholly unreasonable one: there is indeed a sense in which Herodotus is the author of the greatest shaggy-dog story ever written. Back when I first read him, I was less than sensitive to the extraordinarily subtle ordering of themes that gives such underlying unity to his material – but, even then, I could recognize that Herodotus was no leg-puller. He told often fantastical stories, to be sure, but in a spirit of enquiry and openness that struck me as something wholly admirable. 'Now, those who find such things credible must make what they will of the stories told by the Egyptians. My own responsibility, however, as it has been throughout my writing of this entire narrative, is simply to record whatever I may be told by my sources' (2.123).

This seemed – and still seems – to me an estimable approach to the complexities and contradictions of the world. That people from different cultures are likely to have a whole variety of perspectives on the same episode, let alone on how best to order their lives, appeared to Herodotus so significant a truth that he chose to open his work with it. Later in *The Histories*, when he describes how Cambyses, the king of Persia who had conquered Egypt, mocked the religious sensibilities of the Egyptians, he takes for granted that such behaviour was only to be explained by lunacy. 'Everyone believes his own customs to be by far and away the best,' he observes sagely. 'From this, it follows that only a madman would think to jeer at such matters' (3.38). It is a short step from this perspective to an attitude towards 'barbarians' – and towards the Persians in particular – that even on my first reading of *The Histories* I had found arresting. The same imperialists who had conquered Herodotus' own native city of Halicarnassus, and brought bloodshed and fire to mainland Greece, are shown in his narrative to possess striking qualities of nobility and courage. Herodotus notes the premium they set on telling the truth; he admires their hardiness; he freely acknowledges that man for man they are in no way inferior as warriors to the Greeks. Even his portrait of Xerxes, who has come to serve us (in large part thanks to Herodotus himself) as the archetype of the overweening despot, is touched by moments of glory and pathos. Amid all the millions he led against Greece, so Herodotus tells us, there was no one more handsome nor 'better fitted to wield supreme power than Xerxes himself' (7.187). As he watches his army crossing from Asia into Europe, the king feels himself truly blessed – and then he begins to weep. When his uncle asks him the reason for his tears, Xerxes answers that he has been 'musing on how short is human life, and the pity of it pierced me through. All these multitudes here, and yet, in a hundred years' time, not one of them will be alive' (7.46).

That the sentiment expressed by Xerxes owes more to the spirit of tragedy than to anything recognizably Persian in no way diminishes the significance of Herodotus' attempts to see events through eyes other than his own. The truth is that he was both intensely a man of his background, and inexhaustibly curious about the world that lay beyond it. What we get in *The Histories* – as its literal meaning, 'enquiries', suggests – is a heroic attempt to push back the frontiers of knowledge in almost every conceivable sphere. This project, of subjecting the world to *historiê* – 'enquiry' – was one bred of the age. Herodotus lived in an intellectual environment that was heady with a sense of discovery, of an infinitude of wonders waiting to be identified and explained without recourse to the supernatural. Only the Enlightenment, perhaps, can compare. 'I write the truth as I see it – for the tales told by the Greeks are, in my opinion, as laughable as they are plentiful.' So declared Hecataeus, a geographer and genealogist from Miletus. His works have survived only in fragments, but we can be confident that Herodotus, at any rate, knew all about him. As well as featuring in the account of the disastrous Milesian revolt against the Persians, he is the butt of one of the few passages to show Herodotus in a malicious light. When Hecataeus visited Egypt, we are told that the priests dismissed his researches into genealogy – 'a field', Herodotus interpolates with disdainful untruthfulness, 'with which personally I have never bothered' (2.143). The anecdote is telling for two reasons: first, for demonstrating that Herodotus was not the first Greek to extend his enquiries beyond the limits of his own near horizons; and second, for affirming his own sense of what was original and significant about his researches. He wrote *The Histories* in the conviction that they far surpassed anything similar previously attempted. And he was clearly right. In part, this was due to the fact that Herodotus – so far as we can tell – was the first to apply to the study of the past the revolutionary new methods of enquiry that were simultaneously transforming how Greek intellectuals understood the natural world: the beginnings of what we would now call 'science'. The premium that Herodotus set on providing sources for his material is so taken for granted now by historians that it is possible not to recognize just how revolutionary it originally was. In his account of the build-up to the battle of Plataea, he describes what he has been told by a man called Thersander of Orchomenus, who in turn is reporting what he was told at a banquet by a Persian fellow-guest. It is a moment to send a shiver down the spine. Men dead for two and a half thousand years are being given voice. We are witness to the birth-pangs of historical method. History is doubly being made.

Not everything that Herodotus reports, though, can be so readily sourced. If his concern with the means of gathering evidence is something revolutionary, then so too are the sheer scope and range of his interests. No one before him had ever thought to write on such a heroically panoramic scale. Herodotus understood, to a degree that seems to have been exceptional for his time, that he was living in a globalized era. So vast was the empire of the Persians that its king could dream of leaving no lands 'beyond our frontiers for the sun to shine upon' (7.8). It was the world itself, in Herodotus' opinion, that had been at stake in the great war between the Greeks and the Persians. This was the reason why his enquiry, his *historiē*, was of such universal scope. His ambition was an astonishing one: nothing less than to encompass the limits of what could humanly be known. Inevitably, this meant that there were occasions when his ability to determine the truth of information he had come by began to warp and buckle. No one was more aware of this than Herodotus himself. Often, when reporting some wondrous detail, he will hedge it about with qualifications: expressions of uncertainty or open doubt. Reporting the claim of a Phoenician expedition to have circumnavigated Africa (or 'Libya', as he calls it), Herodotus does not conceal his own scepticism. 'One of their claims – which I personally find incredible, although others may not – was that, while sailing round Libya, they had had the sun on their right-hand side' (4.42).

xi

This is precisely the detail, of course, which enables us to know that the Phoenicians were indeed telling the truth and had crossed the Equator. That we have no reports of another naval expedition reaching the Cape of Good Hope until the arrival there in 1488 of the Portuguese serves to remind us at what extremes of knowledge Herodotus was often operating. Unsurprisingly, not all the information he obtained was reliable. What are we to make, for instance, of his report of giant Indian ants, 'midway between dogs and foxes in size' (3.102), who dig up gold, or the griffins 'who stand guard over gold' (4.13) in the mountains beyond Scythia? These are the kind of stories that, while they add hugely to the enjoyment of reading *The Histories*, have resulted in a long tradition of dismissing Herodotus as gullible at best, and at worst a liar. What is astonishing, though, is not that he got his facts about India or the wilds beyond Scythia wrong, but that he had any reports about them at all. Only in the new era of Persian imperialism, which for the first time had brought Herodotus' native city of Halicarnassus and lands fabulously far to the east under the same rule, would he ever have thought to write about either. As it happens, a plausible case has been made for both stories being the result of Chinese whispers – in one case, perhaps, literally so. The giant ants, it has been argued, were in fact a breed of Himalayan marmots, which have been known to expose gold-bearing soil when they dig their holes; the griffins, perhaps, were the weathered skeletons of Protoceratops, a dinosaur whose fossils are to be found scattered everywhere in the Gobi Desert.[1] Or perhaps not. It is as well to admit, as Herodotus himself did on occasion, that we cannot be sure. Sometimes we simply have to acknowledge the limits of our knowledge. *The Histories* serves us as the well-spring of historical wisdom as well as of historical method.

Today, when the entire immensity of the world's learning is available to anyone with an internet connection, it can be harder than ever to think ourselves back into Herodotus' shoes, and a time when the very concept of non-fiction writing was still being developed. Yet that is precisely why, now more than ever, it can be so moving to read him. The process of researching and recording facts on a would-be encyclopaedic scale begins with his history. Anyone who has ever used the internet to check up on a fact stands in a line of descent from him. 'But if I may digress here –' Herodotus says at one point, 'as I have sought opportunities to do from the moment I started this account of my enquiries . . .'

(4.30). This mode of presenting information, which thirty years ago appeared closer in style to *Tristram Shandy* than to any conventional work of history, will nowadays strike most readers as something very familiar. The internet, with its seemingly infinite web of hyperlinks, has provided a whole new metaphor for Herodotus' discursive style of relaying information. When he refers to the capture of Nineveh by the Medes as 'an episode I will recount in a later chapter' (1.106), and then never does so, the frustration for the reader is akin to that of clicking on a broken link. Similarly, the experience of never quite knowing where Herodotus' narrative may lead – to a laugh-out-loud story of a drunk man dancing on a table, perhaps, or to the chilling account of a eunuch's revenge on the man who had him castrated as a child – will be something thoroughly familiar to all who have ever surfed the web. One definition of a classic, wrote Frank Kermode, is that it 'subsists in change, by being patient of interpretation' – and, we might add, patient of translation too. That alone, I hope, is sufficient justification for this new version of *The Histories*. Herodotus, that most ancient of historians, has always had the capacity to renew himself, and to seem fresh to succeeding generations.

I like to think this would not have surprised him. He knew, none better, the sheer scale of what he had embarked upon, and the value of what he had achieved. His ambition, as he declared in the opening sentence of the first work of history ever written, was to ensure that 'human achievement may be spared the ravages of time'. Literally, he spoke of not allowing them to become *exitêla*, a word that could be used in a technical sense to signify the fading of paint from inscriptions or works of art. Today, the colours applied by Herodotus to his portrait of the long-gone world in which he lived remain as fresh and exuberant as ever. The ravages of time have indeed been defied.

Tom Holland

NOTE

1. The marmot theory is to be found in Michel Peissel, *The Ants' Gold: The Discovery of the Greek El Dorado in the Himalayas* (London, 1984). Adrienne Mayor writes about griffins and dinosaurs in *The First Fossil Hunters: Paleontology in Greek and Roman Times* (Princeton, 2000).

Introduction

Herodotus: Historian, Ethnographer, Pluralist, Contemporary[1]

I. THE LIFE

We alas know next to nothing for certain about Herodotus' life as opposed to his work. Biography did not exist as a genre of ancient Greek literature in his fifth-century BC lifetime, and, even if it had, the life of a writer would not have engaged interest in the same way as would those of a politician or general such as his coevals Pericles or Themistocles of Athens. As it was, not even Pericles or Themistocles received biographical treatment in their own day, and indeed the first signs of any kind of properly biographical interest among the ancient Greeks are not detectable until well into the succeeding fourth century BC. It is a fair measure of our general ignorance of Herodotus the man that for such basic details as the names of his parents we are forced to draw upon the 'Herodotus' entry (one of some 30,000 in all) in a tenth-century AD Byzantine dictionary known under the title of *Souda* or 'Fortress'. Any biographical reconstruction therefore necessarily depends on sensible inference from the extant work, which in antiquity attracted the title – not necessarily his own – of *Historiai* ('Enquiries', 'Researches').

Herodotus was almost certainly born and brought up in the Greek city of Halicarnassus, in the region of Caria on the Aegean coast of western Asia Minor (modern Bodrum in Turkey). In most of the surviving medieval manuscripts the opening sentence of the work refers to him in the third person as Herodotus of Halicarnassus. The *Souda* lexicon adds, on unknown authority, that his father was called Lyxes and that he had an uncle called Panyassis; the lexical formation of both those names is Carian. The non-Greek Carians, among whom Halicarnassus was founded by migrants from the Peloponnese somewhere around 1000 BC, are mentioned in the second book of Homer's *Iliad*; but they are pointedly given the epithet 'barbarian-voiced' (*barbarophônoi*, 2.867) to make clear their foreignness. So, if the Byzantine dictionary is right about the names, either Herodotus could have been of mixed Carian–Greek ethnic stock or his family had such close connections with local Carians as to invite the adoption of Carian-style nomenclature.

Exactly when he was born is also unknown, but an educated guess would put his birthdate in the 480s. That would imply that he was born, not in a free and independent Greek city, but in a city that was a tributary subject of the mighty Achaemenid Persian empire. That empire, which at its greatest extent stretched from the Indus valley and Afghanistan to the southern Balkan peninsula and Egypt, had been founded in about 550 BC by Cyrus II 'the Great' (reigned 559–530/29), from a base in southern Iran. Within a decade of its foundation, it had conquered and absorbed the Greek cities of Asia, but just a decade or so before Herodotus' likely birth many of them had risen in a major revolt (499–494), which the Persians had suppressed only with some difficulty. The combination of political subjection to an alien power and close familial commingling with non-Greek people would not have been unhelpful to Herodotus' becoming the sort of acute cross-cultural observer and inclusive historian that he famously would prove to be.

If, as the *Souda* lexicon entry also has it, he found himself exiled in his youth or early adulthood for taking part in a failed attempt to overthrow a local pro-Persian Greek dynast, that too may well have been conducive to the making of the future historian. At any rate, other famous Greek historians, Thucydides and Polybius most notably, found exile a formative experience. But where did he spend his enforced exile? One strong possibility is, at least to begin with, on the nearby Greek offshore island of Samos. Certainly, we could very reasonably infer from his work that he knew Samos intimately. For instance, he records that the local Samian dialect of Ionic Greek differed from that of Chios and Erythrae (1.142), and he is specially well informed on the three surpassing 'wonders' of sixth-century BC engineering that the island boasted: a remarkable kilometre-long water-tunnel bored through a mountain, a massive harbour mole and a great temple of Hera (3.60). He cites by name just three informants in the entire work, and one of these, whom he met in Sparta, as he tells us himself (3.55), had a Samian connection. (The other two personally named informants are the Scythian or Graeco-Scythian Tymnes, 4.76, and the Boeotian Thersander, 9.16.)

The late, uncertifiable evidence on his life includes mention of his receiving a very large sum of money from the Athenians, as a reward for the positive way in which he represented their role in winning the Graeco-Persian Wars (note especially the considered first-person judgement at 7.139). It is in any case likely enough that he would have spent considerable time in Athens, given its role in the fifth century BC as Greek capital of culture, to which all kinds of foreign intellectuals were almost inevitably drawn. It is also quite possible – though again there is no verifiable evidence – that he did indeed recite portions of his *Histories*-in-progress before huge Panhellenic (all- and only-Greek) crowds at one or more celebrations of the quadrennial Olympic Games. The work at any rate gives the strong impression in a number of ways – its strung-together rather than periodic structure, its devotion to story-telling narration and above all its aggressively personal presentation – that it was composed for oral, public recitation, rather than for a private reading audience. In fact all Greek 'literature' for long remained in some sense oral. The two main Greek words for 'to read' meant literally 'to hear' (*akroasthai*) and 'to recognize-again' (*anagignôskein*), the latter implying a process of recognizing visually in writing what had first been received aurally. Literacy rates are of course unknowable in the absence of reliable statistical data, but it is plausibly thought that the proportion of Greeks who were fully literate in both reading and writing will not generally have risen much above ten per cent of any free adult citizen population. Athens, being a democracy in which performing acts of literacy was more regularly required than in other less open polities, may well have achieved a higher rate than was normal in the Greek world.

If we look to the end, Herodotus may have finished his life not in the eastern Aegean of his birth but in southern Italy, in what the Greeks called 'Great Greece'. There is at all events a report that, after being forced to abandon his native Halicarnassus, he at some point became a citizen of the Athenian-led foundation of Thouria (also known as Thourioi, in its Latin form Thurii) in the instep of Italy's heel. This new cosmopolitan city was established in 444/3 on the site of proverbially luxurious Sybaris, which in about 510 had been utterly destroyed by the neighbouring Greek city of Croton. To reflect his change of address and citizenship, a few medieval manuscripts of his work even, as noted, have him refer to himself as Herodotus 'of Thouria' rather than, as the majority do, 'of Halicarnassus'.

2. THE WORK

The subject of Herodotus' work, as he advertises in his ground-breaking first sentence, is his *apodexis* ('revelation', 'display') of his 'enquiries' (*historiai*) into Greek–Barbarian relations, above all relations of outright military conflict, beginning in narrative earnest in the mid-sixth century and continuing down to the year that we call 479 BC. But besides the relatively rare references to pre-550 events, Herodotus also makes some twenty references to post-479 events, the latest of which belongs probably to 430 (7.137). This suggests that it was probably quite soon after that date that the work was somehow made public, which is at least not inconsistent with the date of the earliest likely independent reference to it: the *Acharnians* comedy of Aristophanes of 425 seems to allude parodically to Herodotus' opening discussion of the ultimate causes of the grand East–West conflict. In what form or forms the *Histories* was disseminated, we cannot precisely say. It was, for sure, far too long to have been issued in manuscript copies on papyrus and placed on sale in the Athenian market-square, as we know other, much shorter works were by the end of the fifth century.

What we can say with a degree of certainty, on the other hand, is that the *Histories* was Herodotus' life's work, since there are no other works persuasively attributed to him by any ancient source. We may further plausibly infer that it was composed over a lengthy period, perhaps between about 450 and 430. The circumstance that may well have prompted its termination and 'publication' was the outbreak in 431 of the next major epochal military conflict to engulf the Greek world, the second so-called 'Peloponnesian War'. This, however, was a war not of Greeks (or rather, certain Greeks) against barbarians, but instead one of Greeks against other Greeks, a huge civil war, and not therefore an obvious subject for the kind of celebratory commemoration that Herodotus' project involved. In the event, a very different sort of writer and historian stepped up to take its measure: Thucydides of Athens. He certainly knew Herodotus' work and refers to it dismissively (1.20), but without deigning to name its author, in a typically ancient Greek spirit of agonistic rivalry. Both historians stood in the long shadow cast by Homer, the ultimate Greek literary model for an account of a great war; Herodotus indeed was dubbed 'most Homeric' by the Greek author known as Pseudo-Longinus of a Roman-era work of literary criticism entitled *On the Sublime*. Both historians themselves still cast a long shadow even today (see section 9).

3. TRUTH-TELLING AND EXPLANATION

Herodotus was the historian above all of the Graeco-Persian Wars of 490 and 480–479, from which the Greeks (or rather some Greeks) emerged unexpectedly victorious. However, although one of his stated aims was to celebrate great and wondrous deeds duly so as to prevent their memory from fading, he specified that these were deeds accomplished by both Greeks and non-Greeks, by Greeks and Barbarians, alike. He signally did not succumb to the general wave of Helleno-centric triumphalism that welled up after the unpredictably successful (from a Greek point of view) outcome. Of that triumphalism, the most strikingly obvious and lasting symbol is the Parthenon temple, the construction of which on the Athenian acropolis between 447 and 432 probably coincided more or less exactly with the composition of the *Histories*. That even-handedness is just one of the many glories that increasingly commend Herodotus' historical approach – not only to scholars in the field,[2] but also to historically minded journalists.[3]

Yet Herodotus was more than just a reporter and celebrator of great and memorable events. He was in Cicero's original Latin phrase the *pater historiae*, 'Father of History' (*De legibus*, 'On Laws', 1.5). By Cicero's day (first century BC), History was an established genre or field, and though it meant something rather different for Romans from what it had meant originally for Greeks such as Herodotus and Thucydides (being less analytical and critical, more moralizing and didactic), Cicero's ascription of paternity to Herodotus was a massive compliment. Besides being the first to give an account of a significant past deemed worthy of preservation and study many centuries later, he was also judged to have composed and adorned his version of it in a fitting literary manner.

Modern historians recognize and credit further pioneering achievements. All historiography is dependent ultimately on sources, and Herodotus carefully distinguished between different types of source material on grounds of their intrinsic reliability: first, eyewitness testimony or autopsy (*opsis*, 2.29), then, hearsay evidence (*akoê*, 2.99), finally 'tradition', or in his own phrase *ta legomena*. Indeed, Herodotus explicitly claims his task and duty to be no more (and no less) than to 'state what I am told' (*legein ta legomena*, 7.152), although that elides the fact that he has to a greater or lesser extent shaped the telling of it.

Upon these various sorts of testimony Herodotus exercised his 'reasoning' (*gnômê*, 2.99), more than once referring to the process of reaching judgement in terms of 'weighing up in comparison' (*sumballomenos*, 2.33, 4.87). Rather than accuracy, let alone certainty, Herodotus' more realistic goal was literally 'unerringness' (*atrekêiê*, e.g, 4.152, 7.187).

Finally, modern historians recognize and share their ancient intellectual ancestor's overriding preoccupation with causation: to quote again from the exordium, 'and additionally, and most importantly, to give the reason [*aitiê*]' why the Greeks and barbarians fought one another.

On the whole, Herodotus' standards of verification and certification meet with modern approval, in principle, but there are cases – for instance, the deaths of Great King Cyrus (1.214) and of King Cleomenes of Sparta (6.84) – where his choice of explanation can seem implausible, especially when it is religiously over-determined. One major modern criticism of Herodotus, indeed, is that he can appear too theological, detecting the hand of 'god' or 'the divine' at work where, for example, his immediate successor Thucydides conspicuously did not. For if that view were to be combined with the opinion attributed to Solon (1.32) – 'how jealous the gods are, and how perplexing in their ways' – systematic historical inference and judgement would be exceptionally hard to execute.

Perhaps predictably, in the circumstances, the reception of Herodotus over the centuries has been very mixed. We have already noted Thucydides' competitive scepticism. The seeming tallness of Herodotus' travellers' tales and the depth of his imputed political prejudices also attracted bad notices; Aristotle in his *Poetics*, for example, labelled him the *muthopoios* or 'story-teller', though Herodotus had himself used the word *muthos* only twice (2.23, 45) and on both occasions to mean an unbelievable story. Perhaps the nadir of negative reception is to be found in the usually scholarly Plutarch's rather mean-spirited essay *On the Mean-spiritedness of Herodotus*, but that seems to have been motivated largely by his concern to rehabilitate the reputation of his fellow-Boeotians, which the more broad-minded Herodotus had, it was said, besmirched.[4]

So, besides being praised for allegedly fathering History, Herodotus has had to labour also under the monicker 'Father of Lies', a modern coinage, but the thought behind it can be traced back at least to Petrarch's fourteenth-century *Rerum Memorandarum Libri* (4.26). One recent example of that negative view affects to disbelieve that Herodotus in fact travelled to many (or any) of the far-flung places he claims or implies that he did, or even to relatively accessible Egypt (the subject of a large part of Book 2). But there are good reasons for thinking at least that latter charge to be as false and unjustified as the accusation against Marco Polo that he never travelled to or in China.

4. FATHER OF ETHNOGRAPHY

Herodotus can fairly be hailed also as the Father of Comparative Ethnography, being a generally fair-minded and balanced if at times also rather too credulous ethnographer, both of non-Greek 'others' and, no less remarkably, of his own fellow-Greeks. Herodotus starts off immediately after his Preface with some comparative folklore studies, asking semi-humorously who it was that started the series of Greek–barbarian conflicts which culminated in the Graeco-Persian Wars of 480–479 (1.1–5). Was it the barbarian Easterners, or was it the Greeks? 'Learned' Persian and Phoenician 'authorities' are cited, inconclusively, but Herodotus' tongue, it would appear, is pretty firmly lodged in his cheek. For in his view, women don't just get abducted willy-nilly, so Spartan queen Helen must bear some considerable share of the blame or responsibility for being carried off by the Trojan prince Paris. In any case, if his audience thought Helen was abducted by Paris from Sparta to Troy, as Homer had quite blatantly, unashamedly and unambiguously recounted, well, Herodotus the critical historian is going to make them think again (2.112–16).

Tales of distant antiquity – to which Plato (*Hippias Major* 285d) was to give the collective label of *archaiologia* – were not of course so distant for Herodotus' original readers/auditors, who were fed on a rich diet of Homer. The introduction of such tales by Herodotus right at the start of his work is intended to place the extremely long series of accounts (*logoi*) that follows in a very broad ethnographic context, one that embraces not just the eastern Mediterranean but also a good portion of what we call the Middle East. For apart from his narration and explanation of events and processes, Herodotus describes the ethnicity, customs and beliefs of many 'barbarian' peoples in explicit and elaborate, if not always entirely accurate, detail, beginning with those of the Lydians and Persians in Book 1, going on to dwell in huge detail on those of the Egyptians in Book 2, and in only slightly less detail on those of the various groups of Scythians around the Caspian Sea in Book 4 (to name only his main subjects).

Moreover, Herodotus put his comparative ethnography to keen intellectual use. The *locus classicus* is to be found in Book 3, chapter 38. Here, in what we must assume is an invented dramatic scene, Persian Great King Darius I (reigned 522–486) summons to his presence some Greeks and some Indians who are resident in or at least present at his chief administrative capital city of Susa. He then invites each group to abandon their own traditional funerary customs (cremation in the case of the Greeks, cannibalism for the Indians) and to adopt – for a financial consideration – the customs of the other ethnic group. Both groups rather delightfully express horror at the very thought, the Indians more so even than the Greeks, and declare stoutly that they could not possibly abandon their ancestral customs. At this point, rather than condemning the Indians' funerary cannibalism as morally barbarous, as a typical Greek of his day would surely have done, Herodotus instead passes a benign and universally applicable judgement: that all human groups, not just these two, and including thereby Greeks as well as barbarians, habitually consider their own customs to be not just the best for them, but the best in the whole world, since 'Custom is the King of all'. This is, however, not in itself a relativist position, but rather a pluralist one, since we can be quite sure that Herodotus himself, as a good Greek, did not approve of any form of cannibalism whatsoever, funerary or otherwise.

By contrast, his discourse on Greek ethnicity, customs and beliefs is for the most part implicit. He usually reveals his own views of Greek mores and practices only indirectly, as when, for example, at the beginning of Book 8 he allows his exasperation with the Greeks' tendency to fight against each other, rather than fight shoulder-to-shoulder with their fellow-Greeks against an alien enemy, to show through the surface of his text: 'civil strife among people of the same heritage and race compares as disastrously to a united war effort as does war itself to peace' (8.3).

There is one large and important exception to this general rule of implicit ethnographic indirection in respect of Greeks, namely his treatment of the Spartans. In Book 6, between the description of the Ionian Revolt and the account of the battle of Marathon (490), Herodotus includes a lengthy excursus on the prerogatives of the odd dual kingship of the Spartans (6.51–60). This is followed not long after by a story of the birth of a Spartan king, Demaratus (reigned *c.* 515–490), who was later to play a key role in Herodotus' version of Xerxes' invasion of Greece in Book 7 as an *ex*-king and traitor, since by this time in the narrative he'd been deposed on grounds of his alleged illegitimacy and gone over to the Persian side. To add further spice to the brew, the story of King Demaratus' conception is told teasingly from the point of view of a woman: his anonymous mother (6.63–9).

These two extended passages in Book 6 convey, as forcefully as narrative skill can, two important messages: first, that the Spartans, though Greek, are also in some vital respects 'other' – that is, they depart significantly from otherwise universal Greek norms; and, second, that not the least important way in which they differ from other Greeks is in the role allocated to or assumed by Spartan women, at any rate by royal women. There is a growing consensus among scholars that Herodotus was a master of the art of historiography as embedded narrative. Multiple viewpoints coexist within his narrative, the relations between the different strands shift, and explanations are cumulative rather than competing. Herodotus' account – or rather multiple accounts – of Sparta and Spartans excellently illustrates his narrative mastery.

5. DISSONANCE

The chronological starting-point of the *Histories* in our terms is around 550 BC, when, Herodotus says, the two most powerful mainland Greek cities were Sparta and Athens. But he starts there also because 75 to 100 years constitute the rough upper limit of reliably transmitted human memory, and Herodotus was probably gathering his oral information around 450, about a century or (as he once puts it, 2.142) three generations later. The Spartans allegedly owed their eminence in the first instance to Lycurgus, their famed lawgiver, whom most modern scholars dismiss as a mostly if not wholly mythical figure. Herodotus is thus quite conventional and uncritical in ascribing most of the Spartans' basic political and military institutions to the reforms of Lycurgus, at some unspecified early date (1.65). When he comes to describe the two kings' prerogatives in detail in Book 6, however, he does not mention Lycurgus again, though he does comment sharply on the Spartans' own local tradition about their original settlement of Laconia, saying that in one respect they contradicted all the poets (6.52). From this his audience would have been likely to gain the impression not only that Herodotus was very learned (as was surely his intention) but also that he had gained direct access to local Spartan genealogical and mythical history. In fact, he later tells us himself that he had personally visited Sparta and, as mentioned, names one of his informants there (3.55).

The particular history he wanted to talk with Archias about involved the politico-military expansion of Sparta out of the Greek mainland and into the eastern Aegean around 525 BC. Already by then, so Herodotus has stated earlier (1.68), the Spartans had most of the Peloponnese under their control. This was a prelude to their establishment by 500 of what is conventionally referred to as the Peloponnesian League, the multi-state military alliance that was to be the core of the Greeks' successful resistance to Persia under overall Spartan leadership in 480–479. The League's establishment was presented as a direct consequence of the rash policy of King Cleomenes I in seeking to dominate Athens through military force and the imposition of a quisling tyrant.

Yet Herodotus' account of Cleomenes and his reign is one of the more puzzling, even contradictory, in the whole of the *Histories*. On the one hand, Cleomenes was a great and powerful king, who must have reigned for some thirty years (*c.* 520–490), and at any rate in the late 490s had – for Herodotus (6.61) – the best interests of Hellas at heart. On the other hand, Cleomenes 'did not reign for very long' (5.48), was at least a bit of a madman, only intermittently achieved anything positive in his foreign policy and died horribly by self-mutilation – in entirely just, divinely inflicted retribution (6.84). This was, according to Herodotus, for an act of sacrilege, but here too Herodotus explicitly contradicts the official Spartan version of Cleomenes' end. The explanation of this rather violent narrative dissonance is probably the contradictory nature of his sources – emanating as they did ultimately from the two royal houses that were (as often) at loggerheads with each other. On the one side, there were those who favoured the anti-Persian line taken by Cleomenes, a line that Herodotus himself explicitly approved (6.61); on the other, there were descendants of the 'traitor' king Demaratus (deposed through Cleomenes' machinations and later a favoured courtier of Xerxes), with whom Herodotus could well have conversed in Asia Minor. To this mixture Herodotus brought his own dose of conventional piety through his interpretation of the way Cleomenes allegedly met his end. A similar dissonance may be observed in his treatment of the epoch-making introduction of democracy at Athens (section 7).

6. HERODOTUS THE SCEPTICAL INTELLECTUAL?

There is as yet no scholarly consensus as to whether Herodotus was a cutting-edge intellectual, with perhaps a residual old-fashioned fondness for detecting the hand of god – or rather gods – at work in history (at 8.77, for instance, he seems to express the view that oracles can and do tell only the truth – but that chapter is probably a later addition). Or was he, rather, a conventional religious practitioner and believer (especially in the truth and power of oracles), but one with an unusually enlarged vision and a mind open towards naturalistic or even quasi-scientific explanations of human and natural phenomena? Thus at 7.129 he firmly states his 'scientific' view that the Peneius gorge in Thessaly was due to seismic activity, whether or not one wants to believe that this activity was caused by the Greeks' earthquake-god Poseidon. At any rate, his treatment of the Spartans' religious beliefs and practices is evenhanded. He makes it quite clear that the Spartans were exceptionally religious, and on several occasions – not least, the battles of Marathon and Thermopylae – he reports without comment that the Spartans felt unable to respond immediately or fully to the Persian threats and allied requests for help because they considered they had prior religious obligations to perform. For the Spartans, as he twice puts it (5.63, 9.7), considered the things of the gods more weighty than the things of men. More sceptical or secular modern historians have judged in accordance with their own values and mindset that the Spartans were merely using religion as a self-serving pretext. But Herodotus, in accordance with his usual stated method of reporting what his sources told him (7.152), does not take, or at least does not express, that view.

7. HERODOTEAN JUDGEMENTS

On the other hand, when he comes to choose whether it was Athens or Sparta that contributed the most to saving mainland Greece from total Persian conquest in 480–479, he delivers what he knows will be to many an objectionable judgement, but the one that he considers to be true: namely, that it was the Athenians who – above all by their conduct at the battle of Salamis – were the principal 'saviours of Greece' (7.139). His point was that, had the Greeks lost there, the victorious Persian navy would have sailed on into the Spartans' Peloponnesian backyard and wrapped up the final victory soon enough. Yet that does not mean that Herodotus (unlike some modern historians) slights the critical contribution made by the Spartans to the Persians' decisive defeat – which came on land, in pitched battle, at Plataea in Boeotia in 479. This was, for him, 'the fairest victory of any known to us' (9.64).[5] Even so, the precise mechanics of that crucial victory remain frustratingly obscure. Herodotus was no military historian, to be sure, in any narrowly technical sense.

Likewise, Herodotus' political attitudes are balanced, or perhaps one should say hard to pin down precisely. Pretty clearly, he did not consider absolute, autocratic monarchy – whether in the form of hereditary kingship or of usurped tyranny, whether Greek or non-Greek – to be admirable in itself. It is no coincidence that so many of these sole rulers come to a bad end. He is scathing particularly towards the Egyptians in this regard, since they seemed to him unable 'to live without a king' (2.147). But what sort of a 'republican' was he? Or, to ask that more sharply, to what degree and in what sense was he a democrat?

Though not especially interested in the finer points of constitutional government or revolutionary change, he does bring out forcefully the huge significance of Athens' turn in 508/7 to what the Greeks understood as democracy ('people-power', literally) through the reforms attributed to Cleisthenes. Indeed, he states unequivocally – and controversially – that it was Cleisthenes the Alcmaeonid aristocrat who 'instituted democracy' at Athens (6.131). And when shortly after the now-democratic Athenians managed to inflict twin defeats on their neighbours in Euboea and Boeotia, he comments rather extravagantly that these victories made 'manifest how important it is for everyone in a city to have an equal voice [*isêgoriê*], not just on one level but on all' (5.78). Yet the manner in which Cleisthenes is said to have achieved his reform is bathed in a sharply opportunistic light (5.66). Moreover, when Herodotus related the subsequent decision by the democratic Athenians to support a major revolt of Asiatic Greeks against Persia in 500, he opines (5.97) that this seemed to suggest it was much easier to fool thirty thousand people than a single man (the individual in question being the above-mentioned Spartan king Cleomenes, who, allegedly with the indispensable aid of his shrewd eight- or nine-year-old daughter Gorgo, had rejected outright the Ionian Greeks' request for help, 5.51).

Herodotus himself was probably in some sense a democrat; it seems he did after all consent in the 440s to join the new foundation of Thouria in south Italy, the constitution of which (as drafted by the leading intellectual Protagoras of Abdera) was democratic. But democracy at Athens had moved on in key respects between 508/7 and the 440s, especially through the reforms of Ephialtes and Pericles in 462/1, and it did so even more thereafter, most notably in the increased power of the people's jury-courts. So, while Herodotus was indeed a democrat, he was probably not one of the 'extreme' variety, that is, one favouring the more or less unfettered rule of the (poor) masses over the social, economic and educational elite.

The Spartan who led the Greeks to victory at Plataea in 479, regent Pausanias, was hugely controversial both in Sparta and outside, and both in his own lifetime and after his death. Like Cleomenes before him, he came to an unhappy end – which for Herodotus, like many Greeks, would have been a clear sign that he was fundamentally a bad or at least an ill-fated person (1.32). But unlike Cleomenes, Pausanias predominantly earns plaudits from Herodotus – so key was his role in securing Greek freedom. After victory has been won at Plataea, the historian tellingly uses Pausanias twice as an exemplar of the best Spartan, and therefore by extension Greek, values. In the first instance, a hot-headed Greek from the island-state of Aegina (which in 490 had submitted to Persian suzerainty, but in 480–479 remained true to and fought valiantly in the anti-Persian Greek cause) urges Pausanias to mutilate the corpse of Persian commander Mardonius, in revenge for the mutilation of the corpse of Leonidas by the Persians at Thermopylae the previous year. Pausanias sharply rebukes the Aeginetan and tells him that such barbarity is not the Greek way. Later, when Pausanias is shown the rampant luxuriousness of Mardonius' tent and the vast amounts of lavish food prepared for him and his bloated entourage, he quietly orders his (unfree but Greek) helot attendants to prepare a Laconian – indeed, as we say, 'spartan' – meal in order to demonstrate the superior virtue of Greek self-restraint (9.82).

With that advocacy of human restraint Herodotus coupled a salutary warning that over and above the seemingly limitless range of human choices there rises a superhuman constraint, the inexorable power of fate. This warning Herodotus characteristically places in the mouth of one wise, or at least wised-up, barbarian, ex-king Croesus of Lydia, addressing another, Cyrus, now his master. For, according to his Croesus (1.207):

> The first lesson you should acknowledge is that there is a cycle to human affairs, one that as it turns never permits the same people forever to enjoy good fortune.

That aphorism looks even further forward to another, as far forward as is possible in this life on earth. This time the aphorism is attributed to an exceptionally wise Greek, who once allegedly played the role of adviser to that same barbarian Croesus, then still in his pomp. Herodotus' Solon of Athens gives his Croesus the oriental plutocrat the snappy advice to 'always look to the end', the end in the sense both of terminus and of goal. For, Solon argues (1.32), it is only in light of that end that it will be finally known whether one has lived well. Living well, the condition of *eudaimonia*, was the ultimate goal of the greatest exemplars of ancient Greek culture, such as Aristotle (384–322), who was perhaps the master of them all and himself most happily named (*ariston telos* means 'best end').

Such earthly happiness was, however, constantly placed in jeopardy in the ancient Greek world, above all by the aggressive intensity of internal and interstate politics. It was thus Herodotus' considered view that *stasis emphulios* – civil war within a single people – is as much worse than united war against a foreign enemy as war is worse than peace (8.3). About war as such, indeed, he was at least ambivalent, for in peace sons bury their fathers, whereas in war fathers bury their sons, a reversal of the natural order (1.87). But we should also emphasize, at least as much as his anti-war mindset, his realism. Herodotus was all too well aware that the Hellenic 'tribe' was endemically prone precisely to *stasis emphulios*. It was with a view to pre-empting or at least diminishing that unhappy propensity that he composed a ringing declaration of support for Hellenism and placed it in the mouth of the Athenians, at a critical juncture of the Persian Wars, during the winter of 480/79 (8.144):

> there is the fact that we are all of us Greeks, of one blood and one tongue, united by the temples that we have raised to the gods, and by the way in which we offer them sacrifice, and by the customs that we have in common.

Hellenism, his Athenians thus declare, is a compound of common blood, language and customs – not, it must be noted, a compound including a common political system, for politics has served more often to divide than to unite the Greeks; rather, it was a common culture, one that united not only Athenians with Spartans but also both with Macedonians and all the many other far-flung and heterogeneous Greeks. Herodotus, an eastern Greek in origin who became a western one, and who probably travelled the length and the breadth of the Hellenic world and huge distances outside it too, knew whereof he spoke.

In short, as Edward Gibbon once perceptively observed, Herodotus 'sometimes writes for children, and sometimes for philosophers';[6] that is, he tells rattling good yarns and yet also has something valuable to say to enlightened people of the world who believe that it is both desirable and possible to learn from history.

8. FAMOUS LAST WORDS

The message of moderation, self-restraint or, in Apollo of Delphi's terms, 'nothing to excess', is also exactly the one with which Herodotus chooses to end his whole work, though here it is the founder of the

Persian empire, a pensive and reflective Cyrus the Great, who is credited with delivering it, to his own Persians. He advises them that tough lands produce tough peoples, so, if they wish to retain the empire he has enabled them so spectacularly to gain, they must not even think about removing themselves to some softer, enervating environment. Herodotus was thus both attributing the Greeks' victory over the Persians significantly to their tougher environment (cf. 7.102, 8.111), and at the same time issuing a warning about the difficulty of maintaining imperial power, since, tempting as they are, 'Soft lands are prone to breed soft men', and soft men are likely to have to exchange dominion over others for slavery to them (9.122).

9. LEGACY: HERODOTUS OR THUCYDIDES?

Ever since their lives and works overlapped in the fifth century BC, the twin progenitors of Western historiography, Herodotus (*c.* 484–*c.* 425) and Thucydides (*c.* 460–*c.* 400), have been judged in the light of – and more usually in opposition against – each other. There is even a conjoined, back-to-back marble herm from the Roman period, now in the Naples Museum, that seems physically to embody this contrapuntal conjuncture. It offers idealized depictions of the two literally iconic greats, duly labelled; but they face, fixedly and for ever, in opposite directions.[7] For many years, indeed centuries, the balance of informed opinion from Francesco Guicciardini (1483–1540) to Leopold von Ranke (1795–1886) ran firmly in favour of Thucydides. He was the historian's historian: an acute, disabused, accurate observer, analyst and reporter of the world as it was and is, the world of high politics above all. Over the past twenty years or so, however, as regards both their scholarly and their more general reception, the balance has tilted quite sharply away from Thucydides and towards Herodotus.

For two main reasons, I would suggest: one internal to the practice of historiography, the other a direct reflection of and response to the way the world itself has changed since around 1990, since all history – or rather historiography, the writing of history – is and must be in some way and to some extent contemporary history. First, within the last twenty years the profession of History has experienced a kind of internal crisis and regrouping of forces. Subjected to a barrage from the 'post-modernists', who claimed in essence that there is no such thing as historical objectivity and truth, that History is *what* any historian cares to make of it, and *how* any historian cares to represent it, more traditional historians have fought back by calling attention to the historian's absolute dependence on sources and commitment in principle to telling it how it actually was, within the limits set by the available, reliable source-material.[8] The outcome of that often acrimonious exchange has been a greater liberalization of historiographical norms, and a wider acceptance that even the strictest adherence to conventional protocols regarding sources is compatible with some inevitable subjectivity of perception and some individual freedom in retelling any story about any significant past. Hence, the extremely individualist and pioneering historiographical mode of Herodotus – who claims with apparent modesty only to tell what is told, though he of course tells it the way he sees fit, and whose range of subject-matter is generously comprehensive – is now found more congenial than Thucydides' severe, and somewhat self-deluding, claim (1.20–22) to tell objectively and accurately only the actual facts of the past, and moreover those of a very narrowly defined past consisting of significant political, diplomatic and military events and processes.

Second, and directly connected to the first, the ending in around 1990 of the old East–West, Communist v. 'Free World', Cold War has lessened Thucydides' seemingly paradigmatic authority as an analyst of power relations in a bipolar world divided resolutely along ideological lines. Thucydides is still acknowledged as one of the most powerful such analysts there has ever been, a truly philosophical historian in a Gibbonian sense; but there is now seen to be more scope and greater need for historians of the stamp of Herodotus, who go well beyond political, diplomatic and military history to embrace the history of society, culture, gender, religion and so forth. Herodotus may be more fanciful, less factually reliable and certainly less politically motivated than Thucydides, but these are not now seen necessarily as irremediable defects.

Besides, it is at least arguable, as I have tried briefly to suggest above, that Herodotus was in his own distinctive way a 'philosophical' historian no less than Thucydides. At any rate, whatever Herodotus may or may not have been, or done, his work still lives. Technically, he is of course to be numbered among Bernard Knox's 'oldest dead white

European males', but Knox's correct point in ironically adopting and adapting that semi-humorous label was to emphasize that the influence of such cultural ancestors as these is far from dead, or even moribund, today.[9] In their first rank, more highly regarded now than he has been for many generations, stands the engaged and limitlessly engaging Herodotus of Halicarnassus, *our* contemporary, whose presence has been wonderfully renewed and reinvigorated in this powerfully vibrant new translation.[10]

NOTES

Details of all works cited here are found in the Further Reading.

1. This Introduction is ultimately and now rather remotely based, in part, on a talk I delivered at the Hellenic Embassy, Washington, DC, on 23 September 2009, thanks to the kind invitation of the Society for the Preservation of the Greek Heritage, under its President, Mrs Anna Lea; Dr Brook Manville generously introduced me and my talk. But Stuart Proffitt deserves the major share of the credit for any improvements I have been able to make.

2. See most recently Hamel 2012.

3. Kapuściński 2007; Marozzi 2008; Mendelsohn 2012 (also a Classical scholar).

4. Plutarch, *On the Meanspiritedness of Herodotus* (*c.* 100 AD), ed. A. Bowen as *The Malice of Herodotus* (Warminster, 1992): rev. J. Marincola, *Ploutarchos* 10.2 (May 1994).

5. See Shepherd 2012; Cartledge 2013. The victorious land- and sea-battle of Mycale on the Asiatic coast that followed Plataea under Athenian leadership was more of a mopping-up operation.

6. Edward Gibbon, *The History of the Decline and Fall of the Roman Empire* (London, 1776–1788), ch. XXIV, note 52, in the admirable edition of David Womersley.

7. There is a plaster cast in the Cambridge Classics Faculty's Museum of Classical Archaeology: http://www.classics.cam.ac.uk:8080/collections/casts/double-herm-thucydides-and-herodotus.

8. Evans 2001.

9. Knox 1993.

10. See further Cartledge 1990, 2009a.

Note on Measurements and Currency

LENGTH AND DISTANCE

finger: *c.* 1.9 cm (a finger's breadth, not the length of a finger)

palm: 4 fingers, *c.* 7.6 cm

hand: 5 fingers, *c.* 9.5 cm

foot: 16 fingers, *c.* 32 cm (this is the Olympic foot, supposedly based on the length of Heracles' foot; the Attic foot was *c.* 30 cm)

pygon: 20 fingers, *c.* 38 cm

cubit: 24 fingers, *c.* 46 cm

royal cubit: 27 fingers, *c.* 52 cm

fathom: 6 feet, *c.* 1.9 m

plethron: 100 feet, *c.* 30 m

stade: 600 feet, *c.* 192 m

parasang: (Persian) equivalent to 30 stades, *c.* 5.5 km

schoenus: (Egyptian) variously equivalent to 30, 60 or 120 stades in Egypt; outside Egypt it was most commonly equivalent to 30 stades

VOLUME

cotyle: varies between 210 and 330 ml

choenix: 4 *cotylae*; in Athens, it measured a single man's daily ration of grain

medimnus: 48 *choenixes*

amphora: (of liquid) equivalent to 144 *cotylae*

Laconian quart: (of liquid) estimated at anything between 9 and 25 litres

CURRENCY

drachma: a silver coin roughly equivalent to the daily wage for a skilled worker

stater: a silver coin worth variously 2 or 4 drachmas

Daric stater: a Persian gold coin, worth roughly ten times its silver equivalent

mina: (originally a Near Eastern unit of weight) equivalent in Greece to 100 drachmas

talent: a bar of silver, the value of which depended on the locality issuing it; it also served as a measurement of mass

The Euboïc talent was worth 6,000 drachmas and weighed 26 kg; its Babylonian equivalent weighed in at 30 kg. Herodotus himself (3.89) gives an exchange rate for the Euboic and Babylonian talents of 60:70.

Summary of Contents of The Histories

This overview is after Hamel 2012: 5–6. The Book divisions are not those of Herodotus himself, but ultimately of scholars working in post-Classical Alexandria in Egypt in the third century BC. The Library founded there under either King Ptolemy II (ruled 285–246) or his father Ptolemy I (ruled 305–285) aimed to produce and conserve master copies on papyrus rolls of all then known Greek texts, but much could have happened to H.'s text between *c*. 420 and *c*. 280. The Alexandria editors, however, will have been far better placed than any of their modern successors to decide what H. was most likely to have originally written, even if reading that or consulting it in its papyrus roll form was not at all straightforward. The chapter divisions are much more recent than the third-century BC copy text or texts. Indeed, the original texts did not even distinguish sentences nor did they use diacritical marks such as accents.

Book One

Preface

Book Two

Book Three

Translator's Note on the Text

The edition of Herodotus used for this translation is Charles Hude's *Herodoti Historiae* (Oxford, 1927).

[ ] indicates portions of text that vary from manuscript to manuscript, or are believed to be possible post-Herodotean interpolations, and [. . .] indicates portions of the text that have been lost.

The Histories

BOOK ONE

Herodotus, from Halicarnassus,[1] here displays his enquiries,[2] that human achievement may be spared the ravages of time, and that everything great and astounding, and all the glory of those exploits which served to display Greeks and barbarians[3] alike to such effect, be kept alive – and additionally, and most importantly, to give the reason[4] they went to war.

[1] Well-informed Persian commentators pin the blame for the clash on the Phoenicians. These were a people who originally came from the Red Sea, as we term it, to this sea of ours;[5] and no sooner had they settled in the country which remains their homeland up to the present day than they began investing heavily in the long-distance shipping business, exporting goods from Egypt and Assyria to a wide variety of markets. Pre-eminent among these was Argos,[6] the city which at that time was the leading power, by any reckoning you care to mention, in the land which is now called Greece. There the Phoenicians arrived, in Argos, and duly set out their wares. Five or six days later, with almost everything sold, a large group of women came down to the shore – and among them was the daughter of the king. Inachos, he was called, and his child's name was Io: on that much, at any rate, both the Greek and the Persian sources are agreed. These women were standing around the ship's stern, haggling over the various items that had particularly caught their fancy, when the Phoenicians, who had already tipped the nod to one another, made a sudden rush at them. Most of the women got away, but a few were seized – and one of them was Io. Into the hold the captives were bundled, up came the anchor and off sailed the ship for Egypt.

[2] This, although the Greeks tell a different version of the story, is

3

the Persians' account of how Io came to end up in Egypt – the first of many crimes. Next, they say, came the reprisal: some Greeks docked at the Phoenician city of Tyre, and abducted the king's daughter, Europa.[7] It is likely – although the Persians themselves are not certain as to their identity – that these pirates were Cretan. So far, they say, so even; but then the Greeks committed a second outrage. Off they sailed in a long-ship to Aea in Colchis, to the Phasis river, where they had no sooner completed the mission that had originally brought them there than they were kidnapping the king's daughter, Medea. The king of Colchis sent a herald to Greece to demand his daughter back, along with restitution for her abduction; but the Greeks refused, answering that since no reparations had ever been received from the kidnappers of Io, the Argive princess, they certainly had no intention of handing over any to the Colchians.

[3] A generation now passed, we are told – and then Priam's son, Paris, who had picked up on the story, decided that he might as well steal a Greek wife for himself, since the Greeks, who had never paid reparations to anyone, would hardly be in any position to demand satisfaction from him. The result was the rape of Helen.[8] The Greeks' initial response was to send out the usual messengers, insisting on her return, together with compensation for her kidnapping. No sooner had they made these demands, however, than they were met with the inevit-able riposte: had not Medea likewise been abducted? How could the Greeks possibly expect compensation from others, they were asked, when they had refused point-blank to pay any themselves, and would not even give back Medea, no matter how often the demand was made?

[4] There followed next a massive escalation of what until then had essentially been nothing more serious than a bout of competitive princess-rustling – and the fault was all the Greeks'. Or so the Persians claim, at any rate – for they point out that long before they ever thought of invading Europe, it was the Greeks who invaded Asia. Granted, the Persians acknowledge, stealing women is never acceptable behaviour; but really, they ask, what is the point, once a woman has been stolen, in kicking up a great fuss about it, and pursuing some ridiculous vendetta, when every sensible man knows that the best policy is to affect an utter lack of concern? It is clear enough, after all, that women are never abducted unless they are open to the idea of it in the first place. So it was, the Persians claim, that people in Asia remained pretty much unperturbed by the theft of their women – but the Greeks, simply to get

back the wife of a single Spartan, assembled a huge task-force, invaded Asia and annihilated the empire of Priam. Ever since then, the Persians have viewed the Greeks as a people inveterately hostile to them. Asia and all the various strange-speaking peoples who inhabit it, they think of as belonging to them, but Europe and the Greeks as lying beyond their sphere of influence.

[5] This, then, is the version of events promoted by the Persians,[9] who trace the origin of their hostility towards the Greeks all the way back to the sack of Troy. Regarding Io, however, the Phoenicians do tell a rather different story. Far from bringing her to Egypt by force, they say, there was no need, for she had been sleeping with the ship's captain – and when she found out that she was pregnant, so mortified was she at the thought of having to face her parents that she opted to sail off with the Phoenicians rather than suffer the shame of exposure. So then – these are the stories as told by the Persians and Phoenicians. Far be it from me to say whether they are accurate or not; but what I will do is to name the man who, I myself am convinced, was the first to harm Greek interests, and then, having identified him, carry on with the rest of my account.[10] Human foundations both great and insignificant will need to be discussed – for most of those that were great once have since slumped into decline, and those that used to be insignificant have risen, within my own lifetime, to rank as mighty powers.[11] I will pay equal attention to both, for humans and prosperity never endure side by side for long.[12]

[6] Croesus was a Lydian by birth, the son of Alyattes. He was the ruler of the various peoples who live west of the Halys, a river which flows pretty much in the opposite direction to the north wind, from the south, where it divides Cappadocian Syria from Paphlagonia, all the way to its mouth at the Euxine Sea.[13] This Croesus was the first foreigner on record to establish close relations with the Greeks, forcing some of them to pay him tribute, and offering to others the hand of friendship. Specifically, it was the Ionians, the Aeolians and the Dorians of Asia who were forced to pay him tribute, and the Lacedaemonians[14] who ended up as his friends. Prior to Croesus' reign, all the Greeks had been free.[15] It is true that the Cimmerian invasion of Ionia did take place earlier – but that was only a raid and not a full-blown conquest.

[7] Originally, the Lydian empire had been ruled by the bloodline of Heracles; but then it passed into the hands of Croesus' family, a dynasty

named the Mermnads.[16] This is the story of how it happened. The king of Sardis who is known by the Greeks as Myrsilus was in fact named Candaules, and he was descended from Alcaeus, the son of Heracles. Alcaeus had a son named Belus; his son in turn was Ninus; and Ninus' son was Agron, who was the first of Heracles' line to rule as king of Sardis – just as Candaules, Myrsus' son, was the last. Prior to Agron, the region had been ruled by the descendants of Atys' son, the eponymous Lydus: hence the use of 'Lydians' to describe the people who had originally been known as 'Maeonians'. It was thanks to an oracle that the reins of power ended up being entrusted to the Heraclids, kings who could trace their pedigree back to Heracles himself and to a slave girl owned by Iardanus; and for the next 505 years, twenty-two generations in all, son succeeded father, until at length Candaules, the son of Myrsus, ascended the throne.

[8] Now, it so happened that this Candaules had the most all-consuming obsession with his own wife – so all-consuming, in fact, that he actually believed her to be by far the most beautiful woman in the world.[17] It happened as well that among his bodyguards there was one man, Gyges, Dascylus' son, for whom the king had a particularly soft spot, and whose ear he was endlessly bending, sometimes about weighty affairs of state, and sometimes, to a quite obsessive degree, about the desirability of his wife. In no time at all, indeed, Candaules was being led into making Gyges a fateful – and fatal – proposition. 'I can see that you still need convincing,' he said, 'no matter how much I keep harping on about my wife's stunning looks. Fine – since I suppose it is always easier to trust the evidence of one's own eyes, rather than just believing what one is told – here is what I want you to do: set things up so that you get the chance to see her naked.' 'Master,' cried out Gyges in horror, 'what a monstrous suggestion! Ogle my mistress nude? What – when a woman has only to remove her clothes to shed her sense of self-respect as well? There are certain time-honoured principles that everyone needs to heed – and one of them is this, that a man should always look to his own. I certainly need no convincing that your wife is beautiful beyond compare. But please, I beg you – do not ask me to take this illicit action!'

[9] Yet even as Gyges dug in his heels, terrified of the possible consequences if he did not, the king replied by telling him to show some backbone. 'There is no need to be scared of me, Gyges, or of my wife. I can assure you, I am not doing this to entrap you, and as regards my

wife – well – no harm will come to you from her, I promise. I have a plan, you see – one that will guarantee she never even realizes that you have been spying on her. I am going to station you behind the open door of our bedroom – and then, when I come to bed, my wife will come in close behind me. Right beside the entrance there is a chair – and as my wife starts removing her clothes, garment by garment, and laying them down on it, so will you have the perfect opportunity to look her over in detail. Then, when she crosses from the chair to our bed, with her back still to you, you can slip out through the door – making sure, of course, not to let her spot you.'

[10] Realizing that he was cornered, Gyges gave in. When Candaules judged that he could reasonably retire for the night, he led Gyges to his bedroom – where, sure enough, they were joined a few moments later by Candaules' wife. Gyges watched her come in and disrobe. Then, as she turned her back directly on him, and headed over to the bed, he slipped out from his hiding place. But the woman caught a glimpse of him as he was leaving. She had no illusions about what her husband had been up to – but far from betraying her sense of outrage by screaming, she gave no sign that she had noticed anything untoward. She was already set on making Candaules pay: for among the Lydians, as among most other barbarians, it is such a taboo to be seen naked[18] that even a man considers it a humiliation.

[11] Anyhow, as I mentioned, she held her tongue and gave nothing away – but no sooner had morning come than she put her most trusted house-slaves on stand-by, and sent for Gyges. Since he had long been in the habit of dancing attendance on the queen and her demands, and since it had never crossed his mind that she might have rumbled what had happened, he naturally answered the summons; and the moment he turned up, she came straight to the point. 'Gyges,' she said, 'you have two courses open to you, and which one you opt for is entirely up to you. Either you can kill Candaules, marry me and become the king of Lydia – or else you can be struck down on the spot by this, my dagger, so that I can at least be sure that never again will you be sweet-talked by Candaules into gazing at what is not yours to gaze upon. One of two people must die: either the man whose idea this whole business was, or else the man who saw me naked, in defiance of all propriety.' So astonished was Gyges by this speech that it took him a while to find his tongue; and when he did so at last, he begged the queen not to force him

into making such an impossible choice. She would not be shifted, though, and so Gyges recognized that he really did have only the two options, either to kill his master, or else to be killed in turn. He chose to save himself. But next he had a question. 'Now that you have twisted my arm, and made me swear to kill my master – something I really do not wish to do, I can assure you – answer me this: how do we actually lay our hands on him?' 'In the very room where he put me on display naked,' came the queen's answer, 'that is where you will attack him – and you will do it while he is asleep.'[19]

[12] So the plot was hatched, for Gyges, who knew himself cornered, with no prospect of escape, had realized that either he or Candaules would have to die. At nightfall, Gyges followed the woman into the bed-chamber. She handed him a short sword, then hid him behind the same door as before. Shortly afterwards, as Candaules lay asleep, he crept out and struck. Queen and kingdom, both now belonged to Gyges – that very same Gyges who is commemorated in a poem of iambic trimeters by his contemporary, Archilochus of Paros.[20]

[13] That his hold on power then grew even stronger was due to the oracle at Delphi.[21] The wretchedness of Candaules' fate had not failed to move the Lydians to pity – and indeed, such was the level of outrage that many began dusting down their arms. Gyges' faction, however, succeeded in patching up terms with the other Lydians: the agreement being that if the oracle confirmed Gyges' right to the rule of Lydia he would continue as king, but if not, then the Heraclids would be restored to power. The oracle gave its approval to Gyges – who duly remained on the throne. Nevertheless, the priestess did offer this qualification: that after five generations, the Heraclids would be avenged upon Gyges. But to this prediction, neither the Lydians nor their kings paid the slight-est attention – or, at least, not until it came true.[22]

[14] So that is the story of how the Mermnads wrested power from the dynasty of Heracles. Gyges, now that he was king, showed himself far from ungrateful to Delphi. For of the many silver offerings which currently adorn the oracle, by far the greatest proportion were dedi-cated by him – and that is not even touching on the various golden treasures which he also presented to Delphi, and of which the most memorable are six great bowls. These weigh 30 talents and stand in the Corinthian treasure house (although, properly speaking, it is not the treasure house of the Corinthian people as a whole, but only of Cyp-

selus, Eëtion's son). This Gyges was the first barbarian on record[23] to have presented votive offerings to Delphi, with the single prior exception of the Phrygian king, Midas, Gordias' son. For Midas too made a dedication which is well worth seeking out: the very throne on which he sat in state, and from which he delivered justice, can be found stationed next to Gyges' bowls. The Delphians call the gold and silver presented by Gyges 'The Gygian Treasure', in commemoration of the man who gave them.

[15] Now, once he had seized power, he adopted the time-honoured policy of attacking Miletus and Smyrna, and actually succeeded in capturing the city of Colophon.[24] These, however, were the limits of what he achieved during the course of his thirty-eight-year rule – and so, since there is nothing else to add to the details of his reign, let us move on to another king. And specifically to Ardys, Gyges' son and heir. This king captured Priene[25] as well as invading Miletus, and it was during his time as the master of Sardis[26] that the city was captured by the Cimmerians, a people who had been driven into exile from their own homeland by nomads called the Scythians. Only the acropolis of Sardis succeeded in holding out.

[16] Ardys ruled for forty-nine years in all, and was followed on the throne by his son, Sadyattes, who ruled for twelve. He was succeeded in turn by his own son, Alyattes. This king went to war against the Medes under Cyaxares, the grandson of Deioces; he drove the Cimmerians out of Asia; and he captured Smyrna, a city which had originally been founded by settlers from Colophon.[27] He also attacked Clazomenae – but there, rather than succeeding in his war aims, he was given a bloody nose. There were other accomplishments too that he achieved as king, and which merit rehearsing.

[17] The war against the Milesians, which he had inherited from his father, rumbled on.[28] Leading his troops against Miletus, and putting the city under siege, Alyattes' strategy was to launch his invasion just as the crops were at their ripest. He would march in to the accompaniment of pipes and harps, and flutes both high-pitched and low. Then, once he was on Milesian soil, he and his men would make a point of not demolishing any houses they might come across out in the countryside, nor of setting them on fire, nor even of breaking into them, but instead, across the whole span of their enemy's territory, of letting them stand: for it was the crops and the fruit trees that were Alyattes' targets. The harvest

would go up in smoke, and the invaders would then tramp back home. After all, with the Milesians the masters of the sea, what earthly point would there have been in putting their city under siege?[29] As for the reason why the Lydian king spared their houses – well, it was to ensure that the Milesians would have somewhere to live when the time came for them to sow and work the land, and that he, thanks to all their toil, would have something to destroy when he launched his invasions.

[18] For eleven years, then, this was the way that the war was fought – a period which witnessed two serious Milesian reverses, one a battle fought on their own soil, at Limeneium, and the other on the plain of the River Maeander. For six of those eleven years, it was Sadyattes, the son of Ardys (who was still king of Lydia at the time, and had originally begun the war), who led the campaigns against Miletus, but for the remaining five it was Alyattes, Sadyattes' son, who conducted operations: he had inherited the conflict from his father, as I explained earlier, and really threw himself into its prosecution. As for the other Ionians, they signally failed to come to the support of the Milesians – all, that is, except the Chians,[30] who felt duty bound to help shoulder the burden of the war effort. (This was because the Milesians had previously lent them support in their own war against the Erythraeans.[31])

[19] Twelve years into the war and it so happened that a cornfield was being put to the torch by the invaders. As the crops blazed, sparks were borne on a violent gust of wind towards a temple of Athena. The temple, which stood at a place called Assessus, caught fire and burnt down. At the time, no one thought much of this – but in due course, when back in Sardis with the army, Alyattes fell ill. Time passed and still he remained confined to his sick-bed. At last – perhaps on the advice of others, perhaps on his own initiative – he sent messengers to the oracle at Delphi, to ask Apollo for his diagnosis. When the messengers arrived at Delphi, however, the priestess refused to see them, and warned that they would only be granted a consultation once the temple to Athena had been rebuilt – the same one which had stood outside Miletus at Assessus, and which the Lydians had burned to the ground.[32]

[20] Now I know for a fact that this is what happened, because I heard it directly from the Delphians themselves.[33] The Milesians elaborate further: they say that Periander, the son of Cypselus, and a man who was bound by the most sacred ties of friendship[34] to Thrasybulus (who was the tyrant of Miletus at the time), happened to learn the details of

what the oracle had revealed to Alyattes, and promptly sent a messenger to his friend, letting him in on the secret. Intelligence, after all, is always the key to forward planning.

[21] That, at any rate, is what the Milesians claim. Alyattes, briefed on the news from Delphi, immediately sent a herald to Miletus with the aim of securing a truce with Thrasybulus and the Milesians – but only for so long as it took the temple to be restored. The emissary duly set off for Miletus – where Thrasybulus, armed with reliable inside information, and with a shrewd idea as to Alyattes' likeliest course of action, had come up with a plan of his own. First, he ordered the city's storehouses, from his own to the meanest larder, to be emptied, and all the food to be brought into the market-square; next, he told the Milesians to wait on his signal, and then, when it was given, to crack open the wine and start partying.

[22] There was method behind the seeming madness of these actions and orders, for Thrasybulus' object was to ensure that the herald from Sardis would report back to Alyattes about all the towering stockpiles of food he had seen, and the population dancing in the streets. Sure enough, it all came off as planned. The herald witnessed everything; and once he had delivered the Lydian king's message to Thrasybulus and returned to Sardis, the consequence was indeed, so my sources report, the end of the war. No other explanation will possibly do.[35] Alyattes had been confident that Miletus was in the grip of a severe famine, and that her population had been ground down to an extreme of suffering – but now here was the herald back from Miletus reporting that the actual state of affairs in the city was the very reverse of his assumptions. In due course, by terms of the treaty, each agreed to be the friend and ally of the other; additionally, Alyattes built two temples to Athena at Assessus, rather than just the one, and found himself restored to full health.[36] And that is the story of his war with Thrasybulus and the Milesians.

[23] Periander, the son of Cypselus, and the man who had originally told Thrasybulus about the oracle, was the tyrant of Corinth. It was during his lifetime, so the Corinthians say (and the Lesbians back them up), that something truly astounding happened: Arion of Methymna, the leading musician of his day, a man who could sing and play the cithara with equal proficiency, and who was such a trend-setter that he was, so far as we know, the first to compose a dithyramb,[37] to name it

as such and to have it sung in public, was carried to Taenarum[38] by a dolphin.

[24] Now, although Arion spent the greater part of his career at Periander's court, and produced his dithyramb in Corinth, he had nevertheless always wanted to visit Italy and Sicily. He raked in an absolute fortune touring there, then looked to return to Corinth. For the journey back from Tarentum, he opted to take a ship manned by Corinthians – a reflection of the trust that he had always placed in the people of Corinth. No sooner were they out at sea, however, than the sailors hatched a plot to throw him overboard and take his money. When Arion discovered this, he fell down on his knees before them, offering them all his wealth if they would only spare his life. But his pleas fell on deaf ears. Instead, the sailors told him that he had only two options: either he could kill himself, if he wanted to be buried on dry land, or else he should hurry up and walk the plank. A desperate situation indeed! Arion, recognizing that the sailors were implacable, begged them for permission to stand on the quarterdeck in his full singing regalia, and give them a song – with the proviso that, when the song was over, he would do away with himself. The sailors, who were delighted at the prospect of hearing the best singer in the world, all came hurrying down from the stern into the middle of the ship while Arion, arrayed in his singing robes and clutching his lyre, stood on the quarterdeck. There he sang a haunting hymn in honour of Apollo – and then, when the song was done, hurled himself into the sea, just as he was, still wearing all his robes. The sailors continued on to Corinth; but Arion, it is said, was picked up by a dolphin and borne on its back to Taenarum. There he was able to disembark and make his own way to Corinth, where – without even having changed his clothes – he poured out the full story. So incredible did Periander find it, though, that he ordered Arion to be put under house arrest while a sharp look-out was kept for the sailors. When they duly turned up, he summoned them into his presence and asked them whether they had any news of Arion. 'Oh yes,' they answered, 'he is safe and sound back in Italy. When we left him, he was the toast of Tarentum.' No sooner had they said this, however, than out stepped Arion himself, dressed exactly as he had been when he jumped overboard. Such was the sailors' stupefaction that they could no longer maintain their denials in the face of the on-going cross-examination. This, at any rate, is the story as told by the Corinthians and the Lesbi-

ans – and it is a fact that in a temple in Taenarum there is an offering from Arion, a small bronze statue of a man on the back of a dolphin.

[25] Alyattes of Lydia did not live long after the conclusion of his war against Miletus, dying after a reign of fifty-seven years. He was the second of his dynasty to dedicate an offering to Delphi. For once he had recovered from his illness he presented the oracle with a large silver bowl, complete with a stand made out of welded iron. Even when one bears in mind the great mass of offerings at Delphi, this one is still well worth a look, for it was the handiwork of Glaucus of Chios, the man who single-handedly invented the art of iron-welding.

[26] On Alyattes' death, he was succeeded as king by his son, Croesus, who was then thirty-five years old. The first Greeks whom the new king attacked were the people of Ephesus. It was during the course of his siege that the Ephesians ran a rope from the temple of Artemis[39] to the city wall, and thereby succeeded in dedicating their city to the goddess. (The distance from the old town, which was the part then under siege, and the temple is 7 stades in total.) So far as Croesus was concerned, however, Ephesus was only a beginning: he went on to attack all the Ionian and Aeolian cities one by one. His justification would vary from case to case: whenever he had a serious ground of complaint, he could be sure to make a great fuss about it, but even when one was lacking he would manage to rustle up some flimsy pretext.[40]

[27] In due course, with the Greeks on the Asian mainland all conquered and brought to pay him tribute, Croesus embarked on a programme of shipbuilding, with the intention of taking the attack to the islanders. Just as everything was ready for the shipbuilding to begin, however, Sardis was visited by someone (Bias of Priene, some say, although others claim it was Pittacus of Mytilene) who ended up being responsible for the aborting of the entire project; when asked by Croesus what news there was from Greece, the visitor replied that the islanders were busy buying up horses, ten thousand of them. 'And their plan, my Lord, is to strike at you in Sardis.' 'If only!' exclaimed Croesus, taking the accuracy of this report for granted. 'The very thought of it – that the gods might so delude the islanders as to bring them against my brave Lydians, and perched on horseback too!' 'My Lord,' came the reply, 'the obvious implication of your prayer is that you are keen to catch the islanders while they are in the saddle, here on the mainland. As well you should be. But has it not crossed your mind that the islanders, the

moment they became aware of your plan to prepare a naval campaign against them, might have offered up a corresponding prayer of their own? After all, they would like nothing better than to catch the Lydians out at sea – for then they would be able to pay you back for your enslavement of their countrymen here on the mainland.' Croesus was much amused by the way that this point had been made – not to mention persuaded by its self-evident good sense. The result was the abandonment of his shipbuilding programme, and the signing of a treaty of friendship with those Ionians who lived offshore.[41]

[28] Meanwhile, over the course of time, almost all the peoples living west of the River Halys had been brought to submit to Croesus.[42] The Lycians and the Cilicians excepted, all the others had ended up crushed by him, and absorbed into his empire: the Lydians, the Phrygians, the Mysians, the Mariandynians, the Chalybes, the Paphlagonians, the Thracians (both Thynian and Bithynian), the Carians, the Ionians, the Dorians, the Aeolians and the Pamphylians.[43] In the wake of these conquests, and with Croesus still busy adding to the Lydian empire, Sardis stood at the very height of her prosperity.[44]

[29] All the most learned Greeks of the age were drawn there, each one making the trip in his own way – and one of these visitors was Solon of Athens.[45] He was the man who had been asked by the Athenians to draw up a law-code for them – and now, having completed that, he had gone abroad for ten years. The excuse he gave for embarking on his travels was that he wanted to see the world; but the truth was that he did not want to be pressured into having to repeal any of his recently issued laws. The Athenians themselves were unable to repeal the law-code that Solon had delivered to them, for the reason that they had all solemnly pledged themselves to give it a decade's trial.

[30] This, then – quite apart from any taste for sightseeing – was the reason for Solon's going abroad. In the course of his travels he paid a visit to King Amasis in Egypt, but his prime destination was Sardis, where he was put up by Croesus in the royal palace itself. Three or four days after his arrival, Croesus instructed some servants to give Solon a guided tour of the various treasuries and point out to him how splendid and sumptuous everything was.[46] Then, after Solon had seen and inspected everything, Croesus took the opportunity to ask him a question. 'We have heard a good deal about you, my guest from Athens: you have a reputation as a wise and well-travelled man, as a philosopher

indeed, one who has travelled the world and always kept his eyes wide open. So here is the question I would like to put to you: have you ever come across anyone whose state of contentment would rank head and shoulders above that of everyone else?' In asking this, of course, he was taking for granted that the answer would be himself; but Solon, rather than indulge in flattery, preferred instead to speak what he saw as the truth. 'Yes, my Lord,' he answered. 'An Athenian, by the name of Tellus.' The reply took Croesus aback. 'And why exactly,' he demanded in a heated tone, 'do you reckon this Tellus to have been so happy?' 'There are two reasons,' Solon answered. 'Firstly, he lived at a time when his city was particularly well off, he had handsome, upstanding sons, and he ended up a grandfather, with all his grandchildren making it to adulthood. Secondly, at a time when – by our standards – he was a man of considerable wealth, his life came to an end that was as glorious as its course had previously been happy. What happened was this: the Athenians were fighting a battle against their neighbours at Eleusis, when Tellus stepped into the breach of their crumbling line, and put the enemy to flight. It is true that he himself died, but his death was something beautiful, and the Athenians gave him a state funeral at the very spot where he fell, and awarded him splendid honours.'[47]

[31] This discourse of Solon's, with its cataloguing of all the ways in which Tellus had been truly happy, had certainly served to pique Croesus' interest; and so it was, confident that he would be named the runner-up at least, he asked Solon for the name of the second happiest person on his list. 'Cleobis and Biton,' Solon answered promptly, 'two young men of Argos, because they never lacked for means, and also because of their remarkable physical strength. Not only were they both prize-winning athletes, but there is also the following story told about them. The episode took place during an Argive festival in honour of Hera, when their mother urgently needed to be driven to the temple in their cart, but early in the day, before the oxen had been brought back in from the fields. There being no time to lose, the two young men shouldered the yoke themselves and pulled the cart, with their mother riding on top of it, for a full 45 stades, all the way to the temple. Everyone who had gathered for the festival was a witness to this exploit, and then, in its wake, the two young men died in the best way possible: a divinely authored proof that it is better to be dead than alive. The Argives kept crowding round them, congratulating them on their

strength, and the women of the city kept telling their mother how fortunate she was in her children. In due course, such was the rapture of her joy at her sons' achievement and the fame they had won, that she went to stand before the statue of Hera, and prayed to the goddess that she would bestow upon her children, her Cleobis and Biton, who had brought her such great honour, the greatest blessing that it is possible for mortals to be granted. The mother finished her prayer; and then came the sacrifices and the feasting; and then the young men passed inside the temple and fell asleep, never to wake up again; and in this way their lives were brought to a close. The Argives made statues[48] of them, which were then sent to Delphi – for it was clear that they had been the very best that men can be.'

[32] But Solon's nomination of these two young men for second place in his list of the happiest people known to him threw Croesus into a rage. 'And what of my own happiness, my Athenian friend?' he demanded. 'Is it so beneath contempt that it is not even to be mentioned in the same breath as that of men without rank or title?' 'Croesus,' Solon replied, 'your question was one that touched on the lot of humanity – and I answered it as someone who is all too well aware of how jealous the gods are, and how perplexing in their ways.[49] The longer the span of someone's existence, the more certain he is to see and suffer much that he would rather have been spared. Say that the limit of a man's life is set at seventy years. If you exclude intercalary months, then those seventy years comprise 25,200 days – but if you add a month on to every alternate year, so that the seasons are properly calibrated, then seventy years will give us an additional thirty-five months – which in turn will give us an additional 1,050 days. That means that your seventy years of life will give you 26,250 days in all – and not one of them will resemble the next in terms of what it brings. So you can see, Croesus, how human life is nothing if not subject to the vagaries of chance.[50] Now, to be sure, I can recognize that you are fabulously rich and that you are the king of a great number of people – and yet for all that, I will not be able to say about you what you were anticipating that I would say until I have learned that you died contentedly. Great wealth, after all, is no more guaranteed to bring a man happiness than is daily subsistence – unless, that is, good fortune proves to be the rich man's constant companion, enabling him to keep all his blessings intact, and bringing his life to a pleasant conclusion. But just as there are many men of moderate means

who enjoy the most wonderful luck, so are there many wealthy men who suffer repeated misfortune. Someone who is rich but unlucky is only really better off than a lucky man in two respects, whereas there are many ways in which a lucky man has the advantage of a rich man plagued by ill fortune. It is true that the millionaire is well placed to do whatever he likes and to ride out such disasters as befall him, while the man of moderate means is not; but the latter, if he is only lucky, is far more likely to avoid disasters in the first place, not to mention disfigurement, disease and a whole host of other evils, as well as enjoying parenthood and good looks. And if, in addition to all these advantages, he dies as well as he lived, well, there you have the kind of man you are looking for: one who truly merits the epithet of "happy". But until he is dead, do not go leaping to any conclusions: for he is not yet truly happy, only fortunate. The reality is, of course, that no one can really combine all these blessings, just as no country can produce everything that it needs, for no matter what resources a land may boast, it is bound to be deficient in some, and being the best is simply a matter of being better endowed than the rest. It is the same with mortals: flesh and bone can never be self-sufficient. The man who has one thing will lack another. Whoever is blessed with the most advantages in life, and retains them to the end and dies a peaceful death, that is the man, my Lord, who in my opinion best deserves the title. No matter what, you must always look to the end, look to how it will turn out: for the heavens will often grant men a glimpse of happiness, only to snatch it away so that not a trace of it remains.'

[33] Sentiments such as these were hardly designed to please Croesus, and so he dismissed Solon as a man unworthy of his further attention. Self-evidently, he thought, anyone who told him to disregard the assets of the moment and look instead to the end of everything could only be an idiot.[51]

[34] But after Solon's departure, the noose of a divine and terrible anger began to tighten around Croesus – and this was clearly because he had presumed himself the happiest of men. Almost straightaway, as he slept, a dream laid him in its shadow, one that revealed to him a calamity soon to befall his son – a glimpse of the future destined to come true.[52] Croesus had two sons: one of them was disabled, being both deaf and dumb, but the other, whose name was Atys, was the outstanding figure of his generation, a young man whose talents knew no

bounds. It was Atys whom Croesus had seen in his dream, being killed by a blow from an iron spearhead. When the king woke up, a few moments' reflection on what he had been shown put him into such a panic that he married off his son, and forbade him to go off on any further military expeditions – and this despite the fact that Atys was a commander in the Lydian army. Croesus also had any weapons that might be used in battle – javelins, spears, and so on – removed from the men's quarters, where they had been kept hanging from the ceiling, and had them stashed away instead in the women's bedrooms, so that there would be no risk of them dropping onto his son.[53]

[35] Meanwhile, as he busied himself with the preparations for his son's wedding, there arrived at Sardis a Phrygian, a man of royal descent but one who was nevertheless caught up in the toils of a terrible calamity – for he had blood on his hands. Heading for Croesus' palace, the visitor begged the king to cleanse him of his blood-guilt in accordance with Lydian custom (the ceremony is very similar to the one that is practised in Greece);[54] and Croesus duly set about the process of purification. Then, with the rites formally completed, he asked the man who he was and where he came from. 'We are both of us human, after all,' he said, 'so please, tell me your name. Whereabouts in Phrygia did you live before you ended up here, an asylum-seeker at my hearth? Who did you kill, what man or woman?' 'My Lord,' the stranger replied, 'I am the son of Gordias, the grandson of Midas, and my name is Adrastus. The man I killed was my own brother, in an accident. Driven into exile by my father, and stripped of everything that I ever owned, I have ended up here.' 'Your family and mine have long been allies,' responded Croesus, 'so relax, you are among friends. For as long as you are here in my home, you will want for nothing. Try not to let the burden of your misfortune weigh down on you too heavily – that is the best approach.'

[36] So Adrastus came to live with Croesus. Simultaneously, in Mysia, a great monster of a wild boar appeared on Mount Olympus,[55] and made its lair there, from where it was forever descending to trample the Mysians' crops. Repeated attempts were made to finish it off; but the Mysians' success was in inverse proportion to the damage that kept being inflicted on them by the boar. Finally, as a last resort, they sent a delegation to Croesus. 'My Lord,' the messengers said, 'a great monster of a wild boar has appeared in our country and is ruining our crops. Desperate though we are to capture the brute, the task is beyond us.

Please, we beg you, send us your son and the pick of your young men, your dogs as well, so that we can drive the beast off our land.' Now Croesus, listening to this request, could not help but remember his dream. 'No more talk of my son,' he declared. 'I cannot possibly let him go with you. He has only just got married, and so he has his hands full with that. But you can certainly have the pick of Lydia's huntsmen, not to mention my entire pack of hounds, and I will give them strict instructions to do all they can to clear your lands of this beast.'

[37] This answer was good enough for the Mysians – but not for Atys, who at that very moment came bursting into the room. The young man had heard about the Mysians' request, and now, finding his father obdurate in refusing to let him join them, he wanted his say. 'Father, time was, out on the battlefield or on the hunt,[56] when the fairest and noblest deeds imaginable would be credited to our family, and redound to our honour. Nowadays, however, you forbid me from engaging in either pursuit, even though there has never been any suggestion that I might be a coward or lacking in spirit. What kind of a figure must I cut, then, walking in and out of the city's public places? What will my fellow-citizens make of me? What will my new bride take me for? She must feel that she has been landed with a pretty miserable husband, that is for sure! So I beg you – either let me go on the hunt, or else give me just one reason why what you are doing is for my good!'

[38] 'My dear boy,' answered Croesus, 'my decision is certainly no reflection on you, for I have never detected so much as a hint of coward-ice[57] in you, nor any other failing, come to that. No, I had a dream, a vision which came upon me in my sleep, telling me that your time was almost up, and that your doom was fast approaching in the form of an iron spearhead. That is why I rushed you into getting married, and why I am refusing to let you go on the expedition: my vision. I am deter-mined, for so long as I still have breath, to smuggle you past anything that fate might throw at you. But that requires taking precautions. You are my son! Indeed, my one and only son – for your brother, [deaf and] handicapped as he is, I scarcely count as my child.'

[39] 'Well, I can hardly blame you for trying to protect me, Father,' the young man replied, 'if that was your dream. But there is one thing you have failed to appreciate, one thing you have overlooked – and it is only proper that I point it out to you. You say that your dream revealed to you – and here is the detail which has thrown you into such a panic – that it is

an iron spearhead which is destined to spell my end. But what kind of a boar possesses hands, let alone an iron spearhead? Had you been told that I would be gored to death by a tusk, or something like that, then, yes, you would have been perfectly justified in doing what you are doing. But it was a spear – a spear! It is not as though I am heading into a battle or up against men! So please – let me go!'

[40] 'My dear child,' answered Croesus, 'for some reason which I do not altogether understand, I find myself bowing to the force of your argument about my dream. You win. My mind is changed. You have my permission to go on the hunt.'

[41] The conversation now being over, Croesus sent for Adrastus, and when the Phrygian had come into his presence, said: 'Adrastus, it was to me you came for purification when you found yourself struck down by misfortune, and I have never held it against you. Not only that, but I took you into my house and I spared no expense in setting you up here. You are in my debt: I have shown you every kindness, and now it is your turn to do me a favour. I would like you to become my son's bodyguard on this hunt he is about to embark upon, in case any bandits or villains of that kind attack him while you are out on the road and try to do him harm. And besides, you owe it to yourself to go where you will have the chance to burnish your name: your family is a distinguished one, after all, and you are hardly lacking physically.'

[42] 'My Lord,' answered Adrastus, 'under normal circumstances I would have nothing to do with an exploit of this kind. It is hardly fitting for someone with my record of misfortune to associate with his more successful peers, nor is it something I would wish to do. There are so many reasons for me to show self-restraint. But you keep pressing me – and I can refuse you nothing, not when I reflect how much I owe you for all the kindnesses you have bestowed upon me. I am ready to do as you urge: to serve to the very best of my ability as your son's bodyguard. Rest assured, he will come back to you safe and sound.'

[43] Such was the promise he made to Croesus; and sure enough, not long afterwards, he and Atys set off with a train of hand-picked young men and dogs. On arriving at Olympus, they set to searching the mountain for the beast, and then, once they had tracked it down, they encircled it and let fly with their spears. And now it happened that the single foreigner among them – yes, Croesus' guest, the same man who had been cleansed by him of the stain of blood, the one known as Adrastus – took

aim at the boar with his spear, missed, and hit Croesus' son. Struck by the spearhead, Atys fell to the ground – and the calamity foretold in the dream was fulfilled. The news of what had happened was immediately dispatched to Croesus. The messenger, having run all the way to Sardis, reported to the king how the boar had been fought, and how his son had met his doom.

[44] The death of his child left Croesus utterly prostrated; and what made his cries of anguish all the more terrible was the fact that he himself had cleansed the killer of the taint of bloodshed. Indeed, such was the violence of his grief at his misfortune that he called upon Zeus,[58] as the god of purification, to witness what he had suffered at the hands of the stranger he had welcomed as a friend; and then a second time, but now as the god of hearth and companionship, he invoked the name of Zeus. Why as the god of the hearth? Because, by welcoming Adrastus into his home, Croesus had unwittingly been hosting the killer of his son. And why as the god of companionship? Because, by appointing Adrastus his son's bodyguard, Croesus had in effect recruited to his side a deadly foe.

[45] Time passed, and in due course the Lydians arrived bringing with them the dead body; and in their rear there followed the killer. He stood in front of the corpse, stretched out his hands to Croesus in a gesture of abject submission and told the king to end his life right there, over the body of his son. 'My earlier misfortunes were terrible enough,' he said, 'but now, after I have brought ruin down upon the head of the very man who purified me, why should I wish to live a moment more?' Croesus, when he heard this, was moved to pity, even in the midst of all his own sorrows. 'My friend,' he said, 'this sentence of death which you have pronounced upon yourself is all the justice I desire. You are not to blame for the horror which has overwhelmed me. No – you were nothing but the unwitting agent of some god, whose warnings of what was fated to happen were delivered to me long ago.' And thereupon, in a mighty barrow as befitted a prince, Croesus buried his child. But Adrastus – the son of Gordias, the grandson of Midas, the man who had killed his own brother and dealt a deadly blow to the very man who had purified him – waited until the mourners were gone and the tomb was abandoned to silence; and then, in the firm conviction that of all the men who had ever lived there was no one more crushed by misfortune than himself, he climbed the grave and slit his own throat.[59]

*

[46] For two years, Croesus sat paralysed by grief at the death of his child. But then, after the empire of Astyages, Cyaxares' son, was toppled by Cyrus,[60] the son of Cambyses, the growing might of the Persians led Croesus to put his grief to one side, and begin instead to weigh up his likely prospects for nipping Persian greatness in the bud, and checking the spread of its power. No sooner had he started turning this over in his mind than he decided to test out the efficacy of an assortment of oracles (mainly Greek, although there was one in Libya as well). Emissaries were dispatched to various locations: to Delphi, to Abae in Phocis and to Dodona. Some were sent to Amphiaraus and Trophonius,[61] and some to Branchidae in Miletus. These were the Greek oracles consulted by Croesus' servants; but he also sent men to pay their respects to the oracle of Ammon[62] in Libya. His purpose in doing this was to test just how accurate these oracles truly were; and then, to those which had successfully demonstrated their authenticity, to send messengers a second time, and ask them whether or not he should go to war with Persia.[63]

[47] The instructions he gave to the Lydians before sending them off to test the oracles were very precise. They were to keep a careful track of how many days had passed since their departure from Sardis, and then, on the hundredth day, they were to seek an oracular consultation and ask what King Croesus of Lydia, the son of Alyattes, was doing at that very moment. Each oracle was to give its response; and then, once the answers had been written down, they were to be brought back to him. Now, in every case bar one, we have no record of what the oracles actually said; but we do have the response of Delphi. For there, the moment that the Lydians stepped into the innermost sanctum of the shrine, looking to consult the god and to put the question they had been instructed to ask, the priestess – the Pythia – began to speak as follows, chanting in perfect hexameters:

'I can count an infinitude of grains of sand and I have the measuring
   of the sea,
I understand the talk of the dumb, and I can hear what the
   voiceless say.
A scent wafts through my senses, the scent of a hard-shelled tortoise,
Boiling within bronze, bubbling with lambs' flesh,
Bronze lies beneath it, and bronze is its covering too.'

[48] After the priestess had delivered this pronouncement,[64] the Lydians wrote it down and returned home to Sardis. When the other emissaries too were back, all with their own messages, Croesus opened up the scrolls and looked over what he found written in them. None met his expectations. But then the message from Delphi was read out to him, and immediately he cried out in awestruck wonder, hailing its accuracy and declaring that only Delphi, of all oracles, had the true gift of prophecy – for it alone had identified what he had been up to. Croesus' scheme, you see, following his dispatch of the emissaries to the oracles, had been to arrive at some course of action that no one would ever find out or guess; and so, after keeping a careful track of the calendar for a hundred days, he had taken a tortoise and a lamb, cut them both up and boiled them in a cauldron made of bronze – as was its lid.

[49] So much, then, for the story of what was revealed to Croesus by Delphi. I have been unable to identify the message that was delivered by the oracle of Amphiaraus to the Lydians, once they had completed the traditional rites at the temple: for no record of it has survived. All I will say is that this oracle too proved itself authentic – according to Croesus, at any rate.

[50] Croesus' next move was to propitiate with a magnificent sacrifice the god who speaks at Delphi. First he immolated three thousand animals, an offering of every conceivable breed that might be reckoned acceptable to the heavens, and then he raised a great pyre, heaping up couches overlaid with gold and silver, golden bowls and purple cloaks and tunics, before torching the lot – all in the expectation that this would give him a better chance of winning the god over to his side. He also instructed the Lydians to make their own sacrifices, each according to his means. Then, when these ceremonies had been completed, he melted down an enormous amount of gold and had it moulded into 117 ingots, all of the same size: six palms long, three palms wide and one palm high. Four of the ingots were made of pure gold, and weighed 2½ talents each, while the other ingots were made of an alloy of gold and silver and weighed half a talent less. Croesus also ordered the image of a lion to be fashioned out of pure gold:[65] its weight was 10 talents. (When the temple at Delphi burned down, this same lion fell off the ingots which had been serving as its pedestal, and three and a half talents' worth of its gold melted away: it now weighs 6½ talents, and is to be found in the Corinthian treasury.[66])

[51] Once these offerings had all been made ready, Croesus sent them off to Delphi, along with a number of other gifts. There were two huge mixing-bowls, one of gold, which was placed on the right-hand side of the temple entrance, and another of silver, which was placed on the left. (These also had to be moved when the temple burnt down: the gold one, which weighs 8½ talents and 12 *minae* in all, now stands in the Clazomenaean treasury, while the silver bowl is kept in the corner of the temple's entrance-hall. Its capacity is equivalent to 600 amphoras – a detail which derives from the Delphians' use of it to mix wine at the Festival of the Theophania.[67] The Delphians identify it as the work of Theodorus of Samos – an attribution which I personally am quite content to accept, since it really does seem to me a most extraordinary piece of work.) Croesus also sent four rounded silver jars, which stand in the Corinthian treasury, and he dedicated two basins for the sprinkling of holy water to the service of the god, one of gold and one of silver. (The gold basin has an inscription on it, claiming that it was a votive offering presented by the Lacedaemonians; but this is untrue. Croesus donated it along with all his other gifts, and the inscription was only added later by a Delphian who wished to ingratiate himself with the Lacedaemonians: I could name the guilty person, but will keep my peace.[68] Granted, the boy through whose hand the water trickles was indeed given by the Lacedaemonians – but not the bowls themselves.) Croesus also sent a host of other votive offerings at the same time which lacked inscriptions: these included some casts of silver poured into round moulds, and a gold statue of a woman three cubits high, which ranks as an item of particular interest, because – the Delphians say – it represents the woman who used to bake Croesus' bread.[69] Croesus also made a dedication of his wife's ornamented belts, and of necklaces unclasped from her very throat.

[52] Such were the gifts Croesus sent to Delphi. He also sent votive offerings to the oracle founded by Amphiaraus (the story of whose valour and misfortunes he had come across during the course of his researches): a shield made entirely of gold and a spear likewise fashioned out of solid gold, from the shaft all the way to the tip. In my own lifetime, both these items were still on display in Thebes – in the temple of Ismenian Apollo,[70] to be precise.

[53] The Lydians who were to take the gifts to the shrines were instructed by Croesus to ask the oracles whether he should go to war

with the Persians, and also whether he should attempt to secure an alliance with some other leading military power. Arriving at their destinations, the Lydians duly made a presentation of the votive offerings, and then approached the oracles with their enquiries. 'Croesus, the king of the Lydians and of many other peoples,' they said, 'in the firm conviction that yours are the only true oracles that mankind possesses, has sent you the gifts that your powers of divination merit. Now, here are the questions he wishes to put to you. Should he go to war with the Persians? And should he seek out an alliance with some other military power?' The two oracles, delivering their judgements in response to these questions, were in perfect agreement, for they both predicted that Croesus, if he did go to war with the Persians, would destroy a mighty empire, and they both advised him to identify the strongest military power among the Greeks, and to swear a treaty of friendship with it.

[54] When Croesus was informed of the prophecies that had been brought back to him, he was delighted with the oracles, and secure now in the firm conviction that he would indeed destroy the kingdom of Cyrus, he made enquiries as to the size of Delphi's population, and then, dispatching his ambassadors there again, to the seat of the Pythia, he presented every Delphian with a gift of 2 gold staters. In exchange, the Delphians granted Croesus and the Lydians first place in any queue to put questions to the oracle, waived all consultation fees and reserved them front seats at each and every festival – not to mention the right, granted in perpetuity, of becoming citizens of Delphi if they so wished.

[55] Then, with his bounty duly scattered among the Delphians, Croesus consulted the oracle a third time – for the taste of an authentic prophecy had left him greedy to have his fill of more. On this occasion he asked the god if his reign would be a long one. This was the Pythia's answer:

'Only when a mule has become the ruler of the Medes
Should you flee, Lydian, upon your soft-soled feet, without delay,
By pebbly River Hermus, unashamed to play the coward.'

[56] This response, when it was delivered to Croesus, delighted him more than anything he had yet been told – for the Medes, after all, were hardly likely to replace their human kings with a mule! Confident now that he and his dynasty were destined never to lose power, Croesus next turned his attention to an investigation of the political scene in Greece,

with a view to securing the most formidable states there as his allies. His enquiries soon revealed to him that the two leading powers – the first of Dorian stock, and the second of Ionian – were the Lacedaemonians and the Athenians: none ranked above them. The roots of both were ancient, for the Athenians were sprung from the race of the Pelasgians, and the Lacedaemonians from that of the Hellenes. Unlike the Pelasgians, who were indigenous, the Hellenes had for a long time been inveterate nomads. Back when Deucalion was their king, they dwelt in Phthia; but by the time of Dorus, Hellen's son, they had settled between Mount Ossa and Mount Olympus, in the land known as Histiaeotis. Next, after being driven out of Histiaeotis by the Cadmeians, they settled on Mount Pindus, where they were known as 'Macedonians' – until in due course they set off on yet another migration, this time to Dryopis. Only once they had left there did they finally arrive in the Peloponnese, and come to be known as 'Dorians'.[71]

[57] Working out what language was spoken by the Pelasgians is a problem which defies a definite solution. Perhaps, though – if one must posit an answer – it is reasonable to deduce it from those who have survived into the present day; for there are Pelasgians still living in Creston, in the land of the Tyrrhenians, and who were once the neighbours of the people now known as the Dorians (and who then lived in a land called Thessaliotis), as well as those who were originally the compatriots of the Athenians, and founded Placia and Scylace in the Hellespont, not to mention a whole host of other settlements which once used to rank as Pelasgian, but have since changed their names. On the basis of this evidence, at any rate, it has to be concluded that the language spoken by the Pelasgians was not Greek; and if this is so – and if the inference is one that can be applied equally to all Pelasgians – then it is clear that the Athenians, as a people originally of Pelasgian stock, must at some point in the process of their Hellenization have learned a whole new language: Greek. Certainly, the fact that the Crestonians and the Placians both speak a similar tongue – one which bears no relation to those spoken by their immediate neighbours – strongly suggests that, although they may have changed one homeland for another, they did not change their language, but instead zealously preserved it in its native form.

[58] As for the Greeks,[72] it seems clear to me that they have always spoken the same language, right from their very beginnings. It is true that they were originally of little account at the time when they first

established themselves as a people distinct from the Pelasgians, but since then they have come to encompass a great multitude of different nations, and have long since outgrown their humble beginnings. The Pelasgians themselves were the most notable example of a people who ended up being Hellenized, but there were numerous others as well, all of them originally non-Greek speaking. It is worth reflecting that for as long as the Pelasgians stuck with their own language, they never amounted to much at all.

[59] So, then. Of the two peoples who had been brought to Croesus' attention, one of them, he soon discovered, was riven by internal divisions, for Attica in those days was labouring under the rule of a man who had established himself as a tyrant over the Athenians – Peisistratus,[73] the son of Hippocrates. An extraordinary thing had once happened to this Hippocrates. One day, while he was at the Olympic Games, watching them in a purely private capacity, he had made an offering of sacrificial animals, put the meat into some merchant-ship cauldrons and topped them up with water – only to find the cauldrons, without the fires so much as having been lit, starting to boil and bubble over. It so happened that Chilon the Lacedaemonian was passing at the time, and on witnessing this miracle offered Hippocrates the following advice: that on no account should he bring into his home a wife who might give him children; or failing that, if he already had one, he should immediately send her packing; or failing that, if he should indeed end up with a child, he must disown it on the spot. Hippocrates, however, refused to subscribe to this advice from Chilon[74] – and sure enough, some time afterwards, Peisistratus was born. Peisistratus' aspirations would prove to be of a markedly tyrannical bent; for in due course, at a time when Attica was riven by civil strife, with one faction led by Megacles, the son of Alcmaeon, drawn from the villages along the coast, and a second, led by Lycurgus, the son of Aristolaides, drawn from the lowland settlements further inland, Peisistratus began to pose as the champion of the upland regions, and thereby set himself at the head of a third faction. Next, he put into effect a cunning plan. First he took a knife to himself and his mules, and drove his cart into the city square, claiming to be on the run from enemies who had sought to murder him as he was driving out of town. Then, exploiting the reputation he had won as a general in the campaign against Megara (when he had blazed a whole trail of prodigious feats, including the capture of Nisaea), he asked the people to

supply him with a bodyguard. The mass of the Athenians were well and truly duped, and a hand-picked body of men drawn from the city itself was duly assigned to guard Peisistratus – men who might as well have openly carried spears as the clubs that they actually came to carry. Brandishing their wooden maces, these heavies followed him wherever he went. With their backing, Peisistratus was soon able to stage a coup and seize the Acropolis. From that moment on, and without once having meddled with the existing structure of magistracies or changed the laws, Peisistratus was the master of Athens; and as such, he governed the city with a due respect for constitutional proprieties, ruling it properly and well.

[60] It did not take long, however, for the two factions of Megacles and Lycurgus to make common cause and drive him into exile. So much for Peisistratus' first spell as the tyrant of Athens: he lost power before his regime could put down roots. No sooner had Megacles and Lycurgus succeeded in expelling Peisistratus, however, than they were back at each other's throats. When Megacles found himself having the worst of this faction-fighting, he made contact with Peisistratus, offering to back him as tyrant if he would only first agree to become Megacles' son-in-law. The overture was accepted, an accord was duly drawn up, and then, plotting how best to secure Peisistratus' restoration, the two men came up with quite the most harebrained scheme I have ever heard of, certainly in recent times – and all the more so because the Greeks have long been distinguished from other people by their intelligence and general lack of gullibility, just as the Athenians, who were the victims of the trick, are widely acknowledged to be the most intelligent of the Greeks.[75] In the village of Paeania there was a woman called Phya, who combined stature – she was almost 6 feet tall – with great beauty. The conspirators dressed her up in full armour; then they put her in a chariot, showed her how to hold a striking pose and drove her off to town. Runners were sent ahead, serving her as heralds and broadcasting all the way to Athens a carefully scripted proclamation. 'Athenians,' they cried out, once they had arrived in the city, 'take Peisistratus back into your hearts! For Athena[76] herself has chosen to honour him above all mankind! Why, she is even now escorting him from exile back to her very own acropolis!' Such was the report they delivered all over town – and straightaway the news began to spread like wildfire back out into the countryside that Athena was bringing Peisistratus back home. Meanwhile, in the city itself,

men were so convinced that Phya was indeed the goddess that they received her with their prayers, and Peisistratus with open arms.

[61] So it was that Peisistratus became tyrant again; and just as the agreement with Megacles had obliged him to do, he married Megacles' daughter. Because he already had grown children, however, and because the Alcmaeonid family was supposed to lie under a curse, he did not wish to have any children by his new wife – and so would only have sex with her in a thoroughly illicit way.[77] At first his wife kept this a secret, but in due course she told all to her mother (who may or may not have been pushing her about it in the first place), and she in turn went straight to her husband. Megacles was thrown into such a fury by the way Peisistratus had dishonoured him[78] that he immediately set about patching up his quarrel with his political adversaries. When Peisistratus learned of the moves that were being made against him, he fled the country altogether and made for Eretria,[79] where he held a council of war with his sons. It was the advice of Hippias,[80] who encouraged him to have another stab at the tyranny, which ended up carrying the day; and so they set about raising contributions from each and every state which happened to owe them a debt of gratitude, no matter what it might be. A host of cities duly contributed handsomely to the Peisistratid coffers; but it was Thebes which loosened the purse-strings to most generous effect. Time went by, and (to cut a long story short) eventually all was primed for the attempted return. There were Argive mercenaries, recruited from the Peloponnese; and there was also a volunteer from Naxos,[81] by the name of Lygdamis, a man who had no rivals as an enthusiast for the cause, nor as a provider of funds and men.

[62] Setting out from Eretria, they returned home after ten years and more of exile. The place in Attica they seized as their beach-head was Marathon.[82] Their camp there was soon swelled by an influx of supporters from the city, while others streamed in from the outlying villages: men who preferred the rule of a tyrant to freedom. And so their numbers grew. In the city, meanwhile, Peisistratus' fund-raising, and even his subsequent capture of Marathon, had barely raised an eyebrow among most Athenians; but when they found out that he was advancing from Marathon on the city itself, they abruptly grasped the need to salvage the situation. Out they marched in full force against the returning exiles, and on came Peisistratus and his troops, down the road that led from Marathon to the city – until in due course, at the temple of Athena in

Pallene, the two sides met and took up positions opposite one another. Then it was that the hand of a god revealed itself, for Amphilytus of Acarnania, a man blessed with the gift of second sight, accosted Peisistratus, and spoke to him in hexameters, rhythmic words of prophecy.

'Cast is the fishing-net, and far-flung its meshes,
Tuna, darting through the moon-flecked night, draw near!'

[63] Peisistratus, listening as the god spoke through the seer, and realizing what the prophecy meant, declared his full acceptance of the revelation, and ordered his men into battle. As this was going on, the Athenians from the city had actually been busy with their lunch; and now that they had finished eating, some of them were settling down to play dice and others were curling up for a nap. Peisistratus and his men fell on them and put them to flight. It was at this point that Peisistratus came up with an exceedingly clever ploy to ensure that there would be no prospect of an Athenian rally, and that the fugitives would be scattered for good. His sons were ordered into their saddles and sent galloping off. Then, in accordance with Peisistratus' instructions, every time they overtook a group of fugitives they would cry out to them, telling them that there was no call for anxiety, and urge everyone to go home.

[64] The Athenians fell for it – and Athens, for the third time, was Peisistratus'. This time, the roots of his tyranny were to be planted deep: for he made sure to deploy a large number of mercenaries, and to raise a substantial income for himself,[83] partly from Attica, and partly from his estates on the River Strymon.[84] He also took as hostages the children of those Athenians who had remained in Athens and not immediately fled the city, and packed them off to Naxos (where opposition had similarly been crushed by military means, and which he had handed over to Lygdamis). One final step he took was to follow the advice of an oracle, and lift a curse from the island of Delos:[85] the ritual of purification required him to dig up all the dead bodies which had lain buried within sight of the temple, and transfer them to another part of the island. So it was that Peisistratus ruled as the tyrant of Athens. Many Athenians had fallen in battle against him, and many others fled into exile – the Alcmaeonids most prominent of all.[86]

[65] If this, however, was the state of oppression under which the Athenians were labouring at the time of Croesus' fact-finding mission,

then the condition of the Lacedaemonians[87] told a very different story, for they had left the worst of their troubles well behind them. They had even won the upper hand in their war against Tegea, the one city which – in the days when Leon and Hegesicles were the kings of Sparta – had resisted the rising tide of their good fortune on the battlefield. Even longer ago, the Lacedaemonians had been the worst governed people in the whole of Greece: domestically speaking, their affairs had been a disgrace, while as for external affairs – well – they had simply refused to have any dealings with foreigners at all.[88] Here is the story of how they came to set their constitution on an infinitely better footing. It happened that Lycurgus,[89] a man who was much esteemed among the Spartans, went to consult the oracle in Delphi, and no sooner had he entered the shrine than the Pythia began to address him:

'Here you are, Lycurgus, come to my rich temple,
Dear to Zeus and to all who dwell on Olympus.
Are you man or god? That is more than I can tell,
But on balance I think you must be a god, Lycurgus.'

There are those who say that the Pythia also bequeathed to him the very political order which prevails in Sparta to this day – although the Lacedaemonians themselves claim that he brought it from Crete while he was serving as regent on behalf of his nephew, Leobotas, the king of Sparta. It is certain that the start of his regency marked a major reform of the constitution, and that he took very good care to ensure his new laws would not be sabotaged. In due course, he also set himself to restructuring the state's military apparatus – introducing bands of men all sworn to protect one another, divisional units of thirty and communal messes – and to establishing the civil offices of ephor and City Elder.[90]

[66] As a result of these reforms, the entire constitution was left immeasurably improved; and when Lycurgus died, such was the profound reverence in which his memory was held that a temple was raised to him. Nor did it take long, thanks to the fertility of Lacedaemon and to the size of her population, for her to start expanding and flourishing. The Lacedaemonians soon found themselves scorning the ease of peace; and in the arrogant conviction that they had the measure of the Arcadians, they sought the advice of the Delphic oracle, with a view to grabbing all the Arcadians' land. This was the Pythia's reply:[91]

'You ask me for Arcadia? You ask me for too much!
Arcadia is full of tough nuts, acorn-eaters all,
Men who will block your path. Even so, I hate to be mean.
My gift to you is Tegea: dance there with pounding feet,
And pace out her beauteous plain, measure it with a rope.'

Once the Lacedaemonians had absorbed this response, and having
failed to spot its ambiguity, they decided that they would leave the rest
of Arcadia to its own devices, and go to war against Tegea alone – and
as they marched, so they made sure to take fetters with them, the better
to lead the Tegeans off into slavery.[92] But when the battle came, it was
they who came off second best; and the survivors ended up bound with
the very chains[93] that they themselves had brought, and were put to
work on the Tegean plain, measuring it out with rope. Within my own
lifetime, these same chains – the ones that were used to fetter the Lacedaemonians – were still kept secure in Tegea, hung up around the inside
walls of the temple of Athena Alea.

[67] Nevertheless, even though the early campaigns had gone badly
for the men of Sparta, and seen them repeatedly bested by the Tegeans,
by the time of Croesus, when Anaxandridas and Ariston were kings
in Lacedaemon, it was they who had emerged as victors in the war. This
is how they pulled it off. At a time when they were suffering defeat after
defeat at the hands of the Tegeans, they sent emissaries to Delphi, to ask
which god they would need to propitiate if they were ever to win the
war against Tegea. 'Find the bones of Orestes, Agamemnon's son,' the
Pythia replied, 'and bring them back home.' It proved impossible, however to identify Orestes' grave; and so the Lacedaemonians sent back to
the god, to ask him where the body lay. When this question was put to
the Pythia, she answered:

'On a level plain there stands Arcadian Tegea,
Where two winds roar, nor have any option but so to do.
Blow is met here by counter-blow, and grief is piled on grief.
Its life-giving earth contains the son of Agamemnon.
Bring him home and become the guardian of Tegea.'

This reply, however, brought the Lacedaemonians not a whit closer to
discovering the body. Still they kept on searching, high and low – until
a Spartiate official called Lichas, one of the 'Benefactors', as they are

called, made the breakthrough. (A 'Benefactor' is one of those five citizens who, every year, are required to graduate from the cavalry because they have passed the given age threshold; it is their duty, in the year after their retirement, to serve as agents of the Spartiate community, forever going on missions, wherever they might be sent.[94])

[68] Lichas, then, was one of these officials; and he made his discovery while travelling in Tegea, the result of luck and his own sharp wits. He was there taking advantage of a temporary thaw in relations with the Tegeans, when he happened to enter a forge; inside it he saw the blacksmith hammering out iron, an activity so unfamiliar to him that he was quite stupefied by the sight.[95] When the smith noticed his guest's astonishment, he paused in his work, and said, 'Well now, my Laconian friend, if your jaw is going to drop at the sight of someone working iron, you should have seen what I saw – that really would have made your eyes stand out. There I was, looking to sink a well in my courtyard, and while I'm digging, what should I come across if not a coffin? Seven cubits long, it was! Well, I didn't for a moment think that people back in the past could genuinely have been taller than we are today – but when I opened it, there was the skeleton, and yes, it really was the same size as the coffin! I measured it carefully, then covered it back up with earth.' Such was the smith's account of what he had seen;[96] and as Lichas turned it over in his mind, so it began to dawn on him that everything exactly matched what the oracle had said, and that the body could therefore only have been Orestes'. All the clues seemed to point to the one conclusion. What were the smith's two bellows, for instance, if not the 'winds'? What were his hammer and anvil if not the 'blow' and 'counter-blow'? As for the smith's beating out of the iron, well, it was Lichas' conjecture that this was what the oracle had meant by its allusion to 'grief' being piled on 'grief' – for what had the discovery of iron ever brought to mankind aside from grief?[97] The puzzle was solved – and so Lichas returned to Sparta, to tell the Lacedaemonians the news. There, it was arranged that a fake charge be brought against him; a sentence of banishment was delivered; back Lichas went to Tegea where, after he had first made sure to tell the blacksmith all about his misfortune, he declared his wish to lease the courtyard. The smith, after some initial foot-dragging, was brought to accept the offer. Lichas settled in. He dug up the grave, collected the bones and carted the whole lot back to Sparta[98] – and from that moment on, whenever

there was a trial of strength between the two peoples, it was the Lacedaemonians who proved themselves decisively the superior in battle. Indeed, it did not take them long before they had brought the greater part of the Peloponnese under their control.

[69] All this was duly made known to Croesus; and it prompted him to send heralds to Sparta, emissaries who took with them both gifts and a request for an alliance. 'Croesus, who is the king of the Lydians, and of many other peoples besides, sent us,' the heralds declared on their arrival, making sure to follow the precise script that had been issued to them by their master. 'This is his message to you: "Men of Lacedaemon, it was the divinely sanctioned advice of the oracle that I should make a friend of the Greeks. You, I have been informed, are the leading power among the Greeks. Accordingly, just as the oracle recommended, I extend to you the hand of friendship. Let us be allies – and may our dealings be free of all treachery and deception!"' Such was the message that Croesus delivered through the mouths of his heralds; and the Lacedaemonians, who in truth had already heard all about the oracle's advice to Croesus, were so delighted to receive the Lydians' overtures that they signed up to a treaty of friendship and alliance on the spot. The reason for this was that, some time previously, Croesus had done them certain favours, and so they owed him a debt of gratitude. There was the time, for instance, when the Lacedaemonians had needed gold for a statue of Apollo (the same one which now stands in the Laconian town of Thornax) and had sent agents to Sardis looking to make a purchase; but Croesus had given it to the would-be buyers for free.

[70] Partly for this reason, and partly also because Croesus had ranked them worthy of his friendship above all the other Greeks, the Lacedaemonians signed up to the proposed alliance. They then took two further measures. The first was to declare themselves ready to answer any call for help from Croesus that he might send; the second was to repay his generosity to them by taking him a gift of their own, a bowl made of bronze, lavishly decorated around the outside rim with tiny figures, and with a capacity equivalent to 300 amphoras.[99] In the event, however, the bowl never made it to Sardis – and for this, two conflicting reasons are given. The Lacedaemonian story is that, while the bowl was still on its way to Sardis, and passing through Samian waters, the Samians[100] got wind of what was off their coast, sent out longships in pursuit and stole it. The Samians themselves, however, give a very

different account: they claim that the Lacedaemonians responsible for escorting the bowl were overtaken by events, and that after learning of the fall of Sardis and the capture of Croesus, they sold the bowl in Samos to a group of private citizens, who then placed it as a votive offering in the temple of Hera. If that is indeed what happened, then the men who sold the bowl might very well have claimed on their return to Sparta that it had been stolen from them by the Samians.

[71] So much for the bowl. Meanwhile, because he had failed to grasp the true meaning of the oracle, Croesus was busy with his invasion of Cappadocia, convinced that he was bound to crush the power of Cyrus and the Persians. In the midst of these preparations for the campaign against Persia, however, he received some advice from a Lydian named Sandanis, a man who had always had a name among his countrymen for intelligence, but who now gave that reputation a great boost, such was the quality of his analysis. 'My Lord,' he said, 'bear in mind the kind of men you are planning to attack. Men who wear leather wrapped around their legs – indeed, who never wear anything except for leather. Men whose native land is so unforgiving that they do not consume, they merely subsist. Men who drink no wine but only water, who never so much as get to nibble on a fig, who possess nothing worth having at all. Nothing will come of nothing – so even if you defeat them, what is there in it for you? But should they defeat you, well then – just think how much you stand to lose! Give them a taste of how well we live, and see how they will seize upon the discovery, see how they will resist all our attempts to beat them off. Be grateful to the gods, I say, that they never put it into the Persians' heads to launch a war of aggression against us!' And Sandanis was right, for although Croesus did not take his advice, it is perfectly true that it was indeed the conquest of Lydia which provided the Persians with their first experience of those luxuries which together go to make up the good life.[101]

[72] The Cappadocians are called 'Syrians' by the Greeks, and prior to the rise of the Persians to power, and their acknowledgement of Cyrus as their king, they had ranked as subjects of the Medes. The reason for this was that the frontier between the Median and the Lydian empires was the River Halys, which rises in the uplands of Armenia, flows through Cilicia and then continues with Matiene on its right bank and Phrygia on its left, before leaving those territories behind; it is now that its currents start to battle the gusting of the north wind, and to

separate the Syrian Cappadocians from the Paphlagonians to the west. As a result, the Halys serves to demarcate virtually the whole of western Asia, from the shoreline opposite Cyprus all the way up to the Euxine Sea. It is very much the neck of the peninsula, and it would take a man who was travelling light five whole days to traverse it.[102]

[73] So why did Croesus invade Cappadocia? Well, there was certainly his lust for territory, which had him itching to add to that portion of the world which was already his; but there was also the confidence he had placed in the oracle, and his desire to punish Cyrus for the downfall of Astyages. Astyages, you see, who was the son of Cyaxares, was also Croesus' brother-in-law, and was the king of the Medes; and Cyrus, the son of Cambyses, had defeated him and taken him prisoner. Let me explain how it was that Astyages had ended up related by marriage to Croesus. It all began with a band of nomads, Scythians who been caught up in some tribal blood-feud, and came skulking into Median territory. Media at this point was ruled by Cyaxares, the son of Phraortes, who in turn was the son of Deioces. He treated the Scythians well at first, on the grounds that they had come to him asking for asylum. Indeed, such was the value he put on them that he entrusted some children to their care, so that the boys would pick up their language and their skills in archery. Time passed. Every day the Scythians would go out hunting, and every day they would bring back some trophy. Then one day they brought back nothing. When Cyaxares, who was evidently not the most even-tempered of men, saw that they had returned empty-handed, he had them roughed up and publicly humiliated. So indignant were the Scythians at this treatment, which they felt to have been thoroughly unjustified, that they put their heads together and decided that they would carve up one of their young pupils, dress him for the table exactly as they were accustomed to dress game and then serve the boy up to Cyaxares, as though he were indeed some catch they had hunted down, while they themselves, the moment the dish had been laid before the king, made off at breakneck speed for the court of Alyattes, the son of Sadyattes, in Sardis. All went exactly to plan. Cyaxares and his guests at the banquet tucked into the joint of meat – and the Scythians, their business done, claimed asylum from Alyattes.

[74] The aftermath of this was that Cyaxares demanded their extradition, but Alyattes refused, and so there was war between the Lydians and the Medes. For five years it raged, with the fortunes of battle favour-

ing now the Medes over the Lydians, and now the Lydians over the
Medes. On one occasion, they even fought what can only be described
as a battle at night. Then, in the sixth year of a conflict that until that
point had been thoroughly indecisive, there was yet another engagement, and this time it so happened that, right in the midst of the battle,
the two sides suddenly found themselves fighting in the dark again, even
though it was still the day. The Ionians had been forewarned of this
eclipse by Thales of Miletus, who had pinpointed the date[103] with such
accuracy that he had identified the very year in which it did indeed eventually take place. When the Lydians and the Medes saw that the day was
darkening into night, they not merely broke off the battle, but both
actively committed themselves to securing a long-term peace. Syennesis,
from Cicilia, and Labynetus,[104] a Babylonian, were the two principal
negotiators. Both were keen that a formal treaty should be signed, and
that the two sides be bound by ties of marriage. Accordingly, it was
decided that Alyattes would give the hand of his daughter, Aryenis, to
Astyages, the son of Cyaxares – for everyone knew that treaties rarely
endure unless they are framed by lasting sureties. This compact was
then formalized according to the custom of both peoples, which differs
from Greek practice in only one detail: both parties, after they have
nicked the skin on their own forearms, will then lick up the other's
blood.[105]

[75] It was this same Astyages who was the father of Cyrus' mother
and who, for reasons I will explain later on in my narrative, had been
toppled and imprisoned by his grandson. Perhaps it is no surprise, then,
that Croesus should have regarded Cyrus' actions as a provocation, and
sent messengers to ask the oracles if he should invade Persia; nor, once
the oracle's ambiguous answer had been brought back to him, that he
should have interpreted it favourably for his own ambitions, and pushed
his army directly into the Persian sphere of influence. When Croesus
arrived at the Halys, he used existing bridges to get his troops across the
river – that is my opinion, at any rate, although it is true that the story
as conventionally told by the Greeks[106] holds Thales of Miletus responsible for effecting the crossing. This version presupposes that the bridges
had not yet been built, and that Croesus, arriving at the river with his
army, found himself with no idea how to cross it; Thales, however, who
was present in the camp at the time, was able to make the river flow
on both sides of the army, rather than merely on its left. He achieved

this feat by digging a deep, crescent-shaped trench, starting upstream from the army's encampment and finishing well in its rear, so that the river was diverted from its old course into the new one, flowing on round the camp until in due course it had bypassed it altogether and rejoined the original channel. Instead of one river, there were now two – and both were fordable. Indeed, there are those who say that the original river-bed dried up altogether, a claim which seems to me most improbable[107] – for how then would the return crossing have been made?

[76] Beyond the river, Croesus and his army advanced into a land known as Pteria: this is the most readily defensible region of Cappadocia, and lies more or less in a line with the city of Sinope[108] on the Euxine Sea. Croesus built a camp there, and set himself to ravaging the Syrians' farmland. The main city of the Pterians was captured, its inhabitants enslaved and all its outlying settlements overrun, while the Syrians – who had done absolutely nothing to merit this treatment – were made into refugees. Cyrus, meanwhile, had been mustering his own army, and now he set off to confront Croesus, raising conscripts from among all the peoples he passed along his way. Prior to setting out with his army on this expedition, he had even sent heralds to the Ionians, trying to incite them to rebel against Croesus – but they had resisted his blandishments, and so it was that Cyrus ended up in the region of Pteria, eye-balling Croesus from his camp and then locking with him in a trial of strength. The battle was fierce and the casualties heavy on both sides, but even as dusk began to thicken and the two armies fell back, neither had secured victory, such was the quality of the contest that the rival camps had fought.

[77] To Croesus, of course, this came as a major disappointment; and because the army he had led into battle was much smaller than that of Cyrus, he attributed his lack of success to the fact that he had been outnumbered. So it was, the next day, when Cyrus did not return to the fray, that he ordered a withdrawal to Sardis. Prior to his alliance with the Lacedaemonians, he had arranged a pact with Amasis, the king of Egypt; and it was his intention now to invoke the terms of this treaty with the Egyptians. Nor was that all – for because he had also made an alliance with Labynetus, who was the ruler of Babylon during this period, he similarly planned to summon the Babylonians to his assistance, as well as issuing a specific date for the Lacedaemonians to join

him; then, with these reinforcements secured, and his own army mustered, he aimed to bed down for the winter and to attack the Persians the moment spring arrived. Sure enough, no sooner had he returned to Sardis than he put this plan into action, dispatching heralds round his various allies, instructing them to assemble at Sardis in five months' time. The mercenaries in the army that had already fought the Persians he disbanded and sent home, every last one – for so evenly matched had he and his rival found themselves while going head to head, it never crossed his mind that Cyrus would actually advance on Sardis.

[78] Over and over Croesus turned his plans in his head; and as he did so, all the lower reaches of the city began to swarm with serpents. No sooner had this phenomenon manifested itself than horses out in the fields, interrupting their grazing, came trotting into town and started eating the snakes. Croesus naturally supposed that he was being shown a portent – as indeed he was. Urgently, then, he sent messengers to Telmessus,[109] where there were men qualified to interpret such things. Sure enough, on their arrival, his emissaries were told by the Telmessians precisely what the prodigy meant – but Croesus never got the news. Well before the return voyage to Sardis was over, he had fallen into enemy hands. This was in fact exactly what the Telmessians had said would occur: that Croesus could expect to hear the languages of a foreign army spoken in his land, and would witness its inhabitants conquered by invaders. For what is a snake, after all, if not the offspring of its native earth, and what a horse, if not a creature broken to warfare, and imported from foreign fields? Such was the interpretation provided by the Telmessians. They had delivered their judgement in complete ignorance of the news from Sardis, and of what had happened to Croesus himself, even though he had already been made a captive by that time.

[79] Meanwhile, in the wake of the battle of Pteria, with Croesus in headlong retreat, and with news reaching the Persians that he planned to disband his army on his return home, Cyrus held a council of war, at which it was agreed that the opportunity to march on Sardis as quickly as possible, before the Lydian forces could be mustered a second time, was too good to miss. No sooner had this been decided than it was put into effect. The messenger who brought Croesus the news that the Persians were at his doorstep was none other than Cyrus himself. Nevertheless, despite the fact that Croesus now found himself in desperate straits, with all the assumptions on which he had based his strategy

left in ruins, he still led the Lydians out to battle. Not for nothing was this an era when the Lydians stood unrivalled for courage and prowess in war among the peoples of Asia.[110] Their particular strength lay in their cavalry, for not only were they brilliantly skilful horsemen, but they could handle lances of an unusual length.

[80] The two sides met in front of the city of Sardis, on an immense and treeless plain. (It is watered by a number of rivers, the Hyllus included: all of them are tributaries of the largest river, the Hermus, which rises in the mountain sacred to the mother goddess Dindymene and reaches the sea near the city of Phocaea.) When Cyrus saw the Lydians arrayed for battle, his alarm at the threat posed by their cavalry led him to adopt a suggestion of a Mede, a man called Harpagus: namely, that all the camels which been following in the army's train carrying food and baggage should be divested completely of their loads, formed into a single unit and mounted by men dressed in the clothes of a cavalry unit. Once they had readied themselves, Cyrus commanded these men to advance against Croesus' horsemen, with the rest of his army following behind – his infantry first and then, in the rear, all his cavalry. His orders, given to his entire army as they waited at their battle-stations, were to spare not a single Lydian, but rather to kill all who stood in their way – all, that was, apart from Croesus, who was to be taken alive even if he resisted capture. Such were the instructions that Cyrus issued. As for the reason why he had positioned his camels directly opposite the enemy's cavalry: this was because horses are terrified of camels, and cannot stand the sight of them, nor even to breathe in their scent upon the air. Here was the detail, the crucial detail, upon which the entire stratagem had been founded: it provided Cyrus with a means of disabling Croesus' cavalry, of neutralizing the arm which the Lydian most expected to shine. Sure enough, when battle was joined, the horses had only to smell and see the camels to turn tail, and to trample, as they stampeded, all Croesus' hopes into the dust. Nevertheless, the courage of the Lydians did not fail them; realizing what was happening, they leapt down from their saddles and met the Persians on foot. The slaughter on both sides was prodigious; but it was the Lydians who finally withdrew and fled, back behind the walls of their city, where they now found themselves cooped up by the Persians and put under blockade.

[81] So it was that the invaders settled down to the siege. Croesus,

confident that he would be able to hold out for a good while, sent messengers out from his stronghold to his allies. Whereas his first dispatch had requested them all to assemble in Sardis in four months' time, now, with his capital under siege, he sent a revised appeal: that they should come to his assistance without delay.

[82] This alert was sent to all his allies; but to none of them was it sent with a greater sense of urgency than to the Lacedaemonians. By coincidence, however, the warriors of Sparta were preoccupied at the time with a quarrel of their own, a dispute with Argos over the region known as Thyreae, which they had recently annexed and occupied, despite the fact that it lay within the Argive orbit. (In fact, everything as far west as Malea had once belonged to Argos – not simply the mainland, but the island of Cythera, and all the other islands too.) The Argives, coming to the rescue of their stolen fiefdom, held a parley with the Lacedaemonians, and agreed with them that three hundred men from each side should meet in pitched combat, with Thyreae going to the victors. Meanwhile, the main bodies of both armies were to withdraw back to their own borders, and to remain there for the duration of the contest – thereby ensuring that neither was tempted to come in on the side of its own champions, should it witness them succumbing. Such were the terms on which the two armies parted; and behind them, on the field of battle, the nominated warriors on both sides advanced to the fight. So evenly matched was the clash between them that by the end only three of the six hundred men were left: Alcenor and Chromius for the Argives, and on the Lacedaemonian side, Othryades. These, as night began to fall, were the sole survivors. The two Argives, taking for granted that they were the victors, made off at speed for Argos, but the Lacedaemonian, Othryades, who had been busying himself with the stripping of the Argive dead and the stockpiling of their arms in his camp, refused to abandon his post. The next day, the two armies reappeared, and the story of what had happened was rehearsed in full. For a while, both sides claimed victory: the Argives on the grounds that they had the most champions left standing, and the Lacedaemonians because their own champion – in contrast to the two Argives who had abandoned the battlefield – had remained there all night, despoiling the enemy dead. Finally, so heated did the argument become that the two sides fell to blows. Casualties on both sides were heavy – but it was the Lacedaemonians who came out on top.[111] Ever since then, the Argives have worn

their hair cropped short, in contrast to their previous custom, which was to wear it long; indeed, they passed a law, complete with curses against those who broke it, to the effect that no man in Argos should ever grow out his hair, and no woman wear gold jewellery, until Thyreae was theirs again. The Lacedaemonians also passed a new law, but one that was the mirror image of the one passed in Argos, for whereas previously they had worn their hair short, now they began to wear it long.[112] One other detail – it is said that Othryades, the sole survivor of the three hundred, felt such shame at the thought of returning to Sparta while all his comrades lay dead in the earth of Thyreae, that he killed himself there.[113]

[83] This, then, was the situation in which the Spartan elite were operating when the herald from Sardis arrived, requesting their assistance in helping Croesus to lift the siege. Despite everything, once they had heard the herald out, they showed themselves more than willing to answer the call for help. No sooner had they readied themselves and their fleet[114] for departure, however, than another message came, this time bringing news that the Lydians' stronghold had fallen, and that Croesus himself had been taken alive, and was a prisoner. The Lacedaemonians, with great regret, abandoned their effort immediately.

[84] This is the story of how Sardis fell. Two weeks after bottling Croesus up inside the city, Cyrus sent horsemen touring the lines of his army with a proclamation: the first man over the battlements could expect a rich reward. Prompted by this announcement, soldier after soldier made the attempt, but none succeeded. Then, when everyone else had given up, a Mardian by the name of Hyroeades made an attempt to scale the one point of the acropolis which stood unguarded for so precipitously did it rise, and so impregnably, that it had never crossed anyone's mind that an attack there could possibly succeed. Even Meles, a king of Sardis back in former times, had overlooked it; and he had been told by the Telmessians that a lion borne to him by his concubine, if it were carried around the battlements, would serve to render Sardis forever proof against capture. Meles had duly carried the lion along all those stretches of the walls where the acropolis might be reckoned vulnerable to attack; but the sheerest and most impregnable spot, a cliff on the side of the city which faces Mount Tmolus, he had neglected to tour. It was down the very face of this point on the acropolis, however, that Hyroeades, the previous day, had seen a helmet roll, and then, from the summit, a Lydian descend to retrieve it – a sight which the Mardian had

noted and replayed over and over again in his innermost thoughts. Up
the cliff he went and other Persians quickly began to follow in his wake.
More and more made the climb; and the consequence was the fall of
Sardis and the sacking of the entire city.

[85] And what of the fate of Croesus himself? To answer that question I must mention his son again, the one who despite all his many
other qualities had always been a mute. In the days before the ruin of
his prosperity, Croesus had done all that he could for the young man,
trying this and that, even to the extent of sending emissaries to Delphi
to consult the oracle on his son's behalf. This was the Pythia's reply:

'Such folly, though you are lord of many, Lydian-born Croesus!
Beware what you wish for! That sound you long to hear, in your
home,
Your son finding his tongue – better for you never to hear it.
Know, when he does talk for the first time, that the day will be
an evil one!'

Well – the battlements had been stormed, and one of the Persians was
approaching Croesus to cut him down, not knowing who he was. Even
though Croesus could see the soldier coming, such was the numbing
effect of the catastrophe which had overwhelmed him that he did not
care – for what did it matter to him now if he was struck down and
killed? But his son, the mute, terrified and appalled by the sight of the
Persian bearing down upon his father, suddenly found that his tongue
was sounding out words. 'Please, Sir,' he cried, 'do not kill Croesus!' This
was the very first time that he had spoken – and from that moment on
he could talk with perfect fluency, and continued to do so all his life.[115]

[86] Sardis fell to the Persians, and Croesus into Persian hands, in the
fourteenth year of his reign, and on the fourteenth day of the siege. Just
as the oracle had foretold, he had indeed destroyed a mighty empire –
his own. Now, following his capture, he was led into the presence of
Cyrus, who had him loaded down with chains, and then, accompanied
by the children of some prominent Lydians, fourteen of them in all, placed
on top of a huge pyre, ready built for the occasion. Quite what Cyrus
had in mind, I am not sure: perhaps he was aiming to dedicate the
choicest offerings in his possession to some god or other; or perhaps he
was looking to fulfil a vow; or perhaps he had learned of Croesus' reputation as a god-fearing man, and made him mount the pyre to see if

a supernatural agency of some kind would preserve him from being burned alive. Whatever the explanation,[116] however, Cyrus did what he did; and Croesus, standing there on top of the pyre, and in the full consciousness of his ruin, was suddenly reminded of a maxim that seemed to him now touched by an authentically divine wisdom, for it was the same maxim that had been pronounced by Solon, when he had declared that no one living ranks as happy. The recollection of this prompted Croesus to sigh bitterly, and to utter a groan; and then, breaking a long silence, he repeated, three times over, the name of Solon. Cyrus, overhearing him, ordered the interpreters to approach Croesus and demand of him whom it was he had been calling upon – which they duly did. Although Croesus refused to respond to their questioning at first, an answer was eventually dragged out of him. 'A man so remarkable', he said, 'that I would willingly have paid a fortune to ensure that every ruler in the world be given the chance to listen to him.' This reply, of course, made little sense to the interpreters; and so they pressed him to clarify his meaning. Crowding around Croesus, they kept on badgering him until at last he told them about Solon: how he had come from Athens, how he had made light of all the splendour he had been shown (that had been the gist, at any rate), and about how everything he had warned Croesus might happen had indeed come to pass. 'Nor', said Croesus, 'were his words directed at me alone, for they apply with no less force to men everywhere – and especially to men who consider themselves blessed by fortune.'[117] So he spoke – and all the while the pyre, which had already been torched, was starting to crackle along its edges. But Cyrus, when he learned from his interpreters what Croesus had said, found his heart melting.[118] He reflected that he too was mortal, and yet there he was, burning alive a fellow human being – and one who had previously been no less prosperous than himself. And then too there was his dread of retribution, and his growing consciousness of the mutability of the affairs of men; and so he gave orders that the fire should be extinguished at once, and that Croesus and all those with him should be helped down from the pyre. And yet the flames, despite frantic efforts, could not be mastered.

[87] It was then, so the Lydians say, that Croesus grasped what was happening: that Cyrus had changed his mind, and that his men, despite all their efforts to extinguish the flames, were failing to bring them under control. Seeing this, Croesus raised a desperate appeal to Apollo:

'If ever any offering I have made to you has been acceptable in your sight,' he cried out, 'then please, stand by me now, and redeem me from this danger I face!' Such was his invocation of the god, uttered through his tears; and at once the previously clear and windless sky began to cloud over, and a storm to break, and then rain to lash down so hard that all the flames were put out. Here was proof enough for Cyrus that Croesus was indeed a good man, and a favourite of the gods; and so he had him brought down from the pyre. 'Tell me now, Croesus,' he asked, 'someone must have persuaded you to invade my country, and to be my enemy rather than my friend – who was it?' 'My Lord,' Croesus answered, 'it was all my own doing – to your profit, and to my misfortune. When I launched the invasion, however, it was with the full encouragement of the god of the Greeks – so the ultimate blame, I suppose, should lie with him. For would I otherwise ever have been so foolish as to choose war over peace? In peacetime it is sons who bury their fathers – but in times of war, it is fathers who bury their sons. Somewhere in the heavens there is someone smiling at what has happened.'[119]

[88] Cyrus, impressed by this speech of Croesus', ordered his chains struck off, and commanded him to sit down by his side. Indeed, it was not only Cyrus but his entire entourage who found themselves admiring Croesus' demeanour. Lost in thought, however, the man himself said not a word. Then he turned, watching as the Persians devastated the Lydian capital, and opened his mouth at last. 'O King, should I say what has been on my mind, or is this not an appropriate time to speak?' Cyrus told him not to be afraid, and to say whatever he wished. Croesus responded with a second question. 'What are they doing, all these rampaging hordes?' 'Why,' said Cyrus, 'they are tearing your city to pieces, and carting off your treasures.' But Croesus turned this statement upon its head. 'It is not my city they are tearing to pieces, not my treasures. None of it belongs to me any more. It is you who is being robbed.'

[89] This observation was sufficient to give Cyrus pause; and so he dismissed the rest of his entourage and asked Croesus for his full reading of the situation. 'Since the gods have seen fit to give me to you as a slave,' Croesus replied, 'it is clearly my duty, should I ever have a particular insight, to share it with you. The Persians are naturally prone to violence – and they are poor. If you simply stand by as they plunder and hoard all this staggering wealth, then I can tell you what is likely to happen – the one who grabs the most is bound to end up behind a bid

for power. However, I do have a suggestion to make – and one that I hope will meet with your approval. Put your bodyguards on sentry-duty by all the city gates. Have them confiscate any valuables they see being removed from the city. Give as your pretext the need to offer a tithe to Zeus. If you do that, then you will avoid the obloquy that would otherwise be yours for forcibly stripping people of their plunder – for they will recognize the justice of what you are doing, and willingly forgo what they have.'[120]

[90] Impressed by what he had heard, Cyrus approved this advice wholeheartedly. With much praise for its good sense, he ordered his bodyguards to put the proposal into effect, then turned back to Croesus. 'A king you may once have been,' he said, 'but I see you are no less ready on that account to do me good service and to offer me sound advice. Let me give you something in exchange. Is there anything you want? You only have to ask me for it, and it will be yours straightaway!' 'Master,' Croesus answered, 'nothing would gratify me more than to be allowed to send these chains to the god of the Greeks, whom I honoured above all others, and to ask him if it is his custom to cheat those who serve him well.' When Cyrus asked him what grudge he could possibly hold against the god that he made such a request, Croesus told him the whole story: the plans he had drawn up, the answers he had received from the oracle, the rich gifts he had sent (these were a particular grievance) and the prophecies which had encouraged him to go to war with the Persians. Then, when he had finished his story, he repeated his request for permission to take his reproaches to the god. Cyrus laughed. 'Yes, Croesus,' he said, 'of course you have my permission – not only on this occasion, but whenever else you may have a similar request to make.' The moment Croesus heard this, he dispatched a delegation of Lydians to Delphi. Their orders were to lay the fetters on the threshold of the temple, and then, pointing to them, to ask the oracle if he was not ashamed to have encouraged Croesus to go to war with the Persians, and to believe that Cyrus' hold on power could possibly be destroyed, when the only fruits of such a war were destined to be his chains. All this they were to demand; and then they were to ask whether it was the normal practice of the gods of the Greeks to show such ingratitude.

[91] But when the Lydians arrived in Delphi and obediently repeated Croesus' words, the Pythia, it is said, had a ready retort. 'Not even a god can evade what fate has preordained. Five generations ago, an ancestor

of Croesus, a man who at the time was a guard sworn to the personal protection of the Heraclids, succumbed to the seductions of a woman's treachery, killed his master and stole his throne, an honour to which he had no claim – and now it is Croesus who has paid the debt on that crime.[121] The truth is that Apollo was keen to see Sardis suffer her downfall in the time of Croesus' sons, rather than during the reign of Croesus himself – but the Fates would not be gainsaid. Nevertheless, what little they would allow, the god did secure on Croesus' behalf. The fall of Sardis was delayed by three whole years – and so you should be sure to inform Croesus that he has had three years more of freedom than was originally his lot. Secondly – did the god not come to his rescue when he was on the verge of being burned to ashes? As for the oracle he received, Croesus certainly has no right to find fault with that: attack the Persians, Apollo declared, and you will destroy a great empire. Such an answer should have prompted Croesus to consult his advisers, and then to send men back to ask which empire had been meant: Cyrus' or his own? But because he misinterpreted what had been said, he did not follow it up with the right enquiry – and so he should accept that the fault is his alone. He should also acknowledge that he misread the very last oracle he received – the one in which Apollo alluded to a mule. After all, what else but a mule would you term Cyrus, a man who has both the blue blood of his mother flowing in his veins, and the blood of his father, who came from a quite different country, and was of a much lower social class? For Cyrus' mother was a Mede, and the daughter of Astyages, the king of Media; but his father was a Persian, a vassal of the Medes, and therefore in every way the inferior of the woman he ended up marrying, who should properly have ranked as his mistress as well as his queen.'[122] This was the reply that the Pythia gave to the Lydians; and once they had returned with it to Sardis, and Croesus had listened to them repeat it, he freely acknowledged that he had indeed been culpable, and that the god was not to blame.

[92] Such is the story of Croesus' reign, and of how Ionia came to be conquered for the first time.[123] Greece is full of Croesus' votive offerings, and not only the ones that I have already had cause to mention: in Thebes, in Boeotia, for instance, there is a golden tripod, dedicated to Ismenian Apollo; in Ephesus, it was Croesus who donated the golden cows and most of the pillars; and in 'The Shrine Before the Temple' at Delphi, there is a huge shield of gold. All these dedications were still to

be seen even in my day, although there are others which have not survived. Branchidae, in Miletus, I am told, also boasts offerings presented by Croesus, which are similar to those found in Delphi, and equal in weight. All the gifts he sent to Delphi, and to the shrine of Amphiaraus too, were paid for out of his own household coffers and the patrimony he had inherited from his father; but the rest were funded by the estates of an enemy of his, the same man who had led the faction which was opposed to his becoming king, and backed the right of Pantaleon to the throne. (Pantaleon was the son of Alyattes, but he and Croesus were only half-brothers – for Croesus was born to Alyattes by a Carian woman, whereas Pantaleon's mother was an Ionian.) It was Croesus, of course, who ended up inheriting the throne from his father; and no sooner was he king than he made sure to torture his opponent to death by hauling him over the spikes of a carding-comb.[124] Even prior to this, Croesus had vowed that all his adversary's belongings would be dedicated to the gods, and so they were, just as I previously described – for they were sent to the various shrines I have already listed. So much for the votive offerings made by Croesus.

[93] As far as natural wonders are concerned, Lydia has nothing particularly worthy of record, certainly not in comparison with other countries – the one exception being the gold dust which is washed down from Mount Tmolus. The country can, however, boast a man-made wonder which, with the exception of those built by the Egyptians and the Babylonians, serves to put all others in the shade. This is the tomb of Croesus' father, Alyattes, a monument which consists of a mound of earth raised up on a base of giant stones. Its construction was funded by tradesmen, craftsmen and whores. Even in my day, there were five stone pillars on the summit, each one inscribed with a record of precisely what proportion of the tomb had been funded by these various classes of business; and the figures, when they are added up, prove that the largest contribution of all was made by the whores.[125] (Not that this is surprising: in Lydia, every daughter born to working-class parents will work as a prostitute, and continue to do so until she has raised sufficient money for a dowry, and can secure a husband. This she will arrange on her own terms.) The circumference of the tomb is 6 stades, and it is 13 plethra wide. Beside it is a large lake, named after Gyges, which according to the Lydians never dries up. That is all there is to be said about the tomb of Alyattes.

[94] Their habit of sending their daughters out to work as prostitutes excepted, the Lydians live their lives in a way not dissimilar to the Greeks. So far as we know, they were the first people ever to strike gold and silver coins,[126] and to use them: the result was the invention of shopping. For their own part, the Lydians also claim to have invented the games of which both they and the Greeks are nowadays so fond. The invention of these games, so they say, took place at the same time as the colonization of Tyrrhenia; and they tell a story which explains this conjunction of events. Back in the reign of Atys, the son of Manes, Lydia was afflicted by a terrible famine. For a while, the Lydians endured the pangs of hunger as patiently as they could; but as time went by, and the grip of the famine worsened, so they began to look around for some way to alleviate it, with first one solution and then another being proposed. Among the expedients devised during this period was a whole host of games – dice, knuckle-bones, anything involving balls. (In fact, the only game the Lydians do not claim to have invented themselves is backgammon.) But how, you may ask, did these inventions help the Lydians to cope with the famine? The answer is that every other day they would play their games, and thereby distract themselves from the need to go scrabbling about after food, while on the alternate days they would stop playing games, and concentrate on the demands of their stomachs instead. By this means, they kept going for a full eighteen years. Still, rather than abating, the crisis grew ever more brutal. Eventually, the king divided the entire Lydian people into two, drew lots, and decreed that one half of the population should remain in Lydia, while the other half were to emigrate. As king over those whom fortune had ordained should stay behind, he appointed himself; while as the leader of the emigrants he appointed his son, a man by the name of Tyrrhenus. Once the lots had been cast, the group which was to leave their country made their way down to the coast at Smyrna, built ships for themselves and loaded up all their serviceable possessions, and then set off in search of livelihood and land. Many were the peoples whose countries they sailed past; until in due course they arrived in the land of the Umbrians, and there they settled and put down permanent roots. No longer did they call themselves Lydians; instead, they bore the name of the prince who had led them, and they have come to be known, in witness to his nomenclature, as Tyrrhenians.[127] The Lydians, meanwhile, ended up the slaves of the Persians.[128]

*

[95] It is time now to open up a new chapter in our story. Who was Cyrus, this man who had destroyed the empire of Croesus, and how was it that the Persians had risen to mastery of Asia? I have uncovered four different accounts, and each one serves to shed its own light upon Cyrus. But the version I have chosen to follow is the one told by those Persians who think it more important to get the facts straight than simply to exalt Cyrus.[129] Now, for a period of 520 years, it was the Assyrians who were the masters of Asia; and the first to revolt against their rule were the Medes. In fact, this war of independence proved to be the making of the rebels, for so heroically did they fight the Assyrians that they succeeded in casting off the yoke of slavery altogether and securing their freedom. In the wake of this victory, others too followed the Medes' example.

[96] Yet though the entire continent eventually won its independence, despotism was destined to make a return. There was a Mede named Deioces[130] the son of Phraortes, a man whose lust for power was more than equalled by the keenness of his intellect, and who had come up with a plan. The Medes at this time lived in settlements which were nothing more than villages, and Deioces, who was already a figure of high standing in his own village, began to work harder even than he had been doing previously to establish himself as the very model of fair dealing – for the rule of law was notable by its absence across the whole of Media, and he well understood that to those who value justice there can be no greater enemy than its breakdown. The Medes of his own village, observing his high moral standards, duly appointed him their judge; and Deioces, who was forever focused upon how to win power, made sure to fulfil this office with an unbending show of integrity. Such conduct won him no little praise from his fellow-villagers – so much so, indeed, that the people of other villages began to pick up on his reputation as a man who, uniquely, could be guaranteed to arbitrate between rival plaintiffs with a strict impartiality. No longer willing to tolerate the breakdown of justice, people were inspired by what they had heard about Deioces to approach him, and gladly to submit their cases to his judgement, until, in the end, they refused to turn to anyone else.

[97] Larger and larger grew this body of his loyal clients, men who knew that they could rely upon him to resolve their every lawsuit in accordance with the facts alone. Deioces himself, however, realizing that he was now being called upon by anyone with a legal problem, declared

that he had had enough: no longer would he take his place in the public chair where he had previously sat to deliver his verdicts, and no longer would he operate as a judge. How did it serve his interests, after all, to spend his entire day attending to the business of his neighbours, to the utter neglect of his own? But when the impact of this decision upon the villages proved to be a crime wave worse even than the previous one had been, and a total collapse of law and order, the Medes met in assembly to debate what to do about the situation (a debate in which, I strongly suspect, it was the partisans of Deioces who hogged the floor). 'Only continue as we are', they said, 'and life in this country will become insupportable. We must appoint a king – a king who is one of our own! How else will we ever secure a society governed by the rule of law? What prospect otherwise of getting down to work? Are we all to be swept away upon this rising tide of anarchy?' Such, in their essentials, were the arguments which convinced the Medes of their need for a king.[131]

[98] Which in turn prompted an obvious question: who should they now choose to rule over them? Overwhelmingly the most popular candidate, because the most praiseworthy, was Deioces;[132] and he it was who duly secured the appointment. 'Build me a palace fit for a king!' he then commanded. 'Give me a bodyguard!' The Medes obeyed. Up went a large and well-fortified palace, on a site chosen by Deioces himself, and in came a bodyguard, chosen by the king from among the entire population of Media, without interference from anyone. Then, with his grip on power secure, he compelled the Medes to labour at building a single great conurbation, a project so demanding of their time and effort that everywhere else in Media was left to crumble through neglect. Again the Medes were brought to comply, and so was raised the city known now as Agbatana,[133] an immense and impregnable stronghold enclosed within a series of concentric walls. These are so fashioned that each successive defensive ring serves to rise above the preceding one by the height of its bastions, an effect assisted by Agbatana's hillside situation, to be sure, but which owes much, nevertheless, to careful design. There are seven rings in all – and enclosed within the innermost one are the royal palace and the treasuries. The outermost one is roughly the size of the wall which encircles Athens.[134] The bastions of these various walls have all been painted different colours, so that the cumulative effect is akin to that of a garland of flowers: the first circle is painted

white, the second black, the third purple, the fourth an azure blue and the fifth orange. As for the bastions of the two innermost circles, those of the penultimate one are plated with silver, and those of the last one with gold.

[99] These fortifications were built for the protection of Deioces himself and his palace; everyone else was ordered to settle beyond the walls. Then, with the completion of his various building projects, Deioces set about establishing a wholly novel ceremonial: he forbade people to come into his presence, obliging them instead to communicate with him through intermediaries; he placed an interdict on anyone so much as seeing the king; and he proclaimed it an outrage for anyone to laugh or spit in the royal presence. There was method behind this cocooning of himself within pomp and ritual, for he was looking to be screened from the gaze of his contemporaries, men with whom he had been brought up, and who were not an iota his inferiors in either breeding or courage. No wonder, then, that Deioces should have fretted about provoking them to resentment and conspiracy, and sought, by hiding himself away, to foster a sense of his own mystique.[135]

[100] The introduction of this system of etiquette was not the only way in which he sought to strengthen his autocracy,[136] for he wielded a rod of iron in the field of justice too. Rather than presenting their suits in person, plaintiffs were obliged instead to send them into the palace in written form; Deioces would assess them, then have his verdicts sent back out. Parallel to this manner of resolving lawsuits was a further innovation: anyone reported to be getting above his station would be summoned into the royal presence and slapped down with a punishment appropriate to the offence. Spies were everywhere in the kingdom – Deioces' eyes and ears.

[101] Although it is true that his sway never extended beyond the frontiers of Media, his great achievement was not merely to have forged the Medes into a single people but to have ruled them as one. There is certainly no lack of tribes in Media. The Busae, the Parataceni, the Struchates, the Arizanti, the Budii, the Magians: all are Medes.

[102] Deioces finally died after a reign of fifty-three years, and was succeeded as ruler by Phraortes, his son. The new king, dissatisfied at ranking merely as lord of Media, set himself at the head of a great army. The first people he attacked were the Persians, whom he forced into vassalage. With two powerful peoples now brought under his command, he

then advanced to the conquest of Asia, country by country, until at length he came up against the Assyrians – or to be precise against the Assyrians of Nineveh, that same people who had once been the masters of the world, but who since a revolt by their allies had found themselves shorn of their empire. Nevertheless, they remained a significant power; in the resulting war Phraortes himself and much of his army were wiped out, thereby bringing to an end his reign of twenty-two years.

[103] After Phraortes' death, it was his son, Cyaxares, who was the next of Deioces' line to ascend the throne. Cyaxares, according to reliable report, had even more of a taste for battle than his predecessors. He was the first man in Asia to divide his troops up into separate units, and the first to regiment what had previously been a disorganized rabble into separate lines of battle: spearmen, archers and cavalry. It was also Cyaxares who fought the battle against the Lydians on the day of the eclipse, and who forged all the lands of Asia beyond the River Halys into a single empire, ruled by himself. He took advantage of all the resources this gave him to launch an attack on Nineveh, with the aim of wiping the city out, and thereby avenging his father. He defeated the Assyrians in battle – but then, in the midst of his siege of Nineveh, he was attacked by King Madyes, the son of Protothyes, who came against him at the head of an immense army of Scythians. These invaders had crossed into Asia in hot pursuit of the Cimmerians, a people whom they had previously expelled from Europe, and driven before them in headlong flight. Now the Scythians had arrived in the land of the Medes.

[104] It will take a man travelling light thirty days to cover the distance from Lake Maeëtis to Colchis, on the River Phasis; but to go from Colchis to Media takes no great time at all. There is only the one country to pass through, the land of the Saspeirians – and then comes the Median frontier. The Scythians, however, rather than taking this route, had veered northwards and followed the much longer upland road, keeping the Caucasus mountains on their right. The Scythians met with the Medes in battle and routed them; and so it was, with the consequent collapse of Median power, that the whole of Asia became theirs.

[105] The Scythians' next target was Egypt. Arriving in the region of Syria known as Palestine, they were met there by the king of Egypt, Psammetichus,[137] who alternately bribed and begged them not to continue their advance, and thereby succeeded in turning them back. As the Scythians were retracing their steps through Syria, they came to Ascalon;

and while most of them bypassed the city and left it untouched, a small group separated from the main body of the expedition and fell to plundering the sanctuary of Aphrodite Urania.[138] (An interesting detail that I uncovered during the course of my investigations is that this same sanctuary is the oldest temple to the goddess in existence: even the one in Cyprus derived from it – as the Cypriots themselves freely acknowledge. As for the one in Cythera – well – who could that have been founded by if not the Phoenicians, and from where did the Phoenicians come if not the very region of Syria where the temple at Ascalon stands?)[139] The Scythians who looted the shrine found themselves struck down by the goddess with a disease that transformed them into women:[140] one that their descendants still suffer from even today. This, at any rate, is how the Scythians explain the ailment; and anyone who visits Scythia can see with his own eyes what it is to be an 'Enarean', as the natives term those afflicted by the malady.

[106] The dominion of the Scythians over Asia lasted twenty-eight years – a period during which their violence[141] and arrogance had everything in a state of constant upheaval. When they were not busy extorting the arbitrary taxes they had imposed on everyone, they would gallop around the country, indulging themselves in barefaced robbery. At last, Cyaxares and the Medes hosted a great feast for most of the Scythians, and then, when they had got their guests roaring drunk, put them all to the sword. So it was, with one fell swoop, that the Medes won back their great-power status, and all their former dominions as well. They even succeeded in capturing Nineveh (an episode I will recount in a later chapter),[142] and absorbed the whole of Assyria into their empire – all, that is, except for Babylon and its territories. When Cyaxares finally died, it was after a reign which had lasted – if the Scythian period of rule is included in the tally – for forty years.

[107] His successor on the throne was his son, Astyages. He had a daughter called Mandane, and one night, in his sleep, he imagined that he saw her urinating, making such a flood that it filled his entire city, and drowned the whole of Asia. When Astyages confided the details of this nightmare to those among the Magi[143] who were proficient in the art of reading dreams, the interpretation that they gave him, a full and precise one, chilled his blood. As a result, when Mandane came to be of a nubile age, he did not give her as a wife to any Mede of appropriate status, but instead, haunted still by his dream, married her off to a

Persian named Cambyses – a man whom he knew to be of good family and undemonstrative disposition, but who, in Astyages' opinion, was so lacking in any social standing as to be the inferior by far of a Mede of even mediocre rank.

[108] But then, not a year after Mandane had settled down to married life with Cambyses, Astyages was visited by a second dream of his daughter. This time he saw a vine sprouting out of her intimate parts; and the tendrils of the vine reached so far that they served to put all Asia in their shade. Again, Astyages confided to the dream-readers what he had seen; and then he had his daughter, who was about to give birth, sent from Persia and placed under lock and key. His intention, once the baby had been born, was to have it killed; for the Magi, skilled as they were in the reading of dreams, had interpreted his vision to mean that his daughter's offspring would rule in his place. No wonder, then, that Astyages should have been made uneasy. Sure enough, once Cyrus had been safely delivered, the king summoned a kinsman of his, Harpagus by name, a Mede who served as steward of the entire royal estate and was the loyalest of the loyal, to issue him with some very particular orders. 'If I give you something to do, Harpagus, you are to do it properly. No going behind my back. Side with anyone apart from me, and you will be sure to pay the price. Now then – Mandane has given birth to a child. You are to get hold of it, take it to your house and dispose of it. You can inter the body as you please.' 'O King,' Harpagus replied, 'have you ever had any reason to find fault with me in the past? Can you really doubt just how determined I am not to get your orders wrong in the future? You have told me what you want to see happen. My duty is clear enough. What must be done, must be done.'

[109] Barely had Harpagus given this reply than the child, already wrapped up in a shroud, was handed over to him, to be wetted by his tears and borne by him to his house. On his arrival there, he told his wife everything that Astyages had said. 'What will you do now?' she asked him. 'Not what Astyages ordered,' Harpagus answered, 'that is for sure. He can rant and rave all he likes, but no matter how lunatic his tirades become I refuse to go along with his scheme. Me, the instrument of such a murder? Never! There are any number of reasons why I should refuse to kill the child. Not only is he a relative of mine, but Astyages is old, and has no male heir. Suppose, when he dies, that the person who picks up the reins of power should turn out to be Mandane – mother of

the very child he is getting me to kill. How would my prospects look then? Bleak – very bleak. Of course, it is essential that the child die for my own safety's sake, but it should be one of Astyages' servants who is the killer – not one of mine.'[144]

[110] And putting his words immediately into action, he dispatched a messenger to one of the king's cowherds, a man named Mithridates, who kept his cattle in pasturage ideally suited to Harpagus' purposes – for it was set high up in the mountains, and the mountains were infested with savage beasts. This Mithridates lived with his wife, another slave, who in Greek would have been known as 'Cyno', or 'bitch', for she bore the Median name 'Spako', and *spaka*, in Median, means 'bitch'. (It was beyond Agbatana, where the north wind is met by a range of mountains as it gusts towards the Euxine Sea, that there rose the foothills on which this herdsman set his cattle to graze. Although everywhere else in Media is completely flat, this one part of the country – the mountainous region which borders the land of the Saspeirians – consists of thickly wooded uplands.) When the cowherd, who had scurried to answer the summons, arrived before Harpagus, he was given his orders. 'Astyages has instructed that you are to take this child', Harpagus said, 'and leave it on the very loneliest of mountainsides. He wants it eliminated, and without delay. He has also asked me to pass on to you that should you fail to kill the child, and find some way to spare it, then your death will be a truly excruciating one. I will be watching – for I have my own mission, which is to ensure that the child is indeed exposed.'

[111] With these words still ringing in his ears, the herdsman picked up the child and retraced his steps, all the way back to his hut. It so happened that his wife, who for days had been waiting to go into labour, had given birth at around the same time as the herdsman was making his way to the city – certain proof that a guardian spirit was keeping watch over Cyrus. Husband and wife alike had been fretting about the other: he owing to anxiety about his wife's confinement, and she because of the seemingly unaccountable way in which Harpagus had summoned her husband. On his return home, the sight of him standing before her took the woman by such surprise that she immediately asked him, before the herdsman could so much as open his mouth, why it was that Harpagus had sent him such an urgent summons. 'My dearest wife,' he answered, 'I found something waiting for me in the city that I would give a great deal not to have seen or heard. Our masters are caught up in a terrible

business, and I only wish that it were otherwise. As I went in through Harpagus' doorway, I found that the entire house was echoing to the sound of weeping – and then, no sooner was I inside, than I saw a baby lying there, squirming and bawling, and it was dripping with gold, and dressed in the most exquisite clothes. When Harpagus saw me, he ordered me to pick up the child immediately, and be gone – and he said that I was to take the child with me, and abandon it on a mountainside, at a spot where the wild animals are at their most fierce. These orders, he told me, came directly from Astyages – and he kept on threatening me, over and over again, with what would happen if I let him down. So I picked the baby up and carried it off, taking for granted that the mother was a house-slave. Certainly, it never crossed my mind whose child it really was! What did puzzle me, of course, was the spectacle of the gold and the beautiful clothes – not to mention all those tears that were being shed, quite openly, in Harpagus' house. But then, as I was being shown the way out of the city, the whole story came out. The attendant who was serving as my escort, laying the new-born baby in my arms, told me that its parents were none other than Mandane, Astyages' daughter, and Cambyses, the son of Cyrus. What was more, the orders for its disposal did indeed come from Astyages. And look – here the child is.'

[112] So saying, the herdsman unveiled the infant and showed it to his wife. The sight of such a healthy, good-looking baby immediately had the woman flinging her arms around her husband's knees, and begging him, through floods of tears, not to expose it under any circumstances. 'What alternative do I have?' he replied. 'Harpagus will send spy after spy to check up on me, and I will be put to a terrible death if it is found out that I have disobeyed him.' The woman, however, rather than bowing to her husband's flat refusal, chose instead to try a second approach. 'Clearly,' she said, 'I am not going to be able to dissuade you from exposing the child. Alright, then. If it is absolutely necessary for a baby to be exposed – and to be seen to be exposed – then here is what I suggest you do. My own child, my very own child, came into the world stillborn. Take the body and expose it, and let us bring up the son of Astyages' daughter as if he were our own. It is not as if our masters will be able to catch us out having done anything wrong, is it? And only think how it will work to our advantage! Our own dead boy will be given a funeral fit for a king, while this child, still strong and healthy as he is, will escape execution.'

[113] The herdsman thought that this plan was, under all the circumstances, an excellent one, and so he immediately set about putting his wife's proposal into effect. The baby he had brought with him to be executed he handed over to his wife; his own baby he picked up and laid inside the container which he had earlier been using to transport the living child. Then, once he had adorned the corpse in all the finery previously worn by the other boy, he took it to the very loneliest of the mountains, and left it there. A day passed, and then another. Still the body lay exposed out on the mountainside. Only on the third day, and only after he had made sure to delegate one of his deputies to stand guard over it, did the herdsman head for town, and Harpagus' house. 'The time has come,' he announced, 'to show you the corpse of the infant.' To confirm this claim, Harpagus sent the most trusted members of his personal guard, who duly reported themselves satisfied, and interred the herdsman's child. So it was that the one baby was consigned to its grave, while the other, the boy who would subsequently be known as Cyrus, was adopted by the herdsman's wife and brought up as her own – although not, of course, as Cyrus, but under a quite different name.[145]

[114] Then, however, around the time of his tenth birthday, something happened which led to the revelation of his true identity. He and the other boys of his age were playing out in the main road of the village where they all lived, up amid the meadows where the royal cattle grazed. The game required the children to appoint a make-believe king – and upon whom should their choice fall if not the boy who was supposed to be the herdsman's son. More appointments followed, these ones made by the 'king' himself: some of his friends he set to building houses, and others to shouldering the spears of a bodyguard; one was ordered to serve him as his 'Eye', keeping his kingdom under unblinking surveillance, and another, in a particular mark of honour, to bring him his messages.[146] Not a playmate, in short, but he was given some task to carry out. There was one boy, however, the son of an eminent Mede named Artembares, who refused to do as he was told: a show of disobedience which prompted Cyrus to order his arrest. Once the other children had dutifully grabbed him, Cyrus, not stinting in the slightest, gave the boy a savage flogging. Outraged by what he saw as this insult to his dignity, the boy had no sooner been set free than he was running off down to the city and into his father's house, whining at the top of his

voice about the treatment he had received at the hands of Cyrus.
(Although, of course, he did not actually refer to his assailant as 'Cyrus',
since there was no one yet of that name to complain about, but rather
as 'the son of Astyages' cowherd'.) Artembares, furious at the humiliation suffered by his son, promptly marched him off to Astyages, and
told the king everything. 'You see, my Lord,' he asked, stripping bare the
boy's shoulders, 'how insolently we have been treated? And by one of
your slaves! By the son of a cowherd!'

[115] The story of what had happened, combined with the physical
evidence for it, served to convince Astyages that the boy should indeed
be granted restitution, if only because of the father's rank; and so a summons was duly issued to the herdsman and his son. When the pair had
been brought into his presence, Astyages looked Cyrus over. 'Can it
really be true,' he demanded, 'that you, a slave, and the son of a slave,
had the audacity to mistreat in this appalling manner a boy whose
father is the leading man at my court?' 'Yes, Master,' came the answer,
'it is true – and I was perfectly within my rights. We were all of us – me,
him, the other children in the village – playing a game. The whole point
of this game was to set one of us up as king. I got the vote – because I
was the one that everyone else thought would make the best king. All
the other children did as they were told – but not this one. He refused
to listen, wouldn't even talk. That is why he was punished. But if you
really think that I did something wrong, and that I am the one who
deserves to be in trouble – well, here I am.'

[116] Now, as he spoke these words, so a glimmer of recognition
crossed Astyages' mind. There was something about the way the child's
features resembled his own; the way that the boy's reply seemed better
suited to someone freeborn than to a slave; the way that his age corresponded to the length of time that had passed since the exposure of
Mandane's baby. Indeed, such was Astyages' sense of stupefaction that
for a long while he was left completely dumbstruck, and only with some
difficulty managed to pull himself together again. 'Artembares,' he said
at last, desperate as he was to send the man packing, and get down to
the business of interrogating the herdsman one to one, 'let me take care
of all this. You can rest assured that I will leave neither you nor your son
with any cause for complaint.' With this he dismissed Artembares and
told his servants to take Cyrus inside. Then, when he and the herdsman
were alone together – just the two of them and no one else – Astyages

demanded to be told how it was that the boy had come into the herdsman's possession, and who it was had handed him over. 'The boy is my
own,' the herdsman replied. 'The person who gave me the child was –
still is – my wife.' 'Foolish,' Astyages answered. 'Very, very foolish. Are
you actually looking to find out what a good torturer can achieve?' He
signalled to his guards that they should seize the man, who, as soon as
he found himself being hauled away to the torture-chamber, began to
give a full confession. Right at the beginning he started, telling the whole
truth, and nothing but the truth, until finally, finishing his account, he
fell to his knees and begged Astyages for mercy.

[117] Now that the whole story had come out into the open, Astyages was actually no longer bothered with what the herdsman himself
had done – the focus of all his fury was Harpagus. 'Fetch him,' he
ordered his guards. Harpagus duly came. 'That child I gave you,' Astyages enquired of him, 'the one born to my daughter – do tell me precisely
how you disposed of it, what manner of death you laid on . . .' Harpagus, when he saw that the herdsman was there, inside the palace, realized
that his best course was simply to tell the truth; for if he did not, he was
bound to be caught out and condemned as a liar. 'My Lord,' he said,
'after I took charge of the baby, I began to ask myself whether there
might not be a way for me to carry out what you had in mind, so that
you would have no cause to find fault with me, while simultaneously
avoiding having your daughter – or yourself, indeed – brand me a murderer. So here is what I did. I summoned that herdsman right there, I
handed the baby over to him and I told him that it was your express
command that it be destroyed. Which was nothing more than the truth,
of course – since that was indeed what you had ordered. What is more,
when I gave him the baby, I also gave him exact instructions. He was
told to expose it in a lonely spot in the mountains and to stand guard
over it until it was dead. As for the threats I issued, warning him of what
would happen if he failed to do as he had been told, they could hardly
have been laid on any thicker. And he did indeed do as instructed. And
when the child had breathed its last, I sent my most trustworthy
eunuchs,[147] and they examined the corpse on my behalf, and then they
buried it. Those, my Lord, are the facts of the matter. That is how the
child met with its doom.'

[118] A straightforward enough tale; and Astyages, keeping his fury
at what had happened concealed, first repeated for Harpagus' benefit

the version he had heard from the herdsman, and then, when he was done, finished off by revealing that the child was still alive, and that what had happened was all for the best. 'Thoughts of what might have been done to my grandson were always a source of great distress to me,' Astyages said, 'nor was the breach that it opened up between me and my daughter ever something that I could take lightly. But now, with fate having taken this happy turn, why not send your own child to visit mine, newly restored to me as he is? Also, since it is my intention to reward the gods who were responsible for keeping my grandson safe by offering them up a sacrifice, why not come and join me for the feast?'

[119] This offer prompted a bow of obeisance from Harpagus, who now felt secure in the assurance that his failure had ended up being rewarded, and that the seal set on his good fortune was an invitation to dinner. No sooner had he arrived back home than he was telling his son, his only child, a boy some thirteen years old, to head straight off to Astyages, and to do whatsoever the king might command. Meanwhile, giddy with delight, Harpagus began to spill out the good news to his wife. But Astyages, receiving Harpagus' son into his palace, had the boy butchered, his limbs cut up into joints, his flesh roasted or turned into a stew, and then dressed for the table – a ready meal. The time for the feast arrived. The banqueters – Harpagus included – took their places at table. All the guests, and Astyages himself as well, had mutton placed before them – but not Harpagus. He was served the flesh of his own son, every last scrap of it – all, that is, apart from the head, the hands and the feet, which were kept to one side, in a basket with a lid. Harpagus gnawed away on the joints of meat, until it seemed he had enjoyed his fill – and then it was that Astyages asked him if the meal had been to his taste. 'It was utterly delicious,' Harpagus replied. At this, servants who had been primed beforehand brought in the boy's head, hands and feet, concealed within the basket, and clustered all around him. 'Take off the lid,' they ordered. 'Help yourself to whatever you fancy.' Harpagus did as he had been instructed; he removed the lid; he saw the remains of his son. Maintaining his composure, though, he betrayed not a sign of horror at the sight. 'That meat you've just been eating,' said Astyages. 'Can you guess from what animal it came?' 'Yes,' answered Harpagus, 'I can guess well enough. And what I know as well is that the king can do no wrong.' Such was his answer; and having delivered it, he then scooped up what remained of the meat, and took the scraps home with him – with the

intention, I suppose, of burying as much of his son as could still be assembled in one place.[148]

[120] Fitting justice, in the view of Astyages. So much for Harpagus – next on the king's agenda was Cyrus. Once again, he summoned the Magi who had originally interpreted his dream for him; and once again, after they had all assembled, he asked them for their opinion of his dream. Their response was the same as before: had the child not died – as of course they thought that he had – but continued to live and prosper, then he would inevitably have ended up as king. 'But the child is alive,' Astyages answered. 'Alive and well. He has been growing up out in the country, where all the boys of his village set him up as their king. He played the part perfectly, in every way – almost as though following a script. Appointed bodyguards, sentries, heralds. Gave everyone some role to fill. Ruled for real. So now, tell me – what do you think the implications of that might be?' 'If the child is still alive,' the Magi answered, 'and if he truly has ruled as a king, and if it was all done without any prompting from you, then you have nothing to worry about. In fact, since the boy is hardly likely to rule a second time, you can feel positively optimistic. Sometimes it happens like this, that prophecies attain their fulfilment in mere trivialities, and that dreams, while they come true, simultaneously come to nothing.' 'Then we are very much of the same mind,' Astyages told the Magi. 'My dream was fulfilled the moment that the boy was hailed as king. He holds no terrors for me now. All the same, I would like you all to put your heads together and give me your advice as to what the best course of action is likely to be, both for my dynasty, and for yourselves too.' 'My Lord,' said the Magi in response, 'we do indeed have every incentive for wishing you a long and prosperous reign. The boy is a Persian: should he end up on the throne, then power will pass into the hands of foreigners, and it is we Medes, pushed to the margins, who will end up the slaves, the foreigners. But you are a Mede, just like us. So long as you are king, we too have a stake in the kingdom – and we too, thanks to your patronage, rank among those in power. Come what may, we are bound to look out for your interests – yours, and those of your empire. Believe us, if we had been able to glimpse anything alarming, then we would have let you know. But the dream turned out to be a false alarm – and so our advice to you would be to relax, just as we are. Pack the boy off to his parents in Persia. Get him out of your sight.'

[121] Astyages was delighted by what he heard, and promptly summoned Cyrus. 'I have done you a great wrong, my boy,' he said, 'and all because of a vision in a dream that amounted to nothing. But fortune has kept you safe! Go now to Persia, and prosper there. I will make sure that there are escorts on hand to accompany you – and when you do arrive, and meet with your mother and father, you will find that they are a very different order of person from Mithridates the cowherd and his wife!'

[122] And with these words Astyages packed Cyrus off to Persia. Back in his native land, the boy was taken to the palace of Cambyses, and introduced there to his parents. When they found out that he was their own child, long presumed dead, they opened their arms to him in an ecstasy of joy, and demanded to know how it was that he had survived. 'Up until only a short while ago,' he answered, 'I would not have had a clue. In truth, I was mistaken about almost everything! It was only on the way here that I discovered the full story of my misfortunes. I had always thought that I was the son of a cowherd, the slave of Astyages – but then the escorts who were with me out on the road told me the whole story.' And he went on to describe how he had been brought up by the herdsman's wife, lavishing praise on her, and barely able to continue with his story unless it was to say 'Cyno this' or 'Cyno that'. His parents, anxious that the Persians should have an appreciation of their son's deliverance as something even more miraculous than it actually was, duly seized on the meaning of the woman's name to spread a rumour: that Cyrus, following his exposure, had been brought up by a bitch.[149]

[123] Such was the true origin of the legend – one that has spread far and wide. Now, as he grew up, so Cyrus emerged as the bravest and best-liked man of his generation; and Harpagus, who was longing to take revenge upon Astyages, set about winning him over by plying him with gifts. Harpagus himself, a man wholly lacking any public position of authority, was under no illusion that he would ever obtain his vengeance on Astyages without some form of assistance; and so it was, as he watched the growing maturity of Cyrus (whose sufferings struck him as having been on a very similar scale to his own), that he made every effort to forge a compact with him. Nor was this the first step that Harpagus had taken in his campaign; for already, taking advantage of the harshness of Astyages' treatment of the Medes, he had held meetings

with each of the great men of Media in turn, and convinced them that it would be in their interests to install Cyrus on the throne in place of Astyages. Having accomplished that, and with the conspiracy successfully primed, his next step was to leave Cyrus in no doubt as to what was being purposed; but since Cyrus lived in Persia, and since the roads were heavily guarded, a stratagem was required to get the message through. And so that Harpagus procured a hare, slit open its stomach and carefully, without removing any of its fur or altering its appearance in any way, inserted a letter on which he had jotted down all his musings. Then he sewed up the hare again, handed it to a particularly trusted house-slave, along with some nets to disguise him as a hunter, and packed him off to Persia. The slave's orders, which he had to carry in his head, were to give the hare to Cyrus, and then ask him to dissect it with his own hands – but only when he was quite alone.

[124] Everything went according to plan. Cyrus received the hare; he cut it open; he found the letter inside, pulled it out and set to reading. 'Son of Cambyses,' ran the message, 'the gods must be keeping you in their care, for it is hard to explain otherwise the full measure of your good fortune. The time has come to make Astyages, your would-be killer, pay for his crimes. You would be dead now, had he only had his way; that you are not is thanks to the gods – and to me. I have no doubt that the story of what happened to you is one with which you are thoroughly familiar. Nor do I doubt that you will know all about my own sufferings at the hands of Astyages – inflicted because I refused to kill you and gave you to the herdsman instead. Only take my advice now, and you will end up the lord of Astyages' empire – all of it. Persuade the Persians to revolt – march against the Medes. Suppose that it is me who is appointed by Astyages to the command of the army opposed to you – could your wishes then come any more true? But even if it is some other highly decorated Mede, rest assured that the Median nobility will be the first to desert Astyages' cause, and enlist in your own – for we are all of us committed to bringing about his downfall. Everything here is primed. Please take my advice – and be quick about it!'

[125] With these words echoing in his mind, Cyrus fell to pondering how best he could persuade the Persians to give their backing to a rebellion; and as he pondered, so he arrived at a solution perfectly fitted to their circumstances, which he duly put into action. He wrote down on

a scroll precisely what he needed to say, and then summoned the Persians to a public assembly, where he unrolled the letter and read out to them an announcement – that Astyages had appointed him commander of the Persian army. 'Now, then, men of Persia,' he went on, 'here is what you are to do when you reassemble: come armed with scythes, every last one of you.' These were the instructions he gave them. (In fact, because the Persian people comprise a large number of tribes, it was only the ones exercising a lordship over the less significant tribes who were assembled by Cyrus, and persuaded to revolt against the Medes, namely, the Pasargadae, the Maraphians and the Maspians. Of these three, it is the Pasargadae[150] who have the most eminent pedigree: not for nothing do they include the Achaemenids, the clan which provides the Persians with their kings. The other tribes which constitute the Persians are the Panthialians, the Derousians and the Germanians, all of whom work the arable lowlands, and the Daians, the Mardians, Dropikians and the Sagartians, who live as pastoralists.)

[126] So the Persians all reassembled, scythes in hand. Now it happened that in that same corner of Persia there was a patch of land, some 18 or 20 stades square which was a wilderness of thorns; and these same thorns, Cyrus instructed, were to be cleared in a single day. The job was done – the challenge was met. Then there came a further command: the Persians were to spruce themselves up, and report back for duty the following morning. Meanwhile, all the goats, sheep and cattle that Cyrus had inherited from his father were rounded up, slaughtered and prepared for the enjoyment of the Persian forces; wine was added to the menu and the very best bread. Next morning, no sooner had the Persians turned up than they found themselves relaxing in a meadow, enjoying a sumptuous feast. When they had finished eating, they were asked by Cyrus which they had preferred: the day they had just spent, or the previous one? The two could hardly have been more different, the Persians replied, for the one had brought them nothing but misery, and the other nothing but delight: an answer that Cyrus immediately seized upon. 'Men of Persia,' he told them, no longer bothering to veil his intentions, 'let me spell out the choice confronting you. If you do as I say, all the pleasures you enjoyed today will be yours a thousand times over – no longer will you have to work like slaves. If you disobey me, though, you will be toiling as you did yesterday, for days without number. So follow me. Cast off your chains. That this task is a destiny for which the gods

have fitted me, I do not doubt; nor do I doubt that you are, at the very least, the equals of the Medes – in war no less than in everything else. So there is no time to waste. Down with Astyages!'

[127] The Persians, delighted to find that they had a true leader at last, all duly flocked to the cause of independence, for they had long and profoundly resented their subjugation to Median rule. When news of these events reached Astyages, he dispatched a messenger, summoning Cyrus to appear before him; but Cyrus' only retort was to send the messenger back with a warning. 'I will be with you', the message ran, 'a good deal sooner than you would like.' The receipt of this threat prompted Astyages to order a full-scale mobilization of the Medes; but simultaneously, because the gods had scrambled his brain, he gave command of the army to Harpagus, quite forgetting all that he had inflicted upon the man. When the Medes marched off to war and met the Persians, some of them (those not in on the plot) joined battle; but of the others, some deserted to the Persians, while the greater part deliberately held back from fighting, before taking to their heels.

[128] It was a humiliating rout. But Astyages, when brought the news of how the Median campaign had fared, immediately responded with a fresh vaunt: 'You haven't won yet, Cyrus – I still have your measure!' Braced by this slogan, his first step was to impale all those Magi who had interpreted his dreams for him and convinced him to let Cyrus go; his next was to arm the Medes who were still left to him in the city, boys and old men alike, and lead them out to face the Persians. The result, however, was a second defeat: Astyages' levies were annihilated, and Astyages himself was taken alive.

[129] Harpagus, standing beside the prisoner held at spear-point, gloated, and jeered at him roundly, as though words could serve as darts to pierce Astyages through to the heart: for Harpagus could not forget the meal that he had been given, when he had been feasted on the flesh of his son. 'How does it feel', he demanded, 'to go from being a king to being a slave?'[151] Astyages looked up. 'So then', he retorted, 'you are claiming responsibility for what Cyrus has done?' 'Yes,' Harpagus said. 'I wrote him a letter. It seems fair enough that the consequences be laid at my door.' 'Then truly,' answered Astyages, giving free rein to his tongue, 'you are the stupidest, most unreasonable man I know. The stupidest, because if you are correct, and you are indeed responsible for what has happened, then there was nothing to stop you becoming king yourself,

rather than handing the throne to someone else. The most unreasonable, because, thanks to you, and to your obsession with that one meal, the Median people are now utterly lost to bondage. If you truly felt that you had no recourse but to make someone else king, rather than to sit on the throne yourself, then surely the most certain course of justice would have been to bestow such a prize, not upon a Persian, but upon a Mede? As it is, the Medes, through no fault of their own, have gone from being masters to slaves, and the Persians, their former slaves, now have the whip-hand.'

[130] So it was, after a reign of thirty-five years, that Astyages was toppled from his throne, and the Medes, provoked beyond endurance by the harshness of his rule, bowed their necks to the Persian yoke. A hundred and twenty-eight years, not including the period of Scythian domination, they had ruled over Asia: an empire which consisted of everything beyond the limits of the River Halys. Later on, it is true, in the time of Darius, the Medes regretted their submission, and revolted; but they were defeated in battle once again, and their rebellion was crushed.[152] At the time in question, however, it was the Persians under Cyrus who revolted against the Medes, and as a result secured the rule of Asia.[153] Astyages himself suffered nothing further at the hands of Cyrus, but was kept at the Persian court until he passed away. That, then, is the story of Cyrus' birth and upbringing, and of how he came to be King. The story of how Croesus launched an unprovoked attack against him, and then was overthrown, is one that I have already told. The victory that Cyrus won over Croesus gave him the rule of the whole of Asia.[154]

[131] As regards customs, I have identified a number that are distinctive to the Persians.[155] The setting up of statues, temples and altars is something very alien to them – so much so, in fact, that they regard the entire practice as idiocy, for reasons, I imagine, to do with their gods not being represented in human form, as are the Greek gods.[156] It is a tradition among the Persians that sacrifices to Zeus,[157] whom they identify with the all-embracing dome of the heavens, be made only on the peaks of the very highest mountains. Sacrifices are also offered up to the sun and to the moon, to the earth and to fire, to water and to the winds. In fact, back in the mists of time, these were the only powers to which the Persians ever made sacrifices; but then, in due course, they made a study of

the Assyrians and Arabians, and began to offer up sacrifices to Aphrodite Urania as well. The Assyrian name for Aphrodite is Mylitta, and the Arab name Alilat; the Persians call her Mitra.[158]

[132] As to ritual, the Persians offer up sacrifices to the gods I have just mentioned in a very particular way.[159] They do not build altars, nor, when they are about to perform a sacrifice, do they light a fire; there is no pouring out of libations, nor any playing on flutes; garlands do not feature, neither do grains of spelt. Instead, whenever someone wishes to make an offering to a deity – and no matter who the deity is – he will garland his felt turban with a crown of leaves, usually of myrtle, and then drive the animal to an unsullied spot, where he will invoke the god. The man who actually performs the sacrifice is forbidden to ask for any private or personal benefactions, but prays instead on behalf of the King, and of the Persian people as a whole – among whom, of course, is numbered himself. He cuts up the limbs of the animal he has just killed into pieces; he boils the meat; he makes a bed out of the softest grass he can find – clover, preferably – and then lays all the pieces of meat upon it. Once this is done, a Magus will stand over the sacrifice and sing a hymn relating the story, so it is said, of the birth of the gods. Forget the Magus, and forget the sacrifice: such is the law. Then, after a short pause, the man who performed the sacrifice will remove the meat, and can do with it as he pleases.

[133] Another Persian custom: the celebrating of a person's birthday as the most significant day of his year. Every Persian is obliged to mark it by serving up a quite exceptionally lavish banquet. A person blessed with the resources to do so will lay on an ox roasted whole in an oven, or perhaps a horse, or a camel, or a donkey; someone poorer will rustle up whatever livestock he can spare. Food tends not to be served in large portions: the preference is for smaller dishes, which are then sampled at intervals. This is the custom which has led the Persians to claim that Greeks always leave the table hungry, because they never serve anything worth eating after the main course; if only they did, the Persians say, then they would surely carry on eating. Wine is a particular passion of the Persians – albeit that they regard it as the height of bad manners to vomit or urinate in the presence of others, and are forever on their guard against doing so. Instead, whenever they are drunk, they like to thrash out some weighty issue. Then, the next morning, once they have all sobered up, the head of the house in which the debate took place will

encourage them to go over it once again: if the same decision is arrived at now that they are no longer drunk, it will be approved once and for all; if not, then it is abandoned. Conversely, any debate held in a mood of sobriety will always be re-staged once the participants have got themselves drunk.

[134] Should two Persians happen to meet out on a street, it is always possible to tell whether they are of equal rank, for rather than exchange greetings, they will kiss each other on the lips. Should one of them be of slightly lower rank, then the kissing will be to the cheeks. Should one of them rank very much lower than the other, then he will sink to his knees and prostrate himself before the other.[160] As regards nations, the Persians rank their own immediate neighbours as the fittest to be graced with their respect (always after themselves, of course); then those who lie beyond their immediate neighbours; then those beyond them in turn, and so on, in ever-decreasing order of proximity. Accordingly, it is the peoples who live the furthest away from them who are the most despised. That this is so reflects their presumption that they are the greatest people on the face of the earth, and that the quality of other peoples diminishes the further one travels from Persia, until in the end, on the very margin of things, there is nothing but savagery. In the days of Median power, it was this same principle which actually served to govern the way that the various subject nations related to one another on an administrative level – for although, of course, it was the Medes who had ultimate authority over the empire as a whole, they exercised immediate control only over those nations which directly abutted their own borders, trusting them to exercise a similar control in turn over their own neighbours, and so on, ever outwards. The parallel, in other words, is between the way that the Persians feel a diminished respect for people the further away they are, and the way that under the Medes each successive subject people had the administration of their neighbour.[161]

[135] Distinctive as well is the Persians' relish for adopting the customs of foreign peoples. For instance, they will wear Median fashions rather than their own because they consider them more stylish, and in battle they will sport Egyptian breastplates. Similarly, they only have to learn about some new kind of pleasure, no matter what it may be, and they will start to indulge themselves in it: a notable example, one which they picked up from the Greeks, is their habit of sleeping with boys.[162] Not that the average Persian is ever short of wives – and though the

women who are married to him may be numerous, you can be sure that he will also have acquired an even larger number of concubines.

[136] For a Persian, however, the surest proof of manliness – prowess in battle always excepted – is to father an enormous number of boys. Every year, on the principle that quantity equals might, the man who has notched up the biggest tally of sons receives a prize from the King. The education of a boy will begin at the age of five, and finish when he is twenty, but in all that time he will only ever be taught three things: how to ride a horse, how to fire a bow and how to tell the truth. Prior to the age of five, a boy will live surrounded by women, and never so much as be seen by his father – thereby sparing the father any grief, should his son die before he leaves infancy.

[137] This, in my opinion, is a really excellent custom.[163] So too is the one which forbids even the King himself from imposing the death penalty on a man who has been convicted of only a single offence – a law which also, under the same circumstances, makes it illegal for a master to execute or mutilate any of his house-slaves. Nevertheless, if it is discovered, after due investigation, that the offences committed against someone outweigh in number and gravity any services that may have been rendered him, then he is permitted to give free vent to his anger. As for parricide and matricide, the Persians declare both to exceed the bounds of plausibility, for on every occasion, they say, the cases which appear to contradict such a claim will prove, on closer inspection, to have been the work of either a changeling or someone illegitimate. That parents might truly be killed by children of their own blood is, they insist, a flat impossibility.

[138] Among the Persians, it is prohibited so much as to mention anything that it is forbidden them to do. The worst offence of all that a man can commit, they think, is to tell a lie;[164] the next, to fall into debt. There are many reasons for this, but the principal one is their conviction that any man who owes money is bound to end up telling lies. Should anyone from one of their cities contract leprosy or psoriasis, then he will be obliged to keep to the countryside, and stay in isolation, away from other Persians. Both these afflictions, they say, are a punishment for having offended the sun.[165] Any foreigner who succumbs to them will find himself being run out of the country by a mob; even white doves are driven away, as though they too were guilty of the selfsame crime. It is rivers, however, which are the chief objects of the Persians'

veneration: they will neither urinate in them, nor spit in them, nor use them to wash their hands, nor let anyone else wash in them either.

[139] There is also another peculiarity worth mentioning, one to which the Persians themselves have always been oblivious, although it is perfectly self-evident to us. Their personal names, the meanings of which serve to reflect either physical characteristics or else a general aura of magnificence, all end in the letter 's': *san*, as it is termed by the Dorians, and *sigma* by the Ionians. Only look into the matter yourself, and you will find that it is not just a majority of Persian names which end in the same way, but every one of them.

[140] All of these customs I can vouch for on my own authority. There is one other, however, relating to the handling of the dead,[166] which is only ever talked about in hushed tones, and is therefore shrouded in a degree of mystery: namely, that the body of a male Persian can only be buried once it has first been savaged by a bird or a dog. I know for certain that the Magi dispose of their corpses in this manner, because they, at any rate, are perfectly open about the practice (though nevertheless, a Persian will always make sure, before actually interring a body, to cover it with wax). The Magi are a class of person unlike any other, and quite distinct from the kind of priest you find in Egypt. Unlike the latter, who regard it as taboo to kill any living creature, unless it be as a sacrifice, the Magi are not only willing to kill anything on which they can lay their hands (dogs and humans excepted), but will make a tremendous fuss about it, slaughtering ants, snakes, indeed anything which creeps or flies, with relish. It is an ancient custom; and that being so, one we should no doubt let be.[167] It is now time to pick up the thread of my former narrative.

[141] No sooner had the Persians brought the Lydians crashing to defeat than Ionian and Aeolian messengers were sent to Sardis, looking to secure the same terms of subordination from Cyrus as they had previously enjoyed under Croesus. Cyrus listened to their proposals; and then he told them a story. 'There was once an oboe-player,' he said, 'and one day, when he saw some fish in the sea, this man began to play upon his oboe,[168] in the expectation of coaxing them up onto dry land. But his design came to nothing – and so, taking up a fishing-net, he cast it out over a great shoal of the fish, and hauled them in in that way instead. And as he watched the fish jumping about, he said to them, "It is all very

well your dancing now. The time for that, however, was back when I was playing my oboe – when you refused so much as to shake a fin."' Such was the fable told by Cyrus to the Ionians and the Aeolians: the point of it being that earlier, when Cyrus had sent messengers to the Ionians imploring them to revolt from Croesus, they had refused; now, with the matter settled and their defeat sealed, they were ready to do his bidding. Indeed, such was the anger with which Cyrus expressed himself that, when the news of it was brought back to the Ionians, they immediately set to building walls around their cities, and to holding councils of war at the Panionium[169] – all, that is, apart from the Milesians. With them, and with them alone, Cyrus renewed the treaty that they had previously negotiated with the Lydian king.[170] The other Ionians, however, after a communal vote, all agreed to send emissaries to Sparta, and ask for assistance.

[142] Now, so far as I am aware, there is no other region, not in the whole span of the inhabited world, where the skies are a more beautiful shade of blue, nor the climate finer, than the one in which the Ionians, who share in the Panionium, have founded their cities.[171] Compared to Ionia, the countries which lie further to the north are oppressively cold and wet, while the more southerly regions suffer from an excess of heat and a lack of water. So far as language is concerned, the Ionians have not the one dialect but four. Their southernmost city is Miletus, with Myous and Priene just to the north: all three are in Caria and their inhabitants share an identical manner of speech.[172] Then, in Lydia, you will find the following cities, where the dialect is quite distinct from the one spoken in the settlements just mentioned: namely, Ephesus, Colophon, Lebedus, Teus, Clazomenae and Phocaea. That leaves three further Ionian cities: Samos and Chios, which are situated on islands, and Erythrae, the very last one, which was founded on the mainland. The Chians and the Erythraeans share the same dialect, but the Samians speak one that is distinctively their own.[173]

[143] Which, as I said, makes four in all. Now, of the Ionians who spoke these various dialects, the Milesians were safely out of harm's way, thanks to the treaty that they had sworn with Cyrus, while the islanders had nothing to fear either, for the Phoenicians were yet to be made subjects of the Persian empire, and the Persians themselves were still inveterate landlubbers. Nevertheless, the twelve Ionian cities I have mentioned can indeed all be reckoned to share a common identity

distinct from that of the Ionians who remained in the motherland. There is a single, simple reason for this which reaches back to a period when the power of the entire Greek people was at a very low ebb, and the Ionians, of all the Greeks, were by far the most enfeebled, the most lacking in influence. It is that, Athens aside, they could boast not a single city of any consequence. As a result, the majority of the Ionians – the Athenians included – shrank from applying the name to themselves, and came to scorn the very title of 'Ionian'; even today, in my opinion, the majority remain ashamed of it. The twelve cities founded on the opposite side of the Aegean, however, positively gloried in the name, and established a sanctuary there, for their own exclusive use, which they called 'The Panionium': 'the shrine of all the Ionians'. In fact, they had no wish to give any of the other Ionians a stake in it – and the other Ionians, with the exception of the Smyrnaeans, never actually requested a stake.

[144] A similarly guarded exclusiveness distinguishes the Dorians who come from the region which used to be known as the Six Cities, but is now the Five: they refuse to admit any of the Dorians from the neighbouring towns into their temple, the Triopium. Indeed, should one of their own number break the laws of the sanctuary, then that city too will be excluded and have its stake in the shrine revoked. For instance, in the past, at the games staged in honour of Triopian Apollo, it was the rule that the victors be awarded bronze tripods, which the recipients were forbidden to remove from the temple, but were obliged instead to dedicate as a gift to the god. It happened one day, however, that a man from Halicarnassus by the name of Agasicles, in blatant disregard of this custom, marked his victory by carting off the tripod he had won and nailing it down in his house. This offence prompted five of the six cities – Lindus, Ialysus, Camirus,[174] Cos and Cnidus – to bar the sixth, Halicarnassus, from making further use of the shrine. Such was the penalty imposed by the Five on the errant member of what had previously been the Six.

[145] As to why the Ionians established a league of twelve cities, and set themselves against admitting any other members, the answer, I think, is to be found in the fact that at the time when they lived in the Peloponnese, they constituted twelve distinct communities – just as the Achaeans, the people who expelled them, do today. There is Pellene, which is the nearest Achaean city to Sicyon; then Aegeira; then Aegae, which stands on the banks of the Crathis, a river which never runs dry, and which

gave its name to the river of the same name in Italy; then comes Boura, followed by Helice,[175] where the Ionians took refuge after being defeated by the Achaeans; then Aegium, Rhypes, Patrae, Pharae and Olenus, through which the mighty River Peirus flows; then Dyme; then last of all, and the only one of the twelve not on the coast, Tritaeae.

[146] These, then, are the twelve communities which together constitute what is now Achaea, but was previously Ionia – and this is why it is no coincidence that the cities founded by the Ionians in Asia should also have been twelve in number. Certainly, it is hard to think of anything more ludicrous than the claim that it might have been because they were somehow more Ionian than the other Ionians, or could lay claim to a superior lineage. After all, a not insignificant portion of them were originally Abantians from Euboea, a people who never had any claim even to the name of 'Ionian'. Nor is that the limit of their mongrel character: there were Minyans from Orchomenus, Cadmeians, Dryopians, emigrants from Phocis, Molossians, Pelasgians from Arcadia, Dorians from Epidaurus, and a whole host of other peoples, all mixed up together. Even those who originated from the city hall of Athens, and who therefore consider themselves the most pure-blooded Ionians of all, did not actually bring any women with them on their colonizing venture, but instead married Carian girls whose fathers they had first put to death. It was this murderous behaviour which led the women to pass a law, sworn on solemn oath and handed down from mother to daughter, which prohibited them from ever sitting down to dine with their husbands, or even to address them by name, for these were the killers who, before taking them to bed, had slaughtered their fathers, their husbands, their sons.[176] Miletus was the scene of these events.

[147] Furthermore, there were some Ionians who entrusted power to a Lycian dynasty, kings sprung from the line of Glaucus, the son of Hippolochus; there were others who opted for the Caucones from Pylus, a family which could trace its descent back to Codrus, the son of Melanthus; and there were some who went for both at once. Nevertheless, we should grant that their limpet-like attachment to the name of 'Ionian' is indeed unrivalled, and so perhaps it is best if we leave them to their fantasy of being pure-bred Ionians.[177] In point of fact, however, the name applies to all those who can trace their origin back to Athens, and who keep the Festival of Apatouria. This is a holiday which is celebrated by the Ionians of every city except for those from Ephesus and Colophon:

they, as their excuse for being the only ones not to celebrate the Apatouria, cite some murder or other.

[148] The Panionium is a sanctified spot in the region of Mycale.[178] It faces north and was dedicated, by the common consent of the Ionians, to Poseidon Heliconius. Mycale itself is a promontory which juts out westwards from the mainland in the direction of Samos. It was there that the Ionians from the twelve cities used to congregate so as to celebrate what they called the 'Panionia'. (It is a feature of festivals – not only Ionian ones, but Greek ones in general – that they all end in the same letter. In this, of course, they are just like Persian proper names.)

[149] So much for the cities of the Ionians. Here is a list of their Aeolian equivalents: Cyme, which also goes by the name of Phriconis, Larissa, New Teichos, Temnus, Cilla, Notium, Aegiroessa, Pitane, Aegaeae, Myrina and Gryneium. The roots of these eleven Aeolian cities are ancient. At one time, indeed, there were twelve of them to be found on the mainland, but then one of them, Smyrna, was annexed by the Ionians. As a matter of fact, the land settled by the Aeolians is a good deal more fertile than Ionia, but in terms of climate it can hardly compare.

[150] The story of how the Aeolians lost Smyrna goes like this. Some men from Colophon, outmanoeuvred by a rival faction and driven into exile, had requested asylum – which the Smyrnaeans had duly granted. Then one day, with their hosts beyond the city walls celebrating a festival in honour of Dionysus, the Colophonians spotted their chance. They barred the gates; they seized the town. When all the other Aeolians came to the Smyrnaeans' rescue, an agreement was reached whereby the Ionians would hand over all the Aeolians' personal belongings, and the Aeolians, in return, would abandon Smyrna. Then, once the terms had been carried out, the people of Smyrna were distributed among the eleven remaining cities of Aeolis, and enrolled as citizens of their new homes.

[151] It is these same eleven cities which now constitute the sum of the Aeolian settlements on the mainland (always excluding those found at the foot of Mount Ida, which do not belong to the confederacy). As regards the islands, there are five Aeolian communities on Lesbos, and have been ever since the city of Arisba, which used to be the sixth, was delivered into slavery by the Methymnaeans, in spite of their common ancestry.[179] Tenedos can also boast one city, and the so-called Hundred

Islands another. The Aeolians of Lesbos and Tenedos, like the Ionian islanders, had nothing to fear at this point. As for the other Aeolians, they all took a joint decision to be guided in their policy by the leadership of the Ionians.

[152] Events now began to move fast, and the messengers sent by the Ionians and Aeolians soon arrived in Sparta, where they fixed on a Phocaean by the name of Pythermus to speak on their joint behalf. Pythermus prepared by draping himself in a purple cloak, so as to create a stir among the Spartiates, and to draw as large an audience as possible; then, stepping forward, he delivered a lengthy and heartfelt appeal for assistance.[180] The Lacedaemonians, however, refused to listen: no aid to Ionia was forthcoming. The envoys beat a retreat. Yet the Lacedaemonians, despite their rebuff of the Ionians, still thought fit to dispatch a penteconter, with the intention of reconnoitring what Cyrus was up to, and of keeping an eye on Ionia – or that, at any rate, is how I interpret their mission. The ship duly put in at Phocaea, and a man called Lacrines, the most eminent figure that the expedition could boast, was sent onwards to Sardis. His mission was to deliver a message: a warning to Cyrus that, should he ever dare to trample underfoot the interests of any Greek polity, he would have to answer for it to the Lacedaemonians.

[153] The story goes that Cyrus, once he had heard the herald out, asked some Greeks in his entourage who on earth the Lacedaemonians were, and how substantial their reserves of manpower, that they presumed to issue him with such commands. The answer he was given prompted him to turn back to the Spartiate spokesman. 'Do you really think that I am the kind of man', he said, 'to quake in my boots before people who deliberately set aside an open space in the middle of their city just for the purpose of meeting up to cheat one another on oath? I can assure you – so long as I stay in good health – that it won't be the sufferings of the Ionians which serve to exercise your wagging tongues in the future, but troubles much closer to home.' Cyrus' threat was one targeted at Greeks everywhere, and was provoked by their habit of maintaining town squares for the buying and selling of goods[181] – for the Persians never use these, and indeed lack public squares altogether. When the audience was over, Cyrus appointed a man by the name of Tabalus, a Persian, as governor of Sardis; he put a Lydian, Pactyes, in charge of transporting the gold of Croesus, and that of all the other

Lydians, and then, rather than making the Ionians the focus of his attentions, instead headed off towards Agbatana, taking Croesus along with
him in his train. There were four principal obstacles confronting Cyrus –
Babylon, the people of Bactria,[182] the Sacae[183] and the Egyptians – and
it was his intention to lead the campaigning against these adversaries in
person, while sending a deputy to deal with the Ionians.

[154] No sooner had he left Sardis, however, than Pactyes began to
foment a rebellion, stirring up the Lydians against Tabalus and Cyrus.
Freighted as he was with all the gold of Sardis, he went down to the
coast, where he set about hiring mercenaries and persuading the people
who lived there to sign up to his forces. Then back he came, sweeping
down on Sardis, trapping Tabalus in the acropolis and putting him
under siege.

[155] Cyrus was still on the road when news of the revolt was
brought to him. 'Am I never to be free of this headache?' he exclaimed
to Croesus. 'It is as though the Lydians cannot stop themselves from
stirring up trouble. Bad news for me – but worse news for them. Perhaps the best option would be just to cart them all off into slavery.[184] It
seems to me that my behaviour, at the moment, is like that of someone
who has killed a man with a large brood of children and left the children untouched. After all, here you are, a father and more than a father
to the Lydians, journeying as a prisoner in my train – and all the while,
back in Sardis, the Lydians have had the run of the city. And why?
Because I handed the rule of it over to them myself! And then I think to
wonder that they have risen in revolt against me!' Here were words
spoken from the heart; and Croesus, in terror that Sardis might indeed
be reduced to a wilderness, gave this reply. 'O King, there can be no
doubting that you absolutely have right on your side. Nevertheless, I
would beg you, just to a small degree, to rein in your anger. Please, do
not make a wasteland out of such an ancient city. Sardis is no more to
blame for what is happening now than she was for my own crimes. Just
as it was I who did wrong in the first instance, and must now bear the
taint of my offence like filth daubed across my forehead, so is it Pactyes,
the man to whose rule you entrusted Sardis, who must bear the guilt on
this occasion, and pay you the penalty. But as for the Lydians – please –
let the Lydians be spared. There are still directives you can issue that
should ensure they never rebel again, nor so much as darken your
thoughts. Send a message. Ban them from possessing the kind of

weapons that men of valour would think to keep. Order them to wear tunics under their cloaks and soft slippers laced up around their feet. Make them school their children in the lyre, in the harp, in the requirements of trade. Only do that, my Lord, and you will soon find women where previously there were men, and all danger of them ever staging a rebellion against you gone for good.'

[156] Croesus pushed this suggestion because he had no doubt that it would leave the Lydians better off than if they were all sold into slavery. He was well aware that he would never succeed in changing Cyrus' mind unless he could propose a credible alternative course of action; and what was more, he dreaded that the Lydians, even if they somehow wriggled free of the situation they were currently in, would rise up again at some later point against the Persians and be annihilated. Fortunately, Cyrus liked the idea; his anger began to cool, and he promised Croesus that he would adopt it. He summoned a Mede, a man by the name of Mazares, and instructed him to promulgate what Croesus had suggested – but directly, as orders, to the Lydians. Mazares was also commanded to sell into slavery everyone who had joined the assault on Sardis – everyone, that was, except for Pactyes, who was at all costs to be taken alive and brought to him.

[157] And with this, the plan was set, and Cyrus was able to continue his journey along the high road back to the Persian heartlands. No sooner had Pactyes found out that he was the object of a task-force, and that the task-force was closing in, than he was off, fleeing in a state of high panic to Cyme. By the time that Mazares the Mede, with his contingent of Cyrus' army, came sweeping into Sardis, he found that Pactyes and his followers were already gone. His first step, then, was to force the Lydians to carry out Cyrus' orders: fateful commands indeed, which would transform the entire Lydian way of life. Next, Mazares sent envoys to Cyme with instructions that Pactyes was to be surrendered – which in turn prompted the Cymaeans to send their own envoys to Branchidae,[185] with a request for advice from the god. The oracle there, which lies in Milesian territory on a hill overlooking the harbour of Panormus, had originally been founded back in ancient times, and was one that all the Ionians and Aeolians were in the habit of consulting.

[158] So it was that the Cymaeans sent emissaries to Branchidae, and these envoys asked the priests how best they were to solve the dilemma confronting them: what did the gods want done with Pactyes? Back

came the answer: surrender him to the Persians. Once the oracle's response had been heard out, this recommendation was one that the Cymaeans were perfectly minded to follow – or at least the majority of them were. But then, just as their resolution was about to be put into action, an eminent citizen of Cyme, a man named Aristodicus, the son of Heracleides, stopped them in their tracks: he did not trust the answer that the oracle had supposedly given, and strongly suspected the envoys of lying.[186] Accordingly, a final decision on what to do about Pactyes was postponed while a second embassy was sent to the oracle, with Aristodicus himself among the envoys.

[159] Once they had all arrived at Branchidae, it was Aristodicus who served as their spokesman in addressing the oracle, and in framing their enquiry. 'Lord Apollo,' he said, 'when Pactyes the Lydian fled a hideous death at the hands of the Persians, it was to us that he came, seeking asylum. Now the Persians are demanding his surrender, and ordering us to hand him over. But he is a suppliant, and so – for all our dread of Persian power – we have shrunk from giving him up,[187] at least until the present moment. That is why we need you to spell out unerringly for us which of the two options we should take.' Such was the question asked by Aristodicus; and no sooner was it out of his mouth than back came the answer, the same as had been given before. 'Surrender Pactyes to the Persians.' Aristodicus, who had anticipated this response, refused to rest content with it. Instead, he made a circuit of the temple, and as he went, so he made a cull of all the sparrows in their nests, along with every other kind of bird that was to be found nesting in the temple. It is said that as he was doing this, he was addressed by a voice that reverberated from the very heart of the temple, calling him the most sacrilegious of men, and demanding to know what he was up to. 'You dare to lay hands on these suppliants in my temple?' To which Aristodicus coolly replied, 'And you, Lord Apollo – do you think to come to the rescue of your own suppliants, and yet order the Cymaeans to abandon their own?' 'Indeed,' answered the god. 'You have been given your orders. And why? Because the sooner you are brought to commit such a sacrilege, the sooner you will be brought to ruin – and the sooner you are brought to ruin, then the sooner will I and my priests be free of all your endless questioning about the surrender of suppliants!'

[160] Once news of this ruling had been brought back to Cyme, and

the Cymaeans had heard it out, they found themselves confronted by a dilemma; while they had no wish to surrender Pactyes and be destroyed for it, neither did they wish to keep him and end up being put under siege. Accordingly, they packed him off to Mytilene, a destination to which Mazares' heralds were soon sent as well, with demands for his surrender – demands that the Mytilenaeans were perfectly content to meet. It helped that there was money on offer – although what the precise sum was I am not certain, since the bribe was never paid. This was because, when the Cymaeans discovered what the Mytilenaeans were up to, they sent a boat to Lesbos and evacuated Pactyes to Chios. There he took refuge in the sanctuary of Athena, Guardian of the City;[188] but the Chians dragged him out and delivered him up. The payment they received for this rendition was Atarneus, a place in the region of Mysia opposite Lesbos. So it was that Pactyes fell into the hands of the Persians, who put him under lock and key, eager as they were to see him brought before Cyrus. (For quite a while after this, the Chians made it a point of principle never to scatter barley that had come from Atarneus as an offering to the gods, nor to use grain from the region in their sacrificial cakes. In fact, all produce from Atarneus was off limits to Chian sanctuaries in general.)

[161] Mazares' next step, once the Chians had delivered Pactyes into his hands, was to target all who had played a role in putting Tabalus under siege. First he sold the citizens of Priene into slavery; then he overran the entire floodplain of the Maeander, and allowed his men to strip it bare; then he subjected Magnesia to an identical treatment. No sooner had he done this, however, than he fell sick and died.

[162] Then, with Mazares scarcely cold, another Mede, Harpagus, set out for the western front, to take up the reins of command. This was the same Harpagus who had been feasted by Astyages, the King of the Medes, at the notorious banquet which had so desecrated every conceivable law of hospitality – and who had then gone on to collaborate with Cyrus to secure the kingdom for him. This man, following his appointment by Cyrus to the command of the forces previously led by Mazares, and his arrival in Ionia, set to capturing the cities there through spadework. First, the inhabitants of a given city would be pinned inside their walls; then great mounds of earth would be raised up until they reached the topmost height of the fortifications; then the city would be stormed.[189]

[163] The first Ionians to suffer at his hands were the Phocaeans. These were the Greeks who, before anyone else had thought to do so, began making long-distance journeys by sea; it was they who opened up the Adriatic, Tyrrhenia, Iberia and Tartessus.[190] On these voyages, it was their practice to deploy a war-fleet rather than the broad-bottomed vessels[191] favoured by merchants. When they made contact with Tartessus, they became remarkably friendly with the city's king, a man named Arganthonius, who had the sole rule of Tartessus for eighty years, and who lived to be, at the very least, one hundred and twenty. Indeed, such was the favour with which this man regarded the Phocaeans that initially he told them to quit Ionia altogether and settle wherever they fancied in Tartessian territory; then, when they were unpersuaded, and because they had kept him well informed as to the growing power of the Mede,[192] he provided them with the funding they needed to build fortifications around their city. His contributions were unstinting; not only was the circumference of the wall a pretty lengthy one, but its masonry consisted of huge blocks of stone, very skilfully fitted.

[164] It was to this same ring of fortifications, which would never have been completed without Tartessian gold, that Harpagus marched his troops, to begin the siege of Phocaea. At the same time, he let it be known that all he actually required from the Phocaeans was for them to open a single breach in one of the curtain walls, and to make an offering of one single building to the King. To the Phocaeans, however, so agonizing was the prospect of servitude that they asked for a day's grace to debate the matter before being obliged to give Harpagus their answer; simultaneously, they stipulated that his troops should be pulled back from the wall in the meantime. 'I know perfectly well what you are planning,' Harpagus told them; nevertheless, he gave them permission to deliberate. His troops were duly withdrawn from the foot of the wall; and immediately the Phocaeans set to hauling their warships down into the shallows, where they loaded them with their children, their wives and all their movable possessions, even going so far as to empty the temples of their dedicatory offerings, statues and everything, so that soon there was nothing left in the city at all apart from bronzes, objects carved out of stone and wall-paintings. Then, with everything packed, they took their own places on board, and sailed away to Chios. The Persians had won Phocaea – but a Phocaea that was bereft of men.

[165] The Phocaeans themselves, meanwhile, tried to buy from the

Chians the islands known as the Oenoussae; but the Chians, nervous that the islands would then become a major trading-hub, and that their own island's trade would be embargoed in consequence, refused to sell. So instead, the Phocaeans decided to set their sails for Cyrnus,[193] where twenty years previously, following the advice of an oracle, they had established a colony,[194] a city named Alalia. (By this point, Arganthonius was dead.) Before embarking for Cyrnus, however, the Phocaeans first sailed back down the coast to Phocaea, where they massacred the Persian contingent that had been stationed by Harpagus in the city as its garrison. Then, once the slaughter was done, they sought to make sure that their expedition would be a united one by laying terrible curses upon any of their own number who stayed behind. Additionally, they dropped a lump of iron into the sea, and swore never to return to Phocaea until the lump should reappear.[195] Even as they were preparing to set off on the first leg of their voyage, however, more than half of the citizens were gripped by such a piteous longing for their city, and for the familiar ways of their homeland, that they broke their word, and sailed back to Phocaea. The rest, however, true to their vows, raised anchor and set sail from the Oenoussae.

[166] Five years passed, during which time, following their arrival in Cyrnus, they lived in Alalia alongside the colonists who had originally founded the settlement; and there they raised new sanctuaries. But they also busied themselves with pillaging all the settlements which lay within easy striking distance – to such a degree, indeed, that the Etruscans and the Carthaginians[196] each agreed to man a fleet of sixty ships as a joint reprisal force. The Phocaeans themselves had sixty ships; and once they had all taken up their oars, they stood out to sea, in the waters of what is known as the Sardinian Sea, there to meet the enemy. They won the resulting battle; but it proved a 'Cadmeian' kind of victory.[197] Forty of their own vessels were destroyed, while the rams of the remaining twenty were so badly bent that they were no longer fit for service. The survivors sailed back down the coast to Alalia, where they evacuated their women and children, together with as many of their possessions as they still had room for in their ships; then they sailed for Rhegium,[198] leaving Cyrnus behind for good.

[167] As for the shipwrecked crews, they were divided up between the Carthaginians and the Etruscans – with the larger number ending up in the hands of the Etruscans. The prisoners were then taken out into

the countryside that lay beyond the city of Agylla and stoned to death. From that moment on, the grave to which their battered bodies had been consigned began to cripple anyone from Agylla who happened to pass by: sheep, cart-horses or humans, all alike would fall lame, as though afflicted by a stroke. The Agyllans, desperate to expiate their offence, duly sent to Delphi, where the Pythia instructed them to stage a festival, one that is still celebrated in Agylla to this day: it is marked by the offering up of splendid sacrifices to the shades of the Phocaean dead, and by the staging of athletic contests and chariot races. Not, of course, that all the Phocaeans were killed in the manner I have just described: for the survivors, those who had found a bolt-hole in Rhegium, used it as a base from which to buy a plot in the territory of Oenotria, and there they established a city that is nowadays known as Elea.[199] Its founding owed everything to a man from Posidonia:[200] for he revealed to the Phocaeans that what the Pythia had actually meant by 'Cyrnus' was not the island, but rather a hero to whose worship they were to devote themselves. And that is the story of Phocaea, city of Ionia.

[168] There is a very similar story to be told of the course of action followed by the people of Teus. Once their fortifications were lost to the earthworks raised by Harpagus, the Teians all crowded into their ships and made a get-away to Thrace. There they founded the city of Abdera, on a site which Timesius of Clazomenae had previously tried to settle, but without success because the Thracians had driven him out. Nowadays, this same Timesius is worshipped in Abdera by the Teians as a hero.[201]

[169] The other Ionians, however, did not follow the lead of the Teians and the Phocaeans in preferring the abandonment of their native land to slavery. Although all of them – with the exception of the Milesians – held out against Harpagus with no less commitment than the emigrants had shown, and fought with great courage in defence of their own individual interests, yet defeat, and the fall of the cities, saw them staying where they were, and submitting to Persian rule. The Milesians, meanwhile – as I mentioned previously – had already sworn a treaty with Cyrus himself, and so had no call to fight. All of which meant that the Ionians, for a second time, were reduced to servitude. Indeed, such was the fright that Harpagus' conquest of mainland Ionia gave the Ionian islanders that they too submitted to Cyrus.

[170] Nevertheless, broken though they were, the Ionians continued their practice of meeting at the Panionium – where, so I have it on good authority, a man from Priene named Bias floated a plan so full with potential that the Ionians, had they only adopted it, would surely have ended up the most prosperous of all the Greeks. 'Here is what you must do,' Bias told them. 'Pool your resources. Set sail for Sardinia. Found a single city there, a common home for all Ionians. Do that, and not only will you succeed in casting off your chains, but you will also enjoy the kind of contentment proper to those who inhabit the largest island in the world, and are in a position to lord it over everyone else. Stay in Ionia, however,' he added, 'and what chance freedom then? None that I can see.' A case well made – and it was not the only one put to the Ionians. Bias of Priene had pushed his own proposal in the wake of the Ionians' defeat; and there had been another one suggested even before the conquest of Ionia, by a man originally of Phoenician descent, Thales of Miletus. His recommendation had been that the Ionians should establish a single council chamber, and that it should be at Teus, since this was the city which stood in the very middle of Ionia. The other cities were to continue inhabited, but as demes[202] of Teus.

[171] These were certainly two well-judged plans. But Ionia had been subjected; and Harpagus, once he had mopped up any resistance, and began directing his attacks onto the Carians, the Caunians and the Lycians, made sure to take Ionian and Aeolian contingents with him on his campaigns. The Carians, despite the fact that they are now a mainland people, were originally islanders. In ancient times, when they were subject to King Minos, and were known as 'Leleges', they inhabited the Aegean archipelago. Although the only evidence for such a remote period that I have been able to discover derives from hearsay, it does seem that, rather than pay Minos direct tribute, they would man his ships whenever he so required it. As a result – because Minos conquered a sizeable empire and never enjoyed anything less than good fortune in war – the Carians ended up far and away the most considerable people of the age. (They were also responsible for a triad of innovations, which the Greeks then subsequently adopted: it was the Carians who first worked out how to fasten crests onto helmets, how to emblazon shields with motifs and how to fit handles onto shields. Before this, no shield had ever been fitted with a handle, and anybody who used one would be obliged to manipulate it by means of a leather strap slung around the

neck and over the left shoulder.) Subsequently, many years later, the Carians were driven from the islands by the Dorians and Ionians and pitched up on the mainland – or such, at any rate, is the Cretan version of what happened. The Carians themselves, however, tell a different story: they believe themselves sprung from the soil of the mainland, and never (not once in the entire course of their history) to have been known by any name other than the one that they now bear. In support of their case, they cite the antiquity of the shrine of Carian Zeus at Mylasa. (This is a sanctuary which the Carians permit the Mysians and Lydians to use, as well as themselves, on the grounds that all three peoples are related to one another: Lydus and Mysus, according to the stories told by the Carians, were the brothers of Car. Other peoples, however, unlike the Mysians and Lydians, are banned from the temple – even if they speak a dialect of Carian.)

[172] Now the Caunians, in my opinion, really are indigenous – but they themselves say that originally they came from Crete. Over time, their language has evolved so that now it resembles the language spoken by the Carians. (Or perhaps it happened the other way round – I find it hard to decide for sure which is the likelier.) In their customs and manners, however, they bear no resemblance to the Carians at all, nor indeed to anyone else, for to them the finest thing in life is a large party, one where friends of the same age group all meet, and drink together – men, and women, and even children too. Similarly, although there used to be no lack of foreign cults practised in Caunus, the Caunians ended up intolerant of them, and resolved to worship only the gods who had been worshipped by their forefathers: accordingly, their entire adult male population buckled on armour and began advancing all the way up to the frontier with Calynda, stabbing the air with their spears as they went, and thereby, so they said, driving out the foreign gods.

[173] But enough of the Caunians and their customs. The origins of the Lycians definitely do lie in Crete; indeed, back in ancient times, the whole island was inhabited by barbarians. When a disturbance broke out there, sparked by the rival royal ambitions of the two sons of Europa – Sarpedon and Minos – it was Minos, with the backing of his faction, who seized power, while Sarpedon and his followers were driven into exile. In their banishment, they made for Asia, and specifically for the region of Milyas – this being the ancient name for the land which is nowadays inhabited by the Lycians, in the days when the

Milyans themselves were called Solymians. For a while, during the reign of Sarpedon, the exiles were known by the name which they had brought with them from Crete, and which the neighbours of the Lycians continue to call them to this day: 'Termilaeans'. But then, after another bout of fratricidal strife – this time in Athens – had led to the banishing of Lycus, the son of Pandion, by his brother, Aegeus, and after this Lycus had turned up at the court of Sarpedon, the Termilaeans ended up adopting his name, so that in due course they came to be known as 'Lycians'. As for their laws and customs, these are a fusion of the Cretan and the Carian. There is one practice the Lycians have, however, which is unique to them, and has no parallel anywhere else in the entire record of human custom – for they take their names, not from their fathers, but from their mothers! Suppose that a Lycian asks his neighbour who he is: the neighbour will list his mother's pedigree, complete with all his female ancestors going back through the generations. Suppose as well that a Lycian woman who ranks as a citizen settles down with a slave – any children they have will be considered legitimate. But should a male citizen, be he never so distinguished, have a foreign wife or live-in concubine, then his children will not be granted the rights of citizenship.

[174] Anyway – the display put up by the Carians against Harpagus was a less than brilliant one, with the result that they were soon brought to servitude, for both they and the Greeks who inhabit Caria proved identically ineffectual. Numbered among the latter were the Cnidians, a people who were originally emigrants from Lacedaemon, and who inhabit a coastal region known as Triopium. This, with the exception of one very narrow strip of land which serves to connect it to the Bybassian peninsula, is completely bounded by water: north lies the Ceramic Gulf, while southwards the sea is open as far as Syme and Rhodes. The Cnidians, alarmed by news of Harpagus' conquest of Ionia, and conscious that the neck of their isthmus was barely 5 stades across, began to dig right through it, with the intention of transforming Cnidos into an island. This scheme did not require them to forfeit any of their land: the stretch of the isthmus across which they were digging was precisely the point where their own territory ended and the mainland began. Even as a huge workforce of the Cnidians were setting about this task, however, an unnaturally high number of accidents began to occur, with splinters of rock repeatedly embedding themselves in the flesh of the workmen, and especially in their eyes; and so messengers were sent to

Delphi, to ask what force it was they were up against. The Pythia's response, so the Cnidians claim, was given to them in iambic trimeters, and read as follows:

> 'Neither fortify the isthmus, nor dig it through.
> Zeus would have made an island, had he wished it so.'

This response from the Pythia was sufficient to persuade the Cnidians to bring the excavations to an abrupt halt, and also, on the approach of Harpagus and his army, to surrender without a fight.

[175] Elsewhere, inland from Halicarnassus, lay the land of the Pedasians. Here, whenever there happened to be trouble brewing, either for the Pedasians themselves or for their neighbouring subjects, the priestess of Athena would sprout a bushy beard. Three times in a row this happened. Of all the men who lived in the region of Caria, the Pedasians were the only ones to hold out against Harpagus for any length of time; indeed, the hill-fort that they constructed on the mountain called Lida was the single most formidable challenge that he had to confront.

[176] In due course, however, the Pedasians too were subdued. Then, with Harpagus and his army sweeping into the plain of Xanthus, it was the turn of the Lycians, who, though greatly outnumbered, nevertheless marched out to confront the invaders and meet them in battle – a wonderful show of bravery. After they had been defeated, and found themselves holed up in their city, the Lycians next gathered together their wives, their children, their property and their house-slaves on the acropolis, set fire to it and burned the entire citadel to the ground. They then swore awful blood-oaths, marched back down to face the enemy and were wiped out, right to the very last man. Indeed, almost all the Lycians today who claim to be Xanthians are actually immigrants – with the exception of eighty families who happened to have been abroad at the time of the siege and consequently survived. The outcome, however, was that Xanthus fell into Harpagus' hands, and Caunus too, in much the same way, for the Caunians had followed the example of the Lycians in almost every respect.

[177] Meanwhile, as Harpagus was laying waste the coastal regions of Asia, Cyrus himself was far inland, crushing all the various peoples of the continent, and sparing none. Rather than describe his every campaign, however, it is my intention instead to focus on those that presented

him with the gravest challenges – and me with the themes that most merit elaboration.

[178] There was one land which became the focus of Cyrus' attention only after he had first brought the rest of the continent under his whip-hand: Assyria. There are many great cities to be found there, but there was one which ranked as the most renowned, which could boast the most impressive fortifications, and which had become, after Nineveh's fall, the seat of royal power: Babylon. Here is a description of the city. It lies in an immense plain, its shape is that of a vast square, each side of which measures almost 120 stades, and its total circumference comes to 480 stades. It is not only sheer size which renders Babylon unique, however, but its design as well: the city is unlike any other of which we know. First there comes a moat, deep and broad, filled with water, and enclosing the entire city; then there rises a wall, 50 royal cubits thick and 200 cubits high. (A royal cubit is three fingers longer than a standard one.)

[179] All of which begs a couple of obvious questions: what was done with the earth excavated from the moat, and how did the wall come to be built? The answer is that, even as the ditch was being dug, earth shovelled from the excavation was being moulded into bricks; then, once a sufficient number had been manufactured and fired in kilns, they were laid out in courses, with hot bitumen mortar, and an additional layer, made out of rush matting, inserted after every thirtieth course. The banks of the moat were constructed first; then, by the same method, the wall itself. On top of the wall, lining both its edges, rows of one-room buildings were built, directly facing one another, and separated by a gap sufficiently wide to drive a four-horse chariot along its circuit. The wall also features a hundred gates, fashioned out of solid bronze: door-posts, lintels and all. Now, were you to leave Babylon and travel for eight days, you would come to another city, Is, which shares its name with the river, an insignificant tributary of the Euphrates, next to which it stands. The waters of the River Is are full of lumps of bitumen, which are brought to its surface – and this was the source of the bitumen used in the building of Babylon's wall.

[180] And within the wall – constructed in the manner I have just described – the city is divided into two districts of equal size by a river, one which rises in Armenia and flows into the Red Sea, very wide, deep and fast-flowing: the Euphrates. The wall, when it meets this river, bends

and joins at an angle with another wall, fashioned out of baked brick but without any mortar, which runs all the way through the city, one on each bank. The city itself is packed with houses, all of them three or four storeys high, and laid out so as to form a grid of perfectly straight streets, with some running parallel to the Euphrates and others at right angles descending to the river. When these side-alleys meet with the wall which runs along the bank, access to the river is provided through postern gates, one for each alleyway, and fashioned out of bronze, just as are all the gates set in the main wall.

[181] And if this wall serves the city rather as a breastplate serves to protect a warrior, then so too is there a second wall sheathing Babylon, narrower than the outer bulwark, but hardly any the less formidable. In addition, there is a further walled area in the middle of each of the city's two districts: one, enclosed by a ring of tall and bristling ramparts, constitutes the royal palace, while the second, still standing in my day, is the shrine of Zeus Belus.[203] The gates of this sanctuary are bronze, its shape is square and its sides are each 2 stades long. Right in its centre a tower of solid brick has been constructed, a square stade in size, and on top of this there stands another tower, and on top of that a third in turn, and so it continues, right the way up to the eighth. Sculpted into the exterior of these eight towers, winding its way up to the very summit, is a staircase; and midway up this staircase is a resting place complete with benches, where those who are making the ascent can sit down and catch their breath. In the very topmost tower there is a huge temple; and within this temple are stationed a large couch, adorned with splendid coverings, and beside it a golden table. No cult-statue is to be seen standing there, however – nor, after dark, any mortal. There is one exception to this rule, however, for the god (according to the Chaldaean priests who serve him) will select a single woman, a native of the city, to pass the night in his shrine.

[182] They also make what seems to me the frankly incredible claim that the god frequents the temple in person, and takes his rest on the couch – precisely as happens in Thebes in Egypt, if the Egyptian account is to be believed. (Certainly, it is a fact that a woman does go to bed in the temple of Zeus in Thebes, and that both she and her counterpart in Babylon are said never to have sexual relations with men.) The same is true of the priestess who serves as the mouthpiece of the god at Patara, in Lycia; for there, although the oracle is only seasonal, and the prophetess

herself not always resident, her presence in the temple will always see her shut up inside it, alongside the god, every night.

[183] At a lower level of the sanctuary in Babylon there is another temple, and this does contain a massive figure of a seated Zeus, fashioned out of gold, even down to its pedestal and throne, and with a large table placed beside it, likewise made out of gold. In all, 800 talents' worth was used – or so the Chaldaeans claim. Outside the temple there is an altar which is made of gold as well. Only offerings of unweaned lambs or calves can be made on this, but fully grown livestock are sacrificed on a second altar, which is of a massive size, and on which the Chaldaeans annually burn 1,000 talents of frankincense, to mark the festival of the god. In the time of Cyrus there was also an effigy of solid gold, some 12 cubits high, which stood in the same temple precinct – although I admit that I never actually saw this with my own eyes, but repeat what the Chaldaeans say. Darius, the son of Hystaspes, had designs on this statue, but when the time actually came to remove it his nerve failed him; Xerxes, his son, however, did take it, and when the priest sought to prevent the removal of the effigy, Xerxes had him killed. There are many other adornments in the temple, the offerings of individual benefactors, as well as the ones I have just described.

[184] The strengthening of Babylon's walls and the beautifying of her shrines were the work of a whole sequence of kings who, over time, had succeeded one another on the city's throne – I will offer portraits of them all in my history of Assyria. There were also, however, two female monarchs. Five generations separated the second of these queens from the first, whose name was Semiramis, and who was responsible for the remarkable dykes to be seen on the plain around Babylon. It is these dykes which prevent the river from flooding, as it always used to, and turning the entire landscape into a sea.

[185] The second of Babylon's two queens was called Nitocris,[204] a more intelligent woman than her predecessor. She left as her memorial the monuments that I shall shortly describe; but she also kept a close watch on the mighty and restless empire of the Medes, marking how many other cities had fallen to it, even Nineveh itself, and making sure to ready her own city as best she possibly could. The first precaution that she took was to have channels cut upstream from Babylon, so that the Euphrates, the same river which bisects the city, and which had always previously followed a perfectly straight line, was made instead to wind

backwards and forwards – so much so, indeed, that in one village in Assyria its waters ended up flowing along three quite distinct and separate stretches. The name of this village through which the Euphrates kept coming and going was Ardericca. To this day, those making the journey down from the sea to Babylon will find themselves arriving in the village three times, and three days, in a row. All was the work of Nitocris – as too were the embankments which she raised on either bank of the river, and which are of such a scale and height that they more than merit the title of 'wonder'. She also had the bed of a lake hollowed out, well to the north of Babylon, not far from the river, and following the line of its course; the depth of this lake's basin was determined by the line of the water-level, but it had a breadth of 120 stades. The earth shovelled out from the excavations was used to raise embankments on the river, while the lake itself, once the digging had been completed, was enclosed all the way around its rim by a cladding of stone, which had been transported there especially for the purpose. Both these projects – the diverting of the Euphrates and the deliberate fashioning of a marshland next to it – had the same aim, which was to render its currents more torpid: for not only was the course of the river, and the approach along it to Babylon, transformed into a succession of twists and turns, but any ship making the journey was obliged to circumnavigate the immense lake. It was no coincidence that Nitocris should have deployed her workforce precisely in that part of the country which served as its point of entry, and through which the most direct road out of Media led: her intention was to prevent the Medes from having any contact with her own people, and from gaining intelligence as to her projects.

[186] In turn, this extensive ring of defences fed an additional side-project. Prior to the reign of Nitocris, the division of the city into two halves by the river meant that whenever anyone wanted to cross from one side of Babylon to the other there was no alternative but to take a boat – which was, I am sure, a perpetual source of annoyance. But here too Nitocris showed her foresight. The same labour of excavation that had resulted in the lake-bed being dug out enabled her to raise a second memorial to the feat. First she ordered the quarrying of some massively long stones, and then, once these stones had been prepared and the site of the lake hollowed out, she diverted the course of the river into the excavated basin with such complete success that, as the lake filled up, the original river-bed was left bone dry. Nitocris thereby had an

opportunity to line both the banks of the river and the stairs leading down to it from the postern gates with the same kind of fired brick as had been used in Babylon's walls; and, moreover, to complement this project by fashioning a bridge, more or less in the middle of the city, out of the quarried stones which could now be braced together using iron and lead. At sunrise, square boards of wood would be laid down upon the stones to enable the Babylonians to make the crossing; but at night these boards would be removed, to prevent inhabitants from the opposite sides of the river from stealing from one another. Eventually, with the excavated lake finally filled up by the river, and the design of the bridge brought to completion, Nitocris switched the flow of the Euphrates back out of the lake so that it followed its original courses. As a result, not only did the transformation of the queen's excavations into a marsh serve a useful purpose in its own right; it also provided her fellow-citizens with a bridge into the bargain.

[187] The same queen was also responsible for a notable trick devised against posterity. She had a tomb built for herself over the most frequented gate of the city, embedded within the fabric of the structure itself directly above the lintel, and engraved with the following inscription:

SHOULD ANY KING WHO ASCENDS THE THRONE OF BABYLON AFTER ME FIND HIMSELF SHORT OF TREASURE, THEN LET HIM OPEN MY TOMB AND TAKE AS MUCH AS HE WANTS. ONLY POVERTY, HOWEVER, WILL SUFFICE AS JUSTIFICATION. NO OTHER WILL DO – AND BETTER FOR HIM NOT TO PRESUME OTHERWISE!

This tomb remained undisturbed until the reign of Darius, who, unwilling to use the gate, since it would have required him to drive directly underneath a corpse, thought it insufferable that one of the city gates should be out of bounds to him. On top of that, it struck him as ludicrous not to take the treasure when it was just sitting there, complete with its come-hither inscription – and so he opened up the tomb. Inside it, however, he found no treasure waiting for him, but only the corpse, and one further inscription. It read:

SO THIS IS THE MEASURE OF YOUR LUST FOR TREASURE, AND OF THE DEPTHS TO WHICH YOUR GREED HAS PLUNGED YOU, THAT YOU THINK NOTHING OF FORCING THE TOMB OF THE DEAD.

This is also the measure of what tradition has to tell us about the character of Nitocris.

[188] Cyrus' campaign was directed against the son of this woman by a man named Labynetus, from whom the new king had inherited both his name and the empire of the Assyrians. Now the Great King,[205] whenever he goes to war, will always do so well furnished with corn and herds from his native Persia, not to mention water brought from the Choaspes, a river which flows past Susa, and which is the only one that the King will ever drink from – no other will do. A supply of water from the Choaspes, pre-boiled, is stored in silver vases, and borne in the King's wake by a great train of four-wheeled mule wagons, no matter where he may travel.

[189] In the course of his advance on Babylon, Cyrus came to the Gyndes, a river which rises in Matiene and flows through the land of the Dardanians before it joins with another river, the Tigris – which in turn flows past the city of Opis[206] and on into the Red Sea. Because the Gyndes was too deep to be fordable, it was Cyrus' plan to attempt the crossing using boats, but one of his sacred white horses, wild with overconfidence, plunged into the river with the intention of swimming to the opposite bank; swept underwater, the horse found the currents too strong for it and was borne away. Cyrus' response to this show of brutal arrogance from the river was one of fury – so much so, indeed, that he swore so to enfeeble the Gyndes[207] that in future even a woman would be able to cross it easily, and emerge with her knees perfectly dry. Sure enough, he followed up this threat by abandoning his expedition against Babylon, dividing his army in two, and then marking out on both banks of the Gyndes a hundred and eighty trenches, all of them drawn perfectly straight, and radiating out in every direction. After this, with his men primed for action, Cyrus gave them the order to get digging. The job was duly completed (as was hardly surprising, considering the size of the workforce) but not before the whole of the summer had been used up.

[190] The following spring, however, once Cyrus had been avenged upon the Gyndes, and left the river sliced up into three hundred and sixty channels, he resumed his drive against Babylon. The Babylonians were waiting for him, in a position in advance of their city. At Cyrus' approach, they moved to the attack, but lost the resulting engagement and were forced to retreat behind their walls. Of course, it hardly came

as any great revelation to them that Cyrus was a man of restless ambition, for they had long been tracking the indiscriminate course of his aggression against other peoples far and wide; and so they had taken the precaution of stockpiling food sufficient to last them for very many years. As a result, they viewed the prospect of a siege with equanimity; and indeed, as time dragged by, and everything continued as a stalemate, it was Cyrus who found his position an increasingly precarious one.

[191] In the event, however – either on the suggestion of some adviser or perhaps on his own initiative – he arrived at a solution to his predicament. His entire army was commanded to take up battle-stations, with one contingent drawn up at the point where the Euphrates flows at full pelt into Babylon, and the other on the opposite side of the city, where it exits, both of them with orders to wait until they could see that the river had become traversable, and then to advance along its course into the city. Meanwhile, as his troops moved to follow these instructions and take up their positions, Cyrus himself rode off at the head of all his non-combatant units. His target was the very lake which had been the scene of the Babylonian queen's hydraulic operations, when she had redrawn the course of the Euphrates as well as of the lake itself; and just as Nitocris had done, so now Cyrus did also. The river was channelled along a trench into the marsh that the lake had become, so that the waters flowing along its original course began to subside and ended up fordable. This, of course, was precisely what the Persians stationed on the banks of the Euphrates had been instructed to wait for; and no sooner had the river level subsided to the height of a man's thigh (if that) than they were making their entrance into Babylon. Now, if the Babylonians had only been given forewarning of what Cyrus was up to, or fathomed it for themselves, then they could have turned the entrance of the Persians into their city so completely to their own advantage as to have annihilated the invaders utterly. All they would have had to do was to secure the postern gates that open out onto the river and mount the low walls that run along its banks, and they would have had the Persians caught as if in a trap. As it was, however, the enemy was upon them before they knew what had hit them. Indeed, according to local tradition, such was the size of the city that those who lived in the centre of Babylon had no idea that the suburbs had fallen, for it was a time of festival, and all were dancing, and indulging themselves in pleasures; so

that when they did finally get the news, it was very much the hard way. And that is the story of how, for the first time, Babylon fell.

[192] There are many ways to illustrate the potency of Babylon's resources; and I will start with one in particular. When the Great King divided up his empire into separate regions, it was not only the supply of tribute that was being regulated, but also the provisioning of his household and army. For four months out of twelve, the royal table is furnished by the lands around Babylon, and for the remaining eight by all the rest of Asia. Such is the wealth of Assyria, in other words, that its territory supplies an entire third of the resources of Asia as a whole. The governorship of such a land (or *satrapy*, as the Persians term it) is quite the richest posting there is, as can be seen from the fact that when Tritantaechmes, the son of Artabazus, was graced by the King with the province, it brought him an income of a full *artaba* of silver every day. (An *artaba* is a Persian measure – one that in Attica would be described as three *choenixes* more than a *medimnus*.[208]) In addition, Tritantaechmes had his own private herds of horses, quite distinct from those used by his cavalry: eight hundred stallions in all, and sixteen thousand mares, a ratio sufficient to provide every stud with twenty mating-partners. He kept so many Indian hunting-dogs that the taxes of four large villages in the plain had to be devoted exclusively to keeping them all fed. Such is the measure of the wealth of the governor of Babylon.

[193] The rainfall in Assyria is minimal, barely sufficient to nourish the roots of the wheat. It is the river which waters the crops, and thereby serves to ripen them and make the wheat to grow – not, as in Egypt, where the river rises of its own accord and floods the fields, as a result of any naturally occurring phenomenon, but rather due to artificial irrigation, and the use of swing-buckets. Like Egypt, the landscape around Babylon is one immense lattice-work of canals; the largest of these, which is perfectly navigable by boat, follows the line of the sun as it sets in winter, and extends from the Euphrates to a second river, the Tigris, on which the city of Nineveh was built. To the best of our knowledge, Assyria is wholly without rival as the bread-basket of the world. True, there is no attempt made to grow anything else there, whether figs, or vines, or olives – but so well suited is its soil to the production of cereal crops, those gifts of Demeter, that a sowing will invariably result in a yield two hundred times the original weight of the seed, or even, in an exceptional year, three hundred times. The blades of the wheat and

barley that are grown there are four fingers wide at least, while such is the size of the plants that are grown from millet- and sesame-seeds that I am not even going to touch upon it (a reticence prompted, not by any ignorance on my part, but rather by the scepticism with which those who have never so much as visited the land of Babylon have greeted my account of its fertility). The oil that the Babylonians use is made from sesame-seeds – never from olives. Their palm trees not only grow everywhere across the plain, but most of them bear fruit, which can either be eaten, or else turned into wine or syrup. The method of cultivation used by those who tend the palms corresponds in a number of ways to the methods of growing figs: a particular example is the practice of tying the fruit of what the Greeks term the 'male' palm trees to the date-producing palms, so that gall-flies can then crawl in among the dates, and ripen them, before the fruit drops out of the trees. (For as with wild figs, so with male palm trees – gall-flies are indeed found in their fruit.)

[194] Now I come to what in my own opinion is the greatest wonder of all,[209] with the exception of the city itself: namely, the boats which ply their way down the river to the city, and are both circular and made all of leather. The frames of these are manufactured by the Armenians, who live upstream from the Assyrians, out of branches of willow, over the exterior of which hides are then stretched, so as to form hulls; that the resulting craft are circular, like shields, is due to the fact that they are neither broadened at the stern nor narrowed at the prow. The boats are then fully lined with straw, loaded up with freight (palm-wood casks full of wine, by and large) and launched onto the currents of the river. Steering is undertaken by two men, both equipped with paddles and standing upright: one pulls his paddle towards him, while the other thrusts his out. These boats can be made in a whole range of sizes, right up to the enormous, with the capacity of the very largest actually weighing 5,000 talents. Each boat carries a live donkey – or, if it is a large boat, several donkeys. As a result, once the voyage to Babylon has been completed, and the cargo disposed of, the frame of a boat can immediately be broken up and sold at auction, along with all the straw, while the hides are loaded up onto the donkey, ready for the journey back to Armenia. That the Armenians are obliged to do this, and to build their boats out of hides rather than wood, is due to the speed of the river, which makes it impossible for them to sail back upstream. The donkeys are then

driven back to Armenia – where the Armenians, the moment they are home, can set to building the same kind of boat all over again.

[195] So much for boat design; now for style of dress. A Babylonian's tunic is made of linen, and reaches down to his feet. Over the top of such a tunic he will wear a second tunic made of wool, then wrap himself up in a short white cloak. His sandals will be of a design which, while native to Babylon, is not dissimilar to that of the open slippers which are sported in Boeotia. His hair is worn long, and kept bound up inside a turban. His entire body is soused with perfume. Everyone has his own signet ring and hand-carved staff, each with its own distinctive mark: an apple, perhaps, or a rose, a lily or an eagle, or something else altogether. For a staff not to be emblazoned with such a mark would be a major breach of custom. Such is the way they dress.[210] Now to some of the customs which they have adopted.

[196] The one that I myself rate the cleverest is one that they share with the Eneti, a people from Illyria – so I have learned. Once a year, in every village, this was the scene that would be staged: an assembling of all the girls who had ripened into the full bloom of marriageability. These would then be led in a great throng to a given spot, where a crowd of men would stand around them in a ring. One by one, an auctioneer would raise the girls to their feet, and put them up for sale, starting with the most attractive, and then, once she had been sold for a good price, moving on to whoever was next on the scale. (It should be pointed out that the girls were being bought as wives.) All the rich Babylonians who were in the marriage market would bid furiously against one another for the beauties, while those who were less well off, men who did not demand good looks in a wife, would end up being paid to take the plainer girls. This was because, once the auctioneer had run through the sale of the prettiest lots, he would haul the ugliest girl up to her feet (or even a cripple, if there was one) and auction her off by asking who would accept the smallest amount of money in exchange for taking her as his wife – and whoever accepted the lowest figure would duly get her. The funds for this came from the sale of the attractive girls, thereby ensuring that it was those with good looks who served to provide dowries for their ugly or crippled sisters. It was forbidden a man to arrange the marriage of his daughter on his own whim, nor was anyone who had purchased a girl permitted to take her home without first producing someone prepared to stand surety for him: this was because,

before the man who had bought the girl could lead her away, it had to be formally pledged that he did indeed intend to live with her as a husband. Should a marriage break down, then the law obliged the husband to return the dowry. The opportunity to buy a wife was open even to men who had travelled to the auction from other villages. A wonderful custom, indeed; but one that has since fallen into disuse, and been replaced by another, devised only recently [so as to ensure that the girls of Babylon are not misused too badly, or abducted from their native city]. For such has been the wretchedness of the masses since the conquest, and such their condition of poverty, that the only way for them to make any kind of living at all has been to pimp out their daughters as whores.[211]

[197] Next I come to the custom of theirs that I rank second for ingenuity. Rather than consult a doctor, the Babylonians will instead carry anyone who has fallen ill into the city's main square, where passers-by will give him tips on his ailment, drawn either from personal experience of the sufferer's symptoms, or else from having observed the symptoms in others. Whether the passerby was himself cured of a similar disease, or studied someone else who had been a patient, and had recovered, he will be sure to offer prescriptions and remedies. To walk past an invalid in silence, without asking him what illness he has, is forbidden.

[198] As for the dead, the Babylonians embalm them in honey; and the lamentations that they raise are like those that are heard in Egypt. Whenever a man from Babylon has had sex with his wife, he will fumigate himself by sitting over smouldering incense, while his wife does the same on the far side of the room; then, with the coming of dawn, they will both wash themselves. They will not touch so much as a piece of crockery until these ablutions have been completed. This is a practice that the Arabians hold to as well.

[199] Now I come to the most outrageous of the Babylonians' customs.[212] Once in her life, every native-born woman must go and sit in the shrine of Aphrodite and have sex with a total stranger. Those whose sense of pride has been so puffed up by wealth that they disdain to mingle with the other women there will invariably be driven to the sanctuary in a carriage and pair, veiled behind curtains; and when they do have to stand in the open, a whole retinue of servants will be massed in attendance behind them. These, however, are the exceptions. Most will sit in

the temple precinct with a garland of plaited string round their heads; and everywhere there are women arriving, and women leaving. Gangways, dead straight ones, provide access through the mass of them in a whole range of different directions; and it is along these, up and down, that men who have never before so much as seen the women will go, and make their pick. No woman who has sat herself down there is permitted to go home until a stranger has tossed a silver coin into her lap and led her outside the shrine, there to have sex with her. The man who drops the coin must say, as he does so, 'I summon to your protection the goddess Mylitta' – 'Mylitta' being the Assyrian name for Aphrodite. The coin itself can be of any value: there is no denomination so small that it can legitimately be refused, for the silver, merely by being dropped, has been transmuted into something holy. Similarly, the woman has no right to pick and choose: she must go with the first man who pays her. The moment she has had sex with him, however, she has fulfilled her obligation to the goddess, and can head home; and from that moment on there is no payment, be it ever so great, that will enable someone to get their hands on her again. Good-looking, statuesque women, of course, do not have to wait long to get home; but those who are less pleasing to the eye can find themselves unable to meet the requirement of the law for quite a while. Some, indeed, have been left stranded for up to three or four years. In Cyprus[213] too, there are several places where an almost identical practice is followed.

[200] Such are the customs of the Babylonians. In addition, there are three of their clans who eat nothing but fish: they catch them, dry them in the sun, then grind them up using a pestle and mortar before sieving them through a strip of linen. Next, depending on the preference of those who are to eat it, the powder can either be kneaded into a kind of cake, or else baked in the manner of bread.

[201] With his conquest of the Babylonian people duly completed, Cyrus' next objective was to subdue the Massagetans: a large and warlike tribe, so reports have it, whose homeland lies far to the east, towards the rising of the sun. They live past the River Araxes,[214] opposite the Issedonians. It is said by some that they are of Scythian extraction.

[202] As to whether the Araxes is larger or smaller than the Ister,[215] contradictory claims are made. The large number of islands that are contained within the river are said to approximate to Lesbos in size, and

to be inhabited by people who during the summer subsist on a great variety of grubbed up roots, and during the winter on fruit identified by them as edible, and which, when it was in season, they picked straight from the bough and put into storage. (There is another kind of tree as well which has been found on these islands, whose fruit is truly distinctive. Whenever groups of the islanders get together, they will be sure to light a bonfire, sit around it in a circle and toss this fruit into the flames; for even as the fruit burns, so the scent of it comes to fill their nostrils, until the perfume has made them no less intoxicated than a Greek would be made by wine. Indeed, the more fruit that ends up on the fire, the more intoxicated they become, until eventually they will rise to their feet, dance and burst into song. Such, at any rate, are the reports that are given of this people's lifestyle.) As with the Gyndes, the river which Cyrus divided up into three hundred and sixty separate channels, the River Araxes has its source among the Matienians; it has forty mouths, all but one of which discharge into marshes and lagoons, where it is said that men live who feed on raw fish and wear clothes made out of seal skin. The one stream that does not end up a muddy bog flows into the Caspian Sea. This is a self-contained body of water, one that never mingles with the waters of other seas. The contrast here is with the sea on which the Greeks sail, the entire expanse of it, and with the sea which lies beyond the Pillars of Heracles,[216] the one that is known as the Atlantic, and with the Red Sea: all of these are, in truth, but a single sea.

[203] The Caspian, however, is a sea that stands in isolation. Lengthwise, it would take fifteen solid days of rowing for a ship to complete a crossing of it, while the sea's breadth, at its fullest point, is equivalent to an eight-day voyage.[217] All along its western shore there stretches the Caucasus, the largest chain of mountains in the world, and the one with the highest peaks. The Caucasus is the haunt of any number of different peoples, most of whom live off the fruits of the forest. Also harvested there, it is reported, are the leaves of a certain type of tree which, once they have been pulped and mixed with water, can be used to paint images on clothing. These same images, rather than coming out in the wash, instead age as the wool ages, just as if they had always been woven into the fabric right from the start. It is also said of the people of the Caucasus that they copulate in public, as livestock do.

[204] Westwards, then, of the sea known as the Caspian the Caucasus

rises sheer; while eastwards of it, extending as far as the eye can see, towards the rising of the sun, there stretches a boundless plain. It was a huge portion of this same great plain that constituted the domain of the Massagetans, whom Cyrus was eager to attack. Manifold and weighty were the factors which stirred in him this yearning, and served to goad him on: chief was the seemingly supernatural circumstance of his birth, and secondly the remarkable good fortune that had always been the complement of his campaigns. Certainly, no nation that had found itself the object of Cyrus' ambitions had ever been able to devise a means of escaping him.

[205] Owing to the recent death of the king of the Massagetans, it was his widow, a woman named Tomyris,[218] who sat on the throne at this time. Cyrus, who was keen to make this queen his wife, duly sent her a declaration of courtship; but Tomyris, who knew full well that it was her kingdom rather than herself that was being wooed, rejected his advance. So it was, foiled in his underhand approach, that Cyrus threw himself into a naked assault upon the Massagetans, with an advance upon the Araxes: bridges were built as a means of yoking together the two sides of the river, enabling his army to make the crossing, and on the various boats that were simultanously being deployed to transport his troops, bristling towers were erected.

[206] While all these efforts were going on, however, Tomyris sent an ambassador. 'King of the Medes,' ran her message, 'stop working yourself up into a frenzy over an enterprise that is itself nothing but frenzy. After all, how can you possibly know whether its consequences will work out in your favour? Put a stop to it, rule your own subjects and learn to live with the sight of me ruling mine. But, no, peace is the last thing you want – and so you are bound not to follow my advice. Very well, then. If you are really so desperate to pit your strength against that of the Massagetans, then give up on your exhausting project of bridging the river, and we will withdraw three days' march from the river, so that you can then make the crossing into our territory. Alternatively, if you would rather receive us into your own lands, then you withdraw the same distance.' Cyrus listened to this proposal, and then convened a meeting of all the senior Persians, at which he laid out the options before them and asked for their advice on which he should follow. All were of a single mind: the best course would be to meet with Tomyris and her forces on the Persians' own soil.

[207] From this unanimity, however, there was one dissenter: Croesus the Lydian, who had attended the meeting, and now presented his reasons for disputing the consensus. 'O King,' he said, 'did I not tell you once before, when Zeus delivered me into your hands, that I would do all I could to avert any calamity that I might see menacing your house? The lessons I have absorbed from my own misfortunes are harsh ones. Of course, if you are acting on the assumption that you and the troops you lead are immortal, then there is no point in my spelling them out to you; but if you have come to accept your own mortality, and that of your subjects as well, then the first lesson you should acknowledge is that there is a cycle to human affairs, one that as it turns never permits the same people forever to enjoy good fortune. In consequence, my opinion on this issue differs from that of everyone else here: permit the enemy to cross into your own territory, and you will be running a terrible risk; lose a battle then, and you will lose power as well. After all, should the Massagetans be victorious, they will not return home, but will sweep onwards into your dominions. That is clear enough. And even if you secure a victory, what then? More decisive by far to cross the frontier, to beat the Massagetans on their own territory, and then to pursue them as they flee. The two possibilities I have sketched out here are underpinned by an identical logic: victory, in your case no less than in that of Tomyris, will serve to open up the vitals of empire. Finally, as well as all that, there is one further consideration to bear in mind – how unendurable would it be, and how shameful, were Cyrus the son of Cambyses to cringe before a woman, and give her ground. For all these reasons, it seems best to me that we should cross the river, advance as far as the enemy are prepared to retreat before us, and then attempt to get the better of them by the following ploy – one that has been prompted by my learning how ignorant the Massagetans are of the good things enjoyed by the Persians, and of all that makes life worth living. It is prodigality that will help us to deal with such men. Let us lay out a banquet in our camp, furnished with joints of meat, all of it dressed for the table, and provided on a massive scale, alongside a lavish supply of drinking-bowls, complete with undiluted wine and food of every kind. Next, when all is ready, immediately withdraw the main body of your forces back to the river, while leaving behind in the camp those you can easily spare. Unless I am very much mistaken, the enemy will no sooner catch sight of such an array of fine things than they will fall upon them –

and thereby provide us with an opportunity to make a show of prodigious deeds.'[219]

[208] Confronted by these rival points of view, Cyrus chose to abandon the policy first mooted, and go instead with that of Croesus. Accordingly, he informed Tomyris that it was his intention to cross the frontier, and that she should pull her forces back. This she duly did, just as she had promised she would. As for Croesus, Cyrus entrusted him to the son he had appointed as his heir, Cambyses, together with repeated instructions that the Lydian was to be treated kindly and with respect, even were the expedition against the Massagetans to end in disaster. Then, with his commands clearly on record, Cyrus dispatched Cambyses and Croesus back to Persia together, while he himself led his army across the river.

[209] That same evening, as twilight began to deepen over the land of the Massagetans, and Cyrus, now on the far bank of the Araxes, fell asleep, he was granted a vision. It seemed to him as he dreamt that he was gazing upon the eldest son of Hystaspes, and that this same son had wings growing out of his shoulders, and that one of these wings was serving to put Asia into the shade, and the other Europe. (Hystaspes, the son of Arsames, was an Achaemenid, and his eldest son was Darius, who at the time was around twenty years old, and who, as a consequence of being too young to go on campaign, had been left behind in Persia.) When Cyrus awoke, he mulled this dream over. So portentous did it appear to him that he summoned Hystaspes, and took him to one side. 'Hystaspes,' he said, 'your son has been caught plotting against me and my hold on power. This information admits of no doubt whatsoever – and I will tell you why. Not for nothing am I watched over by the gods, who will always afford me a glimpse of impending danger. So it was, while asleep last night, that I saw your eldest son with wings growing out of his shoulders. One of these wings was serving to put Asia into the shade, the other, Europe. There can be no escaping the implications of such a dream – he is plotting against me. So I want you to return to Persia as fast as you can, and make your son ready, once I am back in the country following my victory here, to be brought before me for interrogation.'

[210] That Cyrus could issue such a prescription reflected his certainty that Darius was indeed guilty. In reality, however, the gods had been illumining a very different truth: namely, that Cyrus' doom was

close at hand, and that the rule of his kingdom was fated to devolve on Darius. 'My Lord,' Hystaspes answered, 'there is not a Persian man born who would think to conspire against you – but should there be one, then he merits immediate death. Why, it was you who found the Persians slaves, and made of them free men – you who found them ruled by others, and made of them the rulers of the world. My son has been plotting revolution[220] against you – that is the message of your dream? Very well, then – I deliver him up into your hands for you to deal with as you will.' And so saying, Hystaspes crossed back over the Araxes and headed for Persia, there to keep watch over his son, Darius, on Cyrus' behalf.

[211] Cyrus himself, meanwhile, advanced onwards from the Araxes, and after a day's journey did as Croesus had suggested. Then, marching all his operational units back to the Araxes, he left behind him the noncombatants of the Persian army, a rump that was promptly attacked by a third of the Massagetan forces, backed into a desperate resistance, and annihilated. It was then, in the wake of this victory, that the Massagetans observed the feast that had been prepared earlier; they duly stretched themselves out, gorged on the food and wine – and fell asleep. Now it was the Persians' turn to launch an ambush; many of the Massagetans were slaughtered, but even more were taken alive, and among these was the son of Queen Tomyris, who had been in command of the Massagetans, and whose name was Spargapises.

[212] Hearing the news of what had happened to her army and her son, Tomyris dispatched a herald to Cyrus. 'Blood-drinker,' her message ran, 'never sated! Proud, are you, Cyrus, of your day's work? Well, you should not be. The fruit of the vine, which bloats you Persians to the point of frenzy, so that the wine, even as it swills down your throats, slips past the abuse that is simultaneously rising in your gullets – that was the poison you deployed, in your underhand way, scorning the honest test of battle, to get the better of my son. Well now, I am going to offer you some good advice, which I strongly advise you to take. Give me back my son, depart my country and I am prepared to overlook the swaggering brutality with which you handled a whole third of the Massagetan army. Refuse, however, and I swear by the sun, the lord of the Massagetans, that, ravening blood-drinker though you may be, yet I will glut your taste for blood.'

[213] The receipt of this message, however, perturbed Cyrus not

a whit. Inebriation, meanwhile, had released the son of Queen Tomyris from its grip; and as he woke up to the full horror of his circumstances, so he begged Cyrus to release him from his chains. His request was granted; but no sooner had he been freed, and given back the use of his hands, than he stabbed himself to death.

[214] Such, then, was the manner in which Spargapises met his end. Meanwhile, because Cyrus had blocked his ears to her terms, Tomyris assembled all the forces she could muster and met with him in battle. The resulting clash was, in my judgement, the most terrible that has ever been fought between two rival barbarian peoples; and the tactics deployed, thanks to my researches,[221] are a matter, not of opinion, but of record. First, so it is said, the two sides rained arrows down upon one another from a distance; then, when all their missiles were spent, they clashed and grappled together in close combat, stabbing with spears, fighting hand to hand with daggers. Time passed; but still the combatants stood locked in battle, neither side willing to cede an inch. Finally, however, it was the Massagetans who gained the upper hand. The greater part of the Persian army was wiped out; and among those who met their end there was Cyrus himself. He had been on the throne for twenty-nine years in all. Tomyris, who had filled a wineskin with human blood, searched among the Persian dead for his corpse; and once she had found it, pushed the head into the wineskin.[222] 'No matter that I am the one left alive,' she said, standing over the desecrated body, 'no matter that I won the battle. When you tricked my son into your hands, you destroyed me. I threatened then that I would glut your thirst for blood. Now – you have your fill.' (Granted, there are many different stories told of how Cyrus met his end – but the one I have related here appears to me the most plausible.)

[215] The Massagetans wear the same kinds of clothing as the Scythians, and share a similar way of life. Some fight on horseback, others on foot (they deploy both cavalry and infantry), and in addition to bows and spears, they have a habit of wielding double-headed axes. They use gold and bronze for everything: bronze for spearheads, arrow-points and the blades of their double-headed axes, gold for head-dresses, belts and the bands around their chests. The same goes for horses: the breast-plates used to protect their chests are made out of bronze, while their bridles, bits and cheek-pieces are all made out of gold. The Massagetans

do not make anything out of iron or silver: supplies of these two metals are non-existent in their country, whereas those of gold and bronze are superabundant.

[216] Now to their customs. Their women, although married to individual husbands, are open to use by anyone. (Despite the fact that the Greeks attribute this custom to the Scythians, I should emphasize that it is most definitely Massagetan.) Should one of their men lust after a particular woman, then he will hang his quiver outside her wagon and take her, without fear of her husband. Because they believe that all people, without exception, have a specific limit set on the span of their lives, the relatives of a person who is very old will gather together and kill him amid much ritual solemnity. Simultaneously, they will offer up cattle as sacrifices; they will then boil up the [human] meat, and feast on it.[223] This, they believe, is the very best way to die – and should one of their number die of an illness, they will bury rather than eat him, and hold it a great cause of sorrow that he did not live long enough to be sacrificed. They have no agriculture, but live off cattle and off fish, which the River Araxes furnishes in great abundance. They also drink milk. The only god they revere is the sun, to whom they sacrifice horses. The thinking behind this ritual is self-evident: the swiftest of mortals is offered up to the swiftest of immortals.

BOOK TWO[1]

[1] The end of Cyrus saw his kingdom pass to Cambyses, his son by Cassandane, who was the daughter of Pharnaspes; her early death had inspired a grief-stricken Cyrus to command that all his subjects go into mourning for her. Being the son of Cyrus by this woman, Cambyses took for granted that the Ionians and Aeolians were his slaves by right of inheritance from his father; accordingly, when he launched an expedition against Egypt, he took contingents drawn from his Greek subjects alongside his other conscripts.

[2] Before the accession of Psammetichus as ruler of their kingdom, the Egyptians used to presume themselves the first-sprung of all men. When Psammetichus became king, however, he wanted to settle the issue of primacy for good – and ever since his reign, the Egyptians have held the Phrygians to be the original race of men, ahead of themselves, whom they rank the second, ahead of everyone else. Not that Psammetichus, in his attempt to identify the primal humans, had been able to discover any worthwhile line of enquiry; and so instead he devised an experiment. He took two new-born infants, selected at random from some family, and gave them to a shepherd, together with instructions that they were to be brought up among a flock of sheep, and a prohibition against uttering so much as a sound within their hearing. They were to be kept in a lonely hut, all by themselves, and the shepherd, as well as attending to whatever else might need doing, was to bring in goats from time to time, to ensure that the infants had their fill of milk. These various arrangements and instructions were issued so that Psammetichus could find out, once the children had passed the stage of meaningless baby-talk, what their first utterance would be. And sure enough, everything went to plan. Two years went by, during which time

the shepherd dutifully stuck to this programme, until one day, as he opened the door of the hut and went inside, the children knelt down before him and reached up with their hands, both of them making the same sound: *bekos*. The first time the shepherd heard this, he made no mention of it; but in due course, after he had found that every visit of his to check up on the children was bringing a repetition of the word, he informed his master, who commanded that the children were to be brought to him. Psammetichus, once he had listened to the evidence of his own ears, set about investigating whether *bekos* was a word in common use anywhere in the world – and sure enough, discovered that in Phrygian it meant 'bread'. Such was the experiment which persuaded the Egyptians to acknowledge that the Phrygians were of a greater antiquity than themselves. That this is the truth of what happened I heard from the priests of Hephaestus at Memphis. (The Greeks tell a whole number of stories – including one which has Psammetichus cutting out the tongues of some women, and then putting the children to live with them – which are just ludicrous.)[2]

[3] This account of how the children were brought up was not, however, the only topic I heard about in Memphis, during the course of my conversations with the priests of Hephaestus.[3] Indeed, the reason that I then went off to Thebes and Heliopolis was because I wanted to know if the priests there would concur with what I had been told in Memphis: the scholars of Heliopolis have a reputation for being the best informed in Egypt. Now, except for the gods' names, I have no desire to pass on any details of what I heard about the dimension of the divine, for in my opinion all men are equal when it comes to a knowledge of the gods. When and if I do touch on the subject, it will only be because I am obliged to by my narrative.[4]

[4] As regards human affairs, however, the priests were all agreed in saying that the Egyptians were the first people to discover what a year is, and to divide up its various seasons into twelve parts. This discovery, they claimed, derived from the stars. Their system, it seems to me, is a much more sophisticated one than the Greek: the Greeks, in order to match their calendar to the seasons, are obliged to insert an intercalary month every other year, whereas the Egyptians, because they have twelve months each of thirty days, need only add another five days onto the year to ensure that the cycle of the seasons returns to its original starting-point.[5] The priests also stated that the Egyptians were the first

to use the names of the twelve gods, and that these were then adopted from them by the Greeks. Other innovations included their allocation of altars, images and temples to the gods, and the carving of figures on stone. Most of these claims they were able to back up with evidence. They also informed me that the first human king of Egypt was Min. In his time the whole of Egypt, with the exception of the province of Thebes, was marshland; indeed, north of Lake Moeris, which is a seven-day voyage upriver from the sea, everywhere that is now dry land lay under water.

[5] The accuracy of what they say about the country seems to me beyond dispute. It should be self-evident even to someone who has not been told it – so long as he has a brain, and eyes to see – that the Egypt to which the Greeks sail is land that has come into the possession of the Egyptians courtesy of the river.[6] The same is true also of the land beyond the lake, up to a distance of three days' voyage; despite the fact that the priests did not think to mention it, this is simply more of the same. Indeed, it is one of the distinguishing physical features of Egypt that if, while approaching it by ship, and with a whole day's sailing still to go, you were to lower a sounding line, you would bring up mud from a depth of 11 fathoms: evidence of just how far the silt extends.

[6] The length of the Egyptian coastline is 60 *schoeni* – or at least it is if we define Egypt as running from the Gulf of Plinthine to Lake Serbonis, in the lea of Mount Casium. It is the distance between these two points which comes to 60 *schoeni*. (People who are short of property measure land in fathoms; those who are slightly better endowed, in stades; those who have lots of property, in *parasangs*; and those with a positive excess of it, in *schoeni*. One *parasang* equals 30 stades, and one *schoenus* – this being the unit of measurement used by the Egyptians – 60 stades. It follows, therefore, that the length of the Egyptian coastline amounts to 3,600 stades.)

[7] Inland from the coast, all the way to Heliopolis, Egypt is one level expanse of water and mud. From the sea to Heliopolis, the road is pretty close in distance to the Athens road which leads from the Altar of the Twelve Gods to the Temple of Olympian Zeus in Pisa.[7] Granted, the equivalence is not absolutely precise, for anyone who does the calculations will find that there is a difference between the two roads of 15 stades: the one from Athens to Pisa is 15 stades short of 1,500, while the one from the sea to Heliopolis is 1,500 stades exactly.

[8] Continuing inland from Heliopolis, Egypt narrows. On one side there stretches the mountain range of Arabia, which runs from the north, where the constellation of the Great Bear rises, to the south, home of the southern wind, before extending without break towards the Red Sea,[8] as it is known. The point where the range changes direction is also where it loses height, and the quarries where the stone was cut for the pyramids at Memphis are found; beyond these, as I just mentioned, the mountains continue onwards to the Red Sea. I discovered that to cross them at their broadest, from east to west, takes two months – and that along their easternmost limit frankincense is produced. So much for the description of these particular mountains; but there is another range, no less rocky, extending along the Libyan side of Egypt – and containing the pyramids – which is sand-covered, and runs parallel to that stretch of the Arabian range which bears south. Consequently, beyond Heliopolis, the land which actually qualifies as a part of Egypt is meagre, with a particularly narrow point, by Egyptian standards, lying four[teen] days' journey upriver by boat. The land between these mountain ranges is perfectly level, with a gap between the Arabian and the Libyan ranges that I would estimate as being, at its narrowest, no more than 200 stades. South of this, however, Egypt broadens out once again.

[9] Such are the land's physical characteristics. The voyage upriver from Heliopolis to Thebes takes nine days, and covers a distance of 4,860 stades, or 81 *schoeni*. All the various measurements which serve to delineate Egypt in stades can now be brought together. The coastline comes to 3,600 stades, as I have already said, while the distance inland from the sea to Thebes is one that I record now as 6,120 stades. From Thebes to the city known as Elephantine it is 1,800 stades.[9]

[10] That a substantial part of the country I have just been describing might be supplementary to the original Egypt is my own personal impression, as well as being what I was told by the priests. Certainly, it struck me that in the gap between the mountain ranges which I mentioned earlier, south of the city of Memphis, there must at some point have existed a gulf of the sea, just as there were once gulfs in the vicinity of Troy, and of Teuthrania, and of Ephesus, and of the plain of the Maeander. Admittedly, this is to compare the small-scale with the great, since none of the rivers silting up these latter regions merits being compared in terms of size with even one of the arms of the Nile – and

the Nile has five in all! There are other rivers as well which, although hardly on the majestic scale of the Nile, have left a palpable, indeed an extensive, residue. Among all the others that I could mention, not the least is the Achelous, which flows through Acarnania, and has already joined up half of the Echinades islands to the mainland.

[11] In Arabia, not far from Egypt, there is a gulf, an extension of the so-called 'Red Sea', very long and narrow, the details of which I shall now describe. In terms of length, a ship that sets out from the inmost point of the gulf will require forty days of rowing to reach the open sea; in terms of width, however, only half a day's voyage is needed, even at the gulf's broadest point. Its waters are tidal, rising and falling daily. Egypt itself, it seems to me, must surely once have constituted just such another gulf, with one stretch of it running from the Northern Sea in the direction of Ethiopia, and another, the Arabian (which I will discuss shortly) bearing from the south up towards Syria. At their extremities, the erosive effects of these gulfs were such that only a narrow strip of land was left between them. Now, suppose the Nile decided to change its course, and to flow into the Arabian Gulf – what would there be to stop that same gulf, over the course of twenty thousand years, from being silted up entirely? Personally, I think that a mere ten thousand years would suffice. That being so, and bearing in mind just how much time has preceded my own coming into the world, it is surely plausible that a gulf even larger than the Arabian could have been silted up – for the Nile is a great river, and capable of working remarkable things.

[12] Those who offer this interpretation of Egypt, then, appear to me wholly convincing – not least because it is so in line with my own conclusions. I have seen with my own eyes how Egypt projects well beyond the coastline of neighbouring lands; how shells appear in the mountains; how salt like the brine of the sea oozes up from the soil, so that even the pyramids are corroded by it; and how the only mountain in Egypt with sand lies above Memphis. A further point – the soil of Egypt is quite unlike that of the adjacent land of Arabia, nor does it resemble the soil of Libya, nor even that of Syria (a point worth making, since the Syrians inhabit the seaboard of Arabia). It is black, and crumbles easily – which suggests that it must originally have beeen alluvial mud, brought down by the river out of Ethiopia. We know that Libyan soil, by contrast, is a reddish deposit overlying sand, while that of Arabia and Syria is clay-like, and rests on a stony base.

[13] One particularly striking piece of evidence that the priests mentioned to me, in relation to their country: in the time of King Moeris, the
river had to rise only a minimum of twelve feet for the land north of
Memphis to be flooded. When I heard this from the priests, Moeris had
been dead for less than nine hundred years. Nowadays, however, unless
the river rises a minimum of 23½ to 24 feet, the region remains
unflooded. It seems to me, then, that should the land continue to rise
and expand at the same rate as it has in the past, those Egyptians who
live north of Lake Moeris, and especially those who inhabit the area
known as 'The Delta', will end up suffering – and permanently – the
very fate that they used to say would be that of the Greeks. For when
they learned that the whole of Greece depends for its water on rainfall,
and not, as in their own country, on the flooding of rivers, they declared
that the day would surely come when the Greeks would find themselves
deceived in all their expectations, and be brought to suffer terribly from
the pangs of starvation.[10] The point they wanted to make was this: that
should the heavens simply see fit to deny the Greeks rain, and afflict us
with a drought, then we would inevitably be wiped out by famine, since
we would have absolutely no means – Zeus aside – of obtaining water.

[14] And when they say this about the Greeks, the Egyptians are certainly not wrong. All the same, let me now spell out the situation which
confronts the Egyptians themselves. The area north of Memphis, as I
mentioned earlier, is piling up with silt. Should the region continue to
increase in height at the same rate as it has done in the past, what will
face the Egyptians who live there once the river is no longer able to
flood their fields, and with no likelihood of rain either, save starvation?
As things stand, of course, there is nowhere else in the entire world, the
rest of Egypt included, where the harvesting of crops requires less effort:
those who live there have no need to toil with a plough, breaking up the
earth into furrows, nor to hoe, nor to labour at any of the tasks which
other men who wish to raise crops are obliged to undertake. Instead,
they simply wait for the river to rise of its own accord and inundate
their fields, after which, once the waters have done their work of irrigation and retreated, each man will sow his own plot; then pigs are
released into the fields to ensure that the seed is trodden down; then
there is another wait. Come the harvest, the pigs are released again –
this time to thresh the grain – and the harvest is brought to storage.

[15] But what of the theories about Egypt that are put forward by the

Ionians? It is their claim that Egypt consists exclusively of the Delta, a region defined by them as extending 40 *schoeni* along the coastline from the so-called 'Watchtower of Perseus' to the salt factories of Pelusium, and inland from the sea as far as the city of Cercasorus, where the waters of the Nile divide to flow onwards either to Pelusium or to Canobus. The other regions of Egypt, according to this definition, belong properly either to Libya or to Arabia. But if we accept this, we are also obliged to accept that there was a time when the Egyptians never had a country at all, as I shall now demonstrate. For let us assume, as I certainly do, that the Egyptians are correct when they claim the Delta to be alluvial – and even, one might go so far as to say, of recent origin. But that would mean that they had no country at all before then – in which case, why all their wasted effort pushing the theory that they might have been the first-born of men? There would certainly have been no call for them to conduct their experiment with the children, to find out which language was spoken first. No, it is my firm conviction that the Egyptians – far from having come into existence simultaneously with what the Ionians call the 'Delta'[11] – have always existed, right the way back to the very first generation of men. As their country grew in extent, there were many who remained where they were; but there were also many, over time, who came to migrate downriver. The truth, then, is that Egypt, back in ancient times, was synonymous with Thebes – a region which has a circumference of 6,120 stades.

[16] Such is my conclusion – and if I am right, then the Ionians must have Egypt badly wrong. Even if the Ionian thesis is correct, I can still demonstrate that the Greeks – the Ionians themselves included – are displaying basic innumeracy when they reckon the entire world to consist of three continents: Europe, Asia and Libya. They need to include in their numbering the Egyptian Delta as a fourth – assuming, that is, that the Delta is indeed neither a part of Asia nor of Libya. At any rate, this is the corollary of the Ionian thesis – for what does it claim, after all, if not that the Nile constitutes the dividing line between Asia and Libya? And what does the Nile do at the apex of the Delta, if not flow around it? And what, then, does this make the Delta, if not a region distinct from Asia and Libya?

[17] But enough of the Ionians' theorizing. Let me spell out my own view on the matter. Egypt constitutes the entirety of the land that is inhabited by the Egyptians – just as Cilicia is the land inhabited by the

Cilicians, or Assyria the land inhabited by the Assyrians – and I certainly know of no border between Asia and Libya that can credibly be defined as such, unless it be the borders of Egypt. Follow the usual Greek reckoning, however, and we would have to envisage the whole of Egypt, right the way from the First Cataract and the city of Elephantine, as consisting of two halves, each one with a different name: one half would be a part of Libya, and the other a part of Asia. From the First Cataract, after all, the Nile flows onwards right the way to the sea – dividing Egypt in two. Up to the city of Cercasorus, the currents form a single stream; beyond it, however, they split and follow three separate courses. The first, known as the 'Mouth of Pelusium', bears eastwards, while the second, the so-called 'Mouth of Canobus', veers west. The third branch does not alter its course: instead, reaching the apex of the Delta from Egypt's interior, its waters sweep onwards, splitting the Delta down the middle before they discharge into the sea. These are certainly not the least in volume, nor is the channel that bears them any less renowned than the other two: the Mouth of Sebennytus, it is called. There are also two other arms, tributaries of the Sebennytic arm, which likewise flow towards the sea: one is known as the Saitic Mouth, and the other as the Mendesian. The Bolbitine and Bucolic Mouths are the result of spadework, and not of natural forces.

[18] One piece of evidence relating to the scale of Egypt, which supports the case I have been making here, was delivered by the oracle of Ammon,[12] and only came to my attention after I had already formed my own opinions. The inhabitants of Marea and Apis, two towns which directly abut Libya, considered themselves to be Libyans rather than Egyptians, for they had taken a strong dislike to certain religious observances, in particular the taboo which prevented them from so much as approaching a cow. Accordingly, they sent an embassy to Ammon. 'We have absolutely nothing in common with the Egyptians,' they declared. 'We live outside the Delta, and share no point of agreement with them. Surely, then, we can have permission to eat whatsoever we like?' But the god refused to let them do as they wished. Instead, he told them that anywhere touched by the flood-waters of the Nile qualified as Egypt, and that anyone who lived north of Elephantine and drank from the river qualified as an Egyptian. A deity had spoken!

[19] At full flood, the Nile inundates not only the Delta, but also great swathes of the land which has been variously identified as either

Libyan or Arabian – to a distance, more or less, of two days' journey on either side. Neither the priests nor anyone else could help me get to grips with the nature of the Nile. One thing I particularly wanted to find out was why, during the summer solstice, the waters of the Nile start to flood as they descend downstream, continue to do so for a hundred days, and then, towards the end of that period, recede again, retreating so far back into the river-bed that they remain shallow for the entire winter, until, once again, the summer solstice comes around. Not one of the Egyptians could help me to understand why this should be so, despite all my efforts to ask them what peculiar attribute the Nile possesses which might cause it to behave so differently to every other river. Nor was this the only enquiry that was repeatedly on my lips. I also wished to know why the Nile, alone of all rivers, should cause no breezes to blow.

[20] It is true that there are certain Greeks, keen to make a name for themselves as intellectuals, who have suggested three different ways to explain the behaviour of the Nile's waters: two of these I wouldn't so much as mention were it not for the fact that I want to sketch them in outline. One explanation attributes the flooding of the river to winds which blow in from the north-west and thereby prevent the Nile from flowing onwards to the sea. The Nile, though, behaves no differently even when the Etesian winds are not blowing; and if the explanation really did lie with these winds, then all the other rivers which flow counter to them would surely have been affected in a similar manner – indeed, bearing in mind how much smaller such rivers are, and how much feebler their currents, to an even greater extent. Yet for all that there are plenty of such rivers in Syria, and in Libya too, not one of them is affected in the same way as the Nile.

[21] The second theory, even more than the one I have just cited, combines ignorance with what is (not to beat about the bush) still more incredible yet: it claims that the Nile functions as it does because its waters flow in from Oceanus, and that the flow of this same Oceanus encircles all the world.

[22] The third explanation, while it may sound by far the most plausible, is also the furthest from the truth. According to this theory, the currents of the Nile derive from melting snow – a claim that makes no more sense than any of the others. Here, after all, is a river which flows from Libya and right through the land of the Ethiopians before it enters

Egypt. That being so, how could its currents possibly derive from snow, when they are flowing from the hottest regions of the world into climates which are, by and large, a good deal cooler? Certainly, to any man capable of rational reflection, it should be obvious that the Nile is most unlikely to derive from snow. The first and most conclusive proof of this is provided by the winds, which, when they blow from Libya and Ethiopia, are hot. Second is the fact that these same countries know neither rain nor frost, and yet it is a firm rule that always, five days after any snow, rain is bound to fall; so the lack of rain in these countries proves that there can be no snow. Thirdly, so scorching is the region that the people who live there are black. It is also a fact that kites and swallows remain there the whole year round, without ever leaving it, and that cranes, in flight from the Scythian winter, migrate there to pass the winter. Yet if it were truly the case that it snowed, even a little, in these countries through which the Nile flows and in which its origins lie, then none of these things would happen[13] – as necessity dictates.

[23] The theory of the man who brings Oceanus into the discussion is impossible to disprove, for it is founded upon a story so resistant to inspection as to be unexaminable. Certainly, from my own point of view, I know of no River Oceanus, and can only suppose that Homer[14] or one of the other poets of earlier times must have come across the name and introduced it into his verse.

[24] Nevertheless, baffling though the whole matter is, after all my criticism of the theories proposed by others I am perhaps obliged to set out my own opinion and to state why I think it is that the Nile floods in summer. To sum up my view as concisely as possible, while leaving nothing out: the sun, during the winter months, is driven by storms off its regular course to the region above Libya. For it stands to reason that it is the country nearest to the sun-god, and most immediately underneath it, which will gasp for water more desperately than any other, just as it is the streams feeding its local rivers which will progressively evaporate.

[25] Now to clarify this theory by setting it out in more detail. When the sun passes over Libya, the atmosphere through which its course takes it is never less than clear, while the land below it is fully exposed to its rays, and untouched by cooling winds. The effect is the same as the one that it invariably has in the summer, when it journeys across the middle of the heavens: the sun draws up water, and then forces it away

inland, where it is borne upon the winds, which scatter the moisture and cause its precipitation. No surprise, then, that the south and south-west winds, the ones which blow from Libya, should be by far the rainiest of all. (That said, it seems probable to me that the sun does not dispose of the entire volume of water which it sucks up each year from the Nile, but retains some of it around itself.) Then, as the storms of winter ease, so the sun resumes its course across the middle of the heavens – from which point on, it draws up water equally from rivers everywhere. Because some of these – those which flow through lands where rain falls and which are scored by gullies – have been swollen by great volumes of rain, they run at flood during the winter; but come the summer, when the rains fail and their waters are being drawn up by the sun, they are greatly enfeebled. But because the Nile is never fed by rain and experiences evaporation by the sun, it is the only river which flows far more shallowly in winter than it does in summer. All of this is logical enough: whereas in summer its waters are being sucked up by the sun to the same degree as those everywhere else, during the winter it alone suffers evaporation. Such are my reasons for deeming that the responsibility lies with the sun.

[26] That the atmosphere there should be so dry is also, in my judgement, due to the sun, for it scorches all in its path; this is why, in upper Libya, it is one perpetual summer. But suppose that there was an alteration in the state of the seasons, with the position in the sky currently occupied by the north wind and the winter being taken over by the south wind and the summer, and the position of the south wind being taken over by the north – if that were to happen, then the sun, as it was driven out of the mid-heavens by the wintery blasts of the north wind, would surely pass over the skies above Europe, just as now it passes over those above Libya. Indeed, I expect that the sun, with the whole of Europe to cover, would affect the Ister as it currently does the Nile.

[27] As to the failure of breezes to blow from the Nile, I have a theory about that as well: namely, that it flies in the face of reason to expect them to blow from anywhere that is characterized by extreme heat. A breeze, after all, tends to blow in from somewhere cold.

[28] But let these phenomena be what they are – and have been since their beginning. Now to the sources of the Nile, a mystery which nobody with whom I came into discussion about the matter, whether Egyptian,

Libyan or Greek, ever professed to have fathomed. The one exception was a man from Sais in Egypt, a clerk who kept the accounts of the temple of Athena[15] – but I had the distinct impression, his claims to a definitive solution notwithstanding, that he was just having a joke. This was what he said: two mountains which have summits rising to a sharp peak, named Crophi and Mophi respectively, lie between the cities of Syene, in the region of Thebes, and Elephantine. In a valley between these two mountains there rise the well-springs of the Nile, which are bottomless: half the water flows into Egypt, in a northerly direction, and half flows into Ethiopia, to the south. It was King Psammetichus[16] of Egypt, so the scribe said, who had found a way to test whether the well-springs were indeed bottomless, by lowering into them a specially fashioned rope, many thousands of fathoms long, which never reached the bottom. But it seems to me that what this story of the scribe's actually demonstrates – if it has any credibility at all – is the presence in the water of powerful whirlpools and a strong counter-current, and that it was because of the battering of the water upon the mountains that the sounding rope, when it was lowered, was unable to plumb the bottom.

[29] There was no further information to be had from anyone; nevertheless, insofar as I was able to push the limits of discovery, I pushed them. Initially I did this as an eyewitness, by travelling as far as the city of Elephantine; beyond there, however, I was dependent for my enquiries upon what I heard from others.[17] Going upriver from the city of Elephantine, the land steepens. Travellers are obliged to tie ropes to their boat, one for each bank of the river, just as they would with an ox, and so proceed. Should one of the ropes snap, the boat is borne away by the force of the currents. It takes a voyage of four days to pass through this terrain, where the Nile twists and turns like the Maeander;[18] the distance that one has to cover in this fashion is 12 *schoeni*. Next you come to a level plain, where the Nile flows round an island named Tachompso. Half of this island is inhabited by Egyptians; but the other half, along with all the country south of Elephantine, is occupied by Ethiopians. Beyond the island lies a great lake, and the Ethiopians who live here around its shores are nomadic. Cross this body of water, and you will rejoin the course of the Nile, which debouches into the lake. Here you must leave your boat and traverse the bank for forty days; this is due to the sharp rocks, some of them sticking out above water and many others forming reefs, which render the Nile unnavigable. Then,

forty days' crossing of this stretch of land once completed, you take another boat for twelve days, at the end of which you come to a great city, said to be the mother city of the whole of Ethiopia, named Meroe. The only gods worshipped here are Zeus and Dionysus,[19] to both of whom the people who live in Meroe pay great honour. They have established an oracle to Zeus, and both the timing and the direction of their military efforts are determined by the oracular commands that this god gives them.

[30] Sail on from this city, and after the same length of time that it takes to get from Elephantine to the mother city of the Ethiopians, you come to a people known as the 'Deserters', or *Asmach* – a word which translates literally into Greek as 'Those who stand on the left hand of the king'. These were a body of 240,000 Egyptians, of the class of the Warriors, who went over to the Ethiopians, for the reason I will now give. Back in the time of King Psammetichus, several border-posts were established: one was in the city of Elephantine, confronting the Ethiopians, another near Pelusium, at Daphnae, opposite the Arabians and the Assyrians, and a third at Marea, facing Libya. (Even in my time, in the Persian era, the same border controls were still operating as under Psammetichus, for there are garrisons maintained by the Persians both at Elephantine and at Daphnae.[20]) Anyway – these Egyptians had spent three years on guard duty with no one to relieve them. After much grumbling about this, they unanimously resolved to desert Psammetichus, and go to Ethiopia. Psammetichus, brought the news, promptly set off in pursuit. He overtook them, and delivered a speech in which, as part of the overall case he was making, he begged them not to abandon the gods of their forefathers, nor their children, nor their wives. At this, it is said, one of the soldiers whipped out his private parts, and said, 'Wherever these go, there'll be both children and women aplenty!' So they made it to Ethiopia, where they offered their services to the Ethiopian king – who duly reciprocated with a gift of his own. 'A rebellion,' the king told them, 'has broken out among some of the Ethiopians. Expel them, and you can settle on their land.' So it was that the Egyptians came to live cheek by jowl with Ethiopians, who absorbed their customs – which served to render them a good deal more civilized.

[31] We can be certain, therefore, that the Nile flows for a distance equivalent to four months' travel by water and land beyond the point where it enters Egypt – do the calculations and you will find that to be

the time, in months, that it takes to get from Elephantine to the Deserters. At this point, the Nile is flowing from the west, and the setting sun. As to what happens beyond that, no one really knows; so scorched by heat is the region that no one lives there.

[32] There is one story, though, that I heard from some men of Cyrene, who told me how once, on a visit to consult the oracle of Ammon, they fell into conversation with Etearchus, the king of the Ammonians; and how during the course of this conversation, when the topic of the Nile and the total mystery of its origins happened to come up, Etearchus mentioned a visit he had once been paid by some Nasamonians (a people from Libya who inhabit the Syrtis and the region a little to its east). Following their arrival, the Nasamonians were asked whether they knew anything more about the deserts of Libya. They replied with a story about the sons of some of their chieftains, young men whose restless ambition to make a name for themselves had led them, on their reaching adulthood, into any number of extravagant escapades. One had been especially hair-raising: after casting lots among themselves, they had chosen five of their number to survey the Libyan desert, on the chance they could see beyond the limits of what had previously been scanned. (The stretch of Libya which borders the sea to the north, beginning at Egypt and ending at Cape Soloeis, is inhabited along its entire length by numerous tribes of Libyans, all except the territory of the Greeks and Phoenicians. Then there comes a stretch inland from the sea and from the people who live alongside it which is infested by wild beasts; and inland from that, there is nothing but sand, where absolutely no water is to be found, and all is desert.) When the young men set off, dispatched by their comrades and well equipped with water and provisions, the first leg of their expedition took them through the inhabited zone of Libya; then, that stretch once completed, they came to the region where the wild animals roam; and from there, with the west wind full in their faces, they made their way across the desert. Day followed day, and sand-dune followed sand-dune, until at last, growing on a plain, they saw some trees. They pressed on, and when they reached the trees, they attempted to pick fruit from the branches. As they were doing so, however, they were set upon by pygmies smaller than humans of average height, who seized them and led them off. The noises made by their captors were totally incomprehensible to the Nasamonians, just as nothing that the Nasamonians said could be understood by their

captors. The Nasamonians were led across huge marshes, until, on the far side, they arrived at a city in which all the inhabitants were the same size as their captors, and black in colour. A huge river flowed beside the city, gliding from west to east, in which crocodiles[21] could be made out.

[33] That pretty much concludes what Etearchus, the king of the Ammonians, had to reveal – except to add that he did say (the Cyrenaeans informed me) that the Nasamonians made it successfully back home, and that the people with whom they had come into contact were all sorcerers. Etearchus had also concluded that the river which flowed by the city was the Nile, which would certainly make perfect sense. For the Nile does, after all, flow from Libya – indeed, it bisects it – so my own conjecture, based on analogy between what is apparent and what is unknown, would be that its length is equivalent to that of the Ister. That river, which splits Europe in two, has its source at the city of Pyrene, in the land of the Celts, who dwell beyond the Pillars of Heracles, and are the neighbours of the Cynetes, the people who live closer to the setting of the sun than any other in Europe. After passing through the middle of Europe, the Ister flows into the Euxine, at Istria, a colony founded by the Milesians, and ends where it meets the sea.

[34] It is because the banks of the Ister are well settled that its course is a matter of common knowledge, whereas the tenantless and desolate character of Libya, through which the Nile flows, precludes anyone from being able to say what its sources might be. I have now recorded all that I have discovered about its course and my investigations can go no further. That the Nile debouches in Egypt, which stands more or less opposite the mountainous region of Cilicia, and that the directest route from there to Sinope on the Euxine Sea will take a man travelling light five days, and that Sinope in turn lies opposite the point where the Ister issues into the sea – these are all reasons, it seems to me, for concluding that the Nile does indeed cross the whole of Libya, and is equivalent to the length of the Ister. But I have talked enough about the Nile.

[35] About Egypt, however, I will have a good deal more to say, for it is a land which boasts an inordinate number of wonders, and possesses more monuments surpassing description than any other in the world. Reason enough, then, to describe it at some length. Certainly, it is not only the climate which renders Egypt unique, nor the fact that the river behaves naturally in a way quite unlike any other river; there is also the

fact that the Egyptians themselves, in almost all their customs and practices, do the exact opposite of the rest of mankind. In Egypt, for instance,
it is the women who go to the market and do business, while it is the
men who stay at home and weave; and while people everywhere else do
their weaving by pushing the weft upwards, the Egyptians push it downwards. Men carry loads on their heads; women on their shoulders.
Women urinate standing up; men squatting down. Their homes they use
for defecating in, while the streets outside are where they eat – this on
the principle that anything which is embarrassing but unavoidable
should be done behind closed doors, while anything that is not a cause
of shame should be done fully in public. Whether a god is male or female
makes no odds, since women are banned from serving as priests, and
only a man may officiate in a temple, be it that of a goddess or of a god.
Sons are under no obligation to care for their parents if they do not wish
to; daughters, however, are under strict obligation to do so, whether
they are willing or not.

[36] Everywhere else, priests in the service of a god will wear their
hair long; but in Egypt they shave themselves bald. Among other nations,
it is the custom for those closest to someone who has just died to mark
their bereavement by cropping their hair; but the Egyptians, who are
clean-shaven as a matter of course, will mark a death by letting both
their hair and their beards grow out. It is otherwise a universal practice
not to mix with animals at home, but the Egyptians habitually live
alongside their livestock. Whereas other people subsist on barley and
the standard strain of wheat, any Egyptian who thought to do so would
be regarded with utter scorn: bread in Egypt is made instead from a specially soft kind of wheat, or *zeia*, as it is sometimes known. Dough is
kneaded with the feet, clay with the hands – and dung as well is picked
up by hand. Other peoples, unless they have come under Egyptian influence, prefer to leave their private parts as they were at birth; in Egypt,
they all circumcise themselves. A man will own two garments, a woman
only one. Whereas conventionally rings and ropes are fastened to the
outside of a sail, in Egypt they are fastened to the inside. Unlike the
Greeks, who move their hands from left to right as they write or do
calculations on an abacus, the Egyptians move their hands from right to
left; not only that, but they claim to be doing the precise opposite, and
insist that they are the ones who are moving their hands to the right,
and the Greeks who are moving theirs to the left. They have two differ-

ent kinds of writing: one is called 'hieroglyphic', and the other 'demotic'.

[37] Far more than people elsewhere, they are religious to an extreme – as is witnessed by any number of customs. For instance, it is a universally accepted practice among them that drinking-cups should be made of bronze, and rinsed not every other day, but on a daily basis. Their wearing of spotlessly laundered clothes of linen verges on the obsessive. A concern with cleanliness is also what explains their enthusiasm for circumcision,[22] since they would rather be hygienic than good-looking. Priests will give themselves a full body-shave every other day: this is done to prevent them from sheltering lice or any other vermin while they minister to the gods. The clothes that priests wear are made only of linen, and their sandals of papyrus. They are permitted no other kind of clothing, nor any other kind of sandal. They wash themselves in cold water twice a day, and twice every night as well. In fact, it would not be too much of an exaggeration to say that the rituals which they are obliged to follow are beyond computation. Nevertheless, it is also the case that the priests enjoy not a few perks. Anything they have that may need replacing is bought for them free of charge, as is anything that they may wish to purchase for themselves. Even their bread, which has a special sacral quality, is baked for them; they are also allocated a generous daily ration of beef and goose, and are provided with wine on top of that. Fish they are not permitted to touch. As for beans, no priest can bear so much as to look at them, for they are held to be an unclean variety of pulse; so much so, indeed, that the Egyptians refuse to cultivate beans at all, nor even to have a nibble on any that grow wild, no matter whether raw or cooked. Each god is served, not by a single priest, but by a whole host of them – one of whom, however, always ranks as the most senior, and whose office, when he dies, passes to his son.

[38] Bulls are believed to be the property of Epaphus, and are in consequence always subjected to a minute inspection. The discovery of even a single black hair on a bull is sufficient to brand it unclean. A priest especially appointed to look for black hairs will examine the beast all over, first having it stand upright, and then getting it on its back; the priest will even pull its tongue out to make sure that it is clear of certain proscribed markings, such as I will describe later on. The priest will also inspect the hairs of the tail to make certain that they have grown precisely as nature intended. Then, if the bull can be certified as pure on all

these counts, the priest will mark it by twisting a band of papyrus around its horns, which he will then seal with clay and stamp with his signet ring. This is the animal led away. The penalty for sacrificing an unstamped bull is death. So much for the inspection of the beast – now to the rituals that govern the sacrifice itself.

[39] Once the animal marked for death has been led to the altar where the sacrifice is to take place, a fire is lit, after which the priests will pour out wine over both altar and sacral victim, raise an invocation to the god and slit the throat of the bull. That done, they will then cut off the head. Unlike the body of the animal, which is flayed, this head is loaded with curses and carted off. Should the priests have a market-place to hand, and should there be any Greek traders in residence, then the head will be taken to the square and sold; but should there be no Greeks present, it will be flung into a river. The curses directed at the head take the form of a prayer: 'May we, who have made this sacrifice, and all of Egypt with us, be spared any evil that threatens – and may it fall instead upon this head!' The practices of pouring out a libation, and then of severing the head of a sacrificial victim, are the same as have been adopted by Egyptians everywhere, no matter what animal is being offered to the gods. For this reason, no Egyptian will have even a tiny bite of a head that has once belonged to a living, breathing beast.

[40] When it comes to the disembowelling and burning of sacral vic-tims, however, the method applied depends on the kind of animal that is being slaughtered. The festival I am going to talk about is Egypt's greatest, staged in honour of the goddess regarded as the very greatest divinity of all. A whole ox is flayed, and after prayers have been raised, all the intestines are removed. (The other innards are left where they are in the carcass, however, together with the lard.) The legs are then cut off, together with the outermost portions of the loin, the shoulders and the neck. That done, the next step is to fill what remains of the bull's body with loaves of ritually purified bread, honey, raisins, figs, frankin-cense, myrrh and other spices; and then, when it has been stuffed, olive oil is poured over the carcass in unstinting quantities, and a burnt offer-ing made of it. Prior to the sacrifice, everyone fasts; then, as the victims are actually being burned, there is a collective beating of chests in lam-entation. Finally, as the laments fade away, the portions of the sacrificial animals that remain unburnt are offered up as a feast.

[41] Now, although it is the universal practice of Egyptians to make

a sacrifice of bulls and calves – so long as they have been certified as pure – it is not permitted to sacrifice cows: these are sacred to Isis. Statues of Isis resemble Greek representations of Io, for they show her as a woman with the horns of a cow; and cows are universally regarded as holy by the Egyptians, to a far greater extent than any other breed of domesticated animal. That is why no Egyptian, male or female, will ever kiss a Greek on the mouth, nor use his knife, his spit or his cooking-pot;[23] indeed, they will even refuse to bring to their lips the flesh of an unblemished bull, if carved with the knife of a Greek. Cattle which die of natural causes are disposed of in a distinctive manner: the Egyptians will throw cows into the river, but bury bulls on the outskirts of which-ever city happens to be near by, making sure to leave one horn, or maybe two, sticking out from the ground as a marker. The carcass will then be left to rot, until, at a fixed time, a barge which has come from an island known as Prosopitis, journeying from city to city, will appear. Prosopitis itself lies in the Delta, has a circumference of 9 *schoeni* and contains a number of settlements. The one from which the barge comes to collect the bulls' bones is called Atarbechis – and in it there stands a shrine of great holiness dedicated to Aphrodite. Many others who live in this town are forever touring the various other cities of Egypt and digging up bones, which they remove and bury together in a single spot. Other farm animals too, when they die, are disposed of in the same manner as bulls. Such is the law – just as it is also the law not to have such animals slaughtered.

[42] Anyone who lives in the province of Thebes, or who may have raised a shrine to Theban Zeus, will keep well clear of sheep, and will only ever sacrifice goats. The Egyptians, you see, do not worship all the gods alike, except for Isis and Osiris (this being their name for Diony-sus). So it is, for instance, in contrast to the Thebans, that those from the province of Mendes, or who may have come by a shrine to Mendes, will abstain from goats and only ever sacrifice sheep. The Thebans, and all those who follow them in having nothing to do with sheep, tell a story to explain how they came to be issued with this prohibition. They say that Heracles longed more than anything to see Zeus, who refused to let him do so. So persistent was Heracles in his demands, however, that Zeus eventually devised a plan. Taking a ram, he skinned it and cut off its head, garbed himself in the fleece and used the head as a mask – then showed himself thus to Heracles. This is why the Egyptians, when they

make statues of Zeus, give him the head of a ram. (The practice has since been adopted from them by the Ammonians, some of whom originally came from Egypt, although other Ammonians came from Ethiopia, which is why the language they speak tends to be a fusion of Egyptian and Ethiopian. Here, then, surely, must also lie the origin of the Ammonians' name; for the name by which the Egyptians know Zeus is 'Amun'.) No wonder, then, that the Thebans do not sacrifice rams, but regard them as holy. That said, on one day every year, during a festival of Zeus, they chop up a single ram into pieces, skin it and dress the statue of Zeus in the fleece, just as the god once dressed himself. They then bring up a statue of Heracles, so that the two of them are face to face. This done, all the worshippers involved in the ceremony beat their breasts in mourning for the ram, which is then laid to rest in a sacral coffin.

[43] This same Heracles, so I heard from the Egyptians, ranks as one of their Twelve Gods. About the other Heracles, however, the one familiar to the Greeks, I heard nothing, despite my best efforts. Nevertheless, it is clear to me that it was not the Egyptians who took the name of Heracles from the Greeks, but rather the Greeks who took it from the Egyptians – and that they then bestowed it upon the child of Amphitryon. The evidence in favour of this is plentiful and suggestive: not least the fact that Amphitryon and Alcmene, the parents of Heracles, were both of Egyptian descent. It is telling as well that the Egyptians claim not to know the names of either Poseidon or the Dioscuri, and that these gods are notable by their absence from the Egyptian pantheon. For surely, had the name of any deity been taken from the Greeks, one of these would have been the one to leave the most significant imprint upon the Egyptian memory, rather than the least? (This is on the assumption that I am correct in my opinion that the Egyptians were making journeys by sea a long time ago, just as some of the Greeks were – for from that it follows that they would certainly have been better acquainted with the names of such gods than with that of Heracles.) Heracles, then, must be a god of the Egyptians – and an ancient one at that. A span of seventeen thousand years, so they themselves claim, separates the reign of Amasis from the time when the Eight Gods became the Twelve – among whom they number Heracles.

[44] Because I wanted to be clear on this particular issue, however, and to broaden my range of informants, I sailed on to Tyre in Phoenicia.

This was because I had heard that there was a sanctuary there sacred to Heracles; and, sure enough, I was able to see with my own eyes just how richly furnished with dedicatory offerings it was. These included two pillars, one of pure gold, and the other of emerald, which gleamed very brightly in the dark. Falling into conversation with the priests of the god, I asked them how much time had passed since the founding of their sanctuary. What I then discovered was a further contradiction of the Greek consensus, for they said that their shrine had been established at the same time as the founding of Tyre – and that Tyre had been settled for two thousand three hundred years in all. There was also another sanctuary that I saw in the city dedicated to Heracles, 'the Thasian' as he was called. So I paid a visit to Thasos too, where I found a sanctuary of Heracles built by the Phoenicians who had sailed off in search of Europa, and ended up colonizing Thasos. (An event which took place a whole five generations before Heracles son of Amphitryon was even born in Greece!) What my researches clearly demonstrate is that Heracles is a very ancient god indeed. Accordingly, it seems to me that the wisest course is pursued by those Greeks who possess an established dual cult: in one, Heracles is sacrificed to as an immortal, and given the cult-title of 'Olympian', while in the other offerings appropriate to a hero are made to him.

[45] But the Greeks are forever making claims without first researching them. There is one particularly foolish myth[24] told of Heracles. On his arrival in Egypt, the Greeks say, the Egyptians crowned him with garlands and led him off in procession, with the intention of sacrificing him to Zeus. For a while, Heracles kept his cool; but then, as they began the rituals of consecration beside the altar, he moved into action, and used his strength to slaughter the lot of them. What this story really tells me is that the Greeks have no understanding at all of either the character or the customs of the Egyptians. How, when the only animals that their religion permits them to sacrifice are sheep, such bulls and calves as have been certified as ritually pure, and geese, could they possibly perform a human sacrifice? What is more, how could Heracles single-handedly have slaughtered thousands upon thousands of people when he was, according to the Greeks' own version of the story, just a human being? But enough of my views on this matter – and I hope that the gods and heroes[25] will look kindly on what I have said.

[46] As I mentioned earlier, there are some Egyptians, the Mendesians,

who will sacrifice neither male nor female goats. Their reason for this is that they hold Pan to be one of the Eight Gods – and that these Eight Gods, they say, are antecedent to the Twelve. Just as the Greeks do, their painters and sculptors portray Pan as having the head and legs of a goat. This is not because they actually believe him to look like one, since in their opinion he is no different in appearance from any of the other gods, but rather for a reason the mere mention of which leaves an unpleasant taste in my mouth. The Mendesians regard all goats as sacred, but especially the males, and the herdsmen who look after them enjoy particular honour. Of the herd, there is always one male goat which is treated with a special reverence, and for which, when it dies, the entire province goes into mourning. In Egyptian, *Mendes* can mean both 'male goat' and 'Pan'. Within my own lifetime, an astonishing incident took place in this province: a male goat had sex, publicly, with a woman. It was quite a spectacle.

[47] The pig is thought by the Egyptians to be an unclean animal. One illustration of this: a passerby has only to brush against a pig and he will immediately head off to the river and plunge into it, fully clothed. Another is that swineherds are the only native Egyptians never to enter an Egyptian sanctuary. Nor is anyone prepared to give his daughter in marriage to a swineherd, nor receive the daughter of one into his own household; swineherds, as a result, marry off their daughters to one another. The only deities to whom the Egyptians consider it acceptable to sacrifice pigs are the Moon and Dionysus; every full moon, at precisely the same moment, pigs will be killed in honour of these two gods, and their flesh feasted upon. Why the Egyptians should shrink from pigs with such horror during other festivals and yet make a sacrifice of them on this one occasion is explained by a story that they tell among themselves, and which I have heard – but do not think it becoming to repeat. The sacrifice of a pig to the Moon follows a set process: once the animal has been killed, the tip of the tail, the spleen and the caul are all laid together, covered with the soft fat which is produced around the animal's stomach, and then given to the god as a burnt offering. All the other meat is eaten on the same day as the sacrificial animal is killed, while the moon is still full in the sky – no one would touch it on any other day. The poor, who have only slender means, shape pigs out of dough, bake them and offer them up in sacrifice.

[48] On the evening before the Festival of Dionysus, right in the

doorway of each person's house, the throat of a young pig is cut; the pig is then given to the swineherd who sold it to the householder in the first place, and who now takes the carcass away. The rest of the Festival of Dionysus the Egyptians celebrate pretty much as the Greeks do, except that they omit the choric dances, and that instead of phalluses they have devised figurines a cubit high and worked by strings. These puppets, which have penises barely smaller than their bodies, jerking up and down, are taken round by women from village to village. A flute-player leads them in procession, and the women, as they follow, sing a hymn to Dionysus. The reason why the penis should be so outsized, and the only part of the puppet to move, is the theme of a sacred tale.

[49] I do not think that Melampous, the son of Amytheon, was ignorant of this sacrificial ritual, but on the contrary was quite familiar with it. After all, it was Melampous who first expounded to the Greeks the name of Dionysus, the sacrifices that should be offered to him and the phallic processions that should be staged in his honour. There were certainly some elements of the story that Melampous omitted or left occluded, elements which then had to be elucidated by such sages as followed in his wake; and yet it was Melampous who showed the way by instituting the phallic procession in honour of Dionysus, and it was from him that the Greeks learned to do what they do. My argument would therefore be that Melampous, who was demonstrably a man of great wisdom, and a self-taught master of the arts of divination, introduced a number of things to the Greeks which he had learned at the feet of the Egyptians – among them, barely altered, the cult of Dionysus. I am not going to claim that the similarities between what the Egyptians do in honour of the god, and what the Greeks do, are mere coincidence: if that were the case, the Greek rites would not appear so alien, nor would they have been so recently introduced. I would also dispute the possibility that the Egyptians could have adopted them or indeed any other custom from the Greeks. No: the likeliest explanation, it seems to me, is that Melampous learned about the worship of Dionysus from Cadmus of Tyre and his companions when they travelled from Phoenicia to the land that is now known as Boeotia.[26]

[50] Indeed, almost all the names of the gods came to Greece from Egypt. That they derived from barbarians was evident enough, I found on investigation – and that they mostly arrived from Egypt seems to me obvious. Excepting Poseidon and the Dioscuri, whose names I have

already mentioned, and Hera, Hestia and Themis, the Graces and the Nereids, there is not one name of a god that has not been known in the land of Egypt since the very dawn of time. Here, I am merely echoing what the Egyptians themselves say. Those gods whose names they do not recognize must, it seems to me, have been given their names by the Pelasgians. The one exception is Poseidon, a god whom the Greeks learned about from the Libyans. The proof of this is that the Libyans are the only people to have used Poseidon's name right from the very beginning, and to have honoured the god without break. One thing the Egyptians do not practise at all is the cult of heroes.

[51] I shall have more to add to my account of all the various customs adopted by the Greeks from the Egyptians. However, it was not from the Egyptians that they learned to make statues of Hermes with an erect penis, but from the Pelasgians. The Athenians were the first to adopt the practice, and all the other Greeks adopted it from them. The Pelasgians, you see, came to settle in Athenian territory at a time when the Athenians themselves had already come to be counted as Greek – and so it was that the Pelasgians began to be regarded as Greeks too. Anyone who has been initiated into the Mysteries of the Cabiri,[27] which are staged on Samothrace, and are Pelasgian in origin, will know what I mean. The reason for this is that the Pelasgians[28] who ended up living alongside the Athenians had previously lived on Samothrace, where they had bequeathed to the Samothracians a knowledge of their rites. All of this serves to demonstrate that it was indeed the Athenians who were the first among the Greeks to make statues of Hermes with an erect penis,[29] and that they learned the practice from the Pelasgians. The Pelasgians themselves told a story about it that touched on matters of great holiness, the details of which are revealed during the Mysteries of Samothrace.[30]

[52] Thanks to what I heard at Dodona,[31] I know for a fact that it was the original practice of the Pelasgians to accompany every sacrifice with prayers to the gods, but without giving any of them titles or proper names, of which the Pelasgians were as yet ignorant. The name they did use was *theoi* – the Greek word for 'gods', which they derived in turn from another Greek word, *ti-themi*, meaning 'to ordain' – on the basis that it was the gods who had ordained what the order of the universe should be, and what its proper arrangement. After a long while had passed, however, the Pelasgians learned of the names used in Egypt for

the gods, and which had since arrived on their shores. (All, that is, except for the name of Dionysus, which they learned about much later.) Then, after more time had gone by, they sought advice concerning these names from the oracle at Dodona, which is held to be the most ancient of Greek oracles (and indeed at the time was the only one in existence). When the Pelasgians asked the oracle whether they should adopt the names that had come from the barbarians, the oracle pronounced that they should. And sure enough, ever since, they have been addressing the gods by their names while making sacrifices. It was from the Pelasgians that these same names were subsequently passed on to the Greeks.

[53] That said, it was only yesterday (to exaggerate just a little – perhaps it was the day before yesterday) that the Greeks learned the answers to a whole number of questions. What were the origins of the various gods? Have they all of them existed forever? What do they look like? My own generation, I reckon, is separated by no more than four hundred years from that of Hesiod and Homer, who were the first to compose for the Greeks an account of the gods' genealogy, to award them their titles, to allot them their honours and particular talents and to signify their forms.[32] Those poets who are said to have lived prior to Hesiod and Homer were actually, it seems to me, born after. Although this is my own personal opinion, for the first part of my argument I have the backing of the priestesses of Dodona.

[54] Speaking of oracles, the Egyptians tell a story about two of them: the one I just mentioned in Greece, and the one in Libya. According to the priests of Theban Zeus, two women, both of them priestesses, were abducted from Thebes by some Phoenicians. It was subsequently discovered that they had been sold on, one to Libya, and one to some Greeks – and that it was these women who had founded the two oracles, one among each of the two peoples. When I asked the priests what grounds they had for being so certain of this story, they explained that they had launched an exhaustive search for the two women, and that, despite their failure to track them down, all the facts had come to light in due course, precisely as I had been told them.

[55] Such, at any rate, is what I heard from the priests at Thebes. But the priestesses who deliver the oracles at Dodona tell a different story. According to them, two black doves took wing from Egyptian Thebes: one flew to Libya and the other one to them. There, perched on an oak tree, the dove cried out in human voice: 'Here, right here, an oracle of

Zeus must be brought into being!' Those who heard this pronouncement presumed it to come from a god, so they did as they had been told. Likewise, the story goes, the dove which had settled in Libya commanded the Libyans to establish the oracle of Ammon – which is also, of course, an oracle of Zeus. I had all this from the priestesses of Dodona, whose names, in descending order of age, are Promeneia, Timarete and Nicandra.[33] Everyone else who lives at Dodona, and is connected to the shrine, concurred.

[56] I have a theory as to what might actually have happened, however. Suppose that the Phoenicians really did abduct the priestesses, and suppose that one of them really was sold in Libya and the other one in Greece. It seems to me that the one who was sold in Greece – or rather Pelasgia, as it was known then – must have been bought by the Thesprotians. Then, as was only natural for someone who had once been an attendant of Zeus in his sanctuary at Thebes but was now a slave, she set up a shrine to Zeus beneath an oak tree, as a memorial of it. Once she had grasped the Greek language, she would have started delivering oracles there, as well as making it known that the same Phoenicians who had sold her had also sold her sister in Libya.

[57] As to why the women should have been called 'doves' by the Dodonaeans, the likeliest explanation, I think, is that they were barbarians, and therefore seemed to the Dodonaeans to be making a noise like birds. The story of the dove that cried out in a human voice derived from the woman's eventual breakthrough in making herself understood – for as long as she was twittering away in her own tongue, she had sounded exactly like a bird to the Dodonaeans. How else to explain the obvious impossibility of a talking dove? The claim of the Dodonaeans that the dove was black surely signifies that the woman was an Egyptian. It is certainly the case that the methods of divination employed at Thebes in Egypt and at Dodona are very similar to one another. It is true as well that the reading of animal entrails to predict the future came from Egypt.

[58] The Egyptians were the first people to meet in large crowds to stage religious festivals, to hold ritual processions and to formulate set approaches for the bringing of gifts to the gods. That these then provided the models for the Greeks seems to me self-evident. Here is the proof: the rites performed in Egypt are manifestly of great antiquity, whereas those in Greece are of recent origin.

[59] Rather than confine themselves to one annual gathering, the

Egyptians stage a whole sequence of festivals. The chief of these, and the one they celebrate most wholeheartedly, is that held in honour of Artemis[34] in the city of Bubastis; second is that held in honour of Isis in the city of Busiris. (The reason for staging it there is that Busiris contains a vast temple of Isis, the goddess known to the Greeks as Demeter. Busiris itself is an Egyptian city located in the middle of the Delta.) Ranked third is the festival in honour of Athena at the city of Sais, and fourth, the Festival of the Sun at Heliopolis. Fifth is the Festival of Leto at Bouto, and sixth the Festival of Ares at Papremis.

[60] When the time comes for the pilgrimage to Bubastis, great crowds of people, men and women together, pack themselves onto barges and sail off. Some of the women have castanets, with which they make a great clacking, and some of the men have flutes, which they play throughout the voyage, while the rest of the men and women sing and clap their hands. Whenever their journey happens to bring them past a city, they steer their barge in close to the bank; some of the women continue to behave as I have already described, but others start screaming abuse at the women onshore, or dancing, or getting to their feet and hitching up their skirts. They repeat this ritual at every city on the river. Then, when they get to Bubastis, the pilgrims celebrate the festival by offering up a prodigious number of animal blood-sacrifices, and by drinking more wine over the course of the festivities than is consumed in the whole of the rest of the year. So many assemble, the locals claim, that the numbers come to 700,000 men and women – but no children.

[61] So that is what people get up to there. The celebrations staged in the city of Busiris serve to honour Isis in the way I have already touched upon. Once the sacrifice is over, all the men and women, countless thousands of people, beat their chests in lamentation – although who it is that they are mourning would be sacrilegious of me to reveal. Any Carians settled in Egypt[35] take this mourning to even greater extremes, hacking their foreheads with knives – and thereby making it clear that they are foreigners, not Egyptians.

[62] In Sais, on one of the nights of the festival, all those who have gathered in the city for the sacrifices ring their houses with a great multitude of lamps, which they then light beneath the open sky. The lamps themselves are saucers filled with salt and olive-oil, with a wick floating on top, which burns the whole night. This is called the Festival of the Lamp Lighting, and even those Egyptians who do not attend in person

all keep watch throughout the night of the sacrifice with their lamps lit. As a result, lights blaze throughout the whole of Egypt, not just in Sais alone. The light and honour given to this one night are explained by a myth of great sacredness.

[63] Those who frequent the festivals at Heliopolis and Bouto offer up sacrifices, and nothing more. At Papremis, however, although the sacrifices and rites are performed precisely as elsewhere, the setting of the sun sees only a few of the priests still busying themselves around the cult-statue; the majority of them, armed with wooden clubs, stand by the entrance to the shrine. There they are confronted by upwards of a thousand men who have massed there in fulfilment of a vow, all of them similarly armed with staves. One day before this, the cult-statue, enclosed within a small wooden shrine sheathed all over with gold, will have been spirited away to a second sacred building. Now the few priests still in attendance put the shrine, with the statue inside it, onto a four-wheeled wagon, which they then haul along themselves. Their colleagues, stationed at the temple entrance-way, refuse the wagon entry; but the votaries, coming to the assistance of the god, start laying about with their clubs the priests who are blocking their way. A ferocious battle with wooden sticks then ensues. The Egyptians insist that no one actually dies during the fighting, but so serious are the wounds inflicted – with broken heads and all – that it seems inconceivable to me that there should not be some fatalities. What are the origins of this custom? The locals have an explanation of the festival. Although Ares[36] himself, they say, was brought up abroad, his mother used to live in the temple; and when Ares grew to manhood, he came to see his mother, with the intention of sleeping with her. The attendants who waited upon the goddess, however, never having seen her son before, refused him entry; and so Ares, unable to get inside, raised reinforcements in a nearby city, and then dealt so brutally with the attendants that he got inside to his mother. And that, so the people of Papremis say, is why they pay their respects to Ares by beating one another up during the festival.

[64] The Egyptians were the first to develop religious scruples about having sex with women inside sanctuaries, and even about going into sanctuaries unwashed after sex. Almost all the peoples in the world – the Egyptians and Greeks only excepted – do still sleep with one another in sanctuaries, and will still enter a sanctuary unwashed after sex with a woman, on the presumption that there is no great difference between

human beings and animals. After all, go into any temple of the gods, or
any sanctuary, and you will see beasts and birds of every stripe copulat-
ing away. Why would animals be doing this, if the gods did not approve?
Such, at any rate, is the line of reasoning – one that I personally find
disagreeable. The Egyptians, however, are utterly scrupulous in adher-
ing to ritual observances, both in this matter and in everything else that
touches on the sacred.

[65] Despite bordering Libya, Egypt is hardly teeming with wildlife.
Every one of the animals that do exist there, however, domestic as well
as wild, is held to be sacred. Any attempt on my part to explain why
animals should have been allocated to the realm of the sacred would
risk plunging me into a discussion of issues that properly pertain to the
gods, the very thing that I have most sought to avoid. (When and if I
have touched upon such matters, it has been only very fleetingly, and
because I had little option.) One custom which relates to wildlife is as
follows. All the various kinds of animal have their own keepers who are
appointed to supervise their maintenance; these keepers, who may be
either men or women, just so long as they are Egyptian, hold ranks
which are passed down on a hereditary basis from parent to child. The
ones who live in cities all make their vows by supplicating the god to
whom the particular creature in their care is sacred; they then shave off
the hair of their children, either the entire scalp, or half of it, or a third,
and weigh the trimmings in a pair of scales, measuring their weight in
silver. The resulting total is then awarded to the creatures' keeper, who
cuts up as much fish as can be purchased with the silver, and gives the
portions to the creatures as food. Such are the arrangements in existence for the upkeep of animals. Anyone who kills an animal deliberately
is sentenced to death; should the killing have been involuntary, however,
then the penalty is whatever fine the priests may set. Only if someone
kills an ibis or a hawk does the degree of intent make no difference: in
these cases there is no alternative but to put the offender to death.

[66] Domestic animals are numerous – and would be even more so,
were it not for something that serves to keep the cat population down.
Female cats which have given birth to kittens will have nothing more to
do with males; the male cats are thereby left as frustrated as they are
needy. This has driven them to devise a cunning plan: they snatch or
steal the kittens from their mother, and then dispose of them. (But

though they kill the kittens, they do not eat them.) The females, bereft of their offspring, and eager for more, due to their love for babies, then return to the males. In the event of a fire, what happens to cats is uncanny in the extreme. The Egyptians, rather than attempting to extinguish the flames, instead form a human chain and keep watch over the cats; the cats, however, slipping through the line of men, or else jumping over it, hurl themselves into the conflagration. An event such as this causes the Egyptians great distress. All the inhabitants of a household in which a cat has died of natural causes will shave off their eyebrows, and nothing else; but if a dog dies, then the entire body and head are shaved.

[67] Following their death, cats are borne away to the city of Bubastis, where they are mummified and buried in sacral pits. Bitches are buried in sanctified tombs as well, but dogs are buried in the town where they came from. The same applies to the burial of mongooses. Field-mice and hawks are taken to the city of Bouto; ibises to Hermopolis.[37] Bears, which are rare, and wolves, which are not much larger than foxes, are buried wherever their bodies are found lying.

[68] Let me now describe the nature of the crocodile. It is a four-legged creature which for four months at a time, all through the depths of winter, eats not a thing. It lives both on dry land and in swampy shallows. It lays and hatches its eggs in earth, and spends most of the day on dry land, but the entire night it spends in the river, because the water is warmer than the dew-sodden air. Of all the living creatures known to us, there is none that grows to such a massive size from such small beginnings. Its eggs are no larger than those of a goose, and its young, when they are hatched, are of course proportionate in size to the eggs. Yet such is its growth that it can end up measuring 17 cubits, or even more. It has eyes like a pig's, and teeth that are huge [relative to its body], with fangs that protrude from its mouth. Alone of creatures, it has no tongue. Unparalleled as well among animals is the way in which it is only the upper jaw of the crocodile which moves up and down, while the lower jaw stays wholly immobile. It has very powerful claws and an impenetrable, scaly hide on its back. In water it can see nothing, but in the open air its sight is piercing. Because of its aquatic lifestyle, the inside of its mouth is completely infested by leeches. While other birds and animals keep well clear of the crocodile, the plover lives alongside it in perfect amity. This is due to the service provided by the bird: whenever the crocodile emerges out of the water onto land, it will almost invariably

turn to the west and give such a yawn that the sandpiper is able to dart inside its mouth and gulp down the leeches. The crocodile, delighted at receiving such assistance, never harms a feather on the plover's head.

[69] To some Egyptians the crocodile is sacred, but there are others who treat it as a deadly foe. Those who live around Thebes and Lake Moeris fervently believe in its holiness. Both communities select one particular crocodile to be reared and trained until it is tame. Rings of glass and gold are inserted in its ears, and bracelets on its front feet. It is granted special portions of food, and even its own sacrificial victims. For as long as it has breath, it is treated with every conceivable care. Then, following its death, it is embalmed and interred in a sacred tomb. The inhabitants of Elephantine and its neighbourhood, however, since they utterly refuse to accept that the crocodile can be sacred, go so far as to eat it. Rather than actually use the word 'crocodile', the Egyptians say *khampsa*. It was the Ionians who first called the animals crocodiles, on the grounds that they resemble the lizards which live among them in dry-stone walls – and which go by the name of *crocodiles*.

[70] There are all sorts of different ways to hunt a crocodile – but since there is one which strikes me as particularly notable, I will stick to writing about that. A hook is baited with the back of a pig, and set to float in the middle of the river; meanwhile, on the riverbank, the hunter has a real live pig, which he wallops. The crocodile, hearing the squeals, makes a rush in the direction of the noise, comes across the bait, gulps it down – and in he is hauled. Once the crocodile has been landed, the first thing the hunter does is to smear mud all over his eyes. Only manage this, and the remaining stages of the crocodile's capture can easily be completed; fail to do it, and there will be trouble.

[71] Hippopotamuses are held sacred in the province of Papremis, but nowhere else in Egypt. They present a most distinctive appearance: four-legged and cloven-hooved, after the manner of a bull, and snub-nosed, with prominent tusks. Not only do they have the mane and tail of a horse, but they neigh like one as well. In size – more or less – they are equivalent to a very large ox. So thick is their hide that the skin, once dried, can be made into the shafts of javelins.

[72] Another river-dwelling animal regarded as holy by the Egyptians is the otter. So too are a couple of fish species: the eel, and one known by the Egyptians as the *lepidotus*. Both, they claim, are sacred to the Nile – as is the fox-goose among birds.

[73] There is another sacred bird, the so-called 'phoenix', which I have never seen in the flesh, but only in a painting. They claim in Heliopolis that it is so rare a visitor to Egypt that it comes only once every five hundred years. It makes its appearance, they go on to say, when its father dies. If it does indeed correspond to the painting, its size and behaviour are as follows. Its feathers are red, but flecked with gold, and the bird it most resembles – in both shape and size – is an eagle. There is one feat attributed to it which I personally find impossible to believe. According to the Egyptians, the phoenix sets out from Arabia for the sanctuary of the Sun, where it buries its father, which it has brought with it sealed up in myrrh. This is how it transports him. First, the phoenix moulds an egg out of myrrh, the very largest that it is capable of carrying; then it practises flying with it; then, after the trial flight, it hollows out the egg, inserts its father and uses additional myrrh to seal over that part of the egg which it has just hollowed out to receive its parent. With the phoenix's father entombed, the egg is back to its original weight; and so, with the egg now sealed up, the phoenix carries it away to Egypt, to the shrine of the Sun. Such, at any rate, is the story that the Egyptians tell of this bird.

[74] In the environs of Thebes, there are snakes which are both holy and harmless to man. They are small in size, with two horns sprouting out of the tops of their heads. Because these snakes, according to the Egyptians, are sacred to Zeus, they are buried in the shrine of the god when they die.

[75] There is a place in Arabia, not far from the city of Bouto, which I visited because I wished to know more about the flying snakes. When I arrived there, I found the bones of these snakes littered everywhere, and their backbones too, piled in numbers beyond my capacity to recount. Some of these piles were massive, some less so, and some – the majority, in fact – only tiny. The spot where these backbones lie scattered is a narrow mountain pass that leads into a large plain, which in turn adjoins the plain of Egypt. Every spring, so report has it, the snakes take wing from Arabia for Egypt; but there, at the pass which would lead them into the country, they are met by ibises, who block their entry and kill them. It is this service, the Arabians say, which explains the great reverence in which the ibis is held by the Egyptians. The Egyptians themselves would not dispute that this is indeed why they honour the bird.

[76] In appearance, the ibis is ink-black all over, has the legs of a

crane and a pronounced hook-beak, and is roughly the size of a corn-crake. At any rate, that is what the black ibises are like, the ones who fight with the snakes; but there is a second kind of ibis as well, which is much more given to congregating where humans live. This ibis is bald, all the way down its neck, with a plumage that is white everywhere except for its head, its neck and the very tips of its wings and its tail, all of which are ink-black. Its legs and its face closely resemble those of the other kind of ibis. The snakes are very like the snakes that live in water, and have featherless wings, most closely resembling those of a bat. But I have said enough now about sacred animals.

[77] And so to the Egyptians themselves. Those who live in the culti-vated region of the country are so concerned to preserve the common memories of mankind that they keep better records than anyone else I have ever come across or questioned. On the distinguishing features of their lifestyle, one is a relish for purgatives: every month, for three days in a row, they attempt to safeguard their health by taking emetics and enemas, convinced that the very food which serves to nourish mankind is simultaneously the cause of all its ailments. In fact, second only to the Libyans, the Egyptians are the healthiest people in the world, thanks (so it seems to me) to the stable climate that they enjoy throughout the year. There is nothing more certain to make people ill than change, after all – and especially change from season to season. They are great eaters of bread, the Egyptians, which they make from emmer wheat, and know by the name of *kyllestis*. All their wine they have to make from barley, since there are no vines in Egypt. Fish they either dry in the sun and eat raw, or else pickle in brine. Among birds, quails are salted, as are ducks and small fowl, then eaten uncooked. The other birds or fish that live alongside the Egyptians – except for those that have been consecrated by them as holy – they roast or boil before eating.

[78] After the meal at any party where the hosts are well-to-do, a man carries round the likeness of a corpse in a coffin, carved out of a block of wood and painted to look as lifelike as possible, which in size can be anything between one and two cubits. Showing it to each guest in turn, he says: 'Look on this carefully as you drink and enjoy yourself, for as it is now, so will you be when you are dead.' Such is the practice at any drinking-party.

[79] In their customs generally, the Egyptians are traditionalists and

have no interest in innovation. Notable among their customs, which are as numerous as they are remarkable, is the 'Linus' song. This Linus is feted in the songs of the Phoenicians, the Cypriots and a whole host of other peoples too – although they each have their own national name for him. Certainly, the person featured in the Egyptian version corresponds to the individual who, in the Greek version, is named Linus. Here, then, amid all the many other wonders of Egypt, is a mystery indeed: where did the Egyptians get the 'Linus' from? It is clearly of very great antiquity. The name that the Egyptians give Linus is 'Maneros'. According to them, this Maneros was the only son of the first king of Egypt. He died before his time, however, and so it was in his honour that they sang this threnody, their first and – at the time – their only song.

[80] In this further custom, there is a point of resemblance between the Egyptians and the Lacedaemonians,[38] alone of the Greeks. Should a younger man meet with someone older on the road, he will step aside; just as, should he be approached by one of his elders while sitting down, he will rise to his feet. On another point, however, Egyptian etiquette is wholly alien to that of all the Greeks: when two people meet out on the street, they do not exchange words but rather lower their hands onto their knees and make a bow.

[81] As for dress, the Egyptians sport linen tunics which they call *kalasiris*, complete with tassels which cover the legs. Over these, they throw white woollen cloaks. Nevertheless, it is strictly against the dictates of their religion to wear any kind of woollen clothing to a shrine, or into a grave. In this, they concur with the practices that are popularly known as Orphic and Bacchic, but are in fact Egyptian and Pythagorean.[39] It is forbidden for any initiate of these rites to be buried in clothes of wool. There is a sacred tale which accounts for this.

[82] Other discoveries were made by the Egyptians as well. It was they, for instance, who found out that each month, each day even, is sacred to one of the gods; and that it is the date of a person's birth which determines his future, his ultimate fate and his character. (Those of the Greeks who are inclined to poetry have often made use of this.) The Egyptians have also been more successful in identifying genuine portents than any other people in the world. Whenever one occurs, they make a note of it, and keep a careful look-out for whatever it may be heralding; then, in due course, should anything similar happen again, they consider themselves well forewarned.

[83] All the same, divination itself is an art which the Egyptians attribute, not to humankind, but to the gods – and even then, only to some. Heracles has an oracular shrine in their country, as do Apollo, Athena, Artemis, Ares and Zeus. Last but decidedly not least is the oracle which they hold in the highest esteem of all: that of Leto, in the city of Bouto. Admittedly, the methods of divination employed do vary from oracle to oracle.

[84] The practice of medicine is highly specialized: individual doctors will treat individual ailments, rather than the whole gamut of diseases. As a result, Egypt positively teems with doctors; some specialize in treating eyes and others heads; some are dentists and others tend to the stomach; some specialize in obscure illnesses.

[85] Now to the manner in which Egyptians mourn and bury their dead.[40] The bereavement of a household in which the departed was a man of repute will see its womenfolk plastering their heads and even their faces with mud; then, leaving the corpse behind them in the house, they and all their female relatives will loosen their clothes and tour the city, beating their naked breasts. Meanwhile, in another part of town, the men will be doing the same: loosening their clothes and beating their chests in mourning. Then, once the lamentations are over, the body is taken to be mummified.

[86] The embalming itself is performed by specialists trained in all the skills required.[41] Whenever a corpse is brought to them, they will show to those who have carried it models of dead bodies, crafted out of wood and painted to look as lifelike as possible. The most highly esteemed method of mummification is said to be sacred to One whose name I feel it would be sacrilege to mention in a context such as this; the next best method unveiled by the embalmers is one that is both cheaper and marginally inferior in quality to the first; the third-best method is the cheapest of all. Then, once they have set out the various options, the embalmers ask their clients which method they want for the corpse. A price is agreed upon; the relatives depart, and the embalmers, left behind in their shop, get down to work. Their first step, when the mummification is being done most conscientiously, is to insert an iron hook through the nostrils and pull out the brain; what cannot be extracted using this method is then sluiced out by pouring in drugs. Next, using an Ethiopian knife of sharp obsidian, the embalmers cut a slit along the soft part of the body, and remove all the intestines from the stomach, which they then clean and rinse out, first with

palm wine and then with crushed spices. After this, they stuff the cavity with pure ground myrrh, cassia and any other kind of sweet-smelling spice you care to mention, excepting only frankincense. Then, once the stomach has been filled, they sew it back up again. After this has been done, they pickle the body by packing it with natron and leaving it, well hidden away, for seventy days. (They are not allowed to leave it any longer than that.) Once the seventy days are up, the embalmers wash the corpse, then wrap the entire body in bandages made from fine linen cut into strips, and smeared on their underside with gum (gum being what the Egyptians use in place of glue). Only now is the corpse reclaimed by relatives of the deceased, who commission a wooden coffin, shaped like a human being, into which it is placed. Finally, they store the body inside a burial chamber, standing it upright against a wall, sealed inside its coffin.

[87] This is the most expensive method of preparing a corpse; but for those who might flinch at the cost there is also a more moderate option. This involves loading a syringe with cedar oil, and then squirting it into the corpse until the stomach is full. No incision is required, no removal of the entrails; instead, the syringe is inserted into the anus, which is then plugged so as to ensure that the liquid does not leak back out. The body is pickled for the prescribed number of days, at the end of which time the embalmers drain off from the guts the same cedar oil which they had previously injected up into the entrails. Such is the potency of this oil that it brings down mixed in with its discharge the stomach and the intestines, both of which it has served to dissolve. Meanwhile, the flesh has been similarly dissolved by the natron, so that all that remains of the corpse is skin and bones. After the procedure has been completed, the embalmers give back the body without any further ado.

[88] There is a third embalming procedure which is used to prepare the bodies of those who lack the means to pay for anything more expensive: the guts are rinsed out with a purgative; then the corpse is embalmed for the customary seventy days and handed back for removal.

[89] When the wife of an eminent man has died, or a woman particularly beautiful or well known, delivery of the body to the embalmers is delayed. Only once three or four days have gone by is it handed over for mummification. The reason for this is that it prevents the embalmers from indulging in necrophilia. One of them, so the embalmers report, was actually caught mounting the fresh corpse of a woman, and was denounced by one of his colleagues.

[90] Should anyone, Egyptian or foreigner, be snatched by a croco-dile, or else be killed by the river itself, it is absolutely incumbent upon the city where the body is eventually washed up to embalm it, to adorn it as handsomely as possible and then to bury it in a consecrated tomb. No one, not even a relative or a friend, is permitted to touch the corpse, for it is believed to have become something more than human – so the only people to handle and bury it are the priests of the Nile themselves.

[91] Greek customs are shunned by the Egyptians – as too, by and large, are those of other peoples. Nevertheless, there is the one excep-tion to this general hauteur. In Chemmis, a large city in the administrative region of Thebes, not far from Neapolis, there stands a square temple which is fringed all around by palm trees and dedicated to Perseus, the son of Danaë. The gateways of this temple are made of stone and rise to an enormous height, as do the two stone statues which stand in front of them. There is a temple within the shrine's enclosure, and within this temple a statue of Perseus. Perseus himself, so the locals say, makes regular appearances across the whole region of Chemmis, not to men-tion inside the shrine, and sometimes will even shed a sandal; tradition says that, should this subsequently be tracked down, all 3 feet of it, the whole of Egypt will enjoy a golden age. So it is claimed, at any rate. In honour of Perseus, certain things are done in the Greek fashion; most notably, an athletics contest is staged with the full range of events, and with prizes of cattle, cloaks and skins. When I asked the people of Chemmis why it was that Perseus was in the habit of materializing among them alone, and why it was that they had differentiated them-selves from the rest of the Egyptians by staging an athletics contest, they answered by claiming that Danaus and Lynceus, before sailing off to Greece, had been natives of Chemmis, and that Perseus, whose lineage they trace from this couple, was therefore one of their own. He origin-ally came to Egypt from Libya, they said, because he was bringing the Gorgon's head – the same reason as is given by the Greeks. It was in the course of this visit that Perseus went to Chemmis, whose name he had earlier learned from his mother, and there acknowledged kinship with his relations. He also instructed them to stage an athletics contest in his honour, which they duly did.

[92] Now, although all the customs I have been describing until now properly relate to the Egyptians who live upriver from the marshlands, those who are settled in the marshes actually live their lives in the same

way as everyone else in Egypt; a man will only ever have the one wife,[42] for instance, just as in Greece. That said, one area in which they have innovated is in the provision of cheap food. An example is their harvesting of the water-lily, the *lotus* as the Egyptians call it, and which grows abundantly in the waters whenever the river is in full spate and floods the plains. They dry the flowers in the sun; then, after crushing the middle of each lotus (which resembles a poppy-head), they make loaves out of it and bake them in a fire. The root of the lotus is edible as well; it is round, the size of an apple, and tastes quite sweet. There is another kind of lily, rather like a rose, which also grows in the river; its fruit, contained within a pod separate from the main growth of the root, resembles nothing quite so much as the honeycomb of a wasp. Inside this fruit is a large quantity of edible seeds, each one about the size of an olive stone, which can be eaten either fresh or dried. There is also papyrus, which the locals uproot from the marshes every year: the upper part of the plant they cut off and use for other purposes, but what remains of the lower reaches of the stalk, about a cubit in all, they eat or sell. Anyone who wants to enjoy papyrus at its very tastiest[43] must be sure to bake it in a red-hot oven before tucking in. Some of the people who live in the marshes, however, subsist entirely on fish, which they catch, gut and dry in the sun. These they then eat dried.

[93] Fish that swim together in shoals are never born in the Delta-arms of the Nile, but rather in lakes, where they grow to adulthood. Then, when the promptings of the breeding season come upon them, they swim out in shoals to the sea. Leading the way are the male fish, ejaculating as they go; following behind them, the females gulp down the sperm and are thereby impregnated. Then, when the time comes to spawn, each shoal makes its way back from the sea to its former haunt. No longer, however, do the males lead the way, but rather the females. As they head the shoal, so they precisely mimic the earlier behaviour of the males, dribbling out eggs – a few at a time, as though scattering seed – which the males, who are following, then gulp down. The reality is, however, that these seeming seeds are fish, and those not gulped down, the survivors, grow to maturity. Any fish which are caught while swimming out to sea are sure to display clear signs of bruising on the left side of their heads, just as any caught while swimming back upriver will have bruising on the right. Why such injuries? Because, as the fish swim out to sea, so they keep close to the bank on their left side, the

same bank they stick to on their return journey, shadowing it as close as they can, grazing it even sometimes, so as not to lose their way upon the currents. When the Nile begins to rise, and water to seep out from the river, the initial overflow trickles into the nearby marshes and low-lying ground. No sooner have these hollows filled up than they start to teem with tiny fish. How do these fish come to be there? I think I understand. The previous year, as the Nile receded, the fish must have laid eggs in the mud, then slipped away with the last of the water. After a time, the waters returned and the eggs promptly hatched into fish. So much for the fish.

[94] For anointing, the Egyptians who live beside the marshes use oil extracted from the fruit of the castor-oil plant, the *kiki* as they call it. This is the same castor-oil plant which grows wild and untended in Greece; but the Egyptians sow it along the banks of rivers and lakes, where it grows prolifically and to foul-smelling effect. At harvest time it is either sliced and pulped, or roasted and boiled down, until there is only a residue left, which is then decanted. The resulting liquid is very thick and ripe smelling, but no less effective than olive oil when used in lamps.

[95] Various methods have been devised by the Egyptians to cope with the swarms of mosquitoes. Those who live south of the marshes benefit from the towers which they climb before going to sleep, for the winds ensure that the mosquitoes fly close to the ground. Those who live beside the marshes, however, have to make other arrangements. Every man among them possesses a net which during the day is used for fishing, but at night-time is put to an alternative use. First, its owner drapes the net over the bed in which he plans to take his rest, then he slips underneath it and goes to sleep. It is no use going to sleep wrapped up in cloth or linen, for mosquitoes can bite straight through them. Through the net, however, they do not even make an attempt.

[96] Cargo boats are made of acacia, which in form is very similar to the Cyrenaean lotus, and weeps a gummy kind of sap. This tree is chopped up into planks of wood some 3 feet long, which are then assembled as though they were bricks. The method used to build such ships never varies: the pieces of wood, all of them 3 feet long, are fastened together with long, thick pins, and then, once the hull has been completed, overlaid with cross-planks. Instead of ribbing, which is never used, the inner fastenings are made secure with ropes of papyrus.

Only a single rudder is made, which is then inserted through the keel. Acacia is used for the mast, and papyrus for the sails. Without a stiff wind, ships of this kind are unable to sail upriver and have to be towed from the bank. When they go downriver, however, they are equipped with a raft, made out of tamarisk wood and lashed together with rush matting, and with a stone, one which weighs upwards of 2 talents and has a hole bored through it. The raft is tied with a rope to the front of the ship, and then released, so that it is borne away by the river, while the stone is attached by a second rope to the stern. The raft, as it is propelled forwards on the current, moves with such speed that it pulls along the *baris* (as this kind of vessel is known), while to the rear of the ship the stone is being dragged along the river-bed, thereby steadying the course. The Egyptians maintain a huge number of such ships, some of them with weights running to many thousands of talents.

[97] When Egypt is flooded by the Nile, nothing is left visible above the waters except for the cities, which closely resemble the islands in the Aegean. While everywhere else in the country is transformed into open sea, the cities alone remain unsubmerged. No wonder, then, that in such conditions people stop ferrying themselves along the course of the river and take to the open plain. To sail from Naucratis to Memphis, for instance, you would no longer follow the conventional route, via the apex of the Delta and the city of Cercasorus, but instead navigate directly past the pyramids themselves. Likewise, when sailing from Canobus on the coast to Naucratis, the journey across the plain would take you past the city of Anthylla, and the city named after Archander.

[98] Of these two places, Anthylla is the one with a particular renown; in the wake of the Persian conquest, it was made over to whomsoever happened to be the wife of the king of Egypt at the time, and was charged with keeping her in slippers. My theory is that the second city was named after the son of Phthius, and the grandson of Achaeus, the Archander who was the son-in-law of Danaus (though even supposing that there was another Archander, the name is certainly not Egyptian).

[99] For my account up to this point, I have drawn upon things that I myself witnessed, upon my own reasoning and upon my research; but from now on, I will be relating information that I heard from Egyptians, supplemented by my own observations.[44] According to the priests, it was Min, the first king of Egypt, who built the dykes which protect

Memphis. The entire length of the river used to flow alongside the chain of sand-covered mountains which abut Libya; until Min, at a point some 100 stades upriver from Memphis, dammed its southern bend, and dried up the original watercourse by diverting the river so that it would henceforward run midway between the mountains. So concerned are the Persians to maintain the dykes which channel the Nile that to this day they keep the closest of watches upon this bend, and repair its defences annually. This is because, should the river ever decide to burst its banks and overflow, there is every risk that the whole of Memphis would be drowned. After all, it too is located in the narrow part of Egypt. It was Min himself, the founder of Egypt's monarchy, who also founded the city which is now called Memphis, following the drying out of the land created by the dykes. Just beyond it to the north and west, he excavated a lake, extending round from the Nile, which skirts the city to its east. One other huge thing well worth mentioning is the shrine of Hephaestus, which he instituted within Memphis itself.

[100] As for Min's successors on the throne, the priests read out a list of their names from a papyrus roll – three hundred and thirty in all. Each of these kings ruled, on average, for the equivalent of a human generation; all of them, with the exception of eighteen Ethiopians, were Egyptian, and all, with the exception of a single native-born woman, were men. The name of this woman, the one who became queen, was the same as that of the queen of Babylon: Nitocris. According to the priests, she took a terrible vengeance on behalf of her brother, whose throne had been conferred on her by the Egyptians after they murdered him while he was still their king. Her vengeance was framed by trickery, and culminated in a great massacre of Egyptians. What she did was construct an immensely long underground chamber, and then, keeping her true intentions to herself, inaugurated it with a formal ceremony. The invitations went out to all the many Egyptians she knew had been most implicated in her brother's murder; she laid on a great banquet for them, and then, as they fell to feasting, sent the river in on them through a large concealed pipe. The only other biographical detail mentioned by the priests relates to the aftermath of this vengeance, and the concern of Nitocris to evade vengeance herself: it is said that she threw herself into a chamber full of ashes.

[101] But with the other kings mentioned by the priests, there was nothing that stuck out, no blaze of great achievement. The only exception

was the very last king, Moeris, who raised as his memorials the northern gateway in the sanctuary of Hephaestus, and some pyramids, around which he dug a lake. I will give the total circumference of this lake, in stades, at a later point, together with the size of the pyramids. Such are reported to have been the accomplishments of Moeris. None of the other kings, though, achieved a thing.

[102] So let me pass them over and commemorate instead their successor, a king by the name of Sesostris. The first thing he did, so the priests informed me, was to set sail from the Arabian Gulf with a fleet of warships, and then to cruise along the coast of the Red Sea, subduing all who lived there, until in due course he came to a stretch of water so shallow that it was no longer navigable. Sesostris duly returned to Egypt; whereupon, according to the priests' account, he assembled a large army and swept across the mainland, subduing every nation in his path. Whenever he happened to meet with a people of particular valour, ferocious in the defence of their liberty, he would erect a number of pillars in their land, on which were inscribed a record of his own name and fatherland, together with an assertion that it was through his own personal might that he had vanquished them. To the peoples whose cities he had conquered easily, without so much as a fight, the same pillars would be raised and inscribed with the very same message as was given to the peoples who had shown themselves true men, but with this one addition: a woman's genitals. These were inscribed because Sesostris wished there to be no doubt as to their lack of courage.

[103] Such was his practice, then, as he continued through the mainland, until in due course he crossed from Asia into Europe, and conquered the Scythians and the Thracians. This, I think, constituted the limit of the Egyptian army's advance. (There are pillars to be seen standing all over Scythia and Thrace, after all, but not a trace of any further on.) Sesostris wheeled round and headed back; and when he arrived on the banks of the River Phasis, one of two things happened, although which I cannot definitively say.[45] Either the king himself, Sesostris, detached a body of troops from his army and left them behind as settlers in the region, or else some of the soldiers themselves, fed up with all his wandering, refused to budge from the region of the Phasis.

[104] Even before I had it confirmed by others that the Colchians are indeed of Egyptian stock, it was so blindingly obvious that I had arrived at the conclusion by myself. When I followed up this insight by asking

both the relevant peoples to confirm it, I found that the Colchians had a much better recollection of the Egyptians than the Egyptians did of the Colchians. The Egyptians said they believed the Colchians to be the descendants of Sesostris' army. My own guess derived from the fact that the Colchians are swarthy and curly-haired, although that can hardly be reckoned conclusive, for so too are a number of other peoples. The clinching detail is that, of all the various peoples of the world, it is only the Colchians, the Egyptians and the Ethiopians who have practised circumcision since the dawn of time. The Phoenicians and the Syrians of Palestine freely concur that they learned the practice from the Egyptians, whereas the Syrians who live between the Thermodon and Parthenius rivers, together with their neighbours, the Macronians, both say that they adopted it not long ago from the Colchians. This is the sum total of the peoples who practise circumcision[46] – and undoubtedly, they have all of them followed the lead of the Egyptians. But the question of whether the Ethiopians are to be numbered among the pupils of the Egyptians, or whether perhaps it was the Egyptians who learned the practice from the Ethiopians, is not one to which I would hazard an answer; the solution is undoubtedly lost in the mists of time. That other peoples, though, were influenced by their contacts with the Egyptians is, in my opinion, demonstrably true: only observe how those among the Phoenicians who have close links with Greece have stopped imitating the Egyptians with regard to their private parts, and do not have their children circumcised.

[105] While I am at it, let me make one further statement about the resemblances between the Colchians and the Egyptians. Not only, exceptionally, do they both work linen, but they do so in the same manner, and their entire ways of life, and their languages too, are all strikingly similar. It is odd, however, that while the Greeks correctly name Egyptian linen after the country of its origin, Colchian linen they name 'Sardonian'.

[106] Most of the pillars which King Sesostris of Egypt raised in the various lands he conquered no longer seem to be standing; but in Palestinian Syria I did see for myself that there were some still in existence, complete with the inscriptions I mentioned earlier, and the women's genitals. In addition, in Ionia, there are two figures of a man carved into the rock, one on the road from Ephesus to Phocaea, and the other between Sardis and Smyrna. In both places, the carvings, which stand

almost 7 feet high, show a man with a spear in his right hand and a bow and arrows in his left; these weapons mix Egyptian with Ethiopian characteristics, as too does the rest of his equipment. Carved across his chest, running from shoulder to shoulder, and written in Egyptian hieroglyphs, these words appear:

IT WAS UPON MY SHOULDERS THAT THE WINNING OF THIS LAND WAS BORNE.

He did not specify on these two occasions his identity and place of origin; but elsewhere he did. Some people who have seen the carvings have guessed them to be likenesses of Memnon, but this is patently wide of the truth.

[107] The return home of Sesostris of Egypt, so the priests informed me, saw him leading a great train of captives, gathered from all the peoples of the many countries that he had vanquished. He happened to pass through Daphnae in Pelusium, where he and all his sons were invited to a banquet by his brother, the man to whom Sesostris had entrusted the regency of Egypt; but the brother, after heaping the outside of the banqueting hall around with brushwood, set it on fire. Sesostris, the moment he found out what had happened, turned to his wife, who is said to have come with him, and asked her what he should do. She advised him to have two of his six sons stretch out across the fire and form a bridge above the flames, over which everyone else could then walk to safety. This was exactly what Sesostris did; and although two of his sons were thus burned to death, all the others were able to make their escape with their father.

[108] Once Sesostris had returned home to Egypt and avenged himself upon his brother, he did not let the great host of prisoners in his train, transported from his various conquests, go to waste. It was they who dragged the massive blocks of stone that were assembed during his reign at the shrine of Hephaestus; and it was they who were forced to dig all the canals that can be seen in Egypt to this day too. They thereby unwittingly rendered the whole country impassable to horses and carts. For, unrelievedly flat though Egypt is, so extensive was the lattice-work of canals that, right from the start, it left the country denuded of horses and carts, when previously it had been full of them. Nevertheless, the king had good reason for dividing up the countryside. Originally, whenever the river retreated, all those Egyptians whose cities lay inland from

it would suffer from drought, and be reduced to drinking brackish water from wells. Hence the scoring of Egypt with canals.

[109] Another thing Sesostris did, so the priests informed me, was to divide the country up into square plots of equal size, portion them out among the entire population of Egypt and then raise revenues from this reform by ordering every plot-holder to pay an annual tax. Anyone with a plot eroded by the river would go to the king and say what had happened. Inspectors would then be sent out to measure the precise extent of the man's loss, so that his future tax-rate could be set at a level appropriate to the reduced size of his holding. It is my theory that this is what lay behind the discovery of geometry,[47] and its subsequent importation into Greece. (The sundial and its pointer, and the division of the day into twelve parts, were learned by the Greeks from the Babylonians.)

[110] Sesostris, who was the only Egyptian king to rule Ethiopia, bequeathed to posterity six stone statues in front of the temple of Hephaestus: two of them, both 45 feet high, were of himself and his wife, and four, each 30 feet high, were of his sons. Many years later, the priest of Hephaestus forbade Darius the Persian from placing a statue of himself in front of them, on the grounds that he had failed to match the achievements of Sesostris the Egyptian: not only had Sesostris won for himself conquests no less extensive than those of Darius, but he had also vanquished the Scythians, whom Darius had failed to subdue. 'That being so,' the priest declared, 'it would not be just for a statue dedicated by you to take precedence over those of a man whose achievements you have not surpassed.'[48] This point, it is said, was conceded by Darius.

[111] The priests also informed me that Sesostris, once he had met his end, was succeeded on the throne by his son, Pheros, a king with no experience of military command, and who happened to have become blind. The occasion was a surge of flood-waters down the Nile that reached up to 27 feet, an unprecedented height; after which, when all the fields were under water, a gale began to blow, so that the river became very choppy. The king, it is said – so enraged that he scorned all propriety – took a spear and hurled it right into the midst of the boiling river, whereupon he was immediately afflicted by a sickness of the eyes and struck blind. For ten years he had no sight; and then, in the eleventh year of his blindness, an oracle arrived from the city of Bouto. 'You have been punished long enough,' it declared. 'Only wash your eyes with the

urine of a woman who has always been faithful to her husband, and never slept with another man, and your sight will be restored.' The first woman put to the test by Pheros was his own wife – but he did not recover his sight. So he carried on, trying the urine of woman after woman until at last his sight was restored. Then he had all the various women he had tested, with the exception of the woman whose urine had bathed his eyes back to full vision, gather in a particular city, the one that nowadays goes by the name of 'The Red Glebe'. Then, once they were gathered there, he burned them all, and the city with them. He took the woman whose urine had bathed his eyes back to full vision as his wife, and marked his deliverance from the suffering that his eyes had caused him by making dedications to all the most celebrated sanctuaries in Egypt. Of these various offerings there is none more noteworthy than the two stone obelisks in the sanctuary of the Sun. Hewn from a single lump of rock, they both rise to a height of 150 feet, and measure 12 full feet across.

[112] Pheros, so the priests said, was followed on the throne by a man from Memphis whose name in Greek was *Proteus*. He built an exquisitely beautiful and well-appointed precinct south of the temple of Hephaestus in Memphis, which stands there to this day. The entire area is known as 'The Tyrians' Camp', after all the Phoenicians from Tyre who have houses clustered round the precinct. Within this precinct built by Proteus there is a shrine dedicated to Aphrodite the Foreigner. Personally, I conjecture that the dedicatee meant by this must be Helen, the daughter of Tyndareus – not only because I've heard it said that she spent some time with Proteus, but also, and even more saliently, because of the epithet given to Aphrodite: 'The Foreigner'. None of the other shrines of Aphrodite bears such a title.

[113] And when I asked the priests about Helen, they gave me their own account of what had happened after she was abducted by Paris, and he set sail for home. As he was crossing the Aegean, so the priests said, a storm blew up, sweeping him off course into the Egyptian sea, until eventually, when the winds refused to abate, he ended up in Egypt itself – or, to be more specific, beside a fish-pickling works in an arm of the Nile, the one that nowadays goes by the name of 'Canobic'. There on the shore, then as now, stood a shrine of Heracles, a sanctuary from which it was forbidden to haul any fugitive slave, no matter whose, once he had had pressed into his flesh a sacred branding-iron, and

thereby given himself over as the property of the god. This law has existed unaltered from the very founding of the sanctuary all the way down to my own time. Paris' servants, the moment they had learned about this law, and how it related to the shrine, slipped away from their master and sat down in the temple, claiming sanctuary of the god; then, eager to do Paris damage, they began to level accusations against him, spilling out the whole story of Helen, and of the wrong he had done to Menelaus. Nor was it only to the priests that they made their case; they also laid their charges before the warden of the estuary, a man named Thonis.

[114] No sooner had Thonis heard them out than he dispatched a message post haste to Proteus in Memphis. 'A stranger,' he reported, 'a Trojan by race, has arrived here from Greece, where he behaved in a most impious way. First he seduced the wife of his friend and host, and then he abducted her, together with an enormous quantity of treasure. Now, thanks to contrary winds, he is here on your soil. Should I let him sail away unharmed, or confiscate what he brought with him?' Back came the response from Proteus: 'No matter who this man may be, this perpetrator of impious deeds, have him arrested and brought to me, so that I may listen to what he has to say.'

[115] On hearing this, Thonis had Paris arrested and his ships impounded, then took Paris and Helen to Memphis, together with all the treasure and the slaves who had claimed sanctuary. On their arrival there, Proteus demanded to know of Paris who he was, and what his course of sailing had been. Paris declared both his lineage and his native land, and gave full details of his voyage, including the place from which he had just arrived. But when Proteus next asked him about Helen, and how he had come by her, Paris refused to give a straight answer. This provoked the suppliants, as they had become, to level accusations against him, and provide a full account of his offence. Finally Proteus delivered his judgement. 'If I did not hold it a matter of pride', he said, 'never yet to have put to death any of the foreigners who have ended up in my country, blown here by contrary winds, I would most certainly have punished you, most wicked of men, on behalf of the Greek whose hospitality you so abused, and against whom you committed such sacrilege. To force yourself upon the wife of your host! And then, as if that were not enough, to provoke her to such a soaring ecstasy of lust that she flew away with you when you escaped! And then, because you were

still not done, to plunder your host's household! And now, here you are – and while I hold to my resolution never to kill foreign guests, I certainly have no intention of handing back this woman to you, nor any of these valuables, just so that you can then make off with them again. No, until such time as your Greek host decides to come and fetch them for himself, I will keep them here for him under lock and key. As for you and those who man your ships, I give you notice that you have three days to weigh anchor and leave my country. Fail to comply, and I shall treat it as a declaration of war.'

[116] Such was the account given to me by the priests of how Helen came to be with Proteus. It seems to me that Homer picked up on the story too; for although it did not lend itself as well to an epic tone as the plot-line that he eventually used, he did demonstrate his awareness of it before setting it aside. For instance, there is an obvious hint in the episode which he added to the *Iliad*, never contradicted elsewhere in the poem, which describes the wanderings of Paris: how Paris was swept off course while carrying away Helen, and how, in the midst of his wandering, he arrived at Sidon, in Phoenicia. The passage can be found in the section which describes the prowess of Diomedes, and runs like this:

> There were gorgeous robes, brocaded, woven by the women
> Of Sidon, that godlike Paris himself had brought
> From there, on the very voyage across the wide seas
> That saw him carry back Helen, Zeus' daughter.

There is also a mention in the *Odyssey*, as follows:

> Very cunning were the drugs that Zeus' daughter had,
> Potent too, gifts from Polydamna, wife of Thon,
> Sprung of Egypt, where the grain-lands teem with strange herbs
> Which, mixed with wine, can either cure, or serve to kill.

Then there is the comment made by Menelaus to Telemachus:

> I yearned for home, marooned in Egypt by the gods,
> For I had failed to sacrifice their due of oxen.

What all these passages[49] clearly serve to demonstrate is that Homer was well aware that the wanderings of Paris had taken him to Egypt, for [as regards the first passage, its significance lies in the fact that] the people who inhabit Sidon are Phoenicians, who live in Syria which borders Egypt.

[117] What these verses and passage[s] clearly demonstrate, beyond all shadow of a doubt, is that Homer could not possibly have been the author of the *Cypria*,[50] and that someone else must therefore have written it. In the *Cypria* it says that Paris reached Troy three days after abducting Helen from Sparta, thanks to a fair wind and a calm sea, whereas in the *Iliad* it says that Paris ended up taking Helen far and wide on his journey home. But enough about Homer and the *Cypria*.

[118] When I asked the priests whether the version told by the Greeks of what had happened at Troy was mere fantasy, they replied with a story which they insisted had been obtained by making enquiries of Menelaus. After the abduction of Helen, a great army of Greeks made for the land of the Trojans to aid him. There they disembarked and set up camp, then sent messengers, one of whom was Menelaus himself, to Troy. Once the embassy had arrived inside the city walls, its delegates demanded the return both of Helen and of all the goods which Paris had stolen and carried off, together with justice for the crimes that had been committed. The Trojans' response was the one which they would never cease to give, under oath or not: namely, that they had neither Helen nor even the goods in question, since the whole lot were in Egypt, and that it would therefore be most unjust if they were obliged to compensate the Greeks for what was actually in the possession of Proteus, the king of Egypt. The Greeks, who assumed that they were being made fun of, promptly put the city under siege, until finally it was theirs; even with the city in their hands, however, there was no sign of Helen. Instead, all the Greeks could uncover was the same story as before; and so, believing it at last, they sent Menelaus himself to visit Proteus.

[119] On his arrival in Egypt, Menelaus duly sailed upriver to Memphis, where he gave a full and truthful account of the affair, received magnificent hospitality from his host, and was reunited with Helen, who was quite unharmed, and all his treasure besides. Even so, in spite of the many favours shown to him, Menelaus behaved criminally towards the Egyptians. Though he was eager to sail off, he nevertheless found himself stranded by contrary winds for day after day after day, until finally he devised a plan fit to appal the gods: he abducted two children from local families and chopped them up in sacrifice. The

discovery of this atrocity filled the Egyptians with revulsion, and they set off after him in pursuit; but Menelaus and his ships took flight and set a course directly for Libya. Where he had headed afterwards the Egyptians could not say. What they had been able to learn, they told me, had been the fruit of research; but as for the events that had taken place in their own land, these they could relate from certain knowledge.

[120] All this I had from the priests of Egypt – and speaking personally, I do not doubt their account as it relates to Helen. For surely, had she indeed been in Troy, then she would have been handed back over to the Greeks, whether Paris wished it or not. Neither Priam nor the rest of his family were so mentally defective as willingly to put themselves, their children and their city in peril, simply so that Paris might live with Helen. And even if we grant that this might perhaps have been their initial attitude, nevertheless (with the onset of hostilities, and a slaughter of Trojans at the hands of the Greeks so prodigious that Priam himself, if the evidence of the epic poets is to be trusted, was losing some two or three or even more of his sons every time battle was joined) my supposition must surely be correct that the effect of these circumstances would have been to convince Priam, had he been the one who was living with Helen, that she simply had to be given back to the Achaeans[51] – for how else, after all, was he to be rid of the evils hemming him in? Nor is it the case that Paris was the heir to the throne, and might therefore conceivably have been operating as regent during Priam's dotage. Rather, it was Hector – both older and more of a man than Paris – who stood to inherit the kingdom upon the death of his father; and so it would hardly have been proper for him to indulge his brother's lawlessness, not when Paris was bringing down such suffering upon the entire Trojan people, and also privately on Hector himself. No, the plain fact is that there was no Helen for the Trojans to return, and, even though the Greeks did not believe them, they had been telling the simple truth: evidence, in my opinion, that events had been shaped by the hand of the divine, so that the utter ruin of the Trojans, and their annihilation, should serve to demonstrate to humanity that terrible crimes will meet with correspondingly terrible punishments from the gods. Such is my belief, and I declare it here.[52]

[121] The king who followed Proteus onto the throne was, according to the priests, Rhampsinitus. He left as his memorials the entrance-gates at the western end of the temple of Hephaestus, and the two statues

which he set up directly facing them. Both statues rise to a height of some 38 feet; the more northerly of the two is called 'Summer' by the Egyptians, and receives both respect and obeisance from them, while the more southerly is called 'Winter' and receives neither.

This Rhampsinitus, it is said, built up a colossal fortune in silver, so vast that none of his successors was ever able so much as to come near it, let alone surpass it. Wishing to ensure the security of all this wealth, Rhampsinitus added a stone extension onto one of the walls of his palace, to serve him as a treasury. The craftsman, however, devised a cunning plan. He so fitted one of the stones that a couple of men, or even one, would easily be able to remove it from its place in the wall. Time went by. The treasury had been completed, and the king's wealth stashed away inside it, when the builder, by now on his deathbed, summoned his two sons to tell them of the foresight he had shown on their behalf: of how, while building the royal treasury, he had devised a scheme to keep them rich for the rest of their lives. He described to them in great detail exactly how the stone should be removed, provided them with its precise location and then admonished them to guard the secret well. 'Do that, and you will be the veritable stewards of the king's exchequer!' The father died, and his sons promptly set to work. They went to the palace by night, found the stone in the treasury wall and removed it with great ease; then they headed out with their massive haul.

The king, when he next opened up the treasury, was startled to see that some of his jars had been pilfered of their riches, but since the seals remained unbroken and the chamber securely locked, found himself at a loss to know whom to blame. A second time he opened it up, and a second time he discovered an obvious diminution of his treasure; on the third occasion, the refusal of the robbers to lay off their depredations had left the jars even more depleted. So the king took action: he ordered snares to be made and set around the jars of money. When the thieves came as usual, one of them slipped into the chamber – and no sooner had he approached a jar than he was caught in one of the traps. The moment he grasped the plight he was in, he called out to his brother, explaining the full situation and ordering him to get inside the chamber as quickly as possible. 'Cut off my head,' the first brother urged, 'otherwise there will be no concealing my identity, and my downfall will spell yours as well.' 'A fair point,' the second brother reflected; and so, duly convinced, he did as had been suggested, then fitted the stone back in its place and set off back home carrying his brother's head.

The next morning, when the king went into the treasury, he was astounded to see the headless corpse of the thief, caught in a trap inside a room that was quite undamaged, even though it had neither an entrance-way nor an exit. Not knowing what else to do, he ordered the thief's body to be hung from the city walls, then posted guards with instructions to arrest anyone they saw in tears or in mourning and to bring him into the royal presence. As it turned out, however, the person prostrated by this gibbeting of the corpse was the mother. She begged and berated her surviving son to come up with whatever plan was needed to get his brother's body cut down and brought back home. 'If you refuse,' she threatened, 'I will go to the king and reveal just who it is has his money.'

So the mother carried on, scolding her surviving son, until eventually, once all his attempts to wriggle free of her demands had failed, he did indeed come up with a plan. Getting hold of some donkeys and skins, he filled the skins with wine and loaded them onto the donkeys, which he then drove along. When he came to the spot where the guards were standing sentinel on the hanging corpse, he gave a pull on the necks of two or three of the skins, so that their fastenings were loosened. Out came the wine; and as it flowed, the young man began to slap the side of his head and to shout loudly, as though uncertain which donkey he should turn to first. The guards meanwhile, seeing the great gushing of wine, all grabbed some jars and ran into the road, catching the wine as it poured out, looking on it as a windfall. The young man put on a great show of outrage, cursing them all roundly, until at last, pretending to have been mollified by the guards' attempt to calm him down, he drove the donkeys to the side of the road and set to rearranging the skins. The conversation between him and the guards continued to flow; and when someone cracked a joke about what had happened and made the young man laugh, he presented them with one of the skins. The guards imme-diately settled themselves down, with the full intention of enjoying a drink right there and then; and as they lolled around, so they tugged on the young man's arm and urged him to stay and drink with them. The young man was persuaded; he stayed. The more the guards drank, the more they began to insist that he was their best friend – and so he gave them yet another skin. Soon enough, such was the prodigious quantity of wine downed by the guards that they all became roaringly drunk, slumped into a stupor and fell sound asleep, right where they were. In the middle of the night, the young man cut down the body of his brother, and then, so as to add insult, shaved the guards' right cheeks. This done, he loaded the corpse up onto the donkeys, and drove back home. 'Mission accomplished!' he could now tell his mother.

When, however, the king was brought the news that the thief's body had been stolen, he was furious, and so all-consuming was his longing to uncover the identity of the man who had pulled off such a trick that he did something which I personally find incredible. He set his daughter up in a brothel, with orders to greet all-comers equally; but he instructed her as well that she was on no account to have sex with a client until she had first obliged him to reveal to her the cleverest and most wicked thing he had done in his life. Should the thief come and make mention of what he had done in his reply, she was to seize him and not to let him go. The girl did as she had been told, but the thief, when he found out what was being done, wished to prove himself the king's superior in cunning. So he cut off the arm of a still-warm corpse at the shoulder, and took it with him under his cloak to visit the king's daughter. Then, when she asked him the question she had been putting to all her clients, he answered her by saying, 'The very wickedest thing I have ever done was to cut off the head of my own brother, when he was caught in a trap in the king's treasury, while the cleverest was to get the guards drunk and to cut down the body of my brother from where it had been gibbeted.' The moment she heard this, the girl naturally made a grab for him, and the thief – under cover of darkness – thrust the corpse's arm at her. She seized it and clung on to it, believing that it was the arm of the thief that she had in her grasp. But he had already abandoned it to her, and was off, fleeing through the doors.

The news of this latest exploit left the king so astounded by the fellow's cunning and audacity that in the end he sent heralds round every city in the kingdom with an offer of amnesty, and the promise of great rewards, if the thief would reveal himself. The young man decided to take the king at his word; he went to Rhampsinitus, who was so impressed by him that he gave him the hand of his daughter in marriage. 'For there is no one', the king declared, 'to compare with him for sheer brains. We Egyptians have been judged the cleverest of peoples, and he is the cleverest of us all!'[53]

[122] Later on, the priests reported, Rhampsinitus descended alive into the realm that is conventionally known by the Greeks as 'Hades', where he played dice with Demeter, sometimes winning, and sometimes losing to her, before returning from the underworld with a gift that had been presented to him by the goddess – a head-dress of gold. This descent and return of Rhampsinitus inspired the Egyptians to stage a festival, or so I was told; the truth is, however, that, even though the festival the priests talked about has indeed continued to be celebrated right into my own time, the question of whether it was really prompted by the story I have just recounted is impossible for me to answer. On the day of the festival, the priests weave a robe;[54] they then bind the eyes of one of their number with a sash, give him the robe to carry, and take him out onto the road which leads to the sanctuary of Demeter. Then, after the others have all gone back, the blindfolded priest is led on by two wolves, it is said, all the way to the sanctuary of Demeter, and then back from the shrine to the place where they first picked him up.

[123] Now, those who find such things credible must make what use they will of the stories told by the Egyptians. My own responsibility, however, as it has been throughout my writing of this entire narrative, is simply to record whatever I may be told by my sources.[55] The rulers of the underworld, so the Egyptians claim, are Demeter and Dionysus. What is more, it was the Egyptians who were the first to propose the doctrine of the immortality of the soul: they maintain that, whenever the body of a human being ceases to be animated by life, its soul will always pass into some other living thing, directly at the point of its conception. Once the soul has been round every creature that walks on dry land, or swims in the sea, or flies in the air, only then will it again pass into the body of a human being, just as it is being born: a process of transmigration which lasts three thousand years. There are some Greeks who have made use of this doctrine, both in the past and more recently, as though it were exclusively their own. I know their names but do not record them.

[124] Now, until the reign of Rhampsinitus, so the priests said, lawfulness was something universal in Egypt, and the entire country enjoyed great prosperity. But when his successor, Cheops, became king,[56] the Egyptians were driven to every extreme of misery. His first act was to close down all the shrines and to forbid animal blood-sacrifices; then he ordered all the Egyptians to do forced labour for him. Some were

assigned the task of hauling blocks of stone from the quarries in the Arabian mountains all the way to the Nile; the blocks were then ferried across the river by boat, and handed over to other gangs who had been assigned the no less remarkable task of dragging them onwards to the Libyan range, as it is called. Gangs totalling a hundred thousand labourers would work in rotation, three months at a time. Time passed, until the Egyptian people had devoted ten years of grinding labour to the construction of the causeway along which the blocks of stone were hauled: an expense of effort hardly less immense, in my opinion, than that required to build the pyramid, bearing in mind that the road is more than half a mile long, 60 feet wide and reaches 48 feet at its highest point, and that it was made of polished stone, complete with carvings of various figures. The ten years that it took to build also saw the construction of the underground chambers commissioned by Cheops to serve him as his burial place, right within the hill on which the pyramids stand, and which he turned into an island by extending a canal from the Nile. The pyramid itself took twenty years to build: it is 800 feet high, and each of its four sides, which together form a square, is 800 feet as well. The pyramid is fashioned of polished blocks of stone, all of them perfectly fitted together, and none less than 30 feet long.

[125] The pyramid was initially so constructed that it resembled a flight of stairs, although several writers have used the image of battlements, and others of altar steps. Once the base had been completed, the builders employed contraptions fashioned out of short timbers to winch up the remaining blocks of stone, lifting each one from the ground up onto the first stage of the stairs. Then, with the block safely arrived, it was loaded onto another contraption positioned on the first tier, and hauled up onto the second level, where it was put into a yet further device. Each level of the stairs must have had its own array of machinery; either that, or else there was a single contraption which was readily transportable, and could be transferred from tier to tier once the stone had been removed from it. (Both methods deserve to be mentioned, since both were relayed to me.) Anyway, it was the uppermost parts of the pyramid which were completed first, then the parts underneath it, and then finally the lowest parts of all, at ground level. There is a notice on the pyramid, written in Egyptian script, which records how much was spent keeping the workforce in radishes, onions and garlic. The total, if I remember correctly what the interpreter who read the notice

told me,[57] was 1,600 talents of silver. If that is so, then how much more, if you think about it, must have been spent on iron[58] for the labourers' tools, and on all their provisions and clothing! Only recollect what I said about how long it took them to build the pyramid – and even then, I suppose, you also have to bear in mind the periods that they spent quarrying the stone and transporting it, and excavating the underground chambers, none of which was exactly short.

[126] Cheops sank to such a nadir of depravity that his solution to a shortage of money was to install his own daughter in a brothel, and command her to charge those who visited her a standard fee of silver (though how much precisely, I was not informed). She did indeed charge the rate set by her father, but she also had a fancy to leave behind a memorial to herself; and so she asked each of her clients to donate a single stone [on the building-site]. It was these stones, I was told, which were used to build the middle pyramid of the three which stand in front of the Great Pyramid. Each one of its sides measures 150 feet.

[127] Cheops reigned for fifty years, according to the Egyptians, and after his death was succeeded on the thone by his brother, Chephren.[59] The new king carried on exactly as his predecessor had done, not least in his taste for pyramid-building – although Chephren's pyramid is on a smaller scale than his brother's. (I know this, because I measured them both myself.) In addition, it lacks both underground chambers and the kind of canal that was built to channel water from the Nile around the middle pyramid, and create the island on which, it is said, Cheops himself lies buried. Chephren's pyramid has a bottom course fashioned of patterned Ethiopian stone, and – excepting the fact that it is 40 feet shorter – was built to the same proportions as the Great Pyramid beside which it was constructed. The pair of them stand on the same hill, which rises to a height of approximately one hundred feet. Chephren was king, it is said, for fifty-six years.

[128] In total, then, there was a period of one hundred and six years when the Egyptians were put to every kind of misery, and in all that time the shrines that had been closed down were never reopened. Indeed, such is the hatred felt by the Egyptians for the very names of Cheops and Chephren that they have no wish to speak them, and even their pyramids they name after the shepherd Philitis, who pastured his flocks in the neighbourhood during the period.

[129] After Chephren, so the priests informed me, his successor as

king of Egypt was Mycerinus,[60] who, despite being the son of Cheops, was a stern critic of his father's policies. Mycerinus reopened the shrines, and permitted the Egyptian people, who had been ground down into a condition of utter wretchedness, to return to their old patterns of work and sacrifice; not only that, but he was also the most scrupulous of all their kings in the exercise of justice. It is for this reason that Mycerinus enjoys a higher reputation among the Egyptians than any of their other kings; quite apart from the fact that his verdicts were invariably just, it was also his practice, should anyone ever object to one of his decisions, to offer restitution from his own personal estate to ensure complete satisfaction. Yet despite this, and despite all the kindness with which he treated his fellow-citizens, he personally suffered no lack of troubles. Of these, the very first was the death of his daughter, his only child. The grief that Mycerinus suffered as a result of this calamity was something terrible; and so it was, because he wished to give his daughter a burial like no other, that he had a wooden cow made, hollow on the inside, and on the outside sheathed all over with gold, within which he entombed his dead child.

[130] Rather than being buried underground, however, this cow was still to be seen in my day in the city of Sais, where it lies inside the palace in a richly decorated chamber. Incense of all kinds is daily burned there in offering, while every night a lamp is kept lit beside it. Close by the cow, in another chamber, there stand statues which, according to the priests of the city of Sais, represent the concubines of Mycerinus. There are around twenty of them standing there, wooden figures of a considerable size, and fashioned, it is true enough, in the likeness of naked women. Whether or not they really represent the concubines of Mycerinus, however, all I can do is to repeat what I was told.

[131] Some tell a quite different story about the cow and the colossal statues: namely, that Mycerinus lusted passionately after his daughter, and forced himself upon her. Such was the girl's distress in the wake of this, it is said, that she hanged herself, prompting Mycerinus to bury her in the cow, and the mother to cut off the hands of the servant-girls who had delivered up their daughter to her father; it is these attendants, supposedly, who are represented by the statues, all of which have suffered an identical fate to their real-life originals. Personally, however, I think that whole story to be nonsense. Not the least ludicrous part of it is its explanation of the statues' missing hands, since I saw them for myself,

and it was perfectly obvious that the hands had just dropped off owing to the effects of time. They are lying there to this day, clearly visible, beside the feet of the statues.

[132] With the exception of its neck and head, which are visible, and are gilded all over with an exceedingly thick layering of gold, the cow is concealed beneath a purple robe. Between its horns there is a representation of the sun, in the form of a golden disc. The cow is in a kneeling posture rather than standing upright, and is lifesize. It is borne from its chamber annually, at the time of year when the Egyptians beat their chests in mourning for the god whose name, in a context such as this, I have no intention of saying,[61] and whose festival provides the cue for the cow to be carried out into daylight. The reason for this, so the story goes, is that Mycerinus' daughter begged her father, on her deathbed, to be allowed once a year to glimpse the sun.

[133] The death of his daughter was not the only calamity to befall the king. An oracle came to him from the city of Bouto, in which it was declared that he had only six years left to live, and that in the seventh he would die. So outraged was Mycerinus by this that he sent a message back to the oracle, bitterly reproaching the god for the injustice by which his father and uncle had both lived to a ripe old age, despite their having closed down the shrines, forgotten the gods and brought untold ruin to their fellow-men, whereas he, despite his piety, would be dying so soon. But from the oracle there came back a second message: 'That is precisely why your life is being cut short! You have failed to do what was required of you! For what you, unlike your two predecessors, failed to grasp, is that it was fated for Egypt to be afflicted by evils for a full one hundred and fifty years!' As Mycerinus listened to this, he realized that his fate was already sealed. Accordingly, he had an immense number of lamps made, which he then had lit at nightfall, enabling him to drink and be entertained without pause, day or night, and to tour pools, and glades, and anywhere else that he had heard might provide him with a pleasant spot for enjoying himself. His ambition in devising this course of action was to show the oracle up as a liar, for by turning night into day, he aimed to turn his six years of life into twelve.

[134] Mycerinus also left a pyramid – a good deal smaller than his father's – each side of whose square base is 280 feet long, and whose lower half is fashioned out of Ethiopian stone. This is the same pyramid which some Greeks say was built by Rhodopis, who was a courtesan;

but they are quite wrong in that particular claim. In fact, it seems to me that such a theory displays a complete ignorance as to who Rhodopis actually was; had they known, its proponents would never have attributed to her the construction of a pyramid on such a scale, and which, it is hardly an exaggeration to say, must have cost thousands upon thousands of talents, beyond the ability to count. What is more, Rhodopis flourished during the reign of Amasis, long, long after the age of the kings who left the pyramids to posterity, and not way back in the time of Mycerinus. Rhodopis herself was a Thracian by birth; she was owned by a man from Samos called Iadmon, the son of Hephaestopolis, who was also the master of Aesop, the fabulist. The clearest proof that Aesop was a slave of Iadmon is what happened when the Delphians, prompted by Apollo, repeatedly announced that anyone who so wished could claim the blood-money from them that was owed following Aesop's murder. Not one person came forward until Iadmon's grandson, who had the same name as his grandfather, laid claim to it – certain proof that Aesop did indeed belong to Iadmon.

[135] It was in the train of Xanthes, a Samian, that Rhodopis came to Egypt. Here, following her arrival, she was set to work; until, at immense cost, she was redeemed from slavery by a man from Mytilene called Charaxus, the son of Scamandronymus and brother of Sappho[62] the poet. Rhodopis, having been freed, stayed on in Egypt, where such was the potency of her sexual allure that she ended up exceedingly wealthy – or rather, I should say, exceedingly wealthy by the standards of the kind of woman that she was, but not so wealthy as to be able to afford a pyramid like that of Mycerinus. There is certainly no point in ascribing great wealth to her – not when it is possible for all those who fancy it to go and see what a tenth part of her estate actually comprised. Rhodopis' ambition, you see, was to leave behind a memorial to herself in Greece, an offering such as no one else had ever thought to make and present to a shrine, and which she looked to dedicate to Delphi, to keep her memory alive there. So she spent a tenth part of her fortune on having ox-roasting spits of iron made for her – as many of them as her tithe could buy her – and sent them all to Delphi. There they still are to this day, piled up in a heap behind the altar which the Chians dedicated, opposite the temple itself. It is a strange thing, but the courtesans of Naucratis[63] have always had a talent for making themselves sexually irresistible. In addition to the courtesan who is the subject of this current

passage – the one who became so famous that every Greek is familiar with the name 'Rhodopis' – there is also a more recent one, Archidice by name, who, despite lacking the all-round celebrity of her counterpart, nevertheless figures in songs far and wide across the Greek world. Charaxus, after he had bought Rhodopis her freedom, returned home to Mytilene, where he was roundly mocked by Sappho in one of her poems. But that is enough about Rhodopis.

[136] According to the priests, the man who succeeded Mycerinus to the throne of Egypt was Asychis: he was the man who added to the sanctuary of Hephaestus the entrance-gate which is aligned to the rising of the sun, and is by far the largest and most beautiful of all the sanctuary's gates. No matter that the others too have figures carved into them, not to mention countless other architectural features well worth seeing, they none of them can rival the eastern gateway. The reign of Asychis, so the priests informed me, was marked by a severe financial crisis, so a law was passed whereby any Egyptian who wished to take out a loan was permitted to do so on the security of his father's corpse. By the terms of an additional provision, however, this law also laid down that the creditor should have complete control over the family vault of the man taking out the mortgage, and that should the loan subsequently default, a penalty would be levied whereby when they died neither the debtor himself, nor any other member of his family, would be permitted burial in their ancestral vault – or indeed in any other. Asychis himself, who aspired to put into the shade all his predecessors on the throne of Egypt, bequeathed as his memorial to posterity a pyramid fashioned out of brick, on which could be read an inscription chiselled out of stone. 'Do not think to compare me unfavourably to the pyramids of stone,' it declared, 'for just as Zeus excels the other gods, so I excel them. A pole was pushed down into a lake, mud clung to this pole, the mud was then scooped up and the fruit of this mud was bricks. And that is how I came to be made.' Such were the achievements of Asychis.

[137] The next king was a blind man called Anysis, who came from a city of the same name. His reign saw an invasion of Egypt by a large force of Ethiopians, under their king, Sabacos. The blind king went and fled into the marshes, and for fifty years the Ethiopian ruled over Egypt – to highly visible effect. Rather than impose the death penalty upon those Egyptians who committed crimes, Sabacos preferred instead to sentence them, for a length of time proportionate to their offences, to

forced labour in whichever city they came from, there to build dykes and embankments. As a result of this, the height of the cities was raised yet further. Originally, of course, earth had been piled up as a result of the canals that were excavated back in the days of King Sesostris; now, with all the excavations that were being carried out under the Ethiopian, the cities became really very elevated indeed. Nevertheless, of all the cities in Egypt which had their height raised in this way, the one which ended up on the highest mound of all, in my estimation, was the city of Bubastis. There is a shrine in Bubastis dedicated to the goddess of the same name, the one who in Greek is called Artemis, and it is most certainly worth describing – for while it may not be the largest sanctuary in existence, nor the most lavishly furnished, it is surely the one which affords the greatest pleasure to anyone who views it.

[138] So, a description of this shrine. Were it not for a single point of access, it would stand on an island; twin canals, both of them 100 feet wide and shaded over by trees, have been channelled from the Nile, right around the shrine and up to its entrance, one on one side, and one on the other, but never meeting. The gateway rises to 60 feet, and is adorned with striking figures, which stand some 9 feet high. The shrine itself is situated in the middle of the city, and the level on which it was originally built has never been altered, despite the fact that the rest of the city has risen and risen, so that one can walk all round the shrine and look down into it from any direction. It is surrounded by a low wall embellished by figures. Beyond this wall, a grove of tall trees has grown up around an enormous temple which houses the statue of the goddess. The total area of the sanctuary is one stade square. There is a road, paved with stones and stretching some 400 feet wide, which extends from the entrance eastwards for approximately 3 stades, through the main square of the city, and onwards to the sanctuary of Hermes. Dotted along the side of this road are trees so tall that they seem to brush the sky. So there it is: a description of the shrine.

[139] In the end, the priests told me, deliverance from the Ethiopian came because of a dream, one in which he imagined that a man was standing over him and advising him to assemble all the priests in one place and then to hack them in two. The response of the Ethiopian to this vision was to run away. 'For it seems to me', he said, 'that the gods can only have sent it to provide themselves with a pretext for taking action against me. They hope to provoke me to sacrilege, and thereby to

bring down upon myself some terrible disaster – if not at the hands of the gods themselves, then through the agency of men. But I will not do it. It was prophesied that I would have the rule of Egypt only for a set time – and now that time has passed, and I must leave.' For it had so happened that, back when Sabacos was in Ethiopia, the oracles consulted by the Ethiopians had pronounced that he was fated to rule as the king of Egypt for fifty years – and the fifty years were now almost up. Add in the disturbing effect upon him of his dream, and it is no wonder that Sabacos should have left Egypt of his own will.

[140] With the Ethiopian gone from Egypt, the blind king returned from the marshes and resumed his reign. For fifty years he had lived on an island raised up out of earth and ashes. Food was one thing that the Egyptians, unbeknown to Sabacos, had been ordered to bring him, and another was a gift of ashes. For seven hundred years, none of the predecessors of Amyrtaeus on the throne was able to find this island, so its location remained a mystery right up to the time of Amyrtaeus. The island itself goes by the name of 'Elbo' and measures 10 stades in diameter.

[141] The next king was a priest of Hephaestus called Sethos. Such was the lack of respect and courtesy that Sethos showed to the warrior class of Egypt that it was as though he imagined he would never have any need of them. One of the ways in which he dishonoured them, for instance, was to confiscate the plots of land – twelve highly productive fields in all – which each warrior had been awarded over the course of earlier reigns. Eventually, when Egypt was invaded by a huge army of Arabians and Assyrians[64] under the leadership of their king, Sennacherib, none of the Egyptian military had any incentive to come to his rescue. Indeed, so desperate were the straits in which Sethos, the priest, found himself that he went into the great hall of the temple and poured out all his unhappiness and forebodings before the statue of the god. Even as he was in the middle of these lamentations he was overcome by a drowsiness, and imagined that he saw the god standing over him, offering him reassurance and a promise that all would be well if only he would march out and meet with the Arab army. 'For I will send you helpers.' Sethos duly put his trust in his dream: he enlisted all the Egyptians who were prepared to follow him, and set up camp at Pelusium, directly in the path of the invasion. With him in his army were shopkeepers, artisans and market-traders – but not one man from the warrior

class. The enemy approached; but then, at night, there came a great swarm of field-mice, which gnawed through the quivers of the invaders, and their bows, and the handles of their shields, so that in the morning they found themselves quite defenceless. They fled and were cut down in great numbers. To this day there is a stone statue of Sethos standing in the sanctuary of Hephaestus, with a field-mouse in his hand. 'Look on me,' declare the letters carved on the statue, 'and revere the gods.'

[142] For everything so far I have depended upon the records of the Egyptians and their priests: records which clearly show that between the first king of Egypt to this last one I just mentioned, the priest of Hephaestus, there were 341 generations in all, and that there was one king, and one high priest, per generation. Now, if three generations are equivalent to a hundred years, then three hundred generations make ten thousand years, with the additional forty-one generations on top of the three hundred totalling 1,340 years – which makes 11,340 in all. Not once during this entire span of time, said the priests, did a single god appear in human form; nor, according to their records, did anything of that kind happen earlier, nor during the reigns of the subsequent kings of Egypt either. They did tell me, though, that there were four occasions during this span when the sun did not rise in the east, but instead rose where it should set, and set where it should rise. They assured me, however, that Egypt was left quite unaffected by this; neither the farmers in the fields nor the fishermen out on the river noticed any changes, nor was there any alteration in the patterns of disease or mortality.

[143] A while ago, one of the visitors to Thebes was Hecataeus, the writer,[65] who was engaged upon genealogy – a field with which personally I have never bothered. Sixteen generations he had traced back his line of descent, through his father's forebears, to a god. The priests of Zeus, however, gave him the treatment that they also gave me. They led me inside to a massive hall, where they showed me large wooden statue after large wooden statue, keeping careful count of each one, until eventually they had arrived at the total I mentioned earlier. It is the invariable practice of each high priest, you see, to set up a likeness of himself in the hall during his own lifetime. As the priests kept up the tally, and pointed out each image, counting back from that of the most recently deceased high priest, and continuing without break until the whole lot had been included in their tour, so they were forever emphasizing that each had

been the son of his predecessor. The priests dismissed out of hand Hecataeus and his own genealogical researches, which had led him back sixteen generations to a divine ancestor; their own approach to genealogy, founded upon totting up the statues in the hall, made it impossible for them to accept that a human being might be descended from a god. Indeed, to emphasize just how much of a rebuttal to Hecataeus their tracing of the high priests' line of descent was, they flatly declared that every one of the three hundred and forty-five figures pointed out by them represented a *piromis*, who was in turn the son of another *piromis* – which meant that none could be the offspring of a god or a hero. (A *piromis*, by the way, is what in Greek would be termed 'a man of quality'.[66])

[144] To reiterate the point that was being made by the priests: all the statues portrayed people who, far from being gods, could hardly have been less divine. Nevertheless, long before their time, there had indeed been gods who governed Egypt, living alongside mortals, who always fully accepted that one of their number should rule supreme. The last of these gods to rule as king was Horus (or Apollo, as he is known by the Greeks), the son of Osiris (which is to say, in Greek, *Dionysus*). It was by overthrowing Typhon[67] that Horus became the last god to sit on the throne of Egypt.

[145] The Greeks hold that Heracles, Dionysus and Pan are the youngest of the gods, but the Egyptians believe that Pan was one of the primal divinities, or the 'Eight', as they are termed, and is therefore very ancient indeed; that Heracles belonged to the second generation of gods, the so-called 'Twelve'; and that Dionysus belonged to the third, the one that was born of the 'Twelve'. I have already given the number of years that separate Heracles from the reign of Amasis, according to the Egyptian account, while Pan is said to be older still; and the span of time between Dionysus and Amasis, although the narrowest of the three, is still reckoned to have been fifteen thousand years. The Egyptians claim their knowledge of these dates to be absolutely precise, derived from a regular addition of the years and an unbroken chronicling of their passage. But the Dionysus who is said to have been the son of Semele, Cadmus' daughter, was born one thousand [and six hundred] years ago; Heracles, the son of Alcmene, some nine hundred years ago; and Pan, the son of Penelope (according to the Greeks, at any rate, who make Pan the son of Penelope and Hermes), approximately eight

hundred years before my time – a shorter period than has elapsed since the Trojan War![68]

[146] As to which of these two different traditions is the more trustworthy, people must decide for themselves, of course; but I certainly know what I think, and have already spelled it out. After all, if it were truly the case that Dionysus the son of Semele, and Pan the son of Penelope, had suddenly appeared in Greece and started ageing, just as Heracles the son of Amphitryon did, then one could certainly argue that they too, like Heracles, were simply men, sprung from a mortal mother, and given the names of gods who had existed long before their time. The fact is, however, that according to the Greeks no sooner had Dionysus been born than Zeus was sewing him up into his thigh, and taking him off to Nysa, in Ethiopia, south of Egypt; while Greek tradition about what happened to Pan after his birth is wholly silent. It seems self-evident to me, then, that the names of these particular gods must have been picked up by the Greeks much later than those of the other gods. It is the various moments in time when this occurred which provided the Greeks with the starting-points from which they subsequently traced the family trees of the respective gods.

[147] Now up until this point I have drawn for my reports exclusively upon what the Egyptians themselves have to say; but henceforward I will relate the consensus of both native and non-Egyptian sources as to what happened in the country, supplemented by some observations of my own. It so happened that following the reign of the priest of Hephaestus, the Egyptians found themselves without a master; but because at no point in the past had they been able to live without a king, they divided up the whole country into twelve separate parts, and established twelve separate kingships. Numerous marriages were then arranged between these various dynasties, and a rule was established that none of them should attempt the overthrow of any of their peers, nor the accumulation of a disproportionate concentration of resources, but that they should instead maintain the friendliest of relations. This arrangement was first negotiated, and then rigorously enforced, because there had been a prophecy, delivered at the very moment when their regimes were established, that whichever of them poured a libation from a bronze bowl inside the temple of Hephaestus would become the king of all Egypt. (It was the practice of the kings to meet together in a whole range of shrines.)

[148] It was also agreed that they should leave a common memorial to themselves, a decision which prompted them to build a labyrinth, in a spot close to the so-called City of the Crocodiles, not far beyond Lake Moeris. It is a wonder beyond description – and I speak as someone who has seen it with his own eyes. Certainly, there can be no doubting that the Labyrinth would have cost more in terms of sweat and gold than all the walls and public monuments built by the Greeks put together (although I grant that the temples of Ephesus and Samos[69] do indeed merit high praise). Now, the pyramids too, of course, are structures which beggar description, with just one of them ranking as equivalent to a whole number of the greatest monuments raised by Greek labour. But even the pyramids come second to the Labyrinth. It has twelve roofed courtyards, each one with a gateway, six of which are set in a straight line along the north side, and six of which directly mirror them along the south side. These courtyards are entirely enclosed by a single exterior wall. The building itself consists of two storeys, one underground and one raised over it, each level containing fifteen hundred rooms – making a total of three thousand rooms in all. Now, because I went on a tour through the ground-level rooms, I saw them for myself, and can therefore speak from first-hand experience; but everything I learned about the underground chambers, I derived from what I was told. According to the officials who are in charge there, the lower level contains the tombs of the kings who built the Labyrinth, and of the sacred crocodiles as well, and it is for this reason that it is absolutely out of bounds. As regards the underground chambers, then, I was dependent on hearsay; but suffice it to say that the chambers on the ground level, which I did see, are on a scale to dwarf every other work of man. Take the corridors which lead from vestibule to vestibule, for instance, or the passages which twist with such intricacy between the various courtyards: these, as we wound our way from a courtyard to some chambers, and then from the chambers to a colonnade, and on from the colonnade into some vestibules, and then from the vestibules back out into a courtyard, provided a source of limitless wonderment to me. The entire complex, roof as well as walls, is fashioned out of stone; the walls are crowded with carved figures, and every courtyard is framed by pillars of exquisitely fitted white limestone. Near the corner where the Labyrinth ends there is a pyramid, 240 feet high, and incised with massive beasts, which can be accessed by means of an underground passageway.

[149] Yet astounding though the Labyrinth is, not even the catalogue of its wonders that I have just been detailing can rival the lake beside which it was built. The circumference of Lake Moeris, as it is known, is as long as the coastline of Egypt itself: 3,600 stades, or 60 *schoeni*. The elongation of the lake runs on an axis from north to south, and its depth, at its very deepest point, is 50 fathoms. Clear evidence that it was excavated by human hand is furnished by the lake itself, for almost in its dead centre there are two pyramids, both of which project above the surface of the water to a height of 50 fathoms, and extend below it an identical distance; both are also surmounted by a seated figure on a throne, colossal in size and made of stone. In all, then, the pyramids measure a total of 100 fathoms – or, since one fathom equals 6 feet, a stade of 600 feet. (It is worth mentioning as well that, bearing in mind one foot equals 4 palms, and a cubit 6 palms, one fathom is equivalent to 4 cubits.) The whole region suffers terribly from drought, so the lake is fed, not by natural springs, but by canals which lead from the Nile. For six months they carry water from the river into the lake, and then for six months they carry water back from the lake into the Nile. Throughout the six-month period when its waters are ebbing away, its fish profit the royal treasury to the tune of a whole talent of silver every day; and every day, as the waters flow back in, it yields 20 *minae*.

[150] According to the locals, the lake also drains westwards into the Gulf of Syrtis in Libya by means of a subterranean passageway which runs inland along the hills to the south of Memphis. One puzzle which nagged at me was the absence, certainly that I could see, of any piles of earth left over from the excavation; and so I asked those who lived right next to the lake where all the mounds left by the diggers might be. Their answer, explaining where the earth had been taken, was one that readily convinced me, for I had heard tell of a very similar occurrence in Nineveh, the capital of Assyria. Sardanapalus,[70] the king of Nineveh, was a man possessed of an immense treasure, which he kept under lock and key in underground vaults – and which some thieves took it into their heads to steal. What they did, starting from their own houses, was to plot the course that a tunnel to the royal palace would have to take – and then they dug. Every night, they would remove the piles of earth from their excavations, and dump it in the Tigris, the river which flows past Nineveh, until they arrived at their target. It was the same method, so I heard, which was deployed in the excavation of the lake in Egypt – albeit that

it was done by day, and not by night. All the earth dug up by the Egyptians was taken by them and dumped into the Nile, which duly bore it away and dispersed it. And that, it is said, is how the lake was excavated.

[151] Now a time came when the twelve kings, all of whom had behaved with great propriety towards one another, met to offer sacrifices in the sanctuary of Hephaestus; and on the last day of the festival, just when they were due to pour out libations, the high priest brought them golden bowls as were always used to make such offerings. But he had miscounted: twelve kings there may have been, but there were only eleven bowls. As a result, Psammetichus, who was last in line, found himself without one; so he took off his bronze helmet, held it out, and used it to pour the libation. No ulterior motive had lurked behind this gesture; all the other kings had been wearing identical helmets of bronze too, as was their custom. Nevertheless, what Psammetichus had done did not escape their notice; nor did the warning of the oracle slip their mind, that whichsoever of their number used a bronze cup for pouring out a libation would be sole king of all Egypt. After a close interrogation, however, which established that Psammetichus had acted without premeditation, they decided that it was hardly reasonable to kill him, and that the best option would therefore be to strip him of the majority of his powers, exile him to the marshes and ban him from ever leaving them, or from having any form of contact with the rest of Egypt.

[152] This was not the first time that Psammetichus had gone into exile, although on the previous occasion (which had followed the execution of his father, Necos, by Sabacos, the Ethiopian) his refuge had been Syria; only after Sabacos was gone, in consequence of the vision shown to him in his dream, had Egyptians from the province of Sais brought Psammetichus back. And now a second time he had been forced into exile, even though he was king, driven into the marshes by his eleven peers – and all because of the business with the helmet. Psammetichus, all too conscious of how disrespectfully he had been treated, kept meditating vengeance on those responsible for his exile. Accordingly, he directed an enquiry to the most trustworthy oracle in the whole of Egypt, [that of Leto] in the city of Bouto; and back duly came its answer. 'Retribution will come from the sea', the oracle declared, 'in the form of men of bronze.' That men of bronze would ever come to his assistance struck Psammetichus as improbable in the extreme. But then,

not long afterwards, it happened that some Ionian and Carian freebooters were swept off-course and forced to land in Egypt, where they duly
stepped ashore, all sheathed in bronze.[71] When an Egyptian, who had
never before seen men wearing bronze armour, made his way into the
marshes, and informed Psammetichus that bronze men had arrived
from the sea and were stripping the plain bare, Psammetichus, who realized that the oracle was in the process of being fulfilled, befriended the
Ionians and the Carians, promising them rich rewards and persuading
them to rally to his cause. Then, having secured their support, he
deployed these new allies alongside his own Egyptian partisans and
overthrew his fellow-kings.

[153] Now master of the whole of Egypt, Psammetichus added a
gateway for Hephaestus in Memphis, facing the winds of the south, and
in front of it built a courtyard sacred to Apis.[72] It is here, whenever Apis
makes an appearance, that the god is looked after. The entire courtyard
is surrounded by a colonnade covered with reliefs and featuring, instead
of pillars, colossal figures some eighteen feet high. Apis is known by the
Greeks as Epaphus.

[154] The reward of the Ionians and the Carians who had helped
Psammetichus to win the throne was to be settled on the banks of the
Nile, the Ionians on one side and the Carians on the other, on plots of
land which together came to be known as 'The Encampments'. Psammetichus also made sure, in addition to this gift of property, to make
good on all the promises that he had made his allies, and to give them
charge of some Egyptian children, who were to be taught fluency in
Greek. Indeed, to such effect did these children end up mastering the
language that all the interpreters in Egypt, right to this very day, trace
descent from them. The lands granted to the Ionians and the Carians,
where they remained based for a considerable time, were located close
to the sea, on an arm of the Nile known as the Pelusiac Mouth, not far
south of the city of Bubastis. Eventually, however, they were deported
from this region by King Amasis, who wanted a bodyguard capable of
keeping his own people in check, and so resettled them in Memphis.
These were the first foreigners ever to put down roots in Egypt; and it is
thanks to their having made the country their home, and thanks to our
own close contacts with them, that we Greeks have had such reliable
information[73] about the progress of events in Egypt from the time of
King Psammetichus onwards. Even in my own day, in the region that

was their base prior to their expulsion, there are still ruins of their homes and traces of their slipways to be seen.

[155] This, of course, is not the first occasion that I have had to mention the Egyptian oracle, and so I will now give the account of it that it properly deserves. The oracle is sacred to Leto and is to be found in a vast city beside the Nile, on what, from the perspective of anyone sailing upriver from the sea, is the right bank of the so-called Sebennytic Mouth. The name of the city that hosts the oracle is Bouto, as I have already said, and in it there is a sanctuary of Apollo and Artemis. The oracle is to be found in the shrine to Leto, which is very large, and has a monumental gateway 60 feet tall. Of all its wonders, however, there is one in particular that I really must mention. Within its precinct is a temple of Leto fashioned out of a single square block of stone, all except its roof! Each of the walls of this cube measures 60 feet by 60. The roof itself consists of another block of stone, complete with 6-foot cornices.

[156] Of all the shrine's sights, this temple was certainly the one that I personally found the most jaw-dropping; but running it second was an island by the name of Chemmis. This island is in the deep lake which stretches beyond the sanctuary in Bouto, and according to the Egyptians it floats. I was stupefied to hear this (all the more so because, speaking for myself, I never once saw it float or move an inch), but was told that, yes, it truly does lack moorings. It has lots of palms growing on it, together with other trees, some of which bear fruit, and some of which do not; there is also a huge temple of Apollo, complete with three altars, on the island. As to why it should float, the Egyptians have a story which they tell in explanation: that once, at a time when it was still secured to the bottom of the lake, there lived in Bouto one of the Eight Gods, Leto, on the very spot where her oracle stands today; that she was entrusted with the care of Apollo by Isis; and that when Typhon, in his desperation to find the son of Osiris, set to roaming the world and ransacking it, she kept Apollo safe by hiding him on the island that to this day is known as 'The Floating Island'. It was Dionysus and Isis, according to the Egyptians, who were the parents of Apollo and Artemis, while Leto was the one who suckled them and kept them safe. The name that the Egyptians give to Apollo is Horus, to Demeter Isis, and to Artemis Bubastis. It was solely thanks to the influence of the tradition I have described here that Aeschylus,[74] the son of Euphorion, took a step that no other poet had ever previously thought to consider, that of mak-

ing Artemis Demeter's daughter. It is this story, according to the Egyptians, which explains why the island floats. Such, at any rate, is their claim.

[157] Psammetichus was on the throne of Egypt for fifty-four years, for twenty-nine of which he was camped out in front of Azotus, a large city in Syria, which he kept under siege until it was his. There is no other city, certainly so far as I am aware, that has ever managed to hold out against a siege[75] for longer than Azotus.

[158] Psammetichus was succeeded as king of Egypt by his son Necos, who was the first to set his hand to the digging of a canal through to the Red Sea, a project that was subsequently completed by Darius of Persia. Lengthwise, this canal is equivalent to a four-day voyage, and in terms of breadth was dug so as to permit two triremes[76] to row side by side. Water, which is channelled into it from the Nile, joins the canal just a little way south of Bubastis, then flows past the Arabian town of Patoumus, and onwards into the Red Sea. The first stretch to be dug was across those parts of the Egyptian plain which abut Arabia, just a little to the north of the mountain range that extends past Memphis, and contains the stone-quarries. The canal then runs parallel to the foothills of this range, in a long line heading from west to east, before passing through a gorge and veering southwards from the mountains, following the direction of the south wind until it enters the Arabian Gulf. As the crow flies, the most direct way to get from the northerly sea to what is known as the Red Sea in the south is to cross from Mount Casium, on the border between Egypt and Syria, down to the Arabian Gulf, a distance of exactly 1,000 stades. This, as I say, would be the shortest route – but the canal, because it jags this way and that, is correspondingly that much longer. The digging of it in Necos' reign cost the lives of 120,000 Egyptians. Midway through the excavations, however, Necos was prompted to abandon the entire project by an oracle, which warned him that all his efforts would end up serving the needs of a barbarian. ('Barbarian', I should explain, is a word applied by the Egyptians to all who do not speak their tongue.)[77]

[159] So it was that Necos gave up on his canal, and devoted his energies instead to military campaigns. He ordered the building of triremes, some on the northern coast and some on the Arabian Gulf near the Red Sea, where the slipways can still be seen; these various ships he deployed as the need arose. Necos also engaged the Syrians by land, defeating them at Magdolus, and pressing on in the wake of this

victory to capture Cadytis, a Syrian town of great significance. The clothes which he had been wearing while performing these deeds he subsequently sent as an offering to Apollo at Branchidae, in the territory of Miletus. Then, after a reign of sixteen years in total, he met his end, leaving the rule of Egypt to Psammis, his son.

[160] It was to this same Psammis, now king of Egypt, that a visit was paid by a deputation of Eleans, who boasted that so fair and flawless was their organization of the Olympic Games that there was no one in the whole world who could conceivably improve upon it, not even the Egyptians themselves, who were quite without peers in wisdom. Following the arrival of the Eleans in Egypt, however, and the announcement of all that they had to say, King Psammis convened a meeting of those said to be the very best minds among his subjects. This panel of Egyptians then interviewed the Eleans, who replied by giving a full account of the regulations which governed their ordering of the games. Once they had completed this exhaustive breakdown, they declared their mission: to find out whether the Egyptians could suggest any improvements which would make the games even fairer. The experts put their heads together, then asked the Eleans whether it was permitted for their own citizens to compete in the games. 'Yes,' came the answer, 'the games are open to any Greek who wishes to enter them – whether he be from Elis or anywhere else.' 'But if you were the ones responsible for that rule,' exclaimed the Egyptians, 'how can that possibly be fair? Suppose one of your fellow-citizens does enter a race. There is absolutely no way that he is not going to benefit from your favouritism, which will then inevitably penalize the foreign contestants. If it is truly the case that you wish to make the games fairer, and that this is why you travelled to Egypt, then what we would propose is this: that all Eleans be banned from taking part in the various events, which should be open instead exclusively to foreign competitors.' Such was the recommendation that the Egyptians made to the Eleans.[78]

[161] A mere six years into his reign, Psammis invaded Ethiopia; but very soon afterwards he died and was succeeded by Apries, his son. This king enjoyed a happier and more prosperous reign than that of any king before him, with the sole exception of Psammetichus, his great-grandfather. Twenty-five years Apries ruled, during which time he attacked Sidon by land, and fought the Tyrians by sea. Nevertheless, it was fated that he should come to a wretched end,[79] a development that had its

origins in an episode which I will describe more fully in my disquisition on Libya, and will therefore only touch upon here. It happened that Apries launched an attack on the Cyrenaeans which met with a reverse as disastrous as the original task-force had been large-scale, and the Egyptians, putting the blame for this calamity on their king, revolted. This was prompted by their conviction that Apries had knowingly sent them off to what was bound to be their doom, calculating that the destruction of the army would enable him to tighten his hold on those of his subjects who remained. So monstrous did this seem to the return-ees, and to those who had been left bereaved by the loss of their friends, that they rose in open rebellion.

[162] When Apries learned what was happening, he dispatched a man called Amasis to argue them into laying down their arms. But no sooner had Amasis arrived, and begun reining in the Egyptians by haranguing them, than one of the rebels who had been standing right behind him put a helmet on his head, and as he did so declared, 'I crown you king!' This coronation, as events would make clear, was certainly not unwelcome to Amasis; for once the rebels had installed him as their candidate to be king of Egypt, he threw himself into preparations for a campaign against Apries. When Apries discovered what had happened, he sent a close adviser of his named Patarbemis, one of the most distin-guished men in all Egypt, with orders to bring Amasis back alive. Patarbemis duly arrived in the rebel camp, and called out Amasis' name; Amasis, though, who was sitting on his horse at the time, rose from his saddle, let rip a fart and told his visitor to take that back to Apries. 'But it is the king who has summoned you,' Patarbemis insisted, 'and so it is only proper that you should go to him!' 'Oh, don't you worry,' answered Amasis, 'I have spent plenty of time getting ready to call on him. Apries will have no cause to complain about my behaviour on that score. I will be there – and I will be bringing others with me too!' After hearing Amasis declare this, and witnessing the sheer scale of his preparations, Patarbemis no longer had any illusions as to what was being planned; and so he hurried off without delay to clarify for the king everything that was afoot. But when Patarbemis came back into his presence with-out Amasis, Apries would not permit him so much as to open his mouth, but instead flew into a towering rage, and ordered his ears and nose cut off.[80] The great mass of the Egyptians, who hitherto had been minded to stay loyal to Apries, were so appalled to see a man of such high reputation

treated in such a shameful and humiliating manner that they promptly went over to the rebels, and put themselves at the disposal of Amasis.

[163] When this news too had been brought to Apries, he armed his mercenaries, a bodyguard of thirty thousand Carians and Ionians. (He also had a palace in the city of Sais, a vast building, well worth seeing).[81] Headlong, Apries advanced against the Egyptians; serried all around him, as he went on the attack, there were foreign troops, and all around Amasis, as he went on the attack, there were men of Egypt. The two sides ended up at the city of Momemphis, and it was there that they readied themselves to put the other to the test.

[164] Now, the people of Egypt are divided up into seven social classes, each one named after a profession; one, for instance, is called the 'priests', another the 'warriors', then there are the 'cowherds', the 'swineherds', the 'tradesmen', the 'interpreters' and the 'steersmen'. The warrior class consists of two further sub-divisions known as the 'Calasiries' and the 'Hermotybies', each of which is drawn from a range of the various provinces into which Egypt is divided.

[165] The provinces from which the Hermotybies derive are Busiris, Sais, Chemmis, Papremis, an island by the name of Prosopitis, and half of Natho. These, and these alone, constitute the home-provinces of the Hermotybies, who at one point, when they were at their most numerous, totalled one hundred and sixty thousand. Such is their devotion to the arts required of a warrior that none has ever bothered himself to learn a manual craft.[82]

[166] The Calasiries are drawn from the remaining provinces: Thebes, Bubastis, Aphthis, Tanis, Mendes, Sebennys, Athribis, Pharbaethus, Thmuis, Onuphis, Anysis and an island opposite Bubastis named Myecphoris. These, and these alone, constitute the home-provinces of the Calasiries, who at one point, when they were at their most numerous, totalled two hundred and fifty thousand. They too, like the Hermotybies, are banned from working in trade, but must instead devote themselves exclusively to the arts of war, with son succeeding father.

[167] Whether this, like so much else, was something that the Greeks picked up from the Egyptians I hesitate to pronounce upon with any certainty; I have noticed that the Thracians too, and the Scythians, the Persians and the Lydians, and almost all the barbarians in fact, hold that those of their countrymen who learn some specialized skill and pass it

on down the generations are dishonoured by it, while those who keep their hands free of handicrafts – and especially if they devote themselves to war – are ranked as the noblest. Indisputably, however, this attitude of contempt towards manual craftsmen is one that all the Greeks have absorbed, with the Lacedaemonians holding to it the most vehemently, and the Corinthians the least.

[168] There were certain privileges enjoyed by the Egyptian warrior class, which they shared exclusively with the priests: each warrior, for instance, would be awarded a tax-exempt plot of land measuring 12 acres. (An acre in Egypt is equivalent to a Samian acre.) Nevertheless, although all warriors received this grant of land as an individual perquisite, the farming of it was done in rotation, so that no one person ever cultivated the same plot two years in a row. Annually, a thousand Calasiries and a thousand Hermotybies would be recruited to serve the king as his bodyguard. Each guard would receive, in addition to the standard plot of land, a daily ration consisting of five pounds of cooked grain, two pounds of beef and four cupfuls of wine. All the royal spear-carriers would receive this ration without fail.

[169] Both sides had arrived in the city of Momemphis – Apries at the head of his mercenaries, and Amasis leading all the Egyptians – and now they met in battle. The foreign troops, despite putting up a good fight, were massively outnumbered, and duly overwhelmed. So much, then, for the confidence of Apries in his hold upon the kingdom, and in his reputed conviction that not even a god could serve to loosen it. Battle saw him brought low: he was captured alive and carted off to the city of Sais, to the very property which had formerly been his own, but was now the palace of Amasis. For a while he was put up in the palace and treated well by Amasis; but eventually criticisms were raised by the Egyptians that justice was being grotesquely ill served by this cosseting of a man who was both a confirmed public enemy and a personal adversary of Amasis himself. Apries was duly placed by Amasis into the hands of the Egyptian people, who strangled him and then consigned him to his ancestral vault. This consisted of a collection of tombs within the sanctuary of Athena, very close to the great hall of the temple, on the left-hand side as one enters. Here, within the temple, is where the people of Sais have buried all the kings who have hailed from their province. In fact, even the tomb of Amasis, though not as close to the great hall as the tombs of Apries and his forefathers, can be found inside the temple

courtyard – a massive columned portico built out of stone, adorned with pillars in the shape of palm trees, and with no expense spared. Set within this colonnade are two doorways, and beyond the doorways the tomb-vault itself.

[170] Also buried in Sais is the One whose name it would be sacrilegious of me to mention in a context such as this; his tomb lies within the sanctuary of Athena, behind the temple, and runs the entire length of one of the sanctuary walls. Also standing within the enclosure are massive stone obelisks,[83] and next to these a lake ornamented with stone around its rim, expertly fashioned along each of its sides, and equal in size, I reckon, to the so-called 'Round Pond' in Delos.

[171] It is this lake which provides the setting for night-time evocations of the god's suffering, to which the Egyptians give the name 'Mysteries'.[84] Now, although I am conversant with these performances, and have a comprehensive grasp of their essence, it is hardly proper for me to betray what is known about them. Likewise, with regard to the rites that are sacred to Demeter, and are called the 'Thesmophoria' by the Greeks, I will breathe not a word, beyond what it is legitimate to report. It was the daughters of Danaus who brought the rite from Egypt, and taught it to the Pelasgian women. Subsequently, in the wake of the ethnic cleansing of the Peloponnese by the Dorians, the knowledge of the Thesmophoria was almost entirely eradicated,[85] and that it survived at all was due entirely to the Arcadians, for they, alone of the Peloponnesians, avoided being uprooted.

[172] With Apries overthrown, it was now Amasis who sat on the throne. He came from the province of Sais, and his hometown was a city called Siouph. He was initially despised by the Egyptians, and held in low esteem, for the simple reason that his background was a humble and undistinguished one; but Amasis, who was certainly not a man to permit any resentment at this to cloud his habitual good sense, in due course won his subjects over. He possessed, among all his countless other treasures, a golden foot-bath which he and his dinner guests were in the habit of using whenever they wished to wash their feet. Amasis had it recycled and made into the statue of a god, which he then installed at the spot in the city most suited to such an image; and the Egyptians, flocking to it day in and day out, treated it with the utmost reverence. When this behaviour of the city's inhabitants was brought to Amasis' attention, he convened an assembly of the Egyptian people, and revealed

to them that the statue which they were now venerating so dutifully had been made from the same foot-bath into which so many of them had once vomited, and urinated, and dunked their dirty feet. 'Me and this foot-bath,' he went on to say, 'we are made of the same clay! Once, after all, I was a man as ordinary as can be, and yet now I am your king. Honour me, then! Show me respect!' And so it was, as a result of this, that Amasis persuaded the Egyptians to accept the reality that they were indeed his slaves.[86]

[173] His daily routine was most distinctive. From dawn until such time as the market-square had filled up with people, he would handle with great conscientiousness all the business that was brought to him; but then, from the mid-morning onwards, he would drink and make jokes with his boozing companions, and clown around with them, and devote himself to having fun. In due course, his friends became so vexed by all this that they delivered him a warning: 'Your Majesty, this lack of self-restraint which your chasing after every idle pleasure betrays is an attribute most ill suited to a king. Far better to sit all day in solemn splendour, framed by the majesty of your throne, attending to affairs of state – for only then will the Egyptians properly appreciate how great a man they have as their ruler. Give heed to your reputation, for your behaviour as it stands is the very opposite of regal!' But to this Amasis had a ready retort. 'It is only when archers need to fire their bows that they bother stringing them. Once the arrows have been shot, they make sure to unstring them again. A bow that was kept strung all the time would surely snap, and what use would it be then to its owner when it was needed once again? Well, so it is with the daily routine of a man. Anyone can play things solemnly all the time and refuse to relax for so much as a moment, if that is what he really wishes, but it is a purblind course of action all the same, which invariably results in breakdowns and debilitating fits. It is precisely because I have grasped this that I choose to divide my time between business and pleasure.' Such was the rebuttal that Amasis delivered to his friends.

[174] Not that Amasis had ever been a man renowned for his sobriety. Even when he was only a private citizen, it is said, he had always been a great one for a drink and a joke. So much so, indeed, that whenever his drinking and partying left him short of funds, he would embark on a round of burglaries. All those who subsequently accused Amasis of harbouring their stolen property would be met by such wide-eyed

protestations of innocence that they would invariably end up hauling him off to the nearest oracular shrine, wherever that might be. However, although there were some oracles which did indeed convict him, so there were some which cleared his name – and this, when Amasis became king, had a strong influence on his policy towards them. The sanctuaries of those gods who had acquitted him of theft could certainly expect no favours from him. Rather, all the funding for their upkeep was cut, nor would Amasis visit them to perform any rites of sacrifice, on the grounds that the gods who inhabited them were mere phantoms, and their seats of prophecy spoke nothing but lies. On the sanctuaries which had convicted him of theft, however, he lavished devotion. For the gods who inhabited them, Amasis explained, were true gods, and the oracles that they delivered had no taint of falsehood.

[175] One particularly striking architectural project of his, a true wonder, was the gateway to the sanctuary of Athena in Sais. It was so towering, and built on such a scale, and fashioned out of such vast and expensively sourced blocks of stone, that it quite overshadowed all the efforts of his rivals. No less striking, however, were the colossal statues and towering, human-headed sphinxes which he presented as dedications to the temple, together with all the restoration work which saw truly massive blocks of stone being transported there. Some of these came from the quarries in Memphis; but others, the very largest of all, came from the city of Elephantine, which it can take a whole twenty days by boat to reach from Sais. There was one wonder more than any other, however, which I found truly astounding: a chamber hollowed out from a single block of stone, and which was brought all the way from the city of Elephantine. Its transportation took three years, and the efforts of two thousand men, all of whom belonged to the class of the steersmen and had been appointed specifically to the task. The external dimensions of this chamber measure 21 cubits along, 14 cubits across and 8 cubits from the ground, while measured from within, and setting the external measurements to one side, the dimensions are 18 cubits and one *pygon* along, 12 cubits across and 5 cubits up. The chamber is to be found by the entrance to the shrine. As to why this should be so, there is a story told which explains the failure to haul it within the sanctuary itself. The chief architect, it is said, as he watched the workmen hauling on the chamber, reflected on how much time had been devoted to the project, and let out a great groan of weariness – which so touched the

heart of Amasis that he forbade the architect to continue with the labour of transportation any further. That said, there are some who tell a different story, and claim that one of the workmen was crushed to death beneath the chamber as he was helping to move it along on rollers, and that this is the reason why the hauling of it was abandoned.

[176] Amasis also contributed astonishingly large additions to all the other sanctuaries of note in Egypt, among which the 75-foot-long recumbent figure in front of the temple of Hephaestus in Memphis is particularly prominent. Flanking it on either side of its base are two other figures, both of them standing upright to a height of twenty feet, and both fashioned out of Ethiopian stone. What is more, in Sais there is a stone figure on the same scale as the one in Memphis, and which lies on its back in an identical manner. Also in Memphis, Amasis built from scratch to finish what is a truly mighty and remarkable sanctuary of Isis.

[177] His reign, so it is reported, saw Egypt attain a pinnacle of prosperity. For the river blessed the land with wealth, and the land likewise blessed its people. So flourishing were its cities that the number of settlements totalled two thousand in all. It was Amasis, moreover, who laid it down as a law of the land that each Egyptian, every year, should make a declaration before the governor of his province as to how he derived his living. The fixed penalty for refusing to do so, or for failing to demonstrate an honest source of income, was instant death. This was a law which was subsequently borrowed from Egypt by Solon of Athens, and imposed upon the Athenians. And long may it remain in force – for, as a law, it can hardly be bettered.[87]

[178] In turn, there was much about the Greeks that Amasis had come to admire, and he displayed this affection for them in various ways. Many benefited from it, but none more so than those who had emigrated to Egypt, for they were granted the city of Naucratis to serve them as a home away from home. To those Greeks who did not want to put down roots, however, but were only occasional visitors to the various harbours of the country, he granted plots of land on which they could set up altars and sanctuaries to their gods. The largest of these sanctuaries, and the most widely talked about and frequented, is called 'The Hellenium',[88] which was instituted as a joint venture by a whole number of cities: of these, Chios, Teus, Phocaea and Clazomenae were Ionian; Rhodes, Cnidos, Halicarnassus and Phaselis were Dorian; of the Aeolian cities, only Mytilene contributed. All of them share in the

ownership of the sanctuary, as well as providing the officials who administer the port. Any other cities which stake a claim to the sanctuary do so under false pretences, for they have no right to it at all. That said, there is a sanctuary of Zeus which was built exclusively by the Aeginetans, a sanctuary of Hera which was built by the Samians and a sanctuary of Apollo for which the Milesians were responsible.

[179] Originally, however, there was no other port of trade in Egypt apart from Naucratis. Whenever anyone turned up in any of the other arms of the Nile, he would be obliged to swear on oath that his arrival there had been involuntary, and then, once his statement had been taken, to sail with his ship to the Canobic Mouth. Alternatively, should contrary winds render the voyage impossible, he would be obliged to convey his cargo around the Delta by barge, until it had docked at Naucratis – a measure of the exclusivity of the privileges that Naucratis enjoyed.[89]

[180] When the temple that pre-dated the current one at Delphi accidentally burned down, and the project of rebuilding it was put out to tender by the Amphictyons,[90] the bill came to a total of 300 talents, of which the Delphians[91] themselves were obliged to foot a quarter. The Delphians accordingly wandered from city to city, soliciting what donations they could – and of these, not the least generous came from Egypt. Amasis contributed 1,000 talents of alum, and the Greeks resident in Egypt 20 *minae*.

[181] Amasis also forged a treaty of friendship and alliance with the Cyrenaeans, and even saw fit to marry one of their women – either because he had set his heart on having a Greek wife, or else because he wished to set the seal on his friendship with the Cyrenaeans. All are agreed that the name of his bride was Ladice, but accounts vary as to whether she was the daughter of Battus, who was the son of Arcesilaus, or of Critobulus, who was one of the pre-eminent men of Cyrene. Whenever Amasis came to sleep with her, however, he found himself quite unable to consummate the marriage, although he had never had any such problem with his other wives. 'Curse you, woman,' he snarled at Ladice, after this had happened once too often; 'you must have fed me some potion! No alternative, then, but to inflict on you the most horrible death that any woman has ever suffered!' Ladice's many denials could not serve to mollify him, and so she raised a silent prayer to Aphrodite, vowing that if only Amasis managed to sleep with her that

night, and so make good the whole disaster, she would send a statue of the goddess to Cyrene. Sure enough, no sooner had she made this promise than Amasis was having his way with her to triumphant effect. Indeed, from that moment on, he only had to be with Ladice to find himself quite unable to keep his hands off her, so besotted with her had he become. Meanwhile, Ladice made sure to fulfil her vow to the goddess: she had a statue fashioned and sent to Cyrene, where it was installed outside the city. (It was still safe and sound there in my time.) In the wake of the Persian conquest of Egypt, Cambyses made enquiries as to the identity of this same Ladice, and had her sent home unharmed to Cyrene.

[182] Amasis presented a number of votive offerings in the Greek world as well. To Cyrene he gave a gilded statue of Athena, and a painted portrait of himself; to the sanctuary of Athena in Lindus, two stone statues and a remarkable linen breastplate; to the sanctuary of Hera in Samos, two wooden statues of himself (still there in my time) positioned behind the doors of the great temple. These latter gifts were presented by Amasis to Samos in acknowledgement of the formal ties of guest-friendship[92] that bound him to Polycrates, the son of Aeaces; the offering made to Lindus, however, was prompted by no such relationship, but rather by the tradition which attributed the founding of the sanctuary of Athena there to the daughters of Danaus, who were supposed to have made a brief landfall on the island during the course of their flight from the sons of Aegyptus.[93] Such, then, was the sum of the offerings made by Amasis. He was also the first man to conquer Cyprus and force it to pay tribute.

BOOK THREE

[1] This, then, was the Amasis against whom Cambyses, the son of Cyrus, was leading an army drawn from all the peoples subject to him, Greeks included – to be specific, Ionians and Aeolians.[1] What lay behind the invasion? Cambyses had made a demand of Amasis, through a herald dispatched to Egypt, that he hand over one of his daughters to him – a demand which had in turn been made on the prompting of an Egyptian with a grudge against Amasis. This physician, alone among his colleagues, had been torn away by royal edict from his wife and children, and packed off to Persia, after Amasis had received a request from Cyrus for the best eye-doctor in Egypt.[2] No wonder, then, that the Egyptian should have been so filled with resentment that he succeeded in pressing (indeed, almost instructing) Cambyses into asking for a daughter from Amasis – who was then confronted by the choice of surrendering his daughter at the cost of deep personal distress, or of rebuffing the request, and making an enemy of Cambyses. Already vexed by the menace of Persian power, Amasis found himself quite unable to answer yes or no. He knew full well that his daughter would be taken by Cambyses not as a wife, but as a concubine;[3] and so it was with this in mind that he finally settled on a course of action. It so happened that the one surviving member of the previous royal house was a daughter of Apries, a strikingly statuesque and handsome girl named Nitetis. Amasis duly arrayed her in fine clothes and gold jewellery, and sent her off to Persia, as though she were his own daughter. In due course, however, when Cambyses happened to address the girl by her father's name, she replied, 'You have no idea, my Lord, just how badly Amasis has abused you. Despite the fact that he dispatched me to you decked out in all this finery, as though it were indeed his own daughter that he had gift-wrapped, the

truth is that I am the daughter of Apries, the one-time master of Amasis, but lately toppled and murdered by him, him and all the Egyptians.' Such was the declaration (and such the provocation that it served to bring to light) which led Cambyses, son of Cyrus, to descend upon Egypt in a towering fury. Or so, at any rate, the Persians report.[4]

[2] The Egyptians, however, claim Cambyses as one of their own, asserting that he was the son of this same daughter of Apries, and that it was Cyrus, not Cambyses, who sent to Amasis for his daughter. In presenting this version of events, however, they are way off the mark. Indeed, since the Egyptians themselves have a better grasp than anyone of how Persian laws function, it can hardly have escaped their attention, firstly, that it is wholly illegal for a bastard to inherit the Persian throne while there is still a legitimate heir alive, and secondly, that Cambyses was the child of Cassandane, the daughter of Pharnaspes, a man of Achaemenid stock, and not an Egyptian at all. The point of the distorted account given by the Egyptians, of course, is to provide them with a feigned link of kinship to the House of Cyrus.

[3] So that is how the matter stands. There is, however, another story – one that I personally do not find persuasive – which relates how a Persian woman came in to visit the wives of Cyrus, and was so impressed by the sight of Cassandane standing there with her tall and handsome offspring that she began to lavish extravagant praise on them. But Cassandane, who was one of Cyrus' wives, only retorted, 'Yes, and see with what a lack of respect Cyrus treats me, despite the fact that I have borne him such children. The only one he has any respect for is his new acquisition from Egypt.' These comments were prompted by Cassandane's resentment of Nitetis; and they were answered by her eldest child, Cambyses. 'That, Mother,' he told her, 'is why, once I am a man, I will turn all Egypt upon its head.' He was barely ten years old when he made this promise, to the great astonishment of the women. He never forgot it, however; and sure enough, no sooner had he come of age and taken possession of the throne,[5] than he was embarking on his invasion of Egypt.

[4] There was another, quite distinct, episode, however, which also contributed to this expedition. One of the mercenaries employed by Amasis was a man named Phanes, who originally came from Halicarnassus, and was both sound in judgement and bold in war. For some reason or other, he developed a grudge against Amasis, and fled Egypt by boat, his aim being to secure an audience with Cambyses. Such had

been his standing among the mercenaries, however, and so detailed the intelligence he had on Egyptian affairs, that Amasis was frantic to capture him, and duly set about hunting him down. He dispatched in a trireme the most trustworthy of his eunuchs,[6] who duly ran his quarry to ground in Lycia. Despite this success, the eunuch did not manage to transport him back to Egypt – for Phanes ran rings round his captor. First he got his guards roaringly drunk; then off he slipped to Persia. When he arrived, he found that Cambyses, despite his enthusiasm for leading his army against Egypt, was at a loss to know which approach to take, for none of the invasion routes offered any water, and so Phanes, in addition to the intelligence that he provided on Amasis, detailed the course that should be taken. 'Make contact with the king of the Arabians,' he advised. 'Ask him for safe passage.'

[5] Certainly, there is no other obvious way into Egypt. The territory between Phoenicia and the limits of the city of Cadytis belongs to Syrians who are known as 'Palestinians'; then from Cadytis (which I would estimate to be almost on the scale of Sardis), the coastal trading-posts as far as the city of Ienysus are subject to the Arabians; beyond Ienysus, and all the way to the Serbonian marsh, where a spur of Mount Casium extends down to the sea, it reverts to Syrian control; onwards from the Serbonian marsh (in which some say Typhon[7] lies hidden), and the crossing has been made into Egypt. The tract of land between the city of Ienysus and Mount Casium and the Serbonian marsh is no small distance, for it takes some three days to cross, and is so ferociously parched as to be quite without water.

[6] I am now going to point out something which few of those who make the voyage to Egypt have thought to reflect upon.[8] Every year there is a constant flow into Egypt of earthenware jars filled with wine, imported from across the Greek world and from Phoenicia – and yet it is hardly an exaggeration to say that empty earthenware wine-jars are never seen. One might well ask, then, what on earth happens to them? This too I can answer. Every headman of a village is required to collect together all the earthenware from his own community and bring it to Memphis; and the people of Memphis must then fill the jars with water, and convey them to the same waterless stretches of Syria. This is the process by which every piece of earthenware imported into Egypt, once it has been emptied, finds its way to Syria to join all the other jars that have been assembled there over time.

[7] Now, it was the Persians, in the immediate wake of their conquest of Egypt, who provisioned the entry route into Egypt with supplies of water, in the manner I have just described; but at the time, there was not a drop to be had. So it was that Cambyses, advised of this by his foreign friend from Halicarnassus, sent messengers with a request for safe passage to the king of the Arabians – who duly answered the pledges given him by granting pledges of his own.

[8] The Arabians,[9] to a degree that few other peoples can match, regard the giving of pledges as a sacred business. Should two parties wish to make a compact, then the procedure is for a third man to stand between them and use a sharp piece of stone to score a light incision along the palms of their hands, just below their thumbs; he will then take a strip of cloth from both men's cloaks, and use the material to anoint with their blood seven stones which have been placed between them; as he does this, so will he invoke Dionysus and Urania. Once the ritual is completed, the man who is giving the pledge will commend the foreigner – or fellow-townsman, as the case may be – to his friends, and these friends will then regard it as their solemn duty to honour the pledge themselves. Apart from Urania, the only god whose existence the Arabians acknowledge is Dionysus;[10] his cropped locks, they say, provide them with the inspiration for the way in which they wear their own hair short: that is, cut in a circle, with the temples shaved. Dionysus is called *Orotalt* by the Arabians, and Urania is *Alilat*.

[9] So it was that the king of the Arabians, after he had given his word to the messengers who had come from Cambyses, devised the following plan. First he filled camel-skins with water and loaded them up onto every living camel he had; then, that done, he drove the camels out into the desert, and there awaited Cambyses' army. Such, at any rate, is the more convincing of the accounts that are given; but there is also a less convincing version which nevertheless, since it does have some plausibility, demands to be told. There is a large river in Arabia, the Corys by name,[11] which flows into the Red Sea, as it is called. The story goes that the king of the Arabians had raw ox-hides and the skins of various other animals stitched together so as to make a pipe, sufficient in length to reach from this same river to the desert; and that he then channelled water through the pipe into large reservoirs which had been dug in the desert for the purpose of receiving and storing the water. It is twelve days' journey from the river to this particular desert. There were

three pipes, and each one conducted the water to one of three locations.

[10] Psammenitus, the son of Amasis, made camp by what is known as the Pelusiac Mouth of the Nile, there to await Cambyses. Amasis himself was no longer alive by the time Cambyses came to invade Egypt, for he had died after a reign that had lasted forty-four years,[12] and never once known any serious calamity. Following his death and mummification, Amasis was laid to rest in the burial-vault that he himself had had built within the shrine. During the reign of his son, Psammenitus, over Egypt, a phenomenon was witnessed which utterly stupefied the Egyptians: rain fell on Egyptian Thebes. This was something that had never happened before; nor, according to the Thebans themselves, has it happened since, up to my own lifetime. Rain is simply not a feature of upper Egypt. On this one occasion, however, it did rain in Thebes: a light drizzle.

[11] Once the Persians had crossed the desert, they took up positions close to the Egyptians, aiming to engage them in battle; whereupon the Greeks and the Carians, who were employed as mercenaries by the Egyptian king, felt so outraged by what Phanes had done in leading an army of gibberish-spouting foreigners against Egypt, that they devised their own riposte. Phanes had children whom he had left behind in Egypt; and these children were now brought to the camp, and into the full view of their father. The mercenaries then set up a mixing-bowl midway between their own and the enemy camp, after which they led out the children one by one, and cut their throats over the mixing-bowl. After the final dispatch of all the children, wine and water were poured into the bowl as well; the mercenaries then gulped down the blood and headed off into battle. Fierce though the fighting was, however, and numerous the casualties on both sides, it was the Egyptians who finally turned tail.

[12] I witnessed something truly extraordinary there, which I was tipped off about by the locals. The site is strewn with the bones of men from both sides who fell in the battle, with those of the Persians quite distinct from those of the Egyptians, just as they were when the fighting originally began; and so brittle are the skulls of the Persians that, should you wish to make a hole in one, you would have only to tap it with a single pebble, whereas those of the Egyptians are so tough that it would be a challenge to smash them through, even if you pounded at them

with a rock. Why should this be so? The locals gave a reason which seems to me eminently plausible: namely, that Egyptians are in the habit of shaving their heads from the very earliest days of their childhood, so that the bone ends up thickened by exposure to the sun. (This also explains why Egyptians never go bald – for it is a fact that the incidence of baldness among Egyptians is the lowest anywhere in the world.) This explanation of the toughness of Egyptian skulls also serves to suggest why Persian skulls should be so brittle: the Persians keep their heads out of the sun from birth by wearing conical felt caps, or *tiaras*. So that is how the matter stands. I saw something very similar at Papremis, when I inspected the skulls of those who had perished at the side of Achaemenes, the son of Darius, at the hands of Inaros the Libyan.[13]

[13] When the Egyptians turned tail from the battlefield, they fled in disarray. Once they were all cornered in Memphis, Cambyses sent a Mytilenaean ship upriver, carrying a Persian herald whose mission it was to summon the Egyptians to negotiate. But the Egyptians, when they saw that the ship had docked in Memphis, came pouring out from behind the fortress in a great mob; they destroyed the ship, butchered and dismembered the crew and carted the remains back inside the walls. They were duly put under siege and eventually brought to surrender. Meanwhile, the Libyans who bordered Egypt were so terrified by what had happened to their neighbour that they surrendered without so much as putting up a fight, accepted tributary status and started to send Cambyses gifts. So too did the people of Cyrene and Barca, whose alarm was no less than that of the Libyans. Although Cambyses looked smilingly upon the gifts he had received from the Libyans, he frowned upon those from the Cyrenaeans – because, I would guess, they were so meagre. All that the Cyrenaeans ever sent was 500 *minae* of silver – which Cambyses scooped up in his hands and tossed out among his troops.

[14] Nine days after taking possession of the fortress of Memphis, Cambyses installed Psammenitus, the king who had reigned over the Egyptians for six months, in the outskirts of the city, with the aim of testing him by offering him insult – Psammenitus and a group of other Egyptians too. First Cambyses had the daughter of the king dressed in the clothes of a slave; then he sent her out with a bucket to fetch water, together with other unmarried girls chosen from among the daughters of Egypt's most prominent men, and dressed in a manner similar to the princess. As the girls went past their fathers, wailing and weeping, so all

the other men, when they saw the humiliation inflicted on their children, wailed and wept in answer; but Psammenitus, the moment he had seen and fathomed what was happening, only bowed his head to the ground. Then Cambyses, once the girls with their water-buckets had gone by, sent out the king's son, together with two thousand other Egyptians of the same age, all of them with ropes tied around their necks and bits placed in their mouths. They were being led to the place where they were to pay the penalty for the massacre of the Mytilenaeans in Memphis, and the destruction of the ship, for it was the decree of the royal judges that, for every casualty that had been inflicted, ten Egyptians of the highest rank should die in return. But when Psammenitus saw the young men come out and pass him by, and learned that his son was being led to execution, he did not weep as all the other Egyptians who were sitting down around him did, nor betray any agony, but instead behaved exactly as he had done while watching his daughter. Once this procession too had gone by, it happened that one of his old dining companions, a man well advanced in years but who had fallen so far from his previous estate that he had been left with nothing more than a beggar might have, came asking for alms among the soldiers, and passed by Psammenitus, the son of Amasis, and all the other Egyptians who were sitting there on the city's outskirts. At the sight of this, Psammenitus let out a great wail of misery, and beat his head, and called to his comrade by name. Now there were men, it seems, who had been set to stand guard over him, and who had been keeping Cambyses informed about Psammenitus' response to all the various processions out of the city. His reactions astounded Cambyses; and so he sent a messenger to Psammenitus with a question. 'Psammenitus,' the messenger said, 'your master, the Lord Cambyses, wants to know why you neither cried out nor sobbed at the sight of your daughter being humiliated and your son going to his death, whereas a beggar who is not even a relation of yours, so he has been informed, solicited marks of respect from you.' To this question Psammenitus answered: 'Son of Cyrus, the evils that have afflicted my own household are too great to be wept over. Tears were, however, an appropriate response to the misery of my old companion, who on the very threshold of old age has been toppled from happiness and wealth, and come to beggary.' When these words were reported back by the messenger, they seemed to those who heard them well said. According to the Egyptians, tears rose to the eyes of Croesus[14] (for he too, as luck would have it, had come to Egypt in Cambyses' train), and to the eyes of all the Persians who were gathered there, and even into Cambyses himself there entered some spark of compassion. And straightaway, he gave orders that the son of Psammenitus should be spared the fate of all the other condemned men, and that Psammenitus himself should be raised up from where he had been sitting, out on the margins of the city, and brought into his presence.

[15] The men who had gone in pursuit of Psammenitus' son discovered that he had been the very first to be hacked down, and was therefore no longer alive; but Psammenitus himself was raised up and led into the presence of Cambyses. There he passed the rest of his days, and had to endure no further brutal treatment. Indeed, had he only had the good sense to avoid meddling, he would surely have had Egypt restored to him, and been appointed its governor, for it is the habitual policy of the Persians to honour the sons of kings, and even to hand back the rule of a kingdom to the sons of those kings who rebel against them. That it is their custom to do so can readily be deduced from a whole host of other examples. Particularly notable are the cases of Thannyras, the son of Inaros, who had the position of authority that his father had lost given back to him, and of Pausiris, the son of Amyrtaeus, who also had the rulership that his father had lost restored to him – and this despite the fact that there was no one who ever did more damage to the Persians than Inaros and Amyrtaeus. As it was, however, Psammenitus paid the price for all his plots and trouble-making: for he was caught red-handed inciting the Egyptians to rebellion. When all was made known to Cambyses, Psammenitus drank the blood of a bull, and promptly dropped down dead. That was the end of him.

[16] From Memphis, Cambyses proceeded to the city of Sais; he was minded to do something there that he did, sure enough, put into practice. No sooner had he arrived in the palace of Amasis than he gave orders that Amasis' corpse was to be exhumed from its resting place, and brought outside. Once this had been done, he commanded his men to whip it, to pluck out its hairs, to stab it and to inflict on it any number of other insults. The corpse, however, because it had been mummified, stood proof against all this and refused to fall to pieces, so once the efforts of his men had brought them to the point of exhaustion, Cambyses ordered the body to be burned. Such a command was sheer sacrilege, for fire is believed by the Persians to be a god. Indeed, the

burning of corpses is contrary to the customs of both peoples: the Persians, following on from what I just said, claim that it is quite wrong to offer up a human corpse to a god, while the Egyptians hold fire to be a living, breathing beast, one that devours everything it gets in its clutches, until it is sated and expires after it has swallowed its final morsel. To give a corpse to any wild beast is absolutely contrary to Egyptian custom – which is why, to make certain that it will not be eaten by worms, they embalm it before laying it to rest. So the orders given by Cambyses broke the laws of both peoples alike.[15] The Egyptians, though, claim that this outrage was inflicted not upon Amasis, but upon some other Egyptian of a similar age – and that it was actually this man whom the Persians were insulting when they believed themselves to be insulting Amasis. The Egyptians say that Amasis had learned from an oracle what was fated to happen to him after death, and that in an effort to ward off what was coming, he had the man whose corpse had been whipped buried right by the doors inside his own tomb, and at the same time ordered his son to place his own corpse as deep as possible in the furthermost recesses of the tomb. It is my own opinion, however, that these supposed instructions of Amasis about how he and the other man were to be buried did not in fact originate with him but were made up by the Egyptians in an effort to save face.

[17] Cambyses' next step was to consult with his advisers on the viability of three separate military ventures: one against the Carthaginians, one against the Ammonians and one against the long-lived Ethiopians who inhabit Libya, beside the Southern Sea. Cambyses' decision was that he should dispatch his war-fleet against the Carthaginians, and a portion of his land-forces against the Ammonians; but that his first move against the Ethiopians should be a campaign of espionage. Under cover of taking gifts to the Ethiopian king, his spies were to reconnoitre all that they could, and in particular to find out whether the reports of Ethiopia's 'Table of the Sun'[16] had any basis in fact.

[18] This Table of the Sun, the story goes, is a meadow situated on the edge of the city, filled with the roasted cuts of every kind of four-footed animal. All those who happen to be serving as the city's officials at a given moment painstakingly deposit the meat there under cover of night; and then, come the day, whoever so wishes can go there and tuck in. The natives, however, say that the meat is generated every night by the earth itself. Such, then, are the claims made for the so-called 'Table of the Sun'.

[19] Cambyses' decision to deploy spies prompted him to issue an immediate summons to the city of Elephantine, to those men among the 'Fish-Eaters'[17] who understood the Ethiopian language. His messengers went off to fetch them, and in the meantime Cambyses gave orders that all those in his war-fleet should set sail against Carthage. The Phoenicians, however, refused to do so: they declared themselves bound by the most solemn oaths, and that it would be the height of impiety for them to launch an assault against their own offspring.[18] This reluctance of the Phoenicians to take part left the rest of the fleet quite inadequate to the task. So it was that the Carthaginians escaped being enslaved by the Persians. Cambyses, you see, did not feel himself justified in bringing force to bear on the Phoenicians, since they had freely submitted to the Persians, and because his entire war-fleet was dependent upon them. (The Cypriots had similarly submitted to the Persians of their own accord, and joined the expedition against Egypt.)

[20] Once the Fish-Eaters had arrived from Elephantine and come into the presence of Cambyses, he dispatched them to the Ethiopians, complete with instructions as to what they were to say, and a whole load of gifts: a purple robe, a necklace of twisted gold, bracelets, an alabaster box of myrrh and a jar of palm wine. It is said that these Ethiopians to whom Cambyses was sending his messengers are the tallest and most handsome men in the world. Their customs are reported to be very different from those of other peoples; and none more so than the one which determines who becomes their king. The man in their city who is judged to be the tallest and strongest in proportion to his height – that is the man who is reckoned worthy of the throne.

[21] These, then, were the people visited by the Fish-Eaters, who duly handed over their gifts to the king, and said: 'Cambyses, the King of the Persians, desirous as he is of tying the knot of friendship and mutual hospitality with you, has sent us with orders to come here for talks, and to make a gift to you of these things in which he himself takes most delight.' But the Ethiopian could tell that they were spies; and told them so. 'You are nothing but liars, come here to spy on my realm! As for these gifts that you have been sent by the Persian King to bring me, they suggest no great desire on his part to establish links of friendship with me, but rather that he has no sense of what is right. How otherwise to explain this longing of his for lands that are not his own, and his hauling into slavery peoples that never did him any wrong? You are to give

him this bow,[19] and repeat these words to him: "From the King of the Ethiopians to the King of the Persians, some advice. Only when the Persians can readily draw bows of an equal size should he think to lead an army against the long-lived Ethiopians – and even then, he should be sure to outnumber us. Meanwhile, let him feel proper gratitude to the gods that they have never turned the minds of the sons of Ethiopia to thoughts of adding other lands to their own."'

[22] And with these words, he unstrung the bow and handed it over to his visitors. Then he took the purple robe, and asked them what it was, and how it had been made. The Fish-Eaters gave him a truthful account of the purple-fish and the dyeing process;[20] but the king only told the men that they were as deceitful as their garments. His second question was about the twisted gold necklace and the bracelets. The Fish-Eaters began to explain that the gold was for decoration; but the king, who thought that the bracelets were fetters, burst out laughing, and declared that the fetters in his own land were stronger by far. The third question was about the myrrh. The visitors described how it was manufactured and used to anoint the body; but the king dismissed it as he had similarly dismissed the robe. When he came to the wine, however, and learned how it was made, he had a drink and was delighted by it. 'What does your king eat,' he went on to ask, 'and what is the maximum span of a Persian man's life?' 'He eats bread,' they answered, and then explained to him how wheat is grown. 'As for the span of a man's life, the fullest measure is set at eighty years.' To this, however, the king declared, 'I do not wonder that your lives should be so short, when all you eat is dung. Indeed, you would not even be able to stay alive for as long as you do, were it not for the restorative powers of this drink.' And so saying, he indicated the wine to the Fish-Eaters. 'For only in this do the Persians leave us trailing.'

[23] Then it was the turn of the Fish-Eaters to ask the king how long his own people lived, and what kind of things they ate. 'The majority', he answered, 'live to be one hundred and twenty, with some living even longer than that. As for our diet – we boil meat and drink milk.' When the spies expressed astonishment at the number of years, the king led them to a spring from which there came a scent like that of violets; and when the spies washed themselves in it, the water left them with a sheen, as though it had been olive oil. So delicate was this spring-water, the spies reported, that nothing could float on its surface: wood, and even

things lighter than wood, just sank to the bottom. (Certainly, if the reports of this water are true, and assuming that the Ethiopians use it for everything, then it would indeed explain their longevity.) From the spring the spies were led to a dungeon full of men, where everyone was shackled with fetters of gold. (This because, among the Ethiopians, it is bronze which ranks as the rarest and most precious of metals.) Then, once they had seen the dungeon, they also saw the so-called 'Table of the Sun'.

[24] After this, and last of all, they saw the Ethiopians' coffins, which are said to be made of a translucent material. What the Ethiopians do with a corpse is to dry it out, either after the Egyptian manner or in some other way, and smear it all over with plaster and adorn it with paint, so as to render it as lifelike as possible; they then enclose it within a hollow column of translucent material (which they mine in great quantities, and which is easy to work). The corpse is now quite visible in the middle of the column, but without giving off any noxious stench, or indeed anything unpleasant at all. This column will be kept by the dead person's closest relatives in their home for a year, during which time they will bring him the first fruits of everything, and offer him up burnt sacrifice. Then, once the year has passed, they will carry it out and set it up among all the other columns which are dotted around the city.

[25] Once the spies had seen everything, they left for home. So angry did their report make Cambyses[21] that he immediately launched an attack on the Ethiopians, without having built up any stockpiles of food, or taken into account that the target of his expedition lay at the very ends of the earth. Instead, mad as he was and quite out of his senses, he had no sooner heard from the Fish-Eaters than he went off with his army, the entire body of his land-forces, all except for the Greeks he had with him in Egypt, who were ordered to stay behind. Once the advance of his army had brought him to Thebes, he ordered a detachment of his men, some fifty thousand in all, to bring him back the Ammonians as slaves and to burn down the oracle of Zeus, while he himself led the rest of his forces onwards against the Ethiopians. The army had not even gone a fifth of the way, however, before everything that they had by way of provisions was gone; nor did it take long, once the food had run out, for the pack-animals to disappear as well, for they too were all consumed. If, once he had grasped the situation, Cambyses had only revised his plan and led his army back, then he would have

compensated for his original mistake, and shown himself a man of good sense; as it was, he took no account at all of what was happening but pressed on regardless. The soldiers, for as long as there was anything in the earth that could be scavenged, kept themselves alive by eating grass, but in due course, after they arrived in the sands, there were some of them who did a truly terrible thing: they cast lots, and devoured every tenth man among them. When Cambyses learned of this, such was his dread of cannibalism that he abandoned his expedition against the Ethiopians and went back; but by the time that he had returned to Thebes, he had lost a large part of his army. From Thebes he went downriver to Memphis, where he dismissed the Greeks and let them sail home.

[26] Such was the fate of the expedition against the Ethiopians. The invasion force sent against the Ammonians set out from Thebes, and was shown a route by guides that indisputably saw it arrive in Oasis, a city inhabited by Samians who are said to belong to the Aeschrionian tribe, and who live seven days' travel away across the sand-dunes from Thebes. (The name of the place, in Greek, is 'The Isles of the Blessed'.) That the army made it as far as Oasis is a matter of record; but beyond Oasis we have no certain information about what happened to the Persians, since they failed to reach the Ammonians, and never made it home either. The only evidence derives, either directly or indirectly, from the Ammonians themselves, who have a story to tell. They claim that in the course of launching its attack against them across the desert from Oasis, the army arrived at a point approximately midway between them and Oasis; and as the Persians were taking their breakfast, a south wind of remarkable strength swept down upon them. Such a mass of sand was this wind carrying that when it deposited its load on the Persians, they were utterly engulfed – and so it was that they came to vanish. That, say the Ammonians, is what happened to the army.[22]

[27] The arrival of Cambyses in Memphis coincided with the manifestation in Egypt of Apis, whom the Greeks call *Epaphus*. No sooner had he made his appearance than the Egyptians began to put on their finest clothes, and to hold street parties. When Cambyses saw what was going on, he jumped to the conclusion that they were celebrating his own failures, so he summoned the prefects of Memphis. Once they had all come into his presence, he fixed them with a glare and asked them, 'Why, when the Egyptians never behaved in this manner the last time I was in Memphis, are they doing so now, after I have lost the greater part

of my army?' The Egyptians explained that a god had appeared to them, and that because these appearances tended to be separated by lengthy intervals of time, it was the practice of all the Egyptians to celebrate each one with festivities. But Cambyses, having heard them out, told them that they were liars – and that he was condemning them to death.

[28] Once the executions had been carried out, he summoned into his presence the priests, who reiterated the earlier explanation. 'So some pet god has turned up in Egypt!' Cambyses exclaimed. 'Then I want to know all about it.' And with this declaration, he ordered the priests to bring him Apis, and they duly went off to fetch him. This Apis (or *Epaphus*) is a calf born of a cow which, from that moment on, evermore carries a barren womb. The Egyptians say that a beam of light descends from the sky onto this cow, and that it is from this light that Apis is born. The calf, which goes by the god's own name, has distinctive markings: although otherwise black, it has a white diamond upon its forehead and the likeness of an eagle upon its back, the hairs of its tail are double and it has a mark shaped like a beetle under its tongue.

[29] The priests brought in Apis, and Cambyses, who was teetering on the edge of madness, drew a dagger and struck at him, aiming for the belly but hitting the thigh instead. Cambyses laughed, then spoke to the priests. 'You poor fools! What kind of god is born a thing like this, nothing but flesh and blood, and vulnerable to a touch of iron? The kind of god, no doubt, that you Egyptians deserve! But do not think you will get away with fooling me!' With these words he commanded those of his men who were responsible for such matters to flog the priests without mercy and to seize and kill any other Egyptians whom they found celebrating the festival. So it was that the Egyptians' festivities were broken up and the priests punished. Apis, struck in the thigh, wasted away where he lay in the shrine. Once he had died of his wound,[23] the priests came and buried him without Cambyses knowing.

[30] The immediate consequence of this crime, the Egyptians claim, was that Cambyses went mad – although even before it he had barely been sane. The first victim of his criminal deeds was his brother Smerdis, who shared with Cambyses both parents, and who had already been packed off from Egypt to Persia. Smerdis had been the one Persian capable of drawing the bow brought back by the Fish-Eaters from the Ethiopian king, which he had pulled a distance equivalent to the length of two fingers, when none of the other Persians had managed even that.

This had provoked Cambyses to much jealous resentment. Then, after Smerdis had left for Persia, Cambyses had a vision as he slept, in which it seemed to him that a messenger came from Persia, and reported to him that Smerdis was sitting on the royal throne, and that his head was brushing the sky. This dream left Cambyses terrified that his brother might kill him, and rule in his place; and so off to Persia he sent Prexaspes, the man whom he trusted more than any other Persian, with orders to eliminate Smerdis. So Prexaspes went up to Susa, and killed him. Some say that he took Smerdis out hunting, and killed him then; others, that he led him down to the Red Sea, and drowned him.

[31] This, then, or so it is reported, was the first of the atrocities committed by Cambyses. His second victim was his sister, who had accompanied him to Egypt, and who not only shared with him both parents, but was his wife too: he had married her despite the fact that until then it had not remotely been the habit of the Persians to set up house with their sisters.[24] It so happened, however, that Cambyses had passionately lusted after another of his sisters, and longed to marry her, despite the fact that what he had set his heart on was quite without precedent. So he had summoned the Royal Judges, as they are known, and asked them whether there might not be some law which obliged a man who wished to marry his sister to do so. (The men who become these Royal Judges are a select band of Persians; they remain in office until they die or else are convicted of some offence. They preside over all the cases brought by the Persians, and are the interpreters of their ancestral statutes: everything is referred to them.) The ruling they gave in response to Cambyses' question satisfied justice without compromising their own security: they declared that, although they had failed to find a law which actually obliged a brother to marry his sister, they had discovered one which permitted the King of the Persians to do as he pleased.[25] So it was that they avoided being intimidated by Cambyses into breaking the law, but not to the point of sacrificing themselves in its defence; for what they had found was a quite additional law, supportive of his desire to marry his sisters. The consequence was that Cambyses had married the one he particularly lusted after; but then, after barely any time at all, he had taken another sister as his wife too. It was the younger of these two sisters who had accompanied him to Egypt – and whom he killed.

[32] As with the death of Smerdis, so with hers – alternative stories are told. Greeks say that Cambyses threw a lion's cub into the ring with

a young dog, and that this wife of his was one of those watching; the puppy was losing, but its brother [another young dog] managed to break free of its leash and came to its rescue, so that the one puppy became two, and the cub was duly vanquished. Cambyses was delighted by the show; but his wife wept as she sat beside him. When he noticed this, Cambyses asked her, 'Why are you crying?' 'I cried', she answered, 'because when I saw the puppy coming to the rescue of its brother, I was reminded of Smerdis, and it struck me that there is now no one to come to your assistance.' It was because of this comment, so Greeks say, that Cambyses killed her. The Egyptian version is that one day, when everyone was sitting down around the table, Cambyses' wife took a lettuce and plucked off all its leaves, and then asked her husband whether the lettuce was more beautiful stripped bare or as it had been when still thick with leaves. 'When thick with leaves,' he said. 'And yet what have you done,' she answered, 'if not strip bare the House of Cyrus, so that it precisely resembles this lettuce?' So angered was Cambyses by this that he leapt on her; and she, who was carrying his child in her womb, suffered a miscarriage, and died.[26]

[33] Such were the ways in which the House of Cambyses was affected by the madness brought on him by the business with Apis – or perhaps, bearing in mind how many ailments there are to which mankind is prone, his lunacy was caused by something else altogether. Indeed, it has been claimed that Cambyses was afflicted from birth by a particularly terrible ailment, called by some the 'sacred disease'.[27] If so, it would hardly be surprising were a man afflicted by such a serious physical malady to be unsound of mind as well.

[34] His madness also affected other Persians. There is the story, for instance, of what he said to Prexaspes, a man whom he had always honoured above all others, appointing him court chamberlain, and his son as pourer of the royal wine – no small honour in itself. 'Prexaspes,' Cambyses is reported to have said, 'what kind of man do the Persians think I am? When they talk about me, what do they say?' 'Master,' Prexaspes answered, 'they praise you to the skies, except when it comes to one thing – for they do say that you take your love of wine to excess.' Cambyses, thrown into a rage by this news of the Persians, answered, 'So now the Persians are saying that I am too fond of wine, are they? That it has driven me mad? That I am not in my right mind? Then what they told me before was just a lie!' He was alluding here to a previous

occasion, when his Persian advisers, and Croesus too, were sitting in council with him, and Cambyses asked them how they rated him as a man, compared to his father. The Persians answered that he was better than his father, 'For you have everything that he had – but you have also won possession of Egypt and the sea.' That was what the Persians had to say; but Croesus, who was also present, judged this answer inadequate, and said to Cambyses, 'In my opinion, son of Cyrus, you are not alike to your father in all respects. This is because you do not yet have a son[28] fit to compare with the son that he left behind in you.' Cambyses, who was delighted to hear this, lavished praise on Croesus' judgement.

[35] This, then, was the episode that he had called to mind. 'Find out for yourself', he raged at Prexaspes, 'whether what the Persians say about me is true, or whether it is they, when they report such things, who have lost their wits. Do you see your son, standing over there, in the antechamber? Well, I am going to shoot him. Now, if I manage to hit him directly in the heart, then that will make it as clear as can be that the Persians have been talking nonsense. But should I miss him, then, yes, report as the truth what is claimed by the Persians, that I am indeed out of my mind!' So saying, he drew his bow to the full and shot the child – who fell to the ground. 'Cut the boy open,' Cambyses ordered, 'and identify where he was hit!' Then, when the arrow was found in the heart, Cambyses was put into such a good mood that he laughed, and said to the father of the child: 'You see, Prexaspes? It is as clear as clear can be. I am not mad! It is the Persians who have lost their wits! But tell me – have you ever seen anyone, anywhere in the world, hit the mark with a shot like that?' Prexaspes, seeing that the man was quite insane, and afraid for his own skin, answered him: 'Master, I doubt that even the god himself could have hit with such pin-point accuracy.' So much, then, for the behaviour of Cambyses on that occasion; on another, he apprehended twelve Persians who were equal in rank to the best, convicted them on some trifling charge and then buried them alive, head first.

[36] These actions prompted Croesus the Lydian to feel that it was his responsibility to have words with Cambyses. 'My Lord,' he said, 'rather than giving free rein to the passions of your youth, you should be keeping them under a tight control and getting a grip on yourself. Prudence is the best policy, just as forethought is the wisest. You are

killing men who are your own fellow-citizens, executing them on the most paltry of charges, even killing children! If you keep on indulging in such behaviour, watch out that the Persians do not rise in revolt against you. As for me, your father Cyrus repeatedly charged and instructed me to offer you criticism, and to recommend to you whatever course of action I should find the fittest.' Such was his advice; but Cambyses, despite the manifest goodwill with which it had been offered, replied: 'You have a nerve, to think to offer me advice! You – who governed your own country to such brilliant effect! You – who gave my father such excellent advice, when you told him to cross the River Araxes and attack the Massagetans, despite the fact that they were perfectly willing to make the crossing into our own territory! It was your incompetence when you were at the head of your native land which brought about your own downfall – just as it was the confidence that Cyrus put in your advice which brought about his. But do not expect to get away with it now! Indeed, I have been waiting a long time for an excuse to get my hands on you!' So saying, Cambyses grabbed a bow, intending to shoot him down; but Croesus leapt to his feet and ran from the room. Cambyses, frustrated in his attempt to use his bow, gave orders instead to his servants that they were to apprehend Croesus and put him to death. The servants, however, familiar with these swings in the royal mood, kept Croesus hidden; they reasoned that, were Cambyses to repent of what he had done and look to have Croesus back, they would be able to unveil him, and would be rewarded for having saved his life; whereas, if Cambyses did not change his mind, and did not come to miss Croesus, they could always finish off the job they had been given. In the event, Cambyses soon longed to have Croesus back, and the servants, once they had become aware of this, let the king know that he was still alive. Cambyses, however, though he acknowledged himself delighted at the survival of Croesus, declared that those responsible for it should not go unpunished, and sentenced them all to death. And put them to death is precisely what he did.

[37] There were many such acts of lunacy committed by Cambyses against the Persians and their allies; indeed, during his stay in Memphis, he broke into ancient tombs and examined the corpses. Similarly, he went so far as to enter the shrine of Hephaestus,[29] and laughed uproariously at the image of the god. This statue of Hephaestus closely resembles the Phoenician *pataici*,[30] which the Phoenicians carry around on the

prows of their triremes. Should anyone never have seen one of these, it is best described, I think, as a likeness of a male pygmy. Cambyses also penetrated the shrine of the Cabiri,[31] which only the priest may lawfully enter. There, he actually had the statues of the gods burned while pouring scorn on them. In appearance, these same statues are very similar to those of Hephaestus; indeed, the Cabiri are said to be his children.

[38] Everywhere you look, it seems to me, the evidence accumulates that Cambyses was utterly deranged, for why otherwise would he have mocked what to others were hallowed customs? Just suppose that someone proposed to the entirety of mankind that a selection of the very best practices be made from the sum of human custom: each group of people, after carefully sifting through the customs of other peoples, would surely choose its own. Everyone believes his own customs to be far and away the best. From this, it follows that only a madman would think to jeer at such matters. Indeed, there is a huge amount of corroborating evidence to support the conclusion that this attitude to one's own native customs is universal. Take, for example, this story from the reign of Darius. He called together some Greeks who were present and asked them how much money they would wish to be paid to devour the corpses of their fathers – to which the Greeks replied that no amount of money would suffice for that. Next, Darius summoned some Indians called Callantians, who do eat their parents, and asked them in the presence of the Greeks (who were able to follow what was being said by means of an interpreter) how much money it would take to buy their consent to the cremation of their dead fathers – at which the Callantians cried out in horror and told him that his words were a desecration of silence.[32] Such, then, is how custom operates; and how right Pindar is, it seems to me, when he declares in his poetry that 'Custom is the King of all'.[33]

[39] At the same time as Cambyses was invading Egypt, the Lacedaemonians were launching their own campaign against Samos, specifically against Polycrates,[34] the son of Aeaces, who had toppled the government there and taken possession of the city. Initially, he had divided it up into three, and given shares to his brothers, Pantagnotus and Syloson; but subsequently, he had put the first of these brothers to death, and driven the younger one, Syloson, into exile, so that the whole of Samos became his. Having done this, he tied the knot of friendship and mutual hospitality[35] with Amasis, the king of Egypt, a pledge that the

two men sealed by the sending and receiving of gifts. And straightaway, in next to no time, the affairs of Polycrates had prospered to such a degree that they were being bruited throughout Ionia, and across the Greek world. No matter where he directed his campaigns, fortune consistently favoured him. He built up a fleet of one hundred penteconters and recruited a thousand archers, raiding and plundering without discrimination – indeed, he used to say that he would earn more gratitude from friends by restoring to them what he had taken from them than he would have done by not taking it in the first place. Many were the islands he conquered, and numerous the cities on the mainland too. Among his victories was the defeat that he inflicted at sea upon the men of Lesbos, who had sent their entire force to the assistance of the Milesians, but now became his prisoners; labouring in chains, they dug the whole of the moat which encircles the walls of Samos.[36]

[40] Now, as may well be imagined, Polycrates' astounding good fortune did not go unnoticed by Amasis, who was unsettled by it. Eventually, with Polycrates' run of luck continuing to bring him ever greater successes, Amasis wrote a letter and sent it off to Samos. 'Here is what Amasis has to say to Polycrates,' it read. 'How pleasant it is to learn that a friend, a man who is bound to one by ties of mutual hospitality, is faring so well. Nevertheless, your astounding good fortune is not a cause of unconfined joy to me – for I well know that the gods are given to envy.[37] What I wish for myself, and for those I care about – if I may put it like this – is a career that blends good fortune with the occasional stumble. Better to go through life experiencing bad as well as good luck than to know nothing but success. I have never yet known nor heard tell of anyone who enjoyed a prosperity so total that he did not ultimately come to a bad end and lose everything that had previously sustained him. That being so, I would advise you, in the face of all your good fortune, to adopt the following policy. Think hard, and identify the object that is most precious to you, the one that it would cause you the most heartache to lose – and then throw it away, some place where there is no chance of its ever coming back into human hands. If, by the time you get to read this, there have still been no disasters to punctuate your run of good fortune, then remedy the situation in the manner that I have here suggested.'

[41] Once Polycrates had read this through, and after reflection had come to appreciate that the advice offered him by Amasis made good

sense, he sought to identify which of his treasures it would most pain him to lose. After much soul-searching, he fixed upon the signet-ring that he habitually wore: its stone, an emerald, was set in gold, and had been worked by Theodorus,[38] the son of Telecles, a Samian. Accordingly, once he had decided that this was the treasure he would throw away, what Polycrates did was to man a penteconter, board it and order it out to the open sea. Next, with the island left far behind, he took off his signet-ring and threw it into the sea, in the full view of everyone on board. Then, that once done, he sailed back to Samos, where he retired to his home and mourned his loss.

[42] It so happened, however, five or six days after this, that a fisherman caught a large and beautiful fish, and thought it only fitting to make a gift of it to Polycrates. He hauled it to the front doors, where he announced that he wished to come into the sight of Polycrates. Permission was granted and the fish handed over. 'My king,' the fisherman said, 'although I am a man who has no living aside from what I catch with my own hands, I knew, when I caught this one, that it would be quite wrong for me to take it to the market-square. Such a fish, it struck me, is really worthy only of you and of your administration – which is why I have brought it here and given it to you.' Polycrates, who was delighted by these words, answered him: 'And excellently well done it is too! I owe you a double debt of gratitude – both for what you have said and for what you have given me. We invite you to come and dine with us this evening.' The fisherman went back home bursting with pride; but the servants, when they sliced open the fish, found in its stomach the very signet-ring of Polycrates! No sooner had they laid their eyes on it and taken it out than they were carrying it into the presence of Polycrates in a state of high excitement; and as they presented him with the signet-ring, they told him how it had been found. And at this, there came into Polycrates' mind a sense of how touched by the numinous the whole business surely was; so he wrote down in a letter a full account of what he had done and what had happened, and then, when he had finished writing, sent it off to Egypt.

[43] When Amasis read the letter that had come from Polycrates, he realized that it was quite impossible for one man to redeem another from something that is inevitably going to happen, and that Polycrates, a man touched by such unfailing good fortune that even those things he threw away were found again, was certainly not someone destined for

a happy end. So Amasis sent a herald to Samos with news that the treaty of mutual friendship between them was dissolved.[39] His motive for doing this was to ensure that when some great and terrible calamity did eventually befall Polycrates, he would not feel in his heart the pain that he would feel for a man who was his friend.

[44] It was against this same Polycrates, the one whose luck knew no bounds, that the Lacedaemonians launched a military offensive, in answer to an appeal from a faction on Samos that would later go on to found Cydonia in Crete.[40] Now, at the time when Cambyses, the son of Cyrus, had been assembling his army for the invasion of Egypt, Polycrates, going behind the Samians' backs, had sent him a herald. 'Send me a request for troops,' Polycrates had requested, 'back here in Samos.' Cambyses, once he had listened to this message, was more than happy to send a message of his own back to Samos, asking Polycrates to dispatch a naval task-force to help him take on Egypt. The townsmen duly nominated by Polycrates, all of whom were on his list of likely subversives, were sent off in forty warships, together with instructions to Cambyses never to send them back.

[45] There are some who say that these Samians packed off by Polycrates never actually made it to Egypt, but only sailed as far as the waters off Carpathos, where they held a council of war and decided that they did not want to continue any further with their voyage. Others claim that they did make it to Egypt, where they were interned, but managed to slip away. Then, as they were making their voyage back to Samos, Polycrates came out to meet them with his fleet, and engaged them in a battle – which was won by the returning exiles. When they landed on the island, however, they had the worst of an infantry battle and this is why they sailed to Lacedaemon. Yet others, however, claim that the Samians who had come back from Egypt did in fact beat Polycrates – a story which seems most implausible to me. Why, after all, would they have needed to ask the Lacedaemonians for assistance if they were capable of overthrowing Polycrates on their own? What is more, it goes against all logic to imagine that a man backed up by hired auxiliaries and a vast squad of archers, recruited from among his own people, could conceivably have been defeated by the few returning Samians. As a safeguard, Polycrates also crammed the wives and children of his subjects into the ship-sheds, ready to set fire to them, ship-sheds and all, should his fellow-townsmen decide to desert to the returning exiles.

[46] When the Samians who had been expelled by Polycrates arrived in Sparta, they came into the presence of the authorities, and spoke at great length, commensurate with their need. The response of the authorities to this first audience, however, was to complain that they could not remember the early section of the speech, and had failed to understand what came after. As a consequence, when the Samians gained a second audience, they simply came in with a sack and said nothing at all, except to comment, 'This sack needs barley-meal.' 'There was no need to say "sack",'[41] came back the reply. The Lacedaemonians resolved, nevertheless, that they would indeed give aid.

[47] So they made their preparations for the campaign against Samos and set off. They did this, according to the Samians, because they owed a debt of gratitude for the naval assistance that the Samians had provided some time previously in their war against the Messenians;[42] but the Lacedaemonians themselves say that they were prompted to launch their campaign less out of any desire to assist the Samians in their hour of need than because they wished to be avenged for the theft of the mixing-bowl which they had been taking to Croesus, and of a breastplate which Amasis, the king of Egypt, had sent them as a gift. It is certainly the case that a year before they stole the bowl the Samians had indeed carried off this same breastplate, which was made of linen, had a large number of figures woven into it and was embroidered with gold and cotton. Most wondrous of all, however, is that each one of the breastplate's threads, fine though it is, consists in turn of three hundred and sixty separate threads, all of them clear to the eye. There is another breastplate, exactly like it, which Amasis presented as an offering to Athena in Lindus.

[48] The Corinthians, because they wished to ensure that the campaign against Samos did go ahead, had enthusiastically joined in: they too, a generation previously, at around the same time as the bowl was stolen, had been grievously insulted by the Samians. Three hundred boys, the sons of the leading men of Corcyra, had been sent by Periander, the son of Cypselus, to Alyattes in Sardis to be castrated. The Corinthians who were escorting the boys put in at Samos; when the whole story came out, and the Samians discovered why the boys were being taken to Sardis, their first step was to instruct the boys to take sanctuary in the shrine of Artemis; next, they refused to turn a blind eye to the attempts that were being made to drag the suppliants away from the

sanctuary; and then, when the Corinthians blocked the boys' food supply, the Samians instituted a festival which they still celebrate to this day
just as it was first established.[43] Every nightfall, for the entire time spent
by the boys in the sanctuary, the Samians so arranged things that unmarried girls and boys would stage dances; and next, having arranged these
dances, they made it a rule that the dancers should carry cakes of sesame and honey, which could then be snatched by the sons of the
Corcyrans to provide them with sustenance. This continued until the
Corinthians who had been guarding the boys gave up and went away –
at which point the Samians took the boys back to Corcyra.

[49] Now had the Corinthians and the Corcyrans been on good
terms with one another after Periander died, such an episode would
hardly have provided the Corinthians with sufficient motivation to join
the campaign. As it was, however, despite their shared kinship, the two
peoples had been at odds with one another ever since the first colonization of the island.[44] No wonder, then, that the Corinthians should have
kept the wrong done them by the Samians very much in their minds. It
was Periander's desire for vengeance that had prompted him to nominate the sons of the leading men of Corcyra for castration, and then to
send them to Sardis, for the Corcyrans, by committing an atrocious
crime against him, had been the ones who first began the feud.

[50] It so happened, after Periander had killed his wife Melissa, that
a very similar misfortune came hard on the heels of the one that had
already befallen him. Melissa had borne him two sons: one of them now
seventeen and the other eighteen years old. They were sent for by Procles, the tyrant of Epidaurus, who was their maternal grandfather, and
who treated them with great kindness – as was only to be expected, of
course, since they were the sons of his daughter. But when Procles came
to send them back, he said, as they parted from him, 'Do you know, my
boys, who it was killed your mother?' This was a question to which the
elder of the two paid not the slightest attention, but which Lycophron,
as the younger was called, found so painful to hear that he refused, on
his arrival in Corinth, to engage his father – as the murderer of his
mother – in conversation; not only that, but he refused to respond to
any of Periander's attempts to talk to him, or to ask him questions.
Eventually, Periander became so infuriated that he threw Lycophron out
of his house.

[51] Then, once he had driven his younger son away, he asked the

older one what the father of their mother had said to them. 'He received us with great kindness,' the son answered, 'but as for his parting words, they have quite slipped my mind. No, I cannot recall them.' Periander, however, persisted with his questioning, arguing that Procles was very unlikely to have made no suggestion to them at all; and then the boy did recall what Procles had said, and repeated it. So it was that Periander grasped what had happened; and, determined not to be swayed by sentiment, he sent a messenger to the people with whom his exiled son had made a new life, and ordered them not to take him in any longer. And so it went on: Lycophron would no sooner find somewhere to stay after he was expelled than he would be kicked out of his new home as well, since all those who opened their doors to him would receive threats from Periander and orders to send him packing. And every time Lycophron was sent packing, he would go to another of his comrades; and they, despite being terrified, would let him in, on the grounds that he was, after all, the son of Periander.

[52] In the end, Periander issued a proclamation, declaring that a fine payable to Apollo, holy in character and set by him at a specific rate, would be imposed upon anyone who might offer shelter to Lycophron or engage him in conversation. Sure enough, as a consequence of this edict, there was no one willing to speak to the boy or to offer him hospitality. Even Lycophron himself thought it wrong to try to defy the prohibitions, and instead, because he still refused to back down, he just hung around the colonnades instead. Three days passed, and on the fourth, seeing how filthy and emaciated his son was, Periander felt such pity that he stifled his anger and approached him. 'My boy,' he said, 'which of these two states is preferable – the one that you are currently in, or the condition of power and plenty that is mine, and which it is yours to inherit if you will only pay the respect that is due your father? You are my son, a prince of this rich and happy city of Corinth – and yet you choose to lead the life of a wandering beggar, and make me, the man who least deserves such treatment, the object of all your hostility and rage. Remember that if something terrible has happened to make you suspicious of me, then I too am caught up in the same business. More so, indeed, than you – for it was I who actually committed the deed. You have learned two lessons both at once: how much better it is to be envied than to be pitied, and what it means to indulge oneself in anger against one's parent and superior. Come, then, return home.' Such was

the attempt made by Periander to win back his son; but the only answer that Lycophron gave was to say, 'You owe the god a fine for having come into conversation with me.' It was now that Periander appreciated just how far gone his son was, and how impregnable his condition of misery; so he sent him out of sight by having him shipped off to Corcyra (which was also then subject to Periander's rule). Next, with Lycophron sent on his way, Periander led an army against the man whom he blamed more than any other for what had happened to him: Procles, his father-in-law. Epidaurus fell, and Procles too, who was taken alive.

[53] Time passed, and as Periander grew older, he was brought to acknowledge that his ability to oversee and manage the affairs of state was no longer what it had been. Accordingly, unable to distinguish any mark of talent in his elder son, who struck him as manifestly lacking in intelligence, Periander sent to Corcyra, summoning Lycophron to take up the reins of supreme power. Even when Lycophron disdained to give the bearer of this message an answer, Periander would still not relinquish his hopes of the young man, but instead, as a second messenger, sent the person whom he calculated would prove more liable to persuade his son than anyone else: his own daughter, the sister of Lycophron. 'Silly boy,' the girl said, on her arrival, 'do you really want supreme power falling into the hands of others? Your patrimony plundered? Would you really rather that than return and have it for yourself? Get back home with you now and stop putting yourself through this torture! Pride is a thing that cripples a man, just as two wrongs do not make a right! Plenty have put pragmatism ahead of the demands of justice. You would hardly be the first to find that the defence of a mother's interests can threaten those dues that are owed him by a father. A tyranny is a precarious thing, much lusted after by others – and besides, he is an old man, long since past his prime. Do not, then, give away to others the good things that are your own!'[45] Nevertheless, despite having been tutored by her father in all these various blandishments, Lycophron's only response to her speech was to declare that he would never come to Corinth so long as he knew that his father was still alive. She duly reported this back. Now Periander dispatched a third emissary, declaring that he himself wished to come to Corcyra, and that Lycophron should come to Corinth and succeed to the tyranny. To these terms his son consented; and Periander duly made ready to leave for Corcyra and his son for Corinth. So anxious, however, were the Corcyrans to

stop Periander from coming to their country, once they had got wind of what was afoot, that they put the young man to death. It was this that prompted Periander to take his vengeance on the people of Corcyra.

[54] The force of Lacedaemonians that came to Samos and began to put it under siege was a formidable one. They launched an attack against the city walls,[46] and managed to scale the tower that stood by the sea, on the outer reaches of the town, only to be driven back when Polycrates himself arrived with a large number of reinforcements. Meanwhile, a sally was launched from the upper tower – the one which stands on the ridge of the mountain – by the mercenaries and the Samians themselves; but although they initially succeeded in holding their own against the Lacedaemonians, they were soon put to flight and cut down by their pursuers.

[55] Now, if all the Lacedaemonians who were there that day had proved the peers of Archias and Lycopas, then Samos would have been taken. For Archias and Lycopas were the only ones to join the Samians as they fled back inside the city walls, and because this left the two of them with their line of retreat blocked off, it saw them perish inside the city of Samos. Once, in his native village of Pitana, I met with another Archias, a man who was the son of Samius and the grandson of the original Archias, and who esteemed the Samians the most of any foreigners; and this Archias told me personally that his father was given the name of 'Samius'[47] because his own father had died a hero's death on Samos. The reason that he so respected the Samians, he explained, was because they had buried his grandfather at public expense.

[56] For forty days Samos was put under siege, until the Lacedaemonians, unable to break the deadlock, returned to the Peloponnese. There is a more far-fetched account, according to which Polycrates used the local mint to strike a large quantity of coins in lead, which he then had covered in gold leaf and gave to the Lacedaemonians, who took them and only then set off. This was the first time that the Lacedaemonians, or indeed any Dorians, had ever launched an expedition against Asia.[48]

[57] Once they realized that the Lacedaemonians were ready to abandon them, the Samians who had joined the campaign against Polycrates sailed off to Siphnos. They were in need of funds, and this was the same period in which Siphnos was at the very peak of her prosperity: the people of Siphnos were the richest of all the islanders, thanks to the gold

and silver mines on their island. Indeed, these mines were so productive that a tenth of the revenue generated from them was sufficient to endow a treasury at Delphi[49] which was the match, in terms of wealth, of any other there. Every year, the people of Siphnos would distribute the proceeds from the mines among themselves; and so it was, as they were building the treasury, that they asked the oracle whether their current prosperity would continue indefinitely. The Pythia replied:

'Well, whenever the town-halls on Siphnos turn to white,
And the market white of brow, then will you need someone
    shrewd
To flag for you a battalion of wood, and a herald of red.'

At the time, both the market-square and the town-hall on Siphnos were clad in Parian marble.[50]

[58] The Siphnians were unable to make any sense of this oracle, either at the time or later when the Samians appeared. The point, however, was that the moment the Samians put in at Siphnos, they sent messengers to the city on board one of their ships – and Samian ships, back in ancient times, were always painted red.[51] It was to this that the Pythia had been alluding when she warned the Siphnians to guard against 'a battalion of wood, and a herald of red'. Sure enough, once the messengers had arrived, demanded a loan of 10 talents from the Siphnians and been rebuffed, the Samians set themselves to stripping the country bare. The Siphnians, the moment they discovered what was happening, went out to the rescue, but were defeated, with many of them being cut off from their city by the Samians, who extorted 100 talents from them.

[59] From the people of Hermione, the Samians took not money but the island of Hydrea off the Peloponnese, which they then entrusted for safe-keeping to the people of Troezen. They themselves, meanwhile, founded Cydonia in Crete, despite the fact that their original purpose in sailing there had not been to colonize it at all, but rather to drive out the Zacynthians from the island. They remained there for five years and prospered to such effect that all the shrines which exist there now, including the temple of Dictynna, were built by them. In the sixth year, however, the Aeginetans combined with the Cretans to defeat the Samians at sea and reduce them to slavery; the boar-shaped prows which the Samians had on their ships were hacked off by the Aeginetans and presented as offerings to the shrine of Athena in Aegina.[52] This the

Aeginetans did because they bore a grudge against the Samians, for in the time when Amphicrates had been king of Samos, the Samians had launched a campaign against the Aeginetans, one which had inflicted great damage (although the Samians too had suffered numerous casualties at the hands of the Aeginetans). The entire episode had stemmed from this.

[60] If I have gone on at some length about the Samians, it is because they were responsible for three construction projects which no other Greeks have ever rivalled.[53] One is a tunnel which leads upwards through a mountain some 150 fathoms high, and has mouths at both ends. The tunnel is 7 stades long,[54] and 8 feet high and wide. Dug out along its entire course there is another channel, 20 cubits deep and 3 feet wide, along which water is channelled through pipes from a great spring and brought to the city. Its architect was a man from Megara: Eupalinus, the son of Naustrophus. If that ranks as the first of the three wonders, then the second is a mole which encloses the harbour from the sea: it reaches down some 20 fathoms at its deepest, and is over 2 stades in length. Third on the list of Samian wonder-works is a temple, the largest known to man.[55] The first architect to work on it was Rhoecus, the son of Phileas, a native of the island. Such is the case for covering the Samians in detail.

[61] Now, as Cambyses, the son of Cyrus, was whiling away his time in Egypt,[56] quite out of his mind, there rose in rebellion against him two brothers, Magians both, one of whom Cambyses had left behind to serve him as the steward of his household. This Magian had been prompted to his coup by the realization that the death of Smerdis had been kept a secret, so that there were very few Persians who actually knew of it, most being under the impression that Smerdis was still alive. These were the circumstances that had set the Magian plotting, and aiming to get his hands on the kingdom. His brother, whom I mentioned as being his partner in the rebellion, was very similar in appearance to Smerdis, the son of Cyrus, whose own brother, Cambyses, had had him executed. Indeed, not only was this Magian similar in appearance to Smerdis, but he even had the same name, Smerdis. 'I will take care of everything for you,' Patizeithes, the Magian, had managed to convince him; and the man was then led by his brother, and seated upon the royal throne. Once that was done, Patizeithes sent heralds off in all directions,

but he made especially sure to send one to Egypt, to announce to the army that they were to take their orders in the future not from Cambyses, but from Smerdis, the son of Cyrus.

[62] Sure enough, this proclamation was delivered by the various heralds, including the one who had been detailed to go to Egypt – although, as things turned out, he found Cambyses and his army in Syria, at Agbatana, where he duly stood up among the soldiers and publicly repeated what he had been told to repeat by the Magian. Hearing what had been said, Cambyses presumed that the herald was telling the truth, and that Prexaspes, the man he had sent to kill Smerdis, had betrayed him by failing to do as instructed. 'Prexaspes,' Cambyses said, fixing him with a glare, 'is this how you carried out the mission I gave you?' 'Master,' Prexaspes answered, 'it is none of it true. Your brother, Smerdis, cannot possibly have risen in revolt against you. You will never have any trouble, no matter where on the scale of danger, from that particular man. I did precisely as you told me to do, and then I buried him – yes, personally, with my own hands. If it is true that the dead are in revolt, then look for Astyages the Mede to rise against you too. If everything continues as it has always done, however, then there is no need for you to fear any injury in the future from your brother. That is why I think the best policy would be to go after this herald and ask him, under interrogation, who it was sent him with this announcement that we should follow the orders of King Smerdis.'

[63] This advice of Prexaspes struck Cambyses as being very sensible, and so the herald was tracked down straightaway and brought back. On his return, Prexaspes questioned him. 'Now, my man, you say that you have come here as the messenger of Smerdis, the son of Cyrus. Tell us the truth, now, and you can be on your way scot-free. Did your orders come directly from Smerdis, in person, or did they come from some underling?' 'I have never once seen Smerdis, the son of Cyrus,' answered the man, 'not since the day that King Cambyses set off on his invasion of Egypt. It was the Magian, the one appointed by Cambyses to be the steward of his household, who gave me this particular mission – although he did say that the order to deliver the speech I gave you came from Smerdis, the son of Cyrus.' All this, delivered to Cambyses and Prexaspes, was of course the simple truth. 'Prexaspes,' Cambyses told him, 'I exonerate you of the charge of disobedience. You are a good man, and you did precisely as ordered. But which Persian can it possibly

be, then, who has risen in rebellion against me, and usurped the name of Smerdis?' 'My Lord,' Prexaspes answered, 'I think I have worked out what has happened. The rebels are a couple of Magians: Patizeithes, the man you left behind as the steward of your household, and his brother Smerdis.'

[64] And it was then, upon hearing the name of Smerdis, that the truth of what Prexaspes had said, and of his own dream, hit Cambyses: for what had he seen in his sleep, if not someone informing him that Smerdis was sitting upon the royal throne, and that his head was brushing the sky? Cambyses realized now that his killing of his brother had been quite needless; so he wept for Smerdis, and then, brushing away his tears, and in agony at the whole wretched business, leapt onto his horse, fully intending to lead his army as fast as he could on Susa, to attack the Magian. As he leapt onto his horse, however, the tip of his scabbard snapped off, and the naked blade of the dagger struck his thigh, wounding him in the very spot where previously he himself had struck Apis, the god of the Egyptians. The wound, Cambyses sensed, was a mortal one; and so he asked, 'What is the name of this city?' Back came the reply: 'Agbatana.' Now, some time previously, the oracle in Bouto had told Cambyses that his life would end in Agbatana. He had concluded from this that he would die an old man in the Median Agbatana, the city which served him as the hub of his administration; but the oracle, it turned out, had been alluding to the Syrian Agbatana. And when, in response to his question, Cambyses came to learn the name of the city, such was the trauma of the misfortune that the Magian had brought upon him, and of his wound, that he quite recovered his sanity and fathomed the meaning of the oracle. 'It is here', he declared, 'that Cambyses, the son of Cyrus, is fated to meet his end.'

[65] And that, at the time, was that; but then, some twenty days later, Cambyses sent for the most eminent Persians in his train, and said to them, 'Men of Persia, I am obliged by circumstances to reveal to you the matter which more than any other I had been hoping to keep a secret. While I was in Egypt, I saw something in my sleep – a vision that I wish that I had never seen. I imagined that there came to me from my palace a messenger, who reported to me that Smerdis was sitting upon the royal throne, and that his head was brushing the sky. Nervous that my own brother might seize power from me, I acted speedily – but not sensibly. Indeed, although I can see now that no man has it within himself

to turn destiny aside,[57] such was my stupidity that I sent Prexaspes off to Susa to kill Smerdis – a terrible deed. Yet once it had been done, I carried on with my life feeling perfectly secure, nor did it so much as cross my mind that with Smerdis out of the way some other man might rise against me. On every count, then, I missed the point of what was to happen – with the consequence that I became the killer of my brother, and quite needlessly so, since I have still ended deprived of my kingdom. You see, the Smerdis whose rebellion I was warned about in my dream, by the agency of the heavens, was none other than the Magian. But I have done what I have done – and you must come to terms with the fact that Smerdis, the son of Cyrus, is no longer among you. The men now in power in this, your kingdom, are the Magians: one, the steward whom I left behind to administer my household, and the other his brother, Smerdis. There is one man, more than any other, who should have avenged the disgrace that these Magians have brought on me – and yet he, by a most cruel twist of fate, has met his end at the hands of his nearest kinsman. My next best option, then – my brother no longer being here – is one that I must of necessity take: namely, to command you, men of Persia, to fulfil my dying wishes. I call now as my witnesses the gods of the royal household, and lay upon all of you here, and especially those of you who are Achaemenids, this charge: never to let supremacy pass back to the Medes. Should they obtain it by means of treachery, then by treachery you must take it back; should it be force that brings them their success, then you must recover it through the exercise of brute force. Do that, and I pray that the earth will be fruitful for you, and your women and cattle fecund – for you will be, and will forever be, free men. Should you not regain power, however, nor make any effort to recover it, then I pray that the opposite befalls you – and more, that every man in Persia meets an end such as has overtaken me.' And even as he said this, Cambyses wept for all he had done.

[66] When the Persians saw their king in tears, they all tore the clothes that they had on, and gave themselves over to uninhibited lamentation. Later, when the bone turned gangrenous and the thigh had rotted, the wound fast carried off Cambyses, after a reign that had lasted in all for seven years and five months. He died quite childless, having fathered neither son nor daughter. Meanwhile, the Persians who had been in attendance on him refused to accept that the Magians could possibly have taken power, for they believed all Cambyses' talk about

the death of his brother to have been mere disinformation, fed to them with the aim of embroiling the whole of Persia in a war against Smerdis.

[67] No wonder, then, that they believed the newly installed king to be Smerdis, son of Cyrus. By now, with Cambyses no longer around, Prexaspes was furiously denying that he had ever killed Smerdis, since it would have been perilous for him to admit that he had the blood of Cyrus' son on his hands. As a result, with Cambyses dead, the Magian had nothing to worry about, but could simply sit on the throne and usurp the role of his namesake, Smerdis, son of Cyrus. Seven months he ruled – which, when combined with the span of Cambyses' reign, made for a total of eight years. His behaviour during his time on the throne was characterized by a great beneficence towards all his subjects, with the consequence that his death was felt as a bereavement by all the various peoples of Asia – the Persians only excepted. For the Magian sent messengers to every nation in his empire, and proclaimed to them a three-year exemption from military service and tribute.

[68] These measures were announced the moment that he had secured his rule; but then, seven months on, the whole deception was brought to light. It so happened that there was a Persian named Otanes,[58] the son of Pharnaspes, and a man who in terms of breeding and wealth was the equal of any of the Persian elite. This Otanes was the first to suspect that the Magian was not in fact Smerdis, son of Cyrus, and to guess at his true identity, by picking up on a key fact: the Magian had never once left his hill-top citadel or summoned into his presence any Persian of high rank. Once his suspicions were raised, Otanes did not let the matter rest there. Cambyses had married his daughter, Phaidymie as she was called, and this woman, along with all the other wives of Cambyses, had subsequently been taken in marriage by the Magian. Accordingly, Otanes sent a message to his daughter, asking her what man it was who shared her bed with her: was it Smerdis, the son of Cyrus, or someone else altogether? Back came her reply: 'I have no idea. I have never seen Smerdis, the son of Cyrus, and so do not really know who my husband is.' Otanes then sent her a second message. 'Even if you personally are unable to recognize Smerdis, the son of Cyrus, you can always ask Atossa[59] who this man is to whom both you and she are married – for there can surely be no doubt that she will know her own brother?' His daughter then sent back another message: 'I can never speak to Atossa,

nor do I ever see any of the other women who live here quartered with me, because when he first took over the kingdom, this man – whoever he is – separated us all into different apartments.'

[69] When Otanes heard this, things became clearer to him. He duly sent a third message in to Phaidymie. 'My daughter, the fact that you are of noble birth obliges you to undertake whatever danger your father may order you into. If this is not Smerdis, son of Cyrus, but rather the man I suspect him to be, then he cannot possibly be allowed to get away with taking you to bed and making the Persians his subjects. No, he must pay the price! So this is what I want you to do. When he is in bed with you, make sure that he is asleep, and then feel for his ears. Should he prove to have some, then you may be confident that your husband is indeed Smerdis, son of Cyrus – but any shortage of ears will mean that you are dealing with Smerdis, the Magian.' Phaidymie, in her reply to this message, pointed out that the plan was a hugely dangerous one: if indeed it chanced that he did not have ears, and she was found groping after them, she had not the slightest doubt that he would dispose of her. 'All the same,' she said, 'I will do it.' So it was that she promised to take part in her father's scheme. The thing was that when Cyrus, son of Cambyses, was king, he had cut off the ears[60] of Smerdis the Magian as punishment for some offence (and a not inconsiderable one either). Sure enough, Phaidymie, daughter of Otanes, completed everything she had promised her father she would do. Because women in Persia sleep with their husbands in rotation,[61] she waited for her turn to visit the Magian, then came and lay beside him until he was fast asleep, whereupon she felt for his ears. It proved a simple matter, not remotely challenging, for her to discover that the man had none; and so at daybreak she sent a message to her father reporting what she had found.

[70] Otanes then took aside Aspathines and Gobryas, both eminent Persians, and friends in whom he placed the utmost trust, and related the whole business to them. As it happened, they had been harbouring suspicions along very similar lines, so they readily accepted everything that Otanes told them. They next resolved that each of them should recruit as a fellow-conspirator whichever man among the Persians struck them as being particularly trustworthy. Otanes duly brought in Intaphrenes, Gobryas brought in Megabyzus, and Aspathines brought in Hydarnes. Then, with the conspirators numbering six, it so happened that Darius, son of Hystaspes, arrived in Susa from Persia, where his

father was the governor; and the six Persians, in the wake of Darius' arrival, decided to co-opt him as well.

[71] So the seven of them held a meeting, where they swapped various pledges and proposals. When the time came for Darius to make his opinion known, he told his fellow-conspirators, 'I thought I was the only one who knew that the man now on the throne was the Magian, and that Smerdis, son of Cyrus, was dead. In fact, that is why I came here at such speed: to arrange for the death of the Magian. But now, since it turns out that you all know what is going on as well as me, I recommend that we act immediately, without delay. There is no alternative.' To this, however, Otanes said, 'You are the child of Hystaspes, the son of a fine father – and it seems to me you have just demonstrated that you are not a whit his inferior. All the same, do not shut your ears to good advice and let the whole enterprise run away with you. Show a bit more prudence and get a grip on things. We need more recruits before we strike.' 'Gentlemen,' Darius answered, addressing everyone present, 'if you follow the course just spelled out by Otanes, then know this: you will all meet with terrible deaths. A desire to make a profit on the side is bound to lead someone to denounce us to the Magian. Your best option would have been to run the risk on your own. It was your choice, however, to bring in more conspirators, and then to communicate everything to me. That being so, either let us act today, or else, if the hours slip by, and today becomes tomorrow, be in no doubt – I will be the first to turn informer. I will go to the Magian, and I will spill the whole business to him myself.'

[72] When Otanes saw how agitated Darius was, he said, 'Very well, since you refuse to allow us any pause and leave us with no option but to move at full speed, elaborate for us, I pray, how precisely we are supposed to breach the royal palace and get to grips with the Magians. Even you must appreciate, from what is reported if not from the evidence of your own eyes, that there are guards stationed there at regular intervals. How on earth are we to get past them?' 'Otanes,' Darius answered, 'there are many things which cannot be explained in words, and yet are practicable, just as there are many things which are brilliant when put into a speech, but not when put into action. We shall have no problem in getting past the duty-guards, just you mark my words. In the first place, they feel such a combination of respect and fear for men of our rank that they will never forbid us entry. What is more, there is a

wonderfully specious story I can tell to get us in. I shall say that I have just come from Persia, and that I wish to communicate a message from my father to the king. A lie that serves a vital purpose, after all, is a lie that should be told.[62] Whether we tell falsehoods or nothing but the truth, we all of us have the same objective: liars are always on the alert for the chance to profit by convincing others of their lies, just as those who tell the truth do so with the aim of ending up more trusted by everyone else, and thereby acquiring profit in their own manner. Different though our means may be, yet we have identical ends. Were there no advantage to be gained, the man who tells the truth might as well tell lies, and the man who tells lies might as well tell the truth. Now, any gatekeeper who is content to wave us past will benefit from doing so in the long run. Anyone who tries to block our path, however, will be branded an enemy on the spot. Then we shove him out of our way, and get down to business.'

[73] It was Gobryas who spoke next. 'Gentlemen,' he said, 'dear friends, will we ever have a better opportunity to regain power, or – failing that – to die in the attempt? We are Persians, but look at us! Ruled by a Mede, a Magian, and worse – a man with no ears! Those of you who attended Cambyses on his sick-bed will surely remember every last word of the curse he laid upon the Persians as his life was nearing its end, should they make no effort to regain their supremacy. At the time, we did not register what was going on. We believed that everything spoken by Cambyses was slander. Now, however, given the way things are, I vote to do as Darius says, and not break up this assembly unless it is to go immediately to attack the Magian.' So argued Gobryas, and all the others concurred.

[74] Now, as fate would have it, this discussion among the conspirators was being paralleled by another development. The Magians too had been putting their heads together and had decided that it would be a good idea to win over Prexaspes to their cause: firstly, because he had suffered so appallingly at the hands of Cambyses, who had shot and killed his son with an arrow; secondly because, as the man who had been personally responsible for the assassination, he was the only one who could be absolutely certain that Smerdis, the son of Cyrus, was indeed dead; and finally because he was someone held in the utmost esteem by the Persians. For all these reasons, they summoned him to a meeting as a friend, and sought to secure his backing by swapping

pledges with him and by swearing him to keep their secret, promising him countless riches if only he would vow in return not to betray to a single soul the deception that they had laid on the Persians. Once they had succeeded in persuading him to do as they asked, and Prexaspes had given them his word, the Magians advanced a second proposal. 'We will summon everyone in Persia to a meeting beneath the wall of the palace,' they said, 'and instruct you to climb to the top of a tower, where you are to announce to everyone that the man who rules them is Smerdis, son of Cyrus, and no one else.' What lay behind this order was the unparalleled trust in which Prexaspes was so clearly held by the Persians, and because he had so often and forthrightly given it as his opinion that Smerdis, son of Cyrus, was indeed still alive, together with strenuous denials that he had killed him.

[75] Once Prexaspes had said that he was willing to do this too, the Magians duly summoned the Persians, had Prexaspes go up a tower and ordered him to deliver his speech. Prexaspes, however, chose to forget everything that they had asked of him, and instead began tracing Cyrus' paternal line, beginning with Achaemenes, then listing all his other forefathers in turn and ending with Cyrus himself. At last, having concluded with an account of all the good things that Cyrus had achieved on behalf of the Persians, Prexaspes was done with his genealogizing – and proceeded to a revelation of the truth. 'On previous occasions,' he said, 'because the danger to me of talking about what had happened was too great, I kept it a secret. Now, however, necessity obliges me to bring it to light.' And so he told them how he had been forced by Cambyses to kill Smerdis, son of Cyrus – and of how the Magians were ruling as kings. Then he called down a great array of curses upon the Persians should they fail to win back power and punish the Magians; and then he threw himself down, head first, from the tower. Such was the end of Prexaspes, a man who all his life had enjoyed the reputation of the best.

[76] Meanwhile, once the Seven Persians had resolved that they should attack the Magians immediately, without delay, they offered up prayers to the gods and set off, quite oblivious of the whole business with Prexaspes. Only when they had gone half way did they find out what had befallen him. The news prompted them to halt by the side of the road and renew their debate. Otanes and his backers stated categorically that delay was essential, and that any notion of launching an attack amid such turmoil was quite out of the question, whereas Darius

and his party insisted on advancing at once and putting their plans into action without delay. In the midst of all this wrangling, there appeared seven pairs of hawks, in pursuit of two pairs of vultures. The hawks were sending the vultures' feathers flying, and shredding their bodies. The sight brought the Seven to give their unanimous backing to the arguments of Darius – and so, emboldened by the birds, they went on towards the palace.

[77] When they came to stand outside the gates, everything happened more or less as Darius had forecast: the guards, confronted by the foremost men in Persia, did indeed cringe before them, never suspecting the divinely appointed mission they were engaged upon, but waving them past and asking them nothing. The Seven made it into the courtyard, where they were met by the eunuchs whose job it was to take messages in to the king, who enquired of them what they wanted, and why they had come. Even as the eunuchs put these questions, however, they were simultaneously threatening to punish the gatekeepers for having admitted the Seven – whose wish to go further into the palace they attempted to obstruct. At this, the Seven yelled encouragement to one another, then drew their daggers, quickly stabbed the men who had been presuming to restrain them and proceeded at full pelt into the men's quarters.

[78] Now it so happened that both the Magians were inside, discussing how to handle the consequences of the Prexaspes affair. Accordingly, when they saw the eunuchs screaming in uproar, they sprang to their feet; and when they realized what was going on, their thoughts turned to resistance. One of them just had time to take down his bow; the other turned and grabbed his spear. Then battle was joined – the two sides, one against the other. So hemmed in by his enemies was the Magian who had picked up his bow and arrows, and so hard pressed by them, that he found his weapons no use at all; but the other Magian, the one who had the spear, defended himself to such good effect that he struck Aspathines in the thigh and Intaphrenes in the eye. (This wound to Intaphrenes, though not fatal, did result in his losing his eye.) Such was the damage that one of the Magians managed to inflict upon his attackers; but the other Magian, when he found his bow and his arrows useless, ran down from the men's quarters into a bedroom which opened directly onto them. His aim was to bar the room's doors; but two of the Seven, Darius and Gobryas, were hot on his heels. Gobryas started to

grapple with the Magian, but it was so dark that Darius, terrified in case he struck Gobryas by accident, stood there beside him, paralysed by indecision. Gobryas, when he saw Darius standing there ineffectually, asked him why he did not lend a hand. 'I am worried,' said Darius, 'in case I hit you.' 'Strike with your sword,' Gobryas answered, 'even if you run both of us through!' Obediently, Darius struck with his dagger – and somehow managed to strike the Magian alone.

[79] Then, having dispatched the Magians, the conspirators cut off their heads. Their own wounded they left behind in the citadel, since it needed guarding, and the wounded were anyway incapacitated; but the remaining five, yelling at the tops of their voices, and taking with them the heads of the Magians, ran outside, calling as they did so on all the other Persians to join them. As they told everyone their news, and brandished the heads, they simultaneously slew each and every Magian who crossed their path. When the Persians learned what the Seven had done, and of the hoax perpetrated by the Magians, they felt themselves perfectly justified in joining in – and so they too drew their daggers, and started to kill any Magian they could find. Indeed, had nightfall not intervened, they would not have left a single Magian alive. This day is now more widely celebrated by the mass of the Persian people than any other in their calendar: they mark it with a great festival which is called by the Persians 'The Slaughter of the Magians', and includes a ban on any Magian appearing by daylight, so that all who belong to the Magians are obliged to keep to their homes the whole day long.

[80] Some five days and more later, when the uproar had subsided, the conspirators against the Magians met to debate the general state of affairs.[63] The speeches that were delivered at this debate, although regarded by some Greeks as incredible, were indeed authentically spoken. It was the recommendation of Otanes that they place the business of government in the midst of the Persian people. 'In my opinion,' he said, 'we should abandon any notion of installing one of us as sole ruler. There is nothing either pleasant or noble about monarchy. You saw for yourselves how far Cambyses went in abusing his power, and you have had some experience as well of the Magian's brutality and arrogance. How can monarchy ever create ordered governance, when a monarch can do what he pleases and not be answerable for it? Install even the very best of men in such a position of authority and his customary personality will be quite transformed. All the good qualities that

he possesses will foster an abusive arrogance in him – and as for envy, well, that is ingrained in men from birth. These twin characteristics will suffice to render him a repository of every kind of evil, and every crime he commits will be traceable to a surfeit of insolence and jealousy. By rights, of course, a man who rules as a tyrant should be proof against envy, bearing in mind all the pleasant things that he enjoys. In reality, however, instinct imbues him with an attitude towards the citizenry which is quite the opposite. Just as he resents the continued existence of the city's elite, so he exults in those who make up its dregs – nor is there anyone quicker to listen to malevolent gossip. A sole ruler is also more prone to violent swings of mood than anyone. Express only a moderate admiration for him, for instance, and your relative lack of deference will throw him into a towering rage – but behave with a creeping subservi-ence and he will grow irate with you for being a flatterer. And that is not all: I now come to mention his gravest offences. A monarch plays havoc with ancestral customs, he rapes women and he executes men without trial. Rule by the majority, on the other hand, bears that fairest of all titles: 'Equality before the law'.[64] Not only that, but it has this second quality: it gives rise to none of the actions which a monarch character-istically takes. Those in office have their authority courtesy of a lottery, and wield it in a way that is strictly accountable. Every policy decision must be referred to the commonality of the people. That is why I give it as my opinion that we should abolish the monarchy and foster the rule of the masses. Everything, after all, is contained within the multitude.' Such was the case made by Otanes.

[81] Megabyzus, however, urged that power be turned over to an oli-garchy. 'While I concur with the criticisms levelled by Otanes against tyranny,' he said, 'I feel that he is seriously wide of the mark in recom-mending that power be transferred to the masses. There is nothing more lacking in intelligence, nor more insolent, than some useless mob. How intolerable that men should escape the haughty brutality of a tyrant, only to succumb to the untempered violence of riff-raff no less haughty or brutal! At least a tyrant, when he does something, understands what he is doing, but a mob lacks even that modicum of knowledge! What can anyone know who has been taught nothing of what is fine and noble, nor possesses any innate sense of it, but only rushes blindly at things, and batters at them like some river in spate? No, leave it to those who bear ill will towards the Persians to deploy the masses in govern-

ment! Let us instead pick a band of the finest men we have and entrust them with power. We ourselves will, after all, be numbered among them – and it is only reasonable to assume that men who rank as the best will devise the best policies as well.' Such was the case made by Megabyzus.[65]

[82] The third person to make known his point of view was Darius. 'In my opinion,' he said, 'the speech that Megabyzus just gave us was very much to the point in its analysis of the masses, but highly misleading when it touched on oligarchy. We have three choices before us. Suppose that each of them functions as well as it possibly can – rule by the people, rule by an elite and rule by a single man.[66] It is this last option, I would argue, which stands head and shoulders above the others. A single individual who cannot be improved upon is self-evidently the best – for the judgement of such a man can be deployed in the governance of his people, without his ever being criticized. Similarly, it serves as the best possible guarantee that plans directed against men opposed to us will be kept confidential. Yes, there are many in an oligarchy with a commitment to civic virtue, and they do indeed practise it in the cause of the common good – and yet how often does that same commitment engender bitter private enmities! Since every oligarch wishes to be foremost, and see his opinions prevail, an eruption of savage feuding is the inevitable consequence – feuding which in turn results in civil strife, which leads to bloodshed, which results in rule by a single man. Proof enough, then, of the degree to which monarchy excels! Then again, wherever the people are in power, corruption is the inevitable consequence. What serves to foster this state of corruption in a commonwealth is the tendency of trouble-makers, not to turn on one another, but rather to form fast friendships and to get things done by ganging up with one another and exploiting the common interest. So it goes on, until in due course someone emerges as a champion of the people and puts a stop to it. The consequence of this, however, is that the people are lost in such admiration for this person that their hero-worship sees him emerge as a monarch. Clear proof again that it is monarchy which is the best! There remains, however, one clinching point to be made. Where did this independence of ours come from? To what do we owe it? To the people, to an oligarchy – or to a monarch? It was an individual, one single individual, who won our liberty for us – and that is why I firmly believe that we should maintain our current

system of government. And that doesn't even touch on a further issue – the excellence of the way that our forefathers ordered things, and which should never be disassembled.[67] There is no alternative.'

[83] Such, then, were the three points of view put forward for consideration – and it was to the last that four of the Seven gave their backing. Otanes, desperate as he had been to see the Persians established as equal before the law, responded to his defeat by making a declaration to the other six. 'My fellow-conspirators,' he said, 'whether it is done by casting lots, or by turning to the Persian people for their choice of candidate, or by some other means altogether, it is evident now that one of us is going to become king. That being so, I will not be a candidate in the contest. I have as little wish to be a ruler as to be ruled. Nevertheless, I renounce my claim to the kingdom on this one condition – that I will not be subject to any of you, neither I nor any of my descendants, in perpetuity.' The other six, once Otanes had delivered these terms, agreed to them; and so he duly stood down from the contest, and withdrew from the meeting. And still, to this day, the House of Otanes ranks as the only free one in all of Persia: though it never breaks the laws of the Persians, it is obedient to the king only to the degree that it wishes to be.

[84] The six remaining conspirators deliberated among themselves as to the fairest way of installing a king. They decided that if one of the others among the Seven became king, Otanes and his descendants should be rewarded as a special privilege with a grant, each and every year, of all the things that the Persians most prize – Median robes included. Behind their decision to give him this award was the fact that he had been the prime mover in the whole business, and had recruited them all to the conspiracy. Then, in addition to the special privileges granted to Otanes, it was resolved that all of the Seven should share a right of unannounced entry to the royal palaces, except when the king happened to be sleeping with one his wives, and that it should be forbidden the king to marry outside the families of his fellow-insurrectionists. As for the method of choosing a king, they resolved that they should all mount their horses out on the margins of the city, and that the kingdom should be given to the rider of whichever horse was the first to neigh after the sun had risen.

[85] Now, Darius had a groom called Oebares, a man who was very clever. Once the meeting had broken up, Darius said to this man, 'Oebares, we have decided how the issue of the kingdom is to be sorted.

We will all of us climb into our saddles, and whoever's horse neighs first as the sun rises will win for his rider the throne. Your brain – is it in good working order? If so, then devise some scheme that will enable us – us, and no one else – to secure this great honour!' 'Master,' Oebares replied, 'if this is really what your prospect of becoming king depends upon, keep your spirits up and rest confident there is no one who will beat you to the throne. I have the perfect plan for success!' 'Well,' said Darius, 'if you really do have a cunning scheme in mind, now is the time to put it into action. No time for delay, because our contest will be held tomorrow morning.' Sure enough, no sooner had Oebares heard this than he set to work as follows. When night fell, he led out a mare, for which Darius' horse had a special partiality, to the limits of the city and tethered her there; he then brought Darius' horse out to the same spot, and walked him round and round and round her, allowing him to draw so close that he brushed against her. Then finally Oebares released the stallion, who mounted the mare.

[86] At the first glimmer of dawn, the six all assembled on horseback, as they had agreed, and rode out to the limits of the city. Then, as they did a circuit, they came to the spot where the mare had been tethered the night before – and immediately Darius' horse galloped up to it and whinnied. Simultaneously, just as the horse was doing this, there was a flash of lightning from the clear blue sky and a clap of thunder. These additional markers, produced as if to order, clinched the contest for Darius: the others all leapt down from their horses and prostrated themselves before him.

[87] But there is another story explaining how Oebares managed to pull off the trick. (In fact, the Persians tell it both ways.) Oebares, according to this second tale, rubbed his hand all over the mare's genitals, and then kept his hand hidden in his trousers. As the sun rose, and the six were about to let their horses go, Oebares whipped out his hand and shoved it under the nostrils of Darius' horse – and no sooner had the horse smelled it than he snorted and whinnied.[68]

[88] So it was that Darius, son of Hystaspes, was proclaimed king – lord, thanks to the conquests of Cyrus, and those subsequently of Cambyses, of all the various peoples of Asia, the Arabians only excepted. (The Arabians, rather than being subjected to slavery by the Persians, had instead come to rank in friendship as their allies, at the time when they had granted Cambyses safe passage into Egypt. Had the Arabians

withheld their support, then the Persians would never have been able to invade Egypt.) The first of the marriages that Darius made to Persian women were to two daughters of Cyrus – Atossa and Artystone. Atossa had been married twice before, first to her brother, Cambyses, and then to the Magian; Artystone was a virgin. Darius also married two other women: one was the daughter of Smerdis, the son of Cyrus, and went by the name of Parmys, while the second was the daughter of Otanes who had exposed the Magian. Darius' power encompassed everything. His first move was to commission and install a stone relief featuring the figure of a man on horseback, together with an inscription:

DARIUS, THE SON OF HYSTASPES, THANKS TO THE EXCELLENCE OF HIS HORSE

– here the name of the horse was inserted –

AND OF OEBARES HIS GROOM, WHO SECURED THE KINGDOM OF PERSIA.

[89] His next step was to organize the Persian empire into twenty provinces, or *satrapies* as the Persians themselves term them. Then, once he had established the provinces and appointed governors to them, he fixed the tribute which was to be paid by all the various peoples of the empire – 'peoples' signifying not only those who were actually named, but those who bordered them as well, while those who lived further afield were assigned to the roster of peoples at random. There now follows an account of how the various provinces were divided up, together with a list of the taxes[69] paid by them each year. The currency that those who paid in silver were told to use was the Babylonian talent, while those who paid in gold had to do so in Euboïc talents. (One Babylonian talent is equivalent to 70 Euboïc *minae*.)[70] During the reign of Cyrus, and of Cambyses his successor, there was no fixed rate of tribute, and people made presentations of gifts instead. Darius, because of the system of tribute that he imposed, and similar measures, was labelled by the Persians 'the Shopkeeper', while they nicknamed Cambyses 'the Despot', and Cyrus 'the Father'. Darius did indeed put a price on everything; Cambyses was indeed cruel and contemptuous of his lessers; and Cyrus was indeed gentle, and all his policies had been devised for the good of his people.

[90] The Ionians, the Magnesians of Asia, the Aeolians, the Carians,

the Lycians, the Milyans and the Pamphylians were all, for the purposes of taxation, assessed as a single unit: the province was listed as Number One on the register, and contributed 400 talents of silver. Province Number Two contributed 500 talents, and consisted of the Mysians, the Lydians, the Lasonians, the Cabalians and the Hytenneans. Province Number Three contributed a tax of 360 talents, and consisted of those who live on the right-hand side of the Hellespont as one sails into it, the Phrygians, the Thracians of Asia, the Paphlagonians, the Mariandynians and the Syrians. Province Number Four consisted of the Cilicians, who contributed 360 white horses, one for each day of the year, and 500 talents of silver; 140 of these talents were used to maintain the cavalry that was deployed on Cilician territory as its garrison, and 360 went to Darius.

[91] Starting at Posideium, a city which was founded on the border between Cilicia and Syria by Amphilochus, the son of Amphiaraus, and extending all the way to Egypt (although not including the area inhabited by the Arabians, who were exempt from taxation), there stretched a region which encompassed the entirety of Phoenicia, the portion of Syria known as Palestine, and Cyprus, and which paid 350 talents: Province Number Five. Province Number Six consisted mainly of Egypt, although other regions too were grouped with it: the adjoining stretches of Libya, together with Cyrene and Barca. The tribute paid by the district came to 700 talents, excluding the revenue generated by the fishing industry of Lake Moeris. Setting this revenue aside, and also setting aside a fixed ration of grain (120,000 measures, issued to the Persians and auxiliary troops who are based in the White Fort in Memphis), the region contributed, as I said, 700 talents. Province Number Seven consisted of the Sattagydae, the Gandarians, the Dadicae and the Aparytians, who between them contributed 170 talents. Province Number Eight, consisting of Susa and the rest of the land of the Cissians, contributed 300 talents.

[92] The next province, Number Nine, consisted of Babylon and the rest of Assyria, and contributed 1,000 talents of silver, and 500 boys to serve as eunuchs. Province Number Ten consisted of the Medes – the people of Agbatana in particular – the Paricanians and the Orthocorybantians, and contributed 450 talents. Province Number Eleven consisted of the Caspians, the Pausicae, the Pantimathi and the Daritae, who jointly paid 200 talents. Province Number Twelve consisted of

Bactria[71] as far as the territory of the Aegli, and paid a tribute of 360 talents.

[93] Province Number Thirteen, which consisted of the lands of the Pactyicans and the Armenians, and everywhere between them and the Euxine Sea, contributed 400 talents. Province Number Fourteen consisted of the Sagartians, the Sarangians, the Thamanaeans, the Outians, the Mycians and all the inhabitants of those islands in the Red Sea where the king settles people who are called 'the Uprooted': jointly, they contributed 600 talents' worth of tribute. The Sacae and the Caspians, who contributed 250 talents, made up Province Number Fifteen, while Province Number Sixteen, which consisted of the Parthians, the Chorasmians, the Sogdians and the Arians, contributed 300 talents.

[94] Province Number Seventeen, which consisted of the Paricanians and the Ethiopians of Asia, contributed 400 talents. The Matienians, the Saspeirians and the Alarodians, who made up Province Number Eighteen, had a tribute of 200 talents imposed on them. Province Number Nineteen, which consisted of the Moschians, the Tibarenians, the Macronians, the Mossynoecians and the Mares, was told to pay 300 talents. Province Number Twenty consisted of the Indians, who have a far larger population than any other people of which we know, and who contributed a larger tribute than everyone else: 360 talents' worth of gold-dust.

[95] The amount paid in Babylonian silver, calculated in Euboïc talents, came to 9,880 talents, while the gold-dust from India, if gold is reckoned to be thirteen times more valuable than silver, will be found to have come to 4,680 Euboïc talents. Add the figures all together, and the sum total of the annual tribute paid to Darius, in Euboïc talents, was 14,560 talents. (I have neglected to include in my calculations any payments made in fractional amounts.)

[96] Such, then, was the tribute levied by Darius from Asia and from a small portion of the continent of Libya. As time went on, however, the Aegean islands also came to contribute taxes, as did peoples in Europe as far as Thessaly. To store all this tribute, what the king does is melt it down and pour it into earthenware jars, and then, once each jar is full, remove the earthenware. Whenever he needs money, he hacks off as much as the occasion requires.

[97] So much for the provinces and the assessments of tribute. The only country I have not mentioned as making a payment is Persia: its inhabitants, the Persians, are exempt from taxes. There were also some

peoples who, although not required to pay any tribute, did contribute gifts: those Ethiopians who border Egypt, and who were conquered by Cambyses in the course of his advance against the long-lived Ethiopians, for instance, and also those Ethiopians who live beside the holy mountain, Nysa, and who celebrate festivals in honour of Dionysus. (These Ethiopians and their neighbours use the same seed as do the Callantian Indians; they also live in homes that are underground.) Every other year – as they still do right into the present – these two peoples jointly bring 2 *choenixes* of unrefined gold, 200 blocks of ebony, 5 Ethiopian boys and 20 large elephant tusks. The Colchians also committed themselves to contributing gifts, as did all the peoples living between them and the Caucasus, a mountain range which constitutes the northernmost limit of Persian rule (for no one beyond it gives the Persians so much as a thought).[72] Every four years, they brought the gifts to which they had committed themselves, and which they still present even today: one hundred boys and one hundred girls. Then there were the Arabians, who contributed 1,000 talents of frankincense every year. Such, then, were the gifts borne to the king, and which were tallied quite distinctly from all the tribute.

[98] As for the gold-dust that I mentioned being brought to the king, that derives from the huge quantity of gold that the Indians procure. Here is how they come by it. There is, in the land of India, towards the rising of the sun, a desert. Indeed, of all the various peoples of Asia whom we might cite, and about whom we have reliable information, it is the Indians who live the furthest east, and the closest to the rising of the sun; east of them there stretches nothing but a wilderness of sand. There are many different tribes of Indians, all of them speaking different languages. Some are nomads, others are not, while some live in swamps next to rivers and eat raw fish, which they catch by going out in boats made of reeds. (Indeed, each boat is made out of a single piece of cane.) These same Indians also wear clothes made out of rushes, which they cut down and harvest from the river, and weave as you might a mat, and then wear in the manner of a breastplate.

[99] East of these,[73] there is another tribe of Indians, named the Padaei, who are nomadic and eat raw meat. These Indians, so it is reported, have a highly distinctive way of treating anyone among their citizens, male or female, who may fall sick. Should the invalid be a man, his closest male friends will kill him, on the grounds that his illness, by eating away at his body, is depriving them of meat. Volubly though he

may protest his good health, they will not pay him the slightest attention, but kill him anyway, and make a feast of him. Should it be a woman who has fallen sick, then her closest female friends will behave towards her precisely as the men do towards a man. They will also sacrifice and feast on anyone who reaches old age. It does not happen very often, however, that anyone comes to be thought of as old. It only requires someone to fall sick before reaching that stage of life, after all, and he or she is killed.

[100] Then again, there are other Indians with a quite different way of life. They kill no living creature, grow no crops and have no tradition of owning a home. All they eat is plants – and in particular a grain about the size of a millet-seed, which grows inside a pod and requires no cultivation. The Indians harvest these seeds, pods and all, then boil them up and eat them. Whenever a member of the tribe happens to fall ill, he will go out into the desert and lie down there. It makes no difference whether he is dead or merely diseased: no one else will give him so much as a second thought.

[101] All the Indians of whom I have spoken mate with one another in public, just as livestock do, and are black in colour from top to toe; in this they are very like the Ethiopians, whom they closely resemble. The semen which they ejaculate into their women is not white like that of other men, but the same shade of black as their skins. (This is also true of the semen ejaculated by Ethiopians.)[74] These particular Indians live far beyond the reach of the Persians, where the south wind has its origins, nor were ever subjects of King Darius.

[102] There are other Indians who live in the northernmost point of India, where the constellation of the Bear shines, on the border between the city of Caspatyrus and the land of Pactyice. Their way of life is very like that of the Bactrians. They are the most warlike of the Indian tribes, and it is they who make expeditions to fetch the gold, out into the sands, where it is impossible actually to live. The sands of this same desert breed ants which are midway between dogs and foxes in size. (There were some that were actually trapped there and brought to the court of the Persian king.) These ants,[75] which in appearance are much like the ants found in Greece, also make their nests underground just as the ants in Greece do, by digging up sand – although, in their case, the excavated sand is flecked with gold. It is this same sand that the Indians are after when they go prospecting in the desert. Each one of them harnesses together three camels, two males and one female: the males do the

actual pulling, like trace-horses, and are positioned on either side of the female, which is placed in the middle and ridden by the Indian. Great care is taken to ensure that the harnessed mare is one that has only just given birth, and has been torn away from her young. The reason for this is that Indian camels are not a whit slower than horses, and far more capable of carrying loads besides.

[103] As for the appearance of the camel, that needs no description from me, since the Greeks are already familiar with it. What I will mention, however, are some details with which Greeks are not familiar: that the camel has two thighs and two knees in each of its hind legs,[76] and that its genitals protrude between its hind legs, and are oriented towards its tail.

[104] Thus the Indians – with their camels harnessed and themselves equipped in the manner I described – ride out in search of the gold; and because the ants disappear underground whenever the weather gets too scorching, the prospectors deliberately time their sally to ensure that their actual seizure of the gold coincides with the most blistering spell of heat. (Unlike in other lands, where the sun is at its hottest at noon, in India the sun is hottest throughout the morning, from sunrise until midday, when the markets shut down. So much hotter is it during this stretch of the day than it is at noon in Greece that the Indians are said to spend the whole time dousing themselves in water. The heat of midday, however, is pretty much the same as it is in other lands, while in the afternoon, the warmth of the sun in India is equivalent to its warmth elsewhere in the mornings. From then on, as the sun heads further and further into the distance, so the day gets ever colder – until at last, by sunset, it is very cold indeed.)

[105] Once the Indians, complete with sacks, have arrived at their destination, they fill up their sacks with the sand, and then go careering off home as fast as they possibly can. The reason for this, as reported by the Persians, is that the ants pick up on their scent, and give them chase. Now, there is nothing in the world quite as fast as these ants, to the degree that none of the Indians, were they to fail in getting a head start while the ants were massing, would make it back to safety. The male camels, because they are not as fleet-footed as the female ones, start to lag, and [may even] end up being cut loose, one after the other; the females, however, with memories of their abandoned young fresh in their minds, do not slacken. And that, so the Persians say, is how the

Indians obtain the greater part of their gold. The rest, a much smaller amount, comes from the country's mines.

[106] Now for some reason, just as fate has blessed Greece with by far the most beautiful mix of seasons, so also has she endowed the furthermost reaches of the inhabited world with the most beautiful things. Take, for instance, India, which lies further east than any other zone of human settlement – a detail which I mentioned before. All the creatures that live there, winged and four-legged ones alike, tower over those of other lands – all except the horses, which must yield place to the Median breed known as 'Nisaean'. What is more, India boasts a superabundance of gold, which is either mined, or borne down on rivers, or else just taken, in the manner I described. There are also trees there which grow wild, and produce as their fruit a wool of such beauty and excellence that it surpasses that of sheep. The Indians use these trees to make their clothes.[77]

[107] Then you could look to Arabia, the country which lies further south than any other inhabited region, and which is the one place in the world where frankincense grows, and myrrh, and cassia, and cinnamon, and rock rose resin. It is no easy matter for the Arabians to collect any of these, myrrh alone excepted. Frankincense they gather by burning styrax resin, which the Phoenicians export to Greece. The Arabians burn the styrax while gathering frankincense, because the bushes on which the frankincense grows are guarded by the same winged snakes as attack Egypt; tiny in size and dappled in colour, the snakes swarm around every bush. Smoke from burning styrax is the only thing that will ever drive them away from the bushes.

[108] The Arabians also claim that the whole world would be filled with these snakes, were it not for something that happens to them which I have known happen to vipers as well. Perhaps it is no surprise that divine providence, wise and far seeing as it is, should have arranged for all creatures which combine timidity with tastiness to breed prolifically, so as to prevent them from being eaten into extinction, while those that are aggressive and dangerous bear only occasional offspring. The hare, for instance, which is hunted by every beast and bird around, not to mention humans, breeds at a prolific rate. Indeed, it is the only creature which can conceive while already pregnant: as a result, it is possible for one of the young in its womb to be covered in fur and to be almost fully formed, while another may have no fur at all and barely have been con-

ceived. But if that is one extreme, then at the other is the lioness, a creature of incomparable strength and courage, which gives birth only the once in her lifetime, and then to a single whelp; even as she gives birth to the cub, so she expels her womb. Why does this happen? Because when the cub, while he is still in the womb, starts to move about, his claws are so much sharper than those of any other animal that he tears at the womb, ripping it ever more to shreds as he continues to grow, until eventually, by the time he is due to be born, not a single patch is left intact.

[109] In the same way, if vipers and the winged snakes of Arabia were able to reproduce themselves as prolifically as it is within their nature to do, it would spell the end of human life. As things are, however, whenever a pair of these snakes comes to mate, and the male is getting the female pregnant, so the female, even as the male is ejaculating his seed into her, fastens onto his neck, and hangs on so tightly that only once she has bitten right through does she finally let him go. So perishes the male, in the manner I have just related – after which the female is brought to pay a blood-price for the male. Her offspring, while still in her womb, avenge[78] their father by devouring their mother's insides, and they enter the world by gnawing their way right out through her stomach. Other snakes, however, because they present no threat to human life, lay eggs, and hatch an immense quantity of offspring. Unlike vipers, which are found across the entire face of the earth, the winged snakes are concentrated in Arabia, and nowhere else. It is this which gives the impression of their being so numerous.

[110] So much for the means by which the Arabians obtain frankincense; now for cassia. Prior to any cassia-hunting expedition, they will wrap themselves up in ox-hides and every other kind of leather – bodies, faces and all, so that only their eyes are showing. The cassia itself grows in ponds: shallow ones, not deep at all. In and around these ponds there roost winged creatures, which resemble bats as much as anything. They are ferociously aggressive and make terrible shrieks. If the cassia is to be plucked, then it is vital that these creatures be kept away from the eyes.

[111] The way that the Arabians collect cinnamon is even more astonishing. Where it comes from, and in what land it grows, they are quite unable to say – although there are those who claim, not at all unreasonably, that it grows in those places where Dionysus was raised. They say that huge birds carry the dry sticks that we, following the

Phoenician example, call 'cinnamon'; and the birds take these sticks to their nests, which are moulded out of mud on the sides of precipitous mountains where no human can possibly get at them. Confronted by this challenge, the Arabians have come up with a very clever solution. They hack off as much as they can of the limbs from oxen and donkeys, and any other beasts of burden that may have died; they then take these chunks of meat to locations near the nests, dump them there and withdraw a safe distance. The birds duly swoop down and carry off the limbs of the various beasts to their nests, which, unable to bear the weight, are sent crashing to the ground – thereby enabling the Arabians to come and pick out what they want. This is how the natives of the region collect cinnamon, which is then exported to countries across the world.

[112] The source of rock rose resin, which the Arabians call *ladanon*, is more remarkable still; the stench of its place of origin is as revolting as its scent is delicious. It is found in the beards of he-goats, where it forms like resin from wood. It is used to make a great many perfumes, and is the incense most commonly burned by the Arabians.

[113] I have now spoken in quite enough detail about spices, the scent of which, perfuming the land of the Arabians, has a truly divine quality of sweetness to it. Also worth mentioning are two remarkable kinds of sheep, neither of which is found anywhere else. One of them has a tail so long – at least 3 cubits!⁷⁹ – that were these sheep permitted to drag their tails behind them, the tails would rub against the ground and end up covered in sores. As it is, however, every shepherd is sufficiently skilled in carpentry to make tiny carts, which he will then fasten under the tails of his flock, so that the tail of each animal is tied to its own individual little cart. The tails of the other kind of sheep are broad – as much as a cubit in width.

[114] Now, track the course of the sun as it crosses the face of the earth, and as it starts to set, so the remotest of those inhabited lands which it traverses will be Ethiopia, a country which produces immense amounts of gold, huge elephants, trees of every kind growing quite untended, ebony, and the tallest, most handsome and longest lived of all men.

[115] These, then, are the outermost limits of Asia and Libya. As regards the west, however, and the extremities of Europe, my information here is unreliable. Personally, I do not accept that there is a river

known to the barbarians as 'Eridanus' which flows into the headwinds of the northern sea, from where amber is said to come; nor that we obtain our tin from 'Tin Islands',[80] which I do not believe exist. The very name *Eridanus*, which is Greek and not barbarian at all, damns itself as the invention of some poet; not only that, but despite all my efforts I have never managed to hear a first-hand account from anyone who has actually confirmed with his own eyes the existence of a sea on the far side of Europe. That said, it is indeed the case that tin and amber do come to us from the margins of the world.

[116] It is also evident that supplies of gold are far more abundant in the northern reaches of Europe than elsewhere. As to how the gold is obtained, that again is a question to which I cannot supply a certain answer – although it is claimed that one-eyed men called Arimaspians snatch it from under the beaks of griffins. It seems to me most implausible that nature might have brought into being a race of one-eyed men who, in all other respects, resemble the rest of humanity. It is probable, however, that the ends of the earth, encompassing the rest of the world as they do, and bounding them in, do possess things which strike us as exceptionally beautiful and rare.

[117] In Asia, there is a plain enclosed by a ring of mountains, broken only by five gorges. This plain once belonged to the Chorasmians, and still serves to demarcate their territory from that of the Hyrcanians, the Parthians, the Sarangians and the Thamanaeans – although, ever since the rise of the Persians to power, it has been the property of the king. There is a mighty river, called the Aces, which flows down from the ring of mountains. Once – at a time when it used to divide into five distinct streams, each one of which would then pass through one of the gorges – this river served to water the lands of all five of the peoples I just mentioned; but now they suffer from a common problem, one which arrived with Persian rule; for the king dammed the gorges through the mountains, and then set a gate in each gorge, thereby blocking off the outward flow of water. As a result, because there was nowhere for the river to flow on to once it had descended from the mountains, the plain enclosed by the mountains became a sea. This has brought great misery to those who were previously in the habit of drawing on the water but now find themselves unable to use it. Granted, in winter they receive no less rain from heaven than does the rest of humanity; but come the summer, when they sow millet and sesame, they are parched. Accordingly,

deprived of water, they travel to Persia, their women too; there, they stand by the gates of the royal palace, raise their voices and howl. Those of the supplicants whose need is greatest then have the doors which block the channel leading down to them opened, on the orders of the king. Only once the earth in their fields has absorbed so much water that it is completely saturated are the gates closed – whereupon the king orders the opening up of more gates for the benefit of those who are the neediest among the peoples left. I gather, from what I have heard, that he charges them an immense fee for this opening of the gates, quite distinct from their regular tribute.[81] Such, then, is how it is organized.

[118] Now, it so happened that immediately after the insurrection, Intaphrenes, one of the Seven who had staged the coup against the Magian, was guilty of such outrageous and brutish behaviour that he was put to death for it. The background to this affair was his wish to enter the palace and talk over various matters with the king – something, indeed, that he was perfectly entitled to do, since all the conspirators against the Magian were permitted to enter the palace unannounced, except on those occasions when the king happened to be having sex with one of his wives. So it was that Intaphrenes, as one of the Seven, assumed that there was no call for him to be announced, but looked to go straight on in. The gatekeeper and the royal courier, however, would not permit it, for, as they told him, 'The king is sleeping with one of his wives.' Intaphrenes, however, assumed that this was a lie; he responded by drawing his scimitar, cutting off their ears and noses, and threading them onto his horse's bridle, which he then fastened around the necks of the two men before sending them packing.

[119] The men then showed themselves to the king, and explained what lay behind the atrocities inflicted upon them. Darius, who was terrified that the other six might jointly have had a hand in the affair, sent for each one in turn, with the aim of knowing their minds, and finding out whether there had been a joint consensus in favour of what had been done. Once he had quite reassured himself that none of the other five was involved, Darius arrested not only Intaphrenes himself, but also his sons and all his kinsmen, in the confident conviction that Intaphrenes and his relatives had been plotting a coup. Then, following these arrests, he had them put in chains, ready to be executed. It was now that the wife of Intaphrenes, her cries of grief choked by sobs, began to haunt

the doors of the palace; and because she returned there day after day, so Darius was moved to pity and sent her a messenger. 'Lady,' he said, 'out of all your kinsmen, King Darius permits you to redeem one from bondage. As to which, the choice is yours.' To this, after due reflection, she replied, 'The king's gift to me is one single life? If so, then out of all those I could have chosen, I choose my brother.' When Darius was informed of this reply, he was so astounded by it that he sent her another message. 'The king asks you, woman, to explain the thinking behind your abandonment of your husband and children, and your decision to reprieve your brother – a man who is neither as close to you as are your children, nor as beloved as is your husband.' 'O King,' she answered, 'I can always have another husband, God willing, and more children, should I lose the ones I have. My father and mother, however, are both dead – and so there is no possibility that I will ever have another brother. That was the thinking behind what I said.'[82] The woman's explanation struck Darius as being very well put – and indeed, so impressed by her was he that he released not only the brother she had been pleading for, but also the eldest of her sons. The rest, however, he had put to death – every last one. That is the story of how, no sooner had the Seven come together, than one of them met his end.

[120] Now to something that took place around the time that Cambyses fell sick. A man named Oroetes, a Persian appointed by Cyrus to the governorship of Sardis, developed an ambition that certainly did not lack for the quality of sacrilege. Despite the fact that he had never before laid eyes on Polycrates, who in turn had never done him any harm, nor ever spoken a single harsh word against him, Oroetes was nevertheless possessed by a longing to capture the Samian, and eliminate him once and for all. His motive? About that, there is widespread agreement. Oroetes and another Persian named Mitrobates, who was governor of the province of Dascyleum, were sitting by the doors of the palace when their conversation degenerated into quarrelling. As they argued over which of them had the better record, Mitrobates taunted Oroetes by asking him why he had failed to secure Samos for the king. 'Call yourself a man? The island is right next to your province! And it isn't as if it would be a challenging place to conquer! Why, one of the natives staged a coup there with the backing of just fifteen hoplites. Not only did he secure the island – he still rules it to this day as its tyrant.' It is said that

Oroetes, when he heard this reproach, was bitterly wounded; but rather than take revenge on the man who had delivered it, he set his heart instead on the utter annihilation of Polycrates, as the man responsible for the stain on his reputation.

[121] A minority of people, however, claim that Oroetes sent a herald to Samos with a request for something or other (precisely what is not recorded), and that Polycrates happened to be lying on a couch in his banqueting hall in the company of Anacreon of Teus. Whether intentionally or purely as a result of fate, he showed Oroetes and his affairs grave disrespect: it so happened that, as the herald of Oroetes approached him and sought to engage him in conversation, Polycrates was facing the wall, and neither turned round nor made a reply.

[122] Such are the two different reasons given for the death of Polycrates: as to which is more convincing, people are at liberty to decide as they will.[83] What is certain, however, is that Oroetes, who had his headquarters in Magnesia, on the heights above the River Maeander, sent a man of Lydia – Myrsus son of Gyges by name – to Samos with a message. He did this because he had learned of Polycrates' designs to found a maritime empire, a plan which, so far as I am aware, Polycrates was the first Greek ever to have had in mind. I make an exception of Minos of Cnossus, and anyone else prior to Minos who may have ruled the seas. Polycrates, however, was undoubtedly the first of what we would term the fully mortal race of men[84] to aim at it; and certainly, he had every expectation that Ionia as well as the offshore islands would come under his rule. It was because of this plan, once he had learned of it, that Oroetes sent his message. 'Oroetes to Polycrates,' the message ran. 'It has come to my attention that you are planning very great things indeed, but that your designs exceed your resources. Only do as I tell you, and not only will you ensure your own success, but you will also save my skin. I say this because I have had utterly reliable information that King Cambyses is planning to have me killed. If you get me out of here right now with all my cash reserves, and if you will let me keep some of them, I will let you have all the rest. If money is capable of securing the rule of all Greece, then that rule will be yours. It is possible, of course, when I refer to money in this way that your suspicions are roused. If so, send the man you most trust, whoever he may be, and I will show him the money.'

[123] Polycrates, who had, it seems, a prodigious love of money, was

delighted to hear this, and more than happy to comply. His first step was to dispatch Maeandrius, son of Maeandrius, a fellow-citizen employed by Polycrates as his secretary, to act for him as his eyes. (This was the same Maeandrius who not long afterwards made a dedication to the temple of Hera of all the various adornments from Polycrates' banqueting hall, which thoroughly deserve a look.) When Oroetes found out that an inspector was expected, he made his preparations. First, he filled eight chests almost up to the top with stones, and covered them with a dusting of gold; then he locked the chests, and kept them ready for inspection. Sure enough, Maeandrius came, peered inside them and then made his report to Polycrates.

[124] Now, there were many seers, and many friends, who sought to dissuade Polycrates from setting out – but still he prepared to go. What is more, his daughter had a vision of her father in a dream, in which she imagined him raised up high in the air, being washed by Zeus and anointed by the Sun. Once she had seen this vision, she went to every length she could to prevent Polycrates from travelling abroad to Oroetes – even going so far as to follow him as he went to his pente-conter, uttering baleful warnings of doom. When Polycrates threatened to make her live as a spinster should he return home safe and sound, she merely prayed that it would happen. 'For I would rather be a maid, no matter how old, than lose my father.'

[125] Polycrates paid not the slightest attention to any of these warn-ings, though, and instead set sail to meet Oroetes. He took with him a large entourage of comrades, among whom was Democedes, son of Calli-phon, a man who hailed from Croton, and who was a physician better skilled in the arts of medicine than any of his contemporaries. On his arrival in Magnesia, Polycrates was butchered in a truly monstrous way, one which no man of his character and vision should have had to suffer; certainly, on the scale of magnificence, there have never been any other Greek tyrants (those of Syracuse only excepted) who have merited com-parison with him. After he had killed Polycrates in a way too appalling for words, Oroetes then had the corpse impaled. He set free the Samians in Polycrates' entourage, having first ordered them to thank him for granting them their liberty; on the other hand, he regarded the foreign-ers and the slaves in the entourage as so much human booty, and kept them. Meanwhile, with the impalement of Polycrates, everything seen by his daughter in her vision had been fulfilled, for he was washed by

Zeus whenever it rained, and anointed by the Sun as the heat made his body ooze out sweat. And so it was [just as King Amasis of Egypt had foretold] that all his good fortune came to an end.[85]

[126] Soon enough, however, divine retribution for the murder of Polycrates was visited on Oroetes. Following the death of Cambyses and the reign of the Magians, Oroetes kept to Sardis, where he lifted not a finger to help the Persians, despite the fact that the empire had been taken from them by the Medes. Not only that, but he took advantage of the troubled times to murder two highly distinguished Persians: Mitrobates, the governor of Dascyleum, who had taunted him about Polycrates, and Cranaspes, son of Mitrobates. Among a whole host of other outrages, not the least shocking was his murder of a courier who had come to him from Darius with a displeasing message. The courier was ambushed on his way home by Oroetes' hirelings; once he was dead, neither he nor his horse was ever seen again.

[127] After Darius had secured the empire, he was eager to avenge himself upon Oroetes for all his many crimes – and for the deaths of Mitrobates and his son in particular. Nevertheless, he did not think it sensible, when he had only recently come to power and everything was still in a state of crisis, to dispatch a force directly against a man so well entrenched as he had learned his target to be: Oroetes had a bodyguard of a thousand Persian spearmen, and ruled the province of Phrygia,[86] in addition to those of Lydia and Ionia. Accordingly, Darius summoned all the most highly regarded Persians to a meeting, and presented his plan. 'Men of Persia,' he demanded, 'which of you is willing to take on a mission for me – one that will require intelligence rather than brute force or weight of numbers? No call for aggression, after all, when it is cunning that is needed. I want Oroetes brought to me dead or alive. So, then, who is game? Oroetes is a man who lifted not a finger to help the Persians, remember, and who has committed any number of crimes. Not only did he dispose of Mitrobates and his son – two Persians of our own class – but he has also murdered the messengers I sent him to summon him.[87] Blatant disobedience, and quite intolerable! We urgently need to topple him, and kill him, before he does the Persians any worse harm.'

[128] Thirty separate men answered this request of Darius' for volunteers to undertake the mission. The competition was such that only a lottery, held on Darius' orders, served to resolve it. The lot fell on Bagaeus, the son of Artontes, who had written a large number of docu-

ments on a range of topics, which he then sealed with the signet-ring of Darius, and took with him when he went to Sardis. When he had arrived and come into the presence of Oroetes, he removed the dispatches from their sheaths and gave them, one by one, to be read by the Royal Secretary (an official that every governor has). Now, the reason why Bagaeus handed over the documents was to find out whether the bodyguards might be minded to turn against Oroetes. When he observed the awestruck respect that they paid to the documents, and to the messages within them even more so, he handed over another one. This time, the words in the document read: 'King Darius forbids you, men of Persia, to serve as the bodyguards of Oroetes.' The guards, when they heard this, dropped their spears onto the ground. At this, seeing how obedient they were to the document's instructions, Bagaeus took his courage into his hands and passed over to the secretary the final document, on which it was written: 'King Darius commands all the Persians present in Sardis to kill Oroetes.' The bodyguards, when they heard this, drew their scimitars, and killed him there and then. And so it was that retribution for the murder of Polycrates the Samian overtook Oroetes the Persian.

[129] All his worldly goods were carted off to Susa, where it so happened, not long after their arrival, that King Darius went out hunting wild game, jumped down from his horse and twisted his ankle. So bad was the sprain that the ankle-bone was quite dislocated from the joint. It had always been the practice of Darius up to this point to keep about him Egyptian doctors, whose reputation had no rival, and it was these he now consulted. They manipulated his ankle with such violence, however, that they only made it worse. For seven days and seven nights Darius was kept awake by the continuous pain; until, on his eighth day of agony, someone from Sardis who had previously heard of the skill of Democedes of Croton sent word of it to the king. Darius gave orders to his servants that he be brought to him without delay. Once they had found Democedes, who had been living quite overlooked in some obscure spot among the slaves of Oroetes, they hauled him off, still wearing rags and dragging his chains behind him, directly into the presence of the king.

[130] So there he stood before Darius, who asked him whether he knew how to practise medicine. Democedes, who was petrified that he would lose forever any prospect of a return to Greece if he did not keep his talents hidden, answered that he did not; but Darius, who could see

that Democedes was patently familiar with the medical arts, and only feigning ignorance, instructed the men who had led him there to bring out whips and cattle-goads. At this, Democedes confessed that although he did not have a specialist's knowledge, 'I did once spend some time with a doctor, and did pick up a few rudimentary principles.' Darius duly put himself into his hands; and Democedes, by employing Greek medical techniques, and by replacing violent with gentle methods, managed to lull him to sleep, and then, in next to no time, to restore to him the full use of a foot that Darius had imagined would be left permanently crippled. Subsequently to this, Darius presented Democedes with two pairs of golden fetters. 'Is this my reward for healing you,' Democedes asked, 'that you deliberately double my punishment?' This witticism delighted Darius, who sent him off to visit his wives. Democedes was led in to see them by the eunuchs, who told the women, 'Here is the man who has restored the king to life!' At this, each one of them plunged a cup into a chest filled with gold, and presented Democedes with a reward so lavish that the house-slave trailing him, whose name was Sciton, himself garnered a considerable fortune just by scooping up all the coins that fell from the cups.

[131] How was it that Democedes had come to leave Croton, and be in the service of Polycrates? In Croton, relations with his father, a man with a truly awful temper, had become so bad as to be unendurable; and so he left and went to Aegina. There he settled, and within a year, despite a complete lack of the tools and instruments necessary for the practice of medicine, he had put all the other doctors completely in the shade. In his second year, he was employed by the Aeginetans as their state physician, on a salary of one talent; in the following year by the Athenians, on a salary of 100 *minae*; and the year after that by Polycrates, on a salary of 2 talents. So it was that he came to be in Samos, where his role in establishing the excellent reputation of doctors from Croton was certainly not insignificant. [I should mention that this was the period which saw physicians from Croton ranked as the best in Greece, with those from Cyrene second. It was around this time too that the Argives had a reputation for being the finest musicians in Greece.]

[132] In Susa, his curing of Darius' injury made him the owner of a huge mansion, and a regular guest at the royal table. Indeed, he lacked for nothing – excepting only a return to Greece. On one occasion, when the Egyptian physicians who had previously tended to the king were

about to be impaled for being shown up by a Greek doctor, he managed
to save them by imploring Darius for mercy. He also rescued a soothsayer from Elis[88] who had served in Polycrates' entourage, and then
been consigned to the oblivion of servitude. In short, Democedes had no
rival as a figure at court.

[133] Then, a short while afterwards, something else happened to
crop up. Atossa, the daughter of Cyrus and wife of Darius, developed a
growth on her breast, which subsequently burst and spread. Ashamed
to show it to anyone, she kept it hidden for as long as it remained unob-
trusive; but then, falling really ill, she sent for Democedes and revealed
the growth to him. He told her that he would be able to make her well
again, but made her solemnly swear in return that she would do for him
whatever favour he might ask of her – having first assured her that it
would be nothing liable to cause her embarrassment.

[134] Sure enough, Atossa was indeed restored to health by his min-
istrations; and soon afterwards, while in bed with her husband, she did
as instructed by Democedes, and badgered Darius with a suggestion.
'All this power you have, my king, and yet you sit idle. You have added
neither to the resources of the Persian people, nor to their subjects.
Surely it is only proper that a man in the prime of his life, and with
prodigious wealth at his command, should accomplish some truly
extraordinary achievement, so that the Persians are in no doubt that
they are ruled by a real man. Indeed, such an undertaking would have a
double advantage: not only would it emphasize to the Persians that they
are ruled by a true man, but it would see them ground down by warfare,
and denied the leisure to plot against you. Now is the time for you to
make your mark – now, while you are young in years! A body still in the
process of growing makes for a growing mind as well – but once the
body ages, so too do the wits, which end up so blunted as to be good for
nothing.' To these words, spoken just as Democedes had instructed,
Darius answered, 'Yes, wife! You have articulated precisely everything I
myself have it in mind to do. My plan it is to yoke this continent to the
other by means of a bridge, and then to launch an invasion of Scythia.
All my preparations will soon be completed.' 'But look,' Atossa said,
'just for the moment, do not make the attack on the Scythians your
priority. They can wait. After all, you can have them whenever you like.
Invade Greece instead. For me! I have had reports about what good
maid-servants Lacedaemonian girls make, and Argives, and Athenians,

and Corinthians, and I want some for myself. And of all the men you could possibly have to serve you as your specialist in Greek affairs, and to act for you as your guide, you have the expert of experts: the man who healed your foot.' 'Well, wife,' Darius answered, 'since you feel that we should first test our mettle against the Greeks, it strikes me that our best course would initially be to dispatch some Persians, together with the man you just mentioned, to reconnoitre the lie of the land. Once they have given us a detailed report on all their discoveries and observations, I will have the information I need to launch my invasion.'[89] No sooner had Darius declared this than he was matching his deeds to his words.

[135] For the next day had only to dawn, you see, and Darius was summoning fifteen men, high-ranking Persians all, and instructing them to go on a tour of the Greek coastline with Democedes, whom they were not to let slip away, but were at all costs to ensure returned. Once he had issued these instructions, he summoned Democedes himself, and requested him to act as a guide for the Persians: he was to show them around the whole of Greece, but then to come back. Darius also told him to gather up all his own personal effects and to take them with him as gifts for his father and brothers, on the assurance that he would be compensated for them many times over. In addition to these gifts, Darius added, they were to be accompanied on their voyage by another: a cargo ship filled with all sorts of valuables. These announcements did not, in my opinion, imply any intention on the part of Darius to catch Democedes out; but Democedes himself, nervous that he was being put to the test, did not rush headlong into accepting everything on offer, informing Darius instead that he would leave his own possessions where they were, so that they would be there for him when he returned. Nevertheless, he said that he would accept the cargo ship promised him by Darius for the transport of gifts to his brothers. Darius then issued him with the same instructions that had been given to the rest of the mission and sent them all on their way to the coast.

[136] Down they travelled to Phoenicia and then, once arrived there, to the city of Sidon, where they promptly set about manning a couple of triremes and loading up a large, round-hulled transport vessel with a whole array of valuables. Then, with everything shipshape, they sailed for Greece, where they surveyed and mapped the coastline, stopping off at various points along the way, until in due course, when most places

of significance had been reconnoitred, they came to Tarentum in Italy. It was here, out of concern for Democedes, that the city's king, Aristophilides, removed the rudders of the Median ships and placed the Persians themselves in detention, on the grounds that they were actually spies. Meanwhile, even as they were being subjected to these indignities, Democedes made it to Croton. Only once he was back in his native land did Aristophilides release the Persians, and restore to them the parts he had removed from their ships.

[137] From Tarentum, the Persians sailed off in pursuit of Democedes; and once they had docked at Croton and found him strolling around the market-square, they seized him. Some of the Crotoniates were in such awe of Persian might that they were quite content to see him taken; but there were others who grabbed hold of Democedes in response, and began cudgelling the Persians, who responded with cries of protest. 'Men of Croton, surely you see what you are doing? This man you are rescuing is a runaway slave of the king's. How can such an insult to Darius possibly increase the royal pleasure? And how will what you are doing – stealing this man from us – benefit you? Whose city, do you imagine, will be higher on our list of invasion targets than yours? Whose population will we try to enslave first, if not yours?' Despite these threats, however, they could not sway the Crotoniates; so the Persians, deprived both of Democedes and of the cargo ship which they had brought with them, sailed back to Asia, no longer bothering, now that they had lost their guide, with trying to visit and inform themselves about the rest of Greece. Even as they were putting out to sea, Democedes gave them an instruction: to inform Darius that he was engaged to marry the daughter of Milon. He did this because the name of Milon, the wrestler, was much bruited at the court of the King;[90] so I would imagine that the reason why Democedes was so keen on this marriage, which it had cost him a good deal of money to arrange, was because he wished to demonstrate to Darius that he was rated as highly in his own native land as in Persia.

[138] At Iapygia,[91] the Persians who had set out from Croton were shipwrecked and sold into slavery; but Gillus, a man from Tarentum who was living there in exile, ransomed them and brought them back to Darius. As his reward for this, he was told by the king that he could have whatever he might desire. Gillus, who had already related the story of his misfortunes, asked to be restored to Tarentum. However, because

he had no wish to embroil the Greek world in the kind of turmoil that would inevitably follow the descent of a large naval force on Italy, he told Darius that he was perfectly content to rely solely upon the Cnidians, who had a special relationship with the Tarentines, as the agents of his return from exile, on the assumption that they were the likeliest of anyone to secure it. Darius gave his word – and kept it. A messenger was sent to the Cnidians with orders from the king that they were to return Gillus to Tarentum. The Cnidians were duly spurred by this into action, but found their own powers of persuasion (not to mention their subsequent resort to force) insufficient to sway the Tarentines. Such, then, is what happened. These were the first Persians to arrive from Asia in the Greek world, and they came as spies, under the circumstances I have just related.

[139] It was in the wake of this episode that King Darius took Samos, the first of all the many cities, Greek and barbarian alike, that would end up under his control.[92] How and why? The answer lies in the invasion of Egypt by Cambyses, the son of Cyrus, and the arrival of large numbers of Greeks in Egypt: some, as was only natural, for the purposes of trade, others to join the invasion and some just to see the sights. Among the latter was Syloson, son of Aeaces and brother of Polycrates, who was in exile from Samos. Now this Syloson had a great slice of good fortune. One day, while in Memphis, he happened to pick up a red cloak, wrap it round himself and go for a stroll in the market-place. There he was spotted by Darius, who at the time was a member of Cambyses' personal guard, and a man of no great significance at all; and Darius was seized by such a longing for the cloak that he went up to Syloson and offered to buy it from him. It was now that Syloson, who could see how eager Darius was for the cloak, was graced by the heavens with a sudden lucky inspiration. 'Not for any amount of money would I sell this cloak,' he said, 'but what I will do, if you absolutely must have it, is give it to you for free.' Darius thanked him lavishly and took the garment – a loss which to Syloson appeared due entirely to his own naivety.

[140] Time passed. Cambyses died, the Seven rose in revolt against the Magians, and Darius, one of the Seven, became king. The man who in Egypt had once been given a cloak by Syloson when he asked for it had now come by the kingdom; and Syloson, when he learned this, travelled up to Susa, sat at the outer doors of the king's palace and declared that he had done Darius a good turn. On hearing this, the gatekeeper

went and reported it to the king, who replied in astonishment, 'I owe a debt of gratitude to a Greek? Me? Says who? I have only just won power, and anyway, there are hardly any Greeks living here. I think I can safely say that I owe nothing to any Greek. Still, bring the man in, so that I may find out what he means by making this claim.' So the gate-keeper led Syloson in, and after he had been taken into the presence of the king, interpreters asked him who he was and what he had done to be able to claim that he had been a benefactor of the king. In reply, Syloson rehearsed the whole story of the cloak, and explained that he was the very man who had made a gift of it. The response of Darius to this was to hail him as the most generous of men. 'For, back then, I was a man quite without power – and yet still you gave me something. Insignificant it may have been – but the sense of gratitude it inspires in me is no less than I would feel now if I received some magnificent gift from somewhere or other. As a reward for it, I offer you gold and silver without limit, so that you may never have cause to repent having done well by Darius, the son of Hystaspes.' But to this, Syloson said, 'It is not gold or silver I am looking for, my Lord, but rather the recovery of my native Samos, which ever since my brother Polycrates was killed by Oroetes has been the fiefdom of one of our slaves. Let there be no bloodshed, no enslavement – but give me Samos.'

[141] When Darius heard this, he dispatched a task-force under the command of Otanes, one of the Seven, with orders to bring about everything that Syloson had requested. So Otanes went down to the coast and prepared his men for the campaign.

[142] Now, power in Samos rested with Maeandrius,[93] son of Maeandrius, who had secured it after being appointed to the regency by Polycrates. His ambition had been to serve as a paragon of just behaviour – but it was not to be. On receiving news of the death of Polycrates, Maeandrius had taken a couple of measures. First, he raised an altar to Zeus the Liberator,[94] and sanctified its surroundings by enclosing them within a wall, which is still to be seen today on the outskirts of the city. This done, he convened an assembly of all the citizens of Samos. 'You know as well as I do', he told them, 'that Polycrates placed his sceptre in my hands, and all his power with it, so that I could easily now be your ruler. However, if I can possibly help it, I will not myself do what I criticize others for doing. It was offensive to me that Polycrates, despite being no different from other men, should have ruled

over you as your master – and I cannot approve of anyone else who does such a thing. The doom of Polycrates is now come – but not mine. I am putting power into the hands of all of you, and announcing publicly that every one of you is equal before the law.[95] I do nevertheless think it only fair that I be granted certain privileges: 6 talents, perquisites drawn from Polycrates' fortune, should be set aside for me, and I also reserve, for myself and my descendants in perpetuity, the priesthood of Zeus the Liberator. I was the one who had that shrine built, after all, just as I am the one who is conferring liberty on you.' This was the speech Maeandrius delivered to the Samians; but one of them, rising to his feet, said, 'What makes you think you are remotely qualified to rule us? You are a low-born and pestilential fraud. In fact, what you should really be doing now is showing us the accounts of all the money you have been handling.'

[143] This was a man – Telesarchus – who was well regarded by his fellow-citizens. It now dawned on Maeandrius that were he to abdicate, someone else would be installed in his place as tyrant; and so he resolved to keep hold of the reins of power. He withdrew to the acropolis, from where he issued summonses to individuals one by one, on the pretext of going over the accounts with them, but in fact to arrest and imprison them. Once they had all been put in chains, however, Maeandrius was struck down by sickness; and his brother, whose name was Lycaretus, presumed that the illness was terminal. Accordingly, to smooth his own takeover of Samos, Lycaretus – who apparently counted their freedom as nothing – killed all the prisoners.

[144] So it was that when the Persians charged with the restoration of Syloson landed on Samos, no one lifted a finger to oppose them; not only that, but Maeandrius himself, and all his faction too, declared themselves ready to evacuate the island, provided that it was under truce. Otanes agreed to this; and once libations had been poured to confirm the agreement, all the highest ranking Persians settled themselves onto seats that had been specially laid out for them facing the acropolis.

[145] Now the tyrant Maeandrius had a brother named Charileos, a near-lunatic who had been chained up in a dungeon for some misdemeanour or other. When Charileos heard what was going on, he leaned out from his prison, and on seeing the Persians sitting down all peaceably together, he raised his voice, and yelled out that he wanted to talk

to Maeandrius. Maeandrius, when he heard this, gave orders for his brother to be released and brought over to him. No sooner had Charileos been led across than he began to abuse Maeandrius, and to insult him, trying to goad him into attacking the Persians. 'You really are the most contemptible of men,' he said. 'Here am I, your own brother, sentenced to be chained up in a dungeon, despite the fact that I have done nothing whatsoever to merit imprisonment. Meanwhile, right before your eyes, sit the Persians, who are driving you from your country and your home. Do you lack the guts to make them pay? It would be easy enough to crush them. If they really scare you so much, lend me your mercenaries and I will take revenge on them for ever having come here. As for you – I am happy to get you off the island.'

[146] So spoke Charileos. Maeandrius took up his suggestion – not, in my opinion, because he was so foolish as to imagine that his own power could overcome that of the Persian king, but rather because he begrudged the fact that Syloson was about to drop the city undamaged into his own lap. Knowing perfectly well that if the Persians suffered any casualties they would vent their fury on the Samians, he aimed to provoke them so that Samos and its society would be crippled when he came to hand over the island; he knew that he personally could make a safe exit from the island whenever he wished, thanks to a secret passageway which he had built, leading from the acropolis to the sea. So Maeandrius sailed away from Samos. Meanwhile, Charileos flung open the gates and sent out his mercenaries, all of whom he had armed, against the Persians, who, because they were under the impression that everything had been settled by treaty, were taken completely by surprise. The mercenaries fell on the Persian elite in their sedan chairs and slaughtered them all. As this was being done, however, the remainder of the Persian force came up to provide reinforcements, pushing the mercenaries back and cooping them up on the acropolis.

[147] When Otanes, the commander-in-chief, saw the atrocities that had been inflicted upon the Persians, he deliberately pushed to the back of his mind that Darius, when giving him the mission, had ordered him on no account to massacre or enslave the Samians, but rather to hand over the island to Syloson without casualties, or indeed collateral damage of any kind. Instead, he ordered his troops to slaughter everyone they could lay their hands on, whether adult male or child. So it was that while some of his forces laid siege to the acropolis, the rest set

themselves to killing all who happened to cross their path, regardless of whether they were in a sanctuary or not.

[148] Maeandrius, meanwhile, was sailing away in headlong flight to Sparta. On his arrival there, he brought with him inland all the belongings that he had taken with him into exile. What he would then do, every so often, was to lay out all his gold and silver drinking-cups, and then, as his servants buffed them up, to engage the king of Sparta, Cleomenes, the son of Anaxandridas, in conversation, and bring him into the house. Cleomenes had only to see the goblets to be dazzled and stupefied by them; whereupon Maeandrius would tell him to take as many of them as he wanted. However, after this offer had been repeated not twice but three times, Cleomenes demonstrated that he was a man of impeccable honesty:[96] not only did he resolve that it would be wrong to take what he was being offered, but he realized that Maeandrius was bound to find other citizens less scrupulous than himself and obtain their backing. Accordingly, he went to the ephors and declared that it would be better for Sparta if the foreigner, their guest from Samos, were to leave the Peloponnese; otherwise either he or some other Spartiate might well be corrupted. The ephors, having listened to this recommendation, duly proclaimed the banishment of Maeandrius.

[149] As for the Persians, they linked arms and formed themselves into a great line, then trawled their way across Samos, so that by the time they came to hand it over to Syloson, the island was emptied of people. In due course, however, Otanes, the commander-in-chief, was prompted by a dream, and by a disease of the genitals that he had contracted, to assist with its resettlement.

[150] It was during the course of this naval campaign against Samos that the Babylonians, who had made very careful preparations, revolted. Such had been the upheavals of the age, what with the rule of the Magian and the consequent insurrection of the Seven, that they had somehow been able to ready themselves for a siege without being noticed. Once their revolt was open, their next step was to send their mothers away, and then, after each man had chosen from his own household one further woman to be put to one side, they rounded up all the remaining women and strangled them. This meant that, for every man, there was one woman left to cook him his food; the others were killed so that they would not use up the men's provisions.

[151] Once he had learned what was happening, Darius mustered all the power he had and launched an expedition against the Babylonians, sweeping down upon the city and putting it under blockade – although its inhabitants did not take the siege seriously at all. Indeed, they used to go up to the buildings on top of the wall, where they would make rude gestures and chant obscenities at Darius and his army. As one of them once put it: 'Why do you hang around here, Persians? Why not go away? Mules will foal before we fall into your hands!' So spoke the Babylonian, in the confident expectation that no mule would ever bear young.

[152] After a year and seven months, Darius and his whole army were in a state of high frustration at their inability to bring the Babylonians to heel. Darius had deployed every kind of stratagem and device against them. Still he could not capture their city, even though among the ploys with which he had experimented was the very one that had delivered Babylon into the hands of Cyrus.[97] There was something ferocious, however, about the determination of the Babylonians not to let slip their guard; and Darius simply could not make their city his.

[153] Then, in the twentieth month of the siege, something astounding happened to Zopyrus, the son of Megabyzus (Megabyzus being one of the Seven who had toppled the Magian): one of the pack-mules belonging to this same Zopyrus gave birth to a foal. When the news was brought to him, he refused to believe it; but then, once he had seen the suckling with his own eyes, he ordered all the various witnesses to keep it to themselves while he pondered what to do. 'Only when mules foal will our walls be breached', such had been the words spoken by the Babylonian at the very start of the siege. 'Surely, then,' Zopyrus reflected, 'the implication of this pronouncement can only be that Babylon is now ripe to be plucked. Some god must have spoken through the Babylonian, and then brought my own mule to foal.'

[154] So, acting on his assumption that the fall of the city and its doom were at hand, he approached Darius and asked him how great a significance he attached to the capture of Babylon. Informed that the king attached the utmost importance to it, Zopyrus pondered anew how to make the project his own, so that he himself would be the man to take the city, for the Persians greatly honour all those who perform services that profit them. The only possible course of action that Zopyrus could devise to secure the city, however, required his own self-mutilation

and desertion to the enemy. So it was, with great imperturbability, that he maimed himself in a way beyond any possibility of being mended: he cut off both his nose and his ears. Then, after he had also shaved his head in a disfiguring manner, and put himself under the whip, he appeared before Darius.

[155] The sight of a man held in such excellent regard, and yet so horribly maimed, quite crushed the king; he rose from his throne with a howl, demanding to know who it was had inflicted such mutilations and why. 'The man with the power to reduce me to such a condition does not exist,' Zopyrus said, 'with the sole exception of yourself. Do not think it was a stranger's hand did this, O King – it was my own. Yes, the deed was mine. Such is the measure of how bitterly I feel the mockery being directed by mere Assyrians at the men of Persia!' To which Darius answered: 'Has there ever been a man so headstrong and foolish? To claim that the people we are besieging prompted you to inflict such irreversible injuries upon yourself is merely to cloak a truly shameful crime beneath a show of fine words. You idiot! Do you really think, just because you are mutilated, that our enemies will rush to surrender? You must have taken leave of your senses to have inflicted such damage on yourself.' 'But if I had confided in you what I intended to do,' Zopyrus said, 'you would never have permitted me to do it. As it was, I shouldered the responsibility all myself, and just got on with it. And the consequence is – unless you refuse me your backing – that Babylon will surely be ours. Here is my plan. I will steal up to the city walls, just as I am, pretending to be a deserter, and claiming that it was you who inflicted all these injuries on me. It seems to me, if I can only convince the Babylonians of this, that I am bound to obtain some position of military responsibility. Meanwhile, ten days after I have slipped in past the walls, you should post a thousand men, all of them readily expendable, by the gates that are named after Semiramis. Seven days after that – so seventeen days in all from now – post another two thousand men by the so-called "Gates of the People of Nineveh". After this, let twenty days go by – thirty-seven days in all from now – and then lead another four thousand men, and station them by the Chaldaean gates, as they are called. Neither the first two contingents, nor this last one, should have any means of defending themselves, saving only their daggers, which they may keep. Then, at dawn the next day, instruct the remainder of

your forces to attack the circuit of the city walls from all sides, but post the Persians by the so-called "Belian" and "Cissian" gates. I am convinced that the Babylonians, once I have shown them I can do great things on their behalf, will put their complete confidence in me – and the keys to their city gates into my hands. From that point on, it will be up to me and the Persian troops to get done what needs to be done.'

[156] Once these instructions had been issued, Zopyrus made his way up to the city gates, glancing back over his shoulder all the time, as though he really were a deserter. The sentries who had been stationed there, when they observed him from the watch-towers, ran down, opened one of the gates ajar and asked him who he was, and what his motive was for being there. 'I am Zopyrus,' he declared, 'and I am deserting to you.' Once they had heard this, the gatekeepers led him into the general assembly, where he stood before the Babylonians, and poured out to them a tale of woe: the injuries that he had inflicted upon himself he blamed upon Darius, claiming that they had been his punishment for advising the king, in view of the manifest impossibility of capturing the city, to lift the siege. 'And now here I am before you, men of Babylon,' he said, pressing on. 'Very good news for you, and very bad news indeed for Darius and his army. Because one thing is certain – he will not go unpunished for maiming me like this. I know all his counsels inside out.' This was what Zopyrus said.

[157] Because the sight of a man so highly esteemed by the Persians without his nose and ears, and encrusted with blood from a whipping, left the Babylonians in no doubt that he was speaking the truth, and was indeed there as an ally, they were happy to trust him with whatever he might ask of them – and what he asked for was an army. Once he had got it from them, he did as had been prearranged with Darius. On the tenth day, he led out his force of Babylonians, surrounded the thousand troops that he had told Darius to post as an initial deployment and wiped them out. When the Babylonians learned that his words were matched by his deeds, they could not have been more delighted, and were ready to oblige him in whatever way they could. The days slipped by – until, as had been fixed with Darius, he led out a picked squad of Babylonians again, and slaughtered two thousand more of Darius' men. When the Babylonians witnessed this feat, the praises of Zopyrus were heard on everyone's lips. Again, the prearranged number of days went

by, and again he led his men out to the agreed spot, where he surrounded the four thousand men, and massacred them. With this culminating feat, Zopyrus became the toast of all Babylon – so much so that he was appointed commander-in-chief of the city's army and the warden of its walls.

[158] But then, when Darius made his assault on the entire circuit of the walls, just as it had been prearranged that he should, the full extent of Zopyrus' trick came to light. Even as the Babylonians, who had mounted the walls, were busy defending them from the onslaughts of Darius' army, Zopyrus threw open the Cissian and Belian gates and let the Persians inside the fortifications. Some of the Babylonians witnessed what he had done, and fled to the shrine of Zeus Belus;[98] but those who failed to observe it remained at their posts until they too discovered that they had been betrayed.

[159] So it was that Babylon was captured a second time; and Darius, once he had mastery of the Babylonians, demolished the entire circuit of their walls and tore out all their gates – both of which were things that Cyrus, when Babylon had originally fallen to him,[99] had neglected to do – and had some three thousand of their most prominent men impaled. He did, however, restore the city to those Babylonians who remained and let them live there. Looking to the future, he also made sure to provide them with women, and thereby ensure that a new generation would be born – for the Babylonians, as I explained initially, had been looking to conserve food, and so had strangled their own wives. All the surrounding peoples were obliged by Darius to send women to Babylon, with a quota set for each one: the total number of women, once they had all assembled in one place, came to five thousand. It was from these same women that the Babylonians of today are descended.

[160] What Zopyrus did was, in the judgement of Darius, the greatest act of service ever rendered by a Persian, whether subsequent to him or preceding, Cyrus alone excepted (for to Cyrus no Persian would ever presume to compare himself). It is said that Darius often stated it as his opinion that he would rather see Zopyrus spared his disfigurements than that he should come by twenty more Babylons, in addition to the one there already was. Great were the honours that Darius paid Zopyrus. Every year, the king made him gifts of all the things that are

most valued by the Persians, granted him Babylon as his own tax-free dominion, for so long as he should live, and gave him many other things besides. This same Zopyrus was the father of the Megabyzus who led the army in Egypt against the Athenians and their allies[100] – and Megabyzus was the father of the Zopyrus who defected from the Persians to the Athenians.

BOOK FOUR

[1] With Babylon captured, the next offensive led by Darius in person[1] was against the Scythians.[2] The population of Asia was flourishing, revenues were flooding in, and so Darius was eager to pay back the Scythians for what they had begun some time previously, when they had launched their unjustified attack on Media,[3] and crushed in battle those who thought to oppose them – for, as I mentioned earlier, the Scythians ruled upper Asia two years short of thirty. It was while in pursuit of the Cimmerians that they invaded Asia and toppled the empire of the Medes, who, prior to the coming of the Scythians, had been the lords of Asia. But after twenty-eight years had passed, during which time the Scythians never once returned to their native land, they finally headed home – where they were met by a challenge no less demanding than that of the Medes. The men of Scythia found a sizeable army blocking their way, for so lengthy had been their absence that their wives had consorted with their slaves.

[2] Now the Scythians are great drinkers of milk – and it is this that leads them to blind all their slaves. What they do is take a blow-pipe made of bone, very like a flute, and then, while one person inserts the pipe into the vagina of a mare and blows on it through his lips, another person will simultaneously do the milking. The reason for this method, they explain, is that the breathing blows up the veins and thereby makes the udder drop down. Then, once the milk has been drawn, they pour it into vessels of hollowed-out wood, station their blind slaves around the vessels and have them stir the milk. The top layer, which is skimmed off, they regard as being the best quality, while the milk that sinks to the bottom they rate less highly. It is this which explains why the Scythians blind everyone they take captive – they are nomads, not tillers of the soil.[4]

[3] So it was, from the union of these slaves with the wives of the Scythians, that there had sprung a whole new generation; and these young men, when they discovered the circumstances of their birth, set themselves to preventing the return of the Scythians from Media. Their first measure was to cut off their country by digging a broad ditch that ran the whole way from the Taurian Mountains to the widest point of Lake Maeëtis; then, taking up defensive positions, they blocked the attempt by the Scythians to force their way through. Engagement after engagement was fought, in none of which were the Scythians able to establish a military superiority, until one of them cried out, 'What are we up to, men of Scythia? These are our own slaves we are fighting against! The more casualties we suffer, the fewer of us are left – and the more casualties we inflict, the fewer of them are left us as our subjects. That is why I think we should put down our spears and our bows, and each one of us pick up our horsewhips and really lay into them with those. For as long as they see us with weapons in our hands, they can fancy themselves our peers, of a birth quite as good as our own. But if they see us carrying whips rather than regular weapons, it will dawn on them that they are our slaves – and then, when they have learned that lesson, it will put an end to all their resistance.'[5]

[4] The Scythians had only to hear this suggestion to act upon it – and sure enough, so panic stricken were the slaves by what was happening that they quite forgot their fighting spirit, and turned on their heels. Such, then, is the story of how the Scythians came to rule Asia and later, following their expulsion by the Medes, to return home. Such is also what lay behind Darius' desire to punish the Scythians and to raise an army against them.

[5] According to the account given by the Scythians themselves[6] of how they came into being, theirs is the most recently sprung of all races.[7] The first man to be born on their soil, which until that moment had been quite uninhabited, was named Targitaus. It is said by the Scythians – although I do not myself believe them, not when they make such a claim – that the parents of this Targitaus were Zeus and a daughter of the River Borysthenes. It was some such union, at any rate, that produced Targitaus, and he in turn fathered three sons: Lipoxaïs, Arpoxaïs and Colaxaïs, who was the youngest. It was while these three were in power that four objects fashioned out of gold – a plough, a yoke, a battleaxe and a cup – were borne down to Scythia from the sky. The first

brother to see these and approach them, intending to seize hold of them, was the eldest; but as he closed in on them, the gold blazed up into flames. He retreated, and then the second brother approached the implements. Again the gold did the same. But now, after the first two brothers had been beaten back by the blaze, the third and youngest approached it, and the fire went out; and so off he carried the objects to his home. The elder brothers, acknowledging the import of this, duly yielded their own stakes in the kingdom so that the youngest brother received it all.

[6] It is from Lipoxaïs that the tribe of Scythians known as the Auchatae trace their descent, while those who are called the Catiari and Traspians descend from Arpoxaïs, the middle brother, and the kings of Scythia – the Paralatae, as they are known – from the youngest brother. Collectively, they are known as 'Scolotians' [a name that derives from that of the king]. 'Scythians' is a name given them by the Greeks.

[7] So that is what the Scythians have to say about their origins; and they claim that in total – that is to say, from the time of Targitaus, their first king, until the invasion of their country by Darius[8] – they have been in existence for a thousand years, and no more. As for the sacred gold, their kings guard it with the utmost care, visiting it once a year and offering it extravagant sacrifices of propitiation. The Scythians claim that anyone during the course of this festival who is outside in the open with the sacred gold and falls asleep, will not live out the year – which is why they will grant him as much land as he can ride around on his horse in a single day. The sheer scale of the country being what it was, Colaxaïs fashioned out of it three kingdoms, one for each of his sons; but one of these kingdoms, the one in which the gold was kept, he made the largest. Owing to a blizzard of feathers, it is impossible to venture, or even to gaze, into the outer reaches of the lands of those who live beyond the Scythians to the north. Both earth and air are filled with feathers, so that visibility is cut to nothing.[9]

[8] But if this is what the Scythians have to say about themselves, and about the regions which lie beyond them, the Greeks inhabiting Pontus[10] tell a different story: that back when the land where the Scythians now live was still uninhabited, it was visited by Heracles. He was driving the cattle of Geryon,[11] whose home lay outside Pontus on an island known to the Greeks as Erytheia, and which is situated near Gades, beyond the Pillars of Heracles, on the edge of Oceanus. (Oceanus, so it is said, has its source where the sun rises, and flows all the way round

the world[12] – but no evidence to back this assertion has ever been produced.) Coming from Erytheia, Heracles arrived in the land now known
as Scythia; and here, overtaken by storms and by the bitter cold, he
covered himself with his lion-skin and fell asleep. It was then that his
mares, which had been grazing while still yoked to his chariot, were
spirited away by some twist of fate.

[9] When Heracles awoke, he roamed the entire country searching
for them, until at length he arrived in the land known as Hylaea. There,
in a cave, he found a creature who was half-maiden and half-viper, a
being two in one: upwards from the buttocks she was a woman, and
below them a serpent. Heracles, after he had gawped at her in astonishment, asked her if she had seen any stray mares about. 'Yes,' she
answered, 'I have them myself. I will give them back to you, but only
after you have slept with me first.' That being her price, Heracles duly
had sex with her; but because she wanted to keep him by her side for as
long as possible, while he just wanted to get hold of his horses and go,
she kept putting off returning them to him. At last, however, she did give
them back, saying, 'When these mares turned up here, I kept them safe
and sound for you, and now you have rewarded me for taking care of
them – for I have three sons by you. Spell out for me what I should do
when they reach adulthood – settle them down here, in this land of
which I am the mistress, or send them off to you?' To this question of
hers, Heracles is said to have replied, 'When you are sure that your children have reached manhood, do as I suggest, and you will not go wrong.
Watch and see if any of them can string this bow, and buckle on this
belt, as I am doing now. He who can, settle him down here in this land.
Whoever cannot complete the tasks I have set, however, send him from
the country altogether. Do this, and not only will your spirits be glad-
dened, but you will be carrying out my instructions as well.'

[10] Heracles drew one of the two bows which up until that moment
he had always carried with him, and showed her the belt, which had a
golden cup hanging from the tip of its buckle; then, after he had handed
them both over, he went on his way. Only once her children had reached
manhood did the mother give them names: one she called Agathyrsus,
the next one Gelonus and the youngest one Scythes. Then, mindful of
the charge she had been given, she did as she had been instructed. In the
event, two of the boys, Agathyrsus and Gelonus, proved unequal to the
challenge set them, and duly left the country, expelled by the very

woman who had given them birth; but Scythes, the youngest, was successful, and so remained in the country. It was from this Scythes, the son of Heracles, that all the succeeding kings of Scythia were descended; just as it was the cup which resulted in every Scythian, even today, carrying a cup attached to his belt. Nothing else achieved by Scythes, however, was due to the contrivances of his mother. Such, at any rate, is the story told by the Greeks of Pontus.

[11] There is yet another version, however, and it was this story, when I heard it, which seemed to me the most plausible. It is claimed that the Scythians, who were nomads at the time, living in Asia, were so hard pressed in a war with the Massagetans that they abandoned their homeland and crossed the River Araxes into the land of the Cimmerians – for the country that the Scythians currently inhabit[13] is said, back in ancient times, to have belonged to the Cimmerians. As the Scythians descended upon them, the Cimmerians, conscious of how vast was the army coming their way, debated what they should do, with sharply polarized and vehemently held opinions being expressed on both sides. But of the two opinions, it was that of the king and his family which was superior. The line of argument advanced by the mass of the people was that there was no alternative to flight, and that they certainly ought not to risk a clash with such a horde, while the king and his family argued that they should stand their ground against the invaders, and fight for their land. Neither side, however, was willing to be persuaded by the other: neither the royal party by the people, nor the people by the royal party. The people planned to abandon their country without a fight, and simply hand it over to the invaders, while the princes held that it would be best to die and be laid to rest in their own land, and not to flee with the mass of the populace; they reflected on all the good things that they had known in their homeland, and on all the evils which were likely to befall them were they to abandon it. Accordingly, once they had resolved this, they divided themselves up into two groups of equal numbers, and fought with one another, until they had all perished in mutual slaughter. They were then laid to rest beside the River Tyras (where their grave can still be seen to this day) by the Cimmerian people,[14] who, after the burials were completed, left the country, so that the Scythians, when they invaded, took possession of what was an empty land.

[12] Even today, in Scythia, there are Cimmerian walls and a

Cimmerian ferry, a whole region named Cimmeria and 'the Cimmerian Bosporus',[15] as it is known. It is perfectly clear that the Cimmerians fled from the Scythians into Asia, and settled in the peninsula where the Greek city of Sinope is now established. Also evident is the fact that when the Scythians, in their pursuit of the Cimmerians, invaded Media, it was because they had taken a wrong turning: at no point during their flight did the Cimmerians leave the coast, whereas the pursuing Scythians kept the Caucasus on their right, and so crossed into Median territory, veering along a road that took them inland. That is the third version of the story, one that is reported by both barbarians and Greeks alike.

[13] Aristeas, the son of Caÿstrobius, a man from Proconnesus, claimed in one of his poems that he had visited the Issedonians while possessed by Apollo.[16] Beyond them, he said, there lived the Arimaspians, a race of one-eyed men, and beyond them the griffins who stand guard over gold, and beyond them, extending right the way to the sea, the Hyperboreans. All these various peoples, from the Arimaspians onwards, and excluding only the Hyperboreans, are perpetually attacking their neighbours: the Issedonians, so Aristeas says, were forced out of their country by the Arimaspians, the Scythians by the Issedonians, and the Cimmerians, who had been settled along the southern coast, were so hard pressed by the Scythians that they abandoned their country. So what the Scythians have to say about their country is contradicted by Aristeas too.

[14] I have already mentioned the origins of Aristeas, the writer of this account; but there is an anecdote I heard about him in Proconnesus and Cyzicus, which I will give you now. The story is that Aristeas, who in terms of breeding was second to none in Proconnesus, visited a fuller's shop in the city, where he promptly died; and that the fuller, after he had locked up his workshop, went off to inform the dead man's family of the news. But as word spread across the city that Aristeas was no more, there arrived from the town of Artake a man of Cyzicus who flatly challenged what was being said, for he claimed to have met with Aristeas heading towards Cyzicus, and to have fallen into conversation with him. Meanwhile, even as he was refusing to brook any contradiction, the relatives of the dead man came to the fuller's shop with everything necessary for the removal of the corpse – but when they unlocked the building, there was not a trace of Aristeas, either dead or

alive.[17] Then, seven years later (so the story goes) he reappeared in Proconnesus, composed the poem that the Greeks today call the *Arimaspeia*,[18] and vanished a second time.

[15] Such is the story told in Proconnesus and Cyzicus – but there is more. Based on evidence marshalled from these two cities, I have calculated that between the second disappearance of Aristeas and an episode that I know for certain took place in Italy, in Metapontion, there was an interval of two hundred and forty years. According to the people of Metapontion, Aristeas himself appeared in their country, and instructed them to set up an altar to Apollo, and to stand alongside it a statue labelled 'Aristeas of Proconnesus'. He told them that they alone, of all the Greeks settled in Italy, had been visited in their land by Apollo, and that he himself, who at the time had been a crow[19] but was now Aristeas, had been in the train of the god. Having delivered this pronouncement, he then disappeared – and so, according to the Metapontines, they sent an embassy to Delphi, to enquire of the god what this apparition of a man might have been. The Pythia answered them that they should do as the phantasm had ordered, and that such obedience would be in their best interests. Taking this advice, the Metapontines duly carried out the instructions they had been given – with the result that there now stands a statue bearing the name of Aristeas next to an altar dedicated to Apollo. The altar itself was set up in the market-place and is surrounded by laurel trees. But that is quite enough on the subject of Aristeas.

[16] About what might lie beyond the land that this account has been side-tracked into discussing, ignorance is universal. Certainly, there is no one from whom I have been able to obtain information who has any claim to accurate knowledge. Not even Aristeas himself, the poet whom I was just now recalling, claimed in his verses to have gone beyond the land of the Issedonians; as he acknowledged, his reports on the regions to the north were pure hearsay, and based on what the Issedonians had told him. Nevertheless, granting that hearsay can only be taken so far, it is my intention to take it to that limit, and to say all that can accurately be said.

[17] Head from the trading-post of the Borysthenites[20] – which, from the perspective of those who live on the coast constitutes the mid-most point of Scythia as a whole – and the first people you will come to are the Callippidae, who are Greek Scythians,[21] and then, beyond them, another tribe, known as the Alazonians. Their way of life, and that of the

Callippidae too, is Scythian in all the essentials, except that they both sow and subsist on grain[22] – not to mention onions, garlic, lentils and millet. Beyond the Alazonians there live Scythians who farm the land, though not with the aim of eating the crops they cultivate, but rather of selling them on. North of them live the Neurians; but beyond them, so far as we have knowledge, there is nothing but emptiness, where only the north wind has breath. These, then, are the tribes along the River Hypanis, to the west of the Borysthenes.

[18] Cross the Borysthenes, however, and immediately inland from the sea is Hylaea, while further inland yet is found the home of Scythian farmers, or Borysthenites, as they are called by those Greeks who live on the River Hypanis – and who refer to themselves as Olbiopolitans.[23] These Scythian farmers inhabit a region that extends three days' journey eastwards, all the way up to a river which goes by the name of Panticapes, and to the north for the equivalent of an eleven-day voyage up the Borysthenes. North of this there stretches a vast and uninhabited region; and in turn, beyond this wilderness, there live the Androphagi,[24] who are a wholly distinctive race of people, and not Scythian at all. Further north yet, and there yawns a true emptiness – one that to the best of our knowledge lacks even a single tribe of humans.

[19] To the east of these agrarian Scythians, across the River Panticapes, there are Scythians who lead a nomadic existence, and who neither sow nor even use a plough. The whole region, with the exception of Hylaea, is devoid of trees. The country occupied by these nomads reaches down to the River Gerrhus, a distance equivalent to fourteen days' journey.

[20] Beyond the Gerrhus are the Royal Lands, as they are known: the Scythians who live in them are braver and more numerous than elsewhere, and take for granted that every other Scythian is their slave. These lands extend south to the Taurian region, and eastwards to the trench that was dug by the offspring of the blind slaves, and to the trading-station on Lake Maeëtis that goes by the name of 'The Cliffs' or Cremni. There is also a stretch which reaches to the River Tanaïs. Beyond the Scythians of the Royal Lands, to the north, live the Melanchlaeni, who are not Scythian, but a separate people. Beyond them is nothing but marshland, where no one lives at all, so far as we know.

[21] Cross the River Tanaïs, and you are no longer in Scythia, but among new divisions of territory, of which the first belongs to the Sau-

romatians; the land they inhabit, that starts at the corner of Lake Maeëtis, and extends northwards for fifteen days' journey, is wholly devoid of either wild or cultivated trees. Beyond the Sauromatians, in the second tract of territory, live the Boudinians, whose land is completely forested with every kind of tree.

[22] Head north, beyond the Boudinians, and the first thing you will come to is a desert that will take you seven days to cross; after the desert, turn just a little eastward, and you will come to the home of the Thyssagetans, a numerous and most distinctive people. They live by hunting. Next to them, in the same stretch of territory, are settled a people known as the Iyrcae, who also live by hunting. Their method is to climb the trees that are plentiful across the entire country, and then wait in hiding. Each man will have trained his horse to lie flat on its stomach, to make it low, in a state of readiness that it shares with the huntsman's dog; then, when an animal is spotted from the tree, the huntsman fires at it with his bow, mounts his horse and gives the quarry chase, as does the hound. Beyond the Iyrcae, in an easterly direction, live yet more Scythians, who came to the land they now inhabit after a rebellion against the Scythians of the Royal Lands.

[23] All the various countries I have been discussing, including that of these Scythians, are level and deep-soiled; but from then on the terrain becomes rocky and uneven. Travel a fair distance across this rugged land, and you will come to the foothills of a lofty mountain range, where there live people who, it is claimed, are all of them bald from birth – men and women alike. Not only that, but they have snub noses and massive chins, speak a private language of their own, wear clothes in the Scythian manner and live off the produce of trees. The name of this tree, the one on which they depend for their sustenance, is the *ponticum*;[25] it is roughly the size of a fig tree. The fruit it bears is like a bean, and contains a stone. When the fruit is ripe, they strain it through strips of cloth and extract from it a thick, black juice. This juice, which they call *aschy*, they either lap up or drink mixed with milk, while the solid residue that gathers at the bottom they knead into cakes and eat. They do this because they have very few cattle – the grazing there not being very good. Each man lives under a tree; when winter comes, he wraps white, waterproof felt around it, which he will then remove in summertime. No other men ever harm them, for they are said to have a quality of the sacred about them – and certainly, they possess no weapons of

war. When differences arise among the surrounding tribes, it is they who act as arbiters – and should any fugitive, no matter who, take refuge with them, no one will lay a hand upon him. They are called the Argippaei.

[24] Our perspective on these bald people, and on the other tribes south of them too, is clear. They often receive visitors: some of these are Scythians, from whom it is not difficult to obtain information, and some are Greeks, whether from the trading-post on the Borysthenes or from others along the Pontic coast. Because any transaction with these tribes has to be made in seven different languages, the Scythians, when visiting them, always take along seven interpreters.

[25] The land of the bald people, however, marks the limit of our certain knowledge: the information that would enable us to discuss with any confidence what lies beyond it is lacking. So towering are the mountains that they constitute an impassable barrier, one which nobody can cross – although, if a claim made by the bald people is to be trusted (which personally I do not think it is), these mountains are inhabited by men with feet like goats, and lead, on their far side, to a people who sleep for six months at a time. This I find quite impossible to accept. What we do know for sure is that the land to the east of the bald people is inhabited by Issedonians; but as for what lies to the north of them, we are wholly ignorant, except for what the bald people themselves, and the Issedonians too, have to say.

[26] The Issedonians are reported to have the following customs. When a man's father dies, all his relatives bring along cattle that are sacrificed and butchered; the joints of meat are then mixed up with chunks of their host's dead father, and the whole lot is served up as a feast.[26] The skull, however, is stripped bare of its flesh and emptied of its brains, then gilded and treated as a thing of great sacredness; once every year, magnificent sacrifices are offered up to it. The son, in performing these for his father, is little different from the Greek who celebrates a memorial day for his ancestor – and in other respects too there is a sense of justice about what the Issedonians do. Their women wield a power no less than that enjoyed by the men.

[27] This too we can know with certainty; but our information regarding what lies beyond the Issedonians derives only from the Issedonians themselves. It is they who report the existence of one-eyed men and griffins that stand guard over gold: stories which were obtained

from them by the Scythians, and from the Scythians by the rest of us. Hence our belief in what, speaking as the Scythians do, we term 'Arimaspians' – *arima* in Scythian means 'one', and *spou* means 'eye'.[27]

[28] The entire region I have been discussing is afflicted by a winter so severe that for eight months it lies in the grip of an unbearable frost, during which time mud will result from lighting a fire rather than pouring out water. The sea freezes over, as too does the whole of the Cimmerian Bosporus, so that the Scythians who live on this side of the trench are able to launch military expeditions across the ice, and to drive their wagons over it into the land of the Sindians. For eight months, then, it is one perpetual winter, while even for the remaining four the region is cold. The winter is quite different in character from the winters that occur in other parts of the world, in that there is no rain worth mentioning during the season, while elsewhere it buckets down, and then in the summer it never stops. Thunderstorms too never happen at the time when elsewhere they are a continuous phenomenon, but instead are common throughout the summer. Indeed, the roll of thunder in winter, should it ever occur, is marvelled at in Scythia as a prodigy. So too is an earthquake, no matter when it might strike, whether in summer or winter. Horses can endure this winter of theirs, while mules and donkeys, which succumb to the first touch of frost, cannot – whereas in other countries it is the horses that succumb to frostbite whenever they stand on icy ground, and the mules and donkeys that are able to cope.

[29] It seems to me that this is also the reason for the breed of cattle in Scythia having no horns, and never growing them. Bearing witness to this theory of mine is a line of Homer's, in the *Odyssey*, which reads: 'And Libya, where no sooner are lambs born than they sprout horns.'[28] This is truly spoken – for in hot climates horns do indeed grow very fast. In bitterly cold ones, however, animals either grow no horns, or, if any at all, only the barest protuberances.

[30] Such, then, is the effect of the cold there. But if I may digress[29] here – as I have sought opportunities to do from the moment I started this account of my enquiries – there are no mules born anywhere in the land of Elis, which I find astounding, since it is hardly a chilly region, nor is there any other obvious explanatory factor. The Eleans themselves attribute to some curse this inability of theirs to breed mules. Accordingly, when their mares come into season, they drive them over the border and allow them to be mounted by donkeys in the territory of

their neighbours, until such time as the mares are made pregnant – after which the Eleans drive them back home.

[31] As for the feathers that, according to the Scythians, so fill the air as to prevent them from either seeing or travelling through the outer reaches of the continent, I have my own theory. North of Scythia, it is forever snowing – although, it goes without saying, less in summer than in winter. Now, anyone who has seen a thick snowfall close at hand will understand what I am saying: for what does the snow resemble, if not feathers? And why are the northern reaches of the continent uninhabitable, if not because of the harshness of the winter? Accordingly, it seems to me that the Scythians and those who live near them, when they speak of feathers, are actually using them as a metaphor for the snow. So much for what is reported about the regions furthermost from us.

[32] About the Hyperborean people, neither the Scythians nor the other nations in the region have anything to say. The Issedonians may be the exception in this, but personally I doubt whether they have any information either; if they did, the Scythians would surely report it, just as they report the stories of the one-eyed people. Hesiod, however, has made mention of the Hyperboreans, and so too has Homer, in the *Epigoni* – presuming that it really was Homer who wrote that particular poem.[30]

[33] By far the majority of the stories told about the Hyperboreans, however, derive from the Delians. According to them, gifts for the gods[31] are wrapped up inside wheat-straw and borne from the land of the Hyperboreans; then, following their arrival among the Scythians, they are received by a succession of neighbouring peoples and transported from Scythia all the way to the Adriatic in the furthest west. From there, they are dispatched south to the Dodonaeans, who are the first among the Greeks to receive them, and from the Dodonaeans down to the Malian Gulf, from where they are carried over to Euboea and passed on from city to city until they arrive in Carystus. The Carystians, however, rather than send them on to Andros, bring them directly to Tenos, from where the Tenians take them to Delos. This, then, is how these sacred offerings are said to come to Delos – although admittedly, on the first occasion, they were carried there by two virgins sent by the Hyperboreans, and whose names, according to the Delians, were Hyperoche and Laodice. Alongside these girls, to keep them from danger and to serve

them as escorts, the Hyperboreans also sent five of their own citizens: men who are nowadays known as the Perphereis, and who enjoy great honour in Delos. When their emissaries failed to return home, however, the Hyperboreans were so appalled at the prospect of those they sent on such missions never coming back that they wrapped up their gifts for the gods in wheat-straw and carried them to their frontier, where they entrusted them to their neighbours, together with instructions that they were to pass on the offerings from their own land to that of some other people. So it was, the Delians say, by means of this constant forwarding, that the offerings came to arrive in Delos. As I well know myself, this is not the only instance of sacred objects being handled in such a manner: whenever the women of Thrace and Paeonia give sacrifice to Queen Artemis,[32] there is never anything performed in her honour unless it be accompanied by an offering wrapped up in wheat-straw.

[34] That these women do this I know for a fact. The sons and daughters of the Delians cut their hair in honour of the young women who were sent by the Hyperboreans and ended up dying on Delos. Any girl, before she gets married, will cut off a lock of her hair, wind it around a spindle and place it on the tomb (which, by the way, lies on the left-hand side of the entrance to the shrine of Artemis[33] and has an olive tree growing out of it). Similarly, a Delian boy will wind some of his hair around a recently sprung shoot, and lay that upon the tomb. Such is the honour paid to Hyperoche and Laodice by those who live on Delos.

[35] The Delians also say that two other Hyperborean girls, Arge and Opis, passed the same peoples on their route as did Hyperoche and Laodice, and indeed arrived before them in Delos. They came bringing with them the tribute that they had vowed to pay Eileithyia[34] in exchange for the easy delivery of Apollo and Artemis in childbirth, and were accompanied on their journey by the gods: so say the Delians, who themselves paid Arge and Opis other honours. The women of Delos, for instance, make a collection for them, and invoke their names by singing the hymn which Olen of Lycia composed in their honour – a practice which was then picked up by the islanders and the Ionians, who likewise hymn the names of Arge and Opis, and make collections for them. (This same man Olen, who came to Delos from Lycia, also composed all the other hymns that have traditionally been sung on the island.) What is more, when thigh-bones are burned on the altar, they say that the

residue of ashes is scattered over the tomb of Opis and Arge, right down to the last handful. This tomb is situated behind the temple of Artemis, facing east, and directly adjacent to the banqueting hall of the Ceans.

[36] But that is quite enough talk about the Hyperboreans. I certainly have no intention of telling the story of Abaris, who is supposed to have been a Hyperborean, and to have carried an arrow the whole way round the world, nor ever to have eaten a thing. Besides, if there are Hyperboreans, then why not Hypernotians? It makes me laugh to observe that of all the multitude of those who have drawn maps of the world, none has ever done it intelligently or convincingly. Oceanus is portrayed as flowing round the edge of the world, which forms so neat a circle it might as well have been drawn with compasses, while Asia is rendered as equal in size to Europe. So let me now briefly clarify the actual size of each continent, and how each of them should properly be represented on a map.[35]

[37] The homeland of the Persians extends all the way south to the body of water known as the Red Sea. Inland from them, their neighbours to the north are the Medes; beyond them in turn are the Saspeirians, and then beyond them the Colchians, who extend as far north as the sea into which the River Phasis empties. These are the four peoples who live between the two bodies of water I just mentioned.

[38] West of this region, projecting out into sea, are two peninsulas, of which I shall now give a description.[36] The northern shoreline of one of them starts at the Phasis, and is bounded by the sea for the entire length of the Euxine and the Hellespont, before ending at Sigeium, in the Troad; meanwhile, the southern shoreline of this same peninsula extends from the Myriandic Gulf, just off Phoenicia, and is flanked by the sea all the way to the Cape of Triopium. The people who inhabit this peninsula constitute thirty nations.

[39] So much for the first peninsula. The second begins in the land of the Persians and extends to the Red Sea, taking in, after Persia, both Assyria and Arabia in succession. It ends, but only as convention would have it,[37] at the Arabian Gulf, into which a canal was channelled by Darius from the Nile. Between the country of the Persians and Phoenicia the land is broad and spacious, but all along the edge of Phoenicia the peninsula is bordered by our sea,[38] reaching down to Egypt, where it ends, by way of Palestinian Syria. In this peninsula there are only three peoples.

[40] So much for the regions of Asia west of the Persians. As to those that lie east of the Persians – the Medes, the Saspeirians and the Colchians, in the direction of the rising of the sun, they are bordered by the Red Sea, and to the north by the Caspian Sea, and by the River Araxes, which flows towards the eastern horizon. Asia is inhabited the whole way up to where the Indians have their home, but beyond that, eastwards of India, all is desert, nor is there anyone who can say what it might be like.

[41] That, then, is the nature and extent of Asia; and Libya too, following on as it does directly from Egypt, is a part of the second peninsula. Now, in Egypt, this peninsula is narrow, since the distance between our sea and the Red Sea is only 100,000 fathoms – which is to say, 1,000 stades.[39] Beyond this narrow stretch, however, the portion of the peninsula that goes by the name of Libya is, as circumstance would have it, extremely wide.

[42] All the more surprising, then, in my opinion, that dividing lines should have been drawn so as to establish Libya, Asia and Europe as distinct entities, since the differences between them are not inconsiderable. So far, indeed, does Europe extend that it is equivalent in distance to the combined lengths of the other two continents, while in terms of width it seems to me incomparably broader. Libya, after all, only excepting the section of it that borders Asia, is self-evidently surrounded by sea: a discovery that was first made, so far as we can tell, by Necos, a king of the Egyptians,[40] who, after he had abandoned his excavation of a canal from the Nile through to the Arabian Gulf,[41] sent crews of Phoenicians off on a naval expedition, with orders that they should return by passing between the Pillars of Heracles back into the Northern Sea, and thence to Egypt. Sure enough, the Phoenicians set off from the Red Sea, and sailed into the Southern Sea. When it turned to autumn, they would make landings and sow whatever stretch of Libyan soil they happened to have come to on their voyage, wait for the harvest, and only then, when the crops were reaped, would they put back to sea. Two years went by; and then, in the course of the third, they turned through the Pillars of Heracles and arrived back in Egypt. One of their claims – which I personally find incredible, although others may not – was that, while sailing round Libya, they had had the sun on their right-hand side.[42]

[43] Such, then, was the original source of our information on Libya, which has since been supplemented by Carthaginian reports – although

not by Sataspes, the son of Teaspes, a man of the Achaemenid clan, who failed to circumnavigate Libya, despite having been dispatched on precisely such a mission: for such were the length and desolate nature of the voyage that he quite lost his nerve and turned back home, thereby failing to meet the challenge that had been laid upon him by his mother. Sataspes, you see, had raped a virgin, the daughter of Zopyrus, the son of Megabyzus; and for this reason he had been condemned by King Xerxes to suffer impalement. Just as the sentence was about to be carried out, however, his mother – who was a sister of Darius – begged for him to be spared, and declared that she would impose on him a harsher penalty than Xerxes had ever done. 'For I will oblige him', she said, 'to sail the whole way round Libya, so that his voyage will see him return to the Arabian Gulf.' After Xerxes had agreed to these terms, Sataspes duly went to Egypt, where he obtained a ship and crew, and set sail for the Pillars of Heracles. Then, once he had passed through them, and rounded the Libyan headland known as Soloeis, he sailed south for many months across an immense expanse of sea; but always there was ever more to cross, and so at length he turned round and sailed back to Egypt. From there he made his way into the presence of Xerxes again, and in his report to the King declared that during the final stage of his voyage he had sailed past tiny men[43] who only ever wore garments fashioned out of palm leaves, and who, whenever his crew drew the ship up onto land, would abandon their cities and flee to the hills. This, he added, was despite the fact that he had never done them any harm, but had only taken from them such cattle as were needed for food. As for his failure to complete the circumnavigation of Libya, the reason he gave for this was that his ship had found itself stuck fast and unable to continue any further. Xerxes, however, refused to accept that Sataspes was telling the truth, and therefore, because he had failed to complete his allotted mission, had him impaled in accordance with the original sentence delivered against him. One of the eunuchs owned by Sataspes, the moment he learned of his master's death, ran away to Samos, taking with him a large sum of money: this subsequently came into the possession of a man from Samos, whose name, although certainly known to me, I choose not to mention.[44]

[44] The greater part of Asia was discovered by Darius, who had wished to know where it was that the sea was joined by the River Indus (this being one of only two in the world which provides a habitat for

crocodiles), and so sent ships with men on board whom he could trust to report back truthfully, including Scylax, a man from Caryanda.[45] These duly set off from the city of Caspatyrus, in the land of Pactyice, and sailed downriver in an easterly direction, towards the rising of the sun, until they met the sea; after that, their voyage took them west across the open waters, until, after sailing for thirty months, they arrived at the very place from which the king of Egypt, as I mentioned previously, had dispatched the Phoenicians to circumnavigate Libya. Once this voyage around Asia had been completed, Darius conquered the Indians and made this sea his lake. So it was that Asia, only excluding those regions which border the rising of the sun, was discovered to be very similar in its characteristics to Libya.

[45] As for Europe, no one really has the foggiest idea whether there is a sea between it and the rising of the sun, or indeed the source of the north wind. Not in doubt, however, is the fact that it is equivalent in length to the combined extent of the other two continents. I cannot compute why something that is a single entity such as the Earth should have been given three distinct names, all of them derived from women,[46] or why the boundaries should have been set at the River Nile in Egypt, and at the Phasis in Colchis (or, according to some, at the River Tanaïs at Lake Maeëtis and at the crossing-point on the Cimmerian straits). I also have no idea as to the identity of those who drew the boundaries, nor whence the continents obtained their names. Nowadays, for instance, most Greeks assert that Libya was named after a woman, a native of the continent who was also called Libya, and Asia after the wife of Prometheus. The Lydians too, however, claim a stake in the name of Asia: they say that it is derived, not from the wife of Prometheus, but from Asies, the son of Cotys and the grandson of Manes, and after whom the Asian tribe from Sardis is similarly named. Europe is mysterious not only in relation to the sea which may or may not surround it, but also because no one knows the origin of its name, or who first pinned the name upon it. (Unless, of course, we accept that it was named after the Europa who came from Tyre, and that prior to her it had been as lacking in a name as were the other two continents. It is evident enough, however, that Europa came from Asia, and never made it to the expanse of land which the Greeks nowadays call Europe, but only from Phoenicia to Crete, and from there to Lycia.) But suffice it to say, the names I use for the continents will be the conventional ones.

[46] The Euxine Sea that Darius was marching against is home to peoples who, the Scythians excepted, are the most ignorant in existence.[47] None of the various peoples within the Euxine stands out as being intelligent, nor do we know of a single man of learning born there: the only exceptions are Anacharsis[48] and (as regards peoples) the Scythians. Now, although in general I do not admire the Scythians as a race, I know of no cleverer solution to the most pressing issue that faces humankind than the one formulated by them. What they have discovered is a way of ensuring that no invader can ever escape them, or overtake them either, unless they should wish to be found. Rather than build cities or walls, they all carry their homes around with them on wagons, practise their archery from horseback and depend for their living on cattle rather than the fruits of the plough. How, then, could they fail to defy every effort made to conquer them or pin them down?

[47] Not only was the lie of the land well suited to this discovery of theirs, but they were helped in making it by the sheer quantity of rivers. The terrain is flat and grassy, and so well watered that the number of rivers flowing across it is equivalent almost to the number of canals in Egypt. Let me give the names of those that merit a mention and are navigable from the sea: the Ister, with its five separate mouths, and then the Tyras, the Hypanis, the Borysthenes, the Panticapes, the Hypacyris, the Gerrhus and the Tanaïs. The courses they follow should also be mentioned.

[48] The unparalleled scale of the Ister – which is the largest river on record, and flows further from the west than any other river in Scythia, with a volume of water that never fluctuates, be it summer or winter – is due to the fact that other rivers feed into it as tributaries. Of those that swell its waters, five flow through Scythia: the river called by the Scythians the Porata and by the Greeks the Pyretus, the Tiarantus, the Ararus, the Naparis and the Ordessus. The first mentioned of these is an immense river which flows in an easterly direction before its waters merge with those of the Ister; the second, the Tiarantus, is further to the west and smaller in scale; the Ararus, the Naparis and the Ordessus all join the Ister midway between the first two rivers on the list. While the course of each of these five rivers never once leaves Scythia before joining that of the Ister, the Maris, which also flows into the Ister, rises in the land of the Agathyrsians.

[49] The currents of three other large rivers, all of which originate

amid the peaks of the Haemus Mountains, flow contrariwise to the north wind before they join with the Ister: namely, the Atlas, the Auras and the Tibisis. The rivers Athrys, Noas and Artanes flow through Thrace and the land of the Crobyzian Thracians before emptying into the Ister. The River Scius descends from Mount Rhodope in the land of the Paeonians, and slices through the middle of the Haemus Mountains before emptying into the Ister. The River Angrus originates in the land of the Illyrians and flows contrary to the north wind until it empties into the Triballic plain, and the River Brongus. Since the Brongus then unites with the Ister in turn, the Ister is effectively joined by the pair of them, mighty rivers both. There are also the rivers Carpis and Alpis, which have their origins north of the land of the Umbrians, and then flow contrariwise to the north wind, until they too merge with the Ister. Bear in mind, after all, that the Ister flows through the whole of Europe: its source lies in the land of the Celts, a people who live further from us, and closer to the setting of the sun, than any other, except for the Cynetes, and only after the Ister has flowed through the whole of Europe, and reached the very edge of Scythia, does it empty into the sea.

[50] In addition to the rivers I have mentioned, there are many others too which add their waters to the Ister, so that in consequence it is the largest river in the world. (Exclude the volume of water that other rivers and streams contribute to it by virtue of being tributaries, however, and the Ister, compared river to river, would be outranked by the Nile.) As for the reason why the flow of the Ister never alters between summer and winter, I think that I may have the solution. During the winter, its waters are those that it would have under any circumstances – or supplemented, perhaps, just a little. The winter rainfall in Scythia, after all, is minimal, with nothing but snow ever falling. During the summer, however, the great drifts of snow that fell during the winter melt and empty into the Ister from all directions. This snow, once it has added to the river, serves to swell its volume, as too do the frequent and violent squalls – for in summer it is perpetually raining. In consequence, more waters merge with those of the Ister during the summer than during the winter; and the degree of disproportion is equivalent to that which separates the volume of water that is evaporated by the sun during the summer and the winter respectively. These differences, striking a perfect balance, serve to cancel each other out; and so it is that the volume of water appears always to be constant.[49]

[51] So much for the Ister, one of the rivers of Scythia. It is followed by the Tyras, which right from its very origins flows as the north wind blows, and has as its source a lake so immense that it serves to demarcate Scythia from the land of the Neurians. Its estuary has been settled by Greeks: the Tyritae, as they are known.

[52] A third river, the Hypanis, originates in Scythia, and flows from a huge lake around which wild white horses graze. Very fittingly, this lake is called the Mother of the Hypanis. From there, where the river rises, its waters continue to flow shallow and sweet for a distance equivalent to five days' voyage; but then, for the four remaining days it takes to reach the sea, they become revoltingly briny. This is because they are joined by the salt waters of a spring which, although their flow is only small, are so brackish that they pollute the Hypanis, despite the fact that it dwarfs most other rivers. The spring is located on the border between the region of Scythia that is worked as farmland and the land of the Alazonians. The name of the spring, which is also the name of the country through which its waters flow, is Exampaeus: a Scythian word, which translates into Greek as 'The Sacred Ways'. The course of the Tyras runs very close to that of the Hypanis throughout the land of the Alazonians, but beyond it they wind away from each other, so that as they flow onwards the space between them widens.

[53] A fourth river, the Borysthenes, is second only to the Ister in size, while in terms of the various uses to which it can be put, I would argue that there is no other river in the world, let alone in Scythia, which can surpass it, the Nile in Egypt excepted. Granting, however, the Nile to be a wholly incomparable river, the Borysthenes certainly has more to offer than all the rest. The pasturage that it provides cattle is the best and most nutritious imaginable; it teems with the most delicious fish; its waters, which flow clear where those of other rivers would turn muddy, are delicious to the taste; the crops that are sown along its banks grow better than anywhere else; even where crops are not grown, the grass is of the lushest. Huge, naturally occurring deposits of salt build up along its estuary mouth. The river also furnishes giant aquatic monsters without spines, which are called sturgeons, and can be pickled, along with many other things that merit wonder. Now the course of the Borysthenes follows the direction of the north wind, and has been charted upriver as far as the land of the Gerrhians, a distance equivalent to a voyage of forty days; beyond that no one can say for sure which peoples

it flows past. It is clear, though, that after it has wound through an empty wilderness it arrives in a land that is inhabited by Scythians who practise agriculture, since these live alongside it for a distance equivalent to a ten-day voyage. The Borysthenes and the Nile are the only two rivers whose sources it is beyond me to identify – but then I reckon no other Greek can identify them either. As the waters of the Borysthenes flow close to the sea, so they merge with those of the Hypanis, and empty into the one single marsh. The estuaries of the two rivers are separated by a headland called the Cape of Hippoles, on which has been raised a shrine to Demeter. Beyond the shrine, on the River Hypanis, stand the homes of the Borysthenites.

[54] Moving on from the details of these rivers, the next one, the fifth, is known as the Panticapes. It too flows southwards from a lake, and the land between it and the Borysthenes is inhabited by agrarian Scythians; beyond them, the river passes into Hylaea, then leaves it behind and merges with the Borysthenes.

[55] A sixth river is the Hypacyris, which originates in a lake and flows through land inhabited by nomadic Scythians; it skirts Hylaea and the so-called 'Racetrack of Achilles', both of which lie on its right bank, before emptying into the sea next to the city of Carcinitis.

[56] Seventh is the River Gerrhus, which branches off from the Borysthenes somewhere in the region where the course of the latter is a mystery. The place where this bifurcation occurs, and which gives its name to the river itself, is Gerrhus; from then on, as it flows towards the sea, it serves as the boundary between the territory of the nomadic tribes and that of the Royal Scythians, until it empties into the Hypacyris.

[57] Eighth is the River Tanaïs, which has as its source a vast lake, and then flows until it empties into an even vaster lake: the name of this lake is Maeëtis, and it separates the Royal Scythians from the Sauromatians. There is also another river, called the Hyrgis, which is a tributary of the Tanaïs.

[58] As can be seen, then, the Scythians are hardly short of noteworthy rivers. Nor do the cattle in Scythia lack for bile, since the grass that grows there produces more of it than any other pastureland on record, as can be gauged by dissecting a Scythian cow.[50]

[59] The Scythians have a ready supply of life's essentials, but they also have various customs which it remains for me to list. The gods they

worship are these, and these alone: Hestia,[51] whom they regard as pre-eminent, then Zeus and Gaia, whom they believe to be husband and wife, followed by Apollo, Aphrodite Urania,[52] Heracles and Ares. All Scythians share in these cults, but [the ones known as] the Royal Scythians offer up sacrifices to Poseidon as well. The name the Scythians give to Hestia is *Tabiti*, while Zeus – quite correctly, in my opinion – they call *Papaeus*, or 'Great Father'. Gaia they name *Api*, Apollo *Goetosyrus*, Aphrodite Urania *Argimpasa* and Poseidon *Thagimasadas*. They have no tradition of fashioning statues, altars or temples, except for Ares, in whose honour they do indeed craft such things.

[60] They perform animal blood-sacrifices in the one identical manner, no matter the rite being celebrated. They tether the front legs of the victim, as it stands in front of the sacrificer; the priest then tugs on the end of the rope, bringing the animal down, and as it falls, so he invokes the god to whom he is making the sacrifice. Next, he wraps a noose around its neck, inserts a stick into the noose and twists it round and round until the animal is strangled. At no point, in other words, does he light a fire, or make any consecration, or pour a libation. Then, once he has throttled and flayed the beast, he boils it.

[61] Now, because there is a terrible lack of trees in Scythia, the Scythians have had to devise their own method for boiling the meat. First they skin the victim, then they fillet the meat from the bones and put it into a cauldron – which, should they happen to have one, will have been manufactured locally, and most closely resembles a Lesbian mixing-bowl, except that it will be that much larger. Then, once the pieces of meat have been dropped in, they cook them by making a fire beneath the cauldron out of the bones of the sacrificed animal. Should they not have a cauldron to hand, they put all the lumps of meat into the stomach of the victim, mix in water and make a fire underneath it out of the bones. These blaze away beautifully, while the stomach, once the bones have been stripped completely bare, can easily hold all the meat. So it is that the ox ends up cooking itself – just as every other kind of sacrificial victim does. Once the meat is boiled, the officiating priest takes some of it, both prime cuts and entrails, and throws it on the ground in front of him as a first offering to the gods. Although all kinds of livestock are sacrificed, the most commonly slaughtered creature is a horse.[53]

[62] These, then, are the methods and the kinds of animal used when

sacrifices are made to the gods – except in the case of Ares. This god has a shrine raised to him in every sub-division of every province,[54] built to a distinctive design. Bundles of brushwood are stacked up in a pile 3 stades long and wide, but not as high. Three of its sides are sheer, one of them can readily be climbed and its summit has a square platform built onto it. Every year, to counter the effects of the terrible weather, which produces a constant subsidence, they add a hundred and fifty wagon-loads of brush to the pile of wood. On top of each of these structures there is set an ancient iron sword, which serves as a symbol of Ares, and to which they offer annual sacrifices of cattle and horses in quantities larger than they offer to any other god. They also sacrifice one in every one hundred prisoners taken in battle – although not as they sacrifice livestock. Rather, their method is to pour wine over each man's head and to cut his throat over a bowl, then to carry the bowls up onto the pile of brushwood where the blood is poured out over the sword. Mean-while, as the bowls are being carried up to the summit of the shrine, something else is being performed down by its side. From hand to shoul-der, the right arms of all the men who have had their throats cut are hacked off and tossed up into the air, whereupon all the other victims are sacrificed as well. Everyone then departs, with the arms left lying wherever they happened to fall and the corpses in a separate pile.

[63] These, then, are the methods of blood-sacrifice established in Scythia. Pigs they never offer in sacrifice; indeed, they are unwilling so much as to rear them on their soil.

[64] War, as practised by the Scythians, has a number of distinctive characteristics. When a Scythian records his first kill, he will gulp down the man's blood. He will also bring the heads of those he has killed in battle to the king, for a head will secure him a share of whatever booty may have been won, whereas no head means no booty. The head itself is scalped: what happens is that the skin is incised all the way around from ear to ear, and then is pinched and worked off the skull. After that, he uses the rib of an ox to scrape it free of any flesh and kneads it with his hands, until it is so soft that he effectively has a napkin that he can fasten to the bridle of the horse he is riding, and take great pride in: the man with the largest number of these napkins [made of skin] is reck-oned to be the bravest. There are many Scythians who wear cloaks fashioned out of scalps, which they stitch together in the manner of shepherds who make cloaks out of leather. A common practice as well

is to take the corpse of an adversary, to skin the right hand, fingernails and all, and then to make it into a cover for an arrow-sheath. (Human skin, it turns out, is thick and has a tremendous sheen, more brilliant, and whiter, than almost any other kind of skin.) There are also many Scythians who will flay men entire, and stretch the hides on wooden frames, which they then carry around with them on their horses.

[65] So much for the customs that govern their behaviour in the field of war. Each of the skulls themselves – if it belonged to a bitter enemy, that is, rather than just to anyone – is sawn in two, with everything below the brow being discarded, and everything above it being scoured clean. If the man doing this is poor, he will simply wrap raw ox-hide around the exterior before using it; if he is wealthy, however, then as well as wrapping raw hide around it, he will also gild the interior and employ it as a drinking-cup. Skulls also derive from family feuds, since these see rivals from the same clans fighting one another to the death before the king. The victor, if he has any distinguished guests to stay, will be sure to pass these skulls around, together with an explanation: that they once belonged to his kinsmen, that these kinsmen made trouble for him and that he succeeded in vanquishing them. Such, to the Scythians, is the very mark of a hero.[55]

[66] Once every year, in every administrative district, the governor will mix a bowl of wine from which all the Scythians who have killed an enemy that year will then take a drink. Those who have not done so do not get to taste the wine, but must instead sit to one side in disgrace.[56] This, to the Scythians, is the ultimate humiliation. Should any of them happen to have killed a particularly large number of men, he will be given two cups, and he can drink from both of these simultaneously.

[67] Soothsayers, who use large numbers of willow rods when they make their divinations, are numerous among the Scythians. What they do is bring large bundles of the rods, which they place on the ground and unroll; they then set these rods aside, one by one, while uttering their prognostications, which they continue to do as they roll the rods back up, one by one again, into a bundle. Such is their ancestral method of divination; but the Enareës, men who are also women, lay claim to another method, a gift from Aphrodite. To make their prophecies they use the bark of a lime tree. First they divide it into three, and then, as they braid and unravel the lime tree bark with their fingers, they pronounce their oracle.

[68] Whenever the king of the Scythians falls sick, he summons the three most reputable of the soothsayers, who then divine the problem using the method related above. Their usual practice is to say something along the lines of, 'Such and such a person swore falsely upon the hearth of the king,' and then identify one of their fellow-citizens – it might be anyone. (It is the prevailing custom of the Scythians, whenever they wish to make a particularly solemn promise, to swear an oath upon the hearth of the king.) Straightaway, the man charged with perjury, whoever he may be, is apprehended and brought in; upon his arrival, the soothsayers charge him with having been exposed in their divinations as someone who swore falsehoods upon the hearth of the king, thereby causing the king to fall sick. The man denies this, insisting that he swore no false oaths, and vehemently protesting his innocence. The king, in the face of these denials, then summons further soothsayers, double the original number. If these too see revealed in their divinations that the man was a perjurer, and convict him, he immediately has his head chopped off, and his goods are divided up among the original three diviners. Should the newly arrived diviners acquit him, however, then other soothsayers are brought in on the case, and others again. Should a majority of these acquit him, then it is considered expedient that the original diviners themselves be put to death.

[69] And the method of execution? First they fill a wagon with brushwood and yoke oxen to it; then, after they have bound the soothsayers hand and foot, and gagged them, they box them up in the middle of the firewood; finally they set light to the firewood, startle the oxen and set the wagon rolling. The oxen are often consumed in the conflagration, together with the soothsayers, but it is not uncommon either – if the pole burns through – for them to escape with only superficial burns. Other offences will also see soothsayers being burned to death in the manner just described, and labelled false prophets. Nor, when a king puts someone to death, are the children necessarily spared: the man's male issue too are killed, although his daughters are left unharmed.

[70] Agreements made on oath between Scythians are sealed by pouring wine into a large earthenware cup, and then mixing it with the blood of those who are swearing the oath[57] – either by jabbing them with an awl, or nicking them superficially somewhere on their bodies with a dagger. After doing this, they dip into the cup a scimitar, some arrows, a battleaxe and a javelin; and then after that they offer up a

large number of prayers. Finally, those who are entering into the agreement, together with the most valued members of their retinues, drain the cup.

[71] The burial places[58] of the kings lie in the land of the Gerrhians, at the point where the Borysthenes becomes navigable. The Gerrhians, when their king dies, dig a large square pit in the ground, while the Royal Scythians slit open the stomach of the corpse, clean it out, fill it with ground aromatic nut-sedge, incense, celery-seeds and aniseed, then sew it back up again and cover it with wax. Next, when everything has been made ready, they lift up the corpse, and convey it by wagon to another tribe. When the people to whom it has been transported receive the corpse, they follow the example of the Royal Scythians and cut off part of their ears, shave off their hair, cut their arms, score their foreheads and noses and stab arrows right through their left hands. Then, with an entourage of those it has already visited, the corpse [of the king] is taken in its wagon to another subject tribe. Once the corpse has been taken on a complete tour of Scythia, they finally come to the Gerrhians, whose settlements are the remotest of all the various tribes in the empire, and to the places of burial. Here, after they have placed the corpse upon a pallet in its tomb, they stick spears along one side of it and then the other, extend planks of wood over them and make a roof for it out of rush matting; next, in the open space still remaining in the tomb, they strangle and bury one of the king's concubines, his cup-bearer, his cook, his groom, his steward and his messenger, some horses, a choice selection of all his other possessions and some golden cups. Nothing made of silver or bronze is ever used. Once that is done, they all furiously compete with one another to raise a huge barrow of earth, as vast as they can possibly make it.

[72] After a whole year has gone by, further action is taken. Of the king's remaining servants, they choose the fifty most suited to their purpose – all of whom, I should add, will be native-born Scythians, since those who serve in the royal household are ordered there by the king himself, rather than being purchased with silver for the purpose – and after they have strangled these servants, together with fifty of his finest horses, they gut them, clean them out, stuff them with chaff and sew them up. Next, they cut a wheel in two and fix both halves on wooden posts, so that the curves are facing the ground, and then fix a whole number of wheels in the same fashion. This done, they drive thick stakes

through the horses, right the way to their necks, which they use to mount the horses on the wheels. The front half of each wheel is used to support a horse's shoulders, and the rear half its stomach, directly next to its thighs. The legs on both sides are left hanging in the air. The horse is also fitted out with a bit and bridle, which is stretched and secured to pegs directly facing it. Each of the fifty young men who have been strangled is mounted on a horse by a stake that is driven straight upwards, in line with the backbone, all the way up to the neck. A portion of this stake, however, is left to project downwards, and is secured to the stake driven through the horse by means of a socket. The horsemen are then set up in a circle around the tomb, and everyone gallops off.

[73] This is how the kings are buried. Any other Scythian, however, when he dies, will be laid in a wagon by his closest relatives and taken on a tour of all his friends, each of whom will welcome the entourage and entertain them – and the corpse will have the same identical portions laid before it as everyone else. For forty days, commoners are taken around in this way and then laid to rest. Once a burial is over, Scythians make sure to purify themselves.[59] They soap and wash their heads; their bodies they cleanse by propping up three poles one against the other and stretching woollen blankets of felt over them, so that as few gaps as possible are left open, and then by placing a dish in the middle of these poles and blankets, and throwing red-hot stones into it.

[74] Now, there is a plant in their country called cannabis, which closely resembles flax, except that it has a thicker stem, and is larger in size. In these respects, cannabis has by far the advantage. It grows both wild and as a result of cultivation, and is even used by the Thracians to make clothes that closely resemble linen. Indeed, only a real specialist can distinguish clothes made from flax from those made from the cannabis plant. Someone who has never seen cannabis before would think the clothes to be linen.

[75] So – what the Scythians do is to take the seeds of a cannabis plant, crawl in under the blankets and cast the seeds onto the glowing stones. As they hit the stones, the seeds flare as though they were incense, and emit a vapour so thick that no steam-bath in Greece could possibly compete with it. The effect of this vapour on the Scythians is to make them howl with delight. It also serves them as the equivalent of a bath, since they never use water to wash themselves. That said, their women do blend water with a mixture of cypress, cedar and frankincense wood,

which is pounded by them with a rough stone until a thick paste is formed, whereupon they plaster the paste all over their bodies and faces. Not only does this endow them with a delicious scent, but when they remove the plaster one day later, it leaves them cleansed and gleaming.

[76] As to foreign practices, the Scythians are another nation who would run a mile rather than adopt the ways of some other people, and of the Greeks in particular – as is clear enough from the case of Anacharsis, and from the later one of Scyles too. Anacharsis, my first example, had seen much of the world, and never ceased to demonstrate how travel can serve to broaden the mind.[60] As he was being taken by ship back to his native haunts in Scythia, and was passing through the Hellespont, he put in at Cyzicus. Here he found the people of the city staging with great magnificence a festival in honour of the Mother of the Gods,[61] to whom he duly raised a prayer, promising that if only he made it back to his homeland safe and sound, he would offer up to her the same sacrifices as he had seen the Cyzicenes making, and would celebrate her rites all night long. So it was, after his return to Scythia, that he stole away down to Hylaea, a region next to the Racetrack of Achilles – and which, as it so happens, is densely forested with every kind of tree. Then, once he had made his way secretly down there, taking with him a drum, and festooned with images of the goddess, Anacharsis went through every last rite in her honour. One of the Scythians, however, spotted what he was up to, and informed Saulius, the king, who came in person, saw Anacharsis performing the rites and shot him dead with an arrow. To this day, should anyone enquire after Anacharsis, the Scythians profess a complete ignorance of him – and all because he went abroad to Greece and adopted foreign customs. I personally have it on the authority of Tymnes,[62] the steward of Ariapeithes, that Anacharsis was the paternal uncle of Idanthyrsus, the Scythian king, and that his father was Gnourus, the son of Lycus and the grandson of Spargapeithes. If this really was his family background, then let him know the truth: that he was killed by his very own brother! Idanthyrsus, after all, was the son of Saulius – and it was Saulius who killed Anacharsis.

[77] Nevertheless, there is another version of this story, which I heard from the Peloponnesians.[63] It has Anacharsis being sent by the Scythian king to see if there was anything to be learned from the example of Greece, and then, on his return home, informing the king who had given him the mission that the Greeks were addicted to every kind of sophistry –

all, that was, except for the Lacedaemonians, with whom alone it was possible to have a sensible exchange of views. But this is just a tall story, fabricated by the Greeks themselves, and does not alter the fact that the man was indeed killed as I described above. Such was the consequence of his foreign ways and his consorting with the Greeks.

[78] Then, very many years later, Scyles, the son of Ariapeithes, suffered a similar fate. Ariapeithes, you see, was the king of the Scythians, and had a number of children, of whom Scyles was but one. Scyles' mother was not a native of Scythia, but a woman from Istria, and she personally taught her son the Greek language and script. Time went by: Ariapeithes met his end thanks to the treachery of Spargapeithes, the king of the Agathyrsians, and Scyles inherited both the kingdom and his father's wife, whose name was Opoea. (This Opoea, who was a native Scythian, had previously borne Ariapeithes a son called Oricus.) Though Scyles was now king of Scythia, he showed not the slightest interest in the Scythian way of life; instead, because of his upbringing, he inclined to all things Greek. What he would do, then, whenever he arrived at the head of a Scythian army outside the city of the Borysthenites (a people who claim to be of Milesian descent), was to leave his army behind on the outskirts, and go himself inside the city walls and lock the gates; then he would take off his Scythian clothes and put on Greek attire instead, and so dressed would frequent the market-place, without any entourage of bodyguards, or indeed any entourage at all. Guards were placed on the gates, however, to ensure that no Scythian would ever see him dressed up as he was, behaving exactly as though he were a Greek – and in particular, worshipping the gods in the manner of the Greeks. Then, when he had spent a month or more like this, he would put back on his Scythian clothes and depart. This was something he did a great deal; indeed, he even built a house in Borysthenes and installed a woman of the city in it as his wife.[64]

[79] But it was inevitable that he would come to a bad end – an end that duly overtook him under the following circumstances. Scyles was eager to be initiated into the rites of Bacchic Dionysus. With everything in hand for the performance of the initiation, however, a truly ominous portent occurred. Scyles, as I just mentioned, owned a house in the city of the Borysthenites: large, luxurious and enclosed within a wall, it had sphinxes and griffins carved of white stone placed all around it. The god struck the house with a lightning-bolt, yet although the entire house

was burned down, Scyles still completed the initiation. Now, the Scythians revile the Greeks for the Bacchic rites, since they argue that it is an offence against reason actively to seek out a god who drives men mad.[65] Accordingly, after Scyles had been initiated into the Bacchic rites, one of the Borysthenites hurried off to the Scythians. 'You Scythians,' he said, 'you laugh at us for our worship of Bacchus, and our possession by the god,[66] but now the spirit of the divine has taken control of your own king! Yes, he is a Bacchic! The madness of the god is upon him! You don't believe me? Come with me and I will show you myself.' So the chiefs among the Scythians followed the Borysthenite, who led them secretly up into a tower where he sat them down. Sure enough, when Scyles went by in wild procession with his fellow-worshippers and the Scythians saw that he was indeed a Bacchic, they had no doubt that this was a calamity on a terrible scale; and so they returned and informed the entire army of what they had seen.

[80] The outcome of this was that even as Scyles was heading back out to his own native stamping-grounds, the Scythians rose in rebellion against him, and set up his brother, Octamasades, the son of Teres' daughter, in his place. Scyles, when he discovered the danger that was brewing, and what lay behind it, fled to the Thracians – and Octamasades, informed of this, duly descended on Thrace. The Thracians met with him on his arrival at the Ister; but Sitalces, just as battle was about to be joined, sent a message to Octamasades. 'Why make a test of each other in this way? You are my own nephew, after all – and you have my brother with you. Give him back to me, and I will hand Scyles over to you. That way, neither of us need put the lives of our men in danger.' (The reason why Sitalces sent a herald with this message was that his brother, who had gone into exile, was in the company of Octamasades.) Agreement was reached: Octamasades handed his uncle over to Sitalces in exchange for his brother, Scyles. Once he had got hold of his brother, Sitalces led him away as a prisoner, but Octamasades had the head of Scyles chopped off right there on the spot – proof indeed of how concerned the Scythians are to maintain their customs,[67] and of the punishment that anyone who supplements them with foreign ways can expect.

[81] One detail I found impossible to discover with any accuracy was the size of the Scythian population, for people kept giving me conflicting tallies. There were those who said that their numbers were very high, while others said that those who ranked as authentic Scythians

were actually very few. Nevertheless, as far as the evidence of my own eyes goes, I was shown one thing of relevance. Between the River Borysthenes and the Hypanis there is a region called Exampaeus, which I mentioned a short while ago[68] when I referred to the salt waters of the spring there that flow into the Hypanis and render it undrinkable. Now, in this same district there is installed a bronze vessel that is at least six times as large as the mixing-bowl at the entrance to the Pontic Sea, the one that was dedicated by Pausanias, son of Cleombrotus.[69] For the benefit of anyone who has not yet seen Pausanias' bowl, however, I will be more specific: the bowl in Scythia could easily hold the equivalent of 600 amphoras, and is 6 fingers thick. It was fashioned, so the locals informed me, out of arrowheads. Because their king, who went by the name of Ariantas, wished to know how many Scythians there were, he gave orders that each one of them was to bring an arrowhead [from his own quiver]; and that should anyone fail to do so, then the penalty would be death. A huge number of arrowheads were duly brought, and the king decided to fashion a monument out of them that he could bequeath to posterity. This was the bronze bowl; and after he had made it using the arrowheads, he presented it to this same place, Exampaeus. That is what I heard touching the size of the Scythian population.

[82] Now, except for the scale and unparalleled number of its rivers, Scythia boasts very few features that inspire wonder. There is one, however, over and above its rivers and the sheer size of its plain, that does deserve a description. I was shown, stamped on a rock beside the River Tyras, a footprint of Heracles – exactly like the footprint of any normal man, except that it was 2 cubits long.[70] So – I have reported what I have reported. Let me now return to the story that was my original theme.[71]

[83] As Darius busied himself with preparations for the invasion of Scythia, and dispatched messengers in all directions, obliging some of his subjects to furnish him with infantry, others to supply him with ships and yet others to bridge the Thracian Bosporus,[72] so did Artabanus, the son of Hystaspes and therefore the brother of Darius, implore him to abandon his expedition against the Scythians, since they were, as Artabanus himself pointed out, impossible to approach. Good advice though this was, however, it failed to convince Darius;[73] Artabanus duly dropped it, and once his army had been completely readied, Darius began to head off at full tilt from Susa.

[84] It was then that Oeobazus – one of the Persians, whose three sons were all serving on the expedition – asked Darius whether one of them might be left behind. 'Since you are my friend,' the King answered him, 'and your request is not excessive, I will leave you all three.' Oeobazus, who presumed from this that his sons were to be discharged from military service, was delighted; but Darius, giving the order to their superiors, had them executed instead. The three children of Oeobazus were left behind all right – but dead.

[85] From Susa, meanwhile, Darius made his way to Chalcedon, and arrived at the stretch of the Bosporus where the bridge had been built; here, he boarded a ship and sailed to the Blue Rocks, as they are nowadays called, but which, according to the Greeks, once used to wander all over the place. There, sitting on a headland, he gazed out over the Euxine – the sea which, more than any other, is a wonder of nature, and rewards the sightseer well. It measures 11,100 stades in length and 3,300 in width at its widest point. The mouth which opens onto this sea is 4 stades wide; it has a neck that goes by the name of the Bosporus and is 120 stades long, over which the bridge was built. The Bosporus extends all the way to the Propontis, which is 500 stades wide and 1,400 stades long, and flows into the Hellespont, which is only 7 stades wide at most, but 400 stades in length. The Hellespont empties out into that broad expanse of sea that is called the Aegean.

[86] How were these measurements arrived at? A ship, on a long day's voyage, will usually cover some 70,000 fathoms, and by night 60,000. Between the mouth of the Euxine and the Phasis, which is where the sea is at its longest, a voyage takes nine days and eight nights. This adds up to 1,110,000 fathoms in all – or 11,100 stades.[74] Meanwhile, at its widest point – that is to say, between the land of the Sindians and Themiscyre, on the River Thermodon – the voyage takes three days and two nights. This comes to 330,000 fathoms – or 3,300 stades. Hence the dimensions I arrived at for the Euxine, the Bosporus and the Hellespont, and which do indeed correspond, just as I have said, to their actual size. There is also a lake attached to the Euxine, flowing into it, and not much smaller than the sea itself, which is called Lake Maeëtis, or else 'Mother of the Euxine'.

[87] Once Darius had viewed the Euxine, he sailed back to the bridge, whose designer had been Mandrocles of Samos, and viewed the Bosporus too. There he erected two marble pillars, and had engraved on

them in both Assyrian[75] and Greek a list of all the peoples in his train –
and not a nation that he ruled, but he had brought a contingent from it.
The complete tally, including cavalry but not those in service with the
fleet, came to seven hundred thousand, together with an assemblage of
six hundred ships. The Byzantines subsequently carted off these pillars
to their city, where they used them for the altar of Artemis Orthosia – all
except for one stone, covered with Assyrian writing, which was left beside
the temple of Dionysus in Byzantium.[76] By my reckoning, the place on the
Bosporus where King Darius had his bridge built was midway between
Byzantium and the sanctuary beside the entrance to the straits.

[88] So delighted was Darius with the bridge of boats that he subsequently lavished its architect, Mandrocles of Samos, with every kind of
gift. Mandrocles used some of these rewards to commission a painting
of the bridging of the Bosporus, with human figures and all: King Darius sat in prime position, with his army depicted in the course of crossing.
Mandrocles then presented this painting as an offering to the temple of
Hera, together with an inscription:

> MANDROCLES, TO COMMEMORATE HIS SPANNING OF THE FISH-
> FILLED BOSPORUS WITH A PONTOON-BRIDGE, DEDICATED THIS TO
> HERA. HIS FEAT WAS TO MAKE REAL THE MIND'S VISION OF KING
> DARIUS, AND EARN FOR HIMSELF A CROWN, AND FOR THE SAMIANS
> GLORY.[77]

Such was the memorial raised by the architect of the bridge.

[89] So it was that Darius crossed over into Europe.[78] As well as
rewarding Mandrocles, he had also sent orders to the Ionians, who were
in command of the fleet with the Aeolians and the Hellespontians, that
they were to sail into the Euxine and proceed as far as the River Ister,
where on their arrival they were to bridge the river and wait for him. So
the navy set off, steering between the Blue Rocks and heading directly
for the Ister; then, leaving the sea behind, they sailed upriver for two
days, and built a bridge over the main body of the Ister, at the point
where it splits into separate arms. Meanwhile, after crossing the Bosporus on the pontoon-bridge, Darius made his way through Thrace
to the springs of the River Tearus, where on arrival he made camp for
three days.

[90] Those who live along the banks of the Tearus claim that its waters
cure scurvy in men and horses (not to mention other diseases) more

effectively than those of any other river. It has thirty-eight springs, some cold and some hot, but all flowing from the same rockface. They are separated from the city of Heraeum, which is near Perinthus, and from Apollonia (the one on the Euxine Sea) by roads that it takes an identical two days to cover. The Tearus empties into the River Contadesdus, the Contadesdus into the Agrianes, the Agrianes into the Hebrus and the Hebrus into the sea, where the city of Aenus stands.

[91] Once Darius had arrived beside the river and pitched camp there, he was so delighted by the Tearus that he had a further pillar erected. The inscription on it read:

NO RIVER CAN BOAST BETTER OR FINER WATERS THAN THOSE FUR-
NISHED BY THE HEADSPRINGS OF THE TEARUS. AND TO THESE
SPRINGS, LEADING AN ARMY AGAINST THE SCYTHIANS, CAME THE
VERY BEST AND FINEST OF ALL MANKIND, DARIUS THE SON OF
HYSTASPES, KING OF PERSIANS AND OF THE ENTIRE CONTINENT.[79]

Such were the words written on the pillar.

[92] From there, Darius continued on his way until he came to another river: this one was called the Artescus, and flowed through the land of the Odrysians.[80] On his arrival there, he ordered every man in his army to file past a spot he had appointed and to place on it a single stone. Then, once his men had finished doing this, Darius and his army marched on – leaving behind them great mounds of stones.

[93] The first people he subdued, before reaching the Ister, were the Getans,[81] who believe themselves to be immortal. The Thracians who occupy Salmydessus, and who live beyond the cities of Apollonia and Mesambria – the Scyrmiadae and the Nipsaei, as they are known – surrendered to Darius without a fight; but the Getans, who are the bravest of the Thracians, and the most sensitive to the demands of just- ice as well, became obstinate, and were promptly enslaved.

[94] The distinguishing feature of their belief in their own immortal- ity is their conviction that, at the point of death, they do not actually die, but instead go to Salmoxis, a divine spirit who is also known by some of them as Gebelëizis. Every five years, one of the Getans is chosen by lot to serve as a messenger, and is sent off to Salmoxis, together with a list of requests appropriate to the moment. The method of dispatch requires three spears to be held by specially nominated men, while others grab the hands and feet of the one who is being sent to Salmoxis;

they toss him up into the air and he is impaled on the points of the spears. Should he die as a result of this skewering, it is believed by the Getans that Heaven will look favourably on their requests. Should he survive, however, then they hold the messenger himself responsible, charging him with being a man of low moral character, and once they have pinned the blame on him, they send another man as messenger. As for the list of requests, that is given to the man while he is still alive. These same Thracians, whenever there is thunder and lightning, fire arrows up into the sky, and shake their fists at Zeus, in the belief that there is no god save their own.

[95] The Greeks who live beside the Hellespont and the Euxine informed me that this Salmoxis was in fact a human being, a slave on Samos, where his master was Pythagoras, son of Mnesarchus.[82] On becoming a free man, he amassed considerable riches; and then, having made his fortune, returned to his native land. Now, the Thracians are a people as backward as their lives are harsh, while Salmoxis, who was familiar with the far more sophisticated lifestyle and customs of the Ionians, had been constantly in the company of Greeks – and in particular of Pythagoras, who was hardly the most backward of sages. Once Salmoxis had furnished a banqueting hall, he played host to all the leading men of the town, and even as he wined and dined them taught them that neither he, nor any of his fellow-drinkers, nor any of their descendants, would ever die, but would instead go to a place where they would exist forever more, and enjoy every kind of blessing. But all the while, even as he was holding the aforementioned banquets and saying these things, he was building an underground lair. Then, once it was fully furnished, he vanished from the sight of the Thracians and went down into his lair, where he lived for three years. The Thracians duly missed him and mourned him as though he were dead. Three years on, however, Salmoxis appeared back before their gaze – thereby confirming everything that he had said. That, so I was informed, is what he did.

[96] I do not myself, however, feel particularly strongly about the credibility or otherwise of this story of the underground lair – indeed, I actually think that Salmoxis lived long before the time of Pythagoras. But no matter whether he really was of mortal origin, or a native deity of the Getans, I take my leave of him. The Getans, whose customs I have just been describing, were defeated by the Persians, and carried off in their wake as just one more contingent in their army.

[97] Once Darius had arrived at the Ister, and with all his land-forces and everyone else had made the crossing, he gave orders that the Ionians should dismantle the pontoon-bridge, and then accompany him overland, together with the troops on board the ships. Just as the Ionians were about to do as they had been instructed, however, and dismantle the bridge, the commander of the Mytilenaeans, Coës, the son of Erxander, spoke up – but only after he had first made sure that Darius was open to receiving the opinions of anyone with a care to give them. 'O King, you are about to invade a land,' Coës said, 'where there is not a trace of tilled fields. Nor are there any cities built there. I would suggest, then, that you let the bridge stay standing where it is, and leave behind as guards the men who assembled it. Should we find the Scythians and fulfil our goal, then our return will be a simple matter – whereas even should we fail to find them, at least our exit will be secure. While it has never concerned me that we might come off second best to the Scythians in pitched battle, I do worry that we might prove unable to find them, and meet with some calamity as we career around. Some will charge that I am saying this out of self-interest, with the aim of staying behind. But I have come to this conclusion, and brought it to your attention, only because it is in your best interests, O King. I myself will follow you, and not be left behind.' Darius wholeheartedly approved this argument, and replied, 'Please, my guest-friend[83] from Lesbos, come into my presence once I am back home safe and sound. I would like to reward your advice in a way fitting to its excellence.'

[98] With these words, he tied sixty knots in a leather thong, and then summoned the Ionian tyrants to a conference. 'Men of Ionia,' he said, 'you should know that I have altered my opinion, and revoked the instructions that I previously gave you about the bridge. Instead, you are to keep this cord, and then, the moment you see me heading off into Scythia, start untying the knots at a rate of one per day. If by the time you have worked your way through the knots so completely that there are no more days to count off, and still I have not returned, you are to sail back to your own land. Until then, however, my change of plan requires you to stand guard over the bridge of boats, and not to stint in your commitment to protecting it and keeping it secure. Do this, and you will be high in my favour.' Having delivered this speech, Darius started briskly on his forward march.

*

[99] Thrace, which precedes the land of Scythia, extends out into the Euxine. Then, as the coastline curves inland, so Scythia begins, and the Ister, its delta facing eastwards, empties from it out into the sea. Taking the Ister as my starting-point, I am now going to describe the coastline of Scythia itself, and give a sense of its scale. Scythia, as originally constituted, began at the Ister, and then continued – its coast oriented southwards, directly facing the south wind – all the way to the city named Carcinitis. From there on, the land that forms the next stretch of coastline, abutting the same sea, becomes mountainous, and protrudes out into the Euxine; the people who inhabit it, the Taurians, do so as far as the 'Rugged Chersonese',[84] as it is known. It sticks out into the sea which lies on the side from where the east wind blows – for there are two stretches of Scythia bordering the sea, you must understand, one facing south and one facing east, just as is the case with Attica. Indeed, the region of Scythia inhabited by the Taurians is very similar to Attica – although only if a people quite distinct from the Athenians were inhabiting the heights of Sunium, and only if the headland of Sunium, from Thoricus round to the deme of Anaphlystus, were jutting out further into the sea, would the analogy be exact. (In giving this description of the land of the Taurians, I am, of course, comparing the small with the large.) For the benefit of anyone who has not sailed along the relevant stretch of Attica, I can provide another clarification. Suppose that in Iapygia it was not the Iapygians who had occupied the headland which begins at the harbour of Brentesium and extends round to Tarentum, but some other people who were living a quite separate existence on it. Indeed, these two examples far from exhaust the parallels to the land of the Taurians that I could have mentioned.

[100] The region just beyond it, inland from the Taurians, and adjacent to the eastern sea, is inhabited by Scythians, as too is the region west of the Cimmerian Bosporus and of Lake Maeëtis, as far as the River Tanaïs, the mouth of which merges with the lake. As for the regions of Scythia beyond the coast, starting from the Ister and bearing inland, these are bounded first by the Agathyrsians, then by the Neurians, then by the Androphagi, and lastly by the Melanchlaeni.

[101] It follows, then, since Scythia is square in shape, and has two of its sides bordered by the sea, that those sides which extend inland must be equivalent in length to its coastline. To journey from the Ister to the Borysthenes takes ten days, you see, and from the Borysthenes to

Lake Maeëtis another ten, while the road that leads inland from the sea past the Scythians to where the Melanchlaeni live takes twenty days in all to cover. I reckon one day's journey to be 200 stades, so Scythia must measure 4,000 stades from east to west, and another 4,000 stades if you measure it along the axis that runs inland. Such are the details of this particular country.

[102] The Scythians, once they had given due reflection to the impossibility of ever repelling the army of Darius in pitched battle by themselves, sent messengers to their neighbours. The kings of these neighbours, in response to the vast force that was bearing down on them, had already convened a council of war. Assembled at this meeting were the kings of the Taurians, the Agathyrsians, the Neurians, the Androphagi, the Melanchlaeni, the Gelonians, the Boudinians and the Sauromatians.

[103] All of these peoples have distinctive customs. It is the practice of the Taurians to sacrifice to the Maiden[85] shipwrecked sailors and Greeks seized at sea. Their method is to perform first rites over their victim, and then to hit him over the head with a club. Some say that they then push the body over the cliff on which the shrine is situated, while sticking the head on a stake; others, while agreeing about what happens to the head, claim that the body is interred rather than being pushed from the cliff. The power to whom they offer these sacrifices, according to the Taurians themselves, is Iphigenia, the daughter of Agamemnon. Should they capture men who are their foes, then the action each Taurian takes is to cut off his enemy's head and carry it back to his dwelling, where he will stick it on a long wooden pole, and so station it that it towers high above the house – usually over the chimney. They claim that these heads, perched aloft, stand sentinel over the whole house. The livelihood of the Taurians is made from rapine and war.

[104] No men enjoy luxury more than the Agathyrsians, who positively drip with gold. They will also sleep with any women around, so as to ensure a shared kinship and that absence of mutual envy and hatred which is the consequence of such a familial relationship. When it comes to other practices, however, they are very like the Thracians.

[105] The customs of the Neurians are Scythian. One generation prior to the invasion of Darius, they were forced by snakes to abandon their country altogether. As well as a huge swarm of serpents that had hatched out from their own soil, an even larger swarm descended on

them from the wastelands to the north, and inflicted such sufferings on them that they evacuated their native land and settled down among the Boudinians. The Neurians are a people who may well possess magical powers. Once a year, according to both the Scythians and the Greeks who live in Scythia, every Neurian becomes a wolf for a few days,[86] and then reverts back to his original form. Personally, I am unconvinced by this particular story, but they insist upon it nevertheless, and will swear to it on oath as they tell it.

[106] The Androphagi, who have no notion of justice nor adhere to any law, are the most uncivilized people in existence. They are nomadic, and dress in a Scythian-like manner, but their language is entirely their own. They are unique among these various tribes for eating people.

[107] The name of the Melanchlaeni derives from the fact that they all wear clothes of black, but in terms of their customs they are Scythians.

[108] The tribe of the Boudinians is a great and a populous one, and all those who belong to it have piercing blue eyes and a ruddy complexion. There is a city in their country made of wood – the name of this city being Gelonus. Each side of its outer wall, which is 30 stades in length, and very high, is fashioned completely out of wood, as are the dwellings and shrines too. There are shrines there sacred to the Greek gods, and furnished in the Greek manner, complete with cult-statues, altars and wooden temples; and every third year a festival is held there in honour of Dionysus, at which Bacchic revels are staged. Originally, you see, the Gelonians were Greeks, who emigrated from their trading-posts, and settled among the Boudinians. The language they use is a mixture of Scythian and Greek.

[109] The Boudinians, however, speak a wholly different language, and their way of life too is quite distinct from that of the Gelonians. The Boudinians, who are sprung from the soil,[87] are nomadic, and the only people in the region who eat pine-seeds, whereas the Gelonians, who are nothing like them in terms of either appearance or complexion, work the land, eat grain and keep gardens. (The Greeks, when they apply the name of 'Gelonian' to the Boudinians as well as to the Gelonians themselves, have it wrong.) The Boudinians live in a country that is entirely covered by trees of every kind. The biggest forest of all contains a large, deep lake, surrounded by bogs and reeds. Otters are trapped in this lake, and beavers, and another kind of wild creature too: it has

a square face, and fur that the Boudinians sew onto their leather jackets as trimming,[88] and testicles which are very useful in treating ailments of the womb.

[110] There is a story told of the Sauromatians, set during the war between the Greeks and the Amazons.[89] (The Amazons are known by the Scythians as the *Oiorpata*, a name that translates into Greek – since *oior* means 'man' in Scythian, and *pata* means 'to kill' – as 'Man Killers'.) The story goes that the Greeks, after their victory at the battle of the Thermodon, sailed away in three ships, and took with them all the Amazons whom they had managed to capture alive; the Amazons set upon the men out at sea, and hacked them down. Because they knew nothing about ships, however, and had no idea how to steer, or use the sails or oars, their massacre of the crews left them adrift, and at the mercy of the waves and the winds. In due course, they turned up on Lake Maeëtis, at Cremni, which stands in the land of the Free Scythians. Here the Amazons disembarked and made their way from the ships to where there was human habitation. The first thing they came across was a herd of horses, which they promptly seized, saddled up and used to plunder all they could from the Scythians.

[111] The Scythians had no idea what had hit them. Indeed, because the looks, dress and race of the mysterious new arrivals were all so unfamiliar, it was presumed that they were men in the first flush of youth. Only once the Scythians had engaged them in battle, and then, in the wake of the battle, come into possession of their dead, did the realization dawn that they were in fact women. The matter was debated, and it was decided by the Scythians no longer to try to kill them, but rather to send their own youngest men after them, in numbers proportionate to the women. The young men were to pitch camp near by, and to copy them in every way. Should the women give them chase, they were not to put up a fight but to retreat until the pursuit was abandoned, when they were to go and pitch camp near the women again. This plan was prompted by the desire of the Scythians to father children on the women.[90]

[112] Sent on their way, the young men duly carried out their instructions. The Amazons, once they realized that the new arrivals meant no harm, let them be. Day by day, the two camps drew closer to one another. Just like the Amazons, the young men had nothing beyond

their weapons and their horses; and just like the Amazons, they devoted their lives to hunting and raiding.

[113] Now, it was the habit of the Amazons, every midday, to split up into ones or twos and head off in different directions to relieve themselves. When the Scythians noticed this, they did exactly the same. One of them sidled up to one of the Amazons who was on her own; and the Amazon, rather than thrusting him away, let him have his way with her. Unable to communicate with him verbally, since neither could understand the other, she gestured instead with her hands that he should come to the same spot the following day, and bring another with him. 'Make it two of you,' she said, using sign language. 'And I will bring a friend of my own.' The young man headed back and reported this to all the others. The following day, he duly went back to the appointed spot, and took another man with him; and at the spot he found the Amazon waiting for him, with a second Amazon. Then the remainder of the young men, when they learned what had happened, came and broke in the remainder of the Amazons.

[114] After the two camps had become one, each man paired up with the woman he had first taken to bed, and they all settled down together. The men found the language of the women impossible to learn, but the women managed to get to grips with that of the men. Once they could all communicate with one another, the men told the Amazons, 'We have parents, and we have our own belongings. No more, then, of this way of life. Let us head back to the main body of our people, and live as they do. You are the wives for us – you and you alone.' To this, however, the Amazons replied, 'We would never be able to settle down with your women. We have no customs in common with them. We have never learned to do women's work.⁹¹ We shoot arrows, throw javelins, ride horses. But what do your women do? None of the things we just listed. They only ever do women's work! They do not go off hunting, or anywhere at all, in fact – they just lurk inside their wagons. So you can see, it would be quite impossible for us to get along. But if you really want us as your wives, and be seen to behave with complete honour as well, go to your parents and take the due share of your possessions. Then, on your return, we can go and set up home together on our own.'

[115] The young men, persuaded by this argument, duly put it into action. However, once they had obtained the allotted share of their

property and had returned to the Amazons, the women said to them, 'We are very nervous at the thought of making our home here in this country – terrified, in fact. Not only have we torn you away from your fathers, but we have wreaked immense damage on the countryside. Our joint course of action, then, since you have thought fit to have us as your wives, should be to get out of this country, and settle down beyond the River Tanaïs.' And once again the young men were persuaded.

[116] So they crossed the Tanaïs, and headed towards the rising of the sun, until three days after they had left the Tanaïs they turned away from Lake Maeëtis and journeyed onwards, with the north wind now blowing directly into their faces, for three further days. In due course, when they came to the country where they are now settled, they made their homes. And from that time to this, the Sauromatian women have kept to their primal way of life: they go out hunting, whether their husbands are with them or not, they go to war and they dress exactly like the men.

[117] The language spoken by the Sauromatians is a mangled form of Scythian, reflecting the original failure of the Amazons to learn it properly. Also distinctive is the custom that forbids any young woman from marrying until she has first killed a man among their enemies.[92] Those who never manage to fulfil this condition die as spinsters of old age.

[118] These peoples I have just listed were those whose kings were in conference when the Scythian messengers arrived, and informed them that the Persian, not content with having made himself the master of one entire continent, had now built a bridge across the neck of the Bosporus and crossed into another – their own. Already, in the wake of this crossing, his ambition to add their continent to his dominions had seen him conquer the Thracians and bridge the River Ister. 'So no matter what,' the Scythians said, 'do not sit to one side and just watch on as we are wiped out. Let us all share in the common resolve – to face this invasion together. And if you won't do this? Then the pressure on us will leave us no choice but to evacuate our country – or else, if we stay, come to terms. Should you refuse to help us, do not doubt what our sufferings will be – nor imagine that you yourselves will get off lightly in their wake. You are in the sights of the Persian just as much as we are. Do you really think, once he has brought us to defeat, that he will be content to leave you alone? The evidence for the case we are making is over-

whelming. After all, if we were truly the sole objects of the Persian's campaign, and if the avenging of his people's one-time enslavement by us were indeed his sole aim, he would surely have bypassed everyone else and invaded our country alone – for that would have made it perfectly clear to everyone that it was the Scythians, and no one else, whom he was targeting. As it is, however, no sooner did he cross over to our continent than he began to trample down all who happened to lie in his path, without exception. Already, he has brought under his sway the Thracians – and among them the Getans, our immediate neighbours.'

[119] Such was the message delivered by the Scythians; but the kings who had come from the various peoples about, when they put it to debate, were divided in their opinions. The kings of the Gelonians, the Boudinians and the Sauromatians, all of whom had arrived at the same conclusion, promised their backing to the Scythians; but those of the Agathyrsians, the Neurians, the Androphagi, the Melanchlaeni and the Taurians gave this response. 'Had it not been you who first wronged the Persians and thereby began the war, then the request you are currently making would seem to us valid, and we would only have had to hear it out to join with you in your endeavour. As it is, it was you, quite without any involvement on our part, who invaded the land of the Persians and ruled as their masters for such time as the heavens granted you; and now, roused by divine promptings in their turn, they are paying you back. But we, who did not wrong these men at all in the past, are not going to wrong them pre-emptively now. Nevertheless, should they invade our lands in addition to yours, we will certainly not put up with any unprovoked aggression. Until we have actually witnessed this for ourselves, however, we will stay where we are, in our own countries. It is our opinion, you see, that the Persians have come, not against us, but solely against those guilty of criminal behaviour.'

[120] When this reply was brought back to the Scythians, and they realized that those who had sent it would not be allying with them, they resolved that, rather than make a stand in the open and fight in pitched battle, they would instead withdraw, retreating at a headlong pace, filling in wells and springs as they went, and scorching the earth – and that they would do this having first divided their forces in two. One of these detachments, made up of the subjects of King Scopasis, was to be reinforced by the Sauromatians. In the event that the Persian swung round in their direction, they were to fall back, retreating in a direct line along

the shore of Lake Maeëtis to the River Tanaïs; and then, when and if the Persian himself fell into headlong retreat, they were to pursue and harry him. So much, then, for one of the two detachments into which the kingdom's forces were divided – their mission being to take the course I just described. Meanwhile, the two other divisions of the kingdom – the large one, which was ruled by Idanthyrsus, and a third sub-division, which had Taxakis as its king – were to join forces, and then, swollen by the Gelonians and the Boudinians, to withdraw as well, keeping one day's march ahead of the Persians, and, as they retreated, putting into effect the plan they had devised. Their initial step would be to head straight for the territories of those who had refused military support, and embroil them in the conflict – thereby leaving them no choice but to join the war against the Persians which they had refused to enter of their own accord. Then, in time – and if, after due deliberation, it seemed for the best – the Scythians would head back to their own country and take the attack to the Persians.

[121] When this had been settled, the Scythians went out to meet Darius' army, sending the elite among their cavalry ahead as the advance guard. Meanwhile, the wagons in which all their women and children lived they dispatched north, with orders to keep going, and never stop. Together with the wagons they also sent on ahead their flocks and herds, all except those they needed as provisions, which they kept behind.

[122] Even as the wagons were heading off with their loads, the Scythian scouts found that the Persians were barely three days' journey from the Ister. This discovery prompted them to camp a day's march ahead of the invaders, and clear the land of everything that grew there. When the Persians saw that the Scythian horsemen had appeared, they set off on the trail of their ever-elusive quarry, making straight for one of the Scythian divisions, and pursuing it eastwards, towards the Tanaïs. After the Scythians had crossed the river, the Persians too made it over the Tanaïs and continued in pursuit, right the way across the land of the Sauromatians, until they arrived in that of the Boudinians.

[123] Now, because the lands of the Scythians and the Sauromatians were so desolate, it was impossible for the Persians to inflict any damage the whole while that they were traversing them. Once they had crossed into Boudinian territory, however, they came upon the town with wooden walls, which had been evacuated by the Boudinians, and emptied of all its contents; this the Persians burned to the ground. That

done, they continued without pause on the trail of the Scythians, until they had crossed the entire region, and fetched up in the wilderness that lies to the north of Boudinian territory, and which has not a trace of human habitation across an expanse equivalent to seven days' journey. Beyond this wilderness is the home of the Thyssagetans; there are four great rivers that flow out of it across the land of the Maeëtians and then issue into Lake Maeëtis, as it is called. The names of these rivers are the Lycus, the Oarus, the Tanaïs and the Syrgis.

[124] So when Darius came to this wilderness, he halted his pursuit of the Scythians, and had his army camp out beside the River Oarus. Then, having taken this step, he set to building eight huge fortressess positioned at regular intervals of some 60 stades, one after the other, which were still in existence (albeit in ruins) right up to my own time. Meanwhile, as Darius was devoting his energies to this project, the Scythians whom he had been pursuing were wheeling northwards on their way back to Scythia. Indeed, they vanished so completely that the Persians could find not a trace of them, and so Darius, abandoning his half-completed fortresses, set off himself, turning back westwards on the assumption that the Scythians had made their escape in the same direction, and that there were no other Scythians elsewhere.

[125] Once Darius and his army, by means of a forced march, had arrived in Scythia, they encountered the two divisions of the Scythians that had been combined into a single force – whereupon he gave them chase. Although his quarry stayed a day's remove ahead of him, Darius never slackened in his pursuit; and so the Scythians continued retreating into the lands of those who had refused them military backing, just as they had agreed that they would do. Their first target was the Melanch-laeni, who were duly thrown into utter confusion by the irruption of the Scythians and the Persians into their land; next, the Scythians made their way into the country of the Androphagi, and created turmoil there as well; then they retreated into the land of the Neurians, where they spread yet further havoc; and then, still retreating, they made for the Agathyrsians. The Agathyrsians, however, who had observed the sham-bles to which their neighbours had been reduced as they fled before the Scythians, sent a herald to the would-be invaders, forbidding them to set foot across the border, and warning them that any attempt at inva-sion would be met with immediate resistance. Once the Agathyrsians had issued this declaration, they went to man the frontier, aiming to

block the invaders' access: an example of valour that the Melanchlaeni, the Androphagi and the Neurians, quite forgetful of all their previous bold talk, had signally failed to adopt when the Persians and Scythians turned up. Indeed, they had been reduced to such a rabble that they just kept on streaming northwards into the wilderness. Rather than attempt to force their way past the obdurate Agathyrsians, the Scythians then led the Persians from the territory of the Neurians down into their own.

[126] Eventually, the chase proved so interminable that Darius sent a horseman to remonstrate with Idanthyrsus, the king of the Scythians: 'Why this endless flight? You have another option, after all. Suppose that you consider yourself capable of opposing all the resources I have at my command. Very well – stop this wandering, make a stand and put up a fight. But should you recognize your own inferiority, there is still no call to run away. Simply send me the gifts of earth and water[93] that are my due as your master, and come into negotiations.'

[127] To this, however, Idanthyrsus, the king of the Scythians, retorted: 'Here is how things are with me, Persian. I have never before fled any man because I was afraid of him – and I am certainly not fleeing you now. In fact, I am doing nothing at the moment that I was not in the habit of doing in times of peace. There is a perfectly good reason why I have not engaged you yet in battle, and I will tell you what it is. We have no cities – nothing that we need worry you might capture. We have no crops – nothing that we need worry you might destroy. Why, then, should we be in any rush to fight with you? If you really want to get to grips with us in a hurry, then there are always the graves of our forefathers. So go ahead – find and desecrate them, if you can! Only attack those graves, and you will soon discover whether we are fighters or not. Until then, however – unless some other motivation seizes us – we will not engage with you in battle. But I have talked quite enough about fighting. As for masters, the only ones I recognize are Zeus, my own ancestor,[94] and Hestia, the queen of the Scythians. You will receive from me a gift, not of earth and water, but such as you deserve. As for your claim to be my master, I tell you this in return – you will not be smiling for long.' [Such were his words – the proverbial 'Scythian address'.[95]]

[128] So the herald went off to deliver this message to Darius, leaving the various kings of Scythia bursting with rage at the mention they had heard of slavery. The division that was stationed with the Sauromatians

under the command of Scopasis was duly dispatched to the Ionians who were standing guard on the bridge over the Ister, and ordered to enter into discussions with them. Meanwhile, those Scythians left behind decided that they would no longer lead the Persians on this dance, but would instead attack them while they were foraging for supplies. Sure enough, whenever the Scythians saw that Darius' men were out gathering food, they would put their plan into action. Again and again, the Scythian horsemen would rout the cavalry, and the Persian horsemen would flee to the side of the infantry who would be coming to their aid. It was then, with the cavalry pegged back, that the Scythians would themselves beat a retreat, for they were afraid of the infantry. The Scythians did not stint in making these kinds of attacks even at night.

[129] There is one thing I must mention, however, which hindered the Scythians in their raids upon Darius' positions, and assisted the Persians – remarkably enough, it was the braying of the donkeys and the appearance of the mules. Neither animal, as I explained earlier,[96] is indigenous to Scythia; and owing to the cold, there is not so much as a single donkey or mule to be found in the entire country. As a result, the appalling din made by the donkeys was a cause of great alarm to the Scythian horses. It would often happen, even as they were charging the Persians, that they would hear the braying of the donkeys and turn in disarray, their ears pricked upright in astonishment, for never before had they heard such a noise, nor beheld such a sight. Because of this the Persians had a slight edge in the fighting.

[130] The Scythians, however, realizing that the Persians were in real trouble, looked to prolong their stay in Scythia, so that the more time they spent there, the lower their supplies would run, and the more desperate their situation would become. Accordingly, every so often the Scythians would leave behind some of their livestock, complete with herdsmen, while they themselves sped off elsewhere. When the Persians then came across the animals and rounded them up, the episode served as a boost to their morale.

[131] In due course, after this had happened a number of times, and the Scythian kings had been informed that Darius was in a desperate way, they sent him a herald bearing gifts: a bird, a mouse, a frog and five arrows.[97] The Persians asked the man carrying these gifts what he meant by such offerings. 'My only orders', he answered, 'were to hand them over, and then immediately depart. If you are smart, however, you will

surely be able to fathom their meaning.' Once they had heard him say this, the Persians fell to debating the matter.

[132] It was the opinion of Darius himself that the Scythians were surrendering not only earth and water, but also objects that served as symbols of themselves: a mouse, he argued, was born of the earth, and fed like men upon its fruits, while a frog lived in water, and a bird was like nothing so much as a horse. 'As for the arrows,' Darius demanded, pressing home his case, 'why hand them over, if not as tokens of Scythian valour?' Gobryas, one of the Seven who had toppled the Magian, disagreed, and argued that the gifts had a quite different significance. 'What they are saying is this: "Unless you should become birds and fly away up into the sky, men of Persia, or become mice and burrow down into the earth, or become frogs and leap into the lakes, you will never make it home – for you will be shot down by our arrows."'

[133] Meanwhile, as the Persians were mulling over what the gifts might mean, the single detachment of Scythians that had originally been detailed to patrol Lake Maeëtis, but had since been sent to hold discussions with the Ionians on the Ister, arrived at the bridge. 'Men of Ionia,' they said, 'the gift we come bearing you, if you will only hear us out, is freedom. We have learned that you were instructed by Darius to stand guard over the bridge for sixty days, and no more – and that once that deadline is past, and supposing that he has still not appeared, you are all to head for home. That being so, why would he censure you simply for doing as you were told? We will not blame you either. Just wait here until the prescribed number of days is up, and then be off.' This the Ionians duly promised they would do; and so the Scythians headed back with all speed.

[134] As for those Scythians who had stayed behind, the receipt by Darius of their gifts saw them marshalling their horsemen and their infantry, and preparing to attack the Persians. But then, between the ranks of the Scythians and their opponents, there suddenly ran a hare. Each and every Scythian, when he saw this hare, gave it chase. Indeed, such was the din made by the Scythians as their lines broke up that Darius demanded to know why his opponents were making such a commotion. Informed that they were chasing a hare, he said to those in whom it was always his habit to confide, 'These Scythians must despise us a great deal. Do you know what? I now think Gobryas was right after all in his interpretation of the gifts they sent me. We need a plan –

and a good one – to get us out of here and back home in safety.' 'I had a pretty good notion', answered Gobryas, 'of just how hard it would be to get to grips with these Scythians, O King, based purely on what I had heard. Now that I am actually here, and have observed how they toy with us, I have an even better understanding. Here, then, is what I think our plan should be. The moment dusk falls, we should light our camp-fires, just as we would normally do. Then, after we have tethered up all our donkeys and left in the dark those troops who are most lacking in fortitude, we should set off by heading straight for the Ister, before the Scythians manage to demolish the bridge – or before the Ionians settle on some measure that will seal our fate.' Such was the opinion of Gobryas – and sure enough, with the coming of night, Darius acted on his advice.

[135] Accordingly, once all the donkeys had been tethered up, he left them behind, right where they were in the camp – together with all the men who were on their last legs, and whose loss would least be felt. Darius had good reason for abandoning the donkeys and those elements of his army that could no longer pull their weight. The donkeys he left behind because he wanted them to raise a tremendous din, and the men because of their enfeebled condition – although what he actually told them was that he and all the able-bodied elements in his army were going to launch an attack on the Scythians, while they spent the time on watch over the camp. Once Darius had delivered this explanation to those he was leaving behind, he lit fires and made off as fast as he could for the Ister. When the donkeys found themselves abandoned by the greater part of the army, their braying was truly exceptional – so the Scythians, when they heard it, never had the slightest doubt that the Persians were still in the camp.

[136] At daybreak, when those who had been left behind realized that Darius had betrayed them, they stretched out their hands in a gesture of submission and explained their circumstances to the Scythians. Once they had heard the suppliants out, the two combined Scythian divisions straightaway joined forces, and together with the Gelonians and the Boudinians and the single division operating alongside the Sauromatians set off for the Ister in hot pursuit of the Persians. Unsurprisingly, since the Persian army consisted mainly of infantry and kept getting lost as a result of the lack of any clear-cut roads, while the Scythians were all on horseback and knew the short-cuts, not only did the two forces miss one another, but the Scythians arrived at the bridge

far in advance of the Persians. When told that the Persians had yet to arrive, they hailed the Ionians on their ships. 'Men of Ionia, the days you were allotted are up, and it is criminal that you are still here! There really is no need for you still to be intimidated into staying. Dismantle the bridge and be off as fast as you please. Revel in your freedom! Give thanks to the gods for it – and to the Scythians. As for your former master, him we shall bring to such a defeat that never again will he lead an army against anyone.'

[137] This prompted much debate among the Ionians. Miltiades of Athens,[98] who was both a seasoned commander and tyrant of the Hellespontine Chersonese,[99] held to the view that they should do as the Scythians were suggesting, and set Ionia free; but he was opposed by Histiaeus of Miletus, who pointed out that none of them ruled as tyrant in his city except by the grace of Darius. 'Should the might of Darius be toppled,' he said, 'then my regime in Miletus will crumble too, and none of the rest of you will stay in power either. Each of our cities would prefer democracy[100] to tyranny.' Sure enough, no sooner had Histiaeus advanced this particular argument than everyone immediately swung round behind it, when previously they had backed that of Miltiades.

[138] Now, all those who had a vote were men highly regarded by the King. There were the tyrants from the Hellespont: Daphnis of Abydus, Hippoclus of Lampsacus, Herophantus of Parium, Metrodorus of Proconnesus, Aristagoras[101] of Cyzicus and Ariston of Byzantium. Then, in addition to these six Hellespontines, there were also the tyrants from Ionia: Strattis of Chios, Aeaces of Samos, Laodamas of Phocaea and Histiaeus of Miletus, who had taken the opposite line to that of Miltiades. The only one of the Aeolians in attendance deserving of a mention was Aristagoras of Cyme.

[139] Once they had opted for the suggestion of Histiaeus, they decided to back it up with deeds as well as words: to dismantle as much of the bridge on the Scythian side as lay within bowshot, aiming to disguise their inactivity beneath a show of action, and also to forestall any attempt by the Scythians to force a crossing of the Ister over the bridge. Meanwhile, even as they were demolishing the Scythian side of the bridge, they would offer an assurance to the Scythians: 'Anything you want us to do, we will do it!' Then, after they had elaborated upon the scheme in this way, Histiaeus acted as spokesman for them all. 'Men of Scythia!' he called out. 'Truly, you have come as the bearers of wonder-

ful news! And just in the nick of time too – so thank goodness you made such speed. The quality of the advice you have given us is perfectly matched by that of the service we are doing you. As you can see, we are dismantling the bridge – and indeed, such is our longing for freedom that there are no limits to our enthusiasm. As we continue with this demolition-work, however, so should you be seizing the moment! Go and look for the Persians! Then, once you have found them, make the punishment fit the crime – not only for your sakes, but for our own!'

[140] The Scythians, convinced a second time that the Ionians were speaking the truth, duly turned round in pursuit of their quarry; but they could find no trace of the Persians, nor of the route that they had taken. For this, the Scythians had only themselves to blame, for it was they who had destroyed all the grass that horses require as provender, and who had filled in all the wells. Had they not done so, it would have been a simple matter for them to track down the Persians as and when they pleased. As it was, the very plan that at the time had struck them as being so brilliant was now a stumbling block, because the Scythians, in their search for their foes, went by that part of their country where there was still fodder for their horses, and water too, under the illusion that the Persians, as they made their retreat, would be taking the self-same route. The Persians, however, were following the path they had taken previously; and although this retracing of their footsteps did not make for an easy journey, it did get them back to the bridge. It was night as they arrived; and when they found the bridge dismantled, they assumed that the Ionians had abandoned them, and so were reduced to the most abject state of dread.

[141] One of the men in Darius' train, however, was an Egyptian who had the loudest voice in the world.[102] Darius ordered him to stand on the very edge of the Ister, and call out for Histiaeus of Miletus – which the man duly did. Histiaeus, alerted by his very first cry, committed the entire fleet to ferrying the army across the river, and repaired the bridge as well.

[142] So it was that the Persians made their escape, and the Scythians, for a second time, failed to track them down. As for the Ionians, Scythian opinion of them depends on whether they are to be judged as free men or as slaves: if the former, say the Scythians, then they are the worst and most unmanly people in the entire world, but if the latter, then they are to be reckoned the very cynosure of loyal and committed

subservience. Such is the insult with which the Scythians put down the Ionians.

[143] Once Darius had made his way through Thrace, he came to Sestus in the Chersonese. From there he passed over to Asia with his ships, but left behind him as the commander of his troops in Europe a Persian named Megabazus. A compliment was once paid by Darius to this man in the full presence of the Persians, which redounded greatly to his honour. Darius, who was preparing to eat some pomegranates, had just split open his first one when his brother, Artabanus, asked him what, if he could have as many of something as there were seeds in a pomegranate, he would wish to have. 'Megabazus,' Darius answered. 'I would rather have a pomegranate's worth of him than the mastery of Greece.' An honour indeed for any man to have been spoken of in such a manner before the Persians by the King – and now he was being left by Darius in command of his army, which numbered eighty thousand in all.

[144] It was this same Megabazus who made a comment that the people of the Hellespont have never forgotten, nor ever will. He happened to be in Byzantium, and learned that the region of Chalcedon had been settled seventeen years earlier than Byzantium. This information prompted him to declare that the Chalcedonians, during that period, must have been blind. 'Why otherwise, when there was such a perfect spot available for a new city, did they choose one far inferior? They could only have been blind!' So there was Megabazus left behind in command of the Hellespont; and he set about conquering all the cities in the region that had refused to collaborate with the Persians.

[145] Meanwhile, as this was going on, a second major military expedition was being launched against Libya, for reasons that I shall explain in due course.[103] First, however, there is another matter to discuss. When the same Pelasgians who had abducted the Athenian women from Brauron[104] drove the descendants of the Argonauts from Lemnos, the exiles set sail for Lacedaemon, where they camped on Mount Taygetus, and lit a fire. The Lacedaemonians, when they saw this, sent a messenger to find out who they were, and where they had come from. 'We are the Minyans,' they said, in answer to the herald's questioning. 'We are descended from the heroes who sailed on the *Argo*,[105] and who put in at Lemnos, where they fathered our line.' After the Lacedaemonians had listened to this account of the Minyan pedigree, they sent a

second messenger to ask the Minyans what their purpose was in coming to Lacedaemon, and why they had lit a fire. 'Exiled by the Pelasgians,' said the Minyans, 'we have come to the land of our fathers. Surely that is only fair? All we ask is to live here among you, sharing in your dues and privileges, and with our own allocation of land.' The Lacedaemonians were content to agree to these requests and terms of the Minyans. What chiefly influenced them to be so obliging was the fact that the sons of Tyndareus[106] had sailed on the *Argo*. So they welcomed the Minyans in, gave them plots of land and divided them up into tribes. The Minyans, meanwhile, immediately started marrying local women, and giving away as brides to their hosts the women they had brought with them from Lemnos.

[146] It did not take very long, however, for the Minyans to start getting above themselves, laying claim to the kingship and offending a whole host of other proprieties. For this, the Lacedaemonians decided, they should pay with their lives; and so they were arrested and flung into prison. Now, whenever the Lacedaemonians have someone to dispose of, the killing is done by night, never by day.[107] Just as they were about to stage the executions, however, the wives of the Minyans, who were all natives of the city and the daughters of prominent Spartiates, requested permission to go into the prison and talk with their husbands, one to one. Permission to enter was duly given, for none of the Lacedaemonians suspected them of anything underhand. Once they had gone inside, though, what the women did was to swap their clothing, every last stitch of it, for what their husbands were wearing, so that the Minyans, now dressed up as their wives, were able to leave the prison posing as women. Then, once they had made their escape in this way, they set up base again on Mount Taygetus.

[147] At the same time as this, preparations for the founding of a colony were being made by Theras, son of Autesion, the son of Tisamenus, the son of Thersander, who was in turn the son of Polynices. This same Theras was of Cadmeian descent,[108] and was the uncle on their mother's side of the two sons of Aristodemus – Eurysthenes and Procles.[109] For as long as these boys remained underage, Theras ruled Sparta as regent; but in due course, when they had reached adulthood and taken over the kingdom, he found it insufferable, having once tasted power, now to be subject to others. Accordingly, he declared that he would no longer stay in Lacedaemon, but sail away to join his kin.

These kinsmen lived on the island that is nowadays called Thera, but in former times was known as Calliste,[110] and were the descendants of a Phoenician, a man called Membliareos, son of Poeciles. It so happened that Cadmus, son of Agenor, while searching for Europa, had put in at the island that today goes by the name of Thera; and once having docked there – either because he found it such a delightful spot, or for some other reason which made him do as he did – he left behind him on the island a whole band of Phoenicians, among whom was his own kinsman, Membliareos. These duly settled on Calliste, as it was originally known – and their descendants were still there, eight generations on, as Theras left Lacedaemon.

[148] So these were the kinsmen upon whom Theras was planning to call, together with recruits from the various tribes of Lacedaemon – not, however, with any aim of dispossessing them, but looking rather to claim them as blood-brothers, and settle in their midst. What is more, when the Minyans staged their breakout from prison and camped on Mount Taygetus, and the Lacedaemonians were set on wiping them out, Theras was so keen to avoid bloodshed that he begged for their lives and promised to take them with him out of the country – an idea to which the Lacedaemonians gave their consent. This is why, as Theras sailed off in three triaconters to join the descendants of Membliareos, he had with him a number of Minyans – although only a few. Most of them, you see, veered off instead towards the land of the Paroreatae and the Caucones, where they drove out the natives, divided themselves up and planted six cities across the region: Lepreum, Macistus, Phrixae, Pyrgus, Epium and Noudium.[111] (Most of these were sacked in my own lifetime by the Eleans.) As for Calliste, that ended up known as 'Thera', after the man who had colonized it.

[149] Theras' own son, though, had refused to join the voyage, and so Theras said that he would leave him behind as a 'sheep among wolves': *oïn en lykoisi*. This saying saw the young man come to be called 'Oeolycus' – a nickname that somehow quite effaced his original name. Oeolycus was the father of Aegeus, after whom the Aegeids,[112] one of the most significant tribes in Sparta, was named. Children born to the men of this tribe always used to die young, until, on the advice of an oracle, they built a shrine to the Furies who had haunted the descendants of Laius and Oedipus.[113] An identical shrine was similarly maintained in Thera after this, by descendants of the same men.

[150] Now up to this point in the story, the Lacedaemonians corroborate exactly what the Therans report; but for subsequent events we are
dependent upon Theran sources alone. What happened, so the Therans
say, is that Grinnus, son of Aesanius, who was king of the island of
Thera by right of descent from Theras, arrived in Delphi, bringing with
him from his capital a hundred cattle for sacrifice. A number of citizens
accompanied him, including one in particular who was a descendant of
a Minyan named Euphemus: Battus,[114] son of Polymnestus. The Pythia,
despite the fact that Grinnus was consulting the oracle on wholly other
matters, informed the king of Thera that he was destined to found a city
in Libya. 'My Lord,' the king responded, 'I am too old – and have put
on too much weight – to go breezing around. Lay this charge of yours
instead upon one of these younger men.' And so saying, he pointed at
Battus. That, however, was as far as it went, and once they were back
home they discounted the oracle altogether. Certainly, none of them had
the faintest idea where in the world Libya actually was,[115] and they
lacked the daring to send a whole party of colonists off into the
unknown.

[151] For seven years after that, however, not a drop of rain fell upon
Thera – until every tree except one had perished of the drought. When the
Therans went to ask advice of the oracle, the Pythia reminded them of
what she had told them about colonizing Libya. So the Therans, recognizing that there was no other solution to the crisis facing them, sent
messengers to Crete in search of any natives or resident foreigners there
who might have visited Libya. These messengers, as they made their way
from place to place, happened to arrive in the city of Itanus. There they
met a man called Corobius, a fisher for purple, who told them that he had
once been swept off course to Libya by winds, and had ended up on the
island of Platea, off the Libyan coast. The Therans duly paid him to come
back with them to Thera, from where a small band of men then made an
initial voyage of reconnaissance. Guided by Corobius, they arrived on
Platea, the island he had mentioned, where they left him,[116] together with
sufficient provisions for a number of months, while they themselves sailed
back to Thera with all speed to tell the Therans the news about the island.

[152] So long did they stay away, however, that the date set for their
return came and went, and Corobius ran out of food. Then it happened
that a ship of Samos, captained by Colaeus, was blown off course while
sailing to Egypt, and ended up at this same Platea. When Corobius gave

the Samians the full story of what had happened, they left him with provisions sufficient for a year. Looking to continue onwards to Egypt, they themselves sailed back out from the island – but were swept away by an easterly wind. The gale did not let up once, not even after they had been driven out through the Pillars of Heracles – until at last, by the favour of the gods, they fetched up in Tartessus. This port was still then a wholly untapped market, and so the profits made by these Samians on their cargo, once they had returned home, were larger than those of any other Greek trader for whom we have reliable information. (This is always excepting, of course, Sostratus of Aegina, the son of Laodamas[117] – with whom no one can compete!) As a tithe on their profits, the Samians set aside 6 talents, and commissioned a bronze mixing-bowl in the Argive style, with a rim that featured protruding griffins' heads. They dedicated this bowl as an offering in the sanctuary of Hera, resting it upon three large, kneeling figures of bronze, each 7 cubits high. It was as a consequence of what the Samians did on this occasion that they first forged their special relationship with the Cyrenaeans and the Therans.

[153] The Therans who had left Corobius on the island returned to Thera and announced to their countrymen the colonization of an island off Libya. The Therans resolved that lots should be drawn, with every other brother being selected, and men chosen from all the various regions of the island. They also resolved that their leader should be Battus, who was to rule as their king. And so they sent two penteconters to Platea.

[154] Such is the Theran version of events – but the Cyrenaeans, despite corroborating the Theran account of what happened subsequently, differ as regards Battus. Indeed, the story they tell bears not the slightest resemblance to that told by the Therans. There was a man, one Etearchus, who ruled a Cretan city called Oaxus, and who had a daughter called Phronime. Because her mother had died and he wanted someone to look after her, Etearchus married another woman; but this newcomer felt perfectly within her rights playing the stepmother in every sense of the word, making her stepdaughter's life a misery, and scheming against her without cease. Eventually, the stepmother accused the daughter of sleeping around – and what is more, convinced her husband of it too. So persuaded was he by the woman that he devised a plot against his daughter, one that offended the heavens themselves. You see, there was

a merchant from Thera there in Oaxus – a man called Themison. Etearchus, who had entered into a solemn compact of mutual guest-friendship with him, made Themison promise on oath that he would do whatever his host might require of him. Once this pledge had been sealed, the king led out his daughter and handed her over, his own child, and gave instructions to Themison that he was to take her away and drop her into the sea. Themison, who was furious at the oath he had been tricked into swearing, broke off all ties of guest-friendship with his host. He did take the girl and sail off with her; but then, once he had reached the open sea, what he did to honour the oath extracted from him by Etearchus was to tie ropes around her and lower her into the sea. Then, once he had hauled her up again, he headed on to Thera.

[155] Subsequently, Phronime was acquired by Polymnestus, a man of high distinction among the Therans, who kept her as his concubine. Time went by, and she bore him a son who, because he was forever stumbling over his words and lisping, was given the name of Battus, 'the Stammerer' – or so, at any rate, both the Therans and the Cyrenaeans say. Personally, I think that he originally had some other name, and then changed it to Battus when he came to Libya, partly as a consequence of the oracle given at Delphi and partly because his adoption of the name brought him such prestige. *Battus*, you see, is the Libyan word for 'king', which is why, I would argue, when the Pythia delivered her oracle, she addressed him in the Libyan tongue – because she knew that he was going to be a king in Libya.[118] He went to Delphi on coming of age, concerning his speech; but when he put his question to the Pythia, she answered him by saying:

'Battus, though for a voice you have come, our lord, Phoebus
    Apollo,
Sends you to Libya – there, amid its sheep, to found a colony.'

In other words, she might just as well have said to him in Greek, '*King*, though for a voice you have come . . .' 'My Lord,' he said by way of reply, 'I came to ask you about my speech, but this oracle you have given me is on a quite different matter. Colonize Libya? Impossible! How do I find the means? How do I get the men?' Despite his protests, however, he could not persuade her to give him a different response. Instead, she just kept repeating her original oracle; so Battus left her in mid-chant and headed back to Thera.

[156] In the wake of this, things began to go badly for Battus, and for all the other Therans too. Ignorant as to the cause of their misfortunes, the Therans sent an embassy to Delphi, to enquire about the ills afflicting them. The Pythia replied that things would improve for them only if they joined Battus in founding Cyrene in Libya. It did not take long for the Therans to send Battus on his way, so he sailed to Libya with two pentekonters. Unsure what else to do, however, he and his crew then sailed back to Thera – where the Therans pelted them with missiles as they sought to disembark, and ordered them to sail back, rather than letting them touch land. With no choice in the matter, back they sailed to Libya, where they founded a colony on the offshore island that went by the name – as I mentioned previously – of Platea. This island, so it is said, was the same size as the city of Cyrene is today.

[157] So there they lived for two years; but because nothing ever went right for them, they left one of their number behind, while all the rest set sail for Delphi. Once they had reached their destination, they consulted the oracle, with the complaint that things had still not improved for them, despite their having founded a colony in Libya and made their homes there. To this, however, the Pythia only answered:

'So you know Libya, that womb of sheep, much better than I do,
When you, unlike me, have never been there? I bow to your lore!'

Battus and his entourage had only to hear this to set sail again. Not until they had actually reached Libya proper, you see, would the god release them from their obligation to found a colony. Back they went to the island, where they picked up the man they had left behind, and founded a colony in Libya itself, in a region called Aziris, directly opposite the island; a river flowed past it on one side and beautiful glades enclosed it on both.

[158] Six years they lived in this place, until, during the seventh, the Libyans begged them to abandon it, declaring that they themselves would lead the way to a much better location – and this convinced the settlers. The Libyans then took them west from Aziris, having carefully calculated the hour of departure to ensure that it would be night-time as the Greeks were being led through the most scenic stretch of the countryside, and so would not get to see it. (This was a region named Irasa.) 'Greeks,' the Libyans said, once they had brought the men to the

so-called 'Spring of Apollo', 'here, where the sky above is rent through with gashes, is the ideal spot for you to settle down.'

[159] Battus, the founder of the colony, ruled[119] for forty years in all, and Arcesilaus, his son, for sixteen; and the span of their lifetimes saw the population of Cyrene stay at much the same level as it had been when the colonists were first sent there. Then, however, during the reign of Battus their third king, who was nicknamed 'the Prosperous', the Pythia issued an oracle in which she urged Greeks everywhere to cross the sea and to join with the Cyrenaeans in colonizing Libya. It was the Cyrenaeans themselves, you see, who had first extended this invitation, together with a promise of land distribution. As the Pythia, in her own pronouncement, put it:

'Whoever arrives in Libya, that much cherished land, too late
For a gift of its soil, will one day be sure to regret it.'

So immense, however, did the concentration of people in Cyrene then become, and such was the appropriation of territory from the neighbouring Libyans, that they and their king – Adicran as he was called – were prompted by the loss of their land, and by the overweening arrogance[120] of the Cyrenaeans, to send a messenger to Egypt, and to place themselves under the protection of the Egyptian king, Apries. He duly mustered a large army of Egyptians, and sent it against Cyrene. The Cyrenaeans marched out to the district of Irasa, and there, at the Spring of Thestê, met with the Egyptians, and defeated them in battle. The Egyptians, who had never tested the mettle of the Greeks before, had sorely underestimated them – and indeed, were wiped out so utterly that only a very few of them ever made it back to Egypt. It was because of this, and because the blame for it was held to lie with Apries, that the Egyptians rose up against him.[121]

[160] This Battus too had a son called Arcesilaus, who began feuding with his brothers the moment he was on the throne, until eventually they walked out on him and made for another region of Libya, where, drawing on their own resources, they founded a city called Barca[122] – the name that it still has today. Even as this city was being established, they incited the Libyans to rise in revolt against the Cyrenaeans. In the wake of this, Arcesilaus launched a strike against the rebel Libyans, who were the same as had harboured his brothers. In their terror of him,

these Libyans fled to those of their compatriots who lived in eastern Libya. Arcesilaus set off after the fugitives, until, in the course of his pursuit across Libya, he came to Leucon, where the Libyans resolved to attack him. When battle was joined, the victory they won over the Cyrenaeans proved so decisive that seven thousand Cyrenaean hoplites fell where they had met. Arcesilaus, who took ill in the wake of this calamity, drugged himself with a potion and was strangled by his brother, Learchus – who in turn was murdered by means of a subterfuge played upon him by the widow of Arcesilaus, whose name was Eryxo.[123]

[161] The heir to Arcesilaus' kingdom was his son, Battus, who was lame, and indeed could barely walk. The Cyrenaeans, meanwhile, were prompted by the disaster that had befallen them to send an enquiry to Delphi, asking what form of institution they should adopt that would best improve their lives. The Pythia instructed them to import an arbitrator from Mantinea, in Arcadia. The Cyrenaeans duly made a request to the Mantineans, who lent them one of their most eminent citizens, a person named Demonax.[124] The first step taken by this man, once he had finished gathering information, was to divide up the Cyrenaeans into three tribes, based on the following allocations: one division he formed out of the Therans and the local Libyans, another out of the Peloponnesians and the Cretans, and a third out of all the islanders. His second measure was to reserve certain sacred precincts and priesthoods for Battus in his role as king, but to assign all the other prerogatives that had hitherto belonged to the monarchy directly to the people.

[162] These arrangements held for as long as Battus remained alive; but during the reign of his son, Arcesilaus, there were furious disagreements about the king's constitutional prerogatives. This was because Arcesilaus – who was the son of Battus 'the Lame' by Pheretime – rejected the framework that had been established by Demonax the Mantinean, and demanded the return of the privileges enjoyed by his ancestors. In the resulting convulsions, Arcesilaus came off worse and fled into exile to Samos, while his mother escaped to Salamis on Cyprus.[125] The ruler of Salamis at this time was Euelthon – the same Euelthon who made a dedication to Delphi of a censer that is well worth seeing and can be found in the treasury of the Corinthians.[126] When Pheretime came before him, she requested military backing for the restoration of her son and herself to Cyrene; but Euelthon, though content to grant her anything else, did not give her an army. 'These presents are all very well,' said Pheretime, as

she took possession of the gifts, 'but it would be even better if you were actually to give me what I asked for – military backing.' Again and again, every time he gave her something, this was what she would repeat – until eventually Euelthon sent her as a gift a golden spindle and distaff, together with some wool for good measure. When Pheretime responded to these with her customary retort, Euelthon declared that they were the gifts appropriate to a woman, but an army was not.

[163] Arcesilaus, meanwhile, was in Samos, where he was busy assembling all the men upon the promise of plots of land. Then, even as recruits were flooding in, he headed off to Delphi to consult the oracle on the matter of his return. 'Loxias',[127] answered the Pythia, 'permits four kings named Battus and four kings named Arcesilaus – eight generations of your dynasty in all – to sit upon the throne of Cyrene. He would advise, however, against attempting to rule for any longer than that. Go back to your native land, and remain quiet. Should you find a kiln full of amphoras, then do not fire them, but send them off upon a fair wind. If you do decide to stoke the kiln, then on no account enter anywhere that is surrounded by water. Disobey, and you will die – you, and the fairest bull that there is.'

[164] Such was the oracle delivered by the Pythia to Arcesilaus. But once he had returned to Cyrene at the head of the men he had mustered in Samos, and seized control of it, Arcesilaus quite forgot the prophecy, and demanded that his political opponents should pay for having forced him into exile. Some of these escaped the country altogether, while others were seized by Arcesilaus and sent off to Cyprus for execution. Blown off course, they were rescued by the Cnidians, who sent them on to Thera. Still others among the Cyrenaeans took refuge in a tall tower that belonged to Aglomachus; but Arcesilaus piled wood around it and burned it down. Once he had done so, he realized that this was surely what the Pythia had foreseen as happening when she had forbidden him to fire any jars that he might find in a kiln; and from that moment on he made sure never to enter the city of Cyrene, since he dreaded to die as the oracle had foretold that he would, were he ever to find himself surrounded by water, and he supposed that by this it was Cyrene that had been meant. Now, he had as his wife one of his own kinswomen, the daughter of the king of Barca, whose name was Alazeir; and it was with this Alazeir that he went to stay. But when the people of Barca, together with some of the exiles from Cyrene, discovered that he was out and

about in the public square, they killed him – him, and his father-in-law Alazeir too. So it was that Arcesilaus, whether wilfully or out of sheer ignorance, missed the point of the oracle, and fulfilled his destiny.

[165] Now, the whole time that he was living in Barca, in the shadow of his self-inflicted ruin, his mother, Pheretime, remained in Cyrene, possessed of her son's prerogatives: to sit in the council and exercise all his other rights. When the news of her son's assassination in Barca reached her, however, she fled to Egypt. She went there because Arcesilaus had done Cambyses, the son of Cyrus, good service; for it was he who had surrendered Cyrene to Cambyses and committed himself to the payment of tribute. Once Pheretime had arrived in Egypt, she sat as a suppliant before Aryandes, urging him to avenge her on the grounds (she claimed) that her son had perished owing to his Persian sympathies.

[166] This Aryandes was the man appointed by Cambyses to be viceroy of Egypt, and would in due course be executed for setting himself up as the equal of Darius. He realized – and indeed saw with his own eyes – that Darius had ambitions to leave behind a memorial to himself such as no other king had ever achieved; and so Aryandes copied his every action until he received his due reward. Darius, you see, had struck coins with gold that he had refined to the finest possible extreme of purity; and Aryandes, when he was ruling Egypt, did the same with silver (indeed even today an *aryandic* is the purest silver coin in existence). When Darius discovered this, he had Aryandes executed – not explicitly for what he had done, but on an alternative charge, that of sedition.

[167] Anyway, when Pheretime arrived in Egypt, Aryandes took pity on her, and put the entire Persian army – land- and sea-forces alike – at her disposal. Amasis, a Maraphian, was appointed to the command of the army, and Badres, who belonged to the tribe of the Pasargadae, to the command of the fleet. Before he launched the campaign, however, Aryandes sent a herald to Barca, to try to discover who the assassin of Arcesilaus had been. He found that the entire population of Barca claimed responsibility, on the grounds that they had suffered numerous miseries at his hands. Aryandes, when he was informed of this, allowed the expedition – and Pheretime with it – to proceed. But despite the nominal charge, which provided the pretext for the dispatch of the expedition, its real purpose, in my opinion, was the conquest of Libya.[128] There were a vast number of different peoples in Libya, after all, and

although a tiny minority of these were subjects of the King, most of them gave Darius not a second thought.

[168] The settlement patterns of the Libyans are as follows. The first Libyan settlements beyond Egypt are those of the Adyrmachidae, whose customs are mostly the same as those of the Egyptians – all except for their style of dress, which differs little from that of the other Libyans. Their women wear a bronze bangle on each ankle. They also grow their hair very long, and should one of them ever find lice on herself, she will get her own back by biting on the lice and tossing them to one side. The Adyrmachidae are the only Libyans who do this. Unique as well is the way in which they parade their nubile young women before their king – and whichever one the king finds the most attractive, he will then deflower. The Adyrmachidae extend from Egypt all the way up to a harbour named Plynos.

[169] Next come the Giligamae, whose settlements reach as far west as the island of Aphrodisias. Platea, the island colonized by the Cyrenaeans, lies off the shore of the central portion of this territory, while on the mainland there is a harbour called Menelaus,[129] and Aziris, where the Cyrenaeans also once lived. It is here that the silphium-growing region[130] begins, reaching from the land opposite the island of Platea to the mouth of the River Syrtis. The customs of the Giligamae are much like those of the other Libyans.

[170] Immediately west of the Giligamae are the Asbystae, who live inland from Cyrene. Due to the occupation of the coastal region by the Cyrenaeans, Asbystian territory does not extend the whole way to the sea. They certainly do not stint when it comes to the driving of four-horse chariots,[131] which they engage in more than any other Libyan people. By and large, however, they follow much the same customs as the Cyrenaeans do.

[171] To the west, the Asbystae are bordered by the Auschisae, who live inland from Barca, and extend down to the sea at Euesperides.[132] In the midst of the land of the Auschisae there live the Bacalians, who are not a numerous people, and whose land reaches as far as Taucheira, a Barcan city on the coast. The Auschisae have the same customs as those who live inland from Cyrene.

[172] To the west of the Auschisae lives the teeming nation of the Nasamonians. Every summer, the Nasamonians leave their livestock by the sea and travel up-country, where they pick dates from the huge,

fruit-hung palm trees that grow in vast numbers there. They also hunt locusts, which they dry in the sun, grind to powder and then sprinkle on draughts of milk. It is their normal practice for each man to have a large number of wives, who are then available, very much in the manner of the Massagetans, to be used sexually by anyone; an erect pole in front of a house serves to signal active copulation. When a Nasamonian first gets married, it is the custom for his bride to spend the wedding night working her way through all the guests. Each man, once he has slept with her, will then give to her as a present whatever he may have brought with him from his own house. As for oaths and divination, when they wish to swear to something, they place their hands on the graves of those men from their past with a proven reputation as the best and most concerned for justice, while those who wish to look into the future will go to the tombs of their ancestors, utter a prayer and there lie down to sleep; whatever they should then happen to see in their dreams is interpreted as revealing the future.[133] When it comes to the giving of pledges, those who wish to exchange them will each hand the other a drink, which they then drain. Should there be nothing liquid available, they will scoop up some dirt from the ground and lick that.

[173] Just along from the Nasamonians are the Psylli[134] – or were, until something occurred that resulted in their complete obliteration. The scouring of the south wind served to dry up their water-holes, and their country, all of which lies within the Syrtis basin, was parched. Deliberations brought the Psylli to a joint resolution: that they would march out to war against the south wind. (Here I am only repeating what the Libyans themselves report.) Arriving amid the dunes, they were engulfed by sand borne on the blowing of the south wind. Their ruination enabled the Nasamonians to take possession of their lands.

[174] Inland from them, in a region infested by wild beasts and from where the south wind blows, live the Garamantes, who shun all human contact and company. They have neither military equipment, nor any knowledge of how to defend themselves.

[175] These live inland of the Nasamonians; but westwards, along the coast, live the Macae, who fashion their hair into crests. They do this by allowing the hair along the middle of the head to grow, but shaving either side of it down to the scalp. When they go to war, they carry shields made out of ostrich-hides. It is through their land that the River Cinyps flows, starting from the so-called 'Hill of the Graces' and empty-

ing into the sea. The Hill of the Graces is thickly wooded, whereas all the other regions of Libya that I was describing earlier are quite bare. The distance from this hill to the sea is 200 stades.

[176] Next to the Macae are the Gindanes, whose women all wear lots of leather anklets; the reason for this, so the story goes, is that each time a woman sleeps with a man, she will fasten a band around her ankle. Accordingly, it is the woman who has the most anklets who is held in the highest esteem, on the grounds that no one has had more men make love to her than she.

[177] A promontory jutting out from the land of the Gindanes into the sea is the home of the Lotus-Eaters, who exist by munching away on nothing save the fruit of the lotus plant. The fruit of the lotus is roughly the size of a mastic berry, and as sweet as a date. The Lotus-Eaters even make wine out of the fruit as well.

[178] Next along the coast from the Lotus-Eaters are the Machlyans, who also make use of the lotus, although not to the degree that those just mentioned do. Their territory extends as far as a large river called the Triton, which empties into an immense lake called Tritonis. There is an island in this lake called Phla, which the Lacedaemonians were reportedly urged by an oracle to colonize.[135]

[179] There is also a story told about Jason: how once the work on the *Argo* had been completed on the lower slopes of Mount Pelion, he loaded it up with a hundred cattle for sacrifice, threw in a bronze tripod for good measure and sailed around the Peloponnese with the aim of reaching Delphi. But when, in mid-voyage, he came to be off Cape Malea, he was overtaken by a north wind[136] and swept off in the direction of Libya. Before he had caught sight of land, however, he found himself stuck in the shallows of Lake Tritonis, and was completely at a loss as how to escape them. The story goes that Triton made an appearance and ordered Jason to give him the tripod. 'I will show you the route out,' he said, 'and send you on your way unharmed.' This was good enough for Jason – and so Triton duly guided the ship's crew through the shallows. The tripod he put in his own shrine – but only after he had first declaimed a prophecy over it, and shared the full details with Jason and his men. 'Should any descendant of a crew-member on the *Argo* carry off this tripod,' he declared, 'it is an utter certainty that one hundred Greek cities will be founded around the lake.' The local Libyans, when they heard this, hid the tripod.

[180] Neighbouring the Machlyans are the Auseans. Like the Machlyans, they live around Lake Tritonis, and the Triton, which flows midway between them, serves as their mutual border. Unlike the Machlyans, who wear their hair long at the back, the Auseans grow their fringes long. Every year, at the Festival of Athena, the unmarried girls among them separate into two groups, and start pelting one another furiously with stones and blocks of wood – by which means, it is said, they discharge an ancestral obligation to the goddess who is the native patron of their land, and whom we know as Athena. Those of the girls who die of their wounds are accused of having lied about their virginity. Before letting them join battle, what the Auseans do, all as one, is to array the girl who ranks as that year's outstanding beauty in a Corinthian helmet and a full outfit of heavy Greek armour, then get her up into a chariot and drive her in a circuit around the lake.[137] What they used when adorning the girls back in the old days, before the Greeks were brought to settle near by, I am in no real position to say – but suspect that it was Egyptian armour. This, I would argue, is because the Greeks derived both their shields and their helmets from Egypt.[138] Athena, the Auseans claim, was the daughter of Poseidon and Lake Tritonis – but for some reason she fell out with her father and put herself under the protection of Zeus, who then adopted her as his own daughter. That is the tale they tell, anyway. They also sleep around with any number of women, rutting in the open like animals rather than living together connubially. Three months on from the birth of a baby, once its features are fully formed, all the men will meet – and whichever of them should happen most to resemble the child, that man is reckoned its father.

[181] Inland of all these various Libyan nomads whom I have been discussing, away from the coastline they inhabit, the central reaches of Libya are infested by wild beasts, while beyond the wild beasts there stretches a ridge of sand, running all the way from Thebes in Egypt to the Pillars of Heracles. Along this ridge, at intervals roughly equivalent to ten days' journey, there are hills formed out of salt that has splintered into great chunks; and on the summit of each hill, welling up from the very depths of the salt, there rises cool and sweet-tasting water. The people who live next to this water, inland from where the wild beasts roam, are the very last before the desert begins. First, at a distance of ten days' journey from Thebes, come the Ammonians,[139] whose sanctuary is an offshoot of the sanctuary of Zeus in Thebes – for there too, as I men-

tioned previously, the statue of Zeus has the head of a ram. It so happens that they have an additional source of water: a spring that is warm as dawn approaches, but cools as the market-square fills up with people. Come midday, the water is icy. (This is the time when they irrigate their gardens.) As the day wanes, however, so the chill fades, until by sunset the water has quite warmed up again. Indeed, the closer to midnight it becomes, the more the water heats up – until, by midnight, it is boiling and bubbling away. Then, with midnight past and dawn approaching, it cools down once again. The name they have given this spring is the Fountain of the Sun.

[182] Onwards from the Ammonians, at a distance of ten further days' travel along the sand bank, there is a hill of salt like the Ammonian one, complete with water and a ring of human settlements. The name of this place is Augila, and it is where the Nasamonians come when they are harvesting dates.

[183] A further ten days' on from Augila, and there is another hill of salt: it too has water and a large number of date-laden palms, just like the previous two. The people who live on it are called the Garamantes, a formidably sizeable tribe who have covered over the salt with earth, which they then sow. It takes thirty days to travel from the Garamantes to the Lotus-Eaters: the shortest cut there is. The Garamantes also breed oxen that walk backwards while grazing. Why do these cattle feed in reverse? Because their horns curve forwards,[140] leaving them no choice but to graze as they do – for, were they to eat while moving forwards, their horns would dig into the earth. Otherwise, however, they differ not a jot from any other breed of cattle – except that their hides do make for exceptionally thick and durable leather. The Garamantes hunt the cave-dwelling Ethiopians, and use four-horse chariots to do so. The reason for this is that these cave-dwelling Ethiopians are the fleetest-footed people in the entire world[141] – at least, of those peoples we hear reported. The diet of these cave-dwellers consists of nothing but reptiles: snakes, lizards, and so on. Their language is quite unlike that spoken by anyone else, and resembles the squeaking of bats.

[184] A further ten days' on from the Garamantes there is another hill of salt, complete with water and a ring of human settlements. The people who live there are called the Atarantians, and they are unique in the world, so far as I know, in having no personal names. Instead, rather than being given names on an individual basis, they are all known by

the one collective name 'Atarantians'. When the sun is high in the sky, and at its most scorching, leaving both the land and the inhabitants utterly debilitated, the Atarantians will curse it roundly, and heap all kinds of foulest abuse upon it. Onwards from them, at a distance of ten days' further travel, there is another hill of salt, complete with water and a ring of human settlements. Close to this particular mound of salt is a mountain called Atlas.[142] It is narrow and forms a perfect circle, and is said to reach so high that no one ever gets to see its peaks, such is the permanency of the cloud cover – in summer as in winter. According to the natives, it is the pillar which holds up the sky. These natives themselves have come to be named after the mountain, for they are known as 'Atlantians'. Apparently, they will never eat anything that has the breath of life, nor in their sleep do they ever see dreams.[143]

[185] When it comes to naming those who live along the ridge, these Atlantians represent the limit of my knowledge. Nevertheless, the ridge does continue onwards, as far as the Pillars of Heracles, and beyond. Travel along the ridge, and at regular ten-day intervals you will come across salt mines and human settlements. Those who inhabit these settlements all have houses made out of blocks of salt, which is possible only because it never rains in that particular stretch of Libya. Of course, if it did rain, the walls of salt would never stand firm. The salt dug up in this particular region is white and purple in colour. The interior of Libya, beyond the ridge and to the south, is nothing but parched desert – without water, wildlife, rain or trees. Nowhere is there so much as a hint of moisture.

[186] As a result, all the Libyans between Egypt and Lake Tritonis are nomadic, eating meat and drinking milk. Cows, however, they do not consume (this for the same reason as the Egyptians), nor do they raise pigs. The women of Cyrene also hold it wrong to eat cows, and this again is because of the Egyptian goddess, Isis, in whose honour they keep fasts and stage festivals. The women of Barca abstain from pigs as well as cows.[144]

[187] Such is the way things are. West of Lake Tritonis, however, the Libyans are no longer nomads, nor do they share the same customs – something that is particularly evident when it comes to how they and the nomads respectively treat their children. The nomads of Libya – although I would not swear to this being true of every last one of them – have a most distinctive practice. Whenever one of their children

turns four, they use hot grease extracted from sheep's wool to cauterize the veins in the child's crown – and sometimes in the temples as well. This has as its aim the long-term prevention of any harmful downflow of phlegm from the head. It is to this that the Libyans attribute their exceptional good health – and it is certainly the case, so far as we can tell, that they are indeed the very healthiest people in the world. Whether their explanation for this is really valid, I am not qualified to say, but the excellence of their health is beyond dispute. Should the process of cauterization induce spasms in a child, then a remedy for that too has been identified: just sprinkle goat's urine on the child, and all will be well. (Here, though, I am only repeating what the Libyans themselves report.)

[188] When they perform animal blood-sacrifices, the first step the nomads take is to remove the ear of a victim and hurl it over their house, and the second is to wring the animal's neck. These sacrifices, across the whole of Libya, are raised exclusively to the sun and moon – although those settled around Lake Tritonis do also sacrifice to Athena, Triton and Poseidon,[145] in that order of precedence.

[189] Now, it seems likely that Athena's clothing and aegis, as shown on her statues, were copied by the Greeks from Libyan women.[146] Aside from the fact that Libyan dresses are made out of leather, and that the tassels on a Libyan aegis consist of thongs rather than snakes, the correspondences are in every other way exact. Indeed, the very name of the clothing worn by the statues of Pallas points to its origins having been in Libya. The tasselled wraps that Libyan women wear over their dresses, although stripped of hair and dyed with madder, are made of goatskins, after all – and the Greek word for goat-skins, *aigeai*, could readily have been changed to *aegis*. What is more, I'm convinced that the invocations uttered during temple rituals also derive from Libya, since Libyan women raise them a great deal, and to very beautiful effect. It is from the Libyans too that the Greeks learned to harness four horses to their chariots.

[190] The nomads bury their dead in the Greek manner[147] – all, that is, except for the Nasamonians, who bury them in a sitting position. They are extremely careful, you see, whenever someone is about to depart this life, to have him seated, so that he does not expire while lying on his back. Their houses are made of asphodel stalks interwoven with rushes, and are readily transportable. Such is the way they do things.

[191] West of the River Triton, and next to the Auseans, are Libyans who plough the land and own property: the Maxyans, as they are called. They wear their hair long on the right side of their heads, and shaved on the left, and they smear their bodies with red ochre. They claim to be descended from men who came from Troy. This particular region, and all the rest of western Libya as well, has a far greater concentration of wild animals and forests than the regions inhabited by nomads. East of the River Triton, which is where the nomads live, you see, Libya is low lying and sandy; but west of the Triton, where the people live as farmers, it is exceedingly hilly, densely forested and infested by wild beasts. There are serpents there of a truly monstrous size, and lions, not to mention elephants, bears, asps and donkeys with horns. There are men with the heads of dogs, and others who have no heads at all, and whose eyes are set in their chests (or so it is claimed by the Libyans), and wild men, and wild women too. Fantastical though these may be, there are certainly many other beasts that are not.[148]

[192] None of them, however, is found in the region inhabited by the nomads. This has its own wildlife: impalas with white rumps, and gazelles, and buffaloes, and donkeys (not the horned kind, but others, donkeys that never – and I mean never – drink a thing), and oryx, the horns of which are used to make the sides of Phoenician lyres (and are themselves beasts on the scale of a bull), and miniature foxes, and hyenas, and porcupines, and wild rams, and kites, and jackals, and panthers, and boryes, and crocodiles – which are about 3 cubits in length, and closely resemble lizards – and ostriches, and tiny snakes, each of them with a single horn. Then, in addition to these creatures, there are the same animals as exist everywhere else, with the exceptions of deer and wild boar, neither of which is found anywhere in Libya. Of mice, there are three different kinds. One is called 'two-legged', another the 'zegeris' (a Libyan name, meaning 'hillock' in Greek), and the third the 'bristly' mouse. There are also weasels that breed among the silphium plants, and are very similar to the weasels of Tartessus. Such is my register of the wildlife indigenous to the land of the Libyan nomads – one that derives from the most wide-ranging research possible.[149]

[193] Next to the Maxyan Libyans live the Zauekes, whose women serve as charioteers in times of war.

[194] Their neighbours in turn are the Gyzantes, whose men are skilled in the craft of making honey. Indeed, they are said to manufac-

ture it in even greater quantities than the region's bees, which themselves produce a tremendous amount. The Gyzantes all smear themselves over with red ochre, and feed on monkeys, which breed in great numbers in the mountainous regions of their territory.

[195] Situated just off this territory, so the Carthaginians report, is an island called Cyrauis, which, although narrow, is 200 stades long; it is also accessible by foot from the mainland, and covered with olive trees and vines. There is a pool on this island, and the local unmarried girls draw up gold-dust from its mud using bird feathers smeared with pitch. I admit I am only writing down what I was told[150] – but even though I cannot personally vouch for the story, it may well be perfectly true. With my own eyes, after all, I once saw pitch being brought to the surface of a lake in Zacynthos. There are quite a number of pools there, the largest of which is 70 feet across in every direction, and 2 fathoms deep. Into this same pool, someone will lower a pole with myrtle tied to the tip, and then, when it is brought back up, the myrtle will be coated in pitch. This, although it reeks like bitumen, is otherwise of much better quality than Pierian pitch. It is poured into a pit that has been excavated beside the lake, and then, when a substantial amount has been collected, they scoop it out of the pit and into jars. Should anything fall into the lake, it will travel underground and reappear in the sea, which is about 4 stades from the lake. So it may well be that the reports from the island off the coast of Libya do indeed approximate to the truth.

[196] The Carthaginians also claim that there is a region in Libya beyond the Pillars of Heracles which is populated by humans, and where, whenever they visit, they unload their cargo, line the goods up in a row along the tideline and then return to their ships, from where they send up smoke-signals. The natives, seeing the smoke, go down to the sea-shore and place gold there as payment for the merchandise, after which they too withdraw, away from the goods. The Carthaginians then disembark to have a look; and should the gold strike them as fitting remuneration for their cargo, they scoop it up and depart. Should they think it inadequate, however, then they climb back into their ships and sit down – whereupon the natives approach once again and deposit more gold, until such time as the Carthaginians are satisfied. There is no cheating on either side. The Carthaginians do not lay hands on the gold until it is equivalent in value to their merchandise, nor do the natives touch the merchandise until the Carthaginians have taken the gold.

[197] Such are the Libyan tribes whose names I am qualified to give. Most of these, then as now, gave the Persian King not a second thought. Let me also supplement my description of Libya by reporting that the peoples who inhabit it are four, and no more than four – at least, so far as we know. Two of these peoples are indigenous, and two of them are not. The Libyans, who live in the north of Libya, and the Ethiopians, who live in the south, are both indigenous, while the Phoenicians and the Greeks are immigrants.

[198] Owing to the poor quality of its soil, Libya is not, in my opinion, fit to stand serious comparison with Asia or Europe. The region that borders the River Cinyps, and takes its name from the river, is the exception. Demeter[151] has endowed this particular area with a fertility equivalent to that of the finest wheat-growing areas in the world – in which it resembles the rest of Libya not at all. Its soil is black and well irrigated by springs; neither drought nor the torrential downpours that can sometimes occur in this stretch of Libya, and leave the ground waterlogged, is a cause for concern. Its yield of crops is on a level with that of Babylon. The land where the Euesperides live is also top quality. Indeed, when the harvests there are at their best, they yield a hundred-fold return (although those in Cinyps are three times better even than that).

[199] The land around Cyrene, which has the highest altitude of all the regions in Libya inhabited by nomads, boasts an astonishing three annual harvests. The crops along the coast are the first to ripen and be ready for harvesting and gathering; once they have been collected, it is the turn of the crops inland from the coast, in the [central] region called 'The Hills', to be collected. Then, once this middle band of crops has been harvested, those in the uplands of the country ripen and enter their prime – so that even as the original crops are being drunk and eaten, the final ones of the year are still being gathered in. The Cyrenaeans are busy with their harvests eight whole months. But enough on such matters – it is time to move on.

[200] Once the Persians sent by Aryandes[152] to avenge Pheretime had arrived at Barca, they put the city under siege, and demanded the surrender of those responsible for the murder of Arcesilaus: a request dismissed by the Barcaeans on the grounds that they all shared in the responsibility. So, for nine months the Persians prosecuted their siege, tunnelling underground[153] in the direction of the walls and launching

a series of powerful assaults. A means of uncovering the tunnels, however, was devised by a man who was a copper-smith: he took a bronze shield and toured the inside of the city wall, holding the shield down to the ground as he did so. For most of the circuit, all was silence; but wherever there were tunnellings the bronze of the shield would ring out. The Barcaeans, capitalizing upon these discoveries, then dug countermines and killed the Persian sappers. As for the direct assaults, these the Barcaeans repulsed.

[201] With time dragging on, and a heavy rate of attrition wearing down both sides – the Persians no less than the Barcaeans – it dawned on Amasis, the commander of the land-forces, that the Barcaeans would never be defeated through the use of brute force. The only prospect of bringing about their downfall was through cunning; and so he duly formed a plan. What he did, under cover of darkness, was to have a wide trench dug, then had it covered over with feeble timbers, and next had the timbers covered over in turn with soil until it was level with the surrounding terrain. As day broke, he invited the Barcaeans to a parley. Delightedly, the people of Barca agreed, and were more than happy to arrive at terms as well. The Barcaeans, it was agreed, would pay an appropriate indemnity to the King, while the Persians would otherwise leave them well alone. Confirmation of this settlement was then sworn to directly over the hidden trench: 'So long as this earth stands firm,' ran the covenant, 'so shall this oath stand firm as well.' Then, confident that the pledge was to be trusted, the Barcaeans emerged from their city, flung open all their gates and permitted any Persians as wished to pass inside their walls to do so. The Persians ran fast to enter the city – but only after they had first smashed up the hidden bridge over the trench. The reason for this demolition of the planks they had laid there was to ensure that there would be no going back on the promise they had given the Barcaeans, since that promise had been to maintain the oath only for so long as the earth stayed in place. Now, with the planks all broken, the oath was demolished as well.

[202] Those Barcaeans most implicated in the murder were handed over by the Persians to Pheretime,[154] who had them impaled along the circuit of the city walls, together with the severed breasts of their wives, which were likewise displayed along the walls at regular intervals. The remaining Barcaeans she instructed the Persians to treat as plunder – the only exceptions being those who belonged to the House of Battus, and

did not have her son's blood on their hands. These Pheretime placed in charge of the city.

[203] Meanwhile, once all the other Barcaeans had been rounded up and sold into slavery, the Persians set off for Egypt. When they reached Cyrene, they stood outside the city, and the Cyrenaeans, proclaiming obedience to some oracle or other, let them pass straight through. 'Now, while we are crossing the city, is our chance to capture it!' So urged Badres, the commander of the fleet; but Amasis, who was in command of the army, refused to countenance it. 'We were sent to capture only the one Greek city – and that was Barca.' Later, however, once they had completed their passage through Cyrene, and were camped out on the hill of Lycaean Zeus,[155] they regretted not taking the city. Accordingly, they tried to enter it a second time, but the Cyrenaeans refused them access. At this, despite the lack of any armed confrontation, the Persians fell into a panic and beat a speedy retreat to a spot some 60 stades from Cyrene, where they sat themselves down. Then, once they had finished staking out a camp, there arrived a messenger from Aryandes, summoning them back home. The Persians asked the Cyrenaeans to supply them with provisions for the journey; once they had loaded these up, they set off for Egypt. Stragglers, as they lagged behind, would be seized by the Libyans and murdered for their clothing and equipment – and so it continued the whole way back to Egypt.

[204] The limit of this particular Persian army's penetration into Libya was Euesperides. The Barcaeans rounded up by the soldiers as slaves were moved onwards from Egypt and sent to King Darius, who gave them a village in the land of Bactria[156] in which to settle. The name they gave this village was Barca – and there were still people living there, on Bactrian soil, in my own day.

[205] As for Pheretime, the fabric of her own life unravelled too. No sooner had she avenged herself on the Barcaeans, and returned from Libya to Egypt, than she suffered a truly hideous death. Her living body became a mass of seething worms, as if to demonstrate to mankind that vengeance, if prosecuted with an excess of savagery, will always arouse the envy of the gods.[157] Such, then, were the scale and the order of the revenge exacted upon the Barcaeans by Pheretime, the daughter of Battus.

BOOK FIVE

[1] The first Hellespontians to be conquered by the Persians who had been left behind by Darius in Europe, and put under the command of Megabazus, were the Perinthians, the people of a city that had never had any wish to be subject to Darius. Once, in their past, they had received some rough treatment at the hands of the Paeonians: this was because the Paeonians from the Strymon had been told by the god in an oracle to march against Perinthus, and then, once the Perinthians were camped out opposite them, to launch an attack if the Perinthians called to them and shouted out their names. (But if the Perinthians shouted nothing at all, they were just to sit on their hands.) So this was what the Paeonians did; and the Perinthians, going eyeball to eyeball with them, made camp in the area in front of their city. There a challenge was issued: that three separate duels, one on one, be fought. Man was pitched against man, horse against horse and dog against dog. When two of these bouts went the way of the Perinthians, they were so overjoyed that they began to chant a victory paean – and at once it dawned on the Paeonians that this had surely been the point of the oracle's words. 'Now the oracle is bound to be fulfilled in our favour!' This, or something like it, was what they told one another. 'Time we got to work!' So it was, because the Perinthians had chanted 'Paean!',[1] that the Paeonians went on the attack – and duly won a victory so crushing that very few Perinthians were left.

[2] This time, though, in contrast to what had happened to them previously at the hands of the Paeonians, the Perinthians proved themselves men valiant in the defence of their freedom; and it was only by the sheer weight of the Persians' numbers that Megabazus succeeded in overwhelming them. Then, with Perinthus vanquished, Megabazus and

337

his army powered their way onwards through Thrace, forcing all the cities and all the peoples who lived there to accept the King's peace. This, you see, was the command that Darius had given them: to conquer Thrace.

[3] Now, second only to the Indians, the Thracians are the most populous nation in the world. Were they only to share a single ruler or a common purpose, they would, in my opinion, be invincible, and put every other nation deep in their shadow. However, since these are eventualities that there is no question of bringing to fruition, the Thracians are perforce enfeebled. The various tribes all sport different names, depending on where they are settled – but, when it comes to the range of their customs, they are all very similar. The Getans, the Trausians and those who live beyond the Crestonians are the only exceptions.

[4] Of these, I have already mentioned[2] the Getans, who believe themselves immortal. The conduct of the Trausians is identical in every way to that of all the other Thracians, except for what they do on the occasion of a male's birth or death. Relatives will sit around a new-born and bewail the evils that are his due now that he has come into the world, and they will rehearse all the various sufferings that afflict mankind. When someone passes away, however, they will rejoice, and cover him with earth as though it were being done in sport, and recite over him all the ills from which he has been freed, and the condition of perfect bliss that he has now entered.

[5] It is the custom among those who live beyond the Crestonians for each man to have a large number of wives. Whenever someone dies, his wives will compete furiously with one another – cheered on as they do so by his friends – to decide which of them it was whom the man had loved the most. Whoever is singled out for the honour is then praised to the skies by men and women alike, before having her throat cut over the grave by her own closest relative, and being interred, dead as she now is, with her husband. All the other wives feel this as a great calamity – since for them there could be no disgrace more terrible.

[6] Elsewhere, it is a custom of the Thracians to sell their children for export.[3] Unmarried girls, rather than being kept on a tight leash, are instead permitted to sleep around with any men they fancy; but wives – who are purchased from their parents for substantial sums of money[4] – are very closely watched indeed. The possession of tattoos is

held to be a sign of breeding, while the lack of them is a mark of low birth. A life free from toil is the life most worth living, whereas nothing could be more humiliating than to work the land as a labourer. The best living is from plunder and war. Such are their most distinctive customs.

[7] The only gods worshipped by ordinary citizens are Ares, Dionysus and Artemis. The exceptions are their kings, who reverence Hermes above all other gods. By him alone do they swear oaths, just as it is from him that they claim their descent.

[8] The Thracians have a particular way of burying their well-to-do. They lay out the corpse for three days, and then, after much prior lamentation, they slaughter all kinds of sacrificial victims, and feast on them. They complete the funerary rites either by cremating the corpse or by burying it in the earth; and then, once they have piled up a tumulus, they stage a wide variety of athletic contests. The best prizes, entirely reasonably, go to those who engage in single combat. Such is the manner in which the Thracians bury their dead.

[9] As regards the people who live to the north of Thrace, no one has any reliable information as to who they might be – although it does seem that the land there, beyond the Ister, is boundless and desolate. In fact, I have only been able to discover one group of people living beyond the Ister: the Sigynnae, they are called. Their clothing is Median in style, and their horses are small, flat-nosed and shaggy all over, with coats that are up to 5 fingers thick. Although incapable of carrying riders, when pulling a cart these horses are as nippy as can be – in consequence, the natives drive around in carts a good deal. Their borders extend almost the whole way to the land of the Eneti[5] on the Adriatic. They are – or at least they claim to be – settlers from Media. Quite how they came to have emigrated from Media, I would not myself like to hazard a guess – but anything is possible, I suppose, with time. *Sigynnae* has the meaning of 'traders' in the language of the Ligurians, who live beyond Massilia,[6] while in Cyprus it means 'spears'.

[10] According to the Thracians, the far banks of the Ister are home to great swarms of bees, and it is this which makes it impossible to travel any further inland. Now, personally speaking, I do not find this claim plausible, since bees are creatures that appear not to like the cold at all – indeed, it seems to me that it is precisely the chilly conditions that explain why the regions towards the Bear[7] are uninhabited. Anyway,

whatever stories may be told about Thrace, the fact is that its coastal regions were being made subject by Megabazus to Persian rule.[8]

[11] Meanwhile, no sooner had Darius crossed the Hellespont and arrived in Sardis than he recalled the good service done him by Histiaeus of Miletus, and the shrewd advice given him by Coës of Mytilene; and so he summoned them both to Sardis and told them to name their reward. Since he already had the Milesians as his subjects, Histiaeus did not ask to rule as tyrant over anywhere else, but requested instead the region of Myrcinus in Edonia, where he intended to found a city. That was his choice; but Coës, who was just an ordinary citizen rather than a tyrant, asked to become tyrant of Mytilene.

[12] Once their wishes had been granted, both of them turned their attentions to making good what they had chosen. Darius, meanwhile, happened to see something which prompted him to order Megabazus to round up the Paeonians, and transport them forcibly from Europe to Asia. There were two Paeonian brothers by the names of Pigres and Mastyes, who had ambitions to rule Paeonia as tyrants; and these men, once Darius had crossed into Asia, turned up in Sardis, bringing with them their statuesque and most attractive sister. They waited until Darius had set up court on the outskirts of the Lydian city, and then went into action: first they arrayed their sister as handsomely as they could, and then sent her off to get water, carrying a jar on her head as she did so, leading a horse with its reins wrapped around her arm and spinning flax. As the woman was passing by Darius, his interest was piqued: her behaviour was typical neither of Persian nor of Lydian women, nor indeed of women anywhere in Asia. Intrigued by her, he sent some of his bodyguards after her with orders to observe what she got up to with the horse. So the guards went off on her trail; and when she got to the river, she watered the horse, and then, once the horse had drunk its fill, filled up the jar with water. After this, she retraced her steps, carrying the water on her head, leading the horse by its reins and turning the spindle round.

[13] The reports of his spies, combined with the evidence of his own eyes, left Darius mightily impressed; and so he ordered the woman to be brought before him. As she was escorted in, her brothers, who had been keeping a close eye on proceedings, came in as well. When Darius asked the woman her place of origin, the young men answered that she was their sister, and that they were all Paeonians. 'And who are the Paeon-

ians,' answered Darius, 'and in what region of the world do they live? And what are your motives in coming to Sardis?' They declared that they had come to offer their submission to him, that Paeonia was a region dotted with settlements on the River Strymon, that the Strymon was not far from the Hellespont, and that the Paeonians were originally Teucrians, colonists from Troy. Once they had delivered this report in its various details, Darius asked them if all the women of their country could match their sister for industriousness. 'Oh, yes,' they answered with great eagerness – for this was precisely the response that their actions had been designed to provoke.

[14] So Darius then wrote a letter to Megabazus, whom he had left in charge of military operations in Thrace, with instructions to uproot the Paeonians from their native land and bring them – women, children and all – to him. A horseman carrying the message immediately sped off to the Hellespont, made the crossing and gave the letter to Megabazus, who, once he had read it, procured some guides from Thrace and set out with an army against Paeonia.

[15] The Paeonians, when they learned that the Persians were advancing against them, mobilized an army and marched off in the direction of the sea, assuming that the Persian invaders were bound to attack them from that direction. Even as the Paeonians were readying themselves to block the advance of Megabazus' army, the Persians discovered that they had massed and were guarding the invasion route from the coast; accordingly, the Persians turned inland, and by using guides they were able to slip past the Paeonians without being noticed, and descend upon their various settlements. These, being empty of men, were easily taken; and the Paeonians, when they learned that their towns had fallen into the hands of the enemy, immediately scattered in all directions. Each band of men, looking to its own, then surrendered separately to the Persians. The consequence of this was that several Paeonian tribes – the Siriopaeonians, the Paeoplians and all the peoples as far as Lake Prasias – were uprooted from their native lands and transported to Asia.

[16] Those who lived around Mount Pangaeum,[9] however, [and the Doberes, Agrianians and Odomantians,] and those who were settled on the shores of Lake Prasias itself, never even came close to being vanquished by Megabazus. This was despite his efforts to subdue them, and the lake-dwellers too. It is a platform made of planks and fixed to tall stakes in the middle of the water that enables the people who actually

inhabit the lake to live the way they do. A single bridge (and a narrow one at that) constitutes the only means of access from the mainland. Back in the distant past, the stakes that support the platform were put in place by all the citizens working together as one; but that has since changed, and there is now a different regulation which determines their planting. Each man, every time he marries a wife, has to bring down three stakes from a mountain called Orbelus, and set them up in the lake – and all these men have a lot of wives. The housing itself is laid out on the platform so that each man has a hut of which he is the absolute master, and in which he lives; he also has a trapdoor which leads down through the platform to the lake. Concerned that their babies might otherwise roll down into the lake, they secure them by their ankles with a rope. For fodder, they give their horses and yoke-animals fish. In fact, the lake is so teeming with fish that anyone who opens a trapdoor and lowers an empty basket into it on a cord will find, in next to no time, as he hauls it back up, that it is full of them. The fish come in two kinds: one they call *paprax*, and the other *tilon*.

[17] Anyway, those Paeonians who had been defeated were transported to Asia, while Megabazus, his victory over them secured, sent a seven-man delegation to Macedonia;[10] it consisted of those Persians who, after himself, ranked highest in his army. Their mission was to demand earth and water for King Darius from Amyntas.[11] Now, from Lake Prasias to Macedonia there is an excellent short cut. First, go past the mine which lies just beyond the lake itself (and which, in more recent times, supplied Alexander[12] with a whole talent's worth of silver every day). Then, with the mine behind you, simply cross the mountain called Dysorum, and you will be in Macedonia.

[18] When, therefore, the Persian delegation arrived where Amyntas was, and came into his presence, they demanded earth and water for King Darius – which Amyntas duly gave them. Then, having invited them to share his hospitality, he had a magnificent banquet prepared, at which the Persians were entertained as his friends. After dinner, they continued with their drinking. 'My dear Macedonian host,' one of them said, 'it is our custom in Persia, whenever we put on a splendid feast like this, to bring in our wives and concubines, and have them sit down beside us. Such has been the enthusiasm with which you have received us, such the scale of your hospitality, and such the readiness with which you have given earth and water to King Darius, that surely you will now

follow us in this custom?' 'While this may indeed be your custom, Persians,' Amyntas answered, 'it is certainly not ours. We keep men and women apart. Nevertheless, you are now our masters, and whatever you require of us shall be done.' So saying, Amyntas sent for the women, who, once they had come at his bidding, sat in a row opposite the Persians. They were all of them very beautiful; and the Persians, after they had looked the women over, informed Amyntas that what he had done was not at all clever. 'Better that the women had never come in the first place,' they explained, 'than that they came and did not sit down beside us. To gaze at them across the room – why, it is torture!' Amyntas, having no choice in the matter, duly told the women to go and sit next to the Persians. The women did as they were instructed, and the Persians, who by now were roaringly drunk, began pawing at their breasts, with one or two even attempting to kiss them.

[19] Despite taking this very badly, Amyntas was so intimidated by the Persians that he watched it all in silence. Also present, however, was his son Alexander, a young man so unversed in life's evils that he found the spectacle quite unbearable, and could not restrain his anger. 'Father,' he said to Amyntas, 'why not obey the promptings of your age? Go and lie down. There is no need to carry on drinking. I will stay here and attend to all the needs of our guests.' Amyntas, who could tell from this that Alexander was plotting something, said, 'So incandescent with rage are you, my boy, that your meaning is not hard to fathom. You aim to send me off so that you can take some drastic step. Please, I beg of you – do not lay violent hands on these men. Otherwise it will spell certain ruin for us. Just watch what is going on, and keep a firm grip on yourself. As for my retiring – I will do as you suggest.'

[20] So Amyntas, having made his appeal, headed off, and Alexander addressed the Persians. 'Dear guests,' he said, 'these women are yours to do with you as you please. Sleep with them all, if you like, or simply take your pick. You have only to snap your fingers! But for the moment, bearing in mind that it is fast approaching bedtime, and that you have clearly had a lot to drink, I suggest – if you have no objection – that you let the women go and have a wash. Then, once they have bathed, you can have them back.' Such was his suggestion – to which the Persians were perfectly amenable. When the women left, though, they were packed off to their quarters. Alexander himself, meanwhile, took the exact same number of smooth-cheeked young men, dressed them up as

women and gave them daggers. Then, as he led them in, he said to the Persians, 'You seem to have enjoyed all the courses of the banquet to the full. Everything we had, everything we could dig up, everything we could procure – it has all been laid on for you. And now, to crown it, the most extravagant gift of all: our very own mothers and sisters! Be in no doubt – you will be treated by us with precisely the degree of honour that you merit. And please, do inform the King who sent you of the hospitality that you received, both bed and board, from his viceroy in Macedonia – a man of Greece.' And so saying, Alexander had the Macedonians dressed as women sit down next to the Persians, man on man; and then, when the Persians began to grope the Macedonians, the Macedonians stabbed the Persians dead.

[21] This, then, was their fate, to be massacred, they and their attendants too – for the Persians had come with wagons, and servants, and any amount of gear. As a result, it was not only they themselves who had to be made to vanish, but everything else as well. Not long afterwards, of course, a major search for the men was launched by the Persians, and was only checked by the wiles of Alexander. He gave large bribes, and the hand of his own sister – Gygaea, she was called – to the Persian in command of the search party, a man by the name of Bubares. So it was, as a result of this cover-up, that the deaths of the Persians were kept a secret.[13]

[22] That the descendants of Perdiccas[14] are indeed Greek, just as they claim to be, is something which I happen to know for a fact (and later in my narrative I will prove it). In this, I am of precisely the same view as the Greeks who officiate at the Olympic Games. When Alexander decided to compete in the games, you see, and stepped down onto the race-track, his Greek fellow-competitors tried to have him disqualified, objecting that the games were open only to Greek contestants, and not to barbarians. Alexander, however, demonstrated that he was in fact an Argive – and was accordingly adjudged to be Greek.[15] He took his place in the line-up, ran the sprint and came equal first. That is how things turned out.

[23] Meanwhile, Megabazus led the Paeonians to the Hellespont, crossed the straits and arrived in Sardis. By this stage, Histiaeus of Miletus was already busy fortifying Myrcinus, the place on the River Strymon that he had asked for from Darius as his reward for keeping the pontoon-bridge secure. Megabazus discovered what Histiaeus was up

to, and had an audience with Darius the moment he arrived in Sardis at the head of the Paeonians. 'Whatever have you done, O King?' he asked. 'You have given permission to a Greek, an underhand and devious man, to found a city in Thrace – a place where there is any amount of timber for building ships, plenty of spars for making oars and silver mines to boot! All those Greeks and barbarians who live there and who between them make up a considerable population, now they have found a leader, will labour day and night to fulfil his commands. You need to put a stop to his activities right now, or you will find yourself with a war directly on your doorstep. Rein him in by sending some diplomatically phrased message – and then, once you have him safely in your hands, make sure that he never again goes anywhere where there are any Greeks.'

[24] Having listened to this forecast of Megabazus, Darius needed no further persuading as to the likelihood of its coming true. It prompted him to send a messenger to Myrcinus: 'Histiaeus, hear the words of King Darius,' ran his dispatch. 'After much pondering, I have come to the conclusion that you are a man more truly devoted to me and my interests than any other I know. Actions speak louder than words – and yours have spoken loudly indeed. Accordingly, since I am planning some major projects, I want you here, no matter what, to talk them over in person.' Histiaeus, trusting in the King's sincerity, and reckoning it a splendid thing to become one of his counsellors, duly came to Sardis. Once he had arrived, Darius said to him, 'Histiaeus, here is why I sent for you. When I came back from Scythia, you were at once lost to my sight. What I soon found myself yearning for – more than anything, in fact – was to see you again, and have you join with me in conversation. I have realized that there is no possession in the whole world which redounds to my honour more than a friend who is intelligent and loyal. That you are a man endowed with both these qualities I am well aware. The service you did my cause, after all, is something for which I can vouch personally. That is why, now you have been so kind as to come here, I would like to make a proposal. Forget about Miletus and this new foundation of yours in Thrace. Follow me to Susa! Everything I have there will be yours. Whether at the table or in the council chamber, you will be constantly at my side.'

[25] So spoke Darius. He then appointed Artaphrenes, his paternal half-brother, to be governor of Sardis, before marching off to Susa and taking Histiaeus with him. He also appointed Otanes[16] to command the

people who lived along the coast. Otanes' father, Sisamnes, had been raised as a judge to the royal bench; but then, because he had taken a bribe in exchange for delivering a crooked verdict, King Cambyses had had him butchered, and flayed from top to toe. Then, when the skinning was finished, thongs had been made from the hide and used to string the chair on which Sisamnes had always sat to deliver his judgements. After this stringing was completed, Cambyses had appointed Sisamnes' own son as judge, in place of the freshly executed and skinned Sisamnes. 'Bear well in mind', Cambyses had instructed him, 'the chair on which you sit as you deliver your judgements.'

[26] It was this same Otanes, with his distinctive chair, who became general in succession to Megabazus. Byzantium, Chalcedon, Antandrus in the Troad and Lamponium: he took them all. He also commandeered ships from the Lesbians and took Lemnos and Imbros – both of which were still inhabited by Pelasgians at the time.

[27] The Lemnians, despite fighting hard and putting up a strong defence, were eventually worsted; and over the survivors the Persians installed as a governor Lycaretus, the brother of Maeandrius, who was once the ruler of Samos. This Lycaretus died while still the ruler of Lemnos [. . .] and for very good reason, since he had sold into slavery and utterly subjected everyone on the island. Some of the Lemnians he had accused of deserting the expedition against the Scythians, and others of preying on Darius' army as it was venturing back from Scythia.

[28] Such, then, were the achievements of Otanes during his tenure as general. There was then a brief abatement of evils – until terrible things befell the Ionians for a second time,[17] courtesy of the Naxians and Milesians. There was no island to rival Naxos for wealth, you see, and at the same period Miletus too stood at the very pinnacle of her own prosperity, the cynosure of Ionia. Before this, however, Miletus had been diseased for two whole generations with the most devastating factional strife, until order had been brought back to the city by some Parians (indeed, the Milesians had chosen the Parians to play the role of arbitrators ahead of all the other peoples of Greece).

[29] To effect the reconciliation, the Parians put their top people on the case. These, once they had arrived in Miletus and witnessed the ravages inflicted on every household there, declared their intention of making a progress throughout the territory. This they duly did; and whenever they saw, in the course of their criss-crossing of the entire

region controlled by Miletus, a well-tended field amid the general desolation of the landscape, they had its owner's name written down. Then, once they had toured the countryside in its entirety, and discovered only a few such men, they returned to Miletus, convened an urgent assembly and appointed to the government of the city all those they had found in possession of well-tended fields. 'For it is our opinion', they declared, 'that they will be as attentive to public needs as they are to their own.' The Parians instructed the other Milesians, who previously had been at one another's throats, to do as they were told by their new rulers.

[30] That is how the Parians brought order to Miletus. But it was then, thanks to this same city, and Naxos, that things began to take a terrible turn for the worse in Ionia – as I shall now explain. Various men, fat cats all, were banished from Naxos by the mass of the people,[18] and went into exile in Miletus. It so happened that the acting governor[19] in Miletus was Aristagoras son of Molpagoras, who was the son-in-law and cousin of Histiaeus son of Lysagoras – the man who had been detained by Darius in Susa. Histiaeus, you see, was actually tyrant of Miletus, but as fate would have it he was in Susa at the time of the arrival of the Naxians, who were long-term guest-friends of his. After they arrived in Miletus, the Naxians asked Aristagoras whether he might perhaps provide them with some military assistance, such as would enable them to be restored to their homes. It struck Aristagoras that their return to their city, if indeed he were to effect it, would bring Naxos under his control; so, using their special friendship with Histiaeus as his pretext, he made them a proposal. 'I personally am unable to provide you with sufficient resources to ensure your restoration – not in the face of the Naxians who currently hold the city. I have ascertained that they have eight thousand men at arms and a great fleet of longships. Nevertheless, I will spare no effort to devise some workable scheme. This is what I would suggest. It so happens that I am a friend of Artaphrenes – the same Artaphrenes who is the son of Hystaspes, the brother of King Darius, the ruler of everyone who inhabits the Asian seaboard, and possessor of a mighty army and a massive fleet. He is a man, I am confident, who will do whatever we may request of him.' When they heard this, the Naxians left it to Aristagoras to move things forward as best he could, and instructed him to promise both gifts and whatever the expenses of the army might be – which, they said, they would defray themselves. They did this fully expecting that when they

appeared in Naxos all the Naxians would jump to obey their orders, and all the other islanders too – none of the [Cycladic] islands, you see, having yet submitted to Darius.

[31] When Aristagoras arrived in Sardis, he told Artaphrenes that Naxos, although not a great island in terms of size, was nevertheless beautiful and fertile, that it was adjacent to Ionia[20] and that it was well endowed with both material resources and people who could be used as slaves. 'You should mount an expedition against the place, and restore these exiles to it. What would be in it for you? Well, firstly, I have set aside a great deal of money, enough to cover all your expenses – in addition, that is, to the funding of the army, which it is only proper that we who are conducting the operation should provide. Secondly, as well as Naxos, you will be obtaining for the King the various islands which it has under its control too – Paros, Andros, and all the others which go by the name of 'the Cyclades'. With these as your base, it will then be a simple matter to target Euboea, a large and prosperous island, no smaller than Cyprus, and very easy to seize.[21] A fleet of a hundred ships should suffice to subdue them all.' 'These suggestions you are making', answered Artaphrenes, 'bode well indeed for the House of the King. Your advice is unfailingly excellent – except for the number of ships. Rather than one hundred ships, have two hundred. They will be ready for you come the spring – always supposing, of course, that the King himself has first given the project his blessing.'

[32] When Aristagoras heard this, he returned to Miletus overjoyed, while Artaphrenes sent news of his proposal to Susa. Once Darius himself had given it his approval, Artaphrenes mobilized two hundred triremes and a vast force of Persians, together with various other contingents of allies. As its commander he appointed a Persian called Megabates, who had Achaemenid lineage, and a man who was a cousin of both himself and Darius. (Years later, so the story goes – although how plausible it is I am not sure – Pausanias of Lacedaemon, the son of Cleombrotus, was so consumed by his passion to rule as a tyrant over Greece[22] that he had himself betrothed to Megabates' daughter.) Once Artaphrenes had appointed Megabates to be its commander, he dispatched the force to Aristagoras.

[33] At Miletus, Megabates picked up Aristagoras, the army of Ionians and the Naxians, before sailing on, ostensibly for the Hellespont – until, arriving at Chios, he docked his ships at Caucasa, aiming to cross to

Naxos with a northerly wind at his back. Since, however, it was ordained that Naxos not fall to the expedition, events obtruded instead. What happened was that Megabates, while making his rounds of the look-outs posted to the fleet, came upon a Myndian ship where, as chance would have it, there were no look-outs stationed at all. Outraged by this, he ordered his personal guards to find the captain of the ship – a man called Scylax – to bind him fast and then to ram him halfway through one of the ship's oar-holes, so that his head was sticking out while his body was left inside. When Scylax had duly been secured in this way, someone informed Aristagoras that Megabates had tied up and humiliated his special friend from Myndus; so Aristagoras approached the Persian and begged him to revoke the sentence. When the request was turned down flat, Aristagoras went and untied the Myndian himself. When Megabates was informed of this, he was so angry with Aristagoras that he flew into a towering rage; but Aristagoras only answered, 'What is any of this to do with you? Didn't Artaphrenes send you with orders simply to obey me and sail where I tell you? Well, then – you mind your own business.' So said Aristagoras; and the indignation of Megabates was such that when night fell he sent men off in a boat to Naxos to tell the Naxians of all that was bearing down upon them.

[34] At no point, you see, had the Naxians had any presentiment that they were the targets of the expedition. Once they had learned the truth, however, they immediately brought everything from the fields inside the city wall, readied themselves for a siege by storing up food and drink and strengthened the ramparts. In all these preparations, their guiding assumption was the imminence of war – so that when the fleet made the crossing from Chios to Naxos, the city it bore down upon was barricaded and the siege dragged on for four months. By this stage, the Persians had exhausted all the money they had brought with them, and Aristagoras too had used up most of his; accordingly, with the costs of the siege still escalating, they built a fortress for the Naxian exiles and set off back to the mainland, their tails between their legs.[23]

[35] It was now impossible for Aristagoras to keep his promise to Artaphrenes. Not only that, but the commitment to fund the campaign was squeezing him, and he was terrified that the whole debacle of the expedition and his falling out with Megabates would mean he was deprived of his rule over Miletus. On all these counts, he was prompted

by his own anxieties to contemplate revolt against Persia – but it also so happened that this was the very moment when there arrived from Histiaeus in Susa the man with the tattoo on his head, signalling to Aristagoras that he should revolt against the King. You see, because the roads were so well policed, Histiaeus had been unable to find any other safe means of communicating with Aristagoras to urge rebellion; so he had shaved the scalp of his most trustworthy slave, tattooed his message onto it and waited for the hair to grow out. Then, the moment it had sprouted fully back, Histiaeus packed the slave off to Miletus, with just a single order: namely, that once he had arrived in Miletus, he should instruct Aristagoras to shave off his hair and examine his scalp. The tattoo pricks, as I have said, spelled out a message urging revolt. Histiaeus' motive in taking this step was his profound resentment at his detention in Susa – since he had every expectation that, in the event of a rebellion, he would be released and sent back to the Aegean. Should revolution[24] not come to Miletus, however, he could see no possible way back for himself.

[36] Such, then, was the plan Histiaeus had in sending the messenger; and it so happened that all these things combined simultaneously to influence Aristagoras. He duly consulted his own supporters, no longer keeping from them either his own opinion or the message that had come from Histiaeus. All of them unanimously declared themselves to be of like mind on the matter, and urged him to rebel – the only exception being Hecataeus, the story-teller, who was at first flatly opposed to making war on the Persian King, and listed all the peoples subject to Darius,[25] and the attributes of Darius' power; and next, when this argument failed to convince, recommended that they should take steps to secure mastery of the sea. Though he was well aware of the depleted condition of Milesian resources, he then went on to say that the only way this would come about, so far as he could see, was if they were to remove from the sanctuary at Branchidae all the treasures that had been dedicated there by Croesus of Lydia. Do that, he said, and he had every confidence of securing mastery of the sea – since not only would they be able to put the treasure to good use, but they would have placed it beyond the plundering reach of the enemy too. (And to be sure, the treasure was indeed immensely valuable, as I showed in the first narrative section[26] of my work.) This proposal did not win approval, but it was decided, nevertheless, to stage a rebellion. It was also agreed that

one of their number should sail to Myous, where the task-force had pitched camp following its withdrawal from Naxos, and make an attempt to arrest the commanders sailing on the ships.

[37] This mission was given to Iatragoras, who successfully duped and apprehended Oliatus of Mylasa, the son of Ibanollis; Histiaeus of Termera, the son of Tymnes; Coës, who was the son of Erxander, and the man to whom Darius had gifted Mytilene; Aristagoras of Cyme, the son of Heracleides; and many others. Aristagoras, now that he was openly a rebel, conspired in every possible way against Darius. His first step was to abdicate, nominally if not in reality, as tyrant, and declare equality under the laws[27] for everyone in Miletus – so hoping to secure the enthusiastic participation of the Milesians in the revolt. He did the same across the rest of Ionia. Some of the tyrants he forced into exile, while those he had seized from the ships that had joined him in the voyage to Naxos he handed over to their respective cities of origin: a gesture calculated to secure those cities' backing. Each tyrant in turn was handed over to his native city.

[38] Now, immediately the Mytilenaeans had Coës, they led him out and stoned him to death; but the Cymaeans let their tyrant go, as too did most of the other Ionians. So it was that tyrants came to be toppled in city after city. Once Aristagoras of Miletus had overthrown the tyrants, he instructed the citizens of each city to appoint a military commander; and then, as his next step, he set off for Lacedaemon on their behalf in a trireme. It was essential, after all, to secure the support of some significant military alliance.

[39] In Sparta, Anaxandridas, the son of Leon, was no longer sitting on the throne, which since his death had been occupied instead by Cleomenes,[28] his son: an inheritance that owed nothing to Cleomenes' personal qualities[29] and everything to his primogeniture. Anaxandridas, you see, had married his own sister's daughter, and she, despite being much adored by him, had failed to bear him any children. This being so, the ephors summoned him. 'Even if you are blind to the problem,' they said, '*we* cannot close our eyes to it. The line of Eurysthenes must not come to an end. Divorce your current wife, barren as she is, and marry another. Do that, and you will be the toast of the Spartiates.' Anaxandridas' response to these two suggestions, however, was a blank refusal – on the grounds that the recommendations were monstrous ones. 'Divorce the wife I currently have, when she has done me no

wrong, and marry someone else – that is your advice? I shall have nothing to do with the suggestion.'

[40] Whereupon the ephors and the elders consulted with one another, and made Anaxandridas a proposal. 'While we can see that you are strongly attached to your wife, do as we suggest and do not oppose us – because otherwise the Spartiates may well decide on a very different resolution to your case. We do not ask you to divorce your current wife. Rather, continue to provide her with everything that you have always given her, but import as well another wife – one who can give you children.' Such was the gist of their proposal – to which Anaxandridas consented. So it was, from that point on, that he had two wives, and divided his time between two households – behaviour that was quite contrary to Spartan custom.[30]

[41] Not long afterwards, his second wife gave birth to the aforementioned Cleomenes. Just as she was bringing into the world an heir to the Spartan kingdom, however, his first wife, who had hitherto been barren, somehow or other became pregnant – a most striking coincidence. The relatives of the second wife, when they learned that the pregnancy was actually genuine, set up a tremendous fuss, declaring her to be full of hot air, and alleging that it was her aim to pass off some other baby as her own. Indeed, they made such trouble that as the woman came to term the ephors did not know who to believe, and so sat in a ring around her, to keep watch on her as she gave birth. Then, the moment she had delivered Dorieus,[31] she immediately conceived Leonidas; and after that, in equally quick succession, Cleombrotus. Indeed, there are those who claim that Cleombrotus and Leonidas were in fact twins.[32] Meanwhile, the second wife, who had given birth to Cleomenes, and was the daughter of Prinetadas,[33] the son of Demarmenus, had no more children at all.

[42] Cleomenes, it is said, was not quite right in the head, to the extent that he was almost a lunatic,[34] while Dorieus was the outstanding figure of his generation. As a result, he never doubted that the kingdom would be his mainly on merit. Indeed, he was so confident of this that, when Anaxandridas died, and the Spartiates, as required by custom, installed his eldest son, Cleomenes, on the throne, Dorieus was outraged and refused to accept that he should be subject to Cleomenes as king. Accordingly, he asked the Spartiates for a band of men, and led them off to found a colony. Rather than consult with the oracle of Del-

phi as to where best he should establish such a settlement, or perform any of the customary actions, he was so irate that he just set off with his ships to Libya, with some men from Thera to serve as his guides. He made it to the River Cinyps, which is the most beautiful stretch of Libya, and founded a colony there[35] on its banks. Two years on, however, he was expelled from the site by the Macae, the Libyans and the Carthaginians, and returned to the Peloponnese.

[43] It was then that a man from Eleon called Antichares suggested to him, on the basis of the oracles of Laius, that he should colonize Heracleia in Sicily. 'The entire land of Eryx', Antichares declared, 'was acquired by Heracles himself, and as a result now properly belongs to his descendants.' When Dorieus heard this, he headed for Delphi to ask the oracle there whether the land he was embarking for would indeed end up as his. The Pythia answered him that it would – and so Dorieus enrolled the group that he had previously led to Libya, and took himself off to Italy.

[44] Even as he was doing this, the people of Sybaris, under the command of Telys, their king, were preparing to make war on Croton, and the Crotoniates (or so the Sybarites report) were reduced to such a state of terror that they asked Dorieus for assistance, a request that hit the mark. Dorieus joined the Crotoniates in an attack on Sybaris, and together they captured the city.[36] This is the version of what Dorieus and his followers got up to as told by the Sybarites, but it is flatly denied by the Crotoniates, who insist that they had no foreign backing in their war against the Sybarites, except for Callias, a soothsayer from Elis, who was one of the Iamids. And what was Callias doing there? He had fled Telys, the tyrant of Sybaris, and deserted to the Crotoniates, because the entrails of the animals he had been sacrificing all foretold that the campaign against Croton was bound to turn out badly. These, then, are the rival versions given.

[45] And both sides can produce corroborative evidence for them. The Sybarites point to the existence of a precinct and temple beside the dry bed of the River Crathis, which they claim were raised there by Dorieus after he had helped them take the city, and which were dedicated to Athena under the title of 'the Crathian'. The most conclusive piece of evidence they cite, however, is the manner of Dorieus' death – proof that his total ruin was the consequence of his ignoring the oracle.[37] Had he not taken on more than he should have done and been side-tracked

from his purpose, the land of Eryx would surely have been his; its conquest would have seen him and his army installed as its occupiers, rather than being wiped out. As for the Crotoniates, they point out that Callias the Elean was granted numerous estates in their territory – estates which were still settled by his descendants in my own time – whereas Dorieus and his descendants received no land at all. Had he really taken part with them in their war against the Sybarites, he would have been granted far more land than Callias. Such is the evidence rehearsed by the respective sides; it is for each individual to decide which is the more persuasive.

[46] Also in the colonizing party that sailed with Dorieus were a number of other Spartiates: Thessalus, Paraebates, Celeës and Euryleon. Despite arriving in Sicily at full strength, they were defeated by the Phoenicians and Egestaeans,[38] and perished in battle – all except for Euryleon, who alone among the band of colonists survived the calamity. He rallied what remained of the expeditionary force, seized the Selinousian colony of Minoa and helped to liberate the Selinousians from the sole rule of Peithagoras. After he had deposed the tyrant, however, he snatched the tyranny of Selinous for himself, and ruled alone – but only for a short while. The Selinousians rose in revolt and killed him, despite the fact that he had fled for refuge to the altar of Zeus, Protector of the City Square.

[47] Also among those of Dorieus' followers who perished alongside him was a citizen of Croton – Philippus, the son of Butacides – who had been banished from his hometown following his betrothal to the daughter of Telys of Sybaris. With his wedding plans frustrated, he had set sail with his very own trireme and a personally funded retinue for Cyrene, from where he had subsequently set out to join Dorieus. Philippus had been a victor in the Olympic Games, and was the most handsome Greek of his day. Indeed, such was his beauty that it won him a unique accolade from the Egestaeans: on his tomb they built a shrine appropriate to a hero, where they would propitiate him with sacrifices.

[48] So perished Dorieus. Had he only put up with having Cleomenes as his king, and stayed in Sparta, he would have become king of Lacedaemon himself, since Cleomenes did not reign for very long[39] and died without having a son (his only child being a daughter – Gorgo[40] by name).

[49] It was while Cleomenes was still in power, however, that

Aristagoras, the tyrant of Miletus, arrived in Sparta. The Lacedaemonians report that during his talks with Cleomenes, he had with him a bronze tablet, on which had been engraved a map of the entire world,[41] right down to the last sea and river. On his arrival for the meeting, Aristagoras said to Cleomenes, 'Do not be startled by my eagerness in coming here. The situation is this: the children of the Ionians, who should properly be free, are slaves. It is of course we who are stung the most painfully by the shame of this – but apart from us, it is you, as the leading people in Greece,[42] who should feel it most. I beg you, then, by the gods of the Greeks, to redeem the Ionians from slavery – men of one blood with you![43] You will easily make a success of the task: these barbarians have no stomach for a fight, whereas you have attained the very pinnacle of prowess in the field of war. Their notion of fighting is to use bows and arrows and short spears. They wear trousers when they go into battle, and funny caps on their heads. So you can see how easy they will be to beat! What is more, the men who live in this particular continent possess more goods than the rest of the world put together – gold above all, but silver too, and bronze, and exquisitely embroidered clothing, and beasts of burden, and people who can be used as slaves. Yours for the taking – as much as you please! As for the sequence of the various peoples who live there, let me give you the details. Here are the Ionians, and here, next to them, are the Lydians, who inhabit a land that is both fertile and rich in silver.' And so saying, he pointed to the map of the earth engraved on the plaque he had brought with him. 'And here,' said Aristagoras, 'just to the east of the Lydians, are the Phrygians, who are possessed of more livestock, and better harvests, than any other people I know. Next to the Phrygians are the Cappadocians – or Syrians, as we call them. They are bordered by the Cilicians, who pay 500 talents to the King every year in tribute,[44] and whose territory extends to this sea here, in which the island of Cyprus is to be found. Here, next to the Cilicians, are the Armenians, who are also exceedingly well endowed with livestock, and here, next to the Armenians, is the land of the Matienians. Next to them, here, is the land of Cissia, and it is on the banks of this river here, the Choaspes, which flows through Cissia, that you will find Susa, where the Great King has his residence, and where the treasure houses containing his wealth stand. Only capture that particular city, and you would not be abashed to compare your wealth with that of Zeus himself! But here, in your country, which is neither sizeable nor particularly fertile,[45] your borders are so constricting that you have to take the risk of fighting the Messenians, whose strength is on a par with yours, and with the Arcadians and the Argives. Do they have gold or silver, the lust for which has moved so many men to fight and die? No! Why, then, when the rule of Asia might easily be yours, would you choose any other course?' So said Aristagoras; and Cleomenes replied, 'My Milesian guest, I shall give you my answer the day after next.'

[50] And that, for the moment, was as far as things went. The day on which Cleomenes had said he would give his answer arrived, however, and after they had met as agreed, Cleomenes asked Aristagoras how many days it took to reach the King's residence from the Ionian coast. Now, hitherto, Aristagoras had been very smart, and pulled the wool completely over Cleomenes' eyes; but here he tripped up badly. What he should have done, since it was his aim to lure the Spartiates away to Asia, was to lie – but instead, when he opened his mouth, it was to declare that the journey up to Susa took three months. At this, despite the fact that Aristagoras still had a good deal more left to say about the journey, and indeed was only warming to his theme, Cleomenes cut him off and said, 'You are to leave Sparta, my Milesian friend, before sunset. What could possibly sound more ridiculous to the Lacedaemonians than this suggestion you are making? Do you really want to lead them three months' journey from the sea?'

[51] And so saying, Cleomenes went home; but Aristagoras, grabbing an olive branch wreathed in wool, followed him there. Then, once inside the house, he played the suppliant, urging Cleomenes to listen to him further after the child who was standing near by – Cleomenes' only daughter, a girl some eight or nine years old by the name of Gorgo – had been sent away. Cleomenes, however, told Aristagoras to say what he wanted, and not to hold back on account of the child. So Aristagoras made his opening gambit: a bribe of 10 talents, if Cleomenes would only do as he asked. Cleomenes shook his head, but Aristagoras did not give up. Higher and higher he raised the figure – until the bribe was 50 talents.[46] It was then that the small child piped up. 'Father,' she said, 'this foreigner will be the ruin of you, unless you get to your feet and leave.' Cleomenes, who was much tickled by this exhortation of his daughter, went into the other room – while Aristagoras left Sparta altogether, and never again got the opportunity to describe the journey inland to the seat of the Great King.

[52] What of the actual road itself? It has staging-posts built by the King along its entire length, and excellent hostels, and the whole road is both well tenanted and secure. The stretch which passes through Lydia and Phrygia has twenty staging-posts, and measures 94½ *parasangs*. Then, after Phrygia, comes the River Halys, where there is a pass which must absolutely be got through before the river itself can be crossed, and where there is a formidable guard house. Beyond the river, the road continues through Cappadocia, past twenty-eight staging-posts, until it reaches the border with Cilicia: a distance of 104 *parasangs*. On this particular frontier, there are two passes to get through, and two watch-posts. Once these have been negotiated, there are three staging-posts as the road makes its way through Cilicia – until, after 15½ *parasangs*, it reaches a river called the Euphrates, which is deep enough to be navigable, and forms the border with Armenia. In Armenia the road covers a distance of 56½ *parasangs*, and features both a watch-post and fifteen staging-posts, where travellers can take a break. From Armenia, the journey continues into Matienian territory, in which there are thirty-four staging-posts, over a distance of 137 *parasangs*. Four rivers navigable by boats flow through Matiene, and the traveller has no choice but to cross these rivers by ferry. The first of them is the Tigris, and the second and third are both called the Zabatus – despite the fact that the two rivers are actually quite distinct, and do not even share the same source, the first-mentioned rising in Armenia, and the next along in Matiene. The fourth river is called the Gyndes,[47] and is the one that Cyrus once divided into three hundred and sixty channels. Beyond the Gyndes, the traveller passes into the land of Cissia, where there are eleven staging-posts. Then, after 42½ *parasangs*, the road reaches the Choaspes, another navigable river, on the banks of which the city of Susa stands. In all, then, the number of staging-posts comes to one hundred and eleven – and not one of these one hundred and eleven posts fails to offer the traveller going up from Sardis to Susa a place to stay overnight.

[53] Now, if the distance of the royal road[48] has been correctly measured in *parasangs*, and if – as indeed is the case – one *parasang* is equivalent to 30 stades, then the distance from Sardis to the so-called Palace of Memnon is 13,500 stades, or 450 *parasangs*. If you assume that it takes one day for a man to cover 150 stades, then it will take exactly ninety days to cover the entire distance.

[54] It follows, then, when Aristagoras of Miletus told Cleomenes the Lacedaemonian it would take three months on the road to reach the King, that his claim was not far wide of the mark. I also have some even more accurate figures to hand should anyone require them – it being necessary, after all, to take into account the stretch from Ephesus to Sardis. I would argue that the total number of stades from the Greek Sea[49] to Susa, as the city of Memnon is known, amounts to 14,040 – it being 540 stades from Ephesus to Sardis. This serves to add three days to the journey of three months.

[55] Once Aristagoras had been driven out of Sparta, he went to Athens, which had been liberated from its tyrants. What had happened was that Hipparchus, the son of Peisistratus, and brother of the reigning tyrant Hippias, had been assassinated by two scions of the Gephyraean family, Aristogeiton and Harmodius – and this despite the fact that Hipparchus had seen very clearly in a dream what was to befall him. Nevertheless, the tyranny continued undiminished for four years[50] in the wake of this assassination – indeed, if anything, it was even harsher than before.

[56] The vision seen by Hipparchus, in a dream during the night before the Panathenaea,[51] was of a tall and handsome man – and this man, so it seemed to Hipparchus, stood over him, and spoke in riddling terms:

'Endure with fortitude, lion, sufferings past endurance;
The man does not exist who can avoid paying for his crimes.'

No sooner had day dawned than Hipparchus made a public deposition to the dream-interpreters concerning these same verses. Subsequently, however, he dismissed the vision from his thoughts, and joined the procession – in which he met his end.

[57] The Gephyraeans, from whom the assassins of Hipparchus were descended, claim originally to have derived from Eretria – but I have found out, on close investigation, that they were actually Phoenicians. To be more specific, they were Phoenicians who came with Cadmus to the land now known as Boeotia, where they settled down in Tanagra, the region that had been granted them as their lot. Following the expulsion of the Cadmeians from Boeotia by the Argives, the Gephyraeans were expelled in their turn by the Boeotians, and made for Athens. The

Athenians took them in and enrolled them as fellow-citizens, the only stipulation being their exclusion from a few rights so insignificant as not to be worth mentioning.

[58] These Phoenicians, the Gephyraeans among them, who came with Cadmus to Boeotia and settled there, brought with them a great number of things which they then taught the Greeks. Most notable of these was the alphabet – which the Greeks, in my opinion, had not possessed up until that point. To begin with, the letters were the same as those used by Phoenicians everywhere; but in due course, as time went by and their language evolved, so too did the form of their script.[52] At this period, the majority of Greek settlements abutting them were Ionian, so it was the Ionians who learned the alphabet from the Phoenicians and appropriated it. They put it to their own ends by adjusting the appearance of a few letters, but they still called the alphabet they were using 'Phoenician' – as was only right and proper, given that it was the Phoenicians who had introduced it to Greece. Also ancient is the Ionian term for papyrus scrolls – 'hides' – which derives from a time when scarcity of papyrus obliged the Ionians to use goat- and sheepskins.[53] Even today, there are many barbarians who write on hides in such a manner.

[59] I have seen examples of the Cadmeian script myself: there were some in the sanctuary of Ismenian Apollo at Thebes in Boeotia, engraved on three tripods, and very similar, by and large, to the Ionian script. One of the tripods had the inscription,

AMPHITRYON DEDICATED ME, TAKEN AS I WAS FROM THE TELEBOAE.

This would date it to the time of Laius,[54] who was the son of Labdacus, the son of Polydorus, the son of Cadmus.

[60] Another of the tripods had lines in hexameters:

SCAEUS THE BOXER, AFTER HIS VICTORY, DEDICATED ME,
AN EXQUISITE OFFERING, TO APOLLO, THE FAR-SHOOTING.

Scaeus must surely be the son of Hippocoön, and therefore roughly contemporaneous with Oedipus, the son of Laius – provided, that is, it really was the son of Hippocoön who made the dedication, and not someone else of the same name.

[61] The third tripod, also in hexameters, read:

LAODAMAS HIMSELF, THE KING, GAVE THIS TRIPOD, AN OFFERING
EXQUISITE INDEED, TO KEEN-EYED APOLLO, PLACING IT HERE.

This Laodamas was the son of Eteocles, and it was during his reign that the Cadmeians, after they had been driven out by the Argives, made for the Encheleans. This left the Gephyraeans stranded, and in due course they were forced by the Boeotians to beat a retreat to Athens. There, they established their own rites, in which no other Athenians play a part, and which are quite unlike the city's other rituals. This is particularly true of the sanctuary of the Achaean Demeter and its Mysteries.

[62] Anyway – now that I have related what Hipparchus saw in his dream, and the origins of the Gephyraeans, the family to which his assassins belonged, I must pick up the narrative that I began earlier and explain how the Athenians were liberated from the rule of their tyrants. With Hippias still firmly in power, and embittered against the Athenians because of the death of Hipparchus, the Alcmaeonids, who were an Athenian family exiled by the sons of Peisistratus,[55] joined with various other Athenian exiles in an attempt to force their way back home; but even though they fortified Leipsydrium, above Paeonia,[56] their effort to return home and liberate Athens met with a decisive reverse, and so failed. From then on, the Alcmaeonids plotted in every way they could against the Peisistratids. They secured a contract from the Amphictyons, for instance, to build and complete the temple at Delphi – the same one that stands there today. Being men of means, and possessed of a distinguished pedigree, the Alcmaeonids finished the temple far more beautifully than had originally been planned – not least by using Parian marble for the façade, when the contract had merely stipulated tufa.

[63] The Athenians claim that the Alcmaeonids, while they were based in Delphi, paid such bribes to the Pythia that, whenever a Spartiate came to consult the oracle, whether on private or public business, the man would be advised by her to set Athens free. The Lacedaemonians, endlessly barraged by this one message, sent a force under Anchimolius,[57] the son of Aster, and a man held in the highest regard by his fellow-citizens, to drive the Peisistratids from Athens – and this despite the fact that the Peisistratids were bound to them by exceptionally close ties of friendship. The considerations of men, however, were as nothing to them compared to those of the god.[58] So the men were sent off – and after crossing the sea, their ships docked at Phalerum, and the

army disembarked. Meanwhile, the Peisistratids, acting on prior intelligence, had summoned auxiliaries from Thessaly, a land with which they had forged an alliance. The consensus of the Thessalians was that they should meet this request by sending a thousand horsemen under their king, Cineas of Conium; once the Peisistratids had these allies with them, they devised an appropriate plan. First, they cleared the plain of Phalerum of trees, so that cavalry would be able to operate freely across it – and then they unleashed their horsemen against the enemy camp. Casualties among the Lacedaemonians as a result of this onslaught were exceedingly high, and included Anchimolius himself, while the survivors were driven back into their ships. Such was the outcome of the first expedition sent from Lacedaemon. The tomb of Anchimolius is at Alopece in Attica, near the shrine of Heracles at Cynosarges.

[64] The next expedition furnished by the Lacedaemonians for dispatch against Athens was a more substantial one. They appointed their king, Cleomenes, the son of Anaxandridas, to the command of the army, and sent it, not by sea as before, but by land. Their opening thrust into Attica was met by the Thessalian cavalry, which was quickly routed, with the loss of some forty men. The survivors immediately headed straight back to Thessaly. Cleomenes, accompanied by those Athenians who aspired to be free, then arrived before the city, placed the tyrants under siege and penned them behind the Pelasgian wall.

[65] Mind you, since the Lacedaemonians had never intended to stage a blockade, and since the Peisistratids had plenty of food and drink, there is no way, all other things being equal, that the former would ever have got hold of the latter. Instead, after a siege lasting no more than a few days, the Lacedaemonians would surely have gone back to Sparta. Fate, however, intervened – to disastrous effect for one side, and as a godsend for the other – when the children of the Peisistratids were taken prisoner as they were being smuggled out of the country. When this occurred, the plans of the Peisistratids were thrown into such confusion that they were reduced to ransoming their children on terms set by the Athenians, who gave them five days to get out of Attica. Once they had gone into exile, they retired to Sigeium on the River Scamander. Their rule over Athens had lasted thirty-six years. Their family originally had come from Pylus; they were descended from Neleus, and were of the same stock as Codrus, and Melanthus, and their people, who long before, and despite being immigrants, had become

kings of Athens. It was to commemorate this that Hippocrates had given his son the name Peisistratus – after the Peisistratus who had been the son of Nestor. So it was that the Athenians were rid of their tyrants.[59] As for the noteworthy things they did after winning their freedom, and those that others did to them – all the way down to the time of the Ionian rebellion against Darius, and the arrival in Athens of Aristagoras the Milesian, with his appeal to them for assistance – it will now be my priority to narrate them.

[66] Great as Athens had been before, once rid of her tyrants she became greater still. There were two power brokers in the city: Cleisthenes an Alcmaeonid, and the man who was said to have bribed the Pythia; and Isagoras, the son of Tisander, whose pedigree, despite the great distinction of his house, I am unable to provide. (That said, relatives of his do offer sacrifices to Carian Zeus.) These two men were embroiled in a power-struggle; and Cleisthenes, when he was having the worst of it, set himself up as a special friend of the people.[60] Next, he replaced the four tribes into which the Athenians had been divided with a tenfold division.[61] The four tribes had been named after the sons of Ion – Geleon, Aegicores, Argades and Hoples – but Cleisthenes abolished these, and replaced them with tribes named after other heroes, all of them natives except Ajax. He was added to the list because, though a foreigner, he had been a neighbour and an ally.

[67] Now, I have a theory that this policy was copied by Cleisthenes from his grandfather on his mother's side, the Cleisthenes who was the tyrant of Sicyon. This Cleisthenes, after he had fought a war against the Argives, halted the rhapsodic contests in Sicyon because they featured the poems of Homer, in which the praises of the Argives and of Argos[62] were continually being sung. Nor is that all. There was (and indeed still is) in the market-square of Sicyon a shrine raised to Adrastus, the son of Talaus – a hero who, because he came from Argos, Cleisthenes was desperate to have banished from Sicyonian territory. So he went to Delphi and asked the oracle for permission to evict Adrastus. The Pythia answered him by saying, 'Adrastus was a king of Sicyon, but all you ever do is stone the Sicyonians to death.' Faced by this refusal of the god to meet his request, Cleisthenes returned home and mulled over whether there might not be some other way he could get rid of Adrastus. When he believed he had the answer, he sent a messenger to Thebes in Boeotia, saying that he wished to introduce Melanippus, the son of Astacus, into

Sicyon – a request which the Thebans granted. Then, once Melanippus had been escorted to Sicyon, Cleisthenes consecrated a precinct to him in the town hall itself, and installed him in its most impregnable spot. (I should explain, at this point, that the reason why Cleisthenes had Melanippus brought to Sicyon was because he had been the deadliest enemy of Adrastus, having killed his brother, Mecisteus, and his son-in-law, Tydeus.) Following the consecration of the precinct, Cleisthenes deprived Adrastus of his sacrificial rites and festivals, and allotted them to Melanippus. Adrastus had always been a particular focus of Sicyonian devotions because Polybus, who used to rule Sicyon, but had no sons, had left the kingdom on his death to Adrastus, who was his grandson by his daughter. Among numerous other marks of respect paid to Adrastus by the Sicyonians were commemorations of his sufferings with tragic choruses, sung in his honour rather than that of Dionysus. Cleisthenes, however, assigned these choruses to Dionysus, and all the other sacrificial rites to Melanippus.

[68] Such was the treatment he meted out to Adrastus. He also changed the names of the Sicyonian tribes, to prevent them from having the same Dorian nomenclature as the tribes of the Argives. Indeed, he made the people of Sicyon into objects of utter ridicule. The tribes, though they still had the customary endings tacked on, had their names changed to 'Swine', 'Donkey' and 'Piggy' – all except his own tribe, which he named the 'Ruler Men', a title awarded them because it derived from the fact of his own rule. The others were the 'Swine Men', the 'Donkey Men' and the 'Piggy Men'. These names were applied to the tribes of Sicyon throughout Cleisthenes' term of rule, and for a further sixty years after his death. Then, however, the Sicyonians put the matter to debate, and changed their names back to the Hylleis, the Pamphylians and the Dymanatae.[63] In addition, they changed the name of the fourth tribe to the Aegialians – so called after Aegialeus, the son of Adrastus.

[69] So these were the policies of Cleisthenes of Sicyon, which Cleisthenes of Athens, who was both his namesake and the son of his daughter, seems to me to have copied – with the aim, contemptuous as the younger Cleisthenes appears to have been of the Ionians, of ensuring that the Athenians would not have tribes as the Ionians did. The evidence for this is that once he and his faction had secured the support of the mass of the Athenian people,[64] who until that point had been kept disenfranchised, he changed the names of the tribes and increased their

number. Whereas previously there had been four tribal leaders, he now created ten, and divided up the demes[65] between them. With the people won over to his side, the members of the opposing faction[66] were put thoroughly in the shade.

[70] It was then the turn of Isagoras, who had come off second best, to devise a counter-plan. What he did was to call in Cleomenes the Lacedaemonian, who, over the course of the siege of the Peisistratids, had become an exceedingly close friend and ally – so much so, indeed, that he was darkly rumoured to have had an affair with Isagoras' wife. Cleomenes' first step was to send a herald to Athens, with a demand that Cleisthenes and a whole host of other Athenians be banished, on the grounds that those he had listed were 'the accursed ones'.[67] In sending such a message, he had been following the instructions of Isagoras, who, unlike the Alcmaeonids and their faction, was innocent of this charge of murder – he and all his allies.

[71] So how did these other Athenians come to be labelled 'the accursed ones'? Well, there was a man of Athens called Cylon, who had won first prize at the Olympic Games, and fancied himself as a tyrant – also he recruited a following of young men his age and tried to seize the Acropolis.[68] When this coup failed, he and his men then sought sanctuary at the foot of Athena's statue. The men in charge of the navy boards, who in those days effectively constituted the government of Athens, persuaded the suppliants to leave – on the assurance that their punishment, whatever else it might be, would not be a capital one. But they were executed all the same, with the Alcmaeonids getting the blame. All this happened before the time of Peisistratus.[69]

[72] Cleisthenes, when confronted by the demand sent by Cleomenes for the banishment of 'the accursed ones', slipped quietly away, but Cleomenes followed this up by appearing in Athens – albeit with no great show of military force. When he arrived, he drove seven hundred Athenian families into exile, all of them nominated by Isagoras. His second step was to attempt a dissolution of the Council, and a transfer of its powers into the hands of Isagoras' three hundred henchmen. The Council dug in its heels, however, and refused to go along with this; and so Cleomenes, backed by Isagoras and his faction, occupied the Acropolis. The remaining Athenians, acting as though of one mind, then put them under siege. Two days went by, until, on the third, a truce was sworn: under its terms the Lacedaemonians were permitted to leave the

country. So was fulfilled the warning that had been given to Cleomenes when, during the course of his occupation of the Acropolis, he had reached its summit and made to go into the temple of Athena to pray. As he was about to pass through the doors, the priestess had risen from her chair and said, 'Back with you, stranger from Lacedaemon – do not go into the shrine. Dorians are prohibited by law from entering here.' 'I am no Dorian, woman,' Cleomenes had answered her, 'but an Achaean.'[70] So he had kept to his purpose, scanted the words of the prophetess and for a second time been slung out on his ear, together with all the other Lacedaemonians. Their comrades-in-arms were fettered fast and readied for death. Among these prisoners was Timesitheus of Delphi, whose unsurpassed feats of strength[71] and courage I could well dwell upon at length.

[73] Once the prisoners had been executed, the Athenians recalled Cleisthenes and the seven hundred families banished by Cleomenes, and sent messengers as well to Sardis – for, knowing as they did how Cleomenes and the Lacedaemonians were set on going to war against them, they wished to forge an alliance with the Persians. The messengers duly arrived in Sardis and launched into what they had been instructed to say – but were interrupted by the city's governor, Artaphrenes, the son of Hystaspes. 'Who are you,' he demanded, 'and from what corner of the world do you come, that you seek to become allies of the Persians?' Once the messengers had supplied him with the requested information, he replied in lapidary manner: 'Give King Darius earth and water, and the Athenians can have their alliance. Refuse him, however, and he orders them begone.' The messengers, eager to secure the alliance, agreed on their own responsibility to hand over the earth and water: an action which, on their return to their own city, saw them severely censured.[72]

[74] Cleomenes, meanwhile, conscious of the grievous insult he had received from the Athenians, in both word and deed, was busy assembling an army from the entire Peloponnese. Although he kept his motives for this mobilization secret, it was his intention to be avenged on the Athenian people, and to install Isagoras, who had left the Acropolis alongside him, as tyrant. By prior arrangement, the Boeotians seized Oenoe and Hysiae, the two outermost demes in Attica, just as Cleomenes was invading Eleusis at the head of a large force, and the Chalcidians, wreaking destruction as they went, advanced across the opposite flank

of Attic territory. The Athenians, despite being attacked from all sides, decided to put the Boeotians and the Chalcidians to the back of their minds, and to take up arms against the Peloponnesians, who had reached Eleusis.

[75] Just as the two camps were about to join battle, however, the Corinthians[73] decided that what they were doing had no possible justification, and they duly headed home. They were only the first to change their minds; next it was the turn of Demaratus, the son of Ariston, who was the other Spartan king,[74] and joint leader of the army that had come from Lacedaemon, and who until that moment had been on perfectly good terms with Cleomenes. (It was as a consequence of this spat that a law was laid down in Sparta forbidding both kings to take to the field together, as they had been doing up to that point. What is more, the fact that one of the kings had been stood down meant that one of the two sons of Tyndareus,[75] both of whom had previously always gone on campaign at the request of the army itself, could likewise be left behind.) The remaining allies at Eleusis, when they saw the kings of the Lacedaemonians at loggerheads, and the Corinthian positions abandoned, also decamped and were gone.

[76] This was the fourth time that Dorians had turned up in Attica. Two of the incursions were hostile, and two were made for the good of the majority of the Athenian people. The first expedition should properly be dated to the time when Codrus was king of Athens, and coincided with the Dorian founding of Megara. The second and third were when they arrived from Sparta on a mission to drive out the Peisistratids, and the fourth was when Cleomenes led the Peloponnesians on the invasion that reached Eleusis. So this last Dorian intrusion into Athens was the fourth one overall.

[77] The inglorious implosion of the army left the Athenians eager for revenge. The initial targets of their campaigning were the Chalcidians; but when a Boeotian relief force came to the support of the Chalcidians, and was observed advancing on the Euripus, the Athenians decided to engage first with the Boeotians rather than the Chalcidians. In the resulting battle, the Athenians won a crushing victory over the Boeotians, killing large numbers of them and taking seven hundred prisoner. Then, on the very same day, the Athenians crossed to Euboea, engaged the Chalcidians, and won a second victory – after

which they left four thousand smallholders settled on the land of the 'Horse-Breeders', as the well-off in Chalcis are known. The captives taken in the second battle were shackled and kept under guard alongside the Boeotian prisoners-of-war – and were eventually only released after the payment of a ransom set at 2 *minae* a head. The chains used to fetter them were hung up on the Acropolis, where they still were in my day, hanging from walls left fire-scorched by the Mede, and facing the sanctuary building angled to the west. A tenth part of the ransom was dedicated to Athena, and used to build a four-horse chariot out of bronze. It stands on the left-hand side of the monumental gateway into the Acropolis, immediately by the entrance. The inscription on it reads:

THE PEOPLES OF BOEOTIA AND OF CHALCIS BOTH WERE MASTERED
BY THE DEEDS IN BATTLE OF THE HEROIC SONS OF ATHENS.
FETTERS DISMAL AND IRON-FORGED SNUFFED OUT ALL THEIR
ARROGANCE.
THESE HORSES, PAID BY A TITHE, WERE DEDICATED TO PALLAS.

[78] So Athens came to flourish – and to make manifest how important it is for everyone in a city to have an equal voice,[76] not just on one level but on all. For although the Athenians, while subjects of a tyrant, had been no more proficient in battle than any of their neighbours, they emerged as supreme by far once liberated from tyranny. This is proof enough that the downtrodden will never willingly pull their weight, since their labours are all in the service of a master – whereas free men, because they have a stake in their own exertions, will set to them with enthusiasm.

[79] Meanwhile, in the wake of these deeds, the Thebans sent emissaries to Apollo, wishing to be avenged[77] on the Athenians. The Pythia told them, however, that retribution would never be secured through their own agency. 'Inform the One With Many Voices,' she instructed, 'and ask for help from those who are closest to you.' So the ambassadors to Delphi returned home, where they convened an assembly and repeated what the oracle had declared; and when the listening Thebans were informed by the speakers that they needed to request help from those who were closest to them, they asked, 'But who? Surely not our immediate neighbours, the Tanagraeans, the Coroneians and the Thespians? They are already our comrades-in-arms, and have always fought

unstintingly in all our wars! So why should we have to request their assistance? Surely the oracle must mean something else?'

[80] As they were mulling things over in this way, though, someone finally fathomed the meaning. 'I think', he said, 'I have worked out what the oracle was aiming to tell us. The story goes that Asopus had two daughters: Thebe and Aegina.[78] That makes them sisters, and is why I conclude that Apollo was advising us to ask the Aeginetans to come to our help.' Since no one else seemed to have any better theory, the Thebans immediately sent an appeal, charging the Aeginetans to do as the oracle had prompted and come to their rescue, on the grounds of their mutual closeness. The Aeginetan response to this appeal for assistance was to permit the messengers who had made it to return with Aeacus and his sons.[79]

[81] Joined by the Aeacids, then, the Thebans ventured an attack on the Athenians – but received very rough handling. Back went the Theban messengers to Aegina, where they returned the Aeacids and asked for men instead. The Aeginetans, buoyed by the sheer scale of their city's prosperity, and mindful as well of their own ancient feud with the Athenians, responded to the Theban request by unleashing a war against the Athenians,[80] which they did not even bother formally to declare. As the Athenians were attacking the Boeotians, the Aeginetans sailed across in their longships to raid Attica, laying waste both Phalerum and a large number of other demes along the coast, and inflicting immense damage on the Athenians.

[82] The grudge held by the Aeginetans against the Athenians came about as follows. It reached back to a time when the land around Epidaurus was so barren of crops that the Epidaurians consulted Delphi about the disaster. The Pythia told them to erect statues of Damia and Auxesia, assuring them that this would serve to improve the situation. The Epidaurians accordingly asked whether the statues should be made of bronze or stone, but the Pythia would not permit the use of either material, and specified instead the wood of a cultivated olive tree. So the Epidaurians asked the Athenians for permission to cut down an olive tree, in the belief that no other would be better suited to such a numinous purpose – and also, according to one story, because there was nowhere else apart from Athens that actually had any olive trees at that time. The Athenians granted the Epidaurians their request, but on one condition: every year they must bring offerings to Athena, the Guardian

of the City, and to Erechtheus.[81] The Epidaurians accepted these terms; they obtained what they had asked for, fashioned the statues out of these olive trees, then set them up. The soil regained its fertility, and the Epidaurians fulfilled the terms of their agreement with the Athenians.

[83] Now, at the time we are talking about, and before it too, the Aeginetans had been obliged to do whatever the Epidaurians told them – and this included, among other things, crossing over to Epidaurus to settle such lawsuits as might arise among themselves. Subsequently, however, the Aeginetans built a navy, and rather than truckle to the Epidaurians any further, seceded from them. In the resulting war, the fact that the Aeginetans had command of the sea[82] enabled them to inflict a number of blows on the Epidaurians – among which was the theft from Epidaurus of the statues of Damia and Auxesia. The Aeginetans took these back to their own island and set them up in its interior, at a place named Oea, some 20 stades from the city of Aegina. Once the statues had been installed in this spot, they were propitiated by means of sacrifices, and filthy jokes told by choruses of women – one chorus per goddess, and both with ten men appointed to their production. The catcalls of these choruses were directed, not at men, but exclusively at the local women. The Epidaurians too had these same rites – together with some others that have never been mentioned.

[84] With the theft of the statues, the Epidaurians terminated their contractual obligations to the Athenians – and when the Athenians sent them an indignant complaint, they made a great show of insisting that they had right on their side. 'As long as we had the statues here in our country,' they explained, 'we kept to our agreement. But it is hardly fair, now that we have been deprived of them, that we should have to continue with the offerings. Go and get your dues instead from the new owners – the Aeginetans.' Prompted by this suggestion, the Athenians duly sent a demand to Aegina for the return of the statues – to which the Aeginetans retorted that it was none of the Athenians' business.

[85] Now, the Athenians' story is that they followed up the demand for the return of the statues by sending on a single longship some of their own citizens, to serve as representatives of the entire community, and that these, upon their arrival in Aegina, sought to uproot the statues from their pedestals, with the aim of taking them back home on the grounds that the wood was theirs. When this method of securing the statues proved a failure, however, the Athenians tied ropes around them

and tugged away; and as they tugged, so there was a clap of thunder, and an earthquake[83] too, even as the thunder was still rolling. The crew of the trireme who had been pulling on the ropes were driven mad by this, and started slaughtering one another as though they were foes. Eventually, out of the entire crew, there was only one left – who then returned to Phalerum.

[86] Such is the Athenian account of what happened; but the Aeginetans report that the Athenians did not come in just a single ship, since if they had done (or come in rather more than one, indeed) then they could easily have been repulsed, even had the Aeginetans not happened to have had a fleet of their own. Instead, so the Aeginetans claim, the Athenians descended upon their island with a large fleet, and forced their surrender, without being engaged at sea. (It is not certain from their account, however, whether this surrender was due to their realizing that they would be vastly outnumbered in any naval battle, or whether it was because their ultimate course of action was already a feature of their plans.) So the Athenians, finding themselves unopposed, disembarked from their ships and made for the statues. Unable to dislodge them from their pedestals, however, the Athenians then bound them with ropes and hauled away, which they continued to do until both statues did exactly the same thing. (Or so the Aeginetans claim – personally, I do not find this credible, but others may.) The statues fell to their knees, you see – and have remained kneeling ever since. That, according to the Aeginetans, is what the Athenians did – while they themselves, because they had been informed that the Athenians were embarking on a campaign against them, had made the Argives stand by in readiness. When the Athenians landed, the Argives duly came to the rescue: slipping across unnoticed from Epidaurus to the island, they fell upon the Athenians, who were taken wholly unawares and cut off from their ships. This was the very point at which the thunder began to roll, and the earth to shake.

[87] So these are the Argive and Aeginetan versions of events, which accord with the Athenian version to this extent – that only one man made it safely back to Attica. Where the two accounts differ, of course, is over the Argives' claim that it was they who wiped out the Athenian task-force of which this man was the sole survivor, since the Athenians attribute the massacre to divine intervention. The Athenians also claim that this sole survivor did not in fact survive for long, but came to a

sticky end. Once he had made it back to Athens, he reported the calamity – and when the wives of the men who had gone on the expedition to Aegina learned of it, they were so appalled that he alone of the entire expedition had been spared that they surrounded the man, grabbed hold of him and stabbed him with the brooches they used to fasten their robes, each of them in turn asking him as they did so where their husband was. So he was dispatched – and not even the calamity on Aegina appeared as terrible a thing to the Athenians as did the action of these wives. At a loss how else to punish the women, they made them adopt an Ionian style of dress, in place of the Dorian fashions which the women of Athens had worn previously and which most closely resemble those of Corinth. As a result of this, the women no longer needed brooches in order to fasten their linen tunics.

[88] To tell the truth, however, this style of dress was not originally Ionian at all, but Carian, since the universal fashion among Greek women back in ancient times was identical to the style we now call Dorian. Some further consequences of the episode were that both the Argives and the Aeginetans passed a law that the pins of brooches in their respective countries be half as long again as the standard measurement, and that women visiting the shrine of the two goddesses make a particular point of dedicating their brooches. It was also laid down that no Attic pottery, and nothing else from Attica either, be taken into the shrine, and that in the future, by law, no one was to drink from any but locally sourced vessels. Even in my day, the women of Argos and Aegina wear brooches just as they have ever since the time of the quarrel with Athens – with lengthened pins.

[89] This, the episode I have just been describing, was where the feud between Athens and Aegina began. No wonder, then, that the Aeginetans, ever mindful of the business with the statues, should have answered the Theban summons with such relish, and leapt to the rescue of the Boeotians by laying waste the coastal regions of Attica. Then, just as the Athenians were deliberating whether to go on the offensive against them, there came this advice from the oracle at Delphi. 'Let thirty years go by,' it said, 'and then, thirty-one years after this act of criminality by the Aeginetans, go to war against them, and – so long as you have first consecrated a sanctuary to Aeacus – all your goals will be met. Go to war immediately, however, and over the course of the next thirty years you will undergo great sufferings, in addition to all your

achievements – although, at the end of this period, you will still emerge triumphant.' The Athenians, once they had listened to this message, did, it is true, consecrate a sanctuary to Aeacus (the one that is now to be found in the agora) – but when they heard mention of thirty years, they found the thought of waiting such a length of time quite insupportable, so appalling had been their sufferings at the hands of the Aeginetans.

[90] Even as they were plotting their revenge, however, a flare-up in their relations with the Lacedaemonians presented them with a stumbling block. The Lacedaemonians, you see, had found out about the conspiracy of the Alcmaeonids with the Pythia,[84] and the trick that the Pythia had played on them and the sons of Peisistratus, and were feeling doubly aggrieved: not only was it by their own doing that men who were friends and allies of theirs had been driven out of Attica, but the Athenians had never shown them so much as a hint of gratitude. What was more, they were motivated by prophecies warning them that the Athenians would be a source of great damage to them – prophecies of which the Lacedaemonians had previously been wholly ignorant, but with which now, because Cleomenes had brought them to Sparta, they were thoroughly familiar. He himself had obtained these prophecies from the shrine on the Acropolis in Athens, where the Peisistratids, who had been their original owners, had left them before heading into exile. It was Cleomenes who had picked them up after they had been discarded.[85]

[91] Additionally, at the same time as they came by these prophecies, the Lacedaemonians could track the growth of Athenian power, and see for themselves that the Athenians would never submit to their own leadership.[86] They had grasped a basic fact: that the people of Attica, once set free, would prove a match for the people of Lacedaemon, whereas having them under the thumb of a tyrant would enfeeble them, and keep them cringing before those in power. The Lacedaemonians therefore sent for Hippias, the son of Peisistratus, from Sigeium on the Hellespont [where the Peisistratids had gone into exile]. Once Hippias had answered this summons of theirs, the Spartiates convened representatives from all their other allies,[87] and addressed the assembled men. 'Friends,[88] a confession – our policy has taken a wrong turn. Under pressure from bogus oracles, we expelled from their homeland allies who were bound to us by exceptionally close ties of friendship – men who were committed to putting the Athenians under our control. Hav-

ing done that, we handed the city over to the masses, who were so unappreciative of the freedom they had obtained from us that, no sooner had they raised their faces from the dirt, they presumed, in their arrogance, to throw us out – us and our king as well. In fact, the more puffed up with pride they become, so the more their power grows – a lesson that their immediate neighbours, the Boeotians and the Chalcidians, have now fully absorbed, and which some others, if they are not very careful, will soon be learning too. So yes, we made a mistake – but now, with your assistance, we aim to try to make up for it. That is why we summoned Hippias here, and you from your various cities – to arrive at a consensus and to join forces, all of us. Hippias must be restored to Athens. We must give back what we took from him.'

[92] Now, this speech of the Spartiates did not go down at all well with the majority of their allies, who nevertheless bit their tongues – all apart from Socleës of Corinth, who spoke as follows:

'So the sky is to be placed below the earth, is it, and the earth to hover above the sky?' he demanded. 'Humans are to gain their livelihood in the sea, are they, and fish in the former haunts of mankind? I only ask because it is you, the Lacedaemonians, who are planning to deny people an equal share of power[89] in their own cities, and to foist tyrannical regimes upon them, when there is nothing more offensive to justice than a tyrant, not in all the affairs of man, nor anyone more steeped in blood! If you really think it such a good idea for cities to be ruled by tyrants, then why not set up a tyranny in your own before trying to establish them elsewhere? As it is, not only do you have no experience of tyrants here in Sparta, but you take the most stringent precautions to ensure that you never will. This is hardly playing fair by your allies! If you only had the experience of tyranny that we have had, the opinions you put forward on the matter might be better informed.

'Take, for instance, the ordering of political life in Corinth. It used to be an oligarchy, and the rulers of the city, a clan named the Bacchiadae, made sure to keep their marriageable daughters firmly in the family. Then one of their number, a man called Amphion, had a cripple for a daughter. The name of this girl was Labda. As none of the Bacchiadae was willing to marry her, she was taken instead by Eëtion, the son of Echecrates, who came from the settlement of Petra, but was descended ultimately from the Lapiths and the descendants of Caineus. Eëtion had no children, neither by his wife nor by anyone else, so he went off to

Delphi, to ask about having a child.[90] The moment he entered there, the Pythia accosted him with these verses:

"Honoured by no one, Eëtion, yet you are rich in honour.
Labda conceives – she bears a rolling boulder! Down it will fall
On those men who rule as monarchs, and set Corinth to rights."

Although delivered to Eëtion, this oracle was somehow reported back to the Bacchiadae, who previously had failed to make sense of an oracle that had come to Corinth, but which in fact had possessed the same meaning as the one given to Eëtion. What it had said was:

"Among the rocks, an eagle conceives, and will spawn a lion,
Mighty, ravening. Many a knee it will serve to loosen.
Heed this warning well, Corinthians, who around beauteous
Peirene are settled, and on the beetling brows of Corinth."

'When the Bacchiadae learned of the oracle given to Eëtion, they immediately realized that it had the same meaning as the earlier oracle, which previously they had found impossible to decipher. Despite having grasped this, however, they kept their peace – since it was their intention to dispose of Eëtion's child once Labda had come to term. Accordingly, as soon as his wife had given birth, they sent ten of their own number over to the village where Eëtion was living to kill the child. These men arrived in Petra, went into the courtyard of Eëtion's house and demanded the baby. Labda, who had no idea what their reason for coming was, and assuming that their request was prompted by their friendship for the father, brought the baby out and placed him in the hands of one of the visitors. Now, it had been agreed on their way there that the first one of them to get hold of the child would dash him to the ground. Providentially, though, even as Labda was carrying and handing him over, the child happened to smile up at the man who had taken hold of him; and when the man observed this smile, he felt such pity that he could not go through with the murder. Instead, affected by compassion, he handed the child over to a second man – who handed him over to a third. On he was passed, through the hands of all ten men – and not a single one of them could bring himself to commit the murder. So they handed the child back to his mother and went outside, where they stood by the gates and tore strips off one another, the particular object of scorn being the first man to have taken the child, since he was the one who had failed to do as had been decided. Then, after a while, they agreed that the best thing would be to go back inside, and share – all of them simultaneously – in the murder.

'Fate would have it that Corinth should derive much suffering from the child of Eëtion. Labda, you see, standing by the same gates as the men, overheard everything they said. Terrified that they would change their minds and kill the baby, were they to lay their hands on him a second time, she took him and hid him in the place which seemed to her the least likely to be discovered, a *cypselus*, or chest. She did this because she was certain that if the men did come back inside and look for the baby, they would turn the house upside down – as indeed duly happened. They barged in and made a thorough search – and when the baby failed to materialize, they decided that their best course of action would be to head back and tell the people who had sent them that all had been done just as instructed. And that, on their return, was precisely what they did say.

'Time went by, and Eëtion's son grew up; and because it was a chest that had kept him out of danger, he was given as a moniker the nickname of "Cypselus". Once he had reached adulthood, he consulted the oracle at Delphi – and, double-edged though the reply was, he placed sufficient trust in it to attack and take control of Corinth. The oracle had said:

> "Fortunate is this man who comes down into my dwelling,
> Cypselus, son of Eëtion, king of far-famed Corinth,
> He and his children both – but not the sons of his children."

Such was the oracle – and as for the kind of man Cypselus made as tyrant, well, he sent many of the Corinthians into exile, deprived many of their property and deprived an even larger number of their lives.

'He ruled for thirty years,[91] and the tapestry of his life was a rich one; he was succeeded as tyrant by Periander, his son. Now, initially, Periander was less brutal than his father, but after he had corresponded by means of a messenger with Thrasybulus, the tyrant of Miletus, he spilled even more blood than Cypselus had done. He dispatched a herald to Thrasybulus, you see, with this enquiry: what system of governance would best and most securely serve to establish his authority over Corinth? Thrasybulus led the man who had come from Periander out of the city and into a field in which there was grain growing; and as he walked through the corn, so he questioned the herald about his reason for coming from Corinth, nor ever ceased his cross-examination. And always, whenever he saw a stalk of grain standing taller than the rest, he would lop off its head and toss it aside, so that all the choicest and tallest stalks, dealt with in this manner, ended up in the dust. Right across the field he went; and then, without having proffered a single word of advice, dismissed the herald. The herald went back home to Corinth, where Periander was eager to learn what Thrasybulus might have recommended. "Nothing," the herald said. "Thrasybulus made no recommendation at all. It astounds me, in fact, that you ever sent me to visit such a man – a lunatic who has no care for what is his own." And then he described what he had seen Thrasybulus doing.

'The significance of these actions was hardly missed by Periander,[92] however – for what Thrasybulus had been recommending, he realized, was that he eliminate all the highest-ranking people in the city. Sure enough, from that moment on, his treatment of his fellow-citizens was marked by every kind of cruelty. Whatever murders Cypselus might have left uncommitted, whatever banishments he might have left unenforced, Periander now brought to fruition. One day, what is more – prompted by his wife, Melissa – he had all the women in Corinth stripped naked. Periander, you see, had sent messengers to Thesprotia, to the oracle of the dead on the River Acheron, to enquire after some money deposited by a friend; Melissa had then materialized and declared that she would neither reveal nor even hint at the location of the treasure. She was cold, she explained, and naked, since the clothes with which Periander had buried her, never having been burned, were of no use to her. "And as proof that I am speaking the truth," she said, "tell Periander this – he put his loaves into an icy oven." The veiled allusion contained in this message, when it was reported back to Periander, did indeed convince him of its truth – the reason being that he had slept with Melissa's corpse. As soon as he had received the message, he issued a proclamation to every woman in Corinth that she should leave her home for the shrine of Hera. The women, assuming that a festival was to be held, dressed up in their finest clothes; but Periander, who had secretly posted his own personal bodyguard at the temple, had them all stripped naked, free and slave women alike. Their clothing was then gathered up and burned in a pit, while Periander offered supplications to Melissa. Once this had been done, and following the dispatch of a second emissary, the shade of Melissa identified the place where his friend had stowed his deposit. So that, you see, Lacedaemonians, is the reality of tyranny.[93] That is how it functions. No wonder we in Corinth, the moment we realized that you were sending for Hippias, felt the utmost astonishment – and now, hearing this speech of yours, we are even more stupefied. We implore you, with the gods of Greece as our witnesses, do not establish tyrannies in our cities. And if you refuse to halt your policy, if you persist in your criminal attempt to restore Hippias? Well, then, you may be assured of this – you will not get the backing of the Corinthians for it!'

[93] Such was the speech delivered by Socleës, the ambassador from Corinth. Hippias, in his reply, invoked as his witnesses the same gods as Socleës, declaring that no one would regret the absence of the sons of Peisistratus more than the Corinthians, when the time came, as it inevitably would, for the Athenians to give them grief.[94] Hippias, in delivering this riposte, spoke as a man whose knowledge of oracles was unrivalled for its accuracy and breadth. But all the remaining allies, who had kept quiet until that moment, were inspired by the freedom with which they had heard Socleës express himself to erupt into yells of support for the Corinthian position, and to beg the Lacedaemonians not to introduce revolution to any Greek city.

[94] So the plan was aborted, and Hippias sent packing. Amyntas of Macedonia offered him Anthemous, and the Thessalians Iolcus; but Hippias opted for neither. Instead, he returned to Sigeium, which Peisistratus had wrested by force from the Mytilenaeans, and then, once he had it under his control, made over to Hegesistratus, a bastard of his by an Argive woman, to rule as tyrant. Hegesistratus, however, did not get to keep this endowment from Peisistratus without a fight. Indeed, the Mytilenaeans, basing themselves in the city of Achilleium, embroiled the Athenians of Sigeium in a protracted conflict. The Mytilenaeans demanded the return of their land – a claim which the Athenians refused to recognize. Instead, they made a great point of insisting that the Aeolians had no more right to a share of the lands of Ilium than they did – or indeed than any of the other Greeks who had joined with Menelaus in avenging the abduction of Helen.[95]

[95] The battles fought during this war contained any number of episodes. In one, for instance, an engagement which the Athenians were in the process of winning, Alcaeus[96] the poet took to his heels – but

although he managed to get away, his shield and armour were seized by the Athenians, and hung up in the temple of Athena in Sigeium. Alcaeus wrote a poem on this debacle, a report which he sent to a man in Mytilene, Melanippus, a comrade of his. It was Periander, the son of Cypselus, who finally made peace between the Mytilenaeans and the Athenians, after they had both turned to him for arbitration. By the terms of the settlement, land was allocated to those already in possession of it – which is how Sigeium came to be Athenian.

[96] Hippias, on his return to Asia from Lacedaemon, stirred up a great deal of trouble by telling damaging lies about the Athenians to Artaphrenes, and doing all he could to ensure that Athens would end up subject to himself and Darius. The Athenians, when they learned what Hippias was up to, sent a messenger to Sardis, forbidding the Persians from listening to the exiles from their city. Artaphrenes, however, delivered the messenger an ultimatum: take back Hippias, or face ruin. Such a message, when it was brought back to Athens, was not one to which the Athenians could consent – and so they delivered a snub to the Persians that amounted, in effect, to a declaration of war.

[97] And this was the very moment, with public opinion as it was, and relations with the Persians at their lowest ebb, that Aristagoras of Miletus, who had been deported from Sparta by Cleomenes[97] the Lacedaemonian, arrived in Athens. Always excepting Sparta, you see, there was no other city more powerful. Appearing before the popular assembly, Aristagoras rehashed the same things he had said in Sparta: about how rich Asia was, and how defeating the Persians, who invariably fought without shields or spears, was easy. On top of this, Aristagoras added that because Miletus was an Athenian colony, it was only right that the greatness of Athens be deployed in her defence. In fact, his need was so pressing that there was nothing he did not promise the Athenians – whom he duly convinced. (This seems to suggest – since the same tricks which had failed Aristagoras, one on one with Cleomenes, had won round thirty thousand Athenians – that a crowd is more easily fooled than a single man.[98]) Once their consent had been secured, the Athenians voted to send twenty ships to the assistance of the Ionians, and to appoint as their commander Melanthius, a man who enjoyed an excellent reputation among his fellow-citizens in all respects. Terrible evils would stem from these ships – both for the Greeks and for the Barbarians.[99]

[98] Aristagoras, meanwhile, had sailed on ahead and arrived in Miletus. There, he came up with a plan that promised the Ionians no advantage at all – nor did he intend it to, since his only aim in adopting it was to aggravate King Darius. He sent a man to Phrygia, to the Paeonians who had been deported there as prisoners-of-war by Megabazus,[100] and given land and a village of their own. 'Men of Paeonia,' said this man, after he had arrived there, 'I have been sent by Aristagoras, the tyrant of Miletus, to suggest how, if you will only be guided by him, you can be redeemed from this place. With the whole of Ionia now in revolt against the King, you have a real opportunity to return safely to your own land. Only get yourselves to the coast, and after that we will take full responsibility for you.' When the Paeonians heard this proposal they welcomed it with open arms; and even though some of them lacked the courage to make the attempt, most gathered together their wives and children, and slipped away to the coast. Then, once by the sea, they crossed over to Chios. Hot on their heels came a large band of Persian horsemen; and these, when they found that the Paeonians had already got across to Chios before they could be overtaken, sent a message to the fugitives, commanding them to return. The Paeonians, however, refused to do as ordered. From Chios, they were taken by the Chians to Lesbos, and the Lesbians then transported them to Doriscus. From there they continued by foot, and so arrived back in Paeonia.

[99] But to return to Aristagoras. When the Athenians docked with their twenty ships, they brought with them five Eretrian triremes, which had joined the expedition not in order to curry favour with Athens, but because of a debt of gratitude they owed the Milesians themselves. (Some time earlier, you see, the Milesians had helped them to shoulder the effort of the war against the Chalcidians – the same conflict in which the Chalcidians had been supported against the Eretrians and Milesians by the Samians.) Now, with their arrival, and with the other allies present too, Aristagoras launched an attack on Sardis – although he himself did not go on the campaign, but stayed behind in Miletus. Instead, he appointed two other men to lead the Milesians to war: his own brother, Charopinus, and another citizen of Miletus, Hermophantus.

[100] Off set the Ionians for Ephesus; and when they arrived there, they left their fleet behind in Ephesian territory, at Coresus, and headed inland in great force, making use of Ephesian guides. After tracking the course of the River Caÿster and crossing Mount Tmolus, they came to

Sardis, which they captured without any opposition. The entire city fell
to them – all except for the acropolis, where, under the personal command of Artaphrenes, a not insignificant squad of men maintained a
resistance.

[101] Despite their successful capture of the city, however, they were
prevented from plundering it. Most of the houses in Sardis were made
of reeds – and even those that were made of brick were thatched with
the same material. No sooner had a soldier torched one of them than
fire began to spread from house to house across the whole span of the
city. As Sardis blazed, and the entire circuit of her suburbs went up in
flames, so the Lydians and such Persians as happened to be there were
cut off, with no means of escape; and so they flooded towards the city
square, and the River Pactolus. (This is the river that brings gold-dust
down from Mount Tmolus – it flows right through the middle of the
square, then joins the River Hermus, and ultimately the sea.) It was by
the Pactolus, then, in the city square, that the Lydians and the Persians
congregated, with no choice but to put up a fight. When the Ionians saw
the stand which was being taken by their adversaries, however, and that
a great crowd of them were advancing to the attack, they retreated in
alarm to the mountain called Tmolus, and from there, under cover of
the night, made back for their ships.

[102] The conflagration that engulfed Sardis also consumed the sanctuary of the native goddess, Cybebe – and it was this that subsequently
provided the Persians with their pretext for the retaliatory burning of
the shrines in Greece.[101] Meanwhile, the Persians in the provinces west
of the River Halys, when informed of what had happened, mobilized
and came to the rescue of the Lydians. On arriving in Sardis, they found
the Ionians already gone; but the Persians followed their trail and
caught up with them at Ephesus. The Ionians took their positions, but
when they joined battle they were utterly routed. The casualties inflicted
by the Persians were extensive, and included, among other distinguished
names, Eualcides, the commander of the Eretrians, and a man much
celebrated by Simonides of Ceos[102] for the numerous crowns that he
had won as an athlete. The survivors of the battle all scattered to their
various cities.

[103] Such was the result of the clash. In its wake, the Athenians
abandoned the Ionian cause altogether, and refused point-blank repeated
appeals from Aristagoras for further assistance. Despite this loss of the

Athenians' backing, however, the sheer scale of what the Ionians had done to Darius was such that they continued to ready themselves for war against the King. They sailed to the Hellespont, where they brought Byzantium and all the other cities in the region[103] under their own control, and then, sailing back out of the Hellespont, secured the backing of most of Caria. Even Caunus, which before the burning of Sardis had been most reluctant to join them, now swelled the roster of their allies.

[104] The Cypriots too – all except the Amathousians – voluntarily joined up, since Cyprus was likewise in a state of revolt against the Medes. This was due to one Onesilus, who was the younger brother of Gorgus, the king of Salamis; he was also the son of Chersis, the son of Siromus, who was the son of Euelthon. This man, even before the Ionian revolt, had repeatedly urged Gorgus to rebel against the King; and now, when he was brought the news from Ionia, he did not hold back from pressing his case. Still, however, Gorgus would not be persuaded – and so Onesilus waited until his brother was absent one day from Salamis, and then, in company with his fellow-partisans, barred the gates against him. Gorgus, deprived of his city, fled to the Medes, while Onesilus took over the rule of Salamis, and set himself to persuading all the other Cypriots[104] to join him in his rebellion. In the event, only the Amathousians spurned these exhortations of his – so he settled down to besiege them.

[105] Now, even as Onesilus was putting Amathous under siege, tidings had been brought to King Darius of the capture and torching of Sardis by the Athenians and Ionians, and of how the chief conspirator – the spider at the centre of the web – was the Milesian, Aristagoras. It is said that the King's initial response to this news was to dismiss the Ionians as being of no account, since he knew full well that they had no prospect of escaping retribution for their insurgency. But the Athenians he *did* ask after; and on being told who they were, he asked for his bow, and when he had it, he fitted an arrow, which he then fired into the heavens. And even as he sent it winging through the air, so he cried, 'Zeus, do not deny me the chance to punish the Athenians!' Having made this appeal, he ordered one of his servants to repeat to him three times, whenever a meal was set before him, 'Master, remember the Athenians.'

[106] After he had given these instructions, he summoned into his presence Histiaeus of Miletus,[105] who by this stage had been detained at

Darius' pleasure a very long time indeed. 'Histiaeus,' he said, 'I have been informed that the man to whom you chose to depute the rule of Miletus has been engaging in insurrectionary activities against me. Not only were the Ionians – who will be made to recompense me for all their actions! – joined by men that he recruited from the mainland opposite, but he then induced the whole gang of them to follow him in robbing me of Sardis. Now, does that strike you as a welcome development? And how exactly, without your scheming, could anything on such a scale ever have happened? You should watch yourself very carefully, if you do not want to catch the blame for it.' But to this Histiaeus said, 'O my King, my King! How could you possibly say such things? I would never plot anything against you – let alone aim to do you serious damage! What conceivable motive would I have for embarking on such a project? Is it as though I want for anything? All that you have is mine. Indeed, so highly do you regard me that I am privy to your innermost counsels. If my deputy has indeed behaved in the manner you suggest, then you may rest assured that he did it on his own account. As it is, I do not myself give any credence to this story that the Milesians and my deputy have rebelled against you. But even if they have done something along those lines, and what you have heard, O King, is actually the truth, then it would only serve to demonstrate what the outcome of your uprooting me from the seaboard has been. It does seem, after all, that what the Ionians have done is to take advantage of being out of my sight to embark on a long-cherished course of action. Had I only been in Ionia, not a single city would have stirred! That being so, you should let me set off now, as fast as possible, back to Ionia. Then I can restore things to the state they were before, and make sure that this schemer I left behind in charge of Miletus ends up in your hands. Whatever you have in mind, I will do it – and then, once I have done it, I vow by the gods who protect the royal house that I will not remove this tunic, which I shall be wearing for the whole length of my trip to Ionia, until I have brought Sardinia, that largest of all islands, to pay you tribute.'

[107] Now, economical with the truth though this speech of Histiaeus' certainly was, it swayed Darius, who let him go. 'And when you have fulfilled all your promises,' Histiaeus was instructed, 'you are to return to Susa.'

*

[108] Parallel to all this – the royal receipt of the news about Sardis, Darius and the business with the bow, his interrogation and release of Histiaeus, and the journeying of Histiaeus to the coast – other things were happening too. As Onesilus of Salamis was laying siege to the Amathousians, for instance, a report reached him that a man called Artybius, a Persian, was expected in Cyprus at the head of an immense seaborne army. This news prompted Onesilus to send heralds all over Ionia with requests for help. The Ionians, after minimal debate on the matter, duly arrived with a substantial force; and this force was present in Cyprus by the time that the Persians made the crossing from Cilicia by ship, and then advanced on Salamis by foot. Simultaneously, the Phoenicians and their fleet were rounding the headland which goes by the name of 'The Keys of Cyprus'.

[109] These were the developments that prompted the tyrants of Cyprus to convene a meeting with the Ionian commanders and say to them, 'Men of Ionia, we Cypriots are going to give you your choice of opponent – either the Persians or the Phoenicians. Should you wish to take up position on land and make a trial of strength with the Persians, then now is the time for you to leave your fleet and form up your infantry, while we get into your ships and grapple with the Phoenicians. Or would you rather that it was you who test the Phoenicians? Whichever course of action you choose, there is only one obligation: to do the best you can to set Ionia and Cyprus free!' To this, the Ionians answered, 'The whole of Ionia, as one, was agreed on our mission. We are here to guard the sea-lanes, not to hand over our ships to Cypriots and fight the Persians on land. So we will make the stand that we were told to make – and to the best of our abilities. As for you, keep alive your memories of all that you suffered as slaves of the Medes. Prove yourselves men of steel!'

[110] Such was the Ionian response. In due course, when the Persians came to the plain of Salamis, the Cypriot kings lined up their forces, with their crack troops – the men of Salamis and Soli – taking up the key position opposite the Persians themselves, and all the other Cypriots facing the remainder of the Persian army. Onesilus deliberately stationed himself opposite Artybius, the Persian general.

[111] Now, Artybius rode a horse that had been trained to rear up at heavy infantry. When Onesilus was informed of this, he consulted his shield-bearer, who was a Carian by birth and brimming with a courage

that was nevertheless only one aspect of his formidable reputation as a warrior. 'I have discovered', Onesilus said, 'that Artybius has a horse which rears up and uses its hooves and teeth to kill anyone it attacks. So weigh your options. Come now, speak! Who do you want to track and make an attack upon – the horse or Artybius himself?' 'My Lord,' the attendant answered, 'I am ready to do both or either – or anything else you command. That said, however, let me explain how I think your interests would best be served. A king and general, I would argue, should only engage with his opposite number. Fell a general, after all, and it will redound greatly to your credit. Alternatively, should *he* kill *you* – which the gods forbid! – then death at the hands of a worthy enemy would rank as only half the calamity it would otherwise be. By the same token, it is for us subordinates to attack other subordinates – even when that subordinate is a horse. So there is no need to worry about the various stunts it can pull. It will not rear up in the face of any man ever again – of that I can assure you!'

[112] No sooner had this conversation been had than the rival camps joined battle, by both land and sea. By sea, it was the Ionians – with the Samians particularly distinguishing themselves – who emerged victorious, and won the day against the Phoenicians. Meanwhile, on land, when the advancing armies crashed into one another, they embroiled the rival commanders in the battle. What happened was that when Artybius galloped up to attack him, Onesilus followed the plan he had agreed with his shield-bearer, and met the attack by striking at Artybius himself. As the horse brought its hooves down onto Onesilus' shield, the Carian slashed at them with a bill-hook, and sliced the horse's hooves right off. Down went the horse – and down with it went Artybius, the Persian general, right there on the spot.

[113] Even as the battle was raging on other fronts, Stesenor, the tyrant of Curium, who had no small number of men by his side, gave up on the fight. (The Curians are said originally to have been colonists from Argos.) No sooner had the Curians deserted than the war-charioteers from Salamis did the same, with the result that it was the Persians who emerged victorious. As the Cypriots turned and fled, they suffered heavy casualties. Among these was Onesilus, the son of Chersis, the very man who had instigated the Cypriot revolt, and Aristocyprus, the king of Soli, and the son of Philocyprus. (This Philocyprus was the tyrant

praised above all others in the poem composed by Solon[106] when the Athenian visited Cyprus.)

[114] To pay Onesilus back for besieging them, the Amathousians cut off his head and took it to Amathous, where they hung it over the city gates. Thus suspended, the head ended up hollowed out and was infested by a swarm of bees, which filled it with honeycombs. When the Amathousians asked an oracle what the significance of this unusual happening might be, they were advised to take the head down and bury it, and offer sacrifices every year to Onesilus as a hero – and that if they did this, their fortunes would enjoy a recovery. The cult of Onesilus was duly maintained – and has been right up to my day.

[115] News was brought to the Ionians who had fought the sea-battle off Cyprus that the affairs of Onesilus had come to utter ruin, and that the cities of Cyprus were under siege – all of them, that was, apart from Salamis, which the city's inhabitants had surrendered to Gorgus, its one-time king. This information prompted the Ionians to sail back immediately to Ionia. The city which held out the longest against its besiegers was Soli: only after four months did the Persians finally manage to tunnel their way under its ring of walls and make it theirs.

[116] So it was, a year after winning their freedom, that the Cypriots were reduced once again to servitude. Meanwhile, Daurises, Hymaeës and Otanes, three Persian generals who were all married to daughters of Darius, pursued the Ionians who had made the attack on Sardis, defeated them in open battle and then harried them into their ships – after which the three generals divided the various cities among themselves, and set to sacking them.

[117] Daurises made for the Hellespont, where he captured the cities of Dardanus, Abydus, Percote, Lampsacus and Paesus. Each city took him a single day to capture. As he was heading on from Paesus for Parium, he received news that the Carians had made common cause with the Ionians, and rebelled against the Persians. So he turned his back on the Hellespont, and made with his army for Caria.

[118] By some means or other, however, news of his approach preceded him to Caria. The Carians assembled at a spot called the White Pillars, on the Marsyas, a river which rises in the region of Idrias, and is a tributary of the Maeander. Once the Carians had all congregated there, they debated what to do, with the best of the many opinions expressed

being, in my view,[107] that of a man from Cindye called Pixodarus, the son of Mausolus and the son-in-law of Syennesis, the king of Cilicia. The essence of this man's suggestion was that the Carians should cross the Maeander and then fight with the river at their backs, so that they would have no line of retreat, and no option but to stand their ground – which would serve to stiffen their natural backbone. This opinion failed to find favour, however, and it was decided instead that if anyone had the Maeander at their backs, it should be the Persians – the reasoning obviously being that, if the Persians were to be defeated in battle and put to flight, they would all plunge into the river and never make it back to safety.

[119] In the event, however, once the Persians had arrived on the scene, they crossed over the Maeander and were met by the Carians on the banks of the Marsyas. The battle fought there was long and fierce – but in the end sheer weight of Persian numbers told. The Persians lost some two thousand men and the Carians some ten thousand. Those Carians who managed to escape ended up cornered at Labraunda, in the shrine of Zeus the Lord of Battles, which consists of a large and numinous grove of plane trees. (So far as we are aware, the Carians are the only people who offer up sacrifices to Zeus the Lord of Battles.) Thus trapped, the survivors debated among themselves what would constitute their best chance of safety: surrender to the Persians, or a complete evacuation from Asia.

[120] Even as they were having this debate, however, the Milesians and their allies came to their assistance – whereupon the Carians abandoned all their previous deliberations and readied themselves to start the war afresh. Although the Carians duly met the Persian advance on the battlefield, they suffered a defeat even more calamitous than the previous one had been. All their contingents suffered heavy casualties – and the Milesians the heaviest of the lot.

[121] Notwithstanding this trauma,[108] though, the Carians picked themselves up, and in due course returned to the fight. Informed that the Persians were setting out to attack their cities, they laid an ambush on the road at Pedasa – and the Persians, when they blundered into it by night, were annihilated. Among the casualties were the three men in command: Daurises, Amorges and Sisimaces. Myrsus, the son of Gyges, also fell. The leader of the ambush was Heracleides, the son of Ibanollis, a man from Mylasa.[109] So that was the end of that particular Persian army.

[122] Meanwhile, another of those engaged in tracking down the

Ionians who had attacked Sardis, Hymaeës, had headed for the Propontis, where he took the Mysian city of Cius. In the wake of its fall, however, he was informed that Daurises had left the Hellespont and was marching on Caria; so he withdrew from the Propontis and led his army to the Hellespont. There, he conquered all the Aeolians who lived in the region of Ilium, and also the Gergithians, who are remnants of the ancient Teucrians. Hymaeës himself, however, while engaged in the conquest of these peoples, fell sick and died in the Troad.

[123] So that was the end of him. Artaphrenes, the governor of Sardis, and Otanes, the third member of the high command, were then given orders to march on Ionia and the adjoining stretch of Aeolis. In Ionia they took Clazomenae, and in Aeolis, Cyme.

[124] The spectacle of these cites being captured, not to mention the seeming impossibility of ever defeating King Darius, led Aristagoras of Miletus, the man who had thrown the whole of Ionia into chaos and set any number of great events in train, to contemplate flight – proof enough that his courage was hardly of the highest order. Accordingly, he summoned his henchmen to a council of war, and declared that their best option would be to prepare a bolt-hole for themselves, in case they should be thrown out of Miletus. But where? Should they build a colony in Sardinia, or should he perhaps lead them to Myrcinus, the town in Edonia that Histiaeus had been fortifying after receiving it as a gift from Darius?[110] Such were the questions put by Aristagoras.

[125] To which of the two destinations should an expedition be dispatched? To neither, argued the story-teller Hecataeus,[111] the son of Hegesander, who was inclined instead to build a stronghold on the island of Leros, and lie low there, in the event of being driven out of Miletus. 'Make Leros your base,' he said, 'and you will be well placed for a return in due course to Miletus.'

[126] Despite this advice from Hecataeus, though, Aristagoras felt that the best option was to make for Myrcinus. Miletus he left in the hands of Pythagoras, an eminent man of the city, while he himself set sail for Thrace, with all the volunteers he could recruit, took possession of the area that was the object of his expedition and set up his base there. His army, however, and Aristagoras himself with it, was wiped out by the Thracians while it was camped out in front of one of their cities – although the Thracians inside the city had been perfectly willing to leave it under truce.

BOOK SIX

[1] So perished Aristagoras, the man behind the Ionian revolt. Mean-while, Histiaeus, the tyrant of Miletus – now that he had been released from Susa by Darius – had turned up in Sardis, and was quizzed by Artaphrenes, the governor of Sardis, as to why he thought the Ionians might have rebelled. Histiaeus professed complete ignorance of every-thing that had been going on – indeed, he claimed that the current state of affairs left him absolutely flabbergasted. Artaphrenes, however, saw through all the Milesian's schemes, and knew full well what really lay behind the revolt. 'Let me tell you the truth of the matter, Histiaeus,' he said. 'Aristagoras merely wore the sandal. The one who stitched it was you.'

[2] This allusion by Artaphrenes to the revolt caused Histiaeus to fear that he had been discovered; and so that very night, the moment it was dark, he slipped away to the coast. He had certainly pulled the wool over Darius' eyes: despite his promise to conquer Sardinia, that largest of islands,[1] for the King, his aim had always been to worm his way to the leadership of the Ionians in their war against Darius. He crossed over to Chios – but the Chians, under the mistaken impression that he was acting as an agent for Darius by fomenting revolution, put him in chains. When they learned the full story, however, and realized that he was an enemy of the King, they let him go.

[3] It was then that the Ionians demanded to know from Histiaeus why he had urged Aristagoras so enthusiastically to revolt against the King – and thereby wrought such havoc across Ionia. Histiaeus, rather than confess the real reason, told them instead that King Darius was planning to uproot the Phoenicians and resettle them in Ionia, and to settle the Ionians in Phoenicia,[2] and that this was why he had given the

389

instructions he did to Aristagoras. In truth, of course, the King had been planning nothing of the kind – but Histiaeus wished to make the flesh of the Ionians creep.

[4] After this, he employed a man from Atarneus called Hermippus as a go-between, and dispatched him to Sardis with missives[3] addressed to various Persians with whom he had already discussed rebellion. Hermippus, however, rather than deliver these letters to their addressees, went instead and put them straight into the hands of Artaphrenes. The governor, apprised now of the entire affair, ordered Hermippus to take the letters sent by Histiaeus and deliver them to everyone on the list of recipients; but then, once he had the replies addressed to Histiaeus, he was to deliver them to himself in person. So the conspiracy was brought to light – whereupon Artaphrenes put a large number of Persians to death.

[5] Histiaeus, with his plans for Sardis thereby confounded, and all his hopes frustrated, successfully requested the Chians to try to engineer his return to Miletus. But the Milesians, delighted to be free of Aristagoras, and relishing the taste of liberty this had given them, were not at all keen to welcome back yet another tyrant to their country. So it was that Histiaeus made his attempt at a restoration to Miletus by night, and backed up by force, only to be wounded in the thigh by one of the Milesians. Thus rebuffed by his own city, he returned to Chios, where he tried to persuade the Chians to give him ships – but in vain. From Chios, then, he crossed over to Mytilene, and here he did persuade some Lesbians to give him a fleet. They manned eight triremes and sailed off with Histiaeus to Byzantium, where they set up base and preyed on ships sailing out of the Euxine Sea. Only if their crews declared themselves ready to submit to Histiaeus were they spared.

[6] Meanwhile, with Histiaeus and the Mytilenaeans thus occupied, the descent of a vast army and fleet upon Miletus was hourly expected. This was because the Persian high command, who reckoned the other cities to be of much less significance, had pooled their resources so as to make a single force, and were advancing fast with it against Miletus. Among the various naval contingents, it was the Phoenicians who were particularly eager; but they were joined as well by recently subjugated Cypriots, Cilicians and Egyptians.

[7] The Ionians, when they learned of the attack being launched against Miletus and the rest of Ionia, sent ambassadors to speak on

their behalf at the Panionium. Once the delegates had arrived there and debated the situation, it was decided that, rather than raise an army to confront the Persians, the best option would be to leave the Milesians themselves to defend the walls of the city – thereby enabling the Ionian fleet to have a full complement of men. At the earliest opportunity, every last ship was to sail with all hands to an assembly point on a small island called Lade, just off the city of Miletus, there to make a stand in defence of Miletus.[4]

[8] So it was, in due course, that a fully crewed Ionian fleet came to be at Lade, together with one contingent of Aeolians from Lesbos. Their order of battle was as follows. On its easternmost wing were eighty ships furnished by the Milesians themselves; next to these, the Prieneans with twelve ships, and then the men of Myous, with three; beside the Myesians were the Teians with seventeen ships, and next to the Teians the Chians, who had a hundred. The position next to them was held by the Erythraeans, who had come with eight ships, and the Phocaeans, who had a contingent of three ships. Beyond the Phocaeans were the Lesbians, who had seventy ships. Finally, positioned on the westernmost wing, were the Samians, with sixty ships. The combined total of these various contingents came to three hundred and fifty-three triremes in all.[5]

[9] Such was the Ionian roster – but that of the Barbarians amounted to six hundred ships. When these too had arrived in Milesian waters, and the entire expeditionary force had taken up position by land as well as at sea, the Persian high command, realizing just how many ships the Ionians possessed, despaired of their prospects of victory; they were terrified that without command of the sea they would not be able to take Miletus, and that terrible punishments would then be inflicted upon them by Darius. With this in mind, they summoned to a meeting the various Ionian tyrants who, toppled from power by Aristagoras of Miletus,[6] had fled to the Medes and opportunistically joined the expedition against Miletus. 'Men of Ionia,' the Persian generals told them, 'now is your chance, every one of you, to stand up and do well by the Royal House. You are each of you to try to detach your fellow-citizens from the main body of the alliance. Press on them the assurance that they can be spared the consequences of their revolt, that their shrines and private property need not be put to the torch and that they do not have to suffer any worse repression than before. Should they refuse to change

their stance, however, and absolutely insist on fighting us, then you are to lay out the full horrors of the servitude that will descend upon them once they have been defeated – for we shall castrate their sons, cart their virgin daughters off to Bactra and make a gift of their lands to others.'

[10] These words prompted each of the Ionian tyrants to pass on the message under cover of darkness to their respective countrymen. Those Ionians who received the communication continued as stubborn as before, though. Each contingent assumed that they and they alone were being contacted by the Persians, and refused to countenance a betrayal of their allies. That, then, is what transpired immediately after the arrival of the Persians before Miletus.

[11] Subsequently, the Ionians who had assembled at Lade held public meetings, at which, among all the many other speakers who no doubt addressed them, one in particular stood out: the Phocaean general, Dionysius.[7] 'Men of Ionia,' he said, 'our fortunes are balanced upon a razor's edge. Are we to be free, or are we to be slaves – and to be treated as runaway slaves at that? If you are prepared in the short term to knuckle down to really tough exercise,[8] it will be gruelling, yes – but it will also enable you to prevail over your opponents and be free. But if you just lounge around without any discipline, there will be no hope whatsoever of escaping the penalty for your rebellion against the King. So do as I say. Put yourselves into my hands. Should the gods only play fair by us, I give you this assurance – that the enemy will either back off from engaging with us altogether, or else, if they do give us battle, will be heavily defeated.'

[12] Once the Ionians had given Dionysius a hearing, they put themselves into his hands. Every morning, he would lead them out on manoeuvres, with the fleet arrayed by column and the marines in full armour, and would set the rowers driving their ships through a line formed of other ships, and exiting the far side of it.[9] Then, for the rest of the day, he would keep the fleet riding at anchor. Thus he kept the Ionians hard at work throughout the day. For seven days the Ionians obeyed him and did as they were ordered; but on the eighth day, unaccustomed to such strenuous activity, and prostrated by their exertions and by the heat of the sun, they began to mutter among themselves. 'We have had our fill of this. Did we tread on the toes of some god, or were we deluded and quite out of our minds, that we put ourselves into the hands of a Phocaean braggart – a man who provided a paltry three

ships? All this maltreatment, now that he has got us into his clutches, will leave us irremediably debilitated. Many of us are already ill. Many more will fall sick in due course. Surely, there are no evils so terrible that they could be worse than those we suffer now? Better to take our chances with the slavery that is to come than be yoked together in the servitude that is our current lot. So come on – for as long as we remain here, let us refuse to do as he says!' And sure enough, no sooner had these words been spoken than there was not a man still willing to obey Dionysius. Instead, as though it were a battle by land that they were facing, they pitched their tents on the island, kept in the shade and refused to board their ships – let alone practise their manoeuvres.

[13] News of what the Ionians were up to reached the Samian admirals when they were already in receipt of messages sent to them by Aeaces, the son of Syloson, in obedience to the Persians, urging them to abandon the Ionian alliance; and now, observing the terrible lack of discipline among the Ionians, they accepted Aeaces' proposals.[10] At the same time, it had become all too obvious to them that there could be no vanquishing the forces available to the King – not when, as they knew full well, even the annihilation of the fleet that lay before them would merely prompt the arrival of another, five times the size. So it was that the Ionian refusal to train provided the Samians with their perfect excuse – and an opportunity, what is more, to ensure the survival of their own shrines and property. This Aeaces, the man from whom they had received the proposition, was the son of Syloson, who was in turn the son of Aeaces – and he had ruled Samos as its tyrant until he was toppled from power by Aristagoras of Miletus, along with all the other Ionian tyrants.[11]

[14] In due course, the Phoenicians began to sail out. The Ionians launched their own ships and advanced in a single column. The two sides closed – and then met. I find it impossible, however, to record with any certainty which of the Ionians proved themselves to be cowards and which to be men of quality[12] in the sea-battle that ensued, for all of them subsequently blamed each other. It is alleged that the Samians, in accordance with what had been agreed with Aeaces, hoisted their sails, deserted their station and made for Samos – all except for eleven ships. The captains of these triremes refused to obey their admirals, but instead stayed where they were and took part in the battle. It was in recognition of this feat that the Samian state granted them the honour of having their

names and patronymics inscribed on a pillar, on the grounds of their outstanding merit. (This same pillar still stands in the market-place there to this day.)[13] The Lesbians, when they saw the ships stationed next to them turning tail, followed the Samian example too – as indeed did most of the Ionians.

[15] Of those who stayed and fought, it was the Chians who performed the most distinguished deeds, and who, because they refused to play the coward, suffered the heaviest losses. Their contingent, as I mentioned earlier, consisted of a hundred ships – and on each of these ships, serving as marines, they had forty men, hand-picked from the ranks of their own citizens. The spectacle of most of their allies giving up on the battle only steeled the Chians not to sink to a similarly contemptible level; abandoned by all but a few of their allies, they repeatedly smashed their way through the enemy line, fighting on and capturing a large number of enemy ships, until most of their own had been lost. Only then did those Chian ships still remaining retreat home.

[16] The Chians whose ships were so badly damaged that they were no longer seaworthy beat a retreat, with the enemy in hot pursuit, to Mycale. There they beached and abandoned their ships, and set out on foot across the mainland. In the course of their journey, the Chians blundered by night into the territory of the Ephesians, their arrival coinciding with the celebration there of the Thesmophoria by the Ephesian women. The Ephesians, who had heard nothing beforehand of how things were going for the Chians, saw only an army that had come crashing onto their land, and jumped to the conclusion that it was a band of robbers looking to steal their women. So out they came to the rescue, every last man of them, and massacred the intruders. Such was the cruel fate that befell the Chians.

[17] Meanwhile, Dionysius of Phocaea, when he realized that the Ionian cause was lost, seized three ships from the enemy and sailed away – although not to Phocaea, which he knew full well was bound to share the servitude of the rest of Ionia. Instead, just as he was, he set sail directly for Phoenicia, where he made a fortune by looting and sinking merchant-shipping, before sailing on to Sicily, and setting himself up there as a pirate, preying on the Carthaginians and Etruscans[14] – but never on any Greeks.

[18] Once the Persians had secured their victory over the Ionian fleet, they invested Miletus both by land and by sea – and by digging mines

under the walls, and by deploying all kinds of siege-engines,[15] they succeeded in capturing the city, acropolis and everything, five years after the
revolt of Aristagoras. The city was reduced to slavery; and in the agony of
Miletus was confirmation of an oracle foretelling what her fate was to be.

[19] The Argives, you see, had once consulted the oracle at Delphi
concerning the security of their city, and had received an answer germane
to others – for, although part of it did indeed relate to the Argives, the
god had appended verses that related to the Milesians. I will discuss the
section concerning the Argives in due course,[16] when I reach the relevant
stage in my narrative; but this – even though they were not present when
the oracle was given! – is what was foretold concerning the Milesians:

> 'Miletus, you deviser of evil deeds, the moment comes
> When whole swarms will batten onto you – a bright prize you
>   shall be.
> A great host of long-haired men will have their feet washed by
>   your wives,
> And others will have the tending of my temple at Didyma.'

And now was the moment when these very things befell the Milesians:
most of the men were slaughtered by the Persians, who did indeed have
long hair;[17] their women and children were reduced to slavery; and the
sanctuary at Didyma – temple and oracular shrine alike – was plundered and put to the torch. (The sheer quantity of valuables in this same
sanctuary is something I have frequently mentioned elsewhere in my
narrative.)[18]

[20] The survivors among the Milesians were led away to Susa. King
Darius did them no further harm, but settled them on the so-called 'Red
Sea', in the city of Ampe, at the point on the River Tigris where it flows
into the sea. Of the actual territory of Miletus, the Persians kept the
stretches around the city for themselves, together with the plain, but
gave the upland reaches to the Carians of Pedasa.

[21] But despite all that the Milesians had suffered at the hands of the
Persians, the people of Sybaris, who were living in Laüs and Scidrus following the theft of their city, failed to pay back the debt of grief that
they owed. When Sybaris was captured by the Crotoniates,[19] you see,
the Milesians, from young to old, had all shaved their heads and put
on the deepest mourning, reflecting the fact that no other cities known
to us had a closer relationship than did these two. The response of the

Athenians, though, was very different. At Miletus' fall they made their grief apparent in many different ways – most notably when Phrynichus wrote and produced a play called *The Fall of Miletus*. So close to home were the evils about which he reminded them that the entire audience fell to weeping and fined the writer 1,000 drachmas. They banned the play from ever being staged again.[20]

[22] So not a Milesian was left in Miletus. Meanwhile, among the Samians, the men of property were less than delighted at the policy that had been adopted by their high command towards the Mede – and these, in the immediate wake of the sea-battle, resolved after due debate not to stay as the slaves of the Persians and the tyrant Aeaces, but rather to sail away before Aeaces could set foot in their country, and to found a colony. By coincidence, you see, the people of Zancle in Sicily had been in constant communication with Ionia, urging the Ionians to come to Fair Shore, where it was their ambition to found a city, and settle it with Ionians. (The beautiful stretch of coast that goes by this name is inhabited by Sicilians,[21] and is in the part of Sicily that faces Tyrrhenia.) So of all the Ionians who had received the invitation, the only ones to take it up were the Samians – together with some refugees from Miletus.

[23] The upshot of their expedition was something like this. The Samians, in the course of their journey to Sicily, came to be in the land of the Epizephyrian Locrians, even as the Zanclaeans themselves – under their king, who went by the name of Scythes – were camped out before a Sicilian city that they were looking to capture. When these circumstances were brought to the attention of Anaxileos, the tyrant of Rhegium, who at the time was at odds with the Zanclaeans, he made contact with the Samians and persuaded them to put Fair Shore, the original object of their voyage, quite from their minds, and to take possession instead of Zancle, since it was then empty of men. The Samians, duly persuaded, seized hold of Zancle – whereupon the Zanclaeans, informed that their city was in enemy hands, hurried back to its rescue. They also appealed to Hippocrates, the tyrant of Gela, on the grounds that he was an ally of theirs. But Hippocrates, when he came with his army to the assistance of the Zanclaeans, first of all put Scythes, their king, into chains, as punishment for the loss of the city, and then chained up his brother, Pythogenes, as well, and packed them both off to the city of Inyx. Then, entering into negotiations with the Samians, he swapped oaths of friendship, and so betrayed all the other Zanclaeans too. His

reward for this, as confirmed by the Samians, was one half of whatever movables and slaves he could seize within the city itself, together with everything out in the fields – all of which was to count as his share. Hippocrates included on the register of slaves most of the Zanclaeans, whom he duly put into chains – but three hundred citizens, the most prominent, he handed over to the Samians to be butchered. The Samians, though, did not slaughter them.

[24] Scythes, the king of the Zanclaeans, ran away from Inyx to Himera, from where he made his way to Asia, and onwards, inland to King Darius. Darius rated Scythes, of all the various refugees from Greece who came to his court, the most highly as a man of honour. The reason for this was that, although Scythes obtained royal permission to return to Sicily, he then came back from there to the King, and eventually met his end in Persia, ripe in years and blessed with great riches. So it was that the Samians escaped the yoke of the Medes, and without so much as having to raise a finger won for themselves the incomparably beautiful city of Zancle.

[25] Once the sea-battle for Miletus was over, the Persians ordered the Phoenicians to restore Aeaces, the son of Syloson, to Samos, as reward for the great services he had done them, and which had proved so invaluable. Because their ships had deserted the battle at sea, the Samians were alone among those peoples who had revolted against Darius in not having either their city or their sanctuaries put to the torch. No sooner had Miletus fallen than the Persians also seized control of Caria, where some cities submitted of their own accord, while others had to be secured by force of arms.

[26] Such was the course of events – news of which was brought to Histiaeus of Miletus in Byzantium, where he was still busy impounding Ionian merchant vessels as they sailed out of the Euxine. The fate of Miletus, however, prompted him to delegate his activities in the Hellespont to Bisaltes, who came from Abydus, and was the son of Apollophanes, while Histiaeus himself sailed with his Lesbians to Chios. There, when a garrison of Chians refused him passage, he met them in battle at a place on the island called 'the Hollows', and inflicted terrible casualties on them. Then, with the backing of his Lesbians, he conquered the remainder of the Chian population, which was still reeling from the after-effects of the battle they had fought at sea, and established his base on Chios, at Polichne.

[27] There is a kind of providence in the affairs of a city, or a people, that is much given to issuing warnings whenever terrible evils threaten – and just such a portent had been delivered to the Chians prior to these events. For instance, they had sent to Delphi a chorus[22] of a hundred young men, of whom a full ninety-eight had then succumbed to a plague and been carried off by it, so that only two had ever made their way home. Again, back in Chios itself, at much the same time, shortly before the sea-battle was fought, the roof had fallen in on a class of one hundred and twenty children as they were learning their letters[23], and only one of the hundred and twenty had been able to escape. It was after the Chians had been given these divine signs that their overwhelming defeat in the sea-battle brought their city to its knees. Then, on top of their losses at sea, came Histiaeus at the head of his Lesbians. No wonder, bloodied as the Chians were, that he should have made an easy conquest of them.

[28] From Chios, Histiaeus then led a sizeable force of Ionians and Aeolians on campaign against Thasos. While he was laying siege to Thasos, however, news reached him that the Phoenicians were sailing north from Miletus against the rest of Ionia. This information prompted him to leave Thasos unsacked, and lead his entire force with all speed to Lesbos. From there, since his army had nothing to eat on Lesbos, he crossed to the mainland with the aim of harvesting the grain in Atarneus, and that belonging to the Mysians in the floodplain of the Caïcus. It so happened, though, that a Persian named Harpagus, a man not lacking military resources, was stationed in this same region, and as Histiaeus was disembarking, Harpagus attacked him, wiped out most of his army and took Histiaeus alive.

[29] How did the capture of Histiaeus come about? Well, the battle between the Greeks and the Persians which took place at Malene, in the territory of Atarneus, was a close- and long-fought one, until the Persian cavalry, which had hitherto been kept in reserve, charged and fell upon the Greeks – an action that proved decisive. Even as the Greeks were being routed, however, Histiaeus remained confident that his continuing offence against the King would not prove a capital one; and so it was, because he loved life, that he snatched after it still. As he was making his escape, a Persian overtook him; this man, as he rode the fugitive down, was on the verge of running him through, when Histiaeus cried out in Persian, and revealed his identity: 'I am Histiaeus of Miletus!'

[30] Now, had his captors, as they escorted him away, only led him to Darius, the King would surely have forgiven him his fault – and so he would not, in my opinion, have come to any harm. It was for precisely this reason, however, and to block off any prospect of his wriggling free and becoming a man of position under the King once again, that Artaphrenes, the governor of Sardis, and Harpagus, his captor, had him brought to Sardis; and then, once he had been delivered, they impaled him on the spot, and had his embalmed head forwarded to King Darius in Susa. When Darius found out what they had done, he berated them soundly for not having brought Histiaeus to him alive; not only that, but he had the head of Histiaeus washed and carefully wrapped, and then buried with the honour due to one who had done both Darius himself and the Persians great service. Such, then, was the fate of Histiaeus.

[31] The following year, after wintering in the neighbourhood of Miletus, the Persian war-fleet put to sea again, and made an easy capture of the islands that lie off the mainland: Chios, Lesbos and Tenedos. Every time the Barbarians took an island, they would mark its capture by trawling it for human prey; this they would do by getting men to join hands so that they formed a line extending from the northern to the southern coast of the island, and then traverse its entire extent, sweeping people up in their net. They also captured cities on the mainland of Ionia with a similar ease – except that here, because it was not practicable to drag-net the inhabitants, the operation was not attempted.

[32] And now it was that the retributions with which the Persian high command had threatened the Ionians, back when the two camps were facing one another, proved to have been no exaggeration. Once they had a city in their power, they would pick out the best-looking children: the boys they would then castrate, cutting off their testicles and making them eunuchs, while any girls of exceptional beauty they would dispatch to the King. The Persians would also, in addition to these actions, burn down entire cities – sanctuaries and all. So it was that the Ionians were reduced to slavery three times: once by the Lydians, and twice in succession by the Persians.

[33] Moving on from Ionia, the war-fleet conquered the entire stretch of land that borders the Hellespont to the north – the southern reaches having already come under the control of the Persians, who had attacked them by land. The regions of Europe that border the Hellespont are the

Chersonese,[24] where there are a large number of cities; Perinthus, and all the other forts on the coast of Thrace; Selymbria; and Byzantium. Now, the Byzantines, rather than wait for the Phoenician fleet to descend upon them, joined with the Chalcedonians, who lived on the opposite shore, in abandoning their homeland and venturing into the Euxine Sea, where they settled in the city of Mesambria. Meanwhile, the Phoenicians, once they had burned down all the places I just mentioned, set course for Proconnesus and Artace, which they likewise put to the torch, and then sailed back to the Chersonese, aiming to capture those cities they had left undamaged on their previous visit. Their fleet did not however target Cyzicus, because the Cyzicenes, even before the embarkation of the Phoenicians, had already negotiated their surrender to the King through Oebares, the son of Megabazus, and the governor of Dascyleum. Nevertheless, the Phoenicians did bring under their control all the cities in the Chersonese – the only exception being Cardia.

[34] The man who up until that point had been ruling these cities as tyrant was Miltiades,[25] the son of Cimon, the son of Stesagoras: an overlordship that had originally been obtained by the Miltiades who was the son of Cypselus, and in the following manner. The Chersonese was occupied by a Thracian people called the Doloncians – who, when a war with the Apsinthians was going badly for them, sent their kings to Delphi to ask about it. 'Invite a man to your country,' the Pythia answered them, 'to serve your people as their Founder. He should be whoever is the first, following your departure from this shrine, to offer you hospitality.' So the Doloncians set off along the Sacred Way; and after they had passed through Phocis and Boeotia without receiving a single invitation, they turned aside to Athens.

[35] Now, this was the period when total power in Athens was wielded by Peisistratus; but also very influential was Miltiades, the son of Cypselus. He came from a dynasty that was wealthy enough to maintain a four-horse chariot,[26] and could trace its origins back to Aeacus and Aegina, although more recently – ever since the time of Philaeus, the son of Ajax, who was the first of his line to have been born an Athenian – it had ranked as Athenian. This Miltiades was sitting in the porch of his house when he saw the Doloncians, dressed outlandishly and carrying spears, passing by; he called out to them, and then, after they had approached him, offered them shelter and hospitality. They accepted his invitation, and duly revealed to him, once they had been given food and

drink, the full story of the oracle. 'So, will you obey the god?' they demanded of him, once all had been disclosed. Miltiades, who was chafing under the rule of Peisistratus, and yearning to be well away from it, had only to hear this question to answer that, yes, indeed he would. Without delay, then, he set off for Delphi, to check with the oracle whether he should do as the Doloncians had requested.

[36] When the Pythia confirmed that he should, Miltiades – son of Cypselus and one-time Olympic victor in the four-horse chariot-race – recruited all the Athenians who wished to take part in the expedition, then set sail with the Doloncians and took over their country. He was installed as tyrant by those who had invited him in. His first step was to wall off the isthmus of the Chersonese between the city of Cardia and Pactya, to prevent the Apsinthians from launching incursions into the region and devastating it. The isthmus is 36 stades wide, while the Chersonese itself, measured from the isthmus, has a total length of 420 stades.

[37] Next, when the building of this wall across the neck of the Chersonese had succeeded in keeping the Apsinthians at bay, Miltiades turned his attentions to those enemies still in the field – the first of which were the people of Lampsacus. The Lampsacenes, however, ambushed him, and took him prisoner. When Croesus of Lydia, on whom Miltiades had made a great impression, learned of this, he sent word to the Lampsacenes that they should let Miltiades go. If they did not, he warned, he would destroy them root and branch 'as though they were a pine tree'. But what had Croesus meant by this threat that he would destroy them root and branch, 'as though they were a pine tree'? The Lampsacenes debated the question round and round until at last, after much mental effort, one of the older citizens hit upon the answer: that the pine is the only tree which, once cut down, produces no shoots, but is destroyed so completely and utterly that it might as well never have been. So it was that the Lampsacenes, who were terrified of Croesus, released Miltiades, and let him go.

[38] Thanks to Croesus, then, Miltiades escaped; and when in due course he died without male issue, his kingdom and possessions passed to Stesagoras, the son of Cimon, who was Miltiades' half-brother on his mother's side. The people of the Chersonese offer sacrifices to the shade of Miltiades such as are traditionally paid to a founder,[27] and have instituted games in his honour: these feature both equestrian and athletic

events, and entry to them is banned to anyone from Lampsacus. In fact, it was during the course of the war against the Lampsacenes that Stesagoras too happened to die childless. He was struck on the head with an axe while in the town hall, by a man who had claimed to be a defector to his side, but was in fact an enemy (and a rather aggressive one at that, as is evident from what he did).

[39] After Stesagoras had perished in this way, the reins of governance in the Chersonese were seized by Miltiades, the son of Cimon, and brother of the recently deceased Stesagoras. He was sent there on a trireme by the Peisistratids, who had been taking good care of him in Athens – quite as though the death of his father were something of which they were perfectly ignorant. (The details of what had actually happened I shall explain elsewhere in my account.)[28] When Miltiades arrived in the Chersonese, he stayed indoors, making a great show of respect for his brother, Stesagoras. When the people of the Chersonese picked up on this, the chiefs of all the various settlements from across the entire region came together and arrived at his house in a single deputation to join him in his grief – whereupon Miltiades imprisoned the lot of them. Then, with the Chersonese his, he acted as patron to five hundred mercenaries, and married Hegesipyle, who was the daughter of the Thracian king, Olorus.

[40] Now, this second Miltiades, the son of Cimon, had not been in the Chersonese long when he was overtaken, new arrival that he was, by circumstances even trickier to negotiate than those that had prevailed before. A couple of years before the events which I have been narrating he had turned tail before the Scythians. This was because, provoked into banding together by King Darius, the nomads among them had swept down as far as the Chersonese – and Miltiades, rather than await their onslaught, had fled. Only when the Scythians had gone did the Doloncians restore him. Then, two years later,[29] he was overtaken by the events that are my current concern.

[41] This was the moment when news of the presence of the Phoenicians in Tenedos led him to load up five triremes with all his worldly goods and set sail for Athens. Embarking from the city of Cardia, he went by way of the Black Gulf – but just as he was about to leave the Chersonese behind, the Phoenicians fell upon him with their fleet. Miltiades himself, together with four of his ships, managed to escape to Imbros; but the fifth was captured by the pursuing Phoenicians. Now, it

so happened that the captain of this particular ship was Metiochus, the eldest son of Miltiades (not, however, by the daughter of Olorus, the Thracian, but by another woman). The Phoenicians, once they had this son of Miltiades and his ship in their hands, and had realized his identity, took him inland to the King, confident that by doing so they would secure for themselves great favour – since back when the Scythians had been urging the Ionians to dismantle the pontoon-bridge and set sail for their own cities, it was Miltiades who had made no bones about his opinion that the Ionians should go along with the Scythian request. Darius, however, when brought Metiochus, the son of Miltiades, by the Phoenicians, did him no harm, but showered him instead with blessings. A house was bestowed upon him, and all sorts of possessions, and a Persian wife, by whom he had children who were themselves ranked as Persian. Miltiades, meanwhile, after leaving Imbros, made it to Athens.

[42] The Persians prosecuted nothing further that year to the detriment of the Ionians; indeed, the policies they did develop over the course of the year tended rather to the benefit of Ionia. Artaphrenes, the governor of Sardis, had envoys sent to him from the various cities, and obliged them to make compacts with one another, to the effect that plundering and looting were no longer to serve as the basis of their relations, but rather the rule of law. This was not all he forced them to do. He measured out the proportions of their respective territories in terms of *parasangs* (this being what the Persians term a length of 30 stades), and then, based on these calculations, taxed each city accordingly – an assessment which would remain constant from that moment on, so that even in my own time it was still being levied according to the prescriptions of Artaphrenes.[30] In point of fact, the level of tribute was not actually so very different from that which had prevailed before.

[43] All these measures helped to restore peace to Ionia. Then, the following spring, after every other commander had been dismissed by the King, Mardonius – a young man who was the son of Gobryas,[31] and had recently married Artozostra, a daughter of King Darius – came down to the coast, bringing with him a large fleet and an even larger army. When Mardonius and this army reached Cilicia, he boarded a ship and continued on his way with the rest of the fleet, while his land-forces advanced to the Hellespont under the command of other officers. It was while sailing along the coast of Asia that Mardonius came to Ionia – and it is at this point that I have something very astounding to

report, a remarkable episode that will confound those Greeks who refuse to accept that Otanes, when he was attempting to win over the other Seven Persians to his point of view, did indeed recommend that Persia be ruled democratically. Mardonius, you see, deposed every single tyrant in Ionia, and placed the cities instead under democratic rule.[32] Then, after taking these steps, he made all speed for the Hellespont. Once a huge fleet had been assembled there, and no less vast an army, the Persians crossed the Hellespont by ship and began to advance through Europe, making for Eretria and Athens.

[44] Nevertheless, although it was these two cities which provided the pretext for the expedition, the Persians were really aiming at the conquest of as many Greek states as they could manage. With their fleet they forced the submission of the Thasians, who lifted not so much as a finger to oppose them, and with their army they added the Macedonians to the ranks of those slaves already in their possession.[33] (All the various peoples east of Macedonia had by this stage come under their sway.) From Thasos, the fleet crossed to the opposite shore and advanced along the mainland, hugging it closely as far as Acanthus; and then, from Acanthus, it set out to round Athos. As it was approaching the headland, however, a violent northerly gale swept down upon the fleet, quite beyond the ability of the Persians to ride out, so that the damage suffered by their ships was terrible, and many were dashed against Athos itself.[34] Around three hundred ships, it is said, were lost, and over twenty thousand men. Some of these casualties were due to the presence in the waters off Athos of an immense number of savage beasts which devoured the Persians, while others were dashed onto the rocks or drowned because they did not know how to swim, or else perished of hypothermia. Such was how the naval wing of the expedition fared.

[45] Meanwhile, on land, Mardonius and his army made camp in Macedonia, where the Brygians, a tribe of Thracians, launched a night attack on them, inflicting substantial casualties, and even wounding Mardonius himself. Nevertheless, not even these assailants could escape the yoke of Persian servitude, since Mardonius refused to withdraw from the region until he had brought them under his control. Once he had conquered them, however, he did indeed pull his forces back, such was the scale of the debacle that his army had suffered at the hands of the Brygians, and the even greater catastrophe that had overwhelmed

his fleet round Athos. In the wake of this disgraceful showing, the task-force limped its way back to Asia.

[46] The following year, because the Thasians had been falsely accused by their neighbours of plotting rebellion, Darius first sent them envoys with orders to demolish their defences and bring their fleet to Abdera. He did this because the Thasians, who combined a recent experience of being put under siege by Histiaeus of Miletus with immense revenues, had put their money to use by building longships, and strengthening the circuit of their city walls. The revenues themselves came from the mainland and from their mines. The gold mines of Scapte Hyle supplied around 80 talents a year, and even though those on Thasos itself did not supply as much, the income from them was still so substantial that Thasian farmers went untaxed: indeed, when revenues from mainland and mines were combined, it helped contribute to an average annual income of 200 talents, rising to 300 at its peak.[35]

[47] I have seen these mines with my own eyes, and by far the most remarkable were those discovered by Thasos and his Phoenicians, after they had colonized the island and supplied it with the name by which it is known today – which derives from Thasos the Phoenician. These Phoenician mines on Thasos are situated midway between the places called Aenyra and Coenyra, opposite Samothrace, and are marked by a great mountain of rubble, where the prospecting was done. But enough now of this.

[48] The Thasians, just as the King had commanded, pulled down their city walls,[36] and brought their entire fleet to Abdera. Next, Darius set about probing the intentions of the Greeks, to find out whether they would fight him or surrender. He dispatched heralds to every corner of Greece, each one of them mandated to visit a different city, and demand of it earth and water. Even as these were being dispatched to Greece itself, however, he was also sending other heralds to all the various tributary cities along the coast, carrying orders to build longships and horse-transports.

[49] Work on these projects was duly set in train; and meanwhile, when the heralds arrived in Greece, many of the mainland cities handed over what the Persian had decreed that he required, as did all the islanders who received his demand. Notable among the islanders who gave earth and water to Darius were the Aeginetans. This gesture provoked an immediate response from the Athenians, who suspected that the

reason the Aeginetans had made the gift was because they were planning to join forces with the Persians in an attack upon them. Delighted to have this pretext to hand, the Athenians headed off to Sparta, where they declared the Aeginetans guilty of having betrayed Greece.[37]

[50] This accusation prompted Cleomenes,[38] the son of Anaxandridas, to cross over to Aegina, with the aim – in his role as king of the Spartiates – of arresting the Aeginetan ringleaders. His attempt to apprehend them, however, provoked widespread opposition from the Aeginetans; the most forthright of these was Crius, the son of Polycritus, who declared that the removal of even a single Aeginetan would have dire consequences. 'Your course of action is clearly provoked by Athenian bribes rather than reflecting the official policy of the Spartiates as a whole. Otherwise you would have come to make your arrests accompanied by the other king.'[39] (This speech had been prompted by a letter from Demaratus.) Cleomenes, obliged to leave Aegina, asked Crius for his name. The answer came back: 'Crius', which means 'ram'. 'Well, Crius,' Cleomenes told him, 'get your horns sheathed in brass, because you are facing terrible danger.'[40]

[51] Meanwhile, back in Sparta, all sorts of muck about Cleomenes was being raked by Demaratus, the son of Ariston, and himself a king of the Spartiates, albeit from the junior house.[41] Both houses actually share an identical ancestry,[42] and the fact that one is junior, and the other – the House of Eurysthenes – enjoys a margin more prestige, is simply due to Eurysthenes having been born first.

[52] Even though no poet has ever corroborated the story, the Lacedaemonians claim that it was not the sons of Aristodemus who led them to the land which they occupy today, but Aristodemus himself, the son of Aristomachus, the grandson of Cleodaeus and the great-grandson of Hyllus. Not long after this, the wife of Aristodemus – Argeia, as she was called – successfully came to term. (She is said to have been the daughter of Autesion, who in turn was the son of Tisamenus, the son of Thersander, the son of Polynices.) According to the Spartans, she had brought twins into the world – even as a mortally sick Aristodemus, after one look at the children, departed it. The Lacedaemonians of the time then consulted together, and decreed that the eldest, as was traditional, should be installed as king – but because the twins were identical in every way, they had no idea which one to choose. When they found

themselves stuck for an answer (and perhaps even at an earlier stage), they tried to solve the puzzle by turning to the woman who had given birth to the twins; but she too declared that she found it quite impossible to tell them apart. (In fact, despite this assurance, she knew full well which one was which – but it was her ambition that they should both of them, by some means, end up on the throne.) So the Lacedaemonians were at a loss; and indeed, such was their perplexity that they sent messengers to Delphi to ask how best to resolve the matter. 'Treat both boys as kings,' the Pythia instructed them, 'but honour the elder one the more.' Concerning the identity of this 'elder one', however, the Pythia's answer gave no hint, and so the Lacedaemonians were left as puzzled as they ever had been. Then it was that a man from Messenia, called Panites, had an idea. The Lacedaemonians, he suggested, should keep a close watch on the mother, and see which of the boys she bathed and fed the first. If she turned out always to follow the same routine, then the mystery would be solved, and they would know all that they needed; but if she varied her routine, and kept changing it, then it would be clear that she was indeed just as much in the dark as they were, and they would have to try some other method. So the Spartiates did as the Messenian had suggested: they kept a close watch on the mother of Aristodemus' children, who never had any suspicion that they were spying on her, and found that she did indeed show one of the boys the honour due a first-born, both when feeding them, and at their bathtime. The Lacedaemonians took this boy, the one his mother had been favouring as her first-born, and brought him up at public expense. Eurysthenes, they called him, while his brother they called Procles. These two, so the Lacedaemonians report, went on to spend their entire adult lives at loggerheads, despite their being brothers; and so it has been with their descendants ever since.[43]

[53] The Lacedaemonians are alone among the Greeks in giving this version of events, so let me now spell out the conventional Greek account, which holds that the list of Dorian kings as traditionally enumerated by the Greeks is correct, and can be traced as far back as Perseus, the son of Danaë – although it skirts the issue of whether his paternity was divine. Not only that, but it demonstrates that the Dorian kings, who even in the time of Perseus were counted as Greeks, must indeed therefore have been Greek. I said 'as far back as Perseus', rather

than fixing on an earlier date, because no mortal is named as having been his father – as Amphitryon, for instance, is named as the father of Heracles. Clearly, then, in using the phrase, I have both accuracy and logic on my side. But were the paternal lineage of Danaë, the daughter of Acrisius, to be traced back through the generations, then the ancestry of the Dorian rulers would indisputably be shown to derive from Egypt.

[54] Besides this Greek genealogy, there is also a version related by the Persians, who claim that Perseus himself was an Assyrian, and that, although he ended up a Greek, his ancestry was not Greek at all. Acrisius and his forefathers were quite unrelated to Perseus, the Persians say, and came from Egypt – a point on which the Persians and the Greeks do concur.[44]

[55] But I have said quite enough on this topic. The question of how, despite being Egyptian, their exploits allowed them to rule as kings over the Dorians has been dealt with by others, so I will leave it well alone. The themes that form my subject are ones that have never been touched upon hitherto.

[56] The Spartiates have bestowed a number of prerogatives upon their kings. They hold two priesthoods, one of Zeus of Lacedaemon, and one of the Heavenly Zeus; they can make war against any country they choose,[45] and no Spartiate is permitted to obstruct them in this, upon pain of being subject to a curse; going into battle, it is the kings who are positioned in the vanguard, and during a withdrawal, in the rear; on campaign, they have a hundred hand-picked men to protect them;[46] as they head off to war, they have the right to take as much livestock as they want, and to be given the hides and backs of every single sacrificial victim.

[57] In addition to these rights, which relate to times of war, they have also been granted prerogatives which apply in times of peace. Whenever there is a public sacrifice, for instance, it is the kings who sit down first to the meal, and receive the first portions, which are for each of them double the size of those received by everyone else at the feast. The kings also pour the first libations, and receive the hides of animals killed in sacrifice. Every new moon, and on the seventh day of every month, both kings are given, at public expense, an animal that has been specially reared for sacrifice to Apollo, together with a *medimnus* of barley-meal and a Laconian quart of wine. At athletics contests, seats are always reserved for them in the front row. They have the right to

appoint as official representatives of foreigners in Sparta whichever citizens they please. Each king also nominates two Pythians: emissaries who are sent to consult Delphi, and who dine at public expense alongside the kings. Should the kings not attend the public mess, then 2 *choenixes* of barley and a *cotyle* of wine are sent to them in their homes; when they are in attendance at the mess, they receive double portions of everything. (The same privilege is afforded them even when they are invited to dine by a private citizen.) The kings are guardians of any oracles that may be given, although the Pythians share in the knowledge of them as well. There are also certain judicial matters which are the exclusive concern of the kings: who should get to marry a virgin heiress whose father has died without first choosing her a husband, for instance; anything to do with public highways; and the adoption of children, which is always performed in the royal presence. When the twenty-eight members of the Gerousia[47] sit in session, so too do the kings – and should they not attend the meeting, their closest relatives among the various members of the Gerousia will wield the royal prerogatives, casting two votes, and then a third one on behalf of themselves.[48]

[58] Such are the rights received from the mass of Spartiates by their kings while alive; but there are privileges bestowed on them in death as well. Whenever a king dies, horsemen tour Laconia,[49] broadcasting the news across the entire territory, while in the city women go up and down, beating on copper cauldrons. This is the compulsory signal for two free persons from every household, a man and a woman, to put on sackcloth and ashes, and anyone who ignores this obligation is subjected to heavy fines. These rituals practised by the Lacedaemonians upon the occasion of the death of their kings correspond precisely to those of the barbarians of Asia – and indeed, by and large, to those of barbarians everywhere, whose customs whenever their own kings die are much the same.[50] This is evident from the fact that it is not only the Spartiates who are required to attend the funeral of a dead king of the Lacedaemonians, but also a number of the subject people who ring the city, and who are drawn from across the entire span of Lacedaemon. Once they, the helots and the Spartiates themselves (thousands upon thousands of men and women all mingling promiscuously together) have congregated in one place, they beat their foreheads in a violence of passion, and give themselves over to endless wails of grief, declaring that the last king to have died in the royal succession was the best there ever

was – no matter who the king. Should he have died in battle, then the Lacedaemonians fashion an image of him, place it on a lavishly appointed bier and carry it out in procession. Following his burial, the city market is closed for ten days, and there are no elections held in all that time, only displays of mourning.

[59] This is not the only way in which the Lacedaemonians resemble the Persians. Whenever a king, on the death of his predecessor, succeeds to the throne, he marks his accession by clearing the debts of any Spartiate indebted either to himself or to the state. Likewise, in Persia, a newly crowned king remits any arrears of tribute which may be owed him by a city, without exception.

[60] There are also the following ways in which the Lacedaemonians resemble the Egyptians.[51] Heralds, flute-players and sacrificial cooks all inherit their respective crafts from their fathers, with flute-player being born to flute-player, sacrificial cook to sacrificial cook and herald to herald. Because heralds, for instance, become what they are by right of birth, not even those with clear and ringing voices can hope to usurp their roles and displace them. That is how things are done.

[61] So while Cleomenes was away on Aegina working for the common good of Greece,[52] there was Demaratus busy stabbing him in the back – not out of any great concern for the Aeginetans, however, but because he was consumed by envy and malice.[53] Cleomenes, once he was back from Aegina, duly turned to pondering how Demaratus might be removed from the throne – and sure enough, by fixing on one particular issue, he found a promising line of attack. Back when Ariston had been king of Sparta, he had married twice, but never had any children. Refusing to acknowledge that he himself might be to blame, however, he instead took a third wife, and under very particular circumstances. He had a friend among the Spartiates, one who was dearer to him than any other citizen. It so happened that the wife of this man was by far the most beautiful woman in all Sparta – despite the fact that she had become the most beautiful having been the ugliest. Indeed, so ill favoured had she been that her nurse, who was alert to the fact that the child was not merely ugly, but the daughter of a very wealthy family, and who could see that the parents regarded her appearance an utter calamity, came up with a well-considered plan. Every day, she would carry the child to the sanctuary of Helen, which stands in a place called Therapne, above the shrine of Phoebus; and every time the nurse carried

her there, she would prop her up against the statue of Helen and beseech the goddess to deliver the child from her ugliness. Once, it is said, as the nurse was leaving the sanctuary, a woman appeared to her and asked what she was carrying in her arms. 'I am carrying a child,' the nurse answered. 'Show her to me,' the woman answered. The nurse refused. 'I have strict instructions from the parents that she is on no account to be shown to anyone.' Still the woman insisted, over and over again, on seeing the child – until the nurse, recognizing how much it meant to the woman to have a look, eventually showed her the child. The woman stroked the girl's head, and then declared: 'You will be the fairest woman in Sparta.' Sure enough, from that day on, the child's looks began to blossom. When she became nubile, she was married to Agetus, the son of Alceides – and the friend of Ariston.

[62] Now, because lust for this woman was an itch that tortured Ariston, he came up with a scheme to scratch it. He promised his comrade, whose wife she was, one of his own possessions as a gift. He should have his pick, anything he liked; and then he urged his comrade to make an identical commitment. The friend, who had no anxieties concerning his wife, because he could see that Ariston too was married, agreed. Once the arrangement had been sealed with solemn oaths, Agetus chose some item or other from Ariston's treasure store, which Ariston duly handed over; and then, when it was the turn of Ariston to make his own corresponding claim, he sought to drag off his friend's wife.[54] Agetus, however, protested that she, alone of all he had, was not covered by the deal. Nevertheless, as he had been tricked and suborned into swearing his oath, he had no choice but to let Ariston lead her away.

[63] Thus it was that Ariston divorced his second wife and came by his third. Not long afterwards, before even ten months had fully passed,[55] his new wife gave birth to a child: this was none other than Demaratus. News of the child's delivery was brought by a household slave to Ariston as he sat in session with the ephors. Knowing the date of his marriage to the mother, and counting off the months on his fingers, Ariston exclaimed with an oath, 'It can't be mine!' The ephors, however, despite hearing him say this, made nothing of the matter at the time. The boy grew up, and Ariston came to regret what he had said; for he no longer had any doubt that Demaratus was indeed his child. Indeed, the very reason that he had named the boy 'Demaratus' – meaning 'Prayed-for-by-the-People' – was that the entire body of the

Spartiates, prior to Demaratus' birth, had prayed for a child to be fathered by Ariston, whom they held in a higher esteem than any other man who had ruled them as king. And that was how Demaratus came by his name.

[64] Time went by, and on the death of Ariston Demaratus succeeded to the kingship. But the whole story, it seems, was fated to come out, and topple Demaratus from his throne; thanks to the withdrawal of the army that Demaratus had staged at Eleusis,[56] he and Cleomenes had already been at each other's throats, and now, after the crossing made by Cleomenes to deal with the medizers on Aegina, relations were even worse.

[65] Casting about for ways to be avenged, Cleomenes struck a deal with Leotychidas, the son of Menares, and grandson of Agis, and who belonged to the same house as Demaratus: by its terms, Cleomenes was to install Leotychidas as king in place of Demaratus, and Leotychidas, in exchange, was to join him in coercing Aegina. Leotychidas was a personal enemy of Demaratus – chiefly because, when Leotychidas had been betrothed to Percalus, the daughter of Chilon and grand-daughter of Demarmenus, Demaratus had schemed to deprive Leotychidas of his marriage and stolen a march on him, by abducting Percalus, and making her his own wife. No wonder, in the wake of this episode, that Leotychidas should have hated Demaratus so; nor that, with the enthusiastic connivance of Cleomenes, he should have sworn on public oath that Demaratus was no son of Ariston, and therefore no legitimate king of Sparta. Leotychidas then followed this sworn declaration by bringing a prosecution in which he dredged up the remark that Ariston had made when, following his slave's announcement that he had a son, he had added up the months, and exclaimed with an oath that the child could not be his. It was on the basis of this comment that Leotychidas built his entire case, and sought to demonstrate – by calling as witnesses the ephors who had happened to be at the meeting, and had heard what Ariston had said – that Demaratus was not the son of Ariston, and therefore had no legal right to the throne of Sparta.

[66] So violently did the arguments rage that in the end the Spartiates decided to consult the oracle at Delphi as to whether Demaratus was the son of Ariston or not. Cleomenes, who had originally suggested that the issue be referred to the Pythia, then promptly suborned Cobon, the son of Aristophantus, and a man who wielded greater influence than

any other in Delphi; whereupon Cobon in turn persuaded Periallus, the priestess who uttered the oracles,[57] to say what Cleomenes wanted to be said. Accordingly, when the messengers sent to Delphi put their question to the Pythia, she gave it as her ruling that Demaratus was not the son of Ariston. In due course, however, after the scandal had become public knowledge, Cobon fled Delphi, and Periallus, the prophetess, was stripped of her sacred office.

[67] So that was how Demaratus came to be deprived of his throne; but it was a more specific insult that led to his fleeing from Sparta into exile among the Medes. In the wake of his deposition, Demaratus did hold an office – but by virtue of election. During the Festival of Naked Boys,[58] which Demaratus was attending as a spectator, a servant was sent over to him by Leotychidas (who by this stage had become king in his place) with a mocking, jeering enquiry: 'How does it feel to be an elected official after having been a king?' Stung to the quick by this question, Demaratus answered, 'At least I have had experience of both – which you have not. But that does not alter the fact that for the Lacedaemonians a whole multitude of evils will be the fruit of your question – either that, or a multitude of blessings.' And so saying, he covered his head and left the theatre for his own house, where he immediately set about preparing to sacrifice an ox to Zeus; and then, once the sacrifice was done, he summoned his mother.

[68] When she had come, he placed into her hands a portion of the entrails, and supplicated her as follows: 'I beg you, Mother, in the name of all the gods, but especially that of Zeus, who guards the limits of our house – tell me the truth. Be straight with me – who is really my father? In the heat of our clashes there was a claim made by Leotychidas that when you became married to Ariston you were already pregnant by your former husband. There are others who bandy even more ridiculous tales and say that you slept with a house-slave, a muleteer, and that he is my father. So I beg you, by the gods – tell me the truth. If, after all, you did the things you are said to have done, then you were hardly the first – many others have done the same. It is common gossip in Sparta that Ariston was unable to father children – the argument being that his first two wives would otherwise surely have become pregnant.'

[69] To these words of Demaratus, his mother answered, 'Such entreaties, my child! Very well. Since you have begged me to give you the truth, that is what I will give you – the truth, and nothing but. Three

nights after Ariston had first led me away to his own house, there came to me a phantasm with the appearance of Ariston, who took me to bed, and then adorned me in the garlands it had been wearing. With this it vanished – and in came Ariston. When he saw me in my garlands, he demanded to know who had given them to me. "You," I answered. He insisted he had not. "But you did," I swore, "and it is hardly noble of you to claim that you did not. You gave me the garlands just a short while back – after you had come in and taken me to bed." It was then that Ariston, realizing that my denials were sworn on oath, recognized in the episode the hand of a god. It was suggestive, for instance, that the garlands turned out to have come from a shrine by the courtyard door – one that belonged to a hero called Astrabacus.[59] Not only that, but we have the assurance of the seers that it was indeed Astrabacus who had visited me. So there you are, my son – the details of everything you wanted to know. Since the night we are talking about was the very one on which I conceived you, either it was this hero who was responsible, in which case your father is Astrabacus – or else your father is Ariston. As for the key piece of evidence deployed by your enemies against you – this charge that Ariston himself, when brought the news of your birth, declared in the full hearing of many that you could not possibly be his, since the allotted span of ten months was yet to be completed – why did he blurt this out? Quite simply, through sheer ignorance of the facts! Women can give birth after nine, even seven months – not all pregnancies last the full ten. As for me, I gave birth to you, my child, after seven months. Even Ariston himself, shortly after, came to appreciate that his comment had been folly. So do not be taken in by any other stories that are told concerning your birth. What you have heard is the complete and unvarnished truth. As for Leotychidas and anyone else who spreads such stories, I only pray that it is their wives who have children by muleteers.'

[70] These words told Demaratus everything that he wished to know; and now, provisioning himself for a journey, and putting it about that he was going to Delphi to consult the oracle, he headed off to Elis. When the Lacedaemonians, who suspected him of attempting to flee the country, set off in pursuit, Demaratus somehow or other managed to stay one step ahead of them, crossing from Elis to Zacynthos, and although the Lacedaemonians also made the crossing and succeeded in depriving him of his servants, their arrest of Demaratus himself was foiled by the people of Zacynthos, who refused to surrender him. There-

after, Demaratus made his way across to Asia to King Darius, who received him with great magnificence, and bestowed on him estates and cities.[60] Such were the twists of fortune that saw the coming to Asia of Demaratus: a man who had won a brilliant name for himself among the Lacedaemonians for his many achievements and force of intellect, and who had once – conferring on his people an accomplishment that no other Spartan king had ever equalled – won an Olympic victory in the four-horse chariot-race.[61]

[71] The successor of Demaratus, after he had been deposed from the throne, was Leotychidas, the son of Menares. He had a son named Zeuxidamus – or Cyniscus, as some of the Spartiates called him. This Zeuxidamus, because he died before Leotychidas, did not become king of Sparta, but he did leave behind a son of his own, Archidamus. Leotychidas, after the loss of Zeuxidamus, married a second time, to Eurydame, a woman who was the sister of Menius, and the daughter of Diactorides. Although she bore him no sons, she did give him a daughter called Lampito, whom Leotychidas gave in marriage to Archidamus,[62] the son of Zeuxidamus.

[72] Not that Leotychidas was to grow old in Sparta. Rather, he would suffer retribution for what he had done to Demaratus. When he led the Lacedaemonians on campaign in Thessaly,[63] he could easily have brought the entire country to heel, had he not accepted as a bribe vast amounts of silver. Caught red-handed, right in the camp, sitting on a glove full of silver, he was put on trial and went into exile, and had his house torn down. He took refuge in Tegea, which was where he died.[64]

[73] But all that was in the future. What happened in the meantime was that Cleomenes, the moment he had brought his business with Demaratus to a successful conclusion, was so consumed by resentment at the high-handed treatment he had received on Aegina that he took Leotychidas with him to Aegina. Now that both kings were coming against them, the Aeginetans decided to resist no longer. Cleomenes and Leotychidas picked out Crius, the son of Polycritus, and Casambus, the son of Aristocrates, who between them were the two most powerful men on the island, together with eight others who for wealth and breeding were pre-eminent among the Aeginetans, and removed them from Aegina. The hostages were brought to Attica and given as a pledge to the bitterest foes that the Aeginetans had: the Athenians.

[74] Subsequently, when the dirty tricks played against Demaratus

came to light, Cleomenes was so gripped by dread of the Spartiates that he slipped away to Thessaly. From there he proceeded to Arcadia, where he stirred up revolution by uniting the Arcadians in a common front against Sparta. He had them swear a whole range of oaths in which they promised to follow him wherever he should lead;[65] but his particular obsession was to get the Arcadian elite to the city of Nonacris, and have them swear by the waters of the Styx. That the waters of the Styx are indeed in this town is a claim made by the Arcadians themselves; and certainly, there is a tiny stream that can be seen to trickle from a rock down into a hollow, surrounded by a wall of unmortared stones. Nonacris, where this spring happens to be situated, is a city in Arcadia, near Pheneus.

[75] When the Lacedaemonians discovered what Cleomenes was up to, they were so alarmed that they restored him to power [in Sparta] on the same terms as before. No sooner was he back, however, than he fell seriously ill: what had previously been mild derangement was now full-blown madness.[66] Whenever he encountered one of the Spartiates, he would hit the man across the face with his staff. This behaviour, and his descent into lunacy, prompted his relatives to lock him up in the stocks. Thus tethered, and seeing that the guard was on his own, standing apart from the others, Cleomenes badgered him for a knife. To begin with, the guard was very reluctant to give him one; but when Cleomenes menaced the man by describing what he would do to him when set free, the guard (who was only a helot, you see) was so intimidated that he did hand over a dagger. With the iron weapon now in his hands, Cleomenes began to hack at himself, beginning at the shins. Strip after strip of his own flesh he sliced off, cutting crossways up from the shins to the thighs, and from the thighs up to the hips and the flanks, until finally, on reaching the stomach, he cut that into ribbons as well – and so expired. The consensus of most Greeks[67] is that it was his bribing of the Pythia to say what she did about Demaratus that brought him to such an end. The Athenians, however, claim that it was because he had cut down the groves in the precinct of the goddess while he was attacking Eleusis. Then there are the people of Argos, who point out that Cleomenes had lured the Argives out from their own sanctuary of Argos, where they had sought refuge after the battle, and hacked them down – and indeed, had shown such a lack of respect for the grove that he had actually had it burned down.

[76] Cleomenes, you see, had consulted the oracle at Delphi, and been told that he would take 'Argos'. Subsequently, at the head of the

Spartiates, he arrived on the banks of a river, the Erasinus, which is said to flow from the Stymphalian Lake (the claim being that this lake drains into an underground chasm and then re-emerges in Argos, from which point on its waters are called by the Argives 'the Erasinus'). On reaching this river, Cleomenes offered sacrifices to it, in an effort to obtain favourable omens for the crossing; but then, when these were not remotely forthcoming, declared that, while he admired the Erasinus for not playing false by its own citizens, it would still not save the Argives. Then, after he had pulled his forces back to Thyreae, he cut the throat of a bull into the sea, and took his men by boat to the region of Tiryns and Nauplia.

[77] News of this prompted the Argives to send a defence force to the coast. When they reached a place called Sepeia, which is near Tiryns, they positioned themselves opposite the Lacedaemonians, a very short distance away. Preying on the minds of the Argives was the prospect not of open battle, but of falling victim to some underhand trick. Their anxiety on this count was due to its having been mentioned by an oracle[68] – the same one as had been given jointly to them and the Milesians by the Pythia, which had run:

'When the female comes to secure a victory over the male,
Taking possession of the field, and glory too, from Argos,
Then will sorrow score the cheeks of many an Argive woman.
And so it will come to be said, by those of a later age,
"Dread though it was, yet the serpent, thrice-coiled, was tamed by
      the spear."'

No wonder, then, with all these things coming together, that the Argives should have been so nervous. Their best option, they decided, was to turn the instructions being issued by the enemy herald to their own advantage, by doing exactly as the Spartiates were being told to do.

[78] But Cleomenes, when he realized that everything the Argives did was prompted by the instructions of his own herald, sent word to his men that the next time the order was given them by the herald to make breakfast, they should take up their weapons and attack the Argives – an order which the Lacedaemonians duly followed to the letter. Even as the Argives, in response to the herald, were getting their breakfast ready, the Lacedaemonians fell upon them; a large number of Argives were killed, and an even larger number took refuge in the grove of Argos, where they were blockaded and watched.

[79] What Cleomenes now did, armed with information from Argive deserters, was to send a herald who called by name on those Argives who were holed up within the sanctuary to come out – and announcing, by way of encouragement, that their ransoms had been received. (The Peloponnesians had set the ransom to be paid out on a prisoner-of-war at 2 *minas* per head.) One after the other, around fifty of the Argives answered this summons of Cleomenes – only to be killed by him as they emerged. Those who were left inside the precinct were for a while oblivious to what was going on, because the trees of the grove were so thick that it was impossible for them to see what was happening to those on the outside – until one of them climbed a tree, and saw precisely. After that, there was no more walking out in answer to Cleomenes' summons.

[80] At this, Cleomenes ordered all the helots to pile up brushwood around the grove, and then, once they had done as instructed, he put it to the torch. As the grove was going up in flames, he asked one of the deserters to which of the gods it was sacred. 'Argos,' came the reply. When he heard this, Cleomenes gave a mighty groan, and cried out to Apollo, 'How terribly, god of prophecy, you deceived me when you foretold that I would capture "Argos"! What else am I to conclude, save that the oracle you gave me has now been fulfilled?'

[81] In the wake of this, Cleomenes dismissed most of his army back to Sparta, but went himself with an elite squad of a thousand men to the temple of Hera to offer animal blood-sacrifice. In his wish to make offerings on the altar, however, he was obstructed by the priest, who declared that it would be sacrilege for a foreigner to perform a sacrifice on such a spot. Cleomenes, however, ordered his helots to drag the priest away from the altar and flog him, while he himself made sacrifice there. Once this was done, he went back to Sparta.

[82] On his return home, his enemies hauled him before the ephors, claiming that he had accepted a bribe to spare Argos capture, even though it had been his to take. Whether, when he answered this charge, he was lying or telling the truth, I cannot say for sure, but certainly, his response was to insist that by capturing the shrine of Argos he had, in his own opinion, fulfilled the oracle given by the god. That being so, he had regarded any attempt to capture the city as most inappropriate, until he had first discovered, by offering up sacrifices, whether the god would make him a gift of the city, or would stand in his way. As he visited the sanctuary of Hera in the hope of receiving a favourable

omen, a spurt of fire had blazed out from the breasts of her statue, thereby revealing to him the certain truth: that he would not take Argos. Had the flame only blazed out from the head of the statue, then the city – acropolis and all – would certainly have been his; but instead, blazing as it had from the breasts, it was clear that anything else he did would fail to meet with the approval of the god. This was his explanation, a defence that seemed to the Spartiates so plausible and reasonable[69] that the prosecution never had any prospect of dragging their quarry down.

[83] As for Argos, such had been the devastation inflicted upon her reserves of manpower[70] that the entire governance and administration of the state passed into the hands of her slaves. Only when the sons of those who had been slaughtered came to manhood did they take back control of the city and throw out the slaves, who, expelled from Argos, seized Tiryns after a battle. Relations between the two sides were, however, for a while perfectly amicable, until there arrived among the slaves a seer called Cleander – a man who was by origin an Arcadian, from Phigaleia. He persuaded the slaves to go on the offensive against their masters. The resulting war dragged on a long time, and was only eventually won by the Argives with much effort.

[84] Such, then, is the explanation given in Argos for the insanity and wretched death of Cleomenes, but the Spartiates themselves deny that the gods had anything to do with his madness. Rather, they say, it was the result of a taste he had picked up, while fraternizing with Scythians, for drinking unmixed wine. What had happened, you see, was that the nomadic Scythians, who were eager to make Darius pay retribution for his invasion of their land, had sent an embassy to Sparta. They aimed to forge an alliance, and to urge a course of action that would see the Scythians themselves attempt an invasion of Persian territory along the River Phasis, while the Spartiates were to set out inland from Ephesus, and then join forces with them. The story goes that Cleomenes, following the arrival of the Scythians on this mission, spent so much time with them that it verged on the scandalous, and he acquired a taste for drinking neat wine. It was this, the Spartiates believe, that drove him mad. Ever since, they report, anyone hankering after stronger liquor has been described as 'doing a Scythian'. So much for the explanation given by the Spartiates for the death of Cleomenes. My own view, however, is that it was divine retribution for his treatment of Demaratus.

[85] When the Aeginetans learned that Cleomenes was dead, they sent messengers to Sparta to denounce Leotychidas for his role in consigning their hostages to Athens. Sure enough, when a court was convened by the Lacedaemonians, it ruled that the treatment of the Aeginetans by Leotychidas had constituted a violation of their status, and sentenced him to be delivered into the hands of the Aeginetans, as requital for the men being held in Athens. Just as the Aeginetans were about to take him off, though, they were addressed by Theasides, the son of Leoprepes, and a man of high repute in Sparta. 'Men of Aegina,' he asked them, 'what on earth do you think you are doing? Do you really intend to remove the king of the Spartiates, just because his fellow-citizens delivered him up into your hands, when that verdict was delivered on the spur of the moment and in the heat of Spartiate anger? If you do remove him, then watch out that at some point in the future the Spartiates do not pay you back for it by bringing about the total ruin of your country.' The Aeginetans who were leading Leotychidas away stopped cold when they heard this – but they did agree, as a compromise, that Leotychidas would come with them to Athens, and recover their men for them.

[86] When Leotychidas arrived in Athens, though, and asked the Athenians for the return of the men who had been left in their safekeeping, they were very reluctant to give back the hostages, and pointed out, to justify themselves, that, having been given possession of the hostages by both kings, it would be quite wrong of them to hand them back to one in the absence of the other.

Leotychidas, however, answered this Athenian refusal by saying, 'Choose one of two options, men of Athens. Do the right thing and give the hostages back – or do the opposite and refuse to return them. And while on the topic of safe-keeping, I would like to tell you about something which took place in Sparta. It so happened, according to a story we Spartiates tell, that three generations before my own there lived in Lacedaemon one Glaucus, the son of Epicydes. This man, so our story goes, had won for himself a pre-eminence in every conceivable field – and was in particular renowned for being a person of the utmost integrity, more so than any other man then alive in Lacedaemon. In the fullness of time, so the story we tell about him goes, there arrived in Sparta a man from Miletus who wished to enter into conversation with Glaucus, and put to him a proposal. "I am a Milesian," this visitor said, "and I have come here, Glaucus, because I wish to have the benefit of your integrity – something that is bruited far and wide across Greece, even as far as Ionia. Two thoughts have struck me: first, how unstable a place Ionia has always been, and how securely, by comparison, things are ordered in the Peloponnese; and secondly, just how apparent it is that wealth is forever changing hands. So it was, bearing all this in mind, and after due reflection, I decided that my best course was to convert half my property into silver, and then to deposit it with you – knowing that to bank it with you is to ensure its safe-keeping. So please, accept this money – and also take and keep these tokens of receipt. Then, if anyone comes to you with matching tokens, and asks for the money back, you will know to return it to him."

'So spoke the stranger from Miletus; and Glaucus duly accepted the deposit on the terms suggested. Then, many years later, the children of the man who had banked his money travelled to Sparta, where they made contact with Glaucus, showed him the tokens and requested the return of the money. His response, however, was to brush them aside. "I have absolutely no recollection of this business. Despite everything you keep telling me, none of it jogs my memory. But let me see if I can call anything to mind. I only ever want to do what is right. If I did indeed take the money, then of course I will return it to you in full. If, on the other hand, I never had it in the first place, then I will deal with you as Greek custom prescribes. That is why I will arrive at a decision on your case in four months' time."

'The Milesians, who regarded this as an outrage, went away convinced that they had been robbed of their money, while Glaucus headed for Delphi to consult the oracle. "Should I swear on oath," he asked the oracle, "so as to rob them of the money?" The Pythia responded with stinging verses:

"In the short term you will profit, Glaucus, son of Epicydes,
Should you win by thieving money with an oath.
So swear your oath – death awaits even the honest man who
   swears one.
But Oath has a nameless child. Without feet he is and without
   hands,
And yet for all that he is swift, and relentless in his pursuit.
A man's descendants and household, all he will seize, all pulverize.
But he who keeps his word – in the long run, his heirs do better."

When Glaucus heard this, he implored the god to forgive him his question. "Between asking permission of a god to commit a deed and the deed itself," answered the Pythia, "there is no difference."

'Glaucus sent for the Milesians, and gave the foreigners back their money. But the moral of the story, men of Athens, and the reason I wanted you to hear it, is this: today, there exists not a single descendant of Glaucus, nor a single household that is reckoned to derive from him. His line has been pulled up from Sparta by the roots, as though it had never been. So always give back a deposit entrusted to you when those who orginally gave it to you demand its return. Should you even contemplate an alternative course of action, no good will come of it.' So spoke Leotychidas; but the Athenians had blocked their ears to him, and so he went away.

[87] The Aeginetans were yet to pay the price for the outrageous offences they had committed some time previously against the Athenians, in support of the Theban cause. Their policy was to cast the Athenians as the villains, and themselves as the injured party – and to plan their revenge. Once every four years the Athenians would hold a festival at Sunium – so the Aeginetans lay in ambush for the state ship, which was full of the leading men of Athens, and then, after they had boarded it, put the delegates in chains.

[88] So wounding was this to the Athenians that they no longer felt any compunction about plotting the total ruin of the Aeginetans. Now, there was in Aegina an eminent man by the name of Nicodromus, the son of Cnoethus, who, because he had once been expelled from the island, nursed a grudge against the Aeginetans. Learning that the Athenians were indeed set on doing Aegina serious harm, he arranged to betray the island to them by alerting them to the day when he would stage a coup, and they would be expected to arrive with reinforcements. Sure enough, sticking to his side of the deal with the Athenians, he duly seized the Old Town, as it is known – but the Athenians failed to appear on time.

[89] What had happened, you see, was that the Athenians, because their own fleet was no match for that of the Aeginetans, had asked the Corinthians to loan them some ships – and the resulting delay had served to doom the whole enterprise. Relations between the Corinthians and the Athenians back in those days were exceedingly good, so the Corinthians had responded to the Athenian request by selling them

twenty ships at a price of 5 drachmas each. (It was illegal for them just to give things away.) Once the Athenians had taken receipt of these ships and combined them with their own, they had seventy ships in all, and a full complement of crews. They duly sailed against Aegina – but arrived there one day later than had been arranged.

[90] This failure of the Athenians to turn up on time caused Nicodromus and his supporters among the Aeginetans to take ship and flee Aegina. The Athenians then settled them in Sunium, from which base they went on to launch raids on the Aeginetans, and thoroughly ravage the island.

[91] But all that was still to come. Back in Aegina, meanwhile, the popular faction that had joined forces with Nicodromus was crushed by the men of substance,[71] who followed up their victory by leading their prisoners out to execution. This brought a curse down on their heads, one they proved quite unable to expiate, despite all their efforts and sacrifices; and when in due course they were exiled from the island, the goddess remained unpropitiated. They had taken prisoner seven hundred of the popular faction, you see, and led them out to execution; and as this was going on, one of the prisoners had slipped his bonds and run down to the gates which led into the temple of Demeter the Lawgiver, where he had grabbed hold of the door handles and clung on to them. When his pursuers, despite all their pulling on him, found it impossible to prise his grip loose, they hacked off his hands, and so were able to lead him away. His hands were left hanging from the door handles.

[92] That was how the Aeginetans managed their internal affairs. The Athenians, meanwhile, when they eventually arrived with their fleet of seventy ships, were met in battle by the Aeginetans, who in the ensuing clash were defeated, and as a result turned for assistance to the people on whom they had previously called: the Argives. This time, however, there was to be no help forthcoming from Argos, whose citizens were riled because the crews of some Aeginetan ships commandeered by Cleomenes had docked in Argive territory, and then joined the Lacedaemonians in launching a raid – an incursion on which the Lacedaemonians had also been joined by men from a Sicyonian squadron. The Argives had then imposed a fine of 1,000 talents on the two cities, 500 from each. The Sicyonians, who acknowledged that they had indeed been in the wrong, had agreed to pay 100 talents to clear the fine; but the Aeginetans, who were altogether more stubborn, had

refused any such compromise. No wonder, then, that their request for help should have received no official response from the Argives. Around a thousand volunteers did answer it, though. Their commander-in-chief was a man called Eurybates, a seasoned pentathlete. Most of the volunteers never made it back home but perished on Aegina fighting the Athenians. Their commander, Eurybates, had a taste for single combat: three times he was victorious, going one on one, but the fourth time, when he came up against Sophanes of Decelea,[72] it was he who was slain.

[93] At sea, however, the Aeginetan fleet caught the Athenians in disarray, and in the resulting victory captured four Athenian ships, crews and all.

[94] Meanwhile, as the Athenians were pursuing their offensive against the Aeginetans, the Persian King had his own designs. 'Remember the Athenians,' his servant was forever reminding him, while at his side there sat members of the Peisistratid clan, casting the Athenians in as bad a light as they possibly could, and providing Darius himself with exactly the pretext he wanted to conquer those Greeks who had refused to give him earth and water. Mardonius, whose own campaign had fared so wretchedly, was relieved of his command, and replaced as leader of the campaign against Eretria and Athens by two other generals: Datis, who by nationality was a Mede, and Artaphrenes, the son of Artaphrenes, who was the nephew of Darius himself. Off they were dispatched, their instructions being to capture Athens and Eretria, and bring the enslaved captives into the royal presence.[73]

[95] Armed with their commissions from the King, the two generals made their way to Cilicia at the head of a vast and well-equipped array of land-forces, and when they arrived set up camp on the Aleian plain. There they were joined by a fleet made up of all the different squadrons which Darius had ordered his various tribute-paying subjects to furnish, and by the transport-ships for horses which he had instructed them to sort out the previous year. Then, once they had loaded the horses onto the transports, and the soldiers onto the fleet of six hundred triremes, they sailed for Ionia. From there, however, rather than have their ships maintain a direct course for the Hellespont and Thrace along the line of the mainland, they set out instead from Samos, making their way by island-hopping across the Icarian Sea – a route prompted more than anything else, I would imagine, by their trepidation at the prospect of sailing

around Athos, where their fleet and crews had slipped up so badly the year before. Also forcing their hand, of course, was the failure of their earlier attempt to capture Naxos.

[96] And sure enough, once past the Icarian Sea, it was to Naxos that the Persians made their way, having decided to make the island the target of their opening attack. Upon their arrival, however, the Naxians, mindful of what had happened previously, went and fled to the mountains rather than stand their ground. The Persians, after enslaving the stragglers, burned both the sanctuaries and city. Then, once they had done that, they put to sea and made for the other islands.

[97] While they were doing this, the Delians too were taking to their heels, abandoning Delos and making for Tenos. The war-fleet swept down, but Datis, who had sailed ahead, ordered his ships to anchor, not off Delos itself, but across the strait at Rhenaea. When he discovered the whereabouts of the Delians, he sent them a herald to make a public announcement. 'Why have you gone and run away, you holy men? You have clearly formed a most mistaken impression of my intentions! Do you really think me such a fool that I would damage the birthplace of the two gods? Even had the King himself not expressly forbidden it, I would never do anything to harm such a place – nor its inhabitants either! So why not come home, and live on your island once more?' Then, once this message had been delivered to the Delians, Datis piled up 300 talents' worth of frankincense on the altar, and burned it as an offering to the gods.

[98] After taking these steps, his next objective was Eretria, to which he sailed at the head of a force that by now included both Ionians and Aeolians. In the wake of his departure, Delos was shaken by an earthquake (so the Delians report): a wholly unprecedented event, and one that in all the time since, right up to the present day, has never been repeated. What was being manifested by it if not a heaven-sent portent, warning mankind of the evils that were to come? For in three consecutive reigns – those of Darius, the son of Hystaspes, and of Xerxes, his son, and of Artaxerxes,[74] his grandson – more evils befell Greece than in all the twenty generations prior to Darius. This was partly due to the Persians, and partly to the battle for supremacy among the leading powers of Greece[75] themselves. It is hardly surprising, then, that Delos, although it had always previously stood motionless, should have been made to tremble. What is more, an oracle was on record as saying,

referring to the island: 'Delos too I will move, though it has never moved before.' (In Greek, the name *Darius* means 'Man of Action', while *Xerxes* means 'Warrior' and *Artaxerxes* 'Great Warrior'. That is what the Greeks, were the names of these kings to be translated correctly into their own language, would call them.)

[99] Moving on from Delos, the Barbarians stopped off at a number of islands, where they press-ganged the men into their army, and took the children of the islanders as hostages. In the course of this cruise from island to island, Datis was also provoked to dock at Carystus by the refusal of the Carystians to give him hostages, or consent to provide troops for an attack on cities that were their neighbours – by which, of course, they meant Eretria and Athens. Only when the Carystians were put under siege and had their land stripped bare were they brought round to the Persian view of the matter.

[100] The news that a Persian army was sailing against them prompted the Eretrians to ask the Athenians to come to their assistance – a request that did not go unregarded by the Athenians, who contributed as auxiliaries the four thousand small-holders who had been allotted the lands of the horse-breeding Chalcidians.[76] The Eretrians' strategy, however, was hardly a sound one: indeed, despite their summoning of the Athenians, they were in two minds as to what it should actually be. Some were in favour of abandoning the city and taking to the mountains of Euboea, while others, in the expectation of profiting from the Persians surreptitiously, were laying the grounds for treachery. When Aeschines, the son of Nothon, and one of the foremost Eretrians, realized just how divided the city was, he spelled out the full state of affairs to the Athenians who had already arrived, and begged them to leave for their own city, so that they at any rate might be spared the ruin of Eretria. The Athenians duly followed this advice of Aeschines.

[101] Over to Oropus they crossed – and safety. Meanwhile, the ships of the Persian fleet were making landfall on Eretrian territory, at Tamynae, Choereae and Aegilia. No sooner had the Persians docked than they began to unload their horses and get ready to go on the offensive against their adversaries. The Eretrians, by contrast, had not the slightest intention of venturing out and offering battle, since now that all talk of abandoning the city had been defeated it was their principal concern to defend their ramparts as best they could. The assault on the city walls proved a ferocious one, and for six days casualties on both sides

were heavy. Then, on the seventh, two distinguished men – Euphorbus, the son of Alcimachus, and Philagrus, the son of Cyneos – betrayed their city to the Persians; once inside Eretria, the Persians not only looted and torched its sanctuaries, in retaliation for those burned down in Sardis, but also rounded up its people as slaves, in compliance with the orders of Darius.

[102] With Eretria now in their hands, the Persians paused for a few days, and then set sail for Attica – where, confident that they would deal with the Athenians just as they had dealt with the Eretrians, they bore down hard. And Hippias,[77] the son of Peisistratus, because there was no better spot in all of Attica for cavalry operations, nor anywhere closer to Eretria, directed them to Marathon.

[103] When news of this reached the Athenians, they too marched out to Marathon. At the head of this rescue-force were ten generals, one of whom was Miltiades,[78] the grandson of Stesagoras, and son of the Cimon who was exiled from Athens by Peisistratus, the son of Hippocrates. It was during the course of this exile that Cimon and his team of four horses took first prize in the games at Olympia – and by so doing, matched the victory won by the Miltiades who was his half-brother on his mother's side. At the next Olympics, however, when he came first again, with the same team of mares, he allowed Peisistratus to be declared the winner: a forfeiture of victory that secured for him the opportunity to return to his own city under cover of a truce. Subsequently, however, after he had won yet another Olympic victory with the same horses (Peisistratus meanwhile having died), Cimon was killed by the sons of Peisistratus, who had employed men to ambush and assassinate him one night at the city hall. Cimon is buried immediately outside the city, beyond the road known as 'Through-the-Hollow'. The mares with which he won his three Olympic victories are buried opposite him. Their record was only ever equalled by the horses of Euagoras, the Spartan[79] – otherwise, no team has matched their deed. Cimon's elder son, Stesagoras, was being brought up in the Chersonese by his uncle, Miltiades, when his father was killed, while the younger one – who had been named Miltiades after the original Miltiades, the one who had first colonized the Chersonese – had been in Athens with Cimon himself.

[104] This was the Miltiades who was now serving as one of the Athenian generals – a man who had arrived in Athens from the

Chersonese, and had twice cheated death. First there was the time when the Phoenicians, setting great store by capturing him and leading him to the King, had pursued him as far as Imbros; the other was when he had escaped the Phoenicians and made it home to Athens, to what he had fondly imagined was safety, when his enemies, who had been lying in wait for him, dragged him through the courts. But the charge they brought against him of having ruled as a tyrant over the Chersonese was thrown out; and Miltiades, in the wake of this second escape, was elected by the Athenian people to the post of general.

[105] The first step the generals took, even before they had left the city, was to send an official envoy off to Sparta, an Athenian citizen and professional long-distance runner called Philippides.[80] While he was in the Mount Parthenium region above Tegea, he was met – according to the story told by Philippides himself, and which he reported back to the Athenians – by Pan.[81] After hailing Philippides by name, Pan then told him to give the Athenians a message. 'Why, when I am so fond of you, do you rebuff me? I have done you many favours in the past – and will do so again in the future.' And sure enough, when things turned out well for the Athenians, they had no doubt that the god had spoken the truth. So they built a sanctuary to Pan under the Acropolis, and every year, in response to his message of support, they display their gratitude by offering him animal blood-sacrifices and staging a torch-race.

[106] But to return to the time when Philippides' story of Pan's appearance was set. The second day after leaving Athens on his mission from the generals, he was already in Sparta.[82] 'Men of Lacedaemon,' he said, once he had come before their officials, 'the Athenians beg you for assistance. Do not, by looking the other way, allow the most ancient city in Greece to fall into bondage and the clutches of barbarians. Already, Eretria has been reduced to slavery, and Greece thereby made the weaker by the loss of a famous city.' This was the message he delivered, just as he had been instructed to do; but the Lacedaemonians, although keen to come to the help of the Athenians, were unable to do so right away, because of a law that they were most unwilling to break.[83] 'It is the ninth day of the month,' they explained, 'and because of that, we are unable to set out until the moon is full.'

[107] So the Lacedaemonians were left waiting for the full moon. Meanwhile, the Barbarians had landed at Marathon, led there by their guide, Hippias, the son of Peisistratus. Only the previous night, he had

had a vision [in a dream], in which he had imagined that he was sleeping with his own mother. He had understood this dream to mean that he would return to Athens, re-establish his rule and die an old man in his native land. At the same time, even as he was holding onto this interpretation of the dream, he had been performing his duties as guide: first, by landing the enslaved prisoners from Eretria onto an island called Aegilia belonging to the Styrians, and then, once the ships had put in at Marathon, by having them drop anchor there, and ordering the troop dispositions of the Barbarians once they were ashore. As he was busy with all this, however, he was seized by a more than usually violent fit of sneezing and coughing. Because he was such an old man,[84] most of his teeth were loose, and one of them was sent flying by the force of his coughing and fell into the sand; though he scrabbled around for it frantically, he was unable to bring it to light. Letting out an audible groan, he turned to those around him, and said, 'This land is not ours – nor will we ever conquer it. The only part of it that is mine is the share of it that my tooth has claimed.'

[108] And so it was, Hippias concluded, that his vision had been fulfilled. Meanwhile, the Athenians, who had taken up position in the sacred precinct of Heracles, were reinforced by the Plataeans, who had come with all their available manpower. The Plataeans did this because they had voluntarily subordinated themselves to the leadership of Athens – while the Athenians in return had always gone to great pains in defence of Plataea. And the reason for the Plataeans' acceptance of Athenian primacy? Well, originally, pressured as they were by the Thebans, and with Cleomenes, the son of Anaxandridas, happening to be in the vicinity at the head of the Lacedaemonians, the Plataeans had sought to place themselves under the leadership of the latter – an offer which the Lacedaemonians had rejected. 'We live too far away from you', they had explained, 'to offer you anything but the most lukewarm support. You might be taken off into slavery any number of times before we even got to hear of it! So what we would advise is this – place yourselves in the hands of the Athenians, who are your neighbours, and men with no small aptitude for providing help.' (Not, however, that the Lacedaemonians made this suggestion out of any concern for the Plataeans, since their aim, rather, was to stir up trouble for the Athenians by setting them and the Thebans at one another's throats.) Anyway, that was the advice the Lacedaemonians gave – and the Plataeans, taking it in good

faith, went to Athens while the Festival of the Twelve Gods was being celebrated, sat themselves down as suppliants before the altar, and pledged themselves to the Athenians. When the Thebans learned what had happened, they went to war against Plataea – and the Athenians came to the rescue. It so happened, however, that the Corinthians were also in the neighbourhood, and they, rather than turning a blind eye to the impending battle, instead persuaded the two sides to accept their arbitration, and brokered a peace deal – by the terms of which a border between the territory of the rival cities was fixed, in exchange for the Thebans agreeing not to lean on those Boeotians who were reluctant to join the Boeotian League.[85] But after the Corinthians had delivered this settlement and gone home, the Thebans set upon the Athenians as they too were withdrawing – an attack that was roundly defeated. The Athenians then crossed the border which the Corinthians had drawn to demarcate the limits of Plataean territory, passed onto Theban soil and fixed the Asopus to serve as a new frontier between the Thebans on the one side, and Plataea and Hysiae on the other. And so it was, in the manner I have just recounted, that the Plataeans came to place themselves under the protection of the Athenians; and so it was too that they came to Marathon to fight in the cause of Athens.

[109] The Athenian generals were split down the middle in their reading of the situation: there were those who refused to countenance giving battle on the grounds that they were too few in number to engage the Medes, while there were others, Miltiades among them, who urged that they should fight. It was then, with opinion evenly divided, but inclining towards the worse of the two options, that Miltiades approached Callimachus of Aphidne,[86] who had been chosen by lot to serve as War Archon, and who therefore – because the Athenians had long since given voting rights to the War Archon equal to those of a general – wielded an eleventh vote. 'It is in your power now, Callimachus,' Miltiades said, 'to condemn Athens to slavery, or to make her free so that the memory of your name will outlive even those of Harmodius and Aristogiton, and last the entire span of human existence. Never before have the Athenians faced a graver peril than they do right now – not since they first came into being. Bow our necks to the Mede, and there can be no doubt how terrible our sufferings will be, once Hippias has us back in his clutches. But should Athens prevail, she will surely emerge as the foremost city in Greece. You may well ask how that could

possibly come about, and why it is that everything should be hanging on your vote. Well – I will now explain. The ten of us on the board of generals[87] are evenly split in our opinions. Some are all for joining battle, and some are not. Now, my own reading is that if we do not fight, serious faction fighting will break out among the Athenians, and shatter their determination not to go over to the Mede. But if we join battle before such defeatism starts to spread among the Athenians, and if the gods do right by us, then we can come out ahead in any clash. So the choice is entirely yours – everything hangs on you. Back my point of view, and your country will be free, your city the first in all Greece. Back the demands of those who are shrinking from battle, however, and you will end up, not with the happy outcome I have just described, but with the opposite.'

[110] Sure enough, this speech of Miltiades served to win Callimachus to his side. The vote of the War Archon was added to those who wanted to give battle – and so the decision was ratified. From then on, as command of the board of generals rotated from day to day, those who were in favour of giving battle would each in turn stand down in favour of Miltiades. Nevertheless, although he always accepted the position, he did not give battle until the official day of his command dawned.[88]

[111] It was then, once his turn had come, that the Athenians drew themselves up ready for battle. Command of the right wing was taken by Callimachus in accordance with Athenian law, which stated that the War Archon should always have command of the right wing. From there – the position of leadership – the tribes stretched away, each one in its numerical position, one after the other. Last of all came the Plataeans, who were stationed on the left wing. (And ever after this battle, when the Athenians make their sacrifices at the public festival they hold every four years, the prayer raised by the Athenian herald asks that blessings rain down equally upon the Athenians and the Plataeans.) So that was how the Athenians were arrayed at Marathon. Their line of battle was equal in length to that of the Medes; and as a consequence it was weakest in the centre, where it was only a few ranks deep, while on the two wings it had strength in depth.

[112] With everyone now at battle-stations, the throats of the sacrificial victims were slit – and then, once these offerings had proved favourable, the signal was given to the Athenians, who advanced

towards the Barbarians at a run. The distance between the two armies was 8 stades[89] at the very least. When the Persians observed the Athenians bearing down on them at full tilt, they set about bracing themselves for the impact; but the truth was, because they could see how few the Athenians were, and because the charge was unsupported by either cavalry[90] or archers, they believed their attackers must be possessed by a death-wish. That, at any rate, was how the Barbarians read the situation; but the Athenians, once the whole mass of them had got to grips with the Barbarians, fought memorably. They were, so far as we can tell, the very first Greeks anywhere to make use of running towards an enemy as a tactic, and the first not to cringe before the sight of Median dress, and the men who wear it. Hitherto, Greeks had only had to hear the name of the Medes to be reduced to a state of terror.[91]

[113] The fighting at Marathon lasted a long time. In the centre, where the Persians themselves and the Sacae were stationed, it was the Barbarians who had the better of it, smashing their way through the Athenian lines, and then pursuing those they had defeated inland. On both the flanks, however, it was the Athenians and the Plataeans who emerged triumphant. The two wings, rather than pursue the routed Barbarians, then used their victory to join forces, and fight those who had broken through the centre – with victory going to the Athenians. As the Persians turned tail, the Athenians set off after them, hacking away, until they reached the sea – at which point they called for fire, and began to grab at the ships.

[114] It was amid all the effort of this that the War Archon, who had shown himself a man of formidable qualities, was killed – as too was one of the generals, Stesileos, the son of Thrasyleos. Another fatality was Cynegeirus,[92] the son of Euphorion, who had reached up to grab the stern ornament of one of the ships and had had his hand chopped off by an axe. There were numerous other celebrated Athenians who also fell.

[115] Seven ships were captured by the Athenians in this manner; but the remainder were got back out to sea by the Barbarians, who picked up the captives from Eretria they had left on the island, and then set sail round Cape Sunium, with the aim of reaching the city before the Athenians did. Blame for first suggesting this strategy to the Persians was pinned by the Athenians on the Alcmaeonids, who are said to have lifted up a shield as a prearranged signal[93] to the Persian fleet while it was out at sea.

[116] Round Cape Sunium it sailed. The Athenians, meanwhile, raced back to the defence of their city[94] as fast as their legs could carry them – and made it there before the Barbarians did. When they arrived, they swapped the sanctuary of Heracles that had been their base at Marathon for another, by setting up camp in the sanctuary at Cynosarges. The Barbarian fleet anchored off Phalerum (which in those days was still the main port of Athens), until at length, after its ships had been moored there for a while, it sailed away back to Asia.

[117] Some 6,400 men fell in the battle at Marathon on the Barbarian side, and on the Athenian, one hundred and ninety-two.[95] Such were the combined casualty figures. An extraordinary thing happened at Marathon to one Athenian, a man called Epizelus, the son of Couphagoras, who had been fighting with great bravery in the very thick of the hand-to-hand combat when suddenly he lost the sight of his eyes. He had taken no wound, nor a blow to anywhere on his body; and yet from that moment on, to the very end of his days, he continued blind. I have heard a story that he used to tell to account for this affliction: that he had imagined himself confronted by a giant man in full armour, whose beard was so bushy that it shadowed his entire shield. This phantom brushed by Epizelus and killed the man standing next to him. Such, I have been reliably informed, is the story he used to tell.

[118] As for Datis, he made his way back to Asia with his army; and while he was at Myconos, he had a vision in his sleep. What exactly he saw in it is not recorded; but the next day, the moment dawn had broken, he made a search of the fleet, until he found a gilded statue of Apollo on one of the Phoenician ships. He demanded to know the shrine from which it had been looted; and then, when he was told, sailed off in his own ship to Delos. There, he deposited the statue in a sanctuary, and instructed the Delians (who by this stage had all returned to the island) to take the image to Delium, a town of the Thebans, on the coast opposite Chalcis. After issuing these orders, Datis continued on his voyage; but the Delians failed to return the image, until, after twenty years had passed, the Thebans were prompted by an oracle to go and bring it back to Delium themselves.

[119] Datis and Artaphrenes, once they had touched Asian soil, took the enslaved Eretrians onwards up to Susa. Before they became the King's prisoners-of-war, the fury felt by Darius towards the Eretrians had been terrible – wronged as he had originally been by their unprovoked

aggression. But when he saw them led into his presence and utterly at his mercy, he inflicted no further miseries on them, but instead settled them in the land of Cissia,[96] on an estate he owned called Ardericca, which stands 210 stades distant from Susa, and 40 stades from a well which yields three distinct products. Asphalt, salt and oil: all of these are extracted from it. As for the means of extraction, the various substances are drawn up using a swipe to which half an animal skin has been attached to serve as a bucket. In goes the swipe and up comes a liquid, which is then poured into a container. From there, it is strained into a further container, and diverted along three different channels. The asphalt and the salt solidify immediately, but the oil [. . .] this *rhadinake*, as the Persians call it, is black,[97] and gives off a revolting stench. This, then, was the neighbourhood where the Eretrians were settled by King Darius – and there they have remained right up to my own time, still making a point of speaking their native tongue. So much for the fate of the Eretrians.

[120] The full moon had arrived, and with it there turned up in Athens a force of two thousand Lacedaemonians, whose eagerness to get there had been such that they had arrived in Attica on only the third day after leaving Sparta. Despite being too late for the battle, however, they were still keen to gaze on the Medes – and so they went on to Marathon, where they surveyed the battlefield. Then, after warmly congratulating the Athenians on their achievement, they headed home.

[121] As for the story told about the Alcmaeonids, that they had arranged to hoist a shield as a signal to the Persians because they wished to see the Athenians under the sway of the Barbarians and of Hippias, I refuse to accept anything so fantastical. It is perfectly self-evident that their loathing of tyrants was at least as great as that of Callias – if not more so. Callias was the son of Phaenippus and the father of Hipponicus, and the only person – on those occasions when Peisistratus was expelled from Athens – who had the nerve to buy Peisistratus' goods when they were put up for sale at public auction. In fact, Callias was forever devising ways to do Peisistratus down.

[122] There are many reasons why Callias deserves never to fade from the collective memory. Quite apart from the one I just mentioned, that he was a man who took a leading role in freeing his country, there is also his record in the Olympic Games, in which his horse was ridden

to victory and he came second in the four-horse chariot-race – and that was having earlier won first prize in the Pythian Games. Expenditure on such a massive scale served to make him a celebrity across the whole of Greece. Finally, there was the business of his three daughters, which showed just the kind of man he was. When they came to be of marriageable age, you see, he gave each one a present no less magnificent than it was welcome to them: the pick of any man in Athens. It made no difference who the object of a daughter's desire might be: the man she chose was the man to whom he gave her away.[98]

[123] The Alcmaeonids were at least the equals of Callias in their loathing of tyrants. That is why I give no credence to the slander, which seems to me a wholly grotesque one, that they lifted up a shield as a signal. They were in exile for the entire length of the tyranny,[99] after all, and it was thanks to them and their manoeuvrings that the sons of Peisistratus were eventually forced from power. Indeed, in my judgement, the role the Alcmaeonids played in the liberation of Athens was vastly more influential than that of Harmodius and Aristogiton.[100] The assassination of Hipparchus, far from bringing the tyranny to an end, served only to turn the surviving Peisistratids rabid, whereas the Alcmaeonids indisputably set Athens free – always assuming, of course, that the explanation I provided earlier, that the Alcmaeonids were the ones who bribed the Pythia to tell the Lacedaemonians to liberate Athens,[101] is indeed correct.

[124] As for the argument that disenchantment with the Athenian people might have led them to betray their country, it surely stands to reason – since there was no one in Athens more respected or admired than the Alcmaeonids – that they could not possibly have had such a motive for making the signal with a shield. No one would deny that a shield was lifted; that it happened is a fact. Concerning the identity of the person who might have lifted it, however, I have nothing further to add to what I have already said.

[125] Now, although the Alcmaeonids had blazed a trail in Athens right from the very beginning, it was Alcmaeon, and Megacles after him, who really served to burnish their lustre. The Lydians who were sent by Croesus from Sardis to the oracle at Delphi found Alcmaeon, the son of Megacles, to be a great help to them, and assiduous in providing assistance; and Croesus, when he learned from those Lydians who had visited the oracle how well Alcmaeon had done by them,

summoned him to Sardis, and then, on his arrival, offered him as a gift as much gold as he could remove on his person in a single go. The nature of this offer being what it was, Alcmaeon came up with a plan which involved him pulling on a tunic so large that it left room for a deep fold, and the loosest-fitting boots that he could find, before heading to the treasury, where he was led into its depths. Once there, he fell upon a mound of gold-dust: first, he stuffed his legs with as much gold as his boots could hold, and then, after he had filled the fold in his tunic brim-full with gold, he sprinkled gold-dust over the hair on his scalp, shoved some more into his mouth and left the treasury barely able to drag his boots along as he went. Indeed, with his mouth filled to bursting, and all the rest of him puffed up as well, he barely looked human. Croesus was overcome by laughter at the sight, and gave Alcmaeon, in addition to all the gold he was already carrying, at least as much again. As a result, the House of the Alcmaeonids became so fabulously rich that Alcmaeon was able to maintain a four-horse chariot, with which he won a victory at Olympia.

[126] After this, one generation later, the family were given such a boost by Cleisthenes, the tyrant of Sicyon, that its name ended up even more widely bruited across Greece than it had been before. It so happened, you see, that Cleisthenes, the son of Aristonymus (who was in turn the son of Myron, and the grandson of Andreas), had a daughter called Agariste. Cleisthenes wanted to identify the best man of all the Greeks, and then to give him his daughter in marriage: an ambition which prompted him, during the same Olympic Games in which he won the four-horse chariot-race, to issue a public announcement. 'Any Greek who considers himself worthy of becoming my son-in-law should get to Sicyon within sixty days at the latest, since it is from that date onwards that I will be making my decision on the marriage – a decision I will arrive at after the passage of a year.' At this, every Greek with an elevated sense of himself and of his lineage headed straight off to Sicyon – where the suitors found a running-track and a wrestling-ground waiting for them, built specially for the purpose by Cleisthenes.[102]

[127] Italy was represented by two men: Smindyrides, the son of Hippocrates, who came from Sybaris, and who, at a time when the city stood at the very peak of its prosperity,[103] lived a life of luxury such as no one had ever attained before; and Damasus, who came from Siris, and whose father was the Amyris whom people had nicknamed 'the

Wise'. Those were the suitors from Italy. Meanwhile, from the Ionian Gulf – or, to be more specific, from Epidamnus on the Ionian Gulf – came Amphimnestus, the son of Epistrophus. From Aetolia came Males, whose brother, Titormus, was the strongest man in Greece, but who had turned his back on human company by going to live in the remotest reaches of the Aetolian countryside. From the Peloponnese came Leocedes, whose father, Pheidon, had been the tyrant of Argos, and established the system of weights and measures[104] used by the Peloponnesians; he had also, in a display of arrogance so overweening that no other Greek has ever matched it, dismissed the Elean stewards of the Olympic Games, and presided over the games himself. There were other Peloponnesians too, as well as the son of Pheidon: Amiantus, the son of Lycurgus, an Arcadian from Trapezous; Laphanes, who was an Azanian from Paeus, and son of the Euphorion who once, according to the tale told in Arcadia, put up the Dioscuri[105] in his house, and from that moment on never refused any man his hospitality; and Onomastus, the son of Agaeus, who came from Elis. Then, alongside these suitors from the Peloponnese, there came two Athenians: Megacles, son of the Alcmaeon who had visited Croesus, and Hippocleides, the son of Tisander, and a man who for wealth and good looks had no superior in Athens. From Eretria, which at this time was highly flourishing, came Lysanias – but no one from the rest of Euboea. Thessaly was represented by one of the Scopadae, Diactorides of Crannon, and the Molossians by Alcon.

[128] So these were the suitors who came to Sicyon; and Cleisthenes, on the day that had been set as the deadline, began by asking them where they all came from, and what the lineage of each was. He then kept them with him for a year, over the course of which he was forever testing the mettle of their qualities as men, their temperaments, their education and their dispositions, both one on one, and collectively. The younger ones he would take out to the gymnasia, but the really key tests came when they all feasted together: for Cleisthenes, in addition to all his other activities over the period of their stay with him, proved a lavishly generous host. Now, it so happened that the suitors who particularly appealed to him were the pair who had arrived from Athens; and of the two of them, he preferred Hippocleides, the son of Tisander. Cleisthenes had been prompted to this judgement both by the many virtues that Hippocleides had as a man, and by the fact that he was related, through his ancestry, to the Cypselids of Corinth.[106]

[129] When the day dawned on which the marriage ceremony was due to be performed, and Cleisthenes was to announce which of the various suitors he had chosen, he sacrificed a hundred oxen and threw a great feast, to which both the suitors themselves and all the Sicyonians were invited. Then, with the meal done, the suitors put on a competitive show of music and public-speaking. As the wine flowed, so Hippocleides, who had established a clear lead over his rivals, ordered the oboe-player to strike up a jig on his oboe; and then, when the oboe-player did as instructed, began to dance. It appeared to the dancer himself that he was cutting a tremendous dash; but Cleisthenes, who was watching the entire performance, was signally unimpressed. In due course, Hippocleides paused in his dancing and ordered someone to bring in a table – on which, once it had duly been fetched, he began to perform some Laconian dance moves, then some different Attic turns, before finally, for his third trick, standing on his head on the table, and moving his feet to the rhythm as though they were his hands. During the first and second of these dance routines, Cleisthenes bit his tongue; appalled though he now was – witnessing such a shameless display of dancing – at the notion of having Hippocleides as his son-in-law, he did not wish to make his displeasure public. The sight of Hippocleides pumping his legs in the air to the music, however, was the final straw. 'Son of Tisander,' he declared, 'you have danced away your marriage.' To which Hippocleides retorted: 'Hippocleides could not care less!' And that was how the celebrated phrase first came to be uttered.

[130] Cleisthenes, after calling for silence, now addressed the assembled suitors. 'To all you men who came here to woo my daughter, I offer my heartiest congratulations. If only I could please everyone, rather than having to choose just one of you as my favourite at the expense of the rest. But, of course, I cannot possibly satisfy you all – not when my deliberations have as their focus a single girl. Consequently, I present to each one of you whose suit has proved unsuccessful the gift of a talent of silver. This is to thank you for the honour you have done me by wishing to marry into my family, and to recompense you for your absence from home. But the man to whom I give the hand of my child, Agariste, is the son of Alcmaeon – Megacles. Let the ceremony be performed, then, in accordance with Athenian custom.' After this, when Megacles had accepted the offer of betrothal, Cleisthenes formally ratified the marriage.

[131] So much for the Judgement of the Suitors: an episode that led to the Alcmaeonids becoming the talk of Greece. The child born of the union of Megacles and Agariste was the same Cleisthenes who organized the tribes in Athens, and instituted democracy there: he was named after his mother's father, Cleisthenes of Sicyon. Megacles also had a second son, Hippocrates, who fathered yet another Megacles, and another Agariste, named after the Agariste who was the daughter of Cleisthenes. This second Agariste married Xanthippus, the son of Ariphron; and while she was pregnant by him, had a dream in which she imagined herself giving birth to a lion. A few days later she bore Xanthippus a son: Pericles.[107]

[132] Now, after the body-blow struck at Marathon, the already considerable reputation enjoyed by Miltiades among the Athenians rose even higher. 'Give me seventy ships,' he asked of them, 'and an army, and money.' Rather than tell the Athenians the country that was to be the object of his expedition, however, he would only say that following him would make them very rich. 'I will lead you', he said, 'to a land where gold is abundant, and easily to be had.' Such was how he couched his request for ships – and to such a pitch of excitement did it bring the Athenians that they gave him what he wanted.

[133] Miltiades, once he had obtained his army, then sailed against Paros; he justified this action by pointing out that the Parians, because they had sent a force by trireme to serve with the Persians at Marathon, had already initiated hostilities. But this was merely a pretext, since his true motive was a grudge he had been nursing against the Parians ever since a native of their island – Lysagoras, the son of Tisias – had blackened his name with Hydarnes of Persia. Once Miltiades had arrived with his fleet at Paros, he and his troops penned the Parians inside the walls of their city; then, while he had them under siege, he sent in a herald with a demand for 100 talents, together with a warning that he and his army would not be going anywhere until the Parians had either paid or lost their city to him. But the Parians, who had no intention of handing over even a single piece of silver to Miltiades, had a whole number of schemes in mind for keeping their city secure – one of which was to build up under cover of night any particularly vulnerable stretch of wall to twice its original height.

[134] Thus far, all the Greeks are agreed; but from this point on in

the story, the account of what happened depends on the Parians. Miltiades, so they say, was rapidly running out of options, when there came to him with a request for a meeting a woman he had taken captive: a native of Paros by the name of Timo, who was a deputy-priestess to the gods of the underworld. 'If you really set such store by capturing Paros,' she told Miltiades, once she was in his presence, 'then I would advise you to do as I recommend.' So she made her suggestion; and after she had done so, Miltiades crossed to the hill in front of the city, to the sanctuary of Demeter the Lawgiver,[108] where, because he could not open the gates, he jumped over the wall. After he had landed, he went up to the temple itself, to do whatever it was he had come to do – either to move what should on no account be moved, or else to attempt something else altogether. When he reached the doors of the temple, however, all of a sudden there came over him such a spasm of terror that he turned on his tracks and leapt back over the wall. As he landed, however, he twisted his thigh – or perhaps, as another version has it, cracked his knee.

[135] Crippled as he now was, Miltiades sailed back to Athens; and despite having put Paros under siege for twenty-six days, and devastated the island, he had failed either to bring any money back with him for the Athenians, or to annex the city. As for the Parians, when they learned of the guidance that Timo, the deputy-priestess of the gods, had provided Miltiades, they wanted to punish her for what she had done; accordingly, once things had calmed down after the siege, they dispatched emissaries to Delphi. The question these messengers were sent to ask was this: should they execute the deputy-priestess of the gods for having told the enemy how her own native city might be captured, and for her revelation to Miltiades of Mysteries that no male was permitted to hear? The answer from the Pythia was 'No': Timo was innocent. It was because Miltiades was fated to come to a wretched end, so the Pythia explained, that Timo had appeared to him, and dragged him down into sacrilege.

[136] Meanwhile, as the Pythia was giving the Parians this oracle, so Miltiades' return home from Paros had set the tongues of the Athenians wagging, his most prominent critic being Xanthippus, the son of Ariphron, who hauled him up before the people on a capital charge of having defrauded them. Miltiades himself, despite his presence in court laid out on a litter, was prevented by the putrid state of his thigh from speaking in his own defence, and so his friends did it for him, reminding the court

in great detail of the battle that had been fought at Marathon, and of the capture of Lemnos: how Miltiades had captured it, punished the Pelasgians and then presented the island to the Athenians. The people were sufficiently won over by this to spare him death; but they still fined him 50 talents for the wrong he had done them. Subsequently, Miltiades' thigh turned so gangrenous that the putrefaction finished him off, and the 50 talents was paid by Cimon, his son.

[137] And how was it that Miltiades, the son of Cimon, had come to seize control of Lemnos? There was a time when the Pelasgians lived in Attica, until they were forced out by the Athenians. As to whether this was a legitimate act or a crime, I cannot comment, beyond reporting what others say. Hecataeus, the son of Hegesander, for instance, claims in his account of the episode that it was a crime. The Athenians, he reports, began to eye up the land under Mount Hymettus which they themselves had given to the Pelasgians as a home, in exchange for building the wall that once ringed the Acropolis. Originally, the land had been of poor quality and lacking any value at all; but when the Athenians saw how the soil had been made to bloom, they were seized by such envy, and such a longing to make it their own, that they drove the Pelasgians out, and gave no pretext for doing so. The Athenians themselves, however, claim that the expulsion had justice on its side – because the Pelasgians, who were settled at the foot of Mount Hymettus, had turned delinquent. Back in those days, you see, the Athenians were like all the other Greeks in having no domestic slaves, and so it was their own [sons and] daughters who would go to fetch water from the Nine Springs; and whenever the girls went, so unrestrained were the Pelasgians in their sexual appetites, and in their contempt for the Athenians, that they would do violence to the girls. Nor was that the limit of the Pelasgians' actions – the final straw being when they were caught red-handed plotting an attack on Athens. The Athenians, after uncovering this plot, could well have put the Pelasgians to death; but they opted not to, and instead, in a way that demonstrated just how much, as a people, they occupied the moral high ground, they ordered the Pelasgians out of the country. As emigrants, the Pelasgians seized control of various places, among which was Lemnos. Such, then, are the two versions of the episode: one as rehearsed by Hecataeus, and the other by the Athenians.

[138] The Pelasgians who were living on Lemnos at the time wanted to be avenged on the Athenians; and accordingly, since they had a

detailed knowledge of Athenian festivals, they obtained some penteconters and laid an ambush at Brauron, where the women of Athens
were celebrating the Festival of Artemis. The Pelasgians bundled a large
number of the women into their ships and then headed back with them
to Lemnos, where the women were kept as concubines. Their bellies
were forever being made to swell with offspring – offspring whom the
women then instructed in both the Attic dialect and the customs of Athens. As a result, their children refused to have anything to do with the
children of the Pelasgian women; and were one of them to be hit by a
Pelasgian child, all the others would join forces and come to his rescue.
What is more, the Athenian children took for granted their right to
order around the other children, and could hardly have been more dom-
ineering. When the Pelasgians realized what was going on, they debated
what to do about it – and as they mulled the issue over, so a terrible
realization began to dawn. If the Athenian children were already set on
discriminating against those children whose mothers were legally married in favour of their own kind, and were wasting no time in their
attempts to gain the upper hand, what on earth would they get up to on
reaching manhood? Accordingly, the Lemnians decided that their best
course would be to kill the children born of the Athenian women. This
they duly did – and murdered the mothers of the children too. It was
this exploit, combined with the earlier one committed by the women of
Lemnos, when they killed Thoas and their own husbands, which has
given rise to the universal practice across Greece of naming any atrocity
'a Lemnian deed'.

[139] Following the murder by the Pelasgians of their children and
their women, their soil would bear no fruit, while both their wives and livestock were rendered barren compared to their former fecund state. So it
was, famished and diminished by childlessness, that the Pelasgians sent
to Delphi to beg release from the evil condition in which they found
themselves. The Pythia ordered them to pay the Athenians whatever
penalty the Athenians themselves should think appropriate. So the
Pelasgians went to Athens, and announced their intention of making
full reparation for their crime. The Athenians adorned a couch in the
town hall with the most beautiful fittings they possessed, and placed
beside it a table covered to overflowing with every good thing to eat,
and then told the Pelasgians to hand over their country when it was in
a similar state. The response of the Pelasgians to this was to declare:

'Only when a ship borne on the north wind completes the voyage from your land to ours in a single day will we hand it over.' Since Attica lies well to the south of Lemnos, they knew, of course, that this was an impossible thing to happen.

[140] And so at the time it proved. Many years later, however, after the Chersonese on the Hellespont had come into Athenian hands, Miltiades, the son of Cimon, took advantage of the prevailing Etesian winds to sail from Elaeous on the Chersonese to Lemnos; and once there, he delivered a speech in which he reminded the Pelasgians of the oracle that they had never dreamt might be fulfilled, and ordered them to leave the island. The people of Hephaestia obeyed, but the people of Myrina, who refused to accept that the Chersonese was indeed part of Attica, had to be put under siege before they would surrender. And that was how the Athenians came to take control of Lemnos,[109] courtesy of Miltiades.

BOOK SEVEN

[1] When news of the battle fought at Marathon reached King Darius, the son of Hystaspes, his exasperation with the Athenians – already considerable because of their attack on Sardis – was raised to a terrible pitch, and left him even more determined to launch an expedition against Greece. Accordingly, he wasted no time in sending messengers to city after city, with instructions to raise troops: requisitions that in every case were more onerous than they had been the last time, and required the supply not only of ships, but of horses, food and transport vessels as well. These demands, which meant the enrolment and ready-ing of the elite of Asia for the campaign against Greece, served to put the continent in a state of upheaval for three whole years. Then, in the fourth year,[1] the Egyptians, who had been reduced to slavery by Cam-byses,[2] rebelled against the Persians. This, however, only made Darius all the more set on attacking both Egypt and Athens.

[2] Now, because it is the Persian custom that a king appoint his suc-cessor before setting out on campaign, his preparations for attacking these two targets provoked much strife among his sons as to which of them had the best claim to supreme power. Before becoming king, you see, Darius had had three sons by his first wife, a daughter of Gobryas; and then, after coming to the throne, had had four more, by Atossa, the daughter of Cyrus. The eldest of the first group of sons was Artoba-zanes, and that of the second Xerxes. Because they had different mothers the rivalry between these two brothers was very bitter: Artobazanes based his claim on the fact that he was the eldest of all Darius' children, and that it was the universal human custom for the eldest son to succeed to a kingdom; Xerxes retorted that his mother, Atossa, was the daughter of Cyrus, who had won the Persians their freedom.

[3] It so happened that the wait for Darius to deliver his judgement on this matter coincided with the journey up to Susa of Demaratus, the son of Ariston, who had been deposed from the Spartan throne, and who after fleeing Lacedaemon had gone into self-imposed exile. This man, when he learned of the dissent between the sons of Darius, is reported to have gone to Xerxes and advised him to point out, in addition to all the other arguments he had been making, that by the time of his own birth Darius had already become King, and Lord of the Persians, whereas Artobazanes had been born while Darius was still in a private position. 'That being so,' Demaratus said, 'it would be neither fitting nor fair for anyone to claim precedence over you. In Sparta, certainly, it is the custom, whenever there is a king whose sons were born to him both before and after his accession to the throne, for the younger son to succeed to the kingdom.'[3] So Xerxes did as Demaratus had suggested; and Darius, recognizing the justice of his case, duly designated him crown prince. Even without this advice, however, it is my own personal opinion that Xerxes would still have had the throne. There was no limit, you see, to the influence wielded by Atossa.[4]

[4] Once Darius had appointed Xerxes his heir as King of the Persians, he turned his attention to the campaigns ahead. It so happened, however, while he was busy with these preparations, and without ever having had the opportunity to avenge himself upon either the rebellious Egyptians or the Athenians, that one year into the Egyptian revolt, and thirty-six years in all after coming to the throne, Darius died. Upon his death, the kingdom passed to his son, Xerxes.

[5] Initially, although Xerxes continued with the mustering of troops for the war against Egypt, he had no great enthusiasm for any campaign against Greece. Always at his side, however, and wielding a greater influence over him than any other Persian, was the son of Gobryas and Darius' sister: his cousin, Mardonius.[5] 'Master,' Mardonius would say, by way of making his case, 'it is quite wrong that the Athenians, after all the grievous harm they have done the Persians, should go unpunished for their actions. For the present, yes, of course – you must complete what you have in hand. Once you have humbled the arrogance of Egypt, though, then mount a campaign against Athens. By doing so, you will not only win for yourself a fine reputation among people everywhere – you will also warn off anyone in the future from launching an attack on your territories.' That was how Mardonius pressed the case for vengeance;

but he would supplement it by pointing out how exceptionally beautiful a land Europe was, how well endowed with every kind of fruit-bearing tree and how fertile in terms of soil.[6] 'What mortal save the King deserves to have it as his own?'

[6] He was motivated to say these things by his relish for novel enterprises, and by his ambition to rule as governor of Greece – and in due course, so vigorous were his promptings that he did indeed persuade Xerxes to do as he wished. There were other factors too which assisted Mardonius in winning Xerxes round. The first of these was the arrival from Thessaly of an embassy from the Aleuadae, the ruling dynasty of the region, calling on the King to come to Greece, and assuring him of their heartfelt support; there were also the Peisistratids, who had journeyed up to Susa, and who, rather than merely echoing the arguments of the Aleuadae, dangled yet additional inducements. Accompanying them on their trip inland was Onomacritus, a man from Athens who, in addition to authoring his own oracles, had also compiled a collection of those delivered by Musaeus.[7] Though since patched up, relations between him and the Peisistratids had previously been exceedingly rocky; this was because Onomacritus had been expelled from Athens by Hipparchus, the son of Peisistratus, after being caught red-handed by Lasus of Hermione doctoring the oracles of Musaeus with a prophecy that the islands offshore of Lemnos were destined to vanish under the sea. It was this that explained why Hipparchus, who previously had made great use of him, had sent him into exile. Now, however, Onomacritus had joined the Peisistratids on their journey inland; and whenever he came into the presence of the King, they would sing his praises in awestruck terms, while Onomacritus himself would declaim his oracles. Any of these that contained portents of calamity to the Barbarians he would omit, choosing instead to recite only the most auspicious ones: how it was destined that the Hellespont be bridged by a man of Persia, and what the course of the advance would be. These oracles chanted by Onomacritus combined with the proposals advanced by the Peisistratids and the Aleuadae to reinforce their arguments.

[7] Now that Xerxes had been persuaded to campaign against Greece, his next step, one year after the death of Darius, was to make an expedition against the rebels. Once they had been crushed, and the whole of Egypt reduced to a slavery even more burdensome than it was in the time of Darius, he appointed as governor a man who was a son of

Darius, and his own brother: Achaemenes. Some time after this, while still serving as governor of Egypt, Achaemenes was assassinated by a Libyan called Inaros,[8] the son of Psammetichus.

[8] With Egypt conquered, and preparations for the expedition against Athens well in hand, Xerxes convened a meeting of the foremost noblemen in Persia, to pick their brains, and keep them all abreast of his intentions.

'Men of Persia,' Xerxes said to them when they had gathered, 'far from binding upon you as law some innovation of my own, I am drawing upon tradition – tradition derived from our elders. We have it from them, after all, that never – not since Cyrus deposed Astyages, and we replaced the Medes as the dominant power – have we sat idly around. Because it is God who serves us as our leader, the more enterprises we embark upon, the better for us it will be. You are all of you so familiar with the achievements of Cyrus, Cambyses and my own father, Darius, that it hardly needs me to list the various peoples they absorbed into our dominion. But what of myself? On succeeding to this throne, I began to ponder how I might avoid failing to measure up to those who had preceded me in this seat of honour, and how I might add to the sway of the Persians on a scale that would, at the very least, match their achievements. Now, after careful reflection, I have decided upon a course that will enable us to win both glory and a land that in size and wealth, let alone fertility, is not inferior to our current possessions – and at the same time to exact vengeance and retribution. That is why I have summoned you all to this meeting – to inform you of the enterprise I have in mind.

'I am going to bridge the Hellespont, and then march an army through Europe and into Greece. My reason for doing this is to punish the Athenians for their actions against the Persians and my father. You saw for yourselves how Darius was planning to launch a direct attack on these same men – but he died before he could bring his vengeance to completion. That is why, for his sake, and for the sake of every other Persian, I shall not rest until I have captured Athens, and put it to the torch. It was the Athenians, after all, who began this – who were the aggressors against my father and myself. First, in the company of Aristagoras of Miletus, that slave of ours, they went to Sardis, and burned down its sacred groves and sanctuaries. Then, after we had landed an army on their own soil, under the command of Datis and

Artaphrenes, they dealt with us in a way with which I am sure all of you are familiar.

'That is why I am resolved to lead an expedition against them – a course that I have calculated will result in a whole number of benefits. For instance, if we conquer them – and those too who live as their neighbours in the land of Pelops the Phrygian – then the limits of Persian territory will be brought to border the sky, the very realm of Zeus.[9] There will be no more lands left beyond our frontiers for the sun to shine upon. You and I, we will together cross the length and breadth of Europe and mould it all into a single land. Once we have subdued the peoples I just mentioned, there will not – so far as I know – be a city or a nation left anywhere on earth capable of meeting us in battle. It is not simply those who have wronged us, you see, who are to bear the yoke of slavery – so too will the innocent.

'So, if you wish to be in my favour, here is what you must do. When you get the signal from me that the time set for you to come has arrived, every last one of you must look to present himself, and not hesitate for a moment. Whoever brings with him the best-equipped contingent of soldiers will be rewarded by me with gifts of the kind that we in our country value most highly. So now you know what is to be done. Nevertheless, because I do not want you thinking that I take no interest in the opinions of people other than myself, let me now throw the discussion open. Should any of you have a point of view that you would like to make public, I command you to reveal it.' And with this, Xerxes fell silent.

[9] Next to speak was Mardonius. 'Not only are you the greatest Persian who has ever lived, Master, but there is no one in the future who will rival you either. With what excellence and truth your speech hit its mark across a whole range of topics! Above all, there was your refusal to allow those Ionians who live in Asia to take us for fools – something they have absolutely no right to do. Did the Sacae, or the Indians, or the Ethiopians, or the Assyrians, or indeed any number of other peoples, many of them very great ones indeed, ever do the Persians any wrong, that we conquered them, and now keep them under us as slaves? No! It was because we wished to widen our dominion! That being so, what a monstrous state of affairs it would be were we not to punish the Greeks for a display of criminality that they themselves initiated.

'What do we have to fear? That they will combine forces to make a large army? That they have deep reserves of money on which to draw? Hardly! We know how they fight – and we know how feeble their resources are. After all, we have already conquered and annexed those of their offspring who settled in our sphere of influence: the Ionians, the Aeolians and the Dorians, as they are called. I myself have already had personal experience of campaigning against these men, when, on the orders of your father, I drove on as far as Macedonia – a region that is hardly any distance from Athens at all! – and not once was I opposed in battle.

'What is more, I am reliably informed that the way of war as invariably practised by the Greeks[10] is, due to their ignorance and general ineptitude, a thoroughly ridiculous one. Whenever they declare war on one another, they will find the best and most level stretch of ground, and then go off to it for a battle – with the result that even the victors only ever leave the field after sustaining massive casualties. As for the losers – a topic I do not want to get started on – they end up utterly annihilated. What the Greeks should do, of course, is take advantage of the fact that they all speak the same language, and use heralds and messengers to settle their differences – anything rather than open warfare. And if, after all, there is no alternative but for them to meet on the battlefield, then they should find a place where there is no possibility of fighting a really decisive battle, and make trial of one another there. But the Greeks are committed to their pointless way of doing things; and that was why, in the course of my own campaigning, I was able to drive as far as Macedonia without its ever even crossing their minds that they might come and engage me in battle.

'So who will there be, O King, when you appear at the head of the hordes of Asia, and all its navies too, to block your way and offer you battle? I very much doubt that Greek courage will extend to such an undertaking. But suppose I turn out to be wrong in that respect, and the foolhardiness of the Greeks does indeed incite them to go into battle with us? Well, they will soon discover that there is no one in the world our equal for prowess in warfare. Let no stone be left unturned. Nothing ever happens of its own accord, after all. Good things will always favour those who put themselves to the test.'

[10] And with this, Mardonius ended a speech that had served to cast the opinions of Xerxes in a most excellent light. All the other Persians, lacking the courage to voice an opinion against the proposal laid before

them, held their tongues, until Artabanus – who was the son of Hystaspes and therefore could draw confidence from the fact that he was Xerxes' uncle – spoke as follows.

'When there is a decision to be made, O King, it is quite impossible to pick the best one, unless a variety of different opinions are aired. If just one single opinion is articulated, it is the only one that can then be adopted. But as with unalloyed gold, whose purity can never be gauged only by reference to itself, but must be rubbed on the touchstone alongside another piece of gold, so with the expressing of different points of view: it enables us to identify quality. I openly told your father, my brother Darius, not to launch a campaign against the Scythians, a people whose refusal to settle down means they lack so much as a single city anywhere in the world. But did he listen to me? No. He was so confident of conquering these nomads, these Scythians, that he went to war against them – only to lose many of his best troops and be forced to retreat. And now you, O King, are about to go to war with men far more formidable than the Scythians, and whose reputation by both land and sea is without parallel. Terrible danger lurks there – and it is only right that I should tell you so.

'You say that you will bridge the Hellespont, and then march an army through Europe and into Greece. But what if you suffer a defeat – by land, by sea, or even by both? These men are said to fight very valiantly, the truth of which we can gauge from the fact that an army as large as the one that went with Datis and Artaphrenes to Attica was wiped out by the Athenians alone.[11] But even supposing they are not victorious by land as well as sea, what then? They only have to launch a naval offensive, and bring us to defeat by sea, and then nothing will stand between them and the dismantling of the bridge beyond a voyage to the Hellespont. And that way grave peril lies, O King!

'It is not because I am blessed with any particular insight of my own that I speculate in this way, but because of the disaster we so nearly suffered on a previous occasion, when your father bridged first the Thracian Bosporus and then the River Ister with pontoons,[12] and crossed over them to invade Scythia. That was the time when the Scythians did all they possibly could to persuade the Ionians, who had been entrusted with the security of the bridges over the Ister, to dismantle the line of retreat. At that point, had Histiaeus, the tyrant of Miletus, gone along with his fellow-tyrants rather than standing up to them, it would have spelled the utter ruin of Persian interests. That everything the King was and did depended upon a single person is a notion too dreadful even to hear put into words!

'You do not want to run a risk like that – not when there is no necessity to do so. So take my advice: dissolve this meeting now. Then in due course, once you have had the chance for some private reflection, and feel the time is right, let us all know what you think your best approach might be. There is nothing quite so advantageous, in my own experience, as a really well-laid plan. True, it can always be stymied by bad luck, but even when things do not turn out as hoped, a sound plan remains a sound plan still. On the other hand, someone who has planned poorly may enjoy a stroke of good fortune and find that something turns up, but his plan is no less a poor one for that.

'You can see for yourself how it is creatures of an overbearing size that God strikes down with his thunderbolts and prevents from flaunting themselves, while the insignificant rile him not in the slightest. You can see for yourself how it is always the largest buildings and the tallest trees that are the targets of his missiles. God, you see, delights in clipping everything that rises high. So if, in his resentment, he should afflict a vast army with panic, or pelt it with thunderbolts, it can easily be wiped out by a smaller force: a fate that, left to its own devices, it would not have merited at all. God, you see, allows no one save himself to entertain grand plans.

'Rush into anything too fast, and you will trip up – most likely with appalling consequences. Good things come to those who pause in their tracks. This may not be immediately obvious, but give it time and you will find it to be so.

'That is my advice to you, O King.[13] As for you, son of Gobryas – put a stop to this nonsense you are spouting about the Greeks, who do not deserve such slander. By disparaging them, you only encourage the King to make war on them. Indeed, it seems to me that all this frantic effort of yours has precisely that as its end. Well, I hope it never happens. Slander is a most terrible thing: two guilty parties teaming up against a single victim. Why two? Because the one who spreads smears is to blame for levelling accusations against someone who is not present, while the other is to blame for believing something before the certain truth of the matter has been confirmed. As for the one absent from the conversation, he is doubly wronged: slandered by the one, and viewed in an evil light by the other.

'But come, Mardonius, if war absolutely must be made against these men, then why not let the King stay here in his customary haunts, while we both pledge our children as sureties? You can hand-pick the men you want, recruit as large an army as you please and lead it off on campaign – and should things turn out for the King as you say they will, then let my children be put to death, and me alongside them too. But should my forecast prove accurate, then let yours be the ones to suffer death – yes, and you too, if indeed you ever make it back home. However, if this is not a bargain you are prepared to strike, and yet still you are absolutely set on leading an army into Greece, then I tell you now that those left behind here in Persia will come to hear of how their country has suffered a terrible calamity, and of how you, Mardonius, the man responsible for it, have been torn to pieces by dogs and birds somewhere in the land of the Athenians, or else of the Lacedaemonians – always provided, of course, that you were not killed earlier on the road. And then you will have a proper understanding of the men whom you are now inciting the King to attack.'

[11] This speech by Artabanus threw Xerxes into a rage. 'Artabanus,' he retorted, 'the only thing that spares you a punishment appropriate to the idiocy of your comments is the fact that you are my uncle. Spineless coward that you are, I hereby sentence you to the humiliation of staying behind with the women,[14] and not accompanying me on the expedition to Greece. I can perfectly well bring my deeds to match my words even without your assistance. Indeed, if I do fail to punish the Athenians, may I no longer rank as the son of Darius, the son of Hystaspes, the son of Arsames, the son of Ariaramnes, the son of Teïspes, the son of Achaemenes[15] – since even were we to sit on our hands, I know full well that there is not the remotest prospect of their doing the same. No, to judge by what they did at the onset of this whole business, when they torched Sardis and invaded Asia, they would soon be on the offensive against our lands. It is simply not an option for either side to back down. We are locked into a contest in which we must either act or die. Either the whole of their lands will end up under the sway of Persians, or ours will end up under that of Greeks.[16] Such is our mutual hatred, there can be no middle position. It is only right and proper, then, that

we, who were the first to suffer injury, should now look to be avenged. Right and proper also that I should explore the nature of this "terrible fate" that I will supposedly endure when I come to advance against these men – men whom even Pelops the Phrygian, who was a slave of my forefathers, brought so utterly to subjugation that right up to the present day both the people and the land itself still bear the name of their conqueror.'

[12] Later, however, once the speeches were done, and darkness was closing in, Xerxes found himself unsettled by the views of Artabanus. That night, as he turned the issue over, he came to the conclusion that it was not, after all, in his interests to invade Greece. Then, in the wake of this about-face, he fell asleep; and that same night, so the Persians report, he had a vision. It seemed to Xerxes that a tall, well-built man was standing over him and saying, 'Why the change of mind, Persian? Did you not just tell the Persians to muster an army, which you were going to lead against Greece? This reversal of policy will benefit you not at all – nor will the one here before you now forgive you for it. Stick to the course of action that you settled upon yesterday.' After delivering these words, the man seemed to Xerxes to fly away.

[13] Rather than dwell on the dream, however, Xerxes greeted the new day by reassembling all the Persians he had previously summoned. 'Men of Persia,' he said, 'forgive me my abrupt change of mind. My powers of reasoning are yet to attain their peak, and those who urged on me the course of action that I adopted yesterday have not left me alone for a single moment. What is more, the instant I heard Artabanus give his opinion, my youthful temper boiled over so violently that I dismissed his words most offensively, and in a manner not at all appropriate to a man of his age. Now, however, I acknowledge that he was right, and have adopted his point of view. Consequently, because I have reversed my policy and will not be invading Greece after all, you may relax.' And the Persians, hearing this, rejoiced and prostrated themselves before him.

[14] When night came, however, and Xerxes fell asleep, he dreamt that the same man as before was standing over him. 'So, son of Darius,' the man said, 'you have appeared before the Persians and cancelled your expedition, have you, dismissing my words as though they were of no account, and spoken by some nobody? Well, know this: if you do not set out at once with your army, then the result will be that though you have

risen swiftly to greatness, yet in no less swift a time will you be cast down again.'

[15] This vision threw Xerxes into such a panic that he leapt out of bed and sent a messenger with a summons for Artabanus. 'Artabanus,' Xerxes declared, once he had arrived, 'there was a short time when I was not thinking straight. I responded to the excellent advice you gave me with rude and foolish words. All the same, it did not take me long to change my mind and to realize that I should adopt the policy you had suggested. Nevertheless, keen though I am to do so, I cannot. Ever since I had my change of heart and reversed my decision, I have been haunted by a phantom in a dream, who absolutely refuses to join with everyone else in praising what I am doing. Indeed, just now, before vanishing, he actually threatened me. Now, if it is a god who is sending this dream, and if there is no satisfying him save by going on campaign against Greece, then the same dream might wing its way to you, and deliver you the very instructions it gave to me. Such a thing might come about, it crossed my mind, were you to take all these clothes of mine, put them on and sit down on my throne, and then in due course go to sleep in my bed.'

[16] Such was the order given by Xerxes; but Artabanus initially refused to obey, not thinking himself worthy to sit on the royal throne, and in the end was only brought to do as he was instructed after being left with no choice in the matter.

'In my judgement,' he told the King, 'it makes no difference whether a good idea comes to a man as the result of his own deliberations, or because he is willing to listen to someone who can offer him sound advice. Your good ideas derive from both sources – but because you also keep bad company, this leads you to stumble. Men say much the same of the sea – that although there is nothing more serviceable to humanity, yet the winds gusting across its surface prevent it from being true to its own nature. It was not the tongue-lashing you gave me that stung most painfully – no, there was something quite else. The Persians had two choices before them – one that would serve to inflate their arrogance, and the other, by pointing out how wrong it is to school the soul in a perpetually acquisitive dissatisfaction with what one has, to curb their conceit. Yet you, faced by these two options, adopted the one more likely to trip you up: you, and the Persians with you.

'And now, just when you have had a change of heart for the better, and opted to abandon the expedition against the Greeks, you say that a dream sent by some god keeps coming to you, forbidding you to abandon the expedition. But this dream of yours, my boy, is not of divine origin. I have lived many more years than you, and so can explain to you the nature of these visions that drift into the minds of men as they sleep. Most of the things we see as flitting presences in our dreams are likely to be the thoughts we had during the day. And what have we had very much in hand over the past few days? Why, this same expedition!

'But what if my interpretation of your dream is wrong, and it does indeed have some aspect of the divine? Well, you have already given the answer to that yourself. Let it come to me, as it did to you, and issue its orders! But the chances of its appearing to me are most unlikely to be improved by my wearing your clothes in place of my own, or by swapping my bed for yours – always assuming, of course, that it wishes to appear to me at all. Whatever this thing may be that is manifesting itself in your sleep, it surely cannot be so simple-minded as to mistake me for you, purely because it has observed that I am dressed up in your clothes! No, what we need to find out is whether I am simply too insignificant to merit a visitation – in your clothes or mine, it will make little difference – and whether instead it comes to you. If it does persist in its visits, then even I would be brought to acknowledge it as divine. So come, then, if this really is what you want to happen, and there is no diverting you from your insistence that I go to sleep in your bed, let us see if it will appear to me as well, once I have done as you ask. But until it does, I will hold to my current opinion.'

[17] With these words, and confident of proving that Xerxes had been talking nonsense, Artabanus did as he had been ordered. He put on Xerxes' clothes and sat on the royal throne, before going to bed; and it was there, as he lay asleep, that he was visited by the same dream that had come to Xerxes. Standing over Artabanus, the figure said, 'So you are the one who has been busily trying to dissuade Xerxes from invading Greece, are you? And all out of concern for him! Well, both now and in the future, your punishment for attempting to divert the inevitable is certain. As for Xerxes, he has been left in no doubt as to the suffering that will be his should he prove disobedient.'

[18] And then, after the figure in the dream had issued these threats, Artabanus imagined that it was coming to burn out his eyes with hot irons. With a loud scream he sprang from the bed and sat down next to

Xerxes, to whom he gave a thorough account of what he had seen in his sleep. 'O King,' he went on to say, 'it was because I am a man who has often seen the humbling of great powers by those much weaker than themselves that I sought to curb the natural instincts of your youth, and because I know, remembering what happened to the expedition led by Cyrus against the Massagetans, and that launched by Cambyses against the Ethiopians, and from my own personal experience of Darius' campaign against the Scythians, how wrong it can be to hanker after too many things.[17] It was my appreciation of this that led me to conclude that a peaceable inactivity would serve to cast you in the happiest light in the eyes of people everywhere. But since there is some supernatural compulsion at work, and since the ruin overtaking the Greeks does indeed appear to be of divine origin, it is I who must now back down and revise my opinion. Inform the Persians of the message you have had from the god, tell them to resume their preparations in accordance with the instructions that you originally gave them, and so match your actions to the god's commands that no aspect of them is neglected.' These words, and the confidence bred in Xerxes by the vision, prompted the King to inform the Persians of what had happened the moment day had dawned, while Artabanus, who previously had been the one dissenting voice to speak publicly, now openly gave his full backing to the enterprise.

[19] So Xerxes was set on war; and in due course there came to him in his sleep a third vision, which the Magi, when they heard it, interpreted[18] to mean that the entire earth, and all the people within it, would be his slaves. This was Xerxes' vision: his head crowned by a wreath made from the bough of an olive tree, the shoots of which enveloped the whole earth, but then vanished. Immediately, once the Magi had given their interpretation of the dream, every last man among the Persians who had assembled for the meeting set off for his own province, and devoted himself with total enthusiasm to fulfilling the orders of the King, whose promise of a reward everyone was keen to win for himself. So it was, by ransacking every corner of the continent, that Xerxes mustered his army.

[20] In the wake of Egypt's conquest, he spent four whole years preparing and provisioning his task-force – and then, in the course of the fifth year, he embarked on his campaign with an immense array of men. Indeed, for sheer scale, no other army of which we know has ever

remotely compared to it: not the one led by Darius against the Scythians; nor the one with which the Scythians, in the course of their pursuit of the Cimmerians, invaded the land of Media, conquered and occupied nearly all the upper regions of Asia and thereby served to provoke Darius' own subsequent invasion; nor the one that, according to our sources,[19] the sons of Atreus led against Troy; nor, prior to the Trojan War, the one that was raised by the Mysians and the Teucrians, and with which they crossed the Bosporus into Europe, conquered the whole of Thrace, descended upon the Ionian Sea and advanced as far south as the River Peneius.

[21] Even if all these armies were combined, and some other ones added as well, they would still not match the total of this one single army. What people of Asia, after all, did Xerxes not lead against Greece? What supply of water, the very great rivers only excepted, did they fail to drink dry? Some supplied ships, and others were conscripted to serve on land; some were ordered to provide cavalry, and others, in addition to serving with the army, provided transport-ships for the horses; some furnished warships for the pontoon-bridges, and others both provisions and ships.

[22] In the first place, prompted by the disaster that had ended the previous attempt to sail round Athos,[20] some three years were spent in readying the area. From Elaeous in the Chersonese, where a host of triremes lay at anchor, men drawn from all the various contingents in the army were set to digging a channel, working in relays and under the whip.[21] The locals who lived in the region of Athos were also set to digging. This work was supervised by two Persians: Bubares, the son of Megabazus, and Artachaeës, the son of Artaeus. As for Athos itself, it is a large and celebrated mountain that runs down to the sea, and is dotted with settlements. At the point where the mountain joins the mainland, it is shaped like a peninsula and forms an isthmus some 12 stades wide. This particular stretch, between the Acanthian Sea and the sea off Torone, is generally level, with hills that are of barely any size at all. It is on this isthmus, where Athos ends, that the inhabitants of Sane, a Greek city, live, while beyond them, on the peninsula of Athos, stand Dion, Olophyxus, Acrothoium, Thyssus and Cleonae: cities whose inhabitants the Persian King was determined to turn from people of the mainland into islanders.

[23] So much for the cities located on Athos. As for the excavations,

what the Barbarians did was to draw a straight line near the city of Sane across the land that was to be dug, and then to allocate a different section of it to each one of the various peoples. Once the canal had reached a certain depth, there were men who would stand right at the bottom and continue with the digging, while others would pass up the earth that was constantly being excavated to others standing on ladders, and they in turn, on receiving it, would pass it on to others, right the way up to the top – where, when it arrived, it would be carted off and flung away. Now, with the exception of the Phoenicians, the various contingents found their workload doubled by the way that the steep sides of the trench kept falling in: something that was bound to happen, since the width of the channel they had dug was the same at the top as it was at the bottom. But the Phoenicians, ever practical, displayed their customary shrewdness on this occasion too: once lots had been taken, and they had been allocated their section of the excavation, they made the top part of their trench twice as wide as the canal itself needed to be, but then, as they dug downwards, allowed the trench progressively to narrow. By the time they reached the bottom, the width of their stretch of the canal was directly equivalent to that dug by the rest of the workforce. There is a meadow, which was converted into a place for the labourers to mix, and buy and sell things. Most of their grain, however, was brought ready-ground from Asia.

[24] I myself have come to the conclusion that it was the sheer scale of Xerxes' relish for magnificence which prompted him to order the digging of the canal: an ambition to flaunt his power and to leave behind him a permanent memorial. It would have been no trouble for him to have had the ships hauled across the isthmus, after all – but instead he commissioned a channel for the sea, wide enough for two triremes to pass through side by side while being rowed.[22] The same men who worked on the excavation were also tasked to join together the two banks of the River Strymon by means of a bridge.

[25] Now, in addition to these projects, Xerxes had the Phoenicians and the Egyptians prepare cables out of papyrus and white flax for the bridges, and lay down supplies of food for the army, so that neither soldiers nor pack-animals would go hungry during the advance on Greece. Then, following information he had obtained about the terrain, he assigned agents to various regions, and had them set up depots in strategic locations, to which provisions were transported by merchant-ship

and ferry from across the whole of Asia. The majority of supplies were brought to a spot in Thrace called the White Cape, while others were allocated variously to Tyrodiza in the territory of Perinthus, to Doriscus, to Eion on the banks of the Strymon, and to Macedonia.

[26] Meanwhile, as the labourers toiled at the projects assigned to them, the entire land-army was setting out with Xerxes from its mustering-point at Critalla in Cappadocia (where all the various military contingents that were to advance overland with Xerxes had been instructed to assemble) and was making its way to Sardis. I am unable to say who received the reward promised by the King to whichever governor brought the best-equipped contingent. Indeed, I do not even know whether a decision was ever made on the matter. Once over the River Halys, the expedition crossed into Phrygia; and as it made its way through Phrygian territory, it came to Celaenae, where the springs of the River Maeander rise. The springs of another river too, which goes by the name of the Catarractes, and is no less in size than the Maeander, rise in Celaenae, right in the very town square, before issuing into the Maeander. Also [in the city] there hangs the skin of Marsyas the Silenus: according to the story told by the Phrygians, he was flayed and his skin was hung there by Apollo.[23]

[27] Waiting in the city was a man from Lydia, Pythius the son of Atys, who received the entire army of the King, and Xerxes himself, with the most lavish hospitality, and then announced himself keen to help fund the war with a financial contribution. Xerxes responded to this offer of money from Pythius by asking some Persians who were present what kind of a man he was, and how much money he possessed, that he could make such a proposal. 'O King,' they answered, 'he is the one who gave your father, Darius, the golden plane tree and vine. He is the richest man any of us have ever heard of, second only to you.'

[28] This last comment so astounded Xerxes that he next asked Pythius directly how much money he had. 'O King,' Pythius answered, 'I will not deceive you, nor will I pretend that I have no idea how much I am worth. I will list the precise details for you. You see, the moment I learned that you were heading down to the Greek Sea[24] it became my ambition to contribute financially to the war – and so I ran a full tally. I found, once all the accounts had been added up, that I have 2,000 talents of silver, and am 7,000 staters short of having four million golden Daric staters. The whole lot I now give to you as a gift. The

income I get from my slaves and estates is quite sufficient to live on.'
Such was the speech he gave – to the delight of Xerxes.

[29] 'You, my Lydian host,' the King said, 'are the first man I have
met since leaving the land of Persia who has looked to provide hospitality to my troops, or has come into my presence and offered me,
voluntarily and quite unprompted, financial assistance with the war.
Not only have you entertained my army lavishly, but this offer of money
you have announced is most generous indeed! So let me, in return, grant
you these privileges. I grant you an official rank as my friend, together
with 7,000 staters from my own purse, so that you will then have a full
four million. Four million, after all, makes for a nice round number – so
rather than leave you short, let me make it up by giving you the seven
thousand. Keep in your possession the things you already have, and
always hold to your current course of behaviour. Do that, and neither
now nor in the future will you ever have cause to regret it.'

[30] Then, once he had made good on these words, Xerxes continued
full tilt with his advance. First, he passed a Phrygian city called Anaua,
then a salt lake, and then he came to Colossae, a large Phrygian city.
This is where the River Lycus plunges into a chasm, and then, some 5
stades after vanishing underground, re-emerges and flows into the Maeander. From Colossae, the army continued on its way to where Phrygia
borders Lydia, and arrived at the city of Cydrara, where the frontier is
marked by an inscription on a pillar that was erected there by Croesus,
and is still solidly fixed in the ground.

[31] So Xerxes crossed from Phrygia into Lydia, and here the road
divided – one fork bearing left to Caria, and the other right to Sardis.
Take the right-hand fork, and the traveller has no choice but to cross the
River Maeander and visit the city of Callatebus, where there are men
who specialize in concocting a honey out of tamarisk and wheat-flour.
This was the road that Xerxes took; and on the way he came across a
plane tree so beautiful that he adorned it with gold, and appointed a
man from the Immortals[25] to stand guard over it. The next day, he
arrived in the Lydian capital.

[32] The first thing he did on coming to Sardis was to send heralds to
Greece with demands for earth and water, and to give notice that meals
were to be readied for the King. These demands for earth were sent
everywhere in Greece – everywhere, that is, except Athens and Sparta.[26]
The reason why Xerxes sent a second demand for earth and water was

that he believed that those who had refused to hand them over the first time, when Darius had sent his messengers, would be so terrified now that they were bound do so. He sent his messengers because he wished to find out if he was right.

[33] After this, he made preparations for the march to Abydus. His men, meanwhile, had been bridging the Hellespont between Asia and Europe. Directly opposite Abydus, there is a rugged promontory which extends from the stretch of the Hellespont that borders the Chersonese, between the city of Sestus and Madytus, down into the sea. (It was here, not long afterwards, that the Athenians, under the command of Xanthippus, the son of Ariphron, captured and nailed alive to a plank a man called Artaÿctes, a Persian who was the governor of Sestus, and who had been committing sacrilegious acts with women brought to him in the sanctuary of Protesilaus in Elaeous.[27])

[34] Culminating at this promontory, and beginning at Abydus, two bridges were built by the contingents charged with the project: the Phoenicians, who used white flax, and the Egyptians, who used papyrus. The distance between Abydus and the shore opposite is seven stades. Once the straits had been bridged, however, a great storm erupted, and smashed the bridges to pieces.

[35] When Xerxes was informed of this, his anger was so terrible that he ordered his men to give the Hellespont three hundred lashes of the whip, and to drop a pair of fetters into the sea. Indeed, I have heard it said that he also sent men with irons to brand the Hellespont. Be that as it may, those who were laying on the lash were certainly ordered to speak to the sea with the insolence so typical of Barbarians.[28] 'O bitter water, this is done to you by your master as punishment for the wrong you did him, despite his never having done you the slightest harm. King Xerxes will cross you, whether you wish it or not. How right people are not to offer sacrifice to you – turbid and briny river that you are!' Such, then, was the punishment inflicted by Xerxes upon the sea – and as for those responsible for the bridging of the Hellespont, he had them beheaded.

[36] Those assigned this abhorrent office duly fulfilled their task, while other engineers rebuilt the bridges. To do this, they joined together a mass of penteconters and triremes to serve the bridges as their underpinnings: three hundred and sixty on the side nearest the Euxine Sea, and three hundred and fourteen on the other side, with an alignment

that was angled obliquely to the Euxine, but parallel to the flow of the Hellespont, so as to maintain the tautness of the cables. Then, once the boats had been placed together, anchors on exceptionally long chains were sunk; this was done so as to counter the winds that blew, on the side facing the Euxine, from the inland sea, and on the other side, the westward one facing the Aegean, from the west and the south. (A narrow gap left between the penteconters and triremes allowed any small ships wishing to sail to or from the Euxine to navigate their way through.) Then, with this stage completed, the engineers extended cables from the shore and wound them taut using wooden windlasses; unlike on the previous occasion, when white flax had been used to cable the one bridge, and papyrus the other, two cables of white flax and four of papyrus were assigned to both bridges. Although, in terms of thickness and quality, there was no distinguishing these cables, it was the flaxen ones – a cubit's length of which weighed one talent – that were proportionately the heavier. Next, with the straits now bridged, they sawed up wood into planks equal in length to the width of the pontoon, arranged them on top of the taut cables and then, once they had been laid out in order, fastened them down. That done, they placed brushwood evenly over the planks, carried earth onto it which they then stamped down, and ran fences along both sides to ensure that the pack-animals [and the horses] would not be frightened by looking over at the sea.

[37] Meanwhile, with the bridges built, and the work around Athos too completed, even down to the moles constructed at the mouths of the canal to serve as breakwaters, and with the announcement that the canal itself had been fully completed, the army wintered at Sardis and prepared itself for the march to Abydus – which, with the coming of spring, it duly began. Just as it was setting off, however, the sun abandoned its place in the heavens and vanished, so that the day, despite being cloudless and unusually clear, turned to night.[29] Xerxes, unsettled by the implications of what he was seeing, asked the Magi what such a phenomenon might portend. 'The god', they answered him, 'is foretelling the abandonment by the Greeks of their cities. The sun symbolizes the prospects of the Greeks, you see, and the moon your own.' When Xerxes heard this, he was overjoyed, and continued with his advance.

[38] As the King was leaving at the head of the invasion force, however, Pythius the Lydian, terrified by the mysterious phenomenon in the

heavens, and emboldened by the generosity shown him, approached Xerxes. 'O Master,' he said, 'I have a favour to ask you, which I hope you will grant me. It would cost you very little, as it happens – but it would mean a great deal to me.' Xerxes, imagining that the request would be for anything rather than what it actually turned out to be, declared that he would indeed grant the favour, and ordered Pythius to state his need. Pythius, when he heard this, took sufficient heart to say, 'O Master, fate has granted me five sons – and all of them are conscripts in your march on Greece. Please, then, O King, take pity on my old age, and discharge from your army just one son of mine, the eldest, to take care of me and my possessions. As for the other four, take them with you – and may you return with all your objectives fulfilled!'

[39] At this, Xerxes grew exceedingly angry. 'You miserable man!' he replied. 'Here am I, leading my army in person against Greece, with my sons, my brothers, my relatives and my friends in my train, and you, my slave, who should properly be following me with your entire household, yes, and your wife as well, you dare to make mention of your son? There is something you should know. It is in the ears that the spirit of a man has its dwelling-place.[30] Only let him hear something good, and his body is suffused with joy – but let him hear the opposite, and then he will swell up with fury. Back when you performed good offices for me, and assured me of more such to come, not all your generosity, I think you will acknowledge, could surpass the generosity that was shown you then by the King. But now that to your abject shame you have taken a wrong turning, you will receive, not your due, but something less. You and four of your sons are spared by virtue of the hospitality you showed me. But the son you most wished to keep by your side – you will pay for that insult with his life.' And straightaway, the moment Xerxes had given this answer, he commanded those responsible for such matters to find the eldest of Pythius' sons, to cut him in half, and then, when they had finished hacking him in two, to place one half on the right-hand side of the road and one half on the left, so that the army would file out midway through.

[40] And so it was done – and the army, as it left, did indeed pass between. In the vanguard were the baggage-carriers and the pack-animals, and after them a mass of soldiers drawn from every nation, mixed up indiscriminately rather than being sorted into divisions. Then, after more than half the army had gone by, there was a gap to ensure

that no contact was had with the King. At the head of his escort there rode a thousand horsemen, the very pick of the Persians. After them marched a thousand similarly hand-picked spearmen, with their spears so held that the heads were turned down to the ground. Next, arrayed in the most beautiful of caparisons, came ten sacred Nisaean horses – so called after a place in Media, a large plain by the name of Nisaea, where these massive horses are bred. The place behind the ten horses was taken by the sacred chariot of Zeus, which was drawn by eight white horses. The reins of these horses were held by the charioteer, and he – because no man is permitted to mount the seat of the chariot – followed them on foot. Behind came Xerxes himself, in a chariot drawn by Nisaean horses. By his side stood his charioteer, a man by the name of Patiramphes, who was the son of a Persian called Otanes.

[41] So that was how Xerxes left Sardis, in a chariot – although, when the fancy took him, he would swap it for a carriage. Behind him were a thousand spearmen, made up of the cream of the Persian nobility, and carrying their spears in the customary manner, followed by another thousand hand-picked Persians, this time on horseback – and then, after the cavalry, there came the remainder of the Persian elite, ten thousand in all, marching on foot. A thousand of them had spear-butts that consisted of golden pomegranates rather than spikes, and these formed a ring encircling the others – the nine thousand on the inside – who had silver pomegranates. The troops whose spears were pointed to the ground also had golden pomegranates, while the ones immediately behind Xerxes had golden apples. The ten thousand infantry were followed by a division of ten thousand further Persians on horseback. Then, 2 stades behind this body of cavalry, the rest of the army followed in a disorganized mass.

[42] From Lydia, the army made its way to the River Caïcus and the land of Mysia, and from the Caïcus, keeping Mount Canê on its left, continued by way of Atarneus to the city of Carene. From there, bypassing Atramytteium and the Pelasgian foundation of Antandrus, it crossed the plain of Thebe. On reaching Ida, it went by the left-hand side of the mountain into the land of Ilium. During its first night there, on the foothills of Ida, violent winds and thunderstorms broke over the army, resulting in a substantial number of casualties.

[43] Next, it reached the Scamander. The waters of this river were the first since the army's departure from Sardis, and its taking to the road,

to fail the thirst of the men and livestock, and to be drunk dry. Xerxes, once he had arrived on the banks of this river, climbed up to the Citadel of Priam,[31] which he was longing to see. Then, once he had surveyed it and been told the full story of what had happened there, he sacrificed a thousand heifers to Athena of Ilium, and the Magi poured out libations to the heroes. The night after these rites had been performed, a great terror seized the entire army. Then, with the coming of dawn, it set off from Ilium, keeping on its left the city of Rhoetium, and Ophryneium too, and Dardanus, which borders Abydus, and on its right, the territory of a Teucrian people called the Gergithians.

[44] And Xerxes, once in Abydus, wished to review his entire task-force. A dais of white stone, built beforehand by the people of Abydus on the orders of the King himself, had already been raised on a hill expressly for him; and Xerxes, as he sat and gazed down from this vantage-point on to the shore, and beheld both his land-forces and his fleet, had a longing to see the ships compete in a race. This contest, when it was duly staged, was won by the Phoenicians from Sidon;[32] and Xerxes was delighted by the sport, and indeed by his entire task-force.

[45] It was then, at the sight of the Hellespont completely covered by his ships, and the entire shoreline and plain of Abydus filled up with his men, that Xerxes considered himself blessed – and afterwards began to weep.

[46] When Artabanus, his uncle, and the man who initially had freely broadcast his opposition to the invasion of Greece, and advised Xerxes against it, saw that his nephew was in tears, he enquired as to the reason. 'What a difference, O King, between your behaviour now, and that of only a short time before. Then you considered yourself blessed – now you weep!' 'Yes,' Xerxes answered, 'for I was musing on how short is human life, and the pity of it pierced me through. All these multitudes here, and yet, in a hundred years' time, not one of them will be alive.' To this Artabanus replied by saying, 'But we mortals experience many other causes of suffering that better merit your compassion. Brief though the span of human life may be, yet there is no man here – no, nor anywhere else either – to whom nature grants such happiness that he will not, and on more than one occasion too, wish for death rather than to continue living. So numerous are the misfortunes that befall us, and so terrible the diseases that afflict us, that life in all its brevity still seems long. Death, to a man whose existence is a burden, provides an escape

very much worth choosing. That God should grant us merely the briefest taste of how sweet life can be serves to demonstrate just how much he begrudges us it.'[33]

[47] 'Enough of this, Artabanus,' Xerxes replied. 'No matter that human existence does indeed very closely match your description of it – let us not dwell on the evils when we have plenty of good things in hand. So tell me this. Had the vision that appeared to you in your sleep not been so unambiguous, would you have clung to your former opinion, and withheld your backing for my invasion of Greece, or would you have changed your mind? Come now, the full truth!' 'O King,' Artabanus answered, 'I only pray that the end result of the vision that appeared in your dream is indeed all that we hope. Yet even now I am still full of anxiety. In fact, when I contemplate all the many perils, I am out of my mind with dread. The main danger I see is this: that the two greatest things in existence are both of them your bitterest enemies.'

[48] 'By the Heavens!' exclaimed Xerxes, in response to this comment, 'you are a most peculiar man! What do you mean by "bitterest enemies"? Is the vast scale of the forces I command by land somehow contemptible? Do you really imagine that the armies of the Greeks will outnumber our own? Or that our fleet will be left trailing in the wake of theirs? Or perhaps both these eventualities? If our resources really do strike you as being inadequate in some way, then let us muster another army as fast as we can.'

[49] 'O King,' Artabanus answered, 'no one in his right mind would think to find fault with the scale of either your army or your fleet. Indeed, were you to gather any more forces, then the two enemies of which I was speaking would become only the more implacable. And their identity? Why, the land and the sea! Take the sea first. Nowhere, so far as I can tell, is there a single harbour capable of providing shelter to your fleet in the event of a storm, and thereby ensuring the preservation of your ships. Yet one harbour would hardly be sufficient: you need harbours along the whole length of the mainland you will be tracking. In the absence of any such havens, however, there is a lesson you need to understand – that events control men, and not the other way round. So much for one of the two enemies I mentioned. Now let me turn to the other. In what sense is the land your adversary? In this sense. Suppose there is no one willing to stand in your way. In that case, you will advance onwards, snatching like a thief after ever more – since the

eagerness of men for success is such that it can never be satisfied. The further you go, though, the more the land will turn against you. That is why I say this: that should you meet with no opposition, then the greater the extent of your conquests, and the longer it takes you to win them, so the more certain it is that starvation will ensue. The best kind of man is one who, as he draws up his plans, is in state of high alarm at the thought of everything that might go wrong with them, but who also, when it comes to putting them into action, behaves with the utmost resolution.'

[50] 'The case you make, Artabanus,' Xerxes replied, 'is a perfectly reasonable one – and yet you should temper your anxieties, and stop focusing on every minor detail. After all, were it your aim always to give equal weight to each and every circumstance as it impinged upon you, then you would never get anything done. Better not to flinch from anything, and suffer terribly for it half the time, than always to imagine that everything will turn out for the worst, and never suffer at all. If you merely dismiss every proposal put forward without yourself demonstrating a risk-free course of action, then you are on no less shaky ground than one whose arguments are the opposite of your own. Indeed, you are both of you more or less equal! And anyway, we are only human – so can anyone say what is truly safe? Not in my opinion. Rewards in life, by and large, go to those who are willing to act, rather than to those who mull everything over and prevaricate. Only look at the expansion of Persian power, after all. Had my predecessors on the throne shared your attitude to things, or even had they not, but been advised by men like yourself, then you would never have seen the Persians go so far. No, it was precisely their willingness to gamble that brought them such returns. Great achievements are never secured save by the taking of great risks. We are simply following in their footsteps. What is more, since this is the perfect time of year for campaigning, and all Europe will soon be ours, we are sure to make it home again without having suffered hunger or anything else untoward. Not only are we taking a plentiful supply of provisions with us on the campaign trail, but we shall also have access to the food of all those peoples through whose lands we pass. The men we are attacking are not nomads, after all, but people who plough the soil.'

[51] Artabanus, in the wake of this speech, replied: 'Very well, then, O King – we will not fret about any aspect of policy. Nevertheless, since

complex matters inevitably require a much greater degree of deliberation, do please accept from me this one piece of advice. Cyrus, the son of Cambyses, conquered all of Ionia, and made it tributary to the Persians – with the sole exception of the Athenians.[34] Accordingly, I would recommend that you on no account lead the Ionians against those who rank as their founding fathers. Even without them, after all, we are more than a match for our enemies – and if they do come as part of your train, they will have no choice but to take the criminal step of enslaving their mother city; or else, if they act according to the dictates of justice, they will join in the securing of her liberty. Should they take the criminal option, then it will be of only minimal benefit to us, whereas should they demonstrate a serious commitment to the cause of justice, then the damage to your army will be very serious. You should take well to heart the wisdom of that ancient saying "In the beginning it is rare to glimpse the end completely".'

[52] 'Artabanus,' Xerxes answered, 'this notion of yours is even more unfounded than all the others you have been airing! Are you truly worried that the Ionians will change sides? The evidence of their worth is irrefutable! You yourself are witness to that – you and all the others who accompanied Darius on his campaign against the Scythians, when it was entirely up to them whether to keep the whole Persian army from ruin or not. The show of duty and loyalty they gave then was of a wholly unblemished order. Besides, because they have left behind their children, wives and property in a land that belongs to us, thoughts of rebellion will never even cross their minds. So that is another thing you can stop worrying about! Be strong in spirit, and keep my household and my tyranny safe. It is to you and to you alone, you see, that I entrust my royal sceptre.'

[53] So saying, Xerxes dispatched Artabanus to Susa, and then summoned the most eminent among the Persians to a meeting. 'Men of Persia,' he said, once they had all convened, 'I have called you here together because I want something from you – proof that you are indeed men of mettle. Mighty and invaluable as the achievements of the Persians have been, do not disgrace them now. Instead, since the cause spurring us on here is the common good of all, let each and every one of us throw himself into the task with relish. That is why I am exhorting you to prosecute the war with all possible vigour. I am told that those we are advancing against are men of impressive quality, and that, if we

can only subdue them, then there will be no other army capable of ever standing up to us. So come, let us pray to the gods who have been allotted the land of Persia as their charge – and make the crossing.'

[54] Preparations for this lasted all day; and then, the next morning, out of a desire to see the sunrise, they waited, as incense of every conceivable kind was burned on the bridges, and the road was strewn with myrtle branches. When the sun did rise, Xerxes poured a libation[35] from a golden cup into the sea, and prayed to it that no mishaps would intervene to stop him from conquering Europe, and reaching the furthermost limits of the continent. Then, when his prayer was done, he threw the cup into the Hellespont, together with a golden mixing-bowl and a type of Persian sword which they call an *akinakes*.[36] Whether he dropped these into the sea as an offering to the sun, or because he had come to regret his flogging of the Hellespont, and wished to make a gift of them to the sea as a way of making amends, I have been unable to determine with any certainty.

[55] Once this had been done, the crossing began, with all the infantry and cavalry taking the bridge nearest the Euxine, and the pack-animals and camp-followers the other bridge, the one facing the Aegean; in the vanguard were the ten thousand Persians, every one of them garlanded, and after them, in a confused mass, came all the various peoples who made up the rest of the army. It took them a whole day to cross; the following day the first to make the crossing were the cavalry and the infantry who carried their spears upside down. These too wore garlands. Then came the sacred horses, and the sacred chariot as well, and then Xerxes himself, with his bodyguard of spearmen, and the thousand cavalry; and then the rest of the army. Simultaneously, the ships were making their way over to the facing shore too. (There is another account I have also heard, according to which it was the King who crossed over last of all.)

[56] Once Xerxes had reached the European shore, he watched his army make the crossing under the whip. Seven days and seven nights it took his forces, without a moment's break. The story goes that a local man, after Xerxes had crossed the Hellespont, exclaimed: 'Why, O Zeus, have you taken on the form of a man from Persia, and swapped your own name for that of Xerxes? And why – if your aim is to devastate Greece – bring the entire world with you? After all, you hardly need their assistance to accomplish that!'

[57] Once the crossing had been completed, and the army had set off along the road, there appeared an extraordinary portent, which Xerxes, despite the self-evident nature of its meaning, dismissed as being of no account: a mare gave birth to a hare. Clearly, what this signified was that Xerxes would cut a most swaggering and splendid figure as he marched his army against Greece, and then would come bolting back to his starting-place, in terror for his life. He had also been given an additional portent, while he was in Sardis, when a mule had foaled another mule that had two pairs of genitals, one male and one female. The male genitals were positioned above the female ones.

[58] But Xerxes read no significance into either of these portents, and instead continued on his way with his land-forces. Meanwhile, the fleet was sailing out of the Hellespont and following the line of the coast, in a direction opposite to that taken by the army. The course of its sailing was a westerly one, and had as its destination Cape Sarpedon, where it had been instructed to head to await the arrival of Xerxes. As for the army (now on the mainland) that headed eastwards across the Chersonese, towards the rising of the sun: the road it took had the tomb of Helle, the daughter of Athamas, on its right, the city of Cardia on its left and passed directly through a town called Agora. Then, after rounding the so-called 'Black Gulf', and crossing the Black River – after which the Black Gulf takes its name, and which had a flow inadequate to the thirst of the Xerxes' forces, who duly drank it dry – the army headed west, passing the Aeolian city of Aenus and the Lake of Stentor, before arriving at Doriscus.

[59] Doriscus is a region in Thrace consisting of a beach and a wide plain, through which there flows a large river called the Hebrus. A royal fortress, the one also called 'Doriscus', had been built there, and a garrison installed in it by Darius, back at the time of his expedition against the Scythians. Well, then, might the place have struck Xerxes as a suitable location in which to parade and count his troops – a reflection which he duly acted upon. Once the entire fleet had arrived at Doriscus, Xerxes ordered the captains to bring their ships to the beach beside the fortress. This beach, which culminates in the celebrated promontory of Serreium, has two cities on it: one, founded by people from Samothrace, called Sale, and another called Zone. Back in ancient times, however, it was the Cicones who held the region. The ships, after they had put in at this beach, were hauled up out of the water so that their keels could dry

and be recoated with pitch. Xerxes, meanwhile, passed his time at Doriscus in aggregating the numbers of his expedition.

[60] Now, what I cannot do (since no one kept a record) is to give the precise amount that each individual contingent furnished[37] towards the total; but as for the total itself, the mass of the land-forces in their entirety came to 1,700,000 men. This was how that number was arrived at: ten thousand men assembled in a single spot, and then, with the men packed together as tightly as possible, a circle was drawn around them. Next, after the line had been drawn, the men were dismissed, and a wall reaching as high as a man's navel was built around the circumference of the circle. Once this was completed, other men were made to cram themselves into the enclosure – and so it went on, until everyone had been added to the roll. Then, once the counting was done, they were drawn up according to nationality.

[61] The contingents which made up Xerxes' army were as follows. First, the Persians and their equipment. They wore soft felt caps called *tiaras* on their heads, long-sleeved, brightly coloured tunics [and corselets] made of iron scales, rather like those of a fish, over their bodies, and trousers over their legs; their shields were not the normal kind, but made of wicker, and had quivers suspended underneath; they had short spears but large bows and arrows made of reed, and each man had a dagger slung from his belt so that it rested against his right thigh. They were commanded by Otanes, whose daughter, Amestris, was married to Xerxes. In ancient times, the Greeks called the Persians the 'Cephenes' – even though the name that they themselves used, and their neighbours too, was the 'Artaei'.[38] Then Perseus, the son of Danaë and Zeus, arrived at the court of Cepheus, the son of Belus, married his daughter Andromeda, and fathered a child whom he named Perses. Perseus left this son behind, because Cepheus had no male offspring. It was from this same Perses that the Persians then derived their name.

[62] The Median levies were equipped in the same manner as the Persians. In fact, it was the Medes, and not the Persians[39] at all, who were the first to adopt that style of dress. The man in command of them was an Achaemenid called Tigranes. Originally, the Medes were known by everyone as 'Arians' – but then Medea of Colchis arrived from Athens, and it was as a result of this, so the Medes themselves report, that they likewise changed their name. The Cissian levies too were equipped and dressed like the Persians – except that they wore turbans instead

of felt caps. Their commander was Anaphes, the son of Otanes. The Hyrcanians were also equipped like the Persians, and were led by Megapanus, who was subsequently the governor of Babylon.

[63] The Assyrian levies wore helmets on their heads which were either bronze or else plaited in a peculiar barbarian style that is not easy to describe; they carried shields, spears and daggers similar to those of the Egyptians, together with wooden clubs studded with iron; and they wore breastplates made of linen. Although the Greeks call them 'Syrians', 'Assyrians' is the name by which the Barbarians know them. [The Chaldaeans were a part of their contingent.] They were led by Otaspes, the son of Artachaeës.

[64] The Bactrian levies wore headgear very similar to that worn by the Medes, and carried their native bows of reed and short spears. The Sacae, a Scythian people, wore on their heads the *kurbasia*, a tall, pointed cap made of stiff material, they sported trousers, and, in addition to their native bows and arrows, carried battleaxes known as *sagareis*. In fact, these Sacae were Scythians from Amyrgium, but were called 'Sacae' because that is the name given by the Persians to all the Scythians. The Bactrians and the Sacae were led by Hystaspes, whose parents were Darius and Atossa, the daughter of Cyrus.

[65] The Indians wore clothes made of cotton, and carried bows and arrows of reed – the arrows being tipped with iron. The Indian levies, so equipped, had been assigned to the command of Pharnazathres, the son of Artabates.

[66] The Arians were equipped like the Bactrians – except for their bows, which were Median in style. They were commanded by Sisamnes, the son of Hydarnes. The Parthian levies too, and the Chorasmians, and the Sogdians, and the Gandarians, and the Dadicae, were all of them fitted out like the Bactrians. The Parthians and the Chorasmians were commanded by Artabazus, the son of Pharnaces; the Sogdians by Azanes, the son of Artaeus; and the Gandarians and Dadicae by Artyphius, the son of Artabanus.

[67] The Caspians wore cloaks made of animal skins, and were armed with their native bows of reed and short swords. So equipped, they had as their commander Ariomardus, the brother of Artyphius. The Sarangians, whose clothes were conspicuous for the bright colours with which they had been dyed, wore knee-high boots, and their bows and spears were like those of the Medes. They were led by Pherendates,

the son of Megabazus. The Pactyes wore cloaks made of animal skins, and were armed with their native bows and daggers. Their commander was Artaÿntes, the son of Ithamitres.

[68] The Outians, Mycians and Paricanians were equipped like the Pactyes. Their commanders were Arsamenes, the son of Darius, who led the Outians and Mycians, and Siromitres, the son of Oeobazus, who led the Paricanians.

[69] The Arabians wore loose belted mantles and carried on their right sides long, tautly strung bows. The Ethiopians tied leopard-skins and lion pelts around themselves, and were armed with bows made from the spines of palm-tree fronds: these bows were immense, 4 cubits long at least, while the arrows were short, and tipped, not with iron, but with sharpened pieces of the kind of stone they use in the engraving of signet rings. Additionally, they had spears with heads made out of gazelle horns sharpened so as to resemble lances, and studded clubs. When going into battle, each warrior would smear half his body with chalk, and the other half with red ochre. In command of the Arabians and the Ethiopians who live south of Egypt was Arsames, whose parents were Darius and Artystone, the daughter of Cyrus. (Darius cherished Artystone above all his other wives,[40] and had a statue of her made of beaten gold.) The Ethiopians from the south of Egypt, then, and the Arabians too: these were the levies commanded by Arsames.

[70] But there were two kinds of Ethiopian in the army – the second kind, whose homeland lay much closer to the rising of the sun, were assigned to serve alongside the Indians. Although these Ethiopians speak a different language from the other kind of Ethiopian, they look no different – with the sole exception of their hair. The eastern Ethiopians have straight hair, you see, whereas the ones from Libya have the woolliest hair in the world. The Ethiopians from Asia were equipped more or less as the Indians were, except that they wore head-dresses scalped from horses, ears and manes included. The manes served them in place of crests, and the horses' ears had been stiffened so that they stood up straight. For frontal protection, they used the skins of cranes rather than shields.

[71] The Libyans came armoured in leather, and used as javelins stakes that had been burned to sharp points. Their commander was Massages, the son of Oarizus.

[72] The levies from Paphlagonia wore plaited helmets on their

heads, were armed with small shields, spears of no great length, and javelins and daggers too, and on their feet wore a native style of boot reaching halfway up their shins. The Ligurian contingent, and the Matienians too, and the Mariandynians, and the Syrians, whom the Persians call 'Cappadocians', were fitted out in the same way as the Paphlagonians. In command of the Paphlagonians and the Matienians was Dotus, the son of Megasidrus, while the commander of the Mariandynians, the Ligurians and the Syrians was Gobryas, the son of Darius and Artystone.

[73] The equipment of the Phrygians was very similar to that of the Paphlagonians, with only minor differences. According to the Macedonians, the Phrygians were known as 'Brigians' for as long as they lived in Europe, adjacent to the Macedonians themselves; but then, when they moved to Asia, they combined their change of country with a change of name [to Phrygians]. The Armenians, who were originally settlers from Phrygia, were equipped exactly as the Phrygians were. Both were under the command of Artochmes, a son-in-law of Darius.

[74] The arms and armour of the Lydians most closely approximated to those of the Greeks. In ancient times, the Lydians were known as 'Maeonians', but then, when they called themselves after Lydus, the son of Atys, their name was changed. The Mysians wore a native style of helmet on their heads, had small shields and used stakes burned to sharp points as javelins. These Mysians were originally settlers from Lydia, and are called 'Olympieni', after Mount Olympus. The Lydians and the Mysians were commanded by the son and namesake of the Artaphrenes who had shared command of the Marathon invasion with Datis.

[75] The headgear of the Thracian levies was made out of fox-skins; on their bodies they wore tunics, over which they then draped brightly patterned mantles, while on their feet and shins they wore boots of fawn-skin. They also carried spears, tiny shields and small daggers. Back when they crossed over to Asia, they were called 'Bithynians'; but originally, according to their own account, they were called 'Strymonians', because they lived beside the Strymon. They report that they were driven out of their original homeland by the Teucrians and the Mysians. The Thracians of Asia were commanded by Bassaces, the son of Artabanus.

[76] Each of the [. . .] had a small shield of raw oxhide and two hunting spears fashioned in the Lycian style, and wore a bronze helmet

on his head. This helmet was surmounted by the ears and horns of an ox, also in bronze, and a crest. The [. . .] wore strips of red cloth wrapped around their shins. There is an oracle of Ares in the land of these men.

[77] The Cabalians, who are of Maeonian stock and also go by the name 'Lasonians', were dressed like Cilicians – and so I will give my account of them when I come to describe the deployment of the Cilicians in my account. The Milyans had short spears and used brooches to fasten their clothes. Some of them had Lycian bows and wore caps made of leather on their heads. The commander of all these various levies was Badres, the son of Hystanes.

[78] The Moschians wore caps made of wood on their heads, and carried shields and short spears. The heads of these spears were very long. The Tibaranians, Macronians and Mossynoecians were fitted out exactly like the Moschian levies. The Moschians and Tibarenians served together under the command of Ariomardus, whose parents were Darius and Parmys, the daughter of Smerdis and grand-daughter of Cyrus, while the Macronians and Mossynoecians were both led by Artaÿctes, the son of Cherasmis, and who served as governor of Sestus on the Hellespont.

[79] The Mares wore their own native style of plaited helmet, and carried small shields made from animal-skins and javelins. The Colchians wore wooden helmets on their heads, carried small shields of raw oxhide and were armed not only with short spears, but with knives as well. The commander of the Mares and the Colchians was Pharandates, the son of Teaspis. The Alarodian and Saspeirian contingents were equipped like the Colchians. They were commanded by Masistius, the son of Siromitres.

[80] The tribes living on the islands in the Red Sea, which are the same islands where the King settles people known as the 'Uprooted', had clothes and equipment very like those of the Medes. The commander of these islanders was Mardontes, the son of Bagaeus, who one year later would be one of the generals at Mycale, and meet his end in the battle.[41]

[81] Such were the peoples whose levies provided the infantry for the campaign by land. The commanders of the army were the ones I have already mentioned, and it was they who organized the divisions, conducted the roll and appointed officers to head units numbering both ten

thousand and one thousand men; the officers with ten thousand men under their command were in turn responsible for appointing further officers to the command of units numbering one hundred, and ten. There were other officers too in charge of various units and tribes.

[82] The generals in command of the divisional commanders I have already mentioned, and of the entire land-army with them, were: Mardonius, the son of Gobryas; Tritantaechmes, whose father, Artabanus, had made public his opposition to the invasion of Greece, and Smerdomenes, the son of Otanes, both of whom were nephews of Darius and cousins of Xerxes; Masistes, whose parents were Darius and Atossa; Gergis, the son of Ariazus; and Megabyzus, the son of Zopyrus.

[83] These generals had command of the entire land-army – all except the Ten Thousand. This particular unit, which consisted of ten thousand hand-picked Persians, was led by Hydarnes, the son of Hydarnes, and was known as the 'Immortals'. Why such a name? Because if ever one of them were killed or fell ill, and thereby created a vacancy, another man would at once be selected – thereby ensuring that the unit was never more nor less than ten thousand.[42] The Persians were not only the most splendidly arrayed men in the entire army, but the best soldiers as well. Their equipment I have already described, but they stood out too by virtue of the prodigious quantities of gold they sported. What is more, they brought their concubines with them in carriages, and great trains of servants complete with any amount of equipment. They also had their own supplies of food, separate from those of the other soldiers, carried by camels and pack-animals.[43]

[84] All these various peoples were riders of horses, but not all of them furnished cavalry. I will now list the ones who did. The Persians on horseback were fitted out exactly like those on foot – except that a certain number of them wore beaten bronze and iron on their heads.

[85] Then there were some nomads, men called Sagartians, a people who count as Persian, and whose language is Persian too, but whose dress blends Persian with Pactyan styles. These provided eight thousand horsemen – armed, as they invariably were, with daggers, but with no other bronze or iron weapons, and with ropes plaited out of thongs. It was these ropes that the Sagartians relied on when they went into battle. What each man would do when he joined with the enemy was to cast his rope, which would have a noose at the end: then, whatever the rope hit, whether horse or man, would be hauled in, struggling impotently to

escape, and dispatched. Such, then, was the way of war adopted by the Sagartians, who were enrolled with the Persian contingent.

[86] The Medes were dressed exactly as their infantry were, and the Cissians too. The Indians were furnished in the same way as their compatriots on foot, but rode swift horses and had chariots, to which they harnessed both horses and wild asses. The Bactrians were dressed like their counterparts in the infantry, the Caspians similarly. The Libyans were dressed no differently from their compatriots on foot, and they too all drove chariots. The equipment worn by the [Caspians?] and Paricanians likewise resembled that of their compatriots on foot. The Arabians too were dressed in the same way as their counterparts in the infantry, and all rode camels, which were no less fast than horses.

[87] These were the only peoples who provided cavalry – which numbered eighty thousand, exclusive of camels and chariots. Now, the horsemen were all of them organized into regiments, with the Arabians stationed in the rear. The reason for this was that horses cannot bear camels,[44] so the Arabians, by serving as the rearguard, ensured that the horses would not be scared.

[88] The men in command of the cavalry were two sons of Datis: Harmamithres and Tithaeus. A third officer who had shared the command with them, Pharnouches, had been left behind in Sardis owing to illness. Just as they were setting out from the city, he had suffered a most unwelcome accident. As he was cantering along, a dog ran under the feet of his horse, which, because it had not seen the dog, took fright, reared up and threw him. Pharnouches began vomiting blood after this fall, and developed consumption. At the time of the original accident, his house-slaves had acted immediately on an instruction from their master by leading the horse to the place where it had thrown him, and cutting off its legs at the knees. That was how Pharnouches came to be discharged from his command.

[89] The number of triremes totalled 1,207 – with the breakdown of those who supplied them being as follows. The Phoenicians and the Syrians of Palestine contributed three hundred. They had helmets on their heads fashioned very much in the Greek style, wore linen breastplates and carried rimless shields and javelins. In ancient times, according to the Phoenicians themselves, they were settled along the Red Sea, but then migrated and made their home instead on the Syrian coast. This particular region of Syria, all the way as far as Egypt, is called Palestine.

The Egyptians contributed two hundred ships. They wore plaited helmets on their heads, and carried hollow shields with wide rims, spears appropriate to marines and massive poleaxes. Most of them also wore breastplates and carried large knives.

[90] So much for Egyptian equipment. The Cypriots furnished a hundred and fifty ships, and although their kings wound turbans around their heads, everyone else wore tunics and other such clothing, all of it Greek in style. The Cypriots, by their own account, originated from any number of places: from Salamis⁴⁵ and Athens, from Arcadia, from Cythnos, from Phoenicia and from Ethiopia.

[91] The Cilicians contributed one hundred ships. They wore a native style of helmet on their heads, used bucklers fashioned out of raw oxhide in place of shields and dressed in woollen tunics. Each man was armed with two javelins and a sword, very similar in make to the Egyptian knife. In ancient times they were called Hypachaeans, but then adopted the name of Cilix, the son of Agenor, who was a man from Phoenicia. The Pamphylians provided thirty ships, and were equipped with Greek arms and armour. The Pamphylians are descended from the Greeks who left Troy with Amphilochus and Calchas, when those who had fought there were scattered in all directions.

[92] The Lycians contributed fifty ships. They wore breastplates and greaves, carried bows of cornel wood and unflighted arrows made of reed and javelins, they slung goat-skins over their shoulders and wore felt caps trimmed with feathers on their heads. They were armed as well with daggers and sickles. The Lycians were originally called Termilians and came from Crete, but then adopted the name of Lycus, the son of Pandion, who was a man from Athens.

[93] The Dorians of Asia, who carried Greek arms and armour, and came from the Peloponnese,⁴⁶ supplied thirty ships. The Carians contributed seventy, and were fitted out exactly like the Greeks, except that they carried sickles and daggers. Their original name is something I have already addressed in the first section of my work.⁴⁷

[94] The Ionians provided a hundred ships, and were equipped in the Greek style. The Ionians, so the Greeks say, were called 'Aegialian Pelasgians' for the entire period that they were settled in the Peloponnese, in what is now called Achaea;⁴⁸ but then, after the arrival in the Peloponnese of Danaus and Xouthus, they came to be called 'Ionians', after Ion, the son of Xouthus.

[95] The islanders furnished seventeen ships, and carried Greek arms and armour. They too were a Pelasgian people who subsequently adopted the name 'Ionian' – and for the same reason as did the twelve cities of the Ionians, the inhabitants of which had come originally from Athens. The Aeolians contributed sixty ships; they too had Greek equipment, and were another people, according to Greek tradition, who originally ranked as Pelasgian. The Hellespontians furnished a hundred ships, their contingent being drawn from the entire region of the Euxine – everywhere, that is, except for Abydus, whose people had been instructed by the King to stay where they were, and guard the bridges. The equipment of the Hellespontians, all of whom were Ionian and Dorian colonists, was Greek in style.

[96] All the ships had Persians, Medes and Sacae serving on board them as marines. The best ships sailing with the fleet were those provided by the Phoenicians – and of these, the elite were the Sidonians. Each of the naval units, and each of the various infantry levies too, had native officers in positions of authority over them; but since the course of my enquiries does not oblige me to provide a list of these, I shall not. Not only was there nothing particularly distinguished about the various officers in command of their respective peoples, you see, but the number of officers was directly proportionate to the number of cities in each country. And, since these officers were just as much slaves[49] as all the other soldiers on the campaign, it was not as though they constituted the high command. The generals who did have power and authority over the various national contingents were all of them ethnic Persians – and these I have already mentioned.

[97] The admirals in command of the fleet were: Ariabignes, the son of Darius; Prexaspes, the son of Aspathines; Megabazus, the son of Megabates; and Achaemenes, the son of Darius. Ariabignes, whose parents were Darius and the daughter of Gobryas, commanded the Ionian and Carian contingents, while the Egyptians were led by Achaemenes, a full brother of Xerxes. The other two admirals were responsible for all the remaining contingents. When triaconters, penteconters, light vessels and transport-ships for horses were added to the total, the fleet was found to number three thousand.

[98] Admirals aside, the most notable men in the fleet were: Tetramnestus, the son of Anysus, who came from Sidon; Matten, the son of Siromus, who was from Tyre; Merbalus, the son of Agbalus, from

Aradus; Syennesis, the son of Oromedon, who was a Cilician; Cyberniscus, the son of Sicas, from Lycia; Gorgus, the son of Chersis, and Timonax, the son of Timagoras, both of whom came from Cyprus; and Histiaeus, the son of Tymnes, Pigres, the son of Hysseldomus, and Damasithymus, the son of Candaules, all of whom were Carian.

[99] Now, as there is no obligation upon me to mention any other captains, I will pass them over – all except Artemisia, whose role in the campaign against Greece was a truly astonishing one for a woman. Following the death of her husband, she had taken over the reins of power; and although she had a grown son, and although there was not the slightest pressure upon her to join the campaign, she was prompted to do so by the formidably masculine cast of her bravery.[50] Artemisia, the daughter of Lygdamis, was her name, of Halicarnassian stock on her father's side and of Cretan on her mother's. She commanded the Halicarnassians, the Coans, the Nisyrians and the Calydnians, and contributed five ships. There was no other squadron in the entire fleet, the Sidonians excepted, more highly esteemed than hers – nor any other ally who gave the King better advice than she. All the cities I listed as subject to her were peopled by Dorians: the Halicarnassians came from Troezen and the others from Epidaurus.

[100] That completes what I have to say about the fleet. As for the army, when the roll-call was done and its organization into divisions completed, Xerxes was filled with a yearning to ride through its ranks and review it in person. And he did just that. He rode in his chariot past people after people, asking questions about each one in turn, and having his secretaries note down the answers, until he had gone from one end of the army to the other, and reviewed cavalry and infantry both. Then, with that done and the ships hauled back down into the sea, Xerxes swapped his chariot for a Sidonian vessel, sat down beneath a golden awning and glided past the prows of the ships, making the same enquiries of each squadron as he had done of the divisions on land, and again having the answers noted down. Each captain had withdrawn his ship to a distance of some 4 plethra from the beach and there dropped anchor; ship after ship, each prow was turned towards the land, and every marine was armed and ready for battle. Gliding between the prows and the beach, Xerxes reviewed the line.

[101] Then, once he had sailed along the whole length and stepped down from the ship, he sent for Demaratus,[51] the son of Ariston, who

was accompanying him on the campaign against Greece, and now came in answer to his summons. 'Demaratus,' Xerxes said, 'there is a question I wish to put to you – one that has been much tickling my fancy. You are a Greek, and your city, judging by what you and the other Greeks I have consulted inform me, is hardly lacking in either importance or strength. So then, tell me this – will the Greeks make a stand and take up arms against me? My own opinion is that not all the Greeks combined, and not all the remaining inhabitants of the West with them, are capable of withstanding my onslaught – unless, that is, they present a united front.[52] Nevertheless, I am interested to learn what your view on the matter might be.' To this question Demaratus replied: 'Do you want a truthful answer, O King, or a pleasing one?' 'A truthful one,' Xerxes instructed; and then assured him that it would in no way be to his disadvantage.

[102] When Demaratus heard this, he told the King, 'So your orders are that I should speak the truth, and nothing but the truth, nor ever be caught out by you at some later point as a person who has been peddling lies.[53] Poverty has always been endemic to Greece, but the courage of its people is a quality that they have acquired for themselves – forged by their wisdom, and by the strength of law. It is this that has enabled them to keep poverty and foreign overlordship at bay. Now, my praise is directed at all those Greeks whose homes lie in Dorian territory – but rather than discuss every last one of them, I am going to confine my comments to the Lacedaemonians. The first point to make is that they will never be open to any proposal of yours which results in the enslavement of Greece – and the second is that they are bound to confront you in battle, even should all the other Greeks take your side. As for the numbers at their command, there is no point in your asking how, with their available manpower, they can possibly adopt such a course of action. It makes no difference whether they have a thousand men on campaign, or more than that, or less – they will fight you still.'

[103] When Xerxes heard this, he laughed. 'Demaratus,' he exclaimed, 'what nonsense this is! A thousand men fight an army the size of mine? Come on! You say that you used to be the king of these people. Tell me, then – would you really be prepared to take on ten men? Surely not! And yet if everything you say about your political system is true, then by rights, as king of these people, you would actually be required by your own laws to take on double the number of opponents as everyone

else! After all – if each one of your fellow-citizens is a match for ten men from my army, then I would expect you to be a match for twenty! At any rate, that is the implication of what you have been saying. But can it really be the case that your compatriots are men of the order and stature that you (and all the other Greeks who have come into conversation with me) like to boast that they are? Watch out that your claims are not just empty brags. Come now: I am going to look at the matter in a wholly objective way. How could a thousand men, or ten thousand, or even fifty thousand come to that, possibly stand up to an army the size of mine, when all of them enjoy a similar degree of liberty, and have no one man in command?[54] Why, presuming that they amount to five thousand, we shall outnumber them by more than a thousand to one! Just perhaps, were they like us in having one man set in authority over them, they might indeed be prompted by their dread of him to conquer their own instincts, and under the compulsion of the whip to advance against a force much larger than themselves. Left to their own devices, though, there is no way that they will do either of these things. In fact, it is my own opinion that, even were their numbers equal to our own, the Greeks would still find the Persians alone more than a match for them. It is actually we [and we alone] who have the qualities you have been mentioning – and even then, not all of us, but only a few. There are certainly Persians in my bodyguard who would be willing to fight three Greeks at once. But what do you know of this? You talk nothing but nonsense.'

[104] 'I knew right from the start, O King,' Demaratus replied, 'that you would not care for my speaking the truth. Nevertheless, you demanded complete honesty – and that, as it relates to the Spartans, is precisely what I have given you. Yet you of all people know perfectly well the current state of my affections for them. Why, they stripped me of my office, my ancestral inheritance, and made me an exile without a city – while your father took me in, and provided me with both livelihood and shelter. No man with his wits about him would ever think to spurn a display of such benevolence, rather than to cherish it with all his heart. I do not commit myself to taking on ten men in combat, or two – or even one, if it were solely down to me. Nevertheless, if I had no choice in the matter, or there were some great issue at stake to motivate me, then I would certainly fight – and nothing would give me greater pleasure than to engage with one of these men who claim to be a match

for three Greeks. So it is with the Lacedaemonians. One on one, they are certainly nobody's inferior – but as a collective, they fight better than any other men on earth. Free though they are, you see, yet they are not altogether free. Set over them as their master is the law[55] – and of that they are far more terrified than ever your men are of you. Certainly, they do what it commands them to do – a command that never alters. No matter how many men may be ranged against them in battle, they are forbidden ever to turn tail, but instead must always maintain their positions, and either triumph or be annihilated. If it does indeed appear to you that I am talking nonsense, then I am perfectly content in the future to hold my peace. I only spoke the way I did because you insisted. But may all your hopes be fulfilled, my Lord.'

[105] Such was the reply given by Demaratus; but Xerxes, far from being angered by it, instead made a joke of the matter, and dismissed him in affectionate terms. Then, when his conversation with Demaratus was over, Xerxes replaced the man whom Darius had appointed to the governorship of Doriscus with Mascames, the son of Megadostes, before marching off with his army through Thrace on his way to Greece.

[106] This Mascames, who was left behind by Xerxes, proved a man of such calibre that he was rated by Xerxes the best of all the governors appointed by either himself or Darius, and was the only man to whom Xerxes regularly sent gifts, year in, year out. In the same vein, Artaxerxes, the son of Xerxes, continued to reward the heirs of Mascames. Even before the invasion, governors had been installed across the entire sweep of Thrace and the Hellespont; afterwards, with the defeat of the Persian army, all the governors in Thrace and the Hellespont were expelled by the Greeks, except for the one in Doriscus. Many tried to conquer [Mascames in] Doriscus – but none succeeded. That is why the King of Persia, whosoever he may be, continues to send gifts there.

[107] Only one of the governors expelled by the Greeks was rated by King Xerxes as a man of quality: Boges, the governor of Eion. Xerxes never stopped singing his praises and loaded his surviving children with honours – and Boges certainly did merit the highest praise. When the Athenians, under the leadership of Cimon, the son of Miltiades, besieged him,[56] he could easily have left under truce and returned home to Asia. This, however, he was unwilling to do, and so, rather than survive at the cost of having the King consider him a coward, he held out to the end. Once all the provisions inside the fortress had been exhausted, he built

a great fire, then cut the throats of his children, his wife, his concubines and his household slaves, and threw their bodies into the flames. After this, he stood on the battlements and scattered all the city's gold and silver into the Strymon; and then, having done this, hurled himself onto the pyre. No wonder, then, even to this day, that the Persians should sing the praises of Boges.

[108] Leaving Doriscus behind, Xerxes continued on his way to Greece; and everyone in his path he forcibly conscripted into his army. You see, as I explained earlier, the entire region as far as Thessaly had been enslaved and brought to pay tribute to the King by two campaigns of conquest: the one led by Megabazus, and the second by Mardonius.[57] The first places Xerxes passed after leaving Doriscus were the forts of Samothrace – the most westerly of which is a city called Mesambria. Midway between Mesambria and the Thasian city of Stryme there flows the River Lissus; its waters were insufficient to cope with the thirst of Xerxes' army and were drunk dry. In ancient times, the region was called Gallaïce, but it is now known as Briantice – although, strictly speaking, it too, like Doriscus, belongs to the Cicones.

[109] After crossing the dried-out bed of the Lissus, Xerxes passed the Greek cities of Maroneia, Dicaea and Abdera. Also close by on his route were two celebrated lakes: Ismaris, which lies between Maroneia and Stryme, and Bistonis, near Dicaea, which is fed by the waters of two rivers, the Trauus and the Compsatus. There was no well-known lake near Abdera for Xerxes to skirt; but he did cross the River Nestus, which flows into the sea there. Then, after these various places, Xerxes' route took him past the cities founded on the mainland by Thasos – near one of which there is a lake some 30 stades in circumference, teeming with fish, and very briny. The pack-animals were the only ones to drink from it – and still they drank it dry! Xerxes skirted the city itself, which is called Pistyrus, and all the other Greek cities along the coast as well, keeping them to his left.

[110] The road then took him through the territory of a number of Thracian tribes: the Paeti, the Cicones, the Bistones, the Sapaei, the Dersaei, the Edonians and the Satrae. The ones who lived on the coast joined him in their ships, while those tribes featuring on my list who lived further inland were all conscripted into the land-army – the Satrae being the only exceptions.

[111] Indeed, to the best of my knowledge, the Satrae have never

been subject to anyone: alone of the Thracians, they have retained their liberty right up to the present day. The reason for this is that they inhabit high mountains, densely covered with every kind of tree, and with snow, and are exceedingly proficient warriors. It is these Thracians who possess the oracular shrine of Dionysus; this oracle stands on one of the very highest mountains, and the Satrae who interpret the shrine's pronouncements are the Bessians. The oracles themselves are delivered by a prophetess, just as at Delphi, rather than by anything more exotic.

[112] Next, after skirting this region, Xerxes passed the fortresses of the Pierians – one of which is called Phagres, and the other Pergamus. His route took him directly below their walls, while to his right rose the lofty mass of Mount Pangaeum, where gold and silver are mined by the Pierians, the Odomantians and in particular the Satrae.

[113] Continuing westwards, Xerxes bypassed the various peoples who live to the north of Pangaeum – the Paeonians, the Doberes and the Paeoplians – and arrived at Eion on the River Strymon, a city which was governed by the same Boges whose story[58] I told a short while back, and who at this stage was still very much alive. The land around Mount Pangaeum is called Phyllis; it extends westwards to a tributary of the Strymon called the Angites, and southwards to the Strymon itself. The Magi, in an attempt to obtain favourable omens, cut the throats of white horses into the Strymon.

[114] Then, once they had performed this and various other rites in honour of the river, they continued on their way over the bridges that they had discovered were spanning the Strymon at Nine Ways, in the land of the Edonians. Informed as to its name – 'Nine Ways' – they buried alive in the ground a matching number of local boys and girls. This practice of burying people alive is very much a Persian custom; indeed, I have been informed that when Amestris, the wife of Xerxes, grew old, she had fourteen children of prominent Persians buried underground as a gift offered on her behalf to the god who is said to dwell beneath the earth.

[115] Leaving behind the Strymon, and still heading daily into the sunset, the army passed a beach on which stands the Greek city of Argilus. This shoreline and the region inland of it are called Bisaltia. From there, keeping the bay off Cape Posideium to his left, Xerxes crossed the so-called 'Plain of Syleus', skirted the Greek city of Stagirus and arrived at Acanthus. As he took this route, so he recruited into his

army all the peoples living along it, and those around Pangaeum too; applying the same principle I described earlier, he obliged those living along the coast to join his navy in their ships, and those living inland to follow him on foot. To my own day, the Thracians neither plough nor sow the road along which King Xerxes marched his army, but instead hold it in the utmost reverence.

[116] On his arrival at Acanthus, Xerxes proclaimed a solemn pact of friendship[59] between himself and the Acanthians, presented them with a gift of Median clothing and lavished them with praise – these compliments being prompted by their enthusiasm for the war, which he could see for himself, and by the work they had put into digging the canal, which he had heard all about.

[117] It so happened, during Xerxes' stay at Acanthus, that Arta-chaeës, the man who had supervised the excavation of the canal, fell sick and died. He was of Achaemenid stock, and held in high regard by Xerxes. Not only was he a mere 4 fingers short of 5 royal cubits, making him the tallest man in Persia, but he also had the loudest voice in the world. Xerxes, who was devastated by this loss, gave him a splendid funeral, and had him buried beneath a mound that the entire army had joined in raising. On the prompting of an oracle, the Acanthians offer sacrifices to this Artachaeës, and hail him by name as a hero. As for King Xerxes, the death of Artachaeës caused him great grief.

[118] The Greeks who served as hosts to the army, and who provided Xerxes with his dinners, were reduced to such desperate straits that it cost them their homes. For instance, when the Thasians, on behalf of their cities on the mainland, entertained the army and furnished Xerxes with his dinner, they charged Antipater, the son of Orgeus, and a man as distinguished as any in the city, with the task; his accounts revealed that the dinner had cost him 400 talents of silver.

[119] Nor were these untypical of the accounts presented in other cities by men with a similar responsibility. The dinner, you see, was something that had been ordered long in advance, and was a very serious matter indeed. No sooner had the inhabitants of the various cities received their instructions from the heralds who were touring the region than they all immediately divided up their grain, and spent months and months in the grinding of wheat-flour and barley-meal. They had made sure to track down the best cattle that money could buy, and fatten them up; to keep birds in cages and water-fowl in ponds, for the delectation

of the troops; and to craft drinking-cups, mixing-bowls and every kind of tableware, all out of gold and silver. (These last, however, were made exclusively for the King and his dinner-guests – the rest of the troops had only to be provisioned with food.) No matter where the army appeared, and although everyone else camped out in the open, there would be a pavilion pitched and ready to serve Xerxes as a resting-place. When the hour came for dinner to be served, it was the hosts who would have to shoulder the entire burden of it; their guests, meanwhile, would eat their fill, pass the night there and then, the next morning, take down the pavilion, pack up all the things they could and set off. Everything would be taken, nothing was left behind.

[120] This was the context for a witty comment made by Megacreon, a man from Abdera, who suggested to the Abderites that they and their wives should go as one to their shrines, and sit there as suppliants, and beg the gods to avert half the evils that might be heading their way in the future, while also expressing their deep gratitude for something already granted them: namely, that King Xerxes was not in the habit of taking a meal twice a day. After all, had the people of Abdera been ordered to prepare a breakfast on the scale of his dinner, then they would have had to flee Xerxes' approach – either that, or stay put and be ground to nothing, more so than any people before them had ever been.

[121] As it was, the various cities did manage to meet all their obligations, crushing though these were. Xerxes, meanwhile, on leaving Acanthus, sent his ships on ahead of him, and instructed the commanders of the fleet to wait for him at Therma. (Therma is the city on the Gulf of Therma from which the gulf itself takes its name.)[60] Xerxes had discovered that it was the shortest route. As regards the army and its marching order, the entire land-force had made the journey between Doriscus and Acanthus, disposed, on Xerxes' instructions, into three divisions. One of these, under the command of Mardonius and Masistes, was detailed to follow the line of the coast and keep in touch with the fleet; another, under the command of Tritantaechmes and Gergis, to take an inland route; and the third division, under the command of Smerdomenes and Megabyzus, and accompanied by Xerxes himself, to follow a course midway between the other two.

[122] The fleet, following Xerxes' directions, sailed right the way along the Athos canal and out into the gulf where the cities of Assa, Pilorus, Singus and Sarte are located. Then, after press-ganging con-

scripts from all four cities, it steered a course for the Gulf of Therma. Round Cape Ampelus, in the land of the Toronaeans, it sailed, and past the Greek cities of Torone, Galepsus, Sermyle, Mecyberna and Olynthus – all of which were obliged to furnish the fleet with ships and troops. This region as a whole goes by the name of Sithonia.

[123] From Cape Ampelus, Xerxes' fleet steered directly to Cape Canastreum, which is the stretch of Pallene that protrudes the furthest into the sea. Here, they recruited ships and men from the various settlements which dot Pallene (or Phlegre, as it was once known): Potidaea, Aphytis, Neapolis, Aege, Therambos, Scione, Mende, and Sane. Then, once it had tracked the shoreline of Pallene, the fleet set sail for its prearranged destination, recruiting as it did so additional troops from the cities adjacent to Pallene and bordering the Gulf of Therma, in the region that is still known as Crossaea: namely, Lipaxus, Combreia, Lisae, Gigonus, Campsa, Smila and Aeneia. From the last-mentioned city on this list, Aeneia, the fleet then sailed into the Gulf of Therma itself, past the land of Mygdonia, and on to its appointed destination, where it docked at Therma, and at the cities of Sindus and Chalestra on the River Axius. (This river marks the border between Mygdonian territory and Bottiaean – on the narrow coastal region of which there stand two cities: Ichnae and Pella.)

[124] So the fleet lay at anchor off the Axius, and the city of Therma, and the cities in between, and there awaited the King. Meanwhile, Xerxes himself and his land-forces were making their way from Acanthus, and heading for their destination of Therma by taking the shortest possible inland route. Their progress took them through Paeonia and Crestonia to the River Echeidorus. (This river has its origins in Crestonia, flows through Mygdonia and issues into the marshland around the River Axius.)

[125] During the course of this journey, the camels in the baggage-train were attacked by lions.[61] Night after night these lions would make their descent, leaving behind their customary haunts, and harming nothing else, whether human or beast, but inflicting carnage solely upon the camels. I can only wonder at the possible reason for this. Why were the lions driven to ignore everything else and attack the camels, when they had never seen such a beast before, nor had any experience of it?

[126] There are a lot of lions in these parts, and also wild oxen, the outsize horns of which are imported into Greece. The range of the lions

is bordered on this side of Europe by the River Nestus, which flows through Abdera, and on the remaining stretch of the continent by the Achelous, which flows through Acarnania. No lions are ever seen east of the Nestus or west of the Achelous: only between these two rivers are they seen.

[127] Once he had arrived in Therma, Xerxes quartered his troops there. The army set up its camp along a stretch of shoreline beginning at the city of Therma and Mygdonia, and continuing the whole way up to the Macedonian frontier with Bottiaeis, where two rivers, the Lydias and the Haliacmon, form a single confluence. During the period of the Barbarians' encampment in this region, only one of the rivers I have mentioned failed to provide the army with a sufficient supply of drinking-water, and ran dry: the Echeidorus, which flows from Crestonia.

[128] From Therma, Xerxes could view the towering mass of Olympus and Ossa, both mountains of Thessaly; and when he learned that a narrow gorge ran midway between them, through which flowed the Peneius, and heard that this same gorge constituted the route of access down into Thessaly, he was anxious to take sail and inspect the mouth of the Peneius. (He had been informed, you see, that his safest option would be to take the high road that led through the inland reaches of Macedonia, and past the city of Gonnus, to Perrhaebia – and so this was what he planned to do.) Accordingly, acting on impulse, Xerxes boarded the Sidonian vessel that he always used whenever he wished to do something of such a kind, and gave signal that the rest of the fleet should put to sea as well, leaving his land-forces where they were. The sight of the Peneius, when Xerxes had arrived at its mouth, astonished him a good deal; and summoning his guides, he asked them if it were possible to divert the river and have it enter the sea some place else.

[129] There is a story that Thessaly, enclosed as it is on every side by towering mountains, was once, back in ancient times, a lake. To the east, it is shut in by Mount Pelion and Ossa, the foothills of which meet and merge; to the north, by Olympus; to the west, by Pindus; and to the south, by Othrys. These same mountains, being equidistant from one another, form the basin that is Thessaly. Any number of rivers flow into it, the five most notable of which are the Peneius, the Apidanus, the Onochonus, the Enipeus and the Pamisus. However, even though all of these descend from the mountains ringing Thessaly under their respective names, once down on the plain they join with one another, and merge their waters into a single river, which then flows out to the sea

through the one, narrow ravine – and the name of the river which prevails over those of the other four, the moment they all converge, and renders them nameless, is the Peneius. The story goes that in ancient times there existed no gorge to provide an outlet, even though the rivers, and Lake Boebeis too (despite lacking their current names) still flowed with no less a volume of water than they do today; and that these torrents served to make the whole of Thessaly into one vast sea. Now, according to the Thessalians, it was Poseidon who made the gorge through which the Peneius flows. This is an entirely plausible suggestion – since anyone who believes that Poseidon is the earth-shaker, and that the rifts made by earthquakes are the work of that particular god, would only have to see the gorge to acknowledge that Poseidon had indeed made it. Certainly, it seems clear to me that the rift in the mountains was the result of an earthquake.[62]

[130] The guides, when Xerxes asked them what alternative outlet into the sea for the Peneius there might be, were able to answer him with absolute certainty that the river had no other way of getting out to the coast. 'There is only this one, my Lord. A chaplet of mountains, you see, rings the whole of Thessaly around.' To this, Xerxes is said to have replied: 'Then the Thessalians are men of good sense indeed. Well did they take the precaution a while ago of conceding to me. One reason stands out from the rest. What could have been easier, after all, or taken less time, than the conquest of their country? All it would have taken was the damming of the gorge. The river would then have been diverted, its currents would have ceased to flow in the direction they now take, its waters would have spilled out across the land and the whole of Thessaly, with the exception of the mountains, would have vanished beneath the waves.' The allusion in this speech was to the sons of Aleuas,[63] and to the fact that they, as Thessalians, had been the very first Greeks to offer their surrender to the King – a gesture of friendship that Xerxes had assumed derived from the Thessalian people as a whole. Then, having delivered his remarks and looked the site over, he sailed back to Therma.

[131] In Pieria, he was delayed a good many days by the efforts of his troops (one third of them in all) to hack a way through the Macedonian mountains, and thereby enable the army as a whole to pass through them into Perrhaebia. Meanwhile, the heralds he had sent across Greece to demand earth were making their return – some of them empty handed, and some with earth and water.

[132] Those who had made their surrender included the Thessalians, the Dolopians, the Eniênians, the Perrhaebians, the Locrians, the Magnesians, the Malians and the Achaeans of Phthiotis. The Thebans also surrendered, together with the rest of the Boeotians – all except for the Thespians and the Plataeans. Those Greeks who stood up to the barbarian onslaught swore an oath against these peoples. By its terms, any Greeks who surrendered to the Persians of their own free will were to be obliged, once the defence of Greece had been brought to a successful conclusion, to hand over a tenth of their possessions to the god of Delphi. Such was the oath made by the Greeks.[64]

[133] To Athens and to Sparta Xerxes sent no heralds, and no demands for earth. The reason? Because, on a previous occasion, when Darius had dispatched just such a mission,[65] one embassy making the demand had been tossed into a pit and the other into a well. 'Fetch earth and water from there for your King,' they had both been told. No wonder, then, that Xerxes did not send anyone to repeat the demand. What unwelcome things happened to the Athenians as a result of their treatment of the heralds I am not in a position to say – unless it were the devastation of their land and city. In my own opinion, however, this had a very different cause.

[134] But upon the Lacedaemonians there fell the wrath of Talthybius, the herald of Agamemnon. Not only was there a shrine of Talthybius in Sparta, you see, but it was also home to his descendants: these are called the Talthybiads, and have always been granted the privilege of serving Sparta as heralds.[66] Such was the aftermath of the incident that the Spartiates found it impossible to obtain favourable omens from their sacrifices – something that went on for a lengthy period of time. Distressed and unsettled by this, the Lacedaemonians convened a whole number of assemblies,[67] and then issued a proclamation, enquiring if there were any among them willing to die for Sparta. At this, Sperthias, the son of Aneristus, and Bulis, the son of Nicolaus, two nobly born Spartiates who had also attained the very highest rank of wealth, volunteered to pay the penalty due to Xerxes for the murder in Sparta of Darius' heralds. So it was that the Spartans sent them off to the Medes – and to their deaths.

[135] The miraculous courage of these men was matched by words quite as admirable. On their way to Susa, they arrived at the court of Hydarnes, a Persian who had the military command of the peoples on

the Asian seaboard. He put them up and feasted them; and while they were all eating together, asked them, 'Why, men of Lacedaemon, do you spurn the friendship of the King? You can see for yourselves how practised he is at rewarding men of good character – after all, just look at me and how I have fared! The same might be true of you, if you would only put yourselves into his hands. In fact, such is the regard in which the King holds you that he would probably give you both the rule of domains on Greek soil.' 'But, Hydarnes,' they answered, 'this advice you are giving us is hardly balanced, is it? You are making a recommendation when you only have half the picture. Granted, with slavery you are perfectly familiar – but not so with liberty. Does it taste sweet, or not? You have no idea! If you did, you would be advising us to fight in its cause, not with spears, but with battleaxes!'

[136] Such was the retort they gave Hydarnes. They then continued on their way up to Susa, and into the royal presence, where the bodyguards initially tried to make them bow down before the King,[68] and do him obeisance – a step which they declared point-blank they would never take, even were they to be hurled face down onto the ground. 'It is not our custom to prostrate ourselves before a human being,' they explained, 'nor have we come here to do so.' Then, having won that battle, they made the following statement (or something along similar lines). 'The Lacedaemonians have sent us, O King of the Medes, to pay compensation for the heralds murdered in Sparta.' But Xerxes, with great generosity of spirit, answered this declaration by stating that he would not ape the Lacedaemonians. 'What you did, after all, when you murdered the heralds, was to contravene a universal human law. I will not repeat the very deed for which I am condemning you – nor will I absolve the Lacedaemonians of their guilt by killing you in exchange.'

[137] So it was, because the Spartiates had done as they did, that the wrath of Talthybius was temporarily abated, even though both Sperthias and Bulis made it back home to Sparta. Many years later, however, during the time of the war between the Peloponnesians and the Athenians, it flared back to life – or so the Lacedaemonians claim. Certainly, what happened does seem to me manifestly to have been of divine agency. That the wrath of Talthybius fell upon heralds, and never came to a stop until it had fully vented itself, was fitting enough. What leaves me in no doubt, however, that the whole business was indeed the work of a god is that it descended upon the sons of those very men who had

been sent up to the King on its account: upon Nicoleös, the son of Bulis, and upon Aneristus, the son of Sperthias, who seized control of Halieis, a colony of Tiryns, after he had docked there in a merchant-ship filled with men. When these two were sent as messengers by the Lacedaemonians to Asia, they were betrayed by Sitalces, the son of Teres, who was the king of the Thracians, and by Nymphodorus, the son of Pytheas, a man from Abdera. Taken prisoner at Bisanthe on the Hellespont, and shipped back to Athens, the pair were put to death by the Athenians, alongside a man from Corinth called Aristeas, the son of Adeimantus. But as these things happened many years after the expedition of the King,[69] I shall now return to my former narrative.

[138] Although the invasion launched by the King ostensibly had Athens as its target, in truth its descent was upon the whole of Greece. No matter that the Greeks themselves had long been aware of this, there was a complete lack of consensus as to how they should respond. Some – those who had given earth and water to the King – were confident that they would suffer nothing untoward at the hands of the Barbarian. Others – those who had given nothing – were in a state of total terror, partly because there were not enough battle-worthy ships in Greece to meet the invader, and partly because so many Greeks had embraced collaboration with the Medes that there were very few left to take an active part in the war.

[139] It is at this stage that I feel obliged to express an opinion which most people will find hard to stomach – but when something seems to me true, I will not shrink from saying it.[70] Had the Athenians been intimidated into abandoning their homeland by the menace that was bearing down upon them, or had they stayed put but surrendered to Xerxes, then no one would have sought to combat the King at sea. And had there been no one to oppose Xerxes at sea, what would have happened on the mainland? Surely, no matter how many walls the Peloponnesians might have strung up across the Isthmus of Corinth in their defence, the Lacedaemonians would still have been betrayed by their allies, not wilfully, but because, with the barbarian fleet capturing their cities one by one, the allies would have had no choice but to abandon the Lacedaemonians; and so the Lacedaemonians themselves, left to stand alone, would doubtless, after displays of prodigious valour, have gone down in a blaze of glory. Alternatively, before such an even-

tuality could occur, they might have witnessed how all the other Greeks were going over to the Medes, and arrived at some accommodation with Xerxes. Either scenario, however, would have resulted in Greece coming under Persian rule. Certainly, I cannot see what possible good the wall built across the Isthmus would have been, had the King had command of the sea. As it is, anyone who proclaims the Athenians the saviours of Greece would hardly be far from the truth. They were bound to tilt the scales in favour of whichever of the two sides they joined. By deciding to help in the preservation of Greek liberty, and backed as they were by the gods, they served to rouse to action everyone else in Greece who had not already gone over to the Medes, and to rout the King. Not even the blood-curdling oracles that had come from Delphi and thrown them into a terrible state of alarm could persuade them to abandon Greece. Instead, they stood their ground, held their nerve and met with the invader of their country.[71]

[140] The Athenians, you see, had sent emissaries to the god at Delphi; and these, after they had performed the customary rites around the shrine, and had come into the inner hall, were sitting down ready to make their consultation, when the Pythia, whose name was Aristonice,[72] began to declaim an oracle.

'Why are you sitting there, you fools? Leave, flee to the ends of
    the earth!
Abandon your homes, and the towering heights that ring your city!
For neither the head nor the body stays securely in its place,
Nor do the feet below, nor the hands, nor anything in between
Endure. Everything is doomed, everything brought crashing to
    the ground
By flames and passion-filled Ares, as he lashes on Syrian-bred
    steeds –
Nor is yours the only towered city he will obliterate.
Many temples of the gods as well will he hand over to fierce fire,
Which stand even now, surely, streaming with the sweat of their
    terror,
And shuddering with dread, while down from the very tops of
    the roofs
There pours, portending evils inescapably to come, black blood.
Go! Leave my sanctum! Shroud your spirits beneath the pall of
    your woes!'

[141] When they heard this, the Athenians sent to consult the god were plunged into an extreme of distress by what the oracle had revealed of the evils that were due them. It was then, however, that Timon, the son of Androboulus, and a man as highly esteemed as any in Delphi, suggested that they pick up some olive-tree boughs, go back in a second time to the oracle and consult it as suppliants – advice which the Athenians took. 'Lord,' they said, 'be moved to compassion by these boughs which come bearing before you as suppliants, and grant our fatherland a more favourable oracle. Otherwise, we shall never leave your inner sanctum, but stay here until the end of our days.' And sure enough, once they had made this statement, the prophetess delivered them a second oracle, which ran as follows:

'Pallas Athena cannot propitiate Olympian Zeus,
No matter how lengthy her prayers, or how cunning her entreaties.
So I tell you again, in words that shall bear no distortion –
While everywhere else will fall that the borders of Cecrops' land
Contain, yes, and the ravines of most holy Cithaeron as well,
Yet to Tritogeneia far-seeing Zeus grants a wooden wall.
Only this will stand defiant, a succour to you and your children.
Do not, then, abide the coming of the cavalry, nor the foot,
Still in the face of the vast, landside host. You must retreat instead,
And turn your backs. And yet, for all that, you shall meet them
    face to face.
Divine Salamis, the sons of women will be destroyed by you
When the grain is scattered – or else, when the harvest is gathered in.'

[142] Because this oracle seemed milder than the previous one (as indeed it was) the messengers sent to consult the god had it transcribed and went back to Athens. On their return, they gave a report to the people, who, in their attempts to make sense of the prophecy, proposed a whole range of interpretations – two of which in particular seemed to be at odds. Some of the older citizens claimed that the god had foretold the survival of the Acropolis, their reasoning being that back in ancient times the Acropolis of Athens had been fenced in by a thorn hedge, and that this [fence] was what had been meant by the 'wooden wall'. Others, however, maintained that the god was alluding to ships, and urged the abandonment of everything else for the sake of fitting out their fleet – though their case that ships were the 'wooden wall' was undermined by

the last two lines the prophetess had spoken: 'Divine Salamis, the sons of women will be destroyed by you/ When the grain is scattered – or else, when the harvest is gathered in.' The view of those who believed ships to be the 'wooden wall' was flatly contradicted by these lines of verse, since the officials who interpreted oracles had taken them to mean that the Athenians, after preparing to fight a battle in the waters off Salamis, would then inevitably lose.

[143] Now, one of the Athenians, a man who had just recently emerged into prominence, was named Themistocles[73] – the son of Neocles, he was called. This man argued that the reading of the oracle given by the interpreters was not altogether the correct one, and pointed out that the verses, had they truly been directed against the Athenians, would never have been couched in such mild terms, but would have read 'Cruel Salamis' rather than 'Divine Salamis' if its inhabitants really were doomed to perish there. On a correct interpretation of the oracle, he argued, it was the enemy who was the object of the god's verses – not the Athenians. That being so, and since the 'wooden wall' meant the fleet, he recommended that they should ready themselves to fight by sea. This explanation of Themistocles, so the Athenians decided, was preferable to that of the interpreters of the oracle, who would rather they did not prepare for any naval campaign – and indeed, if the truth be told, would have had them put up no resistance at all, but abandon Attica and settle in some other land.

[144] There had also been a previous occasion when Themistocles had demonstrated how supreme were his powers of analysis – and at a most opportune moment too, when the public treasury of the Athenians had become flush with revenues from the mines of Laurium,[74] and each and every citizen was due to get 10 drachmas as a personal windfall. It was then that Themistocles had persuaded the Athenians to halt this distribution, and to deploy the funds instead in the building of two hundred ships for use in the war – by which he had meant the war against the Aeginetans. So it was that this conflict, by forcing the Athenians to become mariners, proved in the long run to be the salvation of Greece.[75] Even though the ships were never used for the purpose for which they had been built, they did become available to Greece in her hour of need. What is more, in addition to the ones already built and in service, the Athenians were obliged to construct additional vessels. This was because, in the wake of the oracle, and after due consultation, they had

resolved to do as instructed by the god, and meet the barbarian invasion of Greece by taking to their ships,[76] every last man of them, alongside other such Greeks as wished to join them.

[145] So much for the oracles given to the Athenians. Meanwhile, all those Greeks who had refused to despair of Greece held a meeting in which they exchanged their points of view, and swapped pledges. It was agreed, as a result of their deliberations, that the absolute priority should be to make good their differences, and bring to an end such wars as were being fought among them – of which there were a whole number rumbling on, the one between the Athenians and the Aeginetans being the most serious. Next, informed that Xerxes and his army were at Sardis, they decided to send agents to Asia to spy on the King's affairs, and messengers to Argos, in an attempt to broaden the military alliance against Persia, while other messengers were sent to Gelon, the son of Deinomenes, in Sicily, to Corcyra and to Crete, summoning them to the defence of Greece, with the aim, if possible, of uniting the Greek world around a common identity and purpose – on the grounds that the menace threatened all Greeks equally. (Gelon was said to control immense resources, greater by far than those available to any other Greek power.)

[146] With this agreed upon, and all their various enmities settled, their first move was to send three men to Asia as spies. These, on their arrival in Sardis, made a thorough study of the King's army – but were detected, questioned under torture by the generals of the land-forces and then led away to execution. When Xerxes learned of the death sentence passed against them, however, he strongly criticized the judgement of the generals, and sent some of his personal bodyguards with orders to overtake the spies, if they were still alive, and bring them before him. When the guards found that the spies were indeed still alive, they duly led them into the presence of the King; and Xerxes, once he had discovered their reason for coming to Sardis, ordered his guards to take them on a guided tour of his entire army, both infantry and cavalry, and then, once they had had their fill of looking around, to send them on their way unharmed wherever they chose.

[147] The reasoning behind these orders, so he explained, was that the execution of the spies would have denied the Greeks advance notice of just how colossally his resources surpassed description – and at the derisory cost to his enemies of a mere three men. 'It is my belief', he said, 'that when they get back home to Greece, and the Greeks hear what I

am about, they will surrender these peculiar liberties of theirs before our expedition has taken place – meaning there will be no need for us to go to the trouble of undertaking a campaign against them.' Xerxes expressed a very similar opinion on another occasion too. While at Abydus, he saw ships with cargoes of grain sailing through the Hellespont from the Euxine, bound for Aegina and the Peloponnese. Those at his side, when they realized that the vessels belonged to the enemy, were all ready to seize them, and looked to the King, waiting for him to give the word. 'Where are the ships sailing?' Xerxes asked. 'To your enemies, O Master,' they replied, 'with cargoes of grain.' 'And is that not the destination of our own fleet,' he replied, 'and is not grain included among our supplies? How, then, can it possibly be wrong if they transport corn there for us?'

[148] So the spies, after they had had a good look around, were sent away, and returned back home to Europe. Meanwhile, the Greeks who had entered the sworn league against the Persians[77] followed up their dispatch of the spies by sending messengers to Argos. Now, the Argives themselves claim that, because of intelligence they had received right at the beginning of the Persian mobilization against Greece, and because they had realized, based on this information, that the Greeks would try to enlist them on their side, they had sent messengers to Delphi, to ask the god what their best course of action would be. It was only shortly before, after all, that they had lost six thousand men to the Lacedaemonians, under the command of Cleomenes, the son of Anaxandridas – so well might they have sent messengers to Delphi. In answer to their question, the Pythia replied:

'Detested by your neighbours, and yet dear to the immortal gods,
Keep your spears within your borders, and sit, looking out for
    yourselves.
Protect the head, and the head will be the salvation of the trunk.'

This oracle had been given by the Pythia well before the arrival in Argos of the Greek emissaries, who came into the council chamber and delivered their message as instructed. The Argives replied to what had been said by declaring that they were ready to do as requested, so long as the Lacedaemonians agreed to a thirty-year peace treaty with them, and provided that they were given command of half the allied forces. 'By rights, indeed, command of the entire lot should be ours – but command of half the forces, nevertheless, will do.'

[149] The Council gave this answer, so the Argives say, even though the oracle had forbidden them to join the Greek alliance. Their fear of the oracle was outweighed by their desperation to secure a thirty-year peace – since their sons would then have time to reach manhood. Without such a treaty, they added, there was every chance, should the calamity that had already befallen them[78] be compounded by a savaging at the hands of the Persians, that they would end up permanently subject to the Lacedaemonians. The members of the delegation from Sparta responded to the Council's proposals by saying that they would refer the question of the treaty back to their public assembly, but that, in respect of the command, they had been authorized to point out in reply that they had two kings, while the Argives had only the one. However, although it was out of the question for either of the two from Sparta to give up his post, there was nothing to prevent the Argive king from having a vote equal in weight to each of their two kings. So intolerable did the Argives find this display of selfishness by the Spartiates, they say, that they decided they would rather be ruled by the Barbarians than yield an inch to the Lacedaemonians; and so they announced to the emissaries that they had until sunset to leave Argive territory, or be treated as enemies.

[150] That is the Argive version of events. Elsewhere among the Greeks, however, a very different story is told: that Xerxes sent a herald to Argos before embarking on his invasion of Greece. 'Men of Argos,' this herald is supposed to have said on his arrival, 'here is a message sent you by King Xerxes. We hold ourselves to be descended from Perses, whose father was Perseus, the son of Danaë, and whose mother was Andromeda, the daughter of Cepheus – meaning that we are also descended from you. That being so, it is hardly right for us to make war on our own ancestors – nor for you to oppose us by rallying to the side of others, when instead you should be staying aloof and inactive. After all, if everything happens as I expect it will, there is no one who will stand higher in my estimation than you.' When the Argives heard this, it supposedly gave them such food for thought that for a good while they held their peace, and refrained from insisting on a share of the command until such time as the Greeks sought to enlist them – at which point, because they wanted a pretext for their inactivity, and knowing full well that the Lacedaemonians would never give them a share of the leadership, they presented their demand.

[151] There are certain Greeks who find confirmation of this story in the account of an episode that took place many years later. It so happened that at the same time as an Athenian embassy led by Callias,[79] the son of Hipponicus, was visiting Susa, the city of Memnon, on some separate matter, there was an Argive delegation that had been sent to Susa to ask Artaxerxes, the son of Xerxes, whether the pact of friendship they had entered into with Xerxes still held, or whether he now viewed them as enemies. King Artaxerxes assured them – so these Greeks say – that the pact still very much held, and that he had better relations with Argos than with any other city.

[152] Now, whether Xerxes really did send a herald to Argos with such a message, and whether an Argive embassy really did make its way up to Susa to ask Artaxerxes about the state of their friendship, I cannot state with any certainty – nor am I prepared to advance any version of what happened aside from that given by the Argives themselves. But this much I do know: that if everyone in the world were to make public his own personal problems, with the aim of swapping them for those of his fellow-men, just a single glance at the miseries of his neighbours would see him gladly take back with him the ones that he had brought. Which is to say – the behaviour of the Argives could have been worse. Although it is incumbent on me to state what I am told[80] I am under no obligation to believe it entirely – something that is true for the whole of my narrative. After all – one story even has it that the Argives actually invited the Persians into Greece, because they had been so badly bloodied in their war against the Lacedaemonians that they would have regarded anything as preferable to the state of wretchedness that was theirs at that time!

[153] So that is what people have to say about the Argives. Other messengers, with Syagrus of Lacedaemon the most prominent among them, were sent by the allies to Sicily, to make contact there with Gelon. Gelon's ancestor, although he settled in Gela, came originally from the island of Telos, off Triopium. When the Rhodians from Lindus, under the leadership of Antiphemus, first colonized Gela, there was no leaving this particular man behind. Time went by, and his descendants came to hold, as a hereditary position, the priesthood of the goddesses of the underworld[81] – an office that had originally been acquired by one of their forebears, a certain Telines, in the following manner. Some men were banished from Gela after losing out in a faction fight, and took

refuge in the city of Mactorium, inland from Gela. These men were then restored to Gela by Telines – not by force of human arms, but by the sacred implements of the goddesses. Where he might have obtained these, or whether they were in his possession already, it is beyond me to say – but certainly he put them to use, and duly effected the restoration of the men, on the condition that his descendants be priests of the goddesses. I find it a wonder, in view of what I have learned, that Telines ever managed to accomplish such a feat. After all, exploits of that order are performed, by and large, not by ordinary men but by those who are incomparably spirited, and whose strength marks them out as men in every sense of the word. Telines, by contrast, is said by the inhabitants of Sicily to have been a man of a somewhat soft and womanish disposition.

[154] So that was how Telines came by his office. Meanwhile, when Cleander, the son of Pantares, who had ruled Gela for seven years as its tyrant, met his end at the hands of a man from Gela called Sabyllus, it was his brother, Hippocrates, who took up the reins of the monarchy. During his tyranny, Gelon, who was a descendant of Telines the priest, served alongside Aenesidemus, the son of Pataecus, and many others too, in the bodyguard of Hippocrates. It did not take long, however, for his valour to secure him promotion to the command of the entire cavalry. You see, in all the wars fought by Hippocrates – whether the sieges of Callipolis, Naxos, Zancle and Leontini, or his clashes with the Syracusans and a whole host of Barbarians – it was Gelon who blazed the brightest trail. As for the various cities I just mentioned, not one of them escaped enslavement by Hippocrates – except Syracuse. The Corinthians and the Corcyraeans came to her rescue after she had been defeated in a battle beside the River Elorus. They negotiated a deal whereby the security of the Syracusans was guaranteed in exchange for their surrender to Hippocrates of Camarina, which originally had belonged to Syracuse.

[155] Hippocrates had been tyrant for as many years as Cleander, his brother, when he met with his death at the city of Hybla, while on campaign against the Sicels – whereupon Gelon gave his backing to the sons of Hippocrates, Eucleides and Cleandrus, against their fellow-Geloans, who were no longer content with their subject status. Words were one thing, however, deeds quite another: once Gelon had defeated the Geloans in battle, he usurped the tyranny from the sons of Hippocrates, and ruled himself. This stroke of good fortune was then followed by the expulsion from Syracuse of the so-called 'Gamori', who were forced out

by the mass of the people, and by their own slaves, or 'Cyllyrians',[82] as they are known; and Gelon, by engineering the return home of these Gamori from the city of Casmenae, also managed to bring Syracuse under his control. He had only had to make a move against the people of Syracuse, you see, for them to give up and surrender the city.

[156] Because Syracuse now meant everything to Gelon, the take-over of the city had left him much less interested in Gela; and so he duly turned its governance over to his brother, Hieron, while he himself began to strengthen Syracuse. In no time at all, the city had become a flourishing one. Gelon's first step was to demolish the city of Camarina, deport all the Camarinaeans and enroll them as citizens of Syracuse – measures which he also inflicted on over half the population of Gela. Then there were the Megarians who had settled in Sicily; when these came to terms with Gelon after a siege, he did not execute the men of substance, who had chosen to start the war and so were expecting to be put to death, but instead transported them to Syracuse and enrolled them there as citizens. As for the mass of the Megarian population, who were not responsible for the war and so had not normally anticipated that they might be made to suffer for it, they too were hauled off to Syracuse, where they were sold for export[83] from Sicily. The Euboeans who had settled in Sicily he treated in the same way, and along the same lines. In both cases, he did so because he regarded the masses as people who would foul his house. As a result of such measures, Gelon became a most formidable tyrant.

[157] But back to the occasion of the arrival of the Greek embassy in Syracuse. Going into session with Gelon, the messengers declared, 'We have been sent by the Lacedaemonians and their allies to secure your assistance against the Barbarian. No doubt you have heard all about his invasion of Greece – this man from Persia who is going to bridge the Hellespont, and lead the entire army of the East out of Asia on campaign against Greece. Yes, he justifies himself by saying that Athens is his target – but his real objective is to bring the entire Greek world under his control. Now, you are a man who has gained prodigiously in power. As lord of Sicily, you have no mean portion of the Greek world in your hands. Come to the aid, then, of those of us who are fighting to keep Greece free, and join in our struggle for liberty. If all of us can come together, a united Greece will make for a formidable body of

men – a worthy match for any invader. But should some of us turn traitor, and others have no wish to offer assistance, and only a small part of Greece prove sound, there is an all too present danger that the whole of Greece will fall. Do not expect, should Xerxes defeat us in battle and subdue us, that he will not come calling on you. Act now to guard against it. Come to our aid, and you will be helping yourself. It is, after all, the well-planned action that invariably comes to a happy conclusion.'

[158] The response of Gelon to this speech was one of utter fury. 'Men of Greece,' he said, 'this argument of yours – such self-interest! You presume to come here and summon me to join your alliance against the Barbarian? But only a little while ago, when I was locked in combat with the Carthaginians, it was me asking you for help in taking on a barbarian army! And then there was my urging you to avenge the murder by the Egestaeans of Dorieus, the son of Anaxandridas – and my suggestion that together we liberate the emporia, all of which have proved such a source of advantage and profit to you. But would you come and give me your assistance, or help avenge Dorieus? No! For all you care, the whole of Sicily might as well be under barbarian rule! In the event, things turned out well for us – indeed, they even improved. But now, when the tide of war has turned and is lapping at your feet, suddenly you remember Gelon! Despite the disrespect I have had from you, however, I will not ape it. Instead, I am ready to come to your assistance by providing two hundred triremes and twenty thousand hoplites, together with contingents of horsemen, archers, slingers and lightly armed men to run alongside the cavalry, each of them two thousand strong. I also undertake to provision the entire Greek army with grain for the duration of the war. I offer these guarantees, however, on one condition: that the supreme command of the Greeks against the Barbarian be mine. On no other terms will I come, or send other men either.'

[159] When Syagrus heard this, he could not contain himself. 'How loudly would Agamemnon, the son of Pelops, fall to groaning, were he to learn that the Spartiates had been deprived of their leadership by Gelon and the Syracusans?' he declared. 'So let's have no more of this. The very idea of it – that we should hand over command to you! If you really want to help Greece, then be clear on this point: you will be under the authority of the Lacedaemonians. And if it offends you to follow orders, well then – do not come to our aid.'

[160] The hostility evident in what Syagrus had said prompted Gelon to put his final offer on the table. 'When abuse rains down upon a man,' he said, 'his temper is prone to flare up, my Spartiate guest. Even so, not all the blatant arrogance of your comments will persuade me to start insulting you in return. Though you may be wedded to the leadership, it is hardly surprising that I should hug it to myself even more determinedly, given that I command a vastly larger army, and many more ships. But since my proposal has served to raise your hackles, let me moderate my previous terms. If you command the army, then I command the fleet. If you would rather lead by sea, then I wish to lead by land. And if you do not accept this condition, then you must depart without all these reinforcements that I have listed.'

[161] Such was Gelon's offer; but before the Lacedaemonian representative on the embassy could reply to it, the Athenian had cut in. 'We were not sent by Greece to ask you for a leader, O King of Syracuse,[84] but for an army – and if there is the slightest prospect of your sending one without your also being Greece's commander-in-chief, then you are keeping it well hidden. All you care about is the generalship! As long as you were demanding to lead the Greek forces in their entirety, we Athenians were content to keep our peace, conscious as we were that the Laconian was capable of speaking on behalf of us. But now that you have been forced to stop manoeuvring for overall command, and aim instead for the command of the fleet, let us speak plainly. If the Lacedaemonians themselves do not want it, then it is ours. If the Lacedaemonians do want the command, then we will not stand in their way – but we will not let command of the fleet go to anyone else. After all, what would have been the point of our acquiring the largest naval force in Greece if we Athenians were then to cede command to Syracusans – we, who are the oldest people in Greece, and indeed the only people never to have changed our homeland? It was a man from Athens who was described by Homer, the epic poet, as being the best at deploying and marshalling troops of all those who came to Ilium. That being so, we can hardly be reproached for pointing it out.'

[162] 'Well, my Athenian guest,' answered Gelon, 'it looks as though you have commanders, but will have no one for them to command. Since you refuse to give an inch, but want it all, on your way – and the sooner the better. Go home and tell Greece that the spring has been removed from her year.' [The meaning of this comment, the point Gelon

wished to make, was that what the spring is to the year, his forces were to the Greek army: the most highly regarded part. A Greece deprived of his army, according to this metaphor of his, was like a year from which the spring has been removed.[85]]

[163] So that was the outcome of the negotiations with Gelon, after which the Greek messengers sailed away. The possibility that the Greeks might lack sufficient resources on their own to overcome the Barbarian was certainly a cause of anxiety to Gelon; but as tyrant of Sicily, he found the prospect of going to the Peloponnese and serving under the Lacedaemonians so appalling that he scorned it as a quite intolerable course of action, and opted instead for another. No sooner had he heard that Xerxes was across the Hellespont than he dispatched a man from Cos, Cadmus, the son of Scythes – together with an escort of three pentecoaters, a large sum of money and warm words of friendship – off to Delphi, there to wait and see what the outcome of the war would be. If it was the Barbarian who triumphed, then Cadmus was to give him both the money, and earth and water from the lands that Gelon ruled; but if the Greeks prevailed, then Cadmus was to bring the money back.

[164] Now, some time earlier, this same Cadmus had inherited from his father the tyranny of Cos; but despite the fact that the regime stood on solid foundations, and that Cadmus himself faced no serious opposition, he was prompted by his own sense of justice to abdicate his control of Cos and go to Sicily, where he took the city of Zancle from the Samians,[86] and colonized it with settlers, changing its name to Messana. So that was how Cadmus had come to be in Sicily; and it was because of this, and because Gelon knew him from other circumstances as well to be an upright man, that he was given the mission. Indeed, among all the other various testimonies to the honesty of his dealings, the mission itself was not the least. He had sole charge of the vast amount of money entrusted to him by Gelon, and might easily have appropriated it; but he chose not to, and instead, after the victory of the Greek fleet and the forced retreat of Xerxes, returned to Sicily, bringing the full sum with him.

[165] There is also a story told by those who live in Sicily that Gelon, even though it would have obliged him to serve under Lacedaemonian command, would still have come to the aid of the Greeks, had it not been for the expulsion from the tyranny of Himera of Terillus, the son of Crinippus, by Theron, the son of Aenesidemus, who was the monarch

of Acragas. Even as Xerxes was invading Greece, Terillus brought his own invasion force: three hundred thousand Phoenicians, Libyans, Iberians, Ligurians, Elisycians, Sardinians and Cyrnians. This army was commanded by the Carthaginian king, Hamilcar, the son of Hanno, who was motivated partly by his guest-friendship with Terillus, but above all by the enthusiasm shown for his invasion of Sicily by the tyrant of Rhegium, Anaxileos, the son of Cretines. Anaxileos had married a daughter of Terillus called Cydippe; and now, rallying to his father-in-law's cause, he had handed over his own children as hostages to Hamilcar. It was this, so the Sicilians report, that prevented Gelon from coming to the assistance of the Greeks, and prompted him instead to send the money to Delphi.

[166] What is more, they claim that Gelon and Theron defeated Hamilcar of Carthage in Sicily on the very same day that the Greeks defeated the Persian at Salamis.[87] Hamilcar, whose father was Carthaginian but whose mother was from Syracuse, had become king of Carthage by virtue of his courage; and yet I have been reliably informed that when battle was joined, and he was having the worst of it, he disappeared off the face of the earth and was never seen again, either alive or dead. This was despite the fact that Gelon went to all possible lengths to find him.

[167] The explanation for this given by the Carthaginians themselves (and not implausibly either) is that the battle between the Barbarians and the Greeks [in Sicily] dragged on from dawn until late afternoon, and that Hamilcar stayed for the entire duration of the engagement in the camp, where, in his attempt to secure favourable omens, he offered up the entire bodies of sacrificial victims on a massive pyre; and it so happened, as he was pouring libations onto them, that he saw his troops fleeing, and hurled himself into the blaze. The reason, then, that he was never seen again was that he had been burnt to ashes. Whether Hamilcar really did vanish in this manner, as the Phoenicians report, or in some other way, they certainly offer him sacrifices, and have built memorials to him in all the cities of their various colonies, including the most significant one, Carthage itself. So much for the affairs of Sicily.

[168] Now to what the Corcyraeans said and did in response to the envoys. The messengers who sought to enlist them were the same as had visited Sicily, and the arguments used were the same as had been used on Gelon. The Corcyraeans immediately vowed to send reinforcements;

this was on the grounds that, as they themselves put it, they could not look away when Greece was faced with destruction. 'For if Greece should fall, then there will be no alternative but for us to accept the yoke of slavery the morning after. That being so, we must do all in our power to assist you.' A specious answer – and to be sure, when the time came for the Corcyraeans to send reinforcements, they did indeed man sixty ships, and made a great fuss about putting to sea. Their true intentions, however, were quite different: once they had reached the Peloponnese, they kept their fleet at anchor off Pylus and Taenarum, in the land of the Lacedaemonians, and waited to see how the war would turn out, since they were deeply pessimistic about the likelihood of a Greek victory, assuming that the Persian was bound to win decisively and would come to rule the whole of Greece. Their actions were deliberately designed to enable them to say to the Persian, 'O King, the Greeks sought to enlist us in the war. We are hardly the most minor of powers, after all, and would have provided them with a not insignificant number of ships – indeed, more than anyone else, with the exception of the Athenians. But we did not wish to oppose you or do anything contrary to your will.' They hoped, by delivering this speech, to obtain more favourable treatment than the other Greeks – as well they would have done, in my opinion. They also fabricated an excuse to give the Greeks – which, sure enough, when the Greeks accused them of having failed to come to their aid, they had to deploy. 'We manned sixty triremes,' they insisted, 'but were then prevented from rounding Cape Malea by the Etesian winds. That was why we could not make it to Salamis. Our absence from the battle was certainly not due to any cowardice on our part.' That was how the Corcyraeans sought to deceive the Greeks.

[169] As for the Cretans, when the envoys appointed by the Greeks sought to enlist them, they all jointly took the step of sending messengers to Delphi, to enquire of the god whether it would work to their advantage if they went to the aid of Greece. 'Fools,' answered the Pythia, 'are you such gluttons for punishment that not all the tears you were made to shed by wrathful Minos for giving help to Menelaus sufficed you? Did the Greeks ever assist you in avenging the death of Minos in Camicus? No, they did not! But you – you still rallied to their cause when a woman from Sparta was abducted by a man from a barbarian

land.'[88] When the Cretans heard this reply, they refrained from giving any assistance.

[170] The story goes, you see, that Minos, in the course of his hunt for Daedalus, came to Sicania (as Sicily was then called)[89] where he met with a violent death. In due course, all the Cretans, with the exception of the Polichnitians and the Praesians, were prompted by a god to come with a large force to Sicily, where they laid siege for five years to Camicus (a city which is nowadays inhabited by people from Acragas). Eventually, unable to capture it, and prevented from staying where they were by the pangs of hunger, they abandoned the siege and set off for home. As they were sailing past Iapygia, however, they were overtaken by a terrible storm and cast ashore. Because their ships had been smashed to pieces, and because there did not appear to be any other way of getting passage to Crete, they founded the city of Hyria, and stayed where they were, becoming Messapians from Iapygia instead of Cretans, and mainlanders rather than islanders. From this city of Hyria they then went on to found other colonies, which at a much later date the Tarentines sought to eliminate, and thereby suffered a defeat so crushing that the death-toll was the highest of any Greeks on record, and included, in addition to the Tarentines themselves, the citizens of Rhegium, who had been pressured into coming to the assistance of the Tarentines by Micythus, the son of Choerus – and lost three thousand men in all. As for the Tarentines themselves, there was no counting their losses. Micythus, who was a domestic slave of Anaxileos, had been left behind in charge of Rhegium, and was the Micythus who, after his banishment from Rhegium, settled in Tegea in Arcadia, and dedicated all those statues in Olympia.

[171] But enough about the people of Rhegium and Tarentum, who are a footnote to my account.[90] Back to Crete – which, according to the Praesians, was left desolate and empty, until it was colonized by other people, the majority of whom were Greeks. Then, two generations after Minos had met his end, the Trojan War broke out – and it is clear enough that the help received by Menelaus from the Cretans was not in the least half-hearted. Then, on their return home from Troy, came their reward: both they and their cattle were afflicted by famine and plague, until for a second time Crete was left empty. The Cretans who live there today are a blend of the third group of people to do so and the survivors

of the second. It was by reminding them of all this that the Pythia restrained their wish to assist the Greeks.

[172] The Thessalians, to begin with, collaborated with the Medes only by force of necessity – and no sooner had they learned that the Persian was on the verge of crossing into Europe, than they made clear their distaste for the manoeuvrings of the Aleuadae by sending envoys to the Isthmus. Also gathered at the Isthmus were the nominated representatives of cities from across Greece – or at least, those cities that had the best interests of Greece at heart.[91] On arriving there, the Thessalian envoys addressed these representatives. 'Men of Greece, if Thessaly and the whole of Greece are going to be sheltered from war, then a guard must be placed on the pass by Mount Olympus. We are ready to make our contribution – but only if you too send a sizeable army. If you do not send one, then be in no doubt – we will come to terms with the Persian. Why should we have to stand alone and be annihilated for your sakes, just because we are so much more exposed than the rest of Greece? Only if you wish to help us will you be able to bring pressure to bear. There is no necessity so strong, after all, that it can prevail on people who are powerless. If we are to try to save ourselves, then we will have to rely on our own wits.'

[173] This declaration by the Thessalians prompted the Greeks, after some deliberation, to send a force of infantry by sea to guard the pass. The army duly assembled, and set sail along the Euripus. Then, when the troops arrived at Alus in Achaea, they disembarked and left their ships behind, making their way to Thessaly and arriving at Tempe, the pass down which the River Peneius flows from lower Macedonia into Thessaly, between the two mountains of Olympus and Ossa. There the Greeks made camp: ten thousand hoplites in all, reinforced by the Thessalian cavalry. The general in charge of the Lacedaemonians, who had been selected from among the war-magistrates[92] despite not being of royal birth, was Euaenetus, the son of Carenus, while the Athenian general was Themistocles, the son of Neocles. They stayed there a few days; and then messengers arrived from Alexander of Macedon,[93] the son of Amyntas, advising them to leave and not stay in the pass, or they were sure to be trampled underfoot by the invaders, the sheer scale of whose force, by both land and sea, was made plain. Once this advice had been given, it struck the Greeks as both sound and – since the Macedonian appeared to be very much on their side – persuasive. My own opinion,

however, is that what really swayed them was the horror they felt on discovering that there was another pass into Thessaly, running from inland Macedonia through the land of the Perrhaebians, by way of the city of Gonnus – and which, in the event, was indeed the route by which Xerxes' army invaded. So the Greeks went down to their ships again, and headed back to the Isthmus.

[174] So that was the fate of the expedition to Thessaly, which took place while Xerxes was at Abydus, on the verge of crossing from Asia into Europe. The Thessalians, who were now quite bereft of allies, duly went over to the Medes – and not in any half-hearted manner either, but with such commitment that their deeds served to mark them out as men of the greatest value to the King.

[175] On their return to the Isthmus, the Greeks debated among themselves how and where – in light of what Alexander had told them – they should make their stand.[94] The opinion that prevailed was that they should defend the pass of Thermopylae, on the grounds that it was manifestly narrower than the one that led into Thessaly, and nearer to home as well. Of the path[95] – the one that led to the destruction of the Greeks who fell at Thermopylae – they were wholly ignorant until their arrival there, when they were told about it by the Trachinians. So the decision was made to defend the pass, and thereby prevent the Barbarian from entering Greece. Meanwhile, the fleet was to set sail for Artemisium, in the territory of Histiaea, and thereby ensure that the two forces would be sufficiently close to one another that each would stay abreast of developments.

[176] The lie of the land at these two places is as follows. Artemisium first: between the island of Sciathos and Magnesia, on the mainland, the open expanse of the Thracian sea narrows to a single channel, which is then followed by Artemisium, a beach on the Euboean coast, on which there is a sanctuary of Artemis. The pass which leads through Trachis into Greece is half a *plethron* wide at its narrowest point. Nevertheless, even this is not the narrowest point in the region as a whole, since there are narrower stretches which come both before and after Thermopylae: to its rear, at Alpeni, there is room for only a single wagon to pass, while in front, at the River Phoenix, near the city of Anthela, it narrows again to the width of a single wagon trail. The western flank of Thermopylae consists of a sheer and impassable cliff, very high, which extends all the way to Mount Oeta; while to the east of the road there is nothing but

sea and marshes. The pass itself contains hot springs, which the locals call 'The Pots', and an altar which they raised to Heracles. Additionally, there is a wall built across the pass, which in ancient times had a gate set in it.[96] It was the Phocians who built this wall, out of terror at the arrival of the Thessalians from Thesprotia coming to settle Aeolis – a land which they hold to this day. The Phocians took this pre-emptive measure because the Thessalians were looking to conquer them;[97] they also let the hot water flow directly into the pass, so that the terrain would be scored with gullies, and resorted to every possible contrivance to prevent the Thessalians from invading their land. Now, because the original wall had been built long ago, most of it, over the years, had fallen into ruin; so the Greeks decided to repair it, with the aim of keeping the Barbarian out of Greece. There was also a village very close to the road called Alpeni; and it was from here that the Greeks were planning to obtain their provisions.

[177] These locations, once the Greeks had weighed up every eventuality, and calculated that the Barbarians would be unable to deploy either numbers or cavalry in them, seemed those best suited to their needs; and so they resolved to meet there with the invader of Greece. When news came that the Persian was in Pieria, they duly went their separate ways from the Isthmus: some on foot to Thermopylae, and others by sea to Artemisium.

[178] So off with all speed went those Greeks who were rallying to the cause of Greece, to take up their various battle-stations. But the Delphians meanwhile, terrified for themselves, and for Greece as well, were busy consulting the god, who instructed them, in an oracle, to pray to the winds, 'For they will be formidable allies of Greece.' The first thing the Delphians did, once they had accepted this prophecy as genuine, was to send messengers with news of the oracle they had received to those Greeks who wished to be free – and thereby, since dread of the Barbarian was terrible, to win the undying gratitude of all those to whom the announcement was made. After doing that, the Delphians raised an altar to the Winds at Thyia, and wooed them there with sacrifices. (Thyia is a place that takes its name from Thyia, the daughter of Cephisus, and who has a temple precinct there.) So in accordance with the oracle, the Delphians propitiated the winds – as they have continued to do, right up to the present day.

[179] Meanwhile, the naval wing of Xerxes' task-force was setting

out from the city of Therma; its elite, the ten fastest ships, set a course directly for Sciathos, where three Greek ships, one from Troezen, one from Aegina and one from Athens, were stationed as an advance guard. At the sight of the barbarian ships, these took flight.

[180] Straightaway, the Troezenian vessel, under the command of Praxinus, was captured by the pursuing Barbarians. Finding something auspicious in the fact that the first Greek they had taken captive was also the most handsome, they took this marine – the best-looking of all on board – to the prow of the ship, and there slit his throat. The name of this man who had his throat cut was Leon. It is possible that his name had some bearing on his fate.

[181] The Aeginetan ship, a trireme captained by Asonides, inflicted considerable injury on its pursuers, since one of the marines serving on board it – Pytheas, the son of Ischenous – proved himself that day a man unrivalled for valour. Although the ship had been captured, he continued fighting until he was nothing but mincemeat. Even when he fell, however, he was not dead, but still had the breath of life in him; and so impressed by his prowess were the Persian marines serving on board the ship that they took every measure they could to keep him alive, treating his wounds with myrrh and wrapping them in bandages of the finest linen. Then, once they had arrived back at their own base, they paraded him before the entire force as someone worthy of the utmost admiration, and treated him very well. All the others they had captured on board that ship, though, they treated as slaves.

[182] So it was that two of the ships were lost. The third, a trireme under the command of Phormus, a man from Athens, ran aground at the mouth of the Peneius in the course of its flight; but although the Barbarians captured the ship itself, they failed to capture the crew. This was because, the moment the Athenians had beached their ship, they jumped off it and made their way through Thessaly, all the way back to Athens.

[183] Meanwhile, beacons on Sciathos relayed the news of what had happened to the Greek base at Artemisium. So terror-struck were the Greeks by the information that, although they kept look-outs by day on the heights of Euboea, they switched their anchorage from Artemisium to Chalcis, with the aim of guarding the Euripus. As for the Barbarians, three of their ten ships were wrecked on a reef that lies midway between Sciathos and Magnesia, and goes by the name of 'The Ant'. Accordingly,

the Barbarians ferried a pillar of stone to the reef, and erected it there; and the entire fleet, now that the way ahead had been made clear, sailed out from Therma, eleven days after the King himself had marched out from the same place. The pilot who took the lead in navigating them past the reef was Pammon of Scyros. All day long the Barbarians sailed, until they reached Sepias, in Magnesia – or to be specific, the beach which runs between the city of Casthanaea and Cape Sepias.

[184] Arriving here, and at Thermopylae, the expedition was yet to suffer any casualties: according to my own calculations its numbers at this stage still amounted to the following: 1,207 ships in all had come from Asia, meaning, if we reckon two hundred men to a ship, that the original complement of men, adding all the various nationalities together, amounted to 241,400. In addition to the native crews, each of these ships also carried a further thirty marines, men who were either Persians, Medes or Sacae. These constituted an additional 36,210. To this total, and to the first set of figures as well, I shall add the crews of the penteconters, which – give or take a few – I calculate to have held eighty men each. Now, as I mentioned earlier, there were three thousand of these boats in all – which would mean that they carried a full 240,000 men. So 517,610 was the total number of those who sailed from Asia with the fleet. As for the infantry and the cavalry, they numbered 1,700,000 and 80,000 respectively. To these, I shall add the Arab camel-drivers and the Libyan charioteers: men whom I calculate to have numbered 20,000. Combine the numbers both by sea and by land, then, and the total amounts to a full 2,317,610! And even then, I am only referring to the actual fighting men who were led out of Asia, and have taken no account of the attendants who followed in their train, or the supply ships and those who sailed on them.

[185] I must also add to the sum of the figures already totalled the forces that were brought from Europe, although here I will have to provide an estimate. The Greeks from Thrace and the islands just off Thrace furnished 120 ships. The crews on board these ships amounted to 24,000 men. As for land-forces, I would estimate that some 300,000 of these were furnished by a variety of peoples: the Thracians, the Paeonians, the Eordians, the Bottiaeans, the people of Chalcidice, the Brygians, the Pierians, the Macedonians, the Perrhaebians, the Enianians, the Dolopians, the Magnesians, the Achaeans and the inhabitants of coastal

Thrace. Supplement the numbers from Asia with these various myriads, and the total number of fighting men came to 2,641,610.

[186] I would also estimate, bearing in mind just how many combatants there were, that the servants in their train, and the crews of the small supply-vessels and all the other ships that were sailing alongside the army, would have outnumbered the fighting men, rather than falling short of their total. But suppose I make my calculations based on the presumption that they were neither more nor less, but exactly equivalent, so that for every ten thousand fighting men, there was an equal number of camp-followers – then the number of men led by Xerxes, the son of Darius, to Sepias and Thermopylae would have amounted to 5,283,220.

[187] But if that is the figure you get when you add all the constituent parts of Xerxes' task-force together, then of the precise numbers of women who served in the kitchens and the soldiers' beds, and of the eunuchs, there can be no reckoning. Likewise, in the army's train, so numerous were the yoke-animals and the other beasts of burden, and the Indian hunting-dogs too, that no one could ever possibly set a figure on them. While it is hardly a wonder, then, in my opinion, that the waters of some rivers should have given out, the truly marvellous thing is how on earth all these myriads of people managed to be fed. If you assume that each man was allocated a *choenix* of wheat, and no more, then by my calculations you arrive at a daily consumption rate of 110,340 *medimni* – and that is not even making allowance for the women, the eunuchs, the yoke-animals and the dogs. And yet among all these thousands upon thousands of people, there was no one so handsome or so imposing that he would have been better fitted to wield supreme power than Xerxes himself.

[188] After the fleet had set sail and put in at the beach between the city of Casthanaea and Cape Sepias, in the region of Magnesia, the first ships to arrive there moored directly offshore, while the rest lay at anchor behind them. Because the beach was not a large one, the ships had to moor off it in rows eight deep, with their prows facing out to the sea. All night, under clear skies and in calm weather, they maintained this formation; but then, towards dawn, the sea began to boil, and a terrible storm descended upon them, borne from the north-east by a wind known to those who live in the region as a 'Hellesponter'. Now,

those who had noticed that the winds were building, and whose mooring made it feasible, hauled their ships up onto the beach before the storm hit, and thereby managed to sit it out – they and their ships as well. Of the ships that were caught out on the open sea, however, some were swept onto the rocks of Pelion – the 'Ovens', as they are called – and some onto the beach. Others were wrecked on Cape Sepias itself, or off the city of Meliboea, or were driven ashore at Casthanaea. So violent was the storm, in short, that it was irresistible.

[189] The story goes that the Athenians had called on Boreas, the north wind, for assistance, after being prompted to do so by another oracle that had urged them to appeal to their 'son-in-law' for help. Now Boreas, according to Greek tradition, married an Athenian: Oreithyia, the daughter of Erechtheus. It was on the basis of this kinship, so the tale goes, that the Athenians understood Boreas to be their 'son-in-law' – and as they lay to in the harbour of Chalcis on Euboea, and noticed that the storm was rising, or perhaps even before that, they offered up sacrifices, and called on Boreas and Oreithyia to aid them by destroying the barbarian fleet, as before at Athos. Now, whether or not this was really why Boreas fell upon the Barbarians as they were lying at anchor, I cannot say – but the Athenians do claim, not only that Boreas had come to their rescue previously, but that he did so again on this occasion. The Athenians, on their return home, built a shrine to Boreas beside the River Ilissus.

[190] Even at the lowest estimate, at least four hundred ships were lost in this disaster, together with innumerable men, and wealth beyond the dreams of avarice. One man, a Magnesian called Ameinocles, the son of Cretines, who owned land in the region of Sepias, duly reaped immense profit from all the wreckage. Over the course of time, he picked up any number of gold and silver drinking-vessels as they were washed up onto the shore, discovered Persian treasure-chests and came by more riches [and things of gold] than I can possibly relate. Nevertheless, for all that he became immensely wealthy as a result of his beach-combing, in other respects his luck failed him. He too, you see, suffered his share of grief: the result of a truly appalling accident, in which he killed his own son.

[191] As for the transport-ships for grain and other vessels, there is no counting how many of these were lost. Indeed, such was the damage done to the fleet that its commanders, nervous in case the Thessalians

should attack them, barricaded themselves behind a high palisade fashioned out of the flotsam. For three days the storm raged. Finally, after the Magi had carved up various victims and sought to calm the wind by chanting spells, and made sacrifice as well to Thetis and the Nereids, they brought the storm to ease – either that, or it abated of its own volition. The sacrifices to Thetis were offered because the Ionians had told them the story of how she had been abducted by Peleus from there, and that the whole of Cape Sepias belonged to her and the other Nereids.

[192] On the fourth day the storm stopped for good. And already, only a day after its onset, the look-outs watching up on the Euboean peaks had come rushing down, and given the Greeks a full report on the wrecking of the fleet. After this briefing, the Greeks had raised prayers to Poseidon the Saviour, and poured him libations, and then sped back as fast as they could to Artemisium, in the hope that there would be only a few ships now for them to face. So a second time they made their way to Artemisium and lay at battle-stations there; and it has been the custom, from that day to this, to grace Poseidon with the title of 'Saviour'.

[193] Meanwhile, now that the wind had abated and the swell had eased, the Barbarians hauled their ships back into the sea, and tracked the coast of the mainland, rounding the outermost tip of Magnesia, and then sailing directly into the gulf that leads to Pagasae. There is a place in this gulf, the one in Magnesia, where Heracles is said to have been left behind by Jason and his fellow-Argonauts, in the course of their voyage to Aea [in Colchis]. The Argonauts had sent Heracles to fetch water, because they had been planning to launch themselves (*aphêsein*) out into the open sea only after they had first replenished their stocks of water – which is why the place came to be known as Aphetae. It was here that Xerxes' men dropped anchor.

[194] Now, it so happened that fifteen of the barbarian ships put out to sea much later than the others – and somehow caught sight of the Greeks' ships at Artemisium. The Barbarians, mistaking these ships for their own, set sail towards them and fell into enemy hands. The barbarian ships were commanded by the governor of Cyme in Aeolis, Sandoces, the son of Thamasius, who had previously been a royal judge, before being arrested on the orders of King Darius, and crucified. The charge against Sandoces was that he had accepted a bribe to deliver an unfair ruling in a case. Even as he was hanging from the cross, however, Darius

continued to ponder the matter – and came to the conclusion that the good Sandoces had done the royal house outweighed his crimes. This realization in turn brought Darius to appreciate that he had acted less in wisdom than in haste, so he set Sandoces free. And now this same man had sailed straight into the Greek fleet – and for all that he had had one life back when he escaped death at the hands of King Darius, he was not to escape with his life a second time. The Greeks, you see, when they saw the barbarian squadron bearing down upon them, understood that it had blundered, and, putting out to sea, captured it with ease.

[195] Sailing on board one of the captured ships was Aridolis, the tyrant of Alabanda in Caria, and on another Penthylus, the son of Demonous, a general from Paphus, who had brought twelve ships from the island, lost eleven of them in the storm off Sepias and then sailed in his sole surviving vessel down to Artemisium – where he was taken prisoner. The Greeks, after they had interrogated these two about all the things they wished to discover regarding Xerxes' forces, then sent them in chains to the Isthmus of Corinth.

[196] Nevertheless, these fifteen ships – the ones I just mentioned as being commanded by Sandoces – were the only ones in the barbarian fleet not to reach Aphetae. Three days later, Xerxes and the land-forces, after making their way through Thessaly and Achaea, arrived in Malis. In Thessaly, where Xerxes had been informed that the local horses were the best in Greece, he had tested their mettle by staging a contest between them and his own – a race in which the Greek horses had been left trailing far behind. Now, in Thessaly, the Onochonus was the only river which proved so inadequate to the army's needs as to be drunk dry. In Achaea,[98] however, even the largest river, the Epidanus, was reduced to the barest trickle.

[197] While Xerxes was in Achaea, at Alus, his guides – who were keen to relate to him everything they came across on the road – repeated a story told by the locals about the sanctuary of Laphystian Zeus. In this tale, it was related how, sometime after Athamas, the son of Aeolus, had conspired with Ino to bring Phrixus to his doom, the Achaeans were instructed by an oracle to impose various trials upon Phrixus' heirs. An injunction was laid upon whoever happened to be the senior member of the family at the time, forbidding him entry to the 'Place of the People' (as the Achaeans term their city hall), and which had guards posted on it. If he were to enter it, then there was no possibility that he

could ever leave it, except when about to be sacrificed. Furthermore, the guides continued, those who faced being sacrificed were so terrified that they would be likely to run away, and go to some other country; but any such fugitive, were he to venture back after the passage of time, and be captured, would then, so the guides explained, be sent into the city hall, and prepared for sacrifice by being festooned with garlands, and then led out amid a procession. It is the heirs of Cytissorus, the son of Phrixus, who are put through this ordeal – the reason being that, at the very moment when the Achaeans were about to sacrifice Athamas, the son of Aeolus, in obedience to an oracle that had instructed them to kill him as expiation for their country, this same Cytissorus had arrived from Aea in Colchis, rescued Athamas and by this action brought down upon his descendants the wrath of the god. When Xerxes, after hearing this story, came to the grove, he not only kept clear of it himself, but gave orders that everyone else in the army should do the same; and he treated both the house that belonged to the heirs of Athamas, and their sacred precinct, with exceptional respect.

[198] So much for events in Thessaly and Achaea. From these regions, Xerxes continued into Malis, and followed the coastline of the gulf, in which the tide daily rises and falls. The low-lying land that surrounds it varies from the wide to the very narrow, and is itself surrounded by high and impassable mountains. These mountains enclose the entire land of Malis, and are known as the 'Rocks of Trachis'. Coming from Achaea, the first city on the gulf that one reaches is Anticyra, on the banks of the Spercheius, a river which flows from the land of the Eniênians into the sea. Then, some 20 stades further on, there is another river, called the Dyras, which appeared, according to legend, when it came to the rescue of Heracles as he was burning up.[99] Another 20 stades on from that there is a further river, called the Black River.

[199] Five stades on from this Black River is the city of Trachis. It stands where the stretch of land between the mountains and the sea is at its broadest, on a plain 20,000 *plethra* in extent. South of Trachis, in the mountain range that encloses the city's territory, there is a gorge, and it is through this gorge, past the foothills of the mountains, that the River Asopus flows.

[200] South of the Asopus is another river, not large, called the Phoenix, which flows down from the mountains into the Asopus. This river,

the Phoenix, marks the narrowest point of all; for the road that was built here has room only for a single wagon. From the Phoenix it is fifteen stades to Thermopylae. Lying between the Phoenix and Thermopylae, next to where the Asopus debouches into the sea, is a village called Anthela; it is surrounded by a wide open space on which a shrine dedicated to Demeter of the Amphictyons[100] has been established, together with a seating area for the Amphictyons, and a sanctuary to Amphictyon himself.

[201] King Xerxes made his base at Trachis, in the land of the Malians, while the Greeks were camped out in the pass itself. Although the place is known across most of Greece as Thermopylae, the locals and their immediate neighbours call it Pylae – 'The Gates'. So these were the respective positions of the two sides, with Xerxes in command of everywhere north of Trachis, and the entire mainland to the south under Greek control.

[202] The Greeks who stood awaiting the Persian in this location were as follows. There were 300 hoplites from Sparta, and 1,000 altogether from Tegea and Mantinea, with 500 drawn from each, 120 from Arcadian Orchomenus, and 1,000 from the rest of Arcadia. In addition to the Arcadians, 400 came from Corinth, 200 from Phleious and 80 from Mycenae. These were the contingents from the Peloponnese, while from Boeotia there were 700 Thespians and 400 Thebans.

[203] Swelling these numbers were the Locrians of Opous – who, when the call went out, sent their entire fighting force – and 1,000 Phocians. The summons had come from the Greeks themselves, who had declared through messengers that they were at Thermopylae as the advance guard of all the other allies, that these remaining forces were expected any day and that the sea was being patrolled with unblinking alertness by the Athenians, the Aeginetans and all the various other naval contingents – and so there was nothing to fear. 'After all,' the message continued, 'it is no god who is invading Greece, but only a man. There never was a mortal who did not, right from birth, have misfortune woven into the very fabric of his life – nor will there ever be. Indeed, the greater the man, the greater the misfortunes. The man coming against us is a mortal, and his expectations are accordingly bound to fail him.' Thus reassured, the Locrians and Phocians had come to the assistance of the troops at Trachis.

[204] Now, although each city supplying a contingent had also sent

a man to command it, the one regarded with the greatest awe, and who served as the supreme commander, ahead of all the other generals, was a Lacedaemonian: Leonidas. He was the son of Anaxandridas, and was descended, through Leon, Eurycratidas, Anaxander, Eurycrates, Polydorus, Alcamenes, Teleclus, Archelaus, Hegesilaus, Doryssus, Leobotes, Echestratus, Agis, Eurysthenes, Aristodemus, Aristomachus and Cleodaeus, from Hyllus, who was the son of Heracles. Leonidas had come to be king of Sparta in unexpected circumstances.[101]

[205] Certainly, because he had two brothers older than himself – Cleomenes and Dorieus – it had never crossed his mind that he might end up as king. But then, when Cleomenes died without a male heir, and with Dorieus already dead, having met his end in Sicily, the kingdom did indeed devolve upon Leonides: partly because he was older than Cleombrotus, who was Anaxandridas' youngest son, and partly because he was married to Cleomenes' daughter.[102] So it was Leonidas who came to Thermopylae – escorted, as was the custom, by three hundred handpicked men, all of whom already had sons. On his way there, he also recruited the Thebans whom I mentioned in the roll-call I just gave, and who were commanded by Leontiades, the son of Eurymachus. The reason why Leonidas was so keen to do this, and to single the Thebans out alone among all the Greeks for recruitment, was that they were widely suspected of collaborating with the Medes. By summoning them to war, he wished to discover whether they would indeed supply him with men, or whether they would shrink from lending such open support to the alliance of Greeks. In fact, although the Thebans sent men, their sympathies did indeed incline the other way.

[206] The Spartiates sent Leonidas and his men as an advance guard, so that the other allies would be inspired by the sight to march to war as well, and not go over to the Medes, as they might well have done had they felt that the Spartiates were hanging back. As it happened, the Carneia was indeed holding them up[103] – but it was their intention, the moment the festival was over, to march to the rescue of Leonidas with all their available manpower, leaving behind them only a skeleton holding-force. The rest of the allies too were intending to do much the same thing. In their case, you see, the festival that coincided with the onset of war was the Olympic one.[104] Because they had never imagined that the battle of Thermopylae would be concluded so quickly, they too had sent only advance guards.

[207] So much for their intended course of action. Meanwhile, however, as the Persian bore down upon the pass, so terrified were the Greeks at Thermopylae that they seriously debated withdrawing. The other Peloponnesians were all for heading back to the Peloponnese, and taking the Isthmus as the focus of their resistance; but Leonidas, seeing how enraged the Phocians and the Locrians were by this idea, voted to stay where they were, and send messengers to summon assistance from the various cities, since they themselves were far too few to withstand the army of the Medes.

[208] In the midst of their deliberations, Xerxes sent a scout on horseback to spy out their numbers, and to see what they were up to. Xerxes had already heard, while still in Thessaly, that a tiny force had assembled in the pass, led by the Lacedaemonians under Leonidas – and that Leonidas was of the bloodline of Heracles. The horseman came galloping up to the camp, and duly made his survey – although not of the whole camp, since it was impossible for him to see most of the troops who were stationed behind the wall, which they had repaired and were now garrisoning. Instead, the scout took stock of the men who were out in the open, with their arms and armour piled up in front of the wall, and who at the time, as it happened, were the Lacedaemonians. Some of the men, the scout saw to his astonishment, were exercising naked, and some were combing their hair.[105] Keeping his eyes peeled, however, he added up their numbers; and then, once he had arrived at an accurate total, galloped off unhindered. Rather than pursuing him, everyone treated him with the utmost indifference. So he went back to Xerxes and reported all he had seen.

[209] The King, though, was unable to appreciate the significance of what he was hearing: namely, that the Lacedaemonians were readying themselves to be killed, and to kill in turn as many as they were able. To Xerxes their actions seemed laughable – and so, because he wished to make sense of them, he summoned Demaratus, the son of Ariston, who was there in the camp. After he had duly arrived, Xerxes asked him to explain, point by point, the behaviour of the Lacedaemonians. 'You have already heard me discuss these men,' Demaratus said, 'when we were setting out for Greece. And when you heard what I had to say, you laughed at my forecast of how events in this campaign would unfold – but that was because, O King, when I am in your presence, I have no greater object or aim than to be truthful with you. So hear me out

again. These men have come here to fight us for the pass – and they are getting themselves ready to do just that. It is their custom, you see, whenever they are about to risk their lives, to dress their hair. But rest assured, should you defeat them, and their fellows still in Sparta, my King, then no other people in the world will take up arms against you and stand in your path. For you are about to attack the fairest kingdom[106] in all of Greece – yes, and the bravest men.' To Xerxes, however, these claims seemed wholly incredible; and a second time, he demanded to know how such a tiny force of men was going to fight his own army. 'O King,' Demaratus answered, 'treat me as you would any liar, if things do not turn out for you as I state.' But nothing that he said could make Xerxes believe him.

[210] Confident as Xerxes was that the Greeks were bound to run away at any moment, he let four days go by. Then, on the fifth, when they had still not left, and the seeming impudence and folly of their continued presence there were making him seethe with anger, he sent the Medes and Cissians against them, with orders to take them alive and bring them into his presence. The Medes fell upon the Greeks in a great rush, and although many were slain, others still pressed the attack, and were not driven back, despite terrible losses. It was made clear to everyone, however – and not least to the King himself – that for all the mass of humanity under his command, he had only a very few real men. And all day long the clash continued.

[211] In due course, such was the mauling inflicted on the Medes that they were withdrawn from the attack, and replaced by the Persian 'Immortals', as the men under the command of Hydarnes were termed by the King – and who, it was expected, would have no difficulty completing the task. When they joined battle with the Greeks, however, it was the same story: because they were fighting in a confined space, using spears shorter than those wielded by the Greeks, and unable to press home their weight of numbers, they enjoyed no more success than the Median divisions had done. The Lacedaemonians fought in a manner that richly merits description, and left no one in any doubt that, while they were men who really knew what they were about, their opponents were just amateurs. Every so often, for instance, they would turn tail and give the impression of mass flight, and then, after the Barbarians had raised a cry of triumph at the sight of their retreat, rushed forward to attack them with a great hullabaloo and caught up with

them, the Lacedaemonians would wheel round to confront the Barbarians, and inflict such terrible damage upon the Persians once they had done so that there was no counting the number who fell. Whenever this happened, the Spartiates would suffer their own casualties too – but only a few. The Persians did all they could to force the pass, attacking in formation, and in a whole number of other ways too; but it proved beyond them, and so they retreated.

[212] As these waves of battle were surging forwards, the King is said to have been so alarmed for his army that he leapt up three times from his throne. Nor, the following day, did the contest for the pass go any better for the Barbarians. Once again they joined battle, confident that the Greeks would have suffered so much damage that, given how few they were, they would no longer have it in them to take up arms. The Greeks, however, had organized themselves by their place of origin into separate divisions, and took it in turns to fight – all except for the Phocians, who had been ordered to take up their station on the mountain to guard the path. When the Persians found things unchanged from the day before, they duly retreated.

[213] But then, with the King at a loss how to resolve the impasse he found himself facing, a man from Malis called Epialtes,[107] the son of Eurydemus, came with information for which he had no doubt Xerxes would pay most handsomely, concerning the path over the mountains that led to Thermopylae; and by passing it on, doomed the Greeks who were making their stand there. Subsequently, Epialtes was so terrified of the Lacedaemonians that he fled to Thessaly; and while he was there in exile, the Amphictyons convened a meeting at Pylae, at which a bounty was publicly put on his head by the Pylagorae. Later still, after Epialtes had returned from exile, he was killed in Anticyra by a man from Trachis called Athenades. Despite the fact that Athenades had actually killed Epialtes for another reason altogether (one that I will point out later on in my account)[108] the Lacedaemonians honoured him for the deed nevertheless. So Epialtes, later on, was slain.

[214] There is another version, according to which it was a man from Carystus called Onetas, the son of Phanagoras, and Corydallus of Anticyra who passed on the information to the King, and led the Persians round the mountain – but personally, I find this impossible to believe. There are two decisive reasons for coming to this conclusion: firstly, that it was Epialtes of Trachis, and not Onetas and Corydallus, who had

the bounty put on his head by the Pylagorae, who were speaking on behalf of Greece, and presumably knew all the details. Then there is the fact that the charge laid against Epialtes was, as we know, the reason why he fled into exile. (Admittedly, even though Onetas was not from Malis, he might still have been familiar with the path, had he been a regular visitor to that part of the world.) But no, it was Epialtes who led the Persians along the path round the mountain – and it is as the guilty party that I indict him here.[109]

[215] 'Yes, it will work.' Epialtes had no sooner given this promise to a delighted Xerxes than the King, overjoyed, was sending Hydarnes and his men on the mission. They set off as lights began to blaze across the camp. (The discovery of the path was originally made by local Malians, back at a time when the Phocians had blocked off the pass with their wall, and thereby neutralized the threat of armed incursions – and the Malians, once they had identified the path, guided the Thessalians along it into Phocis. From that moment on, the deadliness of the path was something that no Malian ever had cause to doubt.)

[216] And the course of the path?[110] It begins where the River Asopus flows through a gorge, and then proceeds along the ridge of a mountain called the Anopaea – which is also the name of the path itself. It ends at Alpeni, the first Locrian city one reaches after leaving Malis, near the so-called 'Black Buttocks Stone' and the seats of the Cercopes, where it is at its narrowest.

[217] So that is the lie of the path; and the Persians, after crossing the Asopus, tracked it all through the night, with the mountains of Oeta on their right, and those of Trachis on their left. The coming of dawn saw them on the highest point of the mountain pass. As I mentioned earlier, this stretch of the ridge was being guarded by a thousand hoplites from Phocis, who were there to protect their own territory, and to stand watch over the path. While the pass below was being garrisoned by the men I have already listed, the sentries on the path across the mountains consisted of Phocians who had volunteered themselves to Leonidas for the task.

[218] Now, because the slope of the mountain which the Persians were climbing was covered entirely with oaks, the Phocians did not notice their ascent; but then, once the climb was done, the Phocians realized what was happening. Not a breeze was stirring, and the Persians, as was only to be expected, were making a great noise, because of

all the leaves they were trampling underfoot;[111] but although the Phocians scrabbled to their feet, they were still busy arming themselves when, all of a sudden, the Barbarians were upon them. The Persians themselves were astonished at the sight of men putting on armour, since they had not been expecting to meet any opposition – and now they had run into a sizeable force! Hydarnes, terrified in case the Phocians were Lacedaemonians, asked Epialtes where the force came from – and then, on being set straight, ordered the Persians into battle formation. A thick hail of arrows began to rain down on the Phocians, who – believing that they had been the targets of the expedition right from the beginning – retreated to the top of the mountain, and there prepared to fight to the death. Contrary to their expectations, however, Epialtes, Hydarnes and the Persians paid the Phocians not the slightest attention, but just continued on down the mountainside.

[219] Meanwhile, the first that the Greeks in Thermopylae knew of it was when the soothsayer Megistias, after inspecting the entrails of the sacrificial victims, declared that death would be coming upon them with the dawn. Then, while it was still dark, various deserters brought in news of the Persian flanking action. The third warning arrived at daybreak, when look-outs came running down from the heights. The Greeks then held a council of war, at which opinion was divided. Some argued that they should never abandon their posts, while others took the opposite view. Subsequently, once the meeting had broken up, some began to withdraw and then to scatter in a large number of directions, each to their respective city; others, however, made preparations to stay where they were, alongside Leonidas.

[220] It is also claimed that Leonidas himself sent them away, because he was anxious to ensure their survival, while believing that it would be inappropriate for himself and the Spartiates who were there with him to abandon the position that they had originally come to hold. According to this interpretation, which seems to me by far the likeliest, when Leonidas realized how demoralized his allies were, and how lacking in appetite for sharing in the danger, he dismissed them; but he knew that his own departure would leave a foul stain upon his honour. By holding his ground, he would leave behind him instead a great name,[112] and preserve the prosperity of Sparta from obliteration. You see, at the very first tremors of war, the Spartiates had immediately consulted the oracle; and the Pythia had told them that either Lacedaemon would be

destroyed by the Barbarians, or else their king would die. The oracle that she gave them, in hexameters, was as follows:

'Here is your fate, O you who live in broad-streeted Sparta:
Great and glorious though your city is, yet men bred of Perseus
Will sack it. Either that, or a king sprung from the stock of Heracles
Must perish and be mourned within the borders of Lacedaemon.
For the might of neither the bull nor the lion can check
The Persian, backed as he is by Zeus, face to face. I tell you this:
There can be no holding him, not until one of the two he has rent.'

In my opinion, it was because Leonidas had been mulling this over, and because he wanted to store up glory for the Spartiates alone, that he dismissed the allies, rather than because there was a difference of opinion which then prompted those who left to make a disorderly retreat.

[221] I can offer one further piece of evidence, and not a minor one at that, in support of this view: namely, that Megistias of Acarnania, the soothsayer who had come in the train of the army, and pronounced its fate after looking into the entrails of the sacrificial victims (and who was reputedly descended from Melampous) was instructed quite openly by Leonidas to go, so that he would not share in the general bloodbath. Megistias, however, despite this order to leave, stayed put – but he did in turn send away his son, his only child, who had been serving with the expeditionary force.

[222] So the allies dismissed by Leonidas obediently went off – and with them gone, there remained behind with the Lacedaemonians only the Thespians and the Thebans. Of these two contingents, the Thebans had no choice but to stay, since Leonidas was keeping them there against their will, effectively as hostages; but the Thespians, who had declared that they would rather stay and die by the side of Leonidas and his men than leave and abandon them, were there as volunteers.[113] They were commanded by Demophilus, the son of Diadromes.

[223] Xerxes, who had greeted the sun by performing libations, then delayed launching his offensive until it was roughly the time in the morning when market-squares fill up. Epialtes had told him that he needed to wait only until then, because the route down from the mountain was more direct and took far less time than the ascent and the circuit of it. As Xerxes and the Barbarians under him moved to the attack, so too did Leonidas and his Greeks – indeed, conscious that they

were going out to their deaths, they advanced much deeper into the open stretch of the pass than they had done at first. While on previous days they had stood sentry behind the line of the wall, and made sallies only out into the narrow reaches of the pass, now they joined battle beyond the narrows, where the Barbarians suffered massive casualties. This was due to their officers, who wielded whips and would lash all the men in their respective regiments, urging them ever onwards to the front. There were many also who fell into the sea and were drowned,[114] and even more who were trampled underfoot by their comrades while still alive. Indeed, there was no counting how many perished. The Greeks, you see, because they knew that they were going to die at the hands of the men coming round the mountain, did all they could to demonstrate to the Barbarians the full force of their strength, and fought in a frenzy, without regard for their lives.

[224] Now, by this stage, because most of them had smashed their spears to splinters, they were using their swords to slaughter the Persians. The man who proved himself without peer in this struggle was Leonidas – but then he fell, and with him other celebrated Spartiates too, whose names, as men who well merit commemoration, I have made sure to learn. Indeed, I have learned the names of all the three hundred. On the Persian side too, there fell a whole number of eminent Persians: these included two sons of Darius, Abrocomes and Hyperanthes, born to him by Phratagoune, the daughter of Artanes. (This Artanes was himself the brother of King Darius, the son of Hystaspes, and the grandson of Arsames. He gave the hand of his daughter to Darius, and endowed her with his entire estate, because she was his only child.)

[225] So two of Xerxes' brothers fell in the battle, which raged furiously over the corpse of Leonidas, Persian against Lacedaemonian, until by sheer force of courage the Greeks managed to grab hold of the body, and send their adversaries reeling back four times. This contest continued until the soldiers arrived with Epialtes – at which point, as the Greeks became aware of their coming, the whole character of the fighting changed. The Greeks withdrew back past the wall to where the road was narrow; and there – all of them except for the Thebans – banded together and took up a position on a hillock. On this hillock – which was located in the entrance to the pass, where the stone lion commemorating Leonidas now stands – they defended themselves with daggers, if they still had them, or else with their fists and teeth; meanwhile, the

Barbarians buried them beneath a hail of missiles, pulling down the defensive wall and attacking them head on, with those who had come round the mountain completing the encirclement.

[226] Brave though all the Lacedaemonians and Thespians showed themselves, the man who proved himself the bravest of the lot was a Spartiate called Dieneces. There is a witticism attributed to him, which he made before battle was joined with the Medes. 'So teeming are the Barbarians', someone from Trachis warned him, 'that when they fire their bows, their arrows blot out the sun. That is the measure of their number.' Dieneces, however, far from being unnerved by this, instead took so little account of the vast multitudes of the Medes that he only commented, 'Well, my friend from Trachis, this news of yours is all to the good. If the Medes hide the sun, then we can fight them in the shade rather than in the glare of the day.' This was typical of a whole number of apophthegms attributed to Dieneces of Lacedaemon, and by which he is still remembered to the present.

[227] The Lacedaemonians who ranked next to him for bravery are said to have been two brothers, Alpheus and Maron, who were the sons of Orsiphantus. The most distinguished of the Thespians was a man called Dithyrambus, the son of Harmatides.

[228] They were buried where they had fallen; and over both them and those who had met their ends earlier in the battle, before any of the men dismissed by Leonidas had gone home, an inscription was set. It reads:

HERE IS THE SPOT WHERE ONCE THREE MILLION MEN BATTLED
AGAINST FOUR THOUSAND MEN FROM THE PELOPONNESE.

In addition to this inscription, which is common to all, the Spartiates have their own separate one:

REPORT TO THE PEOPLE OF LACEDAEMON, O STRANGER,
THAT HERE, OBEDIENT TO THEIR ORDERS, WE LIE.

As well as this memorial to the Lacedaemonians, there is also one to the soothsayer:

THIS COMMEMORATES THE FAMOUS MEGISTIAS,
KILLED BY THE MEDES ONCE THEY HAD CROSSED THE SPERCHEIUS:

A SEER WHO KNEW FULL WELL THE FATE THAT WAS NEARING,
BUT COULD NOT BEAR TO ABANDON SPARTA'S LEADERS.

It was the Amphictyons who commissioned these epitaphs and the pillars on which they are written – all except the one to Megistias the soothsayer, which was set up by Simonides,[115] the son of Leoprepes, as a tribute to their guest-friendship.

[229] Two of the three hundred, Eurytus and Aristodemus, are said to have had such chronic eye conditions that they were discharged from the front line, and sent by Leonidas to recuperate in Alpeni, where they could have made common cause, and either headed back together to the safety of Sparta, or else, if they could not bear to go home, perished alongside their comrades. However, although both these options were open to them, they lacked sufficient incentive to agree, and so arrived at different decisions. When Eurytus learned about the Persian flanking action, he demanded his armour, buckled it on and ordered his helot to lead him into battle; the helot duly did so, and though once he had finished escorting Eurytus he then fled, Eurytus himself plunged into the thick of the mêlée, and was killed. Aristodemus, meanwhile, left behind, had passed out. Now, it seems to me that had Aristodemus been the only invalid and then returned home to Sparta, or had both of them together made the journey back, the Spartiates would not have shown such fury. As it was, though, one of the two had died, and one – under circumstances no more extenuating – had shrunk from dying; and so the Spartiates were bitterly angry with Aristodemus, as they were bound to be.

[230] The story that Aristodemus made it back safely to Sparta with the above excuse is complemented by another version, according to which he had been sent from the front line with a message, and could have returned in time for the battle, but had no wish to; instead – although his fellow-messenger did indeed get back in time, and perished in the battle – he lingered on the road, and so survived.

[231] On his return home to Lacedaemon, Aristodemus met with reproaches and disgrace, as follows. The Spartiates humiliated him by refusing to give him kindling for his fire or so much as exchange a word, and taunted him by calling him 'Aristodemus the Trembler'.[116] He did, however, manage to wipe clean the stain of his dishonour at the battle of Plataea.

[232] Another of the three hundred, who had been sent as a messenger to Thessaly, is also said to have survived: his name was Pantites, and so dishonoured was he on his return home to Sparta that he hanged himself.

[233] The Thebans, under the command of Leontiades, were also with the Greeks; but although they did fight the King's army for a while, it was only because they had no choice in the matter. When they saw that the Persians were gaining the upper hand, they split off from Leonidas and the other Greeks during the rush for the hillock, and approached the Barbarians with their hands outstretched in surrender, explaining as they did so the simple truth: namely, that although they had collaborated with the Medes, and been among the first to give earth and water to the King, they had been forced to come to Thermopylae, and so could hardly be held culpable for such injuries as had been inflicted upon the King. This plea – the truth of which was backed up by the Thessalians – saved their lives. Nevertheless, they did not get off entirely free. Some of them, as they approached the Barbarians, were seized and killed, while most of them were branded with the royal mark on the orders of Xerxes – beginning with their commander, Leontiades. (This was the same Leontiades whose son, Eurymachus, was killed many years later by the Plataeans,[117] after he had seized control of their city at the head of four hundred men from Thebes.)

[234] So that was how the Greeks contended for Thermopylae; and afterwards, Xerxes summoned Demaratus, and put a number of questions to him. 'Demaratus,' he began, 'you are a good man. I can appreciate this now because you gave me the truth – everything happened just as you said it would. So, tell me – how many Lacedaemonians are there left? And how many of them are warriors as good as these ones were? Or are all of them that good?' 'O King,' Demaratus answered, 'the Lacedaemonians have a substantial population, and a whole number of cities. To answer your specific question, however – there is a city in Lacedaemon called Sparta, and its manpower comes to around eight thousand. The Spartans are all of them the peers of those who fought here. The other Lacedaemonians do not quite measure up to their standard, but they too are proficient fighters.' 'So, Demaratus,' Xerxes then said, 'how can I best conquer these men with the least amount of trouble? Come, tell me. You became their king, after all – so you must know their intentions inside and out.'

[235] 'O King,' Demaratus answered, 'if you are serious about asking me for my advice, then it is only right and proper that I give you the best I can. You should send three hundred ships from your fleet to Laconia. There is an island there, lying just offshore, called Cythera – about which Chilon, the wisest man ever born in Sparta, once commented, "Better for the Spartiates that it be sunk to the bottom of the sea than that it should continue to stick up above the surface." What he had anticipated, the possibility that was constantly preying on his mind, was the very thing I am now urging on you – not because he specifically predicted your expedition, but out of a general dread of what might be attempted by any troop of men. The island will make a perfect base from which to spread terror among the Lacedaemonians.[118] With a war of their own right on their very doorstep, you need not worry that they will attempt to prevent the rest of Greece from being annexed by your land-forces. And then, once the rest of Greece has been enslaved, Laconia will be left alone and neutralized. But should you not adopt this course of action, what can you expect? The Peloponnese has a narrow isthmus. It is there that you can expect to meet the Peloponnesians, all of whom are sworn to resist you, in battles even more ferocious than anything you have met with so far. But if you only do as I recommend, then this isthmus and the cities beyond it will come over to you without a fight.'

[236] Now, it so happened that Achaemenes, Xerxes' brother and the commander of the fleet, was present at this conversation; and because he was afraid that Xerxes might be convinced to do as Demaratus had suggested, it was he who spoke up next. 'You seem to me, O King, to be swallowing the arguments of a man who resents how well things are going for you, and who may even be a traitor to your cause. That, after all, is just the kind of behaviour that Greeks revel in. They envy the good fortune of others, and hate being put in the shade. If, on top of all the bad luck we have had, which cost us the wreck of four hundred ships, you then send another three hundred from the main body of the fleet to sail round the Peloponnese, your adversaries will be able to meet you on even terms in any battle. Keep the fleet together, however, and they will find it a challenge too far, a match altogether beyond their resources. The fleet, if intact, will be able to assist your land-forces, and your land-forces, advancing in conjunction with your ships, will be able

to assist the fleet – whereas if you split the two arms apart, neither will be able to help the other. Hold to a strategy that best serves your own interests, without concerning yourself with what your enemies are up to – do not worry about where they will take their battle-stations, or what they will do, or how much they number. They can look after all that themselves, while we bother with our own business. And anyway, if the Lacedaemonians do meet the Persians in battle, it will hardly serve to staunch the wound they have been given.'

[237] 'I think you have made some excellent points, Achaemenes,' Xerxes replied, 'and I will act on them. But Demaratus, although his understanding may be trumped by yours, spoke as he did out of a genuine concern for my best interests. I would certainly never accept, as you claim, that he does not have them at heart. I arrive at this conclusion based partly on our previous conversations, and partly on the fact that when one citizen is resentful of another's successes, it is silence that betrays his hostility. Should someone ask a man from the same city for advice, his fellow-citizen would never suggest what seems to him the best course of action unless he had attained a pinnacle of virtue – and such people are very rare. By contrast, there is no relationship more suffused with warm feeling than that between two guest-friends – and the one, if asked by the other for his advice, will always do his best to oblige. So from now on, there will be no more bad-mouthing of Demaratus, who is my guest-friend! That is an order.'

[238] After this declaration, Xerxes made his way through the bodies of the dead; and when the corpse of Leonidas was pointed out to him as that of the king and commander of the Lacedaemonians, he gave orders for its head to be cut off and set on a spike. This seems to me not the least conclusive of a whole number of pieces of evidence clearly demonstrating that Leonidas, while alive, angered King Xerxes more than any other man. Otherwise, the King would never have behaved so sacrilegiously towards his corpse – since under normal circumstances the Persians are more respectful of men who fight bravely than any other people I know. Those whose duty it was to act on the King's commands duly did as instructed.

[239] I shall now return to a point in my narrative where earlier on I omitted something. It was because the Lacedaemonians were the first

people to learn that the King was preparing to invade Greece that they sent messengers to the Delphic oracle, and were duly given the prophecy I mentioned a short while ago. The real wonder, though, was the way they had come by their information. Now, it seems to me – and it certainly stands to reason – that anyone exiled among the Medes, as Demaratus, the son of Ariston, was, would hardly have been well disposed towards the Lacedaemonians; but it is still open to question whether he took the action he did out of concern for them, or as a way of gloating. Demaratus was in Susa when Xerxes decided to invade Greece, and when he heard the news, he wanted to pass it on to the Lacedaemonians. The risk, however, was in being caught – and so, with no other way of communicating his message, he devised the following scheme. Taking a folding writing-tablet, he scraped off the wax and wrote down the King's intentions on the bare wood of the tablet; then, having done this, he covered the lettering back up with melted wax, so that the tablet, while it was being carried along the roads, would appear blank to any guards, and thus not make any trouble. When it arrived in Lacedaemon, the Lacedaemonians could not figure it out at all; but then, eventually, so I have been informed, its secret was fathomed by Gorgo, the daughter of Cleomenes and wife of Leonidas, who suggested that, if they followed her instructions by scraping off the wax, they would find writing scratched into the wood. Sure enough, obedient to her advice, they uncovered the message – which, after reading it, they passed on to the rest of the Greeks. That, at any rate, is what is supposed to have happened.[119]

BOOK EIGHT

[1] I shall now list the Greek contingents that served with the fleet. The Athenians provided one hundred and twenty-seven warships: these were crewed both by the Athenians themselves, and by the Plataeans,[1] whose courage and enthusiasm compensated for their lack of sea legs. The Corinthians provided forty warships and the Megarians twenty. An additional twenty warships, though provided by the Athenians, were crewed by the Chalcidians. The Aeginetans provided eighteen warships, the Sicyonians twelve, the Lacedaemonians ten, the Epidaurians eight, the Eretrians seven, the Troezenians five, the Styrians two, and the Ceans two, together with two penteconters. Additional support was provided by the Locrians of Opous, who came with seven penteconters.

[2] So that is my list, complete with the numbers of the respective contingents furnished, of the ships that went on campaign to Artemisium. The combined total of the ships at Artemisium, excluding the penteconters, came to two hundred and seventy-one. The fleet's supreme commander was provided by the Spartiates: Eurybiadas, the son of Eurycleidas. The reason for this was the refusal of the allies to serve under Athenian leadership, and their declared intention, unless there were a Laconian in command, to disband the expedition altogether.[2]

[3] There had been talk originally, even before the mission went to Sicily to discuss a possible alliance, that the Athenians should be placed in charge of the fleet. When the other allies protested, however, they gave way, because their chief priority was the survival of Greece, and they recognized – correctly – that if they embroiled everyone in a squabble about the command, Greece was doomed. After all, civil strife among people of the same heritage and race compares as disastrously to a united war effort as does war itself to peace.[3] It was because they

understood this that the Athenians backed down without making trouble – but only, as they would subsequently demonstrate, for so long as they had a pressing need of the other Greeks. Once they had repulsed the Persian, and it was his lands that were contested rather than their own, they made the arrogant behaviour of Pausanias a pretext for depriving the Lacedaemonians of their command.[4] But all this happened later on.

[4] At the time in question, when the Greeks who were actually at Artemisium[5] finally saw how many ships were moored at Aphetae, how bristling with men the entire area was and how the fortunes of the Barbarians had turned out to be not at all what they had been led to believe, they were so terrified that they contemplated scuttling from Artemisium to the interior of Greece. When the Euboeans realized what was being planned, they begged Eurybiadas to stay just a short while longer, until they had evacuated their children and servants. But he would not be swayed; and so, changing their tactics, the Euboeans paid Themistocles, the Athenian commander, a bribe of 30 talents to ensure that the Greeks would remain where they were, and fight in the waters off Euboea.

[5] The way that Themistocles got the Greeks to stay was to give Eurybiadas 5 talents, as though the money were drawn from his own reserves, when in fact it came out of the bribe. With Eurybiadas thereby won over,[6] it was left to the Corinthian commander – Adeimantus, the son of Ocytus – to continue the protests, and insist that, rather than stay where he was, he would retreat from Artemisium; but Themistocles, speaking on solemn oath, had words with him. 'You are not going to abandon us! I will give you more money to stay than the King of the Medes would ever send you for deserting your allies.' And so saying, he promptly dispatched 3 talents' of silver to Adeimantus' ship. Eurybiadas and Adeimantus were thereby bribed to change their minds, the Euboeans got what they wanted and Themistocles made a profit – which he was able to do because no one realized that he still had the remainder of the bribe in his possession, and just took for granted that the money had come from Athens for the purpose to which it was put.

[6] So the Greeks remained in Euboea, where their ships duly met with the enemy in battle. What happened was this. Even before the arrival of the Barbarians at Aphetae, which they reached in the early afternoon, they had already been informed that a few Greek ships were

lying off Artemisium; and when the Barbarians saw these for themselves, they were keen to go on the attack so that they might capture the
ships. The time did not seem to them right, however, for making a full
frontal assault, since they were worried that the Greeks, when they saw
ships bearing down on them, might turn and flee, and night descend as
they made their escape. The Greeks would then have got away – and it
was the intention of the Barbarians that no one, not even a fire-bearer,
should escape alive.

[7] Accordingly, they devised a scheme. Two hundred ships were
detached from the main body of the fleet and sent around the far side of
Sciathos, so that they would not be observed by the enemy as they circumnavigated Euboea, past Caphereus, round Geraestus, and into the
Euripus – the point of their going there being to block off the line of
retreat, even as the rest of the fleet launched an attack from the opposite
direction, thereby catching the Greeks in a pincer movement. This being
the plan, then, the designated ships were sent off – but the main fleet
itself had no intention of making a move against the Greeks, not that
day, nor until such time as a prearranged signal should appear marking
the completion of the circumnavigation. Instead, as the two hundred
ships were sent on their way, those left behind at Aphetae conducted
a muster.

[8] Now, coincident with their tallying of the number of ships was the
presence in the Persian camp of a man from Scione called Scyllias, who
was the best diver of his day, and who had managed, while the ships
were being wrecked off Pelion, to recover a large number of possessions
for the Persians, while also getting hold of quite a number for himself;
and although until that moment the opportunity to desert to the Greeks
had never presented itself, it had been his intention for a while to do so.
Although I cannot say precisely how he made it over to the Greeks, I
would be amazed if the story told about it were actually true. It is
claimed, you see, that he dived into the waters off Aphetae, and did not
surface until he reached Artemisium – meaning that he swam some 80
stades underwater![7] (There are lots of other tall stories told about this
man – although there are some that are true as well.) I would like to put
on record my own opinion about this particular episode, which is that he
made it to Artemisium by boat. No sooner had he arrived than he began
to brief the high command on the details of the shipwrecks, and about
the ships that had been dispatched around Euboea.

[9] After hearing this, the Greeks talked things over a good deal. The prevailing opinion was that they should stay where they were for the rest of the day and camp out on the shore, and then, after midnight, put to sea and meet the ships that were sailing around Euboea. In due course, however, when they found that no one was sailing against them, they waited until late afternoon, and then themselves sailed out against the Barbarians – their aim being to test the enemy's performance in battle, and their own skill in driving through its line.

[10] When Xerxes' men and their commanders saw how few were the ships sailing to attack them, they attributed it to lunacy, pure and simple, and put out to sea themselves, confident that they would have no problem in capturing the Greek fleet – a perfectly reasonable expectation, given that it was visibly outnumbered by their own, and less manoeuvrable too. Confident in their own superiority, they formed a circle around the Greeks. Now, those of the Ionians who were backing the Greeks, and only serving with the Persian expedition against their will, felt that the spectacle of the Greek fleet being encircled spelled certain disaster, since they were convinced – given how precarious the situation of the Greeks appeared – that not a man of them would make it home. The rest, though, were delighted by the course of events, and vied with one another to see who would win the reward from the King for being the first to capture an Athenian ship. (In their camp, the Athenians were the main focus of conversation.)

[11] The first thing the Greeks did, on a given signal, was to turn their prows out in the direction of the Barbarians, and to clump their sterns together so as to form a single hub; then, on a second signal, they set to work, despite being tightly hemmed in and fighting face to face. Thirty ships they captured [from the Barbarians] in this engagement, together with a man who was held in particularly high regard by the enemy: Philaon, the son of Chersis and the brother of Gorgus, the king of Salamis. The first Greek to capture an enemy ship (an action which won him the prize for valour) was a man from Athens called Lycomedes, the son of Aeschraeus. Twilight fell with the battle still hanging in the balance – and so the two sides broke off. The Greeks sailed back to Artemisium, and the Barbarians to Aphetae, after a contest that had not gone at all according to Persian expectations. Only one of the Greeks serving with the King had deserted to the Greek side in the course of the

battle: this was Antidorus of Lemnos, who was rewarded for his action by the Athenians with a grant of land on Salamis.[8]

[12] Despite its being the middle of summer, the coming of darkness brought rain, which lashed down with an unseasonable violence all night long, while Mount Pelion shook to crashing thunder. Corpses and flotsam from the wrecked ships began to drift into Aphetae, clogging up the prows of the ships, and obstructing the blades of the oars. The news of this terrified the crews, who were convinced that such were the evils besetting them they were bound to perish. After all, in the wake of the storm that had wrecked the fleet off Mount Pelion, events had repeatedly overtaken them without allowing them even to draw breath: first a gruelling battle, and then torrential rain, flash floods pouring down into the sea and the crashing of thunder.

[13] Bad as their night was, however, those who had been given the task of sailing round Euboea had a far more brutal time of it, since the same nocturnal conditions descended upon them while they were out on the open sea – and with terrible and fatal consequences. The squadron was rounding the Hollows of Euboea when it was hit by the rain and the gales, and was swept away. Those on board had no notion of where they were being carried and were dashed onto the rocks. All this was the doing of the god, to give the Greeks parity, and ensure that the Persians would not have an overwhelming numerical advantage.

[14] So that was how the squadron met with destruction off the Hollows of Euboea. The Barbarians at Aphetae greeted the light of day with open arms, but did not otherwise stir; since their ships were so badly damaged, they were content, as things stood, simply to keep their heads down. Meanwhile, the Greeks were reinforced by fifty-three Athenian warships – and simultaneously, even as their strength was being boosted by these new arrivals, news came too of the storm that had descended upon the Barbarians as they were sailing round Euboea and wiped them out. Then, at the same time of day as before, the Greeks put to sea, fell upon the Cilician squadron and sank it, before sailing back to Artemisium as darkness fell.

[15] The next day but one, so indignant were the Persian high command that such a tiny number of ships should have given them a bloody nose, and so anxious as well about how Xerxes would react, that they no longer waited for the Greeks to initiate hostilities, but instead, in the

middle of the day, ordered all hands to their stations and put out to sea. As coincidence would have it, the battle between the two fleets took place on exactly the same days as witnessed the land-battle at Thermopylae. Just as the struggle at sea was focused entirely on the Euripus, so for Leonidas and his men it was the pass that had to be held. In both cases, the exhortations were the same: on the Greek side, to prevent the Barbarians from getting into Greece, and among the Barbarians, to annihilate the Greeks and secure the passage.

[16] At first, as Xerxes' fleet sailed out in battle formation, the Greeks did not stir from Artemisium. Then the Barbarians adopted a crescent-shaped formation, with the aim of encircling and trapping them. At this point, the Greeks did put to sea and join battle. The two sides in the clash were relatively evenly matched. This was because the sheer size and scale of Xerxes' fleet put it at a disadvantage, with ships crashing into one another, so that all was havoc. Nevertheless, because the prospect of retreating before such a paltry number of ships was a terrible one, it held fast and did not give way. Although the Greeks suffered numerous casualties, ships and men alike, the Barbarians lost many more of both. The struggle ended only when the two sides broke apart.

[17] The best fighters in Xerxes' fleet were the Egyptians, who were conspicuous for a number of impressive feats, among which was the capture of five Greek ships, complete with crews.[9] On the Greek side, it was the Athenians who excelled that day – and none more so than Cleinias, the son of Alcibiades, who at private expense had contributed two hundred men and his own ship.[10]

[18] Once they had disengaged, both sides gladly hurried to make anchorage. As they pulled back after breaking off from the battle, the Greeks had possession of their dead, and their shattered ships; but even so, in light of the rough treatment dealt out to them – not least to the Athenians, half of whose ships had been damaged – there was serious discussion of withdrawing to the Greek hinterland.

[19] Themistocles, however, had been struck by a thought: if they could only detach those of Ionian and Carian stock from the Barbarians, then they would be able to beat the rest. Accordingly, even as the Euboeans were driving their flocks down to the sea, he convened a meeting of the high command, and told them that he had devised a scheme which he was confident would result in the King's best divisions deserting him. That, for the moment, was as much as Themistocles

would lay bare; but he also urged his fellow-commanders (their present circumstances being what they were) to slaughter as many of the Euboeans' flocks as they cared to kill, since it would be better for their own side to have them rather than the enemy. He also recommended that each commander should have his men light a fire. 'As for the precise timing of our departure,' he added, 'leave that to me. I will make sure that we get back to Greece[11] safe and sound.' The others, who were content to do as Themistocles had suggested, promptly lit watch-fires, and then turned to the slaughter of the flocks.

[20] This happened because the Euboeans, who had dismissed an oracle given them by Bacis[12] as plain nonsense, had failed to ready themselves for the looming war by putting their belongings into safe-keeping and stocking up on provisions – which meant that responsibility for their troubles was their own. The relevant oracle of Bacis runs thus:

'Be sure, when a man spouting gibberish yokes the salt-sea with
Papyrus, to move all your loud-bleating goats from Euboea.'

After the Euboeans had failed to put these verses to good use, and with evils either directly on their doorstep or else bearing down hard upon them, there was only one thing left to guide them: their own misfortune.

[21] It was while the Greeks were busy with these matters that the look-out arrived from Trachis. One look-out – Polyas of Anticyra – was at Artemisium, complete with a boat fitted and ready to sail; it was his responsibility to keep the men at Thermopylae informed[13] of any reverses suffered by the fleet. Likewise, stationed with Leonidas, there was an Athenian – Abronichus, the son of Lysicles – ready to jump into a triaconter and bring tidings to the men at Artemisium of any new development that might have overtaken the forces on land. It was this Abronichus, then, who arrived with the news of what had happened to Leonidas and his army. After the briefing, there was no longer any question of the Greeks delaying their withdrawal; so off they set, with each squadron ordered according to its original posting, the Corinthians in the vanguard, and the Athenians bringing up the rear.

[22] The fastest Athenian ships, however, were picked by Themistocles to go with him on a tour of places with drinking-water; and at each one he carved messages onto rocks that the Ionians, when they came to Artemisium the following day, would read. 'Men of Ionia,' the letters

spelled out, 'what you are doing, by making war against the land of your ancestors and enslaving Greece, is a criminal act. Ideally, you should come over to our side. But if it is beyond your power to do so, then from this point on you must retreat to the margins and become neutral – and request the Carians to do the same. Should neither of these options be practicable, and the yoke of compulsion be too heavy for you to cast off, then when it comes to action, and we join in battle, you must play the coward. Just remember this – not only do you derive your ancestry from us, but you were the original cause of the feud between the Barbarian and ourselves.'[14] My own opinion is that Themistocles had a couple of prospects in mind when he wrote this message: either the letters would escape the notice of the King, and possibly induce the Ionians to have a change of heart and come over to the Greek side, or else, if the matter were reported to Xerxes and used to traduce the Ionians, he would stop trusting them and prevent their ships from taking part in combat.

[23] No sooner had Themistocles carved his inscriptions than a man from Histiaea went in a vessel to the Barbarians, and informed them of the Greek retreat from Artemisium. So incredulous were they that they kept the messenger under guard while some fast ships were dispatched to reconnoitre. Then, after these had confirmed the report, the first rays of sun saw the entire fleet set sail as one for Artemisium. There they remained until midday, when they sailed to Histiaea. On their arrival, they seized control of the city itself and overran all the coastal villages in the region of Ellopia, which was the territory belonging to Histiaea.

[24] While they were there, a herald with a message for the fleet arrived from Xerxes, who had been busy making arrangements for the disposal of the war dead. These were the arrangements he had made. Trenches were dug, and in these all but a thousand of the twenty thousand men of his own army who had fallen at Thermopylae were buried; earth was then shovelled over them, and foliage scattered, to prevent their being seen by people from the fleet. So the herald, after he had made the crossing to Histiaea, gathered the entire force in its encampment and addressed the men. 'King Xerxes grants permission to all those of you, our allies, who wish to leave their stations to go and see how he deals in battle with men foolish enough to imagine that they can prevail over his royal might.'

[25] Such was the stampede of those wanting to look in the wake of

this announcement that there were barely any boats left behind. Once the men had crossed over, they wandered about among the corpses, gawping at them. Everyone was convinced that the men lying there were exclusively Lacedaemonians and Thespians – but in fact there were helots on view as well. Nevertheless, no one who made the crossing was fooled by what Xerxes had done with the corpses of his own men. His ploy was far too ridiculous for that. After all, there lay a thousand of their own dead in full view, whereas the corpses of the enemy, four thousand in total, had all been dragged to a single spot and jumbled up together in a heap. This day was devoted to looking around. Then, the following day, the men from the fleet sailed back to Histiaea and their ships, while Xerxes' army set off on their own way.

[26] A few men – Arcadians who were short of money and looking for employment – deserted to the Persian camp. They were brought into the presence of the King, and interrogated by the Persians as to what the Greeks were up to. (One of the Persians led this interrogation on behalf of all the others.) The Arcadians replied that the Greeks were holding the Olympic Festival,[15] and celebrating athletic and equestrian competitions. 'And what do they compete for?' asked the interrogator. 'What prize is at stake?' 'They are given a wreath', replied the Arcadians, 'made of olive leaves.' At this, Tritantaechmes, the son of Artabanus, expressed an opinion that to the King seemed like cowardice, but was in fact noble in the extreme. On learning that a wreath rather than money was the prize, you see, Tritantaechmes could not stop himself from blurting out in front of everyone, 'But this is terrible, Mardonius! What sort of men are these you have brought us to fight against, that they contend with one another, not for financial reward, but for the honour of being the best?'[16]

[27] That was the comment made by Tritantaechmes. Meanwhile, in the immediate wake of the disaster[17] at Thermopylae, the Thessalians sent a herald to the Phocians, prompted by the grudge they had always borne them – and specifically by the most recent reverse they had suffered at Phocian hands. Not that many years before the King's expedition, you see, the Thessalians and their allies had launched a full-scale invasion of Phocis, and been defeated with heavy losses. This had been due to a cunning stratagem devised by Tellias of Elis,[18] who was with the Phocians as their soothsayer when they were cornered on Parnassus. He had the Phocian elite, six hundred men in all, smear both themselves

and their weapons with chalk, and then attack the Thessalians at night, with instructions to kill anyone they saw who was not whitened. The Thessalians – first their sentries, and then the entire body of their army – were so terrified at the sight of what they believed to be not men at all, but rather phantoms of ill omen, that the Phocians ended up masters of four thousand Thessalian corpses and shields. Half of these shields were then presented as a dedication to Abae,[19] and half to Delphi. A tenth of the loot won in the battle was used to fund the giant statues that are contending for the tripod[20] in a contest in front of the temple at Delphi, and which resemble others that were dedicated at Abae.

[28] So that was how the Phocians dealt with the Thessalian infantry that had been blockading them. They also inflicted irreparable damage on the Thessalian cavalry that had invaded their territory. This they did by meeting the Thessalian onslaught in a pass near Hyampolis, where they had dug a wide trench into which they had first put empty wine-jars, and then soil, so as to render the trench indistinguishable from the rest of the terrain. The Thessalians charged, looking to make short work of the Phocians – only to find the jars giving way beneath them. The legs of their horses were broken.

[29] Unsurprisingly, these two defeats rankled a good deal with the Thessalians, and so, when they sent their herald, it was to make the following announcement. 'Now more than ever, O men of Phocis, you must face facts. You are no match for us. After all, at the time when we inclined to the side of the Greeks, they would invariably favour us over you – and now that we have gone over to the Barbarian, such is our influence with him that we could have you stripped of your land and sold into slavery. Nevertheless, for all that we now have you utterly in our power, we bear you no ill will for the wrongs you did us. Fifty talents of silver should serve us as adequate compensation – and in return for that we guarantee to divert the invasion from your territory.'

[30] What lay behind this Thessalian proposal was the fact that the Phocians were the only people in the region not to have collaborated with the Medes – and this in turn, I have concluded, was due to their feud with the Thessalians, and nothing more. Had the Thessalians rallied to the Greek cause, I have no doubt but that the Phocians would have sided with the Medes. As it was, they rebuffed the Thessalian demand for money. 'If we so choose,' they said, 'we can collaborate with

the Medes no less readily than you. For as long as we can avoid it, however, we will never be traitors to Greece.'

[31] This declaration, when it was brought back to the Thessalians, threw them into such a rage that they decided to show the Barbarians the way themselves. The invasion route led from Trachis into Doris, along a narrow strip of Dorian territory some 30 stades wide, which stretches between Malis and Phocis, and in ancient times was called Dryopis. This region was the original motherland of the Dorians of the Peloponnese. The invading Barbarians spared Doris any damage, since the inhabitants had already gone over to their side, and anyway, the Thessalians were not in favour of it.

[32] From Doris they invaded Phocis, but failed to capture the Phocians themselves. Some of the Phocians scaled the heights of Parnassus – the peak of which, known as 'Tithorea', rises near the city of Neon but is otherwise isolated, and can readily accommodate a large crowd of people. It was up this, then, that they went, taking their belongings with them. A majority of the Phocians, however, took refuge with the Ozolian Locrians, in the city of Amphissa, which is located above the Crisaean plain. Meanwhile, the Barbarians – with the Thessalians showing their army the way – overran the whole of Phocis. Wherever they went, they burned and looted everything, torching both cities and sanctuaries.

[33] Everything on the banks of the River Cephisus – the course of which they were tracking – they wiped out: they burned the city of Drymus to the ground, together with Charadra, and Erochus, and Tethronium, and Amphicaea, and Neon, and Pedieis, and Triteis, and Elateia, and Hyampolis, and Parapotamii, and Abae, where there stood a rich sanctuary of Apollo, well provided with treasuries and any number of votive offerings. Then, as now, there was an oracle there – and yet this shrine too they looted and torched. They also chased a group of Phocians near the mountains, took them prisoner and gang-raped the female captives so repeatedly that some of the women died.

[34] Passing by Parapotamii, the Barbarians arrived at Panopeus. Here the army split and went separate ways. The largest and most formidable force, led by Xerxes, set out for Athens by way of Boeotia, and passed into the territory of the Orchomenians. The entire population of Boeotia had gone over to the Medes,[21] and Alexander, looking to keep

THE HISTORIES

their cities out of harm's way, had sent men ahead with responsibility for their security. What these Macedonians did was to make absolutely clear to Xerxes that the Boeotians were indeed backing the Medes.

[35] Meanwhile, the remainder of the Barbarians – those who had taken the other turning – were skirting the left flank of Parnassus as they made their way with their guides to the sanctuary at Delphi. They continued to devastate everywhere in Phocis that they occupied. The cities of Panopeus, Daulis and Aiolis – all were put to the torch. The aim of those taking this route, and who had been split off from the rest of the army for the very purpose, was to plunder the sanctuary at Delphi, and then parade its wealth before King Xerxes. So endlessly had all the noteworthy things in the shrine been on everyone's lips that Xerxes, according to my sources, was more familiar with them than he was with the things he had left behind in his own home – and particularly with the offerings of Croesus,[22] the son of Alyattes.

[36] The news of this plunged the Delphians into such extremes of terror that in a state of blind panic they asked the oracle what they should do with its sacred treasures: bury them in the ground, or move them somewhere else altogether? 'Move nothing,' the god replied. 'I am perfectly capable of looking after my own.' When the Delphians heard this, their thoughts turned next to their own safety. Their children and wives they sent across the gulf to Achaea, while they themselves, for the most part, made their way up to the peaks of Parnassus and took their belongings to the Corycian Cave – although there were some who removed themselves to Amphissa in Locris. The Delphians completely evacuated the city – all except for sixty men, and the prophet.[23]

[37] Then, with the invasion force so close that the Barbarians could actually see the sanctuary in the distance, the prophet – whose name was Aceratus – noticed that the sacred weapons, which it is sacrilege for any human to touch, had been brought out from the inner halls and were lying in front of the temple. He went off to tell the Delphians who still remained there about this prodigy. Meanwhile, the Barbarians, in the course of their onslaught, reached the sanctuary of Athena Before the Temple,[24] where they were greeted by prodigies yet more miraculous. Astounding though it was that weapons of war should have materialized of their own accord outside the temple, it was what happened next that really put every other wonder in the shade. As the barbarian invaders reached the sanctuary of Athena Before the Temple,

thunderbolts began to rain down on them from the heavens, two crags splintered off from Parnassus and came crashing into their ranks with a great din, sweeping away large numbers of them, and from inside the sanctuary of Athena there sounded a yell and a war cry.

[38] Amid the confusion of all these various events, fear descended upon the Barbarians. When news came that they were in full retreat, the Delphians headed down against them and inflicted numerous casualties. The survivors fled straight to Boeotia. My information is that those of the Barbarians who made it back claimed to have seen further god-sent marvels. There had been two hoplites of more than human size who had hunted the fugitives and cut them down.

[39] These, according to the Delphians, were a pair of heroes local to the area, Phylacus and Autonoüs, whose precincts adjoin the sanctuary – the precinct of Phylacus is beside the road above the sanctuary of Athena Before the Temple, while that of Autonoüs is near the Castalian Spring, below the Hyampeian Crag. The boulders that fell from Parnassus still lie to our day in the precinct of Athena Before the Temple, exactly where they came to rest after smashing through the Barbarian ranks. And that was how these men came to depart the shrine.[25]

[40] Meanwhile, at the request of the Athenians, the ships of the Greek fleet who had come from Artemisium put in at Salamis. The Athenians had asked the fleet to dock at Salamis so that they could evacuate their women and children from Attica, and deliberate what course of action they should take. Circumstances were such that they were bound to hold a council of war, since all their expectations had served only to deceive them. Rather than finding, as they had anticipated, every last Peloponnesian warrior camped out in Boeotia, waiting for the Barbarian, they had discovered instead something very different: news had come that the Peloponnesians – whose priority was to ensure their own survival,[26] and who were perfectly happy to let everywhere else go, just so long as the Peloponnese stood protected – were busy building a wall across the Isthmus. It was the discovery of this that had prompted the Athenian request to put in at Salamis.

[41] Unlike the others, however, the Athenians made for their own homes rather than Salamis. When they arrived, they issued a proclamation that every Athenian was to get his children and household to safety as best he could. Most then sent their families to Troezen,[27] while

others opted for Aegina or Salamis. The evacuation was conducted with a marked lack of foot-dragging. Although this was prompted in part by a wish to comply with the oracle, there was also an even more significant motivation. The Athenians, you see, claim that the Acropolis has a guardian, a large serpent that lives in the sanctuary. Nor is this just talk – for every month, on the assumption that it really exists, they present it with an offering. What they give it – month in, month out – is a honey-cake. Never before had one of these honey-cakes been left untouched; but now, on this occasion, it was. Once the priestess[28] had announced this, the Athenians became even more eager to abandon their city, on the grounds that even the goddess had deserted the Acropolis. Then, once the evacuation was complete, they set sail to join the main body of the fleet.

[42] When news reached Troezen that the ships from Artemisium had docked at Salamis, the rest of the Greek fleet (which had mustered, by prior arrangement, at Pogon, the harbour of Troezen) came streaming over to join them. The combined total consisted of many more ships than had fought at Artemisium, and was furnished by a greater number of cities as well. The man in command of the fleet was the same Spartiate – Eurybiadas, the son of Eurycleidas – who had led it at Artemisium, despite his not being of royal blood. By far the largest and best-performing ships were those provided by the Athenians.

[43] Here is the list of those who took part in the campaign. The Peloponnesians first: the Lacedaemonians provided sixteen ships; the Corinthians the same number as they had done at Artemisium; the Sicyonians fifteen; the Epidaurians ten; the Troezenians five; and the Hermioneans three. The Hermioneans excepted, all of these were of Dorian and Macedonian stock; the last stage of their emigration had been from Erineus, Pindus and Dryopis. As for the Hermioneans, they came from Dryopis, and were expelled by Heracles from what is now called 'Doris', together with the Malians.

[44] So much for the Peloponnesians – now to the contingents provided by those who lived on the mainland beyond the Peloponnese. The Athenians provided one hundred and eighty ships, more than anyone else. These were manned exclusively by their own crews, since at Salamis the Plataeans did not serve alongside them. The reason for this was that the Plataeans, during the course of the Greek withdrawal from Artemisium, had disembarked opposite Chalcis on the Boeotian coast, and had

gone off to evacuate their households. Intent upon this rescue mission, they were left out of the muster. (Back when the Pelasgians had possession of what is now called Greece, the Athenians were Pelasgians themselves,[29] and known as 'Cranai'; then, during the reign of Cecrops, as 'Cecropids'; later still, when Erechtheus inherited the throne, they changed their name to 'Athenians'; and when Ion, the son of Xouthus, became their war-leader, they were called 'Ionians' after him.)

[45] The Megarians provided the same number of ships as they had done at Artemisium, while the Ambraciots rallied to the cause with seven ships, and the Leucadians with three. (These were both of Dorian stock, from Corinth.)

[46] Turning to the islanders, the Aeginetans provided thirty ships. They had other ships manned and equipped as well, but these were deployed in defence of their home waters, and it was with their thirty best ships that they fought at Salamis. (The Aeginetans are Dorians from Epidaurus, and the name of their island was formerly Oenone.) After them came the Chalcidians, who provided the same twenty ships as at Artemisium, and the Eretrians, with their seven. Both are Ionians. An unchanged number of ships was also provided by the Ceans, who are of Ionian stock, and originally from Athens. The Naxians provided four ships, which their citizenry, like those of all the other islands,[30] had actually sent to join the Medes; but then, at the urging of one of the captains of their triremes – a man by the name of Democritus, highly regarded in the city – they had disregarded their orders and gone over to the Greeks. The Naxians are Ionians, of Athenian stock. The Styrians provided the same number of ships as they had done at Artemisium, and the Cythnians just one ship, plus a penteconter: both these two peoples were originally Dryopians. Also taking part in the campaign were the Seriphians, the Siphnians and the Melians. These were the only islanders never to have given earth and water to the Barbarian.

[47] All these various contingents came from regions south of Thesprotia and the River Acheron; for even the Ambraciots and the Leucadians, the peoples who had travelled the furthest to join the campaign, only bordered Thesprotia. In fact, no one from further afield came to the assistance of Greece in her hour of danger, saving only the Crotoniates, who sent a single ship, under the command of a man called Phaÿllus, a three-times victor in the Pythian Games.[31] The Crotoniates are of Achaean stock.

[48] Now, all these various contingents consisted of triremes, with

the exception of those sent by the Melians, the Siphnians and the Seriphians, which consisted of penteconters. The Melians (who are of Lacedaemonian stock) sent two, while the Siphnians and the Seriphians (who are of Ionian stock and came originally from Athens) sent one each. The total number of ships – excluding the penteconters – came to three hundred and seventy-eight.

[49] Once the commanders from these cities I have just mentioned had assembled together on Salamis, they held a council of war, at which it was proposed by Eurybiadas that everyone who wished to do so should nominate the location he thought best suited to the fighting of a sea-battle – but that it had to be somewhere under Greek control. By this, he meant one of the places still left to them outside Attica, which had already been given up for lost. The prevailing opinion of those who spoke up was that they should sail for the Isthmus and fight in the waters off the Peloponnese – their reasoning being that, if they remained with their ships at Salamis and suffered a defeat, they would be blockaded on the island without any prospect of assistance, whereas if they fought off the Isthmus they would at least be able to find a friendly refuge.

[50] Then, even as the Peloponnesian commanders were busy pressing this case, there came a man of Athens with news that the Barbarian was on Attic soil, putting everything to the torch as he went. Xerxes and his army, after swinging through Boeotia, and burning down the cities of Thespiae and Plataea – the inhabitants of which had already abandoned them for the Peloponnese – was now in Athens and stripping it utterly bare. (Thespiae and Plataea had been put to the torch because the Thebans had informed Xerxes of their refusal to collaborate.)

[51] From the Hellespont, the starting-point of the Barbarians' march, and which it had taken them a month to cross over to Europe, they had required a further three months to reach Attica – which they did while Calliades was archon at Athens.[32] By the time it fell to them, the city was a ghost town and the only Athenians they found there were a few temple-stewards and indigents in the sanctuary who had barricaded the Acropolis with doors and planks against the invaders – partly because they had lacked the material resources to escape to Salamis, but also because they believed themselves to have fathomed the meaning of the prophecy given by the Pythia, that the wooden wall would never be breached.[33] The safe refuge alluded to by the prophecy was not the ships but where they were.

[52] The Persians put it under siege by taking up position on the knoll that faces the Acropolis and is known in Athens as the 'Areopagus'.[34] What they did was to wrap tow around their arrows, set them alight and then fire them at the barricades. Nevertheless, despite the desperate straits to which the besieged Athenians were brought, and for all that their barricades had let them down, they still held out. Even when the Peisistratids addressed them and offered them terms, they would not surrender, but instead came up with all kinds of other defensive strategies, such as rolling boulders down onto the Barbarians whenever they approached the gates, so that for a long while, unable to capture them, Xerxes was in a quandary.

[53] In due course, however, the Barbarians managed to surmount the challenge and find a way in, as they were bound to – for what had the oracle prophesied, if not that the whole of mainland Attica would come under Persian rule? At the front end of the Acropolis, away from the road that leads up to the gates, there was a stretch standing ungarrisoned, since the approach was so sheer that no one had ever imagined men might actually scale it – and it was here, near the shrine of Aglaurus, the daughter of Cecrops, that the ascent was made. When the Athenians saw that the enemy had reached the summit [of the Acropolis], some of them hurled themselves off the battlements to their deaths, while others fled to the main hall of the temple building. Meanwhile, the Persians who had made the climb headed straight for the gates and opened them, then set to slaughtering the suppliants. Once they had cut down every last one, they looted the sanctuary and torched the whole of the Acropolis.[35]

[54] And now, with Athens completely his, Xerxes sent a messenger on horseback to Susa, updating Artabanus on how well things were going. Then, the day after the dispatch of this herald, he called together all the Athenian exiles in his train, and instructed them to climb the Acropolis and make sacrifice according to their own manner – either in obedience to a vision he had seen in a dream, or perhaps because the burning of the sanctuary had filled him with remorse.[36] The Athenian exiles duly did as they had been commanded.

[55] Now, there is a reason for my mentioning this, which I shall give. On the Acropolis there is a temple to Erechtheus, who is said to have been born of the Earth – and in this temple there is an olive tree and a well filled with salt water, which according to the story told by the

Athenians were put there by Athena and Poseidon respectively, as witnesses to their might, when they were competing with one another for patronage of the region. It so happened that the olive tree had been incinerated by the Barbarians, along with the rest of the sanctuary. The day after it was burned, however, when the Athenians who had been ordered by the King to make sacrifice climbed up to the sanctuary, they saw that a shoot about a cubit long had sprouted from the stump – an occurrence which they duly reported.

[56] When news of what had happened in Athens on the Acropolis reached Salamis, the Greeks were so alarmed that some of the commanders did not even wait for the business they had been discussing to be concluded, but instead looked to make their escape by piling into their ships and hoisting their sails. Meanwhile, those left behind passed a formal resolution that they would give battle in the waters off the Isthmus. As night fell, the council of war broke up and those attending it boarded their ships.

[57] When Themistocles arrived at his ship, an Athenian citizen named Mnesiphilus asked him what decision they had reached – and on learning that the resolution was to head with the fleet for the Isthmus, and fight in defence of the Peloponnese, he urged against it. 'If the ships here do abandon Salamis, they will no longer be fighting for a single fatherland.[37] Instead, each contingent will make for its own city, and neither Eurybiadas nor anyone else will be able to stop the fleet from scattering in all directions. This senseless plan will be the ruin of Greece! By whatever means you can, go and find a way to reverse the decision. Somehow, you have to convince Eurybiadas to change his mind and stay where he is.'

[58] This suggestion appealed very much to Themistocles, who said not a word in reply but headed off instead to Eurybiadas' ship. 'There is something I wish to share with you,' he said on his arrival there, 'on a matter that concerns us both.' 'Come aboard, then,' Eurybiadas told him, 'and talk it over, if you so wish.' So Themistocles sat down beside him, and repeated everything he had heard from Mnesiphilus as though the arguments were his own – and these pleas, together with a whole host of other points, convinced Eurybiadas to leave his ship and summon the commanders to a council of war.

[59] They all duly assembled, but before Eurybiadas could open his

mouth to explain why he had convened the meeting, Themistocles began to press his entreaties on them with the utmost vehemence. He was interrupted in this by the Corinthian commander, Adeimantus, the son of Ocytus: 'In the Games, Themistocles, those who are too quick off the mark earn themselves a beating.'[38] 'Yes,' answered Themistocles, in self-justification, 'but those who get left behind do not win the crown.'

[60] All the same, the tone of his reply to the Corinthian was still at this stage an emollient one; and likewise, in his address to Eurybiadas, he made no mention of what had passed between them earlier, when he had argued that the fleet would scatter in all directions if it abandoned Salamis. After all, it would hardly have been seemly of him to level such a charge in the presence of the allies themselves. So instead he pressed a different case.

'The opportunity is now yours', he told Eurybiadas, 'to be the saviour of Greece – but only if you do as I say. Fight in these waters here, where we are now, and ignore those who are urging you to transfer the fleet to the Isthmus. Hear me out, and then weigh the two options. If you join battle with the enemy off the Isthmus, you will be fighting in open sea, and at a serious disadvantage, since our ships are the more heavily built,[39] and our numbers fewer. Not only that, but even if fortune does favour us, you will still have doomed to ruin Salamis, Megara and Aegina. What is more, the enemy's land-forces are bound to move in parallel with his fleet, so that you yourselves will be the ones responsible for bringing them to the Peloponnese, and thereby putting the whole of Greece at risk.

'Only do as I say, though, and you will find that many benefits follow. Firstly, if our smaller fleet meets with their larger one in the narrows, the logic of war suggests that a decisive victory will be ours. After all – just as fighting on the open seas will work to their advantage, so will a battle in crowded waters work to ours. Additionally, we will ensure the survival of Salamis – the place to which we have evacuated our women and children. And then too – most saliently of all from your perspective – there is this advantage: that if you stay here, you will be fighting no less in defence of the Peloponnese than you would be in a battle off the Isthmus. Surely, then, if you have any sense, you will not draw the enemy to the Peloponnese?

'Should things turn out as I expect, and victory go to our fleet, then the Barbarians will never get to the Isthmus. Instead, they will withdraw in disarray, with Attica the limit of their advance. This in turn will have the advantage of keeping Megara and Aegina intact. Yes, and Salamis too – Salamis, where it has been foretold that we will defeat our enemies! Now, as a rule of thumb, when men come up with a sensible strategy, the outcome will generally be as they have planned. However, let their strategy be a nonsense and they are most unlikely to obtain divine backing for it.'

[61] Once Themistocles had given this speech, Adeimantus of Corinth returned to the attack, commanding him – as a man without a city – to hold his tongue, and urging Eurybiadas not to allow a motion brought by a stateless person to be put to the vote. 'All very well', he insisted, 'for Themistocles to parade his opinions if he can demonstrate that he does indeed have a city – but not otherwise.' (The point of this sneer was, of course, that Athens had fallen and lay under occupation.) Themistocles then laid insultingly into Adeimantus and the Corinthians both, and declared in forthright terms that he and his fellow-citizens most certainly had a city – one larger than Corinth, and more landed too – for as long as they still had two hundred ships, all fully crewed. 'Were we to turn against the Greeks,' he demanded, 'which of them would be able to block us? None!'

[62] Then, having made his meaning clear, he directed his conversation back to Eurybiadas, whom he pressed with an even greater sense of urgency. 'Stay where you are, and your remaining here will be the measure of your quality as a man. Leave, and you will destroy Greece. The entire course of the war depends upon our fleet.[40] So do as I advise. And if you will not – very well, we shall load up the members of our households and make our way to Siris in Italy, which has been ours since ancient times,[41] and where we are fated, so oracles claim, to found a colony. And then, when you find yourself bereft of our support, and quite abandoned, reflect upon what I have said.'

[63] Sure enough, these words of Themistocles brought Eurybiadas to reverse his opinion – the chief factor in bringing about this change of mind being, so I believe, his anxiety that if he did take the fleet off to the Isthmus, the Athenians would desert them.[42] After all, with the Athenians gone, those left behind would no longer be in any position to put up a fight. Accordingly, then, he sided with the argument that they should stay where they were, and settle the issue at sea.

[64] With Eurybiadas now settled on this course, there were no more verbal skirmishings, and instead the fleet made ready to fight at Salamis. Dawn approached; and at the very moment of sunrise, land and sea alike were shaken by an earthquake. The Greeks decided to pray to the gods, and to summon to their aid the descendants of Aeacus: a resolution which they duly put into practice. Once they had offered prayers to all the gods, they called on Ajax and Telamon (both of whom were already present on Salamis) and dispatched an Aeginetan ship to fetch Aeacus and his remaining descendants.[43]

[65] At the same time as this, an Athenian exile whom the Medes had come to rate very highly – a man called Dicaeus, the son of Theocydes – claimed that, with Xerxes' land-forces ravaging an Attica quite emptied of Athenians, he happened to be out with Demaratus of Lacedaemon on the Thriasian plain, and saw coming from Eleusis a swirling of dust, such as some thirty thousand men might kick up. And then, all at once, even as they were wondering who the men responsible for this dust might be, they heard a sound of voices, a cry that seemed to Dicaeus to be the *Iacchus!* of the Mysteries. Demaratus, who was unacquainted with the rites performed at Eleusis, asked him what the noise was. 'There is no helping it, Demaratus,' he answered, 'the King's forces are due some terrible destruction. Clearly, as Attica is empty, something of divine origin must be making this noise – something that is coming from Eleusis to the assistance of the Athenians and their allies. If it drifts down over the Peloponnese, then the King himself and his army here on the mainland are in danger – but if it heads for Salamis, and the ships there, then it is his fleet that the King risks losing. This festival is one that the Athenians celebrate every year in honour of the Mother and the Daughter, and anyone who so wishes, whether from Athens or from elsewhere in Greece, can be initiated into it. As for the cry you heard, it is the *Iacchus!* which is always raised at the festival.'[44] Demaratus' response to this was to urge Dicaeus to keep quiet and not breathe a word of it to anyone else. 'If what you have said gets back to the King, you will lose your head. Neither I nor anyone else will be able to shield you. So keep your peace, and leave the fate of the task-force to the gods.' Such was his advice; and after he had given it, there emerged from out of the swirl of dust and voices a cloud, which rose high into the air and was borne towards the Greek positions on Salamis. So it was they

learned that Xerxes' fleet was doomed. Such, at any rate, is the story told by Dicaeus, the son of Theocydes – and he cited Demaratus, and others too, as men who would corroborate it.

[66] Meanwhile, the crews serving with Xerxes' fleet had crossed back to Histiaea from Trachis, where they had been viewing the disaster inflicted on the Spartans, then paused for three days before sailing on through the Euripus strait, and arrived in Phalerum a further three days after that. By my own reckoning, the numbers involved in the invasion of Attica – both by land and by sea – were not an iota diminished from those that had arrived at Sepias and Thermopylae. This is because I am offsetting those lost to the storm and to the battles fought at Thermopylae and in the waters off Artemisium against those who were yet to join the King's forces: namely, the Malians, the Dorians, the Locrians and the Boeotians, all of whom – if the Thespians and Plataeans are discounted – joined the King's train in full force. Also joining it were the citizens of Carystus, Andros and Tenos, and all the other islanders too, except for those from the five cities I named earlier.[45] The further into Greece the Persian penetrated, you see, the more did peoples follow in his train.

[67] It is true that the Parians, alone among the various squadrons, did not make it to Athens, since they had been left behind on Cythnos and were waiting to see how the war would turn out; but all the others, once their ships had arrived at Phalerum, were paid a visit by Xerxes, who wished to make contact with the men who had just sailed in, and discover what they were thinking. When he arrived, he sat down in the position of pre-eminence and summoned the tyrants of the various peoples who had contributed squadrons, together with their commanding officers, seating them in a manner that reflected the honour in which he held them, with the Sidonian nearest to the royal person,[46] then the Tyrian and then all the rest. Once they had taken their places, and were arranged in due accordance with etiquette, Xerxes sent Mardonius to test their mettle by asking each of them in turn whether or not he should fight at sea.

[68] So Mardonius went round, beginning with the Sidonian; and the opinion of everyone he asked, unanimously expressed, was that yes, Xerxes should indeed engage the enemy fleet. But then up spoke Artemisia.[47]

'Tell the King this from me, Mardonius – and I speak as someone whose record in the battles fought off Euboea was by no means the worst, and whose feats hardly the most contemptible. "It is only proper, Lord, that I give you as my opinion what I truly believe to be in your best interests. Keep your ships in reserve, and do not commit them to battle, for, by sea, the Greek forces will be as superior to yours as men are to women. What earthly need, then, for you to risk your fleet in battle? Not only have you taken Athens, which was the goal of your expedition all along, but the rest of Greece as well. There is no one to stand against you. Those who tried to do so were dealt with as they deserved.

'"Let me tell you how I see things turning out for our adversaries. If you do not rush into fighting them by sea, but instead keep your ships here, close to shore, or perhaps advance on the Peloponnese, you will have no difficulty, my Lord, in meeting your objectives. This is because the Greeks cannot hold out against you for long. Instead, you will soon scatter them in all directions, and send them fleeing to their respective cities. I have information, you see, that they have no provisions on this island. Not only that, but if you should advance with your forces by land against the Peloponnese, it is most unlikely that those who have come from there will be content to do nothing, or to commit their ships on behalf of Athens.

'"If, however, you rush headlong into a naval engagement, I worry that any harm that comes to your fleet will have a concomitant effect on your army. What is more, O King, you should hug to your heart this reflection: that just as bad men tend to have good slaves, so does the reverse apply. No man is better than you – and sure enough, these men you rank as your allies are truly terrible slaves. These Egyptians, Cypriots, Cilicians and Pamphylians – why, they are worse than useless!"'

[69] This speech of Artemisia's to Mardonius greatly alarmed her well-wishers, who assumed that her comments dissuading the King from fighting at sea were bound to lead him to punish her. Conversely, those who resented her, and envied her the honour in which – pre-eminently among the allies – she was held, were delighted by what she had said, as they assumed that it would result in her execution. In fact, when the range of opinions was reported back to Xerxes, he was hugely impressed by Artemisia's take on things, and lavished her with more praise than ever – though she had already stood high in his

estimation before. Nevertheless, he commanded that the majority opinion prevail, since it was his firm conviction that his men had stinted in fighting at their best off Euboea because he had not been there in person, whereas now he was ready to watch his fleet give battle.

[70] So the word was given to put to sea, and the ships headed off for Salamis, where they drew themselves up in lines and adopted battle-stations – all with a minimum of noise. By this stage, the day was almost done, and so, with night by now drawing in, there was no opportunity to engage in battle. Accordingly, they readied themselves for the morrow. The Greeks were now in the grip of dread and panic – the Peloponnesians not least of all. Sitting on Salamis, and faced with fighting for Athenian territory, their nightmare was that they might be defeated, trapped on the island and blockaded, while their own homes were left undefended.

[71] Meanwhile, under cover of night, the barbarian army was setting out for the Peloponnese. Despite this, every possible measure had been taken to block any invasion of the mainland made by the Barbarians. No sooner had the Peloponnesians learned of the death of Leonidas and his men at Thermopylae, you see, than they had all come hurrying from their various cities, and taken up position at the Isthmus, under the command of Cleombrotus, the son of Anaxandridas and the brother of Leonidas. Settling down at the Isthmus, they demolished the Scironian Road, and then, after talking the matter over, decided that their best option would be to build a wall across the Isthmus.[48] Thanks to the presence there of thousands upon thousands of them, and because every last man bent his back, the work proceeded fast. Day and night, those assisting in the task brought in stones, bricks, logs and baskets full of sand, and never had a moment's rest.

[72] The Greeks who had come with all hands to help at the Isthmus were these: the Lacedaemonians; all the Arcadians; the Eleans; the Corinthians; the Sicyonians; the Epidaurians; the Phliasians; the Troezenians; and the Hermioneans. These were the ones who, panic-stricken, rallied to the cause of Greece in her hour of danger. The other Peloponnesians, however, could not be bothered – even though the Olympic Festival and the Carneia were by now over.

[73] Seven ethnic groups have the Peloponnese as their home. Of these, two are aboriginal and still occupy the lands that they have inhabited since primordial times: the Arcadians and the Cynourians. One of the

seven – the Achaeans – have likewise always lived in the Peloponnese, but emigrated from their own homeland to another region. The remaining four peoples – the Dorians, the Aetolians, the Dryopians and the Lemnians – are immigrants. Numerous eminent cities are Dorian, but the only Aetolian one is Elis; Hermione and Asine (the one near Cardamyle in Laconia) are both Dryopian, while the Paroreatae are all of them Lemnian. Although the Cynourians, who live in and around Orneae, appear to be the only aboriginal inhabitants who are Ionian, over the course of time the effect of being ruled by the Argives has been to Dorianize them thoroughly. So, excepting the places I listed, all the remaining cities of these seven peoples adopted a position of neutrality – but this neutrality, if I may speak frankly, equated to collaboration with the Medes.

[74] The Greeks at the Isthmus all went to the effort they did because they knew themselves to be running a life-and-death race – and also because they did not regard the prospects of their fleet as very bright. Meanwhile, their comrades on Salamis, although kept abreast of what was going on, remained extremely jittery – less on their own account than out of anxiety for the Peloponnese. For a while they just whispered to one another, individual to individual, expressing astonishment at the folly of Eurybiadas – but in the end it all erupted into the open. A meeting was convened, at which the same old arguments were rehearsed over and over again – some insisting that it was imperative to set sail for the Peloponnese and risk themselves in its defence, rather than stay and fight for a land that had already fallen to the enemy, while the Athenians, the Aeginetans and the Megarians were for making their stand where they were.

[75] When Themistocles found that his own arguments were being overcome by those of the Peloponnesians, he slipped away unobtrusively from the council of war, and went to find a house-slave of his, his children's tutor, a man named Sicinnus; and after instructing him on what he had to say, dispatched him in a small boat to the camp of the Medes. (Subsequent to these events, Themistocles had him enrolled as a citizen of Thespiae,[49] at a time when the Thespians were accepting new citizens, and made him a wealthy man as well.) Anyway, at this time, Sicinnus landed in his boat and delivered this message to the Barbarian high command: 'Behind the backs of the other Greeks, I have been sent on a mission from the Athenian commander, who is a partisan of the King's, and keen for your cause to triumph over that of the Greeks. He wants to tip you off that the Greeks are panicking and plotting their

escape. What you have now, then – just so long as you do not ignore their flight – is an opportunity to secure a victory so perfect as to put all others in the shade. They are at complete loggerheads and will no longer stand up to you. In fact, as you will see, the only fighting they'll get up to will be among themselves – those on your side against those who are not.' Once he had communicated this to them, he stole away.

[76] The response of the Persians to this message, which seemed to them perfectly credible, was two-fold: first, they landed a large number of men on the islet which lies midway between Salamis and the mainland; and second, with the coming of midnight, they had the western wing of the fleet extend in an arc as far as Salamis, while the ships stationed near Ceos and Cynosoura blocked the channel leading to Mounichia, filling it up completely. The reason the fleet undertook these moves was to ensure that the Greeks, rather than escaping Salamis, would be trapped in the narrows and made to pay for the resistance they had shown at Artemisium. As for the landing of Persians on the tiny island (which goes by the name of Psyttaleia), this was done because it lay directly in the path of the imminent engagement, and therefore, come the battle, was the place where both men and damaged vessels were most likely to be washed ashore – some to be rescued, and some eliminated. Everything was done noiselessly, so as not to alert the enemy. These various preparations ensured that none of the Barbarians got a wink of sleep that night.

[[77] There can certainly be no disputing on my part the truth of oracles – not when, as in the example below, they speak with such transparency that I would shrink from any attempt to discredit them.

'When with their ships they fashion a bridge, and join the holy
    promontory
Of Artemis, she of the golden sword, to sea-girt Cynosoura,
Lunatic with over-confidence, the sackers of gleaming Athens –
Then shall Justice divine quell the strength of that son of Pride,
    Excess,
Despite the terror of his ravening and ambition to gulp down all.
Bronze shall meet and clash with bronze, and Ares with blood
    will dye the sea
Deep crimson. Then it is that a day will dawn for Greece of liberty,
Brought by the far-seeing son of Cronos, and Victory, that holy
    queen.'

In light of how clear verses such as these from Bacis are, I would never presume to challenge the veracity of oracles – nor would I accept anyone else doing it either.][50]

[78] Meanwhile, on Salamis, the commanders were embroiled in the cut and thrust of a most almighty argument. They remained ignorant of their encirclement by the barbarian fleet, and took for granted that it was still stationed where it had been spotted during the day.

[79] While the commanders were busy attacking one another, there arrived from Aegina a man called Aristeides, the son of Lysimachus; he was an Athenian, and although he had been ostracized by the people, I have come to the conclusion, based on what I have learned about his character, that he was the best man in Athens, and the most just too.[51] He presented himself before the council of war, and asked Themistocles to come outside with him, despite the fact that the two men, far from being friends, were the bitterest of rivals. Such was the sheer scale of the present crisis, however, that Aristeides had put all that to one side, and asked Themistocles to leave the meeting because he wished to have a word with him. Aristeides had already heard how keen the Peloponnesians were to withdraw their ships to the Isthmus. Now, once Themistocles had come outside to see him, he declared, 'The issue of who can achieve the most for our country must mark the limit to our rivalry – in every crisis, but the present one especially. Let me tell you this – it makes no difference how much or how little the Peloponnesians talk about sailing away. They will not be able to evacuate their fleets – no matter what the Corinthians, or even Eurybiadas himself, may wish. I can assure you of that based on the evidence of my own eyes. We are surrounded, you see, by a ring of foes. You must go in and make this plain to them.'

[80] 'Your suggestion is as welcome as your news is excellent,' answered Themistocles. 'Precisely what I needed to happen has happened – and here you are, an eyewitness to it. I should explain that these actions of the Medes are my doing. I had no choice, since the Greeks positively refused to stand and fight, except to make them do it. But since you are the one who has come here with this welcome information, you should be the one to report it. If I tell them, you see, they will think that I am making it up and refuse to believe that the Barbarians could possibly be doing such a thing. So please, go in and spell out the situation

to them. Ideally, of course, they should believe what you are telling them – but even if they do not, it is all much the same to us. After all, if what you say is true, and we are indeed completely surrounded, then they will not be going anywhere, no matter what!'

[81] So Aristeides went in to give his briefing, and to report that it was only with the utmost difficulty that he had managed to sail across from Aegina and slip through the enemy blockade. 'The Greek positions are entirely surrounded by Xerxes' fleet. An attack is coming, and I advise you to brace yourselves for it.' With these words he left them; and once again the debate degenerated into a wrangle. Most of the commanders, you see, still refused to believe the news.

[82] But it was then, amid this mood of scepticism, that there arrived a trireme crewed by Tenian deserters, under the command of a man from Tenos called Panaetius, the son of Sosimenes – and the information they brought was both full and accurate. (This was the deed that explains why the Tenians had their names inscribed on the tripod at Delphi listing those who had helped to defeat the Barbarian.[52]) The desertion of this ship at Salamis, combined with the earlier one of the Lemnian ship at Artemisium, brought the total of the Greek fleet to a round three hundred and eighty – a number that previously it had been short of by two.

[83] Once the Greeks had been persuaded of the truth of what the Tenians had to say, they made ready for battle. At the first light of dawn, the marines were called to a meeting, at which the best speech of all was given by Themistocles. The whole way through it, he contrasted the better aspects of human nature and society with the worse. 'Choose what is better!' he exhorted, before winding up his oration by ordering the marines to board their ships. Just as they were doing so, the trireme that had gone to fetch the descendants of Aeacus arrived from Aegina. Then the entire Greek fleet put out to sea – and no sooner had the ships been launched than the Barbarians were upon them.

[84] The Greeks began to back water in the direction of the shore – all except for an Athenian, a man called Ameinias of Pallene, who went crashing headlong into the side of an enemy ship. Because neither vessel could then extricate itself from the other, the rest of the Greek fleet came to Ameinias' assistance, and battle was duly joined. That, at any rate, is the Athenian account of how the fighting came to start, though the Aeginetans claim that it began with the ship which had been sent to

fetch the descendants of Aeacus from Aegina. There are those too who report that a ghostly figure in the form of a woman appeared, and gave a clarion call so ringing that the Greeks could hear it along the entire length of their line – but only after she had first upbraided them for backing water. 'Just how far will you retreat, you lunatics?'

[85] Stationed on the western wing opposite the Athenians, towards Eleusis, were the Phoenicians; and opposite the Lacedaemonians, on the eastern wing towards the Piraeus, the Ionians. Although a few of these did set out to fight badly, as Themistocles had urged them to do, most did not. I could list the names of any number of Ionian trireme captains who captured Greek ships, but shall confine myself to mentioning just two, both Samians: Theomestor,[53] the son of Androdamas, and Phylacus, the son of Histiaeus. I commemorate these two exclusively because Theomestor, as a consequence of his achievements, was installed by the Persians as tyrant of Samos, while Phylacus had his name recorded as a 'Benefactor of the King', and was rewarded with a vast swathe of land. (The Persian word for 'Benefactors of the King' is *orosangai*.)

[86] So that was how those two did – but the vast majority of the ships suffered crippling damage, some at the hands of the Athenians, and others at the hands of the Aeginetans. This was due to the disciplined and ordered manner in which the Greek fleet fought, whereas the Barbarians were so disorganized that they lost all sense of what they were meant to be doing – with consequences that were only to be expected. Nevertheless, their performance that day was a good deal better and more impressive than it had been off Euboea, since each and every man imagined the royal eye fixed directly on him, and this dread of Xerxes spurred everyone to a pitch of effort.

[87] Although I cannot say with any accuracy how individual Barbarians or Greeks might have fared in the contest, there is one exception. Artemisia featured in an encounter that won her an even higher reputation with the King than she had previously enjoyed. As the royal cause collapsed into utter chaos, Artemisia was being pursued in her ship by an Athenian vessel. As the enemy closed in, it so happened that she was trailing other vessels on her own side, which were also serving to block off the escape route ahead of her – and so she decided on a course of action which in the event proved highly effective. With the Athenian ship in hot pursuit, she ploughed straight on and smashed into a ship on her own side, one that was crewed by Calyndians, and had Damasithymus,

the king of Calynda himself, on board. Now, I cannot say whether there might have been some falling out between the two of them when they were both still at the Hellespont, or whether her action was a premeditated one, or whether it was just by chance that the Calyndian ship was in the way. But certainly, her ramming and sinking of the ship proved to be doubly fortunate for her. Firstly, you see, when the captain of the Athenian ship saw her ram a ship crewed by Barbarians, he assumed that she was either a Greek herself or else a defector from the Barbarian cause who was now helping the Greeks, so he changed course and veered off after other vessels.

[88] But her escape and survival were not the limits of her good fortune, since the very damage she had done to Xerxes' cause served to give a massive boost to her reputation at his court. The story goes that the King, as he was watching the battle, noticed her ship execute the ramming. 'Master,' one of his circle exclaimed, 'do you see how well Artemisia is performing in the struggle? She has just sunk an enemy ship!' 'Are you sure that the feat was Artemisia's?' Xerxes demanded. 'Yes,' came the confirmation. 'There is no mistaking the insignia on her ship.' They had assumed, you see, that the destroyed vessel had indeed belonged to the enemy. Nor, in the event, was there anyone to press charges against Artemisia, since – in addition to all the other things I mentioned as going her way – she had one further stroke of luck: the Calyndian ship was lost with all hands. It is claimed that Xerxes' response to what he had been told was to declare, 'My men have become women, and my women men.' That, so the story goes, was what Xerxes said.

[89] One of the commanders killed in the fray was Ariabignes, the son of Darius and brother of Xerxes; but although he was far from being the only well-known Persian or Median casualty, and although there were many other allies too who likewise perished, only a few Greeks lost their lives. This was because they knew how to swim, so that when their ships were destroyed those who had survived the close fighting swam across to Salamis. Most of the Barbarians, however, perished by drowning, because they did not know how to swim. It was when the ships in the front line turned to flee that the carnage was most terrible. This was because the crews in the lines to their rear, who were trying to get past in their ships and demonstrate their own mettle in action to the King, went crashing into the ships of their retreating comrades.

[90] It also happened, amid all the clamour and confusion, that some Phoenicians whose ships had been destroyed came to the King and blamed the loss of their vessels on the Ionians, whom they falsely accused of being traitors. In the event, however, it was not the Ionian commanders who were put to death, but the Phoenicians, who were paid back in fitting coin for their slanders. Even as they were maligning the Ionians, a ship from Samothrace rammed an Athenian one. Then, as the Athenian ship began to capsize, an Aeginetan vessel bore down upon the Samothracians and sank theirs. At this, the Samothracians, armed with javelins, hurled their weapons at the marines on board the ship that had sunk their own and cleared them from the deck, then boarded the vessel and took possession of it. It was as a result of this feat that the Ionians were spared execution. Xerxes, who had witnessed the astounding heroism of the deed, turned to the Phoenicians, and in a towering rage put the blame on them, then ordered them beheaded, so that men who had proved themselves such cowards would never again traduce their betters. (Xerxes, you see, was sitting at the foot of the mountain directly opposite Salamis called Aigaleos – and whenever he saw a trireme on his own side achieve some impressive feat in the battle, he would enquire as to the man responsible, and then have the scribes record the captain's name, his father and his city.) Another factor that contributed to the fate suffered by the Phoenicians was the presence of a man called Ariaramnes, a Persian who was most sympathetic towards the Ionians.

[91] So the Phoenicians were duly dispatched. Meanwhile, those of the Barbarians who turned and sailed in full flight for Phalerum were ambushed in the straits by the Aeginetans, whose feats were so impressive that they fully merit recounting. It was right in the heat of battle, and while the Athenians were disabling both those ships that were still putting up a fight and those that had turned tail, the Aeginetans were doing likewise to those leaving the straits. Flee the Athenians, and a ship would run full tilt into the Aeginetans.

[92] It was at this point that Themistocles' ship, in hot pursuit of an enemy vessel, happened to encounter the ship of a man from Aegina called Polycritus, the son of Crius. This Polycritus had just rammed the very Sidonian vessel that, back in the waters off Sciathos, had captured the Aeginetan patrol-ship, on board which had been Pytheas, the son of Ischenous,[54] whose courage had so astounded the Persians that, after

hacking him down, they had kept him on their ship. But now it was the turn of the Sidonian ship to be captured, and Pytheas' escort of Persians with it – which meant that Pytheas himself ended up safely back in Aegina! As for Polycritus, when he spotted the Athenian vessel, and saw from its insignia that it was the Athenian flagship, he taunted Themistocles by yelling at him, 'So is this what you mean by calling the Aeginetans collaborators with the Medes?' Coming as it did just after the ramming of an enemy ship, the comment was a pointed one to direct at Themistocles. Meanwhile, the Barbarians whose ships had survived the battle ceased their flight only once they had arrived in Phalerum, where their land-forces could give them protection.

[93] The Greeks who won the best name for themselves in the battle were the Aeginetans, followed by the Athenians; and among individuals Polycritus of Aegina, and two Athenians, Eumenes of Anagyrous and Ameinias of Pallene. It was Ameinias who had been pursuing Artemisia – and had he only realized who it was on board the ship, he would never have stopped until he had taken her prisoner or been captured himself. This was because the Athenians held it such a scandal that a woman should be making war on Athens that they had issued specific instructions to the captains of their triremes, with a reward of 10,000 drachmas for anyone who took Artemisia alive. However, as I explained earlier, she managed to escape. She and all the others whose ships had survived the battle were in Phalerum.

[94] At the beginning of the battle, just as the two fleets were closing in on one another, Adeimantus, the Corinthian commander, is said by the Athenians to have lost his nerve so badly that he hoisted his sails and beat a retreat;[55] the Corinthians, when they saw their flagship in full flight, set off in the same way. As they fled, they came to the stretch of Salamis where the sanctuary of Athena Sciras[56] stands; and here they were met by a small boat that they thought could only have been sent by a god, since it was never clear who else might conceivably have sent it, and because the Corinthians, before the encounter, had no idea how things were going with the rest of the fleet. What led them to distinguish divine agency was the fact that the crew of the boat, as it drew near to the ships, called out, 'Adeimantus! Turning your ships in flight is an utter betrayal of the Greeks! But victory over the enemy is even now ensuring that all their prayers are being answered to the letter!' Then,

because Adeimantus did not believe what they had told him, they spoke up again, telling him to take them as hostages and put them to death should it prove that the Greeks were not the victors after all. So he steered his own ship back round, and the rest of the squadron too, and returned to where the fleet was, only to find that everything was over. That, at any rate, is the story put around by the Athenians; but the Corinthians themselves flatly deny it, and hold themselves, on the contrary, to have been among the first to engage the enemy fleet. The rest of Greece supports them in this claim.

[95] As the battle raged off Salamis, an action was being undertaken by a man from Athens called Aristeides, the son of Lysimachus – the same person whose unrivalled qualities I mentioned a little while ago.[57] Taking a sizeable number of the hoplites, Athenian by origin, who had been stationed along the shoreline of Salamis, he led them across to the island of Psyttaleia, and there slaughtered all the Persians who were on the island.

[96] Once the two fleets had disengaged, any wrecks still left at the scene of the battle were hauled ashore onto Salamis by the Greeks, who had no doubt that the King would be deploying the remnants of his fleet against them, and so were bracing themselves for another engagement at sea. Many of the wrecks, however, had been picked up by a westerly wind and swept onto the stretch of the Attic coast that goes by the name of Colias – thereby ensuring that, in addition to all the predictions made about the battle by Bacis and Musaeus, another oracle as well was fulfilled, one that had originally been delivered many years previously by an Athenian soothsayer, a man called Lysistratus, whose prophecy that wrecks would drift ashore there[58] had been quite overlooked by the Greeks.

'The women of Colias will use oars to do their roasting.'

But this happened only after the King had marched away.

[97] Once Xerxes realized the full scale of the disaster[59] that had befallen him, he was nervous that it might occur to the Greeks – or perhaps be suggested to them by some Ionian – to sail to the Hellespont and break up the bridges, thereby leaving him trapped in Europe and at risk of utter annihilation; and so he began to contemplate flight. However, because he did not wish to alert either the Greeks or his own men to this, he had various Phoenician merchant-ships lashed together in an attempt to build a causeway across to Salamis that could serve him as

both a pontoon-bridge and a barrier, and made preparations for battle, as though it were his intention to fight once again by sea. The spectacle of this activity convinced everyone that he had indeed fully committed himself to staying put and continuing the war – everyone, that is, except Mardonius, who knew the workings of Xerxes' mind better than anyone, and so was not taken in.

[98] Simultaneously, Xerxes sent news of the defeat to Persia.[60] Now, the Persians have found a way of sending messages so efficient that there exists nothing mortal possessed of greater speed. There are horses and riders posted at intervals along the entire stretch of a given route,[61] and every day, so it is reported, a fresh horse and rider stand there waiting, ready to undertake that particular day's travel. Neither snow nor rain, neither the heat of day nor the pitch of night, will prevent him from completing his assigned journey in the fastest possible time. One man will come galloping up and hand over his instructions to a second, the second will then hand them over to a third, and so it continues, in a relay – rather like the torch-race which is staged by the Greeks in honour of Hephaestus.[62] The word used by the Persians to describe this horse-post is *angareion*.

[99] The first dispatch to arrive in Susa, announcing that Athens was in Xerxes' hands, had brought such joy to the Persians left behind there that they had spread myrtle branches over all the roads, burned incense and busied themselves with the offering of sacrifices and feasting. But then, when the second message arrived on top of the first, they were so devastated that they all tore their clothes to shreds, howling and wailing without restraint as they did so, and holding Mardonius to blame. The Persians did this less out of any distress for their fleet than because they were terrified for Xerxes.

[100] They continued in this state for the whole time until the return to Susa of Xerxes himself, who duly put a stop to it. Meanwhile, because Mardonius could see that Xerxes was deeply cast down by the result of the sea-battle, and suspected the King was planning to flee Athens, he realized that he himself, as the man responsible for persuading Xerxes to invade Greece, was liable to pay a heavy price for it; this meant that the better option for him would be to raise the stakes still further, and fearlessly risk his life in exchange for the opportunity to conquer Greece. (That said, he had every confidence that he would indeed conquer Greece.) Accordingly, once he had arrived at this conclusion, he made

the following proposal. 'Master, do not be upset, or imagine that what has happened is somehow a great calamity. In the final reckoning, this is a contest that will be decided, not by planks of wood, but by men and horses. These Greeks may imagine that they have won a decisive victory – but will they leave their ships to meet you in battle? No! Nor is there anyone from the mainland who will stand up to you either. All who have sought to do so have paid the price. So if it is your wish now to test the defences of the Peloponnese, then let us do so at once. Alternatively, if you would rather stay where you are, we can do that too. But please – do not be downcast! It is inevitable, wholly inevitable, that the Greeks will be made to pay for both their present and their former actions, and become your slaves. So yes, this would be your best course of action. But even if you are set on retreat and the withdrawal of your forces, I have a plan crafted for that eventuality too. Do not, my Lord, allow the Greeks to make a laughing-stock of the Persians! It was hardly our fault, after all, that your fortunes suffered a reversal – nor can you accuse the Persians of ever having played the coward. Yes, the Phoenicians did, perhaps, and the Egyptians, and the Cypriots, and the Cilicians – but the Persians played no part in this calamity. That being so, and since the Persians are innocent of letting you down, do as I say. If you are resolved not to remain here, then certainly, head off home, and take the bulk of your forces with you. It will then be my responsibility to bring Greece to slavery for you – to which end, let me pick three hundred thousand men from your army.'

[101] Hearing this improved Xerxes' mood no end, and left him as cheerful as could be expected under the circumstances. 'Let me take some soundings,' he told Mardonius, 'and I will then tell you what course of action I intend to adopt.' So he summoned his Persian advisers; and, as he was listening to them, he decided to send for Artemisia as well, and get her advice, since it was clear now that she alone, on the previous occasion, had properly appreciated the course of action that would have served him best. On her arrival, Xerxes dismissed all the other people present – both his Persian advisers and his bodyguards – and told her, 'Mardonius has urged me to stay where I am, and probe the defences of the Peloponnese. He points out that my defeat was hardly the fault of the Persians, or indeed any of my land-forces, and that they are all itching to prove their worth. Alternatively, should I not do as he suggests, then he wishes to have the pick of three hundred

thousand of my men and use them to bring Greece to slavery for me, while I myself, on his urging, march what remains of the army back to my native land. In light of the excellent counsel you gave me before the recent sea-battle, which you told me not to engage in, I would like you now to recommend the course of action I would be best advised to follow.'

[102] 'My Lord,' Artemisia answered, in response to this request for advice, 'it is actually hard to know the best option to recommend. But having said that, and present circumstances being what they are, I think you should probably go back, and leave Mardonius here in Greece, with the men he wants – if indeed he is willing to put his words into action. Look at it this way. Should his conquests measure up to the ambitions he has spoken about, and everything go as he intends, then the achievement, Master, will be yours. The people responsible for it, after all, will have been your slaves. Then again, should events run contrary to Mardonius' expectations, the damage will be strictly limited – just so long as nothing fatal happens to you and the fortunes of your house. After all, if you survive, and your dynasty with you, then the race will be far from over for the Greeks, who will still be engaged in a continuing struggle to the death. But should Mardonius suffer a defeat, well – it will hardly matter. In fact, any victory that the Greeks may win will only be over your slave – and the destruction of a slave is no victory at all. But you yourself, when you put Athens to the torch, achieved what you had set out to do on your campaign – and so now you can be on your way.'

[103] Xerxes was delighted by this advice, since it coincided precisely with his own take on the matter. Indeed, so badly had he lost his nerve that, in my own opinion, he would never have stayed, not even had every man been counselling it – and every woman too. As it was, he praised Artemisia highly, then sent her off to take his children to Ephesus. (Some of his bastards had been in his train, you see.)

[104] The man he sent in charge of these children was a eunuch, originally from Pedasa, called Hermotimus – one more highly placed at the court of the King than any other eunuch. [The Pedasians live inland of Halicarnassus. An interesting thing happens there whenever all those who live in the vicinity of the city are faced by a period of danger: the priestess of Athena in Pedasa sprouts a huge beard. This has happened to them twice now. Hermotimus, then, was one of these same Pedasians.]

[105] Now, no one, so far as we know, has ever paid more terrible a retribution for a wrong done to him than Hermotimus did. When he was sold by the enemy soldiers who had captured him, you see, he was bought by a man from Chios called Panionius, who made his living from the most unholy line of work.[63] Any good-looking boys he could lay his hands on he would castrate, take to Sardis or Ephesus and sell for vast sums – which he could charge because the Barbarians regard eunuchs as being in every way more trustworthy than slaves who have not been castrated, and therefore more valuable. This trade naturally saw Panionius geld a huge number of boys – among whom was Hermotimus. Nevertheless, there was a silver lining to his misfortune: dispatched from Sardis as one of a number of gifts to the King, he ended up, in time, as Xerxes' favourite eunuch.

[106] While the King was at Sardis, preparing to launch the Persian military onslaught against Athens, Hermotimus went down on some business or other to the part of Mysia called Atarneus, where the Chians live – and there he ran into Panionius. Recognizing him, Hermotimus chatted away affably and at great length, listing all the good things that had come his way thanks to Panionius, and promising him a matching number of good things in return, if only he would move with his family to Atarneus – an offer that was welcomed with open arms by Panionius, who duly went there with his children and wife. Then, with the whole family in his grasp, Hermotimus addressed Panionius. 'There is no one in the world who makes a more unholy living than you. What did I or my family ever do to you and yours, that you made me not a man but something neutered? You really thought that the sort of things you did back then would escape the notice of the gods? But they are just, and now their law has caught up with you. Here you are, delivered into my hands as punishment for your unholy behaviour. Do not think to protest, then, that what I do to you is not richly merited.' Then, having spat out this rebuke, he had the children brought into his presence and forced Panionius to castrate all four of his sons – which Panionius, having no choice, duly did. Then, when these operations had been completed, Hermotimus obliged the boys to geld their father in turn. So that was how retribution, in the form of Hermotimus, caught up with Panionius.

[107] Once Xerxes had entrusted Artemisia with responsibility for taking his children to Ephesus, he summoned Mardonius and instructed him to have his pick of men from the army, and then to see if he could

match his actions to his words. Nothing further happened that day; but that night, on the orders of the King, the commanders of his fleet set off from Phalerum and headed back to the Hellespont as fast as each ship could go, with the aim of keeping the pontoons safe for the King to cross over. During the course of this voyage, the Barbarians approached Zoster, where they mistook for ships the thin promontories that jut out from the headland, and fled a considerable distance. Only once they had eventually realized that the ships were in fact headlands did they regroup and continue on their way.

[108] When day came, and the Greeks saw that the army had kept its position, they took for granted that the fleet too was still at Phalerum, and made ready to defend themselves on the assumption that it would attack them again. The moment they discovered that it had gone, however, they decided to set out after it in pursuit. The whole way to Andros, they caught not a glimpse of Xerxes' naval forces – and so, on arriving at Andros, they held a council of war. The case promoted by Themistocles was that they should steer a course through the islands in pursuit of the fleet, and then sail straight for the Hellespont, to break up the bridges. Eurybiadas, however, took the opposite view, declaring that the consequence of any demolition of the pontoons would be the most calamitous one imaginable for Greece. It was his argument that the Persian King, if trapped and obliged to remain in Europe, would not take it passively, since a policy of inactivity would hardly serve Xerxes' interests, nor enable him to find a way home, and would simultaneously doom his army to starvation; if he only grasped the nettle and committed himself fully to the task, then the whole of Europe – city by city and people by people – would surely fall to him, either at sword-point or else as a result of making terms before it came to that. The annual produce of the Greeks would then be the Persians' to consume for evermore. As it was, Eurybiadas continued, he thought it most unlikely that Xerxes would remain in Europe now that his fleet had been defeated. That being so, they should allow him to escape, and withdraw the whole way back to his homeland. 'And from then on, let his country be the one that we fight over.' The other Peloponnesian commanders supported this point of view.

[109] When Themistocles realized he had no chance of persuading the majority to sail for the Hellespont, he too shifted his position; and when he addressed the Athenians – who were especially aggrieved that

the Persians should have escaped, and were perfectly willing to sail for the Hellespont on their own, whether the others wanted to or not – he made these points. 'It is clear, based on a good deal of personal experience, and even more on what I have heard, that when men who have suffered a defeat are cornered they will fight back, and make good their earlier feebleness. We – and all of Greece with us – find ourselves now in a much stronger position than we had anticipated. Why, then, when we have beaten back a veritable swarm of men and they are in full retreat, go after them? The achievement, after all, was not our own. No, it was the work of the gods and the heroes, who begrudged that one man should rule as king over Europe as well as Asia – and a man both impious and overweening at that. After all, this is someone who treated shrines in the same way he did private property, putting them to the torch and hurling down the statues of the gods! He even flogged the sea and cast chains into it![64] As things stand, then, we are best off remaining in Greece, tending to ourselves and our households. Now that we have decisively repulsed the Barbarian, we should all of us be rebuilding our homes, and putting our effort into sowing our fields. The time for descending in our ships upon the Hellespont and Ionia will come with the spring.' His motive for saying this was to build up some credit with Xerxes, as an insurance in case he should ever get into trouble with the Athenians (which, indeed, did happen).[65]

[110] Duplicitous though this speech of Themistocles' was, the Athenians were nevertheless swayed by it. He had long had a reputation for cunning – but now that his cleverness and the brilliance of his counsel had been demonstrated beyond all doubt, the Athenians were ready to follow his directions in everything. The moment Themistocles had won their backing, he dispatched a boat crewed by men whom he could rely upon, even were they to be put to the very extremes of torture, not to reveal the message which he had ordered them to communicate to the King. As before, so now, one of these men was his house-slave Sicinnus. Once they had made landfall in Attica, everyone remained with the boat except for Sicinnus, who headed on to Xerxes, and declared, 'I have been sent by Themistocles, the son of Neocles, who is commander of the Athenians, and the bravest and cleverest of all the allies. He has a message for you. The Greeks wanted to set off in pursuit of your ships, and demolish the bridges over the Hellespont – but Themistocles the Athenian, keen to do you a favour, blocked them from doing so. As a result,

you can now move off in perfect security.' Then, the message delivered, back they sailed.

[111] Now, because the Greeks had decided not to pursue the barbarian fleet any further, nor to sail to the Hellespont and smash the thoroughfare across it, they instead laid siege to Andros, with the aim of capturing it. This was because the Andrians – who were the first of the islanders to have been given a demand for money by Themistocles – had rejected his extortions, which he had framed in the following terms: 'We Athenians have come accompanied by two mighty gods: Persuasion and Compulsion. That being so, you had better produce your cash.' To this, however, the Andrians had replied by declaring: 'It is clearly the measure of Athenian greatness and prosperity that you are blessed with such serviceable gods. We Andrians, however, have attained excellence in nothing save the poverty of our land. We too have a couple of goddesses, you see, who will never abandon us, so constant is their love for our island – but they profit us nothing. Poverty and Helplessness – these are the goddesses that have us in their clutches. It is because of them that we will not give you any money. Powerful though you Athenians may be, yet you will never be as powerful as we Andrians are lacking in power.' And so it was, upon this reply – and their refusal to hand over any money – that the Andrians had been put under siege.[66]

[112] Nor was that the limit of Themistocles' acquisitiveness: for he sent the same emissaries he had used to contact the King to blackmail the other islanders too, demanding money from them, and warning them that if they did not give in to his extortions, he would lead the Greek army against them, put them under siege and capture their cities. As a result of these communications, he raked in vast sums from the Carystians and the Parians, who were so terrified to learn that the Andrians were being besieged as collaborators with the Medes, and that Themistocles enjoyed the highest reputation among the commanders, that they sent him money. As to whether any other islanders made a contribution, I cannot say. (My guess, though, would be that the Carystians and Parians were not alone in paying up, and that some others did as well.) As it happened, the Parians did manage to avoid armed intervention by buying off Themistocles – but the Carystians, despite paying up, failed to keep trouble at bay. So it was that Themistocles, from his base on Andros, and behind the backs of the other commanders, leeched the islanders of money.

*

[113] Meanwhile, in the wake of the sea-battle, Xerxes and his circle let a few days go by before marching back to Boeotia along the road they had come. This was partly because Mardonius had decided to give the King a proper farewell, but also because, given that it was no longer the campaigning season, he thought that it would be better for him to winter in Thessaly, and then make an attempt on the Peloponnese in the spring. Only once he had arrived in Thessaly did Mardonius select his men, with the Persians known as the 'Immortals' his first pick (all of them, that is, except for Hydarnes, their commander, who refused to be parted from the King); then, from among the remainder of the Persians, he chose the heavy infantry and the thousand-strong unit of horse; then the Medes, the Sacae, the Bactrians and the Indians – both their infantry and cavalry. These peoples he picked en masse, but from the other allies he chose only a few: those who cut a good figure, or else already had a proven record. He picked more Persians – men adorned with torques and bracelets – than people from any other nation, with the Medes second. (In fact, in terms of numbers, the Medes were not inferior to the Persians – but they were less formidable.) The grand total, cavalry included, came to three hundred thousand men.

[114] At the same time as Mardonius was choosing his troops, and while Xerxes was still in Thessaly, there came an oracle from Delphi to the Lacedaemonians, telling them to demand from Xerxes blood-satisfaction for Leonidas, and to accept whatever his offer might be. So the Spartiates immediately sent a herald; and once he had caught up with the mass of the army in Thessaly, he came into the presence of Xerxes and delivered this speech: 'The Lacedaemonians and the descendants of Heracles from Sparta[67] demand blood-satisfaction from you, O King of the Medes, for the murder of their king, killed while defending Greece.' At this, Xerxes laughed; and then, after a long pause, he pointed to Mardonius, who happened to be standing beside him, and declared, 'You want satisfaction? Very well, then! Mardonius here will give you all the satisfaction you deserve.'

[115] On receiving this reply the herald departed, while Xerxes left Mardonius behind in Thessaly, and set out himself with all speed for the crossing-point on the Hellespont, which it took him forty-five days to reach at the head of what might, without exaggeration, be described as the merest remnant of his army. Their journey there had seen them seize and devour the crops of everyone in their path – no matter where they

happened to be, and no matter who their hosts. If there were no crops to be found, then they would feed on the grass that was growing in the ground, and eat bark stripped from the trees and leaves ripped off them as well, cultivated and wild alike, leaving nothing behind. This they did because of their terrible hunger. Plague had the army in its grip too, and dysentery, which wrought devastation the whole journey long. The sick were left behind by Xerxes, who would billet them on whatever city they happened to have reached at that stage of their march, there to be cared for and fed – some in Thessaly, some in Macedonia and some at Siris in Paeonia. It was in Siris that Xerxes, while marching on Greece, had left behind the sacred chariot of Zeus; but he was unable to reclaim it on his return journey, because the Paeonians had given it to the Thracians, and told Xerxes, when he demanded it back, that while out grazing the mares had been rustled by some Thracians who lived deep inland, near where the River Strymon has its source.

[116] It was at this stage that the Thracian who ruled as king of the Bisaltians and the land of Crestonia did a truly monstrous thing. Declaring that he had no wish to be the slave of Xerxes, he had taken to the heights of Mount Rhodope, and publicly forbidden his sons from joining the campaign against Greece. But they had paid him no attention (either that, or they were just desperate to witness the war) and had joined the Persian's forces. All six of them made it back in one piece; but their father, to punish them for what they had done, gouged out their eyes.

[117] Such was the coin in which they were paid. Meanwhile, the Persians, after leaving Thrace, arrived at the crossing-point, where they stampeded onto the ships and over the Hellespont to Abydus. The reason for this was their discovery that the pontoons had been loosened in a storm and were no longer securely fastened. The survivors were better provisioned at Abydus, where they stayed a while, than they had been on the road – but even so, the undisciplined way in which they gorged themselves, and the change of water too, meant that many of them perished. The remnants of the army then made it with Xerxes to Sardis.

[118] There is also another story told, according to which Xerxes, after retreating from Athens as far as Eion on the Strymon, abandoned the land route; entrusting Hydarnes with the responsibility for bringing the army to the Hellespont, Xerxes himself continued onwards to Asia

on board a Phoenician ship. During the course of this voyage, he was overtaken by a violent wind – the Strymonian – which whipped the sea up into a frenzy. What made the storm all the more threatening was that the deck of the ship was packed with the numerous Persians who were making the journey with Xerxes. So overcome by terror was the King that he yelled out to the helmsman, demanding to know what, if anything, they could do to be saved. 'Nothing, Master,' he answered. 'Unless, that is, we get rid of all these people on board.' The story goes that Xerxes, when he heard this, made an announcement. 'Now is your chance, men of Persia, to demonstrate the depth of your concern for your king. It would seem, you see, that my salvation is in your hands.' These words of his saw the Persians do him obeisance, and then hurl themselves out into the sea; and the ship, now much lightened, duly made it safely to Asia. What Xerxes did, the moment he had disembarked, was to give the helmsman a golden crown as a reward for saving the life of the King; and then – because he had brought so many Persians to their deaths – to cut off his head.

[119] Personally, however, I give no credence to this alternative account of Xerxes' return, since the story seems entirely bogus to me, in particular what happened to the Persians. For, surely, if the helmsman really spoke to Xerxes as reported, then not even one in ten thousand would dispute what the King's action would have been: namely, to send all those on deck – who were, after all, not simply Persian, but the very elite of Persian society – down into the ship's hold, and to eject a matching number of oarsmen (these, of course, being mere Phoenicians) into the sea. Rather, as I said earlier, he made his return to Asia along the same road as taken by everyone else in his army.

[120] There is one decisive piece of evidence for this. It is perfectly clear that Xerxes' journey back must have brought him to Abdera, since he made a pact of friendship with the Abderites, and presented them with a golden *akinakes* and a *tiara* spangled with gold. The Abderites themselves say (although personally I do not believe the story for one moment) that Xerxes never once loosened his belt the whole time he was making his escape back from Athens, and only in Abdera did he finally feel safe enough to do so. Anyway, the point is that Abdera is located closer to the Hellespont than the Strymon and Eion – which is where he is said to have boarded the ship.

*

[121] Once the Greeks found themselves unable to take Andros, they turned instead to Carystus and laid waste its territory, before returning to Salamis. Now, the first thing they did there was to set aside first-fruits victory-offerings for the gods,[68] among which were three Phoenician triremes: one of them to be dedicated at the Isthmus, where it still remains to my day, one at Sunium and one at Salamis itself, dedicated to Ajax. Then, after they had divided up the booty, they sent first-fruits victory-offerings to Delphi; these paid for a statue of a man, 12 cubits high, holding the beak of a ship in his hand. It stands in the same spot as the gold statue of Alexander the Macedonian.[69]

[122] After the Greeks had sent the first-fruits victory-offerings to Delphi, they all asked the god whether he was pleased by the first fruits he had received, and whether they were adequate. The god answered that he was pleased by the contributions of all the Greeks, excepting only that of the Aeginetans, from whom he demanded the prize for valour awarded them after the battle of Salamis. The Aeginetans, informed of this, duly made a dedication of three gold stars, which can be found attached to a bronze mast in the corner nearest the mixing-bowl dedicated by Croesus.

[123] Once the spoils had been portioned out, the Greeks set sail for the Isthmus to award a prize for valour[70] to the Greek who, over the course of the war, had demonstrated that he best deserved it. On arrival, the commanders cast their votes on the altar of Poseidon for those who, in their opinion, ranked first and second overall. Each commander thought that he personally had proved the best, and accordingly voted for himself – but the consensus of the majority was that Themistocles ranked second. In the first round everyone won only a single vote; but in the second, Themistocles was decisively the winner.

[124] So jealous did this make the other Greeks that they refused to name anyone the winner, and sailed off back to their own cities without having reached a final decision. Yet, for all that, the name of Themistocles was bruited far and wide across the Greek world, nor was there any other man among the Greeks whose reputation for cleverness even remotely approached his. All the same, his victory received no formal ratification from the combatants at Salamis; and so it was, immediately after the vote, that he turned up in Lacedaemon, in the hope of picking up some honours there. And sure enough, the Lacedaemonians gave him the most splendid welcome, and did indeed festoon him with hon-

ours. Granted, they gave the prize for valour, in the form of an olive wreath, to Eurybiadas; but they gave an olive wreath to Themistocles as well, in recognition of his cleverness and the sharpness of his wits. They also presented him with the most beautiful chariot in Sparta. Then, after they had lavished him with praise, three hundred select Spartiates – the 'Horsemen', as they are known[71] – when he left accompanied him as far as the frontier with Tegea. No other man in history, so far as we know, has ever had an escort of Spartiates.[72]

[125] When Themistocles returned to Athens from Lacedaemon, a man from Aphidnae called Timodemus, whose loathing for Themistocles was the only thing that had ever remotely served to distinguish him, was so maddened by envy that he railed at Themistocles, condemning him for his visit to Lacedaemon, and declaring that the honours paid him by the Lacedaemonians were owing to Athens, not himself. Timodemus refused to desist until Themistocles finally put a stop to it by retorting, 'Yes, you are perfectly right – I would never have been honoured by the Spartiates had I come from Belbina.[73] But nor will you be, my friend – even though you come from Athens.'

[126] Artabazus, the son of Pharnaces – a man who had always been held in high regard among the Persians, and whose reputation would stand even higher in the wake of the Plataean campaign[74] – had escorted the King to the crossing-point, together with sixty thousand of the troops chosen by Mardonius. Then, once the King was in Asia, he headed back and stopped at Pallene, where he found the people of Potidaea in revolt. Mardonius was wintering in Thessaly and Macedonia, and because Artabazus himself was in no particular hurry to rejoin the rest of the army, he decided that it was his duty to reduce the Potidaeans to slavery. The Potidaeans, you see, had raised the banner of revolt against the Barbarians the moment the King's retreat had passed them by, and after the flight of the Persian fleet from Salamis. This revolt was general across Pallene.

[127] So Artabazus put Potidaea under siege. He also besieged the Olynthians, whom he suspected of contemplating rebellion against the King. (Olynthus had been seized by the Bottiaeans after their expulsion by the Macedonians from the Gulf of Therma.) Once the siege had secured the city for Artabazus, he led the inhabitants down to a lake and had them massacred, and handed control of the city over to Critobulus

of Torone, and to the people of Chalcidice – which is how the Chalcidians came by Olynthus.

[128] With Olynthus captured, Artabazus devoted all his energies to Potidaea, and prosecuted the siege with such vigour that Timoxeinus, the commander of the Scionaeans, agreed to turn traitor; quite how contact was first established I cannot say, since there is no account of it, but the end result I *can* describe. Whenever Timoxeinus wished to send a letter he had written to Artabazus – or indeed if Artabazus wanted to send one to Timoxeinus – he would wrap the letter around an arrow, at the end where the feathers go, then add feathers to the shaft, and fire the arrow at an agreed spot. Timoxeinus' betrayal of Potidaea was discovered. In due course, you see, one of Artabazus' shots missed its agreed target, and instead struck a man from Potidaea in the shoulder; a crowd of people, as will invariably happen in war when someone is hit, rushed up to the man and gathered around him; then, in quick succession, they grabbed hold of the arrow, noticed the letter and took it to the high command. (Also present were allies from the other cities of Pallene.) Even though the generals were able to identity the traitor by reading the letter, they decided, for the sake of the city of Scione, not to have Timoxeinus executed – since otherwise, the Scionaeans would forever after be considered traitors.

[129] So that was how Timoxeinus came to be found out.[75] Meanwhile, Artabazus had been laying siege to Potidaea for three months when something happened: the sea retreated an immense distance, so that for a long while there was nothing but shallows. When the Barbarians noticed this, they set off over to Pallene. They were only two fifths of the way across, though, with three fifths of the way still to go before they actually made it into Pallene, when the sea came sweeping back with tremendous force – so much so, in fact, that the locals describe the wave as having been bigger than any of the many other such flood-tides. Those who could not swim drowned, while those who could swim were killed by the Potidaeans, who had sallied out in their boats. Demonstrably, the Potidaeans say, the wave and what happened to the Persians are to be explained by the fact that those Persians who ended up in a watery grave were the same as had desecrated the statue of Poseidon in his temple on the edge of the city. Personally, I find this explanation a thoroughly convincing one.[76] As for Artabazus, he led his surviving troops off to Mardonius in Thessaly.

*

[130] So much for the activities of the men who served as escorts to the King. As for the remnants of Xerxes' fleet, their flight from Salamis brought them to Asia, where they ferried the King and his army from the Chersonese across to Abydus, and afterwards wintered in Cyme. Then, the moment the weather began to brighten, early in spring, they assembled at Samos, where some of the fleet had already passed the winter. Most of the marines were either Persians or Medes. Mardontes, the son of Bagaeus, and Artaÿntes, the son of Artachaees, came to serve as their commanders. Also joining the high command, at Artaÿntes' request, was his fraternal nephew, Ithamitres. Because the fleet had suffered a knockout blow, and no one was pressuring them to advance any further west, they kept to their positions in Samos to ensure that the Ionians did not revolt – three hundred ships in all, the Ionian squadrons included. Not that they really thought the Greeks would come to Ionia; instead, extrapolating from the fact that their enemies, far from attempting to pursue them after their flight from Salamis, had seemed relieved to be rid of them, they rather took for granted that the Greeks would be content to patrol their own waters. Nevertheless, even though the morale of the Persians serving with the fleet had taken a beating, they had no doubt that Mardonius would win a decisive victory by land. So they stayed in Samos, plotting among themselves what damage they might do to the enemy, while keeping their ears to the ground for news of how things were faring with Mardonius.

[131] In fact, the coming of spring and the presence of Mardonius in Thessaly did stir the Greeks to action. Although there was still no mustering of the land-forces, the fleet – one hundred and ten ships in all – docked in Aegina. The supreme commander, by land as well as by sea, was Leotychidas, the son of Menares, who was from the other of the two royal houses,[77] and could trace his ancestry back through Hegesileos, Hippocratidas, Leotychidas, Anaxilaus, Archidamus, Anaxandridas, Theopompus, Nicander, Charileos, Eunomus, Polydectes, Prytanis, Euryphon, Procles, Aristodemus, Aristomachus, Cleodaeus and Hyllos to Heracles. All of these – except for the seven listed immediately after Leotychidas – had been kings of Sparta. The Athenian commander was Xanthippus, the son of Ariphron.[78]

[132] With the entire fleet assembled at Aegina, a delegation of Ionians arrived at the Greek base; only a short while before they had visited Sparta, where they had been begging the Lacedaemonians to liberate

Ionia. These messengers – one of whom was Herodotus, the son of Basileïdes[79] – had originally been seven in number: a cell of conspirators whose object had been to assassinate Strattis, the tyrant of Chios. Their plot, though, had been brought to light when one of the group had betrayed the venture; and so the remaining six, after smuggling themselves out of Chios, had gone first to Sparta, and then, as I just mentioned now, to Aegina, where they asked the Greeks to sweep down in their ships upon Ionia. In the event, they did manage to get the Greek fleet as far as Delos – but even that was an effort. To the Greeks, you see, everywhere beyond Delos was unknown territory:[80] they imagined it rife with terrors and positively teeming with the enemy. Why, to the best of their knowledge, Samos was as far distant as the Pillars of Heracles! And so it was that the Barbarians, demoralized as they were, could not muster the courage to sail west of Samos, while the Greeks, despite the appeals of the Chians, refused to venture east of Delos. As a result, fear stood on guard over the middle ground between them.

[133] So the Greeks sailed to Delos. Mardonius, meanwhile, had been wintering in Thessaly. From there, he sent a man from Europus called Mys on a tour of the oracles, with orders to visit all the ones he could and see what answers they gave. What Mardonius was hoping to learn from the oracles when he issued these instructions, I cannot say for sure. There is no tradition of it, you see. That said, it does seem to me that the mission could only have been connected to the prevailing state of affairs.

[134] It is certainly the case that this Mys visited Lebadeia, where he bribed a local man to go down into the cave of Trophonius, and to the oracle at Abae, in Phocis. The first place he visited, though, was Thebes: here, not only did he consult the oracle of Ismenian Apollo (where, as at Olympia, the oracular responses are read in the sacrificial victims), but he also paid someone to go and sleep in the shrine of Amphiaraus. This person was not a Theban, but a foreigner – it being forbidden for the Thebans to consult the oracle there. The reason for this is that Amphiaraus, speaking through his oracle, had ordered them to choose one of two alternatives: either to have him exclusively as an oracle, or else to have him as an ally, but not an oracle. The Thebans opted to have him as an ally – and that is why no one from Thebes is permitted to sleep inside his shrine.

[135] Anyway, at the time in question, so the Thebans report, something happened which I consider a great miracle – and it took place

during the tour that Mys of Europus made of all the oracles, when he came to the temple precinct of Ptoian Apollo. (This particular sanctuary, which is called the Ptoïüm and belongs to the Thebans, stands on the heights above Lake Copaïs, near to the city of Acraephia.) When this man, the one called Mys, visited the shrine, he was accompanied by three men who had been nominated by their fellow-citizens to write down whatever the god might say; and sure enough, the moment they went in, the prophet did indeed begin to speak – but in a barbarian tongue! The Thebans who had come with Mys were astounded to hear a foreign language being spoken rather than Greek, and could make neither head nor tail of what was going on. But Mys of Europus, snatching from their hands the writing-tablet they had brought with them, began writing down what the prophet was saying, which he explained was in Carian;[81] and then, when he had finished transcribing it, he left and headed back to Thessaly.

[136] Once Mardonius had studied what the oracles had to say, he sent a man from Macedonia – Alexander, the son of Amyntas – off to Athens with a message. One reason for appointing him to this mission was that Alexander, in Persian terms, counted almost as family, since his sister – Gygaea, the daughter of Amyntas – had married a man from Persia called Bubares; this couple had a son, Amyntas of Asia, who took his name from his maternal grandfather, and was graced by the King with the revenues of the great Phrygian city of Alabanda. A second reason for sending Alexander was the discovery by Mardonius that he ranked as an official Representative and Benefactor of the Athenian people. Who better, then, Mardonius reflected, to win over the Athenians? Word was, after all, that they were a numerous and valiant people – and it was chiefly thanks to their efforts, as Mardonius well knew, that the Persians had suffered defeat by sea. Only win them to his side, then, and Mardonius expected – perfectly justifiably – that naval supremacy would simply drop into his lap; while by land he reckoned the supremacy already his. That, surely, he thought, would enable him to beat the Greeks. It may be too that this was what he had been told by the oracles, and that they had advised him to forge an alliance with the Athenians. Perhaps, then, it was in obedience to them that he sent Alexander.

[137] Now, this Alexander was descended through seven generations from Perdiccas, who obtained the rule of Macedonia in the following manner. Three brothers of the line of Temenus – Gauanes, Aëropus and

Perdiccas – fled Argos for the land of the Illyrians, from where they crossed into the highlands of Macedonia and arrived in the city of Lebaea. There, they hired themselves out as labourers to the king: one of them looked after the horses at pasture, one served as a cowherd and one – the youngest, Perdiccas – tended to the small stock-animals. Now, back in the days of old, it was not only the common people who lacked the money to throw their weight around, but the very rulers as well. Why, the labourers' food was cooked for them by the king's own wife! Whenever she baked bread, the loaf intended for the young labourer, Perdiccas, would swell up to twice the normal size. Again and again this happened – and so she mentioned it to her husband. As he listened, it immediately dawned upon him that this was a portent, indicating something momentous. He duly summoned the labourers and told them to leave his land. They would go, they replied, once they had been paid the wages they were owed. Now, as the king was listening to their talk of wages, so the rays of the sun were streaming down into the house through the smoke-hole; and the king, unbalanced by some god, pointed to the sunbeams and declared: 'There! I'll give you your wages! They are all the wages you deserve!' The two elder brothers, Gauanes and Aëropus, were so dumbfounded when they heard this that they just stood rooted to the spot; but the boy, who happened to have a large knife with him, declared: 'We accept your gift, O King!' and then, using his knife, traced the circle of sunlight on the floor of the house, drew its light into his lap three times and left with his brothers.

[138] After they had gone, the king's counsellors explained to him the significance of what the boy had done, and with what shrewdness, despite being the youngest of the three, he had accepted the gift. When he heard this, the king was thrown into a rage and sent horsemen after the brothers to kill them. Now, there is a river in the region to which the descendants of the three Argives offer sacrifices – because it was this river[82] that was the saviour of the Temenids. After they had forded it, its currents began to flow with such force that the horsemen proved unable to make the crossing. The brothers reached a different region of Macedonia, and settled there, near the gardens which are said to have belonged to Midas, the son of Gordias, and where roses grow spontaneously, sixty blooms to every bush, and sweeter-smelling than any other flower. It was in these gardens, so the Macedonians claim, that Silenus was captured. They lie at the foot of a mountain called Bermium, which

is so snow-bound as to be inaccessible. The brothers seized control of the region, and then embarked on a career of conquest that secured them the rest of Macedonia too.

[139] This was the Perdiccas from whom Alexander was descended, as follows: Alexander was the son of Amyntas and Amyntas of Alcetas; the father of Alcetas was Aëropus, whose father was Philippus, and his father was Argaeus, who was the son of Perdiccas, the founder of the dynasty.

[140] Such was the lineage of Alexander, the son of Amyntas. When he arrived in Athens on his mission from Mardonius, he delivered this speech. 'Men of Athens, here are the words of Mardonius. "I have received the following message from the King: 'To the Athenians, despite the wrongs they have done me, I grant a total amnesty. This is the course of action, Mardonius, you are to adopt. Restore to them their land, and in addition let them choose another block of territory, whichever one they like – and grant them self-rule. Also, you are to rebuild all the temples of theirs that I burned down – provided, that is, they are indeed willing to come to terms.' I am obliged by the arrival of this message to do as it says – unless, of course, you give me cause to ignore it. So I say to you this. How can you be such utter lunatics as to prosecute a war against the King? You cannot defeat him, nor even hold out against him for any length of time. You saw for yourselves the sheer scale of Xerxes' army, and all that it accomplished. You are familiar as well with my own current weight of arms. Even if you do overcome us and emerge victorious – an eventuality which you would have to be wildly optimistic to think possible! – another task-force, many times the size of ours, will merely replace it. That being so, you will never be a match for the King. Do you really want to have your lands taken away from you, and be on the run for the rest of your lives? No, you must come to terms. And my, what terms they are! The King could not be more favourably inclined towards you! Enter into a military compact with us, then, without treachery, without deceit, and you shall have your freedom."

'That was what Mardonius, men of Athens, instructed me to tell you. As for myself, I am not going to harp upon the goodwill I bear you, since it would hardly be the first time that it has been brought to your attention – but I really do wish that you would do as Mardonius urges. I cannot see what chance you have in the long run of continuing your war against Xerxes – and if I had thought you had any chance at all, then I would never have come to you and urged this case. The power of the King is something more than human, and his reach is exceedingly long. That being so, I fear for you, should you not agree terms right now, when the terms he is willing to offer you are so very favourable. More than any of the other allies, after all, it is you who stand in the line of fire. It is you, and you alone, who will suffer repeated ruin. Why, the land you possess might almost have been designed to serve the opposing forces as a no man's land! So do as you are being urged. How – when the Great King is prepared to forgive you, alone among the Greeks, the harm you have done him, and when he wishes to be your friend – how can it not be worth your while?'

[141] So that was what Alexander had to say. Meanwhile, the news that he had come to Athens with the aim of bringing the Athenians into a compact with the Barbarian had reached the Lacedaemonians, who were reminded by it of oracles[83] which warned that they, and all the other Dorians too, were destined to be cast out of the Peloponnese by the Medes and the Athenians; and so thoroughly alarmed were they at the prospect of the Athenians coming to terms with the Persian that they decided, without delay, to dispatch envoys of their own. In fact, things so fell out that they were introduced simultaneously with Alexander. The reason for this was that the Athenians had been spinning things out and twiddling their thumbs – conscious as they were that the presence of an envoy bringing peace terms from the Barbarian was bound to come to the attention of the Lacedaemonians, and prompt them to send a delegation with all speed. The delay, then, had been quite deliberate, and was designed to demonstrate to the Lacedaemonians the Athenian cast of mind.

[142] Once Alexander had finished his speech, it was the turn of the Spartan envoys to speak. 'We have been sent by the Lacedaemonians', they declared, 'to beg you not to adopt any unsettlingly new strategy that might be detrimental to the Greek cause, and to close your ears to the words of the Barbarian. Such a crime would be a blot upon the people of any city in Greece – but upon you more than any other, and for a whole number of reasons. We did not wish for this war, after all – it was you who went and stirred things up, and whose lands were originally at stake in the contest. Now, the impact of that same struggle is being felt by the whole of Greece. But even setting all that aside, how

intolerable it would be were the Athenians to bear responsibility for the enslavement of Greece, when you have always shown yourselves, since ancient times, to be the liberators of any number of peoples.[84] That said, we do empathize with you in your difficulties – we appreciate that you have already lost two harvests, and that for a long while now your homes have been nothing but rubble. Accordingly, by way of compensation, the Lacedaemonians and their allies make this declaration: that we will maintain your women and all the non-combatant members of your households for as long as this war may last. Alexander of Macedon can present Mardonius' proposals as smoothly as he likes – but do not be taken in! He has no choice but to behave the way he does. Tyrant that he is, after all, he is naturally a tyrant's accomplice. But such a course of action is not for you – not if you have any sense, that is – since barbarians, as you know full well, are not to be trusted, and they never speak the truth.' And that was what the envoys said.

[143] The Athenian response to Alexander was as follows. 'We are well aware that the power of the Mede massively exceeds our own, thank you, and so there is no call to rub our noses in the fact. It diminishes our commitment to freedom not an iota. We shall still defend ourselves to the very limits of our ability. There is no point your trying to persuade us to come to terms with the Barbarian – we shall never change our minds. Go and tell Mardonius that the Athenians have a message for him. "For as long as the sun holds to its current course, we shall never come to terms with Xerxes. Rather, confident in the backing of the gods and heroes for whom he showed such contempt that he burned down their temples and cult-statues, we shall go out and defend ourselves on the field of battle." As for you, never again appear before the Athenians with anything that resembles this proposal. Do you really think that by inciting us to commit sacrilege you are doing us a favour? Representative and friend of the Athenians that you are, we would hate to see you come to any harm at our hands.'

[144] Then, having given this reply to Alexander, they delivered their response to the envoys from Sparta. 'Maybe it was only human for the Lacedaemonians to fear that we would come to an arrangement with the Barbarian. Nevertheless, your anxiety does you no credit, bearing in mind what you know of the Athenian spirit. There is nowhere so rich in gold, not in all the world – no, nor any land so beautiful and fertile, putting all others in the shade – that we would be willing to accept it in

exchange for collaborating with the Medes, and enslaving Greece. Even were we so inclined, there is a whole host of pressing reasons why we could never adopt such a course of action. First and foremost, the cult-statues and temples of the gods have been left as charred rubble. How, when these are crying out to us for vengeance, could we possibly make a settlement with the culprits? On top of that, there is the fact that we are all of us Greeks,[85] of one blood and one tongue, united by the temples that we have raised to the gods, and by the way in which we offer them sacrifice, and by the customs that we have in common. For the Athenians to prove traitors to all this would be a terrible thing. What you should realize – in case it had previously escaped your notice – is that while there still remains even a single Athenian alive, we shall never come to terms with Xerxes. That said, we do appreciate the consideration you have shown us by anticipating the ruin faced by our householders, and by your willingness to support our families. We are full of gratitude! All the same, we will persevere as we are, thank you, and not put you to such trouble. That being the situation, send an army as fast as you can. We doubt that it will take the Barbarian long to get here, since his invasion will come the moment he receives our message and learns that we are rejecting his offer outright. In short, the only way to pre-empt the invasion of Attica is for you to get to Boeotia, and swiftly.'[86] Then, after the Athenians had delivered this reply, the envoys returned to Sparta.

BOOK NINE

[1] On Alexander's return from Athens, he communicated what the Athenians had said to Mardonius, who then promptly set out from Thessaly for Athens at the head of his army. As he went, he drafted everyone who lay along his path. The Thessalian leaders, far from regretting their earlier actions, only cheered on the Persian the more – so much so, indeed, that Thorax of Larissa, who had already accompanied Xerxes on his retreat, had no hesitation at all now about encouraging Mardonius to attack Greece.

[2] When the army, in the course of its advance, came to Boeotia, the Thebans tried to detain Mardonius there by urging upon him that this was by far the best place for him to base his forces, and advised him not to go any further; instead he should stay where he was, and work at conquering all Greece by non-military means. If the Greeks continued to present the same united front as they had done previously, so the Thebans argued, then it would be difficult for anyone – no matter who – to get the better of them by sheer force of arms. 'But if you do as we recommend,' they said, 'you will have no difficulty in foiling all their plans. Send money to the power-brokers in their various cities, and Greece will be riven by factions.[1] It will then be a simple matter for you to subjugate those who remain opposed to you by deploying your partisans against them.'

[3] This advice of theirs, however, failed to sway Mardonius, who had been consumed by a terrible longing to capture Athens a second time – partly out of sheer contumely, and partly because he was picturing in his mind's eye how beacons would blaze across the islands alerting the King, who was then in Sardis, to the fact that Athens was his. Once again, though, on arriving in Attica, the Barbarians found no trace of

the Athenians, most of whom, so Mardonius was informed, were on Salamis with their fleet – with the result that what he captured was a ghost-town. Nine months separated the city's original capture by the King and this subsequent invasion by Mardonius.

[4] While in Athens, he sent a man from the Hellespont called Mury-chides over to Salamis, bearing the same terms that Alexander of Macedon had already conveyed to the Athenians. Mardonius sent this second message because – although in no doubt about the hostile opin-ion held of him by the Athenians – he hoped, now that he had won Attica at spear-point, and the entire region was his, they would abandon their obstinacy. Hence his sending of Murychides to Salamis.

[5] On arrival, Murychides duly delivered Mardonius' message to the Council. One of the Council members, Lycides, then declared that in his view they would be best off welcoming the terms that Murychides had brought them, and submitting the issue to the people. He had been prompted to announce this opinion by a bribe from Mardonius – either that, or by genuine conviction. The Athenians, both the members of the Council and those outside it, were appalled when they learned what Lycides had said – and although the Hellespontine was sent away unharmed, they surrounded Lycides himself and stoned him to death. Indeed, such was the uproar in Salamis over the matter that the women of Athens were alerted to it, with one calling out to another, until a whole lot of women had been recruited; they then descended unbidden upon the house of Lycides, and stoned his wife and children to death.

[6] How was it that the Athenians had crossed over to Salamis? For as long they expected an army from the Peloponnese to assist them, they had remained where they were in Attica. But with the Peloponnesians dragging things out and neglecting to act, news that the invader was actually already in Boeotia prompted the Athenians to stage a mass evacuation of themselves and their property across to Salamis, and then to send an embassy to Lacedaemon with two messages; first, a reproach to the Lacedaemonians for having turned a blind eye to the invasion of Attica rather than accompanying them into Boeotia to confront the Bar-barian; second, a reminder of the various incentives that the Persians had offered them to change sides. 'Refuse to help the Athenians', the messengers were to state, 'and they will find such a bolt-hole as they may.'

[7] Now, at the time, the Lacedaemonians were celebrating a festival –

the Hyacinthia,[2] to be exact – and they felt that it was of the utmost importance to pay the god his due. Simultaneously, the wall they were building across the Isthmus was by this point coming to be topped with battlements. Accordingly, when the messengers from Athens arrived, as part of a delegation that also included Megarians and Plataeans, they came before the ephors, and said:

'The Athenians have sent us to tell you that the King of the Medes is offering to return us our land. Not only that, but he wishes to forge an alliance with us, on fair and equal terms, without treachery or deception, and is willing to give us, as well as our own country, an additional block of land – whichever we choose. But we, rather than coming to an agreement with him, have instead bowed our heads before great Zeus of all the Greeks, and reflected just how terrible a thing it would be to betray Greece. So it was – despite the criminal lack of good faith with which Greeks have been treating us, and our appreciation that it would be far better for us to settle with the Persian rather than to fight him – we turned his offer down. We shall never voluntarily come to terms. In our dealings with the Greeks, what you get is the genuine article.

'As for you – how abject was the state of terror in which you turned up, when you imagined that we might indeed be coming to terms with the Persian! But then, not only did you come to appreciate, beyond all shadow of a doubt, that we were resolved never to betray Greece, but you also drew close to finishing your wall across the Isthmus – with the result that now you pay the Athenians no attention at all. You went back on your word that you would confront the Persian in Boeotia, and you turned a blind eye to the Barbarian's invasion of Attica. No wonder, then, that the Athenians should currently feel such fury towards you! Your behaviour has been utterly unacceptable. That being so, they summon you now to join them by sending an army as fast as you can so that we may meet the Barbarian in Attica. Now that we have lost Boeotia, the best place to give battle is on our territory – in the Thriasian plain.'

[8] Once the ephors had heard this out, they asked for a day to give their reply – and then, when the next day arrived, for another day on top of that. For ten whole days they kept this up, putting things off from day to day. The whole while, all the Peloponnesians were racing as one to finish the wall across the Isthmus – and were almost done. Quite why, when Alexander of Macedon appeared in Athens, they should have got into such a palaver at the prospect of the Athenians going over to the

Medes, whereas now it bothered them not at all, I cannot say – unless it be that by this stage they had completed the wall across the Isthmus and felt they no longer needed the Athenians. When Alexander came to Attica, after all, the building of the wall was yet to be completed, and their terror of the Persians was still keeping them busy at their labours.

[9] Eventually, though, the Spartiates' response was to set out with an army. It came about this way. On the day before what was scheduled to be the final audience, a man from Tegea called Chileos – someone who exerted a greater influence at Sparta than any other foreigner – got from the ephors a full account of what the Athenians had been saying. 'Now, this is the situation, Ephors,' he told them, once he had heard them out. 'If the Athenians break with us and ally themselves to the Barbarian, then no matter how strong the wall we have built across the Isthmus, it makes no difference – the gates to the Peloponnese will still yawn wide open before the Persian. Therefore, listen to the Athenians – and do so before they change their minds and bring about the fall of Greece.'

[10] That was the advice he gave them. They registered his point immediately, and while it was still night,[3] without breathing so much as a word to the messengers who had arrived from the various cities, they dispatched five thousand Spartiates, together with a retinue of helots, seven per man.[4] As commander they appointed Pausanias, the son of Cleombrotus. Strictly speaking, the command belonged to Pleistarchus, the son of Leonidas – but he was still a boy, and Pausanias was both his guardian and his first cousin. (Cleombrotus, the son of Anaxandridas, who was the father of Pausanias, was no longer alive, having died shortly after leading back from the Isthmus the army that had built the wall. The explanation for his withdrawal of the army from the Isthmus was this: as he was offering pre-battle sacrifices against the Persians, the sun had turned dark.[5]) To share the command with him, Pausanias chose a man from his own house: Euryanax,[6] the son of Dorieus. So Pausanias headed off from Sparta, together with his men.

[11] Next day, the messengers – who had no idea that the army had set out – came before the ephors, fully intending themselves to depart, each to his own city. 'You men of Lacedaemon', they said on arrival, 'are just staying right here, celebrating the Hyacinthia, and frolicking like children, letting your allies go hang. This criminal behaviour of yours will leave us Athenians, deserted as we have been by our allies, no choice but to make peace with the Persian as best we can. That we shall indeed

end up allies of the King is self-evident – and then, once the terms are negotiated, we shall go with his forces wherever we are led. In this way, perhaps, the consequences of your inaction will be brought home to you.' So said the messengers – whereupon the ephors declared on oath that the Spartiates, to the best of their knowledge, had already got as far as Orestheum in the course of their march against the 'foreigners'. ('Foreigners' is the word they used to describe non-Greeks.)[7] Their opposite numbers, bemused by this, then asked for an explanation; when this demand resulted in a full report, they were astounded and set off after the Spartiates as fast as they could. Nor were they the only ones to do so, for with them went an elite force of five thousand Lacedaemonians, drawn from the settlements around Sparta.

[12] On, then, they sped to the Isthmus. But the Argives, when they discovered that Pausanias and his men had set out from Sparta, immediately dispatched the fastest long-distance runner they could find as a herald to Attica, since they had earlier given a commitment to Mardonius that they would block any attempt by the Spartiates to leave the Peloponnese. 'Mardonius,' the runner declared, once he had arrived in Athens, 'I have been sent by the Argives to inform you that the youth of Lacedaemon are on their way, and that the Argives lack the strength to stop them from leaving the Peloponnese. That being so, plan wisely – and good luck.'

[13] Then, once he had delivered this message, off he set back home; and Mardonius, with the news ringing in his ears, no longer had any relish for stopping in Attica. Before the briefing, he had deliberately restrained himself, since he had wanted to see what policy the Athenians would adopt – and indeed, expecting that they would come to terms with him, had inflicted no damage, nor ravaged Attica at all. But this had failed to sway the Athenians; and Mardonius, now that he had been given the full picture, duly put Athens to the torch, pulling down any stretch of city wall, house or shrine that had been left standing, until all was rubble, and then, before Pausanias and his force could reach the Isthmus, staged a retreat. This withdrawal had been prompted by the fact that Attica was unsuited to cavalry;[8] additionally, in the event of giving battle and losing, his men would have no line of retreat save for a narrow pass, such that even a tiny force of men would be able to block them. For these reasons, his plan was to pull back to Thebes and give battle there, amid the horse country of a friendly city.

[14] During the course of this slow retreat, while Mardonius was still on the road, there came news that another army – an advance guard of a thousand Lacedaemonians – had arrived at Megara. This information prompted Mardonius to a change of plan, since he wanted if at all possible to take them prisoner. So he turned his army round and led it towards Megara. His cavalry preceded him, and overran the entire territory of Megara. This was the furthest west that Persian forces in Europe ever reached.

[15] Then news reached Mardonius that the Greeks were massed at the Isthmus. He duly went back via Decelea. The leaders of the Boeotians had sent for their near neighbours, the people of the Asopus valley, to show the way – which they did, first as far as Sphendaleis, and from there on to Tanagra. At Tanagra, Mardonius made camp for the night, before the next day heading for Scolus, and crossing onto Theban soil. Here, despite the fact that the Thebans were collaborating with him, he stripped the landscape bare – not with any hostile intent, but rather out of sheer necessity, since it was his ambition to build a stockade around his camp, and thereby provide his men with a place of refuge should his offer of battle disappoint his hopes for it. His army made camp along the River Asopus, with positions which extended from Erythrae, past Hysiae, and all the way into Plataean territory. The stockade itself, however, was not built on this scale; instead, each of its sides was approximately 10 stades long.

While the Barbarians were busy labouring away at it, a man from Thebes called Attaginus, the son of Phrynon, prepared a magnificent banquet, to which he invited Mardonius himself and fifty of the most eminent Persians, who accepted the invitation. The banquet was held in Thebes.

[16] The following story I heard from Thersander of Orchomenus,[9] a man of the highest reputation in his own city. Thersander told me that he too was invited by Attaginus to the banquet, together with fifty men from Thebes, and that the Thebans and the Persians, rather than being kept apart, were instead placed together – one Theban and one Persian to every couch. After the meal was over, they continued drinking; and the Persian who was sharing Thersander's couch asked him, in Greek, where he came from. 'Orchomenus,' answered Thersander. Then the Persian said, 'Now that we have shared a table, and poured a libation from the same cup, I would like to leave you with memorials of my

thoughts. In that way, your eyes will be opened to what is coming, and you will be able to plan ahead, with your own best interests in mind. Just look at these Persians, busy with their banqueting, and gaze upon the army we left camped out along the river. So many to see – and yet, in just a short time, only a fraction of them will survive.' And even as the Persian said this, the tears poured down his cheeks. Thersander, non-plussed by his comments, asked him, 'Should you not be mentioning this to Mardonius, and to the Persians with him who are particularly well regarded?' 'No, my friend,' he answered. 'There is nothing any man can do to avert what the god has decreed. Even if you speak entirely reliably, no one ever wants to believe you. Plenty of Persians have grasped how things stand – but necessity has us fettered, and so we must follow. Of all the miseries to which men are prey, this is the most hateful – to understand something fully but be impotent to affect it.' All this I heard from Thersander of Orchomenus – and he told me too that he informed people about it then and there, well before the battle came to be fought at Plataea.

[17] With Mardonius camped out in Boeotia, all the Greeks who lived in the region and had gone over to the Medes furnished him with troops, just as they had similarly taken part in the invasion of Athens – all, that is, except for the Phocians. These, while firm enough in their backing for the Medes, were collaborating under duress rather than vol-untarily. Not many days after the arrival of Mardonius in Thebes, a thousand Phocian hoplites turned up. They were led by Harmocydes, a man with the highest reputation among his fellow-citizens. Their arrival at Thebes prompted Mardonius to send horsemen with orders that they were to bivouac by themselves out on the plain. This the Phocians did – and all at once, who should appear but the entire mass of Persian cavalry. A rumour began to spread through the Greek contingents camped out with the Medes that Mardonius was going to have the Phocians brought down with javelins – a rumour which also spread through the ranks of the Phocians themselves. It was then that Harmo-cydes, their commander, delivered a rousing speech along these lines: 'It is clear enough, Phocians, that we are staring at annihilation. These men have come to deal us our deaths – prompted, I imagine, by the slanders of the Thessalians.[10] Every last man among you, then, needs now to prove himself a true man. Better, after all, to meet the end of our allotted spans in action, fighting in our own defence, than tamely to hand

ourselves to be slaughtered – a shameful fate indeed! No, we need to teach each one of them what it means to be Barbarians, and to conspire at the murder of men who are Greeks!'

[18] Such was his rallying cry. The horsemen encircled the Phocians and then charged them with seemingly murderous intent, brandishing their weapons as though to hurl them (and one of them, indeed, may actually have done so). The Phocians, meanwhile, stood firm against the attack, banding together on every side and closing ranks as tightly as they could. At this, the cavalry wheeled around and galloped away. Why they did so, I cannot say with any certainty: perhaps the horsemen had come to wipe out the Phocians at the request of the Thessalians, and then, when they saw the Phocians adopt defensive positions, grew so alarmed at the prospect of the damage they would suffer that they pulled back, as instructed by Mardonius; or perhaps their aim was simply to test the Phocians, and get the measure of their spirit. Anyway, once the cavalrymen had withdrawn, Mardonius sent a herald to the Phocians. 'Have no fear,' he told them. 'You have shown yourselves to be men of great courage – which was not what I had been led to expect. Now, throw yourselves wholeheartedly into this war! Any services that you do me or the King will be more than repaid.' So much for the episode involving the Phocians.

[19] The Lacedaemonians, meanwhile, on reaching the Isthmus, made camp there. The news of this, and the sight of the Spartiates actually taking to the field, decided the remainder of the Peloponnesians (or at least those of them who inclined to the nobler cause) that it would be wrong to be left behind in the wake of the Lacedaemonians. Accordingly, once favourable omens had been obtained, they all set out from the Isthmus, and arrived in Eleusis. There, they made sacrifice again; and then, after the omens had once more proved favourable, they continued on their way, accompanied now by the Athenians, who had crossed over from Salamis and joined forces with them at Eleusis. Into Boeotia they came, and it was there, at Erythrae, that they learned of the barbarian encampment along the Asopus – information which prompted them to take up position on the foothills of Mount Cithaeron.

[20] Confronted by the refusal of the Greeks to come down onto the plain, Mardonius sent his entire force of cavalry against them, under the command of Masistius (or 'Macistius', as the Greeks called him),[11] a man who enjoyed a high reputation among the Persians, and who rode

a Nisaean horse so beautifully caparisoned that even the bridle was made of gold. The cavalry then launched themselves, squadron by squadron, against the Greeks,[12] probing now this position and now that, and inflicting in the process considerable damage on the Greeks, whom they roundly excoriated as women.

[21] Now as chance would have it, the most exposed position of all happened to be occupied by the Megarians, and it was they who bore the brunt of the cavalry onslaught. Indeed, they were put under such pressure by the sustained attacks of the horsemen that they sent a herald to the Greek high command, who declared, on his arrival: 'I bring a message from the Megarians. "Allies! In our current position – which is a post we have been occupying from the very beginning – we lack adequate manpower to withstand the Persian cavalry all on our own. So far, thanks to our perseverance and courage, we have been able to stand firm in the face of the pressure. But be in no doubt – unless you send a relief force now to take our place, we will abandon our position."' This message led Pausanias to enquire of the Greeks whether any of them wished to volunteer to move over to the position, and relieve the Megarians of their post. All of them refused to accept the charge, except for the Athenians – or, more precisely, the elite squad of three hundred commanded by Olympiodorus, the son of Lampon.

[22] These, together with a selection of archers, were the men who volunteered to take up a position at Erythrae, on behalf of the other Greeks present. Long and hard they fought – until finally the battle was resolved. It so happened that wave after wave of cavalry had been launching attacks; during one of these assaults, the horse ridden by Masistius, which was well in advance of the others, took an arrow between its ribs, reared up in agony, and threw Masistius. No sooner had he fallen than the Athenians were on top of him. He did try to fight back, but they grabbed hold of his horse and finished him off – although initially, it is true, they were foiled by his armour. Next to his skin, you see, he was wearing a breastplate made of golden scales, and over it a purple tunic. As a result, the Athenians' blows kept glancing off the breastplate, until one of them, realizing the nature of the problem, struck him in the eye. Only then did he slump to the ground and expire. Somehow, though, the rest of the cavalry failed to notice what had happened. They had been too preoccupied with their wheeling and withdrawing, you see, and so had neither seen him fall from his horse

nor witnessed his death. Only when they came to a stop, and found out that there was no one to give them orders, did it immediately dawn on them who was missing. Then, once they knew what had happened, the word was passed through their ranks, and they all of them spurred their horses forwards, with the aim of at least retrieving the corpse.

[23] When the Athenians saw that the cavalry, rather than charging them in waves, was now attacking them in squadrons, they yelled out to the rest of the army. It took a while, however, for the main body of the infantry to come to their assistance, and during this time a bitter battle raged over the corpse. Now, for as long as the three hundred were fighting on their own, they had by far the worst of things, and indeed, were in danger of losing the body. Once they had been reinforced by the full weight of the army, however, the Persian cavalry could no longer hold their ground, nor keep hold of the corpse, but instead themselves suffered numerous casualties. Accordingly, they withdrew a distance of two stades, and tried to settle what their best course of action would be. In the event, they decided – leaderless as they now were – to head back at full gallop to Mardonius.

[24] Once the cavalry was back in the camp, Mardonius and his entire army mourned Masistius with terrible displays of grief, cropping their hair close, shearing their horses and pack-animals of their manes and giving themselves over to ceaseless lamentation.[13] All of Boeotia echoed to the noise – as well it might have done, for the slain man had been held in a greater respect by the Persians and the King than anyone except for Mardonius. So it was that the Barbarians paid honour to the dead Masistius in their own distinctive fashion.

[25] As for the Greeks, the fact that they had not only withstood the cavalry onslaught, but had actually beaten it off, served as a tremendous fillip to morale. Their first step was to put the corpse in a wagon and parade it along their lines. So strapping and handsome was the body that it more than merited being looked at – which, sure enough, was why men kept breaking ranks to go and inspect Masistius. Next, the Greeks decided to head down towards Plataea. Their reason for doing so was that the terrain around Plataea was manifestly better suited to supporting an army than that around Erythrae in a great number of ways, and especially as regards the readier availability of water. Accordingly, they resolved to head for that particular stretch of land, and to the Gargaphian Spring in particular, which rose there, and on arrival to

make camp, with each unit occupying its own separate position. So they picked up all their equipment and journeyed, by way of Hysiae, down from the spurs of Cithaeron onto Plataean soil – where, on arrival, they took up their positions, people by people, beside the Gargaphian Spring and the precinct of the hero Androcrates,[14] on low hills or level ground.

[26] These dispositions provoked a fierce wrangling back and forth[15] between spokesmen for the Tegeans and the Athenians. Both thought that they had the better claim to hold the wing not held by the Lacedaemonians, and both cited in their support recent and long distant achievements. This, for instance, was the case the Tegeans made. 'Always, whenever the Peloponnesians go on a joint expedition, we are the ones, by the common consent of our allies, who are thought the best qualified to hold this position. Nor is this anything recent. No, it reaches back to ancient times, when the descendants of Heracles sought to return to the Peloponnese from exile, following the death of Eurystheus.[16] Which exploit was it that won us the privilege? It was this. Side by side with the Achaeans, and with the Ionians too (who at that point were inhabitants of the Peloponnese), we went to defend the Isthmus. There, we took up a position directly opposite the returning exiles. It was then, so the story goes, that Hyllus made a proclamation. "There is no need", he said, "for the two armies to risk a battle. Instead, let the Peloponnesians select the best fighter they have in their camp, and he can then meet me in single combat – on terms to be arranged." This seemed to the Peloponnesians a reasonable course of action – and so the two sides agreed, on oath, that if Hyllus defeated the Peloponnesian champion, then the descendants of Heracles would return to their ancestral lands, but that if, on the contrary, he were the one defeated, then the descendants of Heracles would go away at the head of their army, and not attempt a return to the Peloponnese for a hundred years. All the allies volunteered – but the one selected was Echemus, the son of Aëropus, and the grandson of Phegeus, who was our king as well as our general, and who fought Hyllus in single combat, and slew him. In consequence of this deed, the Peloponnesians awarded us any number of privileges which we continue to enjoy to this day – and one of these is that, unfailingly, we get to command the wing not commanded by the Lacedaemonians whenever a joint expedition is made.[17] Now, of course, we are hardly going to stand in your way, men of Lacedaemon. Take command of whichever wing you fancy – it is all the same to us. But the other wing – and this is

our point – the command of that wing should come to us, just as it has always done in the past. Why, even setting aside the exploit we just mentioned, we are still more deserving of the position than the Athenians! Many are the struggles in which we have been formidable contenders – and among our adversaries, alongside many others, have been yourselves, you men of Sparta! For all these reasons, then, it is only right that we, and not the Athenians, should have the other wing. After all – what do they have to compare with our record of achievement in either their recent or distant past?'

[27] The Athenians responded to this argument of the Tegeans with one of their own. 'We appreciate that our reason for gathering here is to fight the Barbarians, not make speeches. Nevertheless, since the Tegean spokesman has proposed that we rehearse the brave deeds accomplished by our respective cities over the entire span of time, ancient as well as modern,[18] we are obliged to clarify for you how it is that our people, brave as they are, have come to inherit from their forefathers an unfailing pre-eminence – rather than the Arcadians. Take the descendants of Heracles, for instance, whose champion these Tegeans say they killed at the Isthmus. Previously, the Mycenaeans had been attempting to make them slaves, and when they fled, all the Greeks they approached sent them packing – all, that is, except for us, who alone took them in and toppled the brutal and overweening Eurystheus, and helped defeat in battle those who at the time held the Peloponnese. Then there were the Argives – the ones who marched with Polynices on Thebes, and ended up lying there dead and unburied. It is our proud claim that we went to war with the Cadmeians, recovered the bodies and gave them burial in our own land at Eleusis. Then, what about that time the Amazons swept down from the River Thermodon into the land of Attica? The feats we accomplished then were certainly impressive ones. Likewise, back in the dark days of the Trojan War, we were second to none. But really, what is the point in dredging up all these distant memories? Men who were brave in the past might easily be worthless now, just as those who were worthless once might since have become stronger. So enough of ancient exploits. The truth is, of course, that we have quite as many impressive deeds to our credit as any other city in Greece – but even were we unable to point to anything else, our feat at Marathon would still entitle us to a whole host of honours, this one included. We alone of the Greeks, we alone met the Persians in battle.[19] That was such

a commitment to have undertaken – and yet we survived it, and prevailed over forty-six peoples. Surely, then, that feat in itself entitles us to the position? But really, this is hardly the time to be squabbling over issues of deployment! We are ready to take up position wherever seems best to you, O Lacedaemonians, and face whomsoever you please. No matter where we are posted, we shall do our best to prove our mettle. Command, then, and we shall obey.'

[28] A shout went up from the entire Lacedaemonian camp at this reply,[20] that it was the Athenians and not the Arcadians who deserved the wing. So that was how the Athenians secured it, at the expense of the Tegeans.

Afterwards, the Greeks took up their battle-stations – both those who had arrived late and those who had been with the expedition since the start. The right wing was held by 10,000 Lacedaemonians, of whom 5,000 were Spartiates; each of these was looked after by seven lightly armed helots, amounting to 35,000 in all. Next to themselves the Spartiates positioned the Tegeans, in due recognition of the prestige they enjoyed, and their courage. The Tegean contingent consisted of 1,500 hoplites. Next to them stood 5,000 Corinthians, who in turn – after a successful request put in to Pausanias – had the 300 men from Potidaea, in Pallene, stationed next to them. Then came 600 Arcadians from Orchomenus, followed by 3,000 men from Sicyon. Next came 800 men from Epidaurus. Beyond them were stationed, successively, 1,000 men from Troezen, 200 from Lepreum, 400 from Mycenae and Tiryns and 1,000 from Phleious. Next came 300 men from Hermione. Stationed next to the Hermioneans were 600 Eretrians and Styrians, then 400 men from Chalcis, followed by 500 from Ambracia. Standing next to them were 800 men from Leucas and Anactorium, and then 200 from Pale on Cephallenia. From Aegina 500 men were stationed beyond them and beyond them in turn were stationed 3,000 Megarians. Next to them were 600 men from Plataea. Last of all – or first, if you like – there stood 8,000 Athenians, who were holding the left wing. Their general was Aristeides, the son of Lysimachus.

[29] The sum total of these (all of whom, with the exception of the seven men assigned to each Spartiate, were hoplites) amounted to 38,700. But while that was the total of the heavy infantry who had massed to confront the Barbarian, there were also a number of lightly armed troops – 35,000 of whom were the men stationed alongside the

Spartiates, seven to each man, and all of whom were equipped for battle. There were also 34,500 lightly armed troops drawn from the rest of the Lacedaemonians and Greeks, at a rate of one man to each hoplite. So in total the number of lightly armed troops involved in the battle came to 69,500.

[30] The total number of combatants who had assembled at Plataea – including both hoplites and lightly armed troops – amounted, then, to 1,800 men short of 110,000. But add in the Thespians, who were also present, and the total did come out at 110,000.[21] There were 1,800 Thespians in the camp, you see: men who had escaped with their lives,[22] but without any of the arms and armour of a hoplite.

[31] So that was how the Greek forces were ranged along the Asopus. Meanwhile, once Mardonius and his Barbarians had finished mourning the death of Masistius, the news that the Greeks were at Plataea brought them to the same location – and specifically to the stretch of the Asopus that flows through Plataean territory. On their arrival there, facing the Greeks, Mardonius made his own dispositions. Opposite the Lacedaemonians he stationed the Persians. In fact, so greatly did the Persians outnumber the Lacedaemonians that not only were their lines serried much deeper, but they overlapped the Tegeans as well. Mardonius had organized them very carefully, by posting sections of all the most proficient troops opposite the Lacedaemonians, while stationing the weaker troops opposite the Tegeans. He did this at the prompting of Theban instructors. Next to the Persians he deployed the Medes. These covered the Corinthians, the Potidaeans, the Orchomenians and the Sicyonians. Next to the Medes he stationed the Bactrians. These covered the Epidaurians, the Troezenians, the contingents from Lepreum, Tiryns and Mycenae, and the Phliasians. Next to the Bactrians he posted the Indians. These covered the men of Hermione, Eretria, Styra and Chalcis. Next to the Indians he stationed the Sacae, who covered the Ambraciots, the Anactorians, the Leucadians, the Paleans and the Aeginetans. Next to the Sacae, and facing the Athenians, Plataeans and Megarians, he stationed the Boeotians, the Locrians, the Malians, the Thessalians and the thousand Phocians. (That there were only a thousand was due to the fact that some of the Phocians, rather than going over to the Medes, were instead supporting the Greek cause; these, although pinned down in the region of Parnassus, were sallying out from it to raid and plunder Mardonius' army, and the Greeks on his side as well.) Mardonius also

stationed the Macedonians, and those who lived on the borders of Thessaly, opposite the Athenians.

[32] Only the most formidable of the various peoples deployed by Mardonius, the most prominent and significant of them, have actually been listed here by name. Nevertheless, mixed up among these there were also men of assorted other nationalities, including Phrygians, Mysians, Thracians and Paeonians, as well as Ethiopians and, from Egypt, the so-called 'Hermotybies' and 'Calasiries': warriors – indeed, the only ones in all Egypt – who came armed with knives. In point of fact, these last were marines – but Mardonius had made them disembark from the fleet while still at Phalerum. (The Egyptians, you see, had not been deployed with the land-forces that came to Athens with Xerxes.) The Barbarians, as I explained earlier, numbered 300,000. The number of Greeks allied to Mardonius defies precise computation, since no one ever added them up, of course – but at a guess, I would estimate there to have been some 50,000 of them gathered there. Such was the disposition of the infantry; the cavalry were posted elsewhere.

[33] The day after Mardonius had made all these deployments, nation by nation and squadron by squadron, both sides offered up sacrifices. Officiating for the Greeks was Tisamenus, the son of Antiochus, who had come with the army as its diviner. Despite the fact that he was an Eleian, and belonged to the family of the Iamids, the Lacedaemonians had enrolled him as one of their own citizens. This had come about because of an enquiry made by Tisamenus of the Delphic oracle as to whether he would have children – to which the Pythia had replied that he would win 'the five greatest contests'. Tisamenus, failing to grasp the oracle's meaning, and presuming it to be athletics contests he was due to win, had duly begun devoting himself to athletics – and indeed, so hard did he train for the pentathlon that when he and Hieronymus of Andros ended up contending for victory at the Olympic Games, he missed out on it by a single fall. Meanwhile, the Lacedaemonians had realized that the oracle given to Tisamenus was referring to martial rather than athletic contests – so by means of a bribe they sought to induce him to join their kings, descendants of Heracles, in directing their wars. When Tisamenus saw how much it meant to the Spartiates to procure his friendship, he raised his price, letting them know that he would meet their request only if they made him a fellow-citizen of theirs, with a full share of all that implied – a demand from which he refused

to be shifted. When the Spartiates heard this, they were initially so appalled that they retracted their invitation altogether – but eventually, so great was their terror of the Persian invasion, which by this stage was louring over them, that they gave way and accepted his conditions. After Tisamenus had registered this reversal of policy, he then declared that the conditions on their own were no longer satisfactory to him, and that his brother, Hagias, would have to become a Spartiate as well, on the same terms as himself.

[34] In saying this, he was copying Melampous – if, that is, one may compare the demand for a throne with one for citizenship. After all, when the women of Argos went mad, and the Argives tried to hire Melampous[23] to come from Pylus to heal their wives of their illness, he demanded a half share in the kingship as his fee. So insupportable did the Argives find this that they turned and went away; but then, with more and more of their women going mad, they gave in, and went back to Melampous to meet his demand. Melampous, though, when he saw that they had reversed their position, raised his asking price, declaring that he would do as they wished only if they also gave a third share of the kingship to his brother, Bias. The Argives, cornered by circumstance as they were, consented to this as well.

[35] It was in a very similar manner, then, that the Spartiates, in the desperation of their own need, gave way before Tisamenus' demands. Sure enough, once the terms had been settled, Tisamenus of Elis – now enrolled as a Spartiate – did indeed, by employing the arts of divination, help them to win 'the five greatest contests'. (He and his brother were the only people ever to have been made citizens of Sparta.) The five 'contests' in question were, in chronological order: first, the one at Plataea; then, the battle against the Tegeans and the Argives at Tegea; third, the one at Dipaeeis, which was fought against all the Arcadians, excluding only the Mantineans; then, the victory over the Messenians at Ithome; and finally, the one at Tanagra, over the Athenians and Argives.[24] This last battle was the culmination of the five contests.

[36] So this was the Tisamenus who performed divinations for the Spartiates while they were on Plataean soil. Stay on the defensive, the entrails of the sacrificial victims assured the Greeks, and all would be well – but cross the Asopus to initiate combat, and it would not.

[37] As for Mardonius, although he was itching to start the battle, the sacrificial omens provided him with no support either, but were like-

wise recommending defensive measures. He was having the entrails of sacrificial victims examined just as the Greeks were – the man consulting them, Hegesistratus of Elis, was the most celebrated of the Telliads and had on an earlier occasion inflicted such serious and appalling damage on the Lacedaemonians that they had seized him, chained him up and condemned him to death. It was while he was in this desperate plight, with his life in mortal danger and knowing that execution would come only after the most excruciating torture, that he performed an exploit which defies description. He was being held in stocks that were edged with iron, but when he managed – somehow or other – to get hold of an iron implement that had been smuggled in, he immediately devised a plan of action that required more courage than any other of which we know. He had worked out, you see, that if he hacked off the flat of his own foot, he would be able to ease what was left of it free. This he duly did; and then, because there were guards on watch,[25] he dug a hole through the wall and escaped to Tegea, travelling by night and skulking by day under cover of a wood, so that by the third evening of his journey he had made it to Tegea, despite the full search for him being undertaken by the Lacedaemonians, whose astonishment at his daring was fuelled both by the spectacle of half his foot left lying where it was, and by the fact that they simply could not find him. So it was, then, that he was able to escape the clutches of the Lacedaemonians for a while by fleeing to Tegea, which at the time was not on good terms with the Lacedaemonians. Once he had recovered from his injury and had a wooden foot made for himself, he made no secret from then on of his longing to do the Lacedaemonians harm. Nevertheless, in the long run this loathing for the Lacedaemonians, which became so much a part of him, did not have a happy ending. He was captured while he was acting as a seer at Zacynthos, and put to death.

[38] But the execution of Hegesistratus took place after the events at Plataea – the duration of which he spent on the banks of the Asopus, earning a not inconsiderable sum from Mardonius, and performing sacrifices with great relish, in part because of the money he was making, but also out of loathing for the Lacedaemonians. Still the omens would not countenance the Persians giving battle – nor the Greeks who were on the Persian side either (and who had a seer of their own with them, a man from Leucas named Hippomachus). Meanwhile, with ever more men flooding in to swell the Greek forces, a Theban – a man called

Timagenidas, the son of Herpys – advised Mardonius to set guards on the passes over Cithaeron, pointing out that this would then enable him to apprehend the large numbers of Greeks who were constantly streaming in, day after day.

[39] The two sides had already been confronting one another for eight days when Timagenidas gave this advice to Mardonius. Realizing that the suggestion was an excellent one, Mardonius that evening sent his cavalry to the passes over Cithaeron that lead down to Plataea and are called by the Boeotians 'Three Heads', and by the Athenians 'Oak Heads'. Once the horsemen had reached their objective, the mission was not without success. This was because a wagon-train consisting of five hundred pack-animals and the men in charge of them, which had been bringing provisions from the Peloponnese, was seized as it was making its descent towards the plain. The Persians slaughtered the captives they had taken without mercy, sparing neither man nor beast. Then, when they had had enough of killing, they rounded up the survivors and drove them to Mardonius in his camp.

[40] Two more days went by after this deed, with both sides still reluctant to start the battle. Even though the Barbarians made trial of the Greeks by advancing right to the bank of the Asopus, neither side would actually cross it. That said, Mardonius' cavalry never stopped raiding and harrying the Greeks. This was because the Thebans, wholehearted in their collaboration, were so committed to the effort that they were constantly guiding the cavalry up to the enemy positions, whereupon the Persians and Medes would take over, and leave no one in any doubt as to their courage.

[41] Now, for ten days this was the limit of what occurred. Then, eleven days into the confrontation at Plataea, after the Greek numbers had swelled massively, and with Mardonius chafing at the general lack of action, a discussion was held between Mardonius, the son of Gobryas, and Artabazus, the son of Pharnaces – who was a man held in greater esteem by Xerxes than almost any other Persian. Two opinions were aired in the course of their conference. Artabazus argued that the entire army should strike camp as fast as possible and pull back behind the walls of Thebes, where large supplies of grain had been built up, together with fodder for their pack-animals, and where they could relax and take their ease, while still working to achieve their aims. After all, did they not have great piles of gold – masses of coin, and large quanti-

ties of unminted gold as well – and vast supplies of silver and goblets? Only distribute all that among the Greeks, do so on a lavish scale and target in particular those Greeks who held leading positions in their respective cities, and they would soon be brought to betray their freedom – thereby removing any need for a risky battle. This argument echoed the one that the Thebans had made,[26] and like it drew on a superior measure of understanding; but Mardonius, in giving his own opinion, was forthright and obstinate, and would not compromise. Confident that the Greeks were not remotely a match for his own forces, and having no wish to watch the enemy assemble in numbers even larger than those that had already massed, he aimed to give battle at the earliest opportunity. As for the battle-line sacrifices being made by Hegesistratus, rather than forcing the issue, he was content simply to ignore them, rely on Persian custom and engage with the enemy.

[42] This being his view, there was no one to oppose it – and so it duly carried the day. It was Mardonius, after all, who had been given command of the army by the King, not Artabazus. Accordingly, he summoned the officers in charge of his various regiments, together with the commanders of the Greeks he had with him on his side, and asked them whether they knew of any oracle that foretold an annihilation of Persians in Greece. To this, the officers he had summoned made no answer – some because they genuinely knew of no such oracles, and others (those who were indeed conscious of them) because they did not think it safe to mention them. Accordingly, it was Mardonius himself who spoke. 'Very well – since either you are ignorant or you do not dare speak up, whereas I myself am well informed on the matter, I shall do the talking. There is indeed an oracle, to the effect that Persians are destined to come to Greece and ransack the shrine at Delphi – and then, after the sack, all to perish. In light of that information, however, we shall not be going anywhere near the shrine, still less putting it to the sack[27] – and will thereby be spared destruction. So rejoice, all of you who are loyal to the Persian cause: we shall overcome the Greeks!' Then, having delivered this speech, Mardonius instructed them to get everything ready and in order for dawn the next day, when battle was to be joined.

[43] Now, I know myself for a fact that this oracle, which Mardonius said referred to the Persians, when originally composed was actually alluding to the Illyrians and the army of the Encheleans, and not to the

Persians at all. There was, however, an oracle of Bacis[28] which did refer to the relevant battle:

'By the Thermodon and the grassy banks of the Asopus
A gathering of Greeks, and a great howling of Barbarians.
Many there shall fall, before time, before the hour of their doom,
Among the bow-wielding Medes, when the fateful day arrives.'

These verses – and other, very similar ones by Musaeus as well – do, I know, refer to the Persians. (The Thermodon is a river that flows between Tanagra and Glisas.)

[44] Now that Mardonius had put his questions about the oracles and issued his rallying-cry, night began to fall and the sentries to take up their stations. Then, in the very dead of night, when it seemed that silence was general over both the camps, and almost everyone was fast asleep, there came galloping up to the Athenian look-outs the Persian commander and King of the Macedonians, Alexander, the son of Amyntas, with a request that he be introduced to their high command. A few of the sentries, leaving the rest of their comrades at their posts, hurried off to fetch the generals, and informed them that a man on horseback had arrived from the camp of the Medes, breathing not a word about anything except the names of the commanders themselves, and his wish to enter into a parley with them.

[45] When the commanders heard this, they immediately followed the sentries back to their posts. 'Men of Athens,' Alexander told them once they had got there, 'please take what I am about to say as a pledge of my good faith, and keep it to yourselves, mentioning it to no one save Pausanias, or you will be the ruin of me. After all, I would never be here talking to you if I did not have a profound concern for the whole of Greece. I myself am Greek by descent, and have no wish to see Greece exchange her liberty for servitude. That is why I am informing you that Mardonius and his forces have found it impossible to discover in the sacrificial entrails what they so desperately long to read. Had they been able to, then they would have joined battle long ago. Now, however, Mardonius has decided to ignore the sacrifices, and to join battle anyway, at first light of day. He has done so, I imagine, because he is afraid that otherwise your army will continue to swell. Brace yourselves, then! Indeed, even should Mardonius postpone matters and not join battle, hold tight to your current positions. He has only enough food, you see,

to last him a few more days. And please, if the war does end as you are trusting it will, you must bear me and my own freedom in mind as well. This risky venture which I have undertaken, I have done it for you. It is because I am such an enthusiast for the Greek cause that I wished to alert you to Mardonius' intentions, and prevent the Barbarians from sweeping down on you unawares. I am Alexander the Macedonian.' And so saying, he galloped off back to his post in the Persian camp.

[46] The Athenian commanders crossed to the right wing and repeated to Pausanias what they had heard from Alexander. Nervous as he was of the Persians, his response to their report[29] was to declare: 'Very well, then – since battle is to be joined at dawn, you Athenians must make your stand opposite the Persians, while we take on the Boeotians and the other Greeks who are currently stationed opposite you. Why do I say this? Because you fought the Medes at Marathon, and so are familiar with them and their manner of fighting, while we have never tested ourselves against these men and know nothing about them. Untried though the Spartiates may be against the Medes, however, we have plenty of experience against the Boeotians and Thessalians. So what we should do is gather up our equipment and move over to the left wing, while you swap with us and take this wing here.' The Athenians replied to this by saying: 'Right from the very start, when we observed that the Persians were being deployed opposite you, we have intended to raise precisely the point that you have just beaten us to making. It was only because we were afraid of offending you with our suggestion that we did not mention it. But now, since you yourselves have brought it up, we are delighted with your proposal, and are ready to act on it accordingly.'

[47] So it was, with both sides satisfied, they set about swapping positions at first light of dawn. When the Boeotians realized what was going on, they reported it to Mardonius. The moment he heard the news, he too sought to redeploy his forces, by leading the Persians to face the Lacedaemonians. When Pausanias learned this, and realized that he had failed to prevent his manoeuvre from being detected, he led the Spartiates back to the right wing. Mardonius in turn then led his own men back to the left wing.

[48] It was now, when they were all back in their original positions, that Mardonius sent a herald to the Spartiates. 'Everyone in these parts, O Lacedaemonians,' he said, 'goes on about how you are the bravest of

men; that in battle you never retreat or break ranks, but instead hold fast until either you have annihilated your adversaries, or else yourselves have been annihilated – all this is a cause of great wonder. It turns out, however, not to be true! Why, before battle has even been joined, before we have so much as got to grips with you, we have watched you, with our very own eyes, turn tail and abandon your station, placing the Athenians in the most testing position, while you take up a post opposite our slaves. Is this the behaviour of brave men? Hardly! We have been badly deceived in you! Your glorious reputation being what it is, we were expecting you to send us a herald with a challenge – a declaration of your willingness to fight with the Persians alone. This was something we were ready to do – but now, rather than issuing us with any such challenge, we find you cowering instead. Very well, then. The dialogue that you failed to initiate – we shall open it. Since in terms of numbers we are both a match for the other, why do not we, on behalf of the Barbarians, and you, on behalf of the Greeks – since you are supposed to be the best they have – meet in combat? Everyone else can fight as well, if you like – but later on, once we ourselves have had our battle. Or, if that seems a bad idea to you, and you think it would be sufficient for us to fight things out and no one else, then let us get to it. Whichever one of us secures the victory wins on behalf of their side as a whole.'

[49] The herald paused a short while after making this offer; but then, when no one answered him, he turned on his heels, made his way back to Mardonius and briefed him about what had happened. Mardonius himself was overjoyed by this empty victory, and in his elation unleashed his horsemen against the Greeks. Forward the cavalry surged, inflicting terrible damage with both javelins and arrows on the entire Greek force, which was helpless to get to grips with them, such was the skill with which the archers shot from horseback. They also muddied the Gargaphian Spring, from which the whole Greek army had been drawing its water, and left it heaped over with earth. It was the Lacedaemonians alone who were stationed beside the spring, while the other Greeks had to travel whatever the distance might be from where they happened to be stationed, and were actually closer to the Asopus; the reason they had been going to the spring, though, was that the Asopus had been put out of bounds to them. It had become impossible to draw water from the river on account of the horsemen and the arrows, you see.

[50] Brought to these circumstances, with the Greek forces deprived of water and suffering constant harassment from the cavalry, their commanders crossed to the right wing and met Pausanias to discuss the situation and other matters too. There were additional, even more pressing issues distressing them. Not only had they run out of provisions, but the attendants whom they had sent to the Peloponnese to fetch fresh supplies were cut off by the cavalry, unable to reach their camp.

[51] After due debate, the commanders decided that their best option – supposing that the Persians put off joining battle with them that day – would be to head for the 'island'. (This was located in front of the city of Plataea, at a distance of 10 stades from the Asopus and the Gargaphian Spring, where at this time they had their camp. Had it not been inland, it would have been a real island. There is a river which, in the course of flowing down from Cithaeron to the plain, divides upstream, and then continues along two separate channels for some 3 stades, before merging again. Its name is the Oeroe. The locals claim it to be the daughter of the Asopus.) It was to this place, then, that the commanders decided to shift their position, since it would provide them with a ready supply of water, as well as prevent the cavalry from inflicting on them the casualties they had suffered while directly exposed to attack. It was settled that the move would be made at night, during the second watch, so that the Persians would not spot them setting off and send the cavalry to nip at their heels. It was also agreed that once they had arrived at the new position (the one formed by the bifurcation of Asopus' daughter, Oeroe, as she flows down from Cithaeron), they would dispatch half their force to Cithaeron, under cover of the same night, to pick up the attendants who had gone to fetch provisions. These, you see, were trapped on Cithaeron.

[52] After they had made this decision, the pressure put on them by the cavalry was unrelenting all day long. Then, as daylight faded and the horsemen halted their attacks, night began to deepen, until the hour agreed for departure came, and the bulk of the army, getting to their feet, set off; this was not, however, with any intention of making for the prearranged location, since once they were on the move all they really wanted to do was to escape the cavalry by heading for the city of Plataea, a flight which brought them to the sanctuary of Hera. (This stands at a distance of 20 stades from the Gargaphian Spring, in front of the

city of Plataea.) Once they had reached there, they dumped all their gear down in front of the shrine.

[53] So they set up camp around the sanctuary of Hera; but Pausanias, who had watched them leave their original base, and assumed that they were making for the prearranged location, announced to the Lacedaemonians that they too were to gather up their equipment and follow the lead of the others. Most of the officers were perfectly ready to do as Pausanias had instructed; but Amompharetus, the son of Poliades – who was the commander of the regiment from Pitana, and, since he had been absent from the earlier council of war, was astonished by what he was seeing – declared that he would never retreat from foreigners, nor willingly bring disgrace upon Sparta. Infuriated though Pausanias and Euryanax were by this refusal to obey their orders, what appalled them even more was the prospect of having to abandon the entire division from Pitana – since if Amompharetus persisted in his obduracy, the plan they had agreed upon with the other Greeks would require them to abandon him and all the men with him to their fate. On the basis of this calculation, then, they kept the Laconian force from moving while they sought to persuade Amompharetus that his behaviour was wrong.

[54] Meanwhile, with these attempts to talk Amompharetus round continuing, and the Lacedaemonians and the Tegeans left isolated, what were the Athenians doing? Well – they too were holding fast to their original position,[30] well aware of the Lacedaemonian habit of thinking one thing while saying quite another. Once all the other Greeks had decamped, they sent one of their number on horseback to see whether the Spartiates were really serious about setting off, or whether they had never actually intended to leave – and also to ask Pausanias what they themselves should be doing.

[55] When the Athenian herald reached the Lacedaemonians, he saw that they were stationed in the same spot as ever, and that their leaders had come almost to blows. Because Amompharetus had remained unpersuaded by Euryanax and Pausanias, and their insistence on the dangers that he would face were he, alone of the Lacedaemonians, to remain where he was, the argument had become very heated by the time the Athenian herald arrived in their midst. Indeed, so bitter was the altercation that Amompharetus, picking up a rock with both hands and placing it at the feet of Pausanias, pronounced it to be the pebble with which he was casting his vote against any retreat in the face of the

foreigners. This prompted Pausanias to call Amompharetus mad and simple-minded – after which, in answer to the question that the Athenian had been instructed to ask, he told the herald to explain the difficulties that he was facing, and request the Athenians to join with his own forces, and make their withdrawal in conjunction with the Lacedaemonians.

[56] So back the herald went to the Athenians. When dawn came upon them, and the argument was still raging on, Pausanias, who had remained stationary the whole while, calculated – correctly, as it turned out – that Amompharetus would never allow himself to be left behind were the other Lacedaemonians just to march off; and so he gave the signal, and led all the rest of his men away through the low hills. The Tegeans too went along in their rear. The Athenians did as ordered and went in the opposite direction to the Lacedaemonians. Whereas the latter, nervous of the Persian cavalry, kept to the spurs and foothills of Cithaeron, the Athenians veered down onto the plain.

[57] Initially, because Amompharetus refused to accept that Pausanias would ever dare to leave him behind, he insisted that his men stay where they were and not desert their position. But when Pausanias and his men pressed on, and the unpleasant realization that he was indeed being abandoned dawned on him, he had his regiment collect up their gear, and then led them at a slow pace towards the other column. This had by now covered a distance of some 4 stades, and was waiting for Amompharetus and his regiment at a place called Argiopium on the River Moloeis, where there was also a shrine of Eleusinian Demeter. The reason Pausanias had been waiting there was to ensure that, in the event of Amompharetus and his regiment keeping to the spot where they had been posted rather than leaving it, he would be able to head back to their rescue. Amompharetus and his men came up to join him; and even as they did so, the full force of the barbarian cavalry was breaking against them. The tactics of the cavalry were the same as they had ever been; for, on seeing that the positions occupied by the Greeks over the previous few days had been abandoned, they kept on galloping the whole way forwards until they had caught up with the enemy and could launch an attack on him.

[58] Meanwhile, when Mardonius learned that the Greeks had stolen away under cover of darkness, and saw their positions lying empty, he summoned Thorax of Larissa and his brothers Eurypylus and Thrasydeius.

'Well, you sons of Aleuas,' he asked them, 'what do you have to say now? Look! There is no one out there! You are the neighbours of these Lacedaemonians, and you keep going on about how they never run away from battle, and are men pre-eminent in the business of war. But you watched them earlier, their constant shifting of position – and now we can all see that they used the cover of last night to run away. When they are obliged to meet men who are genuinely the best in the world in battle, they leave no one in any doubt that they are nobodies – mediocre in everything, save for making a show of themselves in front of their fellow-nobodies here in Greece. You, of course, were not familiar with the Persians, and so I at any rate find it perfectly pardonable that you should have lauded the Lacedaemonians – of whom, after all, you did have some knowledge. What I find altogether more astonishing is that Artabazus should have been so terrified of them. Indeed, such was his state of alarm that he made no attempt to conceal this thoroughly cowardly notion of his that we should have struck camp, pulled back to the city of Thebes and withstood a siege there! The Great King will certainly be hearing all about that from me. But that is a reckoning for another time. For now, our responsibility is to ensure that the Greeks do not get away with their current course. We must pursue them, overtake them and make them pay for all the wrongs they have done the Persians.'

[59] So saying, he led the Persians across the Asopus, and then, once they were over it, continued at full tilt on the trail of the Greeks, whom he believed to be running away – although in reality it was only the Lacedaemonians and Tegeans who were his quarry. (This was because the Athenians had swung down onto the plain, and so his view of them was blocked by the ridge.) Meanwhile, when the chiefs of the remaining barbarian divisions saw that the Persians were heading off after the Greeks, immediately they all hoisted their standards, and themselves set off in pursuit – each division going as fast as their feet could carry them, but lacking any discipline or battle order. Confident of making short work of the Greeks, they charged forwards in one great yelling mass.

[60] When Pausanias came under attack from the cavalry, he sent a messenger on horseback to the Athenians. 'Men of Athens,' he said, 'now is the supreme contest come upon us, which will decide whether Greece is to be free or enslaved – and yet, at such a moment, we Lacedaemonians and you Athenians have been betrayed by our allies who took flight last night. It is clear, then, what our course of action must

now be: to defend ourselves to the best of our abilities, and cover our respective backs. Naturally, had the cavalry begun by charging you, then we and the Tegeans – who are still with us, and are certainly no traitors to Greece! – would have been obliged to come to your rescue. As it is, though, it is we who have the whole force bearing down on us, and so it is only right that you should now rally to our defence – we being the division under the greatest pressure. And please, even should circumstances render it impossible for you to come to our assistance, send us your archers, and you will indeed be storing up favour with us. We appreciate that your commitment to this current war has far exceeded that of everyone else – and so we know that you will not block your ears to us now.'

[61] The Athenians, when they learned this news, were all for heading to the rescue, and providing assistance to the full. As they marched off, though, they were set upon by those Greeks who were on the side of the King, and had been stationed opposite them – an attack so bruising as to render the Athenian rescue mission impossible. As a result, the Lacedaemonians (of whom, including the lightly armed troops, there were fifty thousand in total) and the three thousand Tegeans (who had been with the Lacedaemonians the whole time) were left alone to confront Mardonius and the forces he had with him. So they made an offering of the sacrificial animals, but the omens proved unfavourable; and all the while large numbers of them were dropping to the ground, and even more were being wounded. The reason for this was that the Persians had set up a barricade of wicker shields, from behind which they were firing a relentless hail of arrows; and so Pausanias, with the Spartiates desperately hard pressed and the omens unfavourable, turned his gaze towards the shrine of Plataean Hera, and called upon the goddess, begging her not to let their hopes prove false.

[62] Even as he was raising this invocation, the Tegeans began to advance and initiate an attack on the Barbarians – and then, all at once, the very moment when Pausanias had finished his prayer, favourable omens were read in the entrails. Now, at last, the Lacedaemonians advanced against the Persians, who in the face of this attack dropped their bows. To begin with, the wicker barricade was the focus of the battle. Then, once this had been demolished, there was a ferocious struggle around the sanctuary of Demeter, which went on for a long while before at last it came to the final push. The Barbarians, you see,

kept on grabbing the spears and snapping them off. Nor, in terms of spirit and strength, were the Persians in any way inferior to the Greeks – but they lacked protective armour and the training that would have made them a match for the expertise of their opponents. They kept on charging out singly, or else in groups of ten (more or less), and hurling themselves at the Spartiates – who just hacked them down.

[63] Mardonius himself was riding a white horse, surrounded by an elite force of the thousand bravest Persians; and wherever he happened to be, there the fight would be taken with particular vigour to his adversaries. For as long as Mardonius remained alive, the Persians held their ground – and indeed, in the course of defending themselves, inflicted heavy casualties on the Lacedaemonians. But with the death of Mardonius, and the felling of the men stationed with him, who were the most formidable men the Persians had, all the others turned in rout before the Lacedaemonians. One factor more than any other contributed to their ruin: their lack of armour. The contest was one that had pitted lightly armed men against hoplites.

[64] So it was, just as the oracle had foretold,[31] that Mardonius rendered to the Spartiates due recompense for the murder of Leonidas, and the fairest victory of any known to us was won by Pausanias, the son of Cleombrotus, the son of Anaxandridas. (As for his earlier forebears, I listed those when giving the lineage of Leonidas.[32] The two men shared a common ancestry, you see.) Mardonius was killed by Arimnestus, a man highly regarded in Sparta, who was himself killed some time after the war against the Medes, when he and a company of three hundred men took on the entire army of the Messenians in a battle at Stenyclerus, in which both he and the three hundred perished.[33]

[65] When the Persians were routed by the Lacedaemonians at Plataea, they fled in disorder back to their camp and the wooden stockade they had built on Theban territory. Even though the battle had been fought right next to the grove of Demeter, and most of the Persians fell in a ring around the shrine, on unconsecrated ground, not a single one of them, it appears, either entered the actual precinct itself or died in it – something that I find a cause of great wonder. If one absolutely must touch upon the dimension of the divine, then my own interpretation of the matter would be that the goddess refused entry to the men who had burned down the palace[34] at Eleusis.

[66] Now, that was what happened in this battle. As for Artabazus,

the son of Pharnaces, he had thought it a mistake on the part of the King, right from the very beginning, to leave Mardonius behind, and had often spoken out – albeit unsuccessfully – against giving battle. His disapproval of Mardonius' tactics duly led him to adopt the following measures. Because he had no doubt, when battle was joined, what the outcome would be, he led the forty thousand men under his command (a not inconsiderable force!) in tight formation, and ordered them all to follow his lead wherever he went, and at whatever his pace. Then, once he had issued these instructions, he led his troops out as though to battle. He had gone some way down the road, though, when he saw that the Persians were already in flight. He duly changed formation and began to run; making his escape at top speed, he headed not for the wooden stockade or the walls of Thebes but – because it was his intention to get to the Hellespont as fast as he could – for Phocis.

[67] So that was the course taken by Artabazus. Meanwhile, the Greeks who were serving with the King's army all deliberately fought below their best – all, that is, except for the Boeotians, whose clash with the Athenians was protracted. This was because the collaborators among the Thebans had no little relish for taking on the Athenians – and indeed, rather than fighting in a half-hearted manner, an elite force of their three hundred bravest men ended up slain by the Athenians on the battlefield. When the Boeotians were finally routed, they also fled back to Thebes, though they took a different route from the one followed by the Persians, and by the other allies as well – the whole mass of whom had taken to their heels without so much as striking a blow, or achieving anything at all.

[68] So it was the mere sight of the Persians in retreat which prompted the others to make their own escape before they had even joined battle; and this makes it apparent to me that the success or failure of the Barbarian cause was entirely dependent upon the Persians. Thus the only ones who did not flee were the cavalry – the Boeotians included. Indeed, the assistance that these provided to those who were making their escape was immense, since by staying the whole while on the flank closest to the enemy they were able to shield their friends as they fled the Greeks. The victors, you see, were hot on the heels of Xerxes' men, giving chase and slaughtering them.

[69] Meanwhile, in the midst of this rout, reports that a battle had been fought and won by Pausanias and his men reached the other

Greeks – the ones who were stationed by the shrine of Hera, and had taken no part in the fighting. When they heard the news, off they set in a disorganized manner: the Corinthians and those next to them along the road that led most directly to the shrine of Demeter, over various spurs and hills, and the Megarians, the Phliasians and those who were with them by means of the most level route across the plain. The ill-disciplined way in which the Megarians and Phliasians were rushing to close in on the enemy was noticed by the Theban cavalry, under the command of Asopodorus, the son of Timander, who launched a charge. The Thebans fell on them, cutting down six hundred, and then pursuing the remainder and scattering them towards Cithaeron.

[70] So they came to an end quite unworthy of note. In the meantime, the Persians and the rest of the army, who had taken refuge within the wooden stockade, managed to scale the towers before the Lacedaemonians could get to them; and once they had climbed up they did their best to strengthen the fortifications. When the Lacedaemonians attacked, the resulting battle for control of the walls was really very brutal. Indeed, in the absence of the Athenians, the defenders enjoyed a considerable advantage over the Lacedaemonians, who had no expertise in siegecraft. Once the Athenians had arrived to join them, however, the battle for the walls attained a new pitch of ferocity. It lasted a long while, until eventually the courage and perserverance of the Athenians enabled them to scale the fortifications and open up a breach through which the Greeks then poured. First to enter the stockade were the Tegeans; and it was they who plundered Mardonius' tent, including a manger for his horses made entirely of bronze, a remarkable sight. The Tegeans offered up this manger of Mardonius' in the temple of Athena Alea,[35] but the remainder of their takings they placed in the common pot to which all the Greeks contributed. The fall of the palisade saw the Barbarians lose all cohesion, and in their terror abandon any thought of further resistance, as thousands upon thousands of them, pent up in a cramped space, milled about in panic. Such was the opportunity for slaughter presented to the Greeks that out of an army of three hundred thousand – and not counting the forty thousand men who had made their escape with Artabazus – fewer than three thousand survived. The total number of casualties suffered in the battle by the Lacedaemonians from Sparta was ninety-one,[36] by the Tegeans sixteen and by the Athenians fifty-two.

[71] Now, of those on the barbarian side, it was the Persians who performed best of the infantry, the Sacae best of the cavalry and Mardonius, so it is reported, among individuals. On the Greek side, both the Tegeans and the Athenians well proved their worth – but even their valour was put in the shade by that of the Lacedaemonians. The only real justification I have for this assertion (bearing in mind that all of them defeated the opponents they were ranged against) is that the Lacedaemonians were faced with the very toughest of opponents, and prevailed over them. Easily the bravest individual, in my opinion, was Aristodemus – the man who had suffered such abuse and disgrace for being the only one of the three hundred to survive Thermopylae. The next bravest were also Spartiates: Poseidonius, Philocyon and Amompharetus. Nevertheless, when the Spartiates who had been present at the battle themselves debated which of their number had been the bravest, they reckoned that Aristodemus, for all the splendid feats he had achieved, had clearly enough broken ranks as he did, in a frenzy, because the stain on his name had prompted in him a yearning for death – whereas Poseidonius, who had proved himself a man of great heroism despite his lack of a death-wish, was by that measure the braver of the two. Perhaps, though, they only said this out of spite. Of the men I have listed who fell in the battle, all were given special honours, except Aristodemus alone, who received no honours for the reason I just cited – that he had wanted to die.[37]

[72] These, then, were the men who won the greatest renown at Plataea. One I might have listed, except that he did not perish in the actual battle, was Callicrates, who was the most handsome man, not merely in the Greek camp, but of his entire generation[38] – and that is counting all the Greeks, not just the Lacedaemonians. He had been sitting in the ranks while Pausanias was making sacrifice when he was wounded between the ribs by an arrow. He was stretchered away, cursing the prospect of his death; and as the battle raged, so he explained to Arimnestus, a man from Plataea, that while he did not mind dying for Greece, what upset him was that he had seen no action, nor – despite his desperation to perform well – achieved any deed worthy of his capacity.

[73] The Athenian whose reputation was most enhanced, so it is reported, was Sophanes, the son of Eutychides, from the deme of Decelea – whose people, the Athenians themselves say, once did something that has been working to their benefit ever since. For in ancient

times, when the Tyndaridae invaded Attic territory with a sizeable force to fetch back Helen, their ignorance of where she had been hidden led them to turn the various villages upside down; and it was then, so it is said, that the Deceleans (or, according to some, Decelus himself, out of disgust for Theseus' outrageous behaviour,[39] and anxiety for the whole of the land of the Athenians) revealed the full facts of the business to the Tyndaridae, and led them down to Aphidnae, which Titacus, a man born and bred there, then betrayed to them. Right up to the present day, thanks to this deed of theirs, the people of Decelea have never had to pay any dues in Sparta, and are entitled to sit in the front seats at festivals there; and even during the war that was fought many years later between the Athenians and the Peloponnesians, Decelea was spared the devastation that the Lacedaemonians inflicted on the rest of Attica.[40]

[74] So that was the home village of Sophanes, the most heroic of the Athenians that day, and about whom two different stories are told. According to one of these, he used to carry an iron anchor attached by means of a bronze chain to the belt of his breastplate, and which – whenever he closed in on the enemy – he would drop, thereby ensuring that none of the assaults launched at him by his adversaries from their own positions ever served to shift him from his. Should they turn in flight, though, his practice would then be to pick up the anchor and give them chase. In addition to this story, there is a second one which directly contradicts it: according to this version, the anchor was not made of iron and chained to his breastplate, but was something depicted on his shield, which he was forever moving this way and that, so that it never stood still.

[75] Sophanes was also responsible for another glittering deed, when, during the Athenian siege of Aegina, he issued a challenge to the champion pentathlete Eurybates of Argos, and killed him in single combat.[41] Nevertheless, for all that he had proved himself a man of rare courage, death overtook him as well in due course, when the Edonians killed him while he was in joint command of the Athenians with Leagrus, the son of Glaucon, in the battle for the revenue from the gold mines at Datum.[42]

[76] After the Greeks had overwhelmed the Barbarians at Plataea, a woman came to them who was a deserter from the Persian camp. She had been the concubine of Pharandates, the son of Teaspis, a man from Persia. On learning that the Greeks had won and annihilated the Persians, she decked out both herself and her maids in enormous amounts

of gold jewellery, and the most beautiful clothes she had to hand, then stepped down from her covered carriage, and crossed to the Lacedaemonians, who were still busy with their slaughter. When she saw Pausanias directing the whole proceedings, the fact that she was familiar with his name and fatherland from having heard them mentioned so often on previous occasions enabled her to work out his identity; and so she clasped him by his knees and appealed to him as a suppliant. 'O King of Sparta, I beg you, deliver me from the slavery that will otherwise be mine as a prisoner-of-war! You have already helped me, after all, by destroying these people who honour neither divinity nor gods. I am the daughter of Hegetorides, the son of Antagores, and was by birth a Coan. I was kidnapped from there by the Persian, who has held me ever since.' 'Woman,' Pausanias answered, 'you can set your fears at rest. Not only are you my suppliant, but if indeed you are telling the truth, and really are a daughter of Hegetorides of Cos – why, then – it just so happens that he is the closest guest-friend I have in that stretch of the world!' And so saying, he put her into the care of those of the ephors who were present, but only as a short-term measure, since subsequently he sent her on to Aegina at her own request.

[77] No sooner had this woman turned up than there also arrived the Mantineans – just as the action was over. So mortified were they to discover they had come too late for the battle that they announced they deserved to be punished for it. On learning that Artabazus and his Medes were in retreat, the Mantineans were eager to track them as far as Thessaly – but the Lacedaemonians prohibited pursuit of the fugitives. On their return home, the Mantineans sent the commanders of their army into exile. After them, the Eleans also arrived – and they too, like the Mantineans, departed in a state of high mortification, and on their return home banished their leaders. So much for the business of the Mantineans and the Eleans.[43]

[78] One of the men in the Aeginetan contingent at Plataea was a prominent Aeginetan called Lampon, the son of Pytheas. He came rushing up to Pausanias with a truly impious proposal, declaring: 'This feat of yours, O son of Cleombrotus, is an achievement of towering significance and splendour! Thanks to the god, you have rescued Greece and been granted a greater stock of glory than any other Greek known to us. But there are still things left you can do to set the seal on it. These will not only boost your reputation yet further, but make the Barbarians

think twice in future about embarking on any heinous actions against the Greeks. You see, when Leonidas perished at Thermopylae, Mardonius and Xerxes had his head cut off and stuck on a spike.[44] Pay like back with like, then, and what praise will be yours – first from all the Spartans, and then the other Greeks as well! After all, impale Mardonius, and you will be gaining vengeance for Leonidas, your uncle.' To this proposal, however, Pausanias gave an answer that was not at all the favourable response Lampon had been expecting.

[79] 'Impressed though I am, my friend from Aegina, by the high regard you show me, and your concern for my future, you are even so committing a serious error of judgement. First you puff me up high – my achievement and fatherland too – and then you would have me plumb the depths, by urging me to desecrate a corpse. Only do that, you say, and it will do wonders for my good name. But such a deed is better suited to a barbarian than a Greek – and even to them we begrudge it. I would never wish to pander to the Aeginetans in such a way, nor to anyone who finds it acceptable. So long as I do or say nothing that strikes the Spartiates as sacrilege, I am content. As for Leonidas, whom you urge me to avenge, I tell you this: he has been most awesomely avenged! There are souls here beyond numbering that do him honour – him and everyone else who perished at Thermopylae. Never again, therefore, approach me with such a proposal or recommendation – and be grateful this time that you may depart unharmed.'

[80] On hearing this, Lampon made his departure. Pausanias issued a proclamation forbidding anyone to lay a finger on the booty, and ordered the helots to gather up everything of value. They duly dispersed throughout the camp, and came across pavilions adorned with gold and silver, gilded couches and others that were overlaid with silver, and mixing-bowls, shallow bowls and various other kinds of drinking-vessel, all made of gold. The helots also found carts loaded with sacks, which turned out to contain gold and silver cauldrons. From the corpses that lay around they stripped armlets and torques, and short swords made of gold of the kind that the Persians call *akinakes*; but of the brightly patterned items of clothing no account was made. Much was stolen by the helots and sold to the Aeginetans – although there was also a lot that they did produce, since they could not possibly keep everything concealed. This was the origin of what became the prodigious

wealth of the Aeginetans, who bought up gold from the helots at a price equivalent to that of bronze.

[81] Once all the treasure had been assembled, a tithe was allocated to the god at Delphi, and used to dedicate the golden tripod which rests upon the three-headed bronze serpent[45] standing immediately next to the altar; another tithe was allocated to the god of Olympia, and used to dedicate a 10-cubit-high statue of Zeus; a further tithe was allocated to the god of the Isthmus, and used to make a 7-cubit-high statue of Poseidon out of bronze; and the remainder – the Persians' concubines, gold, silver, other valuables and yoke-animals – the Greeks portioned out among themselves, with each contingent receiving its just return. Although it is not recorded what portion of the spoils might have been given to the individuals who had most covered themselves with glory at Plataea, I am sure that they must have been awarded something. Certainly, ten of all the various things of value were set aside and given to Pausanias: women, horses, talents, camels, everything.

[82] It is also reported that Xerxes, when he fled Greece, left all his furnishings to Mardonius. So it was that when Pausanias saw these – the gold, the silver and the brightly patterned curtains with which Mardonius' tent had been fitted out – he commanded the bakers and chefs to cook him a meal of the kind they would have prepared for Mardonius. Once they had done as instructed, Pausanias gazed at the couches of gold and silver with their rich coverlets, and the magnificent feast weighing down the gold and silver tables, and was stupefied by the sheer spread of good things before him – and then, as a joke, he ordered his own servants to prepare a Laconian meal. So great was the contrast between this meal, when it had been readied, and the other, that Pausanias burst out laughing, and sent for the Greek generals. Once they had all assembled, he gestured to the two meals laid out before them[46] and said, 'Men of Greece, the reason I have brought you here together is because I wanted to demonstrate to you the senselessness of the Medes. Here is what their leader enjoyed every day – and yet, for all that, he came to rob us of the miserable portions you see here!' Such were the remarks Pausanias is said to have made to the Greek generals.

[83] For some time afterwards, the Plataeans would regularly come across chests of gold, silver and other valuables. Later on still, something else came to light. By this stage, the corpses were bare of their

flesh; and when the Plataeans came to collect all the bones together in one place, they found a skull that had no suture, but consisted instead of solid bone. There also materialized a jawbone which had sprouted, along the length of its upper jaw, a single tooth made of bone where individual teeth and molars should have been. Also uncovered was the skeleton of a man 5 cubits tall.

[84] Mardonius' corpse was spirited away the day after the battle by someone whom I cannot identify with any precision, since I have heard the names of a whole range of people from various places mentioned as the one who buried him – and I know for a fact that numerous people were lavishly rewarded by Artontes, the son of Mardonius, for the deed. I have found it quite impossible to narrow down which of them it actually was who gathered up the corpse of Mardonius and buried it. But according to one rumour, at any rate, it was Dionysophanes, a man from Ephesus, who buried Mardonius. Such are the details of his burial.

[85] After the division of the spoils, the Greeks buried their dead at Plataea, with separate graves for each contingent. The Lacedaemonians raised three tombs. In one they buried the priests,[47] including Poseidonius, Amompharetus, Philocyon and Callicrates. The next tomb, after this first one which contained the priests, was for the remaining Spartiates, and the third for the helots. But the Tegeans, in contrast to the manner in which the Lacedaemonians buried their dead, buried theirs all together in a mass grave, as did the Athenians, and the Megarians and the Phliasians, when they came to bury those of their men who had fallen victim to the cavalry. All of these various graves, then, were filled. But as for the others – which are likewise landmarks of Plataea – these, so I have found out, are mere empty mounds, raised by those who were ashamed at having missed the battle with the aim of impressing subsequent generations; indeed, there is even one there – the so-called 'tomb of the Aeginetans' – which I have heard was built a full ten years after the battle, at the request of the Aeginetans, by a man from Plataea called Cleades, the son of Autodicus, who was the representative of the Aeginetans in the city.

[86] No sooner had the Greeks buried their dead at Plataea than they held a council of war, at which they resolved to march on Thebes and demand the surrender of those who had been collaborating with the Medes – and in particular Timagenidas and Attaginus, who were the

ringleaders among the city's elite.[48] Should the Thebans refuse to give them up, then they would withdraw from the city only after they had first captured it. Accordingly, with these aims agreed, they arrived before Thebes eleven days after the battle, and started to put it under siege; when the Thebans proved unwilling to do as ordered and hand the men over, the Greeks proceeded to hack down everything in the surrounding countryside and attack the city walls.

[87] Twenty days into this campaign of relentless devastation, Timagenidas addressed the Thebans. 'Men of Thebes, the Greeks are resolved not to lift their siege until they have taken the city, or you have surrendered us to them. The land of Boeotia has had its fill of suffering now, and I would not have us be the cause of any more. It may be, of course, that these demands to hand us over are nothing but veiled extortion. In which case – bearing in mind that, far from acting alone in our collaboration, we had the backing of the whole community for it – let us buy the Greeks off with funds from the public treasury. If, however, we are genuinely the objects of their demands and this siege, then we will hand ourselves over to answer the charges.' The Thebans applauded this speech as an excellent and a timely one; and at once they sent a herald to Pausanias expressing their willingness to surrender the men.

[88] Then, when the two sides had come to agreement on these terms, Attaginus fled the city; and when his children were brought out under arrest, Pausanias absolved them of blame, and declared that the children of collaborators had no share in the guilt of their parents. As for the other people surrendered by the Thebans, it was their presumption that they would be given a trial and have the chance to bribe their way out of trouble. But Pausanias too was alert to this possibility; and so, when he took hold of them, he dismissed all the various allied contingents, and led the prisoners to Corinth, where he executed them. So much for the events at Plataea and Thebes.

[89] Meanwhile, Artabazus, the son of Pharnaces, had already covered a fair distance after fleeing from Plataea. When he arrived in Thessaly, the Thessalians invited him to share in their hospitality, and then – ignorant as they were of what had happened at Plataea – enquired after the rest of the army. Now, Artabazus well knew that any willingness on his part to reveal the full truth about the battle would risk his own and his men's annihilation, since he strongly suspected that all those who learned what had happened would then attack them; and

just as this calculation had led him earlier to keep the Phocians in the dark, so now he said to the Thessalians, 'Men of Thessaly! You have seen the speed with which I am marching to Thrace, the haste with which I am pressing onwards. The reason for this is that I and my men have been sent on a mission on behalf of our forces. Mardonius and his army are directly on our heels, and you should expect them to come marching past any day. Lay on hospitality for him too, and make a show of doing well by him – and in time to come you will certainly not regret it.' So saying, he and his men marched off as fast as they could through Thessaly and Macedonia, heading directly for Thrace – and indeed, so genuine was his hurry that he cut inland. By the time he reached Byzantium, he had lost numerous of his men, either cut down by the Thracians, or else overcome by hunger and exhaustion. From Byzantium, Artabazus made the crossing in boats.[49]

[90] So it was that he, at any rate, made it back to Asia. Now, on the very day that disaster struck at Plataea, so too, by coincidence, did it strike at Mycale, in Ionia. While the Greek squadrons that had arrived at Delos with Leotychidas of Lacedaemon were lying there inactive,[50] you see, three envoys came to them from Samos: Lampon, the son of Thrasycles, Athenagoras, the son of Archestratides, and Hegesistratus, the son of Aristagoras. They had been sent by the Samians without the knowledge of the Persians and the puppet installed by the Persians on Samos as a tyrant, Theomestor, the son of Androdamas. When the messengers came before the Greek commanders, Hegesistratus gave a lengthy speech, listing any number of reasons why the mere sight of the Greek fleet would bring the Ionians to revolt against the Persians, and arguing that the Barbarians themselves would not stand their ground. 'And even supposing they do, why – you will never again come across such easy prey!' Then, invoking the gods that they worshipped in common, Hegesistratus urged his audience to redeem from slavery men who were Greeks, and to hurl back the Barbarians. These objectives, he assured them, would be easy to obtain. 'The Barbarian ships are barely seaworthy – and certainly no match for you in any battle. And if you are worried that we might be leading you into a trap, we are prepared to be boarded as hostages on your ships.'

[91] Then, while the Samian stranger was still desperately making these pleas, Leotychidas asked him a question – perhaps out of a con-

scious desire to obtain an omen, or else by chance, at the prompting of a god. 'What is your name, Samian stranger?' 'Hegesistratus . . .', he answered – but then, before he could complete whatever else he was going to say, he was cut off in mid-flow.[51] 'I accept this omen, Samian stranger,' Leotychidas declared. 'But you and your companions here, before you sail away, must give us a solemn pledge that the people of Samos will indeed be fully committed to their alliance with us.'

[92] No sooner had he spoken than the deed was done: the Samians gave their pledge immediately, and swore oaths of allegiance to the Greeks.[52] The other two Samians then sailed away; but Leotychidas commanded Hegesistratus, in whose name he had identified the omen, to accompany the Greek fleet. They stayed one day in harbour; and then, on the next, favourable auspices were obtained after sacrifices had been made by a man from Apollonia (the Apollonia in the Ionian Gulf, that is)[53] called Deïphonus – the father of whom [Euenius] once had the following events befall him.

[93] There are, in this particular Apollonia, sheep sacred to the sun. By day, they graze beside a river which flows from Mount Lacmon through Apollonian territory out to the sea, by the harbour of Oricum, but by night they are guarded by someone chosen from those among the citizens who are most highly regarded in terms of wealth and lineage – each person nominated doing it for a year. The high value placed by the Apollonians on these sheep is due to a prophecy. The shelter consists of a cave far from the city. It was here that this Euenius – then the man in charge – looked after them. One night, he fell asleep while on his watch, and wolves, slipping into the cave, killed some sixty of the sheep. When Euenius realized what had happened, he bit his tongue and said not a word, having in mind instead to buy substitutes. The Apollonians, though, far from being hoodwinked, found out what had happened; and after hauling him before a court, they sentenced him, for the crime of falling asleep on watch, to be deprived of his eyes. No sooner had they blinded Euenius, however, than their livestock stopped giving birth and their soil turned similarly barren. When the Apollonians asked [the oracles] at Dodona and Delphi the reason for the calamity they were experiencing [, both gave the same answer]: that they had unjustly deprived Euenius, the guardian of the sacred flock, of his sight. For the gods themselves had sent the wolves, and would not cease exacting vengeance on his behalf until the Apollonians had paid reparation to him

for their deed – the choice of what was appropriate resting with Euenius. Then, once that had been settled, they themselves – the gods – would grant Euenius such a gift as most people would regard it a blessing to possess.

[94] These were the oracles delivered to the Apollonian envoys, who kept them secret from everyone else, except for certain of their fellow-citizens whom they commissioned to deal with the matter. The course adopted by these men was as follows. Approaching Euenius while he was sitting on a bench, they sat down beside him and struck up a conversation, which they steered, in due course, to an expression of sympathy on their part for his suffering. Then, after leading him on, they asked him what he would choose as compensation, just supposing, for the sake of argument, that the Apollonians wished to make reparation for what they had done. He, unaware of the oracle, declared that he would settle for the gift of some fields (and indeed, specifically mentioned two citizens whom he knew to own the two finest plots in Apollonia), and a house which was, as he fully appreciated, the best appointed in the city. 'If I ended up with those,' he said, 'then I would feel that I had obtained adequate compensation, and not spend the rest of my days given over to anger.' The people sitting beside him, in reply to these words of his, then said, 'Euenius, these reparations for your blinding will indeed be paid you by the people of Apollonia, in accordance with an oracle they have received.' Euenius, now that he had the full story, was furious, feeling that he had been tricked; but the Apollonians bought the estates and house from their owners anyway, and gave him what he had chosen. And immediately, from that moment on, the gift of prophecy for which he became famous was something instinctive within him.

[95] So this was the Euenius whose son, Deïphonus, had been brought along by the Corinthians to serve the fleet as its diviner. I have also heard that Deïphonus was not in fact his son, but had adopted his name under false pretences, and traded on it to obtain employment across the entire Greek world.

[96] Once the Greeks had obtained favourable omens, the fleet put to sea and headed from Delos towards Samos. On their arrival off Calami on the Samian coast, they dropped anchor by the sanctuary of Hera there, and began to prepare their ships for battle; but the Persians, learning of their approach, themselves put to sea and sailed for the mainland

with their entire fleet – all, that is, except the Phoenicians', which was sent away. The Persians had talked the issue over, you see, and decided – on the grounds that they were no match for the Greeks – not to commit Phoenician ships to battle. The reason they sailed for the mainland was to obtain the protection of their infantry, a force of which had been left behind at Mycale by the main army, on the orders of Xerxes, to stand watch there over Ionia. Sixty thousand strong in number, it was commanded by Tigranes, tallest and most handsome of the Persians. So the commanders of the fleet planned to take refuge beneath the watch of this army by beaching their ships and building a circular stockade to serve as a protection for their ships and as a bolt-hole for themselves.

[97] This, then, was the plan with which they had put to sea. Passing the sanctuary of the Potniae[54] at Mycale, they arrived at Gaeson and Scolopoeis, where the Eleusinian Demeter has a shrine that was built by Philistus, the son of Pasicles, when he accompanied Neileus, the son of Codrus, on his journey to found Miletus; and it was here that the Persians beached their fleet, chopped down some cultivated trees, and built a stockade around their ships using the timber and stones, around which they then fixed stakes. These preparations enabled them to be ready for two eventualities: that they would either be put under siege, or else secure a victory.

[98] Meanwhile, the Greeks were aggrieved to learn that the Barbarians had fled them by departing for the mainland, and were at a loss what to do: whether to make their way home or sail down towards the Hellespont. In the end, they decided to adopt neither course of action, but sail instead for the mainland. Accordingly, once they had stocked up with boarding planks and all the other things required to fight a battle at sea, they set a course for Mycale. When it became obvious, as the Greeks closed in on the enemy camp, that no one was coming out to meet them, and they observed ships beached inside a stockade and a large array of infantry drawn up along the beach, the first thing Leotychidas did was to sail past in his own vessel, getting as close in as he could to the shore, and through a herald issue a proclamation to the Ionians. 'Men of Ionia,' he announced, 'as many of you as can hear me, mark what I have to say. The Persians, after all, will understand nothing of the instructions I am giving you! When battle is joined, keep the thought of freedom uppermost in your minds – and with it the password "Hera". And if you hear this message, please, pass it on to someone

who has not.' The thinking behind this action was the same as Themistocles' at Artemisium.[55] Either the message would mean nothing to the Persians while swaying the Ionians, or else, if it did come to the attention of the Barbarians, it would render them suspicious of the Greeks in their ranks.

[99] Then, after Leotychidas had made his proposal, what the Greeks did next was to bring their ships up to the beach and disembark. They began to draw up their lines; and the Persians, when they saw the Greeks getting ready for battle, and unsettled by the exhortations given to the Ionians, disarmed the Samians as suspected sympathizers with the Greeks. They did this because the Samians had released some Athenian prisoners-of-war left stranded in Attica and captured by Xerxes' forces, and then transported to Samos by the barbarian fleet; indeed, the Samians had not only freed the prisoners, but sent them on their way to Athens complete with provisions. In all, the Samians had liberated some five hundred head of Xerxes' adversaries – and it was this, more than anything, that explained the suspicion in which they were held. A second measure taken by the Persians was to assign the Milesians to guard the passes leading to the summits of Mycale – ostensibly on the grounds that they were the ones most familiar with the terrain, but in reality because they were not wanted in the camp. After taking these precautionary measures against those of the Ionians whom they suspected of wanting to stab them in the back, given the chance, the Persians formed a barrier around themselves by locking together their wicker shields.

[100] Once the Greeks had made their preparations, they advanced against the Barbarians. As they went, so a rumour flew around the entire body of their force, and a herald's staff was seen lying on the very edge of the shore. The rumour passing through the ranks was that the Greeks had defeated Mardonius and his army in a battle in Boeotia. Indeed, here was just one of the many clear proofs of the role played by the divine in mortal affairs: that the disaster at Plataea and the one now threatening at Mycale should both have occurred on the same day,[56] and that a rumour, reaching the Greeks, should have served greatly to boost their morale and render them the keener to brave danger.

[101] One other coincidence: both battles took place beside precincts sacred to Demeter of Eleusis. As I have already mentioned,[57] the one at Plataea was fought right next to the temple of Demeter itself, and the same thing would happen at Mycale too. What is more, by the time the

rumour of the victory won by Pausanias and the Greeks arrived, it was actually true. The action at Plataea took place early in the day, and the one at Mycale in the afternoon. Only when the Greeks made a detailed enquiry into the matter, not long afterwards, did they come to realize that both engagements had taken place on the same day of the same month. Before the arrival of the rumour they had been fearful, not so much for themselves as for the Greeks generally, lest Mardonius bring about the downfall of Greece. After the mysterious winging of the rumour to them, however, they quickened their pace and pressed their attack all the harder. Indeed, with both the islands and the Hellespont as the prizes, the Barbarians as well as the Greeks were keen to join battle.

[102] Now, up to around half of the Greek forces, consisting of the Athenians and those deployed alongside them, were advancing across the beach, over level ground, while the Lacedaemonians and those posted next to them had to traverse a ravine and high ground. Even as these troops were still making their way around, those on the other wing were already busy with the battle. For as long as the Persians were able to keep their wicker shields upright, they put up a good defence, and the battle remained evenly poised. But then, because the Athenians and the contingents alongside them were keen that victory be theirs, and not shared with the Lacedaemonians, they yelled out cries of encouragement to one another, redoubled their efforts and turned the tide of battle. Shoving aside the wicker shields, they fell in a massed onslaught upon the Persians, who – although they continued to stand their ground and fight back for a long time – eventually sought the refuge of their stockade. The Athenians and the various contingents arrayed alongside them – namely, the Corinthians, the Sicyonians and the Troezenians – all joined together in pursuit and launched a combined assault on the palisade. That too fell; and it was then that the Barbarians' courage failed them, and they took to flight – all except the Persians.[58] Even as wave after wave of the Greeks poured in through the fortifications, small pockets of Persians continued to hold out. Two of their commanders fled, and two perished: Artaÿntes and Ithamitres, who were in command of the fleet, both fled, while Mardontes and Tigranes, who held the command by land, both perished in the fighting.

[103] While the Persians were still putting up a fight, the Lacedaemonians and those accompanying them arrived and helped finish off the

men still remaining. Greek casualties in the battle were high, especially among the Sicyonians, who lost their commander, Perileos. The Samian troops, who had been disarmed but were still in the camp of the Medes, and had realized right from the onset of the battle that it might go either way, had not hesitated to do all they could to achieve their aim of assisting the Greeks. The other Ionians too, when they saw the example set by the Samians, likewise revolted against the Persians and attacked the Barbarians.

[104] Meanwhile, the Milesians had been commissioned by the Persians to guard the passes, so that – in the event of a catastrophe such as did indeed overwhelm them – they would have guides able to bring them safely to the heights of Mycale. There was also another reason for the deployment of the Milesians there: to keep them from the Persian camp, and prevent them from stirring up trouble. The Milesians, however, did exactly the opposite of what they had been ordered: they took the fugitives down alternative roads, which led the Barbarians to their enemies, with the result that the Milesians ended up inflicting more casualties on them than anyone, and proving their worst enemies of all. So it was, for the second time, that Ionia revolted against the Persians.

[105] The Greeks who did best in the battle were the Athenians – and of them the best was a specialist pancratiast called Hermolycus, the son of Euthoenus. Some time afterwards, during the war between the Athenians and the Carystians, Hermolycus was killed on Carystian soil in a battle at Cyrnus, and buried on the promontory of Geraestus.[59] Next to the Athenians, the Corinthians, the Troezenians and the Sicyonians were the best.

[106] After the Greeks had finished off most of the Barbarians in the course either of the battle or of the retreat, they torched the ships and the entire stockade – but only after they had first brought out the booty onto the beach and discovered some stashes of treasure. Then, with the fleet and the fortifications both reduced to ashes, they sailed away. On their arrival at Samos, they debated the evacuation of the Ionians, and where in those regions of Greece under their control they should settle the refugees, were they indeed to abandon Ionia to the Barbarians. Certainly, that they lacked the resources to keep a constant watch on Ionia appeared to them self-evident – which being so, they held out not the slightest hope that the Persians would let the Ionians go unpunished. The best option, so the Peloponnesian leaders thought, would be to

empty of their populations the various trading-centres that had collaborated with the Medes, and give their lands to the Ionians to live in; but the Athenians – who took as their starting-point a refusal to countenance any evacuation of Ionia – were not best pleased to have their own colonists a topic of debate among the Peloponnesians. Indeed, so forcefully did they press their objections that the Peloponnesians[60] backed down. So it was that the Athenians came to forge an alliance with the Samians, the Chians, the Lesbians and the various other islanders who had taken the Greek side in the war – all of whom swore to stay faithful to the terms of the treaty,[61] and never to break them. Then, having taken these oaths, away they sailed to demolish the bridges. They did this on the presumption that the bridges were still intact. The fleet duly set sail, then, for the Hellespont.

[107] As for those Barbarians who had escaped and been penned in on the heights of Mycale, they – few as they were – made their way to Sardis. During the course of this journey, Artaÿntes, the commander, was repeatedly insulted by Masistes, the son of Darius,[62] who had been present at the defeat, and said, among other things, that a woman would have made a better commander than him, and that no punishment was too severe for someone who had inflicted such damage on the House of the King. Now, among the Persians, there is no worse insult than to be compared unfavourably to a woman. So often did Artaÿntes have to listen to this that eventually he could take it no more, and drew his scimitar on Masistes, with the intention of killing him. But as he lunged forwards, he was noticed by a man from Halicarnassus called Xeinagoras, the son of Prexileos, who caught him around his midriff, picked him up and flung him down onto the ground. By this stage, Masistes' bodyguards had stepped forwards to screen their master. This action of Xeinagoras won him the gratitude not only of Masistes but of Xerxes as well, because it had saved his brother. Indeed, the King rewarded Xeinagoras for his deed by giving him the whole of Cilicia to rule. Meanwhile, the journey proceeded without further noteworthy incident until they reached Sardis. The King himself had been in Sardis ever since his arrival there in the wake of his defeat in the sea-battle, and his flight from Athens.

[108] During his time in Sardis, Xerxes had fallen passionately in love with Masistes' wife,[63] who was also there. When his messages failed to

win her over, he was prevented by the respect he felt for Masistes as his brother from forcing himself on her – a consideration that had also served to strengthen the resolve of the woman herself, well aware as she was that she would not be raped. Finally, with every other option exhausted, Xerxes arranged for his own son, Darius, to marry the daughter of Masistes and his wife, in the expectation that such a step would improve his own chances of getting his hands on the woman. He duly betrothed the couple, completed the customary marital rites and sped off to Susa. However, after he had arrived and brought Darius' wife into his house, he had a change of heart, and dropped Masistes' wife in favour of his daughter, the wife of Darius – a passion which he brought to consummation. The name of this woman was Artaÿnte.

[109] In time, the whole business came out in the following manner. Amestris, Xerxes' wife, wove him a most wonderful cloak, sweeping and brightly coloured, as a gift. Delighted, he put it on, then headed off to Artaÿnte. After she too had given him great pleasure, he told her to ask for whatever she wanted, in exchange for the services she had just rendered him. 'Demand, and you shall receive.' It was then, because Artaÿnte and her entire house were fated to come to a terrible end, that she said to Xerxes, 'You will really give me whatever I request?' He, never for a moment guessing what she would actually demand, promised on oath – whereupon she, now that he had sworn, coolly asked him for his cloak. This set Xerxes racking his brains: he really did not want to give Artaÿnte the cloak, for the simple reason that he was afraid Amestris, who already had her suspicions about what he was up to, would rumble what was going on. He offered Artaÿnte cities, and inexhaustible supplies of gold, and even sole command of her own army – a classic Persian gift. But still she would not be swayed – and so he gave her the cloak. Artaÿnte, ecstatic at being presented with such a present, then sported it in a mood of triumph.

[110] The fact that she had possession of the cloak soon came to the attention of Amestris. However, rather than bear a grudge against the woman herself when informed what she was up to, Amestris presumed that responsibility for what was going on lay instead with the mother, the wife of Masistes, and plotted *her* destruction. Amestris bided her time until Xerxes, her husband, was celebrating the banquet that is held once every year to mark the royal birthday, and which is known by the Persians as *tukta* – meaning, in Greek, 'complete'. This, the one occasion

when the King anoints his head, is also when he hands out gifts to the Persians. So Amestris waited for the day to come round; and when it did, she asked Xerxes to give her Masistes' wife. Now, to Xerxes, the thought of handing over his brother's wife was both shocking and appalling and all the more so because she was perfectly innocent in the matter. (He had grasped, you see, what lay behind Amestris' request.)

[111] So implacable was his wife, though, and so binding on him the custom that no request made during the course of the royal banquet be refused anyone, that he did eventually – albeit with great reluctance – give Amestris the nod, and make her a present of the woman. 'Do with her what you will,' Xerxes ordered; and then sent for his brother. 'Masistes,' he said, 'not only are you the son of Darius and my own brother, but you are a good man as well. That being so, divorce your current wife. I give you in her stead the hand of my daughter. Marry her. As for the one you have now, she does not seem good to me – dispose of her.' Masistes was astonished by these words. 'O Master,' he said, 'what an unconscionable thing to say! Divorce my wife and marry your daughter – these are seriously your orders? The mother of my children, my young sons and my daughters – one of whom, indeed, you have given in marriage to your own son! A woman with whom I am perfectly compatible! Most honoured though I am, O King, to be thought worthy of your daughter, yet I will not marry her, nor will I divorce my wife. Please, do not resort to compulsion concerning this matter. Some other man will emerge, no less worthy of your daughter than myself. As for me – please, let me continue to live with my wife.' But this answer of his put Xerxes into a fury. 'This is how it is for you, Masistes,' he said. 'Not a moment more will you remain married to your wife – and on top of that, I withdraw the gift I made you of my daughter's hand. That will teach you to accept what you are offered.' When Masistes heard this, he said only, 'Well, Master, at least for now you have not had me killed,' and then out he walked.

[112] Meanwhile, at the same time as this exchange between Xerxes and his brother was taking place, Amestris had summoned Xerxes' bodyguards, and brutally mutilated Masistes' wife. She hacked off the woman's breasts and threw them to the dogs, cut off her nose, her ears, her lips and her tongue,[64] and only then, once she was terribly disfigured, did Amestris send her home.

[113] Of this, Masistes had as yet heard nothing, but expecting that

something terrible had happened, he came bursting into his house at a run. Immediately he had seen his maimed wife, he took counsel with his children, and then set off for Bactria with his sons (and various others as well, no doubt) with the aim of raising the province of Bactria in revolt, and inflicting as much damage on the King as he could. Indeed, I imagine that is exactly what would have happened, had he only made it up to the land of the Bactrians and the Sacae without being intercepted. He was very popular with them, you see, and was the governor of the Bactrians. Xerxes, however, was informed of what he was doing, and dispatched a squad of soldiers who killed Masistes and his children while they were still on the road, and their own men with them. Such was the story of the grand passion of Xerxes and the death of Masistes.

[114] In the meantime, the Greeks who had embarked for the Hellespont from Mycale were initially blown off course by contrary winds, and made anchor off Lectum; from there they proceeded to Abydus, where the bridges they had been expecting to find still securely fastened – and which indeed had been their main reason for coming to the Hellespont – they discovered to be in pieces. It was at this point that the Peloponnesians led by Leotychidas decided to sail back to Greece; but the Athenians and their commander Xanthippus opted instead to stay put, and make an attempt on the Chersonese. As the Peloponnesians sailed away, then, so the Athenians crossed from Abydus over to the Chersonese and put Sestus under siege.

[115] When people from thereabouts heard that the Greeks were in the Hellespont, they all flocked into Sestus, on the grounds that it was the best fortified of any settlement in the region. One man in particular who headed there, from the city of Cardia, was a Persian called Oeobazus, who brought with him the various cables from the bridges. The native inhabitants of Sestus were Aeolians, but there were also Persians, and a great throng of their allies, inside the city.

[116] The governor who ruled the province on behalf of Xerxes was a Persian called Artaÿctes, a man of such cunning and wickedness that he had tricked the King, during the course of the advance on Athens, into allowing him to filch the treasures of Protesilaus,[65] the son of Iphiclus from Elaeous. For, in Elaeous in the Chersonese there stands a precinct containing the tomb of Protesilaus; and the numerous treasures to be found there – gold and silver drinking-bowls, bronze, robes and

various other dedicatory offerings – had all of them been stolen by Artaÿctes, after the King had given him permission to take them. He had hoodwinked Xerxes by telling him, 'Master, there is the house here of some Greek fellow who took part in an invasion of your territory, and met his just deserts by being killed. Give me his house, and it will stand as a warning to everyone against attacking your lands.' This kind of story was bound to persuade Xerxes – who never so much as suspected Artaÿctes' real motives – into giving him a person's house. Artaÿctes' talk of Protesilaus invading the King's lands had been very deliberate, you see. The Persians take for granted that the whole of Asia is theirs: the inalienable property of their kings.⁶⁶ Once Artaÿctes had been made a gift of the treasures, he had them removed from Elaeous to Sestus; he also planted the temple precinct, turned it over to agriculture and used the inner sanctuary – whenever he came to Elaeous in person – in which to have sex with women. But the prospect of the Athenians putting him under siege was something that he had neither anticipated, nor prepared for, and so their descent, when it did come, took him completely unawares.

[117] As it happened, the siege dragged on into the autumn; and the Athenians, who were impatient to get home, and frustrated by their inability to capture the stronghold, demanded that their generals take them back to Athens. The high command, though, refused – not until they had captured the city, or else been recalled by the Athenian people as a whole. Their men were content with this scenario.

[118] Meanwhile, those inside the city walls had been brought to such extremes of desperation that they were boiling up the leather straps from their beds to eat. Then, when even these had been used up, the Persians – Artaÿctes and Oeobazus among them – made their escape under cover of darkness by descending the city walls at their remotest point, where the enemy were at their most sparse. At daybreak, the Chersonesians signalled from the watchtowers to the Athenians what had happened and opened the gates. Some of the Athenians stayed behind to occupy the city, but most of them set off in pursuit of the fugitives.

[119] Now, the escape route taken by Oeobazus was into Thrace, where he was captured by the Apsinthian Thracians; they sacrificed him after their own manner to Pleistorus, a local god, while his companions they put to death in some other fashion. As for Artaÿctes and his men,

who had not been as quick off the mark in making their escape bid, they were overtaken just inland of Aegospotami, where, after a lengthy resistance, all those not killed were taken alive. The prisoners were put into chains by the Greeks and brought back to Sestus – and among them was Artaÿctes himself and his son.

[120] It so happened, according to a portentous tale told by the Chersonesians, that one of the men guarding them was grilling some salted fish, when all of a sudden, even as the fish were lying there in the flames, they began to flop and wriggle about, as though just newly caught. Everyone around the fire was astonished by this; but when Artaÿctes witnessed the extraordinary phenomenon, he called out to the man who was cooking the fish, and said, 'Do not be alarmed by this portent, my Athenian friend. Its manifestation has nothing to do with you. Protesilaus is sending me a sign from Elaeous that, dead and dried up like a salted fish though he may be, yet he has a divinely granted power to punish criminals. Now, that being so, I am willing to make the following recompense – in compensation to the god for the treasures I took from the sanctuary, 100 talents, and as a ransom for myself and my son, should the Athenians let us live, 200 talents.' However, this promise was not enough to sway Xanthippus, the commander. The people of Elaeous, in the cause of securing vengeance for Protesilaus, were demanding that Artaÿctes be put to death – a point of view to which Xanthippus himself was coming round. So they brought Artaÿctes to the headland from which Xerxes had yoked the strait (or, according to some, to the hill which overlooks the city of Madytus), and there they nailed him fast to a plank of wood and crucified him;[67] and then, before his very eyes, they stoned his son to death.

[121] Having taken these measures, the fleet then headed back to Greece, bringing with it – in addition to various other treasures – the cables from the bridges, to be presented as dedicatory offerings to the various sanctuaries. After these events, nothing else happened that year.

[122] The forefather of this Artaÿctes who was crucified was the same Artembares who presented a proposal to the Persians, which they then adopted and brought before Cyrus. 'Since Zeus has bestowed an empire upon the Persians,' the terms of this proposal ran, 'and among individuals, Cyrus, upon you, who toppled Astyages, come, let us emigrate from this small and rugged land of ours, and take ownership of a different and better one. After all, whether on our borders or further

afield, there are any number of countries which we would only have to possess to become objects of even greater wonder than we are at present – any one of them would do. What more natural than that men with power should adopt such a course of action? Nor, it must be said, shall we ever have a better opportunity than now, when so many peoples are our subjects, and we rule the whole of Asia.' But Cyrus, when he heard this proposal, found it less than wonderful; he told the Persians to put it into action by all means, but advised them to prepare themselves, should they go ahead, to be rulers no more, but ruled instead. 'Soft lands are prone to breed soft men. No country can be remarkable for its yield of crops, and at the same time breed men who are hardy in war.'[68] So convinced were the Persians by this argument that they took their leave of Cyrus, and opted – now that his judgement had proved superior to their own – to live in a harsh land and rule rather than to sow a level plain, and be the slaves of others.[69]

Notes

All dates are BC unless stated otherwise. 'H.' is Herodotus.

BOOK ONE

1. *from Halicarnassus*: Some manuscripts have 'from Thouria', since H. – though born in Halicarnassus – later became a citizen of Thouria in south Italy.
2. *enquiries*: In Greek *historiai* (singular *historiê*), the root via Latin *historia* of our 'history'.
3. *barbarians*: All non-Greeks were 'barbarians', a term originally signifying incomprehensible language but later used derogatorily to indicate cultural inferiority. A vision of Greekness, what it was to be Greek, is offered at 8.144.
4. *reason*: The Greek word *aitiê*, translated here as 'reason', could also mean 'responsibility', implying assignation of blame.
5. *Phoenicians . . . sea of ours*: 'Phoenicians' itself meant 'Red Men' in Greek – it is not known what the Phoenicians, from modern Lebanon, called themselves. What the Greeks called the 'Red Sea' is today's 'Persian Gulf'; 'our' sea is the Mediterranean.
6. *Argos*: In Homer, the Greeks' most ancient written source, Greeks were then called 'Argives', 'men of Argos'. But the Argos in question here is the town in the eastern Peloponnese.
7. *Europa*: Note that Europa, who gives her name to 'Europe', was according to this myth by origin Asiatic.
8. *rape of Helen*: This is by no means the only, or the most accepted, version of the origins of the Trojan War. The Greek word *harpagê* meant literally 'seizure' or 'abduction' and was something of a euphemism.
9. *This . . . is the version of events promoted by the Persians*: H. could not himself speak or read Persian, so – if these stories are not indeed pure invention – he must have had them either from a Greek-speaking Persian source or a Persian-speaking Greek source, or sources.
10. *Far be it from me . . . carry on with the rest of my account*: This formulation would support the interpretation of 'reason' in the Preface, at the start of Book 1, as here meaning responsibility or blame.

11. *those that were great once ... mighty powers*: Cyclical processes appealed to H.; see also ch. 207, as mentioned in Introduction 7.

12. *humans and prosperity never endure side by side for long*: Pessimism – or realism? Either way, the implied message to readers/auditors was not to indulge in overconfident expectation.

13. *Euxine Sea*: *Euxine* literally meant 'welcoming to strangers' – a classic case of ancient Greek euphemism, since the environment for shipping and sailors in much of the Black Sea was always at best unpredictable, often actively hostile.

14. *Lacedaemonians*: First mention of the historical Spartans, who were also called 'Lacedaemonians' after the name of both their state and state territory, Lacedaemon. Confusingly, that label might also be applied (e.g. 7.234) to non-Spartan but free residents of the territory, who were politically subordinated and militarily and economically obligated to the Spartans.

15. *all the Greeks had been free*: H. strikes early the note of freedom that will run through the entire work. Here, 'freedom' means autonomy – freedom from external control. Elsewhere it can refer to either personal freedom or the freedom of political self-determination. All types of freedom were deeply cherished by Greeks.

16. *Heracles ... the Mermnads*: Greeks were happy to imagine, in myth, that a Greek hero-god, Heracles, might have sired a non-Greek royal dynasty – descended allegedly from one Mermnas.

17. *Candaules ... believed her to be ... the most beautiful woman in the world*: Candaules' fatal mistake, in Greek eyes, was to allow himself to be overpowered by *erôs* – erotic passion – for his own wife; Greeks normally considered such an emotion was appropriate in adult males only towards boys or prostitutes, but even then it should be kept firmly under control.

18. *taboo to be seen naked*: Nudity was for the Greeks a key cultural marker. They liked to believe that barbarian males did not display their bodies in public because they were ashamed of their flabby flesh, but it would have been no less shameful for a Greek woman than for a Lydian queen to be seen naked, even in private, by a male other than her husband.

19. *'In the very room ... while he is asleep'*: The unnamed queen of Candaules is by no means the last hugely resourceful woman to reverse gender expectations and dominate the opposite sex in the pages of H. The classic case of the type is Artemisia, queen of H.'s own Halicarnassus, at the battle of Salamis.

20. *Archilochus of Paros*: Archilochus, who wrote in the iambic metre, originated on the Cycladic marble island of Paros and migrated to the island of Thasos *c.* 650; unconventional in many ways, at least in his verses, he claimed not to desire the 'tyranny' (absolute sole rule) of Gyges. Gyges gets a mention also in contemporary neo-Assyrian records, under the nomenclature of *Gugu*.

21. *Delphi*: The first mention of the major oracular shrine of the entire Greek world, on a site sacred to Apollo (and Dionysus). *Delphi* literally means 'wombs'. Non-Greeks did occasionally consult the Pythia, Apollo's priestess – for instance, Gyges' distant successor Croesus.

22. *prediction ... came true*: At 8.77, H. apparently writes that all oracular pronouncements were in some sense true – but that passage may be an interpolation.

23. *first barbarian on record*: Greeks were very keen on 'famous firsts'. Phrygia lay inland from the Anatolian coast.

24. *Miletus ... Smyrna ... Colophon*: Three cities of Greek Ionia, the region of Western Anatolia also including Ephesus and another eight cities.

25. *Priene*: Another of the twelve main Ionian cities.

26. *Sardis*: The Lydian capital which lay inland from Ionian Greek Ephesus. Archaeology reveals the extent to which it underwent strong Greek cultural influences. Its burning in 498 by Athenians is given portentous significance by H. at 5.102.

27. *This king went to war ... Colophon*: This sentence implicates Lydia with three quite distinct civilizations: the Medes of northern Iran, the migrant Cimmerians from inland Anatolia and the Ionian Greeks of coastal Colophon.

28. *The war ... rumbled on*: We are now in the first or second quarter of the sixth century.

29. *what earthly point ... putting their city under siege?*: Readers/auditors of the late 430s/early 420s would immediately think of the situation of Athens and its territory in relation to Sparta.

30. *Chians*: People of Chios, another offshore Ionian island in the Eastern Aegean.

31. *Erythraeans*: People of Erythrae, a coastal Ionian city.

32. *When the messengers arrived at Delphi ... Lydians had burned to the ground*: Here readers/auditors would recall the Persians' destructions of Athena's temple on the Athenian acropolis in 480 and 479.

33. *Now I know for a fact ... I heard it directly from the Delphians themselves*: A methodological passage, of a type very common in H. Oral, hearsay evidence was for him primary: see e.g. 2.99.

34. *sacred ties of friendship*: In Athenian Greek this special friendship was called *xenia*, in H.'s Ionic-dialect Greek *xeiniê*; 'ritualized guest-friendship' is a clumsy but accurate rendition.

35. *No other explanation will possibly do*: Modern readers are not necessarily so easily convinced.

36. *Alyattes built two temples ... restored to full health*: Herodotus was always happy to believe, and happier to record, such a divinely inspired convalescence.

37. *dithyramb*: A type of hymn sacred to Dionysus. There is not much in the way of hard evidence underlying this moralizing folktale, but Arion is presumably a historical figure who composed dithyrambs.

38. *Taenarum*: The southernmost point of mainland Europe and notoriously hard to visit (Cape Matapan in more recent times). A reputed entrance to Hades, the Greek underworld or hell, lay near by.

39. *temple of Artemis*: A much later reconstruction of the temple of Artemis at Ephesus was to feature as one of the Seven Wonders of the Ancient World, and Artemis was St Paul's 'Diana of the Ephesians' in Acts.

40. *ground of complaint . . . flimsy pretext*: This distinction between 'ground of complaint' and 'pretext' is a pre-echo of Thucydides 1.23, a famous passage attempting to account for the origins of the Peloponnesian War.

41. *Just as . . . offshore*: The veracity of the anecdote can't be tested, but Bias of Ionian Priene was later reputed one of the 'Seven Sages' of ancient Greece.

42. *all the peoples . . . submit to Croesus*: Croesus' is the first oriental empire which Herodotus discusses, though that of the Medes which he will discuss later (ch. 95ff.) was established earlier.

43. *Lydians . . . Pamphylians*: All but the Ionians, Dorians and Aeolians were 'barbarians'.

44. *height of her prosperity*: Readers/auditors would have been alerted by ch. 5 to expect a fall.

45. *Solon of Athens*: The best attested of all H.'s early characters (*fl. c.* 600), but his visit with Croesus below is alas a factoid.

46. *various treasuries . . . how . . . sumptuous everything was*: Hence the proverbial 'rich as Croesus'.

47. *Tellus . . . splendid honours*: Tellus, whoever he really was – if indeed he ever was – was the ideal-utopian Athenian of everyone's dreams. The moral of his story is told a couple of chapters later – you must always look to the end.

48. *statues*: Two magnificent limestone *kouros* ('male youth') statues of approximately the right date have been excavated and put on display in the museum at Delphi, but their identification as Cleobis and Biton has no authority but H.'s.

49. *your question . . . how perplexing in their ways*: This is a powerful short statement of why the Greeks stood so much in awe of their gods and goddesses, of the divine sphere in general.

50. *human life . . . vagaries of chance*: This could be seen as expressing either pessimism – or realism.

51. *idiot*: The real idiot of course was to be proved to be Croesus.

52. *a dream . . . come true*: Dreams were for Herodotus often divine manifestations, and often truth-telling too.

53. *weapons . . . dropping onto his son*: Shades of the Sleeping Beauty folktale motif here, in which it had been ordered by royal decree that all spindles be removed but to equally little positive effect.

54. *A Phrygian . . . had blood on his hands . . . practised in Greece*: The original audience would have thought at once of Patroclus in the *Iliad*, who had first made the acquaintance of Achilles when admitted by Achilles' father Peleus

to his household as a suppliant-stranger having committed manslaughter. H. shows his usual interest in comparative Greek–non-Greek customs.

55. *in Mysia . . . Mount Olympus*: Not to be confused with the Mt Olympus in Macedonia, mainland Greece.

56. *on the hunt*: Hunting, especially of the fearsome wild boar, was an upper-class Greek craze and virility symbol – much favoured by Alexander the Great.

57. *cowardice*: The word H. uses here for 'cowardice' is *deiliê*; the Greek for bravery or courage, *andreia*, meant literally 'virility' or 'manliness', uniquely used of a woman, Artemisia of Halicarnassus (7.99).

58. *Zeus*: Herodotus regularly 'translates' the names of non-Greek divinities into their Greek nearest equivalents. Croesus, however, who was Philhellenic, might actually have worshipped Zeus *Xenios* (Zeus of Strangers/Guests) as such.

59. *climbed the grave and slit his own throat*: Adrastus thereby achieved a 'good death' – the pre-Christian Greeks did not consider suicide a mortal sin.

60. *Cyrus*: Cyrus II 'the Great' established the Persian empire in about 550, beginning by reversing the domination of the Persians by their kindred Medes.

61. *Amphiaraus . . . Trophonius*: The Amphiareion was at Oropus, the oracle of Trophonius at Lebadeia in Boeotia.

62. *oracle of Ammon*: Egyptian *Amun*, the god of Egyptian Thebes; it was located in the Siwah oasis in the western desert of Egypt.

63. *His purpose . . . was to test . . . whether or not he should go to war with Persia*: Croesus' fatal mistake was, as a mere mortal, to try to second-guess a god. The main god in question, Apollo of Delphi, had his ample revenge.

64. *delivered this pronouncement*: The Pythia, Apollo's priestess and oracular mouthpiece, did not herself prepare her inspired utterances for delivery to consultants, let alone for wider circulation. That was the job of a body of male priests, who rendered them in formal hexameter verses for the sake of memorability and kept written copies of their responses for possible future use. Sceptics, however, both ancient and modern, believe that every single response that is extant in literary form was more or less made up by the priests. H. visited Delphi.

65. *Croesus also ordered the image of a lion . . . out of pure gold*: Croesus' next mistake was to fail to observe the injunction inscribed later on Apollo's very temple at Delphi: 'nothing in excess'.

66. *Corinthian treasury*: Different Greek cities rivalrously set up 'treasuries' at Delphi, as also at Olympia, for the competitive display of specially prized dedications.

67. *silver bowl . . . Festival of the Theophania*: The bowl in which Greeks mixed wine with water, often in a proportion of one to three parts, was called a *kratêr*. Theophania means 'God's or Gods' appearance'.

68. *I could name the guilty person, but will keep my peace*: Herodotus chooses to preserve a sort of holy or religious silence – because he is confident that

the god or gods would themselves have punished such a sacrilege, and to utter the man's name might risk polluting himself.

69. *gold statue of a woman . . . who used to bake Croesus' bread*: One suspects H.'s Delphian guide may have been taking the solemn reporter for a ride.

70. *Thebes . . . Ismenian Apollo*: Oropus, site of the oracular sanctuary of Amphiaraus, lay on the frontier between the territory of Athens and that of the Boeotians. Boeotian Thebes by implication had not scrupled to appropriate the property of Amphiaraus and rededicate these gifts to one of their own chief gods.

71. *come to be known as 'Dorians'*: H.'s would-be historical ethnography is in fact mere mythography, however learned or rational the chains of deductive reasoning apparently are.

72. *Greeks*: What is translated here and throughout as 'Greeks', in deference to standard practice, is in ancient Greek *Hellenes*. We call the Greeks 'Greeks' because the Romans called them *Graeci*. There were ancient Greek *Graikoi*, but they were but a small and unimportant sub-group of the Thessalian peoples.

73. *Peisistratus*: The chronology of Peisistratus' three spells of tyranny at Athens is unclear, but most likely the third and longest lasting began in around 547 or 546, which is shortly before Croesus considered applying to him for aid against Persia.

74. *Hippocrates . . . Chilon*: If – a big 'if' – this encounter were historical, it would have occurred around 590. Chilon, like Bias above, was accounted one of the 'Seven Sages'.

75. *victims of the trick . . . most intelligent of the Greeks*: One of the points of the Trojan Horse story of the fall of Troy was that it showed up the slow-witted Trojans as victims of the wily Greeks.

76. *Athena*: Though technically female, she was distinctly mannish – born of her father not a mother, and given to wearing full masculine arms and armour.

77. *a thoroughly illicit way*: Herodotus is too delicate to spell out whether this was by means of anal intercourse or *coitus interruptus*.

78. *dishonoured him*: One of the very best means of dishonouring a Greek man was through his womenfolk.

79. *Eretria*: On the long island of Euboea, just across the strait from Attica.

80. *Hippias*: Peisistratus' eldest son – and future successor as tyrant.

81. *Naxos*: The marble island of Naxos in the Cyclades was at this period among the richest areas in Greece.

82. *Marathon*: Hippias was to lead a Persian invasion to this very landing-place in 490, in an attempt to have himself restored as tyrant of Athens – under non-Greek control.

83. *he made sure to . . . to raise a substantial income for himself*: Herodotus here switches abruptly into a materialist-historical mode of explanation.

84. *substantial income . . . from his estates on the River Strymon*: Presumably a reference to the gold and silver mines of Mount Pangaeum.

85. *Delos*: After Delphi, the Cycladic island of Delos was Apollo's second most sacred site, the site of his own birth indeed.

86. *the Alcmaeonids most prominent of all*: Herodotus had been told and clearly believed that all members of the prominent aristocratic Alcmaeonid family were in exile throughout the rest of the tyranny of Peisistratus and Hippias (*c.* 546–510); documentary evidence excavated in the agora or civic centre of Athens in the 1930s disproved him.

87. *condition of the Lacedaemonians*: Herodotus tells us himself that he made a visit to Sparta where he talked with one Archias (3.55). Sparta lies some 250 km (150 miles) south-west of Athens, deep in the Peloponnese. In H.'s day it possessed the largest territory of any Greek *polis* or citizen-state, some 8,000 sq. km (3,088 sq. miles). Thucydides (5.68.2) found the Spartan way of life secretive. To less censorious foreigners such as Herodotus, the Spartans were presumably more open, hence giving him privileged access to the material he presents at e.g. 6.51–60.

88. *longer ago, the Lacedaemonians had been the worst governed people in the whole of Greece . . . refused to have any dealings with foreigners at all*: The Spartans' *eunomia*, 'orderliness of governance', was proverbial, as was their *xenophobia*.

89. *Lycurgus*: Modern scholars doubt the very existence of Lycurgus. Plutarch wrote a 'biography' of him *c.* AD 100, but begins it by saying there's nothing asserted of him by one source that is not contradicted by another. Richard Talbert's *Plutarch on Sparta* (Penguin Classics, 2nd edn, 2005) also contains Xenophon's early-fourth-century insider-informed essay on the Spartan way of life.

90. *set himself . . . to establishing the civil offices of ephor and City Elder*: The Board of five ephors, elected annually, served as the chief executive office of the Spartan state; the ephors were advised by a permanent Council of thirty City Elders, twenty-eight of whom were elected, for life, from citizens in good standing aged over sixty, the remaining two members being the two ruling hereditary kings *ex officio*. What Herodotus omits, but later sources dwell upon, is Lycurgus' supposed root and branch reform of Spartan land-holding.

91. *This was the Pythia's reply*: See note 64.

92. *lead the Tegeans off into slavery*: The idea seems to have been to turn the Tegeans into yet more helots.

93. *chains*: A much later pious travel-writer, Pausanias from Magnesia in Asia Minor, claimed still to be able to view them in the third quarter of the second century AD.

94. *A 'Benefactor' . . . wherever they might be sent*: 'Cavalry' literally translates *Hippeis*, but this elite body of three hundred specially selected twenty to

twenty-nine year olds from whom the five Benefactors were drawn served in the army as hoplites or heavy infantry, forming a bodyguard for the commanding king in battle, among other honours.

95. *he saw the blacksmith hammering out iron . . . stupefied by the sight*: This element of the story at least is pure fantasy – metals technology had been well advanced in Sparta since at least 700, even if full Spartan citizens were not themselves permitted to practise it.

96. *Such was the smith's account of what he had seen*: What the smith – if there was such a smith – really discovered was probably the skeleton of a mastodon. The idea of a man being over 10 foot tall was tenable only in the thought-world of heroic mythology.

97. *what had the discovery of iron ever brought . . . aside from grief?*: An allusion perhaps to the early Greek poet Hesiod's wholly negative portrayal of the – current – 'Age of Iron' in his *Works and Days*.

98. *dug up . . . the bones . . . carted the whole lot back to Sparta*: Symbolic transfer of human remains as politically potent relics was by no means a practice confined to pre-Christian antiquity.

99. *bowl made of bronze . . . capacity equivalent to 300 amphoras*: Smiths working in Sparta produced a series of such mixing-bowls or *kratêres*, the most astonishing of which ended up in a Hallstatt-period grave at Vix in Burgundy.

100. *Samians*: People of Samos. Herodotus spent time on the island of Samos, and there is archaeological as well as written evidence for close connections between the men of Sparta and of Samos in the sixth century.

101. *conquest of Lydia . . . the good life*: This motif looks forward to the very end of the *Histories* (9.122), as Herodotus would have expected his alert auditors/readers to realize.

102. *River Halys . . . traverse it*: H.'s interest in geography is palpable but the accuracy of his information does not quite match his interest.

103. *eclipse . . . pinpointed the date*: By our calendar, 585. Thales, the Western world's first intellectual, contended that the world was made up ultimately of water.

104. *Syennesis . . . Labynetus*: 'Syennesis' was in fact a title, not a personal name. 'Labynetus' is the Greek form of *Nabonidus*.

105. *formalized according to the custom of both peoples . . . lick up the other's blood*: Diplomatic treaties in antiquity were sworn, rather than signed, and it was the oaths sworn in the name or names of the god or gods and mutually exchanged by the parties involved which constituted a treaty's binding authority.

106. *the story as . . . told by the Greeks*: This is H.'s way of saying 'those Greek authors whom I have read and/or those Greeks whom I have questioned'.

107. *a claim which seems to me most improbable*: Application of probability reasoning was a standard Greek intellectual ploy.

108. *Sinope*: Modern Sinop on the Black Sea's southern shore.

109. *Telmessus*: Modern Fethiye. It seems to have been a fertile breeding ground for *manteis*, seers; Alexander the Great's pet seer Aristandrus came from here.

110. *Not for nothing was this an era ... among the peoples of Asia*: Note H.'s unstinted praise of these Lydian barbarians.

111. *the warriors of Sparta were preoccupied ... came out on top*: The 'Battle of the Champions' occurred in about 545. So deeply did it wound the psyche of the Argives that in 420 they proposed to the Spartans a rematch on the same terms.

112. *previously they had worn their hair short, now they began to wear it long*: Whether or not the origin of the custom can be so precisely dated, it is the case that Spartan adult males were exceptional in cultivating long hair – to the astonishment of a Persian scout in 480 (7.208).

113. *felt such shame ... that he killed himself there*: This would seem to antici-pate – and perhaps help to explain – the suicide of Pantites, another survivor of a picked Spartan band of three hundred (that at Thermopylae in 480: 7.232).

114. *fleet*: The first mention of a Spartan fleet – but probably this was more of a potential than an actual task-force; the Spartans were notorious land-lubbers.

115. *the very first time that he had spoken ... continued to do so all his life*: Relating such 'wonders' was part of the very essence of H.'s project.

116. *Whatever the explanation*: Herodotus offers a series of complementary, but entirely Greek explanatory options.

117. *men who consider themselves blessed by fortune*: Herodotus thus cleverly enlists Croesus as well as Solon (chs. 30–33) into his cause.

118. *Cyrus ... found his heart melting*: H.'s Cyrus is richly praised (cf. 3.89), yet still not to the same extent as the Cyrus of the Jews, for whom he was noth-ing less than a Messiah.

119. *Somewhere ... what has happened*: The protagonists are both barbarians but their discourse and thought-worlds are entirely Greek – except that a Greek would presumably have been more cautious than Croesus in inter-preting a Delphic response.

120. *'Since the gods have seen fit ... it is clearly my duty ... willingly forgo what they have'*: Croesus has become a familiar Herodotean figure, the wise adviser or warner.

121. *Five generations ago ... Croesus ... paid the debt on that crime*: The biblical 'sins of the fathers visited on the sons' motif has its exact Greek parallel.

122. *Cyrus' mother was a Mede ... queen*: Wonderful Greek snobbery to put down the founder of the Persian empire as a mere half-caste.

123. *for the first time*: Because it would be reconquered in 494 following the crushing of the Ionian Revolt (Book 6).

124. *made sure to torture his opponent ... spikes of a carding-comb*: Herodotus tells this deadpan, without comment, but the inference of despotic oriental cruelty would easily have been drawn by Greeks.

125. *the figures ... prove that the largest contribution of all was made by the whores*: As in his later account of the Great Pyramid (2.125), H.'s leg will have been pulled by local informants.

126. *gold and silver coins*: Actually, the earliest coins struck by the Lydians were made of electrum, a natural alloy of gold and silver.

127. *the group which was to leave their country ... Tyrrhenians*: There is scientific evidence – both human and animal DNA – to back up this claim of origin.

128. *Lydians ... slaves of the Persians*: This is a leitmotif of H.'s discourse – not only were all foreign subjects of Persia slaves, but all Persians too were slaves of the Great King of Persia.

129. *Persians ... get the facts straight than simply to exalt Cyrus*: Persians did not compose written narrative histories of the kind Herodotus is writing, or chronicles along the lines of the 'historical' books of the Bible, or even keep dry documentary archives of significant events.

130. *Deioces*: He comes across more as a glad-handing Greek patronal politician canvassing for votes than as a prospective oriental monarch.

131. *Such ... were the arguments ... need for a king*: Compare and contrast the arguments put forward by Darius for why the Persians should have a king (3.82).

132. *Deioces*: He is a little reminiscent here of Athenian Peisistratus (ch. 59).

133. *Agbatana*: Also commonly known as Ecbatana, a city in Media, one of the four main Achaemenid capitals, (modern Hamadan) besides Susa and Persepolis in Iran, and Babylon.

134. *seven rings in all ... the wall which encircles Athens*: See A. M. Theocharaki, 'The ancient circuit wall of Athens: its changing course and the phases of construction', *Hesperia* 80 (2011), pp. 71–156.

135. *Deioces ... foster a sense of his own mystique*: Byzantine emperors seem to have learned something from Deioces.

136. *autocracy*: Herodotus uses *turannis*, which for a Greek can mean un- or extra-constitutional monarchy.

137. *Psammetichus*: Egyptian *Psamtik*.

138. *Aphrodite Urania*: The Greek version of such eastern goddesses as Philistine Atargatis, Syrian Astarte and Canaanite Ashtoreth.

139. *An interesting detail ... where the temple at Ascalon stands*: A classic piece of comparative theo-archaeology (cf. 2.44).

140. *struck down ... with a disease that transformed them into women*: If this is a reference to impotence, it can only have been temporary – or sporadic.

141. *a period during which their violence*: for a Greek, *hubris*, translated here as 'violence', did not necessarily involve inappropriate relations with, or attitudes towards, the gods but rather violent violations of all kinds of status boundaries.

142. *an episode I will recount in a later chapter*: This promise is not exactly fulfilled in ch. 185.

143. *Magi*: Special kind of priests, both Median and Persian; from their name comes ultimately our 'magic'.

144. *'Not what Astyages ordered ... not one of mine'*: Greeks might be put in mind of the Oedipus story, in which the shepherd entrusted with killing the deformed Oedipus had likewise failed to carry out his royal master's command.

145. *a quite different name*: The Persian original was pronounced something like *Kurash*. Herodotus wrongly believed that all Persian names ended in 's' (ch. 139).

146. *More appointments followed ... bring him his messages*: One notices the reflections of the early career of the Median king/tyrant, Deioces.

147. *eunuchs*: Their name derived from a compound Greek word meaning literally 'keepers of the bed'. They were deemed an indispensable part of the apparatus of an oriental harem-based household (ch. 135). For Greek horror of castration, see 8.105–6 (cf. 3.48).

148. *had the boy butchered ... assembled in one place*: This grisly tale of cannibalism would have reminded Greeks of the feast served up to the gods by impious King Tantalus of his son Pelops; for which abomination Tantalus languished forever in Tartarus, in deepest Hades, permanently tantalized by the sight of food and drink that were always receding from his grasp.

149. *Cyrus ... had been brought up by a bitch*: Connoisseurs of Roman mythology will think at once of twins Romulus and Remus being suckled by a she-wolf.

150. *Pasargadae*: Herodotus interprets this as a tribal name; it was also the site of the real Cyrus' first royal palace.

151. *'How does it feel ... from being a king to being a slave?'*: There's a Greek parallel to this taunt at 6.67 – where the new Spartan king Leotychidas II asks the deposed king he has supplanted, Demaratus, what it feels like to be an official after having been a king.

152. *Later on ... their rebellion was crushed*: Herodotus here looks forward from about 550 to the late 520s.

153. *Asia*: For Herodotus this was synonymous with the Persian empire in Asia.

154. *The victory ... gave him the rule of the whole of Asia*: Not directly so – Cyrus had first to capture Babylon, which he did in 539.

155. *As regards customs ... distinctive to the Persians*: There follow ten whole chapters devoted to them.

156. *their gods not being represented in human form, as are the Greek gods*: See 2.53.

157. *Zeus*: What Herodotus calls *Zeus* would be for the Persians *Ahura Mazda*.

158. *Mitra*: This is a bad mistake. Persian Mithras was male.

159. *in a very particular way*: That is, in a thoroughly non- or un-Greek way.

160. *he will ... prostrate himself before the other*: Prostration, *proskynêsis*, was deemed by Greeks appropriate only for gods – hence the cultural mismatch and standoff at 7.136: the Spartans did not consider it right to prostrate themselves before a mortal man, however powerful. This led, conversely, to Greek misunderstanding of prostration by Persians as a religious rather than a social-political device.

161. *The parallel ... administration of their neighbour*: Herodotus here anticipates his much more detailed description of Persian imperial administration in Book 3.

162. *their habit of sleeping with boys*: In Greek *paiderastia* meant literally 'passionate erotic desire for (male) children', but ancient Greeks were not what we call paedophiles – there were quite strict rules, sometimes legally enforceable, as to the age-grade, sexual maturity and marital status of the partners on either side of the paederastic relationship, and often too, probably, informal taboos regarding physical gratification.

163. *This ... is a really excellent custom*: Herodotus lets slip the mask of objective ethnographer and betrays his humane sympathies.

164. *The worst offence ... is to tell a lie*: Official royal Persian propaganda of Darius I declared the King the implacable enemy of The Lie, by which was meant any religious custom or practice deemed antithetical to the official worship of Ahura Mazda.

165. *offended the sun*: At 7.223 Xerxes, when at Thermopylae, pours libations at sunrise.

166. *customs ... handling of the dead*: For the significance of this as a cultural marker, see 3.38.

167. *It is an ancient custom ... should no doubt let be*: Herodotus implies personal moral disapproval, combined with toleration.

168. *oboe*: The Greek *aulos* is often translated 'flute', but it was a reed instrument, often double in form, hence our 'oboe'.

169. *Panionium*: See the following chapter, and for the term's derivation and meaning, see ch. 143.

170. *Milesians ... negotiated with the Lydian king*: A nice example of the later Roman imperial practice of 'divide and rule', but also a reflection of the Greeks' chronic inability to sink jealously guarded individual political identity within common and communal institutions.

171. *there is no other region ... founded their cities*: A measure of H.'s limited experience, of course, but also the basis of his contrast between the Ionians' ideal environment and the relatively poor civilization they based upon it.

172. *inhabitants share an identical manner of speech*: Herodotus himself was not an Ionian, but a Dorian Greek from Halicarnassus, which also lay within Caria – see Introduction 1 and ch. 144 below.

173. *the same dialect, but the Samians ... distinctively their own*: Herodotus speaks here from deep personal familiarity.

174. *Lindus, Ialysus, Camirus*: Cities of the island of Rhodes; only at the end of the fifth century, probably after H.'s death, was Rhodes town built, and the island politically unified under its sway.

175. *Helice*: Destroyed by an earthquake in 373.

176. *It was this murderous behaviour ... slaughtered ... their sons*: One wonders whether this can, literally, have been the case. It was not usual for Greek wives or daughters to dine with husbands or fathers in the presence of unrelated guests, whatever the ultimate physical or ethnic origins of a particular community, but not even to address them by name seems too extreme. However, H. does well to remind us that it could be murder to found a new Greek settlement in alien territory.

177. *their fantasy of being pure-bred Ionians*: Was Herodotus, one wonders, spurred into this denunciation of the Asiatic Ionians' mongrel nature by aspersions cast on his own – mongrel – pedigree?

178. *a sanctified spot in the region of Mycale*: The exact site is contested. Mycale will come into its own in Book 9, as the site of the final battle of the Persian Wars.

179. *in spite of their common ancestry*: Common ancestry was sometimes put forward as a reason for one community's aiding another, hence H.'s registering the anomaly of Arisba's annihilation by kindred Methymna.

180. *heartfelt appeal for assistance*: This was not the last Spartan embassy to Sardis mentioned in Herodotus (7.134–6). Both were failures.

181. *town squares for the buying and selling of goods*: In a Greek agora, both politics and economic transactions were conducted.

182. *Bactria*: In modern Afghanistan.

183. *Sacae*: Another name for Scythians (7.64).

184. *cart them all off into slavery*: This was a practice later employed by Darius I against the rebel Greeks of both Miletus and Eretria.

185. *Branchidae*: Also known as Didyma, a shrine of the prophecy god Apollo, it was easier to access for Asiatic Greeks than the Delphi HQ. (See also chs. 46 and 92.)

186. *suspected the envoys of lying*: For Herodotus, a divine oracle as such could not lie, but the human priestly intermediaries might well be bribed or otherwise politically suborned, or, as is suspected in this case, have their advice misrepresented.

187. *he is a suppliant ... we have shrunk from giving him up*: Respect for suppliant strangers was hardwired into Greek cultural consciousness.

188. *Guardian of the City*: *Poliouchos*, the same title as the Athena worshipped on both the Athenian and the Spartan acropolis.

189. *inhabitants ... pinned inside their walls ... then the city would be stormed*: This mode of siege warfare originated with the Assyrians; a graphic illustration has been excavated at Paphus on Cyprus, which the Persians put under siege in 498 during the 'Ionian Revolt'.

190. *Tartessus*: Beyond the 'Pillars of Heracles', i.e. the straits of Gibraltar, at the mouth of the Guadalquivir river.

191. *deploy a war-fleet rather than the broad-bottomed vessels*: They therefore sacrificed economy for security, since a round-hulled, sail-driven merchantman required many fewer crew-members than an oared warship.

192. *Mede*: Greeks liked to confuse Medes with Persians. The epitaph of Aeschylus the Athenian tragic playwright included reference to 'the long-haired Mede'.

193. *Cyrnus*: Corsica.

194. *colony*: The Greek word, *apoikiê*, means literally 'home from home', 'settlement abroad'. Such colonies were normally politically independent from the start.

195. *until the lump should reappear*: The allies of Athens, when forming in 478/7 what moderns call the 'Delian League', likewise dropped lumps of iron off the island of Delos – with the same symbolic meaning of unalterable permanence.

196. *Carthaginians*: The people of Carthage; in its own language *Qart-Hadasht*, founded from Phoenician Tyre, was 'New City'. Greeks called it *Carchedon*.

197. *a 'Cadmeian' kind of victory*: The Greek equivalent of a 'Pyrrhic' victory. See 4.147 note on Cadmus.

198. *Rhegium*: Modern Reggio Calabria.

199. *Elea*: In Latin *Velia*, in Campania.

200. *Posidonia*: In Latin *Paestum*.

201. *worshipped . . . as a hero*: There were many kinds of hero, from Heracles or Theseus (of half-divine parentage) down; founders of cities known as *oecists* received the posthumous worship thought appropriate for humans who had achieved great things in life and whose beneficent afterlife presence was sought.

202. *demes*: *Dêmoi*, as in the 139 or 140 that constituted the democratic city of Athens in H.'s day; elsewhere he speaks of Sparta, composed of five villages, as having 'demes' (3.55).

203. *Zeus Belus*: The Babylonians' *Bel-Marduk*.

204. *Nitocris*: Herodotus treats her with the greatest respect, representing her as a kind of female combination of Polycrates and Odysseus.

205. *the Great King*: The title reflects the official Persian title 'King of Kings'.

206. *Opis*: Roughly on the site of modern Baghdad.

207. *Gyndes*: Cyrus' attitude to this river somewhat prefigures that of his grandson Xerxes to the Hellespont (7.35).

208. *choenixes . . . medimnus*: It is interesting that Herodotus chooses as a comparison a dry measure used by the Athenians.

209. *what . . . is the greatest wonder of all*: H.'s standard of narrative worthiness was his personal wonder index. Egypt gets the longest description of all countries because it contains the most wonders.

210. *Babylon . . . the way they dress*: In light of the preceding chapters (178–94) it seems almost unbelievable that anyone should have questioned whether Herodotus had himself personally visited Babylon, but they have.

211. *the only way ... has been to pimp out their daughters as whores*: Quite a sting in the tale.

212. *the most outrageous of the Babylonians' customs*: Once again, the mask of objectivity slips.

213. *Cyprus*: Herodotus does not specify whether he means Greek or non-Greek, Phoenician Cyprus, but presumably the latter.

214. *River Araxes*: H. may have confused it with the Oxus or the Rha (Volga). The Massagetans were semi-nomadic.

215. *Ister*: Danube.

216. *Pillars of Heracles*: The 'Pillars' were natural rocks located on either side of the entrance to the Strait of Gibraltar and named by Greeks after Heracles, in honour of the Labour that had required him to recover the Cattle of Geryon in south-west Spain, near modern Cadiz (Greek *Gadeira*, Latin *Gades*).

217. *The Caspian ... an eight-day voyage*: Herodotus by his error – the proportion of the length to the width is 22:8 not 15:8 – has made it plain that he has not visited and surveyed this area.

218. *Tomyris*: Another of H.'s exceptionally resourceful women rulers, like Nitocris above, and – later – the Greek Artemisia from his own native Halicarnassus.

219. *the enemy will no sooner catch sight ... make a show of prodigious deeds*: Croesus was a better cosmic philosopher than he was a military strategist, alas for Cyrus.

220. *revolution*: The Greek *neoteron ti* (plural *neotera*) means literally 'new(er)' or 'too new thing(s)'; Greeks had ambivalent feelings about novelty and innovation.

221. *thanks to my researches*: How exactly Herodotus 'discovered' what he relates is unclear – he could neither speak nor read any language but Greek, and this was a battle that took place between two barbarian peoples in central Asia almost half a century before his own birth.

222. *Tomyris ... pushed the head into the wineskin*: Rubens' suitably gory 1622/3 painting of this terrible scene may be viewed in the Museum of Fine Arts, Boston.

223. *cattle as sacrifices ... boil up the meat, and feast on it*: Funerary cannibalism will feature again centrally in the emblematic tale about the universality of customary prescription told at 3.38.

BOOK TWO

1. Book Two is easily the longest of the nine – though the division of his work into Books and their subsequent naming after the Nine Muses are not original to H. Some scholars have thought he wrote Book Two as an independent project and only later incorporated it into a larger schema; certainly,

it reads as his masterpiece in the original meaning of that term – the examination piece that demonstrated his mastery of his craft. Reasons for the Book's inordinate length are given at the start of ch. 35; other chapters include the notions of Egypt as agriculturally a utopia (2.14), and culturally the world turned upside down (2.35–6).

2. *The Greeks tell a whole number of stories ... ludicrous*: This comment on the risibility of Greek stories is reminiscent of the Preface to the *Genealogies* of Hecataeus of Miletus, composed *c.* 500. Herodotus knew Hecataeus' work, borrowed from it without acknowledgement and even has a laugh at the author's expense (2.143).

3. *Hephaestus*: Ptah for the Egyptians.

4. *I have no desire to pass on any details ... obliged to by my narrative*: On the gods' names, see ch. 50 and notes.

5. *the Greeks ... cycle of the seasons returns to its original starting-point*: Greek states each had their own calendars, based on a luni-solar system of time-reckoning.

6. *the Egypt to which the Greeks sail ... courtesy of the river*: H. literally speaks of Egypt as 'the gift of the river' (*dôron tou potamou*), a phrase he borrowed from Hecataeus (on whom see ch. 143 etc.).

7. *Altar of the Twelve Gods ... Pisa*: The Altar of the Twelve Gods was located in the Athenian agora or civic centre. Pisa was the area within which lay the sanctuary of Zeus at Olympia, in the north-west Peloponnese; the Zeus Temple was constructed in the 450s and housed a statue by the Athenian Phidias, later accounted one of the Seven Wonders of the World.

8. *Red Sea*: Persian Gulf (see 1.1 and note). The sea we refer to as the Red Sea is described by H. at 2.11.

9. *a distance of ... 1,800 stades*: These figures are designed to give the impression of substantial first-hand experience, but some errors and omissions have led to doubt as to whether Herodotus in fact visited the lands in question.

10. *pangs of starvation*: Herodotus recurs to the poverty of Greece at 7.102 and 8.111.

11. *what the Ionians call the 'Delta'*: Delta is the fourth letter of the Greek alphabet. 'Ionians' certainly includes Hecataeus.

12. *oracle of Ammon*: See 1.46 and note.

13. *Yet if it were truly the case ... none of these things would happen*: H. reasons logically, by his own lights, but the facts of nature are against him.

14. *Homer*: This is the first of several references in H. to Homer, a portmanteau name for the in fact many poets who contributed to the creation of the *Iliad* and *Odyssey*. For H.'s dating of Homer, see ch. 53.

15. *Athena*: Egyptian *Neit*.

16. *Psammetichus*: Egyptian *Psamtik*.

17. *I was dependent ... upon what I heard from others*: H. conducts his own 'enquiries', *historiai* (plural), upon oral tradition/testimony, *akoê*.

18. *Maeander*: The bendy river flows into the sea in western Anatolia/Turkey, in ancient Greek Ionia.

19. *Zeus and Dionysus*: Egyptian *Amun* and *Osiris*.

20. *in the Persian era ... at Daphnae*: Persia conquered Egypt under Cambyses (2.1), in 525; their occupation was often contested but held until the major revolt of 404; the reconquest in 343/2 was short-lived – Alexander took over Egypt in 332 and replaced the native Memphis with Alexandria as the new, alien capital.

21. *crocodiles*: Crocodile, like *pyramid* (a kind of bun) and *obelisk* (little cooking spit), is a Greek slang term – literally meaning 'cowardly yellow' (chs. 68–70).

22. *circumcision*: Greeks found male circumcision unaesthetic and even repugnant. H.'s expression is typically mild.

23. *no Egyptian ... will ever kiss a Greek ... nor use his knife, his spit or his cooking-pot*: In H.'s day Greeks lived in Memphis as well as in the Delta (2.154). Mixed marriages were not uncommon.

24. *foolish myth*: This translates Greek *muthos*, one of H.'s only two uses of that term, both negative (the other at ch. 23).

25. *gods and heroes*: A conventional designation for all the anthropomorphized supernatural powers whom the Greeks worshipped with appropriate rituals of sacrifice, prayers and so forth. See also ch. 53 and note.

26. *I would also dispute the possibility that the Egyptians could have adopted them ... from the Greeks ... Boeotia*: H.'s devotion to the cause of Egyptian religious priority is striking. In his day, Dionysus was indeed widely considered to be in origin a foreign interloper into the Greek pantheon, but his name appears among the earliest examples of Greek written language, the clay tablets inscribed in the 'Linear B' syllabary of the late Bronze Age (fourteenth–twelfth centuries).

27. *initiated into the Mysteries of the Cabiri*: Usually a pair of male gods, one senior, one junior, worshipped in secret by initiates only. Herodotus here identifies them with what are otherwise known as the 'great gods' of Samothrace; see also 3.37, for the Cabiri at Egyptian Memphis.

28. *Pelasgians*: See further 6.137–9 on the Pelasgians in Attica.

29. *statues of Hermes with an erect penis*: Had Herodotus lived to 415, it is conceivable that he would have mentioned the episode of Herm-smashing that cast a pall over the Athenians' expedition to Sicily described vividly by Thucydides in Books 6–7 of his *History*.

30. *details ... revealed during Mysteries of Samothrace*: This implies that H. was himself an initiate.

31. *Dodona*: The oracle was dedicated to Zeus (also at 1.46).

32. *award them their titles ... signify their forms*: The Greeks' gods were famously anthropomorphic – human-formed.

33. *Promeneia ... Nicandra*: Normally, it was deemed inappropriate to reveal the names of respectable women in non-related male company.

34. *Artemis*: There is no one exact or close Egyptian equivalent of Greek Artemis, goddess of wild nature and of childbirth; but see ch. 156, where Herodotus equates her with Bubastis.

35. *Carians settled in Egypt*: A Carian community is attested at Memphis; the Carian immigrants too intermarried with native Egyptians.

36. *Ares*: Greek god of war, but Greeks felt deep ambivalence towards him and he was honoured with very few major shrines, such as that at Acharnae in Attica.

37. *ibises to Hermopolis*: The cemetery at Saqqara is estimated to have held hundreds of thousands of mummified ibises.

38. *Lacedaemonians*: See 1.6 note 14. Herodotus visited Sparta (3.55), and familiarized himself with local custom and lore. (Cf. 6.60.)

39. *practices that are ... Pythagorean*: Pythagoras the mathematician and mystic of the later sixth century came from Samos in the eastern Aegean, but emigrated to 'Great Greece', southern Italy, where his followers formed communities devoted to practising his teachings.

40. *manner in which Egyptians ... bury their dead*: This for H. was a key cultural marker; see the exemplary parable at 3.38.

41. *embalming ... skills required*: The trustworthiness of H.'s account of mummification has been much praised by Egyptologists.

42. *a man will only ever have the one wife*: Greek (in this case Spartan) monogamy is confirmed at 5.40.

43. *papyrus at its very tastiest*: Greeks of H.'s day imported Egyptian papyrus not as a comestible but as an expensive writing material. Locally produced leather, wax, lead or fired clay were cheaper options.

44. *my own observations*: H. always privileges *opsis*, personal visual witness, as a source of certain knowledge (cf. chs. 12, 29); then comes *gnômê*, 'reasoning'; finally *historiê*, 'enquiry'.

45. *I cannot definitively say*: Ouk ekhô atrekeôs eipein, a favourite formula of H. (cf. 3.116, 7.152, 8.87, 9.18).

46. *sum total of the peoples who practise circumcision*: H. was ignorant of the Hebrews/Jews, who clearly also borrowed the custom originally from the Egyptians.

47. *geometry*: Literally 'earth-measurement'.

48. *achievements you have not surpassed*: Darius I's failed Scythian expedition of *c.* 515 is a set piece narrated in Book 4.

49. *all these passages*: Respectively, *Iliad* 6.289–92, and *Odyssey* 4.227–30, 351–2.

50. *the Cypria*: This forms part of the post-Homeric epic tradition, the 'Epic Cycle', a series of poems designed to provide Homer's Trojan War with antecedents and further issue besides the wanderings and homecoming of Odysseus.

51. *Achaeans*: One of Homer's terms for Greeks; others are *Danaans* and *Argives*. *Hellenes* was not yet in use.

52. *Such is my belief, and I declare it here*: H. was not the first rationalist Greek critic of Homer, but he was the first to apply a thoroughgoing historicist rationalism to one of the key elements of the Troy story.

53. *'the cleverest of us all!'*: For a different ethnocentric view as to which people, and which members of it, were the cleverest, see 1.60 (the Athenians had the reputation of being the smartest of all Greeks).

54. *priests weave a robe*: For the claim that in Egypt it is the men who weave, see 2.35.

55. *My own responsibility ... to record whatever I may be told by my sources*: A claim reiterated most generally at 7.152.

56. *when ... Cheops, became king*: H. gets his chronology badly wrong here. Cheops, Chephren and Mycerinus, the builders of the Pyramids of Giza, belonged to the IVth Dynasty (*c.* 2575–2450), a whole millennium and a half before the supposed time of the Trojan War. 'Cheops' is an anglicization of H.'s *Cheopa*; he was known by the Egyptians as *Khufu*.

57. *the interpreter who read the notice told me*: H., as a monoglot Greek-speaker, was always at the mercy of his local interpreters, and here had his leg well and truly pulled. See further 2.154.

58. *iron*: H., so proud of himself for his superior understanding of relative chronology, here confuses (in our terms) the Bronze with the Iron Age.

59. *Chephren*: (known by the Egyptians as *Khafra*) The son of Cheops, not his brother.

60. *Mycerinus*: (known by the Egyptians as *Menkaura*) The son of Chephren, not Cheops.

61. *mourning for the god whose name ... I have no intention of saying*: Most probably Isis.

62. *Charaxus ... Sappho*: Both are real enough (*fl. c.* 600).

63. *Naucratis*: For its status – the Hong Kong or Dejima of ancient Egypt – see further 2.178.

64. *Egypt was invaded by a huge army of ... Assyrians*: Cf. Byron's 'The Assyrian' who 'came down like the wolf on the fold', and 2 Kings 19.

65. *writer*: *Logopoios*, literally 'maker of *logoi*' – narratives or reasoned accounts.

66. *'a man of quality'*: *Kalos kagathos*, literally 'fine (or beautiful) and good (or brave)', a moralizing version of 'upper class'.

67. *Typhon*: Egyptian *Seth*. See also ch. 156.

68. *approximately eight hundred years before my time ... Trojan War*: H. therefore dated the Trojan War before 1250 or so, which – if there ever was a Trojan War – would not have been wildly inappropriate.

69. *temples of Ephesus and Samos*: H. here explicitly uses *nêos*, 'temple'; that of Ephesus was sacred to Artemis, that of Samos to Hera.

70. *Sardanapalus*: Probably a Greek corruption of Assyrian *Ashurbanipal*.

71. *all sheathed in bronze*: A reference to what in Greece is referred to as 'hoplite' armour – minimally consisting of bronze helmet and breastplate, sometimes also bronze greaves.

72. *Apis*: On the sacred bull, see further 3.27–9.

73. *we . . . have had such reliable information*: *Epistametha atrekeôs*, a favourite Herodotean formulation meaning literally 'we know unerringly'.

74. *Aeschylus*: This is H.'s only mention of the great tragic poet, though he does mention Aeschylus' brother Cynegeirus at 6.114.

75. *Azotus . . . hold out against a siege*: It would have been almost three times as long as the siege of Troy.

76. *triremes*: In H.'s day they were the ship-of-the-line, three-banked oared warships, powered by 170 rowers; the design was probably pioneered by the Phoenicians.

77. *'Barbarian' . . . all who do not speak their tongue*: So in this respect at least the Egyptians did as the Greeks.

78. *Such was the recommendation . . . made to the Eleans*: H., who was interested in the cross-cultural significance of the Olympic Games ethos, did not need to add that the Eleans failed to adopt the Egyptians' alleged recommendation.

79. *come to a wretched end*: The conceit 'it was fated that X should come to a wretched end' recurs several times, giving point to the recommendation of Solon to Croesus to 'look to the end', 1.32. For Apries' bad end, by strangulation, see ch. 169.

80. *ears and nose cut off*: The classic oriental punishment for traitors.

81. *He also had a palace . . . well worth seeing*: A non sequitur.

82. *their devotion . . . none has ever bothered himself to learn a manual craft*: This is reminiscent of the Spartans' practice; see ch. 167 for their attitude to manual craftsmanship.

83. *obelisks*: Greek *obeliskos* means literally 'little cooking spit'; here H. uses *oboloi*, 'spits', with the same diminishing meaning.

84. *god's suffering . . . 'Mysteries'*: The unnamed god is Osiris (Dionysus).

85. *knowledge of the Thesmophoria . . . entirely eradicated*: There was a particular reason for H. not to wish to breathe a word about the Thesmophoria – it was a very widely celebrated festival of Demeter, but the celebration was open only to married women.

86. *Amasis persuaded the Egyptians . . . his slaves*: H. habitually refers to subjection to an oriental absolute monarch as 'being enslaved', Greek *douleuein*.

87. *as a law, it can hardly be bettered*: No such law, whether of Solon or not, existed at Athens.

88. *'The Hellenium'*: Literally the 'Greek place'.

89. *a measure of . . . the privileges that Naucratis enjoyed*: Thus Naucratis served as an international port of trade, linking the dissimilar economies

of Egypt and the Greek world, to their mutual benefit, but under the tight control and supervision of the Pharaoh.

90. *Amphictyons*: Literally 'those who possess land round about', the official term for the managers of the shrine of Delphi, who were drawn from a fixed number of central and southern Greek states and peoples, and met in committee at regular stated intervals.

91. *Delphians*: Citizens of the town of Delphi.

92. *acknowledgement of the formal ties of guest-friendship*: Guest-friendship, *xeiniê*, was a semi-sacralized ritual friendship between individuals of different communities and/or cultures, which might have political or diplomatic implications, as here between the Greek Polycrates and the Egyptian Amasis.

93. *flight from the sons of Aegyptus*: The flight of the Danaids was the subject of the earliest surviving Greek tragedy, Aeschylus' *Suppliant Women*, probably of 463/2.

BOOK THREE

1. *Ionians and Aeolians*: In other words, not including Dorian Greeks such as H. himself was. The date is 525; the narrative resumes from 2.1.

2. *best eye-doctor in Egypt*: Egyptian priority in medical skill is unquestionable. Only in the sixth century did Greeks begin to catch up, as the tale of Democedes of Croton (chs. 125, 129–37) exemplifies.

3. *not as a wife, but as a concubine*: H. is unusually alert to the intricate protocols of the Persian royal harem system, which could have major diplomatic implications (cf. 9.108–13).

4. *the Persians report*: By 'the Persians' H. does not of course refer to an official record but to his Greek-speaking Persian informants (cf. ch. 160 note 100).

5. *come of age . . . possession of the throne*: Cyrus died in 529; there seems to have been no dispute over the accession of Cambyses, in contrast to the massive disputes over his behaviour as King and the manner of his demise, below.

6. *eunuchs*: The Egyptian court, like the Persian, relied on such castrated males for essential security services; *eunuch* is a Greek euphemism meaning literally 'guardian of the bed'. Trade in eunuchs was practised by Greeks, to the extreme disgust of H. (8.105, 106; cf. ch. 48).

7. *Typhon*: A mythical hundred-headed monster, Hesiod, *Theogony* 820ff.

8. *I am now going to point out something which few . . . reflect upon*: H. clearly implies that he has made the voyage to Egypt.

9. *The Arabians*: H. digresses, in his usual manner; a second digression on the Arabians follows at chs. 107–13.

10. *Apart from Urania . . . Dionysus*: Actually, pre-Islamic Arabs worshipped several deities, most of them astral.

11. *large river ... Corys by name*: There is no such river in Arabia, nor was there then.

12. *died after a reign that had lasted forty-four years*: Amasis reigned 570–525 and was succeeded by his son by Tentkheta, Psamtik III.

13. *perished at the side of Achaemenes ... at the hands of Inaros the Libyan*: Great King Xerxes was murdered in 465, and the rising of Libyan prince Inaros probably sought to exploit his demise; according to the unreliable Greek chronicler Ctesias, physician to Artaxerxes II, as many as 100,000 were killed under Achaemenes.

14. *tears rose to the eyes of Croesus*: Croesus had had his own share of familial loss (1.34).

15. *absolutely contrary to Egyptian custom ... broke the laws of both peoples alike*: For H.'s preoccupation with the observance of a people's funerary customs, see especially ch. 38.

16. *'Table of the Sun'*: Not clear what or where this is. Possibly Meroë in Sudan.

17. *'Fish-Eaters'*: The later writer, Pausanias (1.33), identified them as Ethiopians from beyond Syene (Aswan).

18. *Phoenicians ... height of impiety ... an assault against their own offspring*: Carthage was traditionally founded from Tyre at a date corresponding to *c*. 800.

19. *give him this bow*: The bow was the symbol of Ethiopia (7.69), and recurs as a motif in several other non-Greek Herodotean stories (chs. 36, 78 and 4.9). Greeks would recall Odysseus' bow from *Odyssey* 19 and 21.

20. *purple-fish and the dyeing process*: Purple dye was extracted from the murex shellfish; for a Greek 'fisher for purple', see 4.151.

21. *So angry did their report make Cambyses*: For the Herodotean theme of the ill-fated anger of oriental monarchs – and Greek tyrants – see 1.73, 141, 156 and ch. 52.

22. *Such a mass of sand was this wind carrying ... what happened to the army*: The priests of Ammon had an interest in spreading news of this miracle, but similar annihilations of caravans by sandstorms have been recently reported.

23. *Apis ... died of his wound*: Killing an Apis bull would have been for the Egyptians the most sacrilegious crime, but there is no support in Egyptian records for this allegation, which must be put down to mere hostile propaganda against the Persian conqueror.

24. *not remotely been the habit ... to set up house with their sisters*: Cambyses was indeed the first but not the last Persian king to practise full brother-sister marriage.

25. *permitted the King of the Persians to do as he pleased*: H. thereby introduces the scandalous notion of Persian kings as absolute rulers above the law.

26. *he leapt on her ... carrying his child in her womb, suffered a miscarriage, and died*: Roman emperor Nero was alleged to have killed Poppaea similarly (Tacitus, *Annals* 16.6).

27. *'sacred disease'*: This is how the Greeks referred to epilepsy.
28. *you do not yet have a son*: Cambyses apparently died without any offspring (ch. 66).
29. *shrine of Hephaestus*: See 2.99, 141, 151, 153, 176.
30. *pataici*: Apotropaic busts in the form of dwarfs.
31. *the Cabiri*: Often a father, mother and son holy trinity; also worshipped on the island of Samothrace (2.51).
32. *Darius summoned some Indians . . . a desecration of silence*: For the exemplary nature of this anecdote, or fable, see Introduction 4. 'India' meant the Punjab/Kashmir, the north-west of today's India.
33. *Pindar . . . 'Custom is the King of all'*: See Introduction 4.
34. *Cambyses . . . Polycrates*: From one, oriental, tyrant H. passes seamlessly to another, Greek, one; the Spartans acquired a reputation as principled tyrant-topplers, but that did not stop them attempting to restore Hippias as tyrant of Athens (5.91ff.).
35. *the knot of friendship and mutual hospitality*: Xenia – in H.'s Greek *xeiniê* – was a long-established custom of ritualized friendship uniting men of power from different cities and, in this case, cultures.
36. *the walls of Samos*: See further ch. 54 and note for the city walls.
37. *the gods are given to envy*: This echoes wise Solon's advice to Croesus at 1.32.
38. *Theodorus*: Certainly a historical figure, and he may have crafted a ring that Polycrates possessed, but the story of the ring that follows is but a local variant on a familiar folktale motif.
39. *the treaty of mutual friendship between them was dissolved*: Far more likely, in hard historical fact, is that Polycrates, concerned for his own position, broke off the friendship as Amasis was about to be attacked by Persia.
40. *the Lacedaemonians launched a military offensive . . . go on to found Cydonia in Crete*: See ch. 59.
41. *'There was no need to say "sack"'*: Such apophthegms, pithy and pointed sayings, were a speciality of the Spartans, whence the generic term 'laconic', derived from one of their other names – *Lakones*.
42. *war against the Messenians*: Presumably the war of reconquest, in the mid-seventh century, known as the Second Messenian War; the original conquest had occurred in the last quarter of the eighth century.
43. *the Samians instituted a festival . . . just as it was first established*: The true origins of this festival may not be exactly as H. was told, but his local knowledge of Samos is evident yet again.
44. *the first colonization of the island*: The traditional date for the foundation of Corcyra, in Greek *Kerkyra*, was 734. The enmity between this metropolis and daughter-city was untypical of such relations in the Greek world generally. It blew up once again in the 430s, and was one of the precipitating factors in the outbreak of the Atheno-Peloponnesian War in 431.

45. *'Silly boy ... the good things that are your own!'*: The sister's speech is a string of platitudes and tropes, but, as such, a compendium of the Greeks' moral-political attitudes, including a characteristic ambivalence towards tyranny.

46. *city walls*: The walled area is about 1.5 km (1 mile) in diameter and the walls a total of nearly 6.5 km (4 miles) in length; even so, three other Samian works were greater than these (ch. 60).

47. *Samius*: Several other Spartans are known to have been given 'ethnic' names to indicate a connection between their family and another city or people. Pitana was rated the poshest of Sparta's four constituent villages; no doubt Archias II acted as H.'s host there. Archias is one of three named informants (cf. 4.76 Tymnes; 9.16 Thersander).

48. *This was the first time that the Lacedaemonians ... launched an expedition against Asia*: Actually, the Spartans got only as far east as the offshore island of Samos, not to the continent of Asia – H.'s formulation reflects his own preoccupation with the duality of Europe and Asia, and contemporary debate over the political status of the Greeks of Asia.

49. *the people of Siphnos were the richest ... endow a treasury at Delphi*: The Siphnians' treasury took the form of a small marble temple in the Ionic order adorned with caryatids and friezes located along the Sacred Way.

50. *Parian marble*: Paros like neighbouring Naxos was basically a marble island.

51. *Samian ships ... always painted red*: With ruddle or red ochre, in Greek *miltos*.

52. *Athena in Aegina*: The goddess' local name was Aphaea; remains of the temple sculptures are now in Munich.

53. *the Samians ... three construction projects which no other Greeks have ever rivalled*: H. here fulfils the promise made in the Preface, since 'exploits' (*erga*) in his usage could cover 'works' as well as 'deeds'.

54. *The tunnel is 7 stades long*: Actually it is 1,050 metres long, rather less than '7 stades' (*c.* 1,250 metres).

55. *Samian ... temple, the largest known to man*: Dedicated to Hera, it measured 52 × 105 metres, and boasted about 136 columns. It was hypaethral, that is, deliberately left open to the sky. Its first architect was Rhoecus (Greek *rhoikos* means 'hunchback'). There was also a Samian sanctuary of Hera at Naucratis (international port of trade in Egypt, 2.178).

56. *Now, as Cambyses ... was whiling away his time in Egypt ...*: Here begins the story of Great King Darius I's ascent to the Achaemenid throne, by way – allegedly – of putting to death a usurper pretending to be Cambyses' younger brother, Smerdis. Historical truth is not ascertainable amid the fog of official propaganda.

57. *no man has it within himself to turn destiny aside*: This was H.'s own view, and a widespread Greek belief.

58. *Otanes*: Soon to star as one of Darius' fellow-conspirators and the supposed advocate of a form of popular governance.

59. *Atossa*: The first mention of this influential daughter of Cyrus the Great, later to be a wife of Darius I.

60. *cut off the ears*: There are other instances of this punishment (ch. 118; 9.112).

61. *women in Persia sleep with their husbands in rotation*: Cf. the experience of the Jewish Esther, wife of Persian king Ahasuerus, Esther 2.15.

62. *'A lie that serves ... should be told'*: Here Darius is made to speak like a Greek rhetorician rather than a future Persian Great King, for whom any form of lying was officially anathema.

63. *met to debate the general state of affairs*: The debate that follows is known generally as 'The Persian Debate' or 'The Debate over the Constitutions'. Its authenticity was queried with particular reference to the first of the three speeches, that of Otanes, which appears to advocate, anachronistically and against the cultural grain, a form of what later came to be called by Greeks 'democracy'. H. defended himself robustly, but unpersuasively, at 6.43.

64. *'Equality before the law'*: Otanes uses the Greek term *isonomiê*, which, though it includes the fundamentally democratic notion of equality, could also be appropriated by non-democrats, e.g. ch. 142; 5.37. It is noticeable that Otanes does not use *demokratia*, though H. himself does at 6.43 ('democratic rule').

65. *the case made by Megabyzus*: Neither Otanes nor Megabyzus has argued specifically against a good, or the best, form of monarchy – which leaves the field open to Darius.

66. *rule by the people ... rule by a single man*: Darius here puts his finger on the theoretical perception underlying the entire debate, that all existing political regimes are a version or variant of either Rule by All or Rule by Some or Rule by One.

67. *the excellence ... should never be disassembled*: Darius in effect plays the Achaemenid card.

68. *according to this second tale ... the horse smelled it ... and whinnied*: It is hardly likely that the Persians themselves would have ascribed Darius' ascension to the throne to a mere cheap trick. That it was not uncontroversial, however, emerges with clarity from the immense trilingual inscription Darius caused to be engraved at Bisitun on the road to Media, as a key part of his legitimating propaganda.

69. *list of the taxes*: The satrapy list that follows (chs. 89–96) has undeniable correspondences with Persian documents but is recast in a Greek order and form.

70. *One Babylonian talent is equivalent to 70 Euboïc minae*: The manuscripts read '70', but 78 would make better sense of the total given for silver paid in tribute at ch. 95.

71. *Bactria*: See 4.204 note 156.

72. *the Caucasus ... (for no one beyond it gives the Persians so much as a thought)*: This is H.'s way of deflating Persian claims to global domination.

73. *East of these*: This conflicts formally with what is said in the previous chapter but H. perhaps means to indicate that these Indians were the most outlandish in a metaphorical as well as a literal-geographical sense.

74. *The semen which they ejaculate . . . same shade of black as their skins. (This is also true of the semen ejaculated by Ethiopians)*: H.'s un-empirical error was justly castigated by Aristotle.

75. *These ants*: It has been argued that H.'s fabulous gold-digging ants were in fact marmots (see note to Translator's Preface).

76. *the camel has . . . two knees in each of its hind legs*: Actually, it does not.

77. *The Indians use these trees to make their clothes*: H. refers to cotton (cf. 7.65).

78. *avenge*: H. uses the religiously inflected word *tisis* for 'vengeance', picking up on his notion of 'divine providence' in the previous chapter.

79. *a tail . . . at least three cubits!*: The exclamation mark indicates H.'s astonishment – but we may be forgiven for doubting the veracity of this report.

80. *'Tin Islands'*: Perhaps a reference to the British Isles; though visited by Pytheas of Massalia, who wrote an account of his travels in the late fourth century, their existence was still doubted in the time of Julius Caesar.

81. *he charges them an immense fee . . . distinct from their regular tribute*: This would tie in with the unflattering tag attached to Darius, 'the Shopkeeper' (ch. 89).

82. *'I can always have another husband . . . the thinking behind what I said'*: The argumentation resembles that used in lines 905–12 of Sophocles' *Antigone* – if indeed those lines are authentic.

83. *Such are the two different reasons . . . decide as they will*: Characteristic Herodotean method. Either way, H. well conveys that the very independence of a wealthy Samos was a standing provocation to the two westernmost satraps.

84. *Polycrates . . . the first of . . . the fully mortal race of men*: H. here divides up the past into two great tranches, the mortal – i.e. the non-mythical and empirically verifiable – and the mythical.

85. *And so it was . . . his good fortune came to an end*: A reference back to ch. 43.

86. *province of Phrygia*: That is, Great Phrygia, inland from Lydia and Ionia, as distinct from Hellespontine Phrygia.

87. *murdered the messengers I sent to summon him*: Alert connoisseurs of H.'s methods might see here a foreshadowing of the Athenians' and Spartiates' murdering of later messengers of Darius (7.133).

88. *a soothsayer from Elis*: Elis had a reputation for the quality of its native soothsayers, *manteis*, the Iamids (cf. 9.33).

89. *'since you feel . . . I need to launch my invasion'*: This anecdote craftily shows Darius to be not only under the influence of a scheming woman but also militarily ill advised, since the Scythian expedition that he in fact undertook next proved a failure.

90. *the name of Milon . . . much bruited at the court of the King*: It is quite unlikely that Darius either knew of or cared much about the superstar status Milon enjoyed in the Greek world, as a multiple winner at the Olympic and many other Greek Games.

91. *Iapygia*: The heel of Italy, including Brentesium (modern Brindisi) and Tarentum (Taranto). H. writes from personal knowledge for a south Italian audience (cf. 4.99).

92. *Samos, the first of . . . cities . . . that would end up under his control*: H. means the first city beyond the existing borders of the empire that Darius conquered, having obtained the throne.

93. *Maeandrius*: First mentioned at ch. 123.

94. *Zeus the Liberator*: The epithet 'Liberator' was attached to Zeus elsewhere in the Greek world, famously at Athens, but here has an especially apt political connotation – liberation from both domestic and external political subjection.

95. *every one of you is equal before the law*: See note 65, *isonomiê*, meaning equality before or under the law.

96. *Cleomenes demonstrated that he was a man of impeccable honesty*: This is not the impression of Cleomenes conveyed by H. at 5.51.

97. *delivered Babylon into the hands of Cyrus*: See 1.188–91.

98. *shrine of Zeus Belus*: The sanctuary and temple of Bel-Marduk; H. naturally translates the chief Babylonian male divinity into his Greek equivalent.

99. *when Babylon had originally fallen to him*: In 539 (1.191).

100. *Megabyzus who led the army in Egypt against the Athenians and their allies*: One of the score of references H. makes to matters 'after the Persian Wars'. The Athenians attempted to wrest Egypt from Persian control between 459 and 454, but the massive expedition ended in total disaster and cost them many ships and lives. Possibly the younger Zopyrus, the genuine defector, served as a major informant for H. on many Persian matters.

BOOK FOUR

1. *led by Darius in person*: Darius would not lead the later Marathon campaign in person.

2. *against the Scythians*: In what follows H. is keen to distinguish between the true Scythians and other Eurasiatic peoples. The ethnographic section proper begins at ch. 46.

3. *their . . . attack on Media*: See 1.103–6.

4. *Scythians . . . are nomads, not tillers of the soil*: H.'s Scythians in many ways function as anti-types to Greek normality; most Greeks were sedentary agriculturalists.

5. *as long as they see us with weapons ... put an end to all their resistance*: This object lesson in the psychology of slave-management was applicable to Greek slavery no less than to Scythian.

6. *the account given by the Scythians themselves*: Since H. did not speak any foreign language, he had this account either from a Greek-speaking Scythian informant or from a Scythian-speaking Greek – see note 62; at chs. 27, 52 and 110, H. claims to know the meanings of Scythian words.

7. *theirs is the most recently sprung of all races*: This was a standard sort of Greek claim to aboriginality.

8. *invasion of their country by Darius*: In about 514.

9. *Owing to a blizzard of feathers ... visibility is cut to nothing*: See also ch. 31.

10. *Pontus*: Simply Greek for 'sea', but it came to be applied specifically to what Greeks otherwise euphemistically called the 'Euxine' ('hospitable') Sea. See 1.6 with note.

11. *Heracles ... driving the cattle of Geryon*: The tenth of Heracles' allotted Labours.

12. *Oceanus ... flows all the way round the world*: Cf. 2.21, 23.

13. *the country ... the Scythians currently inhabit*: A large, fluid territory extending north of the Black Sea from Ukraine as far as the Caspian Sea in south Russia.

14. *Cimmerian people*: Mentioned in Homer, *Odyssey* 11.14–16; see also 1.15 above.

15. *the Cimmerian Bosporus*: The Strait of Kerch; the ferry mentioned is to be located on its northern side.

16. *possessed by Apollo*: Ancient Proconnesus, today's Marmara, was devoted to the worship of Apollo; but to be 'possessed' by him was unusual, for a male, and suggests shamanistic flight. Where exactly the land of the Issedonians was is uncertain: somewhere in central Asia, possibly western Siberia or Chinese Turkestan.

17. *not a trace of Aristeas, either dead or alive*: Aristeas would not have been the only early Greek credited with such a post-mortem disappearance; the disappointed Olympic boxing victor Cleomedes of Astypalaea likewise simply vanished from the face of the earth, allegedly.

18. *the Arimaspeia*: The poem has not survived.

19. *Apollo ... had been a crow*: The crow was especially associated with Apollo; the notion of a bird as the image of the soul again suggests shamanism.

20. *Borysthenites*: People of Borysthenes, modern Berezan island, which took its name from the local river, today's Dnieper.

21. *the Callippidae ... Greek Scythians*: H. seems to mean they are Scythians who have been very thoroughly Hellenized through contact, including perhaps miscegenation, with Greeks.

22. *grain*: The Greek word *sitos* could be used for barley as well as wheat, but the distinguishing feature of agriculture on the black-earth lands north of

the Black Sea was its abundant production of the bread wheat that was exported, by Greek traders, to the Aegean Greek world, not least to populous Athens.

23. *Olbiopolitans*: People of Olbia – so named for its economic abundance and located at the mouth of the River Hypanis (modern Bug).

24. *Androphagi*: The name translates literally as 'Men-eaters'; see further ch. 106.

25. *ponticum*: Perhaps the wild cherry.

26. *the joints of meat . . . served up as a feast*: Such endocannibalism has been doubted, and would have been thoroughly un-Greek – see 3.38; but H. seems keen not to emphasize the outlandishness of this people.

27. *speaking as the Scythians do . . . spou means 'eye'*: H.'s etymologizing goes astray here; the more likely derivation is from the Iranic root *aspa-*, 'horse'.

28. *no sooner are lambs born than they sprout horns*: Odyssey 4.85.

29. *if I may digress . . .* : H. here makes a major statement of method: *prosthêkai*, 'digressions' (literally 'additions') are part of his fundamental plan of exposition.

30. *Hesiod . . . Homer . . . that particular poem*: As at 2.53, H. pairs Hesiod and Homer; as at 2.117, H. casts doubt on the attribution of a work to 'Homer'.

31. *gifts for the gods*: H. maintains a religious silence about their identity.

32. *Queen Artemis*: Bendis to the locals.

33. *shrine of Artemis*: Delos was the reputed birthplace of Artemis and her twin Apollo, children of Leto (ch. 35).

34. *Eileithyia*: A goddess of childbirth, often associated with and sometimes assimilated to Artemis.

35. *let me now briefly clarify . . . represented on a map*: H. opposes his more empirical approach to the theoretical-scientific approach of the Ionian 'physicists', especially Hecataeus of Miletus; see also 2.143 note, 5.49 and note.

36. *two peninsulas . . . give a description*: The region of Colchis, through which the Phasis flowed, was traditionally the eastern limit of the pale of Hellenic settlement at this time.

37. *as convention would have it*: This is a 'learned' reference – actually, few Greeks would have had any views on the subject.

38. *our sea*: This anticipates the Romans' use of *mare nostrum* for the Mediterranean.

39. *the distance between our sea and the Red Sea is only . . . 1,000 stades*: See 2.158. The actual distance was about 115 km (71 miles) rather than H.'s 180 km-plus.

40. *Necos . . . king of the Egyptians*: Reigned 610–595.

41. *excavation of a canal from the Nile . . . to the Arabian Gulf*: See 2.158–9.

42. *sailing round Libya . . . sun on their right-hand side*: This – for H. proof of the tale's falsity – actually proves that the Phoenicians had sailed south of the Equator.

43. *tiny men*: Pygmies (see also 2.32).

44. *I choose not to mention*: H.'s normal reason for suppressing a person's name from the record was religious fastidiousness (e.g. 1.51), but here the reason may be a personal connection to the man's family.

45. *Scylax, a man from Caryanda*: A Carian, whose report of this voyage together with a 'Circumnavigation of the Earth' were preserved and cited in antiquity.

46. *three distinct names ... derived from women*: Europe, Asia and Libya. For the tripartition, ascribed to 'Ionians', see 2.16.

47. *peoples ... the most ignorant in existence*: Here begins the ethnographic section, chs. 46–82, apart from the portion devoted to rivers, chs. 47–58.

48. *Anacharsis*: Dispute continues as to whether Anacharsis was a real person or a Greek figment. H's Philhellenic Anacharsis is at any rate not the usual version.

49. *I think that I may have the solution ... appear always to be constant*: An excellent example of Herodotean 'scientific' geography.

50. *Nor do the cattle in Scythia lack for bile ... gauged by dissecting a Scythian cow*: H. is probably contributing here to learned debate as to whether or not animals of the Black Sea region had bile.

51. *Hestia*: Scythian *Tabiti*; cf. ch. 127.

52. *Aphrodite Urania*: See 1.105 note.

53. *sacrificed ... a horse*: Also practised by the Massagetans (1.216).

54. *Ares ... has a shrine raised to him in ... every province*: Cults of Ares among Greeks were, by contrast, rare, and none involved the human sacrifice described below. In the extant manuscripts H. does not furnish a Scythian equivalent name for Ares.

55. *the very mark of a hero*: H. writes literally 'this they call *andragathiê*', 'manly virtue' (cf. 'personal qualities', 5.39).

56. *the governor will mix a bowl of wine ... sit to one side in disgrace*: One might compare – or contrast – the fate of the Spartan warrior Aristodemus (7.229–31, 9.71).

57. *Agreements ... between Scythians ... swearing the oath*: Other non-Greek peoples sealed oaths with human blood (1.74, 3.8).

58. *burial places*: Kurgans or burial tumuli of the seventh to fourth centuries excavated in southern Russia have yielded skeletons, female as well as male, and accompanying grave goods that corroborate H. in many details. Royal Scythian graves are also mentioned at ch. 127.

59. *Scythians make sure to purify themselves*: Like Greeks, they considered death polluting.

60. *how travel can ... broaden the mind*: In this Anacharsis imitated Athenian Solon (1.30).

61. *Mother of the Gods*: Phrygian Cybele. Her cult flourished at Olbia from the sixth century.

62. *Tymnes*: A non-Greek Carian name, but, like H.'s own father, he could still have been a Greek; H. may have met him at Olbia. For the other two informants named by H. see 3.55 (Archias), 9.16 (Thersander).

63. *Peloponnesians*: By 'Peloponnesians' is meant especially the Spartans, whom H. consistently represents as 'Little Peloponnesians' keen to avoid passing beyond the Isthmus of Corinth, although this avoidance had not been Leonidas' priority.

64. *installed a woman ... as his wife*: Polygamy was characteristic of Eurasian nomadic societies, but very un-Greek (cf. 5.40).

65. *Bacchic rites ... men mad*: H.'s Greek audience would think primarily of female devotees of Bacchus (Dionysus) known as Maenads or 'mad women'.

66. *possession by the god*: H. here alludes to the Greek term for possession by Dionysus/Bacchus, *enthousiasmos*, whence English 'enthusiasm'.

67. *how concerned the Scythians are to maintain their customs*: In this they resembled the Egyptians (2.91), but contrasted sharply with the Persians (1.135).

68. *Exampaeus ... mentioned a short while ago*: See ch. 52.

69. *Pausanias, the son of Cleombrotus*: The first mention of the Spartan regent who commanded the Greeks to victory at Plataea, in 479.

70. *footprint ... 2 cubits long*: Probably a naturally formed depression in calcareous limestone.

71. *Let me now return to ... my original theme*: For similar resumptive formulae, see 1.140, 7.137.

72. *Darius busied himself ... to bridge the Thracian Bosporus*: See chs. 87–8.

73. *Good advice ... failed to convince Darius*: Likewise Artabanus' advice would not be heeded by his nephew, Xerxes, with even more dire results (7.10–19).

74. *Between the mouth of the Euxine and the Phasis ... 11,100 stades*: H. more or less doubles the actual length.

75. *Assyrian*: Probably Old Persian cuneiform.

76. *Byzantium*: This is the first mention of the city on the Golden Horn, founded from Megara c. 700, which over the ages has been transformed successively into Constantinople and now – by the Turks – Istanbul; for its alleged foundation after Chalcedon on the opposite Asiatic shore of the Bosporus, see ch. 144.

77. *HIS FEAT WAS TO ... EARN FOR HIMSELF A CROWN, AND FOR THE SAMIANS GLORY*: Mandrocles represents himself, implausibly, as if on a par with an Olympic victor.

78. *Darius crossed over into Europe*: On the alleged scope of Darius' conquest aims, see ch. 118; for the fort he had built at Doriscus, see 7.59.

79. *THE ENTIRE CONTINENT*: Following Darius' failure to gain 'the entire continent' (of Europe), the Persians restricted their sovereign claim to Asia (1.4).

80. *Odrysians*: There were three main groupings of the Thracian people; the Odrysians were the easternmost.

81. *Getans*: It was among the Getans that the Roman poet Ovid was reputedly exiled in AD 8.

82. *Pythagoras, son of Mnesarchus*: The first mention of this remarkable mathematician and mystic who emigrated to south Italy and left behind there schools of his followers.

83. *guest-friend*: Greek *xeinos*; see Book 2, note 87.

84. *Rugged Chersonese*: Tauric peninsula, modern Crimea.

85. *the Maiden*: H. means Iphigenia, mentioned below, H.'s only mention of her; one version of her myth is enacted dramatically in Euripides' extant tragedy, *Iphigenia among the Taurians*.

86. *every Neurian becomes a wolf for a few days*: Lycanthropy myths are widespread, for instance among Baltic peoples and in the Germanic world; H. remains the sturdy empiricist sceptic.

87. *sprung from the soil*: In Greek *autochthones*, literally 'self-earth people'. Among the Greeks, the Athenians and Arcadians made the same claim for themselves.

88. *another kind of wild creature . . . trimming*: Possibly martens, or mink.

89. *There is a story told . . . Amazons*: Chs. 110–17 give H.'s account of how some Scythians became Sauromatians by way of couplings with Amazon women. There may be some archaeological reality distantly underlying some aspects of the Amazon myth that follows, but it is, essentially, a myth serving chiefly to emphasize the necessity of Greek ideals of marriage and masculinity.

90. *desire . . . to father children on the women*: This sounds euphemistic.

91. *never learned to do women's work*: A thoroughly – masculinist – Greek view.

92. *the custom . . . until she has first killed a man among their enemies*: Tacitus records the identical custom of the Germanic Chatti in his *Germania*, ch. 31.

93. *earth and water*: The first mention (of seven in all) of this symbolic Persian demand from their opponents of total submission.

94. *Zeus, my own ancestor*: Idanthyrsus' 'Zeus' is earlier called Papaeus (ch. 59), father of Targitaus (chs. 5–7).

95. *Scythian address*: A laconic remark or rejoinder leaving no room for hope.

96. *as I explained earlier*: At ch. 28.

97. *a bird . . . and five arrows . . . *: The point of including the anecdote that follows is to highlight the Great King's unfounded confidence.

98. *Miltiades of Athens*: The first mention of the Athenian most closely associated with the victory over the Persians at Marathon, but here figuring, possibly anachronistically, as a hereditary but reluctant tyrant under Persian sway.

99. *Hellespontine Chersonese*: Thracian Chersonese (Greek for 'peninsula') is the Gallipoli peninsula; this is its first mention.

100. *democracy*: H. does not actually use the noun *demokratia* here, but a verb meaning 'to be ruled democratically'.

101. *Aristagoras*: Note the recurrence of this aristocratic name, meaning one who is 'best in the agora', that is in public political speech and debate; this Aristagoras is not to be confused with Aristagoras of Miletus, deputy and successor of Histiaeus.

102. *the loudest voice in the world*: Greeks would be reminded of Homer's Stentor, the herald of the Greeks at Troy – whence our 'stentorian' voice.

103. *I shall explain in due course*: The onward narrative does not resume until ch. 200.

104. *abducted the Athenian women from Brauron*: See further 6.137–40.

105. *heroes who sailed on the Argo*: That is, the Argonauts, Greek for 'sailors on the *Argo*', a magical ship that could speak; they included the cream of pre-Trojan War Greek heroes, such as Jason of Iolcus in Thessaly.

106. *sons of Tyndareus*: Otherwise known as the Dioscuri, Castor and Pollux (Polydeuces in Greek), twin brothers of Helen.

107. *Lacedaemonians ... the killing is done by night, never by day*: H. had visited Sparta in person (3.55), and he knew whereof he spoke; the main objects of these official nocturnal killings were helots.

108. *Cadmeian descent*: Cadmus, a Phoenician from Tyre, was the mythical founder of Boeotian Thebes (5.57–8).

109. *Eurysthenes and Procles*: The supposed ultimate progenitors of the two Spartan royal houses. See 6.51–2 and notes.

110. *Thera ... Calliste*: Modern Santorini, the Venetian name.

111. *Lepreum ... Noudium*: These towns were located in the region of the western Peloponnese known as Triphylia.

112. *Aegeids*: This tribe or clan also had representatives in Cyrene, the foundation story of which colony is told in the following chapters.

113. *Laius and Oedipus*: Father and son, successive kings of mythical Thebes. The Furies were implacable goddesses whose function was to avenge kindred murder, hence their hounding of the descendants of Oedipus, since he had killed his father at a junction in a fit of road rage.

114. *Euphemus ... Battus*: The names are emblematic – Battus 'the Stammerer' (ch. 155), descendant of Euphemus the 'Fine Speaker'.

115. *none of them had the faintest idea where ... Libya actually was*: Cyrene was founded in about 630, so the Therans' ignorance is not of the general whereabouts of the continent of Libya but of where exactly in Libya the colony should be founded. H. uses 'Libya' to mean a continent! (The other two are Europe and Asia.) He gives the boundaries of Libya at 2.15–18.

116. *the island ... where they left him*: Themselves islanders, the Therans felt more comfortable leaving Corobius on land surrounded entirely by water, even though that meant unduly stretching the meaning of 'Libya'.

117. *Sostratus of Aegina, the son of Laodamas*: A stone anchor dedicated by an Aeginetan Sostratus has been discovered at Gravisca, the port of Etruscan Tarquinia; very likely this is the same man.

118. *when the Pythia delivered her oracle . . . she knew that he was going to be a king in Libya*: H. again shows tremendous confidence in an oracle's powers of genuine foresight, as well as huge respect for the Pythia's local knowledge.

119. *Battus . . . ruled*: He and his hereditary successors ruled as 'king', a rare example of the survival of that title and office in post-Homeric Greece; cf. 3.136 for another alleged 'king' of a colony with Spartan associations.

120. *overweening arrogance*: H. uses a verb compounded of *peri*, 'excessive', and *hubris*, 'arrogance'.

121. *the Egyptians rose up against him*: See 2.161–3, 169.

122. *Barca*: Located on high land to west of Cyrene, at a site now called el Merj.

123. *Arcesilaus . . . widow of Arcesilaus, whose name was Eryxo*: Such dynastic dysfunctionality is more reminiscent of an oriental court than a Greek *polis*; but cf. 6.61–9 (Sparta).

124. *Demonax*: The name is an odd compound of the Homeric term for supreme overlord, *anax*, and *demos*, 'people'.

125. *Salamis on Cyprus*: Like Cyrene, Salamis was a Greek city with a hereditary monarch, but that was the norm rather than the exception on Greek Cyprus.

126. *treasury of the Corinthians*: Established by Cypselus, the tyrant of Corinth, *c*. 650–625, and maintained thereafter by the Cypselid family (mentioned at 6.128).

127. *Loxias*: This title of Apollo derives from the Greek for 'crooked', a reference to the sometimes obscure nature of his oracular responses (e.g. at 1.91).

128. *the pretext for the dispatch . . . the conquest of Libya*: H. anticipates Thucydides in distinguishing pretext, *proschêma*, from true cause or explanation, *aitiê*. H. was of the view that the Persian empire was inherently expansionist.

129. *harbour called Menelaus*: It was here, perhaps Marsa Gabes today, that King Agesilaus II of Sparta died in 360/359.

130. *silphium-growing region*: Silphium, highly appreciated in antiquity as a culinary spice and for its medicinal properties, and for those reasons depicted on coins of Cyrene, cannot be certainly identified today (asafoetida?) and may be extinct.

131. *driving of four-horse chariots*: For this peculiarly Libyan skill, see also chs. 183, 189 (allegedly taught to the Greeks), 193; 7.184.

132. *Euesperides*: Euesperides was renamed Berenice in the third century, modern Benghazi.

133. *sleep . . . interpreted as revealing the future*: Such divinatory incubation was also practised in Greece, especially at the shrine of Asclepius at Epidaurus.

134. *Psylli*: Perhaps inhabiting the greater Syrtis.

135. *an island . . . urged by an oracle to colonize*: Presumably this is to be connected with Spartan prince Dorieus' failed Libyan expedition (5.42–3).

136. *off Cape Malea . . . overtaken by a north wind*: Etesian winds off this the southeasternmost cape of mainland Greece are particularly fierce from the north-east, hence the proverb 'Round Malea – and forget your home'.

137. *array the girl . . . circuit around the lake*: Readers might be reminded of Peisistratus' ruse at 1.60.

138. *the Greeks derived both their shields and their helmets from Egypt*: Actually, the Greeks' circular shield was more likely derived from the neo-Assyrians, while the all-over bronze 'Corinthian' helmet was an endogenous Greek invention.

139. *the Ammonians*: Greek *Ammon* represents Egyptian *Amun* (2.42). Amun/ Ammon was a deity of Egyptian Thebes (2.42), equated by Greeks with Zeus.

140. *The Garamantes also breed oxen . . . their horns curve forwards*: Rock paintings at today's Tassili n'Ajjer perhaps gave rise to this story.

141. *cave-dwelling Ethiopians are the fleetest-footed people in the entire world*: Haile Gebrselassie would be interested to learn this, but his Ethiopia is of course not H.'s.

142. *a mountain called Atlas*: H.'s Mt Atlas, wherever exactly it may have been, is located well to the east of today's Atlas Mountains.

143. *'Atlantians' . . . nor in their sleep do they ever see dreams*: The Greeks linked diet to dreams, and H. seems to infer a causal connection between the vegetarian diet and dreamless sleep of the Atlantians.

144. *women of Cyrene . . . as well as cows*: This could be taken as proof of the native Libyan origin of the women married by the first Greek colonists (cf. chs. 153, 164, 168).

145. *Athena . . . Poseidon*: Athena here (cf. ch. 180) may stand for Egyptian *Neit*, Triton and Poseidon for local male water divinities.

146. *it seems likely that Athena's clothing . . . copied by the Greeks from Libyan women*: Diffusionistic theories were dear to H., who tended to favour the notion of Greeks as recipients rather than donors of seemingly shared cultural practices.

147. *nomads bury their dead in the Greek manner*: That is, when Greeks practised inhumation (cf. 3.38); and Greek corpses were stretched out straight, whereas local Libyan corpses were often buried bent.

148. *There are men with the heads of dogs . . . many other beasts that are not*: H. is careful to distance himself from these local tales, but that has not saved him from attack by sceptical readers taking him as believing them uncritically.

149. *the most wide-ranging research possible*: H. is inordinately proud of his *historiê* into the *akoê*, oral tales told him by Cyrenaeans and Greek-speaking Libyans; for the method, cf. 2.29.

150. *I am only writing down what I was told*: Note the explicit reference to H.'s graphic literacy. For his usual method, see 7.152.

151. *Demeter*: H. seems not to be referring here to any particular Libyan earth-mother but just a grain-giving goddess.

152. *Once the Persians sent by Aryandes ... :* Here H. resumes the narrative from ch. 167.

153. *prosecuted their siege, tunnelling underground*: This technique of siegecraft is noted in the surviving fourth-century treatise on the subject by Aeneas the Tactician, ch. 37.

154. *Pheretime*: For her very bad end, see ch. 205 and note 157.

155. *Lycaean Zeus*: The cult of Zeus of Mount Lycaeum was of Arcadian origin, possibly introduced in connection with the reforms of Demonax, an Arcadian from Mantinea (ch. 161).

156. *land of Bactria*: For Bactria, in today's Afghanistan, as a Persian province, see 3.92; for other Greeks transplanted by Darius to Asia as a punishment for revolt, see 6.18–20 (Milesians to the Persian Gulf), 6.119 (Eretrians to Cissia on the Euphrates); other examples at 3.149; 5.14–15, 17, 23, 98.

157. *to demonstrate to mankind that vengeance ... will always arouse the envy of the gods*: H.'s Solon had characterized the divine as vengeful in general (1.32); here the gods' vengeance is linked specifically to the punishment of human immoral excess.

BOOK FIVE

1. *Paean*: A hymn of invocation or thanksgiving, often chanted in honour of Apollo; the non-Greek Paeonians were punning, as often happened in oracular contexts.

2. *I have already mentioned*: 4.93–4; for us this is a different Book, but H. knew no such book divisions, which were imposed on his text for editorial convenience not before the third century.

3. *a custom ... to sell their children for export*: That is, to slave-traders catering to Greek customers.

4. *wives ... for substantial sums of money*: Greeks too had practised bride-price in the Homeric poems, but by H.'s day the normal and near-universal Greek custom was for the prospective groom's family to demand and receive a dowry.

5. *the Eneti*: (from the modern Veneto) Famed for rearing race-horses.

6. *Massilia*: The only mention in H. of the city that is the original of today's Marseille, founded from Phocaea in Ionia *c.* 600.

7. *the Bear*: Ursa Major, the Great Bear constellation; our 'Arctic' comes from *arktos*, the Greek for 'bear'.

8. *Thrace ... coastal regions ... Persian rule*: Thus this was the first toehold of the Persian empire on the continent of Europe.

9. *Mount Pangaeum*: Extremely rich in both gold and silver and so a great prize for any conqueror or other imperial power (such as Athens in the fifth century).

10. *Macedonia*: First mention in H. of this region and kingdom; the kingdom is sometimes called 'Macedon' by scholars to distinguish the political from the geographical entity.

11. *Amyntas*: Amyntas I, father of Alexander I. From this moment on, the Persian empire extended into Europe as far west as the western border of Macedonia and as far south as the northern border with Thessaly; Mt Olympus, abode of the Greeks' gods, was thus now within the Persian empire.

12. *Alexander*: Alexander I, reigned *c.* 498–454; he will play a key role at 8.136–44.

13. *So it was ... kept a secret*: This story is implausible in the extreme – but serves to establish the profile of the future King Alexander I as a good Greek, despite his kingdom's formal submission to Persia.

14. *the descendants of Perdiccas*: They make too abrupt an appearance here; not until 8.139 does H. divulge that it was Perdiccas (I) who established the royal dynasty (H. calls it a 'tyranny') to which Amyntas and Alexander were heirs.

15. *adjudged to be Greek*: On the grounds that Alexander's family's ultimate ancestor, Argeas, had migrated from Argos in the Peloponnese; but note that only members of this royal Macedonian family were adjudged sufficiently certainly Greek by descent to be allowed to compete at Olympia – no other Macedonians were; and there were many Greeks who continued to question the authentic Greekness of the Macedonian people in general.

16. *Otanes*: Not to be confused with either Otanes son of Pharnaspes, 3.68 etc., or Otanes father of Amestris, 7.40 etc.

17. *terrible things ... a second time*: The first time had been when Persia conquered the Ionians (1.169). This second time is what moderns call the 'Ionian Revolt' from Persia, 499–494, of which H. seems to have thoroughly disapproved. See further on the theme of 'evils' ch. 97, 6.98 (Hellas in general).

18. *fat cats all, were banished ... by the mass of the people*: Such a bipartite division – the few rich fat cats against the many poor citizens – was the economic underpinning of what the Greeks called *stasis*, a 'standing-apart' or civil strife.

19. *acting governor*: H. uses the term *epitropos*, which can mean 'regent' or in the private sphere 'guardian'.

20. *it was adjacent to Ionia*: Not so; see also next note.

21. *Euboea ... no smaller than Cyprus ... very easy to seize*: Aristagoras' geography is again awry. Actually, Cyprus measures 9,251 sq. km (3,572 sq. miles), Euboea, which is Greece's second largest island, 3,684 sq. km (1,422 sq. miles). For further geographical difficulties of his, see chs. 49–50.

22. *tyrant over Greece*: Pausanias, the victor of Plataea, was a notoriously ambitious and controversial figure, but tyrant of 'Greece' seems a bit steep, even for him; Thucydides (1.127–35), however, was convinced of the truth of Pausanias' medism.

23. *built a fortress . . . tails between their legs*: The date of the failed attack is *c.* 501.

24. *revolution*: See Book 1 note 220.

25. *listed all the peoples subject to Darius*: This recalls H.'s satrapy list at 3.89ff.

26. *in the first narrative section*: The Greek says 'in the first of the *logoi*'; the precise reference is to 1.92.

27. *equality under the laws*: H.'s *isonomiê*, the very word that he applies to the notional political programme of Otanes in the Persian Debate (3.80); whatever exactly it implied, it was presented as the direct negation of absolute sole rule.

28. *Leon . . . Cleomenes*: Cleomenes I acceded *c.* 520; Leon was last mentioned at 1.65; for a listing of the pedigree of the Agiad royal house, descended ultimately from Heracles via Eurysthenes, see 7.204.

29. *personal qualities*: H.'s *andragathiê*, emphatically repeated at ch. 42 ('merit'), means literally 'manly virtue', a quality which for a Spartan was proved above all in martial combat.

30. *quite contrary to Spartan custom*: And also a flagrant breach of the normal Greek practice of strict monogamy – the template against which H. goes out of his way to mention the plural marriage customs of non-Greek peoples.

31. *Dorieus*: The name is an ethnic one meaning 'the Dorian'; this may account for Cleomenes' alleged vehement retort to the priestess of Athena on the Athenian acropolis (ch. 72) that he was not a Dorian.

32. *twins*: For the most famous Spartan royal twins, see 6.52.

33. *the second wife . . . daughter of Prinetadas*: She was related to the famously wise Chilon, ephor in about 550 (1.59, 7.235).

34. *Cleomenes . . . almost a lunatic*: This is to be read with H.'s description of and judgement upon the manner of Cleomenes' death some thirty years later (6.75, 84); but H.'s somewhat contradictory account of his long reign was not entirely negative, see especially 6.61.

35. *Cinyps . . . founded a colony there*: For the river, see 4.175, for the homonymous region 4.198; the name of the colony is unknown.

36. *they captured the city*: Not only that but in 510 Croton utterly destroyed Sybaris, the site of which was not reoccupied until the foundation in 444/3 of Thuria or Thurii, a city of which H. himself reputedly became a citizen. Sybarites are the eponyms of our 'sybaritic'.

37. *proof . . . of his ignoring the oracle*: H. seems himself to want to endorse this religious explanation.

38. *Phoenicians and Egestaeans*: Both non-Greek, 'Phoenicians' being a reference to the ultimate origin of many settlements in the west of the island, such as Panormus (now Palermo); the latter were to have their day in the

sun in 416/15, when the Athenians answered their call for help against the neighbouring Greek city of Selinous.

39. *did not reign for very long*: Actually Cleomenes reigned for some thirty years, *c.* 520–490.

40. *Gorgo*: An odd name, since it means 'Gorgon', a terrifying snake-haired monster of Greek myth.

41. *a map of the entire world*: The basis of this map has been credited to Anaximander of Miletus, *c.* 610–550; possibly it had been improved by Hecataeus, also of Miletus.

42. *it is you, as the leading people in Greece*: This had been established already in the time of Croesus and Cyrus, *c.* 550 (1.56, 65, 152).

43. *of one blood with you*: For the 'common blood' of the Greeks, see 8.144.

44. *500 talents . . . tribute*: See 3.90.

45. *neither sizeable nor . . . fertile*: By Greek standards, Lacedaemon, the territory of Sparta, was both exceptionally big and exceptionally fertile.

46. *the bribe was 50 talents*: The Spartans, who did not yet produce their own silver coinage, had a bad reputation among other Greeks, not entirely undeserved (6.72), for being easily bribable.

47. *the Gyndes*: See 1.190.

48. *royal road*: It ran from Sardis to Susa, about 2,700 km (1,677 miles).

49. *the Greek Sea*: The Mediterranean, used later (7.28) by a non-Greek speaker from Sardis.

50. *four years*: From 514 to 510.

51. *Panathenaea*: Literally the 'all-Athenian' festival in honour of the city's patron goddess Athena's official birthday; Peisistratus was credited with reorganizing and aggrandizing the festival, by tradition founded in 566.

52. *their script*: The earliest documented Greek alphabetic writing belongs to the third quarter of the eighth century.

53. *goat- and sheepskins*: Besides vellum, Greeks used pottery and lead for everyday messages, bronze and stone for permanent public records.

54. *the time of Laius*: A strictly mythical not human, historical time – see Book 3 note 84.

55. *Athenian family exiled by the sons of Peisistratus*: H. gives the impression that the Alcmaeonid family were exiled throughout the tyranny of Hippias, 527–510, but its head, Cleisthenes (ch. 66ff.), held the archonship in 525/4. H. was somewhat at the mercy of his Alcmaeonid informants.

56. *Paeonia*: H.'s slip for the Attican deme of Paeonidae.

57. *sent a force under Anchimolius*: It is noticeable that, for a naval expedition, the Spartans did not appoint a king as commander; contrast ch. 64.

58. *considerations of men . . . compared to those of the god*: H. more or less repeats this judgement on the Spartans' exceptional piety at 9.7.

59. *the Athenians were rid of their tyrants*: Note that the Athenian ex-tyrants medized; cf. chs. 37–8 for the overthrowing of pro-Persian tyrants in Asia

a decade later, at the outset of the Ionian Revolt which the democratic Athenians – foolishly, in the view of H. (ch. 97) – supported.

60. *a special friend of the people*: H. uses a verb that literally has Cleisthenes making the ordinary citizens of Athens, all of them, his 'comrades'.

61. *he replaced the four tribes ... with a tenfold division*: For the key importance of this tribal reform of 508/7, see 6.131; but H. surely mistakes – 'I have a theory' (ch. 67; cf. ch. 69) – its in fact impersonal motivation.

62. *rhapsodic contests ... of Argos*: Rhapsodes, 'stitchers of songs', were specialist reciters of Homeric epic, in which 'Argives' and 'Argos' were among the terms used for the equivalent of 'Greeks' and 'Greece'.

63. *Hylleis ... Dymanatae*: Hylleis, Pamphylians ('All-tribespeople') and (more usually) Dymanes were the standard names of the three pseudo-kinship tribes in all Dorian cities, for example Sparta.

64. *the support of the mass of the Athenian people*: See note 59.

65. *the demes*: There were in all 139 or 140 of these villages/parishes/wards (same Greek word *demos* as for 'people').

66. *members of the opposing faction*: In Greek *antistasiôtai*.

67. *'the accursed ones'*: The curse attaching hereditarily to the Alcmaeonids was again invoked by the Spartans in 432 – against Pericles, the most important Alcmaeonid of H.'s own time (6.131).

68. *Cylon ... tried to seize the Acropolis*: In about 632.

69. *before the time of Peisistratus*: So put probably because of Peisistratus' temporary alliance with the Alcmaeonid Megacles in the 550s (1.60–61).

70. *'no Dorian ... but an Achaean'*: Cleomenes seems to be claiming this status as a descendant of Heracles; 'Achaean' was a generic name for Greeks in the Homeric poems. See also note 31.

71. *Timesitheus ... unsurpassed feats of strength*: A much later source, Pausanias the traveller-pilgrim of the second century AD, records that Timesitheus was a champion of the *pancration* or 'all-strength' event.

72. *earth and water ... severely censured*: The newly democratic Athenians wanted Persian aid, especially financial, against Sparta, but, mindful also of the Peisistratids' medism, would not accept the Persians' condition of unconditional submission (cf. ch. 96).

73. *Corinthians*: Last heard of energetically supporting the Spartans' expedition against Polycrates of Samos (3.48).

74. *Demaratus ... the other Spartan king*: From the Eurypontid house, first mentioned here by name; for his birth, questionable legitimacy and deposition, see 6.61ff.

75. *two sons of Tyndareus*: The Dioscuri, Castor and Polydeuces, images of whom were taken on campaign as talismans.

76. *equal voice*: H. here uses *isêgoriê*, a variant on *isonomiê* (ch. 37, 3.80), to render democratic equality.

77. *Thebans ... wishing to be avenged*: Thebes was the leading city of the recently defeated Boeotians.

78. *Asopus ... Aegina*: Asopus was the personification of a key Boeotian river, destined to be a major player in the Plataea campaign; 'Thebe and Aegina' are the divine eponyms of those two cities.

79. *permit the messengers ... to return with Aeacus and his sons*: Aegina sent merely token or symbolic aid, in the form of images of the Aeacids; cf. ch. 75 for the Spartans' similar symbolic use of images of the Dioscuri.

80. *war against the Athenians*: This undeclared war beginning c. 505 was still rumbling on in 483 (7.144).

81. *to Athena ... and to Erechtheus*: Athena, as patron goddess of Athens, and Erechtheus, a mythical early king, were jointly worshipped, together with Poseidon, in the shrine on the Acropolis known for short as the Erechtheum.

82. *command of the sea*: H. calls the Aeginetans *thalassokratores*, 'thalassocrats', a position last held in the 530s and 520s by Polycrates (3.39).

83. *clap of thunder ... earthquake*: Thunder was associated with Zeus, earthquakes with Poseidon, and both could be taken as ill divine omens.

84. *the conspiracy of the Alcmaeonids with the Pythia*: See ch. 63.

85. *these prophecies ... after they had been discarded*: The phrasing implies they had been committed to writing; their source is unknowable.

86. *the growth of Athenian power ... their own leadership*: This phraseology would have had immense resonance for H.'s audiences in the 430s, in the run-up to the outbreak of the great Peloponnesian War in 431.

87. *the Spartiates ... all their other allies*: This assembly of c. 505 is arguably the earliest documentation of the existence of the alliance known to moderns as the 'Peloponnesian League' but in antiquity as either 'The Spartans and their allies' or just 'the Peloponnesians'. It may have existed in some form as early as 550 or at least 525.

88. *Friends*: H. uses *summachoi*, 'allies', but a key constituent of their alliances was to swear to 'have the same friends and enemies' as Sparta.

89. *equal share of power*: Isokratiai – akin to but not identical with *isonomiê* and *isêgoriê* (note 75).

90. *went off to Delphi, to ask about having a child*: Cf. Battus of Thera (4.155), another consultant who asks the Pythia about a personal matter only to receive a publicly inflected response.

91. *ruled for thirty years*: Roughly 655–625; Cypselus is the earliest authentic Greek 'tyrant' on record.

92. *significance ... hardly missed by Periander*: Periander's astuteness earned him membership, alongside the Spartan Chilon, in some versions of the club of the 'Seven Sages'.

93. *the reality of tyranny*: Periander is thus made out to conform totally to the negative stereotype of the tyrant, a murderously cruel ruler who exploited

his absolute power to degrade women sexually, and would stop at nothing to satisfy his greed or lust.

94. *the time came ... to give them grief*: A coded reference to the Peloponnesian War, though the Athenians and the Corinthians had already fallen out well before, in the 450s.

95. *abduction of Helen*: See 1.3; but cf. 2.113–20.

96. *Alcaeus*: Alcaeus of Mytilene (*fl. c.* 600), a contemporary of Sappho (2.135).

97. *Aristagoras of Miletus ... deported from Sparta by Cleomenes*: See chs. 51 and 55. H. rather telescopes the chronology, leaping forward from *c.* 504 to 500.

98. *thirty thousand Athenians ... more easily fooled than a single man*: H. quotes what was perhaps the rough total of the citizen population of Athens in *c.* 480 rather than 500, and, to make his contrast more rhetorically effective, assumes they might all have attended an assembly meeting – a physical impossibility.

99. *Terrible evils ... both for the Greeks and for the Barbarians*: H. takes a wholly negative view of the Ionians' and other Asiatic Greeks' attempt to free themselves from Persia, and seems to link Athens' purportedly senseless decision to support the revolt to the fact that it was a democracy.

100. *Paeonians ... deported ... by Megabazus*: Chs. 14–15.

101. *retaliatory burning of the shrines in Greece*: In 480 and again in 479, heinous sacrilege in patriotic Greeks' eyes.

102. *Simonides of Ceos*: A praise-singer blessed with a prodigious memory, much in demand by both individuals and cities, not least the Spartans, during a highly lucrative career centring on the Graeco-Persian Wars of 480–479. He wrote 'Report to the people of Lacedaemon', often rendered as 'Go, tell the Spartans'. He appears again at 7.228.

103. *all the other cities in the region*: Listed at ch. 117 and 6.33.

104. *all the other Cypriots*: H. presumably means only all the other Greek Cypriot cities, not also the Phoenician.

105. *Histiaeus of Miletus*: Last mentioned at ch. 36.

106. *the poem composed by Solon*: Plutarch, *Life of Solon* ch. 26, quotes the poem and assigns Solon's Cyprus visit to a period after the promulgation of his laws at Athens, 594/3.

107. *in my view*: H. perhaps feels constrained to intervene here as the debate was taking place on his own home ground of Caria.

108. *trauma*: H.'s *trôma* means literally 'wound'.

109. *Heracleides ... from Mylasa*: Like H.'s own Greek family, this Carian one combines Greek and native Carian names.

110. *Myrcinus ... a gift from Darius*: Ch. 23.

111. *the story-teller Hecataeus*: H. calls him *logopoios*, here and at ch. 36, perhaps to play down the fact that he was also a serious political actor.

BOOK SIX

1. *promise to conquer Sardinia ... largest of islands*: For the 'promise' see 5.106. Sardinia, the second largest Mediterranean island after Sicily, is 24,090 sq. km (9,300 sq. miles).

2. *to settle the Ionians in Phoenicia*: Not the last time by any means that an exchange of location for Ionian Greeks was mooted (9.106).

3. *missives*: H. uses *bublia*, whence 'bible'; no doubt written on Egyptian papyrus, which had originally reached Greece via Byblos in Phoenicia.

4. *island called Lade ... in defence of Miletus*: The battle of Lade occurred in the summer of 494, the sixth campaigning year of the revolt.

5. *fully crewed Ionian fleet ... three hundred and fifty-three triremes in all*: This catalogue of the ships is a dress rehearsal for Salamis in 480 (8.43–8), where the anti-Persian muster was only slightly larger.

6. *Ionian tyrants ... toppled from power by Aristagoras of Miletus*: See 5.37.

7. *the Phocaean general, Dionysius*: The Phocaeans, like the men of Teos, had collectively upped sticks in 545, but nostalgia caused more than half the émigrés to return home (1.164–9, especially 165).

8. *If you are prepared ... really tough exercise*: There was a stereotype which H. is playing with here of Ionian Greeks as pampered, lazy and self-indulgent.

9. *driving their ships through ... exiting the far side of it*: The technical term for this complicated manoeuvre was *diekplous*.

10. *urging them to abandon the Ionian alliance ... they accepted Aeaces' proposals*: This treachery foreshadows, in reverse, the refusal of the – democratic – Athenians to betray the Greek cause in winter 480/479 (8.143–4).

11. *This Aeaces ... the other Ionian tyrants*: Mentioned in the context of Darius' Scythian expedition at 4.138, but not mentioned by name along with other toppled tyrants at 5.37.

12. *impossible ... to record ... which of the Ionians proved themselves to be cowards and which to be men of quality*: For other rolls of honour after victorious battles, see 8.93 (Salamis), 9.71 (Plataea) and 9.105 (Mycale).

13. *This same pillar ... to this day*: H. yet again reveals his personal knowledge of Samos; the Samians were the leaders of the post-Mycale anti-Persian revolt in 479 (9.106).

14. *preying on the Carthaginians and Etruscans*: This harks back to the piratical activities of Dionysius' forebears on Corsica (1.166).

15. *by digging mines ... deploying all kinds of siege-engines*: Archaeologically, the best-attested example of the Persians' siege techniques occurred at Paphus on Cyprus – not mentioned by H. in his account of the revolt.

16. *I will discuss ... the Argives in due course*: See ch. 77 and note.

17. *the Persians ... long hair*: Aeschylus' epitaph refers to the 'long-haired Mede'.

18. *The sheer quantity of valuables ... frequently mentioned ... in my narrative*: See e.g. 1.92, 5.36.

19. *Sybaris ... captured by the Crotoniates*: See 5.44–5.

20. *The response of the Athenians ... ever being staged again*: Tragedy as an art-form had been invented in the 530s but became a matter of central public concern under the democracy – the first Theatre of Dionysus under the Acropolis dates to about 500. Phrynichus, an older contemporary of Aeschylus, later resumed his career; his *Fall of Miletus* has not survived.

21. *Sicilians*: Greek *Sikeloi*; H. means the native pre-colonial inhabitants (also at 7.155: 'Sicels').

22. *sent a chorus*: It was common practice for Greek cities to send choirs to compete at major interstate festivals of Apollo, such as the four-yearly Pythia Festival at Delphi (as here) or the annual festival on Delos.

23. *children ... learning their letters*: This is one of only a very few early references to formal education in a Greek city.

24. *Chersonese*: Thracian Chersonese, or Gallipoli peninsula.

25. *Miltiades*: For this Miltiades' earlier career, see 4.137, 138.

26. *wealthy enough to maintain a four-horse chariot*: This translates *oikiê hippotrophos* and means exceptionally wealthy enough to race chariots at Olympia and elsewhere (cf. chs. 36, 103).

27. *founder*: Oikistes, the title of the officially designated founder of an *apoikia* ('home from home').

28. *The details ... I shall explain elsewhere in my account*: At ch. 103.

29. *two years later*: 493.

30. *even in my own time ... according to the prescriptions of Artaphrenes*: H. may mean that the original Persian assessment was still being used as the basis of the levies required by the Athenians for their anti-Persian alliance.

31. *Mardonius ... son of Gobryas*: Gobryas was also one of the famous 'Seven Persians' mentioned below (cf. 3.70ff.); this is the first mention of his son Mardonius, the alleged prime mover of the expedition led by Darius' son Xerxes in 480 (7.5).

32. *democratic rule*: Otanes (3.80) had advocated what he called *isonomiê*, which H. rather crudely and anachronistically identifies as *demokratiê*.

33. *added the Macedonians to ... those slaves already in their possession*: See 5.18–20.

34. *damage suffered by their ships ... dashed against Athos itself*: Never again; see 7.22–3 for the canal dug through Athos on the orders of Xerxes.

35. *average annual income ... rising to 300 at its peak*: A staggering sum; in 431 Athens – by then an imperial power commanding some two hundred subordinate allies – was raising only two or three times as much annually in external revenue.

36. *The Thasians ... pulled down their city walls*: H.'s audience would know that in the 460s, as related by Thucydides (1.101), Athens had besieged Thasos, nominally its ally against Persia, because of a dispute over the proper destination of the mining revenues, and after capturing the city ordered its by then rebuilt walls to be pulled down again.

37. *declared the Aeginetans guilty of having betrayed Greece*: The rhetoric of Panhellenism becomes ever more prevalent and shrill, although 'Greece' (Hellas) remained a largely notional concept and ideal for most Greeks most of the time.

38. *Cleomenes*: King Cleomenes I, last mentioned at 5.97.

39. *'Your course of action ... accompanied by the other king'*: Cleomenes and Demaratus had been at loggerheads since the latter's withdrawal from the expedition against Athens of 505 (5.75).

40. *'get your horns sheathed ... facing terrible danger'*: An instance of the characteristically laconic (spartan) mode of repartee, known in Greek as an 'apophthegm'.

41. *Meanwhile, back in Sparta ... the junior house*: Here begins an extraordinarily detailed excursus (chs. 51–9) on the origins and privileges of the two Spartan royal houses and the dual kingship – a unique institution in all Greece that not only piqued H.'s extreme curiosity but caused him to regard certain Spartan regal practices as more oriental than Greek.

42. *Both houses ... share an identical ancestry*: The respective royal pedigrees are rehearsed at 7.204 and 8.131.

43. *so it has been ... ever since*: Not strictly accurate, but certainly true of the joint incumbents in 491.

44. *a point on which the Persians and the Greeks do concur*: The form of argument recalls that at the very opening of the work (1.1–5).

45. *The Spartiates have bestowed ... prerogatives upon their kings ... they can make war against any country they choose*: No longer literally true by the early fifth century, so far as the declaration of war was concerned – that was done by the Spartiates collectively in assembly; but once appointed to the command of an army, a king was more or less an absolute monarch, if only for the duration of the campaign (cf. chs. 72, 84).

46. *a hundred hand-picked men to protect them*: This needs to be distinguished from the elite force of three hundred *hippeis*, 'cavalry' (1.67).

47. *Gerousia*: Literally a Council of Elders; the twenty-eight ordinary members had to be over sixty and of distinguished family and were elected for life. The two kings were members ex officio, making a body of thirty in all.

48. *casting two votes, and then a third one on behalf of themselves*: Thucydides (1.20) scathingly – and plausibly – dismisses this as a gross error.

49. *tour Laconia*: By (literally) 'all the Laconian land' H. means Laconia and Messenia combined, what is called 'Lacedaemon' below.

50. *These rituals ... much the same*: Cf. 4.71 (Scythian kings).

51. *ways in which the Lacedaemonians resemble the Egyptians*: See 2.80.

52. *for the common good of Greece*: A very striking, Panhellenist sentiment.

53. *consumed by envy and malice*: This is not the view of Demaratus that H. provides in Book 7.

54. *Ariston duly handed over . . . sought to drag off his friend's wife*: Cf. 9.108–13 for a somewhat similar tale affecting the Persian court of Xerxes.

55. *before even ten months had fully passed*: Greeks counted inclusively; we would say 'nine months'; see further ch. 69 for the statement, put in the mouth of Demaratus' anonymous mother, that infants could survive even if born after only seven months' gestation.

56. *the withdrawal of the army that Demaratus had staged at Eleusis*: See 5.75.

57. *the priestess who uttered the oracles*: That is, the Pythia, called alternatively *promantis*, 'prophetess', below.

58. *Festival of Naked Boys*: *Gumnopaidiai* could also mean 'Festival of Unarmed Dancing'.

59. *a hero called Astrabacus*: According to the second-century AD religious travel-writer Pausanias (3.16), he was an early hero associated with the cult of Artemis Orthia ('Upright').

60. *King Darius . . . estates and cities*: Demaratus' direct descendants still flourished in north-west Anatolia a generation after H., who could well have interviewed them there.

61. *no other Spartan . . . four-horse chariot race*: Probably *c.* 500; a century later his feat was matched by a Spartan princess, Cynisca, sister of Agesilaus II, who won this event twice running, in 396 and 392, and commemorated her feat very visibly and loudly both at Olympia and in Sparta.

62. *Archidamus*: Archidamus II, reigned *c.* 469–427. 'Lampito' was the name Aristophanes chose for his Spartan character in the *Lysistrata* of 411.

63. *led the Lacedaemonians on campaign in Thessaly*: In 478, when the loyalist Greeks were settling scores with medizers.

64. *suffer retribution . . . where he died*: A good illustration of the maxim expressed by Solon (1.32); in ch. 86 Leotychidas comes across as the very model of financial probity.

65. *he proceeded . . . wherever he should lead*: Cleomenes thus cannily adopted the formula applied normally to relations between Sparta and its subordinate allies of the Peloponnesian League as well as reversing Sparta's habitual policy of dealing with allies on a city-by-city basis rather than as ethnic units.

66. *full-blown madness*: See 5.42.

67. *The consensus of most Greeks*: H. rehearses four possible explanations of Cleomenes' deranged alleged suicide, those given respectively by 'most Greeks', 'the Athenians', 'the Argives' and 'the Spartiates'; oddly, the Spartans alone allegedly preferred a secular explanation, whereas H. himself (ch. 84) piously favours the first – divine retribution for corrupting the Pythia.

68. *mentioned by an oracle*: See ch. 19. The occasion of the unique double oracle addressed to Argos and the Milesians could have been Aristagoras' visit to Sparta in 500.

69. *his explanation . . . so plausible and reasonable*: A glaring illumination of Spartan mentality.

70. *the devastation inflicted upon her reserves of manpower*: If the Sepeia episode (ch. 77ff.; and see 7.148–52) occurred in 494, coincidentally with the destruction of Miletus by the Persians, that would help explain in part the neutrality of Argos during the Persians' invasion fourteen years later.

71. *the popular faction . . . crushed by the men of substance*: This internal binary division is reminiscent of the situation on Naxos in *c.* 500 (5.28–34); these events on Aegina in 493 may be the first documented case of democratic Athens supporting a popular revolution in another city.

72. *Sophanes of Decelea*: A hero of the battle of Plataea (9.73–5).

73. *Off they were dispatched . . . royal presence*: Here begins H.'s account of the Marathon campaign, not actually launched until 490.

74. *Artaxerxes*: Artaxerxes I reigned *c.* 465–425.

75. *the battle for supremacy among the leading powers of Greece*: H. means principally the Peloponnesian War.

76. *allotted the lands of the horse-breeding Chalcidians*: See 5.77.

77. *Hippias*: Ex-tyrant and head of the 'Peisistratid clan' mentioned at ch. 94.

78. *one of whom was Miltiades*: This is H.'s way of proleptically singling him out as the key strategist of the Marathon victory but also recalling chs. 39–41.

79. *Their record was only ever equalled by . . . Euagoras, the Spartan*: Perhaps at the Olympics of 548, 544 and 540.

80. *Philippides*: Readers may be more familiar with the spelling 'Phidippides'.

81. *Pan*: Pan, the goat-man mountain-god and eponym of 'panic', was a native of Arcadia. (For Egyptian Pan, see 2.46.)

82. *The second day . . . he was already in Sparta*: In other words, in more than twenty-four but less than forty-eight hours after leaving Athens he had covered the 250 km (155 miles) from Athens to Sparta; in honour of his feat, and feet, there is today staged annually an ultra-marathon race known as the 'Spartathlon'.

83. *a law that they were most unwilling to break*: See Book 5 note 57.

84. *such an old man*: About eighty.

85. *reluctant to join the Boeotian League*: The Boeotians (like the Arcadians) were both an ethnic group and members of individual cities; but, led by Thebes, they had succeeded in forming a federal state and it was this that the Plataeans, probably in 519, opted out of by allying with Athens

86. *Miltiades approached Callimachus of Aphidnae*: Actually, Callimachus was technically the overall commander-in-chief, and it was in his name, not Militiades', that a major victory-monument was dedicated on the Athenian Acropolis.

87. *the board of generals*: Introduced as a consequence of Cleisthenes' reforms, one general elected per tribe.

88. *he did not give battle until the official day of his command dawned*: His descendants, especially his son Cimon, will have been keen to emphasize his democratic egalitarianism, especially against critics such as Xanthippus (ch. 136) and his son Pericles.

89. *The distance between the two armies was 8 stades*: A highly implausible figure in the August or September heat – perhaps they did really run full-out for a very maximum of one stade after a jogtrot of 7 stades.

90. *unsupported by . . . cavalry*: The absence of the Persians' own cavalry has always seemed strange – perhaps they had been re-embarked, or perhaps they were out of range at the moment chosen by Miltiades – and perhaps the moment of attack was chosen for that very reason.

91. *Greeks had only had to hear the name of the Medes to be reduced to a state of terror*: An implied criticism of Asiatic Greeks, perhaps.

92. *Cynegeirus*: For his brother Aeschylus, see 2.156 and note.

93. *said to have lifted up a shield as a prearranged signal*: Rumours of Alcmaeonid treachery persisted well after 490; for H.'s stout defence, see chs. 121ff.

94. *raced back to the defence of their city*: A distance of some 40 km (25 miles), under arms.

95. *one hundred and ninety-two*: Note the precision. A modern view holds that this figure can be reconciled with the number of heroized human figures depicted in the Parthenon's frieze.

96. *land of Cissia*: See 3.91.

97. *rhadinake . . . is black*: An early reference to the 'black gold' of Iran – the oil from which petroleum is now refined.

98. *There are many reasons . . . gave her away*: The entire chapter has been condemned as a later interpolation.

99. *in exile for the entire length of the tyranny*: Not so – see 5.62 note.

100. *the role the Alcmaeonids played . . . more influential than that of Harmodius and Aristogiton*: In taking this view, H. was contradicting the official foundation myth of the Athenian democracy.

101. *the Alcmaeonids . . . bribed the Pythia to tell the Lacedaemonians to liberate Athens*: See 5.63.

102. *a running-track and a wrestling-ground . . . built specially for the purpose by Cleisthenes*: The date is c. 570; within the previous decade the four major all-Greek athletics festivals – the Olympics and the Pythian, Isthmian and Nemean Games – had been unified into an interlocking 'cycle' or 'circuit' (*periodos*).

103. *the very peak of its prosperity*: Sybaris' later fall in 510 (ch. 21, 5.44–5) thus illustrates H.'s law of inevitable decline (cf. 1.5).

104. *system of weights and measures*: The system known as 'Pheidonian' was named after a king of Argos who would have reigned up to two centuries earlier.

105. *the Dioscuri*: Castor and Polydeuces; the mythical blends with the historical again.
106. *related ... to the Cypselids of Corinth*: An Athenian called Cypselus was eponymous archon in the early sixth century, the name presumably having entered his Athenian family through a guest-friendship and/or marital relationship with the Corinthian tyrant family.
107. *Pericles*: The only mention of the famous Pericles; the lion metaphor was ambivalent and did not necessarily connote Herodotean approval.
108. *Demeter the Lawgiver*: This was the Demeter worshipped throughout most of Greece especially by married women, particularly in the annual Festival of the Thesmophoria.
109. *the Athenians came to take control of Lemnos*: Lemnos, together with the islands of Imbros and Scyros, were considered vital possessions for Athens, not only because of their economic benefits but more especially because of their location on the major sea trade-route from the Hellespont to Athens.

BOOK SEVEN

1. *in the fourth year*: 487. It was also to take Xerxes four years to raise the amphibious expedition that he led against Greece in 480 (ch. 20).
2. *the Egyptians ... reduced to slavery by Cambyses*: See 3.1–16.
3. *it is the custom ... for the younger son to succeed to the kingdom*: This alleged Spartan practice of porphyrogeniture suited Demaratus' – and Xerxes' – case but is not historically corroborated.
4. *the influence wielded by Atossa*: See 3.133–4. Darius had many wives (3.88), but probably only the one queen, Atossa.
5. *Mardonius*: Last mentioned at 6.94, where he was dismissed from his command by Darius in 492.
6. *how exceptionally beautiful ... how fertile in terms of soil*: Mardonius' wishful claims are contradicted at ch. 102, 8.111; his hortatory speech at ch. 9 is no less flawed by wishful thinking.
7. *Musaeus*: A legendary figure often associated in myth with Orpheus. For another collection of oracles, attributed to Bacis, see 8.77.
8. *a Libyan called Inaros*: Mentioned already at 3.12, the rebellion of Inaros occurred in 460, and is noted also by Thucydides (1.104).
9. *the very realm of Zeus*: Xerxes would have said 'Ahura Mazda', the Persians' supreme god of Light and Truth.
10. *the way of war as invariably practised by the Greeks*: Mardonius gives a somewhat caricatural sketch of hoplite phalanx fighting.
11. *by the Athenians alone*: Artabanus echoes Athenian propaganda (9.27) in omitting the Plataeans, who are not omitted by H. (6.108, 111).
12. *bridged first the Thracian Bosporus ... with pontoons*: 4.85–9, 118.

13. *'That is my advice to you, O King'*: Artabanus thus plays to the hilt the dramatic role of the wise adviser, or warner – whose advice and warnings are ignored, with disastrous consequences.

14. *the humiliation of staying behind with the women*: H.'s Xerxes was fond of the trope of womanish men (cf. 'My men have become women, and my women men', 8.88).

15. *the son of Darius ... the son of Achaemenes*: For Xerxes, as for Darius, it was crucial to be able to trace their lineage in the male line directly back to the eponymous Achaemenes; their descent from Cyrus, founder of the Achaemenid empire, was traceable only through Atossa.

16. *'Either the whole of their lands ... end up under that of Greeks'*: H.'s Xerxes is presented as an irrational extremist from the start.

17. *how wrong it can be to hanker after too many things*: Greek had also a single abstract noun to denote this hankering, particularly applicable to an imperial power, *pleonexia*. There may be a contemporary subtext about Athenian imperialism here (cf. note 70).

18. *the Magi ... interpreted*: These Magi held an official priestly office (Book 1 note 137).

19. *according to our sources*: Literally 'according to what is said', *ta legomena* (see also ch. 152: 'what I am told').

20. *the disaster ... round Athos*: See 6.44.

21. *under the whip*: A key contrast between Greek and Persian ways, and presages chs. 35, 56, 103, 223.

22. *wide enough for two triremes ... while being rowed*: Recent scientific exploration has confirmed that the channel was about 30 metres (100 feet) wide at the top and 15 metres (50 feet) at the bottom. Such engineering skill has Assyrian and Babylonian roots.

23. *skin of Marsyas the Silenus ... Apollo*: Silens were brutish attendants of Dionysus; Marsyas unwisely challenged Apollo to a musical contest, with unfortunate results, as told vividly by Ovid in his *Metamorphoses* (6.384–400) and represented famously by Titian in a painting that now hangs in the Archbishop's Palace at Kroměříž, Czech Republic.

24. *the Greek Sea*: The Mediterranean.

25. *the Immortals*: The first mention of this elite force, on which see note 42.

26. *except Athens and Sparta*: The reason for these exceptions is delayed until ch. 133.

27. *Artaÿctes, a Persian ... in the sanctuary of Protesilaus in Elaeous*: A pregnant flash-forward – it is with this episode that H. chooses to end the entire work (9.114–22).

28. *the insolence so typical of barbarians*: Here H. momentarily abandons his even-handed treatment of barbarians, so heinous was the sacrilege of Xerxes in treating a god, the Hellespont, as if he were a mere mortal slave; for what H. hoped was royal repentance, see ch. 54.

29. *the day . . . turned to night*: No such solar eclipse is recorded at this time, April 480.

30. *in the ears . . . its dwelling-place*: In the Greeks' view the 'spirit', *thumos*, resided rather in the liver.

31. *the Citadel of Priam*: The acropolis of New Ilium (modern Turkish Hisarlik), site of the mound primitively excavated by Heinrich Schliemann in his quest for Homer's Troy.

32. *Phoenicians from Sidon*: The Phoenicians provided the core of the Persians' Mediterranean fleet (ch. 96); it was a Sidonian ship that Xerxes used for special purposes (ch. 128).

33. *'What a difference . . . how much he begrudges us it'*: This exchange nicely illustrates how H. writes 'sometimes for philosophers', as Edward Gibbon put it.

34. *conquered all of Ionia . . . with the sole exception of the Athenians*: It was the Athenians' own boast, expressed already by Solon, that they were the oldest city of the Ionians; at ch. 161 the Athenian ambassador to Gelon raises the stakes still higher by claiming that the Athenians are 'the oldest people in Greece'.

35. *poured a libation*: Xerxes' habitual matutinal practice (cf. ch. 223).

36. *akinakes*: A kind of short sword, not a curved scimitar (also at 8.120, 9.80).

37. *what I cannot do . . . is to give the precise amount that each individual contingent furnished*: Here follows H.'s answer to Homer's 'Catalogue of the Ships' at *Iliad* 2 – but whereas Homer had required and invoked the aid of the Muses, H. has to rely on purely secular authority, which he confesses is lacking. His totals (ch. 186) are fantastically too high; modern estimates cut down the land-forces to 200,000 max., the fleet (contra ch. 89) to some 600 ships.

38. *'Artaei'*: Presumably a Greek elaboration of the Old Persian word *arta*, 'correctness, rightness, truth'.

39. *the Medes, and not the Persians*: H. is thus perfectly capable of distinguishing the Medes from the Persians but, like most Greeks, he also often elided the ethnic and cultural distinction.

40. *Darius cherished Artystone above all his other wives*: Perhaps he did, but in the wielding of queenly power she was eclipsed by Atossa (note 4).

41. *Mardontes . . . meet with his end in the battle*: See 9.102.

42. *Immortals . . . the unit was never more nor less than ten thousand*: That may have been so, but in Persian they were not called 'Immortals'; see further chs. 211–18.

43. *Their equipment . . . pack-animals*: H. brilliantly exploits the cultural contrast with Greek manners at 9.80–82.

44. *horses cannot bear camels*: See 1.80.

45. *Salamis*: Not to be confused with the Salamis on Cyprus (4.162).

46. *The Dorians of Asia ... came from the Peloponnese*: They included inhabitants of H.'s own native Halicarnassus, whence came the redoubtable Artemisia, first mentioned at ch. 99.

47. *Their original name is something I have already addressed in the first section of my work*: 'Leleges' (1.171).

48. *what is now called Achaea*: An area of the northern Peloponnese, whereas in Homer 'Achaea' had stood for all mainland Greece.

49. *since these officers were just as much slaves*: H. is keen to insist on this key feature of Persian nomenclature and social–political practice.

50. *the formidably masculine cast of her bravery*: H. with self-conscious paradox attributes to Artemisia the quality that in Greek meant literally 'virility' or 'manliness' – *andreia*. It gives special point to the anecdote at 8.88.

51. *Demaratus*: Last heard of, many years earlier, at ch. 3, which prepares us for Xerxes' treating him as a respected adviser on the Greek campaign.

52. *unless ... they present a united front*: Like Mardonius, Xerxes tends to get his predictions seriously wrong – the Greeks did not present a united front (ch. 138ff.), and yet they won.

53. *speak the truth ... peddling lies*: Demaratus was here playing to the Persians' own culturally inculcated reverence for truth and abhorrence of lies (1.138 and note).

54. *all of them ... have no one man in command*: This recalls Darius at 3.82.

55. *Set over them as their master is the law*: This imputed Spartan reverence for Law, *nomos*, picks up ch. 102, but here 'master', *despotes*, designedly brings out the difference between the Spartans' and the Persians' notions of proper political authority.

56. *the Athenians ... besieged him*: Cimon was then, *c.* 475, leading the forces of the Athenians' anti-Persian naval alliance.

57. *two campaigns of conquest ... led by Mardonius*: See 5.17 (Megabazus), 6.45 (Mardonius).

58. *story*: Here H. uses *logos* – see ch. 107.

59. *solemn pact of friendship*: Xeiniê.

60. *Therma is the city ... takes its name*: H.'s Therma is the site of modern Thessaloniki, originally founded in 316.

61. *attacked by lions*: Macedonia was then still home to mountain-lions; a well-known mosaic from Pella depicts Alexander the Great in combat with one a century and a half later.

62. *it seems clear ... result of an earthquake*: Here speaks H. the rationalist scientist.

63. *the sons of Aleuas*: See also 9.58.

64. *Such was the oath made by the Greeks*: Not by all the Greeks, obviously; H. seems to be using 'the Greeks' here in the same selective sense as it was used by those loyalist Greeks who swore an oath of alliance to resist the Persians and to punish the Greek medizers later. Scholars sometimes speak of this

alliance as the 'Hellenic League' to distinguish it from later supposedly Pan-hellenic, anti-Persian alliances.

65. *on a previous occasion ... just such a mission*: See 6.48–9.
66. *the privilege of serving Sparta as heralds*: See 6.60.
67. *a whole number of assemblies*: H. uses *haliê* for 'assembly'; normally the Spartans would meet in assembly just once a month.
68. *make them bow down before the King*: Such prostration, in Greek *proskunesis*, was for Greeks a religious, for Persians a social, custom.
69. *many years after the expedition of the King*: In 430, according to Thucydides (2.67).
70. *an opinion ... I will not shrink from saying it*: It was unpopular because the Athenians themselves used the claim to have saved Greece in 480–479 as an argument to justify what they considered an alliance but other Greeks thought was a form of despotism.
71. *they stood their ground ... and met with the invader of their country*: All that is indeed true, but overlooks the necessity still to win a decisive land battle, as happened at Plataea in 479, essentially a Spartan victory.
72. *the Pythia ... Aristonice*: A well-omened name, 'Best in Victory'; a marked improvement in principle on her predecessor of *c*. 490, Periallus (6.66).
73. *Themistocles*: The first mention of this key but controversial figure.
74. *revenues from ... Laurium*: Silver-bearing seams of lead, in south-eastern Attica, state-owned but privately worked (with extensive slave-labour); a particularly rich seam was opportunely struck in 483/2.
75. *the salvation of Greece*: Picks up on ch. 139.
76. *taking to their ships*: There is room for dispute over whether the Athenians planned their total evacuation well in advance, or not.
77. *the sworn league against the Persians*: See ch. 132.
78. *the calamity that had already befallen them*: At the hands of Cleomenes (6.77–83).
79. *Callias*: An extremely rich Athenian, his fortune derived significantly from mining revenues.
80. *state what I am told*: In Greek *legein ta legomena*.
81. *the goddesses of the underworld*: Presumably these chthonic divinities are Demeter and Persephone.
82. *the so-called 'Gamori' ... 'Cyllyrians'*: Gamori means 'land-sharers', presumably the old landed aristocracy of colonial Syracuse; the Cyllyrians were part-bondsmen, part-free native Sicilians.
83. *sold for export*: The sale of war-captives into slavery was a regular feature of inter-Greek warfare, the sale of defeated non-combatant civilians was not.
84. *O King of Syracuse*: Gelon was actually tyrant, not 'king' of Syracuse.
85. *a year from which the spring has been removed*: This vivid simile was actually used in a civic funeral oration by Pericles, perhaps in 440/439.
86. *he took the city of Zancle from the Samians*: See 6.23.

87. *on the very same day that the Greeks defeated the Persian at Salamis*: The allegedly exact coincidence of date prompts the thought that the Carthaginians timed their invasion so as to prevent the Sicilian Greeks from receiving help from their kinsmen of old Greece.

88. *a woman from Sparta was abducted by a man from a barbarian land*: See 1.3.

89. *Sicania (as Sicily was then called)*: Besides the Sicels (ch. 155; 6.22, 23), there were natives known to the Greeks as Sicans.

90. *a footnote to my account*: Parentheke, literally parenthesis.

91. *gathered at the Isthmus . . . best interests of Greece at heart*: Presumably it was at the Isthmus in spring 480 that the oath was sworn constituting 'the Greeks' as a loyalist alliance (ch. 132).

92. *from among the war-magistrates*: Five polemarchs commanded the five locally recruited regiments, such as that of Pitana (9.53).

93. *Alexander of Macedon*: Last mentioned at 5.22.

94. *where . . . they should make their stand*: Chs. 175–234 mostly detail the famous last stand at Thermopylae.

95. *the path*: See ch. 216.

96. *wall built across the pass . . . a gate set in it*: Known as the Middle Gate.

97. *the Thessalians were looking to conquer them*: For continuing, contemporary hostility between the Phocians and Thessalians, see 8.30.

98. *Achaea*: Achaea Phthiotis.

99. *Heracles . . . was burning up*: Thanks to the lotion applied mistakenly to his garment by his wife, Deinaeira, on the recommendation of his love-rival Nessus the centaur.

100. *Amphictyons*: See Book 2 note 85.

101. *Leonidas . . . in unexpected circumstances*: See 5.39–41.

102. *Cleomenes' daughter*: The remarkably named Gorgo (ch. 239; also 5.48, 51).

103. *the Carneia was . . . holding them up*: The month in which the festival fell, named Carneius, was a sacred month for all Dorians, not just Spartans. For other delays due to festivals/customs, see 6.106–7 (Marathon), 9.7 (Plataea).

104. *the festival . . . was the Olympic one*: A five-day celebration, normally held to coincide with the second full moon after the summer solstice.

105. *exercising naked . . . combing their hair*: Our word 'gymnasium' comes from the Greek male practice of exercising stark naked, *gumnos*, whence *gumnasion*; on attaining the age of adulthood – twenty – Spartan males let their hair grow long as well as growing a beard, but kept their moustaches shaved off.

106. *the fairest kingdom*: Ex-king Demaratus pointedly calls Sparta a 'kingdom', *basilêiê*.

107. *Epialtes*: Alternatively spelled Ephialtes – the modern Greek word for 'nightmare'; note that Epialtes was from Malis, not either Phocis or Locris, both of which regions were staunchly loyal (ch. 207).

108. *I will point out later on in my account*: An unfulfilled promise.
109. *it is as the guilty party that I indict him here*: H. uses formal legal language, as if he were prosecuting Epialtes on behalf of all Greece as a good Greek patriot.
110. *the course of the path*: The Anopaea path has not been identified!
111. *all the leaves . . . underfoot*: From the previous autumn's fall.
112. *he would leave . . . a great name*: Even Leonidas could not have guessed just how great a name he would bequeath to posterity.
113. *the Thespians . . . were there as volunteers*: The seven hundred Thespian hoplites died to a man; their extraordinary feat of self-sacrifice is commemorated by a modern monument at the battle site.
114. *many . . . were drowned*: The topography of the area has changed greatly since 480; the sea is now about a kilometre distant.
115. *Simonides*: See 5.102 and note.
116. *'the Trembler'*: Possibly the official label for publicly adjudged cowards at Sparta; for Aristodemus' self-sought redemption at Plataea, see 9.71.
117. *Eurymachus . . . killed many years later by the Plataeans*: In 431 (Thucydides 2.2, 5).
118. *a perfect base . . . to spread terror among the Lacedaemonians*: The Athenians captured and used Cythera in this way in 424 (Thucydides 4.54, 5.14).
119. *That . . . is what is supposed to have happened*: If there is any basis to this anecdote, the message would have been sent and deciphered when Gorgo was about twenty-three.

BOOK EIGHT

1. *crewed both by the Athenians . . . and by the Plataeans*: For the Plataeans' first becoming Athenian allies see 6.108.
2. *the refusal of the allies . . . to disband the expedition altogether*: The majority of the thirty-two or thirty-three allies of the Hellenic League were allies of Sparta. All those allies listed in ch. 1 had coastal locations or outlets, but the ten Lacedaemonian ships would have been crewed not by Spartans but by perioeci (free but non-citizen inhabitants of the Spartan state; cf. 7.234) and helots; Eurybiadas may have been the only Spartiate on the water.
3. *civil strife . . . compares as disastrously to a united war effort as does war itself to peace*: See Introduction 4 and 7.
4. *the arrogant behaviour of Pausanias . . . depriving the Lacedaemonians of their command*: See 5.32; Pausanias was replaced at Byzantium by another non-royal Spartan commander in 477, but by then the Athenians had formed on Delos another, naval, anti-Persian alliance.
5. *Artemisium*: Not a town or village but the name of a shrine dedicated to Artemis at the northern end of Euboea.

6. *With Eurybiades thereby won over*: It was often assumed – or alleged – that Spartans would do almost anything for a cash bribe; 5 talents was a seriously huge sum – a millionaire's ransom.

7. *80 stades underwater*: Perhaps he snorkelled . . . ; but the distance is nearer 60 stades.

8. *Salamis*: This Salamis is the islet of Salamis, part of Athens' civic territory, off which the major naval battle was shortly to take place; the Salamis of Philaon and Gorgus, mentioned above, was the one on Cyprus.

9. *five Greek ships . . . with crews*: Anything up to a thousand men all told.

10. *Cleinias . . . had contributed . . . his own ship*: A sign of great wealth (cf. Philippus 5.47); Cleinias was the great-uncle of the famous Alcibiades (*c.* 450–404).

11. *get back to Greece*: An odd expression.

12. *an oracle given them by Bacis*: It is not clear which Bacis is meant, nor is the attribution of oracles to him always reliable; see also ch. 77 and note.

13. *the look-out arrived . . . to keep the men at Thermopylae informed*: H. does intermittently reveal that the interdependence of land and sea operations was a key part of the Greeks' defensive strategy.

14. *the feud between the Barbarian and ourselves*: Presumably a reference back to the Athenians' and Eretrians' decision to aid the Ionian Revolt (5.97, 99).

15. *the Greeks were holding the Olympic Festival*: See 7.206.

16. *not for financial reward, but for the honour of being the best*: Prizes at the Olympics and other 'crown' games were indeed token symbols, but at all other games, for example the Panathenaic at Athens, prizes of material value were on offer.

17. *the disaster*: H. rightly calls it a *trôma*, literally 'wound'.

18. *Tellias of Elis*: Yet another *mantis* from Elis playing a major role outside his native city; see also 5.44; 9.33, 37.

19. *Abae*: For the highly reputed oracular shrine at Abae in Phocis, see ch. 33; 1.46.

20. *the giant statues that are contending for the tripod*: Statues of Heracles and Apollo, the former attempting – unsuccessfully – to steal the sacred object, the latter to prevent him; for the 'tenth', see note 68.

21. *The entire population of Boeotia had gone over to the Medes*: Not strictly true – Thespiae and Plataea had not (ch. 50).

22. *the offerings of Croesus*: See 1.50–51.

23. *the prophet*: The male priest responsible for editing the Pythia's responses for public consumption.

24. *Athena Before the Temple*: Athena *Pronaea*, so named because her temple stood in front of the sanctuary's main temple, that of Apollo.

25. *The boulders that fell . . . how these men came to depart the shrine*: H. peddles the Delphians' own face-saving myth of inviolability; in fact, the Persians sacked and looted Delphi.

26. *the Peloponnesians ... to ensure their own survival*: By 'Peloponnesians' is meant especially the Spartans, but this had not been Leonidas' priority (7.220).

27. *Troezen*: In myth this was where Athens' founder-hero Theseus had grown up; a document found there that was inscribed on stone in the mid-third century purports to contain a record of the actual decree of evacuation passed by the Athenians in summer 480.

28. *the priestess*: The hereditary priestess of Athena *Polias*, 'of the City', the chief religious official of the Athenian state (5.72).

29. *what is now called Greece, the Athenians were Pelasgians themselves*: 'Hellas' is post-Homeric; this identification of Athenians and Pelasgians contrasts with 6.137–40, such is the fluidity of mythography.

30. *all the other islands*: That is, most of the Cycladic islands and those lying off Aegean coasts controlled by Persia.

31. *the Pythian Games*: Held every four years at Delphi in honour of Apollo Pythius; Phaÿllus won twice in the pentathlon, once in the foot-race.

32. *Calliades was archon at Athens*: Calliades held the office of eponymous archon from midsummer 480 to midsummer 479; this is the one precise chronographic notation H. gives in the entire work.

33. *the prophecy ... that the wooden wall would never be breached*: At 7.141.

34. *'Areopagus'*: Literally 'Hill of Ares'.

35. *torched the whole of the Acropolis*: For the first time; they destroyed what was still standing in 479 (9.13).

36. *perhaps because the burning of the sanctuary had filled him with remorse*: Cf. 7.54 for a similar, wishful notion.

37. *a single fatherland*: This use of *patris* seems peculiarly emotive; normally it would refer to a Greek's particular city.

38. *earn themselves a beating*: That is, are disqualified by the judges.

39. *our ships are the more heavily built*: This became very relevant when the battle came to be decided by the smashing together of ships in the confined waters off Salamis.

40. *The entire course of the war depends upon our fleet*: A point of view that H. himself strongly endorsed (7.139).

41. *Siris in Italy ... ours since ancient times*: Siris lay between Tarentum and what had been Sybaris on the instep of Italy; it had been founded from Ionian Colophon – and the Athenians claimed their city as the metropolis of the Ionians.

42. *his anxiety that ... the Athenians would desert them*: Similar anxiety is expressed at ch. 141.

43. *Aeacus and his remaining descendants*: Aeacus, a son of Zeus and Aegina, counted Achilles as well as Ajax among his heroic descendants.

44. *the Iacchus! which is always raised at the festival*: The hymn to this divine congener of Bacchus/Dionysus was sung by initiates in procession to Eleusis every September/October.

45. *the five cities I named earlier*: Naxos, Cythnos, Seriphos, Siphnos and Melos (ch. 46).

46. *the Sidonian nearest to the royal person*: For Sidonian precedence, see 7.96.

47. *up spoke Artemisia*: H.'s Artemisia is as it were the best man in Xerxes' cabinet; see 7.99 and note.

48. *a wall across the Isthmus*: On the strategic question, see 7.139 and note; the Isthmus of Corinth was roughly 8 km (5 miles) wide; on the wall's construction, see further 9.7, 8.

49. *Themistocles had him enrolled as a citizen of Thespiae*: Sicinnus appears from his name to have been a non-Greek, making it all the more remarkable that he was accepted as a citizen of Thespiae, despite the Thespians' recent heavy loss of adult citizen manpower (ch. 25); at Athens, as a freedman, he would have attained only the status of resident alien.

50. *There can certainly be no disputing ... nor would I accept anyone else doing it either*: This entire chapter has been placed within square brackets because it is believed to be a later, non-Herodotean insertion. Once it has been removed, ch. 78 flows naturally on from the end of ch. 76.

51. *Aristeides ... the best man in Athens, and the most just too*: He was to play a major role in the immediate aftermath of the Graeco-Persian Wars, and it was for the fairness of his arrangements for the anti-Persian alliance concluded on Delos in winter 478/7 that he acquired the sobriquet 'the Just'.

52. *the tripod at Delphi listing those who had helped to defeat the Barbarian*: A bronze pillar in the likeness of snake coils issued in three snake-heads supporting a golden cauldron (tripod); on the coils were inscribed the names of thirty-one of the cities or peoples who resisted Persia, beginning with the Spartans; what remains of the 'Serpent Column' is to be found today in the Hippodrome of old Constantinople, whither it had been removed by the eponymous emperor Constantine (d. 337).

53. *Theomestor*: His reign as tyrant did not last long (9.90–92).

54. *Pytheas, the son of Ischenous*: Met at 7.181.

55. *Adeimantus, the Corinthian commander, is said by the Athenians to have lost his nerve ... and beat a retreat*: This is a scurrilous accusation, prompted by the later hostility that developed between the two cities.

56. *Athena Sciras*: This cult of Athena in which women had an especially important role gave its name to the Greek month *Skirophoriôn*.

57. *qualities I mentioned a little while ago*: At chs. 79, 81; this Psyttaleia episode was very minor, and, if not invented, later burnished as part of the propaganda campaign against Themistocles.

58. *Colias ... an Athenian soothsayer ... wrecks would drift ashore there*: Colias cannot be precisely identified but was the site of an important shrine of Aphrodite. Lysistratus, a private-enterprise soothsayer, is otherwise unknown.

59. *the disaster*: H. here uses *pathos*, literally 'suffering', rather than *troma*, 'wound', but both are equally strong.

60. *Xerxes sent news of the defeat to Persia*: This is the scenario of Aeschylus' tragedy *The Persians*, set in Susa and first performed in 472.

61. *a given route*: That is, the Royal Road from Susa to Sardis (5.52).

62. *the torch-race ... in honour of Hephaestus*: Staged as part of the annual Festival of Hephaestus at Athens; a torch-race was featured also at the Festival of Prometheus.

63. *Panionius ... made his living from the most unholy line of work*: H.'s severe condemnation of the immorality of the trade of this Ionian, called 'All-Ionian', contrasts rather with his account of Periander's would-be eunuchization of three hundred Corcyraean boys as revenge for the murder of his son (3.48–53).

64. *'He even flogged the sea and cast chains into it!'*: A reference to Xerxes whipping the Hellespont (7.35).

65. *get into trouble with the Athenians (which, indeed, did happen)*: In about 471 Themistocles was ostracized, made his way to the Persian empire and was granted the governorship of Magnesia on the Maeander, for which treachery he was refused burial in Athenian soil.

66. *the Andrians had been put under siege*: This alleged extortion echoes Miltiades' treatment of Paros (6.133–6) and presages the kind of subsequent imperialist behaviour of the Athenians that led to their unpopularity mentioned at 7.139.

67. *'The Lacedaemonians and the descendants of Heracles from Sparta'*: In other words, the Spartan state collectively and specifically the relatives of Leonidas.

68. *first-fruits victory-offerings for the gods*: Here and immediately below called *akrothinia* or 'top of the heap' offerings, elsewhere a 'tithe', *dekatê* (ch. 27, 5.77).

69. *Alexander the Macedonian*: Soon to be reintroduced in a major role at ch. 136.

70. *prize for valour*: Aristeia, derived from *aristos*, the Greek for 'the best' or 'most valorous'.

71. *the 'Horsemen', as they are known*: Cf. Book 1 note 94.

72. *No other man in history ... an escort of Spartiates*: On the one hand, the Spartans were more generous than any other of the loyalist Greek allies in duly recognizing and honouring Themistocles; on the other hand, they took great care to monitor his movements within the borders of their state.

73. *Belbina*: A tiny island off south-east Attica; in a variant version the island named was Seriphos.

74. *Artabazus ... whose reputation would stand even higher in the wake of the Plataean campaign*: A rather odd comment in the light of 9.66, 89; possibly H. consulted favourable sources at Dascyleum, where Artabazus and his descendants held the satrapy of Hellespontine Phrygia.

75. *that was how Timoxeinus came to be found out*: H. is careful to name and shame traitors to the cause.

76. *I find this explanation a wholly convincing one*: Here H. goes for a religious explanation of a natural phenomenon; cf. 7.129 on the origin of the Peneius gorge; the difference is accounted for by the identity of the human victims of the tsunami.

77. *the other of the two royal houses*: That is, the Eurypontid as opposed to the Agiad, to which Leonidas belonged (7.204); for Leotychidas' controversial accession, see 6.65.

78. *Xanthippus, the son of Ariphron*: And father of Pericles (6.131).

79. *Herodotus, the son of Basileïdes*: Possibly a member of the Ionian priestly family of Basilidae, possibly too a source for our H. of the Strattis story here.

80. *everywhere beyond Delos was unknown territory*: Strictly untrue, or at least an exaggeration, but this generalization did apply particularly to Spartans; cf. 9.90 for Spartan-led delay at Delos in 479 before proceeding to Asia and Mycale.

81. *Carian*: That is, the language of the enquirer.

82. *this river*: Probably the Haliacmon (7.127); perhaps the sacrifices were of horses.

83. *oracles*: Possibly a reference to the oracles obtained by Cleomenes (5.90).

84. *you have always shown yourselves ... the liberators of any number of peoples*: This flattering but ungrounded rhetoric smacks more of post-Persian Wars Athenian propaganda.

85. *the fact that we are all of us Greeks*: This renders two words in the Greek, *to hellênikon*, a combination of the definite article in the neuter gender with the adjective meaning 'Greek'.

86. *swiftly*: One of the main points of H.'s succeeding narrative is that the response of the Spartans was the reverse of swift.

BOOK NINE

1. *'Send money to the power-brokers ... and Greece will be riven by factions'*: This was the tactic employed in 395, and with considerable success, when Sparta was spearheading Greek opposition to Persia; but Mardonius was the last Persian to be persuaded by this Theban advice at this juncture in the campaign.

2. *the Hyacinthia*: A three-day festival in honour of the hero Hyacinthus, associated with the Olympian god Apollo, usually held in early summer and particularly linked with the village of Amyclae, some 5 km (3 miles) south of Sparta, within which the cult-site was located.

3. *while it was still night*: Spartans were trained from a young age to be able to operate under night-time conditions; the point here apparently was to deceive the Argives (ch. 12). But H.'s account contrasts with the version offered by Simonides in a recently recovered elegy on the famous deeds of Pausanias and his men in 479.

4. *five thousand Spartiates, together with a retinue of helots, seven per man*: The number of Spartiates is compatible with the total of eight thousand given by Demaratus to Xerxes (7.234). The figure of 35,000 helots (ch. 28) seems a gross overestimate, even if it does accurately reflect the normal numerical ratio between the two groups and the Spartans' anxiety about leaving Sparta denuded of adult warriors of fighting age.

5. *the sun had turned dark*: There was a partial solar eclipse on 2 October 480.

6. *Euryanax*: His well-omened name, meaning 'King Far and Wide', and a desire perhaps to rehabilitate his father Dorieus, will have influenced Pausanias' choice.

7. *'Foreigners' is the word they used to describe non-Greeks*: The Spartans in other words elided the normal Greek distinction between Greek foreigners (*xeinoi*) and non-Greek foreigners (*barbaroi*). Insofar as they took extreme precautions to prevent contamination even by Greek foreigners, they were literally xeno-phobic.

8. *Attica was unsuited to cavalry*: This was already implied at 5.63–4.

9. *Thersander of Orchomenus*: One of just three named informants (see also 3.55, 4.76).

10. *slanders of the Thessalians*: For Phocian–Thessalian enmity, see 8.30.

11. *as the Greeks called him*: Perhaps by 'as the Greeks' H. means Simonides in particular; for Masistius' first appearance, see 7.79.

12. *The cavalry then launched themselves, squadron by squadron, against the Greeks*: Here, nine or ten days after first mobilizations, begins H.'s account of the preliminaries to the battle of Plataea proper, which occurred four days later, a very messy affair as it is presented by H.

13. *lamentation*: H. uses the same word, *oimôgê*, for Persian lamentation over Salamis (8.99), but also for Spartan grief at the death of a king (6.58).

14. *Androcrates*: Another well-omened name, meaning 'Man-Conquering'.

15. *fierce wrangling back and forth*: H. uses metaphorically the same word, *ôthismos*, that was applied to the pushing and shoving of close-quarter hoplite fighting (ch. 62).

16. *the descendants of Heracles … death of Eurystheus*: The 'Return of the Heraclids' was associated with the Spartan Dorians' migration to their historic homeland (1.56); Eurystheus was the usurping king of Argos who had set Heracles his Twelve Labours.

17. *we get to command … whenever a joint expedition is made*: For the Spartans' conquest of Tegea, see 1.66–8; Tegea's strategic importance to Sparta accounts for its place of honour in allied Peloponnesian campaigns.

18. *ancient as well as modern*: A variation on the division of time drawn at 3.122 and note ('the fully mortal race of men').

19. *We alone of the Greeks … met the Persians in battle*: Standard Athenian propaganda, belied by 6.111.

20. *A shout went up ... at this reply*: In Sparta decisions in the Assembly and in Gerousia (6.57) elections were taken by measuring rival shouts, so possibly the Spartans were asked to decide this issue of precedence by a shouted vote.

21. *the total did come out at 110,000*: Whatever the exact total on the loyalist Greek side may really have been, this was certainly the largest number of Greeks yet assembled on the same side anywhere.

22. *men who had escaped with their lives*: From the destruction of their city by the Persians (8.50), after Thermopylae, where seven hundred Thespian hoplites had perished.

23. *the women of Argos went mad, and the Argives tried to hire Melampous*: The occasions and reasons given for this mythic madness vary; for H.'s take on Melampous, see 2.49.

24. *The five 'contests' ... Athenians and Argives*: They were spread over more than twenty years, from 479 to 458 or 457.

25. *there were guards on watch*: Presumably helots, like the guard of Cleomenes when he was placed in the stocks (6.75).

26. *the one that the Thebans had made*: See ch. 2.

27. *we shall not be ... putting it to the sack*: H.'s Mardonius seems ignorant of the events narrated at 8.35–9.

28. *oracle of Bacis*: See 8.20 and note.

29. *his response to their report*: The whole episode of Alexander's alleged secret mission and Pausanias' extreme reaction to it seems retrospectively trumped up to exonerate Alexander of medism, and to accuse the Spartan high command of gross incompetence.

30. *they too were holding fast to their original position*: The alleged Amompharetus episode above and this report of exemplary Athenian behaviour both look suspiciously *parti pris*.

31. *just as the oracle had foretold*: At 8.114.

32. *the lineage of Leonidas*: See 7.204.

33. *a battle at Stenyclerus ... the three hundred perished*: This would have occurred some time during the war against the revolted Messenian helots that broke out *c.* 464; the 'three hundred' here are presumably a pick-up task-force, like that at Thermopylae, rather than the three hundred 'Horsemen'.

34. *the palace*: 'Palace', *anaktoron*, was the name given to the holy of holies in the temple of Demeter and Persephone.

35. *the temple of Athena Alea*: Other trophy offerings here are reported at 1.66.

36. *The total number of casualties ... was ninety-one*: H. reports only the casualties suffered by the Spartiates – less than half of the one hundred and ninety-two Athenians who died at Marathon (6.117 and note) – not those of the other Lacedaemonians.

37. *except Aristodemus alone, who ... had wanted to die*: It was not the fact that he had in effect committed suicide but rather the manner of his doing

so – breaking ranks and losing self-control – that decided the Spartans against rewarding him.

38. *the most handsome man ... of his entire generation*: A successor in this respect to Philippus of Croton (5.47).

39. *Theseus' outrageous behaviour*: The outrage consisted not in the rape as such (see 1.4 for H.'s easygoing attitude to that), but in the fact that Helen was pre-pubertal and Theseus, according to some accounts, as much as fifty years old.

40. *Decelea was spared the devastation ... inflicted on the rest of Attica*: This could not have been stated as a fact after the Spartans occupied Decelea in 413.

41. *he issued a challenge ... killed him in single combat*: See 6.92.

42. *the Edonians killed him ... in the battle for the ... gold mines at Datum*: Probably the same episode of c. 465 as recounted by Thucydides (1.100, 4.102).

43. *the business of the Mantineans and the Eleans*: The Mantineans, despite fighting at Thermopylae (7.202), are not recorded on the Serpent Column victory-monument (ch. 81), whereas the Eleans, who fought at neither Thermopylae nor Plataea, *are*, presumably because of the key importance of their control of Olympia (cf. ch. 81).

44. *Mardonius and Xerxes had his head cut off and stuck on a spike*: At 7.238 the order is attributed to Xerxes alone.

45. *golden tripod ... three-headed bronze serpent*: See 8.82 note.

46. *the two meals laid out before them*: Cf. the Persians' view of Greek meals (1.133); of course, Spartan meals were peculiarly spartan.

47. *the priests*: The universal reading of the manuscripts has been questioned, but this special treatment comports with the Spartans' noted piety (ch. 7; 5.63).

48. *Timagenidas and Attaginus, who were the ringleaders among the city's elite*: See chs. 15, 16, 38.

49. *From Byzantium, Artabazus made the crossing in boats*: The rest of H.'s battle narrative will concern Asia rather than Europe.

50. *the Greek squadrons ... were lying there inactive*: The fleet had last been mentioned at 8.133, where it is reported as setting sail from Aegina.

51. *he was cut off in mid-flow*: For Spartan dislike of long speeches, see 3.46, also with a Samian connection.

52. *the Samians ... swore oaths of allegiance to the Greeks*: They thus joined what moderns call the 'Hellenic League' (cf. 7.145).

53. *the Apollonia in the Ionian Gulf, that is*: There were several Greek cities called 'Apollonia', in tribute to the god of colonization; besides this one on the Adriatic, H. mentions one on the Black Sea (4.90, 93).

54. *the Potniae*: Literally 'mistresses', and name for Demeter and her daughter.

55. *The thinking behind this action was the same as Themistocles' at Artemisium*: See 8.22.

56. *that the disaster at Plataea and . . . at Mycale should both have occurred on the same day*: See ch. 90.

57. *As I have already mentioned*: At chs. 62, 65.

58. *the Barbarians' courage failed them . . . except the Persians*: H. had likewise singled out for praise the courage of the Persians at Plataea (ch. 62).

59. *Some time afterwards . . . on the promontory of Geraestus*: Perhaps H. mentions his death because Hermolycus, like the Spartan Arimnestus (ch. 64), was killed by his fellow-Greeks.

60. *Peloponnesians*: As before (e.g. 8.40), 'Peloponnesians' means particularly the Spartans (cf. ch. 114: 'the Peloponnesians led by Leotychidas').

61. *swore to stay faithful to the terms of the treaty*: Actually this treaty would have been sworn with 'the Greeks', as the Samians had done in ch. 92, not with the Athenians alone; H. anticipates the later – 477 – withdrawal of the Spartans from anti-Persian naval activity.

62. *Masistes, the son of Darius*: A full brother of Xerxes (7.82), last mentioned at 7.121.

63. *Xerxes had fallen passionately in love with Masistes' wife*: This concluding tale of Masistes' wife (deliberately left unnamed) complements the opening tale of Lydian king Candaules' wife (also anonymous: 1.8–12), but whereas Xerxes lusted after and coveted his brother's wife, Candaules' error had been to fall in love too passionately with his own.

64. *She hacked off the woman's breasts . . . and her tongue*: Mutilation of the nose and ears on the orders of oriental potentates (2.162 Egyptian; 3.118, 154 Persian) as a punishment of males was not unexampled, but Amestris' gendered and personally executed revenge seems excessive.

65. *Protesilaus*: The first Greek to have leapt ashore on Asian soil and to have been killed there during the Trojan War, according to the *Iliad* 2.700–702; in recompense he received worship as a hero, but on the European side of the Hellespont.

66. *the whole of Asia is . . . the inalienable property of their kings*: This harks back to 1.4: 'Asia and all the various strange-speaking peoples who inhabit it, they think of as belonging to them.'

67. *they nailed him fast to a plank of wood and crucified him*: Artaÿctes' unusually cruel fate had been anticipated emphatically at 7.33.

68. *'No country can be remarkable . . . men who are hardy in war'*: This maxim picks up the emphatic theme of Greece's absolute and relative poverty variously expressed at ch. 82; and 1.133, 7.102, 8.111.

69. *rather than . . . be the slaves of others*: H. thus neatly ends his entire work on the motivational grace note of freedom as opposed to slavery.

Maps

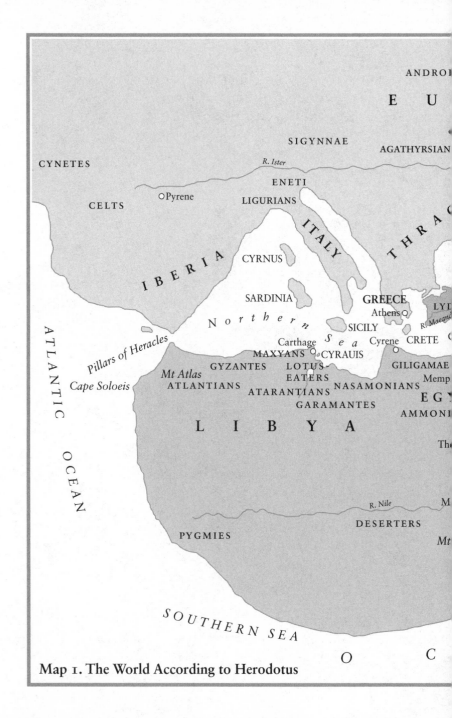

Map 1. The World According to Herodotus

THYSSAGETANS

ARGIPPAEI

IYRCAE

HYPERBOREANS

P E

BOUDINIANS

ARIMASPIANS

ISSEDONIANS

SAUROMATIANS

R. Borysthenes

Lake Maeëtis

A

MASSAGETANS

COLCHIS

Caspian Sea

e Sea

R. Phasis

HYRCANIANS

BACTRIA

AMAZONS

R. Araxes

PADAEI

A

R. Tigris

MEDIA

A S I A

INDIA

BABYLONIA

p. Euphrates

PERSIA

R. Indus

INDIANS

RED SEA

ARABIA

ian Gulf

s

•IA

-LIVED
OPIANS

A

N

U

S

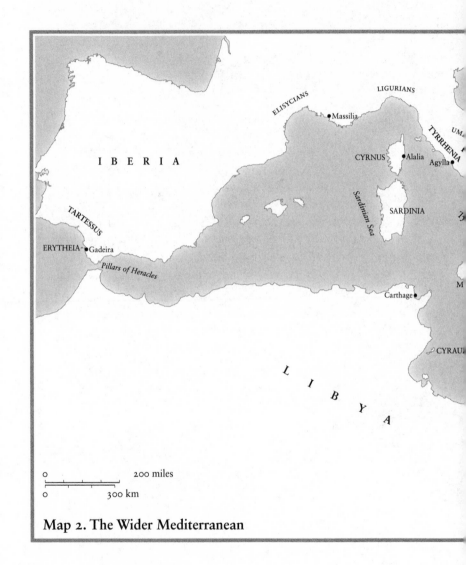

Map 2. The Wider Mediterranean

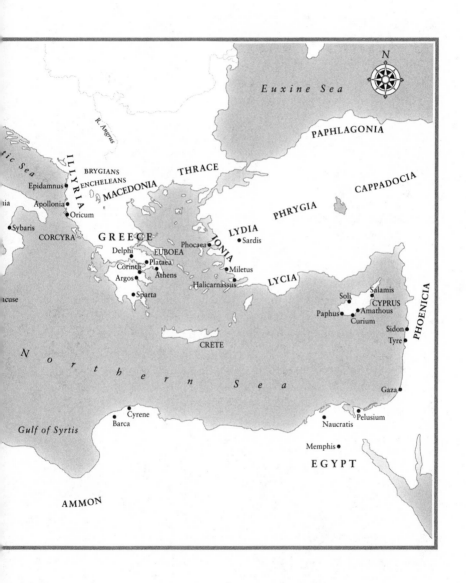

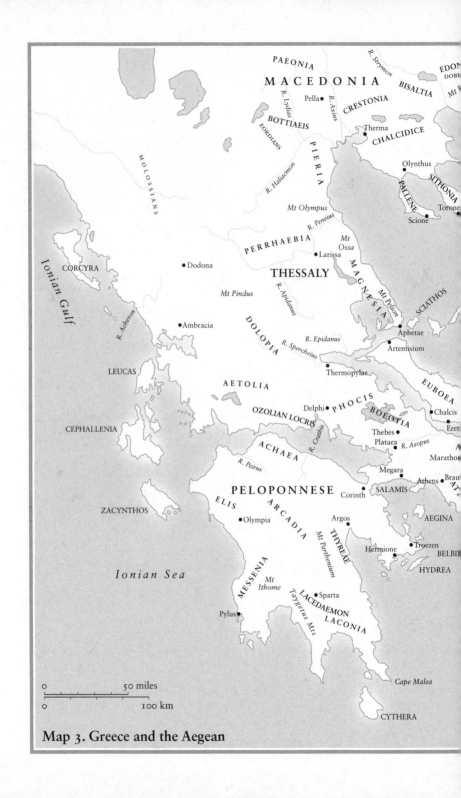

Map 3. Greece and the Aegean

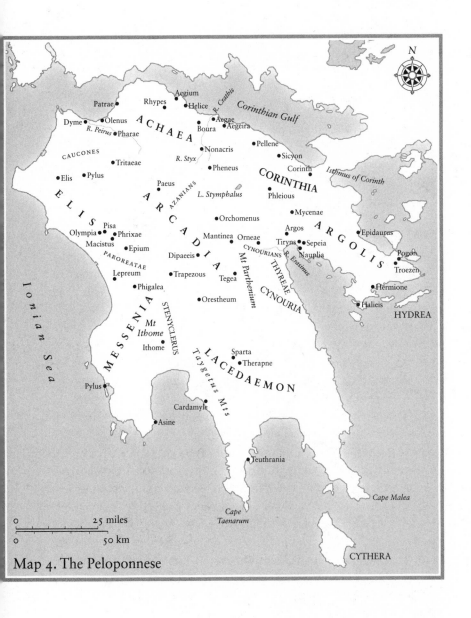

N

Patrae •
Rhypes •
Aegium •
Helice •
R. Crathis
Corinthian Gulf

Dyme •
Olenus •
R. Peirus
Pharae •
ACHAEA
Aegae •
Boura •
Aegeira •

CAUCONES
Tritaeae •
Nonacris •
R. Styx
Pheneus •
Pellene •
Sicyon •
Corinth •
Isthmus of Corinth

Elis •
Pylus •
Paeus •
AZANIANS
L. Stymphalus
CORINTHIA
Phleious •

ELIS
ARCADIA
Orchomenus •
Mycenae •

Pisa •
Olympia • •
Phrixae •
Macistus •
Epium •
PAROREATAE
Mantinea •
Orneae •
Argos •
Tiryns • • Sepeia
Nauplia
R. Erasinus
ARGOLIS
Epidaurus •

Dipaeeis •
CYNOURIANS
Mt Parthenium
THYREAE
Pogon
Troezen •

Lepreum •
Trapezous •
Tegea •
CYNOURIA
Hermione •

Phigalea •
Orestheum •
Halieis •
HYDREA

Ionian Sea
MESSENIA
STENYCLERUS
Mt Ithome
Ithome •
LACEDAEMON
Sparta •
Therapne •

Pylus •
Taygetus Mts
Cardamyle •

Asine •

Teuthrania •

Cape Malea

25 miles
Cape Taenarum

50 km

CYTHERA

Map 4. The Peloponnese

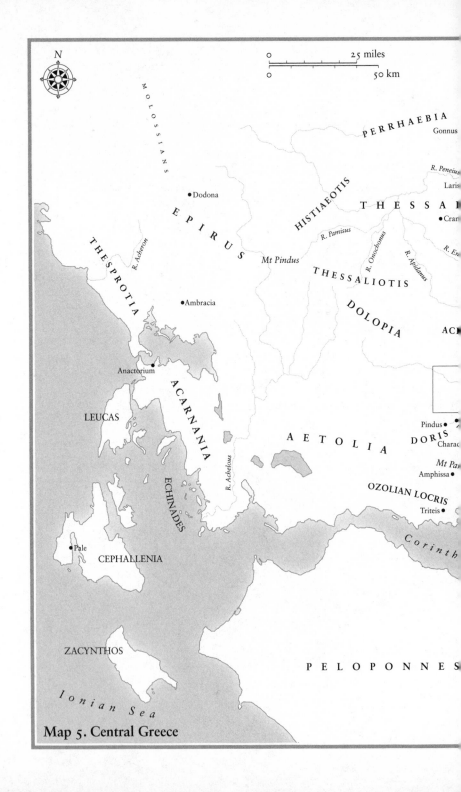

N

0 ____ 25 miles
0 ____ 50 km

M O L O S S I A N S

PERRHAEBIA

Gonnus

R. Peneius

Laris

• Dodona

HISTIAEOTIS

THESSAL

E P I R U S

Mt Pindus

R. Pamisus

• Crar

THESSALIOTIS

R. Onochonus

R. Apidanus

R. En

T H E S P R O T I A

R. Acheron

DOLOPIA

AC

• Ambracia

Anactorium

A C A R N A N I A

A E T O L I A

DORIS

Pindus •

Charac

LEUCAS

Mt Par

Amphissa •

OZOLIAN LOCRIS

R. Achelous

Triteis •

ECHNADES

C o r i n t h

• Pale

CEPHALLENIA

ZACYNTHOS

P E L O P O N N E S

I o n i a n   S e a

Map 5. Central Greece

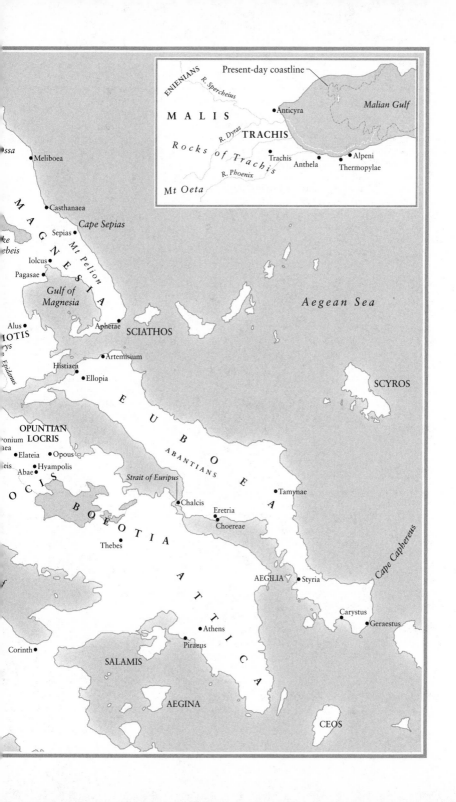

Present-day coastline

ENIENIANS
R. Spercheius
Anticyra
MALIS
Malian Gulf
R. Dyras
TRACHIS
Rocks of Trachis
Trachis   Alpeni
Anthela   Thermopylae
R. Phoenix
Mt Oeta

ssa

Meliboea

MAGNESIA

Casthanaea

Cape Sepias

Sepias

ke
ebeis
Iolcus

Mt Pelion

Pagasae

Gulf of
Magnesia

Alus

IOTIS
rys

Aphetae

SCIATHOS

Aegean Sea

Epidanus

Histiaea

Artemisium

Ellopia

SCYROS

E
U
B
O
E
A

OPUNTIAN
onium LOCRIS
aea
Elateia   Opous
eis   Hyampolis
Abae

ABANTIANS

O
C
I
S

B
O
E
O
T
I
A

Strait of Euripus

Chalcis

Eretria

Choereae

Tamynae

Thebes

A
T
T
I
C
A

AEGILIA   Styria

Cape Caphereus

Carystus

Geraestus

Athens

Piraeus

Corinth

SALAMIS

AEGINA

CEOS

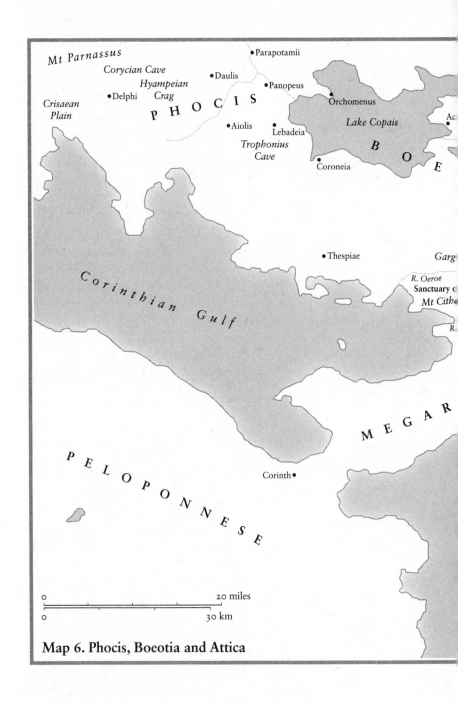

Map 6. Phocis, Boeotia and Attica

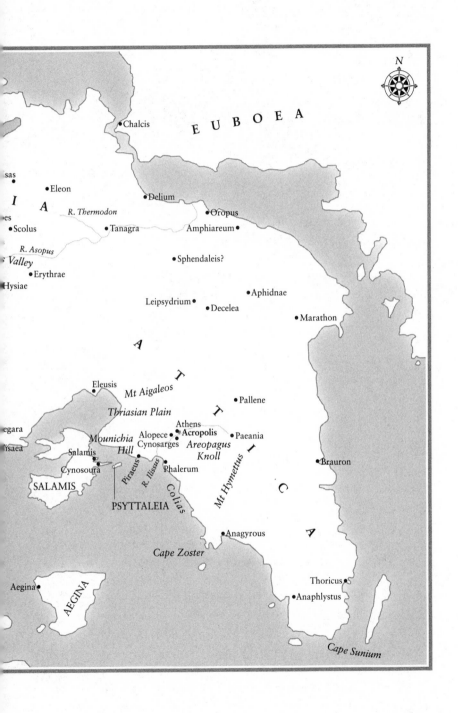

N

•Chalcis

E U B O E A

sas
•

•Eleon

I A

•Delium

R. Thermodon

•Oropus

es

•Scolus

•Tanagra

Amphiareum•

R. Asopus

Valley

•Sphendaleis?

•Erythrae

Hysiae

•Aphidnae

Leipsydrium•

•Decelea

•Marathon

A

Eleusis
•

Mt Aigaleos

•Pallene

T

Thriasian Plain

T

Athens
•

egara

Mounichia

Alopece•

•Acropolis

•Paeania

I

saea

Hill

Cynosarges

Areopagus

Salamis
•

Knoll

Cynosoura

Piraeus

R. Ilissus

Phalerum

•Brauron

C

SALAMIS

Colias

Mt Hymettus

A

PSYTTALEIA

•Anagyrous

Cape Zoster

Thoricus•

Aegina•

AEGINA

•Anaphlystus

Cape Sunium

Map 7. Macedonia and Chalcidice

Mt Orbelus

Mt Rhodope

R. Angites

• Siris

ODOMANTIANS

PAEOPLIANS

• Datum

...mon

BISALTIA

Lake Prasias

EDONIA

DOBERES

...USIANS

Myrcinus •

Mt Pangaeum

Argilus • Eion •

PHYLLIS?

Pergamus •

• Phagres

Thasos •

Aenyra/
Coenyra

THASOS

Syleus Plain

• Stagirus

Acanthian Sea

...A

...HALCIDICE

Acanthus •

Assa •

Dion •

• Olophyxus

A T H O S

Olynthus •

Pilorus •

Thyssus •

• Mecyberna

...otidaea

Galepsus •

• Singus

Cleonae •

• Acrothoium

S I T H O N I A

Mt Athos

...y

• Aphytis

• Sarte

P A L L E N E

Neapolis •

• Aege

Mende •

• Therambos

Torone •

• Scione

Cape Ampelus

Cape Canastreum

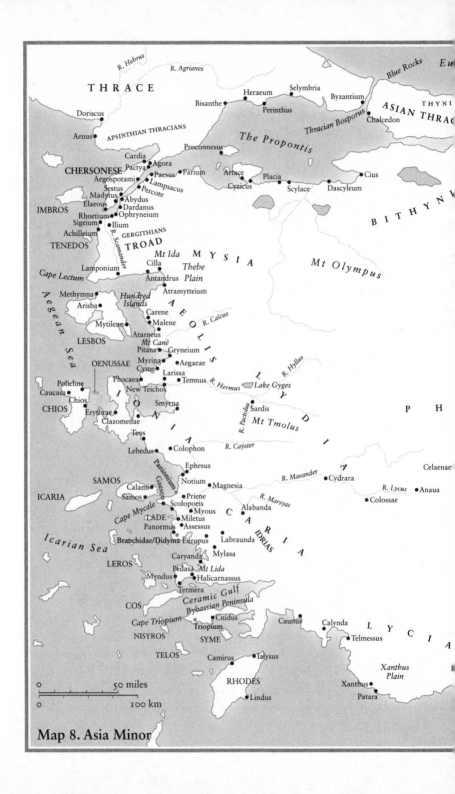

Map 8. Asia Minor

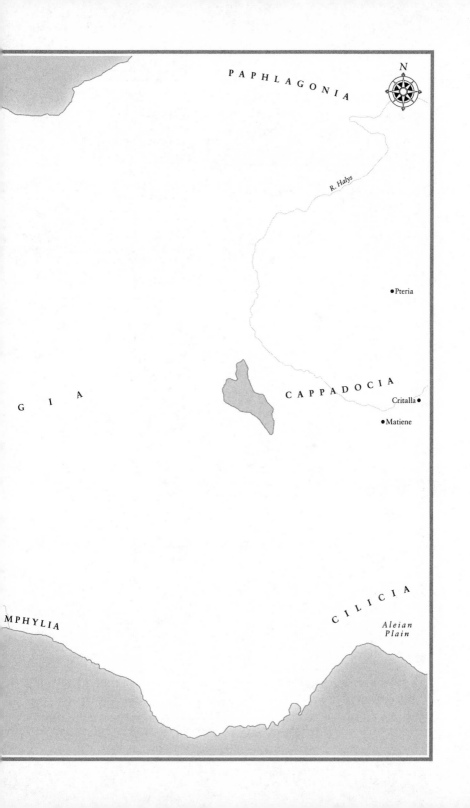

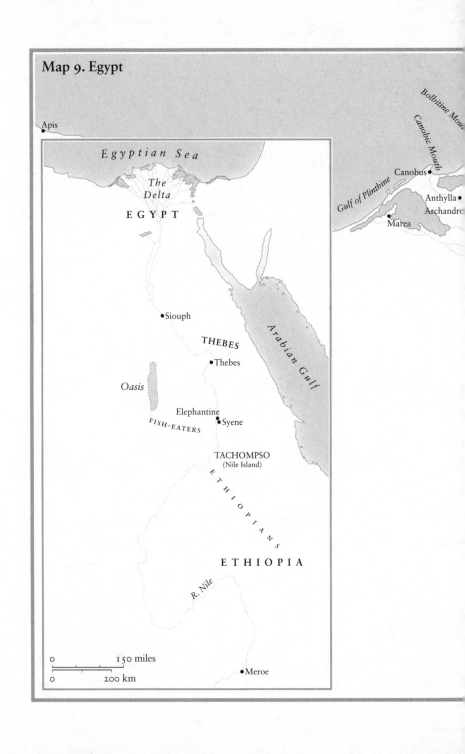

Map 9. Egypt

Apis

Egyptian Sea

The Delta

E G Y P T

Siouph

THEBES

Thebes

Oasis

Elephantine
Syene

FISH-EATERS

TACHOMPSO
(Nile Island)

Arabian Gulf

E
T
H
I
O
P
I
A
N
S

E T H I O P I A

R. Nile

Meroe

Bolbitine Mou...

Canobic Mouth

Canobus

Gulf of Plinthine

Anthylla
Archandr...

Marea

0 ——— 150 miles
0 ——— 200 km

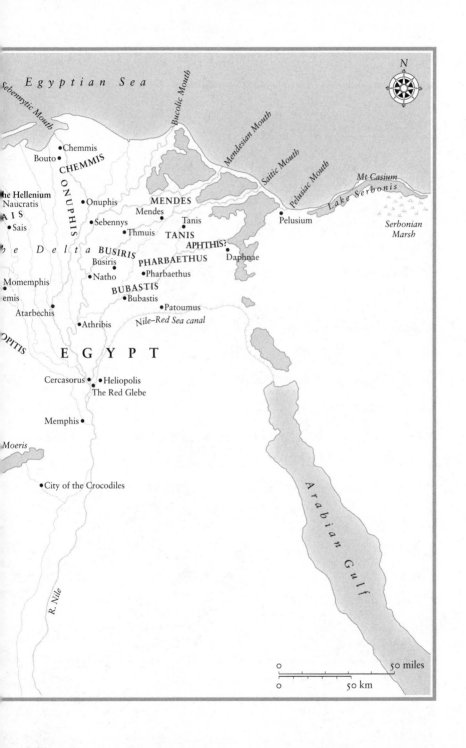

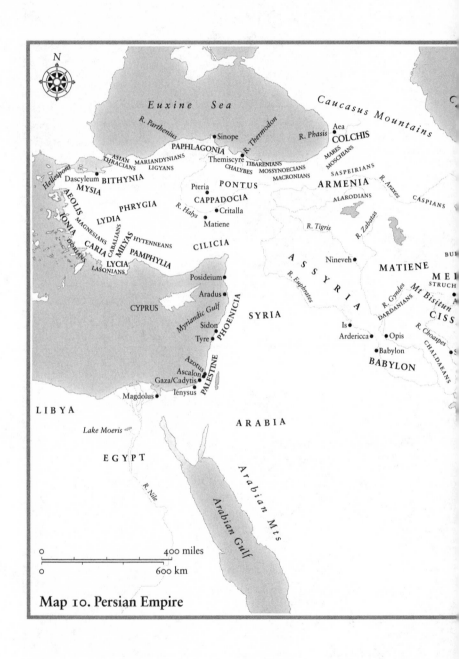

Map 10. Persian Empire

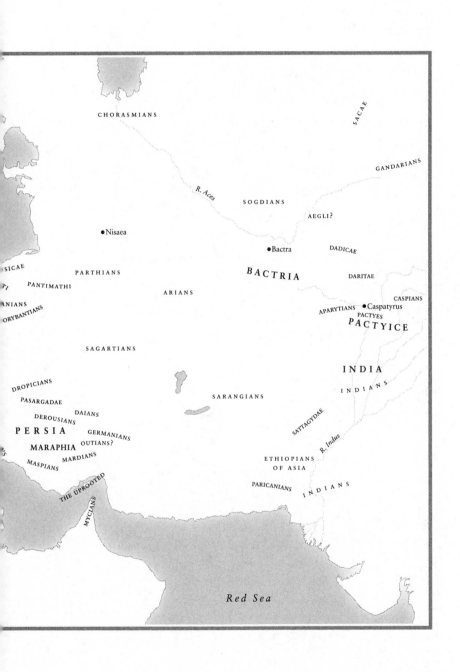

CHORASMIANS

SACAE

GANDARIANS

R. Aces

SOGDIANS

AEGLI?

●Nisaea

●Bactra

DADICAE

SICAE

PARTHIANS

BACTRIA

DARITAE

PANTIMATHI

CASPIANS

ARIANS

APARYTIANS ●Caspatyrus

ANIANS

ORYBANTIANS

PACTYES

PACTYICE

SAGARTIANS

INDIA

DROPICIANS

INDIANS

PASARGADAE

SARANGIANS

DAIANS

DEROUSIANS

PERSIA GERMANIANS

SATTAGYDAE

MARAPHIA OUTIANS?

R. Indus

MASPIANS MARDIANS

ETHIOPIANS
OF ASIA

THE UPROOTED

PARICANIANS INDIANS

MYCIANS

Red Sea

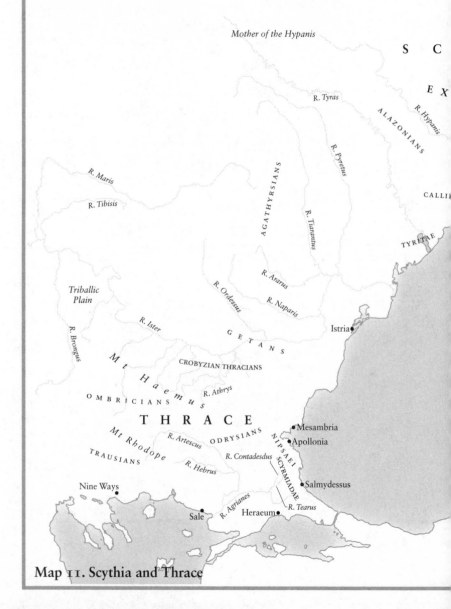

N

100 miles
200 km

NEURIANS

Mother of the Hypanis

S   C

E   X

R. Tyras

ALAZONIANS

R. Hypanis

CALLI

R. Pyretus

R. Maris

AGATHYRSIANS

TYRITAE

R. Tibisis

R. Tiarantus

R. Ordessus

R. Ararus

R. Naparis

Triballic
Plain

R. Ister

Istria

R. Brongus

G E T A N S

Mt Haemus

CROBYZIAN THRACIANS

R. Athrys

OMBRICIANS

T H R A C E

Mesambria

Apollonia

Mt Rhodope

R. Artescus

ODRYSIANS

NIPSAEI

R. Contadesdus

SCYRMIADAE

Salmydessus

TRAUSIANS

R. Hebrus

Nine Ways

R. Agrianes

Sale

Heraeum

R. Tearus

Map 11. Scythia and Thrace

ARGIPPAEI

DROPHAGI

BOUDINIANS

H I A

•Gelonus

R. Hyrgis

MELANCHLAENI

U S

POLITANS

•Panticapes

R. Panticapes

SCYTHIAN FARMERS

enes

EA

BORYSTHENITES

ype of Hippoles

•Careinitis

ck

ypacyris

SCYTHIAN NOMADS

GERRHIANS

ROYAL SCYTHIANS

ROYAL R. Gerrhus

R. Tanaïs

ROYAL LANDS

Cremni

R. Lycus

R. Oarus

Lake Maeëtis

MAEETIANS

SAUROMATIANS

CIMMERIA

Rugged Chersonese

TAURIANS

Cimmerian Bosporus

SINDIANS

Taurian Mts

Euxine Sea

rthenius

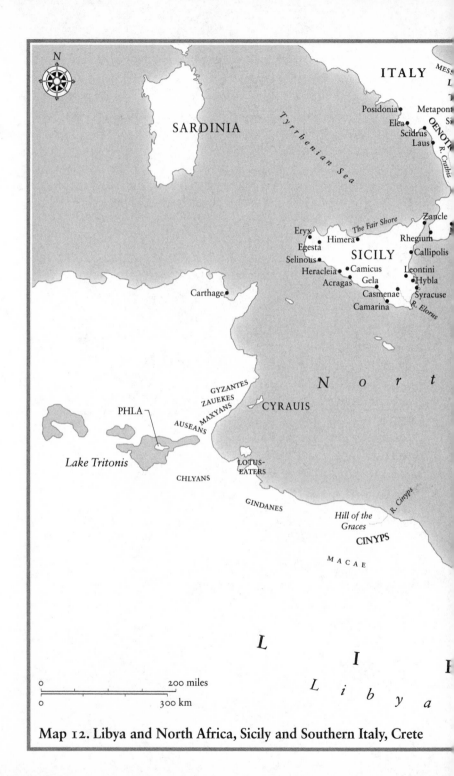

Map 12. Libya and North Africa, Sicily and Southern Italy, Crete

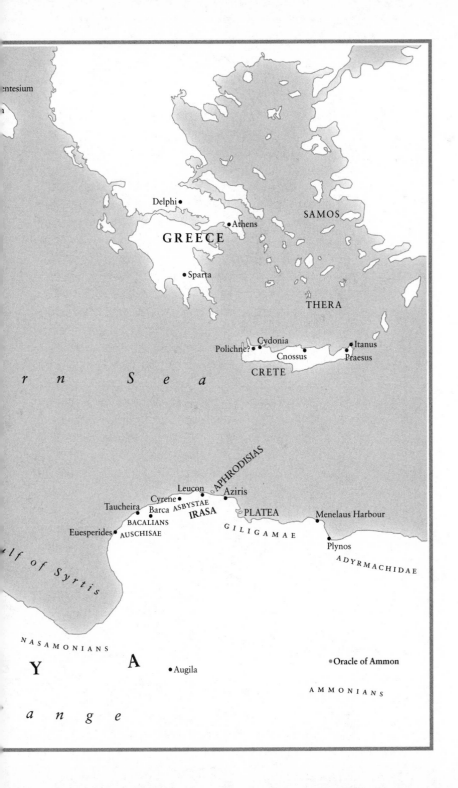

entesium

Delphi •

GREECE

• Athens

SAMOS

• Sparta

THERA

Polichne? •

Cydonia
• •
Cnossus

• Itanus
Praesus

CRETE

r   n   S   e   a

Leucon
•
Cyrene •
Taucheira
•
Barca • ASBYSTAE
BACALIANS
Euesperides •
AUSCHISAE

APHRODISIAS

• Aziris

IRASA

PLATEA

GILIGAMAE

Menelaus Harbour

•
Plynos

ADYRMACHIDAE

lf of Syrtis

NASAMONIANS

Y   A   • Augila

•Oracle of Ammon

AMMONIANS

a   n   g   e

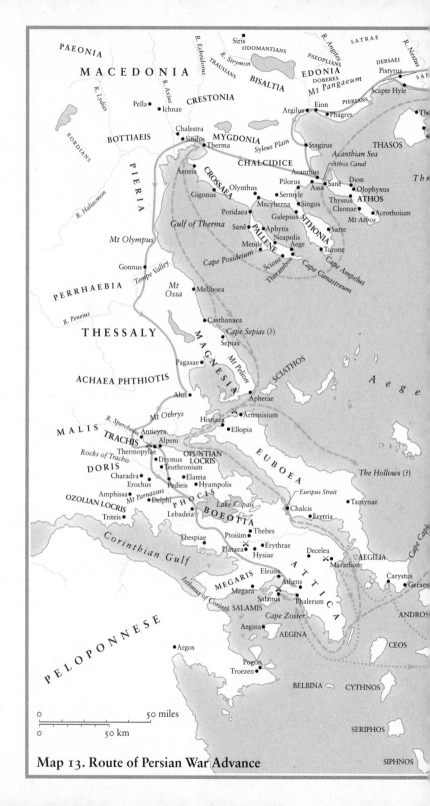

Map 13. Route of Persian War Advance

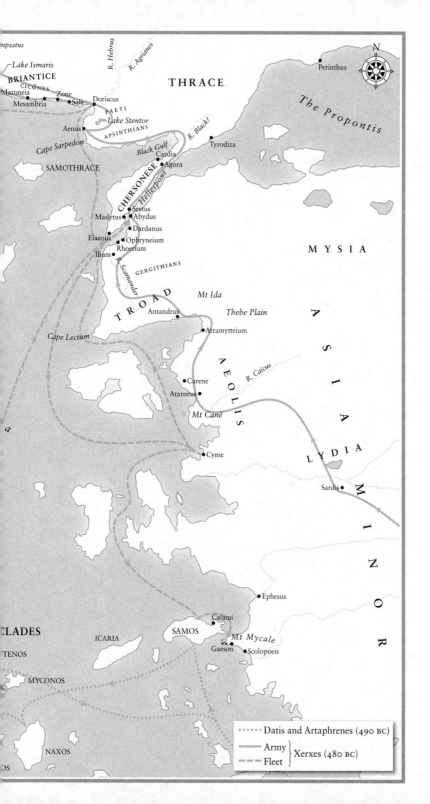

Map Index

Numbers given refer to the map numbers

Further Reading

Briant, P., *From Cyrus to Alexander: A History of the Persian Empire*, tr. P. T. Daniels (Winona Lake, 2002): the definitive modern survey of the Persian empire.

Cartledge, P. A., 'Herodotus and "the Other": a meditation on empire', *Echos du Monde Classique/Classical Views* ns 9 (1990), pp. 27–40.

— *The Greeks: A Portrait of Self and Others* (2nd edn, Oxford, 2002): Herodotus' *Histories* taken as a main medium for reconstructing Classical Greeks' world-view.

— 'Taking Herodotus personally', *Classical World* 102.4 (2009a), pp. 371–82.

— *Ancient Greece: A History in Eleven Cities* (Oxford and New York, 2009b), revised as *Ancient Greece: A Very Short Introduction* (Oxford and New York, 2011): an overview of Greek history from 1400 BC to AD 330.

— *After Thermopylae: The Oath of Plataea and the End of the Graeco-Persian Wars* (New York and Oxford, 2013): a close-up view of the struggle between Athens and Sparta for priority in the commemoration of the great Greek victory in 479 BC.

Derow, P., and R. Parker (eds.), *Herodotus and His World* (Oxford, 2003): a scholarly collection of essays.

Dewald, C., and Marincola, J., 'A Selective Introduction to Herodotean Studies', *Arethusa* 20 (1987), pp. 9–40.

Evans, J. A. S., 'Father of History or Father of Lies: The Reputation of Herodotus', *Classical Journal* 64, 1 (1968), pp. 11–17.

Evans, R. J., *In Defence of History* (2nd edn, London, 2001): a robust rejoinder to 'postmodernist' historiography.

Hamel, D., *Reading Herodotus: A Guided Tour through the Wild Boars, Dancing Suitors, and Crazy Tyrants of* The History (Baltimore, 2012): a useful and lively introductory guide.

Hartog, F., *The Mirror of Herodotus: The Representation of the Other in the Writing of History* (Berkeley, Los Angeles and London, 1988 [French original, *Le Miroir d'Hérodote: Essai sur la représentation de l'autre*, Paris, 1980; reprinted with a new introduction, 1991]): an exceptionally acute reading of Herodotus' representation of non-Greeks, with a special focus on the Scythian story in Book 4.

Holland, Tom, *Persian Fire: the First World Empire and the Battle for the West* (London and New York, 2005): an exciting general account of the Graeco-Persian Wars, firmly based on Herodotus.

Kapuściński, R., *Travels with Herodotus* (London, 2007): the controversial Polish journalist takes inspiration from his reading of Herodotus in hotspots around the globe.

Knox, B., *The Oldest Dead White European Males and Other Reflections on the Classics* (New York, 1993): a leading US historian re-evaluates the Classical legacy.

Kuhrt, A., *The Ancient Near East, c. 3000–330 BC*, 2 vols. (London, 1995): a panoramic survey of the ancient Near East, including Egypt, Assyria, Babylon and Persia.

— *The Persian Empire: A Corpus of Sources from the Achaemenid Period* (London, 2009): for those corners of Persian history that Herodotus doesn't reach.

Luraghi, N. (ed.), *The Historian's Craft in the Age of Herodotus* (Oxford, 2001): a scholarly collection of essays.

Marozzi, J., *The Man who Invented History: Travels with Herodotus* (London, 2008); US edition *The Way of Herodotus: Travels with the Man who Invented History* (2009): A young journalist and travel-writer follows Herodotus' footsteps through Greece and the Middle East.

Mendelsohn, D., *Waiting for the Barbarians: Essays from the Classics to Pop Culture* (New York, 2012): an exceptionally insightful collection of essays and reviews focusing on the Classical tradition.

Momigliano, A. D., 'The Place of Herodotus in the History of Historiography' (1958), reprinted in his *Studies in Historiography* (London, 1966), pp. 127–42.

Pritchett, W. K., *The Liar School of Herodotus* (Amsterdam, 1993): a defence of Herodotus against claims that he didn't really go where he said he did and made it all up on the basis of other people's writings.

Roberts, J. T., *Herodotus: A Very Short Introduction* (Oxford, 2011): one of the best short introductions.

Romm, J. S., *Herodotus* (New Haven, CT, 1998): another excellent short introduction.

Shepherd, W., *Plataea 479 BC: The Most Glorious Victory Ever Seen* (Oxford, 2012): the best short account of the battle, handsomely illustrated.

Acknowledgements

I owe a huge debt of thanks to everyone at Penguin, and especially to Adam Freudenheim, who gave me a wonderfully unexpected opportunity when he invited me to do this translation, and to Stuart Proffitt, who guided it into harbour with the deftest and most experienced of hands. Monica Schmoller braved extreme weather to help polish the prose, Jacob Blandy performed prodigies of research in the cause of making the Glossary Index as comprehensive as it is, and Jeff Edwards produced what are surely the best maps that any edition of Herodotus has ever been able to boast. Ruth Stimson supervised it all with exemplary patience and calm. My profoundest debt of gratitude, though, is to Paul Cartledge, a scholar as renowned for his generosity of spirit as for his great scholarship, and without whom this edition of Herodotus would be immeasurably the poorer. No translator ever had a surer or more hospitable port of call. Sparta is lucky indeed to have him as a citizen. Finally, I must thank my beloved family: my wife, Sadie, and my two daughters, Katy and Eliza, for sharing me so uncomplainingly with Herodotus all these many years, and for making me such a lavish and delicious celebratory feast when at last I finished *The Histories*. Σκοπέειν δὲ χρὴ παντὸς χρήματος τὴν τελευτήν . . .

Tom Holland

Glossary Index

This Glossary Index contains headwords for key concepts, figures and places. Where appropriate, items within entries are in chronological order; otherwise in alphabetical order.

Abae *town in Phocis, location of oracle dedicated to Apollo* oracle tested by Croesus 1.46; oracle offered Thessalian shields by Phocis 8.27; looted and torched by Persians 8.33; Mardonius' envoy visits oracle at 8.134.

Abdera (Abderites) *Greek city on the S coast of Thrace* founded by Teians 1.168; Thasians forced to send their fleet to 6.46, 48; Xerxes' army passes close by 7.109; resources exhausted by Xerxes 7.120; given gifts by Xerxes 8.120.

Abydus *Ionian city on the Hellespont* captured by Persians under Daurises 5.117; Hellespont bridge built from 7.33–4; Xerxes reviews his forces at 7.44; inhabitants responsible for guarding Hellespont bridges 7.95; Greeks find Hellespont bridges in pieces at 9.114.

Acanthus *Greek city on the Athos peninsula* Mardonius' fleet departs from before its shipwreck 6.44–5; honoured by Xerxes with guest-friendship 7.116.

Achaea (Achaeans) *region in the Peloponnese; see also* **Phthiotis** Achaeans have always lived in Peloponnese 8.73; geography, cities 1.145; Pelasgians settle 7.94.

Achaemenes *Persian governor of Egypt (d. 460), son of Darius and Atossa, brother of Xerxes* made governor of Egypt by Xerxes 7.7; commands Egyptian fleet during Xerxes' invasion of Greece 7.97; persuades Xerxes not to send ships to Lacedaemon; rebuked after accusing Demaratus of treachery 7.236–7; killed in battle with Libyans led by Inaros 3.12, 7.7.

Achaemenids *royal Persian patriline; see* **Achaemenes, Ariabignes, Artachaeës, Artaphrenes (1), Artaphrenes (2), Cambyses, Cyrus, Darius, Hystaspes, Megabates, Megabazus, Sataspes, Tigranes, Xerxes**

Achelous *river in Acarnania* western border of European lions' territory 7.126; similarity to Nile 2.10.

Adeimantus *Corinthian admiral* bribed to stay in Artemisium by Themistocles 8.5; unsuccessfully opposes Themistocles' plan to meet Persian fleet at Salamis (1) 8.59–61; alleged by Athenians to have fled before Salamis, returning only after intervention of miraculous boat 8.94.

Adrastus (1) *Phrygian prince, son of Gordias* exiled after accidentally killing brother, admitted into Croesus' home; purified of blood-guilt 1.35–6; commanded by

Croesus to act as Atys' bodyguard 1.41; accidentally kills Atys while hunting Mysian boar 1.43; forgiven by Croesus, commits suicide at Atys' grave 1.45.

Adrastus (2) *legendary Sicyonian king* worship at Sicyon stopped by Cleisthenes (1) 5.67.

Aeacus *legendary Aeginetan hero, son of Zeus, father of Peleus and Telamon, grandfather of Achilles and Ajax; his descendants are known as Aeacids* Miltiades (1) descended from 6.35; Aegina lends images of Aeacus and sons to Thebes (1) during Thebes (1)'s war with Athens 5.80–81; Athenians, on advice of Delphic oracle, consecrate sanctuary to 5.89; Greek fleet carries images of Aeacus and sons during battle of Salamis 8.64, 83–4.

Aegina (Aeginetans) *island in the Saronic Gulf, SW of Athens; also a city on that island* former name; Aeginetans' origins 8.46; Aeginetans found sanctuary of Zeus in Egypt 2.178; war with Samos, resulting feud; enslaves Samians of Cydonia 3.59;

— *rivalry with Athens:* subservient to Epidaurus before seceding; steals statues during resultant war 5.83; conflicting stories of Athens' disastrous attempt to recover statues from 5.84–7; resulting anti-Athenian laws, use of long-pinned brooches 5.88; gives token aid to Thebes (1) before beginning war with Athens 5.80–81; lays waste Attican coast 5.89; captures Athenian statesmen at Sunium 6.87; Aeginetans crush Nicodromus' attempted coup; cursed as result 6.88–91; defeated by Athens, calls on Argives, they refuse to help due to previous Aeginetan attack 6.92; captures Athenian ships 6.93; surrenders to Darius, accused by Athens of betraying Greece 6.49; expels Cleomenes after he tries to arrest Aeginetan leaders 6.50; Cleomenes and Leotychidas arrest Aeginetan leaders 6.73; denounces Leotychidas 6.85;

— *second Persian invasion of Greece:* reaches truce with Athens at meeting of Greeks 7.145; ship captured by Persians at Sciathos despite valour of one of its marines 7.179–81; ships at battle of Artemisium 8.1; *battle of Salamis:* ships at Salamis 8.46, inflict much damage to Persian fleet 8.86; ship captured by Samothracians 8.90; Aeginetans ambush fleeing Persian ships 8.91, ram Sidonian ship, rescue Pytheas; taunt Themistocles 8.92; give prize of valour awarded after Salamis to Delphic oracle on demand of Apollo 8.122; base of Greek fleet after Salamis 8.131; *battle of Plataea:* troops 9.28, 9.31; buy stolen gold cheaply from helots after Plataea 9.80; pay Plataeans to build false burial mound 9.85.

Aeolis (Aeolians) *Greek region on the W coast of Asia Minor* cities 1.149, 151; fertility 1.149; loss of Smyrna to Ionia 1.150; conquered by Croesus 1.28; sends messengers to Sardis to negotiate with Cyrus 1.141; follows the lead of Ionia in regard to Cyrus 1.151; sends emissaries to Sparta 1.152; cities aid Pactyes; sacked by Mazares and Harpagus 1.161–2; made part of Persian Province No. 1 by Darius 3.90; reconquered by Persian army under Hymaeës 5.122; ships and marines in Persian fleet during first Persian invasion of Greece 6.98, during second Persian invasion of Greece 7.95.

Greeks city of Naucratis, coastal sanctuaries 2.178; contributes funds for rebuilding of temple at Delphi 2.180; conquers Cyprus 2.182; gifts to Greek cities 2.182, 3.47; guest-friendship with Polycrates 2.182, 3.39; warning to Polycrates 3.40; dissolves guest-friendship with Polycrates 3.43; visited by Solon of Athens 1.30; *relations with Persia*: sends wrong girl to Cambyses, causing Persian invasion 3.1; dispatches eunuchs on failed mission to capture Phanes 3.4; dies before Cambyses' invasion; his tomb 3.10; Cambyses violates corpse 3.16.

Amazons *legendary tribe of female warriors, said to live in Themiscyre on the S coast of today's Black Sea* escape Greeks after capture, arrive in Scythia, fight then sleep with Scythians leading to birth of Sauromatians 4.110–16; invade Attica 9.27.

Ambracia (Ambraciots) *city in NW Greece* origins; ships at Salamis 8.45; troops at Plataea 9.28, 31.

Amestris *wife of Xerxes, daughter of Otanes* gives Xerxes cloak 9.109; learns of Artaÿnte's possession of cloak; plots against her mother, Masistes' wife; demands Xerxes give her Masistes' wife as gift 9.110; mutilates Masistes' wife 9.112; buries Persian children alive 7.114.

Ammon (Ammonians) *desert town in Libya at the western border of Egypt, location of oracle dedicated to Amun* origins 2.42; founding of oracle 2.54–6; miraculous spring 4.181; oracle proclaims inhabitants of Marea and Apis to be Egyptians 2.18; oracle tested by Croesus 1.46; Persian attack on thwarted by sandstorm 3.26.

Amompharetus *Lacedaemonian commander* argues with Pausanias over Lacedaemonian withdrawal 9.53, 55; abandoned by rest of Lacedaemonians, withdraws pursued by Persian cavalry 9.56–7.

Amphiaraus *legendary seer; an oracular shrine dedicated to him was located on the Attica–Boeotia border and its possession was therefore contested* passes Croesus' test 1.46, 49; Croesus gives gifts to 1.52; Thebans (1) forbidden from consulting; Mardonius' envoy visits 8.134.

Amphictyons *managers of the shrine of Apollo at Delphi* shrine of Demeter near Thermopylae 7.200; put temple rebuilding project out to tender 2.180; contract Alcmaeonids to rebuild temple 5.62; put bounty out on Epialtes 7.213; commission memorial at Thermopylae 7.228.

Amun *ram-horned Egyptian god* adopts Athena 4.180; Cambyses orders destruction of oracle in Ammon 3.25; H. identifies with Zeus; shows himself disguised to Heracles 2.42; oracle at Meroe 2.29; snakes sacred to 2.74; temple at Thebes (2) 1.182, 2.42, of which Ammonian sanctuary an offshoot 4.181.

Amyntas *king of Macedonia, father of Alexander* surrenders to Persians, hosts feast at which Persians drunkenly grope Macedonian women, is unable to prevent Alexander from killing them 5.18–20; offers Hippias city of Anthemous 5.94.

Anacharsis *Scythian prince and philosopher, uncle of Idanthyrsus* intelligence 4.46; travels, observance of Festival of Cybele, murder by own brother 4.76.

daemon over Thyreae; inhabitants wear hair cropped short as result 1.82; conflicting stories of involvement in Athens' disastrous attempt to recover statues from Aegina; its women use long-pinned brooches as result 5.86–8; invaded by Cleomenes and Lacedaemonian army; Argives massacred, tricked by Cleomenes; sacred grove burned down 6.75–80; taken over by slaves, leading to war 6.83; refuses to help Aeginetans because they took part in Cleomenes' raid 6.92; *second Persian invasion of Greece:* in spite of Delphic oracle's warning, proffers alliance with Greece against Xerxes 7.148–9; makes demands, perhaps influenced by Xerxes' supposed earlier message of friendship 7.150; sends runner to Mardonius warning of arrival of Lacedaemonian forces 9.12.

Ariabignes *Persian admiral, son of Darius* commands Carian and Ionian fleet during Xerxes' campaign against Greece 7.97; killed at Salamis 8.89.

Arians *people living in the W of today's Afghanistan* made part of Persian Province No. 16 by Darius 3.93; equipment and commander during Xerxes' campaign against Greece 7.66.

Arimaspians *tribe of one-eyed people said to live beyond Scythia* name's meaning 4.27; relations with neighbours according to Aristeas 4.13, according to the Issedonians 4.27; steal gold from griffins 3.116.

Arion *Lesbian musician* tours Italy and Sicily; sings to murderous sailors, throws himself into sea; carried to Taenarum by dolphin; placed under house arrest by Periander; offers dolphin-statue to temple in Taenarum 1.23–4.

Aristagoras *deputy tyrant of Miletus (r. c. 505–496), leader of the Ionian revolt, cousin and son-in-law of Histiaeus* receives rich Naxian exiles, suggests involving Persians in retaking of island; persuades Artaphrenes (1) to invade 5.30–31; quarrels with Megabates over latter's treatment of friend 5.33; fails to capture Naxos; receives tattooed messenger from Histiaeus urging revolt 5.35; foments revolt after exiling or arresting Ionian tyrants; goes to Lacedaemon to seek alliance 5.36–8; fails to win backing of Cleomenes due to distance to Susa, intervention of Gorgo 5.49–51; persuades Athens to back him 5.97; returns to Miletus, sends emissary to Paeonian prisoners-of-war 5.98; launches Ionian attack on Sardis 5.99; appeals unsuccessfully to Athens to rejoin cause 5.103; considers options at council of war; heads for Thrace at head of army; killed 5.124–6.

Aristeas *legendary poet from Proconnesus* explores Scythia and beyond while possessed by Apollo; twice dies and reappears; statue at Metapontium 4.13–15.

Aristeides *Athenian general (d. c. 467)* H.'s favourable opinion of; arrives at Salamis (1), puts aside rivalry with Themistocles, tells commanders of Salamis (1)'s encirclement 8.79–81; leads Athenians to kill Persians occupying islet off Salamis (1) 8.95; commander of Athenian forces at Plataea 9.28.

Aristodemus *Lacedaemonian warrior* misses Thermopylae due to eye condition, subsequent disgrace 7.229–31; bravery prior to death at Plataea goes unhonoured 9.71.

along 9.15; Greeks assemble along before Plataea 9.31; out-of-bounds to Greek forces 9.49; Persians cross, instigating battle of Plataea 9.59.

Aspathines *Persian nobleman* joins Otanes (1)'s conspiracy against Smerdis (2) 3.70; kills Magians along with fellow-conspirators; wounded in thigh; informs populace 3.77–9.

Assessus *town in Ionia* temple burned down during Alyattes' campaign against Miletus 1.19; temples built by Alyattes 1.22.

Assyria (Assyrians) *land located in N of today's Iraq* geography 4.39; invasion of Egypt under king Sennacherib 2.141; Mylitta (Aphrodite Urania) worshipped in 1.131, 199; Perseus said to be from 6.54; wealth of resources, climate, agriculture 1.192–3; writing 4.87; masters of Asia before Median revolt 1.95; victory over Phraortes and Media 1.102; defeated in battle by Cyaxares 1.103; conquered by Cyrus 1.191; made part of Persian Province No. 9 by Darius 3.92; equipment and commander during Xerxes' campaign against Greece 7.63.

Astyages *last king of Media (r. 585–549), son of Cyaxares, brother-in-law of Croesus, father of Mandane, grandfather of Cyrus* marriage to Alyattes' daughter Aryenis 1.74; succeeds Cyaxares as king of Media; marries Mandane to Cambyses before imprisoning her after she appears in portentous dreams; instructs Harpagus to kill Cyrus 1.107–8; realizes that Cyrus lives; extracts confession from Mithridates 1.116; kills Harpagus' son, cooks and serves up his flesh to Harpagus 1.119; sends Cyrus to Persia on advice of Magi 1.121–2; mobilizes Medes under Harpagus against threat of Cyrus and Persians 1.127; impales Magi who wrongly interpreted his dreams; his defeat and capture by Cyrus; rebukes Harpagus 1.128–9; spends remainder of life as prisoner of Persian court 1.130.

Asychis *king of Egypt (perhaps Sheshonk I, r. c. 945–924, although this does not accord with H.'s chronology)* succeeds Mycerinus; expands temple of Ptah at Memphis; creates laws to deal with financial crisis; pyramid 2.136.

Athena *Greek goddess of wisdom, justice and crafts; see also* **Neit** Aeginetans offer Samian prows to 3.59; Alyattes builds two temples to 1.22; Amasis offers gifts to Lindus' sanctuary of 2.182, 3.47; Assessus' temple of burns down during Lydian attack 1.19; Athenians dedicate bronze chariot to 5.77, discover her burnt olive tree lives after Persian attack 8.55; Athenians offer Alcaeus' shield and armour to Sigeium's temple of 5.95; Auseans worship 4.180; Cleomenes forbidden from entering her shrine 5.72; clothing, aegis based on those of Libyan women 4.189; Cylon seeks sanctuary at statue of 5.71; H. identifies with Egyptian Neit 2.28; Libyans sacrifice to 4.188; Pedasian priestess grows beard at times of peril 1.175, 8.104; Peisistratus disguises woman as 1.60; Persians miraculously killed in Delphi after reaching sanctuary 8.37–9; *Alea:* Tegeans keep Lacedaemonian fetters at temple of 1.66; Tegeans offer bronze manger to 9.70; *Crathian:* Dorieus raises temple to 5.45; *Guardian of the City:* Chios' temple of 1.160; Epidaurians ordered to make offerings to

5.82; *of Ilium:* Xerxes makes sacrifices to 7.43; *Sciras:* Corinthian ships fleeing Salamis meet miraculous boat by sanctuary of 8.94.

Athens (Athenians) *capital city of Attica* acquisition of Lemnos from Pelasgians in recompense for kidnap and murder of Athenian women 6.137–40; first Greek hoplites allegedly to charge into battle at a very long run 6.112; former lack of slaves 6.137; Pelasgian ancestry 1.56, 8.44;

— *rivalry with Aegina:* gives wood to Epidaurus in return for offerings 5.82; conflicting stories of its disastrous attempt to reclaim Epidaurian statues from Aegina 5.85–7; women adopt Ionian dress as a result 5.88; rebuffs Theban (1) attack; attacked by Aegina 5.81; advised by Delphic oracle to suffer Aeginetan raids for thirty years before attacking 5.89; statesmen captured by Aeginetans at Sunium 6.87; hires Corinthian ships; fleet arrives too late to aid Nicodromus' attempted coup in Aegina; later settles Aeginetan rebels in Sunium 6.88–90; victorious and then defeated in sea-battles with Aegina 6.92–3; refuses to return Aeginetan hostages despite Leotychidas' urging 6.86; builds fleet on advice of Themistocles during war with Aegina; subsequent importance of this 7.144;

— *tyranny and democracy:* civil strife during time of Peisistratus 1.59–64; civil strife before overthrowing of Hippias 5.55, 62–5; civil strife during time of Cleisthenes (2) and Isagoras 5.66, 69–72; seeks Persian aid against Lacedaemon 5.73; avoids attack by Peloponnesians under Cleomenes 5.74; defeats Boeotia in battle, invades Chalcis, settles Athenians there; ransoms prisoners, dedicates bronze chariot to Athena 5.77; flourishes under democracy 5.78; refuses to take Hippias back, defying Artaphrenes (1) 5.96;

— *Ionian revolt:* persuaded by Aristagoras to back him against Persia 5.97; fleet arrives in Miletus 5.99; deserts Ionian cause after rout at Ephesus 5.102–3; Athenian grief at Miletus' capture 6.21; later accused by Xerxes of torching Sardis' sanctuaries 7.8;

— *first Persian invasion of Greece:* kills Persian heralds demanding surrender 7.133; sends envoys to Lacedaemon after Aegina surrenders to Darius 6.49; sends aid to Eretrians 6.100; *battle of Marathon:* generals send Philippides to Lacedaemon after Persians land at Marathon 6.105; reinforced by Plataean troops; alliance with Plataea, resulting trouble with Thebes (1) 6.108; senior general persuaded to attack Persians by Miltiades (2) 6.109–10; defeats and harries the Persians 6.111–13; casualties 6.114, 117; captures Persian ships 6.115; lauded by Lacedaemonians 6.120; gives ships, army, money to Miltiades (2) 6.132;

— *second Persian invasion of Greece: Xerxes' campaign:* reaches truce with Aegina at meeting of Greeks 7.145; importance of its involvement in defence of Greece according to H. 7.139; Athenians urged to flee by Delphic oracle; attempt to make sense of later milder message 7.140–43; puts war effort before pride after Greeks refuse to serve under Athenian admiral 8.2–3; marines escape capture by Persians at mouth of R. Peneius 7.182; pray to

Barca (Barcaeans) *Greek city in the N of Libya* founding by Cyrene's king's disgruntled brothers 4.160; gifts to Cambyses 3.13; Barcaeans kill Arcesilaus 4.164; all claim responsibility for killing 4.167; besieged by Persians sent by Aryandes 4.200; tricked by Persians, murdered or enslaved 4.201–3; settled in Bactria by Darius 4.204; made part of Persian Province No. 6 by Darius 3.91.

Bast *cat-headed Egyptian goddess, daughter of Osiris and Isis, called Bubastis by H.* H. identifies with Artemis; worshipped in Bubastis (1) 2.59–60; parentage 2.156; shrine in Bubastis (1) 2.137–8; sanctuary in Bouto 2.155.

Battus *Theran founder and first king of Cyrene* conflicting stories of his selection as leader of Libyan expedition 4.153–6; early botched attempts at founding city in Libya on orders of Delphic oracle, eventual success 4.156–7; tricked by Libyans into relocating colony to Cyrene 4.158.

Bias *Prienean intellectual* allegedly visits Sardis, causes discontinuation of Lydian shipbuilding 1.27; suggests that Ionians establish state in Sardinia 1.170.

Boeotia (Boeotians) *region of central Greece* Boeotians' distinctive footwear 1.59; settled by Cadmus and Phoenicians 5.57; expels Gephyraeans 5.57; attacks Attica 5.74; defeated by Athens 5.78; cities surrender to Xerxes with exception of Plataea and Thespiae 7.132; troops join Persian forces 8.66; Boeotians lead Persians under Mardonius towards Isthmus 9.15; troops at Plataea 9.31, report change of Greek battle-order to Mardonius 9.47, attack Athenians 9.61; best warrior slain; infantry flees to Thebes (1); cavalry's bravery 9.67.

Boges *Persian governor of Eion, Thrace* kills himself, children, wife, concubines, slaves, destroys Eion's gold, silver, during Athenian siege; surviving children honoured by Xerxes 7.107.

Borysthenes *Scythian river (modern Dnieper) flowing through today's Russia, Belarus and Ukraine to today's Black Sea* great size, course, fecundity 4.53; mother of first Scythian 4.5; peoples to the west of 4.17; Scythian kings buried nearby 4.71; tributaries 4.54, 56.

Borysthenites *Greeks living at the mouth of the R. Borysthenes in Scythia* city; claim of Milesian descent, worship of Dionysus; brag to Scythians of Scyles' Bacchic worship 4.78–9; trading-post on the Euxine Sea 4.17.

Bosporus *strait running between Europe and Asia, connecting today's Sea of Marmara and Black Sea* geography 4.85; bridged by Darius with help of Mandrocles 4.83, 87–8.

Boudinians *people of Scythia living N of the Sea of Azov (Lake Maeëtis) perhaps in NE of today's Ukraine* appearance 4.108; land 4.21, 109; language, autochthony, nomadism, diet, wildlife 4.109; ally with Scythians against Darius 4.119; land invaded by Darius and Persians 4.123–4.

Bouto *city in Egypt, location of temples of Horus, Bast and Wadjet (Leto)* Festival of Wadjet 2.59, 63; graveyard of field-mice and hawks 2.67; temple of Wadjet 2.155; *oracle:* Cambyses told he will die in Agbatana 3.64; Mycerinus told he has six years to live 2.133; Pheros recommended odd blindness cure 2.111; Psammetichus questions 2.152.

Branchidae *oracle, also known as Didyma, dedicated to Apollo near Miletus, managed by priests also called Branchidae* location 1.157; Croesus tests 1.46, gives gifts to 1.92; priests twice advise Cyme to surrender Pactyes 1.158–69; receives gifts from Necos 2.159; plundered by Persians after the fall of Miletus 6.19.

Bubastis (1) *city in Egypt* feline graveyard 2.67; Festival of Bast 2.59–60; shrine of Bast 2.137–8.

Bubastis (2) *Egyptian goddess; see* **Bast**

Byzantium (Byzantines) *city (modern Istanbul) on the European coast of the Bosporus* Darius' pillars stolen by 4.87; captured by Ionians 5.103; city abandoned to approaching Phoenician fleet; Byzantines settle on Euxine Sea 6.33.

Cabalians *people of SW Asia Minor* made part of Persian Province No. 2 by Darius 3.90; equipment and commander during Xerxes' campaign against Greece 7.77.

Cadmeians *see* **Cadmus**

Cadmus *legendary Phoenician founder of Thebes (1); his descendants were known as Cadmeians* Cadmeian script at Thebes (1) 5.59–61; Cadmeians drive Hellenes from Thessaly 1.56, expelled from Boeotia by Argives 5.57; Melampous taught about worship of Dionysus by 2.49; Phoenicians left behind on Thera by 4.147.

Cadytis *town (variously identified as modern Gaza or Jerusalem) in Syria* similar in size to Sardis 3.5; captured by Necos 2.159.

Callias (1) *Elean soothsayer* defects from Sybaris to Croton during their war; granted lands by Croton after its victory 5.44–5.

Callias (2) *rich Athenian, son of Phaenippus* hatred of tyranny; dares to buy Peisistratus' goods at auction; takes prizes at Olympic and Pythian Games; allows daughters to choose husbands 6.121–2.

Callimachus *Athenian war archon (d. 490)* casts deciding vote leading to Marathon; commands right wing at battle 6.109–11.

Cambyses *King of Persia (r. 530–522), son of Cyrus and Cassandane* nickname 3.89; Otanes (2)'s father flayed, his skin made into chair on orders of; appoints Otanes (2) in his stead 5.25; escorts Croesus to Persia from Massagetan territory 1.208; succeeds Cyrus as King of Persia 2.1;

— *invasion of Egypt:* sent wrong girl by Amasis, spurring invasion 3.1; requests Polycrates send Samian fleet 3.44; advised by Phanes 3.4; granted safe passage by king of Arabia 3.7; takes Ionians and Aeolians with him 2.1, 3.1; defeats Egyptians at Pelusium 3.11; besieges Memphis after massacre of Mytilenaeans; receives tributes from Libya, Cyrene and Barca 3.13; admits Psammenitus into his court after testing him by humiliation of his children 3.14–15; violates Amasis' corpse 3.16; decides against naval invasion of Carthage after Phoenicians refuse to take part 3.19; sends Fish-Eaters to spy on Ethiopians 3.20; launches rash attack on Ethiopians, loses large part of army 3.25; troops destroyed by sandstorm en route to attack Ammon 3.26;

Greece: ships and marines in Persian fleet 7.93; tyrant captured by Greeks at Artemisium 7.195; Themistocles urges revolt of 8.22.

Carthage (Carthaginians) *Phoenician-founded city-state in N Africa, outside today's Tunis* Phocaeans pillage; launches revenge attack with Tyrrhenians 1.166–7; trade with west-coast Libyans 4.196; expels Dorieus and Lacedaemonians from R. Cinyps 5.42; escapes attack by Cambyses after Phoenicians refuse to take part 3.19; attacks Sicily; beaten in battle; its king Hamilcar disappears 7.165–7.

Carystus (Carystians) *city on Euboea* role in delivery of Hyperboreans' gifts to Delos 4.33; subdued by Persian fleet under Datis 6.99; joins Xerxes' forces 8.66; gives in to Themistocles' demands for money, attacked nonetheless 8.112, 121.

Casium *mountain on Egyptian coast* at border between Egypt and Syria 2.158; on route into Egypt 3.5.

Caspian Sea *land-locked body of water in central Asia* location, size 1.202–3; northern extent of Asia 4.40.

Caspians (1) *people perhaps living on the SE or SW coast of the Caspian Sea* made part of Persian Province No. 11 by Darius 3.92; equipment and commander during Xerxes' invasion of Greece 7.67.

Caspians (2) *people perhaps living in the N of today's Pakistan* made part of Persian Province No. 15 by Darius 3.93; cavalry part of Xerxes' invasion of Greece 7.86.

Cassandane *wife of Cyrus, mother of Cambyses, daughter of Pharnaspes* her jealousy of Cyrus' Egyptian concubine alleged to have inspired Cambyses' invasion of Egypt 3.3; public mourning declared at death 2.1.

cattle *Greece was largely unsuitable for extensive cattle-rearing; Scythia was famed for its herds* Argippaei lack 4.23; Argive brothers pull plough in absence of 1.31; aurochs horns imported into Greece 7.126; bile of Scythian 4.58; Chaldaeans sacrifice unweaned calves in Babylon 1.183; Cretan cattle struck down by plague 7.171; Egyptian bull-god Apis 3.28–9; Egyptian reverence for; sacrifice; burial 2.38–42; Garamantes' long-horned thick-skinned 4.183; Heracles drives Geryon's 4.8; Issedonians sacrifice 4.26; Massagetans sacrifice 1.216; Mycerinus buries daughter in wooden cow 2.129–32; ox-hide helmets worn by unknown contingent of Persian forces 7.76; Persian banquets feature roast ox 1.133; prizes at Chemmis' athletics festival 2.91; Psammenitus commits suicide by drinking bull's blood 3.15; Scythia's hornless 4.29; Scythia's pastures ideal for 4.53; Scythians sacrifice 4.61–2; Scythian use of oxen in executions 4.69; Scythians herd 4.46.

Caucasus *mountain range lying between today's Black and Caspian Seas* largest in the world; inhabitants, their customs 1.203; northernmost extent of Persian rule 3.97.

Caunus (Caunians) *city in Caria* origins, language, cultural differences with Carians; reversion to religion of forebears, driving out of foreign gods 1.172; captured by Harpagus 1.176; joins Ionian revolt 5.103.

Ceos (Ceans) *island off SE Attica* banqueting hall on Delos 4.35; origins 8.46; ships in Greek fleet before battle of Artemisium 8.1, at Salamis 8.46.

Chalcedon (Chalcedonians) *city on the Asian coast of the Bosporus* mocked by Megabazus 4.144; captured by Otanes (2) 5.26; Chalcedonians abandon city to approaching Phoenician fleet, settle on Euxine Sea 6.33.

Chalcidice *peninsula of NE Greece; not to be confused with* **Chalcis** marines in the Persian forces during Xerxes' invasion of Greece 7.185; given Olynthus by Artabazus 8.127.

Chalcis (Chalcidians) *city on Euboea* origins 8.46; attacks Attica 5.74; conquered by Athens, settled with Athenians 5.77; Greek fleet relocates to 7.183; marines crew Athenian ships before battle of Artemisium 8.1; provides same ships at Salamis 8.46; troops at Plataea 9.28, 31.

Chaldaeans *people of Assyria* as priests in Babylon 1.181–3; in Assyrian contingent during second Persian invasion of Greece 7.63.

chariots *although once used by Greeks in war, by H.'s time the use of chariots was largely confined to racing; winning owners, not drivers, were honoured, and the ability to maintain a four-horse chariot was a mark of great wealth and status* Asbystae frequently drive four-horse 4.170; Alcmaeon's great wealth demonstrated by his ability to maintain four-horse 6.125; Auseans parade most beautiful girl of the year around in 4.180; bronze dedicated to Athena in Athens 5.77; Garamantes hunt Ethiopians in four-horse 4.183; Indian chariots pulled by wild-asses 7.86; Libyans learn use of four-horse from Greeks 4.189; women of the Zauekes drive during war 4.193; Miltiades (1)'s family's great wealth demonstrated by their ability to maintain four-horse 6.35–6; Salamis (2)'s use of in war 5.113; Themistocles given most beautiful in Lacedaemon 8.124; Xerxes' drawn by Nisaean horses 7.40; Zeus' in Xerxes' invasion of Greece 7.40; Zeus' stolen by Thracians 8.115; *chariot-races:* Agyllans propitiate Phocaean dead with 1.167; Callias (2) comes second in Olympic four-horse chariot-race, wins that of Pythian Games 6.122; Olympic four-horse chariot-race won by Alcmaeon 6.125, by Cimon 6.103, by Cleisthenes (1) 6.126, by Demaratus 6.70, by Miltiades (1) 6.36.

Chemmis *province and city of the same name (modern Akhmim) in central Egypt* temple of Perseus, Greek-style athletics festival 2.91; home of Egyptian warriors 2.165.

Cheops *king of Egypt (Khufu, r. c. 2609–2584), 'brother' (in fact father) of Chephren* succeeds Rhampsinitus 2.124; closes down shrines, forbids blood-sacrifices 2.124; enslaves Egyptians, puts them to work building road, tomb, pyramid 2.124–5; pimps out own daughter; dies 2.126–7.

Chephren *king of Egypt (Khafre, r. c. 2576–2551), 'brother' (in fact son) of Cheops* succeeds his brother, builds pyramid 2.127.

Chios (Chians) *Ionian island off the W coast of Asia Minor, and a city on that island* dialect 1.142; in Mysia 8.106; refuses to sell islands to Phocaea 1.165; role in Hellenium's founding 2.178; aids Miletus against Lydians under Alyattes 1.18; betrays Pactyes to Mazares, receives Atarneus in return 1.160; *Ionian* *revolt:* briefly imprisons Histiaeus believing him to be agent of Darius 6.2; refuses to supply Histiaeus with ships to help him recapture Miletus 6.5; ships in the Ionian fleet at battle of Lade 6.8; marines' bravery at Lade; unhappy end at Ephesus 6.15–16; conquered by Histiaeus after portents 6.26–7; seized by Persian fleet 6.31; *second Persian invasion of Greece:* conspirators beg Lacedaemonians, Greek fleet to liberate Ionia 8.132; allies with Athens 9.106.

Choaspes *river in Persia* water taken on campaign by Persia for its King to drink 1.188; Susa on banks of 5.49, 52.

Chorasmia (Chorasmians) *region of central Asia S of today's Aral Sea* made part of Persian Province No. 16 by Darius 3.93; plain flooded by Darius 3.117; equipment and commander during Xerxes' invasion of Greece 7.66.

Cilicia (Cilicians) *region of SE Asia Minor* name's origins 7.91; made Persian Province No. 4 by Darius 3.90; among Persian forces during attack on Miletus 6.6; ships and marines in Persian fleet during Xerxes' invasion of Greece 7.91; Cilician squadron sunk by Greeks during battle of Artemisium 8.14; marines adjudged useless by Artemisia 8.68.

Cimmerians *people living N of the Caucasus Mountains before being expelled by Scythians* Scythia formerly occupied by 4.11–13; royals kill each other after Scythian invasion 4.11; Scythians invade Asia in pursuit of 1.103, 4.1, 12, 5.20; raid Ionia 1.6; capture Sardis 1.15; expelled from Asia by Alyattes 1.16.

Cinyps *river in Libya* course 4.175; fertility of surrounding land 4.198; Dorieus' short-lived colony at 5.42.

Cissia (Cissians) *region in the W of today's Iran* well yielding asphalt, salt and oil 6.119; made part of Persian Province No. 8 by Darius 3.91; equipment and commander during Xerxes' invasion of Greece 7.62; cavalry 7.86, deployed at Thermopylae 7.210.

Cithaeron *mountain in Boeotia* foothills base of Greeks before Plataea 9.19; passes guarded by Persians on orders of Mardonius 9.38–9; Greek supply-wagon trapped on 9.50, 51.

City of the Crocodiles *city in Egypt* labyrinth 2.148.

Clazomenae (Clazomenaeans) *city in Ionia* dialect 1.142; role in Hellenium's founding 2.178; treasury in Delphi 1.51; defeats Lydia under Alyattes 1.16; conquered by Persian force under Artaphrenes (1) 5.123.

Cleisthenes (1) *tyrant of Sicyon (r. c. 600–570), son of Aristonymus, grandfather of Cleisthenes (2)* anti-Argive measures in Sicyon, insulting renaming of Sicyonian tribes 5.68; hosts lavish athletics and social etiquette competition; marries daughter to its winner 6.126–30.

Cleisthenes (2) *reformer of Athens (d. after 507), grandson of Cleisthenes (1)* secures support of Athenian people over Isagoras, reforms Athenian tribal divisions 5.66, 69; flees Athens after intervention of Cleomenes on instructions of Isagoras 5.70, 72; restored after failure of Isagoras' coup 5.73.

Cleombrotus *Lacedaemonian royal (d. 480), son of Anaxandridas and first wife, brother of Dorieus and Leonidas, half-brother of Cleomenes, father of*

Pausanias born to Anaxandridas' first wife shortly after birth of Cleomenes to his second 5.41; leads Greek forces at Isthmus of Corinth 8.71; dies having led Lacedaemonian army back from Isthmus of Corinth after eclipse 9.10.

Cleomenes *king of Lacedaemon (r. c. 520–c. 490), son of Anaxandridas and second wife, half-brother of Dorieus, Leonidas and Cleombrotus* birth to Anaxandridas' second wife quickly followed by birth of Dorieus and then Leonidas and Cleombrotus to first 5.41; Maeandrius offers gifts to; rejects them, banishes him 3.148; mental illness 5.42; Peisistratid prophecies revealed to Lacedaemonians by 5.90; Plataeans seek alliance; recommends they ask Athens 6.108; refuses to aid Aristagoras with Ionian revolt 5.49–51; Scythian embassy gives taste for neat wine to 6.84;

— *campaigns against Athens:* leads Lacedaemonian attack on Hippias' Athens, besieges city; overthrows him after capture of Peisistratid children 5.64–5; orders banishment of Cleisthenes (2) on instructions of Isagoras 5.70; arrives in Athens, occupies Acropolis, besieged by Athenians, sent back to Lacedaemon 5.72; invades Attica with Peloponnesian army with intention of installing Isagoras as tyrant 5.74; lays waste shrine of Demeter and Corê at Eleusis 6.75; deserted by Corinthians, fellow-king Demaratus and other allies 5.75;

— *campaign against Argos:* attacks Argos after misunderstanding Delphic oracle; tricks Argives into leaving sacred grove; kills them, burns sacred grove 6.76–80; offers blood-sacrifices to Hera, flogs priest who attempts to prevent him 6.81; convinces Lacedaemonians he acted correctly in not taking Argos 6.82;

— *downfall:* Crius prevents him from arresting Aeginetan collaborators 6.50; replaces Demaratus with Leotychidas, after bribing Delphic oracle's priestess 6.65–7; returns to Aegina with Leotychidas, arrests Aeginetan collaborators, delivers them to Athens 6.73; plotting against Demaratus discovered, flees to Arcadia, incites revolt against Lacedaemon; restored to power by alarmed Lacedaemonians 6.74–5; suicide; possible reasons for this 6.75–84.

Cnidus (Cnidians) *Dorian city in Caria* bans Halicarnassus from using Triopium 1.144; doomed attempts to turn Cnidus into an island; embassy to Delphic oracle and surrender to Harpagus 1.174; geography 1.174; role in Hellenium's founding 2.178; unsuccessful attempt to effect Gillus' return to Tarentum 3.138.

Coës *Mytilenaean nobleman, guest-friend of Darius* advises Darius not to dismantle bridge over R. Ister 4.97; made tyrant of Mytilene by Darius in reward 5.11; arrested by Aristagoras, stoned to death by Mytilenaeans 5.38.

Colchis (Colchians) *region in the W of today's Georgia* circumcision 1.104; Egyptian origins 2.104–5; geography 4.37; king demands return of daughter Medea after kidnap by Greeks 1.2; four-yearly gift of children to Darius 3.97; equipment and commander during Xerxes' invasion of Greece 7.79.

Colophon *Ionian city in Lydia* captured by Gyges 1.15; dialect 1.142; inhabitants found Smyrna 1.16, refuse to celebrate Apatouria 1.147; inhabitants' role in Ionia's gain of Smyrna from Aeolis 1.150.

Corcyra (Corcyraeans) *island (modern Corfu) in the Ionian Sea* boys saved from castration by Samians 3.48; intercedes in Gela's siege of Syracuse 7.154; sends ships promised to Greek fleet to anchor off Pylus and Taenarum to await Persian victory with aim of winning Xerxes' favour 7.168.

Corinth (Corinthians) *city in NE Peloponnese* allies with Lacedaemon against Samos 3.48; arbitrates in dispute between Thebes (1) and Athens 6.108; castration of Corcyraean boys foiled by Samians 3.48; deserts Cleomenes' invasion of Athens 5.75; intercedes in Gela's siege of Syracuse 7.154; loans ships to Athens 6.89; origins 8.43; sailors plan to murder Arion 1.23; under Cypselus and Periander 5.92; *second Persian invasion of Greece:* troops at Thermopylae 7.202; ships at battle of Artemisium 8.1, lead withdrawal 8.21; ships at Salamis 8.43, alleged by Athenians to have fled before battle, returning only after intervention of miraculous boat 8.94; troops at Plataea 9.28, 31, attempt disorganized attack after Pausanias' victory 9.69; troops rout Persians at Mycale 9.102; adjudged next-best to Athenians 9.105; *Isthmus of:* Greeks' base during Xerxes' invasion 7.172, 177; prisoners sent to 7.195; walled by Peloponnesians 8.40, 71–2, 74, 9.7–8; Greek commanders at Salamis (1) debate returning to 8.49, 56–64; trireme captured during battle of Salamis dedicated at 8.121; Greeks muster at 9.15; statue of Poseidon installed after Plataea 9.81.

Cos (Coans) *Dorian island off the W coast of Asia Minor* bans Halicarnassus from using Triopium 1.144; commanded by Artemisia during second Persian invasion of Greece 7.99; former tyrant of Cos sent by Gelon to monitor second Persian invasion of Greece 7.163; Coan concubine of Persian warrior aided by Pausanias, later sent to Aegina 9.76.

Crete (Cretans) *Greek island in the S Aegean* Carians', Caunians', Lycians' origins in 1.172–4; enslaves Samian colony 3.59; Europa's kidnappers alleged to have been Cretan 1.2; Samians found colony 3.44; Therans send envoys 4.151; refuses to join Greece against Xerxes after Delphic oracle cites its desolation after death of Minos, involvement in Trojan War 7.169–71.

crocodiles *H. mentions both the Nile Crocodile and the smaller Mugger Crocodile of NW India* City of the Crocodiles' sacred labyrinth 2.148; Egyptian name 2.69; Egyptians revere corpses of those killed by 2.90, worship, eat 2.69, hunt 2.70; H. describes 2.68; Indus 4.44; Ionian's give name 2.69; Libyan 4.191; nearby Pygmies' city 2.32.

Croesus *king of Lydia (r. c. 560–546), son of Alyattes, father of Atys* Alcmaeon given gold by 6.125; first foreigner to establish close relations with Greeks 1.6; gifts to Greek temples 1.92; kingdom 1.6; Lampsacenes ordered to free Miltiades (1) by 6.37; pillar at Phrygia–Lydia border 7.30; Xerxes familiar with Delphi's treasures of 8.35;

— *rise to power:* succeeds Alyattes 1.26; tortures opponents on taking throne 1.92; attacks Ephesus and Ionian and Aeolian cities; abandons ship-building programme, signs treaty of friendship with Ionian islanders; conquests 1.26–8; discusses happiness with Solon 1.30–33; dreams of Atys' death; attempts to protect him 1.34; admits Adrastus (1) into home, purifies him 1.35–6; persuaded by Atys to allow him to hunt Mysian boar; commands Adrastus (1) to act as Atys' bodyguard 1.37–41; grief-stricken at death of Atys, forgives Adrastus (1) 1.44–5;

   — *downfall:* stirred from grief by growing power of Cyrus; tests efficacy of oracles 1.46–8; excessively propitiates Apollo 1.50–51; sends gifts to oracle of Amphiaraus 1.52; consults oracles, misunderstands prophecies 1.53, 55; considers alliance with Lacedaemon and Athens 1.56; allies with Lacedaemon 1.69–70; invasion of Cappadocia 1.71, 73, 76; ignores advice of Sandanis 1.71; lust for territory, confidence in Delphic oracle, desire to punish Cyrus 1.73; disappointed at stalemate, withdraws to Sardis after battle; alliance with Amasis, Labynetus 1.77; repeatedly calls on Babylonians, Egyptians, Lacedaemonians for aid 1.77, 81; asks Telmessians to interpret portent 1.78; defeated by Cyrus at Sardis due to horses' fear of camels 1.80; besieged by Cyrus 1.80–81, 84; captured, fulfilling Delphic oracle's prophecy 1.85; brought to Cyrus in chains, placed on pyre; cites Solon's take on happiness 1.86; saved by Apollo 1.87;

   — *prisoner of Persia:* advises Cyrus 1.87–9; sends Lydians to reproach Apollo 1.90–91; accepts oracle's explanation 1.91; taken to Agbatana by Cyrus 1.153; persuades Cyrus to spare Lydians after Pactyes' revolt 1.155–6; advises Cyrus to attack Tomyris and Massagetans on Massagetan soil 1.207; escorted by Cambyses back to Persia 1.208; in Egypt with Cambyses, weeps at plight of Psammenitus 3.14; pleases Cambyses with sycophantic response to question 3.34; hidden by servants after angering Cambyses with well-meant advice 3.36.

crops *barley and wheat were the staple crops in H.'s Greece; barley was eaten largely by the poor, while wheat was imported from abroad as well as grown at home; various vegetables were also cultivated* Alazonian 4.17; Alyattes destroys Milesian harvest 1.17; Artaÿctes turns temple precinct over to growing 9.116; Assyrian 1.193; Callippidae 4.17; Cyrus argues living in fertile land leads to poor warriors 9.122; Darius dams Chorasmian river ruining harvest 3.117; Delphic oracle references Salamis (1)'s 7.141; Egyptian 2.14, 92, 94, 168; Epidaurians advised by Delphic oracle after harvest fails 5.82; Gelonian 4.109; Indians do not grow 3.100; Libyan 4.191, 198–9; Lydian harvest best in the world according to Aristagoras 5.49; Massagetans do not grow 1.216; Mysian harvest destroyed by boar 1.36; Persian army returning from Greece seizes en route 8.115; Phoenicians circumnavigating Libya grow en route 4.42; Scythian 4.17–18, 53; Scythians do not grow 4.2, 19, 46, 97, 127; Thasian farmers go untaxed 6.46; Thracians cease to grow on road used by Xerxes and his army 7.115; *barley:* Assyrian 1.193; Egyptian wine made from 2.77; Egyptians do not eat 2.36; Lacedaemonian kings offer to Apollo 6.57; *wheat:* Assyrian 1.193; Egyptian bread made from emmer 2.36, 77; Fish-Eaters explain cultivation to long-lived Ethiopian king 3.22; Lydians make 'honey' out of tamarisk and 7.31; Persian army's rations 7.187; *grain:* Alazonians subsist on 4.17; Callippidae subsist on 4.17; Chians cease using grain from Atarneus in religious practices 1.160; Egypt gives to Persian empire 3.91; Egyptian warriors' rations 2.168; Gelon offers to provision Greek army in return for supreme command 7.158; Gelonians eat 4.109; Greek cities prepare to host Persian army by stockpiling 7.119; Histiaeus captured after landing in Asia Minor to harvest 6.28; Indians harvest wild 3.100; Persian army's bought ready-ground from Asia 7.24, grain-transport ships wrecked in storm off Sepias 7.191; Persian sacrifice does not feature offerings 1.132; Thebes (1)'s supplies during second Persian invasion of Greece 9.41; Thrasybulus breaks tallest stalks to teach lesson to Periander 5.92; Xerxes allows Greek grain-transport ships to escape 7.147.

Croton (Crotoniates) *Greek city (modern Crotone) in the S of Italy* origins 8.47; prevents Persian spies from arresting Democedes 3.137; conflicting claims of Dorieus' involvement in its capture of Sybaris 5.44–5; ship in the Greek fleet at Salamis 8.47.

Cyaxares *king of Media (r. 615–585), son of Phraortes, father of Astyages* offers Scythians asylum before humiliating them; fed Median boy in revenge 1.73; succeeds Phraortes as king of Media; love of war; modernizes army, unites Asia Minor, attacks Assyrians, besieges Nineveh 1.103; attacked and defeated by Scythians 1.103–4; gets Scythians drunk; kills them, reclaims power; dies 1.106.

Cyclades *island chain off the SE coast of Greece; see* **Andros, Ceos, Cythnos, Delos, Naxos, Paros, Seriphos, Siphnos, Tenos, Thera**

Cyme (Cymaeans) *city in Aeolis, also known as Phriconis* sends embassy to Branchidae to ask for advice on Pactyes 1.157; second embassy sent after Aristodicus doubts message of first; receives same answer 1.158–9; evacuates Pactyes to Mytilene, then to Chios after Mytilenaeans threaten to betray him 1.160; conquered by Persian army 5.123.

Cyprus (Cypriots) *island off the S coast of Asia Minor, peopled by Greeks and Phoenicians* origins 7.90; temple of Aphrodite Urania 1.105; women's sex with strangers at temple of Aphrodite Urania 1.199; conquered by Amasis 2.182; Cypriots take part in Persian invasion of Egypt 3.19; made part of Persian Province No. 5 by Darius 3.91; joins Ionian revolt 5.104; attacked by Persia and Phoenicia 5.109; defeated in battle by Persia after desertions 5.113; cities besieged, conquered 5.115–16; takes part in Persian attack on Miletus 6.6; ships and marines in Persian fleet during Xerxes' invasion of Greece 7.90; Cypriots adjudged useless by Artemisia 8.68.

Cypselus *first tyrant of Corinth (r. c. 655–625), son of Eëtion, father of Periander* prophecies preceding birth of; narrowly escapes death as baby; consultation of Delphic oracle, cruelty of rule as tyrant 5.92; treasure house in Corinth 1.14.

Cyrene (Cyrenaeans) *Greek city in N Libya* H. told of visit to Ammon by some men of 2.32; land's fertility 4.199; women's taboo on cows, worship of Isis 4.186; founding by Therans, events leading up to 4.150–58; first kings, influx of settlers 4.149; attacked unsuccessfully by Apries 2.161, 4.159; defeated in battle by Libyans 4.160; alliance with Egypt under Amasis sealed by his marriage to Ladice; receives statue of Aphrodite from her 2.181; calls in Mantinean arbitrator on advice of Delphic oracle; divided into tribes; meagre gifts to Cambyses 3.13; attacked by Arcesilaus; Cyrenaeans flee 4.164; escape attack by Persians sent by Aryandes 4.203; made part of Persian Province No. 6 by Darius 3.91.

Cyrnus (Cyrnians) *modern Corsica* site of Phocaean colony Alalia 1.165; in Carthaginian army in attack on Sicily 7.165.

Cyrus *first King of Persia (r. c. 550–530/529), founder of the Achaemenid Persian empire, son of Cambyses, grandson of Astyages, father of Cambyses* grief at wife's death 2.1; legend concerning his upbringing by a bitch 1.122–3; nickname 3.89; Persians told to prepare for slavery should they move to better land by 9.122; supplies taken to war by 1.188; threatens Greeks after Lacedaemonian warning 1.153;

— *rise to power:* portentous dreams preceding birth of 1.107–8; survives early peril; secretly adopted by Mithridates and Spako 1.108–13; plays king in children's game revealing true identity 1.114–16; sent to Persia by Astyages on advice of Magi; learns truth of birth, meets true parents 1.121–2; grows up to be brave and popular 1.123; receives message from Harpagus concealed in dead hare urging revolt against Media 1.124; proclaims himself head of Persian army, musters troops, hosts feast, leads successful revolt 1.125–8; defeats and captures Astyages 1.73, 128;

— *invasion of Lydia:* fails to incite Ionians to rebel against Croesus; meets Croesus in battle at Pteria 1.76; marches on Sardis; disables Lydian cavalry using camels; besieges Sardis 1.80–81; offers reward to first man over battlements leading to Sardis' capture 1.84–6; places Croesus on pyre, hears of Solon's take on happiness; attempts to extinguish flames 1.86; takes Croesus' advice 1.87–9; angry at Ionian and Aeolian messengers 1.141; renews Croesus' treaty with Milesians 1.141; appoints Tabalus governor of Sardis, Pactyes transporter of Lydian gold before returning to Agbatana 1.153; persuaded by Croesus to spare Lydians after Pactyes' revolt 1.155–6; commands Mazares to deal with Pactyes' revolt 1.156; lays waste to inland Asia 1.177;

— *invasion of Assyria:* sacred horse drowned crossing R. Gyndes; abandons campaign, redirects river 1.189; engages Babylonians in battle; besieges city 1.190; captures Babylon through diversion of Euphrates 1.191;

— *campaign against Massagetans:* launches campaign after Tomyris rejects advances; bridges and fortifies R. Araxes 1.205; persuaded by Croesus to attack Tomyris on Massagetan soil 1.206–8; sends back to Persia Croesus escorted by Cambyses 1.208, Hystaspes following portentous dream concerning Darius 1.209; ambushes drunken Massagetans on advice of Croesus, captures Spargapises; unperturbed by Tomyris' threats 1.211–13; killed in battle; corpse desecrated by Tomyris 1.214.

Cythnos (Cythnians) *island in the W Cyclades* origins; ships at Salamis 8.46; Parians left behind on 8.67.

Cyzicus *Greek city in Mysia on the S shore of Propontis* Aristeas seen on road to 4.14; Festival of Cybele witnessed by Anacharsis 4.76; negotiates surrender to Darius 6.33.

Dadicae *people living in NE of today's Afghanistan* made part of Persian Province No. 7 by Darius 3.91; equipment and commander during Xerxes' invasion of Greece 7.66.

Daphnae *city in NE Egypt* border-post established by Psammetichus 2.30; hosts banquet at which Sesostris' brother attempts to murder Sesostris and his sons 2.107.

Darius *King of Persia (r. 521–486), son of Hystaspes, father of Xerxes* Aryandes executed for sedition on orders of 4.166; Bel-Marduk's statue taken by 1.183; Chorasmian plain flooded by 3.117; Memphis' priests forbid from erecting statue of himself 2.110; name's meaning 6.98; Necos' Red Sea canal completed by 2.158, 3.39; nickname 3.89; Nitocris (1)'s tomb opened by 1.187; Persian judge spared from crucifixion by 7.194; questions Greeks, Callantians on funerary cannibalism 3.38; Scylax sent to explore Asia by 4.44; supplicants 3.117; tribute-storing method 3.96;

— *rise to power:* appears in Cyrus' portentous dream 1.209; member of Cambyses' guard in Egypt; given cloak by Syloson 3.139; joins Otanes (1)'s anti-Magian conspiracy 3.70; urges immediate attack on Smerdis (2) 3.71–3; having learned of Prexaspes' denunciation of Magians, convinces others to attack after portentous bird-on-bird attack 3.76; along with fellow-conspirators, kills Patizeithes and Smerdis (2), informs populace 3.77–9; successfully advocates monarchy in debate with fellow-conspirators 3.82; gains throne through Oebares (1)'s cunning scheme 3.85–7; marries Cyrus' daughters Atossa and Artystone, Smerdis (2) and Otanes (1)'s daughters; instals stone relief 3.88; *early reign:* organizes Persian empire into twenty provinces, fixes rates of tribute 3.89; executes Intaphrenes and kinsmen believing them to have plotted coup; releases Intaphrenes' wife's brother and eldest son 3.119; has Oroetes killed 3.127–9; rewards Democedes after successful treatment of dislocated ankle 3.129–30; persuaded by Atossa to send spies to Greece instead of invading Scythia 3.134; orders Cnidians to effect Gillus' return to Tarentum 3.138; agrees to give Syloson Samos in return for cloak; dispatches task-force under Otanes (1) to effect this 3.140–41;

— *campaign against Babylon:* besieges Babylon after revolt 3.151–3; rebukes Zopyrus for self-mutilation, hears his plan to recapture city 3.155; recaptures Babylon, destroys walls, gates, impales noblemen, reprovides with women 3.159; rewards Zopyrus 3.160;

— *invasion of Scythia:* prepares for invasion, ignores Artabanus' advice 4.83; executes Oeobazus' sons 4.84; inspects Euxine 4.85, Bosporus; erects pillars 4.87; his forces 4.87; sends Ionians to bridge R. Ister, enters Thrace 4.89; erects pillar commending R. Tearus 4.91; conquers Getans, Scyrmiadae, Nipsaei 4.93;

halts dismantling of R. Ister bridge on advice of Coës 4.97–8; invades Scythia, pursues Scythians through neighbouring lands 4.122–5; demands Scythians fight or surrender 4.126; misunderstands Scythian kings' cryptic gifts 4.132; realizes gifts' significance, abandons donkeys and sick troops on advice of Gobryas 4.134–5; arrives at R. Ister, escapes Scythians, returns to Asia 4.141–3;

— *Ionian revolt:* appoints much-admired Megabazus head of Persian forces in Europe 4.143; rewards Histiaeus and Coës 5.11; impressed by Paeonian woman, orders Megabazus to capture and transport Paeonians to him 5.12–14; sends message to Histiaeus recalling him to Sardis 5.24; appoints Artaphrenes (1) governor of Sardis and Otanes (2) general; returns to Susa, taking Histiaeus with him 5.25; approves Persian invasion of Naxos 5.32; learns of Ionian revolt, vows revenge against Athenians 5.105; convinced by Histiaeus, allows him to return to Ionia to put down revolt 5.106–7; esteem for Zanclaean king 6.24; rebukes Artaphrenes (1) after execution of Histiaeus; has Histiaeus' head properly buried 6.30; treats Miltiades (2)'s captured son kindly 6.41; orders Thasos destroy its walls, surrender fleet 6.46;

— *first Persian invasion of Greece:* demands surrender of Greek cities; orders building of ships 6.48; encouraged to invade Athens by Peisistratids; replaces Mardonius with Datis and Artaphrenes (2) 6.94; settles enslaved Eretrians in Cissia 6.119; angry at Athenians after Persian defeat; musters troops 7.1; sons' rivalry 7.2; makes Xerxes heir on advice of Demaratus; dies 7.3–4.

Dascyleum *capital city of Hellespontine Phrygia* governed by Mitrobates 3.120, by Oebares (2) 6.33.

Datis *Median commander of Persian forces* appointed co-leader of campaign against Athens and Eretria by Darius during first Persian invasion of Greece 6.94; musters troops in Cilicia, conquers Naxos, reassures Delians 6.95–7; heads for Eretria, press-ganging islanders en route; subdues Carystus 6.99; captures Eretria 6.101; lands in Attica, heads for Marathon on advice of Hippias 6.102; defeated by Athens and Plataea at Marathon 6.112–13; fails to get to Athens before Athenians; returns to Asia 6.115–16; returns statue of Apollo to Delos 6.118; takes enslaved Eretrians to Susa 6.119.

Deioces *first king of Media, father of Phraortes* quits judiciary with view to taking power 1.95–7; becomes king, demands palace, bodyguards; has Agbatana built 1.98; institutes etiquette system to separate himself from subjects 1.99; legal system; punishment; spies 1.100; death 1.102.

Delos (Delians) *island in the central Cyclades, sacred to Apollo* curse lifted by Peisistratus 1.64; Hyperborean emissaries visit; resultant traditions; continued receipt of Hyperboreans' offerings 4.34–5; Delians flee on approach of Persian fleet under Datis; are reassured 6.97; hit by earthquake portending evils to come 6.98; fail to take statue of Apollo looted by Phoenicians to Delium 6.118; Greek fleet goes to 8.132.

Delphi (Delphians) *city in Phocis, location of important sanctuary and oracle dedicated to Apollo* solicit funds for the rebuilding of temple 2.180; *second*

invasion 7.239; discusses Greek bravery with Xerxes 7.101–4; questioned by Xerxes about Lacedaemonians 7.209; advises Xerxes to capture Cythera; accused of treachery by Achaemenes, defended by Xerxes 7.234–7; advises silence after he and Athenian exile witness portentous Bacchic dust-cloud 8.65.

Demeter *Greek goddess of fertility, especially agricultural; see also* **Isis** gifts of cereal crops 1.193; H. identifies with Egyptian Isis 2.59; Scythian shrine 4.53; *Achaean:* shrine in Athens; its Mysteries 5.61; *Amphictyonic:* shrine in Malis 7.200; *Eleusinian:* shrine in Argiopium 9.57, 101; shrine at Eleusis desecrated by Cleomenes 6.75 Persian desecrators of palace refused entry to 9.65; shrine in Mycale 9.97, 101; *Lawgiver:* temple in Aegina 6.91, in Paros 6.134; Egyptian origins of Thesmophoria; upholding by Arcadians 2.171.

Democedes *Crotoniate doctor, son of Calliphon* rows with father, moves to Aegina, works as doctor 3.131; goes with Polycrates to Magnesia (2), enslaved by Oroetes 3.125; treats Darius' dislocated ankle, handsomely rewarded 3.129–30; saves Egyptian doctors from impalement, frees Elean soothsayer 3.132; cures Atossa's breast cancer 3.133–4; sent to Greece as guide of Persian spies, flees to Croton 3.135–6; protected by Crotoniates; gets engaged to daughter of famous wrestler 3.137.

democracy *literally 'people power'; H. is among the first Greek writers to preserve the term, applying it retrospectively to the regime introduced by the reforms of Cleisthenes (2) at Athens in 508/7 and, questionably, to the regimes instituted by Mardonius in Greek Ionia in 493* Otanes (1) advocates (under name 'isonomia'); Megabyzus compares Otanes' 'isonomia' unfavourably to tyranny 3.81; Cleisthenes (2) institutes in Athens 6.131; Athens flourishes under 5.66, 78, 91; H. criticizes 5.97; Mardonius deposes Ionian tyrants, institutes 6.43.

Didyma *see* **Branchidae**

Dionysius *Phocaean general* makes speech to Ionians before battle of Lade; harsh regime causes Ionians to mutiny 6.11–12; becomes a pirate in Phoenicia, then Sicily 6.17.

Dionysus *Greek god of wine and ritual madness; see also* **Osiris** birth 2.145; Borysthenites worship 4.79; Byzantium's temple of 4.87; Cleisthenes (1) replaces worship of Adrastus with 5.67; H. identifies with Osiris 2.42, 144; Melampous introduces to Greece 2.49; origins 2.146; phallic processions 2.48–9; worshipped by Ethiopians 3.97, Gelonians 4.108, Thracians 5.7, 7.111; youngest of the gods 2.145; *Arabian 'Orotalt':* H. identifies with Dionysus 3.8.

Dioscuri *also known as Tyndaridae, Castor and Pollux (Greek Polydeuces), legendary twin brothers of Helen, sons of Tyndareus* Argonaut status causes Lacedaemonians to welcome Minyans 4.145; Helen rescued from Theseus by 9.73; hosted by father of suitor of Cleisthenes (1)'s daughter 6.127; Lacedaemon takes their images on campaign 5.75; unknown to Egyptians 2.43.

disposal of the dead *specific rites and disposal methods were thought necessary to ensure the soul's successful transition to the afterlife; in H.'s Greece burial was the norm, but cremation was also considered acceptable* Amasis' burial 3.10;

Ephesus (Ephesians) *city in Ionia* dialect 1.142; refuses to celebrate Apatouria 1.147; seized by Croesus in spite of Ephesians' dedication of city to Artemis 1.26; Persians rout Ionians at 5.102; kill Chian troops, believing them to be robbers 6.16.

Epialtes *native of Malis* informs Xerxes about alternative route to Thermopylae; later flees to Thessaly, killed 7.213; guilt affirmed by H. 7.214; tells Hydarnes of Phocians' identity 7.218.

Epidaurus (Epidaurians) *city in the E Peloponnese* origins; restore land's fertility on advice of Delphic oracle using statues crafted from Athenian wood; give offerings to Athens in return 5.82; cease offerings after statues are stolen by Aeginetans 5.83–4; captured by Periander 3.52; ships before battle of Artemisium 8.1, at Salamis 8.43; rallies to defence of Peloponnese at Isthmus of Corinth 8.72; troops in Greek army at Plataea 9.28, 31.

Eretria (Eretrians) *city on Euboea* origins 8.46; Peisistratus' base during exile from Athens 1.61–2; ships join Ionian revolt, repaying debt to Milesians 5.99; alarmed by approaching Persian fleet, asks Athens for aid; muddled strategy 6.100; betrayed by eminent Eretrians, captured by Persia 6.101; Darius enslaves, settles in Cissia 6.119; ships before battle of Artemisium 8.1, at Salamis 8.46; troops at Plataea 9.28, 31.

Erythrae (1) (Erythraeans) *city in Ionia* dialect 1.142; war with Chios 1.18; ships in the Ionian fleet at battle of Lade 6.8.

Erythrae (2) (Erythraeans) *city in Boeotia* Persians camp at before Plataea 9.15; Lacedaemonians learn of Persian presence 9.19; Athenians fight Persians 9.22; Plataea's territory better than 9.25.

Ethiopia *land S of Egypt* circumcision 2.104; gold, elephants, flora, ebony 3.114; invasion of Egypt under Sabacos 2.137, 139; conquered by Cambyses; annual gift to Darius 3.97; equipment and commander during Xerxes' invasion of Greece 7.69; troops at Plataea 9.32; *peoples:* handsomeness 3.114; cave-dwelling Ethiopians, their speed, diet, language 4.183; Ethiopians of Asia, made part of Persian Province No. 17 by Darius 3.94, equipment and commander during Xerxes' invasion of Greece 7.70; long-lived Ethiopians, their height, handsomeness, method of choosing kings 3.20, longevity, diet, funerary customs 3.23–4, 'Table of the Sun' 3.18, king recognizes Fish-Eater emissaries as spies, rebukes Cambyses, dismisses all gifts with exception of wine, discusses longevity, diet 3.21–3.

Etruria *see* **Tyrrhenia**

Euboea (Euboeans) *large island off the E coast of Boeotia and Attica* role in delivery of Hyperboreans' gifts to Delos 4.33; said by Aristagoras to be easy to seize 5.31; Greek look-outs on heights of 7.183, 192; bribe Themistocles to remain at Artemisium and fight Persians 8.4–5; part of Persian fleet wrecked off 8.13; flocks killed by Greeks after Euboeans fail to heed Bacis 8.19–20.

Euelthon *king of Salamis (2)* refuses to give Pheretime military backing for attack on Barca; annoyed, gives her golden spinning implements 4.162.

Euenius *Apollonian seer* blinded after failing to look after sacred sheep, receives gift of second sight after reparations paid by Apollonians 9.93–4.

Euphrates *Assyrian river, flowing from Armenia through today's Syria and Iraq before joining the R. Tigris* course 1.179; redirected and fortified by Nitocris (1) 1.185; diverted by Cyrus in order to capture Babylon 1.191.

Europa *Phoenician princess, mother of Minos and Sarpedon* kidnapped by Greeks in revenge for kidnap of Io 1.2.

Europe *one of the three continents recognized by H., along with Libya and Asia* gold of northern extremities 3.116; lions 7.126; Mardonius talks up 6.5; mysteries 4.45; name 4.45; R. Ister in relation to 2.33, 4.49; size 4.42, 45; western extremities, purported rivers, islands 3.115.

Euryanax *Lacedaemonian royal, son of Dorieus* junior commander of Lacedaemonian army sent to Athens after Mardonius' invasion 9.10; infuriated by Amompharetus' refusal to obey orders 9.53.

Eurybates *Argive commander and pentathlete* survives war with Athens over Aegina 6.92; later killed in single combat with Sophanes 6.92, 9.75.

Eurybiadas *Lacedaemonian commander* made supreme commander of Greek fleet after Greeks refuse to serve under Athenian 8.2; plans to flee Artemisium before being bribed by Themistocles 8.4–5; commands Greek fleet at Salamis (1) 8.42; fears Athenians will desert; persuaded by Themistocles to meet Persian fleet off Salamis (1) 8.58–63; argues that Greeks should not break up Hellespont bridges 8.108; honoured with olive wreath on return to Lacedaemon 8.124.

Eurytus *Lacedaemonian warrior* discharged from Lacedaemonian force prior to Thermopylae due to eye condition, orders helot to lead him into battle, dies 7.229.

Euxine Sea *today's Black Sea* geography, size 4.85–6; stupidity of its peoples 4.46; surrounding lands 4.99; ships sailing out of subject to Histiaeus' piracy 6.5, 26; Greek inhabitants contribute ships to Xerxes 7.95.

Fish-Eaters *Ethiopian people living in Elephantine (today's Aswan), S Egypt* sent by Cambyses to spy on Ethiopia under pretence of diplomacy, recognized as spies 3.20–21.

funeral, burial customs *see* disposal of the dead

Gandarians *people living in E of today's Afghanistan* made part of Persian Province No. 7 by Darius 3.91; equipment and commander during Xerxes' invasion of Greece 7.66.

Gela *Greek city on the S coast of Sicily* colonization 7.153; tyrant Hippocrates betrays Zanclaean allies, imprisons Zancle's king, delivers city to Samians 6.23.

Gelon *tyrant of Gela (r. c. 491–485), son of Deinomenes* lineage 7.153; resources 7.145; bravery in bodyguard of Gela's tyrant; seizes Gela; takes control of Syracuse 7.154–5; consolidates power; sells Megarian civilians into slavery 7.156; refuses to join Greece against Xerxes after envoys reject his demands to lead fleet or army; sends money-laden ship to Delphi in case of Persian victory

7.157–63; said to have been prevented from joining up due to Carthaginian invasion 7.165–6.

Gelonus (Gelonians) *city in Boudinian territory, perhaps in NE of today's Ukraine* crops, diet 4.109; Greek-style shrines, Festival of Dionysus, Greek origins 4.108; allies with Scythians against Darius and Persians 4.119.

Gephyraeans *Athenian family* Phoenician origins; expelled from Boeotia; settle in Athens, retain own rites 5.57–8, 5.61; Hipparchus killed by two scions of 5.55–6.

Getans *Thracian people living W of Euxine (today's Black) Sea in today's Romania and Bulgaria* belief in own immortality; god Salmoxis, his origins; human sacrifice 4.94–6; enslaved by Darius 4.93, 96.

Gobryas *Persian nobleman* joins Otanes (1)'s anti-Magian conspiracy 3.70; convinced by Darius, urges immediate attack on Smerdis (2) 3.73; with fellow-conspirators, kills Patizeithes and Smerdis (2), informs populace 3.77–9; correctly understands Scythian kings' cryptic gifts 4.132.

gold *rare in Greece, where it was mined on the Aegean islands of Siphnos and Thasos; Asia Minor had larger resources, for example that panned in the R. Pactolus at Sardis* Aeginetans offer Delphic oracle 8.122; Agathyrsians gold rich 4.104; Agbatana's wall 1.98; Amasis sends Apries' daughter to Cambyses after adorning her 3.1; Amasis' foot-bath 2.172; Argive women cease to wear until Thyreae is reclaimed 1.82; Arimaspians steal from griffins 3.116; Artabazus advises bribing Greeks 9.41; Artaÿnte rejects Xerxes' offer 9.109; Artemis' sword 8.77; Asia Minor gold rich according to Miltiades (2) 6.132; Bel-Marduk's temple, Babylon, artefacts 1.181, 183; Boges destroys Eion's 7.107; Cambyses sends Ethiopians necklace 3.20; Carthaginians trade with Libyans 4.196; Cleomenes rejects Maeandrius' offer of goblets 3.148; concubine adorns herself and maids 9.76; Croesus burns couches, bowls in propitiation of Apollo, sends to Delphi, sends shield, spear to oracle of Amphiaraus 1.50–52, gives to Delphians 1.54, to Lacedaemonians 1.69, to Alcmaeon 6.125, tripod at Thebes (1), cows at Ephesus 1.92; Cyrauis islanders method of collecting 4.195; Cyrus adorned as a baby 1.111; Darius presents Democedes with fetters; rewards him with 3.130, strikes coins 4.166; Darius' statue of wife 7.69; Egyptian kings make offerings using bowls 2.151; Egyptian sacred crocodile 2.69; Elaeous' tomb of Protesilaus contains bowls 9.116; Ethiopia gold rich 3.114; Ethiopians two-yearly contribution to Persia 3.97; gold-dust washes down from Mt Tmolus, Lydia 1.93, 5.101; griffins guard 3.116, 4.13, 27; Gyges offers Delphic oracle 1.14; helots sell to Aeginetans 9.80; Heracles' cup 4.10; Heracles' Phoenician shrine's pillar 2.44; India gold rich 3.106; Indians contribute yearly tribute of gold-dust to Persia 3.94, 98, steal from giant ants 3.102–5; long-lived Ethiopians make shackles 3.23; Lydians first to strike coins 1.94; Magnesian (1) salvages Persian 7.190; Mardonius' furnishings 9.82; Masistius' breastplate 9.22, horse's tack 9.20; Massagetan territory gold rich; uses 1.215; mine at Datum 9.75, at Mt Pangaeum 7.112, at Scapte Hyle 6.46, on Siphnos 3.57, on Thasos 6.46–7; Mycerinus buries his daughter in wooden cow sheathed with 2.129–32; Northern Europe gold rich 3.116; Oroetes fools Maeandrius with fake display 3.123; Pactyes defects with Croesus' gold 1.153–4; Papremis' cult-statue's shrine 2.63; Persian empire gold rich according to Aristagoras 5.49; Persian furnishings 9.80, gold apportioned out among Greeks after Plataea 9.81, Immortals wear much 7.83, spears adorned with 7.41, taxes paid in Euboïc talents of 3.89; Pheretime given spinning tools 4.163; Plataeans discover 9.83; Polycrates alleged to have paid off Lacedaemonians with gilded leaden coins 3.56, discards signet-ring 3.41; Pythius' 7.27–8; Rhampsinitus returns from Hades with head-dress 2.122; Samians steal linen breastplate embroidered with 3.47; Scythian kings buried with cups 4.71; Scythian sacred 4.5, 7; silver less valuable than 3.95; statue of Alexander 8.121; Syloson rejects Darius' offer 2.140; Thasians' tableware 7.119; touchstone used to test 7.10; tripod atop serpent column at Delphi 9.81; Xerxes adorns tree with 7.31; Xerxes' awning 7.100; Xerxes gives to Abderites 8.120, gives helmsman crown of 8.118, offers Hellespont bowl 7.54.

Gorgo *Lacedaemonian princess, daughter of Cleomenes* only child 5.48; convinces Cleomenes not to aid Aristagoras 5.51; works out Demaratus' secret message 7.239.

Gorgus *king of Salamis (2), brother of Onesilus* deposed by Onesilus, flees to Persia 5.104; restored after Persian victory over Cyprus 5.115.

Greece (Greeks) *the entire Greek world (H.'s Hellas): as well as occupying much of modern Greece, Greek peoples had also established extensive colonies throughout the Mediterranean and Euxine (today's Black) Sea; these territories by no means constituted a coherent nation-state* Amasis' admiration for 2.178; Amazons captured by, kill 4.110; Cleisthenes (1) holds contest to identify best man in 6.126–30; dependency on rainfall for water; dangers thereof 2.13; Egyptian views on 2.13; Europa and Medea kidnapped by, refuse to return Medea 1.2; former weakness 1.143; geography skills criticized by H. 2.16–17; geometry learned from Babylonians 2.109; in Scythia 4.17–18, 24, 51; intellectuals make for Lydia 1.29; intelligence and scepticism 1.60; language 1.58; linen, names for 2.105; Psammetichus according to 2.2; residents of Egypt contribute money towards rebuilding of Delphi's temple 2.180; Thracian god Salmoxis, according to 4.95; Trojan War accounts disputed by Egyptian priests 2.118; war with Troy 1.3–4; warfare according to Mardonius 7.9; writing and calculation compared to Egyptian 2.36; alphabetic writing learned from Phoenicians 5.58; *customs and religion:* armour use learned from Egyptians 4.180; calendar 2.4; Carian innovations adopted by 1.171; customs learned from Egyptians, Pelasgians 2.49–52; diet 1.133; Dionysus' worship learned from Melampous 2.49; etiquette compared to Egyptian 2.80; fondness for games 1.94; gods learned about only recently 2.53, represented in human form 1.131, 2.53, Egyptian origins 2.4, 49–50, 58, 145–6; Heracles compared to Egyptian, Phoenician 2.43–5; Linus song 2.79; manual crafts, contempt for 2.167; monogamy 2.92; paedophilia 1.135; reincarnation, belief in 2.123; rituals, chariot techniques learned from Libyans 4.189; sanctuaries kept pure 2.64; slaves, former lack of 6.137;

— *early relations with Croesus and Persia:* origins of Persian hostility towards Greece 1.1–5; Croesus establishes close relations 1.6, conquers Greeks of Asia 1.27, investigates political scene 1.56; Cyrus mocks public spaces, threatens 1.153; Darius quizzes Greeks on funerary cannibalism 3.38, urged by Atossa to invade 3.134, sends spies 3.135–8, sends heralds demanding surrender 6.48–9;

— *second Persian invasion: Xerxes' campaign:* vows to force surrendering Greek states to pay tributes to Delphi once Xerxes defeated 7.132; lack of consensus as to how to respond to invasion 7.138; free states swap pledges, declare truces, send spies to Sardis, messengers to Argos and colonies 7.145; spies detected, tortured, taken to Xerxes; given guided tour of his forces, sent home 7.146–8; fails to win alliance of Gelon after envoys reject his leadership demands 7.157–63, of Corcyra and Crete 7.168–9; sends force to guard Tempe pass on Thessalians' urging; returns to Isthmus of Corinth on Alexander's advice 7.172–3; decides to make stand at Thermopylae; sends fleet to Artemisium 7.175, 177; told by Delphians to propitiate winds 7.178; three ships lost to Persian fleet at Sciathos 7.179–82; alarmed fleet moves from Artemisium to Chalcis 7.183; forces at Chalcis learn of wrecking of Persian fleet, pray to Poseidon, return to Artemisium 7.192; captures errant Persian ships, interrogates their generals 1.194–5; *battle of Thermopylae:* forces at Thermopylae 7.202–3, terrified at Persian approach, debate fleeing, but stay on account of Leonidas 7.207, hold out in face of attack by Medes, Cissians, Immortals 7.210–12, betrayed by Epialtes 7.213; warned by soothsayer of Persian approach; some Greeks flee or are sent home by Leonidas, others stay 7.219–20; forces initially repel Persians before being overcome 7.223–5; bravery; memorial inscription 7.226–8; betrayed by Thebans (1) 7.233; *battle of Artemisium:* fleet before battle; Eurybiadas supreme commander after allies refuse to serve under Athenian 8.1–3; plans to flee after seeing Persian force, prevented by Euboeans' and Themistocles' bribery 8.4–5; told by Scyllias the diver about wreck of Persian fleet, its plan of attack; fleet sails out to test Persians 8.8–9, captures thirty Persian ships, returns to Artemisium 8.11, reinforced by Athenian ships; learns of Persian wreck, destroys Cilician squadron 8.14, attacked by Persians, battle of Artemisium taking place at same time as Thermopylae; comes off better 8.15–16; Athenians its best fighters 8.17; commanders debate withdrawing to mainland 8.18; fleet withdraws after learning of Leonidas' defeat at Thermopylae 8.21; *battle of Salamis:* fleet docks at Salamis (1) to evacuate Athenian women and children; reinforced by new ships 8.42; fleet before battle 8.43–8; commanders hold council of war, plan to meet Persians at Isthmus of Corinth, before learning of Xerxes' arrival in Attica 8.49–50; some commanders flee; Themistocles persuades rest to remain at Salamis (1); prayers and preparations 8.56–64; commanders argue over whether to withdraw to Peloponnese 8.74, 79, persuaded of Persian encirclement by Aristeides, Tenian deserters 8.81–2; marines exhorted to choose what is better by Themistocles; fleet meets Persians in battle; marines upbraided by ghostly voice 8.83–4; fleet's battle order; ships captured by Ionians 8.85; good organization sees Greece have the better of the Persians 8.86; mariners survive sinking due to ability to swim 8.89; best commanders 8.93; fleet pursues Persians as far as Andros, holds war-council 8.108, besieges Andros after Themistocles' blackmail 8.111, sacks Carystus, returns to Salamis (1); dedicates triremes at Isthmus of Corinth, Sunium and Salamis (1), sends offerings to Delphi 8.121; commanders vote for most valorous among them; jealous after Themistocles wins, return to their respective homes 8.123–4;

— *second Persian invasion: Mardonius' campaign:* fleet assembles at Aegina 8.131, urged by Chian conspirators to liberate Ionia, gets as far as Delos 8.132; *battle of Plataea:* army's base on foothills of Mt Cithaeron 9.19, attacked by Persian cavalry 9.20, parades corpse of Masistius, heads for Plataea 9.25; army's battle-order, numbers before battle 9.28–30; told to stay on defensive by sacrificial omens 9.36; supplies seized by Persians on Mt Cithaeron 9.39; army harried by Persian cavalry 9.40, attacked by Persian cavalry, water-source destroyed; provisions exhausted, reinforcements cut off 9.49–50; commanders decide to withdraw to 'island' outside Plataea, attempt rescue of attendants trapped on Cithaeron 9.51; continually harassed by Persian cavalry, majority of army flees to Plataea instead 9.52; Greek allies of Persians fight deliberately badly 9.67; forces stationed by Shrine of Hera (those who had fled to Plataea in 9.52) learn of Pausanias' victory, attempt disorganized attack; routed by Theban (1) cavalry 9.69; forces dedicate spoils to Apollo at Delphi, Zeus at Olympia, Poseidon at Isthmus of Corinth, portion rest out among themselves after victory 9.81, bury dead 9.85; army besieges Thebes (1) demanding surrender of collaborators 9.86–8; *battle of Mycale:* fleet at Delos urged by rebel Samians to overthrow Persian-installed governor 9.90–91, sets off after favourable sacrificial omens 9.92, heads for Mycale after flight of Persian fleet 9.98; Greeks land at Mycale and get ready for battle; learn of victory at Plataea on same day; advance on Persians 9.99–100; sustain high casualties 9.103; torch Persian ships, sail to Samos; debate evacuation of Ionians; sail to Hellespont 9.106; fleet finds Hellespont bridges destroyed; separates 9.114.

Gyges *king of Lydia, formerly Candaules' bodyguard, son of Dascylus* persuaded by Candaules to observe latter's wife naked 1.8–10; offered choice by wife of Candaules; kills Candaules, marries wife, becomes king 1.11–12; approved as king by Delphic oracle; offers gifts to Delphic oracle; conquests 1.13–15.

Gyndes *Assyrian river* course; flow altered by Cyrus after sacred horse is drowned 1.189.

Halicarnassus (Halicarnassians) *Dorian city in Caria* banned from using Triopium after Halicarnassian steals tripod 1.144; role in Hellenium's founding 2.178; Troezenian origins of; commanded by Artemisia during second Persian invasion of Greece 7.99.

Halys *river of Asia Minor* course 1.6, 72; Median empire's western limit 1.130; pass, guard house 5.52; Thales possibly redirects; Croesus crosses 1.75; Xerxes' army crosses 7.26.

Hamilcar *king of Carthage, son of Hanno* leads attack on Sicily, defeated by Gelon; disappears, perhaps due to self-immolation 7.165–7.

Harpagus *Median nobleman, kinsman of Astyages* fails to kill Cyrus as commanded by Astyages; instructs Mithridates to kill Cyrus 1.108–10; brought before Astyages, learns that Cyrus lives 1.117–18; sends son to Astyages, unknowingly eats son's flesh, learns truth 1.119; gives Cyrus gifts with a view to getting revenge on Astyages, foments revolt in Media; sends Cyrus message concealed in dead hare 1.123; leads Median army against Persia, defects; gloats over captured Astyages, is rebuked 1.129; suggests use of camels in Cyrus' war with Croesus 1.80; takes over task-force on death of Mazares, captures Ionian cities through siege warfare 1.162; besieges Phocaea, captures city but not Phocaeans 1.164; besieges Teus 1.168; lays waste Asia Minor coast with help of Ionians and Aeolians 1.171, 174–6.

Hecataeus *Milesian mythographer and ethnographer* called 'story-teller' by H. 5.36, 125; on Athenian expulsion of Pelasgians 6.137; study of genealogy, visit to Thebes (2) 2.143; urges caution before Ionian revolt 5.36; advises Aristagoras to lie low on Leros 5.125.

Hegesistratus *Elean soothsayer in the employ of Persia* imprisoned by Lacedaemonians; mutilates foot, escapes; later captured by Lacedaemonians and executed; carries out sacrifices before Plataea, urges caution 9.37–8; interpretations ignored by Mardonius 9.41.

Helen *legendary princess of Lacedaemon, daughter of Tyndareus, sister of the Dioscuri, wife of Menelaus* rescued from Decelea by Dioscuri after being kidnapped by Theseus 9.73; kidnapped by Paris 1.3; shrine at Memphis 2.112; with Proteus after arrest and imprisonment of Paris 2.115–16.

Heliopolis *city in the Nile Delta* H. visits; scholars the wisest in Egypt 2.3; Festival of the Sun 2.59, 63.

Hellenes *ancient and current name for the Greek people* ancestors of Macedonians, Dorians and Lacedaemonians 1.56, wanderings; language 1.58; Greekness defined 8.144.

Hellenium *Panhellenic sanctuary at Naucratis, Egypt* institution in the reign of Amasis, administration 2.178.

Hellespont *strait (modern Dardanelles) connecting today's Sea of Marmara with the Aegean* geography 4.85; inhabitants of its Asian coast made part of Persian Province No. 3 by Darius 3.90; tyrants in the Ionian forces during Darius' invasion of Scythia 4.138; cities of its European coast conquered by Megabazus 4.144; cities captured by Ionians 5.103; cities sacked by Persian army under Daurises 5.117; Aeolian inhabitants conquered by Persian army under Hymaeës 5.122; cities razed by Phoenician fleet 6.33; bridged in preparation for Xerxes' invasion of Greece; bridges destroyed by storm 7.33–4; Xerxes orders its physical and verbal chastisement 7.35; re-bridged with boats 7.36; offered gifts by Xerxes 7.54; inhabitants' ships and marines in Persian fleet during Xerxes' invasion of Greece 7.95.

helots *hereditary, serf-like Greek subject-people of Lacedaemon (Laconia and Messenia)* role in Lacedaemonian mourning 6.58; helot guard intimidated by Cleomenes into giving him dagger 6.75; prepare Argive sacred grove for burning; flog its priest 6.80–81; Eurytus' helot leads him into battle at Thermopylae 7.229; dead displayed by Xerxes after Thermopylae 8.25; seven per Lacedaemonian warrior at Plataea 9.10, 28; ordered by Pausanias to collect Persian valuables; sell gold cheaply to Aeginetans 9.80; buried separately from Lacedaemonian warriors and priests in aftermath of Plataea 9.85.

Hephaestus *Greek god of fire and craftsmanship; see also* **Ptah** Greeks honour with torch-races 8.98.

Hera *Greek goddess of women and marriage, sister-wife of Zeus* Amasis offers two wooden statues of himself to Samos' temple 2.182; Argive temple 1.31; Cleomenes offers blood sacrifice 6.81–2; Maeandrius dedicates Polycrates' furnishing 3.123; Mandrocles dedicates painting 4.88; Naucratis' Samian-built temple 2.178; Pausanias invokes 9.61; Periander strips Corinthian women at shrine 5.92; Plataea's sanctuary 9.52; Samian sanctuary 3.60, 9.96; Samians dedicate bowl 4.152; Samians offer Croesus' bowl 1.70; unknown to Egyptians 2.50.

Heracles *legendary hero of Twelve Labours fame, son of Zeus and Alcmene, worshipped as a god in Egypt and elsewhere* abandoned by Jason at Aphetae 7.193; birth 2.145; footprint at R. Tyras 4.82; Geryon's cattle stolen by; journeys to Scythia, loses cattle, fathers Scythes 4.8–11; Lydia ruled by descendants 1.7; myth of his slaughter of Egyptians 2.45; origins 2.43, 146; R. Dyras aids 7.198; worshipped in Egypt, Tyre and Thasos 2.43–4.

Hermione (Hermioneans) *city in E Peloponnese* origins 8.43; Hermionean island of Hydrea seized by Samian dissidents 3.59; ships at Salamis 8.43; rallies to defence of Peloponnese at Isthmus of Corinth 8.72; troops at Plataea 9.28, 31.

Hermotimus *Pedasan eunuch* bought and castrated by Panionius, sent to Susa; becomes Xerxes' favourite eunuch; later forces Panionius to castrate his sons, forces sons to castrate Panionius 8.105–6; sent to Ephesus with Artemisia in charge of Xerxes' children 8.103–4.

Hermus *Lydian river (modern Gediz)* source, course, tributaries 1.80.

Herodotus *Halicarnassian historian (c. 484–c. 425)* aims 1.0; digression 4.30; historical method 2.99, 123, 142, 147, 7.152;

— *calculates:* distance between Mediterranean and Susa 5.54; size of Egypt 2.6–9, Euxine 4.85–6, Greek forces in Persian army before Plataea 9.32, Lake Moeris 2.149, Scythia 4.101, Xerxes' force before Salamis 8.66, before Thermopylae 7.184–7; tribute levied by Persian empire under Darius 3.95;

— *compares:* Egypt and various gulfs 2.10; Lacedaemonian kings to Egyptians, Persians 6.58–60; Nile and various rivers 2.10; Scythia to Attica, Iapygia 4.99;

— *discreet about:* Delphian sycophant who added inscription of Croesus' basin in Corinthian treasury at Delphi 1.51; Babylon's fertility, due to scepticism of audience 1.193; Egyptian god to whom mummification is sacred 2.86, god's ritual 2.132, Mysteries 2.171, relationship with pigs 2.47, take on divinity 2.3; Greek adherents to reincarnation 2.123; Samian who came into Sataspes' money 4.43; Thesmophoria 2.171;

— *dubious about:* Abderite claims of close friendship with Xerxes 8.120; Aeginetan statues' transformation 5.86; Alcmaeonid treachery at Marathon 6.121, 123–4; Argippaei's story of goat-footed men 4.25; Carystian betraying Greeks before Thermopylae 7.214; Cassandane's hatred for Egyptian concubine inspiring Cambyses' invasion of Egypt 3.3; claims that copulation in sanctuaries is fine as animals do likewise 2.64; Europe's extremities 3.115; first-born Scythian's parentage 4.5; genealogy 2.143; Hyperboreans' existence 4.32, 36; Ister's bees 5.10; Neurian lycanthropy 4.105; Phoenician circumnavigation of Libya 4.42; phoenix's life-cycle 2.73; Rhampsinitus' pimping of own daughter 2.121; Salmoxis' slave origins 4.95–6; Scyllias the diver's underwater swim 8.8; Xerxes' throwing overboard of Persian nobles 8.119;

— *considers miraculous:* Gela's capture by effeminate priest 7.153; Persians killed by tidal wave 8.129, outside shrine of Demeter at Argiopium 9.65; Theban (1) oracle's use of Carian in addressing Mardonius' envoy 8.135;

— *investigates:* Arabian mountains 2.8; Ascalon's plunder 1.105; Cyrus' origins 1.95; flying snakes of Arabia 2.75; Gephyraeans' origins 5.57; Heracles' cult in Thasos and Tyre 2.44; Ister's northern reaches 5.9; labyrinth at City of the Crocodiles 2.148; Lake Moeris 2.149–50; Nile's flooding, breezes 2.19–27, source 2.28–34; Persian and Egyptian skulls 3.12; Persian customs 1.131–40; Plataea's bogus tombs 9.85; pyramids 2.124–7; Thermopylae, names of the three hundred at 7.224;

— *opinions:* Aristeides best man in Athens 8.79; Cleisthenes (2)'s policies copied from Cleisthenes (1) 5.67; Croesus first foreigner to harm Greek interests 1.5; Deioces' supporters dominated during crimewave debate 1.97; Democedes' marriage way of proving himself to Darius 3.137; good fortune is fleeting 1.5; Homer not author of *Cypria* 2.117; Ionian sky's blue most beautiful 1.142; Lacedaemon sent ships during Ionian revolt to spy on Cyrus and Ionia 1.152; Masistes would have raised revolt against Xerxes had he made it to Bactria 9.113; Peisistratus' trick harebrained 1.60; Scythian nomadism admirable 4.46; on Trojan War 2.120; *Babylon:* coracles amazing 1.194; division by R. Euphrates annoying 1.186; wife-auctions and medical system clever 1.196–7; *Egypt:* calendar more sophisticated than Greece's 2.4; Egyptians have been making sea-voyages for a long time 2.43; Nile would silt up Arabian Gulf if it changed course 2.11; once had a gulf 2.10; *Persian invasions of Greece:* Aristodemus bravest at Plataea 9.71; Athens saved Greece during second Persian invasion 7.139; Epialtes was indeed betrayer of Greece at Thermopylae 7.214; Eurybiadas changed his mind about battle of Salamis because he wanted to keep Athenians on side 8.63; Lacedaemonians best at Plataea 9.71; Leonidas did indeed dispatch Greeks from Thermopylae 7.220–21; Peloponnese neutrality equated to collaboration 8.73; Isthmus wall would have proven ineffective during second Persian invasion 7.139; Phocians sided with Greeks because Thessalians sided with Persians 8.30; Scyllias the diver got to Artemisium by boat 8.8; Xerxes' lack of confidence such that he would have returned to Persia even if advised to stay in Greece 8.103, reasons for digging of Athos canal 7.24;

— *named informants:* Archias of Pitana, on grandfather's heroism at Samos 3.55; Thersander of Orchomenus, on weeping Persian at Theban (1) banquet 9.16; Tymnes, steward of Ariapeithes, on Scythian royal family 4.76;

— *theories about:* Aphrodite the Foreigner 2.112; Athena's clothing's origins 4.189; Battus' real name 4.155; circumcision 2.104; creatures' birth-rates 3.108; Dionysus 2.146, his introduction to Greece 2.49; Dodonaean oracle's founding 2.56–7; Egypt's scale 2.15–18; Greeks' adoption of phallus-adorned Hermes statues 2.51; Ister's steady flow 4.50; legendary poets 2.53; Nile's fish, seemingly spontaneous generation of 2.93, flooding 2.24–6, lack of breezes 2.27, source 2.28; origins of Colchians 2.104–5, Greek armour 4.180, Greek gods 2.43, 49–50, Greek rituals 4.189, Greek writing 5.58–61, Macedonians 5.22; Persian religion 1.131; Rhodopis 2.134–5; Scythian 'feathers' meaning 4.31;

— *visits:* Arabia 2.75; Cyzicus 4.14; Dodona 2.52; Egypt: 2.3, 12, 29, 148, 3.12; Lacedaemon 3.55; Proconnesus 4.14; Scythia 4.81–2; Thasos 2.44, 6.46; Tyre 2.44; Zacynthos 4.195.

Hipparchus *Athenian of Peisistratid tyrant family (d. 514), son of Peisistratus, younger brother of Hippias* role in murder of Cimon, father of Miltiades (2) 6.103; exiles Onomacritus from Athens for doctoring oracles 7.6; assassination by Gephyraeans preceded by portentous dream 5.55–6.

Hippias *tyrant of Athens (r. 527–510), son of Peisistratus, brother of Hipparchus* role in murder of Cimon, father of Miltiades (2) 6.103; advises father to become tyrant again 1.61; retains power after assassination of Hipparchus in spite of Alcmaeonid plotting 5.62; calls on Thessalian cavalry, clears Phalerum's plain of trees, repels Lacedaemonian attack 5.63; besieged by Lacedaemonians; exiled to Sigeium after capture of Peisistratid children 5.64–5; summoned to Lacedaemon with view to his restoration to Athens as tyrant 5.91; fails to convince Lacedaemonians to restore him 5.93; returns to Sigeium 5.94; urges Artaphrenes (1) to attack Athens 5.96; advises Persian forces to head to Marathon 6.102; portentous dream of sleeping with his mother fulfilled 6.107.

Hippocleides *Athenian nobleman, son of Tisander* drunkenly dances away his marriage to Cleisthenes (1)'s daughter before uttering famous phrase 6.127–9.

Histiaea *city in N Euboea near Artemisium* Histiaean tells Persians of Greek withdrawal; seized by Persians 8.23.

Histiaeus *tyrant of Miletus (c. 515–493), cousin and father-in-law of Aristagoras; depicted by H. as the instigator of the Ionian revolt* convinces Ionians not to dismantle Ister bridge during Darius' campaign against Scythia 4.137; given city in Edonia by Darius in reward 5.11; *Ionian revolt:* his fortification of city reported to Darius 5.23; taken to Susa by Darius 5.25; sends tattooed messenger to Aristagoras urging revolt 5.35; convinces Darius to let him return to Ionia to put down revolt 5.106–7; returns to Sardis, flees to Chios after being accused by Artaphrenes (1) of being behind Ionian revolt 6.1–2; lies to Ionians about reasons for his fomentation of revolt 6.3; betrayed by messenger, his scheming discovered by Artaphrenes (1) 6.4; rebuffed by Milesians, sets himself up as pirate using Mytilenaean ships 6.5; learns of Ionian defeat at Miletus, conquers Chios 6.26–7; besieges Thasos before learning of Phoenician advance 6.28; captured by Persians, his army wiped out, after crossing to mainland to harvest crops 6.28–9; executed by Artaphrenes (1), his embalmed head sent to Darius 6.30.

Homer *legendary poet, the traditional author of the* Iliad *and the* Odyssey: aware of Paris' visit to Egypt 2.116; cited by Athenian envoy in praise of Athenian command 7.161; Cleisthenes (1) bans recitations of poems 5.67; first, along with Hesiod, to codify Greek theology 2.53; H. refutes supposed authorship of the *Cypria* 2.117; Hyperboreans discussed in the *Epigoni* 4.32; introduces concept of R. Oceanus 2.23; lambs' horns discussed in the *Odyssey* 4.29.

horses *mounted warfare had become common by H.'s time, but it was far from a Greek speciality: among Greek states only Boeotia and Thessaly had the resources to maintain large cavalry units; in Asia Minor the Lydians were noted for their horsemanship; see also* **chariots** Ahura Mazda's chariot pulled by sacred white 7.40; Artybius' horse trained to rear up in battle 5.111–12; camels frighten 1.80, 7.87; camels just as fast as 3.102, 7.86; cavalry of Xerxes' forces during second Persian invasion of Greece 7.84–7; Cilicians contribute to Persia each year 3.90; Cimon's three-time Olympic-winning horses buried opposite him 6.103; Darius orders building of horse transport-ships 6.48, 7.1, twists ankle dismounting horse 3.129; Darius' horse honoured in stone relief 3.88; Egyptian canals make country impassable to 2.108; Ethiopians wear horse-scalp head-dresses 7.70; Greek horsemanship derided by Croesus 1.27; horse-fight organized by Paeonians and Perinthians 5.1; Iyrcae train horses to lie flat while hunting 4.22; Lydians skilled horsemen 1.79; Magi sacrifice to R. Strymon 7.113; Mardonius' eat from bronze manger 9.70; Massagetan tack made from bronze and gold 1.215; Massagetans sacrifice to sun god 1.216; Nisaean horse of Masistius 9.20; Nisaean bigger than giant Indian horses 3.106; Nisaean in Xerxes' army 7.40; Otanes (1)'s anti-Magian conspirators choose king of Persia by seeing whose horse neighs first 3.84–7; Pausanias receives ten after victory at Plataea 9.81; Persian horses shorn after death of Masistius 9.24; Persian postal system uses horse-relays 8.98; Persians roast horses and donkeys at feasts 1.133; Persians teach horse-riding to boys 1.136; Pharnouches' horse killed after throwing him 7.88; Phocian booby-traps break Thessalian horses' legs 8.28; private herds belonging to Babylon's governor

1.192; sacred horse belonging to Cyrus killed in R. Gyndes 1.189; Scythian horses seized by Amazons in attack on Scythia 4.110; Scythian horses withstand winter unlike mules and donkeys 4.28; Scythian horses' fear of donkeys and mules 4.129; Scythian sacrifice 4.61–2, 72; Scythian wild 4.52; Scythians bury with their kings; later sacrifice on his behalf 4.71–2; Scythians practise archery from horseback 4.46; Sigynnae horses small, long-haired, fast 5.9; snakes eaten by horses portending Croesus' fall 1.78; Thessalian horses pitted against Persian by Xerxes 7.196; Thracians living on Lake Prasias feed fish to 5.16; Xerxes dismisses portentous birth of freakish foals 7.57–8; *donkeys:* Arabs use donkey corpses to obtain cinnamon from giant birds 3.111; Armenia-to-Babylon shipping industry employs 1.194; Cleisthenes (1) renames Sicyonian tribe 'Donkey Men' 5.68; Elean mares impregnated by neighbouring 4.30; Libya's horned and non-drinking 4.191–2; Persians trick Scythians using 4.134–5; Rhampsinitus burgled by clever thief using 2.121; Scythian horses scared of 4.129; *mules:* Delphic oracle alludes metaphorically to mule in regard to Cyrus 1.55, 91; Elis' dearth of 4.30; foal born to mule portending fall of Babylon 1.151, 153; mule wagons carry special water drunk by Persian Kings 1.188; Peisistratus mutilates 1.59; Scythian horses scared of 4.129.

Hydarnes *Persian general, son of Hydarnes satrap of Lydia,* receives Spartan envoys 7.135; commander of Immortals 7.83; sent by Xerxes to investigate Epialtes' mountain path to Thermopylae 7.215; attacks Phocians after mistaking them for Lacedaemonians 7.217–18; refuses to be parted from Xerxes after Mardonius selects Immortals for his force 8.113.

Hymaeës *Persian general, son-in-law of Darius* pursues and defeats Ionians at sea after battle of Cyprus 5.116; seizes Cius, conquers Ilium's Aeolians; dies 5.122.

Hyperboreans *people believed to live in the far N of Europe* H.'s general scepticism of; hero Abaris 4.36; mentioned by Hesiod and Homer 4.32; offerings sent to Delos, initially via emissaries 4.33, 35.

Hyrcanians *people of central Asia, inhabiting region S of the Aral Sea* nearby plain flooded by Darius 3.117; equipment and commander during Xerxes' invasion of Greece 7.62.

Hystaspes *governor of Persia, son of Arsames, father of Darius* sent back to Persia from Massagetan land to arrest Darius following Cyrus' portentous dream 1.209–10.

Iamids *clan of Elean soothsayers: see* **Callias, Tisamenus**

Idanthyrsus *Scythian king, son of Saulius* family 4.76; ruler of largest division of Scythia 4.120; rebukes Darius 4.127.

Ilium *city in NW Asia Minor, also known as Troy* Aeolian inhabitants conquered by Hymaeës 5.122; storm-struck as Persian army marches through; Xerxes sacrifices cattle to Athena at 7.42–3; *Trojan War:* according to Egyptian priests 2.118–20; Athenians cite their supremacy during 9.27; Magi make offerings to heroes of 7.43; Persian hostility towards Greeks goes back to 1.5; Xerxes' army bigger than Greek forces during 7.20.

Imbros *island in the Aegean Sea (today's Gokceada)* conquered by Otanes (2) using Lesbian ships 5.26.

incense and spices *mostly produced in Arabia, and often used in ritual* Babylonians soused in perfume 1.195; cinnamon stolen from giant birds by Arabians 3.111; rock rose resin collected from goats' beards by Arabians 3.112; scent pervades Arabia 3.113; silphium cultivated in Libya 4.169; *cassia bark:* collected from ponds by leather-clad Arabians in face of attack by bat-like creatures 3.110; used in embalming 2.86; *frankincense:* burned by Chaldaeans 1.183, by Datis in offering to gods 6.97; collected by Arabians in face of attack by winged snakes 3.107; given to Persia each year by Arabia 3.97; produced in Arabian mountains 2.8; used in Scythian baths 4.75; used to stuff sacral bulls in Egypt 2.40; *myrrh:* given as gift by Cambyses to Ethiopian king 3.20; used in embalming 2.86, to seal phoenix egg 2.73, to stuff sacral bulls in Egypt 2.40, to treat wounds 7.181.

India (Indians) *land roughly corresponding to today's Punjab* black semen 3.101; climate 3.104; geography 3.98; large population 3.94; Scylax explores on orders of Darius 4.44; steal gold from giant ants 3.102–5; wildlife's large size 3.106; *customs:* boats 3.98; cannibalism 3.99; cotton, use of 3.106; diets 3.98, 99, 100; funerary cannibalism of Callantians 3.38; funerary customs 3.100; public copulation 3.101; styles of dress 3.98; *under Persian rule:* made part of Persian Province No. 20 by Darius 3.94; yearly tribute of gold dust 3.94, 98; equipment and commander during Xerxes' invasion of Greece 7.65; cavalry's equipment 7.86; hunting-dogs 7.187; infantry and cavalry selected by Mardonius for his invasion 8.113, at Plataea 9.31.

Intaphrenes *Persian nobleman* joins Otanes (1)'s anti-Magian conspiracy 3.70; along with fellow-conspirators kills Patizeithes and Smerdis (2), informs populace 3.77–9; loses eye in attack on Smerdis (2) 3.78; executed by Darius after maiming courtiers 3.118–19.

Io *Argive princess, daughter of Inachos* resemblance to Isis 2.41; kidnapped by Phoenicians, taken to Egypt 1.1; made pregnant by ship's captain 1.5.

Ionia (Ionians) *Greek region on the W coast of Asia Minor* cities 1.142, 145; climate 1.142; dialects 1.142; Egypt's geography according to 2.15–16; law passed by Ionian women prohibiting social contact with husbands after colonizers kill wives' fathers 1.146; Magi told Thetis' story by 7.191; mixed allegiances 1.147; mongrel heritage 1.146; name for letter 's' differs from Dorian 1.139; Panionium 1.143; pride at Ionian identity 1.143; Smyrna gained from Aeolis by 1.150;
— *under Croesus and Persian rule:* conquered by Croesus 1.28; refuses to rebel against Croesus at urging of Cyrus 1.76, Croesus reminds messengers of this 1.141; builds defensive walls around cities; holds war-councils at Panionium 1.141; Lacedaemon refuses to aid 1.152; cities, sacked by Mazares and Harpagus after aiding Pactyes, submit to Persian rule 1.161–2, 169; made part of Persian Province No. 1 by Darius 3.90;

before being overcome 7.223–5; troops' bravery; memorial inscription 7.226–8; survivors of Thermopylae; their subsequent disgrace 7.229–32; *battles of Artemisium and Salamis*: rallies to defence of Peloponnese at Isthmus of Corinth 8.72; ships at Artemisium 8.1; ships at Salamis 8.43, 85;

— *second Persian invasion of Greece: Mardonius' campaign*: sends herald to Xerxes demanding blood-satisfaction for Leonidas; told to seek it from Mardonius 8.114; begs Athens not to surrender to Xerxes 8.142; rebuked by Athenians for doubting them, urged to dispatch its army posthaste 8.144; *battle of Plataea*: slow to send forces due to festival, completion of Isthmus of Corinth wall; rebuked by Athenian envoys 9.7; set out without telling envoys after much delay 9.8–11; troops arrive at Isthmus inspiring rest of Peloponnese to join up 9.19; troops at Plataea 9.28, 31; gives control of wing to Athenians despite Tegean protests 9.26–8; twice swap wings with Athenians 9.46–7; troops, mocked by Mardonius for vacillating, do not respond when challenged to take on Persians alone 9.48–9, left isolated while Amompharetus and Pausanias argue over their withdrawal 9.54, split after Pausanias abandons Amompharetus 9.56–7, attacked by Persians; sacrificial omens unfavourable until Pausanias appeals to Hera; attack Persians, overcome them after death of Mardonius 9.60–63; troops besiege Persians, rout them after arrival of Athenians; casualties 9.70; bravery at Plataea, individuals honoured 9.71; bury dead separately according to status 9.85; *battle of Mycale*: fleet at Mycale 9.102–3; afterwards returns to Peloponnese with Leotychidas 9.114.

Laconia *region of the SE Peloponnese; with Messenia it constituted the Spartan state of* **Lacedaemon**

Lade *small island off Miletus, W Asia Minor, today landlocked* battle of Lade 6.7–18.

Ladice *Cyrenaean wife of Amasis, daughter of Battus or Critobulus* sends statue of Aphrodite to Cyrene after goddess causes Amasis to consummate their marriage; sent back to Cyrene by Cambyses 2.181.

Lampon *Aeginetan* suggests that Pausanias put Mardonius' head on a spike; rebuked by Pausanias 9.78–9.

Lampsacus (Lampsacenes) *Ionian city on the Hellespont* captures Miltiades (1), releases him on orders of Darius; thus forbidden from taking part in Chersonese Games 6.37–8; captured by Persians under Daurises 5.117.

Lasonians *people of Lycia* made part of Persian Province No. 2 by Darius 3.90; said to be the same as Cabalians 7.77.

Lemnos (Lemnians) *island in the Aegean Sea* conquered by Otanes (2); accused of treachery, sold into slavery 5.26–7; acquired by Athens from Pelasgians thanks to Miltiades (2) 6.137–40.

Leonidas *king of Lacedaemon (r. c. 490–480), son of Anaxandridas and first wife, brother of Dorieus and Cleombrotus, half-brother of Cleomenes, husband of Gorgo* lineage 7.204; born to Anaxandridas' first wife shortly after birth of Cleomenes to second 5.41; succeeds Cleomenes, marries Gorgo 7.205; *battle of*

marriage customs, oath-making, prophecy 4.172; nomadic Libyans' diet, taboos on cows and pigs, child-rearing methods, blood-sacrifices, gods 4.186–8, funerary practices 4.190; Psylli, their former land, war on the south wind, obliteration 4.173; west coast Libyans, their trade with Carthaginians 4.196; Zauekes, their female charioteers 4.193;

— *after Greek colonization:* trick Battus and Therans into relocating to Cyrene 4.158; king begs Apries and Egyptians to intervene against Cyrene 4.159; revolt against Cyrene at urging of Barca's founders, defeat Cyrenaean forces 4.160; expel Dorieus and Lacedaemonians from R. Cinyps 5.42; in Carthaginian army in attack on Sicily 7.165;

— *under Persian rule:* Cambyses gladly receives gifts from 3.13; eastern region made part of Persian Province No. 6 by Darius 3.91; infantry's equipment and commander during Xerxes' invasion of Greece 7.71, 86.

Lindus *Dorian city on Rhodes* bans Halicarnassus from using Triopium 1.144; sanctuary of Athena receives gifts from Amasis 2.182, 3.47; colonization of Gela 7.153.

linen *woven from the flax plant, linen was expensive; as well as tunics, it was used to make light strong breastplates* Athenian women wear tunics of 5.87; Babylonian tunics made of 1.195; bandages used by Persians 7.181, used to wrap mummies in Egypt 2.86; breastplate offered by Amasis to Athena 2.182; breastplate stolen by Samians 3.47; breastplates worn by Assyrian troops 7.63, by Phoenician and Syrian marines 7.89; Colchians produce 2.105; Egyptian priests wear spotless 2.37; Egyptian tasselled tunics 2.81; Egyptians produce 2.105; Greek confusion about origin 2.105; hemp indistinguishable from 4.74; mosquitoes can bite through 2.95.

lions *not wholly unfamiliar to Greeks; lions still lived in N Greece and adjoining Thrace* Cambyses pits cub against puppy 3.32; camels attacked by during Xerxes' invasion of Greece 7.125; European range 7.126; golden lion created on orders of Croesus offered to Delphi 1.50; Leonidas commemorated with stone 7.225; Libyan 4.191; reproductive habits 3.108; Sardis' king uses cub in attempt to proof city against capture 1.84; skins worn by Ethiopians 7.69; Xanthippus' wife dreams she gives birth to, portending birth of Pericles 6.131.

Locris (Locrians) *region of central Greece divided into E and W districts, the former N and the latter SW of Phocis* colonizer of Epizephyrian Locris, Italy 6.23; surrenders to Xerxes 7.132; Locrians of Opous fight alongside Greeks at Thermopylae 7.203, enraged by Peloponnesian desire to flee 7.207; ships of Locrian Opous in Greek fleet at battle of Artemisium 8.1; other Locrians join Persian forces 8.66, fight alongside Persians at Plataea 9.31.

Lycia (Lycians) *region of SW Asia Minor* Cretan origins, complicated changes of name 1.173, 7.92; laws and customs, practice of matrilineal descent 1.173; made part of Persian Province No. 1 by Darius 3.90; ships and marines in Persian fleet during Xerxes' invasion of Greece 7.92.

Lycurgus *Lacedaemonian lawgiver* proclaimed a god by Delphic oracle; reforms constitution, restructures military while serving as regent 1.65; temple raised to him upon death 1.66.

Lydia (Lydians) *region of W Asia Minor* Asia's name according to 4.45; culture of prostitution 1.93; currency invented by 1.94; famine; games invented as famine-distraction 1.94; fertility, silver-rich according to Aristagoras 5.49; horsemen's brilliance 1.79; manual crafts, contempt for 2.167; name 7.74; nudity taboo 1.10; troops' courage and prowess in war 1.79; wonders, natural and man-made 1.93; under Gyges 1.13–15; campaigns against Miletus 1.15–22; war with Media ended by eclipse 1.74; meets Persians under Cyrus in battle at Pteria 1.76; defeated by Persians at Sardis due to horses' fear of camels 1.80; envoys sent to Delphi by Croesus 1.90–91; revolts at urging of Pactyes 1.154; spared by Cyrus at pleading of Croesus 1.155–6; forced to adopt emasculating laws after Pactyes' revolt 1.157; made part of Persian Province No. 2 by Darius 3.90; Lydians of Sardis saved from Ionians by Persians 5.101–2; equipment and commander during Xerxes' invasion of Greece 7.74.

Macedonia (Macedonians) *region of NE Greece* disputes over heritage of its people 5.22; Perdiccas' accession to throne preceded by portents 8.137–8; surrenders to Persia 5.17–21, 6.44; troops in Persian army 7.185, at Plataea 9.31.

Macronians *people inhabiting the S coast of Euxine (today's Black) Sea* circumcision 2.104; made part of Persian Province No. 19 by Darius 3.94; equipment and commander during Xerxes' invasion of Greece 7.78.

Maeander *river of Asia Minor, flowing into the Aegean at Miletus* similarities to R. Nile 2.29; source 7.26; tributaries 5.118, 7.26, 30; Milesians beaten by Lydians at 1.17; floodplain overrun by Mazares 1.161; crossed by Xerxes' army 7.31.

Maeandrius *tyrant of Samos, brother of Lycaretus* sent by Polycrates to Magnesia (2) to assess Oroetes' offer 3.123; becomes tyrant; raises altar to Zeus, requests money and hereditary priesthood in return for stepping down, is rebuffed 3.142; arrests Samians, falls ill; succeeded by Lycaretus 3.143; aids Persian task-force under Otanes (1) in seizing Samos 3.144; persuaded by mad brother to provoke Persians; flees Samos 3.145–6; banished from Lacedaemon by Cleomenes after offering him gifts 3.148.

Maeëtis *Scythian lake (modern Sea of Azov) located between today's Russia and Ukraine* similar in size to Euxine 4.86; trading station 4.20; tributaries 4.57, 123.

Magi (Magus) *priestly caste of Media and Persia* funerary customs 1.140; role in Persian sacrifice 1.132, 140; interpret Astyages' dreams of Mandane 1.107–8; reinterpret Astyages' dreams in light of Cyrus' survival; advise him to send Cyrus to Persia 1.120; impaled by Astyages for incorrectly interpreting dreams 1.128; interpret Xerxes' dream 7.19; interpret eclipse as favourable to Persians 7.37; make offerings to heroes of Trojan War 7.43; sacrifice horses to R. Strymon; bury Thracian children alive 7.113–14; sacrifice to Thetis in attempt to calm storm at Sepias 7.191.

Magians *tribe of Media; see also* **Parizeithes, Smerdis (2)** massacred by Persians after uncovering of Smerdis (2)'s usurpation; forbidden from appearing by daylight during Persian festival celebrating massacre 3.79.

Magnesia (1) (Magnesians) *region of E Thessaly* surrenders to Xerxes 7.132; in Persian army 7.185; Magnesian (1) landowner salvages Persian wrecks 7.190.

Magnesia (2) (Magnesians) *Aeolian city on the R. Maeander in Ionia* sacked by Mazares after Pactyes' revolt 1.161; made part of Persian Province No. 1 by Darius 3.90.

Malis (Malians) *small coastal region of E central Greece* geography 7.198–200; surrenders to Xerxes 7.132; ships join Persian fleet before Salamis 8.66; troops at Plataea 9.31.

Mandane *Median princess, daughter of Astyages, wife of Cambyses, mother of Cyrus* Astyages' first portentous dream of; marries Cambyses 1.107; Astyages' second portentous dream of; gives birth to Cyrus 1.108.

Mandrocles *Samian architect* rewarded by Darius for bridging Bosporus; dedicates painting to Hera 4.88.

Mantinea (Mantineans) *city in Arcadia* sends arbitrator to Cyrene 4.161; troops at Thermopylae 7.202; troops miss Plataea; prevented from pursuing Persians by Lacedaemonians, depart in shame; commanders later exiled 9.77.

Marathon *coastal town in Attica* seized as beach-head by Peisistratus 1.62; site of Persian invasion under Datis and Artaphrenes (2) 6.102, 107;
— *battle of Marathon:* 6.107–17. *See also entries under* **Athens, Persia**

Mardonius *Persian general, son of Gobryas, nephew of Darius, cousin of Xerxes*
— *first Persian invasion of Greece:* deposes Ionian tyrants, institutes democracy; heads for Greece via Hellespont 6.43; conquers Thasos, Macedonia; fleet wrecked at Athos, marines eaten by sharks 6.44; conquers aggressive Thracian tribe; returns to Asia 6.45; relieved of command by Darius 6.94;
— *second Persian invasion of Greece:* influence over Xerxes; convinces him to attack Greece 7.5–6; praises Xerxes, dismisses Greek chances; rebuked by Artabanus 7.9–10; general of Persian army 7.82; leads third of Persian army along coastal route into Greece 7.121; asks commanders if they think Xerxes should fight at sea 8.68; not fooled by Xerxes' feigned battle preparations after defeat at Salamis 8.97; urges Xerxes either to stay in Greece or to give him command of Persian army with view to conquest 8.100; given pick of army by Xerxes 8.107; selects troops 8.113; overwinters in Thessaly and Macedonia 8.126; sends envoys on tour of oracles 8.133; mulls over oracles' messages; sends Alexander on mission to win over Athenians 8.136; leads army towards Athens after Athenians refuse to surrender 9.1; urged by Thebans (1) to conquer Greece by non-military means; his desire to capture Athens precludes this; seizes empty Athens 9.2–3; sends envoy to Salamis (1) urging Athenian surrender 9.4; warned by Argos of approaching Lacedaemonian forces 9.12; razes Athens, heads to Boeotia 9.13–14; *battle of Plataea:* denudes Theban (1) lands en route to Isthmus; builds stockade along R. Asopus; attends lavish banquet

9.15; impressed by bravery of Phocian troops in face of apparent Persian cavalry attack 9.18; sends Persian cavalry to attack Greek forces 9.20; mourns Masistius 9.24; deploys his army at Plataea 9.31–2; unable to attack due to sacrificial omens urging caution 9.37, 38; has Mt Cithaeron's passes guarded 9.38–9; ignores Artabazus' advice and sacrifices of Hegesistratus; attacks Greeks 9.41; rubbishes oracles foretelling Persian destruction in Greece 9.42; taunts Lacedaemonians for vacillating over battle-order, challenges them to take on Persian troops 9.48; deploys cavalry against Greeks 9.49; believing Greeks to have fled, mocks Thorax and his brothers for lauding Lacedaemonians, leads Persian army in pursuit 9.58–9; killed in battle by Lacedaemonians, fulfilling oracle; his killer 9.63–4; best among individuals in Persian army at Plataea 9.71; tent looted by Tegeans 9.70; burial 9.84.

Marea *town in W Egypt* inhabitants question the oracle at Ammon regarding their nationality 2.18; border-post established by Psammetichus 2.30.

Mares *people living in today's central Georgia* made part of Persian Province No. 19 by Darius 3.94; equipment and commander during Xerxes' invasion of Greece 7.79.

Mariandynians *people living on the SW coast of Euxine (today's Black) Sea* conquered by Croesus 1.28; made part of Persian Province No. 3 by Darius 3.90; equipment and commander during Xerxes' invasion of Greece 7.72.

marriage customs *Greeks practised monogamy (with one Spartan exception) whereas other cultures practised varying forms of polygamy or polykoity* Babylonian marriage auctions 1.196; Cleisthenes (1) holds athletics contest to decide who marries his daughter 6.126–30; Delians cut locks of hair in honour of Hyperboreans before marrying 4.34; Enetian marriage auctions 1.196; Lydian blood oaths 1.74; Massagetan married women's promiscuity 1.216; Median blood oaths 1.74; Nasamonian brides sleep with all men at wedding 4.172; Persian conspirators forbid king from marrying outside the group 3.84; Persian polygamy 1.135; Persians don't traditionally practise sibling-marriage 3.31; Sauromatian women forbidden from marrying until they have killed enemy 4.117; Thracian grooms must retrieve stakes from mountain 5.16; Thracian polygamy 5.5; Thracian wives closely watched in contrast to unmarried women 5.6.

Masistes *Persian general and governor of Bactria, son of Darius, brother of Xerxes* general of Persian army during Xerxes' invasion of Greece 7.82; leads third of Persian army along coastal route into Greece 7.121; nearly killed by Artaÿntes after comparing him unfavourably to a woman 9.107; ordered by Xerxes to divorce wife 9.111; wife mutilated by Amestris 9.112; heads to Bactria with sons to foment revolt; killed en route on Xerxes' orders 9.113.

Masistius *Persian general* commands Alarodian and Saspeirian troops during Xerxes' invasion of Greece 7.79; *battle of Plataea:* leads Persian cavalry at Plataea riding Nisaean horse 9.20; killed by Athenians in spite of special armour 9.22; mourned by Mardonius and Persians; corpse paraded by Greeks 9.24–5.

Massagetans *semi-nomadic people living E of the Caspian Sea on the central Asian steppe* territory 1.201–2, 204; weaponry; gold and bronze, use of 1.215; *customs*: diet; elderly killed; funerary cannibalism; sun-worship; women's promiscuity 1.216; *invaded by Cyrus*: their queen Tomyris responds to Cyrus' threats 1.205–6; kill Persian non-combatants, enjoy feast before being ambushed 1.211; defeat Cyrus and Persians in battle 1.214.

Matiene (Matienians) *land in the NW of today's Iran* made part of Persian Province No. 18 by Darius 3.94; equipment and commander during Xerxes' invasion of Greece 7.72.

Mazares *Median general* heads task-force to deal with Lydian revolt on orders of Cyrus, enforces adoption of emasculating laws 1.156–7; imprisons Pactyes after bribing Mytilenaeans and Chians 1.160; targets Sardis' attackers, sells Prieneans into slavery, sacks R. Maeander's floodplain and Magnesia (2); dies 1.161.

Media (Medes) *region in the N of today's Iran* geography 1.110, 4.37; name's origins 7.62; tribes 1.101; eclipse brings end to war with Lydia 1.74; successfully revolts again Assyrian rule 1.95; Deioces takes control 1.96–7, reforms 1.98–101; conquered by Cyrus 1.127–30; unsuccessfully revolts against Darius 1.130; made part of Persian Province No. 10 by Darius 3.92; equipment and commander during Xerxes' invasion of Greece 7.62; cavalry 7.86; marines 7.96, 184; troops sent into battle at Thermopylae, beaten back 7.210–11; infantry and cavalry selected by Mardonius for his force 8.113; troops at Plataea 9.31.

medicine *undeveloped in Greece (the Crotoniate physician Democedes the exception rather than the rule), but more advanced in Egypt* Babylonian medical system 1.197; Democedes cures Darius' ankle; as state physician of Aegina 3.129–31; Democedes cures Atossa's breast cancer 3.133–4; Egyptian doctors fail to cure Darius' ankle 3.129; Egyptian eye-doctor sent to Cyrus by Amasis 3.1; Egyptian medical system highly specialized 2.84; Libyans cauterize heads of children with lanolin, sprinkle with goat-urine in event of spasm 4.187.

medizing *Greek collaboration with Persia (not Media: the term reflects Greek use of 'Medes' to mean 'Persians'); motivations might include fear of conquest or a desire to be on the winning side* Aeginetan 6.64; Aeginetans accused of 8.92; Athenian refusal to medize 8.144; Greeks terrified due to extent of 7.138; H. believes Greek states' neutrality akin to 7.73; Megabazus conquers Hellespont's non-medizing Greek cities 4.144; Pausanias declared children of medizers free of guilt 9.88; Peloponnesians advocate stripping medizing Ionian cities of their people 9.106; Phocis medizes under duress 9.17; Phocis' reasons for not 8.30; Theban (1) 7.205, 233, 9.15, 40, 67; Thebans (1) tell Xerxes of Thespiae and Plataea's refusal to medize 8.50; Thebes (1) besieged by Greek forces for 9.86–8; Themistocles blackmails medizing islanders 8.112; Thessalian 7.172.

Megabates *Persian general, cousin of Darius and Artaphrenes (1)* appointed commander of Artaphrenes (1)'s planned invasion of Naxos 5.32; quarrels with

Aristagoras after mistreating his friend; warns Naxians of invasion, leading to siege 5.33–4.

Megabazus *Persian general, father of Oebares (2), Bubares and Pherendates* much admired by Darius, appointed head of Persian troops in Europe 4.143; comment on Chalcedon; conquers western Hellespontine cities 4.144, Perinthus; marches along Thrace coast 5.1–2; captures Paeonians, transports them to Asia on Darius' orders 5.14–15; sends delegation to Macedonia to receive its surrender; members killed after groping Macedonian women 5.17–21; returns to Sardis bringing warning of Histiaeus' activities 5.23.

Megabyzus *Persian nobleman, father of Zopyrus* joins Otanes (1)'s anti-Magian conspiracy 3.70; along with fellow-conspirators, attacks and kills Patizeithes and Smerdis (2), informs populace 3.77–9; unsuccessfully advocates aristocratic oligarchy in debate with fellow-conspirators 3.81.

Megacles *eminent Athenian, son of Alcmaeon* leader of faction before Peisistratus' tyranny 1.59; unites with Lycurgus to drive Peisistratus out of Athens; fights with Lycurgus, plots with Peisistratus, restores him to power 1.60; deposes Peisistratus after he marries and dishonours daughter 1.61.

Megara (Megarians) *city in Megaris* Dorian-founded 5.76; attacked by Peisistratus 1.59; settlers on Sicily sold into slavery by Gelon 7.156; ships at battle of Artemisium 8.1, at Salamis 8.45; in Athenian embassy to Lacedaemon 9.7; territory overrun by Persians under Mardonius 9.14; troops relieved by Athenians after Persian cavalry attack at Erythrae (2) 9.21, at Plataea 9.28, 31; launch disorganized attack after Pausanias' victory; routed by Theban (1) cavalry 9.69; bury dead after battle 9.85.

Melampous *legendary Greek soothsayer, son of Amytheon* introduces cult of Dionysus to Greece having learned of it from Cadmus 2.49; strikes a hard bargain with the Argives after they ask him to cure wives 9.34.

Melanchlaeni *people of Scythia living in E of today's Ukraine* land 4.20; style of dress 4.107; refuse to ally with Scythians against Darius 4.119; invaded by Scythians and Persians, flee northwards 4.125.

Melanippus *legendary Theban (1) hero* his image brought to Sicyon by Cleisthenes (1) to stop worship of Adrastus (2) 5.67.

Memphis *old capital city of Egypt* Carians and Ionians resettled in 2.154; flooding, silting up of 2.13–14; H. visits 2.3; Min founds 2.99; role in provisioning of Syria with water 3.6; shrine of Ptah 2.99; shrines expanded by various kings 2.112, 121, 153, 176; source of stone for Amasis' temple expansion 2.175; Trojan War according to priests of; H.'s opinion thereof 2.118–20; captured by Persians under Cambyses after massacre of Mytilenaeans 3.13–14; prefects condemned to death by Cambyses following appearance of Apis 3.27.

Messenia *region of the SW Peloponnese: with Laconia it constituted the Spartan state of* **Lacedaemon**

Midas *king of Phrygia, father of Gordias* first non-Greek to offer gifts to Delphic oracle 1.14; rose-gardens in Macedonia 8.138.

Miletus (Milesians) *Ionian city in Caria* construction of sanctuary of Apollo in Egypt 2.178; wars with Lydia 1.15–22; renews treaty with Cyrus 1.141; factional strife, restoration of order by Parian arbitrators 5.28–9; troops join Carians in battle against Persian army, suffer heavy defeat 5.120; repels Histiaeus when he attempts to return as tyrant 6.5; ships in the Ionian fleet at battle of Lade 6.8; captured by Persia, Milesians enslaved; fall foretold by Delphic oracle 6.18–19; surrounding hills given to Pedasa; surviving inhabitants settled in Persia 6.20; grief at capture of Sybaris 6.21; troops in Persian fleet suspected of treachery, sent to guard passes before battle of Mycale 9.99, rebel during battle 9.104.

Miltiades (1) *Athenian nobleman and tyrant of Thracian Chersonese, son of Cypselus, uncle of Miltiades (2)* wealth; descent from Aeacus; becomes tyrant on invitation of Doloncians, fortifies region against Apsinthians 6.35–6; taken prisoner by Lampsacus, released on orders of Croesus 6.37; dies, people of Chersonese worship his ghost 6.38.

Miltiades (2) *Athenian general and tyrant of Thracian Chersonese (c. 550–489), son of Cimon, nephew of Miltiades (1)* Lemnos acquired by Athens due to cunning of 6.137–40; marriage to Thracian princess 6.39; Peisistratus murders father after feud 6.103; seizes power after brother's death 6.39; argues unsuccessfully that Ionians should dismantle Ister bridge 4.137; flees Chersonese before Scythian invasion 6.40; pursued by Phoenicians, escapes; son captured, delivered to Darius 6.41; heads Athenian forces at Marathon; made general 6.103–4; persuades senior general to attack Persians 6.109–10; given ships, army, money by Athens, besieges Paros; injured after foolishly approaching sanctuary of Demeter; returns to Athens empty-handed 6.132–4; accused of fraud by Xanthippus, unable to speak in own defence; found guilty, fined; dies 6.136.

Milyas (Milyans) *region of Lycia* made part of Persian Province No. 1 by Darius 3.90; equipment and commander during Xerxes' invasion of Greece 7.77.

Min *legendary first king of Egypt (Menes)* first human ruler of Egypt 2.4; redirects Nile, builds dykes, founds Memphis 2.99; successors 2.100.

Minos *legendary king of Crete, son of Zeus and Europa* banishes brother leading to formation of Lycia 1.173; Carians serve 1.171; death in Sicily cited by Delphic oracle in advising Crete not to join Greece against Xerxes 7.169–70.

Minyans *Lemnian descendants of the Argonauts* exiled by Pelasgians; escape from Lacedaemon after imprisonment 4.145–46; settle in Thera 4.148.

Mithridates *Median cowherd* ordered to kill Cyrus by Harpagus 1.110; exposes stillborn son in Cyrus' stead, secretly adopts Cyrus 1.113; confesses to Astyages 1.116.

Mitrobates *Persian governor of Dascyleum* taunts Oroetes 3.120; murdered along with son by Oroetes 3.126.

Moeris *man-made lake in Egypt* canals 2.149–50; construction 2.150; crocodiles worshipped 2.69; geography, pyramids 2.149; location 2.4.

Moschians *people living on the E coast of today's Black Sea* made part of Persian Province No. 19 by Darius 3.94; equipment and commander during Xerxes' invasion of Greece 7.78.

Mossynoecians *people living on the S coast of today's Black Sea* made part of Persian Province No. 19 by Darius 3.94; equipment and commander during Xerxes' invasion of Greece 7.78.

Mycale *mountainous peninsula on the Ionian coast, W Asia Minor* location of Panionium 1.148; Chians pursued by Persians to 5.16;
— battle of Mycale: 9.96–107. *See also entries under* **Athens, Greece, Persia**

Mycenae (Mycenaeans) *city in the NE Peloponnese* attempts to enslave Heraclids 9.27; troops at Thermopylae 7.202, Plataea 9.28, 31.

Mycerinus *king of Egypt (Menkaure, r. c. 2551–2523), 'son' (actually grandson) of Cheops* succeeds Chephren, reopens shrines, liberates Egyptians 2.129; reign's justness 2.129; daughter's death and tomb 2.129–32; reproaches oracle at Bouto after being told he has six years to live, prepares for death 2.133; pyramid 2.134.

Mycians *people living on the tip of today's Oman and in the Makran Mountains opposite* made part of Persian Province No. 14 by Darius 3.93; Mycian infantry's equipment and commander during Xerxes' invasion of Greece 7.68.

Myous (Myesians) *Ionian city in Caria* dialect 1.142; ships in the Ionian fleet at battle of Lade 6.8.

Mysia (Mysians) *region of NW Asia Minor* relationship to Carians and Lydians 1.171; conquered by Croesus 1.28; appeals to Croesus for help with monstrous boar 1.36; made part of Persian Province No. 2 by Darius 3.90; equipment and commander during Xerxes' invasion of Greece 7.74; troops at Plataea 9.32.

Mytilene (Mytilenaeans) *Aeolian city on Lesbos* role in Hellenium's founding 2.178; bribed by Mazares; prevented from giving up Pactyes 1.160; war with Peisistratids over Sigeium 5.94–5; massacred by Egyptians at Memphis during Cambyses' invasion 3.13; stone Coës to death 5.38; supplies ships to Histiaeus for use in piracy 6.5.

Naucratis *Greek city in the west of the Nile Delta, Egypt* courtesans 2.135; granted to Greeks by Amasis; location of Hellenium, Aeginetan-constructed sanctuary of Zeus, Samian sanctuary of Hera, Milesian sanctuary of Apollo; privileged position 2.178–9.

Naxos (Naxians) *Ionian island in the Cyclades* origins 8.46; wealth 5.28; conquered by Peisistratus, given to Lygdamis 1.64; rich exiles to Miletus ask Aristagoras for military backing; he advises Persians to invade 5.30–31; warned of invasion by Megabates, withstands Persian siege 5.34–5; conquered by Persian fleet under Datis and Artaphrenes (2) 6.96; sends ships to join Xerxes' fleet; these defect to Greeks 8.46.

Necos *king of Egypt (Necho II, r. c. 610–595), son of Psammetichus, father of Psammis* succeeds father; abandons construction of canal connecting Nile to

Red Sea on advice of oracle 2.158; sends Phoenicians to circumnavigate Libya 4.42; campaign against Syria; gifts to oracle at Branchidae; death 2.159.

Neit *Egyptian goddess of war and hunting* Amasis gives Cyrenaeans statue 2.182; identified with Athena by H. 2.28; festival at Sais 2.59, 62; oracular shrine 2.83; temple at Sais 2.169–70, expanded by Amasis 2.175.

Neurians *people of Scythia, living NW of Euxine (today's Black) Sea in the S of Belarus* land 4.17, 51; forced by snakes to flee territory; lycanthropy 4.105; refuse to ally with Scythians against Darius and Persians 4.119; flee after land invaded by Scythians and Persians 4.125.

Nile *river in Egypt* canal to Red Sea begun by Necos, completed by Darius 2.158; course into Ethiopia and beyond 2.29, 31; divides at Cercasorus 2.15; Egypt's fertility depends upon 2.5; estuaries and mouths 2.10, 17, 18; flooding 2.13, 19, 97; flooding, lack of breezes, failed attempts to explain these, H. attempts to do so 2.19–27; Libya bisected by 2.33; Min redirects 2.99; power 2.11; R. Ister similar 2.33–4; sacred fish 2.72; source, mysteries of 2.28; *Delta*: fish's spawning 2.93; Ionians consider to be whole of Egypt 2.15–16; Nile at full flood inundates 2.19; silt 2.13, 15.

Nineveh *capital city of Assyria* king's treasure stolen by tunnelling thieves 2.150; inhabitants kill Phraortes, halt Median conquest of Asia 1.102; besieged by Cyaxares and Media, saved by Scythian invasion 1.103; captured by Media 1.106.

Nitocris (1) *queen of Babylon, mother of Labynetus* redirects and fortifies Euphrates; builds artificial marsh to protect Babylon from Medes; builds bridge between two halves of Babylon; tomb, opened by Darius 1.185–7.

Nitocris (2) *queen of Egypt* drowns brother's murderers, commits suicide 2.100.

Oceanus *river believed by some in H.'s time to encircle the world* as explanation of Nile's mysteries 2.21; H.'s scepticism of 2.23, 4.36.

Oebares (1) *Darius' groom* secures Darius' rule over Persia with cunning scheme 3.85–7; honoured in stone relief 3.88.

Oebares (2) *Persian governor of Dascyleum, son of Megabazus* negotiates surrender of Cyzicus 6.33.

oligarchy *the 'rule of the few': a small number of individuals held power and free citizens might be denied the right to hold office or to vote* Corinth formerly a narrow, dynastic oligarchy 5.92; Darius criticizes 3.82; Megabyzus proposes Persia be governed by 3.81.

Olympia *sanctuary in the NW Peloponnese managed by Elis, site of oracle and Olympic Games* oracle's responses read in sacrificial victims 8.134; statues dedicated by Micythus 7.170; statue of Zeus installed after Plataea 9.81; *Olympic Games*: Alexander allowed to compete 5.22; chariot-race won by Alcmaeon 6.125, Cimon 6.103, Cleisthenes (1) 6.126, Demaratus 6.70, Miltiades (1) 6.36; Eleans boast of organization 2.160; horse-race won by Callias 6.122; Persians non-plussed by prizes 8.26; Pheidon dismisses stewards, presides over 6.127; Tisamenus competes in pentathlon 9.33.

Olympus (1) *highest mountain in Greece, home of the chief Greek gods and goddesses* viewed by Xerxes; geography 7.128–9; Tempe pass guarded by Greek forces on urging of Thessalians 7.172–3.

Olympus (2) *mountain in Mysia* Atys killed at 1.43; monstrous wild boar lives on 1.36; Mysians named after 7.74.

Onesilus *king of Salamis (2), brother of Gorgus* seizes Salamis (2) from Gorgus, persuades most Cypriots to rebel against Persia, besieges Amathous 5.104; appeals to Ionians for help in face of Persian attack 5.108; kills Persian general in single combat with help of shield-bearer; dies 5.111–13; cult in Amathous 5.114.

oracles *holy sites at which questions could be asked of gods, goddesses or legendary heroes; their responses (taking various unintelligible forms – at Delphi the Pythia gibbered, at Dodona oak leaves rustled and doves cooed), cryptically interpreted by priests or priestesses, were also called oracles; see* **Abae, Ammon, Amphiaraus, Bacis, Bouto, Branchidae, Delphi, Dodona, Olympia, Trophonius**

Oroetes *Persian governor of Sardis* desire to kill Polycrates, capture Samos 3.120–22; fools Polycrates with begging message and display of wealth 3.122–3; kills Polycrates horribly, enslaves Democedes 3.125; fails to aid Persians during reign of Smerdis (2), kills Persian noblemen, messenger 3.126; killed by bodyguards on orders of Darius 3.128.

Osiris *Egyptian god of the underworld, father of Horus* H. identifies with Dionysus 2.42, 144; king of Hades 2.123; Meroe's people worship 2.29; phallic processions 2.48–9; pigs sacrificed 2.47; tomb, rites in Sais 2.170–71.

Otanes (1) *Persian nobleman, son of Pharnaspes, father-in-law of Cambyses* uncovers Smerdis (2)'s deception after daughter confirms his lack of ears 3.68–9; forms anti-Magian conspiracy 3.70; outvoted after urging caution in attack on Smerdis (2) 3.71–3; learning of Prexaspes' denunciation, urges caution; overruled after portentous bird-on-bird attack 3.76; along with fellow-conspirators kills Patizeithes and Smerdis (2), informs populace 3.77–9; unsuccessfully advocates democracy in debate with fellow-conspirators 3.80; rules himself out of kingship, awarded special privileges 3.83–4; heads task-force to Samos on orders of Darius 3.141, 144; orders Samians' slaughter after unexpected attack 3.146–7, 149; resettles Samos prompted by portentous dream; genital disease 3.149.

Otanes (2) *Persian governor, son of Sisamnes* made a judge after father's skin is turned into chair by Cambyses; appointed general by Darius 5.25; conquests 5.26; harries Ionians after defeat of Cyprus 5.116; conquers Clazomenae and Cyme 5.123.

Outians *people of Persia* made part of Persian Province No. 14 by Darius 3.93; equipment and commander during Xerxes' invasion of Greece 7.68.

Pactolus *Lydian river, flowing through Sardis* brings gold-dust down from Mt Tmolus 5.101.

Pactyes *Lydian nobleman* put in charge of transporting Lydian gold by Cyrus; foments revolt, hires mercenaries, besieges Sardis 1.153–4; flees to Cyme in face of Mazares' task-force 1.157; evacuated to Mytilene, then Chios; betrayed by Chians, imprisoned by Persians 1.160.

Pactyicans *people of Armenia* made part of Persian Province No. 13 by Darius 3.93; equipment and commander during Xerxes' invasion of Greece 7.67.

Paeonia (Paeonians) *land in today's Macedonia and Bulgaria* Artemis worshipped by 4.33; lake-dwellers, their homes, marital customs, fishing techniques 5.16; Perinthus attacked on advice of oracle 5.1; *under Persian rule:* surrender to Megabazus, transported to Asia on Darius' orders 5.15; prisoners-of-war flee to Chios at urging of Aristagoras' emissary, return home 5.98; in Persian army 7.185; Xerxes' chariot of Ahura Mazda lost to Thracians by 8.115; troops at Plataea 9.32.

Palestine (Palestinians) *coastal region of ancient Syria* geography 3.5, 4.39; invaded by Scythians 1.105; practice of circumcision 2.104; pillars raised by Sesostris at 2.106; made part of Persian Province No. 5 by Darius 3.91; ships, marines in Persian fleet during Xerxes' invasion of Greece 7.89.

Pallene (1) *W peninsula of Chalcidice, formerly known as Phlegre* cities; inhabitants conscripted by Xerxes 7.123; revolts against Persian rule 8.126.

Pallene (2) *town in Attica* site of battle between Peisistratus and Athenians 1.62; heroic Ameinias from 8.84, 93.

Pamphylia (Pamphylians) *region on the S coast of Asia Minor* origins 7.91; conquered by Croesus 1.28; made part of Persian Province No. 1 by Darius 3.90; in Persian fleet during Xerxes' invasion of Greece 7.91; adjudged useless by Artemisia 8.68.

Pan *half-goat Greek god of nature* birth, origins 2.145–6; Egyptian attitudes towards 2.46; Philippides meets; subsequently worshipped in Athens 6.105; youngest of the gods 2.145.

Pangaeum *mountain in Edonia, SW Thrace* surrounding lands 7.113; inhabitants of surrounding lands resist Megabazus' attempted conquest 5.16; mined for gold and silver by Pierians and Thracian tribes 7.112.

Panionium *Ionian shrine on Mycale peninsula* founding 1.143; location; festival 1.148; Ionian war-councils held 1.141, 6.7.

Panionius *Chian slaver* buys and castrates Hermotimus; later forced by Hermotimus to castrate his sons before being castrated himself, by them 8.105–6.

Paphlagonia (Paphlagonians) *land on the S coast of Euxine (today's Black) Sea* conquered by Croesus 1.28; made part of Persian Province No. 3 by Darius 3.90; equipment and commander during Xerxes' invasion of Greece 7.72.

Papremis *city in the Nile Delta* Festival of Ares 2.59, 63; inhabitants' worship of the hippopotamus 2.71.

papyrus *aquatic plant put to many uses by the Egyptians; the Greeks used it only for writing* bridge-cables 7.25, 34, 36; bulls marked pure using 2.38; food, harvest 2.92; Ionians call papyrus scrolls 'hides' 5.58; ropes, sails 2.96; sandals of Egyptian priests 2.37.

Paricanians *people perhaps living in the S of today's Afghanistan* made part of Persian Province No. 17 by Darius 3.94; equipment and commander during Xerxes' invasion of Greece 7.68; cavalry 7.86.

Paris *legendary prince of Troy, son of Priam* kidnaps Helen 1.3; blown off course on return with Helen, lands in Egypt 2.113; imprisoned by Proteus 2.115.

Parnassus *mountain NE of Delphi, location of sacred Corycian Cave* Phocians surrounded by Thessalians 8.27, seek refuge during Xerxes' invasion 8.32; Delphian men seek refuge during Xerxes' invasion; struck by lightning during Persian attack on Delphi 8.36–7; Phocians attack Persians from 9.31.

Paros (Parians) *Ionian island in the central Cyclades* sends arbitrators to restore order to Miletus 5.28–9; besieged by Miltiades (2) 6.133; sends emissaries to Delphic oracle asking if priestess should be punished 6.135; remains neutral during Xerxes' invasion of Greece 8.67; blackmailed by Themistocles 8.112.

Parthians *people of central Asia, living S of today's Aral Sea* made part of Persian Province No. 16 by Darius 3.93; nearby plain flooded by Darius 3.117; equipment and commander during Xerxes' invasion of Greece 7.66.

Patizeithes *Magian steward of Cambyses, brother of Smerdis (2)* hatches plot to have brother impersonate his murdered Persian lookalike/namesake, sends heralds to sow confusion among army 3.61–2; plots with brother to use Prexaspes to consolidate their power; denounced by Prexaspes 3.74–5; killed by Otanes (1)'s anti-Magian conspirators 3.78.

Pausanias *Lacedaemonian royal, son of Cleombrotus* dedicates bowl at entrance to Euxine Sea 4.81; *battle of Plataea:* commander of Lacedaemonian army dispatched to Athens after Mardonius' invasion 9.10; sends Athenian troops to relieve Megarians in face of Persian cavalry attack 9.21; told of Alexander's secret visit, twice reorganizes battle-order 9.46–7; plans to withdraw Greek army to 'island' outside Plataea 9.50–51; argues with Amompharetus over Lacedaemonian withdrawal 9.53, 55; withdraws with Tegeans and Athenians leaving Amompharetus behind 9.56; troops attacked by Persian cavalry, appeals to Athenians for backup 9.60; invokes Hera, leading to good omens 9.61–2; looks after Cos-born Persian concubine, daughter of guest-friend 9.76; rebukes Lampon after he suggests Mardonius' head be displayed atop spike 9.78–9; orders helots to gather Persian valuables 9.80; given ten of all things of value after battle; contrasts Lacedaemonian and Persian meals 9.81–2; declares Theban (1) collaborators' children free of blame, executes collaborators 9.88.

Pedasa (Pedasians) *city in Caria* priestess of Athena grows beard at sign of trouble 1.175, 8.104; captured by Harpagus 1.175–6; Persian army en route to ambushed by Carians 5.121; given Miletus' surrounding hills 6.20.

Peisistratids *family of Athenian tyrants; see also* **Hipparchus, Hippias, Peisistratus** lineage 5.65; plotted against by Alcmaeonids 5.62, 6.123; with aid of Thessalians, repel Lacedaemonian attempt to drive them from Athens 5.63; exiled to Sigeium after their children captured by Lacedaemonians 5.65, having left prophecies at Acropolis before exile 5.91; send Miltiades (2) to Chersonese 6.39; urge Darius to invade Greece 6.94, Xerxes to invade Greece 7.6, Athenians to surrender during Xerxes' siege 8.52.

Peisistratus (c. 600–527), *three-time tyrant of Athens, son of Hippocrates, father of Hippias and Hipparchus, patriarch of Peisistratid family* father witnesses miracle at Olympic Games, ignores warning regarding his offspring; head of upland faction during Attican civil strife; dupes Athenians, seizes power 1.59; driven out by Megacles and Lycurgus; plots with Megacles, regains power after duping Athenians again 1.60; marries Megacles' daughter, has sex with her in illicit way; flees to Eretria when this is discovered, raises funds, musters mercenaries; returns to Attica, captures Marathon, meets Athenian troops at Pallene (2) 1.61–2; attacks Athenians during their postprandial relaxation on advice of seer; sons dupe Athenians 1.63; becomes tyrant of Athens for third time, consolidates power through deployment of mercenaries, raising of income, hostage-taking; lifts curse from Delos 1.64; feud with Cimon, father of Miltiades (2) 6.103.

Pelasgians *Greek people sometimes identified as the indigenous ancestors of historical Greeks, sometimes regarded as foreigners* Athenians descendants of 1.56, 8.44; live in Crestonia; language 1.57; origins, religion; provide names for certain Greek gods; teach Greeks to make statues of Hermes with erect penis; adopt names of Egyptian gods on advice of oracle at Dodona 2.50–52; Thesmophoric rites learned from Egyptians 2.171; drive Argonauts from Lemnos 4.145; live in Lemnos and Imbros 5.26; expelled from Attica after raping Athenian girls, settle on Lemnos 6.137; kidnap Athenian women, later kill them and their children 6.138; cursed, promise to surrender Lemnos to Athens when a ship sails south from Athenian territory 6.139; much later surrender Lemnos to Athens after Miltiades (2) sails there from Athenian Chersonese 6.140.

Peloponnese (Peloponnesians) *large peninsular region of S Greece* Dorian ethnic cleansing of 2.171; ethnic groups 8.73; weights and measures 6.127; large part conquered by Lacedaemon 1.68; allies of Lacedaemon under Cleomenes desert him during failed invasion of Attica 5.74–5, reject its call to restore Hippias to Athens as tyrant 5.93; *second Persian invasion of Greece: Xerxes' campaign*: troops at Thermopylae 7.202, vote to flee 7.207; build wall across the Isthmus of Corinth 8.40, 71; despair of safety of homeland 8.70; many remain neutral during Xerxes' invasion, H. compares this to collaboration 8.72–3; commanders of Greek fleet urge withdrawal to defence of Peloponnese 8.74, 78; *Mardonius' campaign*: troops head to Boeotia before Plataea 9.19; commanders advocate evacuation of Ionia after Mycale 9.106, fleet returns home with Leotychidas 9.114.

Pelusium *city in NE Egypt* location of salt factories 2.15; site of battle between Egypt and Persia 3.11.

Peneius *river flowing through the Tempe pass between Mts Ossa and Olympus (1) from S Macedonia into Thessaly* inspected by Xerxes; course, tributaries, creation by Poseidon 7.128–30; pass guarded by Greek forces on urging of Thessalians 7.172–3; Athenian ship runs aground at mouth 7.182.

penteconter *a fifty-oared galley, used in trade as well as in war* Battus sails to Libya in two 4.156; Gelon sends three to await outcome of Xerxes' invasion of Greece 7.163; Greek fleet's during second Persian invasion 8.1, 46, 48; Lacedaemon sends to spy on Cyrus and Ionia 1.152; Pelasgians kidnap Athenian women using 6.138; Persian fleet's during second invasion of Greece 7.97, 148; Polycrates builds fleet of 3.39; used by Polycrates 3.41, 124, by Therans to colonize Libya 4.143, by Xerxes to bridge Hellespont 7.36.

Periander *tyrant of Corinth (r. c. 625–585), son of Cypselus* Arion arrested by, sailors interrogated by 1.24; mediates between Mytilene and Athenian exiles 5.95; Thrasybulus told of Delphic oracle's response to Alyattes' emissaries by 1.20; succeeds father as tyrant, behaves cruelly following example of Thrasybulus; sleeps with wife's corpse, supplicates her ghost by stripping Corinthian women 5.92; feuds with son over wife's murder; attacks Epidaurus; son's exile to Corcyra, refusal to return, murder 3.50–53; planned castration of Corcyraean boys foiled by Samians 3.48.

Perrhaebia (Perrhaebians) *region of N Thessaly* surrenders to Xerxes 7.132; troops in Persian army 7.185.

Perseus *legendary hero, son of Zeus and Danaë* first Dorian king; claims as to Assyrian ancestry of 6.53–4; in Egypt after killing Medusa; worshipped at Chemmis; related customs and beliefs 2.91; in Persia 7.61.

Persia (Persians) *land in the S of today's Iran, heartland of Persian empire; H. often uses 'Medes' and 'Barbarians' to mean Persians* Asia regarded as property of 1.4, 9.116; castrated slaves favoured 8.105; fathering boys sign of virility 1.136; geography 4.37; Greece, hostility towards 1.1–5; leather worn 1.71; model of governance 1.134; name changed after arrival of Perseus 7.61; personal names 1.139; poor warriors according to Aristagoras 5.49; postal system 8.98; poverty 1.89; restoration of conquered lands' kings 3.15; royal road between Sardis and Susa 5.52–4; skulls, fragility of 3.12; tribes 1.125; unfavourable comparison to woman considered particularly insulting 9.108; violence, proneness to 1.89; wealth according to Aristagoras 5.49; *customs and religion:* attitudes towards leprosy, psoriasis 1.138, lying 1.138; banquets 1.133; birthdays 1.133, royal 9.110; conjugal visits, rotation of 3.69; death penalty 1.137; debate, love of 1.133; disbelief in parricide and matricide 1.137; education 1.136; etiquette 1.134; festival celebrating slaughter of Magians 3.79; foreign customs, fashions, enthusiasm for 1.135; funerary customs 1.140, 3.16; hedonism 1.135; human sacrifice 7.114, 180; manual crafts, contempt for 2.167; pederasty 1.135; rivers venerated 1.138; royal judges 3.31; sacrifice 1.131–2; wine, love of 1.133; xenophobia 1.134;

— *under Cyrus:* conquered by Media under Phraortes 1.102; troops mustered by Cyrus, urged to revolt 1.125–6; defeats Media under Astyages twice in battle 1.127–8; growing power 1.46; sees off Lydia in battle at Pteria 1.76; defeats after neutralizing cavalry with camels; besieges Sardis 1.80–81; captures Sardis after soldier scales cliff 1.84–6; captures Babylon after Cyrus redirects Euphrates 1.188–91; *campaign against Massagetans:* Persian non-combatants killed by Massagetans before army attacks 1.211; army wiped out by Massagetans under Tomyris 1.214;

— *conquest of Egypt under Cambyses:* invades Egypt via Arabia and defeats in first battle 3.11; captures Memphis after siege 3.13; moved by Psammenitus' dignity 3.14; force sent to destroy Ammon disappears, another starves en route to attack Ethiopians 3.25–6;

— *under Smerdis (2):* noblemen warned by Cambyses before his death; lament at his weeping; disbelieve Cambyses' talk of Magian usurpation 3.65–6; Persians summoned by Smerdis (2) and Patizeithes to hear Prexaspes' speech 3.75; massacre Magians after Smerdis (2)'s usurpation revealed 3.79;

— *under Darius:* empire's provinces 3.89–96; Persians exempted from paying tax 3.97; spies sent to Greece by Darius 3.134–8; task-force under Otanes (1) sent to Samos 3.141, captures Samos apparently bloodlessly 3.144, kills Samians after slaughter of elite by mercenaries 3.146–7, clears Samos 3.149; *Babylonian revolt:* army besieges Babylon 3.151–3; recaptures Babylon through cunning of Zopyrus 3.153–9; *invasion of Scythia:* army travels from Susa, crosses Bosporus via boat-bridge 4.83–5, 89; leaves cairn at R. Artescus, conquers Thracian peoples 4.92–3; conquers Getans 4.96; crosses R. Ister 4.97; pursues Scythians through neighbouring lands 4.121–5; harassed by Scythian cavalry; donkeys scare Scythian horses 4.128–9; seizes Scythian live-stock, falsely boosting morale 4.130; commanders confused by Scythian kings' gifts 4.132; flees Scythia after abandoning donkeys and sick troops 4.134–6; makes escape 4.142; *attack on Libya:* force captures Barca after siege 4.200–202; fails to capture Cyrene, returns to Egypt on Aryandes' orders 4.203–4; *Ionian revolt:* army routs Ionians at Ephesus 5.102; attacks and defeats Cyprus 5.108–13; captures Hellespontine cities 5.117; beats Carians twice over in battle before being ambushed, annihilated 5.119–21; captures further Hellespontine, Ionian, Aeolian cities 5.122–3; marches on Miletus 6.6; generals order deposed Ionian tyrants to incite Ionian troops to betrayal 6.9–10; victory over Ionian fleet secured, captures Miletus, enslaves Milesians 6.18; restores tyrant of Samos, captures Caria 6.25; punishes Ionians 6.31–3; policies restore peace to Ionia 6.42–3;

— *first Persian invasion of Greece: Mardonius' campaign:* fleet heads for Greece; wrecked at Athos, marines eaten by sharks 6.44; army attacked by Thracians in Macedonia; conquers them before returning to Asia 6.45; *Artaphrenes (2) and Datis' campaign:* heralds demand surrender of Greeks 6.48–9; troops muster in Cilicia; conquers Naxos 6.95–6; heads for Eretria, press-ganging islanders en route; subdues Carystus 6.99; captures Eretria; destroys sanctuaries in revenge for destruction of Sardis' during Ionian revolt 6.101; *battle of Marathon:* lands in Attica, heads for Marathon on advice of Hippias 6.102; defeated by Athens at Marathon 6.112–13; fleet fails to get to Athens before Athenians; returns to Asia 6.115–16; casualties 6.117;

Pheretime *wife of Battus 'the Lame', mother of Arcesilaus* flees to Salamis (2) after Arcesilaus demands return of royal privileges; fails to persuade its king to back her militarily 4.162; flees to Egypt after Arcesilaus killed by Barcaeans, asks Aryandes for support 4.165; kills captured Barcaeans after their conquest by Persia 4.202; returns to Egypt, dies horribly 4.205.

Pheros *legendary king of Egypt, son of Sesostris* succeeds father, struck blind after abusing Nile 2.111; sight restored on advice of oracle at Bouto; murders unfaithful wife, remarries woman whose urine cured his blindness, makes offerings to Egyptian temples 2.111.

Phleious (Phliasians) *city in the NE Peloponnese* troops at Thermopylae 7.202, rally to defence of Peloponnese at Isthmus of Corinth 8.72, at Plataea 9.28, 31, launch disorganized attack after Pausanias' victory; routed by Theban (1) cavalry 9.69; bury dead after Plataea 9.85.

Phocaea (Phocaeans) *Ionian city* long-distance sea journeys; friendship with Arganthonius, king of Tartessus, fortification using his funds 1.163; role in Hellenium's founding 2.178; besieged by Harpagus; flee to Chios 1.164; fail to buy islands from Chians; head for Cyrnus after massacring Persian garrison, swearing oath not to return; half break oath, return home 1.165; in Alalia, pillage Tyrrhenian and Carthaginian settlements; win battle against Tyrrhenians and Carthaginians, losing many ships, flee to Rhegium; captured by Tyrrhenians and Carthaginians after shipwreck, stoned to death at Agylla 1.166–7; buy land in Oenotria, establish city of Elea 1.167; ships in Ionian fleet at battle of Lade 6.8; flee to Phoenicia and Sicily and become pirates under Dionysius 6.17.

Phocis (Phocians) *region of central mainland Greece* build wall across Thermopylae pass in fear of Thessalian invasion 7.176; disguised as ghosts vanquish Thessalian invaders, break their horses' legs with booby-traps 8.27–8; *battle of Thermopylae:* troops at Thermopylae 7.203, enraged by Peloponnesian desire to flee 7.207, guard mountain path during battle 7.212, attacked by Persians 7.217–18; reject Thessaly's demand for money 8.29–30; take refuge from Persian invasion on Parnassus and in Locris; cities and sanctuaries destroyed by Persians; Phocians raped and killed 8.32–3; *battle of Plataea:* collaborate unwillingly with Persians under Mardonius; troops join Persian forces; bravery in face of apparent attack by Persian cavalry impresses Mardonius 9.17–18; troops at Plataea; others support Greeks, harass Persians 9.31.

Phoenicia (Phoenicians) *land corresponding to the coastal regions of today's Syria and Lebanon* Argos, trade with 1.1; circumnavigation of Libya on orders of Necos 4.42; Io kidnapped by 1.1; origins 1.1; alphabetic script taught to Greeks by Cadmus' Phoenicians 5.58; shipping-trade 1.1; *under Persian rule:* refuses to take part in Cambyses' invasion of Carthage 3.19; made part of Persian Province No. 5 by Darius 3.91; attacks Cyprus 5.108; defeated at sea by Ionia 5.112; defeats Ionians at battle of Lade 6.14; fleet sails north against Ionia 6.28; razes cities in southern Thrace, Chersonese 6.33; shrewdness in digging of Athos canal 7.23; prepare cables for R. Strymon bridge 7.25; bridge Hellespont 7.34; wins race between Xerxes' ships 7.44; ships and marines in Persian fleet during Xerxes' invasion of Greece 7.89; part of Carthaginian army in attack on Sicily 7.165; ships oppose Athenians at Salamis 8.85; commanders put to death by Xerxes after accusing Ionians of treachery 8.90.

Phraortes *king of Media, son of Deioces, father of Cyaxares* succeeds father; defeats Persians; defeated and killed by Assyrians at Nineveh 1.102.

Phrygia (Phrygians) *region of central Asia Minor* Egyptians think Phrygians firstborn men 2.2; European origins 7.73; livestock, fertility according to Aristagoras 5.49; conquered by Croesus 1.28; made part of Persian Province No. 3 by Darius 3.90; Xerxes marches through 7.26, 30; equipment and commander during Xerxes' invasion of Greece 7.73; troops at Plataea 9.32.

Phthiotis *region of Greece S of Thessaly, its S lands occupied by Achaeans, thus often called Achaea by H.* surrenders to Xerxes 7.132; in the Persian army 7.185; rivers drunk dry by Xerxes' forces; sanctuary of Zeus treated respectfully by Xerxes 7.196–7.

Pierians *people inhabiting Edonia and S Macedonia* fortresses in Edonia bypassed by Xerxes 7.112; in the Persian army 7.185.

pigs *taboo in Egypt, but not in Greece, where they were reared for food and frequently offered in sacrifice, especially in cults of the fertility goddess Demeter* Barcaean women abstain from eating 4.186; Cleisthenes (1) renames a Sicyonian tribe 'Swine Men', 'Piggy Men' 5.68; Egyptians use to prepare fields 2.14, sacrifice, think unclean 2.47–8, use as bait in crocodile hunting 2.70; Egypt's 'swineherds' caste 2.164; Libyans think unclean 4.186; Scythians have no use for 4.63; *wild boar:* Libya devoid of 4.192; monster wild boar ravages Mysia, leading to death of Atys 1.36–43; Samian ships' boar-shaped prows 3.59.

Plataea (Plataeans) *city in Boeotia* geography 9.51; sends troops to help Athenians at Marathon; alliance with Athens recommended by Lacedaemon causing trouble with Thebes (1) 6.108; refuses to surrender to Xerxes 7.132; marines aboard Athenian ships before battle of Artemisium 8.1; return home to evacuate their city, missing Salamis 8.44; sacked by Xerxes after Thebans (1) inform him of refusal to collaborate 8.50; in Athenian embassy to Lacedaemon 9.7; Greek forces relocate to 9.25;

— *battle of Plataea:* 9.20–70; Plataean troops at 9.31; find Persian treasure, freakish bones in aftermath 9.83; site of false burial mounds built by ashamed Greeks 9.85. *See also entries under* **Aegina, Athens, Greece, Lacedaemon, Mardonius, Masistius, Pausanias, Persia, Phocis, Tegea**

Polycrates *tyrant of Samos (r. c. 535–522), son of Aeaces, brother of Pantagnotus and Syloson* shares Samos with brothers before killing one, exiling the other; builds up forces; conquers islands and mainland cities; enslaves Lesbians 3.39; guest-friendship with Amasis 2.182, 3.39; warned by Amasis; ring, jettisoned on advice of Amasis, recovered from fish's belly 3.40–42; Amasis dissolves guest-friendship 3.43; sends Samian dissidents to Cambyses as naval task-force, they defect to Lacedaemon 3.44–6; ambition to found maritime empire 3.122; sends Maeandrius to Magnesia (2); fooled by Oroetes' begging message and display of wealth 3.122–3; travels to see Oroetes in spite of warnings, daughter's portentous dream; killed horribly 3.124–5.

Poseidon *Greek god of the sea and earthquakes* absent from Egyptian pantheon 2.43; Athens' salt-water well created by 8.55; Ausean take on 4.180; Libyan origins of 2.50; Libyans sacrifice to 4.188; Persians killed by tidal wave after desecrating his statue in Potidaea 8.129; R. Peneius' gorge created by 7.129; statue made after battle of Plataea 9.81; *Heliconius:* Panionium dedicated to 1.148; *Saviour:* prayed to by Greeks after Sepias storm 7.192; *Scythian 'Thagimasadas':* sacrificed to 4.59.

Potidaea (Potidaeans) *city in Pallene (1)* revolts against Persian rule, besieged by Artabazus 8.126–9; in Greek army at Plataea 9.28, 31.

Prexaspes *chamberlain of Cambyses* dispatched to Susa by Cambyses to murder Smerdis (1) 3.30; son murdered by Cambyses 3.34–5; accused by Cambyses of failing to murder Smerdis (1); questions Smerdis (2)'s herald, discovers truth 3.62–3; denies murder of Smerdis (1) 3.67; agrees to Patizeithes and Smerdis (2)'s plan to consolidate power 3.74; instead extols Cyrus, tells Persians truth about murder of Smerdis (1) before committing suicide 3.75.

Priam *legendary king of Troy, father of Paris* his empire annihilated 1.4; would have returned Helen to Greeks had she been in Troy 2.120; Xerxes inspects Citadel of 7.43.

Priene (Prieneans) *Ionian city in Caria* captured by Ardys 1.15; sold into slavery by Mazares following Pactyes' revolt 1.161; ships in Ionian fleet at battle of Lade 6.8.

Propontis *inland sea (modern Marmara) separating Euxine (today's Black) Sea from the Aegean* geography, size 4.86; Hymaeës invades 5.122.

Proteus *legendary king of Egypt* succeeds Pheros, expands temple of Ptah at Memphis 2.112; imprisons Paris; spends time with Helen 2.115–16.

Psammenitus *king of Egypt (Psamtik III, r. c. 526–525), son of Amasis* succeeds father; defeated by Persians under Cambyses at Pelusium 3.10–11; flees to Memphis, besieged after massacre of Mytilenaeans 3.13; tested by Cambyses with humiliation of children; admitted to court; plots against Cambyses; drinks bull's blood, dies 3.14–15.

Psammetichus *king of Egypt (Psamtik I, r. c. 664–610), father of Necos* border-posts established at Elephantine, Daphnae and Marea; fails to prevent guards from deserting to Ethiopia 2.30; experiments on children prove Phrygians to be the first-born men 2.2; Greek stories about 2.2; Ptah's temple at Memphis expanded by 2.153; attempts to fathom wellsprings of Nile 2.28; reign 2.157; Scythians prevented from attacking Egypt by bribes and begging 1.105; exiled after accidentally fulfilling prophecy at sanctuary of Ptah 2.151; plots revenge, questions oracle at Bouto, regains throne with help of Carian and Ionian freebooters 2.152; settles Carians and Ionians in Egypt 2.154; besieges Azotus for twenty-nine years 2.157;

Psammis *king of Egypt (Psamtik II, r. c. 595–589), son of Necos, father of Apries* succeeds father; advises Eleans on Olympics 2.160; invades Ethiopia; dies 2.161.

Ptah *Egyptian god of craftsmanship, called Hephaestus by H.* Cambyses mocks statue of 3.37; Memphis' shrine 2.2–3, 99, Darius forbidden from erecting statue at 2.110, Egyptian kings sacrifice at 2.151, expanded by Moeris 2.101, by Sesostris 2.108, 110, by Proteus 2.112, by Rhampsinitus 2.121, by Asychis 2.136, by Psammetichus 2.153, by Amasis 2.176; Sethos inspired by 2.141.

Pygmies *people of the Libyan Desert* language, capture of the Nasamonians, city 2.32; observed during attempted circumnavigation of Libya 4.43.

Pytheas *Aeginetan marine, son of Ischenous* captured, grievously wounded, after bravely fighting Persians at Sciathos; restored to health by his captors, honoured 7.181; rescued by Aeginetans during battle of Salamis 8.92.

Pythia *oracular priestess of Apollo; see* Delphi

Pythius *wealthy Lydian* hosts Xerxes and Persian army, contributes war-funds; rewarded by Xerxes 7.27–9; alarmed by eclipse, angers Xerxes by asking him to discharge eldest son from his army; son killed horribly 7.38–9.

Red Sea *H.'s term for today's Persian Gulf, Gulf of Oman and Arabian Sea* as one with Mediterranean and Atlantic 1.202; Egypt surrounded by 2.8; geography 4.37, 39–41; H. uses to refer to today's Red Sea 2.11; Milesians settled by Darius on 6.20; Phoenicians' original homeland 1.1, 7.89; Sesostris has coast explored 2.102; Smerdis (1) drowned in 3.30; 'Uprooted' tribes inhabit islands 3.93, 7.80.

Rhampsinitus *legendary king of Egypt* and the clever thief 2.121; visit to Hades 2.122; succeeds Proteus; constructs gates at temple of Ptah at Memphis 2.121.

Rhegium *Greek city (modern Reggio Calabria) in the toe of Italy* settled by Phocaeans 1.166; tyrant persuades Samians to seize Zancle 6.22; seeks to wipe out Cretan colonies, suffers terrible losses 7.170.

Rhodes (Rhodians) *Dorian island off the coast of W Asia Minor* part in founding Hellenium 2.178.

Rhodopis *Thracian ex-slave, courtesan in Egypt* her owner, connection to Aesop 2.134; brought to Egypt by Xanthes, freed by Charaxus brother of Sappho; becomes wealthy off back of sexual allure; offers iron roasting spits to Delphi 2.135.

Sabacos *Ethiopian king of Egypt (perhaps Shabaka, r. c. 716–702)* invades Egypt, supplants Anysis; introduces new justice system, builds up cities 2.137; flees Egypt after portentous dream 2.139.

Sacae *wide-ranging nomadic people of Scythian origin, extending from the N of the Black Sea as far as today's Iran and Afghanistan* made part of Persian Province No. 15 by Darius 3.93; at Marathon 6.113; equipment and commander during Xerxes' invasion of Greece 7.64; marines 7.96, 184; infantry and cavalry selected by Mardonius for his force 8.113; troops at Plataea 9.31; cavalry best among Mardonius' army at Plataea 9.71.

sacrifice *a key ritual within Greek religion: animals sacrificed were generally sheep, goats, pigs or cattle, but poultry was also used, especially in extispicy (divination through inspection of sacrificial entrails); human sacrifice is documented by H. among non-Greeks* Babylonian 1.183; Cheops forbids blood-sacrifice 2.124; Cleomenes offers blood-sacrifices to Hera, flogs priest who attempts to prevent him 6.81; Egyptian 2.38–41, 42–3, 47–8, 60–63, 69, 151; Greeks unable to attack Persians due to sacrificial omens urging caution 9.38; Lacedaemonian 6.57; Libyan 4.186–8; Magi 1.132, 140, 7.113–14, 191; Massagetan 1.216; oracle's responses read in sacrificial victims at Olympia, Thebes (1) 8.134; Paeonian 4.33; Persian 1.131–2; Persians' sacrificial omens urging caution 9.37; Scythian 4.59, 61–2, 71–2; Thracian 4.33; Xerxes sacrifices cattle to Athena in Ilium 7.43–5; *human:* Apsinthians sacrifice Oeobazus 9.119; Cyrus intends to sacrifice Croesus, Lydian children, by burning 1.86; Getan to Salmoxis 4.94; Magi bury Thracian children alive 7.114; Persians bury people alive 7.114, sacrifice handsome Troezenian marine 7.180; Scythian retainer sacrifice after king's death 4.71–2; Scythian to Ares 4.62; Taurian to Iphigenia 4.103; Thracian wife-sacrifice after husband's death 5.5.

Sagartians *people of SE Persia* made part of Persian Province No. 14 by Darius 3.93; cavalry's equipment during Xerxes' invasion of Greece 7.85.

Sais *province and city in the western Nile Delta, Egypt* Festival of Neit 2.59, 62; temple of Neit 2.169–70, expanded by Amasis 2.175; tomb of Mycerinus' daughter 2.130–32; tombs of Amasis, Apries and forefathers 2.169.

Salamis (1) *small island off W coast of Attica* Delphic oracle alludes to; Themistocles deduces meaning 7.141–3; sole deserter to Greek side during battle of Artemisium granted land on 8.11; Greek fleet evacuates Athenian women and children from 8.40; Athenian fleet's base during second Persian invasion of Greece 9.3; *battle of Salamis:* 8.78–96, takes place on the same day as Carthaginian attack on Sicily 7.166; Phoenician trireme captured during battle later dedicated to Ares at Salamis (1) 8.121. *See also entries under* **Aegina, Athens, Greece, Persia, Themistocles, Xerxes**

Salamis (2) *Greek city on Cyprus* King Euelthon refuses to back Pheretime militarily 4.162; revolt under Onesilus 5.104; inhabitants oppose Persians during battle of Cyprus 5.110; war-charioteers flee 5.113; surrenders to Gorgus 5.115.

Samos (Samians) *Ionian island off W Asia Minor, and a city on that island* Aegina, war with; resulting feud 3.59; Amasis gives gifts to 2.182; assist Theran founding of city in Libya, make money in Tartessus, gift bowl to sanctuary of Hera 4.152; Corinthians, enmity with 3.49; dialect 1.142; engineering feats 3.60; Periander's planned castration of Corcyraean boys foiled 3.48; steal breastplate sent by Amasis to Lacedaemon 3.47; steal or buy Lacedaemonian bowl intended for Croesus 1.70, 3.47;

Cyaxares in battle at Nineveh, seize whole of Asia 1.103–4; arrogant dominion over Asia; made drunk then killed by Cyaxares and Medes 1.106; return
home to find their women have taken up with slaves 4.1; defeat slaves using
horsewhips 4.3–4;

— *Persian invasion:* invaded by Darius; hold war-council with neighbours
4.102, 118–19; plan battle tactics 4.120; send women, children, flocks north,
attack Persians 4.121; lead Persians into land of Boudinians, back through
Scythia and into lands of tribes refusing to ally with them 4.122–5; king's
response to Darius 4.127; harass Persian cavalry, hindered by their horses'
fear of donkeys 4.128–9; kings' cryptic gifts to Darius 4.131; parley with
Ionians guarding Ister bridge 4.133; muster forces 4.134; tricked by Darius;
head for Ister bridge, arrive before him, order Ionians to leave 4.135–6; tricked
by Ionians; unable to find Darius 4.139–40.

Sepias *beach in Magnesia (1)* used as harbour by Persian fleet 7.183, 188; hit by
storm, wrecking Persian ships 7.188–92.

Seriphos (Seriphians) *island in the W Cyclades* origins; ship in the Greek fleet at
Salamis 8.48.

Sesostris *legendary king of Egypt, his story drawing on both Senwosret I (r. c.
1961–1916) and Senwosret III (r. c. 1873–1854)* carvings in Ionia 2.106;
compared to Darius; statues at Memphis 2.110; conquests in Asia 2.102;
conquers Scythia and Thrace 2.103; soldiers left behind in Colchis 2.104;
triumphant return to Egypt; brother's attempts to murder sons 2.107; revenge
upon brother; use of prisoners to transport stone, dig canals 2.108; divides
land, institutes tax system 2.109.

Sestus *Aeolian city in the Thracian Chersonese* geography 7.33; besieged by Athenians under Xanthippus 9.114–19.

Sethos *priest of Ptah and king of Egypt (Shabatka, r. c. 702–690)* succeeds Anysis,
dishonours warrior class; inspired by Ptah, repels Sennacherib's invasion with
help of tradesmen, mice; statue at Memphis 2.141.

sheep and goats *a common livestock in H.'s Greece, supplying meat, milk, skins
and wool (the Mediterranean's main cloth); they were also frequently used in
sacrifice* Agyllan sheep struck lame due to curse 1.167; Apollonian sheep
sacred to sun 9.93; Arabian long- and fat-tailed sheep 3.113; Chaldaeans sacrifice unweaned lambs in Babylon 1.183; Crius' nickname means 'ram' 6.50;
Egyptian taboo on sheep and goats 2.42, 46; Euboean sheep slaughtered after
they ignore oracle 8.19–20; goat-footed men 4.25; Indian 'wool' (cotton) surpasses sheep's 3.106; Ionians formerly used goat- and sheep-skin instead of
papyrus 5.58; Libyan lambs quickly grow horns according to Homer 4.29;
Libyan women's goat-skin cloaks 4.189; Libyans use lanolin to cauterize children's heads; sprinkle goat's urine in event of spasms 4.187; Lycian soldiers
wear goat-skins 7.92; Psammetichus has children raised by sheep 2.2; rock
rose resin collected from goats' beards 3.112; Zeus disguises himself with
ram-skin 2.42.

Sicily *island off the toe of Italy* Minos dies in, attacked by Cretans 7.170; attempted colonization by Dorieus 5.43–6; base of Phocaean general Dionysius' piracy operation 6.17; colonized by Samians 6.22–4; under Hippocrates and Gelon 7.153–7; attacked by Carthage and allies 7.165–7.

Sicyon (Sicyonians) *city in the Peloponnese, W of Corinth* origins 8.43; under Cleisthenes (1) 5.68; take part in Lacedaemonian attack on Argive territory 6.92; ships at battle of Artemisium 8.1, at Salamis 8.43; rally to defence of Peloponnese at Isthmus of Corinth 8.72; troops in Greek army at Plataea 9.28, 31; rout Persians at Mycale, sustain heavy casualties 9.102–3; best after Athenians at Mycale 9.105.

Sidon (Sidonians) *city in Phoenicia* Apries attacks 2.161; Democedes visits 3.136; Paris' experiences according to Homer 2.116; *second Persian invasion of Greece:* win Xerxes' boat-race at Abydus 7.44; ships best in Xerxes' fleet 7.96; ship exclusively used by Xerxes 7.100, 128; commander seated next to Xerxes 8.67; ship carrying Pytheas captured by Aeginetans 8.92.

Sigeium *Athenian-founded city in NW Asia Minor* Peisistratus' illegitimate son Hegesistratus installed as tyrant, leading to war between Athenian exiles and Mytilenaeans 5.94–5; Hippias and Peisistratids exiled to 5.65; seized by Hippias 5.94.

silver *mined on the island of Siphnos and at Mt Pangaeum in Thrace; H. states it was worth thirteen times less than gold* Agbatana's wall 1.98; Alyattes offers Delphic oracle bowl 1.25; Artabazus advises bribing Greeks 9.41; Aryandes casts coins 4.166; Babylon's governor paid 1.192; Boges destroys Eion's 7.107; Cleomenes rejects Maeandrius' offer 3.148; coin dropped in Mylitta's shrine transmutes into something holy 1.199; Croesus burns couches in propitiation of Apollo, offers to Delphic oracle 1.50–51; Cyrenaeans offer Cambyses small amount 3.13; Egyptian animal keepers paid 2.65; Elaeous' tomb of Protesilaus contains bowls 9.116; gold more valuable than 3.95; Gyges offers Delphic oracle 1.14; Leotychidas caught taking bribe 6.72; Lydia silver-rich according to Aristagoras 5.49; Lydians first to strike coins 1.94; Magnesian (1) salvages 7.190; Mardonius' furnishings 9.82; Massagetans have no use for 1.125; Milesian converts property into 6.86; mine at Lake Prasias 5.17, at Mt Pangaeum 7.112, on Siphnos 3.57, in Thrace 5.23; Persia silver-rich according to Aristagoras 5.49; Persian furnishings 9.80, king's water stored in silver vases 1.188, silver apportioned out among Greeks after Plataea 9.81, spears silver-adorned 7.41, taxes paid in Babylonian talents 3.89; Plataeans discover 9.83; Pythius' 7.28; Rhampsinitus silver rich 2.121; Scythians do not use in burying their kings 4.71; Syloson rejects Darius' offer 2.140; Thasians' tableware 7.119.

Siphnos (Siphnians) *island in the W Cyclades* origins 8.48; wealth, endowment of treasury at Delphi; questioning of oracle 3.57; raided by Samian dissidents, fulfilling oracle 3.58; ship in Greek fleet at Salamis 8.48.

slavery *an integral part of Greek and non-Greek life; in Greece chattel slavery was the usual model, but see also helots* Argives' slaves run Argos after Lacedaemonian invasion, attempt to take over 6.83; Arisba destroyed and inhabitants delivered into by Methymna 1.151; Artemisia says that bad men have good slaves and vice versa 8.68; Athenians formerly lacked house-slaves 6.137; Barcaeans sold into after revolt, resettled in Bactria 4.203–4; Boges' slaves killed during Persian siege 7.107; Cyrus contemplates enslaving Lydians 1.155–6, raised by slaves 1.110–22, says better to be free in harsh land 9.122; Darius' house-slave becomes rich after collecting coins dropped by Democedes 3.130; Demaratus rumoured to be slave's son 6.68; Egyptian noblewomen dressed as slaves by Cambyses 3.14; Eretrian slaves settled in Cissia 6.119; Eretrians enslaved by Persians on orders of Darius 6.101; fugitive slaves may free themselves through branding at Egyptian shrine of Heracles 2.113; Getan god originally Pythagoras' slave 4.95; Harpagus' house-slave carries secret messages 1.123; Heraclid dynasty's matriarch a slave girl 1.7; Histiaeus' slave carries secret messages to Aristagoras tattooed on his scalp 5.35; Lacedaemonians enslaved by Tegeans after unsuccessful invasion 1.66; Lemnians sold by Lycaretus into 5.27; Lycian matrilineal descent means slaves may father legitimate children 1.173; Milesians enslaved by Persians after revolt 6.18–19; Persian army's commanders no more than slaves 7.96; Persian law outlaws execution or mutilation of 1.137; Persian spies shipwrecked and sold 3.138; Persians favour castrated slaves 8.105; Pharnouches' slaves cut off his horse's legs 7.88; Prieneans sold by Mazares 1.161; Thracian slave girl Rhodopis becomes concubine in Egypt 2.135; Samians enslaved by Aeginetans and Cretans 3.59; Scythians blind slaves 4.2; Scythians' slaves take up with their wives, take over during Scythian conquest of Media 4.1, 3–4; Sicilian slaves expel their masters 7.155; Sicilians enslaved by Hippocrates 7.154; Tarentine former slave dedicates statues in Olympia 7.170; Themistocles' slave acts as his messenger, is later made citizen of Thespiae 8.75, 110; Xerxes' intention to enslave all of Europe 7.8; Zanclaeans enslaved by Hippocrates 6.23. See also helots

Smerdis (1) *brother of Cambyses, son of Cyrus the Great and Cassandane* great strength; murdered on orders of Cambyses 3.30; death kept secret 3.61.

Smerdis (2) *Magian usurper (d. 521), brother of Patizeithes* ears cut off in punishment during reign of Cyrus 3.69; impersonates murdered Persian lookalike/namesake at urging of brother, seizes throne 3.61; beneficent rule 3.67; deception uncovered by Otanes (1) after his daughter confirms lack of ears 3.68–9; plots with brother to use Prexaspes to consolidate power 3.74; denounced by Prexaspes 3.75; killed by Otanes (1)'s anti-Magian conspirators 3.78.

Smyrna (Smyrnaeans) *Ionian city on the W Asia Minor coast* attacked by Gyges; captured by Alyattes 1.15–16; Lydians sent to found new colony build boats at 1.94; does not seek to join Panionium 1.143; lost by Aeolis to Ionia 1.149–50.

snakes *associated with the underworld, and often envisaged as guardians of sacred places* Acropolis guarded by giant 8.41; Ethiopian cave-dwellers eat 4.183; Heracles sleeps with snake-woman 4.9; horses eat in Sardis, portending Croesus' downfall 1.78; Libya's monstrous; tiny horned 4.192; Magi sacrifice 1.140;

6.28; conquered by Mardonius 6.44; forced by Darius to destroy its walls, sends fleet to Abdera after being falsely accused of plotting revolt 6.46, 48.

The Uprooted *inhabitants of islands in today's Persian Gulf, resettled there by Persian kings* made part of Persian Province No. 14 by Darius 3.93; equipment and commander during Xerxes' invasion of Greece 7.80.

Thebes (1) (Thebans) *leading city of Boeotia* contributes funds to Peisistratus 1.61; shrine of Apollo; examples of Phoenician script 5.59–61; receives token aid from Aegina before unsuccessful attack on Athens 5.79–81; attacks Plataea and Athens after they ally 6.108; recovers statue of Apollo looted by Phoenicians from Delium 6.118;

— *second Persian invasion of Greece: Xerxes' campaign:* surrenders to Xerxes 7.132; *battle of Thermopylae:* troops fight alongside Greeks at Thermopylae 7.202, sympathies lean toward Persia 7.205, kept as hostages at Thermopylae by Leonidas after other Greeks are dismissed 7.222, surrender to Persians at first chance; some killed, rest branded 7.233; inform Xerxes of Thespiae and Plataea's refusal to collaborate 8.50;

— *second Persian invasion of Greece: Mardonius' campaign:* amazed after oracle at Ptoiüm speaks in Carian language to Mardonius' envoy 8.135; urge Mardonius to base himself in Thebes (1), conquer Greece by non-military means 9.2; lands denuded by Persians under Mardonius 9.15; troops aid Persian cavalry in harrying Greeks 9.40.

Thebes (2) (Thebans) *city, located in province of the same name, on the Nile in central Egypt* crocodile worship 2.69; Amun, Festival of 2.42, shrine of 4.181; Egypt once synonymous with 2.15; genealogy studied by its priests 2.142–3; geography 2.9, 28; H. visits 2.3; taboo on sheep 2.42; unprecedented rain following death of Amasis 3.10.

Themistocles *Athenian admiral and politician (c. 528–462)* persuades Athenians to build fleet during war with Aegina; subsequent importance of this; suggests Delphic oracle refers not to Athens but to Persians 7.143–4; bribed by Euboeans to fight Persians, bribes Eurybiadas and Adeimantus to do the same 8.4–5; hatches plan to get Carians and Ionians to desert; urges fellow-commanders to slaughter Euboean sheep, light watch-fires 8.19; has messages left on Euboea urging Ionians and Carians to defect or refuse to fight 8.23; *battle of Salamis:* persuades Eurybiadas to meet Persian fleet off Salamis (1) by threatening Athenian desertion 8.57–63; sends slave to tip off Persians that Greeks are about to withdraw 8.75; pleased to learn from Aristeides of Salamis (1)' encirclement 8.80; inspires Greek marines before battle 8.83; taunted by Aeginetans for doubting them 8.92; having failed to persuade Greek commanders to break up Hellespont bridges, makes duplicitous speech to Athenians advocating the opposite 8.108–9; sends slave to tell Xerxes he has prevented breaking up of bridges 8.110; besieges Andros after Andrians refuse to give him money; blackmails Paros and Carystus 8.111–12; never ratified as most valorous Greek due to jealousy of fellow-commanders; visits Lacedae-

triaconter *a thirty-oared galley, used in trade as well as in war* used by Persian fleet during second invasion of Greece 7.97, by Theras to colonize Libya 4.148.

Triopium *cape on the SW coast of Asia Minor, location of a Dorian shrine of the same name* geography 1.174, 4.38; shrine's laws 1.144.

trireme *a warship with three banks of oars on each side* used by Aeginetans with images of Aeacids before Salamis 8.83, by Aristagoras to sail to Lacedaemon 5.38; Artaphrenes (1) mobilizes two hundred against Miletus 5.32; Athenian trireme captured by Persians during second Persian invasion of Greece 7.181, runs aground at mouth of R. Peneius 7.182; Athenian trireme's crew driven mad, kill one another 5.85; Corcyraeans claim to have sent sixty to join Greek fleet during second Persian invasion 7.168; Crotoniate sails to Cyrene in personal 5.47; Eretrian triremes aid Athens 5.99; Gelon offers Greeks triremes in return for supreme command during second Persian invasion 7.158; Greek fleet's before Salamis 8.43–8; Histiaeus uses Lesbian triremes for piracy 6.5; Ionian fleet's before battle of Lade 6.9; Ionian captains' triremes at Salamis 8.85; Miltiades (2) flees to Athens with five 6.41; Miltiades (2) sent to Chersonese by 6.39; Necos orders building of 2.159; Persian fleet's before first invasion of Greece 6.95, during second invasion of Greece 7.89, off Elaeous before second invasion of Greece 7.22; Persian spies man triremes in Phoenicia 3.136; Phanes pursued by eunuch-commanded trireme 3.4; Phoenician triremes dedicated to gods after Salamis 8.121; Phoenician triremes' figureheads 3.37; Samian triremes' valour at battle of Lade 6.14; Tenian trireme joins Greek fleet before Salamis 8.82; two to row side by side in Nile canal 2.158, in Athos canal 7.24; Xerxes bridges Hellespont using triremes 7.36, notes names of valorous trireme captains during battle of Salamis 8.91.

Tritantaechmes *Persian general, son of Artabanus* general of Persian army during Xerxes' invasion of Greece 7.82; alarmed after learning of Greeks' competition for token prizes in Olympics; thought a coward by Xerxes 8.26.

Troezen (Troezenians) *city in the E Peloponnese* origins 8.43; looks after Hydrea for Samos 3.59; ship captured by Persians at Sciathos; handsome marine sacrificed 7.180; ships before battle of Artemisium 8.1; base of reinforcing Greek ships before Salamis 8.42; ships at Salamis 8.43; rallies to defence of Peloponnese at Isthmus of Corinth 8.72; troops in Greek army at Plataea 9.28, 31, rout Persians at Mycale 9.102; troops next-best after Athenians at Mycale 9.105.

Trophonius *legendary hero; an oracular shrine dedicated to him was located in W Boeotia* tested by Croesus 1.46; Mardonius' envoy bribes local to consult 8.134.

Troy, Trojan War *see* Ilium

Tymnes *steward of Ariapeithes, informant of H.* tells H. about Idanthyrsus' family 4.76.

Assyrians 7.63; Carian invention of helmet-crests 1.171; leather of Milyans 7.77; of Mysians 7.74; of Cilicians 7.91; plaited of Egyptians 7.89, of Marians 7.79; wooden of Moschians 7.78; *shields:* Alcmaeonids alleged to have used to signal to Persian fleet 6.115, 121, 123; Barcaeans use to detect Persian miners 4.200; Carian invention of decoration, handles 1.171; crane-skin of Asiatic Ethiopians 7.70; Croesus offers to Amphiaraus 1.52, Delphi 1.92; Greek derived from Egypt 4.180; hollow of Egyptians 7.89; of Moschians 7.78; of Phoenicians and Palestinians 7.89; ostrich-skin of Macae 4.175; ox-hide bucklers of Cilicians 7.91; small animal-skin of Marians 7.79; small ox-hide bucklers of Colchians 7.79; small of Paphlagonians 7.72; small of Mysians 7.74; Thessalians' dedicated to Abae and Delphi by Phocians 8.27; tiny of Thracians 7.75; wicker of Persians 7.61, used to create barrier 9.61, 99, 102; *spears, javelins:* Caunians use spears to drive out foreign gods 1.172; Croesus offers golden spear to Amphiaraus 1.52; gazelle-horn spears of Ethiopians 7.69; Getan human sacrifice uses spears 4.94; hippopotamus-skin javelins of Egyptians 2.71; javelins of Cilicians 7.91, of Libyans 7.71, of Lycians 7.92, of Marians 7.79, of Mysians 7.74, of Phoenicians and Palestinians 7.89, of Samothracians 7.90, of Paphlagonians 7.72; lances of Lydian cavalry 1.79; short long-headed spears of Moschians 7.78; short spears of Bactrians 7.64, of Colchians 7.79, of Milyans 7.77, of Persian Immortals make fighting difficult 7.211; spear-butts in the form of golden and silver pomegranates, apples of Persians 7.41; spears of Egyptians 7.89, of Thracians 7.75; *swords, daggers:* daggers of Pactyes 7.67, of Paphlagonians 7.72, of Persians 7.61, of Sagartians 7.85, of Thracians 7.75; daggers, sickles of Carians 7.93, of Lycians 7.92; knives of Colchians 7.79; scimitars of Persians 3.118, 128, 9.107; Scythians' shrine to war-god marked by iron swords 4.62; short swords of Caspians 7.67, of Persians 9.80, offered by Darius to Hellespont 7.54; swords of Cilicians 7.91.

wine *drunk diluted with water in H.'s Greece; drinking neat wine was thought to be physically and mentally ruinous and a habit of barbarian peoples* Babylonians make from palm-tree fruit, import from Armenia 1.193–4; Cambyses said to be too fond of 3.34; Cambyses sends gift of palm-wine to Ethiopians 3.20, 22; Cleomenes driven mad after acquiring Scythian habit of drinking neat 6.84; clever thief steals from Rhampsinitus using 2.121; Croesus warned that Persians never drink 1.71; Cyrus serves to Persians to give them taste of good life 1.126; Delphians use giant bowl to mix during festival 1.51; Egyptian priests drink 2.37, use in sacrificial rites 2.39; Egyptian warriors receive in their rations 2.168; Egyptians drink great quantities of during festival at Bubastis (1) 2.60, fill corpses' stomachs with palm-wine during embalming 2.86, import from Greek world, use wine-jars to store water 3.6, make from barley 2.77; Greek mercenaries drink mixed with children's blood before battle 3.11; Hippocleides gets drunk on, performs dances 6.129; Lacedaemonian kings given each month 6.57; Lotus-Eaters make from lotus 4.178; Persian passion for, abhorrence of drunkenness 1.133; Persians get Massagetans

warned of Ionians' divided loyalties; sends Artabanus to Susa as regent 7.47–53; prevents capture of grain-bearing Greek cargo ships 7.147; prepares for crossing, offers gifts to Hellespont 7.53–4; *in Europe:* watches army cross Hellespont; mistaken for Zeus by local man 7.55–6; dismisses births of freakish foals portending failure 7.57–8; counts forces 7.60; army and fleet 7.61–99; reviews forces 7.100; discusses Greek bravery with Demaratus, scoffs at his answers 7.101–4; route through Thrace, conscription of Thracian tribes 7.108–10, 112–13; crosses R. Strymon 7.114; route to Acanthus, conscription of Thracian tribes 7.115; proclaims guest-friendship with Acanthians; buries Artachaeës 7.116–17; places great strain on hosts 7.118–20; separation of land-forces into three divisions 7.121; route to Therma 7.124; views Mts Olympus (1) and Ossa, inspects R. Peneius 7.128; muses on ease of flooding Thessaly by damming river 7.130; held up by forces' difficulty in passing Macedonian Mts; receives surrender of many Greek regions 7.131–2; *battle of Thermopylae:* arrives in Malis after staging horse-races in Thessaly, treating sacred grove of Achaea Phthiotis respectfully 7.196–7; makes base at Trachis 7.201; sends spy to Thermopylae, who confused by Lacedaemonians' behaviour; questions Demaratus, scoffs at his answer 7.208–9; angry when Greeks fail to leave, sends Medes and Cissians to attack them; recalls these and deploys Immortals; alarmed at failure to defeat Greeks 7.210–12; told by Epialtes of mountain path to Thermopylae 7.213; sends Hydarnes and Immortals to investigate 7.215; attacks remaining Greek forces; brothers killed 7.223–4; questions Demaratus about how best to conquer Lacedaemon, advised to send ships to capture Cythera; persuaded otherwise by Achaemenes, defends Demaratus' honour 7.234–7; displays Leonidas' head on spike 7.238; invites fleet to view dead at Thermopylae, concealing Persian dead 8.24–5; thinks Tritantaechmes a coward after he is alarmed by token prizes on offer in Olympics 8.26; *battle of Salamis:* reaches Attica three months after leaving Hellespont 8.50–51; captures Athens; sends messenger updating Artabanus; commands Athenian exiles to sacrifice at Acropolis 8.52–4; visits fleet, holds war-council; has Mardonius ask commanders if they think Greeks should be engaged at sea 8.67; impressed by Artemisia's critical answer, decides to fight at Salamis (1) anyway 8.69; mistakenly impressed at Artemisia's ship's ramming of friendly vessel 8.88; executes Phoenicians after they accuse Ionians of treachery; impressed by Samothracian heroism; keeps list of heroic captains during battle 8.90; *withdrawal from Greece:* worried that Greeks will destroy Hellespont bridges after Persian defeat at Salamis; feigns battle preparations, sends news of defeat to Susa 8.97–8; urged by Mardonius either to stay in Greece or to give him command over portion of army with view to conquest; advised by Artemisia to take latter course; sends her to Ephesus with his children 8.100–103; allows Mardonius to pick out troops, sends fleet commanders to Hellespont to protect bridges 8.107; told by Themistocles' slave that Themisto-

THE STORY OF PENGUIN CLASSICS

Before 1946 . . . "Classics" are mainly the domain of academics and students; readable editions for everyone else are almost unheard of. This all changes when a little-known classicist, E. V. Rieu, presents Penguin founder Allen Lane with the translation of Homer's *Odyssey* that he has been working on in his spare time.

1946 Penguin Classics debuts with *The Odyssey*, which promptly sells three million copies. Suddenly, classics are no longer for the privileged few.

1950s Rieu, now series editor, turns to professional writers for the best modern, readable translations, including Dorothy L. Sayers's *Inferno* and Robert Graves's unexpurgated *Twelve Caesars*.

1960s The Classics are given the distinctive black covers that have remained a constant throughout the life of the series. Rieu retires in 1964, hailing the Penguin Classics list as "the greatest educative force of the twentieth century."

1970s A new generation of translators swells the Penguin Classics ranks, introducing readers of English to classics of world literature from more than twenty languages. The list grows to encompass more history, philosophy, science, religion, and politics.

1980s The Penguin American Library launches with titles such as *Uncle Tom's Cabin* and joins forces with Penguin Classics to provide the most comprehensive library of world literature available from any paperback publisher.

1990s The launch of Penguin Audiobooks brings the classics to a listening audience for the first time, and in 1999 the worldwide launch of the Penguin Classics Web site extends their reach to the global online community.

The 21st Century Penguin Classics are completely redesigned for the first time in nearly twenty years. This world-famous series now consists of more than 1,300 titles, making the widest range of the best books ever written available to millions—and constantly redefining what makes a "classic."

The Odyssey continues . . .

The best books ever written

PENGUIN  CLASSICS

SINCE 1946

Find out more at www.penguinclassics.com

Visit www.vpbookclub.com